BRITISH HIT SINGLES

12TH EDITION

GUINNESS PUBLISHING

Acknowledgements

Managing Editor
Karen O'Brien

Chief Consultant
Dave McAleer

Design
Robert Hackett

Editor
Jane Bolton

Assistant Editor
Ben Keith

Proofreader
Sue Harper

Cover Design
Dominic Sinesio and Leslie Horowitz,
Office Group, NYC

Pre-production Manager
Patricia Langton

Publishing Director
Ian Castello-Cortes

With thanks to:
Andy Gregory, Justin Lewis, John Tobler, Helen
Weller, Greg King, David Roberts, Mark Bennett,
Paul Easton at Music Choice, Brian Henson, James
Bath, Catherine Bonifassi and John Philibert

Contents

Our **Top 100 Singles of All Time** are profiled with illustrations throughout the book,
starting with No 1 on page 8 and finishing with No 100 on page 436

Introduction

It has been 22 years since **Guinness British Hit Singles** first hit the shelves. Now in its 12th edition, it has come to be regarded as the 'bible' of the UK singles charts by both the record-buying public and the music industry at large. With 1999 marking the 50th birthday of the 7-inch single, there has never been a better time to add new information and features to the book

by Dave McAleer

Tamperer featuring Maya: Newcomer in 1998

This new-look 12th edition of **Guinness British Hit Singles** offers not only a comprehensive listing of every UK chart hit from 1952–1998, but also a whole range of new facts and features. With more than 2000 new hits and 500 new artists added since the 11th edition in 1997, the book now contains a total of 32000 chart hits and 6500 acts.

Brand-new items: New to this edition is the **News and Reviews** section (Section 1), which offers a round-up of the major musical events of 1997 and 1998, as well as feature articles on the histories of the single and the singles chart. The traditional Facts and Feats section has now been renamed **Records** (Section 2) and has been expanded to include new categories and listings, as well as **redesigned** to make information more easily accessible at a glance. In the main alphabetical-by-artist listing (Section 3) we have added **mini-biographies** for every act that has spent more than 100 weeks on the chart. We have also introduced new **symbols** to denote music genres for the 3000+ acts that have reached the Top 20, as well as symbols to show which hits have been UK million sellers, US No 1s and UK entries at No 1. Furthermore, we have included profiles of our **Top 100 Singles of All Time**, which feature illustrated fact-packed run-downs of why these records have earned a place in musical history.

Our new points system: Another improvement to the book is the new points-based system which is used in the Records section to calculate chart success for singles and artists. This method has been carefully developed from our previous points system to ensure even greater accuracy and is used concurrently with our usual 'weeks on [the chart]' method. From a fan's point of view, it is interesting to note the different results that can be produced by the points system and the 'weeks on' method: the former approach better reflects a single's sales success, and the latter its total time on the chart. For example, ABBA fans will prefer the points system because it puts the Scandinavian superstars at No 13 in the Top 50 Artists of All Time (page 36), whereas Artists With Most Weeks on Chart (page 54) shows them at No 41. However, Frank Sinatra aficionados will be happier with the 'weeks on' method, which shows Ol' Blue Eyes as No 8 in Artists With Most Weeks on Chart, compared with No 33 in the Top 50 Artists of All Time.

Chart news since the last edition: Looking back over the charts since the last **Guinness British Hit Singles** was published in 1997, it is clear that, despite predictions to the contrary, the UK singles market is going from strength to strength. A record 1127 singles entered the Top 75 in 1997, and an unprecedented 20 singles sold more than 500000 copies each in 1998. Record companies have got singles marketing down to a fine art (pre-release build-up, discounted first-week pricing, timing of release, etc.), and it is now commonplace for a label's 'top priority' single to enter the charts at No 1 and to be replaced the following week by another company's 'top priority'. The proof of this is that more than 40 per cent of the records that have entered at No 1 since 1952 have done so during the last two years. Sometimes, when a single enters at No 2, the record label sees this as an indication that the artist has peaked and no longer deserves 'top priority' status.

Every year the turnaround on the pop chart accelerates, and the term 'chart climber' is now almost as archaic as '7-inch single'. It was not long ago that a chart entry at No 21 or No 41 meant that a record was assured of a Top 20 or Top 40 placing the following week. Nowadays, it means that the single is dead in the water; if a record does not make the Top 20 or Top 40 during its first week on the chart, it will probably never do so. Strange as this may be though, the UK chart is still preferable, in our view, to the recently overhauled US system, where it is now no longer necessary for a single to be released in order to make the chart. Since 80 per cent of chart points are now calculated from radio airplay, a track can reach the US Top 10 without one single being sold.

We hope that you enjoy the new-look, improved **Guinness British Hit Singles**, the UK's ultimate chart reference.

The Corrs: Newcomers in 1997/98

How to use this book

Below are typical extracts from Sections 3 and 4, with descriptions of what each part of an entry signifies and a key for any abbreviations or symbols used. For more detailed explanations, see the introductions to the individual sections

Section 3: Alphabetical-by-artist

music-genre symbol
(see key on page 7)

artist name

date of chart entry

hit symbol (see key on page 7)

alternative label credit

cross-reference

mini-biography (for artists with more than 100 weeks on chart)

total weeks on chart

weeks on chart

highest position reached on chart

refers to numbered footnote

still on chart on 31 Dec, 1998

hit symbol (see key on page 7)

label and catalogue number

CHER ⊘ *Perennially popular vocalist. b. Cherilyn LaPierre, 20 May, 1946, California. She was half of the most successful husband/wife duo ever. Sonny and Cher, and had an equally stunning run of solo smashes. Her No 1s now span a record 33 years, and at the age of 52 she is the oldest female solo singer to top the chart* **180 wks**

19 Aug 65	● ALL I REALLY WANT TO DO *Liberty LIB 66114*	9	10
31 Mar 66	● BANG BANG (MY BABY SHOT ME DOWN) *Liberty LIB 66160*	3	12
4 Aug 66	I FEEL SOMETHING IN THE AIR *Liberty LIB 12034*	43	2
22 Sep 66	SUNNY *Liberty LIB 12083*	32	5
6 Nov 71	● GYPSIES TRAMPS AND THIEVES *MCA MU 1142* ▲	4	13
16 Feb 74	DARK LADY *MCA 101* ▲	36	3
13 Apr 91	★ THE SHOOP SHOOP SONG (IT'S IN HIS KISS) *Epic 6566737*	1	15
13 Jul 91	● LOVE AND UNDERSTANDING *Geffen GFS 5*	10	8
12 Oct 91	SAVE UP ALL YOUR TEARS *Geffen GFS 11*	37	5
7 Dec 91	LOVE HURTS *Geffen GFS 16*	43	5
18 Apr 92	COULD'VE BEEN YOU *Geffen GFS 19*	31	4
14 Nov 92	OH NO NOT MY BABY *Geffen GFS 29*	33	4
16 Jan 93	MANY RIVERS TO CROSS *Geffen GFSTD 31*	37	3
6 Mar 93	WHENEVER YOU'RE NEAR *Geffen GFSTD 32*	72	1
15 Jan 94	I GOT YOU BABE *Geffen GFSTD 64* [1]	35	3
28 Oct 95	WALKING IN MEMPHIS *WEA WEA 021CD1*	11	7
20 Jan 96	● ONE BY ONE *WEA WEA 032CD*	7	9
27 Apr 96	NOT ENOUGH LOVE IN THE WORLD *WEA WEA 052CD*	31	2
17 Aug 96	THE SUN AIN'T GONNA SHINE ANYMORE *WEA WEA 071CD*	26	3
31 Oct 98	★ BELIEVE *WEA WEA 175CD* ■	1†	9

[1] Cher with Beavis and Butt-Head

See also SONNY and CHER

6

Key to music-genre symbols

☺	Alternative Dance	ℭ	Easy Listening
♪	Classical/Opera	◉	Pop
🤠	Country	✎	Punk
☺	Dance	🌴	Reggae
🎸	Disco	🎸	Rock
♂	Folk	🎻	Rock'n'roll
✈	Heavy Metal	♪	Rhythm & Blues
🧢	Hip Hop/Rap	R&B	R & B
☹	Indie	🎤	Soul
🎷	Jazz	🌐	World

Abbreviations for mini-biographies

b – born		**syn** – synthesizer	
d – died		**t** – trumpet	
b – bass guitar		**v** – vocals	
d – drums		**MOR** – Middle	
fl – flute		of the Road	
g – guitar			
k – keyboard			
prc – percussion			
prog – programming			
s – saxophone			

Key to hit symbols

★ UK No 1
● UK Top 10
◆ UK million seller
■ UK entry at No 1
▲ US No 1

Section 4: Alphabetical-by-title

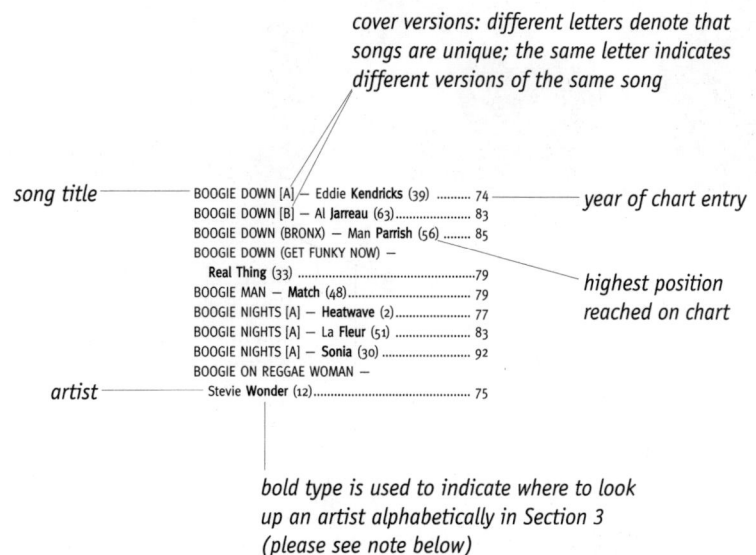

cover versions: different letters denote that songs are unique; the same letter indicates different versions of the same song

song title

BOOGIE DOWN [A] — Eddie **Kendricks** (39) .... 74 — *year of chart entry*
BOOGIE DOWN [B] — Al **Jarreau** (63)..................... 83
BOOGIE DOWN (BRONX) — Man **Parrish** (56) 85
BOOGIE DOWN (GET FUNKY NOW) —
   Real Thing (33) 79
BOOGIE MAN — **Match** (48).................................. 79
BOOGIE NIGHTS [A] — **Heatwave** (2) 77
BOOGIE NIGHTS [A] — La **Fleur** (51) 83
BOOGIE NIGHTS [A] — **Sonia** (30) 92
BOOGIE ON REGGAE WOMAN —

artist — Stevie **Wonder** (12)................................. 75

highest position reached on chart

bold type is used to indicate where to look up an artist alphabetically in Section 3 (please see note below)

Alphabetical order and music-genre symbols

Alphabetical order in Sections 3 and 4 is governed by the following rules. Act names that begin with a number appear as though the number were spelt out. For example, the group '4 Non-Blondes' is filed as though it were 'Four Non-Blondes', and the song '007' is filed as though it were 'Double-O Seven'. Individual artists are ordered according to their surnames, while bands are ordered according to their entire names. Thus Marti Webb the individual can be found under 'W', whereas Max Webster the band will be filed under 'M'. Individuals who have a single letter for their surname, will be filed according to the usual rules. Thus, Mel B and Leila K will be found under 'B' and 'K' respectively.

The **music-genre symbols** are not intended to provide an absolute or final categorisation of an artist's or act's sound, but rather aim to give a general impression of an artist's or act's style of music.

What: *Rock Around the Clock* **1**
Who: Bill Haley and His Comets
When: 1955 (17), 1955 (1), 1956 (5), 1968 (20), 1974 (12)
Which: Launched rock'n'roll around the world and helped to change the face of popular music. The record had five separate UK chart runs and amassed world sales of more than 25 million

What: *Bohemian Rhapsody* **2**
Who: Queen
When: 1975 (1), 1991 (1)
Which: Was the only record to top the UK chart on two separate occasions, selling more than one million copies each time. It is a genuine pop classic and one of the first hit singles to benefit from an outstanding video

What: *Relax* **3**
Who: Frankie Goes to Hollywood
When: 1983 (1), 1993 (5)
Which: Topped the chart thanks partly to a BBC ban. This controversial dance favourite sold almost two million copies in the UK and spent 22 weeks in the Top 10 as well as more than one year in total on the chart

What: *You've Lost That Lovin' Feeling* **4**
Who: Righteous Brothers
When: 1965 (1), 1969 (10), 1977 (42), 1990 (3)
Which: Is regarded as one of the classic pop records of all time. This Phil Spector production became the first single to reach the UK Top 10 on three separate occasions

1 - News and reviews

In this new section of **Guinness British Hit Singles**, we round up all the major musical happenings during the two years since the 11th edition was published. As well as coverage of music awards, festivals, regional scenes and much more, we also have features on the history of the single and the charts, and an in-depth look at what's been happening in the DJ world.

Contents:

Lauryn Hill: Winner of a record four Grammy Awards in 1999

The history of the single

The 45 celebrates its 50th birthday in 1999. To commemorate, we chart the history of the single, from the first phonograph and cylinder records to the latest MP3 digital technology

Although **Thomas Edison** is usually credited with the invention of the **phonograph** (record player) in 1877, the French inventor Charles Cros started his recording career some months before Edison cut the classic 'Mary Had a Little Lamb'. However, it was Edison who was first to patent the machine, on Christmas Eve, 1877, and who went on to form the first record company in 1878.

The first **cylinder records** were introduced in 1889 and led to the emergence of 'phonograph parlours', where patrons paid to hear well-known marches or popular songs on the miraculous 'talking machines'. Despite the obvious distortion of the sounds being played, audiences were enthralled by the technology of the Victorian era and flocked to these parlours for several years.

Rio PMP300 portable music player

The battle of music formats began in the mid-1890s, when the flat 12-inch wax-coated zinc disc appeared and challenged the cylinder. By the advent of World War I, cylinders had been assigned to the scrap heap, and **double-sided discs** became the standard format. Astonishingly, it was about this time that the first LPs were released, but they attracted few buyers, and the idea was quickly shelved.

Radio arrived in style in the 1920s and altered the playing field once again – it was an entertainment medium that seemed ideal for record promotion. Radio may have killed the music-hall star, but it boosted record sales to undreamed of quantities. Things developed quickly, and by the mid-1920s the introduction of the **microphone** meant that performers no longer had to sing into horns. With this advance came the first **electronically recorded discs**.

An attempt at **stereo** output around 1933 failed, as did further attempts at producing LPs in the mid-1920s and the Depression-hit early 1930s. **Albums** began to catch on in the mid-1940s, but were then just a collection of 10-inch or 12-inch 78rpm singles in a folder similar to a photo album (hence the name). In June 1948, Columbia unveiled the long-playing **microgroove** record, which for the next 35 years became the standard format for albums.

The **tape recorder** was perfected in Germany during World War II, and, shortly after the guns stopped firing, tape machines were introduced to recording studios worldwide. Domestic tape recorders first appeared in the early 1950s but were quite exclusive due to their high cost – in the region of £80.

The first **7-inch 45rpm single** (tagged 'doughnut discs' by the media) reached the US marketplace in 1949, and by the mid-1950s accounted for the bulk of sales there. However, in the UK, they were not in common use until 1957 (and were then usually available only two weeks after the 78rpm versions had been released). By 1959, the vinyl 45 had replaced its breakable forerunner, the 10-inch 78, and would remain king of the singles format until 1990.

The fact that both the 45rpm single and the LP could only be played on electric record players signalled the end of 'wind-up' gramophones, which required constant replacement of their needles (styli).

EMI first announced the arrival of 'Stereosonic' records in 1955. However, the first **stereo** albums did not arrive in the UK until spring 1958. Stereo was not an overnight success and mono remained the master format, at least for singles, until the late 1960s.

Pre-recorded tapes first appeared in the USA in the mid-1950s, but did not really take off until the mid/late-1960s when the **cassette** format was launched in Europe, and the bulky **eight-track tape** variant did big business in the USA. Cassettes won out as the dominant format, and by 1985 were even outselling vinyl records.

The 1970s witnessed the introduction of **Dolby**, the rise and fall of **Quad Sound**, and the development of superior-sounding metal tapes. By 1975, the **12-inch single** had arrived, but it would be 1991 before it managed to outsell the 7-inch. Portable music came into its own in 1980, thanks to the launch of the **Walkman personal stereo**, a lightweight cassette player fitted with headphones. In 1983 a new format, the **compact disc**, hit the market and revolutionized the way the world listened to music.

During the past ten years various new music formats have challenged the CD: **DAT**, **DCC** and **MiniDisk** (which made a strong revival in 1998) have all been unveiled as The Next Big Format. Today **DVD**, which promises eight hours of top quality music on one disc, is being touted as a strong competitor. However, many feel that the winner could be MP3 technology, which downloads digital music files directly from the Internet. Diamond Multimedia has developed the

Rio PMP300, a portable music player that is similar to a Walkman or MiniDisk player, only much lighter and smaller. The Rio does not require a tape or a record and has no moving parts, which means no skipping, even when subject to vibrations. The impact that this new technology will have on the music industry as a whole looks set to be revolutionary, and may mean the end of the single as we know it.

Glossary:
7-inch, 10-inch, 12-inch: types of vinyl single
CD: compact disc
DAT: digital audio tape
DCC: digital compact cassette
Dolby: peripheral noise reduction system
DVD: digital versatile disc
LP: long-playing (record)
MiniDisk: magneto-optical recording disc
mono: one-channel sound
MP3: digital music format
Quad Sound: surround-sound using four speakers
rpm: revolutions per minute
stereo: two-channel sound

The history of the singles chart

The UK Top 75 has become the world's fastest-moving chart, with the average chart life of a single diminishing rapidly, and new records being set on a regular basis

The first UK singles chart appeared in *New Musical Express* on 14 November, 1952. This date was not chosen randomly; the recently launched *NME* saw it as another weapon in its circulation war with *Melody Maker*, which celebrated its 1000th edition on the same day. *NME*'s first chart was a Top 12, which contained 15 records (there were three tied positions). It was based on a telephone poll of a couple of dozen record dealers, and only three British acts were represented.

The Beatles

Any listing of record-breaking feats from the 1950s would have to include the five simultaneous Top 20 chart entries by Ruby Murray in 1955 and Bill Haley in 1956, as well as Elvis Presley's seven simultaneous singles in the *NME* Top 30 in 1957. Elvis, incidentally, was the only artist in that decade to have a record enter the chart at No 1: 'Jailhouse Rock' in 1958.

By the early 1960s, the public were buying more records, and the chart expanded accordingly. The trade magazine *Record Retailer* started its Top 50 in March, 1960, which became available to the public when it was also published in *Record Mirror* in March, 1962. In the 1950s, US recordings had ruled the roost, but the arrival of the Beatles heralded a new dawn for British artists, and in March, 1964, UK acts hogged all the Top 10 slots for the first time.

Three singles entered the chart at No 1 in the 1960s (one each by Cliff Richard, Elvis Presley and the Beatles), and in the following decade the tally increased to four (one by Gary Glitter and an impressive three by Slade). The chart was extended to a Top 75 in 1978, and it has remained the same size ever since.

During the 1980s, The Jam had a record 13 simultaneous chart entries, Madonna finally forced the chart door wide open for female artists, charity records became commonplace, and 14 singles entered the chart at No 1. Among the most notable feats achieved in the 1990s were the six chart-toppers scored with their first six releases by the Spice Girls, and the extraordinary fact that 93 records (so far) have entered the chart at No 1.

Before the 1990s, the average Top 20 hit entered the chart, climbed until it peaked, and slowly descended. The following list shows how the gradual increase in number of hits per year, and a corresponding decrease in the average number of weeks spent in the Top 20, changed drastically in the current decade.

Years	Top 20 entries	Average weeks in Top 20
1957/58	243	8.45
1967/68	298	6.93
1977/78	354	5.96
1987/88	464	4.48
1997/98	757	2.76

From these figures it is clear that more than three times as many records reach the upper echelons today than in the 1950s, and that their chart span has been reduced proportionately. Interestingly, the number of new acts entering the chart has always remained the same – about one third of all acts.

Before the 1990s, a Top 40 chart entry was a good indication that a record was bound for the Top 10. Nowadays, if it does not enter the Top 10 during its first week, it has little chance of ever doing so. Record company marketing strategies are so geared towards the first seven days of release that the odds are stacked against any single climbing higher than its debut position. It is similarly amazing to consider the number of records that entered in the Top 10 during the period covered by this book (1977–98). Almost 400 achieved that once remarkable feat in 1997/98 – ten times more than in 1987/88, and 392 more than managed it in 1957/58. The fallout from this trend has been that the kudos associated with entering the chart at No 1 has now been greatly devalued, as it has become virtually the norm and not the exception. In 1998, a record-breaking 27 of the 31 (another record) UK chart-toppers entered at No 1.

Charts in other countries are more stable than the UK Top 75, which has become the world's fastest-moving chart. This fact is underlined when our chart is compared to the US chart. In the USA, only 179 singles reached the Top 20 in 1997/98 (compared to the UK's 757), and each of those US entries spent an average of 11 weeks on the chart – a feat that only six per cent of UK Top 20 entries can even match, let alone surpass.

The outlook for the future is interesting: to date, the number of singles entering the Top 75 peaked at 1127 in 1997, but indications are that unless recent chart trends change, we could be facing the extraordinary situation whereby the entire Top 10 changes on a weekly basis.

Elvis Presley

Music awards

During 1998 music awards received more commercial sponsorship and media coverage than ever, with the Mercury Music Prize and the Mobo Awards creeping up on the BRITs for lead position among the British music awards. On the alternative front, the *NME* Brats became the *NME* Premier Awards, and Jonathan King organized the world's biggest audience-polled music event, the Britannia Award. Meanwhile, on the other side of the Atlantic, the Grammies hailed 1998 the year of the female artist

BRITS (16 Feb, 1999)

Best Female . . . . .Des'ree
Best Male . . . . .Robbie Williams
Best Group . . . . .Manic Street Preachers
Best Album . .*This Is My Truth Tell Me Yours,* Manic Street Preachers
Best Newcomer .Belle & Sebastian
Best Dance Act . . . . .Fatboy Slim
Best Single . . . .*Angels,* Robbie Williams

Best Video . . . .*Millennium,* Robbie Williams
Best International Female . . . . .Natalie Imbruglia
Best International Male . . . . .Beck
Best International Group .The Corrs
Best International Newcomer . . . . .Natalie Imbruglia
Best Soundtrack/Cast Recording . . . .*Titanic*

Mobo Awards (14 Oct, 1998)

Best Drum & Bass Act . . . . .4 Hero
Best Reggae Act . . . . .Glamma Kid
Best International Reggae Act . . . . .Beenie Man
Best Hip Hop Act . . . . .Phoebe 1
Best International Hip Hop Act . . . . .Noreaga
Best R&B Act . . . . .Beverley Knight
Best Dance Act . . . . .Stardust
Best Jazz Act . . . . .Jazz Steppers
Best Gospel Act .David & Carrie Grant
Best Video Award . . . .*Under the Bridge*, All Saints
Best International Act . . . . .Puff Daddy & The Family
Best International Single . . . .*Ghetto Supastar*, Pras Michel
Best Single Award . . . .*Freak Me*, Another Level
Best Album Award . . . .*Colours*, Adam F
Best Newcomer Award . . . . .Lynden David Hall
Best Night Club Award . . . .
. . . . .Rotation @ Subterrania (Femi Fem & Chris Crooks)
Outstanding Achievement Award . . . . .Puff Daddy
Contribution to Black Music Award . .Carl Macintosh, Loose Ends
Lifetime Achievement Award . . . . .B B King

Beverley Knight:
Best R&B Act, Mobos

*Robbie Williams: Best Male, Best Single,
Best Video at BRITs; Best Solo at NME
Premier Awards; Best Male at MTV Europe*

MTV Europe Music Awards (12 Nov, 1998)

Best Female . . . . .Madonna
Best Male . . . . .Robbie Williams
Best Group . . . . .Spice Girls
Best Breakthrough Artists . . . . .All Saints
Best Album . . . .*Ray of Light*, Madonna
Best Single . . . .*Torn*, Natalie Imbruglia
Best Dance Act . . . . .Prodigy
Best Rock Act . . . . .Aerosmith
Best Video . . . .*Teardrop*, Massive Attack

Music awards (continued)

Q Magazine Music Awards (31 Oct, 1998)

Best Single ....*Road Rage*, Catatonia
Best New Act ....Gomez
Best Album ....*Mezzanine*, Massive Attack
Best Producer.....................................Norman Cook
Lifetime Achievement Award...R.E.M.
Classic Songwriter ....Paul Weller
Best Act in the World Today....................Manic Street Preachers
The Q Inspiration Award ....Blondie

Country Music Assoc. Awards (23 Sept, 1998)

Entertainer of the Year ....Garth Brooks
Male Vocalist of the Year ....George Strait
Female Vocalist of the Year.............................Trisha Yearwood
Horizon Award..Dixie Chicks
Vocal Group of the Year...Dixie Chicks
Single of the Year ....*Holes in the Floor of Heaven*, Steve Wariner
Vocal Duo of the Year ....Kix Brooks & Ronnie Dunn
Album of the Year ....*Everywhere*, Tim McGraw
Musician of the Year...Brett Mason

MTV Video Music Awards (12 Nov, 1998)

Best Video of the Year...............................*Ray of Light*, Madonna
Best Rock Video...*Pink*, Aerosmith
Best R&B Video ....
.......*Gone Till November*, Wyclef Jean featuring the Refugee Allstars
Best Rap Video.............................*Gettin' Jiggy Wit It*, Will Smith
Best Direction ....*Ray of Light*, Madonna
Best Female Video ....*Ray of Light*, Madonna
Best New Artist ....*Torn*, Natalie Imbruglia
Best Group Video.............................*Everybody*, Backstreet Boys
Best Male Video ....*Just the Two of Us*, Will Smith
Best Dance Video ....*Smack My Bitch Up*, Prodigy
Best Breakthrough Video ....*Smack My Bitch Up*, Prodigy
Best Alternative Music Video ....*Time of Your Life*, Green Day
Best Art Direction ....*Bachelorette*, Björk
Best Special Effects ....*Frozen*, Madonna
Best Cinematography ....*Criminal*, Fiona Apple

Mercury Music Prize (16 Sept, 1998)

Gomez . . . . *Bring It On*

Gomez: Mercury Music Prize; Best New Band, Session of the Year at NME Premier Awards

Muzik Magazine Dance Awards (1 Oct, 1998)

Best Album ....*Moon Safari*, Air
Best Single ....*Music Sounds Better With You*, Stardust
Best Small Club ....Basics, Leeds
Best Large Club ....Gatecrasher, Sheffield
Best Ibiza Club ....Ministry of Sound at Pacha
Best New Artist Album...........................*Jurassic 5*, Jurassic 5
Best British DJ ....Tall Paul
Best International DJ ....Deep Dish
Best New DJ.....................................Pure Science
Best Band ....Freestylers
Best Compilation ....*Brothers Gonna Work It Out*, Chemical Brothers
Best Remixer....................................Norman Cook
Best Independent Label.......................Hooj Choons
Best Major Label..................................AM:PM
Best Essential Mix................Carl Cox at Space, Ibiza
Best Radio Show ....Judge Jules, Radio One
Best Live Act....................................Faithless
Event of the Year..................Megadog Beach Festival
Best Video ....*Smack My Bitch Up*, Prodigy
Outstanding Contribution to Dance Music ....Danny Rampling

Britannia Record of the Year (19 Dec, 1998)

Boyzone .... *No Matter What*

NME Premier Awards (25 Jan, 1999)

Best Single ....
.. *If You Tolerate This Your Children Will Be Next*, Manic Street Preachers
Best Band ....Manic Street Preachers
Best Solo Art .... Robbie Williams
Best Music Video...................................
.. *If You Tolerate This Your Children Will Be Next*, Manic Street Preachers
Best Album .. *This Is My Truth Tell Me Yours*, Manic Street Preachers
Best New Band .... Gomez
Best Radio Show................. Mark Radcliffe, Radio 1
Session of the Year........................... Gomez
Best Dance Act .... Fatboy Slim
Best Dance Record........... *Rockafeller Skank*, Fatboy Slim
The Godlike Genius Award for Unique Services to Music .....
.... Massive Attack
Musical Event of the Year............. Glastonbury Festival
Best Venue .... Brixton Academy, London

Kerrang! (25 Aug, 1998)

Best New British Band .... Stereophonics
Best British Live Act..................... Cradle of Filth
Best International Newcomer .... Soulfly
Best International Live Act .... Green Day
Best Single .. *The Impression That I Get*, Mighty Mighty Bosstones
Classic Songwriter Award .... Lemmy
Best Video .... *Genius*, Pitchshifter
Best Album..................... *Around the Fur*, Deftones
Best British Band .... Bush
Best Band in the World................. Marilyn Manson
The Kerrang! Hall Of Fame .... AC/DC

41st Grammy Awards (Feb 24, 1999)

Record of the Year........... *My Heart Will Go On*, Celine Dion
Album of the Year ... *The Miseducation of Lauryn Hill*, Lauryn Hill
Song of the Year .... *My Heart Will Go On*, Celine Dion
Best New Artist .... Lauryn Hill
Best Female Pop Vocal Performance ....
.... *My Heart Will Go On*, Celine Dion
Best Male Pop Vocal Performance.. *My Father's Eyes*, Eric Clapton
Best Dance Recording............... *Ray of Light*, Madonna
Best Pop Album .... *Ray of Light*, Madonna
Best Rap Album .... *Vol 2...Hard Knock Life*, Jay-Z
Best R&B Album .... *The Miseducation of Lauryn Hill*, Lauryn Hill
Best Rock Album .... *The Globe Sessions*, Sheryl Crow
Best Country Album .... *Wide Open Spaces*, Dixie Chicks
Best Rock Song................ *Uninvited*, Alanis Morissette
Best R&B Song............ *Doo Wop (That Thing)*, Lauryn Hill
Best Country Song....................................
... *You're Still the One*, Robert John, Mutt Lange and Shania Twain
Best Alternative Music Performance .. *Hello Nasty*, Beastie Boys
Best Metal Performance........... *Better Than You*, Metallica
Best Hard Rock Performance.......................
.... *Most High*, Jimmy Page and Robert Plant

Eurovision Song Contest (9 May, 1998)

Dana International (Israel)........................ *Diva*

1998 Festivals and gigs

1998 was an anxious year for the festivals scene, with bad weather, the World Cup, and a glut of identical events and line-ups being blamed for poor ticket sales. However, although the Phoenix, Universe 98, and Gay Pride festivals were cancelled, Glastonbury and WOMAD sold out, and the ubiquitous Robbie Williams was the star of the stage wherever he played

What: Reading
Where: Richfield Avenue, Reading, Berkshire
When: August 28–30
Cost: Weekend: £75
Per day: £30
Headliners: Page & Plant, Ash, Beastie Boys, Prodigy, Garbage, New Order
Crowd: 55000 per day
Highs: Bonus acts from cancelled Phoenix festival
Lows: Prodigy and Beastie Boys sparring on stage

What: V98
Where: Chelmsford, Essex, and Temple Newsham, Leeds
When: August 22–23
Cost: Weekend: £55
Per day: £30
Headliners: The Verve, The Seahorses, Green Day, The Charlatans, Texas, Robbie Williams
Crowd: 55000 per day
Highs: Robbie Williams
Lows: Sanitized, corporate atmosphere

What: Glastonbury
Where: Worthy Farm, Pilton, Shepton Mallet, Somerset
When: June 26–28
Cost: £80
Headliners: Primal Scream, James, Blur, Robbie Williams, Pulp, Bob Dylan
Crowd: 100000
Highs: Blur, Robbie Williams, Spiritualized
Lows: Weather, mud, wellies for sale at £45, rumours of E-coli infection

What: Womad
Where: Rivermead, Reading, Berkshire
When: July 24–26
Cost: Weekend: £53
Fri: £17; Sat/Sun: £27.50
Headliners: Te Vaka, Chumbawamba, Istanbul Oriental Ensemble, Faithless, Oliver Mutukudzi, Carlo Nunez
Crowd: 34350
Highs: Musafir Gypsies of Rajasthan, sunshine
Lows: None, apparently

Shirley Manson from Garbage: Reading and T in the Park

What: T in the Park
Where: Balado, near Kinross, Scotland
When: July 11–12
Cost: Weekend: £54; Per day: £29.50
Headliners: Prodigy, The Seahorses, Robbie Williams, Pulp, Beastie Boys, Garbage
Crowd: 45000 per day
Highs: Robbie Williams
Lows: Rain, mud, Chumbawamba's non-appearance

What: Creamfields
Where: Matterly Estate, near Winchester, Hampshire
When: May 2–3
Cost: Weekend: £37.50
Headliners: Primal Scream, Finely Quaye, Run-DMC, Money Mark, Beth Orton, Laurent Garnier
Crowd: 35000
Highs: Run-DMC
Lows: Empty dance tents by 4am on Sunday

What:	Radio 1 Live
Where:	Cardiff
When:	September 13
Cost:	Free
Headliners:	Ash, Robbie Williams, The Divine Comedy, The Shirehorses, Manic Street Preachers, Republica
Crowd:	10000
Highs:	Free, covered concert
Lows:	Over too soon

What:	The Beach Festival
Where:	Carlyon Bay, St Austell, Cornwall
When:	August 14–16
Cost:	£60
Headliners:	Asian Dub Foundation, Bentley Rhythm Ace, Dreadzone, Basement Jaxx, Laurent Garnier
Crowd:	12000
Highs:	Sun, sea, sand; DIY ethos
Lows:	Displeased locals; freeloaders

What:	Party in the Park
Where:	Hyde Park, London
When:	July
Cost:	£15
Headliners:	All Saints, Boyzone, Natalie Imbruglia, Tom Jones
Crowd:	100000
Highs:	All Saints
Lows:	No alcohol allowed

What:	Notting Hill Carnival
Where:	Notting Hill Gate, London
When:	August 30–31
Cost:	Free
Headliners:	Junior Delgado, Pops Mohammed, Abdul Tee Jay, Beverley Knight, Lynden David Hall, Jurassic Five
Crowd:	Two million
Highs:	Beverley Knight
Lows:	Overcrowding

Best concerts of 1998:
- Morcheeba, London, March
- Spiritualized, London, March
- Massive Attack, London, April
- Garbage, London, June
- Ocean Colour Scene, Stirling Castle, August
- Depeche Mode, London, September
- Fun Lovin' Criminals, London, October
- Radiohead, Paris, December
- Björk, Manchester, December
- Lilith Fair, London, December
- P J Harvey, London, December

Best outdoor gigs of 1998:
Verve, Wigan, May
Madness, London, June
Stereophonics, Cardiff, June
Pulp, Finsbury Park, July
Paul Weller, London, August

1998 cancellations:
Essential
Gay Pride
Universe 98
Tribal Gathering
Phoenix Festival
Rolling Stones UK Tour

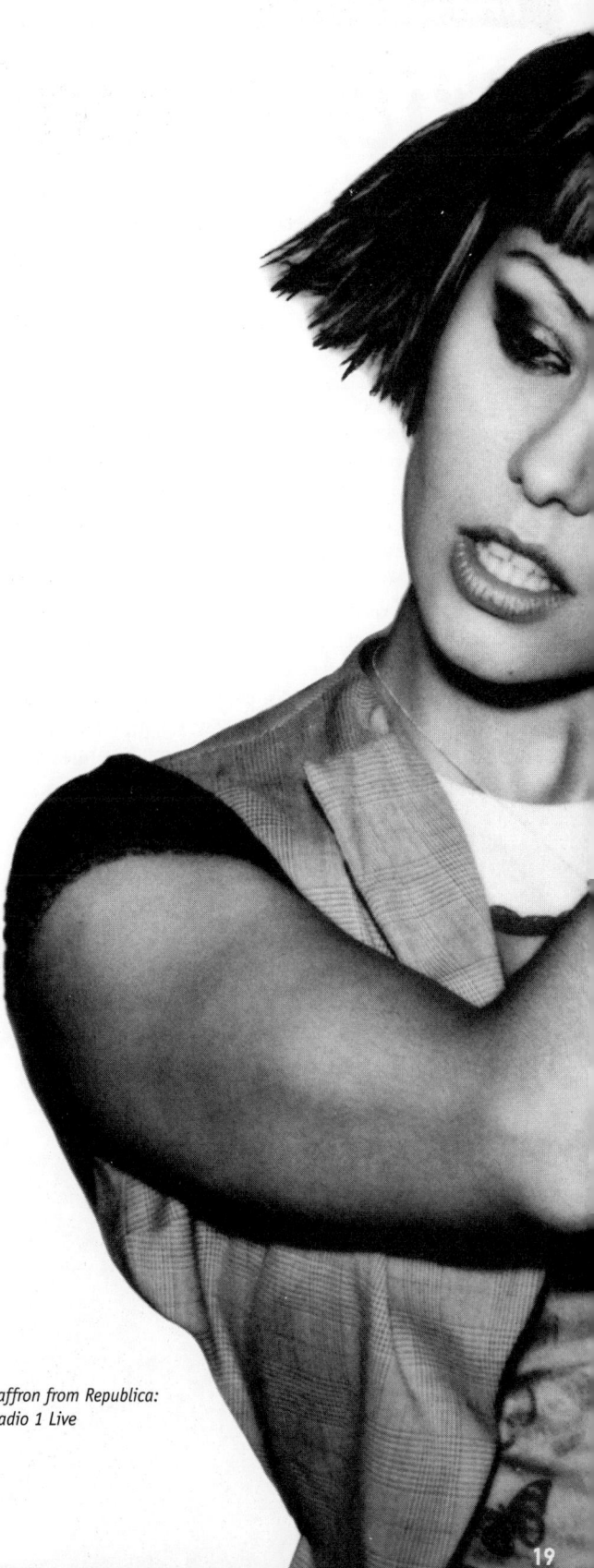

Saffron from Republica: Radio 1 Live

British regional scenes

With Wales, Scotland and Ireland all offering a host of exciting new acts, and Radio 1 planning to expand Steve Lamacq's *The Evening Session* programme to include variant regional broadcasts, 1997/98 was the year of proud music regionalism

Ireland

No other overseas country made more of an impact on the UK charts in 1998 than Ireland. The Irish invasion heralded a host of new pop acts, and although established bands such as **Boyzone** continued to break records for sales and longevity, they also made room for energetic girl group **B*Witched**, who scored three No 1s with their first three releases. Still on the teenage theme, **Ronan Keating**'s protégés **WestLife** were groomed for stardom, fellow Dublin boy band **OTT** were lingering just outside the Top 10 (before being dropped by their label), and on an alternative note the capital's girl-punk-trio, **Chicks**, provided a breath of fresh air. Meanwhile, **The Corrs** were among the most significant newcomers to the UK charts in 1998. They had three Top 10 hits – 'Dreams', 'What Can I Do', and 'So Young' – and sold a phenomenal two million copies of their album 'Talk on Corners' in the UK alone.

Northern Ireland

David Holmes was the most exciting and highest profile DJ to come out of Ireland (North or South) and placed the Belfast dance scene on the map with his cinematic soundscapes inspired by urban living and street-level encounters. Northern Ireland also continued to foster its strong tradition of guitar rock, with **Ash**'s edgy youth earning them three chart hits in 1997/98. **Neil Hannon** refined his dedadent posturing with **The Divine Comedy**, and Northern Ireland's answer to Metallica, **Therapy?**, continued their long run of chart success, bringing their total number of hit singles up to 13.

Scotland

While Edinburgh's **Shirley Manson** continued to take **Garbage** into a world-class league, Glasgow-based lo-fi collective **Belle & Sebastian** struck another blow for Scotland when they snatched the 1999 BRIT Best Newcomer Award from under the noses of mega-pop outfits such as Steps and Another Level. Also carrying the indie baton for Scotland were disco-flavoured **Bis**, guitar rock'n'rollers **Mogwai**, and brooding Glaswegians **the delgadoes**, while melodic dance/pop group **The Lanterns** were waiting in the wings to make an entrance.

The Manic Street Preachers

Wales

The **Manic Street Preachers** went from strength to strength, walking off with Best Group and Best Album at the 1999 BRITS. After their chart and festival success last year, **Catatonia** became the primary promoters of a new Welsh music scene and sang about thanking God daily for their national identity. Newcomers **The Stereophonics** had six hit singles in 1997/98 and played a sell-out show to 10000 people at Cardiff Castle, while **The Super Furry Animals** consolidated Wales' raw rock output. Additionally, a 165-acre festival site has been bought near Ffairfach, and plans are under way for a three-day live-music event in July, 2000.

London: The Asian Underground

The burgeoning Asian Underground scene – growing out of London's East End – has been one of the most innovative music scenes to emerge from Britain in recent years. Musicians such as **Talvin Singh**, **Nitin Sawhney** and **Cornershop** fused classical Indian traditions with western music technology and explored the contradictions of what it meant to be British and Asian. Record labels Outcaste and Nation opened doors for artists, while club dancefloors felt the force of angry young radicals **Asian Dub Foundation**, funky DJ **Milky Bar Kid**, raga-trip-hopper **Amar** and tabla'n'bass sensations **State of Bengal**, **Badmarsh & Shri** and **Black Star Liner**.

Talvin Singh: **"As far as music is concerned, if you go to India, they say:**

— Talvin Singh

'You're not Indian, you're British.' Then you go to England and it's like you ain't nothing, cos you ain't English."

Overseas acts in UK charts

The UK charts have never been so open to overseas music as in 1997/98. A French disco-house explosion reshaped how England viewed European music, and opened minds and pockets to sounds from the Continent, Scandinavia and the rest of the world

LHOOQ

France

In 1998 UK dancefloors were burning up to the sound of French disco-house. From **Stardust**'s infectious club anthem of the year, 'Music Sounds Better With You' (produced by **Thomas Bangalter**, half of **Daft Punk**), to **Air**'s ambient album, *Moon Safari*, the UK pop charts were invaded by the French. This explosion brought us Parisian producers **Cassius**, DJ and label pioneer **Laurent Garnier**, psychedelic hip-hopster **Kid Loco**, rapper **MC Solaar**, and purveyors of kitsch electronica **Super Discount**. Such was the sheer coolness attached to all things French that it resulted in British dance acts such as Jacques Lu Cont, aka Les Rythmes Digitales, even pretending to be French.

Iceland

Since **Björk** paved the way for Icelandic music to be taken seriously by the rest of the world, numerous acts have taken full advantage of her trail-blazing tactics and followed suit into the UK charts. **Alda**'s cartoon pop gave her two Top 20 singles in 1998 ('Real Good Time' and 'Girls' Night Out'), while electronic collective **GusGus** also charted with 'Polyesterday.' Other hotly tipped Icelandic acts include Uma-Thurman lookalike **Móa**, quirky all-girl pop outfit **Bellatrix**, and brooding groovers **LHOOQ**.

Japan

Engineering a hybrid of western pop and eastern technology, Japanese club pop was big in 1998 and looks set for an even higher profile in 1999. Following **DJ Krush** into the charts were **Pizzicato 5** with their quirky brand of retro pop, and **Towa Tei** with his much-hyped techno collaboration with Kylie Minogue, 'German Bold Italic.' Meanwhile, bubbling under the charts were *Planet of the Apes*-obsessed surf-rocker and studio-whizz **Cornelius** and dance duo **Boom Boom Satellites**.

Following the 41st Annual Grammy Awards, 1999 was being billed as the year of women after **Lauryn Hill**, **Celine Dion** and **Madonna** walked off with most of the major awards. Although British artists had, arguably, their worst year in the USA since 1963 (the year before the Beatles made it there), US artists from all areas of the musical spectrum continued to thrive in the UK, with R&B and rap acts scoring especially well. In fact, many of the UK's boy bands and girl groups have styled themselves on US R&B acts. Meanwhile, the US *Billboard* Hot 100 singles chart (started in 1958) underwent a radical shake-up when it revamped its methodology to further prioritize radio airplay and to include tracks not released as singles.

The Cardigans

Sweden

Leading the way in Sweden's ever-growing musical export industry were plastic popsters **Aqua**, ice-cool pop-turning-rock band **The Cardigans**, and reggae-tinged foursome **Ace of Base**. However, these established bands were only the tip of an iceberg of exciting new acts. **Meja** had a Top 20 hit with her debut single 'All 'Bout the Money', while the **Wannadies** and **Whale** continued to build on their UK chart success. As the talent continues to flow out of Stockholm in 1999, watch out for rockers **Fungus**, house-techno duo **Antiloop**, and kitsch covers-starlet **Stina Nordenstam**.

Jamaica

Legendary Jamaican toaster and rapper **Beenie Man** led the way in the UK charts with three hits in 1997/98, including a Top 10 single with 'Who Am I.' Also making waves were rising young stars and reggae innovators such as **Sizzla**, **Red Rat** and sound-system collective **Scare Dem Crew**. Chart regulars **Chaka Demus & Pliers** and **Shaggy** continued to score hits, while veterans **Sly & Robbie** and **Prince Buster** made welcome returns to the charts.

Cult of the DJ

It's taken ten years, but the art of the DJ has finally moved from the underground to the overground and gained recognition as a legitimate form of musicianship. As far back as 1979, David Bowie was anticipating the future of music when he declared: "I am a DJ, I am what I play." Now that 1998 has been hailed as the year of the great British DJ, we take a look at the major players

In recent years, the DJ has been transformed from underground club pioneer to major player in the commercial charts. DJ-ing (or 'turntablism') is no longer confined to the use of two decks and a mixer, but has developed into an art form that is finally gaining recognition outside of the club circuit as a legitimate form of musicianship. DJs now often compose, produce and perform their own music as well as playing other people's tunes, and are becoming standard in band line-ups in the dance music scene. Pushing the boundaries of electronic equipment, DJs now often work with as many gadgets, pedals and effects as any other musician. The art of turntablism has become much less about parasitic pastiche and more about original sonic composition.

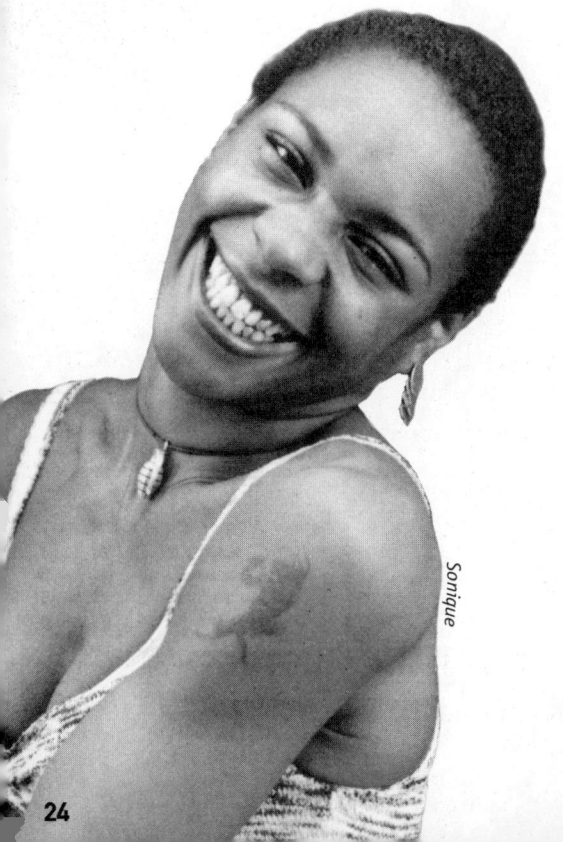

Sonique

Norman Cook, aka **Fatboy Slim**, is the primary example of the new palatability of the DJ. Pioneer of the **Brighton big beat** scene, his repetitive hooks appeal to music fans of all ages, and it was difficult to escape his catchy "funksoul brother" tune, 'Rockafella Skank', in 1998. Cook's meteoric rise means that he has come closer to being a household name than any club DJ ever has, as well as being the most sought-after remixer in the country and one of the privileged British acts to break the US music charts. After his No 1 remix of Cornershop's 'Brimful of Asha', he had so many offers of work that among the artists he had to turn down were Madonna, Pet Shop Boys and Aerosmith. Cook's celebrity status was consolidated by his recent engagement to Radio 1 DJ **Zoë Ball**. Together, these cheeky, down-to-earth chancers have become a tabloid sensation and the 'First Couple' of the DJ world.

Voted the most powerful person in the UK music industry by *Musik* magazine, Radio 1's **Pete Tong** has become so integral to British dance culture that his name recently entered the *Oxford Dictionary of Slang* as a synonym for "wrong". As well as managing A&R for acts such as All Saints and Goldie, his *Essential Selection* remix albums are top performers in the dance music charts.

A legendary co-founder of balearic beats and acid house, **Paul Oakenfold** was voted 'Best DJ in the World' in 1998 by *DJ* magazine's annual Top 100 DJs poll and entered the 1999 *Guinness Book of Records* as the 'Most Successful Club DJ'. Earning a cool £250000 each year, he also owns the Perfecto label and has sold one million records worldwide. Among the many other British DJs on the thriving dance scene are **'Tall Paul' Newman** (voted Best British DJ of 1999 by *Musik* magazine), **Darren Emerson** (who helped to create the electronic sound of Underworld), **David Holmes** (Belfast's purveyor of cinematic soundscapes), **Basement Jaxx** (Brixton-based saviours of deep house) and **Adam Freeland** (founder of new skool breakbeat).

Dialogue and interaction with overseas club scenes has never been so flourishing. In addition to the traditional transatlantic traffic between clubs and DJs, cross-fertilization is now occuring between

Norman Cook, 1998: **"I've realized now that what I do is dumb-arse, repetitive sample- and breakbeat-based dance music. I'm not an actor, I'm not a dancer, I'm not attractive to look at, so I don't play live and I don't appear in videos."**

repetitive sample- and breakbeat-based dance music. I'm not an actor, I'm not a dancer, I'm not attractive to look at, so I don't play live and I don't appear in videos."

British and other European dance music scenes. Among the many DJs from mainland Europe who are becoming well known in Britain are France's **Laurent Garnier** and **Dimitri from Paris**, as well as Austria's inventive remix duo, **Kruder & Dorfmeister**.

But in all of this, a glass ceiling remains in place: for women. In *DJ* magazine's Top 100 poll only one female made the Top 50, **Sonique** (at No 18), and only five women were included in the selection overall. Similarly, in *Musik* magazine's rundown of the Top 50 most powerful people in British dance music, only two women were featured. But trends are changing and numbers of female DJs are steadily growing with the likes of early drum'n'bass pioneers **DJ Rap** and **Kemistry & Storm**, as well as **Andrea Parker**, **Smokin' Jo**, **Lisa Unique**, **DJ Heaven**, **Lisa Loud** and **Donna Dee**.

Paul Oakenfold, 1998: **"Divisions in music are breaking down. Kids who buy Oasis also buy the Chemical Brothers, my mix of U2 outsells the original, turntables outsell guitars by three to one and, musically, everyone's eyes are on England."**

Newcomers, comebacks and splits

1997/98 was a period of polarity in the charts: talented teenagers vied with golden oldies and comeback queens for the No 1 spot. Meanwhile, as shake-ups in the record industry filtered down, it meant the end of the road for other acts

Newcomers

Not only did middle age prove to be an asset for a chart career in 1997/98, but extreme youth was also in style. With a resurgence of pure pop in the charts, teenage acts were in high demand. **Billie** shot to stardom at the age of 15 and had two consecutive No 1s with her first two releases. US teenager **Britney Spears** kept Blur from No 1 in March, 1999, and 12-year-old **Charlotte Church** caused a major stir in classical circles. New acts in 1997/98 included pop sensations **B*Witched**, **Steps**, **Five** and **The Corrs**; R&B groups **All Saints**, **Another Level** and **Honeyz**; and indie bands **Catatonia**, **Gomez**, **Belle & Sebastian**, **theaudience**, **Embrace** and **Puressence**. **Roni Size** and Reprazent took drum'n'bass into a new dimension, while **Finley Quaye** fused reggae, soul and funk. Pioneer of big beat, **Fatboy Slim**, was everywhere, although the king of aliases was not exactly a newcomer, but merely Norman Cook in a new guise.

Comebacks

1998 was the year of comebacks, with a veritable invasion of the charts by older acts and blasts from the past. At the age of 52 **Cher** became the oldest solo female artist to score a No 1 single, and stayed there for seven weeks with the best-selling record of 1998, 'Believe'. In February, 1999, **Blondie** had their first No 1 since 1980 with 'Maria', and 53-year-old singer Deborah Harry found her star status restored to its former glory. The return of 1980s acts to the limelight reached its zenith in November, 1998, when the top four chart positions were held by **Cher**, **George Michael**, **U2** and **Culture Club** – with an average age of 40, they became the oldest top four acts ever. **Duran Duran** hosted a sell-out concert at Wembley Arena, and The Big Rewind Tour brought together **ABC**, **The Human League** and Culture Club. There were also a flurry of *Best of* compilations for eighties acts such as **The Style Council**, **Phil Collins** and **OMD**; new material from **UB40**, **Ringo Starr** and **Cliff Richard**; and recovered material from **John Lennon** and **Bruce Springsteen**. Even **Elvis** managed a comeback with a virtual concert projected onto giant screens at Wembley Arena. Elsewhere, **Iron Maiden** and **Echo and the Bunnymen** were back in town, and rumours circulated that the **Stone Roses** might be revived. Shaun Ryder brought the **Happy Mondays** together again, and Jason Nevin's remix of 'It's Like That' started the ball re-rolling for **Run-DMC**.

Massive Attack: rumoured split

Splits

Northern pop-punkers **Kenickie** split up in style when they announced their demise at a shambolic final gig at London's LA2 in October, 1998. The band blamed record company pressures – most likely a result of poor album and single sales. Similar pressures were behind the dissolution of indie veterans **Sleeper**, and, elsewhere, indie-pop group **Boo Radleys** called it a day after ten years together. Rumoured splits surrounded **Massive Attack**, **Elastica**, and the **Spice Girls**, but the crises were averted in the end. Some bands lost key members but resolved to soldier on: singer Kelli Dayton left the **Sneaker Pimps**; guitarist Bernard Butler moved on from **Suede**; **Geri Halliwell** took her leave from the Spice Girls; frontman The Wrekked Train (aka Dave Randall) walked out on the **Lo-Fidelity All-Stars**; Kéllé Bryan split from **Eternal**; songwriter and co-producer Billy Reeves got fed up with **theaudience**; and Nicole Appleton left and returned to **All Saints** after a sensational bust-up. Other musicians took time out from their bands for solo projects, including **Graham Coxon** from Blur (who set up his own label, Transcopic Records, and put out an album, *The Sky Is Too High*), Liam Howlett from **Prodigy** (who put together his favourite records on a DJ mix album, *The Dirtchamber Sessions: Vol 1*), **Mel B** from the Spice Girls (who teamed up with Missy 'Misdemeanour' Elliott for 'I Want You Back'), and **Mel C** (who sang a duet with Bryan Adams for 'When You're Gone').

Sneaker Pimps: frontwoman Kelli Dayton left

Artists departed from their labels	
Kavana	Virgin
Dannii Minogue	MCA
Kylie Minogue	Deconstruction
OTT	Epic
Sleeper	RCA
Gorky's Zygotic Mynci	Mercury

27

News and reviews

Obituaries

Age at time of death appears in brackets

Wally Whyton (Vipers) (67) . . . . .22 Jan 1997
Billy McKenzie (Associates) (39) . . . . .23 Jan 1997
Brian Connolly (Sweet) (48) . . . . .9 Feb 1997
Michael Menson (Double Trouble) (29) . . . . .13 Feb 1997
Notorious B.I.G. (24) . . . . .9 Mar 1997
Harold Melvin (Bluenotes) (57) . . . . .24 Mar 1997
Jeff Buckley (30) . . . . .4 Jun 1997
John Denver (53) . . . . .12 Oct 1997
Michael Hutchence (INXS) (37) . . . . .22 Nov 1997
Floyd Cramer (64) . . . . .31 Dec 1997
Sonny Bono (62) . . . . .5 Jan 1998
Carl Perkins (65) . . . . .19 Jan 1998
Carl Wilson (51) . . . . .6 Feb 1998
Falco (40) . . . . .7 Feb 1998
Judge Dread (53) . . . . .13 Mar 1998
Rob Pilatus (Milli Vanilli) (32) . . . . .3 Apr 1998
Cozy Powell (50) . . . . .5 Apr 1998
Tammy Wynette (55) . . . . .6 Apr 1998
Wendy O Williams (The Plasmatics) (48) . . . . .6 Apr 1998
Dorothy Squires (83) . . . . .14 Apr 1998
Linda McCartney (55) . . . . .17 Apr 1998
Frank Sinatra (82) . . . . .14 May 1998
Tony De Vit (40) . . . . .2 Jul 1998
Karl Denver (67) . . . . .25 Dec 1998
Johnny Moore (Drifters) (64) . . . . .30 Dec 1998
David McComb (Triffids) (37) . . . . .2 Feb 1999
Gwen Guthrie (48) . . . . .3 Feb 1999
Dusty Springfield (59) . . . . .2 Mar 1999

Collaborations

1998 was the year of weird and wonderful collaborations, with artists using samples and fusing genres in ways not done before. Leading the way were US R&B and rap stars, who collaborated with just about everybody including each other. **Busta Rhymes** invited **Ozzy Ozbourne** to play on his new album, **Puff Daddy** used the legendary **Jimmy Page** for 'Come With Me', and **Wu-Tang Clan** revamped 'Say What You Want' for **Texas**. Divas **Mariah Carey** and **Whitney Houston** laid to rest rumours of rivalry by teaming up, **Brandy** and **Monica** played up their competition and **Mel B** worked with **Missy 'Misdemeanour' Elliott**. Other power unions included **Celine Dion** with the **Bee Gees**, and **Elton John** with **LeAnn Rimes**, while **Space** and **Cerys** from Catatonia gave us a peculiarly British duet with 'The Ballad of Tom Jones'. One to watch out for in 1999 is a rumoured collaboration between **Björk** and **The Artist Formerly Known As Prince**. A virtual form of collaboration, sampling turned out many inspired re-interpretations of old genres and tunes in 1998: **Pras Michel** reworked Dolly Parton and Kenny Rogers' old country classic 'Islands in the Stream' for 'Ghetto Supastar That Is What You Are', **Jay-Z** sampled the musical *Annie* for 'Hard Knock Life', **Puff Daddy** took on The Police's 'Every Breath You Take' for a tribute to Notorious B.I.G., and **Busta Rhymes** lifted the theme from TV series *Knight Rider* for 'Fire It Up'. However, many observers felt that the sampling mania went too far, resulting in not only lazy musicianship, but also cases of blatant bootlegging.

Mel B and Missy Elliot: collaborations

Scandal

In the bad behaviour stakes there were plenty of candidates for the No 1 rock'n'roll scandal. Guns'n'Roses frontman **Axl Rose** was charged with disorderly conduct at an airport, **Ian Brown** was jailed for threatening to cut off an air stewardess's hands, and **Mark Morrison** served time when charged with possession of a weapon. **Marilyn Manson** faced charges for the alleged assault of a journalist, as well as damage to a hotel room. In November, 1998, **Coolio** made two court appearances in different countries in the same week for charges including theft, assault, carrying a concealed weapon, being an unlicensed driver and possession of marijuana. Wu-Tang Clan's **Ol' Dirty Bastard** spent much of 1998 in and out of court because of his threats against his ex-girlfriend, and The Fall's **Mark E Smith** was charged with assault of his girlfriend. **George Michael** had to do community service after being charged with "lewd behaviour" in a Los Angeles toilet in April 1998, but cleverly and humorously integrated the whole experience into his new song, 'Outside'. Meanwhile, **Liam Gallagher** maintained his bad boy image with assault charges in Australia, a life ban from using Cathay Pacific Airlines for unruly behaviour, and fisticuffs with a press photographer in London.

George Michael: scandal

Pop stars and politics

Taking the most direct action on the political front was Chumbawamba's **Danbert Nobacon**, who threw a bucket of water over politician John Prescott's table at the 1998 BRIT Awards. **Bono** picked up the political torch at the 1999 BRITs when he officially unveiled Jubilee 2000, a campaign to abolish Third World debts by the year 2000. Elsewhere, Pulp's **Jarvis Cocker** and Creation Records boss **Alan McGee** spoke out against what Labour's 'New Deal' meant for musicians on the dole, and Manic Street Preachers' **Nicky Wire** offered to take the place of disgraced Welsh Foreign Secretary Ron Davies. **Drugstore** protested against the release of Chilean dictator General Pinochet, and ex-Spice Girl **Geri Halliwell** took up a new job as United Nations goodwill ambassador. **Noel Gallagher**, **The Boo Radleys** and **Ocean Colour Scene** joined Who legend **Pete Townshend** at a fundraiser for Liverpool dockers, while **Placebo**, **Ash**, **Stereophonics**, **Space**, **James**, **Bernard Butler** and **Jools Holland** lent their support to Greenpeace.

Pop wars

Public slanging matches broke out between Nicole Appleton from **All Saints** and Sophie Ellis-Bextor from **theaudience** after the latter insulted the former's fiancé, Robbie Williams. A dispute also occurred between All Saints and the **Spice Girls** about the merits of each band. Meanwhile, the **Beastie Boys** and **Prodigy** went to war over which band's lyrics were the most misogynstic, after the Beastie Boys asked Prodigy to drop 'Smack My Bitch Up' from their Reading Festival set.

Romance

Nicole Appleton (All Saints) and **Robbie Williams**' fiery on-off relationship fed the tabloids' hunger for celebrity dramas, as did **Natalie Appleton**'s troubles with **Jamie Theakston** (TV presenter). Other romances included **Zoë Ball** (Radio 1 DJ) and **Norman Cook** (Fatboy Slim), **Saffron** (Republica) and **Fast** (Fun Lovin' Criminals), **Gwen Stefani** (No Doubt) and **Gavin Rossdale** (Bush), and **Leeroy Thornfield** (Prodigy) and **Sara Cox** (TV presenter). **Mel B** (Spice Girls), **Louise** and **Ronan Keating** (Boyzone) each got married, as did **Shane Lynch** (Boyzone) to **Easther Bennett** (Eternal). Splits that rocked the rock world were **Justine Frischmann** (Elastica) and **Damon Albarn** (Blur), **Mick Jagger** and **Jerry Hall**, and **Rod Stewart** and **Rachel Hunter**. Liam Gallagher and **Patsy Kensit** were on and off, and **Noel Gallagher**'s PR wife **Meg Matthews** was rarely out of the limelight.

theaudience: pop wars

Pop stars and the movies

Increasingly, pop stars were making serious forays into the world of cinema. Glam-rock tribute *Velvet Goldmine* boasted **Placebo**, while **Shaun Ryder** and **Edwyn Collins** made their debuts as gangsters in *The Avengers* and *Media Darlings* respectively, and **Henry Rollins** played a convict in *Morgan's Ferry*. **Baby Spice** landed the lead in *Sleeping Beauty*, while **Posh Spice** was lined up as one of the next James Bond girls. In the band biopic league, 1997's *Spiceworld: The Movie* made a big impact at the box office, while Radiohead's *Meeting People Is Easy* made a quieter entrance in 1998. Documentaries in the making include a short film about singer/songwriter Elliot Smith, and *Boyzone: The Movie*. Wim Wenders will be directing *The Million Dollar Hotel*, a film based on a story written by U2's **Bono**, and **All Saints**' Nicole Appleton is to star in *Saving Grace*, directed by Mick Jagger and shot in Cornwall. Meanwhile, all of All Saints, bar Shaznay Lewis, were cast in the lead roles of former Eurythmic **Dave Stewart**'s new film, *Honest*. Pulp's **Jarvis Cocker** displayed serious directing ambition, **Marilyn Manson** worked on ideas for his own film, and **Courtney Love** shot *The Man on the Moon* alongside actor Jim Carrey. Norwegian playwright Dean Testerman wrote a play based around **Radiohead** lyrics, while the brother of **Manic Street Preachers**' bassist Nicky Wire incorporated Manics' lyrics into his play *Everything Must Go*. **Goldie** chose to tread the boards in London's West End alongside actor Andrew McCarthy in *Volunteer Man* and also played a gangster in *Everybody Loves the Sunshine*. Other DJ debuts included cameos from **Carl Cox** and **Tony De Vit** in *Human Traffic*, **Andrew Weatherall** in *Hard Men*, and **Dave Pearce** on TV soap *Brookside*.

> **Banned videos**
> *Satan* (1997) . . . . .Orbital
> *Smack My Bitch Up* (1997) . . . . .Prodigy
> *Alarm Call* (1998) . . . . .Björk
> *Rabbit in Your Headlights* (1998) . .UNKLE
> *My Favourite Game* (1998) . .The Cardigans

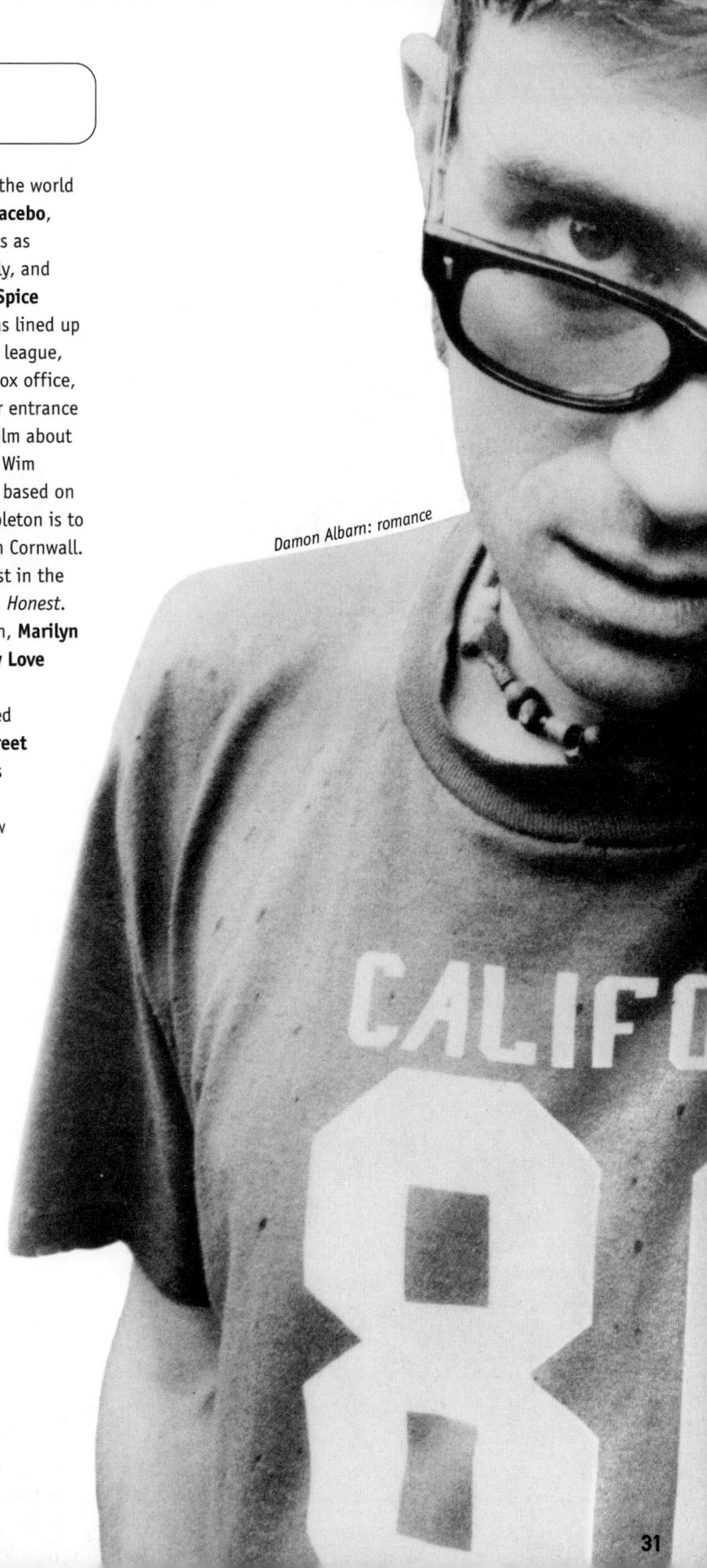

Damon Albarn: romance

What: *I Believe* 5
Who: Frankie Laine
When: 1953 (1)
Which: Spent a record 18 (non-consecutive) weeks at the top of the UK chart. The semi-religious ballad, which was composed for Jane Froman, returned to No 1 in 1995 with a recording by Robson and Jerome

What: *You're the One That I Want* 6
Who: John Travolta and Olivia Newton-John
When: 1978 (1), 1998 (4)
Which: Appeared in the classic film *Grease*. This transatlantic No 1 returned to the pinnacle 20 years after debuting, and was also heavily featured in the 1990 Top 5 hit *Grease Megamix*

What: *Albatross* 7
Who: Fleetwood Mac
When: 1969 (1), 1973 (2)
Which: Is the biggest-selling instrumental chart hit, and almost became the first record to reach No 1 twice. Despite the group's enormous US popularity, this hypnotic gem surprisingly never made the Top 100 there

What: *Sailing* 8
Who: Rod Stewart
When: 1975 (1), 1976 (3), 1987 (41)
Which: Became a football-terrace favourite and this popular performer's anthem. Its quick return to the UK Top 3 in 1976 was due to its inclusion in the successful BBC TV series *Sailor*

2 - Records

Points system: The following listings (except for the 'most weeks' charts) are calculated via a computer-generated points system. A single receives 6 points for every week spent in the Top 20, and 12 points for every week spent in the Top 10. Every week's No 1 gets a further 20 points, every week's No 2 gets 19 points, and so on down to each week's No 20, which receives one extra point. Peak bonus points are given for singles that peak in the Top 20 (1000 for a No 1, 850 for a No 2, 800 for a No 3, 750 for a No 4, right down to 200 for a No 20 peak). A further 10 points are given for every week a single spends at No 1. If there are any ties, singles are listed in order of: highest peak position, most weeks at No 1 (if applicable), then most weeks in the Top 10, Top 20 and Top 75. The system is weighted in favour of hits that spent a long time at the top end of the chart (in one or more runs), and allows for the fact that fewer sales were needed to reach No 1 in early years.

Collaborations: When two or more artists combine for a hit, such as Elton John and George Michael, each receives the total points for the record concerned, whereas recognised duos, such as Simon and Garfunkel, are counted as a separate act, and their points are listed independently from any hits that the members may also have as solo artists.

Ties: Where acts have tied for a position in a top ten or top twenty listing, subsequent positions are omitted to accommodate the tie.

Credits: If an act or a member of an act has had hits under an alternative name, the additional credit appears in brackets but is *not* counted in the overall total for that act. Thus, in 'Most number one hits' on page 38, Freddie Mercury's solo hit is listed but not counted in the total number of hits for Queen.

See also 'How to Use This Book' (pp 6–7)

Contents:

Madonna: Most successful female artist

Top 100 singles of all time

Our Top 100 Singles of all time are listed here and are also profiled with illustrations throughout the book, starting at No 1 on page 8 and finishing at No 100 on page 436

1 ROCK AROUND THE CLOCK Bill Haley and His Comets
2 BOHEMIAN RHAPSODY Queen
3 RELAX Frankie Goes to Hollywood
4 YOU'VE LOST THAT LOVIN' FEELIN' Righteous Brothers
5 I BELIEVE Frankie Laine
6 YOU'RE THE ONE THAT I WANT
     John Travolta and Olivia Newton-John
7 ALBATROSS Fleetwood Mac
8 SAILING Rod Stewart
9 TAKE MY BREATH AWAY Berlin
10 (EVERYTHING I DO) I DO IT FOR YOU Bryan Adams
11 BLUE MONDAY 1988 New Order
12 YOUNG GIRL Union Gap featuring Gary Puckett
13 DO THEY KNOW IT'S CHRISTMAS Band Aid
14 HE AIN'T HEAVY, HE'S MY BROTHER Hollies
15 LOVE IS ALL AROUND Wet Wet Wet
16 HOLIDAY Madonna
17 I WILL SURVIVE Gloria Gaynor
18 YOU SEXY THING Hot Chocolate
19 SHE LOVES YOU Beatles
20 REET PETITE Jackie Wilson
21 IMAGINE John Lennon
22 YOU TO ME ARE EVERYTHING Real Thing
23 SPACE ODDITY David Bowie
24 TAINTED LOVE Soft Cell
25 ALL RIGHT NOW Free
26 SECRET LOVE Doris Day
27 CARS Gary Numan
28 I HEARD IT THROUGH THE GRAPEVINE Marvin Gaye
29 TWO TRIBES Frankie Goes to Hollywood
30 RIVERS OF BABYLON/BROWN GIRL IN THE RING Boney M

31 YOUNG AT HEART Bluebells
32 THINK TWICE Celine Dion
33 CRAZY FOR YOU Madonna
34 TEARS Ken Dodd
35 I WILL ALWAYS LOVE YOU Whitney Houston
36 I FEEL LOVE Donna Summer
37 A WHITER SHADE OF PALE Procol Harum
38 LET'S TWIST AGAIN Chubby Checker
39 LEADER OF THE PACK Shangri-Las
40 WHEN A MAN LOVES A WOMAN Percy Sledge
41 WHEN I FALL IN LOVE Nat 'King' Cole
42 CARA MIA David Whitfield
43 THE LAST WALTZ Engelbert Humperdinck
44 REACH OUT I'LL BE THERE Four Tops
45 Y.M.C.A. Village People
46 UNCHAINED MELODY Righteous Brothers
47 HEY JUDE Beatles
48 SUGAR SUGAR Archies
49 TEMPTATION Heaven 17
50 GOOD VIBRATIONS Beach Boys
51 DANCING QUEEN Abba
52 I'LL DO ANYTHING FOR LOVE (BUT I WON'T DO THAT)
     Meat Loaf
53 CHAIN REACTION Diana Ross
54 IN THE AIR TONIGHT Phil Collins
55 IT'S NOT UNUSUAL Tom Jones
56 THE POWER OF LOVE Frankie Goes to Hollywood
57 OH MEIN PAPA Eddie Calvert
58 LAST CHRISTMAS/EVERYTHING SHE WANTS Wham!
59 BABY LOVE Supremes
60 ISRAELITES Desmond Dekker and the Aces

Shakespears Sister: #62

Top 50 artists of all time

All EPs, double singles and records that appeared in the chart as double-sided hits have been treated as standard singles and allocated points accordingly

Cliff Richard: Top 50 #1

1	Cliff Richard	**21**	Hollies
2	Elvis Presley	**22**	Shadows
3	Madonna	**23**	U2
4	Michael Jackson	**24**	Tom Jones
5	Beatles	**25**	Lonnie Donegan
6	Rod Stewart	**26**	Shakin' Stevens
7	Queen	**27**	UB40
8	Elton John	**28**	Diana Ross
9	David Bowie	**29**	Erasure
10	Paul McCartney	**30**	Everly Brothers
11	Rolling Stones	**31**	Madness
12	Status Quo	**32**	Prince
13	Abba	**33**	Frank Sinatra
14	Bee Gees	**34**	Whitney Houston
15	Stevie Wonder	**35**	Perry Como
16	Kylie Minogue	**36**	Take That
17	Frankie Laine	**37**	Roy Orbison
18	George Michael	**38**	Supremes
19	Pet Shop Boys	**39**	Kinks
20	Slade	**40**	T Rex
		41	Phil Collins
		42	Wet Wet Wet
		43	Pat Boone
		44	Manfred Mann
		45	Hot Chocolate
		46	Electric Light Orchestra
		47	Janet Jackson
		48	Duran Duran
		49	Beach Boys
		50	Celine Dion

Most hit singles (by artist)

Double-sided hits, double singles, EPs and albums only count as one hit each time. Re-issues and re-entries do not count as new hits, nor do re-mixes if the same vocal track is used. If the named act on the label has not gone into the studio (or onto the stage) to make a new record, then there is no new hit. (Additional act hits under other credits are listed in brackets)

1 Cliff Richard 120
2 Elvis Presley 112
3 Elton John 73
4 David Bowie 60
5 Diana Ross (+ 18 with Supremes
    and 2 with Supremes and
    Temptations) 58
6 Rod Stewart (+ 5 with the Faces,
    1 with Python Lee Jackson and
    1 with Glass Tiger) 57
7 Stevie Wonder 53
8 Status Quo 52
9 Paul McCartney/Wings 50
10 Michael Jackson 49
11 Queen 49
12 Madonna 47
13 Rolling 46
14 Prince 45
15 UB40 44
16 Bee Gees 37
17 Shakin' Stevens 37
18 Donna Summer 37
19 Frank Sinatra 36
20 Depeche Mode 35

Elvis Presley: Most hits #2

Most number one hits (by artist)

Beatles (Paul McCartney + 4 solo, John Lennon + 3 solo and George Harrison + 1 solo) **17**	Shadows (+ 7 with Cliff Richard. Hank Marvin + 1 with Cliff Richard and the Young Ones) **5**
Elvis Presley **17**	Boyzone **4**
Cliff Richard **13**	Jason Donovan **4**
Abba **9**	Everly Brothers **4**
Madonna **8**	Whitney Houston **4**
Rolling Stones (Mick Jagger + 1 with David Bowie) **8**	Frank Ifield **4**
Spice Girls (Melanie B + 1 with Missy Elliott) **8**	Jam **4**
Take That (Gary Barlow + 2 solo and Robbie Williams + 1 solo) **8**	Elton John **4**
Michael Jackson (+ 1 with Jacksons) **7**	Frankie Laine **4**
George Michael (+ 4 with Wham) **7**	Paul McCartney (+ 17 with Beatles) **4**
Slade **6**	Kylie Minogue **4**
Rod Stewart **6**	Guy Mitchell **4**
Bee Gees **5**	Oasis **4**
Blondie **5**	Pet Shop Boys **4**
David Bowie **5**	Shakin' Stevens **4**
Police **5**	T Rex **4**
Queen (Freddie Mercury + 1 solo) **5**	Wham! (George Michael + 7 solo) **4**

Most weeks at number one (by artist)

Elvis Presley **73**	Rolling Stones (Mick Jagger + 1 with David Bowie) **18**
Beatles (Paul McCartney + 17 solo, John Lennon + 7 solo) **69**	Rod Stewart **18**
Cliff Richard **44**	Frank Ifield **17**
Frankie Laine **32**	Paul McCartney **17**
Abba **31**	George Michael **17**
Wet Wet Wet **23**	Bryan Adams **16**
Spice Girls (Melanie B + 1 with Missy Elliott) **21**	Whitney Houston **16**
Take That (Gary Barlow + 2 solo and Robbie Williams + 1 solo) **21**	Elton John **16**
Queen (Freddie Mercury + 2 solo) **20**	Shadows **16**
Slade **20**	T Rex **16**
Everly Brothers **19**	John Travolta and Olivia Newton-John (Olivia Newton-John + 2 with Electric Light Orchestra) **16**
Madonna **19**	

Most weeks at number one (by an artist in one calendar year)

1953	Frankie Laine **27**	1984	Frankie Goes to Hollywood **15**
1961	Elvis Presley **18**	1994	Wet Wet Wet **15**
1991	Bryan Adams **16**	1958	Connie Francis **12**
1963	Beatles **16**	1962	Frank Ifield **12**
1978	John Travolta and Olivia Newton-John **16**	1964	Beatles **12**
1962	Elvis Presley **15**	1976	ABBA **12**

Most weeks at number one (by one disc)

I BELIEVE Frankie Lane (1953 – two chart runs)	18	**CARA MIA** David Whitfield (1954)	10
(EVERYTHING I DO) I DO IT FOR YOU Bryan Adams (1991)	16	**I WILL ALWAYS LOVE YOU** Whitney Houston (1993–94)	10
LOVE IS ALL AROUND Wet Wet Wet (1994)	15	**HERE IN MY HEART** Al Martino (1952–53)	9
BOHEMIAN RHAPSODY Queen (1975–76 and 1991–92)	14	**OH MEIN PAPA** Eddie Calvert (1954)	9
ROSE MARIE Slim Whitman (1955)	11	**SECRET LOVE** Doris Day (1954)	9

Most weeks at number one (by one song)

I BELIEVE (two versions)	22	**MARY'S BOY CHILD** (two versions)	11
(EVERYTHING I DO) I DO IT FOR YOU (one version)	16	**ROSE MARIE** (one version)	11
LOVE IS ALL AROUND (one version)	15	**YOUNG LOVE** (two versions)	11
BOHEMIAN RHAPSODY (one version)	14	**ANSWER ME** (two versions)	10
UNCHAINED MELODY (three versions)	14	**CARA MIA** (one version)	10

Most number one hits (in a year)

Only twelve acts have amassed three or more chart-toppers in a calendar year

1953	I BELIEVE, HEY JOE, ANSWER ME	Frankie Lane
1961	ARE YOU LONESOME TONIGHT, WOODEN HEART, LITTLE SISTER/HIS LATEST FLAME, SURRENDER	Elvis Presley
1962	ROCK-A-HULA BABY/CAN'T HELP FALLING IN LOVE, GOOD LUCK CHARM, SHE'S NOT YOU, RETURN TO SENDER	Elvis Presley
1963	FROM ME TO YOU, SHE LOVES YOU, I WANT TO HOLD YOUR HAND	Beatles
1964	CAN'T BUY ME LOVE, A HARD DAY'S NIGHT, I FEEL FINE	Beatles
1965	TICKET TO RIDE, HELP!, DAY TRIPPER/ WE CAN WORK IT OUT	Beatles
1973	CUM ON FEEL THE NOIZE, SKWEEZE ME PLEEZE ME, MERRY XMAS EVERYBODY	Slade
1976	MAMMA MIA, FERNANDO, DANCING QUEEN	ABBA
1980	ATOMIC, CALL ME, THE TIDE IS HIGH	Blondie
1984	RELAX, TWO TRIBES, THE POWER OF LOVE	Frankie Goes to Hollywood
1989	ESPECIALLY FOR YOU, TOO MANY BROKEN HEARTS, SEALED WITH A KISS	Jason Donovan
1989	SWING THE MOOD, THAT'S WHAT I LIKE, LET'S PARTY	Jive Bunny and the Mastermixers
1993	PRAY, RELIGHT MY FIRE, BABE	Take That
1996	WANNABE, SAY YOU'LL BE THERE, 2 BECOME 1	Spice Girls
1997	MAMA/WHO DO YOU THINK YOU ARE, TOO MUCH, SPICE UP YOUR LIFE	Spice Girls
1998	NEVER EVER, UNDER THE BRIDGE/ LADY MARMALADE, BOOTIE CALL	All Saints

George Michael: see Most number one hits (by artist), Most weeks at number one (by artist)

Singles entering at number one

Chemical Brothers: 1996

14 Nov 1952	**HERE IN MY HEART**	. . . . Al Martino
24 Jan 1958	**JAILHOUSE ROCK**	. . . . Elvis Presley
4 Nov 1960	**IT'S NOW OR NEVER**	. . . . Elvis Presley
1 Jun 1961	**SURRENDER**	. . . . Elvis Presley
12 Jan 1962	**THE YOUNG ONES**	. . . . Cliff Richard
26 Apr 1969	**GET BACK**	. . . . Beatles and Billy Preston
3 Mar 1973	**CUM ON FEEL THE NOIZE**	. . . . Slade
30 Jun 1973	**SKWEEZE ME PLEEZE ME**	. . . . Slade
17 Nov 1973	**I LOVE YOU LOVE ME LOVE**	. . . . Gary Glitter
15 Dec 1973	**MERRY XMAS EVERYBODY**	. . . . Slade
22 Mar 1980	**GOING UNDERGROUND**	. . . . Jam
27 Sep 1980	**DON'T STAND SO CLOSE TO ME**	. . . . Police
9 May 1981	**STAND AND DELIVER**	. . . . Adam and The Ants
13 Feb 1982	**TOWN CALLED MALICE/PRECIOUS**	. . . . . . Jam
4 Dec 1982	**BEAT SURRENDER**	. . . . Jam
26 Mar 1983	**IS THERE SOMETHING I SHOULD KNOW**	
		. . . . Duran Duran
16 Jun 1984	**TWO TRIBES**	. . . . Frankie Goes to Hollywood
15 Dec 1984	**DO THEY KNOW IT'S CHRISTMAS?**	. . . . Band Aid
7 Sep 1985	**DANCING IN THE STREET**	. . . .
		. . . . .David Bowie and Mick Jagger
4 Apr 1987	**LET IT BE**	. . . . Ferry Aid
20 May 1989	**FERRY 'CROSS THE MERSEY**	. . . . . . .Marsden/
	McCartney/Johnson/Christians/Stock Aitken Waterman	
10 Jun 1989	**SEALED WITH A KISS**	. . . . Jason Donovan
16 Dec 1989	**LET'S PARTY**	. . . . . Jive Bunny and The Mastermixers
23 Dec 1989	**DO THEY KNOW IT'S CHRISTMAS?**	. . Band Aid II
5 Jan 1991	**BRING YOUR DAUGHTER TO THE SLAUGHTER**	
		. . . . Iron Maiden
26 Jan 1991	**INNUENDO**	. . . . Queen
2 Nov 1991	**THE FLY**	. . . . U2
23 Nov 1991	**BLACK OR WHITE**	. . . . Michael Jackson
7 Dec 1991	**DON'T LET THE SUN GO DOWN ON ME**	. . . . .
		. . . . George Michael/Elton John
21 Dec 1991	**BOHEMIAN RHAPSODY/THESE ARE THE**	
	DAYS OF OUR LIVES	. . . . Queen

Spice Girls: 1996/1997/1998

Singles entering at number one

(continued)

12 Oct 1996	**SETTING SUN** . . . . .Chemical Brothers		8 Feb 1997	**AIN'T NOBODY** .LL Cool J
19 Oct 1996	**WORDS** . . . . .Boyzone		15 Feb 1997	**DISCOTHEQUE** U2
26 Oct 1996	**SAY YOU'LL BE THERE** . . . . .Spice Girls		22 Feb 1997	**DON'T SPEAK** . . . . .No Doubt
9 Nov 1996	**WHAT BECOMES OF THE BROKEN HEARTED**		15 Mar 1997	**MAMA/WHO DO YOU THINK YOU ARE** . .Spice Girls
	. . . . .Robson Green and Jerome Flynn		5 Apr 1997	**BLOCK ROCKIN' BEATS** . . . . . .Chemical Brothers
23 Nov 1996	**BREATHE** . . . . .Prodigy		3 May 1997	**BLOOD ON THE DANCE FLOOR** . .Michael Jackson
7 Dec 1996	**I FEEL YOU** .Peter André		10 May 1997	**LOVE WON'T WAIT** . . . . .Gary Barlow
14 Dec 1996	**A DIFFERENT BEAT** . . . . .Boyzone		17 May 1997	**YOU'RE NOT ALONE** . . . . .Olive
21 Dec 1996	**KNOCKIN' ON HEAVEN'S DOOR/THROW**		31 May 1997	**I WANNA BE THE ONLY ONE** . . . .
	THESE GUNS AWAY . . . . .Dunblane			. . . . .Eternal Featuring Bebe Winans
28 Dec 1996	**2 BECOMES 1** . . . . .Spice Girls		7 Jun 1997	**MMMBOP** . . . . .Hanson
25 Jan 1997	**YOUR WOMAN** . . . . .White Town		28 Jun 1997	**I'LL BE MISSING YOU** . .Puff Daddy and Faith Evans
1 Feb 1997	**BEETLEBUM** . . . . .Blur		19 Jul 1997	**D'YOU KNOW WHAT I MEAN?** . . . . .Oasis

No Doubt: 1997

16 Aug 1997	**MEN IN BLACK** .Will Smith
13 Sep 1997	**THE DRUGS DON'T WORK** . . . . .Verve
20 Sep 1997	**CANDLE IN THE WIND 1997/SOMETHING ABOUT THE WAY YOU LOOK TONIGHT** . . . . .Elton John
25 Oct 1997	**SPICE UP YOUR LIFE** . . . . .Spice Girls
29 Nov 1997	**PERFECT DAY** . . . . .Various
13 Dec 1997	**TELETUBBIES SAY EH-OH!** . . . . .Teletubbies
27 Dec 1997	**TOO MUCH** . . . . .Spice Girls
24 Jan 1998	**ALL AROUND THE WORLD** . . . . .Oasis
31 Jan 1998	**YOU MAKE ME WANNA** . . . . .Usher
7 Feb 1998	**DOCTOR JONES** .Aqua
21 Feb 1998	**MY HEART WILL GO ON** . . . . .Celine Dion
28 Feb 1998	**BRIMFUL OF ASHA** . . . . .Cornershop
7 Mar 1998	**FROZEN** . . . . .Madonna
21 Mar 1998	**IT'S LIKE THAT** . . . . .Run-Dmc vs Jason Nevins
2 May 1998	**ALL THAT I NEED** . . . . .Boyzone
9 May 1998	**UNDER THE BRIDGE/LADY MARMALADE** . . . . .All Saints
16 May 1998	**TURN BACK TIME** . . . . .Aqua
6 Jun 1998	**C'EST LA VIE** .B*Witched
20 Jun 1998	**3 LIONS '98** Baddiel and Skinner and Lightning Seeds
11 Jul 1998	**BECAUSE WE WANT TO** . . . . .Billie
18 Jul 1998	**FREAK ME** . . . . .Another Level
25 Jul 1998	**DEEPER UNDERGROUND** . . . . .Jamiroquai
1 Aug 1998	**VIVA FOREVER** . . . . .Spice Girls
15 Aug 1998	**NO MATTER WHAT** . . . . .Boyzone
5 Sep 1998	**IF YOU TOLERATE THIS YOUR CHILDREN WILL BE NEXT** . . . . . . .Manic Street Preachers
12 Sep 1998	**BOOTIE CALL** . . . . .All Saints
19 Sep 1998	**MILLENNIUM** . . . . .Robbie Williams
26 Sep 1998	**I WANT YOU BACK** . .Melanie B featuring Missy Elliott
3 Oct 1998	**ROLLERCOASTER** . . . . .B*Witched
17 Oct 1998	**GIRLFRIEND** . . . . .Billie
24 Oct 1998	**GYM AND TONIC** . . . . .Spacedust
31 Oct 1998	**BELIEVE** . . . . .Cher
19 Dec 1998	**TO YOU I BELONG** . . . . .B*Witched
26 Dec 1998	**GOODBYE** . . . . .Spice Girls

Mick Hucknall (Simply Red): 1995

Records / Number ones

1950s

The number one hits for each year are listed chronologically and contain the date the hit entered chart, title of hit, artist name, number of weeks spent at No 1, and UK entry at No 1 if applicable

1952

NME publishes the first ever chart, a Top 12

14 Nov   **HERE IN MY HEART** Al Martino ■ 9

1953

16 Jan   **YOU BELONG TO ME** Jo Stafford 1
23 Jan   **COMES A-LONG A-LOVE** Kay Starr 1
30 Jan   **OUTSIDE OF HEAVEN** Eddie Fisher 1
6 Feb   **DON'T LET THE STARS GET IN YOUR EYES** Perry Como. 5
13 Mar   **SHE WEARS RED FEATHERS** Guy Mitchell. 4
10 Apr   **BROKEN WINGS** The Stargazers 1
17 Apr   **(HOW MUCH IS) THAT DOGGIE IN THE WINDOW** Lita Roza 1
24 Apr   **I BELIEVE** Frankie Laine. 9
26 Jun   **I'M WALKING BEHIND YOU** Eddie Fisher featuring
      Sally Sweetland 1
3 Jul   **BELIEVE** Frankie Laine 6
14 Aug   **MOULIN ROUGE** Mantovani 1
21 Aug   **I BELIEVE** Frankie Laine. 3
11 Sep   **LOOK AT THAT GIRL** Guy Mitchell 6
23 Oct   **HEY JOE** Frankie Laine 2
6 Nov   **ANSWER ME** David Whitfield 1
13 Nov   **ANSWER ME** Frankie Laine 8
      (**ANSWER ME** by David Whitfield returned to number one
      for one week on 11 Dec, 1953, to share the top spot with
      Frankie Laine's version)

1954

Top 20 began 1 Oct, 1954

8 Jan   **OH MEIN PAPA** Eddie Calvert 9
12 Mar   **I SEE THE MOON** Stargazers 5
16 Apr   **SECRET LOVE** Doris Day 1
23 Apr   **I SEE THE MOON** Stargazers 1
30 Apr   **SUCH A NIGHT** Johnnie Ray 1
7 May   **SECRET LOVE** Doris Day 8
2 Jul   **CARA MIA** David Whitfield with chorus,
      and Mantovani and his orchestra 10
10 Sep   **LITTLE THINGS MEAN A LOT** Kitty Kallen 1
17 Sep   **THREE COINS IN THE FOUNTAIN** Frank Sinatra. 3
8 Oct   **HOLD MY HAND** Don Cornell. 4
5 Nov   **MY SON MY SON** Vera Lynn 2
19 Nov   **HOLD MY HAND** Don Cornell 1

26 Nov   **THIS OLE HOUSE** Rosemary Clooney 1
3 Dec   **LET'S HAVE ANOTHER PARTY** Winifred Atwell 5

1955

7 Jan   **FINGER OF SUSPICION** Dickie Valentine 1
14 Jan   **MAMBO ITALIANO** Rosemary Clooney 1
21 Jan   **FINGER OF SUSPICION** Dickie Valentine 2
4 Feb   **MAMBO ITALIANO** Rosemary Clooney 2
18 Feb   **SOFTLY SOFTLY** Ruby Murray 3
11 Mar   **GIVE ME YOUR WORD** Tennessee Ernie Ford. 7
29 Apr   **CHERRY PINK AND APPLE BLOSSOM WHITE** Perez Prado. 2
13 May   **STRANGER IN PARADISE** Tony Bennett 2
27 May   **CHERRY PINK AND APPLE BLOSSOM WHITE** Eddie Calvert. . . . 4
24 Jun   **UNCHAINED MELODY** Jimmy Young 3
15 Jul   **DREAMBOAT** Alma Cogan. 2
29 Jul   **ROSE MARIE** Slim Whitman 11
14 Oct   **THE MAN FROM LARAMIE** Jimmy Young 4
11 Nov   **HERNANDOS HIDEAWAY** Johnston Brothers 2
25 Nov   **ROCK AROUND THE CLOCK** Bill Haley and His Comets 3
16 Dec   **CHRISTMAS ALPHABET** Dickie Valentine 3

1956

Top 30 began 13 April, 1956

6 Jan   **ROCK AROUND THE CLOCK** Bill Haley and His Comets 2
20 Jan   **SIXTEEN TONS** Tennessee Ernie Ford 4
17 Feb   **MEMORIES ARE MADE OF THIS** Dean Martin 4
16 Mar   **IT'S ALMOST TOMORROW** Dreamweavers. 2
30 Mar   **ROCK AND ROLL WALTZ** Kay Starr with
      the Hugo Winterhalter Orchestra 1
6 Apr   **IT'S ALMOST TOMORROW** Dreamweavers 1
13 Apr   **POOR PEOPLE OF PARIS** Winifred Atwell 3
4 May   **NO OTHER LOVE** Ronnie Hilton 6
15 Jun   **I'LL BE HOME** Pat Boone 5
20 Jul   **WHY DO FOOLS FALL IN LOVE**
      Teenagers featuring Frankie Lymon 3
10 Aug   **WHATEVER WILL BE WILL BE** Doris Day 6
21 Sep   **LAY DOWN YOUR ARMS** Anne Shelton 4
19 Oct   **A WOMAN IN LOVE** Frankie Laine 4
16 Nov   **JUST WALKIN' IN THE RAIN** Johnnie Ray 7

1957

4 Jan   **SINGING THE BLUES** Guy Mitchell 1
11 Jan   **SINGING THE BLUES** Tommy Steele and the Steelmen 1
18 Jan   **SINGING THE BLUES** Guy Mitchell 1
25 Jan   **THE GARDEN OF EDEN** Frankie Vaughan. 4
      (**SINGING THE BLUES** by Guy Mitchell returned to
      number one week to share the top spot with
      GARDEN OF EDEN by Frankie Vaughan on 1 Feb, 1957)
22 Feb   **YOUNG LOVE** Tab Hunter 7
12 Apr   **CUMBERLAND GAP** Lonnie Donegan 5
17 May   **ROCK-A-BILLY** Guy Mitchell 1
24 May   **BUTTERFLY** Andy Williams 2
7 Jun   **YES TONIGHT JOSEPHINE** Johnnie Ray 3
28 Jun   **GAMBLIN' MAN/PUTTING ON THE STYLE**
      Lonnie Donegan. 2
12 Jul   **ALL SHOOK UP** Elvis Presley. 7

UK entry at No 1 ■

1958

1959

Doris Day: 1954 / 1956

1960s

1960

Change from NME chart to record retailer: Top 50 began 10 Mar, 1960

29 Jan	**STARRY EYED** Michael Holliday	1
5 Feb	**WHY** Anthony Newley	4
10 Mar	**POOR ME** Adam Faith	1
17 Mar	**RUNNING BEAR** Johnny Preston	2
31 Mar	**MY OLD MAN'S A DUSTMAN** Lonnie Donegan	4
28 Apr	**DO YOU MIND** Anthony Newley	1
5 May	**CATHY'S CLOWN** Everly Brothers	7
23 Jun	**THREE STEPS TO HEAVEN** Eddie Cochran	2
7 Jul	**GOOD TIMIN'** Jimmy Jones	3
28 Jul	**PLEASE DON'T TEASE** Cliff Richard and the Shadows	2
4 Aug	**SHAKIN' ALL OVER** Johnny Kidd and the Pirates	1
11 Aug	**PLEASE DON'T TEASE** Cliff Richard and the Shadows	2
25 Aug	**APACHE** Shadows	5
29 Sep	**TELL LAURA I LOVE HER** Ricky Valance	3
20 Oct	**ONLY THE LONELY** Roy Orbison	2
3 Nov	**IT'S NOW OR NEVER** Elvis Presley ■	8
29 Dec	**I LOVE YOU** Cliff Richard and the Shadows	2

1961

12 Jan	**POETRY IN MOTION** Johnny Tillotson	2
26 Jan	**ARE YOU LONESOME TONIGHT** Elvis Presley	4
23 Feb	**SAILOR** Petula Clark	1
2 Mar	**WALK RIGHT BACK/EBONY EYES** Everly Brothers	3
23 Mar	**WOODEN HEART** Elvis Presley	6
4 May	**BLUE MOON** Marcels	2
18 May	**ON THE REBOUND** Floyd Cramer	1
25 May	**YOU'RE DRIVING ME CRAZY** Temperance Seven	1
1 Jun	**SURRENDER** Elvis Presley ■	4
29 Jun	**RUNAWAY** Del Shannon	3
20 Jul	**TEMPTATION** Everly Brothers	2
3 Aug	**WELL I ASK YOU** Eden Kane	1
10 Aug	**YOU DON'T KNOW** Helen Shapiro	3
31 Aug	**JOHNNY REMEMBER ME** John Leyton	3
21 Sep	**REACH FOR THE STARS/CLIMB EV'RY MOUNTAIN** Shirley Bassey	1
28 Sep	**JOHNNY REMEBER ME** John Leyton	1
5 Oct	**KON-TIKI** Shadows	1
12 Oct	**MICHAEL** Highwaymen	1
19 Oct	**WALKIN' BACK TO HAPPINESS** Helen Shapiro	3
9 Nov	**LITTLE SISTER/HIS LATEST FLAME** Elvis Presley	4
7 Dec	**TOWER OF STRENGTH** Frankie Vaughan	3
28 Dec	**MOON RIVER** Danny Williams	2

1962

11 Jan	**THE YOUNG ONES** Cliff Richard and the Shadows ■	6
22 Feb	**ROCK-A-HULA BABY/CAN'T HELP FALLING IN LOVE** Elvis Presley	4
22 Mar	**WONDERFUL LAND** Shadows	8
17 May	**NUT ROCKER** B Bumble and the Stingers	1
24 May	**GOOD LUCK CHARM** Elvis Presley	5
28 Jun	**COME OUTSIDE** Mike Sarne with Wendy Richard	2
12 Jul	**I CAN'T STOP LOVING YOU** Ray Charles	2
26 Jul	**I REMEMBER YOU** Frank Ifield	7
13 Sep	**SHE'S NOT YOU** Elvis Presley	3
4 Oct	**TELSTAR** Tornados	5
8 Nov	**LOVESICK BLUES** Frank Ifield	5
13 Dec	**RETURN TO SENDER** Elvis Presley	3

1963

3 Jan	**THE NEXT TIME/BACHELOR BOY** Cliff Richard and the Shadows (BACHELOR BOY listed from 10 Jan, 1963, only)	3
24 Jan	**DANCE ON!** Shadows	1
31 Jan	**DIAMONDS** Jet Harris and Tony Meehan	3
21 Feb	**WAYWARD WIND** Frank Ifield	3
14 Mar	**SUMMER HOLIDAY** Cliff Richard and the Shadows	2
28 Mar	**FOOT TAPPER** Shadows	1
4 Apr	**SUMMER HOLIDAY** Cliff Richard and the Shadows	1
11 Apr	**HOW DO YOU DO IT** Gerry and the Pacemakers	3
2 May	**FROM ME TO YOU** Beatles	7
20 Jun	**I LIKE IT** Gerry and the Pacemakers	4
18 Jul	**CONFESSIN'** Frank Ifield	2
1 Aug	**(YOU'RE THE) DEVIL IN DISGUISE** Elvis Presley	1
8 Aug	**SWEETS FOR MY SWEET** Searchers	2
22 Aug	**BAD TO ME** Billy J Kramer and the Dakotas	3
12 Sep	**SHE LOVES YOU** Beatles	4
10 Oct	**DO YOU LOVE ME** Brian Poole and the Tremeloes	3
31 Oct	**YOU'LL NEVER WALK ALONE** Gerry and the Pacemakers	4
28 Nov	**SHE LOVES YOU** Beatles	2
12 Dec	**I WANT TO HOLD YOUR HAND** Beatles	5

1964

16 Jan	**GLAD ALL OVER** Dave Clark Five	2
30 Jan	**NEEDLES AND PINS** Searchers	3
20 Feb	**DIANE** Bachelors	1
27 Feb	**ANYONE WHO HAD A HEART** Cilla Black	3
19 Mar	**LITTLE CHILDREN** Billy J Kramer and the Dakotas	2
2 Apr	**CAN'T BUY ME LOVE** Beatles	3
23 Apr	**WORLD WITHOUT LOVE** Peter and Gordon	2
7 May	**DON'T THROW YOUR LOVE AWAY** Searchers	2
21 May	**JULIET** Four Pennies	1
28 May	**YOU'RE MY WORLD** Cilla Black	4
25 Jun	**IT'S OVER** Roy Orbison	2
9 Jul	**HOUSE OF THE RISING SUN** Animals	1
16 Jul	**IT'S ALL OVER NOW** Rolling Stones	1
23 Jul	**HARD DAY'S NIGHT** Beatles	3
13 Aug	**DO WAH DIDDY DIDDY** Manfred Mann	2
27 Aug	**HAVE I THE RIGHT** Honeycombs	2
10 Sep	**YOU REALLY GOT ME** Kinks	2
24 Sep	**I'M INTO SOMETHING GOOD** Herman's Hermits	2
8 Oct	**OH PRETTY WOMAN** Roy Orbison	2
22 Oct	**(THERE'S) ALWAYS SOMETHING THERE TO REMIND ME** Sandie Shaw	3
12 Nov	**OH PRETTY WOMAN** Roy Orbison	1
19 Nov	**BABY LOVE** Supremes	2
3 Dec	**LITTLE RED ROOSTER** Rolling Stones	1
10 Dec	**I FEEL FINE** Beatles	5

UK entry at No 1 ■

1965

Date	Title	Artist	Weeks
14 Jan	**YEH YEH** Georgie Fame and the Blue Flames		2
28 Jan	**GO NOW** Moody Blues		1
4 Feb	**YOU'VE LOST THAT LOVIN' FEELIN'** Righteous Brothers		2
18 Feb	**TIRED OF WAITING FOR YOU** Kinks		1
25 Feb	**I'LL NEVER FIND ANOTHER YOU** Seekers		2
11 Mar	**IT'S NOT UNUSUAL** Tom Jones		1
18 Mar	**THE LAST TIME** Rolling Stones		3
8 Apr	**CONCRETE AND CLAY** Unit Four Plus Two		1
15 Apr	**THE MINUTE YOU'RE GONE** Cliff Richard		1
22 Apr	**TICKET TO RIDE** Beatles		3
13 May	**KING OF THE ROAD** Roger Miller		1
20 May	**WHERE ARE YOU NOW (MY LOVE)** Jackie Trent		1
27 May	**LONG LIVE LOVE** Sandie Shaw		3
17 Jun	**CRYING IN THE CHAPEL** Elvis Presley		1
24 Jun	**I'M ALIVE** Hollies		1
1 Jul	**CRYING IN THE CHAPEL** Elvis Presley		1
8 Jul	**I'M ALIVE** Hollies		2
22 Jul	**MR TAMBOURINE MAN** Byrds		2
5 Aug	**HELP!** Beatles		3
26 Aug	**I GOT YOU BABE** Sonny and Cher		2
9 Sep	**(I CAN'T GET NO) SATISFACTION** Rolling Stones		2
23 Sep	**MAKE IT EASY ON YOURSELF** Walker Brothers		1
30 Sep	**TEARS** Ken Dodd		5
4 Nov	**GET OFF OF MY CLOUD** Rolling Stones		3
25 Nov	**THE CARNIVAL IS OVER** Seekers		3
16 Dec	**DAY TRIPPER/WE CAN WORK IT OUT** Beatles		5

1966

Date	Title	Artist	Weeks
20 Jan	**KEEP ON RUNNING** Spencer Davis Group		1
27 Jan	**MICHELLE** Overlanders		3
17 Feb	**THESE BOOTS ARE MADE FOR WALKIN'** Nancy Sinatra		4
17 Mar	**THE SUN AIN'T GONNA SHINE ANYMORE** Walker Brothers		4
14 Apr	**SOMEBODY HELP ME** Spencer Davis Group		2
28 Apr	**YOU DON'T HAVE TO SAY YOU LOVE ME** Dusty Springfield		1
5 May	**PRETTY FLAMINGO** Manfred Mann		3
26 May	**PAINT IT BLACK** Rolling Stones		1
2 Jun	**STRANGERS IN THE NIGHT** Frank Sinatra		3
23 Jun	**PAPERBACK WRITER** Beatles		2
7 Jul	**SUNNY AFTERNOON** Kinks		2
21 Jul	**GET AWAY** Georgie Fame and the Blue Flames		1
28 Jul	**OUT OF TIME** Chris Farlowe and the Thunderbirds		1
4 Aug	**WITH A GIRL LIKE YOU** Troggs		2
18 Aug	**YELLOW SUBMARINE/ELEANOR RIGBY** Beatles		4
15 Sep	**ALL OR NOTHING** Small Faces		1
22 Sep	**DISTANT DRUMS** Jim Reeves		5
27 Oct	**REACH OUT I'LL BE THERE** Four Tops		3
17 Nov	**GOOD VIBRATIONS** Beach Boys		2
1 Dec	**GREEN GREEN GRASS OF HOME** Tom Jones		7

1967

Date	Title	Artist	Weeks
19 Jan	**I'M A BELIEVER** Monkees		4
16 Feb	**THIS IS MY SONG** Petula Clark		2
2 Mar	**RELEASE ME** Engelbert Humperdinck		6
13 Apr	**SOMETHING STUPID** Nancy Sinatra and Frank Sinatra		2
27 Apr	**PUPPET ON A STRING** Sandie Shaw		3
18 May	**SILENCE IS GOLDEN** Tremeloes		3
8 Jun	**WHITER SHADE OF PALE** Procol Harum		6
19 Jul	**ALL YOU NEED IS LOVE** Beatles		3
9 Aug	**SAN FRANCISCO (BE SURE TO WEAR SOME FLOWERS IN YOUR HAIR)** Scott McKenzie		4
6 Sep	**THE LAST WALTZ** Engelbert Humperdinck		5
11 Oct	**MASSACHUSETTS** Bee Gees		4
8 Nov	**BABY NOW THAT I'VE FOUND YOU** Foundations		2
22 Nov	**LET THE HEARTACHES BEGIN** Long John Baldry		2
6 Dec	**HELLO GOODBYE** Beatles		7

1968

Date	Title	Artist	Weeks
24 Jan	**BALLAD OF BONNIE AND CLYDE** Georgie Fame		1
31 Jan	**EVERLASTING LOVE** Love Affair		2
14 Feb	**MIGHTY QUINN** Manfred Mann		2
28 Feb	**CINDERELLA ROCKEFELLA** Esther and Abi Ofarim		3
20 Mar	**THE LEGEND OF XANADU** Dave Dee, Dozy, Beaky, Mick and Tich		1
27 Mar	**LADY MADONNA** Beatles		2
10 Apr	**CONGRATULATIONS** Cliff Richard		2
24 Apr	**WHAT A WONDERFUL WORLD/CABARET** Louis Armstrong		4
22 May	**YOUNG GIRL** Union Gap featuring Gary Puckett		4
19 Jun	**JUMPING JACK FLASH** Rolling Stones		2
3 Jul	**BABY COME BACK** Equals		3
24 Jul	**I PRETEND** Des O'Connor		1
31 Jul	**MONY MONY** Tommy James and the Shondells		2
14 Aug	**FIRE** Crazy World of Arthur Brown		1
21 Aug	**MONY MONY** Tommy James and the Shondells		1
28 Aug	**DO IT AGAIN** Beach Boys		1
4 Sep	**I'VE GOTTA GET A MESSAGE TO YOU** Bee Gees		1
11 Sep	**HEY JUDE** Beatles		2
25 Sep	**THOSE WERE THE DAYS** Mary Hopkin		6
6 Nov	**WITH A LITTLE HELP FROM MY FRIENDS** Joe Cocker		1
13 Nov	**THE GOOD THE BAD AND THE UGLY** Hugo Montenegro and His Orchestra and Chorus		4
11 Dec	**LILY THE PINK** Scaffold		3

1969

Date	Title	Artist	Weeks
1 Jan	**OB-LA-DI OB-LA-DA** Marmalade		1
8 Jan	**LILY THE PINK** Scaffold		1
15 Jan	**OB-LA-DI OB-LA-DA** Marmalade		2
29 Jan	**ALBATROSS** Fleetwood Mac		1
5 Feb	**BLACKBERRY WAY** Move		1
12 Feb	**(IF PARADISE IS) HALF AS NICE** Amen Corner		2
26 Feb	**WHERE DO YOU GO TO, MY LOVELY** Peter Sarstedt		4
26 Mar	**I HEARD IT THROUGH THE GRAPEVINE** Marvin Gaye		3
16 Apr	**THE ISRAELITES** Desmond Dekker and the Aces		1
23 Apr	**GET BACK** Beatles with Billy Preston ■		6
4 Jun	**DIZZY** Tommy Roe		1
11 Jun	**THE BALLAD OF JOHN AND YOKO** Beatles		3
2 Jul	**SOMETHING IN THE AIR** Thunderclap Newman		3
23 Jul	**HONKY TONK WOMEN** Rolling Stones		5
30 Aug	**IN THE YEAR 2525 (EXORDIUM AND TERMINUS)** Zager and Evans		3
20 Sep	**BAD MOON RISING** Creedence Clearwater Revival		3
11 Oct	**JE T'AIME…MOI NON PLUS** Jane Birkin and Serge Gainsbourg		1
18 Oct	**I'LL NEVER FALL IN LOVE AGAIN** Bobbie Gentry		1
25 Oct	**SUGAR SUGAR** Archies		8
20 Dec	**TWO LITTLE BOYS** Rolf Harris		6

UK entry at No 1 ■

1970s

1970

31 Jan	**LOVE GROWS (WHERE MY ROSEMARY GOES)** Edison Lighthouse	5
7 Mar	**WAND'RIN' STAR** Lee Marvin	3
28 Mar	**BRIDGE OVER TROUBLED WATER** Simon and Garfunkel	3
18 Apr	**ALL KINDS OF EVERYTHING** Dana	2
2 May	**SPIRIT IN THE SKY** Norman Greenbaum	2
16 May	**BACK HOME** England World Cup Squad	3
6 Jun	**YELLOW RIVER** Christie	1
13 Jun	**IN THE SUMMERTIME** Mungo Jerry	7
1 Aug	**THE WONDER OF YOU** Elvis Presley	6
12 Sep	**TEARS OF A CLOWN** Smokey Robinson and the Miracles	1
19 Sep	**BAND OF GOLD** Freda Payne	6
31 Oct	**WOODSTOCK** Matthews' Southern Comfort	3
21 Nov	**VOODOO CHILE** Jimi Hendrix Experience	1
28 Nov	**I HEAR YOU KNOCKIN'** Dave Edmunds	6

1971

9 Jan	**GRANDAD** Clive Dunn	3
30 Jan	**MY SWEET LORD** George Harrison	5
6 Mar	**BABY JUMP** Mungo Jerry	2
20 Mar	**HOT LOVE** T Rex	6
1 May	**DOUBLE BARREL** Dave and Ansil Collins	2
15 May	**KNOCK THREE TIMES** Dawn	5
19 Jun	**CHIRPY CHIRPY CHEEP CHEEP** Middle of the Road	5
24 Jul	**GET IT ON** T Rex	4
21 Aug	**I'M STILL WAITING** Diana Ross	4
18 Sep	**HEY GIRL DON'T BOTHER ME** Tams	3
9 Oct	**MAGGIE MAY** Rod Stewart	5
13 Nov	**COZ I LUV YOU** Slade	4
11 Dec	**ERNIE (THE FASTEST MILKMAN IN THE WEST)** Benny Hill	4

1972

8 Jan	**I'D LIKE TO TEACH THE WORLD TO SING (IN PERFECT HARMONY)** New Seekers	4
5 Feb	**TELEGRAM SAM** T Rex	2
19 Feb	**SON OF MY FATHER** Chicory Tip	3
11 Mar	**WITHOUT YOU** Nilsson	5
15 Apr	**AMAZING GRACE** The Pipes and Drums and Military Band of the Royal Scots Dragoon Guards	5
20 May	**METAL GURU** T Rex	4
17 Jun	**VINCENT** Don McLean	2
1 Jul	**TAKE ME BAK 'OME** Slade	1
8 Jul	**PUPPY LOVE** Donny Osmond	5
12 Aug	**SCHOOL'S OUT** Alice Cooper	3
2 Sep	**YOU WEAR IT WELL** Rod Stewart	1
9 Sep	**MAMA WEER ALL CRAZEE NOW** Slade	3
30 Sep	**HOW CAN I BE SURE** David Cassidy	2
14 Oct	**MOULDY OLD DOUGH** Lieutenant Pigeon	4
11 Nov	**CLAIR** Gilbert O'Sullivan	2
25 Nov	**MY DING-A-LING** Chuck Berry	4
23 Dec	**LONG HAIRED LOVER FROM LIVERPOOL** Little Jimmy Osmond	5

1973

27 Jan	**BLOCKBUSTER** Sweet	5
3 Mar	**CUM ON FEEL THE NOIZE** Slade ■	4
31 Mar	**TWELFTH OF NEVER** Donny Osmond	1
7 Apr	**GET DOWN** Gilbert O'Sullivan	2
21 Apr	**TIE A YELLOW RIBBON ROUND THE OLD OAK TREE** Dawn featuring Tony Orlando	4
19 May	**SEE MY BABY JIVE** Wizzard	4
16 Jun	**CAN THE CAN** Suzi Quatro	1
23 Jun	**RUBBER BULLETS** 10cc	1
30 Jun	**SKWEEZE ME PLEEZE ME** Slade ■	3
21 Jul	**WELCOME HOME** Peters and Lee	1
28 Jul	**I'M THE LEADER OF THE GANG (I AM)** Gary Glitter	4
25 Aug	**YOUNG LOVE** Donny Osmond	4
22 Sep	**ANGEL FINGERS** Wizzard	1
29 Sep	**EYE LEVEL** Simon Park Orchestra	4
27 Oct	**DAYDREAMER/THE PUPPY SONG** David Cassidy	3
17 Nov	**I LOVE YOU LOVE ME LOVE** Gary Glitter ■	4
15 Dec	**MERRY XMAS EVERYBODY** Slade ■	5

1974

19 Jan	**YOU WON'T FIND ANOTHER FOOL LIKE ME** New Seekers	1
26 Jan	**TIGER FEET** Mud	4
23 Feb	**DEVIL GATE DRIVE** Suzi Quatro	2
9 Mar	**JEALOUS MIND** Alvin Stardust	1
16 Mar	**BILLY DON'T BE A HERO** Paper Lace	3
6 Apr	**SEASONS IN THE SUN** Terry Jacks	2
4 May	**WATERLOO** ABBA	2
18 May	**SUGAR BABY LOVE** Rubettes	4
15 Jun	**THE STREAK** Ray Stevens	1
22 Jun	**ALWAYS YOURS** Gary Glitter	1
29 Jun	**SHE** Charles Aznavour	4
27 Jul	**ROCK YOUR BABY** George McCrae	3
17 Aug	**WHEN WILL I SEE YOU AGAIN** Three Degrees	2
31 Aug	**LOVE ME FOR A REASON** Osmonds	3
21 Sep	**KUNG FU FIGHTING** Carl Douglas	3
12 Oct	**ANNIE'S SONG** John Denver	1
19 Oct	**SAD SWEET DREAMER** Sweet Sensation	1
26 Oct	**EVERYTHING I OWN** Ken Boothe	3
16 Nov	**GONNA MAKE YOU A STAR** David Essex	3
7 Dec	**YOU'RE THE FIRST THE LAST MY EVERYTHING** Barry White	2
21 Dec	**LONELY THIS CHRISTMAS** Mud	4

1975

18 Jan	**DOWN DOWN** Status Quo	1
25 Jan	**MS. GRACE** Tymes	1
1 Feb	**JANUARY** Pilot	3
22 Feb	**MAKE ME SMILE (COME UP AND SEE ME)** Steve Harley and Cockney Rebel	2
8 Mar	**IF** Telly Savalas	2
22 Mar	**BYE BYE BABY** Bay City Rollers	6

UK entry at No 1 ■

3 May	**OH BOY** Mud	.2
17 May	**STAND BY YOUR MAN** Tammy Wynette	.3
7 Jun	**WHISPERING GRASS** Windsor Davies and Don Estelle	.3
28 Jun	**I'M NOT IN LOVE** 10cc	.2
12 Jul	**TEARS ON MY PILLOW** Johnny Nash	.1
19 Jul	**GIVE A LITTLE LOVE** Bay City Rollers	.3
9 Aug	**BARBADOS** Typically Tropical	.1
16 Aug	**CAN'T GIVE YOU ANYTHING (BUT MY LOVE)** Stylistics	.3
6 Sep	**SAILING** Rod Stewart	.4
4 Oct	**HOLD ME CLOSE** David Essex	.3
25 Oct	**I ONLY HAVE EYES FOR YOU** Art Garfunkel	.2
8 Nov	**SPACE ODDITY** David Bowie	.2
22 Nov	**D.I.V.O.R.C.E.** Billy Connolly	.1
29 Nov	**BOHEMIAN RHAPSODY** Queen	.9

1976

31 Jan	**MAMMA MIA** Abba	.2
14 Feb	**FOREVER AND EVER** Slik	.1
21 Feb	**DECEMBER '63 (OH WHAT A NIGHT)** Four Seasons	.2
6 Mar	**I LOVE TO LOVE (BUT MY BABY LOVES TO DANCE)** Tina Charles	.3
27 Mar	**SAVE YOUR KISSES FOR ME** Brotherhood of Man	.6
8 May	**FERNANDO** Abba	.4
5 Jun	**NO CHARGE** J J Barrie	.1
12 Jun	**COMBINE HARVESTER (BRAND NEW KEY)** Wurzels	.2
26 Jun	**YOU TO ME ARE EVERYTHING** Real Thing	.3
17 Jul	**THE ROUSSOS PHENOMENON (EP)** Demis Roussos	.1
24 Jul	**DON'T GO BREAKING MY HEART** Elton John and Kiki Dee	.6
4 Sep	**DANCING QUEEN** Abba	.6
11 Oct	**MISSISSIPPI** Pussycat	.4
13 Nov	**IF YOU LEAVE ME NOW** Chicago	.3
4 Dec	**UNDER THE MOON OF LOVE** Showaddywaddy	.3
25 Dec	**WHEN A CHILD IS BORN (SOLEADO)** Johnny Mathis	.3

1977

15 Jan	**DON'T GIVE UP ON US** David Soul	.4
12 Feb	**DON'T CRY FOR US ARGENTINA** Julie Covington	.1
19 Feb	**WHEN I NEED YOU** Leo Sayer	.3
12 Mar	**CHANSON D'AMOUR** Manhattan Transfer	.3
2 Apr	**KNOWING ME KNOWING YOU** ABBA	.5
7 May	**FREE** Deniece Williams	.2
21 May	**I DON'T WANT TO TALK ABOUT IT / FIRST CUT IS THE DEEPEST** Rod Stewart	.4
18 Jun	**LUCILLE** Kenny Rogers	.1
25 Jun	**SHOW YOU THE WAY TO GO** Jacksons	.1
2 Jul	**SO YOU WIN AGAIN** Hot Chocolate	.3
23 Jul	**I FEEL LOVE** Donna Summer	.4
20 Aug	**ANGELO** Brotherhood of Man	.1
27 Aug	**FLOAT ON** Floaters	.1
3 Sep	**WAY DOWN** Elvis Presley	.5
8 Oct	**SILVER LADY** David Soul	.3
29 Oct	**YES SIR I CAN BOOGIE** Baccara	.1
5 Nov	**NAME OF THE GAME** ABBA	.4
3 Dec	**MULL OF KINTYRE/GIRLS' SCHOOL** Wings	.9

1978

Top 75 began 6 May, 1978

4 Feb	**UP TOWN TOP RANKING** Althia and Donna	.1
11 Feb	**FIGARO** Brotherhood of Man	.1

18 Feb	**TAKE A CHANCE ON ME** Abba	.3
11 Mar	**WUTHERING HEIGHTS** Kate Bush	.4
8 Apr	**MATCHSTALK MEN AND MATCHSTALK CATS AND DOGS** Brian and Michael	.3
29 Apr	**NIGHT FEVER** Bee Gees	.2
13 May	**RIVERS OF BABYLON** Boney M	.5
17 Jun	**YOU'RE THE ONE THAT I WANT** John Travolta and Olivia Newton-John	.9
19 Aug	**THREE TIMES A LADY** Commodores	.5
23 Sep	**DREADLOCK HOLIDAY** 10cc	.1
30 Sep	**SUMMER NIGHTS** John Travolta and Olivia Newton-John	.7
18 Nov	**RAT TRAP** Boomtown Rats	.2
2 Dec	**DA YA THINK I'M SEXY** Rod Stewart	.1
9 Dec	**MARY'S BOY CHILD/OH MY LORD** Boney M	.4

1979

6 Jan	**Y.M.C.A.** Village People	.3
27 Jan	**HIT ME WITH YOUR RHYTHM STICK** Ian and the Blockheads	.1
3 Feb	**HEART OF GLASS** Blondie	.4
3 Mar	**TRAGEDY** Bee Gees	.2
17 Mar	**I WILL SURVIVE** Gloria Gaynor	.4
14 Apr	**BRIGHT EYES** Art Garfunkel	.6
26 May	**SUNDAY GIRL** Blondie	.3
16 Jun	**RING MY BELL** Anita Ward	.2
30 Jun	**ARE 'FRIENDS' ELECTRIC?** Tubeway Army	.4
28 Jul	**I DON'T LIKE MONDAYS** Boomtown Rats	.4
25 Aug	**WE DON'T TALK ANYMORE** Cliff Richard	.4
22 Sep	**CARS** Gary Numan	.1
29 Sep	**MESSAGE IN A BOTTLE** Police	.3
20 Oct	**VIDEO KILLED THE RADIO STAR** Buggles	.1
27 Oct	**ONE DAY AT A TIME** Lena Marten	.3
17 Nov	**WHEN YOU'RE IN LOVE WITH A BEAUTIFUL WOMAN** Dr Hook	.3
8 Dec	**WALKING ON THE MOON** Police	.1
15 Dec	**ANOTHER BRICK IN THE WALL (PART II)** Pink Floyd	.5

Slade: 1971 / 1972 / 1973

1980s

1980

19 Jan	**BRASS IN POCKET** Pretenders		2
2 Feb	**THE SPECIAL AKA LIVE! (EP)** Specials		2
16 Feb	**COWARD OF THE COUNTY** Kenny Rogers		2
1 Mar	**ATOMIC** Blondie		2
15 Mar	**TOGETHER WE ARE BEAUTIFUL** Fern Kinney		1
22 Mar	**GOING UNDERGROUND/DREAMS OF CHILDREN** Jam ■		3
12 Apr	**WORKING MY WAY BACK TO YOU** Detroit Spinners		2
26 Apr	**CALL ME** Blondie		1
3 May	**GENO** Dexy's Midnight Runners		2
17 May	**WHAT'S ANOTHER YEAR** Johnny Logan		2
31 May	**THEME FROM M*A*S*H (SUICIDE IS PAINLESS)** Mash		3
21 Jun	**CRYING** Don McLean		3
12 Jul	**XANADU** Olivia Newton-John and Electric Light Orchestra		2
26 Jul	**USE IT UP AND WEAR IT OUT** Odyssey		2
9 Aug	**THE WINNER TAKES IT ALL** Abba		2
23 Aug	**ASHES TO ASHES** David Bowie		2
6 Sep	**START** Jam		1
13 Sep	**FEELS LIKE I'M IN LOVE** Kelly Marie		2
27 Sep	**DON'T STAND SO CLOSE TO ME** Police ■		4
25 Oct	**WOMAN IN LOVE** Barbra Streisand		3
15 Nov	**THE TIDE IS HIGH** Blondie		2
29 Nov	**SUPER TROUPER** Abba		3
20 Dec	**(JUST LIKE) STARTING OVER** John Lennon		1
27 Dec	**THERE'S NO-ONE QUITE LIKE GRANDMA** St Winifred's School Choir		2

1981

10 Jan	**IMAGINE** John Lennon		4
7 Feb	**WOMAN** John Lennon		2
21 Feb	**SHADDAP YOU FACE** Joe Dolce Music Theatre		3
14 Mar	**JEALOUS GUY** Roxy Music		2
28 Mar	**THIS OLEHOUSE** Shakin' Stevens		3
18 Apr	**MAKING YOUR MIND UP** Bucks Fizz		3
9 May	**STAND AND DELIVER** Adam and the Ants ■		5
13 Jun	**BEING WITH YOU** Smokey Robinson		2
27 Jun	**ONE DAY IN YOUR LIFE** Michael Jackson		2
11 Jul	**GHOST TOWN** Specials		3
1 Aug	**GREEN DOOR** Shakin' Stevens		4
29 Aug	**JAPANESE BOY** Aneka		1
5 Sep	**TAINTED LOVE** Soft Cell		2
19 Sep	**PRINCE CHARMING** Adam and the Ants		4
17 Oct	**IT'S MY PARTY** Dave Stewart and Barbara Gaskin		4
14 Nov	**EVERY LITTLE THING SHE DOES IS MAGIC** Police		1
21 Nov	**UNDER PRESSURE** Queen and David Bowie		2
5 Dec	**BEGIN THE BEGUINE (VOLVER A EMPEZAR)** Julio Iglesias		1
12 Dec	**DON'T YOU WANT ME** Human League		5

1982

16 Jan	**LAND OF MAKE BELIEVE** Bucks Fizz		2
30 Jan	**OH JULIE** Shakin' Stevens		1
6 Feb	**THE MODEL/COMPUTER LOVE** Kraftwerk		1
13 Feb	**A TOWN CALLED MALICE/PRECIOUS** Jam ■		3
6 Mar	**THE LION SLEEPS TONIGHT** Tight Fit		3
27 Mar	**SEVEN TEARS** Goombay Dance Band		3
17 Apr	**MY CAMERA NEVER LIES** Bucks Fizz		1
24 Apr	**EBONY AND IVORY** Paul McCartney with Stevie Wonder		3
15 May	**A LITTLE PEACE** Nicole		2
29 May	**HOUSE OF FUN** Madness		2
12 Jun	**GOODY TWO SHOES** Adam Ant		2
26 Jun	**I'VE NEVER BEEN TO ME** Charlene		1
3 Jul	**HAPPY TALK** Captain Sensible		2
17 Jul	**FAME** Irene Cara		3
7 Aug	**COME ON EILEEN** Dexy's Midnight Runners with Emerald Express		4
4 Sep	**EYE OF THE TIGER** Survivor		4
2 Oct	**PASS THE DUTCHIE** Musical Youth		3
23 Oct	**DO YOU REALLY WANT TO HURT ME** Culture Club		3
13 Nov	**I DON'T WANNA DANCE** Eddy Grant		3
4 Dec	**BEAT SURRENDER** Jam ■		2
18 Dec	**SAVE YOUR LOVE** Renée and Renato		4

1983

15 Jan	**YOU CAN'T HURRY LOVE** Phil Collins		2
29 Jan	**DOWN UNDER** Men at Work		3
19 Feb	**TOO SHY** Kajagoogoo		2
5 Mar	**BILLIE JEAN** Michael Jackson		1
12 Mar	**TOTAL ECLIPSE OF THE HEART** Bonnie Tyler		2
26 Mar	**IS THERE SOMETHING I SHOULD KNOW** Duran Duran ■		2
9 Apr	**LET'S DANCE** David Bowie		3
30 Apr	**TRUE** Spandau Ballet		4
28 May	**CANDY GIRL** New Edition		1
4 Jun	**EVERY BREATH YOU TAKE** Police		4
2 Jul	**BABY JANE** Rod Stewart		3
23 Jul	**WHEREVER I LAY MY HAT (THAT'S MY HOME)** Paul Young		3
13 Aug	**GIVE IT UP** KC and the Sunshine Band		3
3 Sep	**RED RED WINE** UB40		3
24 Sep	**KARMA CHAMELEON** Culture Club		6
5 Nov	**UPTOWN GIRL** Billy Joel		5
10 Dec	**ONLY YOU** Flying Pickets		5

1984

14 Jan	**PIPES OF PEACE** Paul McCartney		2
28 Jan	**RELAX** Frankie Goes to Hollywood		5
3 Mar	**99 RED BALLOONS** Nena		3
24 Mar	**HELLO** Lionel Richie		6
5 May	**THE REFLEX** Duran Duran		4
2 Jun	**WAKE ME UP BEFORE YOU GO GO** Wham!		2
16 Jun	**TWO TRIBES** Frankie Goes to Hollywood ■		9
18 Aug	**CARELESS WHISPER** George Michael		3
8 Sep	**I JUST CALLED TO SAY I LOVE YOU** Stevie Wonder		6
20 Oct	**FREEDOM** Wham!		3
10 Nov	**I FEEL FOR YOU** Chaka Khan		3
1 Dec	**I SHOULD HAVE KNOWN BETTER** Jim Diamond		1
8 Dec	**THE POWER OF LOVE** Frankie Goes to Hollywood		1
15 Dec	**DO THEY KNOW IT'S CHRISTMAS** Band Aid ■		5

UK entry at No 1 ■

1985

Date	Title / Artist	Weeks
19 Jan	I WANT TO KNOW WHAT LOVE IS Foreigner	3
9 Feb	I KNOW HIM SO WELL Elaine Paige and Barbara Dickson	4
9 Mar	YOU SPIN ME ROUND (LIKE A RECORD) Dead or Alive	2
23 Mar	EASY LOVER Philip Bailey (duet with Phil Collins)	4
20 Apr	WE ARE THE WORLD USA for Africa	2
4 May	MOVE CLOSER Phyllis Nelson	1
11 May	19 Paul Hardcastle	5
15 Jun	YOU'LL NEVER WALK ALONE Crowd	2
29 Jun	FRANKIE Sister Sledge	4
27 Jul	THERE MUST BE AN ANGEL (PLAYING WITH MY HEART) Eurythmics	1
3 Aug	INTO THE GROOVE Madonna	4
31 Aug	I GOT YOU BABE UB40, guest vocals by Chrissie Hynde	1
7 Sep	DANCING IN THE STREET David Bowie and Mick Jagger ■	4
5 Oct	IF I WAS Midge Ure	1
12 Oct	THE POWER OF LOVE Jennifer Rush	5
6 Nov	A GOOD HEART Feargal Sharkey	2
30 Nov	I'M YOUR MAN Wham!	2
14 Dec	SAVING ALL MY LOVE FOR YOU Whitney Houston	2
28 Dec	MERRY CHRISTMAS EVERYONE Shakin' Stevens	2

1986

Date	Title / Artist	Weeks
11 Jan	WEST END GIRLS Pet Shop Boys	2
25 Jan	THE SUN ALWAYS SHINES ON TV A-Ha	2
8 Feb	WHEN THE GOING GETS TOUGH, THE TOUGH GET GOING Billy Ocean	4
8 Mar	CHAIN REACTION Diana Ross	3
29 Mar	LIVING DOLL Cliff Richard and the Young Ones	3
19 Apr	A DIFFERENT CORNER George Michael	3
10 May	ROCK ME AMADEUS Falco	1
17 May	THE CHICKEN SONG Spitting Image	3
7 Jun	SPIRIT IN THE SKY Doctor and the Medics	3
28 Jun	THE EDGE OF HEAVEN Wham!	2
12 Jul	PAPA DON'T PREACH Madonna	3
2 Aug	THE LADY IN RED Chris de Burgh	3
23 Aug	I WANT TO WAKE UP WITH YOU Boris Gardiner	3
13 Sep	DON'T LEAVE ME THIS WAY Communards	4
11 Oct	TRUE BLUE Madonna	1
18 Oct	EVERY LOSER WINS Nick Berry	3
8 Nov	TAKE MY BREATH AWAY Berlin	4
6 Dec	THE FINAL COUNT DOWN Europe	2
20 Dec	CARAVAN OF LOVE Housemartins	1
27 Dec	REET PETITE Jackie Wilson	4

1987

Date	Title / Artist	Weeks
24 Jan	JACK YOUR BODY Steve 'Silk' Hurley	2
7 Feb	I KNEW YOU WERE WAITING (FOR ME) Aretha Franklin and George Michael	2
21 Feb	STAND BY ME Ben E King	3
14 Mar	EVERYTHING I OWN Boy George	2
28 Mar	RESPECTABLE Mel and Kim	1
4 Apr	LET IT BE Ferry Aid ■	3
25 Apr	LA ISLA BONITA Madonna	2
9 May	NOTHING'S GONNA STOP US NOW Starship	4
6 Jun	I WANNA DANCE WITH SOMEBODY (WHO LOVES ME) Whitney Houston	2
20 Jun	STAR TREKKIN' Firm	2
4 Jul	IT'S A SIN Pet Shop Boys	3
25 Jul	WHO'S THAT GIRL Madonna	1
1 Aug	LA BAMBA Los Lobos	2
15 Aug	I JUST CAN'T STOP LOVING YOU Michael Jackson with Siedah Garrett	2
29 Aug	NEVER GONNA GIVE YOU UP Rick Astley	5
3 Oct	PUMP UP THE VOLUME/ANITINA (THE FIRST TIME I SEE SHE DANCE) M/A/R/R/S	2
17 Oct	YOU WIN AGAIN Bee Gees	4
14 Nov	CHINA IN YOUR HAND T'Pau	5
19 Dec	ALWAYS ON MY MIND Pet Shop Boys	4

1988

Date	Title / Artist	Weeks
16 Jan	HEAVEN IS A PLACE ON EARTH Belinda Carlisle	2
30 Jan	I THINK WE'RE ALONE NOW Tiffany	3
20 Feb	I SHOULD BE SO LUCKY Kylie Minogue	5
26 Mar	DON'T TURN AROUND Aswad	2
9 Apr	HEART Pet Shop Boys	3
30 Apr	THEME FROM S EXPRESS S Express	2
14 May	PERFECT Fairground Attraction	1
21 May	WITH A LITTLE HELP FROM MY FRIENDS/SHE'S LEAVING HOME Wet Wet Wet/Billy Bragg with Cara Tivey	4
18 Jun	DOCTORIN' THE TARDIS Timelords	1
25 Jun	I OWE YOU NOTHING Bros	2
9 Jul	NOTHING'S GONNA CHANGE MY LOVE FOR YOU Glenn Medeiros	4
6 Aug	THE ONLY WAY IS UP Yazz and the Plastic Population	5
10 Sep	A GROOVY KIND OF LOVE Phil Collins	2
24 Sep	HE AIN'T HEAVY HE'S MY BROTHER Hollies	2
8 Oct	DESIRE U2	1
15 Oct	ONE MOMENT IN TIME Whitney Houston	2
29 Oct	ORINOCO FLOW Enya	3
19 Nov	FIRST TIME Robin Beck	3
10 Dec	MISTLETOE AND WINE Cliff Richard	4

1989

Date	Title / Artist	Weeks
7 Jan	ESPECIALLY FOR YOU Kylie Minogue and Jason Donovan	3
28 Jan	SOMETHING'S GOTTEN HOLD OF MY HEART Marc Almond with Gene Pitney	4
25 Feb	BELFAST CHILD Simple Minds	2
11 Mar	TOO MANY BROKEN HEARTS Jason Donovan	2
25 Mar	LIKE A PRAYER Madonna	3
15 Apr	ETERNAL FLAME Bangles	4
13 May	HAND ON YOUR HEART Kylie Minogue	1
20 May	FERRY 'CROSS THE MERSEY Christians, Holly Johnson, Paul McCartney, Gerry Marsden and Stock Aitken Waterman ■	3
10 Jun	SEALED WITH A KISS Jason Donovan ■	2
24 Jun	BACK TO LIFE (HOW EVER DO YOU WANT ME) Soul II Soul featuring Caron Wheeler	4
22 Jul	YOU'LL NEVER STOP ME LOVING YOU Sonia	2
5 Aug	SWING THE MOOD Jive Bunny and the Mastermixers	5
9 Sep	RIDE ON TIME Black Box	6
21 Oct	THAT'S WHAT I LIKE Jive Bunny and the Mastermixers	3
11 Nov	ALL AROUND THE WORLD Lisa Stansfield	2
25 Nov	YOU GOT IT (THE RIGHT STUFF) New Kids on the Block	3
16 Dec	LET'S PARTY Jive Bunny and the Mastermixers ■	1
23 Dec	DO THEY KNOW IT'S CHRISTMAS Band Aid II ■	3

UK entry at No 1 ■

1990s

1990

Date	Title	Artist	Weeks
13 Jan	**HANGIN' TOUGH** New Kids on the Block		2
27 Jan	**TEARS ON MY PILLOW** Kylie Minogue		1
3 Feb	**NOTHING COMPARES 2 U** Sinead O'Connor		4
3 Mar	**DUB BE GOOD TO ME** Beats International featuring Lindy Layton		4
31 Mar	**THE POWER** Snap		2
14 Apr	**VOGUE** Madonna		4
12 May	**KILLER** Adamski		4
9 Jun	**WORLD IN MOTION** Englandneworder		2
23 Jun	**SACRIFICE/HEALING HANDS** Elton John		5
28 Jul	**TURTLE POWER** Partners in Kryme		4
25 Aug	**ITSY BITSY TEENY WEENY YELLOW POLKA DOT BIKINI** Bombalurina		3
15 Sep	**THE JOKER** Steve Miller Band		2
29 Sep	**SHOW ME HEAVEN** Maria McKee		4
27 Oct	**A LITTLE TIME** The Beautiful South		1
3 Nov	**UNCHAINED MELODY** Righteous Brothers		4
1 Dec	**ICE ICE BABY** Vanilla Ice		4
29 Dec	**SAVIOUR'S DAY** Cliff Richard		1

1991

Date	Title	Artist	Weeks
5 Jan	**BRING YOUR DAUGHTER…TO THE SLAUGHTER** Iron Maiden ■		2
19 Jan	**SADNESS PART I** Enigma		1
26 Jan	**INNUENDO** Queen ■		1
2 Feb	**3 AM ETERNAL** KLF featuring Children of the Revolution		2
16 Feb	**DO THE BARTMAN** Simpsons		3
9 Mar	**SHOULD I STAY OR SHOULD I GO** Clash		2
23 Mar	**THE STONK** Hale and Pace and the Stonkers		1
30 Mar	**THE ONE AND ONLY** Chesney Hawkes		5
4 May	**SHOOP SHOOP SONG (IT'S IN HIS KISS)** Cher		5
8 Jun	**I WANNA SEX YOU UP** Color Me Badd		3
29 Jun	**ANY DREAM WILL DO** Jason Donovan		2
13 Jul	**(EVERYTHING I DO) I DO IT FOR YOU** Bryan Adams		16
2 Nov	**THE FLY** U2 ■		1
9 Nov	**DIZZY** Vic Reeves and the Wonder Stuff		2
23 Nov	**BLACK OR WHITE** Michael Jackson ■		2
7 Dec	**DON'T LET THE SUN GO DOWN ON ME** George Michael and Elton John ■		2
21 Dec	**BOHEMIAN RHAPSODY/ THESE ARE THE DAYS OF OUR LIVES** Queen ■		5

1992

Date	Title	Artist	Weeks
25 Jan	**GOODNIGHT GIRL** Wet Wet Wet		4
22 Feb	**STAY** Shakespears Sister		8
18 Apr	**DEEPLY DIPPY** Right Said Fred		3
9 May	**PLEASE DON'T GO/GAME BOY** KWS		5
13 Jun	**ABBA-ESQUE (EP)** Erasure ■		5
18 Jul	**AIN'T NO DOUBT** Jimmy Nail		3
8 Aug	**RHYTHM IS A DANCER** Snap		6
19 Sep	**EBENEEZER GOODE** Shamen		4
17 Oct	**SLEEPING SATELLITE** Tasmin Archer		2
31 Oct	**END OF THE ROAD** Boyz II Men		3
21 Nov	**WOULD I LIE TO YOU** Charles and Eddie		2
5 Dec	**I WILL ALWAYS LOVE YOU** Whitney Houston		10

1993

Date	Title	Artist	Weeks
13 Feb	**NO LIMIT** 2 Unlimited		5
20 Mar	**OH CAROLINA** Shaggy		2
3 Apr	**YOUNG AT HEART** Bluebells		4
1 May	**FIVE LIVE EP** George Michael and Queen with Lisa Stansfield ■		3
22 May	**ALL THAT SHE WANTS** Ace of Base		3
12 Jun	**(I CAN'T HELP) FALLING IN LOVE WITH YOU** UB40		2
26 Jun	**DREAMS** Gabrielle		3
17 Jul	**PRAY** Take That ■		4
14 Aug	**LIVING ON MY OWN** Freddie Mercury		2
28 Aug	**MR. VAIN** Culture Beat		4
25 Sep	**BOOM! SHAKE THE ROOM** Jazzy Jeff and the Fresh Prince		2
9 Oct	**RELIGHT MY FIRE** Take That featuring Lulu ■		2
23 Oct	**I'D DO ANYTHING FOR LOVE (BUT I WON'T DO THAT)** Meat Loaf		7
11 Dec	**MR BLOBBY** Mr Blobby		1
18 Dec	**BABE** Take That		1
25 Dec	**MR BLOBBY** Mr Blobby		2

1994

Date	Title	Artist	Weeks
8 Jan	**TWIST AND SHOUT** Chaka Demus and Pliers with Jack Radics and Taxi Gang		2
22 Jan	**THINGS CAN ONLY GET BETTER** D:Ream		4
19 Feb	**WITHOUT YOU** Mariah Carey ■		4
19 Mar	**DOOP** Doop		3
9 Apr	**EVERYTHING CHANGES** Take That ■		2
23 Apr	**THE MOST BEAUTIFUL GIRL IN THE WORLD** Prince		2
7 May	**THE REAL THING** Tony Di Bart		1
14 May	**INSIDE** Stiltskin		1
21 May	**COME ON YOU REDS** Manchester United Football Squad		2
4 Jun	**LOVE IS ALL AROUND** Wet Wet Wet		15
17 Sep	**SATURDAY NIGHT** Whigfield ■		4
15 Oct	**SURE** Take That ■		2
29 Oct	**BABY COME BACK** Pato Banton		4
26 Nov	**LET ME BE YOUR FANTASY** Baby D		2
10 Dec	**STAY ANOTHER DAY** East 17		5

1995

Date	Title	Artist	Weeks
14 Jan	**COTTON EYE JOE** Rednex		3
4 Feb	**THINK TWICE** Celine Dion		7
25 Mar	**LOVE CAN BUILD A BRIDGE** Cher, Chrissie Hynde and Neneh Cherry with Eric Clapton		1
1 Apr	**DON'T STOP (WIGGLE WIGGLE)** Outhere Brothers		1
8 Apr	**BACK FOR GOOD** Take That ■		4
6 May	**SOME MIGHT SAY** Oasis ■		1
13 May	**DREAMER** Livin' Joy ■		1

UK entry at No 1 ■

Date	Song	Weeks
20 May	UNCHAINED MELODY/(THERE'LL BE BLUE BIRDS OVER) THE WHITE CLIFFS OF DOVER Robson Green and Jerome Flynn ■	7
8 Jul	BOOM BOOM BOOM Outhere Brothers	4
5 Aug	NEVER FORGET Take That ■	3
26 Aug	COUNTRY HOUSE Blur ■	2
9 Sep	YOU ARE NOT ALONE Michael Jackson	2
23 Sep	BOOMBASTIC Shaggy ■	1
30 Sep	FAIRGROUND Simply Red ■	4
28 Oct	GANGSTA'S PARADISE Coolio featuring LV ■	2
11 Nov	I BELIEVE/UP ON THE ROOF Robson and Jerome ■	4
9 Dec	EARTH SONG Michael Jackson ■	6

1996

Date	Song	Weeks
20 Jan	JESUS TO A CHILD George Michael ■	1
27 Jan	SPACEMAN Babylon Zoo ■	5
2 Mar	DON'T LOOK BACK IN ANGER Oasis ■	1
9 Mar	HOW DEEP IS YOUR LOVE Take That ■	3
30 Mar	FIRESTARTER Prodigy ■	3
20 Apr	RETURN OF THE MACK Mark Morrison	2
4 May	FASTLOVE George Michael ■	3
25 May	OOH AAH... JUST A LITTLE BIT Gina G ■	1
1 Jun	THREE LIONS (THE OFFICIAL SONG OF THE ENGLAND FOOTBALL TEAM) Baddiel and Skinner and the Lightning Seeds ■	1
8 Jun	KILLING ME SOFTLY Fugees ■	4
6 Jul	THREE LIONS (THE OFFICIAL SONG OF THE ENGLAND FOOTBALL TEAM) Baddiel and Skinner and the Lightning Seeds	1
13 Jul	KILLING ME SOFTLY Fugees	1
20 Jul	FOREVER LOVE Gary Barlow ■	1
27 Jul	WANNABE Spice Girls ■	7
14 Sep	FLAVA Peter Andre ■	1
21 Sep	READY OR NOT Fugees	2
5 Oct	BREAKFAST AT TIFFANY'S Deep Blue Something	1
12 Oct	SETTING SUN Chemical Brothers ■	1
19 Oct	WORDS Boyzone ■	1
26 Oct	SAY YOU'LL BE THERE Spice Girls ■	2
9 Nov	WHAT BECOMES OF THE BROKEN HEARTED/ UP ON THE ROOF/YOU'LL NEVER WALK ALONE Robson and Jerome ■	2
23 Nov	BREATHE Prodigy ■	2
7 Dec	I FEEL YOU Peter Andre ■	1
14 Dec	A DIFFERENT BEAT Boyzone ■	1
21 Dec	KNOCKIN' ON HEAVEN'S DOOR – THROW THESE GUNS AWAY Dunblane ■	1
28 Dec	2 BECOME 1 Spice Girls ■	3

1997

Date	Song	Weeks
18 Jan	PROFESSIONAL WIDOW (IT'S GOT TO BE BIG) Tori Amos	1
25 Jan	YOUR WOMAN White Town ■	1
1 Feb	BEETLEBUM Blur ■	1
8 Feb	AIN'T NOBODY LL Cool J ■	1
15 Feb	DISCOTEQUE U2 ■	1
22 Feb	DON'T SPEAK No Doubt ■	3
15 Mar	MAMA/WHO DO YOU THINK YOU ARE Spice Girls ■	3
5 Apr	BLOCK ROCKIN' BEATS Chemical Brothers ■	1
12 Apr	I BELIEVE I CAN FLY R Kelly	3
3 May	BLOOD ON THE DANCE FLOOR Michael Jackson ■	1
10 May	LOVE WON'T WAIT Gary Barlow ■	1
17 May	YOU'RE NOT ALONE Olive ■	2
31 May	I WANNA BE THE ONLY ONE Eternal featuring Bebe Winans ■	1
7 Jun	MMMBOP Hanson ■	3
28 Jun	I'LL BE MISSING YOU Puff Daddy and Faith Evans ■	3
19 Jul	D'YOU KNOW WHAT I MEAN? Oasis ■	1
26 Jul	I'LL BE MISSING YOU Puff Daddy and Faith Evans	3
16 Aug	MEN IN BLACK Will Smith ■	4
13 Sep	THE DRUGS DON'T WORK Verve ■	1
20 Sep	CANDLE IN THE WIND 1997/SOMETHING ABOUT THE WAY YOU LOOK TONIGHT Elton John ■	5
25 Oct	SPICE UP YOUR LIFE Spice Girls ■	1
1 Nov	BARBIE GIRL Aqua ■	4
29 Nov	PERFECT DAY Various ■	2
13 Dec	TELETUBBIES SAY EH-OH! Teletubbies ■	2
27 Dec	TOO MUCH Spice Girls ■	2

1998

Date	Song	Weeks
10 Jan	PERFECT DAY Various	1
17 Jan	NEVER EVER All Saints	1
24 Jan	ALL AROUND THE WORLD Oasis ■	1
31 Jan	YOU MAKE ME WANNA Usher ■	1
7 Feb	DOCTOR JONES Aqua ■	2
21 Feb	MY HEART WILL GO ON Celine Dion ■	1
28 Feb	BRIMFUL OF ASHA Cornershop ■	1
7 Mar	FROZEN Madonna ■	1
14 Mar	MY HEART WILL GO ON Celine Dion	1
21 Mar	IT'S LIKE THAT Run-DMC vs Jason Nevins ■	6
2 May	ALL THAT I NEED Boyzone ■	1
9 May	UNDER THE BRIDGE/LADY MARMALADE All Saints ■	1
16 May	TURN BACK TIME Aqua ■	1
23 May	UNDER THE BRIDGE/LADY MARMALADE All Saints	1
30 May	FEEL IT Tamperer featuring Maya	1
6 Jun	C'EST LA VIE B*Witched ■	2
20 Jun	3 LIONS '98 Baddiel and Skinner and Lightning Seeds ■	3
11 Jul	BECAUSE WE WANT TO Billie ■	1
18 Jul	FREAK ME Another Level ■	1
25 Jul	DEEPER UNDERGROUND Jamiroquai ■	1
1 Aug	VIVA FOREVER Spice Girls ■	2
15 Aug	NO MATTER WHAT Boyzone ■	3
5 Sep	IF YOU TOLERATE THIS YOUR CHILDREN WILL BE NEXT Manic Street Preachers ■	1
12 Sep	BOOTIE CALL All Saints ■	1
19 Sep	MILLENNIUM Robbie Williams ■	1
26 Sep	I WANT YOU BACK Melanie B featuring Missy Elliott ■	1
3 Oct	ROLLERCOASTER B*Witched ■	2
17 Oct	GIRLFRIEND Billie ■	1
24 Oct	GYM AND TONIC Spacedust ■	1
31 Oct	BELIEVE Cher ■	7
19 Dec	TO YOU I BELONG B*Witched ■	1
26 Dec	GOODBYE Spice Girls ■	1

UK entry at No 1 ■

Most weeks on chart

Artists with most weeks on chart

1	Elvis Presley	1155
2	Cliff Richard	1124
3	Elton John	558
4	Michael Jackson (+ 235 as a Jackson)	479
5	Madonna	477
6	Rod Stewart (+ 46 with Faces)	465
7	Beatles	456
8	Frank Sinatra	439
9	David Bowie	433
10	Diana Ross (+ 197 as a Supreme, 27 with the Supremes and Temptation)	429
11	Stevie Wonder	410
12	Status Quo	408
13	Paul McCartney	405
14	Queen	393
15	Rolling Stones	366
16	Shadows (+ 404 backing Cliff Richard)	359
17	Tom Jones	356
18	Bee Gees	349
19	Roy Orbison	345
20	Everly Brothers (Phil Everly had six more solo and 18 with Cliff Richard)	337
21	UB40	324
22	Shirley Bassey	323
23	Jim Reeves	322
24	Lonnie Donegan	321
25	Four Tops	318
	Hollies	318
27	Supremes	306
28	Donna Summer	298
29	Pat Boone	296
30	Perry Como	294
	Prince	294
32	Hot Chocolate	283
33	Beach Boys	281
	Billy Fury	281
	Frankie Laine	281
36	Slade	277
	Shakin' Stevens	277
38	Oasis	273
39	Madness	258
40	Electric Light Orchestra	255
41	ABBA	252
42	Adam Faith	251
43	Petula Clark	247
	Who (+ 4 as High Numbers)	247
45	Connie Francis	241
46	Whitney Houston	238
47	Nat 'King' Cole	237
48	Engelbert Humperdinck	235
	Jacksons	235
	T Rex	235

Whitney Houston: Artists with most weeks on chart #46

Most weeks on chart (by recording)

Entries are listed by title, artist, number of chart runs and weeks on chart

MY WAY Frank Sinatra	10	124	
AMAZING GRACE Judy Collins	8	67	
RELAX Frankie Goes to Hollywood	3	59	
ROCK AROUND THE CLOCK Bill Haley and His Comets	8	57	
RELEASE ME Engelbert Humperdinck	1	56	
STRANGER ON THE SHORE Mr Acker Bilk	1	55	
BLUE MONDAY New Order	5	53	
I LOVE YOU BECAUSE Jim Reeves	2	47	
WHATEVER Oasis	8	47	
WHITE LINES (DON'T DO IT) Grandmaster Flash and Melle Mel	5	46	
ALL RIGHT NOW Free	5	44	
LET'S TWIST AGAIN Chubby Checker	5	44	
TAINTED LOVE Soft Cell	5	44	
BROWN GIRL IN THE RING Boney M	2	43	
DECK OF CARDS Wink Martindale	5	41	
RIVERS OF BABYLON Boney M	1	40	
A SCOTTISH SOLDIER Andy Stewart	2	40	
TIE A YELLOW RIBBON ROUND THE OLD OAK TREE Dawn	2	40	
HE'LL HAVE TO GO Jim Reeves	3	39	
SOMEWHERE MY LOVE Mike Sammes Singers	2	38	

Most weeks on chart (by a song)

Entries are listed by title, number of versions and weeks on chart

MY WAY (5 – all vocal) 167
UNCHAINED MELODY (8 – 7 vocal, 1 instrumental) 96
AMAZING GRACE (2 – 1 vocal, 1 instrumental) 94
ROCK AROUND THE CLOCK (3 – all vocal) 70
CAN'T HELP FALLING IN LOVE (5 – all vocal) 68
I BELIEVE (4 – all vocal) 68

ONLY YOU (6 – all vocal) 66
STRANGER ON THE SHORE (2 – 1 vocal, 1 instrumental) 65
THEME FROM 'THE THREEPENNY OPERA' / MACK THE KNIFE (6 – all vocal) 62
RELAX (1, vocal) 59

Most consecutive weeks on chart (by disc)

RELEASE ME Engelbert Humperdinck 56
STRANGER ON THE SHORE Mr Acker Bilk 55
RELAX Frankie Goes to Hollywood 48
MY WAY Frank Sinatra 47
RIVERS OF BABYLON Boney M 40
I LOVE YOU BECAUSE Jim Reeves 39
TIE A YELLOW RIBBON ROUND THE OLD OAK TREE Dawn 39
A SCOTTISH SOLDIER Andy Stewart 38
WHITE LINES DON'T DO IT Grandmaster Flash and Melle Mel 38
LOVE IS ALL AROUND Wet Wet Wet 37

David Bowie: Artists with most weeks on chart #9

World's biggest-selling single

In the last three months of 1997, Elton John's tribute to Diana, Princess of Wales, 'Candle in the Wind 1997', sold more than 33 million copies around the world. It topped the chart in almost every corner of the globe and broke records for the biggest-selling and fastest-selling single in numerous countries, including the UK and the USA. In the UK, the song that Elton performed at the Princess's funeral (on 6 September, 1997), sold 658000 on its first day, 1.5 million in week one, 2 million in eight days, 3 million in 15 days, and had passed 5.4 million by the sixth week. In the USA, there were record-shattering advance orders of 8.7 million and a first week ship-out of 3.4 million. In total, it achieved a grand total of 11 million sales in the USA. In Canada, the single debuted at No 1 on 22 September, 1997, and had already earned 19 Canadian platinum discs by Christmas. Amazingly, it was still in the Canadian Top 3 in March 1999 – 17 months later. In total, it spent 45 weeks as the Canadian No 1.

It is estimated that the initial worldwide pressing was 21 million copies and that this figure had passed 30 million in just five weeks. Before the end of 1997, it had earned more than 140 platinum discs around the world, and Sir Elton was presented with a certificate from *The Guinness Book of Records* officially recognising his song as the World's Biggest-Selling Single.

Sir Elton John

Most weeks in the Top 20

1 Elvis Presley	.634	
2 Cliff Richard	.580	
3 Frankie Laine	.259	
4 Beatles	.257	
5 Madonna	.255	
6 Michael Jackson (+ 76 as a Jackson)	.235	
7 Lonnie Donegan	.219	
8 Elton John	.209	
9 Rod Stewart (+ 23 with Faces and 7 with Python Lee Jackson)	.204	
10 Pat Boone	.198	
11 Everly Brothers	.196	
12 Perry Como	.193	
13 Queen	.180	
14 Shadows (+ 267 with Cliff Richard)	.179	
15 Status Quo	.176	
16 David Bowie	.174	
17 Paul McCartney (+ 257 as a Beatle)	.173	
18 Rolling Stones	.170	
19 Bee Gees	.167	
20 Tom Jones	.164	
David Whitfield	.164	

Longest Top 20 chart span

Entries are listed by act name, year span and number of years on chart

1 Louis Armstrong (1952–1994) .... .42
2 Elvis Presley (1956–1997) .... .41
3 Shirley Bassey (1957–1997) .... .40
Perez Prado (1955–1995) .... .40
Cliff Richard (1958–1998) .... .40
6 Nat 'King' Cole (1952–1991) .... .39
7 Petula Clark (1954–1988) .... .34
8 Beatles (1963–1996) .... .33
Rolf Harris (1960–1993) .... .33
10 Frank Sinatra (1954–1986) .... .32

Louis Armstrong: Longest Top 20 chart span #1

Most Top 20 entries

1 Cliff Richard .... .89
2 Elvis Presley .... .79
3 Madonna .... .50
4 Michael Jackson (+ 14 as a Jackson) .... .42
5 Queen .... .39
6 Elton John .... .38
7 Rod Stewart (+ 4 with Faces, + 1 with Python Lee Jackson) .... .36
Status Quo .... .36
9 David Bowie .... .34
10 Paul McCartney (+ 31 as a Beatle) .... .33

Most weeks in the Top 10

1	Elvis Presley	359
2	Cliff Richard	321
3	Beatles	192
4	Frankie Laine	187
5	Madonna	176
6	Michael Jackson (+ 44 as a Jackson)	143
7	Rod Stewart (+ 9 with The Faces, + 5 with Python Lee Jackson)	117
8	Guy Mitchell	115
9	Abba	114
10	Everly Brothers	112
11	Lonnie Donegan	111
	Elton John	111
13	Rolling Stones	107
	Shadows (+ 183 with Cliff Richard)	107
15	Queen	104
16	Pat Boone	103
17	David Bowie	102
18	Perry Como	101
19	Paul McCartney (+ 192 as a Beatle)	100
20	David Whitfield	92

Most Top 10 hits

Re-entries and re-mixes are counted towards totals if they reached the Top 10 during completely separate chart runs

1	Cliff Richard	63
2	Elvis Presley	57
3	Madonna	46
4	Michael Jackson (+ 12 as a Jackson)	38
5	Beatles	28
6	Rod Stewart (+ 3 with The Faces and 1 with Python Lee Jackson)	27
7	Queen	25
8	David Bowie	24
	Elton John	24
	Paul McCartney (+ 28 as a Beatle)	24
11	Status Quo	22
12	Rolling Stones	21
13	Abba	19
	Bee Gees	19
	Frankie Laine	19
	U2	19
	Stevie Wonder	19
18	Hollies	18
	George Michael (+ 9 with Wham! and 1 with Boogie Box High)	18
	Pet Shop Boys	18

Most consecutive Top 10 hits

1	Madonna	35
2	Cliff Richard	26
3	Beatles	23
	Elvis Presley	23
5	Rolling Stones	19
6	Abba	18
7	Boyzone	13
	Kylie Minogue	13
9	Mariah Carey	12
	Shadows (+ 11 with Cliff Richard)	12
	Slade	12
	Take That	12

Most hits without a Top 10

Entries are listed by year, act, title of highest placed hit, its peak position and act's total number of hits

1988	AC/DC **HEATSEEKER** (12)	26
1983	Alarm **68 GUNS** (17)	16
1987	Mission **WASTELAND** (11)	16
1985	Lloyd Cole **LOST WEEKEND** (17)	15
1986	Julian Cope **WORLD SHUT YOUR MOUTH** (19)	15
1987	Cult **LI'L DEVIL** (11)	15
1992	Inspiral Carpets **DRAGGING ME DOWN** (12)	15
1985	Killing Joke **LOVE LIKE BLOOD** (16)	15
1981	Saxon **AND THE BANDS PLAYED ON** (12)	15
1994	The The **DISINFECTED EP** (17)	15

Most Top 10 hits in the 1990s

1	Madonna	24
2	Michael Jackson	15
	Mariah Carey	15
4	Take That	13
	Celine Dion	13
	Boyzone	13
7	Eternal	12
	George Michael	12
	East 17	12
10	Oasis	10
	Blur	10
	Janet Jackson	10
	M People	10

Kylie Minogue: Most consecutive Top 10s #7

59

Most weeks on chart in each year

1952	Vera Lynn	.10
1953	Frankie Laine	.84
1954	Frankie Laine	.84
1955	Ruby Murray	.80
1956	Bill Haley and His Comets	.110
1957	Elvis Presley	.108
1958	Elvis Presley	.70
1959	Russ Conway	.79

1960	Cliff Richard	.79
1961	Elvis Presley	.88
1962	Chubby Checker	.73
1963	Beatles	.68
1964	Jim Reeves	.73
1965	Seekers	.51
1966	Dave Dee, Dozy, Beaky, Mick and Tich	.50
1967	Engelbert Humperdinck	.97
1968	Tom Jones	.58
1969	Marvin Gaye	.60
1970	Elvis Presley	.59
1971	Elvis Presley	.66
1972	T Rex	.58
1973	David Bowie	.55
1974	Wombles	.65
1975	Mud	.45
1976	Rod Stewart	.48
1977	Elvis Presley	.51
1978	John Travolta	.60
1979	Donna Summer	.46
1980	Madness	.46
1981	Adam and the Ants	.91
1982	Soft Cell	.49
1983	Michael Jackson	.60
1984	Frankie Goes to Hollywood	.68
1985	Madonna	.84
1986	Madonna	.59
1987	Madonna	.41
1988	Kylie Minogue	.54
1989	Bobby Brown	.52
1990	New Kids on the Block	.56
1991	REM	.36
1992	Michael Jackson	.38
1993	Whitney Houston	.50
1994	Mariah Carey	.45
1995	Oasis	.65
1996	Oasis	.134
1997	Spice Girls	.49
1998	Leann Rimes	.39

Marvin Gaye: Most weeks on chart in 1969

Most weeks on chart in one year (by artist)

1996	Oasis	.134
1956	Bill Haley and His Comets	.110
1957	Elvis Presley	.108
1967	Engelbert Humperdinck	.97
1981	Adam and the Ants	.91
1961	Elvis Presley	.88
1953	Frankie Laine	.84
1957	Pat Boone	.84
1985	Madonna	.80
1955	Ruby Murray	.80

Most consecutive years on chart

Elvis Presley (1956–1985)	30
Elton John (1971– 1998)	28
Diana Ross (1970–1996) (+ 6 with Supremes 1964–1969)	27
Cliff Richard (1979 –1998)	20
Status Quo (1973–1992)	20
Cliff Richard (1958–1974)	17
UB40 (1980–1995)	16
Stranglers (1977–1992)	16
David Bowie (1972–1987)	16
Hot Chocolate (1970–1984)	15
Madonna (1984–1998)	15
Prince (1983–1997)	15
Andy Williams (1962–1976)	15

Chubby Checker: Most weeks on chart in 1962

Top 50 acts of the 1990s

1	Madonna	26	Whitney Houston
2	Michael Jackson	27	M People
3	Take That	28	Prince
4	Boyzone	29	Rod Stewart
5	Mariah Carey	30	New Kids on the Block
6	Celine Dion	31	Simply Red
7	East 17	32	Peter Andre
8	George Michael	33	Guns 'n' Roses
9	Janet Jackson	34	Backstreet Boys
10	Spice Girls	35	REM
11	Kylie Minogue	36	Manic Street Preachers
12	Eternal	37	Jamiroquai
13	Oasis	38	Ace of Base
14	U2	39	R Kelly
15	Prodigy	40	KLF
16	Bryan Adams	41	Robbie Williams
17	2 Unlimited	42	911
18	Blur	43	Cher
19	Wet Wet Wet	44	Shamen
20	Erasure	45	Sash!
21	Elton John	46	Cliff Richard
22	Pet Shop Boys	47	Suede
23	Bon Jovi	48	Roxette
24	Queen	49	Beautiful
25	Snap	50	All Saints

Top 50 singles of the 1990s

1	**(EVERYTHING I DO) I DO IT FOR YOU** Bryan Adams	15	**I'LL BE MISSING YOU** Puff Daddy and Faith Evans
2	**LOVE IS ALL AROUND** Wet Wet Wet	16	**WANNABE** Spice Girls
3	**I'LL BE THERE FOR YOU** Rembrandts	17	**GANGSTA'S PARADISE** Coolio featuring LV
4	**YOU GOT THE LOVE** Source featuring Candi Staton	18	**NO LIMIT** 2 Unlimited
5	**THE BEST THINGS IN LIFE ARE FREE** Luther Vandross and Janet Jackson	19	**BARBIE GIRL** Aqua
6	**THINK TWICE** Celine Dion	20	**KILLING ME SOFTLY** Fugees
7	**I WILL ALWAYS LOVE YOU** Whitney Houston	21	**UNCHAINED MELODY/WHITE CLIFFS OF DOVER** Robson Green and Jerome Flynn
8	**THINGS CAN ONLY GET BETTER** D:Ream	22	**RETURN OF THE MACK** Mark Morrison
9	**IT MUST HAVE BEEN LOVE** Roxette	23	**BABY COME BACK** Pato Banton
10	**I'LL DO ANYTHING FOR LOVE (BUT I WON'T DO THAT)** Meat Loaf	24	**DREAMER** Livin' Joy
11	**STAY** Shakespears Sister	25	**PLEASE DON'T GO/GAME BOY** KWS
12	**CANDLE IN THE WIND 1997/SOMETHING ABOUT THE WAY YOU LOOK TONIGHT** Elton John	26	**MY HEART WILL GO ON** Celine Dion
13	**RHYTHM IS A DANCER** Snap	27	**THE SHOOP SHOOP SONG (IT'S IN HIS KISS)** Cher
14	**NEVER EVER** All Saints	28	**SATURDAY NIGHT** Whigfield
		29	**COTTON EYE** Joe Rednex
		30	**END OF THE ROAD** Boyz II Men

East 17: Top 50 acts of the 1990s #7

Round-up of 1997

It was a musically mixed twelve months. The top two singles were very different tributes to recently deceased icons, while a Danish ditty about the top-selling pre-teen doll, 'Barbie', and a record by pre-school toddlers' idols, the Teletubbies, were among the other chart-toppers. More than half of the Top 20 singles featured female vocals, and a record four acts made their chart debuts at No 1, including White Town (artist's real name Jyoti Mishra) with 'Your Woman', which was recorded in his bedroom. It was a year when girl bands flexed their muscles, with outfits such as the The Spice Girls and Eternal more than holding their own against male equivalents such as the USA's teen sensations the Backstreet Boys and Hanson, and Britain's Boyzone and 911. In fact, in 1997 The Spice Girls scored their sixth No 1 with their sixth release (thus doubling the previous record). There was also room on the charts for rock and rap, with acts such as U2, Blur, Verve, Texas, No Doubt and Cast clicking alongside US rap superstars Puff Daddy, LL Cool J and Will Smith. Nonetheless 1997 will be best remembered in musical history as the year that Elton John's tribute to Diana, Princess of Wales, 'Candle in the Wind 1997' sold more than five million copies in the UK and 33 million around the globe.

Chumbawamba:
Top 20 singles 1997 #11

Top 20 artists of 1997

1 Backstreet Boys
2 Spice Girls
3 U2
4 911
5 George Michael
6 Sash!
7 Blur
8 Eternal
9 Boyzone
10 Hanson
11 Verve
12 Puff Daddy
13 Texas
14 No Doubt
15 No Mercy
16 LL Cool J
17 Peter Andre
18 Shola Ama
19 Cast
20 Gary Barlow

Natalie Imbruglia:
Top 20 singles 1997 #12

Top 20 singles of 1997

1 CANDLE IN THE WIND 1997 / SOMETHING ABOUT
   THE WAY YOU LOOK TONIGHT Elton John
2 I'LL BE MISSING YOU Puff Daddy and Faith Evans
3 BARBIE GIRL Aqua
4 I BELIEVE I CAN FLY R Kelly
5 DON'T SPEAK No Doubt
6 MEN IN BLACK Will Smith
7 PERFECT DAY Various
8 I WANNA BE THE ONLY ONE Eternal featuring Bebe Winans
9 MMMBOP Hanson
10 MAMA/WHO DO YOU THINK YOU ARE Spice Girls
11 TUBTHUMPING Chumbawamba
12 TORN Natalie Imbruglia
13 SPICE UP YOUR LIFE Spice Girls
14 YOU'RE NOT ALONE Olive
15 THE DRUGS DON'T WORK Verve
16 TOO MUCH Spice Girls
17 PROFESSIONAL WIDOW (IT'S GOT TO BE BIG) Tori Amos
18 WHERE DO YOU GO No Mercy
19 YOUR WOMAN White Town
20 TELETUBBIES SAY EH-OH! Teletubbies

Round-up of 1998

The term 'girl power' may have become passé by 1998, but it was the year when women overtook men in the chart race, with four of the first five and indeed eight of the first ten singles of the year featuring female vocalists. The Spice Girls, who, together with Eternal, had made British girl groups fashionable around the globe, continued to add to their impressive tally of No 1s. However, top honours of the year went to fellow female outfits, All Saints and B*Witched, who each achieved three No 1 singles. In terms of nationalities, the overall Top 20 acts hailed from seven different countries and the only US act to make it to the Top 10 was the relative veteran Madonna.

1998 will be remembered as the year in which teenaged vocalists – such as Britain's Billie and Cleopatra, and the USA's Brandy and Usher – made their first real chart impression and when, believe it or not, 52-year-old Cher reached No 1. Other noteworthy events included Five replacing Boyzone as the top boy band, Robbie Williams dethroning Gary Barlow as the ex-Take That member of choice and the Bee Gees' songs being back in demand again. Additionally, this was the year in which Steps showed that there was still room for an Abba-styled vocal group, The Corrs joined the growing legion of Irish hitmakers and Celine Dion enchanted the whole world with a beautiful ballad from the year's most successful film, *Titanic*.

Aqua: Top 20 artists 1998 #6
Top 20 singles 1998 #8

Top 20 artists of 1998

1 All Saints
2 Robbie Williams
3 Five
4 B*Witched
5 Boyzone
6 Aqua
7 Madonna
8 Steps
9 Spice Girls
10 Billie
11 Celine Dion
12 Will Smith
13 Pras Michel
14 Another Level
15 Cleopatra
16 Savage Garden
17 Sash!
18 Brandy
19 Corrs
20 Mase

Billie: Top 20 artists 1998 #10
Top 20 singles 1998 #17, #20

Top 20 singles of 1998

1 NEVER EVER All Saints
2 MY HEART WILL GO ON Celine Dion
3 BELIEVE Cher
4 IT'S LIKE THAT Run-DMC vs Jason Nevins
5 C'EST LA VIE B*Witched
6 NO MATTER WHAT Boyzone
7 FEEL IT Tamperer featuring Maya
8 DOCTOR JONES Aqua
9 UNDER THE BRIDGE/LADY MARMALADE All Saints
10 VIVA FOREVER Spice Girls
11 GHETTO SUPERSTAR THAT IS WHAT YOU ARE
   Pras Michel featuring Ol' Dirty Bastard
   and introducing Mya
12 FREAK ME Another Level
13 ROLLERCOASTER B*Witched
14 3 LIONS '98 Baddiel and Skinner and Lightning Seeds
15 FROZEN Madonna
16 BRIMFUL OF ASHA Cornershop
17 BECAUSE WE WANT TO Billie
18 MILLENNIUM Robbie Williams
19 YOU MAKE ME WANNA Usher
20 GIRLFRIEND Billie

European acts with most weeks on chart

(excluding UK and Ireland)

1	ABBA (Sweden/Norway)	252	6	Ace of Base (Sweden)	77
2	Roxette (Sweden)	135	7	Julio Iglesias (Spain)	75
3	A-Ha (Norway)	131	8	Black Box (Italy)	74
4	Snap (Germany)	115	9	Kraftwerk (Germany)	69
5	2 Unlimited (Holland)	112	10	Cappella (Italy)	68

Australian acts with most weeks on chart

1	Kylie Minogue	217	4	INXS	121
2	Jason Donovan	137	5	Seekers	120
3	AC/DC	125			

Top 1990s boy bands with most weeks on chart

1	East 17	162	4	New Kids on the Block	90
2	Take That	158	5	Backstreet Boys	85
3	Boyzone	138			

Top girl groups with most weeks on chart

1	Supremes	306	6	Sister Sledge	111
2	Bananarama	202	7	Bangles	94
3	Eternal	130	8	Nolans	90
4	Spice Girls	126	9	En Vogue	89
5	Three Degrees	112	10	Pointer Sisters	87

Eternal: Top girl group #3

Top football team chart acts

1 Manchester United FC
2 England World Cup Squad
3 Liverpool FC
4 Scotland World Cup Squad
5 Tottenham Hotspur FC

Top-scoring football records

1 **THREE LIONS** Baddiel and Skinner and Lightning Seeds
2 **BACK HOME** England World Cup Squad
3 **WORLD IN MOTION** Englandneworder
4 **COME ON YOU REDS** Manchester United Football Squad
5 **3 LIONS '98** Baddiel and Skinner and Lightning Seeds

Most successful charity hit

1 **DO THEY KNOW IT'S CHRISTMAS** Band Aid
2 **CANDLE IN THE WIND 1997** Elton John
3 **SACRIFICE/HEALING HANDS** Elton John
4 **BOHEMIAN RHAPSODY/THESE ARE THE DAYS OF OUR LIVES**
   Queen
5 **WITH A LITTLE HELP FROM MY FRIENDS/SHE'S LEAVING HOME**
   Wet Wet Wet/Billy Bragg

Most successful soap stars

1 Kylie Minogue
2 Jason Donovan
3 Danii Minogue
4 Michelle Gayle
5 Natalie Imbruglia

Band Aid: Most successful charity hit #1

Biggest film hits

Title songs (or songs played over credits) that were not hits prior to release of film

1 (EVERYTHING I DO) I DO IT FOR YOU Bryan Adams
   (*Robin Hood: Prince of Thieves* – 1991)
2 LOVE IS ALL AROUND Wet Wet Wet
   (*Four Weddings and a Funeral* – 1994)
3 I WILL ALWAYS LOVE YOU Whitney Houston (*The Bodyguard* – 1992)
4 CHERRY PINK AND APPLE BLOSSOM WHITE Perez Prado
   (*Underwater* – 1955)
5 THE GOOD, THE BAD and THE UGLY Hugo Montenegro
   (*The Good, The Bad and The Ugly* – 1968)

Most successful family act

1 Bee Gees
2 Everly Brothers
3 Jacksons / Jackson Five
4 Five Star
5 Carpenters
6 Sister Sledge
7 Osmonds
8 Gladys Knight and the Pips
9 Isley Brothers
10 Tavares

Sexiest records

Biggest hits with 'sex' in the title

1 YOU SEXY THING Hot Chocolate
2 I WANNA SEX YOU UP Color Me Bad
3 DO YA THINK I'M SEXY? Rod Stewart
4 I'M TOO SEXY Right Said Fred
5 LET'S TALK ABOUT SEX Salt-n-Pepa
6 SEX ON THE BEACH T-Spoon
7 I WANT YOUR SEX George Michael
8 SEXY EYES Dr Hook
9 SEXCRIME (NINETEEN EIGHTY FOUR) Eurythmics
10 (SEXUAL) HEALING Marvin Gaye

Youngest chart-toppers

1 Little Jimmy Osmond . . . . .9 years 8 months – 1972
2 Frankie Lymon .13 years 9 months – 1956
3 Donny Osmond . . . . .14 years 6 months – 1972
4 Helen Shapiro .14 years 10 months – 1961
5 Billie . . . . .15 years 2 months – 1998

Biggest posthumous hit

1 IT DOESN'T MATTER ANYMORE Buddy Holly
2 WAY DOWN Elvis Presley
3 BOHEMIAN RHAPSODY (1991) Queen (Freddie Mercury)
4 REET PETITE Jackie Wilson
5 IMAGINE John Lennon

Most successful Eurovision Song Contest hits

1 SAVE YOUR KISSES FOR ME Brotherhood of Man . . . . .UK – 1976
2 PUPPET ON A STRING Sandie Shaw .UK – 1967
3 OOH AAH…JUST A LITTLE BIT Gina G . . . . .UK – 1996
4 MAKING YOUR MIND UP Bucks Fizz . . . . .UK – 1981
5 ALL KINDS OF EVERYTHING Dana . . . . .Eire – 1970
6 CONGRATULATIONS Cliff Richard . . . . .UK– 1968
7 WATERLOO Abba . . . . .Sweden – 1974
8 WHAT'S ANOTHER YEAR Johnny Logan . . . . .Eire – 1980
9 A LITTLE PEACE Nicole . . . . .Germany – 1982
10 BEG STEAL OR BORROW New Seekers . . . . .UK –1972

Top singles by film/tv actors and actresses

Artists who had achieved some film/TV fame before charting

1 **YOU'RE THE ONE THAT I WANT**
John Travolta (and Olivia Newton-John)
2 **UNCHAINED MELODY/WHITE CLIFFS OF DOVER**
Robson Green and Jerome Flynn
3 **GRANDAD** Clive Dunn
4 **DON'T GIVE UP ON US** David Soul
5 **SILVER LADY** David Soul
6 **I SHOULD BE SO LUCKY** Kylie Minogue
7 **YOUNG LOVE** Tab Hunter
8 **WAND'RIN' STAR** Lee Marvin
9 **ESPECIALLY FOR YOU** Kylie Minogue and Jason Donovan
10 **I BELIEVE/UP ON THE ROOF** Robson Green and Jerome Flynn

Most successful rap singles

1 **I'LL BE MISSING YOU** Puff Daddy and Faith Evans
2 **GANGSTA'S PARADISE** Coolio featuring LV
3 **IT'S LIKE THAT** Run-DMC vs Jason Nevins
4 **BOOM BOOM BOOM** Outhere Brothers
5 **MEN IN BLACK** Will Smith
6 **ICE ICE BABY** Vanilla Ice
7 **DON'T STOP (WIGGLE WIGGLE)** Outhere Brothers
8 **BOOM! SHAKE THAT ROOM** Jazzy Jeff and the Fresh Prince
9 **TURTLE POWER** Parnters in Kryme
10 **READY OR NOT** Fugees

Top singles by non-humans

1 **SUGAR SUGAR** Archies (cartoon characters)
2 **REMEMBER YOU'RE A WOMBLE** Wombles (furry litter-gatherers)
3 **SWING THE MOOD** Jive Bunny and the Mastermixers (cartoon rabbit)
4 **DO THE BARTMAN** Simpsons (cartoon family)
5 **MR BLOBBY** Mr Blobby (blobby character)

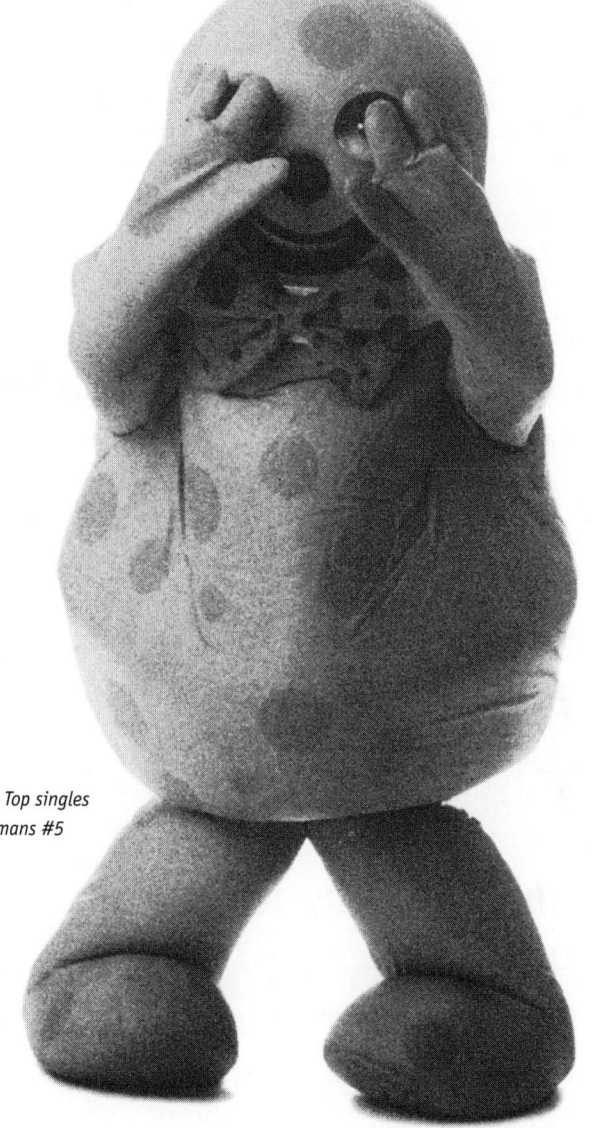

Mr Blobby: Top singles by non-humans #5

Most successful TV advert hits

Singles that charted due to TV adverts – calculated from chart success after a record (or sound-alike version) was used in advert

1 I'D LIKE TO TEACH THE WORLD TO SING New Seekers (Coca-Cola)
2 YOUNG AT HEART Bluebells (Volkswagen)
3 HE AIN'T HEAVY, HE'S MY BROTHER Hollies (Miller Lite)
4 THE FIRST TIME Robin Beck (Coca-Cola)
5 STAND BY ME Ben E King (Coca-Cola)
6 INSIDE Stiltskin (Levi's)
7 THE JOKER Steve Miller Band (Levi's)
8 SHOULD I STAY OR SHOULD I GO Clash (Levi's)
9 GUAGLIONE Perez Prado (Guinness)
10 BLUE VELVET Bobby Vinton (Nivea)

Most successful one-off duet hits

Two hit-making solo artists who teamed together on one chart single

1 THE BEST THINGS IN LIFE ARE FREE Luther Vandross and Janet Jackson
2 I KNOW HIM SO WELL Elaine Paige and Barbara Dickson
3 ESPECIALLY FOR YOU Kylie Minogue and Jason Donovan
4 SOMETHIN' STUPID Nancy and Frank Sinatra
5 SOMETHING'S GOTTEN HOLD OF MY HEART
   Marc Almond and Gene Pitney
6 DANCING IN THE STREET David Bowie and Mick Jagger
7 EBONY AND IVORY Paul McCartney and Stevie Wonder
8 DON'T LET THE SUN GO DOWN ON ME George Michael and Elton John
9 I KNEW YOU WERE WAITING (FOR ME)
   Aretha Franklin and George Michael
10 THE BOY IS MINE Brandy and Monica

Most successful reggae-oriented record

1 ISRAELITES Desmond Dekker and the Aces
2 OH CAROLINA Shaggy
3 I WANT TO WAKE UP WITH YOU Boris Gardiner
4 TWIST AND SHOUT Chaka Demus and Pliers / Jack Radics / Taxi Gang
5 EVERYTHING I OWN Ken Boothe

Biggest banned hit

RELAX Frankie Goes to Hollywood (1984)

Shortest stay Top 5 hits

Records that entered chart in Top 5 and dropped out of Top 20 the following week (position drop indicated at end of each entry)

1 YOU DON'T CARE ABOUT US Placebo (1998) 5–26
2 PEACOCK SUITE Paul Weller (1996) 5–25
3 BARREL OF A GUN Depeche Mode (1997) 4–23
4 NO SURPRISES Radiohead (1998) 4–22
5 ON YOUR OWN Blur (1997) 5–22
6 THIS IS A CALL Foo Fighters (1995) 5–21
   STREET SPIRIT (FADE OUT) Radiohead (1996) 5–21
   PERSEVERANCE Terrorvision (1996) 5–21

Instrumental number ones

1953	**MOULIN ROUGE** Mantovani	1962	**NUT ROCKER** B Bumble and the Stingers
1954	**OH MEIN PAPA** Eddie Calvert	1962	**TELSTAR** Tornados
1954	**LET'S HAVE ANOTHER PARTY** Winifred Atwell	1963	**DANCE ON** Shadows
1955	**CHERRY PINK AND APPLE BLOSSOM WHITE** Perez Prado	1963	**DIAMONDS** Jet Harris and Tony Meehan
1955	**CHERRY PINK AND APPLE BLOSSOM WHITE** Eddie Calvert	1963	**FOOT TAPPER** Shadows
1956	**POOR PEOPLE OF PARIS** Winifred Atwell	1968	**THE GOOD, THE BAD AND THE UGLY** Hugo Montenegro and His Orchestra
1958	**HOOTS MON** Lord Rockingham's XI	1969	**ALBATROSS** Fleetwood Mac
1959	**SIDE SADDLE** Russ Conway	1972	**AMAZING GRACE** Royal Scots Dragoon Guards
1959	**ROULETTE** Russ Conway	1972	**MOULDY OLD DOUGH** Lieutenant Pigeon
1960	**APACHE** Shadows	1973	**EYE LEVEL** Simon Park Orchestra
1961	**ON THE REBOUND** Floyd Cramer	1994	**INSIDE** Stiltskin
1961	**KON-TIKI** Shadows		
1962	**WONDERFUL LAND** Shadows		

Placebo: Shortest stay #1

UK million sellers

This alphabetical list features every single that has sold more than one million copies in the UK

Bryan Adams
   (EVERYTHING I DO) I DO IT FOR YOU
All Saints
   NEVER EVER
Paul Anka
   DIANA
Aqua
   BARBIE GIRL
Babylon Zoo
   SPACEMAN
Band Aid
   DO THEY KNOW IT'S CHRISTMAS
Beatles
   SHE LOVES YOU
   DAY TRIPPER/WE CAN WORK IT OUT
   I FEEL FINE
   CAN'T BUY ME LOVE
   I WANT TO HOLD YOUR HAND
Harry Belafonte
   MARY'S BOY CHILD
Mr Acker Bilk
   STRANGER ON THE SHORE
Blondie
   HEART OF GLASS
Boney M
   MARY'S BOY CHILD/OH MY LORD
   RIVERS OF BABYLON/BROWN GIRL IN THE RING
Boyzone
   NO MATTER WHAT
Brotherhood of Man
   SAVE YOUR KISSES FOR ME
Cher
   BELIEVE
Coolio featuring LV
   GANGSTA'S PARADISE
Bing Crosby
   WHITE CHRISTMAS
Culture Club
   KARMA CHAMELEON
Dexy's Midnight Runners
   COME ON EILEEN
Celine Dion
   MY HEART WILL GO ON
   THINK TWICE
Ken Dodd
   TEARS

Frankie Goes to Hollywood
   TWO TRIBES
   RELAX
Fugees
   KILLING ME SOFTLY
Art Garfunkel
   BRIGHT EYES
Gary Glitter
   I LOVE YOU LOVE ME LOVE
Robson Green and Jerome Flynn
   UNCHAINED MELODY/WHITE CLIFFS OF DOVER
   I BELIEVE/UP ON THE ROOF
Bill Haley and His Comets
   ROCK AROUND THE CLOCK
Whitney Houston
   I WILL ALWAYS LOVE YOU
Human League
   DON'T YOU WANT ME
Engelbert Humperdinck
   THE LAST WALTZ
   RELEASE ME (AND LET ME LOVE AGAIN)
Frank Ifield
   I REMEMBER YOU
Michael Jackson
   EARTH SONG
Elton John
   CANDLE IN THE WIND 1997/SOMETHING ABOUT
      THE WAY YOU LOOK TONIGHT
Tom Jones
   GREEN GREEN GRASS OF HOME
John Lennon
   IMAGINE
Paul McCartney
   MULL OF KINTYRE/GIRLS' SCHOOL
George Michael
   CARELESS WHISPER
Olivia Newton-John and John Travolta
   SUMMER NIGHTS
   YOU'RE THE ONE THAT I WANT
Simon Park Orchestra
   EYE LEVEL

Pink Floyd
   ANOTHER BRICK IN THE WALL (PT 2)
Elvis Presley
   IT'S NOW OR NEVER
Puff Daddy and Faith Evans
   I'LL BE MISSING YOU
Queen
   **BOHEMIAN RHAPSODY/THESE
   ARE THE DAYS OF OUR LIVES**
Cliff Richard
   THE YOUNG ONES
Run-DMC vs Jason Nevins
   IT'S LIKE THAT
Jennifer Rush
   THE POWER OF LOVE
Seekers
   THE CARNIVAL IS OVER
Slade
   MERRY XMAS EVERYBODY
David Soul
   DON'T GIVE UP ON US
Spice Girls
   **WANNABE
   2 BECOME 1**

Steps
   HEARTBEAT/TRAGEDY
Teletubbies
   TELETUBBIES SAY EH-OH!
John Travolta and Olivia Newton-John
   **YOU'RE THE ONE THAT I WANT
   SUMMER NIGHTS**
Various
   PERFECT DAY
Village People
   Y M C A
Wet Wet Wet
   LOVE IS ALL AROUND
Wham!
   LAST CHRISTMAS/EVERYTHING SHE WANTS
Whigfield
   SATURDAY NIGHT
Robbie Williams
   ANGELS
Stevie Wonder
   I JUST CALLED TO SAY I LOVE YOU

All Saints: UK million-sellers

Transatlantic (UK and US) number ones

This list, ordered alphabetically by act, features every single that has made it to the No 1 spot in both the UK and the USA. Duets are listed under both acts, and the year indicates when single topped UK chart

ABBA
   DANCING QUEEN (1976)
Bryan Adams
   (EVERYTHING I DO) I DO IT FOR YOU (1991)
Animals
   HOUSE OF THE RISING SUN (1964)
Paul Anka
   DIANA (1957)
Archies
   SUGAR SUGAR (1969)
Rick Astley
   NEVER GONNA GIVE YOU UP (1987)

Bangles
   ETERNAL FLAME (1989)
Beach Boys
   GOOD VIBRATIONS (1966)
Beatles
   SHE LOVES YOU (1963)
   I WANT TO HOLD YOUR HAND (1963)
   CAN'T BUY ME LOVE (1964)
   A HARD DAY'S NIGHT (1964)
   I FEEL FINE (1964)
   TICKET TO RIDE (1965)
   HELP! (1965)
   PAPERBACK WRITER (1966)
   ALL YOU NEED IS LOVE (1967)
   HELLO GOODBYE (1967)
   HEY JUDE (1968)
   GET BACK (1969)
Bee Gees
   NIGHT FEVER (1978)
   TRAGEDY (1979)
Berlin
   TAKE MY BREATH AWAY (1986)
Chuck Berry
   MY DING-A-LING (1972)
Blondie
   HEART OF GLASS (1979)
   CALL ME (1980)
   THE TIDE IS HIGH (1980)
David Bowie
   LET'S DANCE (1983)
Boyz II Men
   END OF THE ROAD (1992)
Byrds
   MR TAMBOURINE MAN (1965)

Puff Daddy

Belinda Carlisle
HEAVEN IS A PLACE ON EARTH (1988)
Ray Charles
I CAN'T STOP LOVING YOU (1962)
Chicago
IF YOU LEAVE ME NOW (1976)
Rosemary Clooney
THIS OLE HOUSE (1954)
Phil Collins
GROOVY KIND OF LOVE (1988)
Commodores
THREE TIMES A LADY (1978)
Perry Como
DON'T LET THE STARS GET IN YOUR EYES (1953)
Coolio featuring LV
GANGSTA'S PARADISE (1995)
Crickets
THAT'LL BE THE DAY (1957)
Culture Club
KARMA CHAMELEON (1983)
Bobby Darin
MACK THE KNIFE (1959)
Doris Day
SECRET LOVE (1954)
Kiki Dee and Elton John
DON'T GO BREAKING MY HEART (1976)
John Denver
ANNIE'S SONG (1974)
Dexy's Midnight Runners
COME ON EILEEN (1982)
Celine Dion
MY HEART WILL GO ON (1998)
Carl Douglas
KUNG FU FIGHTING (1974)
Duran Duran
THE REFLEX (1984)
Tommy Edwards
IT'S ALL IN THE GAME (1958)
Faith Evans and Puff Daddy
I'LL BE MISSING YOU (1997)
Everly Brothers
ALL I HAVE TO DO IS DREAM / CLAUDETTE (1958)
CATHY'S CLOWN (1960)
Falco
ROCK ME AMADEUS (1986)
Eddie Fisher
I'M WALKING BEHIND YOU (1953)
Tennessee Ernie Ford
SIXTEEN TONS (1956)
Foreigner
I WANT TO KNOW WHAT LOVE IS (1985)
Four Seasons
DECEMBER '63 (OH WHAT A NIGHT) (1976)
Four Tops
REACH OUT I'LL BE THERE (1966)

Aretha Franklin and George Michael
I KNEW YOU WERE WAITING (FOR ME) (1987)
Seidah Garrett and Michael Jackson
I JUST CAN'T STOP LOVING YOU (1987)
Marvin Gaye
I HEARD IT THROUGH THE GRAPEVINE (1969)
Gloria Gaynor
I WILL SURVIVE (1979)
Bill Haley and His Comets
ROCK AROUND THE CLOCK (1955)
Hanson
MMMBOP (1997)
George Harrison
MY SWEET LORD (1971)

Celine Dion

Transatlantic (UK and US) number ones (continued)

Highwaymen
MICHAEL (1961)
Whitney Houston
SAVING ALL MY LOVE FOR YOU (1985)
I WANNA DANCE WITH SOMEBODY (WHO LOVES ME) (1987)
I WILL ALWAYS LOVE YOU (1992)
Human League
DON'T YOU WANT ME (1981)
Tab Hunter
YOUNG LOVE (1957)
Terry Jacks
SEASONS IN THE SUN (1974)

Michael Jackson
BILLIE JEAN (1983)
BLACK OR WHITE (1991)
YOU ARE NOT ALONE (1995)
Michael Jackson (duet Seidah Garrett)
I JUST CAN'T STOP LOVING YOU (1987)
Elton John
**CANDLE IN THE WIND 1997 / SOMETHING ABOUT
THE WAY YOU LOOK TONIGHT (1997)**
Elton John and Kiki Dee
DON'T GO BREAKING MY HEART (1976)
Elton John / George Michael
DON'T LET THE SUN GO DOWN ON ME (1991)
Kitty Kallen
LITTLE THINGS MEAN A LOT (1954)
John Lennon
(JUST LIKE) STARTING OVER (1980)
Los Lobos
LA BAMBA (1987)
Madonna
PAPA DON'T PREACH (1986)
WHO'S THAT GIRL (1987)
LIKE A PRAYER (1989)
VOGUE (1990)

Coolio

Manfred Mann
DO WAH DIDDY DIDDY (1964)
Marcels
BLUE MOON (1961)
Dean Martin
MEMORIES ARE MADE OF THIS (1956)
Al Martino
HERE IN MY HEART (1952)
Paul McCartney and Stevie Wonder
EBONY AND IVORY (1982)
George McCrae
ROCK YOUR BABY (1974)
Meat Loaf
I'LL DO ANYTHING FOR LOVE (BUT I WON'T DO THAT) (1993)
Men at Work
DOWN UNDER (1983)
George Michael
CARELESS WHISPER (1984)
George Michael / Elton John
DON'T LET THE SUN GO DOWN ON ME (1991)
George Michael and Aretha Franklin
I KNEW YOU WERE WAITING (FOR ME) (1987)
Smokey Robinson and the Miracles
THE TEARS OF A CLOWN (1970)
Guy Mitchell
SINGING THE BLUES (1957)
Monkees
I'M A BELIEVER (1967)

New Kids on the Block
HANGIN' TOUGH (1990)
Olivia Newton-John and John Travolta
YOU'RE THE ONE THAT I WANT (1978)
Nilsson
WITHOUT YOU (1972)
Sinead O'Connor
NOTHING COMPARES 2 U (1990)
Roy Orbison
OH PRETTY WOMAN (1964)
Tony Orlando (Dawn)
KNOCK THREE TIMES (1971)
TIE A YELLOW RIBBON ROUND THE OLD OAK TREE (1973)

Paul McCartney

Transatlantic (UK and US) number ones (continued)

Pet Shop Boys
WEST END GIRLS (1986)
Peter and Gordon
A WORLD WITHOUT LOVE (1964)
Pink Floyd
ANOTHER BRICK IN THE WALL (PART 2) (1979)
Platters
SMOKE GETS IN YOUR EYES (1959)
Police
EVERY BREATH YOU TAKE (1983)
Perez Prado
CHERRY PINK AND APPLE BLOSSOM WHITE (1955)
Elvis Presley
ALL SHOOK UP (1957)
JAILHOUSE ROCK (1958)

IT'S NOW OR NEVER (1960)
ARE YOU LONESOME TONIGHT? (1961)
SURRENDER (1961)
GOOD LUCK CHARM (1962)
Johnny Preston
RUNNING BEAR (1960)
Puff Daddy and Faith Evans
I'LL BE MISSING YOU (1997)
Lionel Richie
HELLO (1984)
Righteous Brothers
YOU'VE LOST THAT LOVIN' FEELIN' (1965)
Tommy Roe
DIZZY (1969)
Rolling Stones
(I CAN'T GET NO) SATISFACTION (1965)
GET OFF OF MY CLOUD (1965)
PAINT IT BLACK (1966)
HONKY TONK WOMEN (1969)
Leo Sayer
WHEN I NEED YOU (1977)
Del Shannon
RUNAWAY (1961)

Paul Anka

Simon and Garfunkel
BRIDGE OVER TROUBLED WATER (1970)
Frank Sinatra
STRANGERS IN THE NIGHT (1966)
Nancy Sinatra
THESE BOOTS ARE MADE FOR WALKIN' (1966)
Nancy and Frank Sintra
SOMETHIN' STUPID (1967)
Sonny and Cher
I GOT YOU BABE (1965)
David Soul
DON'T GIVE UP ON US (1977)
Spice Girls
WANNABE (1996)
Jo Stafford
YOU BELONG TO ME (1953)
Kay Starr
ROCK AND ROLL WALTZ (1956)
Starship
NOTHING'S GONNA STOP US NOW (1987)
Ray Stevens
THE STREAK (1974)
Rod Stewart
MAGGIE MAY (1971)
DA YA THINK I'M SEXY (1978)
Barbra Streisand
WOMAN IN LOVE (1980)
Supremes
BABY LOVE (1964)

Survivor
EYE OF THE TIGER (1982)
Tiffany
I THINK WE'RE ALONE NOW (1988)
Tornados
TELSTAR (1962)
John Travolta and Olivia Newton-John
YOU'RE THE ONE THAT I WANT (1978)
Conway Twitty
IT'S ONLY MAKE BELIEVE (1958)
Bonnie Tyler
TOTAL ECLIPSE OF THE HEART (1983)
UB40
(I CAN'T HELP) FALLING IN LOVE (1993)
USA for Africa
WE ARE THE WORLD (1985)
Vanilla Ice
ICE ICE BABY (1990)
Anita Ward
RING MY BELL (1979)
Wham!
WAKE ME UP BEFORE YOU GO GO (1984)
Paul McCartney and Stevie Wonder
EBONY AND IVORY (1982)
Stevie Wonder
I JUST CALLED TO SAY I LOVE YOU (1984)
Zager and Evans
IN THE YEAR 2525 (EXORDIUM and TERMINUS) (1969)

Rolling Stones

What: *Take My Breath Away* **9**
Who: Berlin
When: 1986 (1), 1988 (52), 1990 (3)
Which: Was heard in hit movie *Top Gun*. A noteworthy Giorgio Moroder production and composition that headed the UK/US charts and won an Oscar for Best Film Song of 1986

What: *(Everything I Do) I Do It For You* **10**
Who: Bryan Adams
When: 1991 (1)
Which: Broke longevity records for No 1 in many countries including the UK, where it stayed at the top for 16 consecutive weeks. This song from the movie *Robin Hood: Prince of Thieves* sold more than three million units in the USA alone

What: *Blue Monday* **11**
Who: New Order
When: 1983 (12), 1983 (9), 1988 (3 – remix), 1995 (17 – 2nd remix)
Which: Is the biggest-selling 12-inch single of all time and has spent more than 200 weeks in the UK Top 200. Quincy Jones supervised the 1988 remix, which topped the US club chart

What: *Young Girl* **12**
Who: The Union Gap featuring Gary Puckett
When: 1968 (1), 1974 (6)
Which: Returned to the UK Top 10 six years after heading the transatlantic charts and three years after the group had disbanded. In 1968 they replaced The Beatles as the most successful group in the USA

3 - Alphabetical-by-artist

In this section of **Guinness British Hit Singles**, we list every record that has hit the UK singles chart from 14 November, 1952, to 26 December, 1998. The information is presented **alphabetically** by artist, and then **chronologically** for each artist. Each hit single is catalogued with the following information: **date** disc first hit the chart, **title** of hit, **label** and **catalogue** number, highest **position** the hit reached on the chart, and total **number of weeks** spent on the chart.

Hits: Records which were not hits are not listed. A record is a hit if it appears in the charts even for just one week at No 75, the lowest position listed.

Dates: It should be noted that the date given for the entry of a disc into the chart is the **week ending date,** which is the way that the charts have traditionally been dated. For example, 'Too Much' by the Spice Girls entered the chart in the week ending 27 December 1997, which means that its first day of chart action was 21 December 1997, thus making it the Christmas No 1.

Symbols: No 1 records are indicated by a star symbol, other top ten records by a dot, and a dagger indicates hits still on the chart at the end of 1998. Also, for the first time, symbols are included for records that sold one million copies in the UK, entered the UK chart at No 1, or topped the US chart. Additionally, a **mini-biography** is provided for every artist who has spent 100 weeks or more on the chart, and a **music-genre** symbol for each of the 3000+ artists who have had Top 20 entries. A **key** to hit symbols appears at the bottom of each page, and a key to the music-genre symbols appears on the 'How to Use This Book' feature at the beginning of the book (see pp 6–7).

Collaborations: We have credited **collaborative hits** under the entries of all the artists involved. So, for example, you will find Celine Dion and The Bee Gees' 1998 Top 5 hit, 'Immortality', listed twice – once under Celine Dion and once under Bee Gees. There is no separate entry for them as a new act, and the weeks that this record spent on the chart are credited to both sets of artists.

Credits: A numbered **box** after the catalogue number of any hit indicates that the **credit** on the label of the hit is different from the other hits of that artist. At the foot of each act's list is an explanation of all alternative label credits.

See also 'How to Use This Book' (pp 6–7)

John Lennon

A

A *UK, male vocal / instrumental group* **4 wks**

7 Feb 98	FOGHORN *Tycoon TYCD 5*........................	63	1
11 Apr 98	NUMBER ONE *Tycoon TYCD 6*....................	47	1
27 Jun 98	SING-A-LONG *Tycoon TYCD 7*...................	57	1
24 Oct 98	SUMMER ON THE UNDERGROUND *Tycoon TYCD 8*	72	1

A versus B *UK, male production duo* **1 wk**

9 May 98	RIPPED IN 2 MINUTES *Positiva CDTIV 89*..........	49	1

AALIYAH R&B *US, female vocalist* **32 wks**

2 Jul 94	BACK AND FORTH *Jive JIVECD 357*...............	16	5
15 Oct 94	(AT YOUR BEST) YOU ARE LOVE *Jive JIVECD 359*.....	27	2
11 Mar 95	AGE AIN'T NOTHING BUT A NUMBER *Jive JIVECD 369* ...	32	2
13 May 95	DOWN WITH THE CLIQUE *Jive JIVECD 377*	33	2
9 Sep 95	THE THING I LIKE *Jive JIVECD 382*	33	2
3 Feb 96	I NEED YOU TONIGHT *Big Beat A 8130CD* [1]	66	1
24 Aug 96	IF YOUR GIRL ONLY KNEW *Atlantic A 5669CD*.....	21	2
23 Nov 96	GOT TO GIVE IT UP *Atlantic A 5632CD*........	37	2
24 May 97	IF YOUR GIRL ONLY KNEW / ONE IN A MILLION *Atlantic A 5610CD*	15	3
30 Aug 97	4 PAGE LETTER *Atlantic AT 0010CD1*	24	2
22 Nov 97	THE ONE I GAVE MY HEART TO / HOT LIKE FIRE *Atlantic A 0017CD*	30	2
18 Apr 98	JOURNEY TO THE PAST *Atlantic AT 0026CD*	22	3
12 Sep 98	ARE YOU THAT SOMEBODY? *Atlantic AT 0047CD* ...	11	4

[1] Junior MAFIA featuring Aaliyah

ABBA ☻ *The most successful Swedish recording act in UK: Bjorn Ulvaeus (g/v), Benny Andersson (k/v), Agnetha Faltskog (v), Anni-Frid (Frida) Lyngstad (v). 'Waterloo' was the first Scandinavian No 1 in the UK and the biggest-ever Eurovision Song Contest hit in the USA* **252 wks**

20 Apr 74	★ WATERLOO *Epic EPC 2240*	1	9
13 Jul 74	RING RING *Epic EPC 2452*.................	32	5
12 Jul 75	I DO I DO I DO I DO I DO *Epic EPC 3229*	38	6
20 Sep 75	● S. O. S. *Epic EPC 3576*	6	10
13 Dec 75	★ MAMMA MIA *Epic EPC 3790*	1	14
27 Mar 76	★ FERNANDO *Epic EPC 4036*	1	15
21 Aug 76	★ DANCING QUEEN *Epic EPC 4499* ▲	1	15
20 Nov 76	● MONEY MONEY MONEY *Epic EPC 4713*........	3	12
26 Feb 77	★ KNOWING ME KNOWING YOU *Epic EPC 4955* ...	1	13
22 Oct 77	★ THE NAME OF THE GAME *Epic EPC 5750*	1	12
4 Feb 78	★ TAKE A CHANCE ON ME *Epic EPC 5950*	1	10
16 Sep 78	● SUMMER NIGHT CITY *Epic EPC 6595*..........	5	9
5 May 79	● DOES YOUR MOTHER KNOW *Epic EPC 7316*	4	9
14 Jul 79	● ANGELEYES / VOULEZ-VOUS *Epic EPC 7499*	3	11
20 Oct 79	● GIMME GIMME GIMME (A MAN AFTER MIDNIGHT) *Epic EPC 7914*	3	12
15 Dec 79	● I HAVE A DREAM *Epic EPC 8088*	2	10
2 Aug 80	★ THE WINNER TAKES IT ALL *Epic EPC 8835*	1	10
18 Jul 81	● LAY ALL YOUR LOVE ON ME *Epic EPC A 1314*....	7	7
12 Dec 81	● ONE OF US *Epic EPC A 1740*................	3	10
20 Feb 82	HEAD OVER HEELS *Epic EPC A 2037*	25	7
23 Oct 82	THE DAY BEFORE YOU CAME *Epic EPC A 2847*.....	32	6
11 Dec 82	UNDER ATTACK *Epic EPC A 2971*	26	8
12 Nov 83	THANK YOU FOR THE MUSIC *CBS A 3894*	33	6
5 Sep 92	DANCING QUEEN (re-issue) *Polydor PO 231*	16	5

ABBACADABRA *UK, male/female vocal/instrumental group* **1 wk**

5 Sep 92	DANCING QUEEN *PWL International PWL 246*	57	1

Russ ABBOT ℂ *UK, male vocalist* **22 wks**

6 Feb 82	A DAY IN THE LIFE OF VINCE PRINCE *EMI 5249*	61	1
20 Feb 82	A DAY IN THE LIFE OF VINCE PRINCE (re-entry) *EMI 5249* ...75	75	1
29 Dec 84	● ATMOSPHERE *Spirit FIRE 4*	7	13
13 Jul 85	ALL NIGHT HOLIDAY *Spirit FIRE 6*	20	7

Gregory ABBOTT 𝄞 *US, male vocalist* **13 wks**

22 Nov 86	● SHAKE YOU DOWN *CBS A 7326* ▲	6	13

ABC ☻ *UK, male vocal/instrumental duo* **93 wks**

31 Oct 81	● TEARS ARE NOT ENOUGH *Neutron NT 101*	19	8
20 Feb 82	● POISON ARROW *Neutron NT 102*	6	11
15 May 82	● THE LOOK OF LOVE *Neutron NT 103*	4	11
4 Sep 82	● ALL OF MY HEART *Neutron NT 104*	5	8
15 Jan 83	THE LOOK OF LOVE (re-entry) *Neutron NT 103*	71	1
5 Nov 83	THAT WAS THEN THIS IS NOW *Neutron NT 105*	18	4
21 Jan 84	S.O.S. *Neutron NT 106*	39	5
10 Nov 84	HOW TO BE A MILLIONAIRE *Neutron NT 107*	49	4
6 Apr 85	BE NEAR ME *Neutron NT 108*	26	4
15 Jun 85	VANITY KILLS *Neutron NT 109*	70	1
16 Jan 86	OCEAN BLUE *Neutron NT 110*	51	3
6 Jun 87	WHEN SMOKEY SINGS *Neutron NT 111*	11	10
5 Sep 87	THE NIGHT YOU MURDERED LOVE *Neutron NT 112*....	31	4
28 Nov 87	KING WITHOUT A CROWN *Neutron NT 113*	44	3
27 May 89	ONE BETTER WORLD *Neutron NT 114*	32	4
23 Sep 89	THE REAL THING *Neutron NT 115*.............	68	1
14 Apr 90	THE LOOK OF LOVE (re-mix) *Neutron NT 116*	68	1
27 Jul 91	LOVE CONQUERS ALL *Parlophone R 6292*........	47	2
11 Jan 92	SAY IT *Parlophone R 6298*	42	3
22 Mar 97	STRANGER THINGS BLATANT *Deconstruction 453632* ...57	57	1

The act was a UK, male vocal/instrumental group for first six hits, and a UK/US, male/female vocal/instrumental group for the next four

Paula ABDUL ☻ ☺ *US, female vocalist* **67 wks**

4 Mar 89	● STRAIGHT UP *Siren SRN 111* ▲	3	13
3 Jun 89	FOREVER YOUR GIRL *Siren SRN 112* ▲	24	6
19 Aug 89	KNOCKED OUT *Siren SRN 92*	45	3
2 Dec 89	(IT'S JUST) THE WAY THAT YOU LOVE ME *Siren SRN 101*	74	1
7 Apr 90	● OPPOSITES ATTRACT *Siren SRN 124* [1] ▲	2	13
21 Jul 90	KNOCKED OUT (re-mix) *Virgin America VUS 23*	21	5
29 Sep 90	COLD HEARTED *Virgin America VUS 27* ▲	46	3
22 Jun 91	● RUSH RUSH *Virgin America VUS 38* ▲	6	11
31 Aug 91	THE PROMISE OF A NEW DAY *Virgin America VUS 44* ▲ ...52	52	2
18 Jan 92	VIBEOLOGY *Virgin America VUS 53*	19	6
8 Aug 92	WILL YOU MARRY ME *Virgin America VUS 58*......	73	1
17 Jun 95	MY LOVE IS FOR REAL *Virgin America VUSCD 91* ...	28	3

[1] Paula Abdul with the Wild Pair

ABI *UK, male vocalist* **2 wks**

13 Jun 98	COUNTING THE DAYS *Kuku CDKUKU 1*	44	2

ABIGAIL *UK, female vocalist* **4 wks**

16 Jul 94	SMELLS LIKE TEEN SPIRIT *Klone CDKLONE 25*......	29	4

Colonel ABRAMS ☺ 𝄞 *US, male vocalist* **35 wks**

17 Aug 85	● TRAPPED *MCA MCA 997*...................	3	23
7 Dec 85	THE TRUTH *MCA MCA 1022*.................	53	3
8 Feb 86	I'M NOT GONNA LET YOU (GET THE BEST OF ME) *MCA MCA 1031*	24	7
15 Aug 87	HOW SOON WE FORGET *MCA MCA 1179*	75	2

ABSOLUTE *US, male production / instrumental duo* **3 wks**

18 Jan 97	I BELIEVE *AM:PM 5820752* [1]	38	2
14 Mar 98	CATCH ME *AM:PM 5825032*	69	1

[1] Absolute featuring Suzanne Palmer

ABSOLUTELY FABULOUS – See PET SHOP BOYS

AC/DC ✈
Internationally acclaimed Australia-based quintet: Angus Young (g), Malcolm Young (g), Bon Scott (v) (d. 1980), Cliff Williams (b), Phillip Rudd (d). Brian Johnson (ex-Geordie) replaced Scott in 1980. Surprisingly, these top album sellers never had a UK Top 10 single **125 wks**

10 Jun 78	ROCK 'N' ROLL DAMNATION *Atlantic K 11142*	24	9
1 Sep 79	HIGHWAY TO HELL *Atlantic K 11321*	56	4
2 Feb 80	TOUCH TOO MUCH *Atlantic K 11435*	29	9
28 Jun 80	DIRTY DEEDS DONE DIRT CHEAP *Atlantic HM 2*	47	4
28 Jun 80	HIGH VOLTAGE (LIVE VERSION) *Atlantic HM 1*	48	3
28 Jun 80	IT'S A LONG WAY TO THE TOP (IF YOU WANNA ROCK 'N' ROLL) *Atlantic HM 3*	55	3
28 Jun 80	WHOLE LOTTA ROSIE *Atlantic HM 4*	36	8
13 Sep 80	YOU SHOOK ME ALL NIGHT LONG *Atlantic K 11600*	38	6
29 Nov 80	ROCK 'N' ROLL AIN'T NOISE POLLUTION *Atlantic K 11630*	15	8
6 Feb 82	LET'S GET IT UP *Atlantic K 11706*	13	6
3 Jul 82	FOR THOSE ABOUT TO ROCK (WE SALUTE YOU) *Atlantic K 11721*	15	6
29 Oct 83	GUNS FOR HIRE *Atlantic A 9774*	37	4
4 Aug 84	NERVOUS SHAKEDOWN *Atlantic A 9651*	35	5
6 Jul 85	DANGER *Atlantic A 9532*	48	4
18 Jan 86	SHAKE YOUR FOUNDATIONS *Atlantic A 9474*	24	5
24 May 86	WHO MADE WHO *Atlantic A 9425*	16	5
30 Aug 86	YOU SHOOK ME ALL NIGHT LONG (re-issue) *Atlantic A 9377*	46	4
16 Jan 88	HEATSEEKER *Atlantic A 9136*	12	6
2 Apr 88	THAT'S THE WAY I WANNA ROCK 'N' ROLL *Atlantic A 9098*	22	5
22 Sep 90	THUNDERSTRUCK *Atco B 8907*	13	5
24 Nov 90	MONEYTALKS *Atco B 8886*	36	3
27 Apr 91	ARE YOU READY *Atco B 8830*	34	3
17 Oct 92	HIGHWAY TO HELL (LIVE) *Atco B 8479*	14	4
6 Mar 93	DIRTY DEEDS DONE DIRT CHEAP (LIVE) *Atco B 6073CD*	68	1
10 Jul 93	BIG GUN *Atco B 8396CD*	23	3
30 Sep 95	HARD AS A ROCK *Atlantic A 4368CD*	33	2
11 May 96	HAIL CAESAR *East West 7559660512*	56	1

Richard ACE *Jamaica, male vocalist* **2 wks**

2 Dec 78	STAYIN' ALIVE *Blue Inc. INC 2*	66	2

ACE ✔ *UK, male vocal/instrumental group* **10 wks**

9 Nov 74	HOW LONG *Anchor ANC 1002*	20	10

ACE OF BASE ☺
Sweden, male/female vocal/instrumental group **88 wks**

8 May 93	★ ALL THAT SHE WANTS *London 8612702*	1	16
28 Aug 93	WHEEL OF FORTUNE *London 8615452*	20	6
13 Nov 93	HAPPY NATION *London 8619272*	42	3
26 Feb 94	● THE SIGN *London ACECD 1* ▲	2	11
11 Jun 94	● DON'T TURN AROUND *London ACECD 2*	5	11
15 Oct 94	HAPPY NATION (re-issue) *London 8610972*	40	3
14 Jan 95	LIVING IN DANGER *London ACECD 3*	18	4
11 Nov 95	LUCKY LOVE *London ACECD 4*	20	5
27 Jan 96	BEAUTIFUL LIFE *London ACECD 5*	15	6
25 Jul 98	● LIFE IS A FLOWER *London ACECD 7*	5	11
10 Oct 98	● CRUEL SUMMER *London ACECD 8*	8	5
19 Dec 98	ALWAYS HAVE, ALWAYS WILL *London ACECD 9*	12†	2

ACEN *UK, male producer* **4 wks**

8 Aug 92	TRIP II THE MOON *Production House PNT 042*	38	3
10 Oct 92	TRIP II THE MOON (re-mix) *Production House PNT 042RX*	71	1

ACES – See Desmond DEKKER and the ACES

Tracy ACKERMAN – See Q

ACT *UK/Germany, male/female vocal/instrumental group* **2 wks**

23 May 87	SNOBBERY AND DECAY *ZTT ZTAS 28*	60	2

ACT ONE *US, male/female vocal/instrumental group* **6 wks**

18 May 74	TOM THE PEEPER *Mercury 6008 005*	40	6

A.D.A.M. featuring AMY ☺ ☺
France, male/female vocal/instrumental duo **11 wks**

1 Jul 95	ZOMBIE *Eternal YZ 951CD*	16	11

Arthur ADAMS *US, male vocalist* **5 wks**

24 Oct 81	YOU GOT THE FLOOR *RCA 146*	38	5

Bryan ADAMS ✔
Globally successful rock singer/songwriter/guitarist, b. 5 November, 1959, Ontario. He has had more UK hits than any other Canadian artist and was the biggest-selling singles artist in the UK in 1991 **196 wks**

12 Jan 85	RUN TO YOU *A&M AM 224*	11	12
16 Mar 85	SOMEBODY *A&M AM 236*	35	7
25 May 85	HEAVEN *A&M AM 256*	38	5
10 Aug 85	SUMMER OF '69 *A&M AM 267*	42	7
2 Nov 85	IT'S ONLY LOVE *A&M 285* [1]	29	6
21 Dec 85	CHRISTMAS TIME *A & M AM 297*	55	2
22 Feb 86	THIS TIME *A & M AM 295*	41	7
12 Jul 86	STRAIGHT FROM THE HEART *A & M AM 322*	51	3
28 Mar 87	HEAT OF THE NIGHT *A & M ADAM 2*	50	2
20 Jun 87	HEARTS ON FIRE *A & M ADAM 3*	57	3
17 Oct 87	VICTIM OF LOVE *A & M AM 407*	68	2
29 Jun 91	★ (EVERYTHING I DO) I DO IT FOR YOU *A & M AM 789* ◆ ▲	1	24
14 Sep 91	CAN'T STOP THIS THING WE STARTED *A & M AM 612*	12	6
23 Nov 91	THERE WILL NEVER BE ANOTHER TONIGHT *A & M AM 838*	32	3
28 Dec 91	(EVERYTHING I DO) I DO IT FOR YOU (re-entry) *A & M AM 789*	73	1
22 Feb 92	● THOUGHT I'D DIED AND GONE TO HEAVEN *A & M AM 848*	8	7
18 Jul 92	ALL I WANT IS YOU *A & M AM 879*	22	5
26 Sep 92	DO I HAVE TO SAY THE WORDS *A & M AM 0068*	30	3
30 Oct 93	● PLEASE FORGIVE ME *A & M 5804232*	2	16
15 Jan 94	● ALL FOR LOVE *A & M 5804772* [2] ▲	2	13
22 Apr 95	● HAVE YOU EVER REALLY LOVED A WOMAN *A & M 5810282* ▲	4	9
11 Nov 95	ROCK STEADY *Capitol CDCL 763* [3]	50	2
1 Jun 96	● THE ONLY THING THAT LOOKS GOOD ON ME IS YOU *A & M 5813692*	6	7
24 Aug 96	● LET'S MAKE A NIGHT TO REMEMBER *A & M 5815672*	10	8
23 Nov 96	STAR *A & M 5820252*	13	4
8 Feb 97	● I FINALLY FOUND SOMEONE *A & M 5820832* [4]	10	7
19 Apr 97	18 TIL I DIE *A & M 5821852*	22	3
20 Dec 97	BACK TO YOU *A & M 5824752*	18	7
21 Mar 98	I'M READY *A & M 5825352*	20	4
10 Oct 98	ON A DAY LIKE TODAY *Mercury MERCD 516*	13	5
12 Dec 98	● WHEN YOU'RE GONE *A & M 5828212* [5]	3†	6

[1] Bryan Adams and Tina Turner [2] Bryan Adams, Rod Stewart and Sting
[3] Bonnie Raitt and Bryan Adams [4] Barbra Streisand and Bryan Adams
[5] Bryan Adams featuring Melanie C

Cliff ADAMS *UK, orchestra* **2 wks**

28 Apr 60	LONELY MAN THEME *Pye International 7N 25056*	39	2

Gayle ADAMS *US, female vocalist* **1 wk**

26 Jul 80	STRETCHIN' OUT *Epic EPC 8791*	64	1

Marie ADAMS – See Johnny OTIS SHOW

Oleta ADAMS 🎷 ☺ *US, female vocalist* **36 wks**

24 Mar 90	RHYTHM OF LIFE *Fontana OLETA 1*	52	2
3 Nov 90	RHYTHM OF LIFE (re-entry) *Fontana OLETA 1*	56	3
12 Jan 91	● GET HERE *Fontana OLETA 3*	4	12
13 Apr 91	YOU'VE GOT TO GIVE ME ROOM/RHYTHM OF LIFE (re-issue) *Fontana OLETA 4*	49	3
29 Jun 91	CIRCLE OF ONE *Fontana OLETA 5*	73	1
28 Sep 91	DON'T LET THE SUN GO DOWN ON ME *Fontana TRIBO 1*	33	5
25 Apr 92	WOMAN IN CHAINS (re-issue) *Fontana IDEA 16* [1]	57	1
10 Jul 93	I JUST HAD TO HEAR YOUR VOICE *Fontana OLECD 6*	42	3
7 Oct 95	NEVER KNEW LOVE *Fontana OLECD 9*	22	3
16 Dec 95	RHYTHM OF LIFE (re-mix) *Fontana OLECD 10*	38	2

10 Feb 96	WE WILL MEET AGAIN *Mercury OLECD 11*	51	1

[1] Tears For Fears featuring Oleta Adams

The original release of 'Woman in Chains' credited Tears For Fears only

ADAMSKI ☺ ⊗ *UK, male instrumentalist/producer* — 39 wks

20 Jan 90	N-R-G *MCA MCA 1386*............................	12	6
7 Apr 90	★ KILLER *MCA MCA 1400*...........................	1	18
8 Sep 90	● THE SPACE JUNGLE *MCA MCA 1435*.............	7	8
17 Nov 90	FLASHBACK JACK *MCA MCA 1459*..................	46	2
9 Nov 91	NEVER GOIN' DOWN/BORN TO BE ALIVE *MCA MCS 1578* [1] ...51		2
4 Apr 92	GET YOUR BODY *MCA MCS 1613* [2]	68	1
4 Jul 92	BACK TO FRONT *MCA MCS 1644*	63	1
11 Jul 98	ONE OF THE PEOPLE *ZTT ZTT 101CD* [3]	56	1

[1] Adamski featuring Jimi Polo/Adamski featuring Soho
[2] Adamski featuring Nina Hagen [3] Adamski's Thing

Featured vocalist on 'Killer' was Seal

ADDAMS and GEE *UK, male instrumental duo* — 1 wk

20 Apr 91	CHUNG KUO (REVISITED) *Debut DEBT 3108*	72	1

ADDIS BLACK WIDOW *US, male rap duo* — 2 wks

3 Feb 96	INNOCENT *Mercury Black Vinyl MBVCD 1*	42	2

ADDRISI BROTHERS *US, male vocal duo* — 3 wks

6 Oct 79	GHOST DANCER *Scotti Brothers K 11361*................	57	3

ADEVA 🎤 ☺ *US, female vocalist* — 66 wks

14 Jan 89	RESPECT *Cooltempo COOL 179*	17	9
25 Mar 89	MUSICAL FREEDOM (MOVING ON UP) *Cooltempo COOL 182* [1]	22	8
12 Aug 89	WARNING *Cooltempo COOL 185*	17	8
21 Oct 89	I THANK YOU *Cooltempo COOL 192*	17	7
16 Dec 89	BEAUTIFUL LOVE *Cooltempo COOL 195*	57	1
28 Apr 90	TREAT ME RIGHT *Cooltempo COOL 200*	62	2
6 Apr 91	RING MY BELL *Cooltempo COOL 224* [2]	20	5
19 Oct 91	IT SHOULD'VE BEEN ME *Cooltempo COOL 236* ...	48	3
29 Feb 92	DON'T LET IT SHOW ON YOUR FACE *Cooltempo COOL 248*.....34		4
6 Jun 92	UNTIL YOU COME BACK TO ME *Cooltempo COOL 254*	45	3
17 Oct 92	I'M THE ONE FOR YOU *Cooltempo COOL 264*	51	2
11 Dec 93	RESPECT (re-mix) *Network NWKCD 79*	65	1
27 May 95	TOO MANY FISH *Virgin America VUSCD 89* [3] 34		2
18 Nov 95	WHADDA U WANT (FROM ME) *Virgin America VUSCD 98* [3] ...36		2
6 Apr 96	DO WATCHA DO *Avex UK AVEXCD 24* [3]	54	1
4 May 96	I THANK YOU (re-mix) *Cooltempo CDCOOLS 318*	37	2
12 Apr 97	DO WATCHA DO (re-issue) *Distinctive DISNCD 28* [4]	60	1
26 Jul 97	WHERE IS THE LOVE?/THE WAY THAT YOU FEEL *Distinctive DISNCD 31*................	54	1

[1] Paul Simpson featuring Adeva [2] Monie Love vs Adeva [3] Frankie Knuckles featuring Adeva [4] Hyper Go Go and Adeva

ADICTS *UK, male vocal/instrumental group* — 1 wk

14 May 83	BAD BOY *Razor RZS 104*	75	1

ADIEMUS *UK, male instrumental duo* — 2 wks

14 Oct 95	ADIEMUS *Venture VEND 4*	48	2

Larry ADLER – See Kate BUSH

ADONIS featuring 2 PUERTO RICANS, A BLACK MAN AND A DOMINICAN *US, male vocal/instrumental group* — 4 wks

13 Jun 87	DO IT PROPERLY ('NO WAY BACK')/NO WAY BACK *London LON 136*	47	4

ADRENALIN M.O.D. *US, male vocal/instrumental group* — 5 wks

8 Oct 88	O-O-O *MCA RAGAT 2*.........................	49	5

ADULT NET *UK/US, male/female vocal/instrumental group* — 2 wks

10 Jun 89	WHERE WERE YOU *Fontana BRX 2*..............	66	2

ADVENTURES ⊗ *UK, male vocal/instrumental group* — 24 wks

15 Sep 84	ANOTHER SILENT DAY *Chrysalis CHS 2000*........	71	2
1 Dec 84	SEND MY HEART *Chrysalis CHS 2001*...........	62	4
13 Jul 85	FEEL THE RAINDROPS *Chrysalis AD 1*..........	58	3
9 Apr 88	BROKEN LAND *Elektra EKR 69*................	20	10
2 Jul 88	DROWNING IN THE SEA OF LOVE *Elektra EKR 76*.....	44	4
13 Jun 92	RAINING ALL OVER THE WORLD *Polydor PO 211*......	68	1

ADVENTURES OF STEVIE V ☺ *US, male producer and vocalist* — 22 wks

21 Apr 90	● DIRTY CASH *Mercury MER 311*	2	13
29 Sep 90	BODY LANGUAGE *Mercury MER 331*.............	29	5
2 Mar 91	JEALOUSY *Mercury MER 337*..................	58	3
27 Sep 97	DIRTY CASH (re-mix) *Avex Trax AVEXCDX 57*	69	1

ADVERTS ⊗ *UK, male/female vocal/instrumental group* — 11 wks

27 Aug 77	GARY GILMORE'S EYES *Anchor ANC 1043*	18	7
4 Feb 78	NO TIME TO BE 21 *Bright BR 1*	34	4

AEROSMITH ✈ *US, male vocal/instrumental group* — 75 wks

17 Oct 87	DUDE (LOOKS LIKE A LADY) *Geffen GEF 29*	45	5
16 Apr 88	ANGEL *Geffen GEF 34*	69	2
9 Sep 89	LOVE IN AN ELEVATOR *Geffen GEF 63*	13	8
24 Feb 90	DUDE (LOOKS LIKE A LADY) (re-issue) *Geffen GEF 72*	20	5
14 Apr 90	RAG DOLL *Geffen GEF 76*	42	4
1 Sep 90	THE OTHER SIDE *Geffen GEF 79*	46	2
10 Apr 93	LIVIN' ON THE EDGE *Geffen GFSTD 35*	19	4
3 Jul 93	EAT THE RICH *Geffen GFSTD 46*	34	3
30 Oct 93	CRYIN' *Geffen GFSTD 56*	17	6
18 Dec 93	AMAZING *Geffen GFSTD 63*	57	3
2 Jul 94	SHUT UP AND DANCE *Geffen GFSTD 75*	24	4
20 Aug 94	SWEET EMOTION *Columbia 6604492*	74	1
5 Nov 94	CRAZY / BLIND MAN *Geffen GFSTD 80*	23	4
8 Mar 97	FALLING IN LOVE (IS HARD ON THE KNEES) *Columbia 6640752*..................	22	4
21 Jun 97	HOLE IN MY SOUL *Columbia 66645012*	29	2
27 Dec 97	PINK *Columbia 6648722*	38	2
12 Sep 98	I DON'T WANT TO MISS A THING *Columbia 6664082* ▲ ....4†		16

AFRICAN BUSINESS *Italy, male vocal/instrumental group* — 1 wk

17 Nov 90	IN ZAIRE *Urban URB 64*	73	1

AFTER 7 *US, male vocal group* — 3 wks

3 Nov 90	CAN'T STOP *Virgin America VUS 31*	54	3

AFTER THE FIRE *UK, male vocal/instrumental group* — 12 wks

9 Jun 79	ONE RULE FOR YOU *CBS 7025*.................	40	6
8 Sep 79	LASER LOVE *CBS 7769*......................	62	2
9 Apr 83	DER KOMMISSAR *CBS A 2399*.................	47	4

AFTERNOON BOYS – See Steve WRIGHT

AFTERSHOCK ☺ *US, male vocal/instrumental duo* — 8 wks

21 Aug 93	SLAVE TO THE VIBE *Virgin America VUSCD 75*........11		8

AGE OF CHANCE *UK, male/female vocal/instrumental group* — 13 wks

17 Jan 87	KISS *Fon AGE 5*	50	6
30 May 87	WHO'S AFRAID OF THE BIG BAD NOISE! *Fon VS 962*	65	2
20 Jan 90	HIGHER THAN HEAVEN *Virgin VS 1228*	53	5

AGE OF LOVE ☺ *Italy, male instrumental / production duo* — 6 wks

5 Jul 97	THE AGE OF LOVE – THE REMIXES *React CDREACT 100* 17		4
19 Sep 98	AGE OF LOVE *React CDREACT 135*	38	2

AGENT 00 *UK, male production duo*   **1 wk**

7 Mar 98	THE MAGNIFICENT *Inferno CDFERN 002*	65	1

AGENT PROVOCATEUR
UK, male / female vocal / production group   **1 wk**

22 Mar 97	AGENT DAN *Epic AGENT 3CD*	49	1

AGNELLI and NELSON *Ireland, male DJ duo*   **4 wks**

15 Aug 98	EL NINO *Xtravaganza 0091575 EXT*	21	4

A-HA ⊗ *Norway's biggest-selling act: Morten Harket (v), Pal Waaktaar (g), Magna Furuholmen (k). This teen-targeted trio were one of the world's most popular acts in the 1980s. Noted for their videos and stage shows, they attracted big and enthusiastic audiences globally*   **131 wks**

28 Sep 85 ●	TAKE ON ME *Warner Bros. W 9006* ▲	2	19
28 Dec 85 ★	THE SUN ALWAYS SHINES ON TV *Warner Bros. W 8846*	1	12
5 Apr 86 ●	TRAIN OF THOUGHT *Warner Bros. W 8736*	8	8
14 Jun 86 ●	HUNTING HIGH AND LOW *Warner Bros. W 6663*	5	10
4 Oct 86 ●	I'VE BEEN LOSING YOU *Warner Bros. W 8594*	8	7
6 Dec 86 ●	CRY WOLF *Warner Bros. W 8500*	5	7
28 Feb 87	MANHATTAN SKYLINE *Warner Bros. W 8405*	13	6
4 Jul 87 ●	THE LIVING DAYLIGHTS *Warner Bros. W 8305*	5	9
26 Mar 88 ●	STAY ON THESE ROADS *Warner Bros. W 7936*	5	6
18 Jun 88	THE BLOOD THAT MOVES THE BODY *Warner Bros. W 7840*	25	4
27 Aug 88	TOUCHY! *Warner Bros. W 7749*	11	7
3 Dec 88	YOU ARE THE ONE *Warner Bros. W 7636*	13	10
13 Oct 90	CRYING IN THE RAIN *Warner Bros. W 9547*	13	7
15 Dec 90	I CALL YOUR NAME *Warner Bros. W 9462*	44	5
26 Oct 91	MOVE TO MEMPHIS *Warner Bros. W 0070*	47	2
5 Jun 93	DARK IS THE NIGHT *Warner Bros. W 0175CD*	19	4
18 Sep 93	ANGEL *Warner Bros. W 0195CD*	41	3
26 Mar 94	SHAPES THAT GO TOGETHER *Warner Bros. W 0236CD*	27	3

AHMAD *US, male rapper*   **2 wks**

9 Jul 94	BACK IN THE DAY *Giant 74321212042*	64	2

AIR ☺ ⊗ *France, male instrumental / production duo – Benoit Dunkel, Nicolas Godin*   **10 wks**

21 Feb 98	SEXY BOY *Virgin VSCDT 1672*	13	4
16 May 98	KELLY WATCH THE STARS *Virgin VSCDT 1690*	18	3
21 Nov 98	ALL I NEED *Virgin VSCDT 1702*	29	3

AIR SUPPLY ⊗ *UK/Australia, male vocal/instrumental group*   **17 wks**

27 Sep 80	ALL OUT OF LOVE *Arista ARIST 362*	11	11
2 Oct 82	EVEN THE NIGHTS ARE BETTER *Arista ARIST 474*	44	4
20 Nov 93	GOODBYE *Giant 74321153462*	66	2

AIRHEAD *UK, male vocal/instrumental group*   **10 wks**

5 Oct 91	FUNNY HOW *Korova KOW 47*	57	3
21 Dec 91	COUNTING SHEEP *Korova KOW 48*	35	5
7 Mar 92	RIGHT NOW *Korova KOW 49*	50	2

AIRSCAPE *Belgium / Holland male instrumental/production group*   **3 wks**

9 Aug 97	PACIFIC MELODY *Multiply CDMULTY 22*	27	2
29 Aug 98	AMAZON CHANT *Xtravaganza 0091605 EXT*	46	1

See also CUBIC 22

Laurel AITKEN and the UNITONE
Jamaica/Cuba, male vocal/instrumental group   **3 wks**

17 May 80	RUDI GOT MARRIED *I-Spy SEE 6*	60	3

AKA *UK, male vocal group*   **2 wks**

12 Oct 96	WARNING *RCA 74321360662*	43	2

Jewel AKENS *US, male/vocalist*   **8 wks**

25 Mar 65	THE BIRDS AND THE BEES *London HLN 9954*	29	8

AKIN *UK, female vocal duo*   **1 wk**

14 Jun 97	STAY RIGHT HERE *WEA WEA 117CD*	60	1

ALABAMA 3 *UK, male vocal/instrumental group*   **3 wks**

22 Nov 97	SPEED AT THE SOUND OF LONELINESS *Elemental ELM 42CDS 1721*	72	1
11 Apr 98	AIN'T GOIN' TO GOA *Elemental ELM 45CDS1*	40	2

ALANA – See MK

ALARM ✎ *UK, male vocal/instrumental group*   **64 wks**

24 Sep 83	68 GUNS *IRS PFP 1023*	17	7
21 Jan 84	WHERE WERE YOU HIDING WHEN THE STORM BROKE *IRS IRS 101*	22	6
31 Mar 84	THE DECEIVER *IRS IRS 103*	51	4
3 Nov 84	THE CHANT HAS JUST BEGUN *IRS IRS 104*	48	4
2 Mar 85	ABSOLUTE REALITY *IRS ALARM 1*	35	6
28 Sep 85	STRENGTH *IRS IRM 104*	40	4
18 Jan 86	SPIRIT OF '76 *IRS IRM 109*	22	5
26 Apr 86	KNIFE EDGE *IRS IRM 112*	43	3
17 Oct 87	RAIN IN THE SUMMERTIME *IRS IRM 144*	18	5
12 Dec 87	RESCUE ME *IRS IRM 150*	48	2
20 Feb 88	PRESENCE OF LOVE (LAUGHERNE) *IRS IRM 155*	44	3
16 Sep 89	SOLD ME DOWN THE RIVER *IRS EIRS 123*	43	3
4 Nov 89	A NEW SOUTH WALES/THE ROCK *IRS EIRS 129*	31	5
3 Feb 90	LOVE DON'T COME EASY *IRS EIRS 134*	48	3
27 Oct 90	UNSAFE BUILDING 1990 *IRS ALARM 2*	54	2
13 Apr 91	RAW *IRS ALARM 3*	51	2

'A New South Wales' features Morriston Orpheus Male Voice Choir

Morris ALBERT ☾ *Brazil, male vocalist*   **10 wks**

27 Sep 75 ●	FEELINGS *Decca F 13591*	4	10

ALBERTA *Sierra Leone, female vocal*   **1 wk**

26 Dec 98	YOYO BOY *RCA 74321640602*	49†	1

ALBERTO Y LOST TRIOS PARANOIAS
UK, male vocal/instrumental group   **5 wks**

23 Sep 78	HEADS DOWN NO NONSENSE MINDLESS BOOGIE *Logo GO 323*	47	5

ALCATRAZ ☺ *US, male instrumental/production duo*   **4 wks**

17 Feb 96	GIV ME LUV *AM:PM 5814332*	12	4

ALDA ⊗ *Iceland, female vocalist*   **8 wks**

29 Aug 98	REAL GOOD TIME *Wildstar CDWILD 7*	7	7
26 Dec 98	GIRLS NIGHT OUT *Wildstar CDWILD 10*	20†	1

Cali ALEMAN – See Tito PUENTE Jr and the LATIN RHYTHM featuring
Tito PUENTE, INDIA and Cali ALEMAN

ALESSI ⊗ *US, male vocal duo*   **11 wks**

11 Jun 77 ●	OH LORI *A & M AMS 7289*	8	11

ALEX PARTY ☺
Italy/UK, male/female vocal/instrumental group   **28 wks**

18 Dec 93	SATURDAY NIGHT PARTY *Cleveland City Imports CCICD 17000*	49	6
28 May 94	SATURDAY NIGHT PARTY (READ MY LIPS) (re-entry) *Cleveland City Imports CCICD 17000*	29	4
18 Feb 95 ●	DON'T GIVE ME YOUR LIFE *Systematic SYSCD 7*	2	13
18 Nov 95	WRAP ME UP *Systematic SYSCD 22*	17	3
19 Oct 96	READ MY LIPS (re-mix) *Systematic SYSCD 30*	28	2

'Read My Lips' in 1996 is a remix of the first hit with added vocals

ALEXIA ⊗ ☺ *Italian, female vocalist*   **15 wks**

21 Mar 98 ●	UH LA LA LA *Dance Pool ALEX 1CD*	10	9

| 13 Jun 98 | GIMME LOVE *Dance Pool ALEX 2CDZ* | 17 | 4 |
| 10 Oct 98 | THE MUSIC I LIKE *Dance Pool ALEX 3CD* | 31 | 2 |

ALFI and HARRY (
US, male vocalist – David Seville under two false names **5 wks**

| 23 Mar 56 | THE TROUBLE WITH HARRY *London HLU 8242* | 15 | 5 |

See also David SEVILLE

John ALFORD ☉ *UK, male vocalist* **12 wks**

17 Feb 96	SMOKE GETS IN YOUR EYES *Love This LUVTHISCD 7*	13	5
25 May 96 ●	BLUE MOON/ONLY YOU *Love This LUVTHISCD 9*	9	4
23 Nov 96	IF/KEEP ON RUNNING *Love This LUVTHISCD 15*	24	3

ALI *UK, male vocalist* **2 wks**

| 23 May 98 | LOVE LETTERS *Wild Card 5698092* | 63 | 1 |
| 24 Oct 98 | FEELIN' YOU *Wild Card 5676992* | 63 | 1 |

ALI and FRAZIER *UK, female vocal duo* **4 wks**

| 7 Aug 93 | UPTOWN TOP RANKING *Arista 74321158842* | 33 | 4 |

Tatyana ALI (R&B) ☉ *US, female vocalist* **5 wks**

| 14 Nov 98 ● | DAYDREAMIN' *Epic 6665462* | 6 | 5 |

ALIBI *UK, male vocal duo* **2 wks**

| 15 Feb 97 | I'M NOT TO BLAME *Urgent 74321434762* | 51 | 1 |
| 7 Feb 98 | HOW MUCH I FEEL *Urgent 74321548472* | 58 | 1 |

ALICE IN CHAINS ⌁ *US, male vocal/instrumental group* **14 wks**

23 Jan 93	WOULD *Columbia 6588882*	19	3
20 Mar 93	THEM BONES *Columbia 6590902*	26	3
5 Jun 93	ANGRY CHAIR *Columbia 6593652*	33	2
23 Oct 93	DOWN IN A HOLE *Columbia 6597512*	36	2
11 Nov 95	GRIND *Columbia 6626232*	23	2
10 Feb 96	HEAVEN BESIDE YOU *Columbia 6628935*	35	2

ALIEN VOICES *UK, male producer – Andreas Georgiou* **1 wk**

| 26 Dec 98 | LAST CHRISTMAS *Wildstar CDWILD 15* [1] | 54† | 1 |

[1] Alien Voices featuring Three Degrees

ALISHA *US, female vocalist* **2 wks**

| 25 Jan 86 | BABY TALK *Total Control TOCO 6* | 67 | 2 |

ALISHA'S ATTIC ☉ *UK, female vocal duo* **35 wks**

3 Aug 96	I AM I FEEL *Mercury AATCD 1*	14	10
2 Nov 96	ALISHA RULES THE WORLD *Mercury AATCD 2*	12	6
15 Mar 97	INDESTRUCTIBLE *Mercury AATCD 3*	12	6
12 Jul 97	AIR WE BREATHE *Mercury AATCD 4*	12	6
19 Sep 98	THE INCIDENTALS *Mercury AATCD 5*	13	7

ALL ABOUT EVE ☉ ☹
UK, female/male vocal/instrumental group **47 wks**

31 Oct 87	IN THE CLOUDS *Mercury EVEN 5*	47	5
23 Jan 88	WILD HEARTED WOMAN *Mercury EVEN 6*	33	4
9 Apr 88	EVERY ANGEL *Mercury EVEN 7*	30	5
30 Jul 88 ●	MARTHA'S HARBOUR *Mercury EVEN 8*	10	8
12 Nov 88	WHAT KIND OF FOOL *Mercury EVEN 9*	29	4
30 Sep 89	ROAD TO YOUR SOUL *Mercury EVEN 10*	37	4
16 Dec 89	DECEMBER *Mercury EVEN 11*	34	5
28 Apr 90	SCARLET *Mercury EVEN 12*	34	2
15 Jun 91	FAREWELL MR SORROW *Mercury EVEN 14*	36	2
10 Aug 91	STRANGE WAY *Vertigo EVEN 15*	50	3
19 Oct 91	THE DREAMER *Vertigo EVEN 16*	41	2
10 Oct 92	PHASED (EP) *MCA MCS 1688*	38	2
28 Nov 92	SOME FINER DAY *MCA MCS 1706*	57	1

Tracks on Phased (EP): Phased / Mine / Infra Red / Ascent-Descent

ALL-4-ONE (R&B) ☉ *US, male vocal group* **23 wks**

2 Apr 94	SO MUCH IN LOVE *Atlantic A 7261CD*	60	1
18 Jun 94 ●	I SWEAR *Atlantic A 7255CD* ▲	2	18
19 Nov 94	SO MUCH IN LOVE (re-mix) *Atlantic A 7216CD*	49	2
15 Jul 95	I CAN LOVE YOU LIKE THAT *Atlantic A 8193CD*	33	2

ALL SAINTS ☉ (R&B) *UK/Canada, female vocal group* **61 wks**

6 Sep 97 ●	I KNOW WHERE IT'S AT *London LONCD 398*	4	8
22 Nov 97 ★	NEVER EVER *London LONCD 407* ◆	1	24
9 May 98 ★	UNDER THE BRIDGE/LADY MARMALADE		
	London LONCD 408 ■	1	14
12 Sep 98 ★	BOOTIE CALL *London LONCD 415* ■	1	11
5 Dec 98 ●	WAR OF NERVES *London LONCD 421*	7†	4

ALL SEEING I ☉ ☺ *UK, male vocal/production group* **7 wks**

| 28 Mar 98 | BEAT GOES ON *ffrr FCD 334* | 11 | 7 |

ALL STAR CHOIR – See Donna SUMMER

ALL-STARS – See Louis ARMSTRONG

ALL-STARS – See Junior WALKER and the ALL-STARS

ALL SYSTEMS GO *UK, male vocal/instrumental group* **2 wks**

| 18 Jun 88 | POP MUZIK *Unique NIQ 03* | 63 | 2 |

Richard ALLAN *UK, male vocalist* **1 wk**

| 24 Mar 60 | AS TIME GOES BY *Parlophone R 4634* | 44 | 1 |

Steve ALLAN *UK, male vocalist* **2 wks**

| 27 Jan 79 | TOGETHER WE ARE BEAUTIFUL *Creole CR 164* | 67 | 1 |
| 10 Feb 79 | TOGETHER WE ARE BEAUTIFUL (re-entry) *Creole CR 164* | 70 | 1 |

Donna ALLEN ☺ 🎤 *US, female vocalist* **27 wks**

18 Apr 87 ●	SERIOUS *Portrait PRT 650744 7*	8	12
3 Jun 89 ●	JOY AND PAIN *BCM BCM 257*	10	10
21 Jan 95	REAL *Epic 6610992*	34	2
11 Oct 97	SATURDAY *AM:PM 5823752* [1]	29	3

[1] East 57th Street featuring Donna Allen

Keith ALLEN – See BLACK GRAPE; Joe STRUMMER

ALLISONS ☉ *UK, male vocal duo* **27 wks**

23 Feb 61 ●	ARE YOU SURE *Fontana H 294*	2	16
18 May 61	WORDS *Fontana H 304*	34	5
15 Feb 62	LESSONS IN LOVE *Fontana H 362*	30	6

ALLNIGHT BAND *UK, male instrumental group* **3 wks**

| 3 Feb 79 | THE JOKER (THE WIGAN JOKER) *Casino Classics CC 6* | 50 | 3 |

ALLURE (R&B) *US, female vocal group* **8 wks**

| 14 Jun 97 | HEAD OVER HEELS *Epic 6645942* [1] | 18 | 3 |
| 10 Jan 98 | ALL CRIED OUT *Epic 6652715* | 12 | 5 |

[1] Allure featuring NAS

ALMIGHTY *UK, male vocal/instrumental group* **22 wks**

30 Jun 90	WILD AND WONDERFUL *Polydor PO 75*	50	2
2 Mar 91	FREE 'N' EASY *Polydor PO 127*	35	2
11 May 91	DEVIL'S TOY *Polydor PO 144*	36	2
29 Jun 91	LITTLE LOST SOMETIMES *Polydor PO 151*	42	2
3 Apr 93	ADDICTION *Polydor PZCD 261*	38	2
29 May 93	OUT OF SEASON *Polydor PZCD 266*	41	2
30 Oct 93	OVER THE EDGE *Polydor PZCD 298*	38	2
24 Sep 94	WRENCH *Chrysalis CDCHS 5014*	26	2
14 Jan 95	JONESTOWN MIND *Chrysalis CDCHS 5017*	26	3
16 Mar 96	ALL SUSSED OUT *Chrysalis CDCHS 5030*	28	2
25 May 96	DO YOU UNDERSTAND *Raw Power RAWX 1022*	38	1

Marc ALMOND ☺ *Distinctive vocalist who first found fame fronting chart regulars Soft Cell, b. 9 July, 1956, Lancashire, UK. His only No 1 also gave co-vocalist Gene Pitney his first ever British chart-topper and sold more than one million copies in Europe alone* **112 wks**

2 Jun 83	BLACK HEART *Some Bizarre BZS 19* [1]	49	3
2 Jun 84	THE BOY WHO CAME BACK *Some Bizarre BZS 23*	52	5
1 Sep 84	YOU HAVE *Some Bizarre BZS 24*	57	3
20 Apr 85 ●	I FEEL LOVE (MEDLEY) *Forbidden Fruit BITE 4* [2]	3	12
24 Aug 85	STORIES OF JOHNNY *Some Bizarre BONK 1*	23	5
26 Oct 85	LOVE LETTER *Some Bizarre BONK 2*	68	3
4 Jan 86	THE HOUSE IS HAUNTED (BY THE ECHO OF YOUR LAST GOODBYE)		
	Some Bizarre GLOW 1	55	3
7 Jun 86	A WOMAN'S STORY *Some Bizarre GLOW 2* [3]	41	3
18 Oct 86	RUBY RED *Some Bizarre GLOW 3*	47	3
14 Feb 87	MELANCHOLY ROSE *Some Bizarre GLOW 4*	71	1
3 Sep 88	TEARS RUN RINGS *Parlophone R 6186*	26	7
5 Nov 88	BITTER SWEET *Some Bizarre R 6194*	40	3
14 Jan 89 ★	SOMETHING'S GOTTEN HOLD OF MY HEART		
	Parlophone R 6201 [4]	1	12
8 Apr 89	ONLY THE MOMENT *Parlophone R 6210*	45	2
3 Mar 90	A LOVER SPURNED *Some Bizarre R 6229*	29	4
19 May 90	THE DESPERATE HOURS *Some Bizarre R 6252*	45	2
23 Mar 91	SAY HELLO WAVE GOODBYE '91 *Mercury SOFT 1* [5]	38	3
18 May 91 ●	TAINTED LOVE *Mercury SOFT 2* [5]	5	8
28 Sep 91	JACKY *Some Bizarre YZ 610*	17	6
11 Jan 92	MY HAND OVER MY HEART *Some Bizarre YZ 633*	33	5
25 Apr 92 ●	THE DAYS OF PEARLY SPENCER *Some Bizarre YZ 638*	4	7
27 Mar 93	WHAT MAKES A MAN A MAN (LIVE) *Some Bizarre YZ 720CD*	60	2
13 May 95	ADORED AND EXPLORED *Some Bizarre MERCD 431*	25	3
29 Jul 95	THE IDOL *Some Bizarre MERCD 437*	44	2
30 Dec 95	CHILD STAR *Some Bizarre MERCD 450*	41	1
28 Dec 96	YESTERDAY HAS GONE *EMI Premier CDPRESX 13* [6]	58	1
11 Jan 97	YESTERDAY HAS GONE (re-entry)		
	EMI Premier CDPRESX 13 [6]	69	1

[1] Marc and the Mambas [2] Bronski Beat and Marc Almond [3] Marc Almond and the Willing Sinners [4] Marc Almond featuring special guest star Gene Pitney [5] Soft Cell/Marc Almond [6] PJ Proby and Marc Almond

I Feel Love medley comprises: I Feel Love / Love to Love You Baby / Johnny Remember Me
'Say Hello Wave Goodbye' 1991 is a re-recording of a Soft Cell hit

ALOOF *UK, male vocal/instrumental group* **6 wks**

19 Sep 92	ON A MISSION *Cowboy RODEO 5*	64	1
18 May 96	WISH YOU WERE HERE... *East West EW 038CD*	61	1
30 Nov 96	ONE NIGHT STAND *East West EW 067CD*	30	2
1 Mar 97	WISH YOU WERE HERE... (re-mix) *East West EW 083CD1*	43	1
29 Aug 98	WHAT I MISS THE MOST *East West EW 179CD1*	70	1

Herb ALPERT ♔ *Leader of the USA's biggest-selling instrumental act, The Tijuana Brass, b. 31 March, 1935, Los Angeles. Multi-talented trumpet-toting star, whose band had four albums simultaneously in the US Top 10 in the mid-1960s. He sold his A&M label for $300 million in 1989* **106 wks**

3 Jan 63	THE LONELY BULL *Stateside SS 138* [1]	22	9
9 Dec 65 ●	SPANISH FLEA *Pye International 7 N 25335* [2]	3	20
24 Mar 66	TIJUANA TAXI *Pye International 7 N 25352* [2]	37	4
27 Apr 67	CASINO ROYALE *A & M AMS 700* [2]	27	14
3 Jul 68 ●	THIS GUY'S IN LOVE WITH YOU *A & M AMS 727* ▲	3	16
26 Mar 69	THIS GUY'S IN LOVE WITH YOU (re-entry) *A & M AMS 727*	47	1
9 Apr 69	THIS GUY'S IN LOVE WITH YOU (2nd re-entry)		
	A & M AMS 727	49	1
7 May 69	THIS GUY'S IN LOVE WITH YOU (3rd re-entry)		
	A & M AMS 727	50	1
18 Jun 69	WITHOUT HER *A & M AMS 755* [2]	36	5
12 Dec 70	JERUSALEM *A & M AMS 810* [2]	47	1
2 Jan 71	JERUSALEM (re-entry) *A & M AMS 810* [2]	42	2
13 Oct 79	RISE *A & M AMS 7465* ▲	13	13
19 Jan 80	ROTATION *A & M AMS 7500*	46	3
21 Mar 87	KEEP YOUR EYE ON ME *Breakout USA 602*	19	9
6 Jun 87	DIAMONDS *Breakout USA 605*	27	7

[1] Tijuana Brass [2] Herb Alpert and the Tijuana Brass

Alpert provides vocals on 'This Guy's in Love With You' and 'Without Her'
Janet Jackson provides uncredited vocals on 'Diamonds'

ALPHABETA – See Izhar COHEN and ALPHABETA

ALPHAVILLE ☺ *Germany, male vocal/instrumental group* **13 wks**

18 Aug 84 ●	BIG IN JAPAN *WEA Int. X9505*	8	13

Gerald ALSTON *US, male vocalist* **1 wk**

15 Apr 89	ACTIVATED *RCA ZB 42681*	73	1

ALTERED IMAGES ☺
UK, male/female vocal/instrumental group **60 wks**

28 Mar 81	DEAD POP STARS *Epic EPC A 1023*	67	2
26 Sep 81 ●	HAPPY BIRTHDAY *Epic EPC A 1522*	2	17
12 Dec 81 ●	I COULD BE HAPPY *Epic EPC A 1834*	7	12
27 Mar 82	SEE THOSE EYES *Epic EPC A 2198*	11	7
22 May 82	PINKY BLUE *Epic EPC A 2426*	35	6
19 Mar 83 ●	DON'T TALK TO ME ABOUT LOVE *Epic EPC A 3083*	7	7
28 May 83	BRING ME CLOSER *Epic EPC A 3398*	29	6
16 Jul 83	LOVE TO STAY *Epic EPC A 3582*	46	3

ALTERN 8 ☺ *UK, male instrumental/production duo* **34 wks**

13 Jul 91	INFILTRATE 202 *Network NWK 24*	28	7
16 Nov 91 ●	ACTIV 8 (COME WITH ME) *Network NWK 34*	3	9
8 Feb 92	FREQUENCY *Network NWKT 37*	41	1
11 Apr 92 ●	EVAPOR 8 *Network NWK 38*	6	6
4 Jul 92	HYPNOTIC ST-8 *Network NWK 49*	16	4
10 Oct 92	SHAME *Network NWKTEN 56* [1]	74	1
12 Dec 92	BRUTAL-8-E *Network NWK 59*	43	5
3 Jul 93	EVERYBODY *Network NWKCD 73*	58	1

[1] Altern 8 vs Evelyn King

ALTHIA and DONNA ⚑ *Jamaica, female vocal duo* **11 wks**

24 Dec 77 ★	UP TOWN TOP RANKING *Lightning LIG 506*	1	11

ALVIN and the CHIPMUNKS – See CHIPMUNKS

ALY-US *US, male vocal/instrumental group* **2 wks**

21 Nov 92	FOLLOW ME *Cooltempo COOL 266*	43	2

Shola AMA ♪ R&B *UK, female vocalist* **35 wks**

19 Apr 97 ●	YOU MIGHT NEED SOMEBODY *WEA WEA 097CD1*	4	14
30 Aug 97 ●	YOU'RE THE ONE I LOVE *WEA WEA 121CD1*	3	8
29 Nov 97	WHO'S LOVING MY BABY *WEA WEA 145CD1*	13	7
21 Feb 98	MUCH LOVE *WEA WEA 154CD1*	17	3
11 Apr 98	SOMEDAY I'LL FIND YOU/I'VE BEEN TO A MARVELLOUS PARTY		
	EMI CDTCB 001 [1]	28	3

[1] Shola Ama and Craig Armstrong / Divine Comedy

Eddie AMADOR *US, male DJ/producer* **2 wks**

24 Oct 98	HOUSE MUSIC *Pukka CDPUKKA 18*	37	2

AMAZULU ☺ *UK, female/male vocal/instrumental group* **57 wks**

6 Jul 85	EXCITABLE *Island IS 201*	12	13
23 Nov 85	DON'T YOU JUST KNOW IT *Island IS 233*	15	11
15 Mar 86	THE THINGS THE LONELY DO *Island IS 267*	43	6
31 May 86 ●	TOO GOOD TO BE FORGOTTEN *Island IS 284*	5	13
13 Sep 86	MONTEGO BAY *Island IS 293*	16	9
10 Oct 87	MONY MONY *EMI EM 32*	38	5

AMBASSADORS OF FUNK featuring MC MARIO ☺ ☺ 🎧
UK, male DJ and rapper – Simon Harris and Einstein **8 wks**

31 Oct 92 ●	SUPERMARIOLAND *Living Beat SMASH 23*	8	8

AMEN CORNER ☺ *UK, male vocal/instrumental group* **67 wks**

26 Jul 67	GIN HOUSE BLUES *Deram DM 136*	12	10

UK No 1 ★   UK Top 10 ●   UK million seller ◆   UK entry at No 1 ■   US No 1 ▲

11 Oct 67		WORLD OF BROKEN HEARTS *Deram DM 151*	24	6
17 Jan 68	●	BEND ME SHAPE ME *Deram DM 172*	3	12
31 Jul 68	●	HIGH IN THE SKY *Deram DM 197*	6	13
29 Jan 69	★	(IF PARADISE IS) HALF AS NICE *Immediate IM 073*	1	11
25 Jun 69	●	HELLO SUZIE *Immediate IM 081*	4	10
14 Feb 76		(IF PARADISE IS) HALF AS NICE (re-issue)		
		Immediate IMS 103	34	5

AMEN UK ☺ *UK, male / female vocal / production group*   6 wks

8 Feb 97		PASSION *Feverpitch CDFVR 1015*	15	4
28 Jun 97		PEOPLE OF LOVE *Feverpitch CDFVR 18*	36	2

AMERICA ✍ *US, male vocal/instrumental group*   20 wks

18 Dec 71		HORSE WITH NO NAME *Warner Bros. K 16128* ▲	49	2
8 Jan 72	●	HORSE WITH NO NAME (re-entry) *Warner Bros. K 16128* ...	3	11
25 Nov 72		VENTURA HIGHWAY *Warner Bros. K 16219*	43	4
6 Nov 82		YOU CAN DO MAGIC *Capitol CL 264*	59	3

AMERICAN BREED *US, male vocal/instrumental group*   6 wks

7 Feb 68		BEND ME SHAPE ME *Stateside SS 2078*	24	6

AMERICAN MUSIC CLUB *US, male vocal/instrumental group*   4 wks

24 Apr 93		JOHNNY MATHIS' FEET *Virgin VSCDG 1445*	58	2
10 Sep 94		WISH THE WORLD AWAY *Virgin VSCDX 1512*	46	2

AMES BROTHERS ☾ *US, male vocal group*   6 wks

4 Feb 55	●	NAUGHTY LADY OF SHADY LANE *HMV B 10800*	6	6

AMIRA *US, female vocalist*   3 wks

13 Dec 97		MY DESIRE *VC VCRD 27*	51	1
8 Aug 98		MY DESIRE (re-mix) *VC Recordings VCRD 36*	46	2

AMNESIA – See Frank'o MOIRAGHI featuring AMNESIA

AMOS ☺ *UK, male vocalist*   12 wks

3 Sep 94		ONLY SAW TODAY – INSTANT KARMA *Positiva CDTIV 16*	48	2
25 Mar 95		LET LOVE SHINE *Positiva CDTIV 24*	31	2
7 Oct 95		CHURCH OF FREEDOM *Positiva CDTIV 38*	54	1
12 Oct 96		STAMP! *Positiva CDTIV 65* [1]	11	5
31 May 97		ARGENTINA *Positiva CDTIV 74* [1]	30	2

[1] Jeremy Healy and Amos

Tori AMOS ✪ *US, female vocalist*   63 wks

23 Nov 91		SILENT ALL THESE YEARS *East West YZ 618*	51	3
1 Feb 92		CHINA *East West YZ 7531*	51	2
21 Mar 92		WINTER *East West A 7504*	25	4
20 Jun 92		CRUCIFY *East West A 7479*	15	6
22 Aug 92		SILENT ALL THESE YEARS (re-issue) *East West A 7433*	26	4
22 Jan 94	●	CORNFLAKE GIRL *East West A 7281CD*	4	6
19 Mar 94	●	PRETTY GOOD YEAR *East West A 7263CD*	7	4
28 May 94		PAST THE MISSION *East West YZ 7257CD*	31	3
15 Oct 94		GOD *East West A 7251CD*	44	2
13 Jan 96		CAUGHT A LITE SNEEZE *East West 5524CD1*	20	3
23 Mar 96		TALULA *East West A 8512CD1*	22	2
3 Aug 96		HEY JUPITER/PROFESSIONAL WIDOW *East West A 5494CD*	20	9
9 Nov 96		BLUE SKIES *Perfecto PERF 130CD1* [1]	26	2
11 Jan 97	★	PROFESSIONAL WIDOW (IT'S GOT TO BE BIG) (re-mix)		
		East West A 5450CD	1	10
2 May 98		SPARK *Atlantic AT 0031CD*	16	3

[1] BT featuring Tori Amos

AMPS *US, male/female vocal/instrumental group*   1 wk

21 Oct 95		TIPP CITY *4AD BAD 5015CD*	61	1

AMY – See A.D.A.M. featuring AMY

AND WHY NOT? ✪ R&B *UK, male vocal/instrumental group*   18 wks

14 Oct 89		RESTLESS DAYS (SHE CRIES OUT LOUD) *Island IS 426*	38	7
13 Jan 90		THE FACE *Island IS 444*	13	8
21 Apr 90		SOMETHING YOU GOT *Island IS 452*	39	3

Angry ANDERSON ✪ *Australia, male vocalist*   13 wks

19 Nov 88	●	SUDDENLY *Food For Thought YUM 113*	3	13

John ANDERSON BIG BAND *UK, big band*   5 wks

21 Dec 85		GLENN MILLER MEDLEY *Modern GLEN 1*	63	2
11 Jan 86		GLENN MILLER MEDLEY (re-entry) *Modern GLEN 1*	61	3

Glenn Miller Medley comprises the following tracks:
In the Mood / American Patrol / Little Brown Jug / Pennsylvania 65000

ANDERSON BRUFORD WAKEMAN HOWE
UK, male vocal/instrumental group   2 wks

24 Jun 89		BROTHER OF MINE *Arista 112379*	63	2

Carl ANDERSON *US, male vocalist*   4 wks

8 Jun 85		BUTTERCUP *Streetwave KHAN 45*	49	4

Carleen ANDERSON R&B *US, female vocalist*   17 wks

12 Feb 94		NERVOUS BREAKDOWN *Circa YRCDG 112*	27	4
28 May 94		MAMA SAID *Circa YRCD 114*	26	4
13 Aug 94		TRUE SPIRIT *Circa YRCD 118*	24	3
14 Jan 95		LET IT LAST *Circa YRCD 119*	16	3
7 Feb 98		MAYBE I'M AMAZED *Circa YRCD 128*	24	2
25 Apr 98		WOMAN IN ME *Circa YRCD 129*	74	1

Gillian ANDERSON – See HAL featuring Gillian ANDERSON

Laurie ANDERSON ✪ ☺
US, female vocalist/multi-instrumentalist   6 wks

17 Oct 81	●	O SUPERMAN *Warner Bros. K 17870*	2	6

Leroy ANDERSON and his POPS CONCERT ORCHESTRA
US, orchestra   4 wks

28 Jun 57		FORGOTTEN DREAMS *Brunswick 05485*	28	1
12 Jul 57		FORGOTTEN DREAMS (re-entry) *Brunswick 05485*	30	1
6 Sep 57		FORGOTTEN DREAMS (2nd re-entry) *Brunswick 05485*	24	2

Lynn ANDERSON ✿ *US, female vocalist*   20 wks

20 Feb 71	●	ROSE GARDEN *CBS 5360*	3	20

Moira ANDERSON *UK, female vocalist*   2 wks

27 Dec 69		THE HOLY CITY *Decca F 12989*	43	2

Peter ANDRE ✪ *UK, male vocalist*   82 wks

10 Jun 95		TURN IT UP *Mushroom D 1000*	64	1
16 Sep 95		MYSTERIOUS GIRL *Mushroom D 11921*	53	2
16 Mar 96		ONLY ONE *Mushroom D 1307*	16	3
13 Apr 96		ONLY ONE (re-entry) *Mushroom D 1307*	69	1
1 Jun 96		MYSTERIOUS GIRL (re-issue) *Mushroom D 2000* [1]	2	18
14 Sep 96	★	FLAVA *Mushroom D 2003* ■	1	9
7 Dec 96	★	I FEEL YOU *Mushroom D 1521* ■	1	9
1 Mar 97		I FEEL YOU (re-entry) *Mushroom D 1521*	65	1
8 Mar 97	●	NATURAL *Mushroom DX 1577*	6	8
15 Mar 97		I FEEL YOU (2nd re-entry) *Mushroom D 1521*	74	1
10 May 97		NATURAL (re-entry) *Mushroom DX 1577*	58	1
24 May 97		NATURAL (2nd re-entry) *Mushroom DX 1577*	68	2
9 Aug 97	●	ALL ABOUT US *Mushroom MUSH 5CD*	3	8
8 Nov 97	●	LONELY *Mushroom MUSH 16CD*	6	5
3 Jan 98		LONELY (re-entry) *Mushroom MUSH 16CD*	71	4
24 Jan 98		ALL NIGHT ALL RIGHT *Mushroom MUSH 21CD* [2]	16	4
25 Jul 98		KISS THE GIRL *Mushroom MUSH 34CDSX*	9	5

[1] Peter Andre featuring Bubbler Ranx   [2] Peter Andre featuring Warren G

Chris ANDREWS ◎ *UK, male vocalist* — **36 wks**

7 Oct 65	●	YESTERDAY MAN *Decca F 12236*	..3	15
2 Dec 65		TO WHOM IT CONCERNS *Decca F 22285*	..13	10
14 Apr 66		SOMETHING ON MY MIND *Decca F 22365*	45	1
28 Apr 66		SOMETHING ON MY MIND (re-entry) *Decca F 22365*	41	2
2 Jun 66		WHATCHA GONNA DO NOW *Decca F 22404*	40	4
25 Aug 66		STOP THAT GIRL *Decca F 22472*	36	4

Eamonn ANDREWS ℂ *Ireland, male vocalist* — **3 wks**

20 Jan 56		SHIFTING WHISPERING SANDS (PARTS 1 & 2) *Parlophone R 4106*	18	3

Hit is credited: 'with Ron Goodwin and his Orchestra and Chorus'

ANEKA ◎ *UK, female vocalist* — **16 wks**

8 Aug 81	★	JAPANESE BOY *Hansa HANSA 5*	1	12
7 Nov 81		LITTLE LADY *Hansa HANSA 8*	50	4

Dave ANGEL *UK, male DJ / producer* — **1 wk**

2 Aug 97		TOKYO STEALTH FIGHTER *Fourth & Broadway BRCD 355*	58	1

Simone ANGEL *Holland, female vocalist* — **1 wk**

13 Nov 93		LET THIS FEELING *A & M 5803652*	60	1

ANGELETTES *UK, female vocal group* — **5 wks**

13 May 72		DON'T LET HIM TOUCH YOU *Decca F 13284*	35	5

ANGELHEART *UK, female producer* — **2 wks**

6 Apr 96		COME BACK TO ME *Hi-Life 5776312* [1]	68	1
22 Mar 97		I'M STILL WAITING *Hi-Life 5735452* [2]	74	1

[1] Angelheart featuring Rochelle Harris [2] Angelheart featuring Aletia Bourne

ANGELIC UPSTARTS
UK, male vocal/instrumental group — **30 wks**

21 Apr 79		I'M AN UPSTART *Warner Bros. K 17354*	31	8
11 Aug 79		TEENAGE WARNING *Warner Bros. K 17426*	29	6
3 Nov 79		NEVER 'AD NOTHIN' *Warner Bros. K 17476*	52	4
9 Feb 80		OUT OF CONTROL *Warner Bros. K 17558*	58	3
22 Mar 80		WE GOTTA GET OUT OF THIS PLACE *Warner Bros. K 17576*	65	2
2 Aug 80		LAST NIGHT ANOTHER SOLDIER *Angelic Upstarts Z 7*	51	4
7 Feb 81		KIDS ON THE STREET *Angelic Upstarts Z 16*	57	3

Bobby ANGELO and the TUXEDOS
UK, male vocal/instrumental group — **6 wks**

10 Aug 61		BABY SITTIN' *HMV POP 892*	30	6

ANGELS *US, female vocal group* — **1 wk**

3 Oct 63		MY BOYFRIEND'S BACK *Mercury AMT 1211* ▲	50	1

ANGELS OF LIGHT – See PSYCHIC TV

ANGELWITCH
UK, male vocal/instrumental group — **1 wk**

7 Jun 80		SWEET DANGER *EMI 5064*	75	1

ANIMAL *US, puppet vocal and instrumental – drums* — **3 wks**

23 Jul 94		WIPE OUT *BMG Kidz 74321219532*	38	3

ANIMAL NIGHTLIFE
UK, male/female vocal/instrumental group — **22 wks**

13 Aug 83		NATIVE BOY (UPTOWN) *Innervision A3584*	60	3
18 Aug 84		MR. SOLITAIRE *Island IS 193*	25	12
6 Jul 85		LOVE IS JUST THE GREAT PRETENDER *Island IS 200*	28	6
5 Oct 85		PREACHER, PREACHER *Island IS 245*	67	1

ANIMALS ✍ *Groundbreaking Newcastle band: Eric Burdon (v), Alan Price (k), Brian 'Chas' Chandler (b) (d. 1996), Hilton Valentine (g), John Steel (d). They were the first hit act produced by Mickie Most and the first UK group to top the US chart after The Beatles* — **147 wks**

16 Apr 64		BABY LET ME TAKE YOU HOME *Columbia DB 7247*	21	8
25 Jun 64	★	HOUSE OF THE RISING SUN *Columbia DB 7301* ▲	1	12
17 Sep 64	●	I'M CRYING *Columbia DB 7354*	8	10
4 Feb 65	●	DON'T LET ME BE MISUNDERSTOOD *Columbia DB 7445*	3	9
8 Apr 65	●	BRING IT ON HOME TO ME *Columbia DB 7539*	7	11
15 Jul 65	●	WE GOTTA GET OUT OF THIS PLACE *Columbia DB 7639*	2	12
28 Oct 65	●	IT'S MY LIFE *Columbia DB 7741*	7	11
17 Feb 66		INSIDE – LOOKING OUT *Decca F 12332*	12	8
2 Jun 66	●	DON'T BRING ME DOWN *Decca F 12407*	6	8
27 Oct 66		HELP ME GIRL *Decca F 12502* [1]	14	10
15 Jun 67		WHEN I WAS YOUNG *MGM 1340* [1]	45	3
6 Sep 67		GOOD TIMES *MGM 1344* [1]	20	11
18 Oct 67	●	SAN FRANCISCAN NIGHTS *MGM 1359* [1]	7	10
14 Feb 68		SKY PILOT *MGM 1373* [1]	40	3
15 Jan 69		RING OF FIRE *MGM 1461* [1]	35	5
7 Oct 72		HOUSE OF THE RISING SUN (re-issue) *RAK RR 1*	25	6
18 Sep 82		HOUSE OF THE RISING SUN (re-entry of re-issue) *RAK RR 1*	11	10

[1] Eric Burdon and the Animals

ANIMOTION ✍ *US/UK, male/female vocal/instrumental group* — **12 wks**

11 May 85	●	OBSESSION *Mercury PH 34*	5	12

Paul ANKA ◎ *Celebrated Canadian singer/songwriter, b. 30 July, 1941, Ottawa. He topped the UK and US charts aged 16 and was the youngest transatlantic chart regular of the 1950s. He also penned big hits for Buddy Holly, Tom Jones, Donny Osmond and Frank Sinatra ('My Way')* — **134 wks**

9 Aug 57	★	DIANA *Columbia DB 3980* ◆ ▲	1	25
8 Nov 57	●	I LOVE YOU BABY *Columbia DB 4022*	3	15
8 Nov 57		TELL ME THAT YOU LOVE ME *Columbia DB 4022*	25	2
31 Jan 58	●	YOU ARE MY DESTINY *Columbia DB 4063*	6	13
30 May 58		CRAZY LOVE *Columbia DB 4110*	26	1
26 Sep 58		MIDNIGHT *Columbia DB 4172*	26	1
30 Jan 59	●	(ALL OF A SUDDEN) MY HEART SINGS *Columbia DB 4241*	10	13
10 Jul 59	●	LONELY BOY *Columbia DB 4324* ▲	3	17
30 Oct 59	●	PUT YOUR HEAD ON MY SHOULDER *Columbia DB 4355*	7	12
26 Feb 60		IT'S TIME TO CRY *Columbia DB 4390*	28	1
31 Mar 60		PUPPY LOVE *Columbia DB 4434*	33	4
14 Apr 60		IT'S TIME TO CRY (re-entry) *Columbia DB 4390*	47	1
5 May 60		PUPPY LOVE (re-entry) *Columbia DB 4434*	37	3
15 Sep 60		HELLO YOUNG LOVERS *Columbia DB 4504*	44	1
15 Mar 62		LOVE ME WARM AND TENDER *RCA 1276*	19	11
26 Jul 62		A STEEL GUITAR AND A GLASS OF WINE *RCA 1292*	41	4
28 Sep 74	●	(YOU'RE) HAVING MY BABY *United Artists UP 35713* [1] ▲	6	10

[1] Paul Anka featuring Odia Coates

ANNETTE – See VARIOUS ARTISTS (EPs & LPs) – Further Adventures of North (EP)

ANOTHER LEVEL ◎ (R&B) *UK, male vocal group* — **29 wks**

28 Feb 98	●	BE ALONE NO MORE *Northwestside 74321551982*	6	9
18 Jul 98	★	FREAK ME *Northwestside 74321582362* ■	1	12
7 Nov 98	●	GUESS I WAS A FOOL *Northwestside 74321621202*	5†	8

ANOUCHKA – See Terry HALL

Adam ANT ◎ ✎ *Warpaint-wearing, colourfully costumed 'Antmusic' innovators: included Stuart (Adam Ant) Goddard (v) and Marco Pirroni (g). The London-based act was 1981's top chart act with nine hits. Also in that year, they amassed 91 chart weeks – a total not bettered until 1996* — **199 wks**

2 Aug 80		KINGS OF THE WILD FRONTIER *CBS 8877* [1]	48	5
11 Oct 80	●	DOG EAT DOG *CBS 9039* [1]	4	16
6 Dec 80	●	ANTMUSIC *CBS 9352* [1]	2	18
27 Dec 80	●	YOUNG PARISIANS *Decca F13803* [1]	9	13
24 Jan 81		CARTROUBLE *Do It DUN 10* [1]	33	9
24 Jan 81		ZEROX *Do It DUN 8* [1]	45	9
21 Feb 81	●	KINGS OF THE WILD FRONTIER (re-entry) *CBS 8877* [1]	2	13

9 May 81 ★	STAND AND DELIVER *CBS A 1065* [1] ■	1	15
12 Sep 81 ★	PRINCE CHARMING *CBS A 1408* [1]	1	12
12 Dec 81 ●	ANT RAP *CBS A 1738* [1]	3	10
27 Feb 82	DEUTSCHER GIRLS *Ego 5* [1]	13	6
13 Mar 82	THE ANTMUSIC EP (THE B-SIDES) *Do It DUN 20* [1]	46	4
22 May 82 ★	GOODY TWO SHOES *CBS A 2367*	1	11
18 Sep 82 ●	FRIEND OR FOE *CBS A 2736*	9	8
27 Nov 82	DESPERATE BUT NOT SERIOUS *CBS A 2892*	33	7
29 Oct 83 ●	PUSS 'N BOOTS *CBS A 3614*	5	11
10 Dec 83	STRIP *CBS A 3589*	41	6
22 Sep 84	APOLLO 9 *CBS A 4719*	13	8
13 Jul 85	VIVE LE ROCK *CBS A 6367*	50	4
17 Feb 90	ROOM AT THE TOP *MCA MCA 1387*	13	7
28 Apr 90	CAN'T SET RULES ABOUT LOVE *MCA MCA 1404*	47	2
11 Feb 95	WONDERFUL *EMI CDEMS 366*	32	3
3 Jun 95	GOTTA BE A SIN *EMI CDEMS 379*	48	2

[1] Adam and the Ants

Tracks on The Antmusic EP (The B-sides): Friends / Kick / Physical

ANT and DEC – *See PJ and DUNCAN*

Mark ANTHONI – *See FIRE ISLAND*

Billie ANTHONY ℂ *UK, female vocalist*   16 wks

15 Oct 54 ●	THIS OLE HOUSE *Columbia DB 3519*	4	16

Marc ANTHONY – *See Louie VEGA and Marc ANTHONY*

Miki ANTHONY *UK, male vocalist*   7 wks

3 Feb 73	IF IT WASN'T FOR THE REASON THAT I LOVE YOU *Bell 1275*	27	7

Ray ANTHONY ℂ *US, orchestra*   2 wks

4 Dec 53 ●	DRAGNET *Capitol CL 13983*	7	1
8 Jan 54	DRAGNET (re-entry) *Capitol CL 13983*	11	1

Richard ANTHONY ℂ *France, male vocalist*   15 wks

12 Dec 63	WALKING ALONE *Columbia DB 7133*	37	5
2 Apr 64	IF I LOVED YOU *Columbia DB 7235*	48	1
23 Apr 64	IF I LOVED YOU (re-entry) *Columbia DB 7235*	18	9

ANTHRAX ✓ *US, male vocal/instrumental group*   37 wks

28 Feb 87	I AM THE LAW *Island IS LAW 1*	32	5
27 Jun 87	INDIANS *Island IS 325*	44	4
5 Dec 87	I'M THE MAN *Island IS 338*	20	6
10 Sep 88	MAKE ME LAUGH *Island IS 379*	26	3
18 Mar 89	ANTI-SOCIAL *Island IS 409*	44	3
1 Sep 90	IN MY WORLD *Island IS 470*	29	2
5 Jan 91	GOT THE TIME *Island IS 476*	16	4
6 Jul 91	BRING THE NOISE *Island IS 490* [1]	14	5
8 May 93	ONLY *Elektra EKR 166CD*	36	3
11 Sep 93	BLACK LODGE *Elektra EKR 171CD*	53	2

[1] Anthrax featuring Chuck D

ANTI-NOWHERE LEAGUE
UK, male vocal/instrumental group   10 wks

23 Jan 82	STREETS OF LONDON *WXYZ ABCD 1*	48	5
20 Mar 82	I HATE . . . PEOPLE *WXYZ ABCD 2*	46	3
3 Jul 82	WOMAN *WXYZ ABCD 4*	72	2

ANTI-PASTI – *See EXPLOITED*

ANTICAPPELLA
Italy/UK, male/female vocal/instrumental group   12 wks

16 Nov 91	231 *PWL Continental PWL 205*	24	4
18 Apr 92	EVERY DAY *PWL Continental PWL 220*	45	2
25 Jun 94	MOVE YOUR BODY *Media MCSTD 1980* [1]	21	3
1 Apr 95	EXPRESS YOUR FREEDOM *Media MCSTD 2048*	31	2

25 May 96	231 / MOVE YOUR BODY (re-issue of re-mix) *Media MCSTD 40037*	54	1

[1] Anticappella featuring MC Fixx It

ANTONIA – *See BOMB THE BASS*

ANTS – *See Adam ANT*

ANUNA – *See Bill WHELAN featuring ANUNA and the RTE CONCERT ORCHESTRA*

APACHE INDIAN 🏝 ☺ *UK, male vocalist*   33 wks

28 Nov 92	FE' REAL *Ten TEN 416* [1]	33	3
2 Jan 93	ARRANGED MARRIAGE *Island CID 544*	16	6
27 Mar 93	CHOK THERE *Island CID 555*	30	4
14 Aug 93 ●	NUFF VIBES EP *Island CID 560*	5	10
22 Oct 93	MOVIN' ON *Island CID 580*	48	2
7 May 94	WRECKX SHOP *MCA MCSTD 1969* [2]	26	2
11 Feb 95	MAKE WAY FOR THE INDIAN *Island CID 586* [3]	29	2
22 Apr 95	RAGGAMUFFIN GIRL *Island CID 606* [4]	31	2
29 Mar 97	LOVIN' (LET ME LOVE YOU) *Coalition COLA 002CD*	53	1
18 Oct 97	REAL PEOPLE *Coalition COLA 019CD*	66	1

[1] Maxi Priest featuring Apache Indian [2] Wreckx-N-Effect featuring Apache Indian [3] Apache Indian and Tim Dog [4] Apache Indian with Frankie Paul

The listed flip side of 'Fe' Real' was 'Just Wanna Know' by Maxi Priest. Tracks on Nuff Vibes (EP): Boom Shack a Lak / Fun / Caste System / Warning

APHEX TWIN
UK, male instrumentalist/producer – Richard James   9 wks

9 May 92	DIGERIDOO *R&S RSUK 12*	55	2
27 Nov 93	ON *Warp WAP 39CD*	32	3
8 Apr 95	VENTOLIN *Warp WAP 60CD*	49	1
26 Oct 96	GIRL/BOY (EP) *Warp WAP 78CD*	64	1
18 Oct 97	COME TO DADDY *Warp WAP 94CD*	36	2

Tracks on Girl/Boy (EP): Girl/Boy Song / Milkman / Inkey $ / Beatles Under My Carpet. The EP was incorrectly listed in the chart and, because of its length, should have been considered an album
See also POLYGON WINDOW

APHRODITE'S CHILD *Greece, male vocal/instrumental group*   7 wks

6 Nov 68	RAIN AND TEARS *Mercury MF 1039*	29	7

APOLLO – *See HOUSE OF VIRGINISM*

APOLLO FOUR FORTY ☺
UK, male instrumental/production group   39 wks

22 Jan 94	ASTRAL AMERICA *Stealth Sonic SSXCD 2* [1]	36	2
5 Nov 94	LIQUID COOL *Stealth Sonic SSXCD 3* [1]	35	2
25 Mar 95	(DON'T FEAR) THE REAPER *Stealth Sonic SSXCD 4* [1]	35	2
27 Jul 96	KRUPA *Stealth Sonic SSXCD 5*	23	4
28 Sep 96	KRUPA (re-entry) *Stealth Sonic SSXCD 5*	24	4
15 Feb 97 ●	AIN'T TALKIN' 'BOUT DUB *Stealth Sonic SSXCDX 6*	7	7
5 Jul 97	RAW POWER *Stealth Sonic SSXCD 7*	32	3
11 Jul 98	RENDEZ-VOUS '98 *Epic 6661102* [2]	12	6
8 Aug 98 ●	LOST IN SPACE *Stealth Sonic SSX 9CD*	4	9

[1] Apollo 440 [2] Jean Michel Jarre and Apollo 440

Kim APPLEBY ✪ *UK, female vocalist*   31 wks

3 Nov 90 ●	DON'T WORRY *Parlophone R 6272*	2	10
9 Feb 91	G.L.A.D. *Parlophone R 6281*	10	6
29 Jun 91	MAMA *Parlophone R 6291*	19	8
19 Oct 91	IF YOU CARED *Parlophone R 6297*	44	3
31 Jul 93	LIGHT OF THE WORLD *Parlophone CDR 6352*	41	2
13 Nov 93	BREAKAWAY *Parlophone CDR 6362*	56	1
12 Nov 94	FREE SPIRIT *Parlophone CDR 6397*	51	1

See also MEL and KIM

APPLEJACKS ✪ *UK, male/female vocal/instrumental group*   29 wks

5 Mar 64 ●	TELL ME WHEN *Decca F 11833*	7	13

| 11 Jun 64 | LIKE DREAMERS DO *Decca F 11916* | .20 | 11 |
| 15 Oct 64 | THREE LITTLE WORDS *Decca F 11981* | .23 | 5 |

APPLES *UK, male vocal/instrumental group* — 1 wk

| 23 Mar 91 | EYE WONDER *Epic 6566717* | .75 | 1 |

Charlie APPLEWHITE Ⓒ *US, male vocalist* — 1 wk

| 23 Sep 55 | BLUE STAR (THE MEDIC THEME) *Brunswick 05416* | .20 | 1 |

Helen APRIL – *See John DUMMER and Helen APRIL*

APRIL WINE *Canada, male vocal/instrumental group* — 9 wks

| 15 Mar 80 | I LIKE TO ROCK *Capitol CL 16121* | .41 | 5 |
| 11 Apr 81 | JUST BETWEEN YOU AND ME *Capitol CL 16184* | .52 | 4 |

AQUA ☉ *Denmark, male/female vocal/instrumental group* — 62 wks

25 Oct 97	★ BARBIE GIRL *Universal UMD 80413* ◆	.2	24
7 Feb 98	★ DOCTOR JONES *Universal UMD 80457* ■	.1	14
25 Apr 98	BARBIE GIRL (re-entry) *Universal UMD 80413*	.66	2
16 May 98	★ TURN BACK TIME *Universal UMD 80490* ■	.1	10
1 Aug 98	● MY OH MY *Universal UMD 85058*	.6	9
17 Oct 98	MY OH MY (re-entry) *Universal UMD 85058*	.66	2
26 Dec 98	GOOD MORNING SUNSHINE *Universal UMD 85086*	18†	1

AQUARIAN DREAM
US, male/female vocal/instrumental group — 1 wk

| 24 Feb 79 | YOU'RE A STAR *Elektra LV 7* | .67 | 1 |

ARAB STRAP *UK, male vocal/instrumental duo* — 3 wks

13 Sep 97	THE GIRLS OF SUMMER (EP) *Chemikal CHEM 017CD*	.74	1
4 Apr 98	HERE WE GO/TRIPPY *Chemikal CHEM 20CD*	.48	1
10 Oct 98	(AFTERNOON) SOAPS *Chemikal CHEM 27CD*	.74	1

*Tracks on The Girls of Summer (EP): Hey! Fever/Girls of Summer/
The Beautiful Barmaids of Dundee/One Day After School*

ARCADIA ☉ *UK, male vocal/instrumental group* — 13 wks

26 Oct 85	● ELECTION DAY *Odeon NSR 1*	.7	7
25 Jan 86	THE PROMISE *Odeon NSR 2*	.37	4
26 Jul 86	THE FLAME *Odeon NSR 3*	.58	2

Tasmin ARCHER ☉ *UK, female vocalist* — 37 wks

12 Sep 92	★ SLEEPING SATELLITE *EMI EM 233*	.1	15
2 Jan 93	SLEEPING SATELLITE (re-entry) *EMI EM 233*	.67	1
20 Feb 93	IN YOUR CARE *EMI CDEMS 260*	.16	6
29 May 93	LORDS OF THE NEW CHURCH *EMI CDEM 266*	.26	4
21 Aug 93	ARIENNE *EMI CDEM 275*	.30	4
8 Jan 94	SHIPBUILDING *EMI CDEM 302*	.40	4
23 Mar 96	ONE MORE GOOD NIGHT WITH THE BOYS *EMI CDEM 401*	.45	2

ARCHIES ☉ *US, male/female cartoon vocal group* — 26 wks

| 11 Oct 69 | ★ SUGAR SUGAR *RCA 1872* ▲ | .1 | 26 |

Jann ARDEN *Canada, female vocalist* — 2 wks

| 13 Jul 96 | INSENSITIVE *A & M 5812652* | .40 | 2 |

Tina ARENA ☉ *Australia, female vocalist* — 30 wks

15 Apr 95	● CHAINS *Columbia 6611255*	.6	11
12 Aug 95	HEAVEN HELP MY HEART *Columbia 6620975*	.25	5
2 Dec 95	SHOW ME HEAVEN *Columbia 6626975*	.29	3
3 Aug 96	SORRENTO MOON (I REMEMBER) *Columbia 6635435*	.22	4
27 Jun 98	WHISTLE DOWN THE WIND *Really Useful 5672192*	.24	5
24 Oct 98	IF I WAS A RIVER *Columbia 6665605*	.43	2

ARGENT ✍ *UK, male vocal/instrumental group* — 27 wks

| 4 Mar 72 | ● HOLD YOUR HEAD UP *Epic EPC 7786* | .5 | 12 |
| 10 Jun 72 | TRAGEDY *Epic EPC 8115* | .34 | 7 |

| 24 Mar 73 | GOD GAVE ROCK AND ROLL TO YOU *Epic EPC 1243* | .18 | 8 |

See also SAN JOSE featuring Rodriguez ARGENTINA; SILSOE

ARIEL *UK, male/female vocal/instrumental group* — 3 wks

| 27 Mar 93 | LET IT SLIDE *Deconstruction 74321134512* | .57 | 2 |
| 21 Jun 97 | DEEP (I'M FALLING DEEPER) *Wonderboy WBOYD 005* | .47 | 1 |

ARIZONA – *See Zeitia MASSIAH*

Ship's Company and Royal Marine Band of H.M.S. ARK ROYAL
UK, male choir and Marine band — 6 wks

| 23 Dec 78 | THE LAST FAREWELL *BBC RESL 61* | .46 | 6 |

ARKARNA *UK, male vocal/instrumental/production group* — 3 wks

| 25 Jan 97 | HOUSE ON FIRE *WEA WEA 088CD1* | .33 | 2 |
| 2 Aug 97 | SO LITTLE TIME *WEA WEA 108CD1* | .46 | 1 |

Joan ARMATRADING ♂ ✍ *UK, female vocalist* — 53 wks

16 Oct 76	● LOVE AND AFFECTION *A & M AMS 7249*	.10	9
23 Feb 80	ROSIE *A & M AMS 7506*	.49	5
14 Jun 80	ME MYSELF I *A & M AMS 7527*	.21	11
6 Sep 80	ALL THE WAY FROM AMERICA *A & M AMS 7552*	.54	3
12 Sep 81	I'M LUCKY *A & M AMS 8163*	.46	5
16 Jan 82	NO LOVE *A & M AMS 8179*	.50	5
19 Feb 83	DROP THE PILOT *A & M AMS 8306*	.11	10
16 Mar 85	TEMPTATION *A & M AM 238*	.65	2
26 May 90	MORE THAN ONE KIND OF LOVE *A & M AM 561*	.75	1
23 May 92	WRAPPED AROUND HER *A & M AM 877*	.56	2

ARMIN *Holland, male DJ producer* — 1 wk

| 14 Feb 98 | BLUE FEAR *Xtravaganza 0091485 EXT* | .45 | 1 |

ARMOURY SHOW *UK, male vocal/instrumental group* — 6 wks

25 Aug 84	CASTLES IN SPAIN *Parlophone R 6079*	.69	2
26 Jan 85	WE CAN BE BRAVE AGAIN *Parlophone R 6087*	.66	1
17 Jan 87	LOVE IN ANGER *Parlophone R 6149*	.63	3

Craig ARMSTRONG – *See Shola AMA*

Louis ARMSTRONG ✍ Ⓒ
US, male jazz-band leader, vocalist/instrumentalist – trumpet — 93 wks

19 Dec 52	● TAKES TWO TO TANGO *Brunswick 04995*	.6	10
13 Apr 56	● THEME FROM THE THREEPENNY OPERA *Philips PB 574* [1]	.8	11
15 Jun 56	TAKE IT SATCH (EP) *Philips BBE 12035* [1]	.29	1
13 Jul 56	THE FAITHFUL HUSSAR *Philips PB 604* [1]	.27	2
6 Nov 59	MACK THE KNIFE *Philips PB 967* [1]	.24	1
4 Jun 64	● HELLO DOLLY *London HLR 9878* ▲	.4	14
7 Feb 68	★ WHAT A WONDERFUL WORLD/CABARET *HMV POP 1615*	.1	29
26 Jun 68	SUNSHINE OF LOVE *Stateside SS 2116*	.41	7
16 Apr 88	WHAT A WONDERFUL WORLD (re-issue) *A & M AM 435*	.53	5
19 Nov 94	● WE HAVE ALL THE TIME IN THE WORLD *EMI CDEM 357*	.3	11
18 Mar 95	WE HAVE ALL THE TIME IN THE WORLD (re-entry) *EMI CDEM 357*	.66	2

[1] Louis Armstrong with his All-Stars

*Take It Satch (EP) tracks: Tiger Rag/Mack the Knife/The Faithful Hussar/Back
O'Town Blues. 'Mack the Knife' is a re-issue of 'Theme From Threepenny Opera'
under a different title*
'Cabaret' was not listed with 'What a Wonderful World' until 14 Feb, 1968

ARMY OF LOVERS *Sweden/France, male/female vocal/group* — 12 wks

17 Aug 91	CRUCIFIED *Ton Son Ton WOK 2007*	.47	5
28 Dec 91	OBSESSION *Ton Son Ton WOK 2009*	.67	1
15 Feb 92	CRUCIFIED (re-issue) *Ton Son Ton WOK 2017*	.31	5
18 Apr 92	RIDE THE BULLET *Ton Son Ton WOK 2018*	.67	1

UK No 1 ★   UK Top 10 ●   UK million seller ◆   UK entry at No 1 ■   US No 1 ▲

ARNEE and the TERMINATERS ✪
UK, male vocal/instrumental group **7 wks**

| 24 Aug 91 | ● I'LL BE BACK *Epic 6574177* | 5 | 7 |

ARNIE'S LOVE *US, male/female vocal/instrumental group* **3 wks**

| 26 Nov 83 | I'M OUT OF YOUR LIFE *Streetwave WAVE 9* | 67 | 3 |

David ARNOLD – See BJORK; David McALMONT; PROPELLERHEADS

Eddy ARNOLD ⬥ *US, male vocalist* **21 wks**

17 Feb 66	● MAKE THE WORLD GO AWAY *RCA 1496*	8	17
26 May 66	I WANT TO GO WITH YOU *RCA 1519*	49	1
9 Jun 66	I WANT TO GO WITH YOU (re-entry) *RCA 1519*	46	2
28 Jul 66	IF YOU WERE MINE MARY *RCA 1529*	49	1

PP ARNOLD ⚲ *US, female vocalist* **37 wks**

4 May 67	FIRST CUT IS THE DEEPEST *Immediate IM 047*	18	10
2 Aug 67	THE TIME HAS COME *Immediate IM 055*	47	2
24 Jan 68	(IF YOU THINK) YOU'RE GROOVY *Immediate IM 061*	41	4
10 Jul 68	ANGEL OF THE MORNING *Immediate IM 067*	29	11
24 Sep 88	BURN IT UP *Rhythm King LEFT 27* [1]	14	10

[1] Beatmasters with PP Arnold

ARPEGGIO *US, male/female vocal group* **3 wks**

| 31 Mar 79 | LOVE AND DESIRE (PART 1) *Polydor POSP 40* | 63 | 3 |

ARRESTED DEVELOPMENT ⬥
US, male/female vocal/instrumental group **39 wks**

16 May 92	TENNESSEE *Cooltempo COOL 253*	46	4
11 Jul 92	TENNESSEE (re-entry) *Cooltempo COOL 253*	54	3
24 Oct 92	● PEOPLE EVERYDAY *Cooltempo COOL 265*	2	14
9 Jan 93	● MR. WENDAL/REVOLUTION *Cooltempo CDCOOL 268*	4	9
3 Apr 93	TENNESSEE (re-issue) *Cooltempo CDCOOL 270*	18	6
28 May 94	EASE MY MIND *Cooltempo CDCOOL 293*	33	3

Steve ARRINGTON 🎤 ☺ *US, male vocalist* **19 wks**

27 Apr 85	● FEEL SO REAL *Atlantic A 9576*	5	10
6 Jul 85	DANCIN' IN THE KEY OF LIFE *Atlantic A 9534*	21	8
7 Sep 85	DANCIN' IN THE KEY OF LIFE (re-entry) *Atlantic A 9534*	75	1

ARRIVAL ✪ *UK, male/female vocal/instrumental group* **20 wks**

| 10 Jan 70 | ● FRIENDS *Decca F 12986* | 8 | 9 |
| 6 Jun 70 | I WILL SURVIVE *Decca F 13026* | 16 | 11 |

ARROLA – See RUFF DRIVERZ

ARROW *Montserrat, male vocalist* **15 wks**

28 Jul 84	HOT HOT HOT *Cooltempo ARROW 1*	59	5
13 Jul 85	LONG TIME *London LON 70*	30	7
3 Sep 94	HOT HOT HOT (re-mix) *The Hit Label HLC 7*	38	3

ARROWS ✪ *US/UK, male vocal/instrumental group* **16 wks**

| 25 May 74 | ● A TOUCH TOO MUCH *RAK 171* | 8 | 9 |
| 1 Feb 75 | MY LAST NIGHT WITH YOU *RAK 189* | 25 | 7 |

ARSENAL F.C. ✪
UK, male football team vocal group **15 wks**

8 May 71	GOOD OLD ARSENAL *Pye 7N 45067* [1]	16	7
15 May 93	SHOUTING FOR THE GUNNERS *London LONCD 342* [2]	34	3
23 May 98	● HOT STUFF *Grapevine AFCCD 1*	9	5

[1] Arsenal FC First Team Squad [2] Arsenal FA Cup Squad featuring Tippa Irie and Peter Hunnigale

ART COMPANY ✪ *Holland, male vocal/instrumental group* **11 wks**

| 26 May 84 | SUSANNA *Epic A 4174* | 12 | 11 |

ART OF NOISE ✪ ☺
UK, male/female instrumental/production group **64 wks**

24 Nov 84	● CLOSE (TO THE EDIT) *ZTT ZTPS 01*	8	19
13 Apr 85	MOMENTS IN LOVE/BEAT BOX *ZTT ZTPS 02*	51	4
9 Nov 85	LEGS *China WOK 5*	69	1
22 Mar 86	● PETER GUNN *China WOK 6* [1]	8	9
21 Jun 86	PARANOIMIA *China WOK 9* [2]	12	9
18 Jul 87	DRAGNET *China WOK 14*	60	4
29 Oct 88	● KISS *China CHINA 11* [3]	5	7
12 Aug 89	YEBO *China CHINA 18* [4]	63	3
16 Jun 90	ART OF LOVE *China CHINA 23*	67	1
11 Jan 92	INSTRUMENTS OF DARKNESS (ALL OF US ARE ONE PEOPLE) *China WOK 2012*	45	5
29 Feb 92	SHADES OF PARANOIMIA *China WOK 2014*	53	1

[1] Art of Noise featuring Duane Eddy [2] Art of Noise featuring Max Headroom [3] Art of Noise featuring Tom Jones [4] Art of Noise featuring Mahlathini and the Mahotella Queens

ART OF TRANCE *UK, male instrumentalist / producer* **1 wk**

| 31 Oct 98 | MADAGASGA *Platipus PLAT 43CD* | 69 | 1 |

ARTEMESIA *Holland, male producer – Patrick Prinz* **3 wks**

| 15 Apr 95 | BITS + PIECES *Hooj Choons HOOJ 31CD* | 46 | 2 |
| 23 Sep 95 | BITS + PIECES (re-entry) *Hooj Choons HOOJ 31CD* | 75 | 1 |

See also ETHICS; MOVIN' MELODIES; SUBLIMINAL CUTS

Neil ARTHUR *UK, male vocalist* **2 wks**

| 5 Feb 94 | I LOVE I HATE *Chrysalis CDCHSS 5005* | 50 | 2 |

ARTIST – See PRINCE

ARTISTS UNITED AGAINST APARTHEID
International, male/female vocal/instrumental charity assembly **8 wks**

| 23 Nov 85 | SUN CITY *Manhattan MT 7* | 21 | 8 |

ASAP *UK, male vocal/instrumental group* **4 wks**

| 14 Oct 89 | SILVER AND GOLD *EMI EM 107* | 60 | 2 |
| 3 Feb 90 | DOWN THE WIRE *EMI EM 131* | 67 | 2 |

ASCENSION *UK, male / female vocal / DJ / production group* **1 wk**

| 5 Jul 97 | SOMEONE *Perfecto PERF 141CD* | 55 | 1 |

ASH ☺ *UK, male vocal/instrumental group* **34 wks**

1 Apr 95	KUNG FU *Infectious INFECT 21CD*	57	1
12 Aug 95	GIRL FROM MARS *Infectious INFECT 24CD*	11	5
21 Oct 95	ANGEL INTERCEPTOR *Infectious INFECT 27CD*	14	4
27 Apr 96	● GOLDFINGER *Infectious INFECT 39CD*	5	5
6 Jul 96	● OH YEAH *Infectious INFECT 41CD*	6	7
28 Sep 96	OH YEAH (re-entry) *Infectious INFECT 41CD*	69	1
25 Oct 97	● A LIFE LESS ORDINARY *Infectious INFECT 50CD*	10	5
3 Oct 98	JESUS SAYS *Infectious INFECT 59CD*	15	4
5 Dec 98	WILD SURF *Infectious INFECT 61CDS*	31	2

ASH – See QUENTIN and ASH

ASHA *Italy, female vocalist* **2 wks**

| 8 Jul 95 | JJ TRIBUTE *Ffrreedom TABCD 228* | 38 | 2 |

ASHAYE *UK, male vocalist* **3 wks**

| 15 Oct 83 | MICHAEL JACKSON MEDLEY *Record Shack SOHO 10* | 45 | 3 |

Tracks on medley: Don't Stop Til You Get Enough / Wanna Be Startin' Something / Shake Your Body Down to the Ground / Blame It on the Boogie

John ASHER ✪ *UK, male vocalist* **6 wks**

| 15 Nov 75 | LET'S TWIST AGAIN *Creole CR 112* | 14 | 6 |

ASHFORD and SIMPSON ♫ US, male/female vocal duo | | 22 wks

18 Nov 78	IT SEEMS TO HANG ON Warner Bros. K 17237	48	4
5 Jan 85 ●	SOLID Capitol CL 345	3	15
20 Apr 85	BABIES Capitol CL 355	56	3

ASHTON, GARDNER AND DYKE ✪
UK, male vocal/instrumental group | | 14 wks

16 Jan 71 ●	THE RESURRECTION SHUFFLE Capitol CL 15665	3	14

ASIA UK, male vocal/instrumental group | | 13 wks

3 Jul 82	HEAT OF THE MOMENT Geffen GEF A2494	46	5
18 Sep 82	ONLY TIME WILL TELL Geffen GEF A2228	54	3
13 Aug 83	DON'T CRY Geffen A 3580	33	5

ASIA BLUE UK, female vocal group | | 2 wks

27 Jun 92	ESCAPING Atomic WNR 882	50	2

ASIAN DUB FOUNDATION UK, male vocal/instrumental group | | 4 wks

21 Feb 98	FREE SATPAL RAM ffrr FCD 326	56	1
2 May 98	BUZZIN' ffrr FCDP 335	31	2
4 Jul 98	BLACK WHITE ffrr FCD n337	52	1

ASSEMBLY ✪ UK, male vocal/instrumental group | | 10 wks

12 Nov 83 ●	NEVER NEVER Mute TINY 1	4	10

ASSOCIATES ✪ UK, male vocal/instrumental group | | 47 wks

20 Feb 82 ●	PARTY FEARS TWO Associates ASC 1	9	10
8 May 82	CLUB COUNTRY Associates ASC 2	13	10
7 Aug 82	LOVE HANGOVER/18 CARAT LOVE AFFAIR Associates ASC 3	21	8
16 Jun 84	THOSE FIRST IMPRESSIONS WEA YZ 6	43	6
1 Sep 84	WAITING FOR THE LOVEBOAT WEA YZ 16	53	4
19 Jan 85	BREAKFAST WEA YZ 28	49	6
17 Sep 88	HEART OF GLASS WEA YZ 310	56	3

'18 Carat Love Affair' listed until 28 Aug only. Act was duo on 1982 hits

ASSOCIATION US, male vocal/instrumental group | | 8 wks

22 May 68	TIME FOR LIVING Warner Bros. WB 7195	23	8

Rick ASTLEY ✪ UK, male vocalist | | 91 wks

8 Aug 87 ★	NEVER GONNA GIVE YOU UP RCA PB 41447 ▲	1	18
31 Oct 87 ●	WHENEVER YOU NEED SOMEBODY RCA PB 41567	3	12
12 Dec 87 ●	WHEN I FALL IN LOVE/MY ARMS KEEP MISSING YOU RCA PB 41683	2	10
27 Feb 88 ●	TOGETHER FOREVER RCA PB 41817 ▲	2	9
24 Sep 88 ●	SHE WANTS TO DANCE WITH ME RCA PB 42189	6	10
26 Nov 88 ●	TAKE ME TO YOUR HEART RCA PB 42573	8	10
11 Feb 89 ●	HOLD ME IN YOUR ARMS RCA PB 42615	10	8
26 Jan 91 ●	CRY FOR HELP RCA PB 44247	7	7
30 Mar 91	MOVE RIGHT OUT RCA PB 44407	58	2
29 Jun 91	NEVER KNEW LOVE RCA PB 44737	70	1
4 Sep 93	THE ONES YOU LOVE RCA 74321160142	48	2
13 Nov 93	HOPELESSLY RCA 74321175642	33	2

Before 9 Jan, 1988, 'When I Fall in Love' was listed by itself. After that date 'My Arms Keep Missing You' was the side listed

ASTRO TRAX UK, male/female vocal/production trio | | 1 wk

24 Oct 98	THE ENERGY (FEEL THE VIBE) Satellite 74321622052	74	1

ASWAD ♫ UK, male vocal/instrumental group | | 80 wks

3 Mar 84	CHASING FOR THE BREEZE Island IS 160	51	3
6 Oct 84	54-46 (WAS MY NUMBER) Island IS 170	70	3
27 Feb 88 ★	DON'T TURN AROUND Mango IS 341	1	12
21 May 88	GIVE A LITTLE LOVE Mango IS 358	11	8
24 Sep 88	SET THEM FREE Mango IS 383	70	2
1 Apr 89	BEAUTY'S ONLY SKIN DEEP Mango MNG 105	31	6
22 Jul 89	ON AND ON Mango MNG 708	25	8
18 Aug 90	NEXT TO YOU Mango MNG 753	24	6
17 Nov 90	SMILE Mango MNG 767 ☐1	53	2
30 Mar 91	TOO WICKED EP Mango MNG 771	61	2
31 Jul 93	HOW LONG Polydor PZCD 252 ☐2	31	5
9 Oct 93	DANCE HALL MOOD Bubblin' CDBUBB 1	48	2
18 Jun 94 ●	SHINE Bubblin' CDBUBB 3	5	14
17 Sep 94	WARRIORS Bubblin' CDBUBB 4	33	3
18 Feb 95	YOU'RE NO GOOD Bubblin' CDBUBB 5	35	3
5 Aug 95	IF I WAS Bubblin' CDBUBB 6	58	1

☐1 Aswad featuring Sweetie Irie ☐2 Yazz and Aswad

Tracks on Too Wicked EP: Best of My Love/Warrior Re-Charge/Fire/I Shot The Sheriff

Gali ATARI – See MILK AND HONEY featuring Gali ATARI

ATGOC Italy, male instrumentalist/producer | | 2 wks

21 Nov 98	REPEATED LOVE Wonderboy WBOYD 012	38	2

Chet ATKINS US, male instrumentalist – guitar | | 2 wks

17 Mar 60	TEENSVILLE RCA 1174	46	1
5 May 60	TEENSVILLE (re-entry) RCA 1174	49	1

ATLANTA RHYTHM SECTION
US, male vocal/instrumental group | | 4 wks

27 Oct 79	SPOOKY Polydor POSP 74	48	4

ATLANTIC OCEAN ☺ Holland, male instrumental duo | | 14 wks

19 Feb 94	WATERFALL Eastern Bloc BLOCCD 001	22	6
2 Jul 94	BODY IN MOTION Eastern Bloc BLOCCD 009	15	4
26 Nov 94	MUSIC IS A PASSION Eastern Bloc BLOCCDX 017	59	1
30 Nov 96	WATERFALL (re-mix) Eastern Bloc BLOC 104CD	21	3

ATLANTIC STARR ✎ ☺
US, male/female vocal/instrumental group | | 48 wks

9 Sep 78	GIMME YOUR LOVIN' A & M AMS 7380	66	3
29 Jun 85	SILVER SHADOW A & M AM 260	41	6
7 Sep 85	ONE LOVE A & M AM 273	58	4
15 Mar 86 ●	SECRET LOVERS A & M AM 307	10	12
24 May 86	IF YOUR HEART ISN'T IN IT A & M AM 319	48	4
13 Jun 87 ●	ALWAYS Warner Bros. W 8455 ▲	3	14
12 Sep 87	ONE LOVER AT A TIME Warner Bros. W 8327	57	3
27 Aug 94	EVERYBODY'S GOT SUMMER Arista 74321228072	36	2

ATMOSFEAR UK, male vocal/instrumental group | | 7 wks

17 Nov 79	DANCING IN OUTER SPACE MCA 543	46	7

ATOMIC ROOSTER ✎ UK, male vocal/instrumental group | | 25 wks

6 Feb 71	TOMORROW NIGHT B & C CB 131	11	12
10 Jul 71 ●	THE DEVIL'S ANSWER B & C CB 157	4	13

ATTRACTIONS – See Elvis COSTELLO

Winifred ATWELL ✪ The 'Queen of the Ivories' (and Elton John's early idol), b. 27 April, 1914, Trinidad, d. 28 February, 1983. Britain's all-time top female instrumentalist, who earned a couple of gold discs for her popular party medleys and hosted a very successful TV series in 1957 | | 117 wks

12 Dec 52	BRITANNIA RAG Decca F 10015	11	1
9 Jan 53 ●	BRITANNIA RAG (re-entry) Decca F 10015	5	5
15 May 53	CORONATION RAG Decca F 10110	12	1
29 May 53 ●	CORONATION RAG (re-entry) Decca F 10110	5	5
25 Sep 53	FLIRTATION WALTZ Decca F 10161	12	1
9 Oct 53 ●	FLIRTATION WALTZ (re-entry) Decca F 10161	10	1
6 Nov 53	FLIRTATION WALTZ (2nd re-entry) Decca F10161	12	1
4 Dec 53 ●	LET'S HAVE A PARTY Philips PB 213	2	9
23 Jul 54 ●	RACHMANINOFF'S 18TH VARIATION ON A THEME BY PAGANINI (THE STORY OF THREE LOVES) Philips PB 234	9	9
1 Oct 54	RACHMANINOFF'S 18TH VARIATION ON A THEME BY PAGANINI (THE STORY OF THREE LOVES) (re-entry) Philips PB 234	19	2
26 Nov 54 ★	LET'S HAVE ANOTHER PARTY Philips PB 268	1	8

UK No 1 ★   UK Top 10 ●   UK million seller ◆   UK entry at No 1 ■   US No 1 ▲

26 Nov 54	LET'S HAVE A PARTY (re-entry) *Philips PB 213*	14	6
4 Nov 55 ●	LET'S HAVE A DING DONG *Decca F 10634*	3	10
16 Mar 56 ★	POOR PEOPLE OF PARIS *Decca F 10681*	1	16
18 May 56	PORT AU PRINCE *Decca F 10727* [1]	18	6
20 Jul 56	LEFT BANK *Decca F 10762*	14	7
26 Oct 56 ●	MAKE IT A PARTY *Decca F 10796*	7	12
22 Feb 57	LET'S ROCK 'N ROLL *Decca F 10852*	28	2
15 Mar 57	LET'S ROCK 'N ROLL (re-entry) *Decca F 10852*	24	2
6 Dec 57 ●	LET'S HAVE A BALL *Decca F 10956*	4	6
7 Aug 59	SUMMER OF THE SEVENTEENTH DOLL *Decca F 11143*	24	2
27 Nov 59 ●	PIANO PARTY *Decca F 11183*	10	7

[1] Winifred Atwell and Frank Chacksfield

Various hits listed above were medleys as follows: Let's Have a Party: Boomps a Daisy / Daisy Bell / If You Knew Suzie / Knees Up Mother Brown / The More We Are Together / She Was One of the Early Birds / That's My Weakness Now / Three O'Clock in the Morning. Let's Have Another Party: Another Little Drink / Broken Doll / Bye Bye Blackbird / Honeysuckle and the Bee / I Wonder Where My Baby Is Tonight / Lily of Laguna / Nellie Dean / Sheik of Araby / Somebody Stole My Gal / When the Red Red Robin. Let's Have a Ding Dong: Happy Days Are Here Again / Oh Johnny Oh Johnny Oh / Oh You Beautiful Doll / Ain't She Sweet / Yes We Have No Bananas / I'm Forever Blowing Bubbles / I'll Be Your Sweetheart / If These Lips Could Only Speak / Who's Taking You Home Tonight. Make It a Party: Who Were You With Last Night / Hello Hello Who's Your Lady Friend / Yes Sir That's My Baby / Don't Dilly Dally On the Way / Beer Barrel Polka / After the Ball / Peggy O'Neil / Meet Me Tonight in Dreamland / I Belong To Glasgow / Down at the Old Bull and Bush. Let's Rock 'n' Roll: Singin' the Blues / Green Door / See You Later Alligator / Shake Rattle and Roll / Rock Around the Clock / Razzle Dazzle. Let's Have a Ball: Music Music Music / This Ole House / Heartbreaker / Woody Woodpecker / Last Train to San Fernando / Bring a Little Water Sylvie / Puttin' On the Style / Don't You Rock Me Daddy-O. Piano Party: Baby Face / Comin' Thru' the Rye / Annie Laurie / Little Brown Jug / Let Him Go Let Him Tarry / Put Your Arms Around Me Honey / I'll Be With You in Apple Blossom Time / Shine On Harvest Moon / Blue Skies / I'll Never Say 'Never Again' Again / I'll See You In My Dreams

See also VARIOUS ARTISTS (EPs & LPs) – All Star Hit Parade

THE AUDIENCE – see THEAUDIENCE

AUDIOWEB ○ ✎ *UK, male vocal/instrumental group*   11 wks

14 Oct 95	SLEEPER *Mother MUMCD 69*	74	1
9 Mar 96	YEAH *Mother MUMCD 72*	73	1
15 Jun 96	INTO MY WORLD *Mother MUMCD 76*	42	1
19 Oct 96	SLEEPER (re-mix) *Mother MUMCD 78*	50	2
15 Feb 97	BANKROBBER *Mother MUMCD 85*	19	2
24 May 97	FAKER *Mother MUMCD 91*	70	1
25 Apr 98	POLICEMAN SKANK... (THE STORY OF MY LIFE) *Mother MUMCD 100*	21	2
4 Jul 98	PERSONAL FEELING *Mother MUMCD 104*	65	1

Brian AUGER – See Julie DRISCOLL, Brian AUGER and the TRINITY

AURRA ☺ ✎ *US, male/female vocal/instrumental group*   18 wks

4 May 85	LIKE I LIKE IT *10 TEN 45*	51	5
19 Apr 86	YOU AND ME TONIGHT *10 TEN 71*	12	8
21 Jun 86	LIKE I LIKE IT (re-issue) *10 TEN 126*	43	5

David AUSTIN *UK, male vocalist*   3 wks

21 Jul 84	TURN TO GOLD *Parlophone R 6068*	68	3

Patti AUSTIN ✎ *US, female vocalist*   20 wks

20 Jun 81	RAZZAMATAZZ *A & M AMS 8140* [1]	11	9
12 Feb 83	BABY COME TO ME *Qwest K 15005* [2] ▲	11	10
5 Sep 92	I'LL KEEP YOUR DREAMS ALIVE *Ammi AMM 101* [3]	68	1

[1] Quincy Jones featuring Patti Austin   [2] Patti Austin and James Ingram
[3] George Benson and Patti Austin

AUTECHRE *UK, male instrumental duo*   1 wk

7 May 94	BASSCAD *Warp WAP 44CD*	56	1

AUTEURS *UK, male/female vocal/instrumental group*   8 wks

27 Nov 93	LENNY VALENTINO *Hut HUTCD 36*	41	2

23 Apr 94	CHINESE BAKERY *Hut HUTDX 41*	42	2
6 Jan 96	BACK WITH THE KILLER AGAIN *Hut HUTCD 65*	45	3
24 Feb 96	LIGHT AIRCRAFT ON FIRE *Hut HUTCD 66*	58	1

AUTUMN *UK, male vocal/instrumental group*   6 wks

16 Oct 71	MY LITTLE GIRL *Pye 7N 45090*	37	6

Peter AUTY and the SINFONIA OF LONDON
UK, male vocalist with UK orchestra   9 wks

14 Dec 85	WALKING IN THE AIR *Stiff LAD 1*	42	5
19 Dec 87	WALKING IN THE AIR (re-issue) *CBS GA 3950*	37	4

Label credits the Snowman featuring Peter Auty
See also DIGITAL DREAM BAB

AVALON BOYS – See LAUREL and HARDY with the AVALON BOYS featuring Chill WILLS

Frankie AVALON ○ *US, male vocalist*   15 wks

10 Oct 58	GINGERBREAD *HMV POP 517*	30	1
24 Apr 59	VENUS *HMV POP 603* ▲	16	6
22 Jan 60	WHY *HMV POP 688* ▲	20	4
28 Apr 60	DON'T THROW AWAY ALL THOSE TEARDROPS *HMV POP 727*	37	4

AVERAGE WHITE BAND ♀ *UK, male vocal/instrumental vocal group*   47 wks

22 Feb 75 ●	PICK UP THE PIECES *Atlantic K 10489* ▲	6	9
26 Apr 75	CUT THE CAKE *Atlantic K 10605*	31	4
9 Oct 76	QUEEN OF MY SOUL *Atlantic K 10825*	23	7
28 Apr 79	WALK ON BY *RCA XC 1087*	46	4
25 Aug 79	WHEN WILL YOU BE MINE *RCA XB 1096*	49	5
26 Apr 80	LET'S GO ROUND AGAIN PT.1 *RCA AWB 1*	12	11
26 Jul 80	FOR YOU FOR LOVE *RCA AWB 2*	46	4
26 Mar 94	LET'S GO ROUND AGAIN (re-mix) *The Hit Label HLC 5*	56	2

Kevin AVIANCE *US, male vocalist*   1 wk

13 Jun 98	DIN DA DA *Distinctive DISNCD 42*	65	1

AVONS ○ *UK, male/female vocal group*   22 wks

13 Nov 59 ●	SEVEN LITTLE GIRLS SITTING IN THE BACK SEAT *Columbia DB 4363*	3	13
7 Jul 60	WE'RE ONLY YOUNG ONCE *Columbia DB 4461*	49	1
21 Jul 60	WE'RE ONLY YOUNG ONCE (re-entry) *Columbia DB 4461*	45	1
27 Oct 60	FOUR LITTLE HEELS *Columbia DB 4522*	45	2
1 Dec 60	FOUR LITTLE HEELS (re-entry) *Columbia DB 4522*	49	1
26 Jan 61	RUBBER BALL *Columbia DB 4569*	30	4

AWESOME *UK, male vocal group*   2 wks

8 Nov 97	RUMOURS *Universal MCSTD 40145*	58	1
21 Mar 98	CRAZY *Universal MCSTD 40195*	63	1

AWESOME 3 *UK, male/female vocal/instrumental group*   8 wks

8 Sep 90	HARD UP *A & M AM 591*	55	3
3 Oct 92	DON'T GO *Citybeat CBE 1271*	75	1
4 Jun 94	DON'T GO (re-mix) *Citybeat CBX 771CD*	45	2
26 Oct 96	DON'T GO (2nd re-mix) *XL XLS 78CD* [1]	27	2

[1] Awesome 3 featuring Julie McDermott

Hoyt AXTON *US, male vocalist*   4 wks

7 Jun 80	DELLA AND THE DEALER *Young Blood YB 82*	48	4

AXUS *UK, male/female vocal/production duo*   1 wks

26 Sep 98	ABACUS (WHEN I FALL IN LOVE) *INCcredible INCRL 8CD*	62	1

Roy AYERS *US, male vocalist/instrumentalist – vibraphone*   13 wks

21 Oct 78	GET ON UP, GET ON DOWN *Polydor AYERS 7*	41	4

13 Jan 79	HEAT OF THE BEAT *Polydor POSP 16* [1]	43	5
2 Feb 80	DON'T STOP THE FEELING *Polydor STEP 6*	56	3
16 May 98	EXPANSIONS *Soma Recordings SOMA 65CDS* [2]	68	1

[1] Roy Ayers and Wayne Henderson [2] Scott Grooves featuring Roy Ayers

AZ *US, male rapper – Anthony Cruz*　　　　　　1 wk

| 30 Mar 96 | SUGARHILL *Cooltempo CDCOOL 315* | .....67 | 1 |

AZ YET ✏ (R&B) *US, male vocal group*　　　　　10 wks

| 1 Mar 97 | LAST NIGHT *LaFace 74321423202* | .....21 | 3 |
| 21 Jun 97 ● | HARD TO SAY I'M SORRY *LaFace 74321481482* | .....7 | 7 |

Charles AZNAVOUR ℂ *France, male vocalist*　　　29 wks

22 Sep 73	THE OLD FASHIONED WAY *Barclay BAR 20*	50	1
20 Oct 73	THE OLD FASHIONED WAY (re-entry) *Barclay BAR 20*	38	12
22 Jun 74 ★	SHE *Barclay BAR 26*	1	14
27 Jul 74	THE OLD FASHIONED WAY (2nd re-entry) *Barclay BAR 20*	47	2

AZTEC CAMERA ◎ *UK, male vocal/instrumental group*　74 wks

19 Feb 83	OBLIVIOUS *Rough Trade RT 122*	47	6
4 Jun 83	WALK OUT TO WINTER *Rough Trade RT 132*	64	4
5 Nov 83	OBLIVIOUS (re-issue) *WEA AZTEC 1*	18	11
1 Sep 84	ALL I NEED IS EVERYTHING/JUMP *WEA AC 1*	34	6
13 Feb 88	HOW MEN ARE *WEA YZ 168*	25	9
23 Apr 88 ●	SOMEWHERE IN MY HEART *WEA YZ 181*	3	14
6 Aug 88	WORKING IN A GOLDMINE *WEA YZ 199*	31	5
8 Oct 88	DEEP AND WIDE AND TALL *WEA YZ 154*	55	3
7 Jul 90	THE CRYING SCENE *WEA YZ 492*	70	3
6 Oct 90	GOOD MORNING BRITAIN *WEA YZ 521* [1]	19	8
18 Jul 92	SPANISH HORSES *WEA YZ 688*	52	3
1 May 93	DREAM SWEET DREAMS *WEA YZ 740CD1*	67	2

[1] Aztec Camera and Mick Jones

'Jump' only listed from 22 Sep to end of chart run

AZURE *Italy/US, male/female vocal/DJ duo*　　　1 wk

| 25 Apr 98 | MAMA USED TO SAY *Inferno CDFERN 005* | .....56 | 1 |

AZYMUTH ♪ *Brazil, male instrumental group*　　8 wks

| 12 Jan 80 | JAZZ CARNIVAL *Milestone MRC 101* | .....19 | 8 |

Bob AZZAM *Egypt, singing orchestra*　　　　　14 wks

| 26 May 60 | MUSTAPHA *Decca F 21235* | .....23 | 14 |

B

Derek B *UK, male rapper*　　　　　　　　　15 wks

27 Feb 88	GOODGROOVE *Music Of Life 7NOTE 12*	16	6
7 May 88	BAD YOUNG BROTHER *Tuff Audio DRKB 1*	16	6
2 Jul 88	WE'VE GOT THE JUICE *Tuff Audio DRKB 2*	56	3

Eric B and RAKIM *UK, male DJ/rap duo*　　　26 wks

7 Nov 87	PAID IN FULL *Fourth & Broadway BRW 78*	15	6
20 Feb 88	MOVE THE CROWD *Fourth & Broadway BRW 88*	53	2
12 Mar 88	I KNOW YOU GOT SOUL *Cooltempo COOL 146*	13	6

2 Jul 88	FOLLOW THE LEADER *MCA MCA 1256*	21	5
19 Nov 88	THE MICROPHONE FIEND *MCA MCA 1300*	74	1
12 Aug 89	FRIENDS *MCA MCA 1352* [1]	21	6

[1] Jody Watley with Eric B and Rakim

Howie B *UK male instrumentalist/producer*　　4 wks

19 Jul 97	ANGELS GO BALD: TOO *Polydor 5711672*	36	2
18 Oct 97	SWITCH *Polydor 5717112*	62	1
11 Apr 98	TAKE YOUR PARTNER BY THE HAND *Polydor 5693272* [1]	74	1

[1] Howie B featuring Robbie Robertson

JAZZIE B – See Maxi PRIEST; SOUL II SOUL

Jon B *US, male vocalist*　　　　　　　　　2 wks

| 17 Oct 98 | THEY DON'T KNOW *Epic 6663975* | .....32 | 2 |

Lisa B *US, female vocalist*　　　　　　　　9 wks

12 Jun 93	GLAM *ffrr FCD 210*	49	2
25 Sep 93	FASCINATED *ffrr FCD 218*	35	3
8 Jan 94	YOU AND ME *ffrr FCD 226*	39	4

Lorna B *UK, female vocalist*　　　　　　　6 wks

28 Jan 95	DO YOU WANNA PARTY *Steppin' Out SPONCD 2* [1]	36	3
1 Apr 95	SWEET DREAMS *Steppin' Out SPONCD 3* [1]	37	2
15 Mar 97	FEELS SO GOOD *Avex UK AVEXCD 53* [2]	69	1

[1] DJ Scott featuring Lorna B [2] Zero Vu featuring Lorna B

Melanie B (R&B) *UK, female vocalist*　　　　9 wks

| 26 Sep 98 ★ | I WANT YOU BACK *Virgin VSCDT 1716* [1] ■ | .....1 | 9 |

[1] Melanie B featuring Missy 'Misdemeanor' Elliott

See also SPICE GIRLS

B REAL – See LL COOL J; COOLIO; METHOD MAN; Busta RHYMES

Sandy B ☺ *US, female vocalist*　　　　　　8 wks

20 Feb 93	FEEL LIKE SINGIN' *Nervous SANCD 1*	60	1
18 May 96	MAKE THE WORLD GO ROUND *Champion CHAMPCD 322*	73	1
24 May 97	MAKE THE WORLD GO ROUND (re-mix) *Champion CHAMPCD 327*	35	2
8 Nov 97	AIN'T NO NEED TO HIDE *Champion CHAMPCD 331*	60	1
28 Feb 98	MAKE THE WORLD GO ROUND (2nd re-mix) *Champion CHAMPCD 333*	20	3

Stevie B ◎ *US, male vocalist*　　　　　　　9 wks

| 23 Feb 91 ● | BECAUSE I LOVE YOU (THE POSTMAN SONG) *Polydor PO 126* ▲ | .....6 | 9 |

Tairrie B *US, female rapper*　　　　　　　2 wks

| 1 Dec 90 | MURDER SHE WROTE *MCA MCA 1455* | .....71 | 2 |

B*WITCHED ◎ *Ireland, female vocal group*　34 wks

6 Jun 98 ★	C'EST LA VIE *Glow Worm 6660532* ■	1	19
3 Oct 98 ★	ROLLERCOASTER *Epic 6664752* ■	.....1†	13
19 Dec 98 ★	TO YOU I BELONG *Glow Worm 6667712* ■	.....1†	2

B-CREW *US, female vocal group*　　　　　　1 wk

| 20 Sep 97 | PARTAY FEELING *Positiva CDTIV 78* | .....45 | 1 |

B-MOVIE *UK, male vocal/instrumental group*　7 wks

| 18 Apr 81 | REMEMBRANCE DAY *Deram DM 437* | .....61 | 3 |
| 27 Mar 82 | NOWHERE GIRL *Some Bizarr JDDe BZZ 8* | .....67 | 4 |

B-TRIBE *Spain, male/female vocal/instrumental group*　4 wks

| 25 Sep 93 | ¡FIESTA FATAL! *East West YZ 770CD* | .....64 | 4 |

What: *Do They Know It's Christmas*   **13**
Who: Band Aid
When: 1984 (1), 1985 (3)
Which: Helped millions and inspired many similar projects. This crucially significant charity record, masterminded by Bob Geldof, was a worldwide success and sold more than 3.6 million copies in the UK alone

What: *He Ain't Heavy, He's My Brother*   **14**
Who: Hollies
When: 1969 (3), 1988 (1)
Which: Thanks to a beer commercial, finally hit the top almost 19 years after first entering the charts. The track features the distinctive piano-playing of Elton John in his pre-hit days

What: *Love Is All Around*   **15**
Who: Wet Wet Wet
When: 1994 (1)
Which: Headed the chart for 15 consecutive weeks – a record for a British act. It notched up more than 1.6 million UK sales, putting it in the all-time Top 10 best sellers list

What: *Holiday*   **16**
Who: Madonna
When: 1984 (6), 1985 (2), 1991 (5)
Which: Gave pop's First Lady her debut hit and had three Top 10 runs – a record for a female artist. In 1985, only another Madonna single, 'Into the Groove', managed to stop this dance jewel from topping the chart

Alice BABS *Sweden, female vocalist*   **1 wk**

| 15 Aug 63 | AFTER YOU'VE GONE *Fontana TF 409* | 43 | 1 |

BABY BUMPS ☺ *UK, male/female vocal/instrumental duo*   **4 wks**

| 8 Aug 98 | BURNING *Delirious DELICD 10* | 17 | 4 |

BABY D ☺ ☺ *UK, male/female vocal/instrumental group*   **40 wks**

18 Dec 93	DESTINY *Production House PNC 057*	69	1
23 Jul 94	CASANOVA *Production House PNC 065*	67	1
19 Nov 94 ★	LET ME BE YOUR FANTASY *Systematic SYSCD 4*	1	14
3 Jun 95 ●	(EVERYBODY'S GOT TO LEARN SOMETIME) I NEED YOUR LOVING *Systematic SYSCD 11*	3	12
13 Jan 96 ●	SO PURE *Systematic SYSCD 21*	3	7
6 Apr 96	TAKE ME TO HEAVEN *Systematic SYSCD 26*	15	5

BABY JUNE *UK, male vocalist – Tim Hegarty*   **1 wk**

| 15 Aug 92 | HEY! WHAT'S YOUR NAME *Arista 115271* | 75 | 1 |

BABY O *US, male/female vocal/instrumental group*   **5 wks**

| 26 Jul 80 | IN THE FOREST *Calibre CAB 505* | 46 | 5 |

BABY ROOTS *UK, male vocalist*   **1 wk**

| 1 Aug 92 | ROCK ME BABY *ZYX ZYX 68027* | 71 | 1 |

BABYBIRD ☺ *UK, male vocal/instrumental group*   **28 wks**

10 Aug 96	GOODNIGHT *Echo ECSCD 24*	28	2
12 Oct 96 ●	YOU'RE GORGEOUS *Echo ECSD 26*	3	16
1 Feb 97	CANDY GIRL *Echo ECSCD 31*	14	3
17 May 97	CORNERSHOP *Echo ECSCD 33*	37	2
9 May 98	BAD OLD MAN *Echo ECSCD 60*	31	2
22 Aug 98	IF YOU'LL BE MINE *Echo ECSCX 65*	28	3

BABYFACE ✎ R&B *US, male vocalist*   **23 wks**

9 Jul 94	ROCK BOTTOM *Epic 6601832*	50	4
1 Oct 94	WHEN CAN I SEE YOU *Epic 6606592*	35	3
9 Nov 96	THIS IS FOR THE LOVER IN YOU *Epic 6639352*	12	5
8 Mar 97	EVERYTIME I CLOSE EYES *Epic 6642492*	13	4
19 Jul 97	HOW COME, HOW LONG *Epic 6646202* [1]	10	5
25 Oct 97	SUNSHINE *Northwestside 743215281702* [2]	25	2

[1] Babyface featuring Stevie Wonder [2] Jay-Z featuring Babyface and Foxy Brown

BABYLON ZOO ☺

UK, male vocalist/multi-instrumentalist – Jas Mann   **19 wks**

27 Jan 96 ★	SPACEMAN *EMI CDEM 416* ◆ ■	1	14
27 Apr 96	ANIMAL ARMY *EMI CDEM 425*	17	3
5 Oct 96	THE BOY WITH THE X-RAY EYES *EMI CDEMS 440*	32	2

BABYS *US/UK, male vocal/instrumental group*   **3 wks**

| 21 Jan 78 | ISN'T IT TIME *Chrysalis CHS 2173* | 45 | 3 |

BACCARA ♫ ☺ *Spain, female vocal duo*   **25 wks**

| 17 Sep 77 ★ | YES SIR I CAN BOOGIE *RCA PB 5526* | 1 | 16 |
| 14 Jan 78 ● | SORRY I'M A LADY *RCA PB 5555* | 8 | 9 |

Burt BACHARACH ℂ *US, orchestra and chorus*   **11 wks**

| 20 May 65 ● | TRAINS AND BOATS AND PLANES *London HL 9968* | 4 | 11 |

BACHELORS ℂ *Irish vocal/instrumental trio, who were one of the few popular non-rock groups of the 1960s: brothers Declan and Con Cluskey and John Stokes. This Dublin act had hits on both sides of the Atlantic with revivals of popular pre-rock ballads*   **187 wks**

24 Jan 63 ●	CHARMAINE *Decca F 11559*	6	19
4 Jul 63	FARAWAY PLACES *Decca F 11666*	36	3
29 Aug 63	WHISPERING *Decca F 11712*	18	10
23 Jan 64 ★	DIANE *Decca F 11799*	1	19
19 Mar 64 ●	I BELIEVE *Decca F 11857*	2	17
4 Jun 64 ●	RAMONA *Decca F 11910*	4	13
13 Aug 64 ●	I WOULDN'T TRADE YOU FOR THE WORLD *Decca F 11949*	4	16
3 Dec 64 ●	NO ARMS CAN EVER HOLD YOU *Decca F 12034*	7	12
1 Apr 65	TRUE LOVE FOR EVER MORE *Decca F 12108*	34	6
20 May 65 ●	MARIE *Decca F 12156*	9	12
28 Oct 65	IN THE CHAPEL IN THE MOONLIGHT *Decca F 12256*	27	10
6 Jan 66	HELLO DOLLY *Decca F 12309*	38	4
17 Mar 66 ●	THE SOUND OF SILENCE *Decca F 12351*	3	13
7 Jul 66	CAN I TRUST YOU *Decca F 12417*	26	7
1 Dec 66	WALK WITH FAITH IN YOUR HEART *Decca F 22523*	22	9
6 Apr 67	OH HOW I MISS YOU *Decca F 22592*	30	8
5 Jul 67	MARTA *Decca F 22634*	20	9

Randy BACHMAN – *See BUS STOP*

BACHMAN-TURNER OVERDRIVE ✈

Canada, male vocal/instrumental group   **18 wks**

| 16 Nov 74 ● | YOU AIN'T SEEN NOTHING YET *Mercury 6167 025* ▲ | 2 | 12 |
| 1 Feb 75 | ROLL ON DOWN THE HIGHWAY *Mercury 6167 071* | 22 | 6 |

BACK TO THE PLANET

UK, male/female vocal/instrumental group   **2 wks**

| 10 Apr 93 | TEENAGE TURTLES *Parallel LLLCD 3* | 52 | 1 |
| 4 Sep 93 | DAYDREAM *Parallel LLLCD 8* | 52 | 1 |

BACKBEAT BAND *US, male vocal/instrumental group*   **5 wks**

26 Mar 94	MONEY *Virgin VSCDX 1489*	48	3
23 Apr 94	MONEY (re-entry) *Virgin VSCDX 1489*	73	1
14 May 94	PLEASE MR. POSTMAN *Virgin VSCDX 1502*	69	1

BACKBEAT DISCIPLES – *See Arthur BAKER*

BACKROOM BOYS – *See Frank IFIELD*

BACKSTREET BOYS ☺ *US, male vocal group*   **85 wks**

28 Oct 95	WE'VE GOT IT GOIN' ON *Jive JIVECD 386*	54	1
16 Dec 95	I'LL NEVER BREAK YOUR HEART *Jive JIVECD 389*	42	3
1 Jun 96	GET DOWN (YOU'RE THE ONE FOR ME) *Jive JIVECD 394*	14	8
24 Aug 96 ●	WE'VE GOT IT GOIN' ON (re-issue) *Jive JIVECD 400*	3	7
16 Nov 96 ●	I'LL NEVER BREAK YOUR HEART (re-issue) *Jive JIVECD 406*	8	8
18 Jan 97 ●	QUIT PLAYING GAMES (WITH MY HEART) *Jive JIVECD 409*	2	10
29 Mar 97 ●	ANYWHERE FOR YOU *Jive JIVECD 416*	4	6
2 Aug 97 ●	EVERYBODY (BACKSTREET'S BACK) *Jive JIVECD 426*	3	11
11 Oct 97 ●	AS LONG AS YOU LOVE ME *Jive JIVECD 434*	3	19
14 Feb 98 ●	ALL I HAVE TO GIVE *Jive JIVECD 445*	2	12

BAD ANGEL – *See BOOTH and the BAD ANGEL*

BAD BOYS INC. ☺ *UK, male vocal group*   **31 wks**

14 Aug 93	DON'T TALK ABOUT LOVE *A & M 5803412*	19	5
2 Oct 93	WHENEVER YOU NEED SOMEONE *A & M 5804032*	26	3
11 Dec 93	WALKING ON AIR *A & M 5804692*	24	6
21 May 94 ●	MORE TO THIS WORLD *A & M 5806072*	8	7
23 Jul 94	TAKE ME AWAY (I'LL FOLLOW YOU) *A & M 5806912*	15	5
17 Sep 94	LOVE HERE I COME *A & M 5807752*	26	4

BAD COMPANY ✈ *UK, male vocal/instrumental group*   **23 wks**

1 Jun 74	CAN'T GET ENOUGH *Island WIP 6191*	15	8
22 Mar 75	GOOD LOVIN' GONE BAD *Island WIP 6223*	31	6
30 Aug 75	FEEL LIKE MAKIN' LOVE *Island WIP 6242*	20	9

BAD ENGLISH *UK/US, male vocal/instrumental group*   **3 wks**

| 25 Nov 89 | WHEN I SEE YOU SMILE *Epic 655347 1* ▲ | 61 | 3 |

BAD MANNERS ☺ ✈ *Good-time ska band fronted by shaven-headed Buster Bloodvessel (b. Douglas Trendle, 6 September, 1958, London). Spent more weeks on UK chart in 1980 (45) than anyone bar Madness. Even after the hits, they remained a popular live attraction*   **111 wks**

| 1 Mar 80 | NE-NE NA-NA NA-NA NU-NU *Magnet MAG 164* | 28 | 14 |

UK No 1 ★   UK Top 10 ●   UK million seller ◆   UK entry at No 1 ■   US No 1 ▲

14 Jun 80		LIP UP FATTY *Magnet MAG 175*	15	14
27 Sep 80	●	SPECIAL BREW *Magnet MAG 180*	3	13
6 Dec 80		LORRAINE *Magnet MAG 181*	21	12
28 Mar 81		JUST A FEELING *Magnet MAG 187*	13	9
27 Jun 81	●	CAN CAN *Magnet MAG 190*	3	13
26 Sep 81	●	WALKING IN THE SUNSHINE *Magnet MAG 197*	10	9
21 Nov 81		BUONA SERA *Magnet MAG 211*	34	9
1 May 82		GOT NO BRAINS *Magnet MAG 216*	44	5
31 Jul 82	●	MY GIRL LOLLIPOP (MY BOY LOLLIPOP) *Magnet MAG 232*	9	7
30 Oct 82		SAMSON AND DELILAH *Magnet MAG 236*	58	3
14 May 83		THAT'LL DO NICELY *Magnet MAG 243*	49	3

BAD NEWS UK, male vocal group — 5 wks

12 Sep 87		BOHEMIAN RHAPSODY *EMI EM 24*	44	5

BAD RELIGION US, male vocal/instrumental group — 2 wks

11 Feb 95		21ST CENTURY (DIGITAL BOY) *Columbia 6611435*	41	2

BAD SEEDS – See Nick CAVE and the BAD SEEDS

BAD YARD CLUB – See David MORALES

Wally BADAROU France, male instrumentalist – keyboards — 6 wks

19 Oct 85		CHIEF INSPECTOR *Fourth & Broadway BRW 37*	46	6

BADDIEL – See LIGHTNING SEEDS

BADDIEL and SKINNER – See LIGHTNING SEEDS

BADFINGER ◑ UK, male vocal/instrumental group — 34 wks

10 Jan 70	●	COME AND GET IT *Apple 20*	4	11
9 Jan 71	●	NO MATTER WHAT *Apple 31*	5	12
29 Jan 72	●	DAY AFTER DAY *Apple 40*	10	11

See also VARIOUS ARTISTS (EPs & LPs) – The Apple (EP)

BADMAN UK, male producer – Julian Brettle — 3 wks

2 Feb 91		MAGIC STYLE *Citybeat CBE 759*	61	3

Erykah BADU ✎ US, female vocalist — 11 wks

19 Apr 97		ON & ON *Universal UND 561117*	12	4
14 Jun 97		NEXT LIFETIME *Universal UND 56132*	30	3
29 Nov 97		APPLE TREE *Universal UND 56150*	47	1
11 Jul 98		ONE *Elektra E 3833CD1* [1]	23	3

[1] Busta Rhymes featuring Erykah Badu

Joan BAEZ ♂ US, female vocalist — 47 wks

6 May 65		WE SHALL OVERCOME *Fontana TF 564*	26	10
8 Jul 65	●	THERE BUT FOR FORTUNE *Fontana TF 587*	8	12
2 Sep 65		IT'S ALL OVER NOW BABY BLUE *Fontana TF 604*	22	8
23 Dec 65		FAREWELL ANGELINA *Fontana TF 639*	35	3
20 Jan 66		FAREWELL ANGELINA (re-entry) *Fontana TF 639*	49	1
28 Jul 66		PACK UP YOUR SORROWS *Fontana TF 727*	50	1
9 Oct 71	●	THE NIGHT THEY DROVE OLD DIXIE DOWN *Vanguard VS 35138*	6	12

Carol BAILEY UK, female vocalist — 2 wks

25 Feb 95		FEEL IT *Multiply CDMULTY 3*	41	2

Philip BAILEY ◑ ✎ US, male vocalist — 20 wks

9 Mar 85	★	EASY LOVER *CBS A 4915* [1]	1	12
18 May 85		WALKING ON THE CHINESE WALL *CBS A 6202*	34	8

[1] Philip Bailey (duet with Phil Collins)

Merril BAINBRIDGE Australia, female vocalist — 1 wk

7 Dec 96		MOUTH *Gotham 74321431012*	51	1

Adrian BAKER ◑ UK, male vocalist — 8 wks

19 Jul 75	●	SHERRY *Magnet MAG 34*	10	8

See also GIDEA PARK

Anita BAKER ✎ US, female vocalist — 22 wks

15 Nov 86		SWEET LOVE *Elektra EKR 44*	13	10
31 Jan 87		CAUGHT UP IN THE RAPTURE *Elektra EKR 49*	51	5
8 Oct 88		GIVING YOU THE BEST THAT I GOT *Elektra EKR 79*	55	3
30 Jun 90		TALK TO ME *Elektra EKR 111*	68	2
17 Sep 94		BODY & SOUL *Elektra EKR 190CD*	48	2

Arthur BAKER US, male producer/multi-instrumentalist — 7 wks

20 May 89		IT'S YOUR TIME *Breakout USA 654* [1]	64	2
21 Oct 89		THE MESSAGE IS LOVE *Breakout USA 668* [2]	38	5

[1] Arthur Baker featuring Shirley Lewis [2] Arthur Baker and the Backbeat Disciples featuring Al Green

See also Wally JUMP Jr and CRIMINAL ELEMENT

Hylda BAKER and Arthur MULLARD
UK, female/male vocal duo — 6 wks

9 Sep 78		YOU'RE THE ONE THAT I WANT *Pye 7N 46121*	22	6

George BAKER SELECTION ◑
Holland, male/female vocal/instrumental group — 10 wks

6 Sep 75	●	PALOMA BLANCA *Warner Bros. K 16541*	10	10

BALAAM AND THE ANGEL UK, male vocal/instrumental group — 2 wks

29 Mar 86		SHE KNOWS *Virgin VS 842*	70	2

Long John BALDRY ◑ UK, male vocalist — 36 wks

8 Nov 67	★	LET THE HEARTACHES BEGIN *Pye 7N 17385*	1	13
28 Aug 68		WHEN THE SUN COMES SHININ' THRU *Pye 7N 17593*	29	7
23 Oct 68		MEXICO *Pye 7N 17563*	15	8
29 Jan 69		IT'S TOO LATE NOW *Pye 7N 17664*	21	8

Edward BALL UK, male vocalist — 2 wks

20 Jul 96		THE MILL HILL SELF HATE CLUB *Creation CRESCD 233*	57	1
22 Feb 97		LOVE IS BLUE *Creation CRESCD 244*	59	1

Kenny BALL and his JAZZMEN ♪ Top UK trad jazz-band leader,
b. 22 May, 1930, Essex. His Dixieland band were at the forefront of the
early 1960s jazz revival. Their biggest hit, 'Midnight in Moscow',
reached runner-up spot on both sides of the Atlantic — 136 wks

23 Feb 61		SAMANTHA *Pye Jazz Today 7NJ 2040*	13	15
11 May 61		I STILL LOVE YOU ALL *Pye Jazz 7NJ 2042*	24	6
31 Aug 61		SOMEDAY (YOU'LL BE SORRY) *Pye Jazz 7NJ 2047*	28	6
9 Nov 61	●	MIDNIGHT IN MOSCOW *Pye Jazz 7NJ 2049*	2	21
15 Feb 62	●	MARCH OF THE SIAMESE CHILDREN *Pye Jazz 7NJ 2051*	4	13
17 May 62	●	THE GREEN LEAVES OF SUMMER *Pye Jazz 7NJ 2054*	7	14
23 Aug 62		SO DO I *Pye Jazz 7NJ 2056*	14	8
18 Oct 62		THE PAY OFF *Pye Jazz 7NJ 2061*	23	6
17 Jan 63	●	SUKIYAKI *Pye Jazz 7NJ 2062*	10	13
25 Apr 63		CASABLANCA *Pye Jazz 7NJ 2064*	21	11
13 Jun 63		RONDO *Pye Jazz 7NJ 2065*	24	8
22 Aug 63		ACAPULCO 1922 *Pye Jazz 7NJ 2067*	27	6
11 Jun 64		HELLO DOLLY *Pye Jazz 7NJ 2071*	30	7
19 Jul 67		WHEN I'M SIXTY FOUR *Pye 7N 17348*	43	3

Michael BALL ℭ UK, male vocalist — 39 wks

28 Jan 89	●	LOVE CHANGES EVERYTHING *Really Useful RUR 3*	2	14
28 Oct 89		THE FIRST MAN YOU REMEMBER *Really Useful RUR 6* [1]	68	2
10 Aug 91		IT'S STILL YOU *Polydor PO 160*	58	2
25 Apr 92		ONE STEP OUT OF TIME *Polydor PO 206*	20	2
12 Dec 92		IF I CAN DREAM (EP) *Polydor PO 248*	51	1
26 Dec 92		IF I CAN DREAM (EP) (re-entry) *Polydor PO 248*	68	1
11 Sep 93		SUNSET BOULEVARD *Polydor PZCD 293*	72	1

30 Jul 94	FROM HERE TO ETERNITY *Columbia 6606905*	36 3
17 Sep 94	THE LOVERS WE WERE *Columbia 6607972*	63 2
9 Dec 95	THE ROSE *Columbia 6614535*	42 4
17 Feb 96	(SOMETHING INSIDE) SO STRONG *Columbia 6629005*	40 2

[1] Michael Ball and Diana Morrison

Tracks on If I Can Dream (EP): If I Can Dream / You Don't Have to Say You Love Me / Always on My Mind / Tell Me There's a Heaven

BALTIMORA ☺ *Ireland, male vocalist* — 12 wks

10 Aug 85 ●	TARZAN BOY *Columbia DB 9102*	3 12

Charli BALTIMORE *US, female rapper* — 4 wks

1 Aug 98	MONEY *Epic 6662272*	12 4

BAM BAM *US, male vocalist/multi-instrumentalist* — 2 wks

19 Mar 88	GIVE IT TO ME *Serious 7OUS 10*	65 2

Afrika BAMBAATAA *US, male vocalist* — 27 wks

28 Aug 82	PLANET ROCK *21 POSP 497* [1]	53 3
10 Mar 84	RENEGADES OF FUNK *Tommy Boy AFR 1* [1]	30 4
1 Sep 84	UNITY (PART 1 – THE THIRD COMING) *Tommy Boy AFR 2* [2]	49 5
27 Feb 88	RECKLESS *EMI EM 41* [3]	17 8
12 Oct 91	JUST GET UP AND DANCE *EMI USA MT 100*	45 3
17 Oct 98	GOT TO GET UP *Multiply CDMULTY 42*	22 4

[1] Afrika Bambaataa and the Soul Sonic Force [2] Afrika Bambaataa and James Brown [3] Afrika Bambaataa and Family featuring UB40

BAMBOO ☺ ☺ *UK, male producer* — 12 wks

17 Jan 98 ●	BAMBOOGIE *VC Recordings VCRD 29*	2 10
4 Jul 98	THE STRUTT *VC Recordings VCRD 35*	36 2

BANANARAMA ☺ *Britain's most charted female group: Sarah Dallin, Keren Woodward, Siobhan Fahey. The London-based trio were also best sellers in the USA, where 'Venus' topped the chart. Fahey, who married Eurythmic Dave Stewart, left in 1988 to form Shakespears Sister* — 202 wks

13 Feb 82 ●	IT AIN'T WHAT YOU DO IT'S THE WAY THAT YOU DO IT *Chrysalis CHS 2570* [1]	4 10
10 Apr 82 ●	REALLY SAYING SOMETHING *Deram NANA 1* [2]	5 10
3 Jul 82 ●	SHY BOY *London NANA 2*	4 11
4 Dec 82	CHEERS THEN *London NANA 3*	45 7
26 Feb 83 ●	NA NA HEY HEY KISS HIM GOODBYE *London NANA 4*	5 10
9 Jul 83 ●	CRUEL SUMMER *London NANA 5*	8 10
3 Mar 84 ●	ROBERT DE NIRO'S WAITING *London NANA 6*	3 11
26 May 84	ROUGH JUSTICE *London NANA 7*	23 7
24 Nov 84	HOTLINE TO HEAVEN *London NANA 8*	58 2
24 Aug 85	DO NOT DISTURB *London NANA 9*	31 6
31 May 86 ●	VENUS *London NANA 10* ▲	8 13
16 Aug 86	MORE THAN PHYSICAL *London NANA 11*	41 5
14 Feb 87	TRICK OF THE NIGHT *London NANA 12*	32 5
11 Jul 87	I HEARD A RUMOUR *London NANA 13*	14 9
10 Oct 87 ●	LOVE IN THE FIRST DEGREE *London NANA 14*	3 12
9 Jan 88	I CAN'T HELP IT *London NANA 15*	20 6
9 Apr 88 ●	I WANT YOU BACK *London NANA 16*	5 10
24 Sep 88	LOVE, TRUTH AND HONESTY *London NANA 17*	23 8
19 Nov 88	NATHAN JONES *London NANA 18*	15 9
25 Feb 89 ●	HELP *London LON 222* [3]	3 9
10 Jun 89	CRUEL SUMMER (re-mix) *London NANA 19*	19 6
28 Jul 90	ONLY YOUR LOVE *London NANA 21*	27 4
5 Jan 91	PREACHER MAN *London NANA 23*	20 6
20 Apr 91	LONG TRAIN RUNNING *London NANA 24*	30 5
29 Aug 92	MOVIN' ON *London NANA 25*	24 5
28 Nov 92	LAST THING ON MY MIND *London NANA 26*	71 2
20 Mar 93	MORE MORE MORE *London NACPD 27*	24 4

[1] Fun Boy Three and Bananarama [2] Bananarama with Fun Boy Three [3] Bananarama/La Na Nee Nee Noo Noo

The listed flip side of 'Love in the First Degree' was 'Mr Sleaze' by Stock Aitken Waterman. Act was a duo for last two hits

BAND ✎ *Canada/US, male vocal/instrumental group* — 18 wks

18 Sep 68	THE WEIGHT *Capitol CL 15559*	21 9
4 Apr 70	RAG MAMA RAG *Capitol CL 15629*	16 9

BAND AID ☺ *International, male/female vocal/instrumental charity assembly* — 26 wks

15 Dec 84 ★	DO THEY KNOW IT'S CHRISTMAS? *Mercury FEED 1* ■	1 13
7 Dec 85 ●	DO THEY KNOW IT'S CHRISTMAS? (re-entry) *Mercury FEED 1*	3 7
23 Dec 89 ★	DO THEY KNOW IT'S CHRISTMAS? *PWL/Polydor FEED 2* [1] ■	1 6

[1] Band Aid II

BAND AKA *US, male vocal/instrumental group* — 12 wks

15 May 82	GRACE *Epic EPC A 2376*	41 5
5 Mar 83	JOY *Epic EPC A 3145*	24 7

BAND OF GOLD *Holland, male/female vocal/instrumental group* — 11 wks

14 Jul 84	LOVE SONGS ARE BACK AGAIN (MEDLEY) *RCA 428*	24 11

BAND OF THIEVES – See Luke GOSS and the BAND OF THIEVES

BANDERAS ☺ *UK, female vocal/instrumental duo* — 16 wks

23 Feb 91	THIS IS YOUR LIFE *London LON 290*	16 10
15 Jun 91	SHE SELLS *London LON 298*	41 6

BANDWAGON – See Johnny JOHNSON and the BANDWAGON

Honey BANE *UK, female vocalist* — 8 wks

24 Jan 81	TURN ME ON TURN ME OFF *Zonophone Z 15*	37 5
18 Apr 81	BABY LOVE *Zonophone Z 19*	58 3

BANG *UK, male vocal duo* — 2 wks

6 May 89	YOU'RE THE ONE *RCA PB 42715*	74 2

BANGLES ☺ *US, female vocal/instrumental group* — 94 wks

15 Feb 86 ●	MANIC MONDAY *CBS A 6796*	2 12
26 Apr 86	IF SHE KNEW WHAT SHE WANTS *CBS A 7062*	31 7
5 Jul 86	GOING DOWN TO LIVERPOOL *CBS A 7255*	56 3
13 Sep 86 ●	WALK LIKE AN EGYPTIAN *CBS 650071 7* ▲	3 19
10 Jan 87	WALKING DOWN YOUR STREET *CBS BANGS 1*	16 6
18 Apr 87	FOLLOWING *CBS BANGS 2*	55 3
6 Feb 88	HAZY SHADE OF WINTER *Def Jam BANGS 3*	11 10
5 Nov 88	IN YOUR ROOM *CBS BANGS 4*	35 6
18 Feb 89 ★	ETERNAL FLAME *CBS BANGS 5* ▲	1 18
10 Jun 89	BE WITH YOU *CBS BANGS 6*	23 8
14 Oct 89	I'LL SET YOU FREE *CBS BANGS 7*	74 1
9 Jun 90	WALK LIKE AN EGYPTIAN (re-issue) *CBS BANGS 8*	73 1

Tony BANKS – See FISH

BANNED *UK, male vocal/instrumental group* — 6 wks

17 Dec 77	LITTLE GIRL *Harvest HAR 5145*	36 6

BANSHEES – See SIOUXSIE and the BANSHEES

Buju BANTON *Jamaica, male vocalist* — 1 wk

7 Aug 93	MAKE MY DAY *Mercury BUJCD 2*	72 1

Pato BANTON ☙ ☺ *UK, male vocalist* — 31 wks

1 Oct 94 ★	BABY COME BACK *Virgin VSCDT 1522*	1 18
8 Apr 95	BUBBLING HOT *Virgin VSCDT 1530* [1]	15 7
20 Jan 96	SPIRITS IN THE MATERIAL WORLD *MCA MCSTD 2113* [2]	36 2
27 Jul 96	GROOVIN' *IRS CDEIRS 195* [3]	14 4

[1] Pato Banton with Ranking Roger [2] Pato Banton with Sting [3] Pato Banton and the Reggae Revolution

The sleeve of 'Baby Come Back' credits Ali and Robin Campbell
See also STING

BAR CODES featuring Alison BROWN
UK, male/female vocal group   **1 wk**

| 17 Dec 94 | SUPERMARKET SWEEP *Blanca Casa BC 101CD* | 72 | 1 |

BAR-KAYS *US, male vocal/instrumental group*   **15 wks**

23 Aug 67	SOUL FINGER *Stax 601 014*	33	7
22 Jan 77	SHAKE YOUR RUMP TO THE FUNK *Mercury 6167 417*	41	4
12 Jan 85	SEXOMATIC *Club JAB 10*	51	4

Chris BARBER'S JAZZ BAND ✍
UK, male jazz band, Chris Barber – trombone   **30 wks**

13 Feb 59 ●	PETITE FLEUR *Pye Nixa NJ 2026*	3	22
31 Jul 59	PETITE FLEUR (re-entry) *Pye Nixa NJ 2026*	22	2
9 Oct 59	LONESOME (SI TU VOIS MA MERE) *Columbia DB 4333* [1]	27	2
4 Jan 62	REVIVAL *Columbia SCD 2166*	50	2
1 Feb 62	REVIVAL (re-entry) *Columbia SCD 2166*	43	2

[1] Chris Barber featuring Monty Sunshine

BARBRA and NEIL – See Barbra STREISAND; Neil DIAMOND

BARCLAY JAMES HARVEST
UK, male vocal/instrumental group   **9 wks**

2 Apr 77	LIVE EP *Polydor 2229 198*	49	1
16 Apr 77	LIVE EP (re-entry) *Polydor 2229 198*	49	1
26 Jan 80	LOVE ON THE LINE *Polydor POSP 97*	63	2
22 Nov 80	LIFE IS FOR LIVING *Polydor POSP 195*	61	3
21 May 83	JUST A DAY AWAY *Polydor POSP 585*	68	2

Tracks on Live EP: Rock'n'Roll Star / Medicine Man (Parts 1 & 2)

BARDO ◎ *UK, male/female vocal duo*   **8 wks**

| 10 Apr 82 ● | ONE STEP FURTHER *Epic EPC A2265* | 2 | 8 |

BAREFOOT MAN *Germany, male vocalist*   **4 wks**

| 5 Dec 98 | BIG PANTY WOMAN *Plaza PZACD 082* | 21† | 4 |

Gary BARLOW ◎ *UK, male vocalist*   **40 wks**

20 Jul 96 ★	FOREVER LOVE *RCA 74321397922* ■	1	16
10 May 97 ★	LOVE WON'T WAIT *RCA 74321470842* ■	1	7
26 Jul 97	SO HELP ME GIRL *RCA 74321501202*	11	7
9 Aug 97	LOVE WON'T WAIT (re-entry) *RCA 74321470842*	67	1
20 Sep 97	SO HELP ME GIRL (re-entry) *RCA 74321501202*	64	4
15 Nov 97 ●	OPEN ROAD *RCA 74321518292*	7	5

Gary BARNACLE – See BIG FUN; SONIA

BARNBRACK *UK, male vocal/instrumental group*   **7 wks**

| 16 Mar 85 | BELFAST *Homespun HS 092* | 45 | 7 |

Jimmy BARNES – See INXS

Richard BARNES *UK, male vocalist*   **10 wks**

23 May 70	TAKE TO THE MOUNTAINS *Philips BF 1840*	35	6
24 Oct 70	GO NORTH *Philips 6006 039*	49	1
7 Nov 70	GO NORTH (re-entry) *Philips 6006 039*	38	3

BARRACUDAS *UK/US, male vocal/instrumental group*   **6 wks**

| 16 Aug 80 | SUMMER FUN *EMI-Wipe Out Z 5* | 37 | 6 |

Wild Willy BARRETT – See John OTWAY and Wild Willy BARRETT

Amanda BARRIE and Johnny BRIGGS
UK, female/male vocal duo   **3 wks**

| 16 Dec 95 | SOMETHING STUPID *EMI Premier CDEMS 411* | 35 | 3 |

The listed flip side of 'Something Stupid' was 'Always Look on the Bright Side of Life' by the Coronation Street Cast

J. J. BARRIE ℭ *Canada, male vocalist*   **11 wks**

| 24 Apr 76 ★ | NO CHARGE *Power Exchange PX 209* | 1 | 11 |

Featured vocalist is Vicki Brown

Ken BARRIE *UK, male vocalist*   **15 wks**

10 Jul 82	POSTMAN PAT *Post Music PP 001*	44	8
25 Dec 82	POSTMAN PAT (re-entry) *Post Music PP 001*	54	3
24 Dec 83	POSTMAN PAT (2nd re-entry) *Post Music PP 001*	59	4

BARRON KNIGHTS ◎ *UK, male vocal/instrumental group*   **94 wks**

9 Jul 64 ●	CALL UP THE GROUPS *Columbia DB 7317*	3	13
22 Oct 64	COME TO THE DANCE *Columbia DB 7375*	42	2
25 Mar 65 ●	POP GO THE WORKERS *Columbia DB 7525*	5	13
16 Dec 65 ●	MERRY GENTLE POPS *Columbia DB 7780*	9	7
1 Dec 66	UNDER NEW MANAGEMENT *Columbia DB 8071*	15	9
23 Oct 68	AN OLYMPIC RECORD *Columbia DB 8485*	35	4
29 Oct 77 ●	LIVE IN TROUBLE *Epic EPC 5752*	7	10
2 Dec 78 ●	A TASTE OF AGGRO *Epic EPC 6829*	3	10
8 Dec 79	FOOD FOR THOUGHT *Epic EPC 8011*	46	6
4 Oct 80	THE SIT SONG *Epic EPC 8994*	44	4
6 Dec 80	NEVER MIND THE PRESENTS *Epic EPC 9070*	17	8
5 Dec 81	BLACKBOARD JUMBLE *CBS A 1795*	52	5
19 Mar 83	BUFFALO BILL'S LAST SCRATCH *Epic EPC A 3208*	49	3

Joe BARRY *US, male vocalist*   **1 wk**

| 24 Aug 61 | I'M A FOOL TO CARE *Mercury AMT 1149* | 49 | 1 |

John BARRY ORCHESTRA ℭ
UK, male instrumental group/orchestra   **78 wks**

10 Mar 60 ●	HIT AND MISS *Columbia DB 4414* [1]	10	12
28 Apr 60	BEAT FOR BEATNIKS *Columbia DB 4446*	40	2
9 Jun 60	HIT AND MISS (re-entry) *Columbia DB 4414* [1]	45	1
14 Jul 60	NEVER LET GO *Columbia DB 4480*	49	1
18 Aug 60	BLUEBERRY HILL *Columbia DB 4480*	34	3
8 Sep 60	WALK DON'T RUN *Columbia DB 4505* [1]	49	1
22 Sep 60	WALK DON'T RUN (re-entry) *Columbia DB 4505* [1]	11	13
8 Dec 60	BLACK STOCKINGS *Columbia DB 4554*	27	9
2 Mar 61	THE MAGNIFICENT SEVEN *Columbia DB 4598* [1]	48	1
16 Mar 61	THE MAGNIFICENT SEVEN (re-entry) *Columbia DB 4598* [1]	45	2
6 Apr 61	THE MAGNIFICENT SEVEN (2nd re-entry) *Columbia DB 4598* [1]	50	1
8 Jun 61	THE MAGNIFICENT SEVEN (3rd re-entry) *Columbia DB 4598* [1]	47	1
26 Apr 62	CUTTY SARK *Columbia DB 4806* [1]	35	2
1 Nov 62	JAMES BOND THEME *Columbia DB 4898*	13	11
21 Nov 63	FROM RUSSIA WITH LOVE *Ember S 181*	44	1
19 Dec 63	FROM RUSSIA WITH LOVE (re-entry) *Ember S 181*	39	2
11 Dec 71	THE PERSUADERS *CBS 7469*	13	15

[1] John Barry Seven

Len BARRY ◎ *US, male vocalist*   **24 wks**

| 4 Nov 65 ● | 1-2-3 *Brunswick 05942* | 3 | 14 |
| 13 Jan 66 ● | LIKE A BABY *Brunswick 05949* | 10 | 10 |

Michael BARRYMORE *UK, male vocalist*   **4 wks**

| 16 Dec 95 | TOO MUCH FOR ONE HEART *EMI CDEM 412* | 25 | 4 |

Lionel BART *UK, male vocalist*   **3 wks**

| 25 Nov 89 | HAPPY ENDINGS (GIVE YOURSELF A PINCH) *EMI EM 121* | 68 | 1 |
| 23 Dec 89 | HAPPY ENDINGS (GIVE YOURSELF A PINCH) (re-entry) *EMI EM 121* | 71 | 2 |

BAS NOIR *US, female vocal duo*   **1 wk**

| 11 Feb 89 | MY LOVE IS MAGIC *10 TEN 257* | 73 | 1 |

Rob BASE and DJ E-Z ROCK ◄ *US, male rap/DJ duo*   **19 wks**

| 16 Apr 88 | IT TAKES TWO *Citybeat CBE 724* | 24 | 6 |

14 Jan 89		GET ON THE DANCE FLOOR *Supreme SUPE 139*	14	7
4 Mar 89		IT TAKES TWO (re-entry) *Citybeat CBE 724*	49	3
22 Apr 89		JOY AND PAIN *Supreme SUPE 143*	47	3

BASEMENT BOYS – See ULTRA NATE

BASEMENT JAXX ☺ *UK, male DJ / producer duo*   **3 wks**

31 May 97		FLY LIFE *Multiply CDMULTY 21*	19	3

BASIA *Poland, female vocalist*   **9 wks**

23 Jan 88		PROMISES *Epic BASH 4*	48	4
28 May 88		TIME AND TIDE *Epic BASH 5*	61	3
14 Jan 95		DRUNK ON LOVE *Epic 6611582*	41	2

Count BASIE – See Frank SINATRA

Toni BASIL ◑ *US, female vocalist*   **16 wks**

6 Feb 82	●	MICKEY *Radialchoice TIC 4* ▲	2	12
1 May 82		NOBODY *Radialchoice TIC 2*	52	4

Alfie BASS – See Michael MEDWIN, Bernard BRESSLAW, Alfie BASS and Leslie FYSON

BASS BOYZ *UK, male producer – James Salmon*   **1 wk**

28 Sep 96		GUNZ AND PIANOZ *Polydor 5753432*	74	1

See also PIANOMAN

BASS BUMPERS

Germany/UK, male/female vocal/instrumental group   **4 wks**

25 Sep 93		RUNNIN' *Vertigo VERCD 78*	68	1
5 Feb 94		THE MUSIC'S GOT ME *Vertigo VERCD 84*	25	3

Fontella BASS ♀ *US, female vocalist*   **15 wks**

2 Dec 65		RESCUE ME *Chess CRS 8023*	11	10
20 Jan 66		RECOVERY *Chess CRS 8027*	32	5

BASS-O-MATIC ☺ *UK, male multi-instrumentalist*   **19 wks**

12 May 90		IN THE REALM OF THE SENSES *Virgin VS 1265*	66	3
1 Sep 90	●	FASCINATING RHYTHM *Virgin VS 1274*	9	11
22 Dec 90		EASE ON BY *Virgin VS 1295*	61	4
3 Aug 91		FUNKY LOVE VIBRATIONS *Virgin VS 1355*	71	1

Shirley BASSEY ℂ *Internationally acclaimed vocalist and cabaret entertainer, b. 8 January, 1937, Cardiff, Wales. With 30 hit singles (spanning a record 40-year period) and 33 hit albums, she is Britain's most successful female chart artist*   **323 wks**

15 Feb 57	●	BANANA BOAT SONG *Philips PB 668*	8	10
23 Aug 57		FIRE DOWN BELOW *Philips PB 723*	30	1
6 Sep 57		YOU YOU ROMEO *Philips PB 723*	29	2
19 Dec 58		AS I LOVE YOU *Philips PB 845*	27	2
26 Dec 58	●	KISS ME HONEY HONEY KISS ME *Philips PB 860*	3	17
9 Jan 59	★	AS I LOVE YOU (re-entry) *Philips PB 845*	1	17
31 Mar 60		WITH THESE HANDS *Columbia DB 4421*	38	2
21 Apr 60		WITH THESE HANDS (re-entry) *Columbia DB 4421*	31	2
12 May 60		WITH THESE HANDS (2nd re-entry) *Columbia DB 4421*	41	2
4 Aug 60	●	AS LONG AS HE NEEDS ME *Columbia DB 4490*	2	30
11 May 61	●	YOU'LL NEVER KNOW *Columbia DB 4643*	6	17
27 Jul 61	★	REACH FOR THE STARS / CLIMB EV'RY MOUNTAIN *Columbia DB 4685*	1	16
23 Nov 61	●	I'LL GET BY *Columbia DB 4737*	10	8
23 Nov 61		REACH FOR THE STARS / CLIMB EV'RY MOUNTAIN (re-entry) *Columbia DB 4685*	40	2
15 Feb 62		TONIGHT *Columbia DB 4777*	21	8
26 Apr 62		AVE MARIA *Columbia DB 4816*	31	4
31 May 62		FAR AWAY *Columbia DB 4836*	24	13
30 Aug 62	●	WHAT NOW MY LOVE *Columbia DB 4882*	5	17
28 Feb 63		WHAT KIND OF FOOL AM I? *Columbia DB 4974*	47	2
26 Sep 63	●	I (WHO HAVE NOTHING) *Columbia DB 7113*	6	20
23 Jan 64		MY SPECIAL DREAM *Columbia DB 7185*	32	7
9 Apr 64		GONE *Columbia DB 7248*	36	5

15 Oct 64		GOLDFINGER *Columbia DB 7360*	21	9
20 May 65		NO REGRETS *Columbia DB 7535*	39	4
11 Oct 67		BIG SPENDER *United Artists UP 1192*	21	15
20 Jun 70	●	SOMETHING *United Artists UP 35125*	4	21
2 Jan 71		THE FOOL ON THE HILL *United Artists UP 35156*	48	1
23 Jan 71		SOMETHING (re-entry) *United Artists UP 35125*	50	1
27 Mar 71		(WHERE DO I BEGIN) LOVE STORY *United Artists UP 35194*	34	9
7 Aug 71		FOR ALL WE KNOW *United Artists UP 35267*	46	1
21 Aug 71	●	FOR ALL WE KNOW (re-entry) *United Artists UP 35267*	6	23
15 Jan 72		DIAMONDS ARE FOREVER *United Artists UP 35293*	38	6
3 Mar 73	●	NEVER NEVER NEVER *United Artists UP 35490*	8	18
14 Jul 73		NEVER NEVER NEVER (re-entry) *United Artists UP 35490*	48	1
22 Aug 87		THE RHYTHM DIVINE *Mercury MER 253* [1]	54	2
16 Nov 96		'DISCO' LA PASSIONE *East West EW 072CD* [2]	41	1
20 Dec 97		HISTORY REPEATING *Wall of Sound WALLD 036* [3]	19	7

[1] Yello featuring Shirley Bassey [2] Chris Rea and Shirley Bassey [3] Propellerheads featuring Miss Shirley Bassey

BASSHEADS ☺ *UK, male/female vocal/instrumental group*   **19 wks**

16 Nov 91	●	IS THERE ANYBODY OUT THERE *Deconstruction R 6303*	5	8
30 May 92		BACK TO THE OLD SCHOOL *Deconstruction R 6310*	12	4
28 Nov 92		WHO CAN MAKE ME FEEL GOOD *Deconstruction R 6326*	38	2
28 Aug 93		START A BRAND NEW LIFE (SAVE ME) *Deconstruction CDR 6353*	49	2
15 Jul 95		IS THERE ANYBODY OUT THERE (re-mix) *Deconstruction 74321293882*	24	3

BATES *Germany, male vocal/instrumental group*   **1 wk**

3 Feb 96		BILLIE JEAN *Virgin International DINSD 151*	67	1

Mike BATT with the NEW EDITION ◑
UK, male vocalist with male/female vocal group   **8 wks**

16 Aug 75	●	SUMMERTIME CITY *Epic EPC 3460*	4	8

BAUHAUS ☹ ✐ *UK, male vocal/instrumental group*   **35 wks**

18 Apr 81		KICK IN THE EYE *Beggars Banquet BEG 54*	59	3
4 Jul 81		THE PASSIONS OF LOVERS *Beggars Banquet BEG 59*	56	2
6 Mar 82		KICK IN THE EYE (EP) *Beggars Banquet BEG 74*	45	4
19 Jun 82		SPIRIT *Beggars Banquet BEG 79*	42	5
9 Oct 82		ZIGGY STARDUST *Beggars Banquet BEG 83*	15	7
22 Jan 83		LAGARTIJA NICK *Beggars Banquet BEG 88*	44	4
9 Apr 83		SHE'S IN PARTIES *Beggars Banquet BEG 91*	26	6
29 Oct 83		THE SINGLES 1981-83 *Beggars Banquet BEG 100E*	52	4

Tracks on Kick in the Eye (EP): Kick in the Eye (Searching for Satori) / Harry / Earwax

Les BAXTER ℂ *US, orchestra and chorus*   **9 wks**

13 May 55	●	UNCHAINED MELODY *Capitol CL 14257*	10	9

BAY CITY ROLLERS ◐ *Tartan teen sensations from Edinburgh: Leslie McKeown (v), Eric Faulkner (g), Stuart Wood (g), Alan Longmuir (b), Derek Longmuir (d). They were the first of many acts heralded as 'Biggest Group Since The Beatles' and one of the top teeny-bop groups of the 1970s*   **116 wks**

18 Sep 71	●	KEEP ON DANCING *Bell 1164*	9	13
9 Feb 74	●	REMEMBER (SHA-LA-LA) *Bell 1338*	6	12
27 Apr 74	●	SHANG-A-LANG *Bell 1355*	2	10
27 Jul 74	●	SUMMERLOVE SENSATION *Bell 1369*	3	10
12 Oct 74	●	ALL OF ME LOVES ALL OF YOU *Bell 1382*	4	10
8 Mar 75	★	BYE BYE BABY *Bell 1409*	1	16
12 Jul 75	★	GIVE A LITTLE LOVE *Bell 1425*	1	9
22 Nov 75	●	MONEY HONEY *Bell 1461*	3	9
10 Apr 76	●	LOVE ME LIKE I LOVE YOU *Bell 1477*	4	9
11 Sep 76	●	I ONLY WANNA BE WITH YOU *Bell 1493*	4	9
7 May 77		IT'S A GAME *Arista 108*	16	6
30 Jul 77		YOU MADE ME BELIEVE IN MAGIC *Arista 127*	34	3

DUKE BAYSEE *UK, male vocalist*   **6 wks**

3 Sep 94		SUGAR SUGAR *Bell 74321228702*	30	4
21 Jan 95		DO YOU LOVE ME *Double Dekker CDDEK 1*	46	2

UK No 1 ★   UK Top 10 ●   UK million seller ◆   UK entry at No 1 ■   US No 1 ▲

B B and Q BAND *US, male vocal/instrumental group*   **15 wks**

18 Jul 81	**ON THE BEAT** *Capitol CL 202*	.41	5
6 Jul 85	**GENIE** *Cooltempo COOL 110* [1]	.40	4
20 Sep 86	**(I'M A) DREAMER** *Cooltempo COOL 132*	.35	5
17 Oct 87	**RICOCHET** *Cooltempo COOL 154*	.71	1

[1] Brooklyn Bronx and Queens

BBC CONCERT ORCHESTRA, BBC SYMPHONY CHORUS
cond. Stephen JACKSON *UK, orchestra, chorus and conductor*   **3 wks**

22 Jun 96	**ODE TO JOY (FROM BEETHOVEN'S SYMPHONY NO. 9)** *Virgin VSCDT 1591*	.36	3

BBE ☺ *France/Italy, male instrumental group*   **20 wks**

28 Sep 96	**SEVEN DAYS AND ONE WEEK** *Positiva CDTIV 67*	.3	9
29 Mar 97 ●	**FLASH** *Positiva CDTIV 73*	.5	5
14 Feb 98	**DESIRE** *Positiva CDTIV 87*	.19	3
30 May 98	**DEEPER LOVE (SYMPHONIC PARADISE)** *Positiva CDTIV 93*	.19	3

BBG *UK, male vocal/instrumental group*   **10 wks**

28 Apr 90	**SNAPPINESS** *Urban URB 54* [1]	.28	5
11 Aug 90	**SOME KIND OF HEAVEN** *Urban URB 59*	.65	2
23 Mar 96	**LET THE MUSIC PLAY** *MCA MCSTD 40029* [2]	.46	1
18 May 96	**SNAPPINESS (re-mix)** *Hi-Life 5762972*	.50	1
5 Jul 97	**JUST BE TONIGHT** *Hi-Life 5738972* [2]	.45	1

[1] BBG featuring Dina Taylor   [2] BBG featuring Erin

BBM *UK, male vocal/instrumental group*   **2 wks**

6 Aug 94	**WHERE IN THE WORLD** *Virgin VSCD 1495*	.57	2

BC-52s – *See B-52s*

BE BOP DELUXE *UK, male vocal/instrumental group*   **13 wks**

21 Feb 76	**SHIPS IN THE NIGHT** *Harvest HAR 5104*	.23	8
13 Nov 76	**HOT VALVES EP** *Harvest HAR 5117*	.36	5

Tracks on Hot Valves EP: *Maid in Heaven / Blazing Apostles / Jet Silver and the Dolls of Venus / Bring Back the Spark*

BEACH BOYS ☺ *Arguably the most successful and consistently popular US group of the rock era: Brian Wilson (b/k/v), Mike Love (v), Carl Wilson (g/v) (d. 1998), Al Jardine (g/v), Dennis Wilson (d/v) (d. 1983). This influential California-based family band has a legendary vocal sound*   **281 wks**

1 Aug 63	**SURFIN' USA** *Capitol CL 15305*	.34	7
9 Jul 64 ●	**I GET AROUND** *Capitol CL 15350* ▲	.7	13
29 Oct 64	**WHEN I GROW UP (TO BE A MAN)** *Capitol CL 15361*	.44	2
19 Nov 64	**WHEN I GROW UP (TO BE A MAN) (re-entry)** *Capitol CL 15361*	27	5
21 Jan 65	**DANCE DANCE DANCE** *Capitol CL 15370*	.24	6
3 Jun 65	**HELP ME RHONDA** *Capitol CL 15392* ▲	.27	10
2 Sep 65	**CALIFORNIA GIRLS** *Capitol CL 15409*	.26	8
17 Feb 66 ●	**BARBARA ANN** *Capitol CL 15432*	.3	10
21 Apr 66 ●	**SLOOP JOHN B** *Capitol CL 15441*	.2	15
28 Jul 66 ●	**GOD ONLY KNOWS** *Capitol CL 15459*	.2	14
3 Nov 66 ★	**GOOD VIBRATIONS** *Capitol CL 15475* ▲	.1	13
4 May 67 ●	**THEN I KISSED HER** *Capitol CL 15502*	.4	11
23 Aug 67 ●	**HEROES AND VILLAINS** *Capitol CL 15510*	.8	9
22 Nov 67	**WILD HONEY** *Capitol CL 15521*	.29	6
17 Jan 68	**DARLIN'** *Capitol CL 15527*	.11	14
8 May 68	**FRIENDS** *Capitol CL 15545*	.25	7
24 Jul 68 ★	**DO IT AGAIN** *Capitol CL 15554*	.1	14
25 Dec 68	**BLUEBIRDS OVER THE MOUNTAIN** *Capitol CL 15572*	.33	5
26 Feb 69 ●	**I CAN HEAR MUSIC** *Capitol CL 15584*	.10	13
11 Jun 69 ●	**BREAK AWAY** *Capitol CL 15598*	.6	11
16 May 70 ●	**COTTONFIELDS** *Capitol CL 15640*	.5	17
3 Mar 73	**CALIFORNIA SAGA – CALIFORNIA** *Reprise K 14232*	.37	7
3 Jul 76	**GOOD VIBRATIONS (re-issue)** *Capitol CL 15875*	.18	7
10 Jul 76	**ROCK AND ROLL MUSIC** *Reprise K 14440*	.36	4
31 Mar 79	**HERE COMES THE NIGHT** *Caribou CRB 7204*	.37	8
16 Jun 79 ●	**LADY LYNDA** *Caribou CRB 7427*	.6	11
29 Sep 79	**SUMAHAMA** *Caribou CRB 7846*	.45	4
29 Aug 81	**BEACH BOYS MEDLEY** *Capitol CL 213*	.47	4
22 Aug 87 ●	**WIPEOUT** *Urban URB 5* [1]	.2	12
19 Nov 88	**KOKOMO** *Elektra EKR 85* ▲	.25	9
2 Jun 90	**WOULDN'T IT BE NICE** *Capitol CL 579*	.58	1
29 Jun 91	**DO IT AGAIN (re-issue)** *Capitol EMCT 1*	.61	2
2 Mar 96	**FUN FUN FUN** *PolyGram TV 5762972* [2]	.24	4

[1] Fat Boys and the Beach Boys   [2] Status Quo with the Beach Boys

Walter BEASLEY *US, male vocalist*   **3 wks**

23 Jan 88	**I'M SO HAPPY** *Urban URB 14*	.70	3

BEASTIE BOYS 🔄 *US, male rap group*   **51 wks**

28 Feb 87	**(YOU GOTTA) FIGHT FOR YOUR RIGHT (TO PARTY)** *Def Jam 650418 7*	.11	11
30 May 87	**NO SLEEP TILL BROOKLYN** *Def Jam BEAST 1*	.14	7
18 Jul 87	**SHE'S ON IT** *Def Jam BEAST 2*	.10	8
3 Oct 87	**GIRLS/SHE'S CRAFTY** *Def Jam BEAST 3*	.34	4
11 Apr 92	**PASS THE MIC** *Capitol 12CL 653*	.47	2
4 Jul 92	**FROZEN METAL HEAD (EP)** *Capitol 12CL 665*	.55	1
9 Jul 94	**GET IT TOGETHER/SABOTAGE** *Capitol CDCL 716* ...	.19	4
26 Nov 94	**SURE SHOT** *Capitol CDCLS 726*	.27	3
4 Jul 98 ●	**INTERGALACTIC** *Grand CDCL 803*	.5	7
7 Nov 98	**BODY MOVIN'** *Grand Royal CDCLS 809*	.15	4

Tracks on Frozen Metal Head (EP): *Jimmy James / Jimmy James (Original) / Drinkin' Wine / The Blue Nun*

BEAT 🌐 ☂ *UK, male vocal/instrumental group*   **92 wks**

8 Dec 79 ●	**TEARS OF A CLOWN/RANKING FULL STOP** *2 Tone CHSTT 6*	.6	11
23 Feb 80 ●	**HANDS OFF – SHE'S MINE** *Go Feet FEET 1*	.9	9
3 May 80 ●	**MIRROR IN THE BATHROOM** *Go Feet FEET 2*	.4	9
16 Aug 80	**BEST FRIEND/STAND DOWN MARGARET (DUB)** *Go Feet FEET 3*	.22	9
13 Dec 80 ●	**TOO NICE TO TALK TO** *Go Feet FEET 4*	.7	11
18 Apr 81	**DROWNING/ALL OUT TO GET YOU** *Go Feet FEET 6*	.22	8
20 Jun 81	**DOORS OF YOUR HEART** *Go Feet FEET 9*	.33	6
5 Dec 81	**HIT IT** *Go Feet FEET 11*	.70	1
17 Apr 82	**SAVE IT FOR LATER** *Go Feet FEET 333*	.47	4
18 Sep 82	**JEANETTE** *Go Feet FEET 15*	.45	3
4 Dec 82	**I CONFESS** *Go Feet FEET 16*	.54	3
30 Apr 83 ●	**CAN'T GET USED TO LOSING YOU** *Go Feet FEET 17*	.3	11
2 Jul 83	**ACKEE 1-2-3** *Go Feet FEET 18*	.54	4
27 Jan 96	**MIRROR IN THE BATHROOM (re-mix)** *Go Feet 74321232062*	.44	2

See also VARIOUS ARTISTS (EPs & LPs) – The Two Tone EP

BEAT SYSTEM *UK, male vocal/instrumental group*   **3 wks**

3 Mar 90	**WALK ON THE WILD SIDE** *Fourth & Broadway BRW 163*	.63	2
18 Sep 93	**TO A BRIGHTER DAY (O' HAPPY DAY)** *ffrr FCD 217*	.70	1

BEATLES ☺ ✒ *World's most successful group: John Lennon (v/g) (d. 1980), Paul McCartney (v/g), George Harrison (g), Richard 'Ringo Starr' Starkey (d). The Liverpool legends who changed the face of music hold countless records, including most No 1 singles and albums in the UK and the USA, and have sold an estimated one billion records*   **456 wks**

11 Oct 62	**LOVE ME DO** *Parlophone R 4949* ▲	.17	18
17 Jan 63 ●	**PLEASE PLEASE ME** *Parlophone R 4983*	.2	18
18 Apr 63 ★	**FROM ME TO YOU** *Parlophone R 5015*	.1	21
6 Jun 63	**MY BONNIE** *Polydor NH 66833* [1]	.48	1
29 Aug 63 ★	**SHE LOVES YOU** *Parlophone R 5055* ◆ ▲	.1	31
5 Dec 63 ★	**I WANT TO HOLD YOUR HAND** *Parlophone R 5084*	.1	21
26 Mar 64 ★	**CAN'T BUY ME LOVE** *Parlophone R 5114*	.1	14
9 Apr 64	**SHE LOVES YOU (re-entry)** *Parlophone R 5055*	.42	2
14 May 64	**I WANT TO HOLD YOUR HAND (re-entry)** *Parlophone R 5084* ◆ ▲	.48	1
11 Jun 64	**AIN'T SHE SWEET** *Polydor 52 317*	.29	6
9 Jul 64	**CAN'T BUY ME LOVE (re-entry)** *Parlophone R 5114* ◆ ▲	.47	1
16 Jul 64 ★	**A HARD DAY'S NIGHT** *Parlophone R 5160* ▲	.1	13
3 Dec 64 ★	**I FEEL FINE** *Parlophone R 5200* ◆ ▲	.1	13
15 Apr 65 ★	**TICKET TO RIDE** *Parlophone R 5265* ▲	.1	12
29 Jul 65 ★	**HELP!** *Parlophone R 5305* ▲	.1	14

9 Dec 65	★ DAY TRIPPER/WE CAN WORK IT OUT *Parlophone R 5389* ◆ ▲ ..1	12
16 Jun 66	★ PAPERBACK WRITER *Parlophone R 5452* ▲ 1	11
11 Aug 66	★ YELLOW SUBMARINE/ELEANOR RIGBY *Parlophone R 5493* 1	13
23 Feb 67	● PENNY LANE/STRAWBERRY FIELDS FOREVER	
	Parlophone R 5570 2	11
12 Jul 67	★ ALL YOU NEED IS LOVE *Parlophone R 5620* ▲ 1	13
29 Nov 67	★ HELLO GOODBYE *Parlophone R 5655* ▲ 1	12
13 Dec 67	● MAGICAL MYSTERY TOUR (DOUBLE EP)	
	Parlophone SMMT/MMT 1 2	12
20 Mar 68	★ LADY MADONNA *Parlophone R 5675* 1	8
4 Sep 68	★ HEY JUDE *Apple R 5722* ▲ 1	16
23 Apr 69	★ GET BACK *Apple R 5777* [2] ■ ▲ 1	17
4 Jun 69	★ BALLAD OF JOHN AND YOKO *Apple R 5786* 1	14
8 Nov 69	● SOMETHING/COME TOGETHER *Apple R 5814* ▲ 4	12
14 Mar 70	● LET IT BE *Apple R 5833* ▲ 2	9
24 Oct 70	LET IT BE (re-entry) *Apple R 5833* 43	1
13 Mar 76	● YESTERDAY *Apple R 6013* ▲ 8	7
27 Mar 76	HEY JUDE (re-entry) *Apple R 5722* 12	7
27 Mar 76	PAPERBACK WRITER (re-entry) *Parlophone R 5452* 23	5
3 Apr 76	GET BACK (re-entry) *Apple R 5777* [2] 28	5
3 Apr 76	STRAWBERRY FIELDS FOREVER (re-entry)	
	Parlophone R 5570 32	3
10 Apr 76	HELP! (re-entry) *Parlophone R 5305* 37	3
10 Jul 76	BACK IN THE U.S.S.R. *Parlophone R 6016* 19	6
7 Oct 78	SGT. PEPPER'S LONELY HEARTS CLUB BAND – WITH	
	A LITTLE HELP FROM MY FRIENDS *Parlophone R 6022* ..63	3
5 Jun 82	● BEATLES MOVIE MEDLEY *Parlophone R 6055* 10	9
16 Oct 82	● LOVE ME DO (re-entry) *Parlophone R 4949* 4	7
22 Jan 83	PLEASE PLEASE ME (re-entry) *Parlophone R 4983* 29	4
23 Apr 83	FROM ME TO YOU (re-entry) *Parlophone R 5015* 40	4
3 Sep 83	SHE LOVES YOU (2nd re-entry) *Parlophone R 5055* 45	3
26 Nov 83	I WANT TO HOLD YOUR HAND (2nd re-entry)	
	Parlophone R 5084 62	2
31 Mar 84	CAN'T BUY ME LOVE (2nd re-entry) *Parlophone R 5114* ...53	2
21 Jul 84	A HARD DAY'S NIGHT (re-entry) *Parlophone R 5160* 52	2
8 Dec 84	I FEEL FINE (re-entry) *Parlophone R 5200* 65	1
20 Apr 85	TICKET TO RIDE (re-entry) *Parlophone R 5265* 70	2
30 Aug 86	ELEANOR RIGBY/YELLOW SUBMARINE (re-entry)	
	Parlophone R 5493 63	1
28 Feb 87	PENNY LANE/STRAWBERRY FIELDS FOREVER (2nd re-entry)	
	Parlophone R 5570 65	1
18 Jul 87	ALL YOU NEED IS LOVE (re-entry) *Parlophone R 5620* 47	3
5 Dec 87	HELLO GOODBYE (re-entry) *Parlophone R 5655* 63	1
26 Mar 88	LADY MADONNA (re-entry) *Parlophone R 5675* 67	1
10 Sep 88	HEY JUDE (2nd re-entry) *Apple 5722* 52	2
22 Apr 89	GET BACK (2nd re-entry *Apple R 5777* [2] 74	1
17 Oct 92	LOVE ME DO (2nd re-entry) *Parlophone R 4949* 53	1
1 Apr 95	● BABY IT'S YOU *Apple CDR 6406* 7	6
8 Jul 95	BABY IT'S YOU (re-entry) *Apple CDR 6406* 71	1
16 Dec 95	● FREE AS A BIRD *Apple CDR 6422* 2	8
16 Mar 96	● REAL LOVE *Apple CDR 6425* 4	7

[1] Tony Sheridan and the Beatles [2] Beatles with Billy Preston

Tracks on Magical Mystery Tour (EP): Magical Mystery Tour/Your Mother Should Know/I Am the Walrus/Fool on the Hill/Flying/Blue Jay Way

BEATMASTERS ☺ *UK, male/female instrumental group*　　　47 wks

9 Jan 88	● ROK DA HOUSE *Rhythm King LEFT 11* [1] 5	11
24 Sep 88	BURN IT UP *Rhythm King LEFT 27* [2] 14	10
22 Apr 89	● WHO'S IN THE HOUSE *Rhythm King LEFT 31* [3] 8	9
12 Aug 89	● HEY DJ – I CAN'T DANCE (TO THAT MUSIC YOU'RE PLAYING)/	
	SKA TRAIN *Rhythm King LEFT 34* [4] 7	11
2 Dec 89	WARM LOVE *Rhythm King LEFT 37* [5] 51	2
21 Sep 91	BOULEVARD OF BROKEN DREAMS *Rhythm King 6573617* 62	1
16 May 92	DUNNO WHAT IT IS (ABOUT YOU) *Rhythm King 6580017* [6] ..43	3

[1] Beatmasters featuring the Cookie Crew [2] Beatmasters with PP Arnold
[3] Beatmasters featuring Merlin [4] Beatmasters featuring Betty Boo
[5] Beatmasters featuring Claudia Fontaine [6] Beatmasters featuring Elaine Vassell

BEATS INTERNATIONAL ☺
UK, male/female vocal/instrumental group　　　30 wks

| 10 Feb 90 | ★ DUB BE GOOD TO ME *Go.Beat GOD 39* [1] ....1 | 13 |

12 May 90	● WON'T TALK ABOUT IT *Go.Beat GOD 43* 9	7
15 Sep 90	BURUNDI BLUES *Go.Beat GOD 45* 51	3
2 Mar 91	ECHO CHAMBER *Go.Beat GOD 51* 60	2
21 Sep 91	THE SUN DOESN'T SHINE *Go.Beat GOD 59* 66	2
23 Nov 91	IN THE GHETTO *Go.Beat GOD 64* 44	3

[1] Beats International featuring Lindy Layton

BEAUTIFUL PEOPLE *UK, male instrumental/sampling group*　　　1 wk

| 28 May 94 | IF 60S WERE 90S *Essential ESSX 2037* ....74 | 1 |

BEAUTIFUL SOUTH ☻

Ex-Housemartins Paul Heaton (v/g) and Dave Hemmingway (v) (from the beautiful north of England) formed this band that featured Briana Corrigan (v) (replaced by Jacqui Abbot in 1994). Heaton and Dave Rotheray (g) write the witty and ironic songs that made them 1990s favourites　　　130 wks

3 Jun 89	● SONG FOR WHOEVER *Go! Discs GOD 32* 2	11
23 Sep 89	● YOU KEEP IT ALL IN *Go! Discs GOD 35* 8	8
2 Dec 89	I'LL SAIL THIS SHIP ALONE *Go! Discs GOD 38* 31	8
6 Oct 90	★ A LITTLE TIME *Go! Discs GOD 47* 1	14
8 Dec 90	MY BOOK *Go! Discs GOD 48* 43	6
16 Mar 91	LET LOVE SPEAK UP ITSELF *Go! Discs GOD 53* 51	2
11 Jan 92	OLD RED EYES IS BACK *Go! Discs GOD 66* 22	6
14 Mar 92	WE ARE EACH OTHER *Go! Discs GOD 71* 30	3
13 Jun 92	BELL BOTTOMED TEAR *Go! Discs GOD 78* 16	5
26 Sep 92	36D *Go! Discs GOD 88* 46	2
12 Mar 94	GOOD AS GOLD *Go! Discs GODCD 110* 23	5
4 Jun 94	EVERYBODY'S TALKIN' *Go! Discs GODCD 113* 12	8
3 Sep 94	PRETTIEST EYES *Go! Discs GODCD 119* 37	3
12 Nov 94	ONE LAST LOVE SONG *Go! Discs GODCD 122* 14	5
18 Nov 95	PRETENDERS TO THE THRONE *Go! Discs GODCD 134* 18	4
12 Oct 96	● ROTTERDAM *Go! Discs GODCD 155* 5	9
14 Dec 96	DON'T MARRY HER *Go! Discs GODCD 158* 8	10
29 Mar 97	BLACKBIRD ON THE WIRE *Go! Discs 5821252* 23	5
5 Jul 97	LIAR'S BAR *Go! Discs 5822492* 43	1
3 Oct 98	● PERFECT 10 *Go! 5664832* ....2†	13
19 Dec 98	DUMB *Go! Discs 5667532* ....16†	2

BEAVIS and BUTT-HEAD – *See CHER*

Gilbert BECAUD Ⓒ *France, male vocalist*　　　12 wks

| 29 Mar 75 | ● A LITTLE LOVE AND UNDERSTANDING *Decca F 13537* ......10 | 12 |

BECK ☺ ✒ *US, male vocalist*　　　22 wks

5 Mar 94	LOSER *Geffen GFSTD 67* 15	6
29 Jun 96	WHERE IT'S AT *Geffen GFSTD 22156* 35	2
16 Nov 96	DEVIL'S HAIRCUT *Geffen GFSTD 22183* 22	2
8 Mar 97	THE NEW POLLUTION *Geffen GFSTD 22205* 14	5
24 May 97	SISSYNECK *Geffen GFSTD 22253* 30	2
8 Nov 97	DEADWEIGHT *Geffen GFSTD 22293* 23	3
19 Dec 98	TROPICALIA *Geffen GFSTD 22365* ....39†	2

Jeff BECK ✒ *UK, male vocalist/instrumentalist – guitar*　　　57 wks

23 Mar 67	HI-HO SILVER LINING *Columbia DB 8151* 14	14
2 Aug 67	TALLYMAN *Columbia DB 8227* 30	3
28 Feb 68	LOVE IS BLUE *Columbia DB 8359* 23	7
9 Jul 69	GOO GOO BARABAJAGAL (LOVE IS HOT) *Pye 7N 17778* [1] 12	9
4 Nov 72	HI-HO SILVER LINING (re-issue) *RAK RR 3* 17	11
5 May 73	I'VE BEEN DRINKING *RAK RR 4* [2] 27	6
9 Oct 82	HI-HO SILVER LINING (re-entry of re-issue) *RAK RR 3* 62	4
7 Mar 92	PEOPLE GET READY *Epic 6577567* [2] 49	3

[1] Donovan with the Jeff Beck Group [2] Jeff Beck and Rod Stewart

Robin BECK ☻ *US, female vocalist*　　　13 wks

| 22 Oct 88 | H FIRST TIME *Mercury MER 270* ....1 | 13 |

Peter BECKETT – *See Barry GRAY ORCHESTRA*

BEDAZZLED *UK, male vocal/instrumental group*　　　1 wk

| 4 Jul 92 | SUMMER SONG *Columbia 6581627* ....73 | 1 |

UK No 1 ★　UK Top 10 ●　UK million seller ◆　UK entry at No 1 ■　US No 1 ▲

BEDLAM AGO GO UK, male vocal/instrumental group — 1 wk

| 4 Apr 98 | SEASON NO. 5 Sony S2 BDLM 2CD | 57 | 1 |

BEDROCK featuring KYO
UK, male/female vocal/instrumental group — 4 wks

| 1 Jun 96 | FOR WHAT YOU DREAM OF Stress CDSTR 23 | 25 | 3 |
| 12 Jul 97 | SET IN STONE/FORBIDDEN ZONE Stress CDSTR 80 [1] | 71 | 1 |

[1] Bedrock

BEDROCKS ✶ UK, male vocal/instrumental group — 7 wks

| 18 Dec 68 | OB-LA-DI OB-LA-DA Columbia DB 8516 | 20 | 7 |

Celi BEE and the BUZZY BUNCH
US, male/female vocal/instrumental group — 1 wk

| 17 Jun 78 | HOLD YOUR HORSES BABE TK TKR 6032 | 72 | 1 |

BEE GEES ☮ ♫ All-time top family recording act. Group nucleus: British-born and Australian-raised Barry, Robin and Maurice Gibb. Among other achievements, they have composed ten UK No 1s, and in 1978 penned four consecutive US chart-toppers — 349 wks

27 Apr 67	NEW YORK MINING DISASTER 1941 Polydor 56 161	12	10
12 Jul 67	TO LOVE SOMEBODY Polydor 56 178	50	1
26 Jul 67	TO LOVE SOMEBODY (re-entry) Polydor 56 178	41	4
20 Sep 67	★ MASSACHUSETTS Polydor 56 192	1	17
22 Nov 67	● WORLD Polydor 56 220	9	16
31 Jan 68	● WORDS Polydor 56 229	8	10
27 Mar 68	JUMBO/THE SINGER SANG HIS SONG Polydor 56 242	25	7
7 Aug 68	★ I'VE GOTTA GET A MESSAGE TO YOU Polydor 56 273	1	15
19 Feb 69	● FIRST OF MAY Polydor 56 304	6	11
4 Jun 69	TOMORROW TOMORROW Polydor 56 331	23	8
16 Aug 69	● DON'T FORGET TO REMEMBER Polydor 56 343	2	15
28 Mar 70	I.O.I.O. Polydor 56 377	49	1
5 Dec 70	LONELY DAYS Polydor 2001 104	33	3
29 Jan 72	MY WORLD Polydor 2058 185	16	9
22 Jul 72	● RUN TO ME Polydor 2058 255	9	10
28 Jun 75	● JIVE TALKIN' RSO 2090 160 ▲	5	11
31 Jul 76	● YOU SHOULD BE DANCING RSO 2090 195 ▲	5	10
13 Nov 76	LOVE SO RIGHT RSO 2090 207	41	4
29 Oct 77	● HOW DEEP IS YOUR LOVE RSO 2090 259 ▲	3	15
4 Feb 78	● STAYIN' ALIVE RSO 2090 267 ▲	4	12
15 Apr 78	★ NIGHT FEVER RSO 002 ▲	1	20
13 May 78	STAYIN' ALIVE (re-entry) RSO 2090 267	63	6
25 Nov 78	● TOO MUCH HEAVEN RSO 25 ▲	3	13
17 Feb 79	★ TRAGEDY RSO 27 ▲	1	10
14 Apr 79	LOVE YOU INSIDE OUT RSO 31 ▲	13	9
5 Jan 80	SPIRITS (HAVING FLOWN) RSO 52	16	7
17 Sep 83	SOMEONE BELONGING TO SOMEONE RSO 96	49	4
26 Sep 87	★ YOU WIN AGAIN Warner Bros. W 8351	1	15
12 Dec 87	E.S.P. Warner Bros. W 8139	51	5
15 Apr 89	ORDINARY LIVES Warner Bros. W 7523	54	3
24 Jun 89	ONE Warner Bros. W 2916	71	1
2 Mar 91	● SECRET LOVE Warner Bros. W 0014	5	11
21 Aug 93	PAYING THE PRICE OF LOVE Polydor PZCD 284	23	5
27 Nov 93	● FOR WHOM THE BELL TOLLS Polydor PZCD 299	4	14
16 Apr 94	HOW TO FALL IN LOVE PART 1 Polydor PZDD 311	30	4
1 Mar 97	● ALONE Polydor 5735272	5	9
21 Jun 97	I COULD NOT LOVE YOU MORE Polydor 5712232	14	3
8 Nov 97	STILL WATERS (RUN DEEP) Polydor 5718892	18	3
18 Jul 98	● IMMORTALITY Epic 6661682 [1]	5	12

[1] Celine Dion with Bee Gees

BEENIE MAN ✶ Jamaica, male vocalist/toaster/rapper — 7 wks

20 Sep 97	● DANCEHALL QUEEN Island Jamaica IJCD 2018 [1]	70	1
7 Mar 98	● WHO AM I Greensleeves GRECD 588	10	5
8 Aug 98	FOUNDATION Shocking Vibes SVJCDS1	69	1

[1] Cherelle Franklyn / Beenie Man

B.E.F. – See Lalah HATHAWAY

BEGGAR and CO ♪ UK, male vocal/instrumental group — 15 wks

| 7 Feb 81 | (SOMEBODY) HELP ME OUT Ensign ENY 201 | 15 | 10 |
| 12 Sep 81 | MULE (CHANT NO 2) RCA 130 | 37 | 5 |

BEGINNING OF THE END US, male vocal/instrumental group — 6 wks

| 23 Feb 74 | FUNKY NASSAU Atlantic K 10021 | 31 | 6 |

BEIJING SPRING UK, female vocal duo — 5 wks

| 23 Jan 93 | I WANNA BE IN LOVE AGAIN MCA MCSTD 1709 | 43 | 3 |
| 8 May 93 | SUMMERLANDS MCA MCSTD 1761 | 53 | 2 |

BEL CANTO UK, male vocal/instrumental group — 1 wk

| 14 Oct 95 | WE'VE GOT TO WORK IT OUT Good Groove CDGG 2 | 65 | 1 |

Harry BELAFONTE ☾ US, male vocalist — 87 wks

1 Mar 57	● BANANA BOAT SONG HMV POP 308	2	18
14 Jun 57	● ISLAND IN THE SUN RCA 1007	3	25
6 Sep 57	SCARLET RIBBONS HMV POP 360	18	6
1 Nov 57	★ MARY'S BOY CHILD RCA 1022	1	12
22 Aug 58	LITTLE BERNADETTE RCA 1072	16	7
28 Nov 58	● MARY'S BOY CHILD (re-entry) RCA 1022 ◆	10	6
12 Dec 58	SON OF MARY RCA 1084	18	4
11 Dec 59	MARY'S BOY CHILD (2nd re-entry) RCA 1022	30	1
21 Sep 61	HOLE IN THE BUCKET RCA 1247 [1]	32	2
12 Oct 61	HOLE IN THE BUCKET (re-entry) RCA 1247 [1]	34	6

[1] Harry Belafonte and Odetta

BELL BOOK and CANDLE
German, male / female vocal / instrumental group — 1 wk

| 17 Oct 98 | RESCUE ME Logic 74321616882 | 63 | 1 |

Archie BELL and the DRELLS ♪
US, male vocal/instrumental group — 33 wks

7 Oct 72	HERE I GO AGAIN Atlantic K 10210	11	10
27 Jan 73	THERE'S GONNA BE A SHOWDOWN Atlantic K 10263	36	5
8 May 76	SOUL CITY WALK Philadelphia Interna PIR 4250	13	10
11 Jun 77	EVERYBODY HAVE A GOOD TIME Philadelphia Interna PIR 5179	43	4
28 Jun 86	DON'T LET LOVE GET YOU DOWN Portrait A 7254	49	4

Freddie BELL and the BELLBOYS ♪
US, male vocal/instrumental group — 10 wks

| 28 Sep 56 | ● GIDDY-UP-A-DING-DONG Mercury MT 122 | 4 | 10 |

Maggie BELL ♪ UK, female vocalist — 12 wks

15 Apr 78	HAZELL Swansong SSK 19412	37	3
13 May 78	HAZELL (re-entry) Swansong SSK 19412	74	1
17 Oct 81	HOLD ME Swansong BAM 1 [1]	11	8

[1] B.A. Robertson and Maggie Bell

William BELL ♪ US, male vocalist — 22 wks

29 May 68	TRIBUTE TO A KING Stax 601 038	31	7
20 Nov 68	● PRIVATE NUMBER Stax 101 [1]	8	14
26 Apr 86	HEADLINE NEWS Absolute LUTE 1	70	1

[1] Judy Clay and William Bell

BELL BIV DEVOE (R&B) US, male vocal group — 29 wks

30 Jun 90	POISON MCA MCA 1414	19	11
22 Sep 90	DO ME MCA MCA 1440	56	3
15 Aug 92	● THE BEST THINGS IN LIFE ARE FREE Perspective PERSS 7400 [1]	2	13
9 Oct 93	SOMETHING IN YOUR EYES MCA MCSTD 1934	60	2

[1] Luther Vandross and Janet Jackson with special guests BBD and Ralph Tresvant

★ UK No 1   ● UK Top 10   ◆ UK million seller   ■ UK entry at No 1   ▲ US No 1

BELL and JAMES US, male vocal duo — 3 wks

31 Mar 79	LIVIN' IT UP (FRIDAY NIGHT) *A & M AMS 7424* 68	1
14 Apr 79	LIVIN' IT UP (FRIDAY NIGHT) (re-entry) *A & M AMS 7424* 59	2

BELLAMY BROTHERS 🐦 US, male vocal duo — 29 wks

17 Apr 76 ●	LET YOUR LOVE FLOW *Warner Bros. K 16690* ▲ 7	12
21 Aug 76	SATIN SHEETS *Warner Bros. K 16775* 43	3
11 Aug 79 ●	IF I SAID YOU HAVE A BEAUTIFUL BODY WOULD YOU HOLD IT AGAINST ME *Warner Bros. K 17405*.........3	14

BELLBOYS – See Freddie BELL and the BELLBOYS

Regina BELLE 🎤 US, female vocalist — 13 wks

21 Oct 89	GOOD LOVIN' *CBS 655230* 73	1
11 Dec 93	A WHOLE NEW WORLD (ALADDIN'S THEME) *Columbia 6599002* [1] ▲ 12	12

[1] Regina Belle and Peabo Bryson

BELLE and SEBASTIAN
UK, male/female vocal/instrumental group — 5 wks

24 May 97	DOG ON WHEELS *Jeepster JPRCDS 001* 59	1
9 Aug 97	LAZY LINE PAINTER JANE *Jeepster JPRCDS 002* 41	2
25 Oct 97	3... 6... 9 SECONDS OF LIGHT *Jeepster JPRCDS 003* 32	2

BELLE and the DEVOTIONS ⦿ UK, female vocal group — 8 wks

21 Apr 84	LOVE GAMES *CBS A 4332* 11	8

La BELLE EPOQUE 📀 France, female vocal duo — 14 wks

27 Aug 77	BLACK IS BLACK *Harvest HAR 5133* 48	1
10 Sep 77 ●	BLACK IS BLACK (re-entry) *Harvest HAR 5133* 2	13

BELLE STARS ⦿ UK, female vocal/instrumental group — 42 wks

5 Jun 82	IKO IKO *Stiff BUY 150* 35	6
17 Jul 82	THE CLAPPING SONG *Stiff BUY 155* 11	9
16 Oct 82	MOCKINGBIRD *Stiff BUY 159* 51	3
15 Jan 83 ●	SIGN OF THE TIMES *Stiff BUY 167* 3	11
16 Apr 83	SWEET MEMORY *Stiff BUY 174* 22	9
13 Aug 83	INDIAN SUMMER *Stiff BUY 185* 52	3
14 Jul 84	80s ROMANCE *Stiff BUY 200* 71	1

BELLINI ☺ Germany, male vocal / production group — 7 wks

27 Sep 97 ●	SAMBA DE JANEIRO *Virgin DINSD 165* 8	7

BELLY US, male/female vocal/instrumental group — 9 wks

23 Jan 93	FEED THE TREE *4AD BAD 3001CD* 32	3
10 Apr 93	GEPETTO *4AD BAD 2018CD* 49	2
4 Feb 95	NOW THEY'LL SLEEP *4AD BAD 5003CD* 28	2
22 Jul 95	SEAL MY FATE *4AD BAD 5007CD* 35	2

BELMONTS – See DION

BELOVED ⦿ ☺ UK, male/female vocal/instrumental duo — 47 wks

21 Oct 89	THE SUN RISING *WEA YZ 414* 26	7
27 Jan 90	HELLO *WEA YZ 426* 19	7
24 Mar 90	YOUR LOVE TAKES ME HIGHER *East West YZ 463* 39	3
9 Jun 90	TIME AFTER TIME *East West YZ 482* 46	4
10 Nov 90	IT'S ALRIGHT NOW *East West YZ 541* 48	3
23 Jan 93 ●	SWEET HARMONY *East West YZ 709CD* 8	10
10 Apr 93	YOU'VE GOT ME THINKING *East West YZ 738CD* 23	4
14 Aug 93	OUTERSPACE GIRL *East West YZ 726CD* 38	2
30 Mar 96	SATELLITE *East West EW 034CD* 19	3
10 Aug 96	EASE THE PRESSURE *East West EW 058CD* 43	2
30 Aug 97	THE SUN RISING *East West EW 122CD1* 31	2

Act was male-only before 1993

BELTRAM US, male producer – Joey Beltram — 4 wks

28 Sep 91	ENERGY FLASH (EP) *R&S RSUK 3* 52	2

7 Dec 91	THE OMEN *R&S RSUK 7* [1] 53	2

[1] Program 2 Beltram

Tracks on Energy Flash (EP): Energy Flash / Psycho Bass / My Sound / Sub-Base Experience

Pat BENATAR ✎ US, female vocalist — 53 wks

21 Jan 84	LOVE IS A BATTLEFIELD *Chrysalis CHS 2747* 49	5
12 Jan 85	WE BELONG *Chrysalis CHS 2821* 22	9
23 Mar 85	LOVE IS A BATTLEFIELD (re-issue) *Chrysalis PAT 1* 17	10
15 Jun 85	SHADOWS OF THE NIGHT *Chrysalis PAT 2* 50	4
19 Oct 85	INVINCIBLE (THEME FROM 'THE LEGEND OF BILLIE JEAN') *Chrysalis PAT 3* 53	3
15 Feb 86	SEX AS A WEAPON *Chrysalis PAT 4* 67	3
2 Jul 88	ALL FIRED UP *Chrysalis PAT 5* 19	10
1 Oct 88	DON'T WALK AWAY *Chrysalis PAT 6* 42	5
14 Jan 89	ONE LOVE *Chrysalis PAT 7* 59	3
30 Oct 93	SOMEBODY'S BABY *Chrysalis CDCHS 5001* 48	1

David BENDETH Canada, male vocalist and multi-instrumentalist — 5 wks

8 Sep 79	FEEL THE REAL *Sidewalk SID 113* 44	5

BENELUX and Nancy DEE
Belgium/Holland/Luxembourg, female vocal group — 4 wks

25 Aug 79	SWITCH *Scope SC 4* 52	4

Eric BENET US, male vocalist — 1 wk

22 Mar 97	SPIRITUAL THANG *Warner Bros. W 0390CD* 62	1

Nigel BENN – See PACK featuring Nigel BENN

BENNET UK, male vocal/instrumental group — 3 wks

22 Feb 97	MUM'S GONE TO ICELAND *Roadrunner RR 22853* 34	2
3 May 97	SOMEONE ALWAYS GETS THERE FIRST *Roadrunner RR 22983* 69	1

Boyd BENNETT and his Rockets 🎻
US, male vocalist and male vocal/instrumental group — 2 wks

23 Dec 55	SEVENTEEN *Parlophone R 4063* 16	2

Chris BENNETT – See MUNICH MACHINE

Cliff BENNETT and the REBEL ROUSERS ⦿
UK, male vocal/instrumental group — 23 wks

1 Oct 64	ONE WAY LOVE *Parlophone R 5173* 9	9
4 Feb 65	I'LL TAKE YOU HOME *Parlophone R 5229* 42	3
11 Aug 66 ●	GOT TO GET YOU INTO MY LIFE *Parlophone R 5489* 6	11

Peter E. BENNETT with the CO-OPERATION CHOIR
UK, male vocalist and choir — 1 wk

7 Nov 70	THE SEAGULL'S NAME WAS NELSON *RCA 1991* 45	1

Tony BENNETT ⦿ US, male vocalist — 61 wks

15 Apr 55 ★	STRANGER IN PARADISE *Philips PB 420* 1	16
16 Sep 55	CLOSE YOUR EYES *Philips PB 445* 18	1
13 Apr 56	COME NEXT SPRING *Philips PB 537* 29	1
5 Jan 61	TILL *Philips PB 1079* 35	2
18 Jul 63	THE GOOD LIFE *CBS AAG 153* 27	13
6 May 65	IF I RULED THE WORLD *CBS 201735* 40	5
27 May 65	I LEFT MY HEART IN SAN FRANCISCO *CBS 201730* 46	2
30 Sep 65	I LEFT MY HEART IN SAN FRANCISCO (re-entry) *CBS 201730* 40	5
9 Dec 65	I LEFT MY HEART IN SAN FRANCISCO (2nd re-entry) *CBS 201730* 25	7
23 Dec 65	THE VERY THOUGHT OF YOU *CBS 202021* 21	9

Gary BENSON ⦿ UK, male vocalist — 8 wks

9 Aug 75	DON'T THROW IT ALL AWAY *State STAT 10* 20	8

UK No 1 ★   UK Top 10 ●   UK million seller ◆   UK entry at No 1 ■   US No 1 ▲

George BENSON
Grammy-winning guitarist/vocalist, b. 22 March, 1943, Pennsylvania. This one-time child prodigy topped the US chart in 1976 with the triple platinum album Breezin'. *He was also a major live attraction in Britain during the 1980s*   **143 wks**

25 Oct 75	SUPERSHIP *CTI CTSP 002* [1]	.30 6
4 Jun 77	NATURE BOY *Warner Bros. K 16921*	.26 6
24 Sep 77	THE GREATEST LOVE OF ALL *Arista 133*	.27 7
31 Mar 79	LOVE BALLAD *Warner Bros. K 17333*	.29 9
26 Jul 80 ●	GIVE ME THE NIGHT *Warner Bros. K 17673*	.7 10
4 Oct 80 ●	LOVE X LOVE *Warner Bros. K 17699*	.10 8
7 Feb 81	WHAT'S ON YOUR MIND *Warner Bros. K 17748* [2]	.45 5
19 Sep 81	LOVE ALL THE HURT AWAY *Arista ARIST 428* [2]	.49 3
14 Nov 81	TURN YOUR LOVE AROUND *Warner Bros. K 17877*	.29 11
23 Jan 82	NEVER GIVE UP ON A GOOD THING *Warner Bros. K 17902*..14 10	
21 May 83	LADY LOVE ME (ONE MORE TIME) *Warner Bros. W 9614*	.11 10
16 Jul 83	FEEL LIKE MAKIN' LOVE *Warner Bros. W 9551*	.28 7
24 Sep 83 ●	IN YOUR EYES *Warner Bros. W 9487*	.7 10
17 Dec 83	INSIDE LOVE (SO PERSONAL) *WEA Int. W 9427*	.57 5
19 Jan 85	20/20 *Warner Bros. W 9120*	.29 9
20 Apr 85	BEYOND THE SEA (LA MER) *Warner Bros. W 9014*	.60 3
16 Aug 86	KISSES IN THE MOONLIGHT *Warner Bros. W 8640*	.60 4
29 Nov 86	SHIVER *Warner Bros. W 8523*	.19 9
14 Feb 87	TEASER *Warner Bros. W 8437*	.45 4
27 Aug 88	LET'S DO IT AGAIN *Warner Bros. W 7780*	.56 3
5 Sep 92	I'LL KEEP YOUR DREAMS ALIVE *Ammi AMMI 101* [3]	.68 1
11 Jul 98	SEVEN DAYS *MCA MCSTD 48083* [4]	.22 3

[1] George 'Bad' Benson [2] Aretha Franklin and George Benson [3] George Benson and Patti Austin [4] Mary J Blige featuring George Benson

BENTLEY RHYTHM ACE ☺ *UK, male instrumental duo*   **4 wks**

6 Sep 97	BENTLEY'S GONNA SORT YOU OUT *Parlophone CDRS 6476*....17 4	

Brook BENTON *US, male vocalist*   **18 wks**

10 Jul 59	ENDLESSLY *Mercury AMT 1043*	.28 2
6 Oct 60	KIDDIO *Mercury AMT 1109*	.42 3
3 Nov 60	KIDDIO (re-entry) *Mercury AMT 1109*	.41 3
16 Feb 61	FOOLS RUSH IN *Mercury AMT 1121*	.50 1
13 Jul 61	BOLL WEEVIL SONG *Mercury AMT 1148*	.30 9

BENZ *UK, male rap/vocal group*   **9 wks**

16 Dec 95	BOOM ROCK SOUL *Hacktown 74321329652*	.62 2
16 Mar 96	URBAN CITY GIRL *Hacktown 74321348732*	.31 3
25 May 96	MISS PARKER *Hacktown 74321377292*	.35 2
29 Mar 97	IF I REMEMBER *Hendricks CDBENZ 1*	.59 1
9 Aug 97	ON A SUN-DAY *Hendricks CDBENZ 2*	.73 1

Ingrid BERGMAN – See Dooley WILSON

BERLIN ☻ *US, male/female vocal/instrumental group*   **39 wks**

25 Oct 86 ★	TAKE MY BREATH AWAY (LOVE THEME FROM 'TOP GUN')	
	CBS A 7320 ▲	.1 15
17 Jan 87	YOU DON'T KNOW *Mercury MER 237*	.39 6
14 Mar 87	LIKE FLAMES *Mercury MER 240*	.47 3
20 Feb 88	TAKE MY BREATH AWAY (LOVE THEME FROM 'TOP GUN')	
	(re-entry) *CBS A 7320*	.52 3
13 Oct 90 ●	TAKE MY BREATH AWAY (re-issue) *CBS 656361 7*	.3 12

Elmer BERNSTEIN ℂ *US, orchestra*   **11 wks**

18 Dec 59 ●	STACCATO'S THEME *Capitol CL 15101*	.4 10
10 Mar 60	STACCATO'S THEME (re-entry) *Capitol CL 15101*	.40 1

Leonard BERNSTEIN, ORCHESTRA and CHORUS
US, male conductor, orchestra and chorus   **4 wks**

2 Jul 94	AMERICA – WORLD CUP THEME 1994	
	Deutsche Grammophon USACD 1	.44 4

BERRI ☺ ☻ *UK, female vocalist*   **22 wks**

26 Nov 94	THE SUNSHINE AFTER THE RAIN	
	Ffrreedom TABCD 223 [1]	.26 6

2 Sep 95 ●	THE SUNSHINE AFTER THE RAIN (re-mix)	
	Ffrreedom TABCD 232	.4 11
2 Dec 95	SHINE LIKE A STAR *Ffrreedom TABCD 239*	.20 5

[1] New Atlantic / U4EA featuring Berri

LaKiesha BERRI *US, female vocalist*   **1 wk**

5 Jul 97	LIKE THIS AND LIKE THAT *Adept ADPTCD 7*	.54 1

Chuck BERRY ♪ *US, male vocalist/instrumentalist – guitar*   **91 wks**

21 Jun 57	SCHOOL DAY *Columbia DB 3951*	.24 2
12 Jul 57	SCHOOL DAY (re-entry) *Columbia DB 3951*	.24 2
25 Apr 58	SWEET LITTLE SIXTEEN *London HLM 8585*	.16 5
11 Jul 63	GO GO GO *Pye International 7N 25209*	.38 6
10 Oct 63 ●	LET IT ROCK/MEMPHIS TENNESSEE *Pye International 7N 25218*..6 13	
19 Dec 63	RUN RUDOLPH RUN *Pye International 7N 25228*	.36 6
13 Feb 64	NADINE (IS IT YOU) *Pye International 7N 25236*	.27 6
2 Apr 64	NADINE (IS IT YOU) (re-entry) *Pye International 7N 25236*.....43 1	
7 May 64 ●	NO PARTICULAR PLACE TO GO *Pye International 7N 25242*.....3 12	
20 Aug 64	YOU NEVER CAN TELL *Pye International 7N 25257*	.23 8
14 Jan 65	PROMISED LAND *Pye International 7N 25285*	.26 6
28 Oct 72 ★	MY DING-A-LING *Chess 6145 019* ▲	.1 17
3 Feb 73	REELIN' AND ROCKIN' *Chess 6145 020*	.18 7

Dave BERRY ☻ *UK, male vocalist*   **76 wks**

19 Sep 63	MEMPHIS TENNESSEE *Decca F 11734* [1]	.19 13
9 Jan 64	MY BABY LEFT ME *Decca F 11803* [1]	.41 1
23 Jan 64	MY BABY LEFT ME (re-entry) *Decca F 11803* [1]	.37 8
30 Apr 64	BABY IT'S YOU *Decca F 11876*	.24 6
6 Aug 64 ●	THE CRYING GAME *Decca F 11937*	.5 12
26 Nov 64	ONE HEART BETWEEN TWO *Decca F 12020*	.41 2
25 Mar 65 ●	LITTLE THINGS *Decca F 12103*	.5 12
22 Jul 65	THIS STRANGE EFFECT *Decca F 12188*	.37 6
30 Jun 66 ●	MAMA *Decca F 12435*	.5 16

[1] Dave Berry and the Cruisers

Mike BERRY ☻ *UK, male vocalist*   **51 wks**

12 Oct 61	TRIBUTE TO BUDDY HOLLY *HMV POP 912* [1]	.24 6
3 Jan 63 ●	DON'T YOU THINK IT'S TIME *HMV POP 1105* [1]	.6 12
11 Apr 63	MY LITTLE BABY *HMV POP 1142* [1]	.34 7
2 Aug 80 ●	THE SUNSHINE OF YOUR SMILE *Polydor 2059 261*	.9 12
29 Nov 80	IF I COULD ONLY MAKE YOU CARE *Polydor POSP 202*.......37 9	
5 Sep 81	MEMORIES *Polydor POSP 287*	.55 5

[1] Mike Berry with the Outlaws

Nick BERRY ☻ *UK, male vocalist*   **24 wks**

4 Oct 86 ★	EVERY LOSER WINS *BBC RESL 204*	.1 11
27 Dec 86	EVERY LOSER WINS (re-entry) *BBC RESL 204*	.72 2
13 Jun 92 ●	HEARTBEAT *Columbia 6581517*	.2 8
31 Oct 92	LONG LIVE LOVE *Columbia 6587597*	.47 3

Adele BERTEI – See JELLYBEAN

BEST COMPANY *UK, male vocal duo*   **1 wk**

27 Mar 93	DON'T YOU FORGET ABOUT ME *ZYX ZYX 69468*	.65 1

BEST SHOT *UK, male rap group*   **2 wks**

5 Feb 94	UNITED COLOURS *East West YZ 795CD*	.64 2

BEVERLEY SISTERS ℂ *UK, female vocal group*   **34 wks**

27 Nov 53	I SAW MOMMY KISSING SANTA CLAUS *Philips PB 188*..........11 1	
11 Dec 53 ●	I SAW MOMMY KISSING SANTA CLAUS (re-entry)	
	Philips PB 188	.6 4
13 Apr 56	WILLIE CAN *Decca F 10705*	.23 4
1 Feb 57	I DREAMED *Decca F 10832*	.24 2
13 Feb 59 ●	LITTLE DRUMMER BOY *Decca F 11107*	.6 13
20 Nov 59	LITTLE DONKEY *Decca F 11172*	.14 7
23 Jun 60	GREEN FIELDS *Columbia DB 4444*	.48 1

7 Jul 60	GREEN FIELDS (re-entry) *Columbia DB 4444*	29	2

See also VARIOUS ARTISTS (EPs and LPs) – All Star Hit Parade No 2

Frankie BEVERLY – See MAZE featuring Frankie BEVERLY

BEYOND *UK, male vocal/instrumental group* **1 wk**

21 Sep 91	RAGING EP *Harvest HARS 530*	68	1

Tracks on Raging (EP): Great Indifference / Nail / Eve of My Release

B-52s 🌀 ◢ *US, male/female vocal/instrumental group* **60 wks**

11 Aug 79	ROCK LOBSTER *Island WIP 6506*	37	5
9 Aug 80	GIVE ME BACK MY MAN *Island WIP 6579*	61	3
7 May 83	(SONG FOR A) FUTURE GENERATION *Island IS 107*	63	2
10 May 86	ROCK LOBSTER/PLANET CLAIRE (re-issue) *Island BFT 1*	12	7
3 Mar 90 ●	LOVE SHACK *Reprise W 9917*	2	13
19 May 90	ROAM *Reprise W 9827*	17	7
18 Aug 90	CHANNEL Z *Reprise W 9737*	61	2
20 Jun 92	GOOD STUFF *Reprise W 0109*	21	6
12 Sep 92	TELL IT LIKE IT T-I-IS *Reprise W 0130*	61	3
9 Jul 94 ●	(MEET) THE FLINTSTONES *MCA MCSTD 1986* [1]	3	12

[1] BC-52s

'Planet Claire' only listed from 17 May, 1986

BG THE PRINCE OF RAP *Germany, male rapper* **2 wks**

18 Jan 92	TAKE CONTROL OF THE PARTY *Columbia 6576330*	71	2

BIBLE *UK, male vocal/instrumental group* **8 wks**

20 May 89	GRACELAND *Chrysalis BIB 4*	51	4
26 Aug 89	HONEY BE GOOD *Ensign BIB 5*	54	4

BIBLE OF DREAMS – See Johnny PANIC and the BIBLE OF DREAMS

Matt BIANCO 🌀 *UK, male vocalist* **65 wks**

11 Feb 84	GET OUT OF YOUR LAZY BED *WEA BIANCO 1*	15	8
14 Apr 84	SNEAKING OUT THE BACK DOOR/MATT'S MOOD		
	WEA YZ 3	44	7
10 Nov 84	HALF A MINUTE *WEA YZ 26*	23	10
2 Mar 85	MORE THAN I CAN BEAR *WEA YZ 34*	50	7
5 Oct 85	YEH YEH *WEA YZ 46*	13	10
1 Mar 86	JUST CAN'T STAND IT *WEA YZ 62*	66	2
14 Jun 86	DANCING IN THE STREET *WEA YZ 72*	64	3
4 Jun 88	DON'T BLAME IT ON THAT GIRL/WAP-BAM-BOOGIE		
	WEA YZ 188	11	13
27 Aug 88	GOOD TIMES *WEA YZ 302*	55	3
4 Feb 89	NERVOUS/WAP BAM BOOGIE (re-mix) *WEA YZ 328*	59	2

'Matt's Mood' only credited from 5 May, 1984. Act was a UK/Poland male/female vocal/instrumental group on first five hits

BIDDU ◢ *UK, orchestra* **13 wks**

2 Aug 75	SUMMER OF '42 *Epic EPC 3318*	14	8
17 Apr 76	RAIN FOREST *Epic EPC 4084*	39	4
11 Feb 78	JOURNEY TO THE MOON *Epic EPC 5910*	41	1

BIG APPLE BAND – See Walter MURPHY and the BIG APPLE BAND

BIG AUDIO DYNAMITE ☺ ✑
UK/US, male vocal/instrumental group **27 wks**

22 Mar 86	E=MC2 *CBS A 6963*	11	9
7 Jun 86	MEDICINE SHOW *CBS A 7181*	29	5
18 Oct 86	C'MON EVERY BEATBOX *CBS 650147*	51	3
21 Feb 87	V THIRTEEN *CBS BAAD 2*	49	5
28 May 88	JUST PLAY MUSIC *CBS BAAD 4*	51	3
12 Nov 94	LOOKING FOR A SONG *Columbia 6610182* [1]	68	2

[1] Big Audio

BIG BAD HORNS – See LITTLE ANGELS

BIG BAM BOO *UK/Canada, male vocal/instrumental duo* **2 wks**

28 Jan 89	SHOOTING FROM MY HEART *MCA MCA 1281*	61	2

BIG BEN BANJO BAND ℂ *UK, instrumental group* **6 wks**

10 Dec 54 ●	LET'S GET TOGETHER NO. 1 *Columbia DB 3549*	6	4
9 Dec 55	LET'S GET TOGETHER AGAIN *Columbia DB 3676*	19	1
30 Dec 55	LET'S GET TOGETHER AGAIN (re-entry) *Columbia DB 3676*	18	1

These hits were both medleys as follows: Let's Get Together No 1: I'm Just Wild About Harry / April Showers / Rock-a-Bye Your Baby / Swanee / Darktown Strutters Ball / For Me and My Gal / Oh You Beautiful Doll / Yes Sir That's My Baby. Let's Get Together Again: I'm Looking Over a Four-leafed Clover / By the Light of the Silvery Moon / Oh Susannah / Baby Face / I'm Sitting on Top of the World / My Mammy / Dixie's Land / Margie

BIG BOPPER 🎵 *US, male vocalist* **8 wks**

26 Dec 58	CHANTILLY LACE *Mercury AMT 1002*	30	1
9 Jan 59	CHANTILLY LACE (re-entry) *Mercury AMT 1002*	12	7

BIG COUNTRY ✑ 🌀 *Distinctive folk-influenced rock quartet from Dunfermline, Scotland: Stuart Adamson (v/g, ex-Skids), Bruce Watson (g), Tony Butler (b), Mark Brzezicki (d). These frequent early-1980s chart visitors achieved five Top 10 albums including the 1984 No 1 Steeltown* **102 wks**

26 Feb 83 ●	FIELDS OF FIRE (400 MILES) *Mercury COUNT 2*	10	12
28 May 83	IN A BIG COUNTRY *Mercury COUNT 3*	17	7
3 Sep 83 ●	CHANCE *Mercury COUNT 4*	9	9
21 Jan 84 ●	WONDERLAND *Mercury COUNT 5*	8	8
29 Sep 84	EAST OF EDEN *Mercury MER 175*	17	6
1 Dec 84	WHERE THE ROSE IS SOWN *Mercury MER 185*	29	7
19 Jan 85	JUST A SHADOW *Mercury BCO 8*	26	4
12 Apr 86	LOOK AWAY *Mercury BIGC 1*	7	8
21 Jun 86	THE TEACHER *Mercury BIGC 2*	28	4
20 Sep 86	ONE GREAT THING *Mercury BIGC 3*	19	6
29 Nov 86	HOLD THE HEART *Mercury BIGC 4*	55	2
20 Aug 88	KING OF EMOTION *Mercury BIGC 5*	16	5
1 Oct 88	KING OF EMOTION (re-entry) *Mercury BIGC 5*	74	1
5 Nov 88	BROKEN HEART (THIRTEEN VALLEYS) *Mercury BIGC 6*	47	4
4 Feb 89	PEACE IN OUR TIME *Mercury BIGC 7*	39	3
12 May 90	SAVE ME *Mercury BIGC 8*	41	3
21 Jul 90	HEART OF THE WORLD *Mercury BIGC 9*	50	2
31 Aug 91	REPUBLICAN PARTY REPTILE (EP) *Vertigo BIC 1*	37	2
19 Oct 91	BEAUTIFUL PEOPLE *Vertigo BIC 2*	72	1
13 Mar 93	ALONE *Compulsion CDPULSS 4*	24	3
1 May 93	SHIPS (WHERE WERE YOU) *Compulsion CDPULSS 6*	29	3
10 Jun 95	I'M NOT ASHAMED *Transatlantic TRAX 1009*	69	1
9 Sep 95	YOU DREAMER *Transatlantic TRAD 1012*	68	1

Tracks on Republican Party Reptile (EP): Republican Party Reptile / Comes a Time / You and Me and the Truth

BIG DADDY *US, male vocal/instrumental group* **8 wks**

9 Mar 85	DANCING IN THE DARK *Making Waves SURF 1033*	21	8

BIG DADDY KANE *US, male vocalist* **6 wks**

13 May 89	RAP SUMMARY/WRATH OF KANE *Cold Chillin' W 2973*	52	2
26 Aug 89	SMOOTH OPERATOR *Cold Chillin' W 2804*	65	1
13 Jan 90	AIN'T NO STOPPIN' US NOW *Cold Chillin' W 2635*	44	3

BIG DISH *UK, male vocal/instrumental group* **5 wks**

12 Jan 91	MISS AMERICA *East West YZ 529*	37	5

BIG FAMILY – See JT and the BIG FAMILY

BIG FUN 🌀 *UK, male vocal group* **33 wks**

12 Aug 89 ●	BLAME IT ON THE BOOGIE *Jive JIVE 217*	4	11
25 Nov 89 ●	CAN'T SHAKE THE FEELING *Jive JIVE 234*	8	9
17 Mar 90	HANDFUL OF PROMISES *Jive JIVE 243*	21	6
23 Jun 90	YOU'VE GOT A FRIEND *Jive CHILD 90* [1]	14	6
4 Aug 90	HEY THERE LONELY GIRL *Jive JIVE 251*	62	1

[1] Big Fun and Sonia featuring Gary Barnacle

BIG MOUNTAIN ♥ ☺
US, male/female vocal/instrumental group　　　**15 wks**

4 Jun 94 ●	BABY I LOVE YOUR WAY *RCA 74321198062*	2 14
24 Sep 94	SWEET SENSUAL LOVE *Giant 74321234642*	51 1

BIG ROLL BAND – *See Zoot MONEY and the BIG ROLL BAND*

BIG SOUND – *See Simon DUPREE and the BIG SOUND*

BIG SOUND AUTHORITY
UK, male/female vocal/instrumental group　　　**12 wks**

19 Jan 85	THIS HOUSE (IS WHERE YOUR LOVE STANDS)	
	Source BSA 1	21 9
8 Jun 85	A BAD TOWN *Source BSA 2*	54 3

BIG SUPREME *UK, male vocal group*　　　**5 wks**

20 Sep 86	DON'T WALK *Polydor POSP 809*	58 3
14 Mar 87	PLEASE YOURSELF *Polydor POSP 840*	64 2

BIG THREE *UK, vocal/instrumental group*　　　**17 wks**

11 Apr 63	SOME OTHER GUY *Decca F 11614*	37 7
11 Jul 63	BY THE WAY *Decca F 11689*	22 10

Barry BIGGS ♥ *Jamaica, male vocalist*　　　**46 wks**

28 Aug 76	WORK ALL DAY *Dynamic DYN 101*	38 5
4 Dec 76 ●	SIDESHOW *Dynamic DYN 118*	3 16
23 Apr 77	YOU'RE MY LIFE *Dynamic DYN 127*	36 4
9 Jul 77	THREE RING CIRCUS *Dynamic DYN 128*	22 8
15 Dec 79	WHAT'S YOUR SIGN GIRL *Dynamic DYN 150*	55 7
20 Jun 81	WIDE AWAKE IN A DREAM *Dynamic DYN 10*	44 6

Ronald BIGGS – *See SEX PISTOLS*

Ivor BIGGUN *UK, male vocalist*　　　**15 wks**

2 Sep 78	WINKER'S SONG (MISPRINT)	
	Beggars Banquet BOP 1 1	22 12
12 Sep 81	BRAS ON 45 (FAMILY VERSION) *Dead Badger BOP 6* 2	50 3

1 Ivor Biggun and the Red Nosed Burglars 2 Ivor Biggun and the D Cups

BILBO *UK, male vocal/instrumental group*　　　**7 wks**

26 Aug 78	SHE'S GONNA WIN *Lightning LIG 548*	42 7

Mr. Acker BILK and his PARAMOUNT JAZZ BAND ✐ ☾
First UK act to top US chart in 1960s, b. 28 January, 1929, Somerset. Band leader/clarinettist/vocalist was at forefront of UK trad-jazz revival. 'Stranger on the Shore' spent more than one year on chart and was voted No 1 Instrumental of 1962 in the USA　　　**171 wks**

22 Jan 60 ●	SUMMER SET *Columbia DB 4382*	5 19
9 Jun 60	GOODNIGHT SWEET PRINCE *Melodisc MEL 1547*	50 1
18 Aug 60	WHITE CLIFFS OF DOVER *Columbia DB 4492*	30 9
8 Dec 60	BUONA SERA *Columbia DB 4544*	7 18
13 Jul 61 ●	THAT'S MY HOME *Columbia DB 4673*	7 17
2 Nov 61	STARS AND STRIPES FOREVER/CREOLE JAZZ	
	Columbia SCD 2155	22 10
30 Nov 61 ●	STRANGER ON THE SHORE	
	Columbia DB 4750 1 ◆ ▲	2 55
15 Mar 62	FRANKIE AND JOHNNY *Columbia DB 4795*	42 2
26 Jul 62	GOTTA SEE BABY TONIGHT *Columbia SCD 2176*	24 9
27 Sep 62	LONELY *Columbia DB 4897* 1	14 11
24 Jan 63	A TASTE OF HONEY *Columbia DB 4949* 1	16 9
21 Aug 76 ●	ARIA *Pye 7N 45607* 2	5 11

1 Mr. Acker Bilk with the Leon Young String Chorale 2 Acker Bilk, his Clarinet and Strings

BILL *UK, male vocalist*　　　**1 wk**

23 Oct 93	CAR BOOT SALE *Mercury MINCD 1*	73 1

BILLIE ♪ *UK, female vocalist*　　　**24 wks**

11 Jul 98	BECAUSE WE WANT TO *Innocent SINCD 2* ■	1 12
17 Oct 98	GIRLFRIEND *Innocent SINCD 3* ■	1 10
19 Dec 98	SHE WANTS YOU *Innocent SINDXX 6*	3† 2

BILLIE – *See H20*

BIMBO JET ♪ *France, male/female vocal/instrumental group*　　　**10 wks**

26 Jul 75	EL BIMBO *EMI 2317*	12 10

BINARY FINARY *UK, male production duo*　　　**3 wks**

10 Oct 98	1998 *Positiva CDTIV 98*	24 3

Umberto BINDI *Italy, male vocalist*　　　**1 wk**

10 Nov 60	IL NOSTRO CONCERTO *Oriole CB 1577*	47 1

BIOHAZARD *US, male/instrumental group*　　　**4 wks**

9 Jul 94	TALES FROM THE HARD SIDE *Warner Bros. W 0254CD*	47 2
20 Aug 94	HOW IT IS *Warner Bros. W 0259CD*	62 2

La BIONDA *Italy, male/female vocal group*　　　**4 wks**

7 Oct 78	ONE FOR YOU ONE FOR ME *Philips 6198 227*	54 4

BIOSPHERE
Norway, male instrumentalist – Ger Jenssen, keyboards　　　**2 wks**

29 Apr 95	NOVELTY WAVES *Apollo APOLLO 20CDX*	51 2

BIRDLAND *UK, male vocal/instrumental group*　　　**7 wks**

1 Apr 89	HOLLOW HEART *Lazy LAZY 13*	70 1
8 Jul 89	PARADISE *Lazy LAZY 14*	70 1
3 Feb 90	SLEEP WITH ME *Lazy LAZY 17*	32 3
22 Sep 90	ROCK 'N' ROLL NIGGER *Lazy LAZY 20*	47 1
2 Feb 91	EVERYBODY NEEDS SOMEBODY *Lazy LAZY 24*	44 1

BIRDS *UK, male vocal/instrumental group*　　　**1 wk**

27 May 65	LEAVING HERE *Decca F 12140*	45 1

Jane BIRKIN and Serge GAINSBOURG ☻
UK/France, female/male vocal duo　　　**34 wks**

30 Jul 69 ●	JE T'AIME. . . MOI NON PLUS *Fontana TF 1042*	2 11
4 Oct 69 ★	JE T'AIME. . . MOI NON PLUS (re-issue) *Major Minor MM 645*	1 14
7 Dec 74	JE T'AIME. . . MOI NON PLUS (2nd re-issue) *Antic K 11511*	31 9

BIS *UK, male/female vocal/instrumental group*　　　**8 wks**

30 Mar 96	THE SECRET VAMPIRE SOUNDTRACK (EP)	
	Chemikal Underground CHEM 003CD	25 2
22 Jun 96	BIS VS THE DIY CORPS (EP) *Teen-C SKETCH 001CD*	45 1
9 Nov 96	ATOM POWERED ACTION (EP) *Wiiija WIJ 55CD*	54 1
15 Mar 97	SWEET SHOP AVENGERZ *Wiiija WIJ 67CD*	46 1
10 May 97	EVERYBODY THINKS THAT THEY'RE GOING TO GET THEIRS	
	Wiiija WIJ 69CD	64 1
14 Nov 98	EURODISCO *Wiiija WIJ 86CD*	37 2

Tracks on The Secret Vampire Soundtrack (EP): Kandy Pop/Secret Vampires/Teen-C Power/Diska. Tracks on Bis vs The DIY Corps (EP): This is Fake DIY/Burn the Suit/Dance to the Disco Beat. Tracks on Atom Powered Action (EP): Starbright Boy/Wee Love/Team Theme/Cliquesuck

Elvin BISHOP *US, male instrumentalist – guitar*　　　**4 wks**

15 May 76	FOOLED AROUND AND FELL IN LOVE *Capricorn 2089 024*	34 4

Hit has vocal (uncredited) by Mickey Thomas

BITI – *See DEGREES OF MOTION featuring BITI*

BIZARRE INC ☺ *UK, male/female vocal/instrumental group*　　　**47 wks**

16 Mar 91	PLAYING WITH KNIVES *Vinyl Solution STORM 25R*	43 5

14 Sep 91		SUCH A FEELING *Vinyl Solution STORM 32S*	13 9
23 Nov 91	●	PLAYING WITH KNIVES (re-issue) *Vinyl Solution STORM 38S*	4 8
3 Oct 92	●	I'M GONNA GET YOU *Vinyl Solution STORM 46S* [1]	3 12
2 Jan 93		I'M GONNA GET YOU (re-entry)	
		Vinyl Solution STORM 46S [1]	72 1
27 Feb 93		TOOK MY LOVE *Vinyl Solution STORM 60CD* [1]	19 5
23 Mar 96		KEEP THE MUSIC STRONG *Some Bizarre MERCD 451*	33 2
6 Jul 96		SURPRISE *Some Bizarre MERCD 462*	21 3
14 Sep 96		GET UP SUNSHINE STREET *Some Bizarre MERCD 471*	45 2

[1] Bizarre Inc featuring Angie Brown

BIZZ NIZZ ☻ ☺
US/Belgium, male/female vocal/instrumental group **11 wks**

31 Mar 90	●	DON'T MISS THE PARTYLINE *Cooltempo COOL 203*	7 11

BIZZI *UK, male vocalist* **1 wk**

6 Dec 97	BIZZI'S PARTY *Parlophone Rhythm CDRHYTHM 7*	62 1

BJORK ☺ ☻ *Iceland, female vocalist* **67 wks**

27 Apr 91		OOOPS *ZTT ZANG 19* [1]	42 3
19 Jun 93		HUMAN BEHAVIOUR *One Little Indian 112 TP7CD*	36 2
4 Sep 93		VENUS AS A BOY *One Little Indian 122 TP7CD*	29 4
23 Oct 93		PLAY DEAD *Island CID 573* [2]	12 6
4 Dec 93		BIG TIME SENSUALITY *One Little Indian 132 TP7CD*	17 8
19 Mar 94		VIOLENTLY HAPPY *One Little Indian 142 TP7CD*	13 4
6 May 95	●	ARMY OF ME *One Little Indian 162 TP7CD*	10 5
26 Aug 95		ISOBEL *One Little Indian 172 TP7CD*	23 4
25 Nov 95	●	IT'S OH SO QUIET *One Little Indian 182 TP7CD*	4 15
24 Feb 96	●	HYPERBALLAD *One Little Indian 192 TP7CD*	8 4
9 Nov 96		POSSIBLY MAYBE *One Little Indian 193 TP7CD*	13 3
1 Mar 97		I MISS YOU *One Little Indian 194 TP7CDL*	36 2
20 Dec 97		BACHELORETTE *One Little Indian 212 TP7CD*	21 5
17 Oct 98		HUNTER *One Little Indian 222 TP7CD*	44 1
12 Dec 98		ALARM CALL *One Little Indian 232 TP7CDL*	33 2

[1] 808 State featuring Bjork [2] Bjork and David Arnold

BJORN AGAIN *Australia, male/female vocal/instrumental group* **8 wks**

24 Oct 92	ERASURE-ISH (A LITTLE RESPECT/STOP!)	
	M & G MAGS 32	25 3
12 Dec 92	SANTA CLAUS IS COMING TO TOWN *M & G MAGS 35*	55 4
27 Nov 93	FLASHDANCE...WHAT A FEELING *M & G MAGCD 50*	65 1

BLACK ☻ *UK, male vocalist – Colin Vearncombe* **35 wks**

27 Sep 86		WONDERFUL LIFE *Ugly Man JACK 71*	72 1
27 Jun 87	●	SWEETEST SMILE *A & M AM 394*	8 10
22 Aug 87	●	WONDERFUL LIFE *A & M AM 402*	8 9
16 Jan 88		PARADISE *A & M AM 422*	38 3
24 Sep 88		THE BIG ONE *A & M AM 468*	54 4
21 Jan 89		NOW YOU'RE GONE *A & M AM 491*	66 2
4 May 91		FEEL LIKE CHANGE *A & M AM 780*	56 2
15 Jun 91		HERE IT COMES AGAIN *A & M AM 753*	70 1
5 Mar 94		WONDERFUL LIFE (re-issue) *PolyGram TV 5805552*	42 3

'Wonderful Life' on A & M is a re-recording. It was re-issued on PolyGram TV in 1994

BLACK & WHITE ARMY *UK, 250 male vocalists* **2 wks**

23 May 98	BLACK & WHITE ARMY *Toon TOON 1CD*	26 2

Cilla BLACK ☻ *Undoubtedly one of Britain's favourite female vocalists/ entertainers this century, b. Priscilla White, 27 May, 1943, Liverpool. After handing in her Top 20 season ticket, she has become an award-winning and extremely popular TV presenter* **194 wks**

17 Oct 63		LOVE OF THE LOVED *Parlophone R 5065*	35 6
6 Feb 64	★	ANYONE WHO HAD A HEART *Parlophone R 5101*	1 17
7 May 64	★	YOU'RE MY WORLD *Parlophone R 5133*	1 17
6 Aug 64	●	IT'S FOR YOU *Parlophone R 5162*	7 10
14 Jan 65	●	YOU'VE LOST THAT LOVIN' FEELIN' *Parlophone R 5225*	2 9
22 Apr 65		I'VE BEEN WRONG BEFORE *Parlophone R 5269*	17 8

13 Jan 66	●	LOVE'S JUST A BROKEN HEART *Parlophone R 5395*	5 11
31 Mar 66	●	ALFIE *Parlophone R 5427*	9 12
9 Jun 66	●	DON'T ANSWER ME *Parlophone R 5463*	6 10
20 Oct 66		A FOOL AM I *Parlophone R 5515*	13 9
8 Jun 67		WHAT GOOD AM I *Parlophone R 5608*	24 7
29 Nov 67		I ONLY LIVE TO LOVE YOU *Parlophone R 5652*	26 11
13 Mar 68	●	STEP INSIDE LOVE *Parlophone R 5674*	8 9
12 Jun 68		WHERE IS TOMORROW *Parlophone R 5706*	39 3
12 Feb 69	●	SURROUND YOURSELF WITH SORROW *Parlophone R 5759*	3 12
9 Jul 69	●	CONVERSATIONS *Parlophone R 5785*	7 12
13 Dec 69		IF I THOUGHT YOU'D EVER CHANGE YOUR MIND	
		Parlophone R 5820	20 9
20 Nov 71	●	SOMETHING TELLS ME (SOMETHING IS GONNA HAPPEN TONIGHT)	
		Parlophone R 5924	3 14
2 Feb 74		BABY WE CAN'T GO WRONG *EMI 2107*	36 6
18 Sep 93		THROUGH THE YEARS *Columbia 6596982*	54 1
30 Oct 93		HEART AND SOUL *Columbia 6598562* [1]	75 1

[1] Cilla Black with Dusty Springfield

BLACK CONNECTION
Italy, male/female vocal/production group **3 wks**

14 Mar 98	GIVE ME RHYTHM *Xtravaganza/Edel 0091465 EXT*	32 2
24 Oct 98	I'M GONNA GET YA BABY *Xtravaganza 0091615 EXT*	62 1

BLACK EYED PEAS *US, male rap trio* **1 wk**

10 Oct 98	JOINTS & JAMS *Interscope IND 95604*	53 1

Frank BLACK *US, male vocalist* **4 wks**

21 May 94	HEADACHE *4AD BAD 4007CD*	53 1
20 Jan 96	MEN IN BLACK *Dragnet 6627862*	37 2
27 Jul 96	I DON'T WANT TO HURT YOU (EVERY SINGLE TIME)	
	Dragnet 6634635	63 1

Jeanne BLACK *US, female vocalist* **4 wks**

23 Jun 60	HE'LL HAVE TO STAY *Capitol CL 15131*	41 4

BLACK BOX ☺ ☻ *Italy, male/female vocal/instrumental group* **74 wks**

12 Aug 89	★	RIDE ON TIME *Deconstruction PB 43055*	1 22
17 Feb 90	●	I DON'T KNOW ANYBODY ELSE *Deconstruction PB 43479*	4 8
2 Jun 90		EVERYBODY EVERYBODY *Deconstruction PB 43715*	16 5
3 Nov 90	●	FANTASY *Deconstruction PB 43895*	5 11
15 Dec 90		THE TOTAL MIX *Deconstruction PB 44235*	12 8
6 Apr 91		STRIKE IT UP/RIDE ON TIME (re-mix)	
		Deconstruction PB 44459	16 8
14 Dec 91		OPEN YOUR EYES *Deconstruction PB 45053*	48 4
14 Aug 93		ROCKIN' TO THE MUSIC *Deconstruction 74321158122*	39 2
24 Jun 95		NOT ANYONE *Mercury MERCD 434*	31 2
20 Apr 96		I GOT THE VIBRATION/A POSITIVE VIBRATION	
		Manifesto MERCD 459 [1]	21 3
22 Feb 97		NATIVE NEW YORKER *Manifesto FESCD 18* [1]	46 1

[1] Blackbox

BLACK CROWES *US, male vocal/instrumental group* **28 wks**

1 Sep 90		HARD TO HANDLE *Def American DEFA 6*	45 5
12 Jan 91		TWICE AS HARD *Def American DEFA 7*	47 3
22 Jun 91		JEALOUS AGAIN/SHE TALKS TO ANGELS	
		Def American DEFA 8	70 1
24 Aug 91		HARD TO HANDLE (re-issue) *Def American DEFA 10*	39 4
26 Oct 91		SEEING THINGS *Def American DEFA 13*	72 1
2 May 92		REMEDY *Def American DEFA 16*	24 3
26 Sep 92		STING ME *Def American DEFA 21*	42 2
28 Nov 92		HOTEL ILLNESS *Def American DEFA 23*	47 3
11 Feb 95		HIGH HEAD BLUES/A CONSPIRACY *American 74321258492*	25 2
22 Jul 95		WISER TIME *American 74321298272*	34 2
27 Jul 96		ONE MIRROR TOO MANY *American 74321398572*	51 1
7 Nov 98		KICKIN MY HEART AROUND *American Recordings 6666665*	55 1

BLACK DIAMOND *US, male vocalist* **1 wk**

17 Sep 94	LET ME BE *Systematic SYSCD 1*	56 1

UK No 1 ★ UK Top 10 ● UK million seller ◆ UK entry at No 1 ■ US No 1 ▲

111

BLACK DUCK UK, male rapper   5 wks

17 Dec 94	WHIGGLE IN LINE *Flying South CDDUCK 1*	33	5

BLACK GORILLA UK, male/female vocal/instrumental group   6 wks

27 Aug 77	GIMME DAT BANANA *Response SR 502*	29	6

BLACK GRAPE ☹ ☺ UK, male vocal/instrumental group   25 wks

10 Jun 95	●	REVEREND BLACK GRAPE *Radioactive RAXTD 16*	9	5
5 Aug 95	●	IN THE NAME OF THE FATHER *Radioactive RAXTD 19*	8	4
2 Dec 95	●	KELLY'S HEROES *Radioactive RAXTD 22*	17	5
25 May 96	●	FAT NECK *Radioactive RAXTD 24*	10	3
29 Jun 96	●	ENGLAND'S IRIE *Radioactive RAXTD 25* [1]	6	4
1 Nov 97		GET HIGHER *Radioactive RAXTD 32*	24	3
7 Mar 98		MARBLES *Radioactive RAXTD 33*	46	1

[1] Black Grape featuring Joe Strummer and Keith Allen

BLACK LACE ◑ UK, male vocal/instrumental group   83 wks

31 Mar 79		MARY ANN *EMI 2919*	42	4
24 Sep 83	●	SUPERMAN (GIOCA JOUER) *Flair FLA 105*	9	18
30 Jun 84	●	AGADOO *Flair FLA 107*	2	30
24 Nov 84	●	DO THE CONGA *Flair FLA 108*	10	9
1 Jun 85		EL VINO COLLAPSO *Flair LACE 1*	42	5
7 Sep 85		I SPEAKA DA LINGO *Flair LACE 2*	49	4
7 Dec 85		HOKEY COKEY *Flair LACE 3*	31	6
20 Sep 86		WIG WAM BAM *Flair LACE 5*	63	3
26 Aug 89		I AM THE MUSIC MAN *Flair LACE 10*	52	3
22 Aug 98		AGADOO *NOW CDWAG 260*	64	1

BLACK MACHINE ☺ ◉
France/Nigeria, male vocal/instrumental duo   5 wks

9 Apr 94	HOW GEE *London LONCD 348*	17	5

BLACK MAGIC US, male producer – Lil' Louis   2 wks

1 Jun 96	FREEDOM (MAKE IT FUNKY) *Positiva CDTIV 51*	41	2

See also LIL' LOUIS

BLACK RIOT US, male producer   3 wks

3 Dec 88	WARLOCK/A DAY IN THE LIFE *Champion CHAMP 75*	68	3

'A Day in the Life' only listed from 17 Dec, 1988

BLACK SABBATH ☈ UK/US, male vocal/instrumental group   70 wks

29 Aug 70	●	PARANOID *Vertigo 6059 010*	4	18
3 Jun 78		NEVER SAY DIE *Vertigo SAB 001*	21	8
14 Oct 78		HARD ROAD *Vertigo SAB 002*	33	4
5 Jul 80		NEON KNIGHTS *Vertigo SAB 3*	22	9
16 Aug 80		PARANOID (re-issue) *Nems BSS 101*	14	12
6 Dec 80		DIE YOUNG *Vertigo SAB 4*	41	7
7 Nov 81		MOB RULES *Vertigo SAB 5*	46	4
13 Feb 82		TURN UP THE NIGHT *Vertigo SAB 6*	37	5
15 Apr 89		HEADLESS CROSS *IRS EIRS 107*	62	1
13 Jun 92		TV CRIMES *IRS EIRSP 178*	33	2

Group UK only for first three hits and re-issue of 'Paranoid'

BLACK SHEEP US, male rap duo   1 wk

19 Nov 94	WITHOUT A DOUBT *Mercury MERCD 417*	60	1

BLACK SLATE ☈ UK/Jamaica, male vocal/instrumental group   15 wks

20 Sep 80	●	AMIGO *Ensign ENY 42*	9	9
6 Dec 80		BOOM BOOM *Ensign ENY 47*	51	6

BLACK UHURU Jamaica, male vocal/instrumental group   9 wks

8 Sep 84	WHAT IS LIFE? *Island IS 150*	56	6
31 May 86	THE GREAT TRAIN ROBBERY		
	Real Authentic Sound RAS 7018	62	3

Band of the BLACK WATCH ☾ UK, military band   22 wks

30 Aug 75	●	SCOTCH ON THE ROCKS *Spark SRL 1128*	8	14
13 Dec 75		DANCE OF THE CUCKOOS		
		(THE 'LAUREL AND HARDY' THEME)		
		Spark SRL 1135	37	8

Bill BLACK'S COMBO US, male instrumentalist – bass   8 wks

8 Sep 60	WHITE SILVER SANDS *London HLU 9090*	50	1
3 Nov 60	DON'T BE CRUEL *London HLU 9212*	32	7

Tony BLACKBURN UK, male vocalist   7 wks

24 Jan 68	SO MUCH LOVE *MGM 1375*	31	4
26 Mar 69	IT'S ONLY LOVE *MGM 1467*	42	3

BLACKBYRDS US, male vocal/instrumental group   6 wks

31 May 75	WALKING IN RHYTHM *Fantasy FTC 114*	23	6

BLACKFOOT US, male vocal/instrumental group   5 wks

6 Mar 82	DRY COUNTY *Atco K 11686*	43	4
18 Jun 83	SEND ME AN ANGEL *Atco B 9880*	66	1

J. BLACKFOOT US, male vocalist   4 wks

17 Mar 84	TAXI *Allegiance ALES 2*	48	4

BLACKFOOT SUE ◉ UK, male vocal/instrumental group   15 wks

12 Aug 72	●	STANDING IN THE ROAD *Jam 13*	4	10
16 Dec 72		SING DON'T SPEAK *Jam 29*	36	5

BLACKGIRL US, female vocal group   3 wks

16 Jul 94	90s GIRL *RCA 74321217882*	23	3

BLACKHEARTS – See Joan JETT and the BLACKHEARTS

Honor BLACKMAN – See Patrick MACNEE and Honor BLACKMAN

BLACKNUSS Sweden, male / female vocal / instrumental group   1 wk

28 Jun 97	DINAH *Arista 74321479762*	56	1

BLACKSTREET [R&B] US, male vocal group   46 wks

19 Jun 93		BABY BE MINE *MCA MCSTD 1772* [1]	37	3
13 Aug 94		BOOTI CALL *Interscope A 8250CD*	56	1
11 Feb 95		U BLOW MY MIND *Interscope A 8222CD*	39	2
27 May 95		JOY *Interscope A 8195CD*	56	2
19 Oct 96	●	NO DIGGITY *Interscope IND 95003* [2] ▲	9	7
8 Mar 97		GET ME HOME *Def Jam DEFCD 32* [3]	11	5
26 Apr 97	●	DON'T LEAVE ME *Interscope IND 95534*	6	10
27 Sep 97	●	FIX *Interscope IND 97521*	7	5
13 Dec 97		(MONEY CAN'T) BUY ME LOVE *Interscope IND 95563*	18	6
27 Jun 98		THE CITY IS MINE *Northwestside 74321588012* [5]	38	2
12 Dec 98	●	TAKE ME THERE *Interscope IND 95620* [4]	7†	3

[1] Blackstreet featuring Teddy Riley [2] Blackstreet featuring Dr. Dre [3] Foxy
Brown featuring Blackstreet [4] Blackstreet and Mya featuring Mase and Blinky
Blink [5] Jay-Z featuring Blackstreet

BLACKWELLS US, male vocal group   2 wks

18 May 61	LOVE OR MONEY *London HLW 9334*	46	2

BLAGGERS I.T.A. UK, male vocal/instrumental group   7 wks

12 Jun 93	STRESSS *Parlophone CDITA 1*	56	2
9 Oct 93	OXYGEN *Parlophone CDITA 2*	51	2
8 Jan 94	ABANDON SHIP *Parlophone CDITA 3*	48	3

BLAHZAY BLAHZAY US, male rap duo   1 wk

2 Mar 96	DANGER *Mercury Black Vinyl MBVCD 2*	56	1

Vivian BLAINE © *US, female vocalist* — **1 wk**

10 Jul 53	**BUSHEL AND A PECK** *Brunswick 05100*	12	1

BLAIR – See Terry HALL

BLAIR *UK, male vocalist* — **5 wks**

2 Sep 95	**HAVE FUN GO MAD** *Mercury MERCD 443*	37	3
6 Jan 96	**LIFE** *Mercury MERCD 447*	44	2

Peter BLAKE *UK, male vocalist* — **4 wks**

8 Oct 77	**LIPSMACKIN' ROCK 'N' ROLLIN'** *Pepper UP 36295*	40	4

BLAME *UK, male instrumental/production duo* — **2 wks**

11 Apr 92	**MUSIC TAKES YOU** *Moving Shadow SHADOW 11*	48	2

BLAMELESS *UK, male vocal/instrumental group* — **5 wks**

4 Nov 95	**TOWN CLOWNS** *China WOKCD 2046*	56	1
23 Mar 96	**BREATHE (A LITTLE DEEPER)** *China WOKCD 2070*	27	3
1 Jun 96	**SIGNS...** *China WOKCD 2077*	49	1

BLANCMANGE © *UK, male vocal/instrumental group* — **71 wks**

17 Apr 82	**GOD'S KITCHEN/I'VE SEEN THE WORD** *London BLANC 1*	65	2
31 Jul 82	**FEEL ME** *London BLANC 2*	46	5
30 Oct 82 ●	**LIVING ON THE CEILING** *London BLANC 3*	7	14
19 Feb 83	**WAVES** *London BLANC 4*	19	9
7 May 83 ●	**BLIND VISION** *London BLANC 5*	10	8
26 Nov 83	**THAT'S LOVE, THAT IT IS** *London BLANC 6*	33	8
14 Apr 84 ●	**DON'T TELL ME** *London BLANC 7*	8	10
21 Jul 84	**THE DAY BEFORE YOU CAME** *London BLANC 8*	22	8
7 Sep 85	**WHAT'S YOUR PROBLEM?** *London BLANC 9*	40	5
10 May 86	**I CAN SEE IT** *London BLANC 11*	71	2

Billy BLAND ♀ *US, male vocalist* — **10 wks**

19 May 60	**LET THE LITTLE GIRL DANCE** *London HL 9096*	15	10

BLAST featuring VDC
Italy, male/female vocal/instrumental group — **5 wks**

18 Jun 94	**CRAYZY MAN** *UMM MCSTD 1982*	22	3
12 Nov 94	**PRINCES OF THE NIGHT** *UMM MCSTD 2011*	40	2

BLESSID UNION OF SOULS *US, male vocal/instrumental group* — **6 wks**

27 May 95	**I BELIEVE** *EMI CDEM 374*	29	5
23 Mar 96	**LET ME BE THE ONE** *EMI CDEM 387*	74	1

BLESSING *UK, male vocal/instrumental group* — **13 wks**

11 May 91	**HIGHWAY 5** *MCA MCS 1509*	42	6
18 Jan 92	**HIGHWAY 5 (re-mix)** *MCA MCS 1603*	30	6
19 Feb 94	**SOUL LOVE** *MCA MCSTD 1940*	73	1

Mary J BLIGE [R&B] *US, female vocalist* — **63 wks**

28 Nov 92	**REAL LOVE** *Uptown MCS 1721*	68	2
27 Feb 93	**REMINISCE** *Uptown MCSTD 1731*	31	4
12 Jun 93	**YOU REMIND ME** *Uptown MCSTD 1770*	48	3
28 Aug 93	**REAL LOVE (re-mix)** *Uptown MCSTD 1922*	26	4
4 Dec 93	**YOU DON'T HAVE TO WORRY** *Uptown MCSTD 1948*	36	2
14 May 94	**MY LOVE** *Uptown MCSTD 1972*	29	3
10 Dec 94	**BE HAPPY** *Uptown MCSTD 2033*	30	4
15 Apr 95	**I'M GOIN' DOWN** *Uptown MCSTD 2053*	12	4
29 Jul 95 ●	**I'LL BE THERE FOR YOU – YOU'RE ALL I NEED TO GET BY** *Def Jam DEFDX 11* [1]	10	5
30 Sep 95	**MARY JANE (ALL NIGHT LONG)** *Uptown MCSTD 2088*	17	4
16 Dec 95	**(YOU MAKE ME FEEL LIKE A) NATURAL WOMAN** *Uptown MCSTD 2108*	23	3
30 Mar 96	**NOT GON' CRY** *Arista 74321358252*	39	2
1 Mar 97	**CAN'T KNOCK THE HUSTLE** *Northwestside 74321447192* [2]	30	2
17 May 97	**LOVE IS ALL WE NEED** *Uptown MCSTD 48053*	15	4

16 Aug 97 ●	**EVERYTHING** *MCA MCSTD 48059*	6	9
29 Nov 97	**MISSING YOU** *MCA MCSTD 48071*	19	3
3 Jan 98	**MISSING YOU (re-issue)** *MCA MCSTD 16CD*	72	1
31 Jan 98	**MISSING YOU (re-entry)** *MCA MCSTD 48071*	74	1
11 Jul 98	**SEVEN DAYS** *MCA MCSTD 48083* [3]	22	3

[1] Method Man featuring Mary J Blige [2] Jay-Z featuring Mary J Blige
[3] Mary J Blige featuring George Benson

BLIND MELON ♂ *US, male vocal/instrumental group* — **13 wks**

12 Jun 93	**TONES OF HOME** *Capitol CDCL 687*	62	2
11 Dec 93	**NO RAIN** *Capitol CDCL 699*	17	6
9 Jul 94	**CHANGE** *Capitol CDCL 717*	35	3
5 Aug 95	**GALAXIE** *Capitol CDCLS 755*	37	2

BLINK *Ireland, male vocal/instrumental group* — **1 wk**

16 Jul 94	**HAPPY DAY** *Lime CDR 6385*	57	1

BLINKY BLINK – See BLACKSTREET; MASE

BLOCKHEADS – See Ian DURY and the BLOCKHEADS

Kristine BLOND *Denmark, female vocalist* — **3 wks**

11 Apr 98	**LOVE SHY** *Reverb BNOISE 1CD*	22	3

BLONDIE © ✎ *Influential New York-based quintet, fronted by ex-Bunny Girl Deborah Harry (v) (b. 1 July, 1945, New York) and fiancé Chris Stein (g). Few acts were more popular internationally 1978-1981, and no other US act in the 1980s matched their three successive No 1s. The band made an impressive comeback in 1999 with new material* — **154 wks**

18 Feb 78 ●	**DENIS** *Chrysalis CHS 2204*	2	14
6 May 78 ●	**(I'M ALWAYS TOUCHED BY YOUR) PRESENCE DEAR** *Chrysalis CHS 2217*	10	9
26 Aug 78	**PICTURE THIS** *Chrysalis CHS 2242*	12	11
11 Nov 78 ●	**HANGING ON THE TELEPHONE** *Chrysalis CHS 2266*	5	12
27 Jan 79 ★	**HEART OF GLASS** *Chrysalis CHS 2275* ◆ ▲	1	12
19 May 79 ★	**SUNDAY GIRL** *Chrysalis CHS 2320*	1	13
29 Sep 79 ●	**DREAMING** *Chrysalis CHS 2350*	2	8
24 Nov 79	**UNION CITY BLUE** *Chrysalis CHS 2400*	13	10
23 Feb 80 ★	**ATOMIC** *Chrysalis CHS 2410*	1	9
12 Apr 80 ★	**CALL ME** *Chrysalis CHS 2414* ▲	1	9
8 Nov 80 ★	**THE TIDE IS HIGH** *Chrysalis CHS 2465* ▲	1	12
24 Jan 81	**RAPTURE** *Chrysalis CHS 2485* ▲	5	8
8 May 82	**ISLAND OF LOST SOULS** *Chrysalis CHS 2608*	11	9
24 Jul 82	**WAR CHILD** *Chrysalis CHS 2624*	39	4
3 Dec 88	**DENIS (re-mix)** *Chrysalis CHS 3328*	50	3
11 Feb 89	**CALL ME (re-mix)** *Chrysalis CHS 3342*	61	2
10 Sep 94	**ATOMIC (re-mix)** *Chrysalis CDCHS 5013*	19	4
8 Jul 95	**HEART OF GLASS (re-mix)** *Chrysalis CSCHS 5023*	15	3
28 Oct 95	**UNION CITY BLUE (re-mix)** *Chrysalis CDCHS 5027*	31	2

See also Deborah HARRY

BLOOD SWEAT AND TEARS
US/Canada, male vocal/instrumental group — **6 wks**

30 Apr 69	**YOU'VE MADE ME SO VERY HAPPY** *CBS 4116*	35	6

BLOODHOUND GANG
US, male/female vocal/instrumental group — **1 wk**

23 Aug 97	**WHY'S EVERYBODY ALWAYS PICKIN' ON ME?** *Geffen GFSTD 22252*	56	1

BLOODSTONE *US, male vocal/instrumental group* — **4 wks**

18 Aug 73	**NATURAL HIGH** *Decca F 13382*	40	4

Bobby BLOOM © *US, male vocalist* — **24 wks**

29 Aug 70 ●	**MONTEGO BAY** *Polydor 2058 051*	3	14
12 Dec 70	**MONTEGO BAY (re-entry)** *Polydor 2058 051*	42	3
9 Jan 71	**HEAVY MAKES YOU HAPPY** *Polydor 2001 122*	31	5
9 Jan 71	**MONTEGO BAY (2nd re-entry)** *Polydor 2058 051*	47	2

What: *I Will Survive*   **17**
Who: Gloria Gaynor
When: 1979 (1), 1993 (5 – remix)
Which: Is one of the most popular club and party records of all time. Surprisingly, this feminist anthem, which topped charts on both sides of the Atlantic, started out as a B-side

What: *You Sexy Thing*   **18**
Who: Hot Chocolate
When: 1975 (2), 1987 (10 – remix), 1997 (6 – 2nd remix)
Which: Entered the Top 10 in three different decades. Although never a No 1, it has appeared on two of the band's chart-topping albums. This club classic was also the group's biggest US hit

What: *She Loves You*   **19**
Who: Beatles
When: 1963 (1), 1983 (45)
Which: Had record advance orders of more than 300000 and sold 1.6 million in the UK. This was one of the record-breaking five Beatles hits that simultaneously occupied the US Top 5 in 1964

What: *Reet Petite*   **20**
Who: Jackie Wilson
When: 1957 (6), 1986 (1)
Which: Took a record 29 years and 42 days to top the chart after first debuting. It was the first chart entry for both the singer and its composer, Motown founder, Berry Gordy Jr

BLOOMSBURY SET *UK, male vocal/instrumental group* **3 wks**

25 Jun 83	HANGING AROUND WITH THE BIG BOYS *Stiletto STL 13*	56	3

Tanya BLOUNT *US, female vocalist* **1 wk**

11 Jun 94	I'M GONNA MAKE YOU MINE *Polydor PZCD 315*	69	1

Kurtis BLOW *US, male rapper* **23 wks**

15 Dec 79	CHRISTMAS RAPPIN' *Mercury BLOW 7*	30	6
11 Oct 80	THE BREAKS *Mercury BLOW 8*	47	4
16 Mar 85	PARTY TIME (THE GO-GO EDIT) *Club JAB 12*	67	1
15 Jun 85	SAVE YOUR LOVE (FOR NUMBER 1) *Club JAB 14* [1]	66	2
18 Jan 86	IF I RULED THE WORLD *Club JAB 26*	24	8
8 Nov 86	I'M CHILLIN' *Club JAB 42*	64	2

[1] René and Angela featuring Kurtis Blow

BLOW MONKEYS ☯ *UK, male vocal/instrumental group* **46 wks**

1 Mar 86	DIGGING YOUR SCENE *RCA PB 40599*	12	10
17 May 86	WICKED WAYS *RCA MONK 2*	60	2
31 Jan 87 ●	IT DOESN'T HAVE TO BE THIS WAY *RCA MONK 4*	5	8
28 Mar 87	OUT WITH HER *RCA MONK 5*	30	6
30 May 87	(CELEBRATE) THE DAY AFTER YOU *RCA MONK 6* [1]	52	2
15 Aug 87	SOME KIND OF WONDERFUL *RCA MONK 7*	67	2
6 Aug 88	THIS IS YOUR LIFE *RCA PB 42149*	70	2
8 Apr 89	THIS IS YOUR LIFE (re-mix) *RCA PB 42695*	32	5
15 Jul 89	CHOICE? *RCA PB 42885* [2]	22	6
14 Oct 89	SLAVES NO MORE *RCA PB 43201* [2]	73	2
26 May 90	SPRINGTIME FOR THE WORLD *RCA PB 43623*	69	2

[1] Blow Monkeys with Curtis Mayfield [2] Blow Monkeys featuring Sylvia Tella

BLU PETER *UK, male DJ/producer* **1 wk**

21 Mar 98	TELL ME WHAT YOU WANT / JAMES HAS KITTENS *React CDREACT 285*	70	1

BLUE ☯ *UK, male vocal/instrumental group* **8 wks**

30 Apr 77	GONNA CAPTURE YOUR HEART *Rocket ROKN 522*	18	8

Babbity BLUE *UK, female vocalist* **2 wks**

11 Feb 65	DON'T MAKE ME (FALL IN LOVE WITH YOU) *Decca F 12053*	48	2

Barry BLUE ☯ *UK, male vocalist* **48 wks**

28 Jul 73 ●	(DANCING) ON A SATURDAY NIGHT *Bell 1295*	2	15
3 Nov 73 ●	DO YOU WANNA DANCE *Bell 1336*	7	12
2 Mar 74	SCHOOL LOVE *Bell 1345*	11	9
3 Aug 74	MISS HIT AND RUN *Bell 1364*	26	7
26 Oct 74	HOT SHOT *Bell 1379*	23	5

See also CRY SISCO!

BLUE ADONIS featuring Lil' Miss Max
Belgium, male production duo, female vocalist **3 wks**

17 Oct 98	DISCO COP *Serious SERR 002CD*	27	3

BLUE AEROPLANES *UK, male/female vocal/instrumental group* **3 wks**

17 Feb 90	JACKET HANGS *Ensign ENY 628*	72	1
26 May 90	. . . AND STONES *Ensign ENY 632*	63	2

BLUE AMAZON *UK, male production duo / female vocalist* **1 wk**

17 May 97	AND THEN THE RAIN FALLS *Sony S2 BAS 301 CD*	53	1

BLUE BAMBOO *Belgium, male producer – Johan Gielen* **4 wks**

3 Dec 94	ABC AND D. . . *Escapade CDJAPE 6*	23	4

BLUE BOY ☺ *UK, male producer* **16 wks**

1 Feb 97 ●	REMEMBER ME *Pharm CDPHARM 1*	8	13
23 Aug 97	SANDMAN *Sidewalk CDSWALK 001*	25	3

BLUE FEATHER *Holland, male vocal/instrumental group* **4 wks**

3 Jul 82	LET'S FUNK TONIGHT *Mercury MER 109*	50	4

BLUE FLAMES – See Georgie FAME

BLUE GRASS BOYS – See Johnny DUNCAN and the BLUE GRASS BOYS

BLUE HAZE *UK, male vocal/instrumental group* **6 wks**

18 Mar 72	SMOKE GETS IN YOUR EYES *A & M AMS 891*	32	6

BLUE JEANS – See Bob B SOXX and the BLUE JEANS

BLUE MELONS *UK, male/female vocal/instrumental group* **1 wk**

8 Jun 96	DO WAH DIDDY DIDDY *Fundamental FUNDCD 1*	70	1

BLUE MERCEDES *UK, male vocal/instrumental duo* **18 wks**

10 Oct 87	I WANT TO BE YOUR PROPERTY *MCA BONA 1*	23	11
13 Feb 88	SEE WANT MUST HAVE *MCA BONA 2*	57	2
23 Jul 88	LOVE IS THE GUN *MCA BONA 3*	46	5

BLUE MINK ☯ *UK/US, male/female vocal/instrumental group* **83 wks**

15 Nov 69 ●	MELTING POT *Philips BF 1818*	3	15
28 Mar 70 ●	GOOD MORNING FREEDOM *Philips BF 1838*	10	10
19 Sep 70	OUR WORLD *Philips 6006 042*	17	9
29 May 71 ●	BANNER MAN *Regal Zonophone RZ 3034*	3	14
11 Nov 72	STAY WITH ME *Regal Zonophone RZ 3064*	11	13
17 Feb 73	STAY WITH ME (re-entry) *Regal Zonophone RZ 3064*	43	2
3 Mar 73	BY THE DEVIL (I WAS TEMPTED) *EMI 2007*	26	9
23 Jun 73 ●	RANDY *EMI 2028*	9	11

BLUE NILE *UK, male vocal/instrumental group* **4 wks**

30 Sep 89	THE DOWNTOWN LIGHTS *Linn LKS 3*	67	1
29 Sep 90	HEADLIGHTS ON THE PARADE *Linn LKS 4*	72	1
19 Jan 91	SATURDAY NIGHT *Linn LKS 5*	50	2

BLUE OYSTER CULT ⅄ *US, male vocal/instrumental group* **14 wks**

20 May 78	(DON'T FEAR) THE REAPER *CBS 6333*	16	14

BLUE PEARL ☺ *UK/US, male/female vocal/instrumental group* **29 wks**

7 Jul 90 ●	NAKED IN THE RAIN *Big Life BLR 23*	4	13
3 Nov 90	LITTLE BROTHER *Big Life BLR 32*	31	5
11 Jan 92	(CAN YOU) FEEL THE PASSION *Big Life BLR 67*	14	6
25 Jul 92	MOTHER DAWN *Big Life BLR 73*	50	2
27 Nov 93	FIRE OF LOVE *Logic 74321170292* [1]	71	1
4 Jul 98	NAKED IN THE RAIN '98 *Malarky MLKD 7*	22	2

[1] Jungle High with Blue Pearl

See also VARIOUS ARTISTS (EPs & LPs) – Gimme Shelter (EP)

BLUE RONDO A LA TURK *UK, male vocal/instrumental group* **9 wks**

14 Nov 81	ME AND MR SANCHEZ *Virgin VS 463*	40	4
13 Mar 82	KLACTOVEESEDSTEIN *Diable Noir VS 476*	50	5

BLUE ZOO ☯ *UK, male vocal/instrumental group* **17 wks**

12 Jun 82	I'M YOUR MAN *Magnet MAG 224*	55	3
16 Oct 82	CRY BOY CRY *Magnet MAG 234*	13	10
28 May 83	I JUST CAN'T (FORGIVE AND FORGET) *Magnet MAG 241*	60	4

BLUEBELLS ☯ *UK, male vocal/instrumental group* **49 wks**

12 Mar 83	CATH *London LON 20*	62	2
9 Jul 83	SUGAR BRIDGE (IT WILL STAND) *London LON 27*	72	1
24 Mar 84	I'M FALLING *London LON 45*	11	12
23 Jun 84 ●	YOUNG AT HEART *London LON 49*	8	12
1 Sep 84	CATH (re-issue) *London LON 54*	38	7
9 Feb 85	ALL I AM (IS LOVING YOU) *London LON 58*	58	3
27 Mar 93 ★	YOUNG AT HEART (re-issue) *London LONCD 338*	1	12

BLUENOTES – See Harold MELVIN and the BLUENOTES

UK No 1 ★   UK Top 10 ●   UK million seller ◆   UK entry at No 1 ■   US No 1 ▲

BLUES BAND *UK, male vocal/instrumental group* — 2 wks

12 Jul 80	BLUES BAND (EP) *Arista BOOT 2*	68	2

Tracks on Blues Band (EP): Maggie's Farm / Ain't it Tuff / Diddy Wah Diddy / Back Door Man

BLUES BROTHERS ☻ ♥ *US, male vocal duo* — 8 wks

7 Apr 90	EVERYBODY NEEDS SOMEBODY TO LOVE *East West A7591*	12	8

For the first two weeks, the flip side of 'Everybody Needs Somebody to Love' – 'Think' by Aretha Franklin – was listed

BLUETONES ☹ ☻ *UK, male vocal/instrumental group* — 35 wks

17 Jun 95	ARE YOU BLUE OR ARE YOU BLIND *Superior Quality BLUE 001CD*	31	2
14 Oct 95	BLUETONIC *Superior Quality BLUE 002CD*	19	3
3 Feb 96 ●	SLIGHT RETURN *Superior Quality BLUE 003CD*	2	8
11 May 96 ●	CUT SOME RUG / CASTLE ROCK *Superior Quality BLUE 005CD*	7	5
20 Jul 96	CUT SOME RUG / CASTLE ROCK (re-entry) *Superior Quality BLUE 005CD*	73	1
28 Sep 96 ●	MARBLEHEAD JOHNSON *Superior Quality BLUE 006CD*	7	6
21 Feb 98 ●	SOLOMON BITES THE WORM *Superior Quality BLUED 007*	10	3
9 May 98	IF... *Superior Quality BLUED 009*	13	5
8 Aug 98	SLEAZY BED TRACK *Superior Quality BLUED 010*	35	2

Colin BLUNSTONE ☻ *UK, male vocalist* — 29 wks

12 Feb 72	SAY YOU DON'T MIND *Epic EPC 7765*	15	9
11 Nov 72	I DON'T BELIEVE IN MIRACLES *Epic EPC 8434*	31	6
17 Feb 73	HOW COULD WE DARE TO BE WRONG *Epic EPC 1197*	45	2
14 Mar 81	WHAT BECOMES OF THE BROKEN HEARTED *Stiff BROKEN 1* [1]	13	10
29 May 82	TRACKS OF MY TEARS *PRT 7P 236*	60	2

[1] Dave Stewart. Guest vocals: Colin Blunstone

See also Neil MacARTHUR

BLUR ☹ ☻ *Prime movers of Britpop: Damon Albarn (v/k), Graham Coxon (g), Alex James (b), Dave Rowntree (d). They won a record four BRIT Awards in 1995, and their first No 1 caused a media storm when it outpaced 'Roll With It' by major rivals Oasis* — 102 wks

27 Oct 90	SHE'S SO HIGH *Food FOOD 26*	48	3
27 Apr 91 ●	THERE'S NO OTHER WAY *Food FOOD 29*	8	8
10 Aug 91	BANG *Food FOOD 31*	24	4
11 Apr 92	POPSCENE *Food FOOD 37*	32	2
1 May 93	FOR TOMORROW *Food CDFOODS 40*	28	4
10 Jul 93	CHEMICAL WORLD *Food CDFOODS 45*	28	4
16 Oct 93	SUNDAY SUNDAY *Food CDFOOD 46*	26	3
19 Mar 94 ●	GIRLS AND BOYS *Food CDFOODS 47*	5	5
11 Jun 94	TO THE END *Food CDFOODS 50*	16	5
3 Sep 94 ●	PARKLIFE *Food CDFOOD 53*	10	7
19 Nov 94	END OF A CENTURY *Food CDFOOD 56*	19	3
26 Aug 95 ★	COUNTRY HOUSE *Food CDFOODS 63* ■	1	11
9 Sep 95	COUNTRY HOUSE *Food FOODS 63*	57	1
25 Nov 95 ●	THE UNIVERSAL *Food CDFOODS 69*	5	9
24 Feb 96 ●	STEREOTYPES *Food CDFOOD 73*	7	5
11 May 96 ●	CHARMLESS MAN *Food CDFOOD 77*	5	6
1 Feb 97 ★	BEETLEBUM *Food CDFOODS 89* ■	1	5
19 Apr 97	SONG 2 *Food CDFOODS 93*	2	5
26 Apr 97	BEETLEBUM (re-entry) *Food CDFOODS 89*	59	2
28 Jun 97 ●	ON YOUR OWN *Food CDFOOD 98*	5	5
27 Sep 97	MOR *Food CDFOOD 107*	15	3

Chart rules allow for a maximum of three formats; the 7-inch of 'Country House', already available on 2 CDs and cassette, was therefore listed separately

BMU *US/UK, male vocal group* — 2 wks

18 Feb 95	U WILL KNOW *Mercury MERCD 420*	23	2

BOB and EARL ♥ *US, male vocal duo* — 13 wks

12 Mar 69 ●	HARLEM SHUFFLE *Island WIP 6053*	7	13

BOB and MARCIA ⬩ *Jamaica, male/female vocal duo* — 25 wks

14 Mar 70 ●	YOUNG GIFTED AND BLACK *Harry J HJ 6605*	5	12
5 Jun 71	PIED PIPER *Trojan TR 7818*	11	13

BOBBYSOCKS *Norway/Sweden, female vocal duo* — 4 wks

25 May 85	LET IT SWING *RCA PB 40127*	44	4

Andreas BOCELLI – *See Sarah BRIGHTMAN*

Karen BODDINGTON and Mark WILLIAMS
Australia, female/male vocal duo — 1 wk

2 Sep 89	HOME AND AWAY *First Night SCORE 19*	73	1

BODY COUNT *US, male rap/instrumental group* — 4 wks

8 Oct 94	BORN DEAD *Rhyme Syndicate SYNDG 4*	28	2
17 Dec 94	NECESSARY EVIL *Virgin VSCDX 1529*	45	2

BODYSNATCHERS *UK, female vocal/instrumental group* — 12 wks

15 Mar 80	LET'S DO ROCK STEADY *2 Tone CHSTT 9*	22	9
19 Jul 80	EASY LIFE *2 Tone CHSTT 12*	50	3

Humphrey BOGART – *See Dooley WILSON*

Hamilton BOHANNON ⬩
US, male vocalist/instrumentalist – drums — 38 wks

15 Feb 75	SOUTH AFRICAN MAN *Brunswick BR 16*	22	8
24 May 75 ●	DISCO STOMP *Brunswick BR 19*	6	12
5 Jul 75	FOOT STOMPIN' MUSIC *Brunswick BR 21*	23	6
6 Sep 75	HAPPY FEELING *Brunswick BR 24*	49	3
26 Aug 78	LET'S START THE DANCE *Mercury 6167 700*	56	4
13 Feb 82	LET'S START TO DANCE AGAIN *London HL 10582*	49	5

BOILING POINT *US, male vocal/instrumental group* — 6 wks

27 May 78	LET'S GET FUNKTIFIED *Bang BANG 1312*	41	6

Marc BOLAN – *See T REX*

CJ BOLLAND ☺ *UK, male producer* — 8 wks

5 Oct 96	SUGAR IS SWEETER *Internal LIECD 35*	11	5
17 May 97	THE PROPHET *ffrr FCD 300*	19	3

See also RAVESIGNAL III

Michael BOLTON ☻ *Soulful rock balladeer/songwriter who initially recorded under his real name, Michael Bolotin (b. 26 February, 1953, Connecticut) and fronted recording groups The Nomads and Blackjack. He is one of the best-selling male vocalists of the 1990s* — 113 wks

17 Feb 90 ●	HOW AM I SUPPOSED TO LIVE WITHOUT YOU *CBS 655397 7* ▲	3	10
28 Apr 90 ●	HOW CAN WE BE LOVERS *CBS 655918 7*	10	10
21 Jul 90	WHEN I'M BACK ON MY FEET AGAIN *CBS 656077 7*	44	5
20 Apr 91	LOVE IS A WONDERFUL THING *Columbia 6567717*	23	8
27 Jul 91	TIME LOVE AND TENDERNESS *Columbia 6569897*	28	7
9 Nov 91	WHEN A MAN LOVES A WOMAN *Columbia 6574887* ▲	8	6
8 Feb 92	STEEL BARS *Columbia 6577257*	17	6
9 May 92	MISSING YOU NOW *Columbia 6579917* [1]	28	4
31 Oct 92	TO LOVE SOMEBODY *Columbia 6584557*	16	6
26 Dec 92	DRIFT AWAY *Columbia 6588557*	18	5
13 Mar 93	REACH OUT I'LL BE THERE *Columbia 6588972*	37	4
13 Nov 93	SAID I LOVED YOU BUT I LIED *Columbia 6598762*	15	8
26 Feb 94	SOUL OF MY SOUL *Columbia 6601772*	32	3
14 May 94	LEAN ON ME *Columbia 6604132*	14	7
9 Sep 95 ●	CAN I TOUCH YOU...THERE *Columbia 6624385*	6	9
2 Dec 95	A LOVE SO BEAUTIFUL *Columbia 6627092*	27	5
16 Mar 96	SOUL PROVIDER *Columbia 6629812*	35	3
8 Nov 97	THE BEST OF LOVE / GO THE DISTANCE *Columbia 6652802*	14	4

[1] Michael Bolton featuring Kenny G

BOMB THE BASS ☺ ☺ *UK, male producer – Tim Simenon* — 50 wks

Date	Title	Pos	Wks
20 Feb 88 ●	BEAT DIS *Mister-ron DOOD 1*	2	9
27 Aug 88 ●	MEGABLAST/DON'T MAKE ME WAIT *Mister-ron DOOD 2* [1]	6	9
26 Nov 88 ●	SAY A LITTLE PRAYER *Rhythm King DOOD 3* [2]	10	10
27 Jul 91 ●	WINTER IN JULY *Rhythm King 6572757*	7	9
9 Nov 91	THE AIR YOU BREATHE *Rhythm King 6575387*	52	3
2 May 92	KEEP GIVING ME LOVE *Rhythm King 6579887*	62	2
1 Oct 94	BUG POWDER DUST *Stoned Heights BRCD 300* [3]	24	3
17 Dec 94	DARKHEART *Stoned Heights BRCD 305* [4]	35	3
1 Apr 95	1 TO 1 RELIGION *Stoned Heights BRCD 313* [5]	53	1
16 Sep 95	SANDCASTLES *Fourth & Broadway BRCD 324* [6]	54	1

[1] Bomb The Bass featuring Merlin and Antonia/Bomb The Bass featuring Lorraine
[2] Bomb The Bass featuring Maureen [3] Bomb The Bass featuring Justin Warfield
[4] Bomb The Bass featuring Spikey Tee [5] Bomb The Bass featuring Carlton
[6] Bomb The Bass featuring Bernard Fowler

BOMBALURINA ☺ *UK, male/female vocal group* — 20 wks

Date	Title	Pos	Wks
28 Jul 90 ★	ITSY BITSY TEENY WEENY YELLOW POLKA DOT BIKINI *Carpet CRPT 1*	1	13
24 Nov 90	SEVEN LITTLE GIRLS SITTING IN THE BACKSEAT *Carpet CRPT 2* [1]	18	7

[1] Bombalurina featuring Timmy Mallett

BOMBERS *Canada, male/female vocal/instrumental group* — 10 wks

Date	Title	Pos	Wks
5 May 79	(EVERYBODY) GET DANCIN' *Flamingo FM 1*	37	7
18 Aug 79	LET'S DANCE *Flamingo FM 4*	58	3

BON JOVI ✎ *Globally popular New Jersey band: Jon Bon Jovi (v), Richie Sambora (g), David Bryan (k), Alec John Such (b), Tico Torres (d). The UK's biggest-selling album act of 1994, who have sold in excess of 75 million albums worldwide* — 177 wks

Date	Title	Pos	Wks
31 Aug 85	HARDEST PART IS THE NIGHT *Vertigo VER 22*	68	1
9 Aug 86	YOU GIVE LOVE A BAD NAME *Vertigo VER 26* ▲	14	10
25 Oct 86 ●	LIVIN' ON A PRAYER *Vertigo VER 28* ▲	4	15
11 Apr 87	WANTED DEAD OR ALIVE *Vertigo JOV 1*	13	7
15 Aug 87	NEVER SAY GOODBYE *Vertigo JOV 2*	21	5
24 Sep 88	BAD MEDICINE *Vertigo JOV 3* ▲	17	7
10 Dec 88	BORN TO BE MY BABY *Vertigo JOV 4*	22	7
29 Apr 89	I'LL BE THERE FOR YOU *Vertigo JOV 5* ▲	18	7
26 Aug 89	LAY YOUR HANDS ON ME *Vertigo JOV 6*	18	6
9 Dec 89	LIVING IN SIN *Vertigo JOV 7*	35	6
24 Oct 92 ●	KEEP THE FAITH *Jambco JOV 8*	5	6
23 Jan 93	BED OF ROSES *Jambco JOVCD 9*	13	6
15 May 93 ●	IN THESE ARMS *Jambco JOVCD 10*	9	7
7 Aug 93	I'LL SLEEP WHEN I'M DEAD *Jambco JOVCD 11*	17	5
2 Oct 93	I BELIEVE *Jambco JOVCD 12*	11	6
26 Mar 94 ●	DRY COUNTY *Jambco JOVCD 13*	9	6
24 Sep 94 ●	ALWAYS *Jambco JOVCD 14*	2	18
17 Dec 94 ●	PLEASE COME HOME FOR CHRISTMAS *Jambco JOVCD 16*	7	6
25 Feb 95 ●	SOMEDAY I'LL BE SATURDAY NIGHT *Jambco JOVDD 15*	7	7
4 Mar 95	PLEASE COME HOME FOR CHRISTMAS (re-entry) *Jambco JOVCD 16*	46	4
10 Jun 95 ●	THIS AIN'T A LOVE SONG *Mercury JOVCD 17*	6	9
30 Sep 95 ●	SOMETHING FOR THE PAIN *Mercury JOVCD 18*	8	7
25 Nov 95 ●	LIE TO ME *Mercury JOVCD 19*	10	8
9 Mar 96 ●	THESE DAYS *Mercury JOVCD 20*	7	6
6 Jul 96	HEY GOD *Mercury JOVCD 21*	13	5

See also Jon BON JOVI

Jon BON JOVI ✎ *US, male vocalist/instrumentalist* — 27 wks

Date	Title	Pos	Wks
4 Aug 90	BLAZE OF GLORY *Vertigo JBJ 1* ▲	13	8
10 Nov 90	MIRACLE *Vertigo JBVJ 2*	29	5
14 Jun 97 ●	MIDNIGHT IN CHELSEA *Mercury MERCD 488*	4	7
30 Aug 97 ●	QUEEN OF NEW ORLEANS *Mercury MERCD 493*	10	4
15 Nov 97	JANIE, DON'T TAKE YOUR LOVE TO TOWN *Mercury 5749872*	13	3

See also BON JOVI

Ronnie BOND *UK, male vocalist* — 5 wks

Date	Title	Pos	Wks
31 May 80	IT'S WRITTEN ON YOUR BODY *Mercury MER 13*	52	5

Gary 'U.S.' BONDS ♪ *US, male vocalist* — 39 wks

Date	Title	Pos	Wks
19 Jan 61	NEW ORLEANS *Top Rank JAR 527* [1]	16	11
20 Jul 61 ●	QUARTER TO THREE *Top Rank JAR 575* [1] ▲	7	13
30 May 81	THIS LITTLE GIRL *EMI America EA 122*	43	6
22 Aug 81	JOLE BLON *EMI America EA 127*	51	3
31 Oct 81	IT'S ONLY LOVE *EMI America EA 128*	43	3
17 Jul 82	SOUL DEEP *EMI America EA 140*	59	3

[1] U.S. Bonds

BONE *UK, male vocal/instrumental duo* — 1 wk

Date	Title	Pos	Wks
2 Apr 94	WINGS OF LOVE *Deconstruction 74321176282*	55	1

BONE THUGS-N-HARMONY ◀ *US, male rap group* — 22 wks

Date	Title	Pos	Wks
4 Nov 95	1ST OF THA MONTH *Epic 6625172*	32	2
10 Aug 96 ●	THA CROSSROADS *Epic 6635502* ▲	8	11
9 Nov 96	1ST OF THA MONTH (re-issue) *Epic 6638505*	15	4
15 Feb 97	DAYS OF OUR LIVEZ *East West A 3982CD*	37	2
26 Jul 97	LOOK INTO MY EYES *Epic 6647862*	16	3

Elbow BONES and the RACKETEERS
US, male group leader and female backing group — 9 wks

Date	Title	Pos	Wks
14 Jan 84	A NIGHT IN NEW YORK *EMI America EA 165*	33	9

BONEY M ◀ ✆

Internationally successful West Indian vocal group: Bobby Farrell, Marcia Barrett, Liz Mitchell, Maisie Williams. This German-based quartet were assembled by producer Frank Farian (later behind controversial duo Milli Vanilli), and were chart regulars in the 1970s — 167 wks

Date	Title	Pos	Wks
18 Dec 76 ●	DADDY COOL *Atlantic K 10827*	6	13
12 Mar 77 ●	SUNNY *Atlantic K 10892*	3	10
25 Jun 77 ●	MA BAKER *Atlantic K 10965*	2	13
29 Oct 77 ●	BELFAST *Atlantic K 11020*	8	13
29 Apr 78 ★	RIVERS OF BABYLON/BROWN GIRL IN THE RING *Atlantic/Hansa K 11120* ◆	1	40
7 Oct 78 ●	RASPUTIN *Atlantic/Hansa K 11192*	2	10
2 Dec 78 ★	MARY'S BOY CHILD – OH MY LORD *Atlantic/Hansa K 11221* ◆	1	8
3 Mar 79 ●	PAINTER MAN *Atlantic/Hansa K 11255*	10	6
28 Apr 79 ●	HOORAY HOORAY IT'S A HOLI-HOLIDAY *Atlantic/Hansa K 11279*	3	9
11 Aug 79	GOTTA GO HOME/EL LUTE *Atlantic/Hansa K 11351*	12	11
15 Dec 79	I'M BORN AGAIN *Atlantic/Hansa K 11410*	35	7
26 Apr 80	MY FRIEND JACK *Atlantic/Hansa K 11463*	57	5
14 Feb 81	CHILDREN OF PARADISE *Atlantic/Hansa K 11637*	66	2
21 Nov 81	WE KILL THE WORLD (DON'T KILL THE WORLD) *Atlantic/Hansa K 11689*	39	5
24 Dec 88	MEGAMIX/MARY'S BOY CHILD (re-mix) *Ariola 111947*	52	3
5 Dec 92 ●	BONEY M MEGAMIX *Arista 74321125127*	7	9
17 Apr 93	BROWN GIRL IN THE RING (re-mix) *Arista 74321137052*	38	3

'Brown Girl in the Ring' only listed with 'Rivers of Babylon' from 5 Aug, 1978, peaking at No 2. 'El Lute' only listed with 'Gotta Go Home' from 29 Sep, 1979. The 1992 megamixes are different

Graham BONNET ☺ *UK, male vocalist* — 15 wks

Date	Title	Pos	Wks
21 Mar 81 ●	NIGHT GAMES *Vertigo VER 1*	6	11
13 Jun 81	LIAR *Vertigo VER 2*	51	4

Graham BONNEY ☺ *UK, male vocalist* — 8 wks

Date	Title	Pos	Wks
24 Mar 66	SUPERGIRL *Columbia DB 7843*	19	8

BONO ✎ *Ireland, male vocalist* — 23 wks

Date	Title	Pos	Wks
25 Jan 86	IN A LIFETIME *RCA PB 40535* [1]	20	5
10 Jun 89	IN A LIFETIME (re-issue) *RCA PB 42873* [1]	17	7

4 Dec 93 ●	I'VE GOT YOU UNDER MY SKIN *Island CID 578* [2]	4	9
9 Apr 94	IN THE NAME OF THE FATHER *Island CID 593* [3]	46	2

[1] Clannad featuring Bono [2] Frank Sinatra with Bono [3] Bono and Gavin Friday

I've Got You Under My Skin was the listed B-side of 'Stay (Faraway So Close)' by U2.
See also U2

BONZO DOG DOO-DAH BAND ⊙
UK, male vocal/instrumental group **14 wks**

6 Nov 68 ●	I'M THE URBAN SPACEMAN *Liberty LBF 15144*	5	14

Betty BOO ⊙ ☺ *UK, female rapper* **55 wks**

12 Aug 89 ●	HEY DJ I CAN'T DANCE TO THAT MUSIC YOU'RE PLAYING		
	Rhythm King LEFT 34 [1]	7	11
19 May 90 ●	DOIN' THE DO *Rhythm King LEFT 39*	7	12
11 Aug 90 ●	WHERE ARE YOU BABY *Rhythm King LEFT 43*	3	10
1 Dec 90	24 HOURS *Rhythm King LEFT 45.*	25	8
8 Aug 92	LET ME TAKE YOU THERE *WEA YZ 677*	12	8
3 Oct 92	I'M ON MY WAY *WEA YZ 693*	44	3
10 Apr 93	HANGOVER *WEA YZ 719CD*	50	3

[1] Beatmasters featuring Betty Boo

BOO RADLEYS ☹ ⊙ *UK, male vocal/instrumental group* **27 wks**

20 Jun 92	DOES THIS HURT/BOO! FOREVER *Creation CRE 128*	67	1
23 Oct 93	WISH I WAS SKINNY *Creation CRESCD 169*	75	1
12 Feb 94	BARNEY (. . . & ME) *Creation CRESCD 178*	48	2
11 Jun 94	LAZARUS *Creation CRESCD 187*	50	2
11 Mar 95 ●	WAKE UP BOO! *Creation CRESCD 191*	9	8
13 May 95	FIND THE ANSWER WITHIN *Creation CRESCD 202*	37	3
29 Jul 95	IT'S LULU *Creation CRESCD 211*	25	2
7 Oct 95	FROM THE BENCH AT BELVIDERE *Creation CRESCD 214*	24	2
17 Aug 96	WHAT'S IN THE BOX (SEE WATCHA GOT)		
	Creation CRESCD 220	25	2
19 Oct 96	C'MON KIDS *Creation CRESCD 236*	18	2
1 Feb 97	RIDE THE TIGER *Creation CRESCD 248X*	38	1
17 Oct 98	FREE HUEY *Creation CRESCD 299X*	54	1

BOO-YAA T.R.I.B.E. *US, male rap group* **6 wks**

30 Jun 90	PSYKO FUNK *Fourth & Broadway BRW 179*	43	3
6 Nov 93	ANOTHER BODY MURDERED *Epic 6597942* [1]	26	3

[1] Faith No More & Boo-Yaa T.R.I.B.E.

BOOGIE BOX HIGH ⊙ *UK, male vocal/instrumental duo* **11 wks**

4 Jul 87 ●	JIVE TALKIN' *Hardback 7BOSS 4*	7	11

BOOGIE DOWN PRODUCTIONS *US, male rap/scratch duo* **2 wks**

4 Jun 88	MY PHILOSOPHY/STOP THE VIOLENCE *Jive JIVEX 170*	69	2

BOOKER T. and the M.G.'s ♥ *US, male instrumental group* **43 wks**

11 Dec 68	SOUL LIMBO *Stax 102*	30	9
7 May 69	TIME IS TIGHT *Stax 119.*	4	18
30 Aug 69	SOUL CLAP '69 *Stax 127.*	35	4
15 Dec 79 ●	GREEN ONIONS *Atlantic K 10109*	7	12

BOOM BOOM ROOM *UK, male vocal/instrumental group* **1 wk**

8 Mar 86	HERE COMES THE MAN *Fun After All FUN 101*	74	1

BOOMTOWN RATS ✐ ⊙ *New-wave group named after a band in*
a Woody Guthrie novel. Fronted by charismatic Bob Geldof (b. 5 October,
1954, Dublin), who was later knighted for organising Live Aid. This
punk-inspired outfit achieved five Top 10s in less than 18 months **123 wks**

27 Aug 77	LOOKING AFTER NO. 1 *Ensign ENY 4*	11	9
19 Nov 77	MARY OF THE 4TH FORM *Ensign ENY 9*	15	9
15 Apr 78	SHE'S SO MODERN *Ensign ENY 13*	12	11
17 Jun 78 ●	LIKE CLOCKWORK *Ensign ENY 14*	6	13
14 Oct 78 ★	RAT TRAP *Ensign ENY 16*	1	15
21 Jul 79 ★	I DON'T LIKE MONDAYS *Ensign ENY 30*	1	12
17 Nov 79	DIAMOND SMILES *Ensign ENY 33.*	13	10

26 Jan 80 ●	SOMEONE'S LOOKING AT YOU *Ensign ENY 34*	4	9
22 Nov 80 ●	BANANA REPUBLIC *Ensign BONGO 1*	3	11
31 Jan 81	THE ELEPHANT'S GRAVEYARD (GUILTY) *Mercury BONGO 2*	..26	6
12 Dec 81	NEVER IN A MILLION YEARS *Mercury MER 87*	62	4
20 Mar 82	HOUSE ON FIRE *Mercury MER 91*	24	8
18 Feb 84	TONIGHT *Mercury MER 154*	73	1
19 May 84	DRAG ME DOWN *Mercury MER 163*	50	3
2 Jul 94	I DON'T LIKE MONDAYS (re-issue) *Vertigo VERCD 87*	38	2

Daniel BOONE ⊙ *UK, male vocalist* **25 wks**

14 Aug 71	DADDY DON'T YOU WALK SO FAST		
	Penny Farthing PEN 764	17	15
1 Apr 72	BEAUTIFUL SUNDAY *Penny Farthing PEN 781*	48	1
15 Apr 72	BEAUTIFUL SUNDAY (re-entry) *Penny Farthing PEN 781*	21	9

Debby BOONE *US, female vocalist* **2 wks**

24 Dec 77	YOU LIGHT UP MY LIFE *Warner Bros. K 17043* ▲	48	2

Pat BOONE ⊙ ℭ *Major rival to Elvis in late 1950s, b. 1 June, 1934,*
Florida. This clean-cut vocalist was voted the World's Outstanding
Male Singer in the UK in 1957. He was seldom absent from the UK
or US charts during the early rock'n'roll years **308 wks**

18 Nov 55 ●	AIN'T THAT A SHAME *London HLD 8173*	7	9
27 Apr 56 ★	I'LL BE HOME *London HLD 8253*	1	22
27 Jul 56	LONG TALL SALLY *London HLD 8291*	27	3
17 Aug 56	I ALMOST LOST MY MIND *London HLD 8303*	14	7
24 Aug 56	LONG TALL SALLY (re-entry) *London HLD 8291*	18	4
7 Dec 56 ●	FRIENDLY PERSUASION *London HLD 8346*	3	21
11 Jan 57	AIN'T THAT A SHAME (re-entry) *London HLD 8173*	22	2
11 Jan 57	I'LL BE HOME (re-entry) *London HLD 8253*	19	2
1 Feb 57 ●	DON'T FORBID ME *London HLD 8370*	2	16
26 Apr 57	WHY BABY WHY *London HLD 8404*	17	7
5 Jul 57 ●	LOVE LETTERS IN THE SAND *London HLD 8445* ▲	2	21
27 Sep 57 ●	REMEMBER YOU'RE MINE/THERE'S A GOLDMINE		
	IN THE SKY *London HLD 8479*	5	18
6 Dec 57 ●	APRIL LOVE *London HLD 8512* ▲	7	23
13 Dec 57	WHITE CHRISTMAS *London HLD 8520*	29	1
4 Apr 58 ●	A WONDERFUL TIME UP THERE *London HLD 8574*	2	17
11 Apr 58 ●	IT'S TOO SOON TO KNOW *London HLD 8574*	7	12
27 Jun 58 ●	SUGAR MOON *London HLD 8640*	6	12
29 Aug 58	IF DREAMS CAME TRUE *London HLD 8675*	16	11
5 Dec 58	GEE BUT IT'S LONELY *London HLD 8739*	30	1
16 Jan 59	I'LL REMEMBER TONIGHT *London HLD 8775*	28	1
6 Feb 59	I'LL REMEMBER TONIGHT (re-entry) *London HLD 8775*	21	1
20 Feb 59	I'LL REMEMBER TONIGHT (2nd re-entry) *London HLD 8775.*	..18	7
10 Apr 59	WITH THE WIND AND THE RAIN IN YOUR HAIR		
	London HLD 8824	21	3
22 May 59	FOR A PENNY *London HLD 8855.*	28	3
26 Jun 59	FOR A PENNY (re-entry) *London HLD 8855*	19	6
31 Jul 59	'TWIXT TWELVE AND TWENTY *London HLD 8910.*	18	6
18 Sep 59	'TWIXT TWELVE AND TWENTY (re-entry) *London HLD 8910.*	..26	1
23 Jun 60	WALKING THE FLOOR OVER YOU *London HLD 9138*	40	2
14 Jul 60	WALKING THE FLOOR OVER YOU (re-entry)		
	London HLD 9138	46	1
4 Aug 60	WALKING THE FLOOR OVER YOU (2nd re-entry)		
	London HLD 9138	39	2
6 Jul 61	MOODY RIVER *London HLD 9350* ▲	18	10
7 Dec 61 ●	JOHNNY WILL *London HLD 9461*	4	13
15 Feb 62	I'LL SEE YOU IN MY DREAMS *London HLD 9504*	27	9
24 May 62	QUANDO QUANDO QUANDO *London HLD 9543*	41	4
12 Jul 62 ●	SPEEDY GONZALES *London HLD 9573*	2	19
15 Nov 62	THE MAIN ATTRACTION *London HLD 9620*	12	11

'There's a Goldmine in the Sky' was only listed for the week of 27 Sep, 1957.
It peaked at No 23

BOOM – *See Boris DLUGOSCH presents BOOM*

BOOT ROOM BOYZ – *See LIVERPOOL FC*

Duke BOOTEE – *See GRANDMASTER FLASH, Melle MEL and the FURIOUS FIVE*

BOOTH and the BAD ANGEL
UK/US, male vocal/instrumental duo   **4 wks**

| 22 Jun 96 | | I BELIEVE *Fontana BBCD 1* | 25 | 3 |
| 11 Jul 98 | | FALL IN LOVE WITH ME *Mercury MERCD 503* | 57 | 1 |

Ken BOOTHE 🌴 *Jamaica, male vocalist*   **22 wks**

| 21 Sep 74 | ★ | EVERYTHING I OWN *Trojan TR 7920* | 1 | 12 |
| 14 Dec 74 | | CRYING OVER YOU *Trojan TR 7944* | 11 | 10 |

BOOTHILL FOOT-TAPPERS
UK, male/female vocal/instrumental group   **3 wks**

| 14 Jul 84 | | GET YOUR FEET OUT OF MY SHOES *Go! Discs TAP 1* | 64 | 3 |

BOOTSY'S RUBBER BAND *US, male vocal/instrumental group*   **3 wks**

| 8 Jul 78 | | BOOTZILLA *Warner Bros. K 17196* | 43 | 3 |

BOOTZILLA ORCHESTRA – See Malcolm McLAREN

BOSS *US, male producer – David Morales*   **1 wk**

| 27 Aug 94 | | CONGO *Cooltempo CDCOOL 296* | 54 | 1 |

See also David MORALES AND THE BAD YARD CLUB

BOSTON *US, male vocal/instrumental group*   **13 wks**

| 29 Jan 77 | | MORE THAN A FEELING *Epic EPC 4658* | 22 | 8 |
| 7 Oct 78 | | DON'T LOOK BACK *Epic EPC 6653* | 43 | 5 |

Eve BOSWELL ☾ *Hungary, female vocalist*   **13 wks**

30 Dec 55	●	PICKIN' A CHICKEN *Parlophone R 4082*	9	7
2 Mar 56		PICKIN' A CHICKEN (re-entry) *Parlophone R 4082*	16	3
6 Apr 56		PICKIN' A CHICKEN (2nd re-entry) *Parlophone R 4082*	20	3

La BOUCHE *US, male/female rap/vocal duo*   **12 wks**

24 Sep 94		SWEET DREAMS *Bell 74321223912*	63	1
15 Jul 95		BE MY LOVER *Arista 74321265402*	27	4
30 Sep 95		FALLING IN LOVE *Arista 74321305102*	43	2
2 Mar 96		BE MY LOVER (re-mix) *Arista 74321339822*	25	4
7 Sep 96		SWEET DREAMS (re-issue) *Arista 74321398542*	44	1

Judy BOUCHER 🌴 *St Vincent, female vocalist*   **23 wks**

| 4 Apr 87 | ● | CAN'T BE WITH YOU TONIGHT *Orbitone OR 721* | 2 | 14 |
| 4 Jul 87 | | YOU CAUGHT MY EYE *Orbitone OR 722* | 18 | 9 |

Peter BOUNCER – See SHUT UP AND DANCE

BOUNCING CZECKS *UK, male vocal/instrumental group*   **1 wk**

| 29 Dec 84 | | I'M A LITTLE CHRISTMAS CRACKER *RCA 463* | 72 | 1 |

BOURGEOIS TAGG *US, male vocal/instrumental duo*   **6 wks**

| 6 Feb 88 | | I DON'T MIND AT ALL *Island IS 353* | 35 | 6 |

BOURGIE BOURGIE *UK, male vocal/instrumental group*   **4 wks**

| 3 Mar 84 | | BREAKING POINT *MCA BOU 1* | 48 | 4 |

Toby BOURKE – See George MICHAEL

Aletia BOURNE – See ANGELHEART

BOW WOW WOW ✏
UK / Burma female/male vocal/instrumental group   **54 wks**

26 Jul 80		C30, C60, C90, GO *EMI 5088*	34	7
6 Dec 80		YOUR CASSETTE PET *EMI WOW 1*	58	6
28 Mar 81		W.O.R.K. (N.O. NAH NO NO MY DADDY DON'T) *EMI 5153*	62	3
15 Aug 81		PRINCE OF DARKNESS *RCA 100*	58	4
7 Nov 81		CHIHUAHUA *RCA 144*	51	4
30 Jan 82	●	GO WILD IN THE COUNTRY *RCA 175*	7	13
1 May 82		SEE JUNGLE (JUNGLE BOY)/TV SAVAGE *RCA 220*	45	3

5 Jun 82	●	I WANT CANDY *RCA 238*	9	8
31 Jul 82		LOUIS QUATORZE *RCA 263*	66	2
12 Mar 83		DO YOU WANNA HOLD ME *RCA 314*	47	4

Your Cassette Pet listed as Louis Quatorze on 6 Dec, 1980 only. Tracks on Your Cassette Pet (available only as a cassette) are: Louis Quatorze / Gold He Said / Umo-Sex-Al Apache / I Want My Baby On Mars / Sexy Eiffel Towers / Giant Sized Baby Thing / Fools Rush In / Radio G String. RCA 263 is disc version of track on EMI WOW 1 Cassette

BOWA featuring MALA *US, male/female vocal/instrumental duo*   **1 wk**

| 7 Dec 91 | | DIFFERENT STORY *Dead Dead Good GOOD 8* | 64 | 1 |

David BOWIE 🎤 *Unique singer/songwriter and pop chameleon,*
b. David Jones, 8 January, 1947, London. One of the most popular, important and influential artists of the rock era, who received the BRIT award for Outstanding Contribution to British Music in 1996   **433 wks**

6 Sep 69		SPACE ODDITY *Philips BF 1801*	48	1
20 Sep 69	●	SPACE ODDITY (re-entry) *Philips BF 1801*	5	13
24 Jun 72		STARMAN *RCA 2199*	10	11
16 Sep 72		JOHN I'M ONLY DANCING *RCA 2263*	12	10
9 Dec 72	●	THE JEAN GENIE *RCA 2302*	2	13
14 Apr 73	●	DRIVE-IN SATURDAY *RCA 2352*	3	10
30 Jun 73	●	LIFE ON MARS *RCA 2316*	3	13
15 Sep 73	●	THE LAUGHING GNOME *Deram DM 123*	6	12
20 Oct 73	●	SORROW *RCA 2424*	3	15
23 Feb 74	●	REBEL REBEL *RCA LPBO 5009*	5	7
20 Apr 74		ROCK 'N' ROLL SUICIDE *RCA LPBO 5021*	22	7
22 Jun 74		DIAMOND DOGS *RCA APBO 0293*	21	6
28 Sep 74	●	KNOCK ON WOOD *RCA 2466*	10	6
1 Mar 75		YOUNG AMERICANS *RCA 2523*	18	7
2 Aug 75	★	FAME *RCA 2579* ▲	17	8
11 Oct 75	★	SPACE ODDITY (re-issue) *RCA 2593*	1	10
29 Nov 75	●	GOLDEN YEARS *RCA 2640*	8	10
22 May 76		TVC 15 *RCA 2682*	33	4
19 Feb 77	●	SOUND AND VISION *RCA PB 0905*	3	11
15 Oct 77		HEROES *RCA PB 1121*	24	8
21 Jan 78		BEAUTY AND THE BEAST *RCA PB 1190*	39	3
2 Dec 78		BREAKING GLASS (EP) *RCA BOW 1*	54	7
5 May 79	●	BOYS KEEP SWINGING *RCA BOW 2*	7	10
21 Jul 79		D.J. *RCA BOW 3*	29	5
15 Dec 79		JOHN I'M ONLY DANCING (AGAIN) (1975)/ JOHN I'M ONLY DANCING (1972) *RCA BOW 4*	12	8
1 Mar 80		ALABAMA SONG *RCA BOW 5*	23	5
16 Aug 80	★	ASHES TO ASHES *RCA BOW 6*	1	10
1 Nov 80	●	FASHION *RCA BOW 7*	5	12
10 Jan 81		SCARY MONSTERS (AND SUPER CREEPS) *RCA BOW 8*	20	6
28 Mar 81		UP THE HILL BACKWARDS *RCA BOW 9*	32	6
14 Nov 81	★	UNDER PRESSURE *EMI 5250* [1]	1	11
28 Nov 81		WILD IS THE WIND *RCA BOW 10*	24	10
6 Mar 82		BAAL'S HYMN (EP) *RCA BOW 11*	29	5
10 Apr 82		CAT PEOPLE (PUTTING OUT FIRE) *MCA 770*	26	4
27 Nov 82	●	PEACE ON EARTH – LITTLE DRUMMER BOY *RCA BOW 12* [2]	3	8
26 Mar 83	★	LET'S DANCE *EMI America EA 152* ▲	1	14
11 Jun 83	●	CHINA GIRL *EMI America EA 157*	2	8
24 Sep 83	●	MODERN LOVE *EMI America EA 158*	2	8
5 Nov 83		WHITE LIGHT, WHITE HEAT *RCA 372*	46	3
22 Sep 84	●	BLUE JEAN *EMI America EA 181*	6	8
8 Dec 84		TONIGHT *EMI America EA 187*	53	4
9 Feb 85		THIS IS NOT AMERICA (THE THEME FROM 'THE FALCON AND THE SNOWMAN') *EMI America EA 190* [3]	14	7
8 Jun 85		LOVING THE ALIEN *EMI America EA 195*	19	6
27 Jul 85		LOVING THE ALIEN (re-entry) *EMI America EA 195*	67	1
7 Sep 85	★	DANCING IN THE STREET *EMI America EA 204* [4] ■	1	12
15 Mar 86	●	ABSOLUTE BEGINNERS *Virgin VS 838*	2	9
21 Jun 86		UNDERGROUND *EMI America EA 216*	21	6
8 Nov 86		WHEN THE WIND BLOWS *Virgin VS 906*	44	4
4 Apr 87		DAY-IN DAY-OUT *EMI America EA 230*	17	6
27 Jun 87		TIME WILL CRAWL *EMI America EA 237*	33	4
29 Aug 87		NEVER LET ME DOWN *EMI America EA 239*	34	6
7 Apr 90		FAME (re-mix) *EMI-USA FAME 90*	28	4
22 Aug 92		REAL COOL WORLD *Warner Bros. W 0127*	53	1
27 Mar 93	●	JUMP THEY SAY *Arista 74321139422*	9	6

12 Jun 93		BLACK TIE WHITE NOISE *Arista 74321148682* [5]	36	2
23 Oct 93		MIRACLE GOODNIGHT *Arista 74321162262*	40	2
4 Dec 93		BUDDHA OF SUBURBIA *Arista 74321177052* [6]	35	3
23 Sep 95		THE HEART'S FILTHY LESSON *RCA 74321307032*	35	2
2 Dec 95		STRANGERS WHEN WE MEET/THE MAN WHO SOLD THE WORLD		
		(LIVE) *RCA 74321329402*	39	2
2 Mar 96		HALLO SPACEBOY *RCA 74321353842*	12	4
8 Feb 97		LITTLE WONDER *RCA 74321452072*	14	3
26 Apr 97		DEAD MAN WALKING *RCA 74321475852*	32	2
30 Aug 97		SEVEN YEARS IN TIBET *RCA 74321512542*	61	1
21 Feb 98		I CAN'T READ *Velvet ZYX 87578*	73	1

[1] Queen and David Bowie [2] David Bowie and Bing Crosby [3] David Bowie and the Pat Metheny Group [4] David Bowie and Mick Jagger [5] David Bowie featuring Al B Sure! [6] David Bowie featuring Lenny Kravitz

Tracks on Breaking Glass (EP): Breaking Glass / Art Decade / Ziggy Stardust. All three versions of 'John I'm Only Dancing' are different. Tracks on Baal's Hymn (EP): Baal's Hymn / The Drowned Girl / Remembering Marie / The Dirty Song / Ballad of the Adventurers

George BOWYER *UK, male vocalist* — 2 wks

| 22 Aug 98 | | GUARDIANS OF THE LAND *Boys BYSCD 01* | 33 | 2 |

BOX TOPS ☺ ✎ *US, male vocal/instrumental group* — 33 wks

13 Sep 67	●	THE LETTER *Stateside SS 2044* ▲	5	12
20 Mar 68		CRY LIKE A BABY *Bell 1001*	15	12
23 Aug 69		SOUL DEEP *Bell 1068*	22	9

BOY GEORGE ☺ *UK, male vocalist* — 46 wks

7 Mar 87	★	EVERYTHING I OWN *Virgin BOY 100*	1	9
6 Jun 87		KEEP ME IN MIND *Virgin BOY 101*	29	4
18 Jul 87		SOLD *Virgin BOY 102*	24	5
21 Nov 87		TO BE REBORN *Virgin BOY 103*	13	7
5 Mar 88		LIVE MY LIFE *Virgin BOY 105*	62	2
18 Jun 88		NO CLAUSE 28 *Virgin BOY 106*	57	3
8 Oct 88		DON'T CRY *Virgin BOY 107*	60	2
4 Mar 89		DON'T TAKE MY MIND ON A TRIP *Virgin BOY 108*	68	2
19 Sep 92		THE CRYING GAME *Spaghetti CIAO 6*	22	4
12 Jun 93		MORE THAN LIKELY *Gee Street GESCD 49* [1]	40	3
1 Apr 95		FUNTIME *Virgin VSCDG 1538*	45	2
1 Jul 95		IL ADORE *Virgin VSCDX 1543*	50	2
21 Oct 95		SAME THING IN REVERSE *Virgin VSCDT 1561*	56	1

[1] PM Dawn featuring Boy George

See also CULTURE CLUB

BOY MEETS GIRL ☺ *US, male/female vocal duo* — 13 wks

| 3 Dec 88 | ● | WAITING FOR A STAR TO FALL *RCA PB 49519* | 9 | 13 |

Jimmy BOYD ☾ *US, male vocalist* — 22 wks

8 May 53	●	TELL ME A STORY *Philips PB 126* [1]	5	15
11 Sep 53		TELL ME A STORY (re-entry) *Philips PB 126* [1]	12	1
27 Nov 53	●	I SAW MOMMY KISSING SANTA CLAUS		
		Columbia DB 3365 ▲	3	6

[1] Frankie Laine and Jimmy Boyd

Jacqueline BOYER *France, female vocalist* — 2 wks

| 28 Apr 60 | | TOM PILLIBI *Columbia DB 4452* | 33 | 2 |

BOYS *US, male vocal group* — 5 wks

| 12 Nov 88 | | DIAL MY HEART *Motown ZB 42245* | 61 | 2 |
| 29 Sep 90 | | CRAZY *Motown ZB 44037* | 57 | 3 |

BOYS NEXT DOOR – See June HUTTON and Axel STORDAHL with the BOYS NEXT DOOR

BOYSTOWN GANG ◢ *US, male/female vocal group* — 20 wks

| 22 Aug 81 | | AIN'T NO MOUNTAIN HIGH ENOUGH – REMEMBER ME (MEDLEY) | | |
| | | *WEA DICK 1* | 46 | 6 |

| 31 Jul 82 | ● | CAN'T TAKE MY EYES OFF YOU *ERC 101* | 4 | 11 |
| 9 Oct 82 | | SIGNED SEALED DELIVERED (I'M YOURS) *ERC 102* | 50 | 3 |

BOYZ – See HEAVY D and the BOYZ

BOYZ II MEN ♪ R&B *US, male vocal group* — 81 wks

5 Sep 92	★	END OF THE ROAD *Motown TMG 1411* ▲	1	21
19 Dec 92		MOTOWNPHILLY *Motown TMG 1402*	23	6
27 Feb 93		IN THE STILL OF THE NITE (I'LL REMEMBER)		
		Motown TMGCD 1415	27	4
3 Sep 94	●	I'LL MAKE LOVE TO YOU *Motown TMGCD 1431* ▲	5	12
26 Nov 94		ON BENDED KNEE *Motown TMGCD 1433* ▲	20	3
24 Dec 94		I'LL MAKE LOVE TO YOU (re-entry)*Motown TMGCD 1431*	57	3
22 Apr 95		THANK YOU *Motown TMGCD 1438*	26	3
8 Jul 95		WATER RUNS DRY *Motown TMGCD 1443*	24	3
9 Dec 95	●	ONE SWEET DAY *Columbia 6626035* [1] ▲	6	11
20 Jan 96		HEY LOVER *Def Jam DEFCD 14* [2]	17	4
20 Sep 97		4 SEASONS OF LONELINESS *Motown 8606992* ▲	10	6
6 Dec 97		A SONG FOR MAMA *Motown 8607372*	34	2
25 Jul 98		CAN'T LET HER GO *Motown 8607952*	23	3

[1] Mariah Carey and Boyz II Men [2] LL Cool J featuring Boyz II Men

BOYZONE ☺ *Irish 'boy band' vocal quintet who became international teen idols: Ronan Keating, Stephen Gately, Mikey Graham, Keith Duffy, Shane Lynch. They achieved the best-ever start to a UK singles career with 13 consecutive Top 5 singles* — 143 wks

10 Dec 94	●	LOVE ME FOR A REASON *Polydor 8512802*	2	13
29 Apr 95	●	KEY TO MY LIFE *Polydor PZCD 342*	3	8
12 Aug 95	●	SO GOOD *Polydor 5797732*	3	6
25 Nov 95	●	FATHER AND SON *Polydor 5775762*	2	16
9 Mar 96	●	COMING HOME NOW *Polydor 5775702*	4	9
19 Oct 96	●	WORDS *Polydor 5755372* ■	1	11
14 Dec 96	★	A DIFFERENT BEAT *Polydor 5732052* ■	1	9
1 Mar 97		A DIFFERENT BEAT (re-entry) *Polydor 5732052*	74	1
15 Mar 97		A DIFFERENT BEAT (re-entry) *Polydor 5732052*	62	4
22 Mar 97	●	ISN'T IT A WONDER *Polydor 5735472*	2	7
2 Aug 97	●	PICTURE OF YOU *Polydor 5713112*	2	18
6 Dec 97	●	BABY CAN I HOLD YOU / SHOOTING STAR *Polydor 5691672*	2	14
2 May 98	★	ALL THAT I NEED *Polydor 5698732* ■	1	10
18 Jul 98		ALL THAT I NEED (re-entry) *Polydor 5698732*	49	4
15 Aug 98	●	NO MATTER WHAT *Polydor 5675672* ◆ ■	1	15
5 Dec 98	●	I LOVE THE WAY YOU LOVE ME *Polydor 5631992*	2†	1

BRAD *US, male vocal/instrumental group* — 1 wk

| 26 Jun 93 | | 20TH CENTURY *Epic 6592482* | 64 | 1 |

Scott BRADLEY *UK, male vocalist* — 1 wk

| 15 Oct 94 | | ZOOM *Hidden Agenda HIDDCD 1* | 61 | 1 |

Paul BRADY *UK, male vocalist* — 1 wk

| 13 Jan 96 | | THE WORLD IS WHAT YOU MAKE IT *Mercury PBCD 5* | 67 | 1 |

Billy BRAGG ☺ ✎ *UK, male vocalist* — 51 wks

16 Mar 85		BETWEEN THE WARS (EP) *Go! Discs AGOEP 1*	15	6
28 Dec 85		DAYS LIKE THESE *Go! Discs GOD 8*	43	5
28 Jun 86		LEVI STUBBS TEARS *Go! Discs GOD 12*	29	5
15 Nov 86		GREETINGS TO THE NEW BRUNETTE *Go! Discs GOD 15* [1]	58	2
14 May 88	★	SHE'S LEAVING HOME *Childline CHILD 1* [2]	1	11
10 Sep 88		WAITING FOR THE GREAT LEAP FORWARDS *Go! Discs GOD 23*	52	3
8 Jul 89		WON'T TALK ABOUT IT *Go.Beat GOD 33* [3]	29	4
6 Jul 91		SEXUALITY *Go! Discs GOD 56*	27	5
7 Sep 91		YOU WOKE UP MY NEIGHBOURHOOD *Go! Discs GOD 60*	54	3
29 Feb 92		ACCIDENT WAITING TO HAPPEN (EP) *Go! Discs GOD 67*	33	3
31 Aug 96		UPFIELD *Cooking Vinyl FRYCD 051*	46	1
17 May 97		THE BOY DONE GOOD *Cooking Vinyl FRYCD 064*	55	1

[1] Billy Bragg with Johnny Marr and Kirsty MacColl [2] Billy Bragg with Cara Tivey [3] Norman Cook featuring Billy Bragg

Tracks on Between the Wars (EP): Between the Wars / Which Side Are You On / World Turned Upside Down / It Says Here. Tracks on Accident Waiting to Happen (EP):

UK No 1 ★   UK Top 10 ●   UK million seller ◆   UK entry at No 1 ■   US No 1 ▲

Accident Waiting to Happen / Revolution / Sulk / The Warmest Room. 'She's Leaving Home' was listed with the flip side 'With a Little Help From My Friends' by Wet Wet Wet. 'Won't Talk About It' was listed with the flip side 'Blame It on the Bassline' by Norman Cook featuring MC Wildski

BRAIDS US, female vocal duo   3 wks

2 Nov 96	BOHEMIAN RHAPSODY *Atlantic A 5640CD*	21	3

BRAINBUG ☺ *Italy, male producer: Alberto Bertapelle*   7 wks

3 May 97	NIGHTMARE *Positiva CDTIV 76*	11	5
22 Nov 97	BENEDICTUS/NIGHTMARE *Positiva CDTIV 86*	24	2

Wilfrid BRAMBELL and Harry H. CORBETT
UK, male vocal duo   12 wks

28 Nov 63	AT THE PALACE (PARTS 1 & 2) *Pye 7N 15588*	25	12

Bekka BRAMLETT – See Joe COCKER

BRAN VAN 3000 *Canada, male/female vocal/instrumental group*   2 wks

6 Jun 98	DRINKING IN L.A. *Capitol CDCL 802*	34	2

BRAND NEW HEAVIES 🎤 ☺
UK/US, male/female vocal/instrumental group   63 wks

5 Oct 91	NEVER STOP *ffrr F 165*	43	3
15 Feb 92	DREAM COME TRUE *ffrr F 180*	24	4
18 Apr 92	ULTIMATE TRUNK FUNK EP *ffrr F 185*	19	6
1 Aug 92	DON'T LET IT GO TO YOUR HEAD *ffrr BNH 1*	24	4
19 Dec 92	STAY THIS WAY *ffrr BNH 2*	40	5
26 Mar 94	DREAM ON DREAMER *ffrr BNHCD 3*	15	4
11 Jun 94	BACK TO LOVE *ffrr BNHCD 4*	23	4
13 Aug 94	MIDNIGHT AT THE OASIS *ffrr BNHCD 5*	13	6
5 Nov 94	SPEND SOME TIME *ffrr BNHCD 6*	26	4
11 Mar 95	CLOSE TO YOU *ffrr BNHCD 7*	38	3
12 Apr 97	SOMETIMES *ffrr BNHCD 8*	11	5
28 Jun 97	YOU ARE THE UNIVERSE *ffrr GNHCD 9*	21	3
18 Oct 97	YOU'VE GOT A FRIEND *London BNHCD 10*	9	8
10 Jan 98	SHELTER *London BNHCD 11*	31	4

All the above hits are credited 'featuring N'Dea Davenport' on either the sleeve or the label. Tracks on Ultimate Trunk Funk EP: Never Stop / Stay This Way / Mr Tanaka. BNH 2 is a re-mixed version of the track on the Ultimate Trunk Funk EP

Johnny BRANDON Ⓒ *UK, male vocalist*   12 wks

11 Mar 55 ●	TOMORROW *Polygon P 1131* [1]	8	6
29 Apr 55	TOMORROW (re-entry) *Polygon P 1131* [1]	16	2
1 Jul 55	DON'T WORRY *Polygon P 1163*	18	4

[1] Johnny Brandon and the Phantoms

BRANDY (R&B) *US, female vocalist*   41 wks

10 Dec 94	I WANNA BE DOWN *Atlantic A7217CD*	44	3
3 Jun 95	I WANNA BE DOWN (re-mix) *Atlantic A 7186CD*	36	3
3 Feb 96	SITTIN' UP IN MY ROOM *Arista 74321344012*	30	4
6 Jun 98 ●	THE BOY IS MINE *Atlantic AT 0036CD* [1] ▲	2	20
10 Oct 98	TOP OF THE WORLD *Atlantic AT00 46CD* [2]	2	8
12 Dec 98	HAVE YOU EVER? *Atlantic AT 0058CD*	13†	3

[1] Brandy and Monica [2] Brandy featuring Mase

Laura BRANIGAN ◉ *US, female vocalist*   33 wks

18 Dec 82 ●	GLORIA *Atlantic K 11759*	6	13
7 Jul 84 ●	SELF CONTROL *Atlantic A 9676*	5	17
6 Oct 84	THE LUCKY ONE *Atlantic A 9636*	56	3

BRASS CONSTRUCTION *US, male vocal/instrumental group*   35 wks

3 Apr 76	MOVIN' *United Artists UP 36090*	23	6
5 Feb 77	HA CHA CHA (FUNKTION) *United Artists UP 36205*	37	5
26 Jan 80	MUSIC MAKES YOU FEEL LIKE DANCING *United Artists UP 615*	39	6
28 May 83	WALKIN' THE LINE *Capitol CL 292*	47	3
16 Jul 83	WE CAN WORK IT OUT *Capitol CL 299*	70	2

7 Jul 84	PARTYLINE *Capitol CL 335*	56	4
27 Oct 84	INTERNATIONAL *Capitol CL 341*	70	2
9 Nov 85	GIVE AND TAKE *Capitol CL 377*	62	3
28 May 88	MOVIN' 1988 (re-mix) *Syncopate SY 11*	24	4

BRAT ◉ *UK, male vocalist – Roger Kitter*   8 wks

10 Jul 82	CHALK DUST – THE UMPIRE STRIKES BACK *Hansa SMASH 1*	19	8

BRAVADO *UK, male/female vocal/instrumental group*   3 wks

18 Jun 94	HARMONICA MAN *Peach PEACHCD 5*	37	3

BRAVO ALL STARS
UK/US, male/female vocal/instrumental group   2 wks

29 Aug 98	LET THE MUSIC HEAL YOUR SOUL *Edel 0039335 ERE*	36	2

Artists featured: Backstreet Boys, Aaron Carter, Scooter, 'N Sync, Caught in the Act, The Boyz, Blumchen, Gil, Squeezer, Mr President, Touche, R'N'G and the Moffatts

Dhar BRAXTON *US, female vocalist*   8 wks

31 May 86	JUMP BACK (SET ME FREE) *Fourth & Broadway BRW 47*	32	8

Toni BRAXTON 🎤 (R&B) *US, female vocalist*   72 wks

18 Sep 93	ANOTHER SAD LOVE SONG *LaFace 74321163502*	51	2
15 Jan 94 ●	BREATHE AGAIN *LaFace 74321185442*	2	12
2 Apr 94	ANOTHER SAD LOVE SONG (re-issue) *LaFace 74321196682*	15	8
9 Jul 94	YOU MEAN THE WORLD TO ME *LaFace 74321214702*	30	5
3 Dec 94	LOVE SHOULDA BROUGHT YOU HOME *LaFace 74321249412*	33	3
13 Jul 96 ●	YOU'RE MAKIN' ME HIGH *LaFace 74321395402* ▲	7	11
2 Nov 96 ●	UN-BREAK MY HEART *LaFace 74321410632* ▲	2	19
24 May 97	I DON'T WANT TO *LaFace 74321468612*	9	8
8 Nov 97	HOW COULD AN ANGEL BREAK MY HEART *LaFace 74321531982* [1]	22	4

[1] Toni Braxton with Kenny G

BRAXTONS *US, female vocal group*   7 wks

1 Feb 97	SO MANY WAYS *Atlantic A 5469CD*	32	2
29 Mar 97	THE BOSS *Atlantic A 5441CD*	31	3
26 Jul 97	SLOW FLOW *Atlantic AT 0001CD*	26	2

BREAD ◉ *US, male vocal/instrumental group*   46 wks

1 Aug 70 ●	MAKE IT WITH YOU *Elektra 2101 010* ▲	5	14
15 Jan 72	BABY I'M A WANT YOU *Elektra K 12033*	14	10
29 Apr 72	EVERYTHING I OWN *Elektra K 12041*	32	6
30 Sep 72	THE GUITAR MAN *Elektra K 12066*	16	9
25 Dec 76	LOST WITHOUT YOUR LOVE *Elektra K 12241*	27	7

BREAK MACHINE ◉ ☺ *US, male vocal/dance group*   32 wks

4 Feb 84 ●	STREET DANCE *Record Shack SOHO 13*	3	14
12 May 84 ●	BREAKDANCE PARTY *Record Shack SOHO 20*	9	8
14 Jul 84	BREAKDANCE PARTY (re-entry) *Record Shack SOHO 20*	65	2
11 Aug 84	ARE YOU READY? *Record Shack SOHO 24*	27	8

BREAKBEAT ERA *UK, male/female drum and bass trio*   2 wks

18 Jul 98	BREAKBEAT ERA *XL Recordings XLS 95CD*	38	2

BREAKFAST CLUB *US, male vocal/instrumental group*   3 wks

27 Jun 87	RIGHT ON TRACK *MCA MCA 1146*	54	3

BREATHE ◉ *UK, male vocal/instrumental group*   27 wks

30 Jul 88 ●	HANDS TO HEAVEN *Siren SRN 68*	4	12
22 Oct 88	JONAH *Siren SRN 95*	60	3
3 Dec 88	HOW CAN I FALL *Siren SRN 102*	48	7
11 Mar 89	DON'T TELL ME LIES *Siren SRN 109*	45	5

Freddy BRECK *Germany, male vocalist*   4 wks

13 Apr 74	SO IN LOVE WITH YOU *Decca F 13481*	44	4

BRECKER BROTHERS US, male vocal/instrumental group — 5 wks

4 Nov 78	EAST RIVER Arista ARIST 211	34	5

BREEDERS US/UK, female/male vocal/instrumental group — 6 wks

18 Apr 92	SAFARI (EP) 4AD BAD 2003	69	1
21 Aug 93	CANNONBALL (EP) 4AD BAD 3011CD	40	3
6 Nov 93	DIVINE HAMMER 4AD BAD 3017CD	59	1
23 Jul 94	HEAD TO TOE (EP) 4AD BADD 4012	68	1

Tracks on Safari (EP): Do You Love Me Now/Don't Call Home/Safari/So Sad About Us. Tracks on Cannonball (EP): Cannonball/Cro-Aloha/Lord of the Thighs/900. Tracks on Head to Toe (EP): Head to Toe/Shocker In Gloom Town/Freed Pig

BREEKOUT KREW US, male vocal duo — 3 wks

24 Nov 84	MATT'S MOOD London LON 59	51	3

Ann BREEN Ireland, female vocalist — 2 wks

19 Mar 83	PAL OF MY CRADLE DAYS Homespun HS 052	69	1
7 Jan 84	PAL OF MY CRADLE DAYS (re-entry) Homespun HS 052	74	1

BRENDON ♪ UK, male vocalist — 9 wks

19 Mar 77	GIMME SOME Magnet MAG 80	14	9

Maire BRENNAN Ireland, female vocalist — 2 wks

16 May 92	AGAINST THE WIND RCA PB 45399	64	2

Rose BRENNAN Ireland, female vocalist — 9 wks

7 Dec 61	TALL DARK STRANGER Philips PB 1193	31	9

Walter BRENNAN US, male vocalist — 3 wks

28 Jun 62	OLD RIVERS Liberty LIB 55436	38	3

Tony BRENT © UK, male vocalist — 52 wks

19 Dec 52	● WALKIN' TO MISSOURI Columbia DB 3147	9	2
2 Jan 53	● MAKE IT SOON Columbia DB 3187	9	4
9 Jan 53	● WALKIN' TO MISSOURI (re-entry) Columbia DB 3147	7	5
23 Jan 53	GOT YOU ON MY MIND Columbia DB 3226	12	1
13 Mar 53	● MAKE IT SOON (re-entry) Columbia DB 3187	9	3
30 Nov 56	CINDY OH CINDY Columbia DB 3844	16	6
8 Feb 57	CINDY OH CINDY (re-entry) Columbia DB 3844	30	1
28 Jun 57	DARK MOON Columbia DB 3950	17	14
28 Feb 58	THE CLOUDS WILL SOON ROLL BY Columbia DB 4066	24	3
9 May 58	THE CLOUDS WILL SOON ROLL BY (re-entry) Columbia DB 4066	20	2
5 Sep 58	GIRL OF MY DREAMS Columbia DB 4177	16	7
24 Jul 59	WHY SHOULD I BE LONELY Columbia DB 4304	24	4

Bernard BRESSLAW © UK, male vocalist — 11 wks

5 Sep 58	● MAD PASSIONATE LOVE HMV POP 522	6	11

See also Michael MEDWIN, Bernard BRESSLAW, Alfie BASS and Leslie FYSON

Teresa BREWER © US, female vocalist — 53 wks

11 Feb 55	● LET ME GO LOVER Vogue/Coral Q 72043	9	10
13 Apr 56	● A TEAR FELL Vogue/Coral Q 72146	2	15
13 Jul 56	● SWEET OLD-FASHIONED GIRL Vogue/Coral Q 72172	3	15
10 May 57	NORA MALONE Vogue/Coral Q 72224	26	2
23 Jun 60	HOW DO YOU KNOW IT'S LOVE Coral Q 72396	21	11

BRIAN and MICHAEL © UK, male vocal duo — 19 wks

25 Feb 78	★ MATCHSTALK MEN AND MATCHSTALK CATS AND DOGS Pye 7N 46035	1	19

BRICK US, male vocal/instrumental group — 4 wks

5 Feb 77	DAZZ Bang 004	36	4

Edie BRICKELL and the NEW BOHEMIANS
US, female/male vocal/instrumental group — 10 wks

4 Feb 89	WHAT I AM Geffen GEF 49	31	7
27 May 89	CIRCLE Geffen GEF 51	74	1
1 Oct 94	GOOD TIMES Geffen GFSTD 78 [1]	40	2

[1] Edie Brickell

Alicia BRIDGES US, female vocalist — 11 wks

11 Nov 78	I LOVE THE NIGHT LIFE (DISCO ROUND) Polydor 2066 936	32	10
8 Oct 94	I LOVE THE NIGHT LIFE (DISCO ROUND) (re-mix) Mother MUMCD 57	61	1

Johnny BRIGGS – See Amanda BARRIE and Johnny BRIGGS

BRIGHOUSE AND RASTRICK BRASS BAND ©
UK, male brass band — 13 wks

12 Nov 77	● THE FLORAL DANCE Transatlantic BIG 548	2	13

Bette BRIGHT UK, female vocalist — 5 wks

8 Mar 80	HELLO I AM YOUR HEART Korova KOW 3	50	5

Sarah BRIGHTMAN © ♪ UK, female vocalist — 95 wks

11 Nov 78	● I LOST MY HEART TO A STARSHIP TROOPER Ariola/Hansa AHA 527 [1]	6	14
7 Apr 79	THE ADVENTURES OF THE LOVE CRUSADER Ariola/Hansa AHA 538 [2]	53	5
30 Jul 83	HIM Polydor POSP 625 [3]	55	4
23 Mar 85	● PIE JESU HMV WEBBER 1 [4]	3	8
11 Jan 86	● THE PHANTOM OF THE OPERA Polydor POSP 800 [5]	7	10
4 Oct 86	● ALL I ASK OF YOU Polydor POSP 802 [6]	3	16
10 Jan 87	● WISHING YOU WERE SOMEHOW HERE AGAIN Polydor POSP 803	7	11
11 Jul 92	AMIGOS PARA SIEMPRE (FRIENDS FOR LIFE) Really Useful RUR 10 [7]	11	11
24 May 97	● TIME TO SAY GOODBYE (CON TE PARTIRO) Coalition COLA 003CD [8]	2	14
23 Aug 97	WHO WANTS TO LIVE FOREVER Coalition COLA 014CD [9]	45	1
6 Dec 97	JUST SHOW ME HOW TO LOVE YOU Coalition COLA 035CD [9]	45	1
14 Feb 98	STARSHIP TROOPERS Coalition COLA 040CD [10]	58	1

[1] Sarah Brightman and Hot Gossip [2] Sarah Brightman and the Starship Troopers [3] Sarah Brightman and the Royal Philharmonic Orchestra [4] Sarah Brightman and Paul Miles-Kingston [5] Sarah Brightman and Steve Harley [6] Cliff Richard and Sarah Brightman [7] Jose Carreras and Sarah Brightman [8] Sarah Brightman and Andrea Bocelli [9] Sarah Brightman & the LSO featuring Jose Cura [10] United Citizen Federation featuring Sarah Brightman

The listed flip side of 'Wishing You Were Somehow Here Again' was 'The Music of the Night' by Michael Crawford. COLA 040CD is a dance re-mix of AHA 527

BRIGHTON AND HOVE ALBION F.C.
UK, male football-team vocalists — 2 wks

28 May 83	THE BOYS IN THE OLD BRIGHTON BLUE Energy NRG 2	65	2

BRILLIANT UK, male/female vocal/instrumental group — 13 wks

19 Oct 85	IT'S A MAN'S MAN'S MAN'S WORLD Food FOOD 5	58	5
22 Mar 86	LOVE IS WAR Food FOOD 6	64	4
2 Aug 86	SOMEBODY Food FOOD 7	67	4

Danielle BRISEBOIS US, female vocalist — 1 wk

9 Sep 95	GIMME LITTLE SIGN Epic 6610782	75	1

Johnny BRISTOL ♪ US, male vocalist — 16 wks

24 Aug 74	● HANG ON IN THERE BABY MGM 2006 443	3	11
19 Jul 80	MY GUY – MY GIRL (MEDLEY) Atlantic/Hansa K 11550 [1]	39	5

[1] Amii Stewart and Johnny Bristol

BRITS – See VARIOUS ARTISTS (MONTAGES)

UK No 1 ★   UK Top 10 ●   UK million seller ◆   UK entry at No 1 ■   US No 1 ▲

BROCK LANDARS *UK, male vocal/production duo* — 2 wks

11 Jul 98		SMDU *Parlophone CDBLUE 001*	49	2

BROKEN ENGLISH ☺ ✎ *UK, male vocal/instrumental group* — 13 wks

30 May 87		COMIN' ON STRONG *EMI EM 5*	18	10
3 Oct 87		LOVE ON THE SIDE *EMI EM 55*	69	3

BRONSKI BEAT ☺ *UK, male vocal/instrumental group* — 78 wks

2 Jun 84	●	SMALLTOWN BOY *Forbidden Fruit BITE 1*	3	13
22 Sep 84	●	WHY? *Forbidden Fruit BITE 2*	6	10
1 Dec 84		IT AIN'T NECESSARILY SO *Forbidden Fruit BITE 3*	16	11
20 Apr 85	●	I FEEL LOVE (MEDLEY) *Forbidden Fruit BITE 4* 1	3	12
30 Nov 85	●	HIT THAT PERFECT BEAT *Forbidden Fruit BITE 6*	3	14
29 Mar 86		COME ON, COME ON *Forbidden Fruit BITE 7*	20	7
1 Jul 89		CHA CHA HEELS *Arista 112331* 2	32	7
2 Feb 91		SMALLTOWN BOY (re-mix) *London LON 287* 3	32	4

1 Bronski Beat and Marc Almond 2 Eartha Kitt and Bronski Beat 3 Jimmy Somerville with Bronski Beat

Tracks on medley: I Feel Love/Love to Love You Baby/Johnny Remember Me

Jet BRONX and the FORBIDDEN
UK, male vocal/instrumental group — 1 wk

17 Dec 77		AIN'T DOIN' NOTHIN' *Lightning LIG 50*	49	1

BROOK BROTHERS ✎ *UK, male vocal duo* — 35 wks

30 Mar 61	●	WARPAINT *Pye 7N 15333*	5	14
24 Aug 61		AIN'T GONNA WASH FOR A WEEK *Pye 7N 15369*	13	10
25 Jan 62		HE'S OLD ENOUGH TO KNOW BETTER *Pye 7N 15409*	37	1
16 Aug 62		WELCOME HOME BABY *Pye 7N 15453*	33	6
21 Feb 63		TROUBLE IS MY MIDDLE NAME *Pye 7N 15498*	38	4

Bruno BROOKES – See Liz KERSHAW and Bruno BROOKES

BROOKLYN BOUNCE *Germany, male production duo, and male/female vocal/industrial group* — 1 wk

30 May 98		THE MUSIC'S GOT ME *Club Tools 0064795 CLU*	67	1

BROOKLYN, BRONX and QUEENS – See B B and Q Band

Elkie BROOKS ☺ ✎ *UK, female vocalist* — 91 wks

2 Apr 77	●	PEARL'S A SINGER *A & M AMS 7275*	8	9
20 Aug 77	●	SUNSHINE AFTER THE RAIN *A & M AMS 7306*	10	9
25 Feb 78		LILAC WINE *A & M AMS 7333*	16	7
3 Jun 78		ONLY LOVE CAN BREAK YOUR HEART *A & M AMS 7353*	43	5
11 Nov 78		DON'T CRY OUT LOUD *A & M AMS 7395*	12	11
5 May 79		THE RUNAWAY *A & M AMS 7428*	50	5
16 Jan 82		FOOL IF YOU THINK IT'S OVER *A & M AMS 8187*	17	10
1 May 82		OUR LOVE *A & M AMS 8214*	43	5
17 Jul 82		NIGHTS IN WHITE SATIN *A & M AMS 8235*	33	5
22 Jan 83		GASOLINE ALLEY *A & M AMS 8305*	52	5
22 Nov 86	●	NO MORE THE FOOL *Legend LM 4*	5	16
4 Apr 87		BREAK THE CHAIN *Legend LM 8*	55	3
11 Jul 87		WE'VE GOT TONIGHT *Legend LM 9*	69	1

Garth BROOKS ⚓ *US, male vocalist* — 14 wks

1 Feb 92		SHAMELESS *Capitol CL 646*	71	1
22 Jan 94		THE RED STROKES/AIN'T GOING DOWN *Liberty CDCLS 704*	13	5
16 Apr 94		STANDING OUTSIDE THE FIRE *Liberty CDCL 712*	28	4
18 Feb 95		THE DANCE/FRIENDS IN LOW PLACES *Capitol CDCL 735*	36	3
17 Feb 96		SHE'S EVERY WOMAN *Capitol CDCL 767*	55	1

Mel BROOKS ☺ *US, male vocalist* — 10 wks

18 Feb 84		TO BE OR NOT TO BE (THE HITLER RAP) *Island IS 158*	12	10

Meredith BROOKS ☺ ✎ *US, female vocal/instrumentalist* — 13 wks

2 Aug 97	●	BITCH *Capital CDCL 790*	6	10
6 Dec 97		I NEED *Capital CDCLS 794*	28	2
7 Mar 98		WHAT WOULD HAPPEN *Capital CDCL 798*	49	1

Norman BROOKS ℂ *US, male vocalist* — 1 wk

12 Nov 54		A SKY BLUE SHIRT AND A RAINBOW TIE *London L 1228*	17	1

BROS ☺ *UK, male vocal/instrumental group* — 84 wks

5 Dec 87		WHEN WILL I BE FAMOUS *CBS ATOM 2*	62	2
9 Jan 88	●	WHEN WILL I BE FAMOUS (re-entry) *CBS ATOM 2*	2	13
19 Mar 88	●	DROP THE BOY *CBS ATOM 3*	2	10
18 Jun 88	★	I OWE YOU NOTHING *CBS ATOM 4*	1	11
17 Sep 88	●	I QUIT *CBS ATOM 5*	4	8
3 Dec 88	●	CAT AMONG THE PIGEONS/SILENT NIGHT *CBS ATOM 6*	2	8
29 Jul 89	●	TOO MUCH *CBS ATOM 7*	2	7
7 Oct 89	●	CHOCOLATE BOX *CBS ATOM 8*	9	6
16 Dec 89	●	SISTER *CBS ATOM 9*	10	6
10 Mar 90		MADLY IN LOVE *CBS ATOM 10*	14	4
13 Jul 91		ARE YOU MINE *Columbia 6569707*	12	5
21 Sep 91		TRY *Columbia 6574047*	27	4

Act was duo for last six hits

BROTHER BEYOND ☺ *UK, male vocal/instrumental group* — 58 wks

4 Apr 87		HOW MANY TIMES *EMI EMI 5591*	62	3
8 Aug 87		CHAIN-GANG SMILE *Parlophone R 6160*	57	3
23 Jan 88		CAN YOU KEEP A SECRET *Parlophone R 6174*	56	4
30 Jul 88	●	THE HARDER I TRY *Parlophone R 6193*	2	14
5 Nov 88	●	HE AIN'T NO COMPETITION *Parlophone R 6193*	6	10
21 Jan 89		BE MY TWIN *Parlophone R 6195*	14	6
1 Apr 89		CAN YOU KEEP A SECRET (re-mix) *Parlophone R 6197*	22	5
28 Oct 89		DRIVE ON *Parlophone R 6233*	39	4
9 Dec 89		WHEN WILL I SEE YOU AGAIN *Parlophone R 6239*	43	5
10 Apr 90		TRUST *Parlophone R 6245*	53	2
19 Jan 91		THE GIRL I USED TO KNOW *Parlophone R 6265*	48	2

BROTHER LOVE – See PRATT and McCLAIN with BROTHERLOVE

BROTHERHOOD *UK, male rap group* — 1 wk

27 Jan 96		ONE SHOT/NOTHING IN PARTICULAR *Bite It BHOODD 3*	55	1

BROTHERHOOD OF MAN ☺ *UK, male/female vocal group* — 97 wks

14 Feb 70	●	UNITED WE STAND *Deram DM 284*	10	9
4 Jul 70		WHERE ARE YOU GOING TO MY LOVE *Deram DM 298*	22	10
13 Mar 76	★	SAVE YOUR KISSES FOR ME *Pye 7N 45569* ◆	1	16
19 Jun 76		MY SWEET ROSALIE *Pye 7N 45602*	30	7
26 Feb 77	●	OH BOY (THE MOOD I'M IN) *Pye 7N 45656*	8	12
9 Jul 77	★	ANGELO *Pye 7N 45689*	1	12
14 Jan 78	★	FIGARO *Pye 7N 46037*	1	11
27 May 78		BEAUTIFUL LOVER *Pye 7N 46071*	15	12
30 Sep 78		MIDDLE OF THE NIGHT *Pye 7N 46117*	41	6
3 Jul 82		LIGHTNING FLASH *EMI 5309*	67	2

BROTHERS ☺ *UK, male vocal group* — 9 wks

29 Jan 77	●	SING ME *Bus Stop Bus 1054*	8	9

BROTHERS FOUR *US, male vocal group* — 2 wks

23 Jun 60		GREENFIELDS *Philips PB 1009*	49	1
7 Jul 60		GREENFIELDS (re-entry) *Philips PB 1009*	40	1

BROTHERS GRIMM – See JAZZ and the BROTHERS GRIMM

BROTHERS IN RHYTHM ☺
UK, male instrumental/production duo — 12 wks

16 Mar 91		SUCH A GOOD FEELING *Fourth & Broadway BRW 228*	64	2
14 Sep 91		SUCH A GOOD FEELING (re-issue) *Fourth & Broadway BRW 228 210*	14	8

UK No 1 ★   UK Top 10 ●   UK million seller ◆   UK entry at No 1 ■   US No 1 ▲

123

| 30 Apr 94 | FOREVER AND A DAY *Stress CDSTR 36* [1] | 51 | 2 |

[1] Brothers in Rhythm present Charvoni

BROTHERS JOHNSON ✏ ♥ *US, male vocal/instrumental duo* — 34 wks

9 Jul 77	STRAWBERRY LETTER 23 *A & M AMS 7297*	35	5
2 Sep 78	AIN'T WE FUNKIN' NOW *A & M AMS 7379*	43	6
4 Nov 78	RIDE-O-ROCKET *A & M AMS 7400*	50	4
23 Feb 80	● STOMP *A & M AMS 7509*	6	12
31 May 80	LIGHT UP THE NIGHT *A & M AMS 7526*	47	4
25 Jul 81	THE REAL THING *A & M AMS 8149*	50	3

BROTHERS LIKE OUTLAW featuring Alison EVELYN
UK, male/female vocal group — 1 wk

| 23 Jan 93 | GOOD VIBRATIONS *Gee Street GESCD 44* | 74 | 1 |

Edgar BROUGHTON BAND *UK, male vocal/instrumental group* 10 wks

18 Apr 70	OUT DEMONS OUT *Harvest HAR 5015*	39	5
23 Jan 71	APACHE DROPOUT *Harvest HAR 5032*	49	1
6 Feb 71	APACHE DROPOUT (re-entry) *Harvest HAR 5032*	35	2
13 Mar 71	APACHE DROPOUT (2nd re-entry) *Harvest HAR 5032*	35	1
27 Mar 71	APACHE DROPOUT (3rd re-entry) *Harvest HAR 5032*	33	1

Alison BROWN – See BAR CODES featuring Alison BROWN

Angie BROWN – See BIZARRE INC; MOTIV 8

Crazy World of Arthur BROWN ✏
UK, male vocal/instrumental group — 14 wks

| 26 Jun 68 | ★ FIRE *Track 604 022* | 1 | 14 |

Bobby BROWN [R&B] ☺
Swingbeat superstar, b. 5 February, 1969, Massachusetts, who married Whitney Houston in 1992. This energetic entertainer has seen several of his hits chart again when re-mixed. He joined a re-formed New Edition in 1996, the vocal group in which he topped the chart with 'Candy Girl' at the age of 14 — 123 wks

6 Aug 88	DON'T BE CRUEL *MCA MCA 1268*	42	7
17 Dec 88	● MY PREROGATIVE *MCA MCA 1299* ▲	6	17
25 Mar 89	DON'T BE CRUEL (re-issue) *MCA MCA 1310*	13	8
20 May 89	● EVERY LITTLE STEP *MCA MCA 1338*	6	9
15 Jul 89	● ON OUR OWN (FROM GHOSTBUSTERS II) *MCA MCA 1350*	4	9
23 Sep 89	ROCK WIT'CHA *MCA MCA 1367*	33	6
25 Nov 89	RONI *MCA MCA 1384*	21	7
9 Jun 90	THE FREE STYLE MEGA-MIX *MCA MCA 1421*	14	7
30 Jun 90	SHE AIN'T WORTH IT *London LON 265* [1] ▲	12	9
22 Aug 92	HUMPIN' AROUND *MCA MCS 1680*	19	6
17 Oct 92	GOOD ENOUGH *MCA MCS 1704*	41	4
19 Jun 93	THAT'S THE WAY LOVE IS *MCA MCSTD 1783*	56	2
22 Jan 94	SOMETHING IN COMMON *MCA MCSTD 1957* [2]	16	5
25 Jun 94	TWO CAN PLAY THAT GAME *MCA MCSTD 1973*	38	3
1 Apr 95	● TWO CAN PLAY THAT GAME (re-entry) *MCA MCSTD 1973*	3	12
8 Jul 95	● HUMPIN' AROUND (re-mix) *MCA MCSTD 2073*	8	6
14 Oct 95	MY PREROGATIVE (re-mix) *MCA MCSTD 2094*	17	3
3 Feb 96	EVERY LITTLE STEP (re-mix) *MCA MCSTD 48004*	25	2
22 Nov 97	FEELIN' INSIDE *MCA MCSTD 48067*	40	1

[1] Glenn Medeiros featuring Bobby Brown [2] Bobby Brown and Whitney Houston

Carl BROWN – See DOUBLE TROUBLE

Dennis BROWN ▽ *Jamaica, male vocalist* — 18 wks

3 Mar 79	MONEY IN MY POCKET *Lightning LV 5*	14	9
3 Jul 82	LOVE HAS FOUND ITS WAY *A & M AMS 8226*	47	6
11 Sep 82	HALFWAY UP HALFWAY DOWN *A & M AMS 8250*	56	3

Diana BROWN and Barrie K. SHARPE
UK, female/male vocal duo — 11 wks

| 2 Jun 90 | THE MASTERPLAN *ffrr F 133* | 39 | 6 |
| 1 Sep 90 | SUN WORSHIPPERS (POSITIVE THINKING) *ffrr F 144* | 61 | 2 |

| 23 Mar 91 | LOVE OR NOTHING *ffrr F 152* | 71 | 1 |
| 27 Jun 92 | EATING ME ALIVE *ffrr F 190* | 53 | 2 |

Errol BROWN ☺ ◢ *UK, male vocalist* — 13 wks

4 Jul 87	PERSONAL TOUCH *WEA YZ 130*	25	8
28 Nov 87	BODY ROCKIN' *WEA YZ 162*	51	2
14 Feb 98	IT STARTED WITH A KISS *EMI CDHOT 101* [1]	18	3

[1] Hot Chocolate featuring Errol Brown

Foxy BROWN 🔙 [R&B] *US, female rapper* — 20 wks

21 Sep 96	TOUCH ME TEASE ME *Def Jam DEFCD 18* [1]	26	3
8 Mar 97	GET ME HOME *Def Jam DEFCD 32* [2]	11	5
10 May 97	AIN'T NO PLAYA *Northwestside 74321474842* [3]	31	2
21 Jun 97	● I'LL BE *Def Jam 5710432* [4]	9	5
11 Oct 97	BIG BAD MAMMA *Def Jam 5749792* [5]	12	3
25 Oct 97	SUNSHINE *Northwestside 74321528702* [6]	25	2

[1] Case featuring Foxy Brown [2] Foxy Brown featuring Blackstreet [3] Jay-Z featuring Foxy Brown [4] Foxy Brown featuring Jay-Z [5] Foxy Brown featuring Dru Hill [6] Jay-Z featuring Babyface and Foxy Brown

Gloria D. BROWN *US, female vocalist* — 3 wks

| 8 Jun 85 | THE MORE THEY KNOCK, THE MORE I LOVE YOU *10 TEN 52* | 57 | 3 |

Horace BROWN [R&B] *US, male vocalist* — 7 wks

25 Feb 95	TASTE YOUR LOVE *Uptown MCSTD 2026*	58	1
18 May 96	ONE FOR THE MONEY *Motown 8605232*	12	4
12 Oct 96	THINGS WE DO FOR LOVE *Motown 8605712*	27	2

Ian BROWN ☹ *UK, male vocal/instrumentalist* — 11 wks

24 Jan 98	● MY STAR *Polydor 5719872*	5	4
4 Apr 98	CORPSES *Polydor 5696552*	14	4
20 Jun 98	CAN'T SEE ME *Polydor 5440452*	21	3

James BROWN ✏ ♥
'Soul Brother No 1', b. 3 May, 1933, South Carolina. The most charted R&B performer of all time has influenced numerous musical styles since the mid-1950s. This multi-award-winning entertainer's act has inspired countless performers down through the years, including Michael Jackson, Prince and Mick Jagger — 101 wks

23 Sep 65	PAPA'S GOT A BRAND NEW BAG *London HL 9990* [1]	25	7
24 Feb 66	I GOT YOU *Pye International 7N 25350* [1]	29	6
16 Jun 66	IT'S A MAN'S MAN'S MAN'S WORLD *Pye International 7N 25371* [1]	13	9
10 Oct 70	GET UP I FEEL LIKE BEING A SEX MACHINE *Polydor 2001 071*	32	7
27 Nov 71	HEY AMERICA *Mojo 2093 006*	47	3
18 Sep 76	GET UP OFFA THAT THING *Polydor 2066 687*	22	6
29 Jan 77	BODY HEAT *Polydor 2066 763*	36	4
10 Jan 81	RAPP PAYBACK (WHERE IZ MOSES?) *RCA 28*	39	5
2 Jul 83	BRING IT ON . . . BRING IT ON *Sonet SON 2258*	45	4
1 Sep 84	UNITY (PART 1 – THE THIRD COMING) *Tommy Boy AFR 2*	49	5
27 Apr 85	FROGGY MIX *Boiling Point FROG 1*	50	3
1 Jun 85	GET UP I FEEL LIKE BEING A SEX MACHINE (re-issue) *Boiling Point POSP 751*	47	5
25 Jan 86	● LIVING IN AMERICA *Scotti Brothers A 6701*	5	10
1 Mar 86	GET UP I FEEL LIKE BEING A SEX MACHINE (re-entry of re-issue) *Boiling Point POSP 751*	46	4
18 Oct 86	GRAVITY *Scotti Brothers 650059 7*	65	2
30 Jan 88	SHE'S THE ONE *Urban URB 13*	45	3
23 Apr 88	THE PAYBACK MIX *Urban URB 17*	12	6
4 Jun 88	I'M REAL *Scotti Brothers JSB 1* [3]	31	4
23 Jul 88	I GOT YOU (I FEEL GOOD) (re-issue) *A & M AM 444*	52	3
16 Nov 91	GET UP (I FEEL LIKE BEING A) SEX MACHINE (2nd re-issue) *Polydor PO 185*	69	2
24 Oct 92	I GOT YOU (I FEEL GOOD) (re-mix) *FBI FBI 9* [4]	72	1
17 Apr 93	CAN'T GET ANY HARDER *Polydor PZCD 262*	59	2

[1] James Brown and The Famous Flames [2] Afrika Bambaataa and James Brown

'Froggy Mix' is a medley of twelve James Brown songs. The listed flip side of 'I Got You (I Feel Good)' was 'Nowhere to Run' by Martha Reeves and the Vandellas

Joanne BROWN – See Tony OSBORNE SOUND

Jocelyn BROWN ☺ 🎤 *US, female vocalist*　　　62 wks

21 Apr 84	SOMEBODY ELSE'S GUY *Fourth & Broadway BRW 5*	13	9
22 Sep 84	I WISH YOU WOULD *Fourth & Broadway BRW 14*	51	3
15 Mar 86	LOVE'S GONNA GET YOU *Warner Bros. W 8889*	70	1
29 Jun 91 ●	ALWAYS THERE *Talkin Loud TLK 10* 1	6	9
14 Sep 91	SHE GOT SOUL *A & M AM 819* 2	57	3
7 Dec 91 ●	DON'T TALK JUST KISS *Tug SNOG 2* 3	3	11
20 Mar 93	TAKE ME UP *A & M AMCD 210* 4	61	1
11 Jun 94	NO MORE TEARS (ENOUGH IS ENOUGH) *Ding Dong 74321209032* 5	13	7
8 Oct 94	GIMME ALL YOUR LOVIN' *Ding Dong 74321231322* 5	22	3
13 Jul 96 ●	KEEP ON JUMPIN' *Manifesto FESCD 11* 6	8	6
10 May 97	IT'S ALRIGHT, I FEEL IT! *Talkin Loud TLCD 22* 8	26	2
25 Oct 97	I AM THE BLACK GOLD OF THE SUN *Talkin Loud TLCD 26* 8	31	2
22 Nov 97	HAPPINESS *Sony S3 KAMCD 2* 7	45	1
2 May 98	FUN *INCcredible INCRL 2CD* 9	33	2
29 Aug 98	AIN'T NO MOUNTAIN HIGH ENOUGH *INCcredible INCRL 7CD*	35	2

1 Incognito featuring Jocelyn Brown 2 Jamestown featuring Jocelyn Brown
3 Right Said Fred. Guest vocals: Jocelyn Brown 4 Sonic Surfers featuring Jocelyn Brown 5 Jocelyn Brown and Kym Mazelle 6 Todd Terry featuring Martha Wash and Jocelyn Brown 7 Kamasutra featuring Jocelyn Brown 8 Nuyorican Soul featuring Jocelyn Brown 9 Da Mob featuring Jocelyn Brown

Joe BROWN and the BRUVVERS ⊙
UK, male vocal/instrumental group　　　92 wks

17 Mar 60	DARKTOWN STRUTTERS BALL *Decca F 11207*	34	6
26 Jan 61	SHINE *Pye 7N 15322* 1	33	6
11 Jan 62	WHAT A CRAZY WORLD WE'RE LIVING IN *Piccadilly 7N 35024*	37	2
17 May 62 ●	A PICTURE OF YOU *Piccadilly 7N 35047*	2	19
13 Sep 62	YOUR TENDER LOOK *Piccadilly 7N 35058*	31	6
15 Nov 62 ●	IT ONLY TOOK A MINUTE *Piccadilly 7N 35082*	6	13
7 Feb 63 ●	THAT'S WHAT LOVE WILL DO *Piccadilly 7N 35106*	3	14
21 Feb 63	IT ONLY TOOK A MINUTE (re-entry) *Piccadilly 7N 35082*	50	1
27 Jun 63	NATURE'S TIME FOR LOVE *Piccadilly 7N 35129*	26	6
26 Sep 63	SALLY ANN *Piccadilly 7N 35138*	28	9
29 Jun 67	WITH A LITTLE HELP FROM MY FRIENDS *Pye 7N 17339* 1	32	4
14 Apr 73	HEY MAMA *Ammo AMO 101* 1	33	6

1 Joe Brown

Kathy BROWN – See PRAXIS

Miquel BROWN *US, female vocalist*　　　7 wks

18 Feb 84	HE'S A SAINT, HE'S A SINNER *Record Shack SOHO 15*	68	4
24 Aug 85	CLOSE TO PERFECTION *Record Shack SOHO 48*	63	3

Peter BROWN *US, male vocalist*　　　9 wks

11 Feb 78	DO YA WANNA GET FUNKY WITH ME *TK TKR 6009*	43	4
17 Jun 78	DANCE WITH ME *TK TKR 6027*	57	5

Polly BROWN *UK, female vocalist*　　　5 wks

14 Sep 74	UP IN A PUFF OF SMOKE *GTO GT 2*	43	5

Roy 'Chubby' BROWN ⊙ *UK, male comedian*　　　22 wks

13 May 95	LIVING NEXT DOOR TO ALICE (WHO THE F**K IS ALICE) *N.O.W. CDWAG 245* 1	64	2
12 Aug 95 ●	LIVING NEXT DOOR TO ALICE (WHO THE F**K IS ALICE) (re-entry) *N.O.W. CDWAG 245* 1	3	17
21 Dec 96	ROCKIN' GOOD CHRISTMAS *PolyStar 5732612*	51	3

1 Smokie featuring Roy 'Chubby' Brown

Sam BROWN ⊙ *UK, female vocalist*　　　35 wks

11 Jun 88	STOP *A & M AM 440*	52	3
4 Feb 89 ●	STOP (re-entry) *A & M AM 440*	4	12
13 May 89	CAN I GET A WITNESS *A & M AM 509*	15	7
3 Mar 90	WITH A LITTLE LOVE *A & M AM 539*	44	4
5 May 90	KISSING GATE *A & M AM 549*	23	8
26 Aug 95	JUST GOOD FRIENDS *Dick Bros. DDICK 014CD1* 1	63	1

1 Fish and Sam Brown

BROWN SAUCE ⊙ *UK, male/female vocal group*　　　12 wks

12 Dec 81	I WANNA BE A WINNER *BBC RESL 101*	15	12

BROWN SUGAR – See SEX CLUB featuring BROWN SUGAR

Sharon BROWN *US, female vocalist*　　　11 wks

17 Apr 82	I SPECIALIZE IN LOVE *Virgin VS 494*	38	9
26 Feb 94	I SPECIALIZE IN LOVE (re-mix) *Deep Distraxion OILYCD 025*	62	2

Duncan BROWNE *UK, male vocalist*　　　8 wks

19 Aug 72	JOURNEY *RAK 135*	23	6
22 Dec 84	THEME FROM 'THE TRAVELLING MAN' *Towerbell TOW 64*	68	2

Jackson BROWNE 🎸 *US, male vocalist*　　　14 wks

1 Jul 78	STAY *Asylum K 13128*	12	11
18 Oct 86	IN THE SHAPE OF A HEART *Elektra EKR 42*	66	2
25 Jun 94	EVERYWHERE I GO *Elektra EKR 184CD1*	67	1

Ronnie BROWNE – See SCOTTISH RUGBY TEAM with Ronnie BROWNE

Tom BROWNE 🎺 🎤 *US, male vocalist*　　　24 wks

19 Jul 80 ●	FUNKIN' FOR JAMAICA (N.Y.) *Arista ARIST 357*	10	11
25 Oct 80	THIGHS HIGH (GRIP YOUR HIPS AND MOVE) *Arista ARIST 367*	45	5
30 Jan 82	FUNGI MAMA (BEBOPAFUNKADISCOLYPSO) *Arista ARIST 450*	58	4
11 Jan 92	FUNKIN' FOR JAMAICA (re-mix) *Arista 114998*	45	4

BROWNS 🎸 *US, male/female vocal group*　　　13 wks

18 Sep 59 ●	THE THREE BELLS *RCA 1140* ▲	6	13

BROWNSTONE R&B *US, female vocal group*　　　24 wks

1 Apr 95 ●	IF YOU LOVE ME *MJJ 6614135*	8	12
15 Jul 95	GRAPEVYNE *MJJ 6620942*	16	4
23 Sep 95	I CAN'T TELL YOU WHY *MJJ 6623775*	27	2
17 May 97	5 MILES TO EMPTY *Epic 6640962*	12	4
27 Sep 97	KISS AND TELL *Epic 6649852*	21	2

BROWNSVILLE STATION *US, male vocal/instrumental group*　　　6 wks

2 Mar 74	SMOKIN' IN THE BOYS' ROOM *Philips 6073 834*	27	6

Dave BRUBECK QUARTET 🎹 *US, male instrumental group*　　　30 wks

26 Oct 61 ●	TAKE FIVE *Fontana H 339*	6	15
8 Feb 62	IT'S A RAGGY WALTZ *Fontana H 352*	36	3
17 May 62	UNSQUARE DANCE *CBS AAG 102*	14	12

Tommy BRUCE and the BRUISERS ⊙
UK, male vocal/instrumental group　　　21 wks

26 May 60 ●	AIN'T MISBEHAVIN' *Columbia DB 4453*	3	16
8 Sep 60	BROKEN DOLL *Columbia DB 4498*	36	4
22 Feb 62	BABETTE *Columbia DB 4776* 1	50	1

1 Tommy Bruce

Claudia BRUCKEN *Germany, female vocalist*　　　2 wks

11 Aug 90	ABSOLUT(E) *Island IS 471*	71	1
16 Feb 91	KISS LIKE ETHER *Island IS 479*	63	1

BRUISERS UK, male instrumental group — 7 wks

| 8 Aug 63 | BLUE GIRL Parlophone R 5042 | 31 | 6 |
| 26 Sep 63 | BLUE GIRL (re-entry) Parlophone R 5042 | 47 | 1 |

See also Tommy BRUCE

Frank BRUNO UK, male vocalist — 4 wks

| 23 Dec 95 | EYE OF THE TIGER RCA 74321336282 | 28 | 4 |

BRUNO and LIZ – See Liz KERSHAW and Bruno BROOKES

Tyrone BRUNSON US, male instrumentalist – bass — 5 wks

| 25 Dec 82 | THE SMURF Epic EPC A 3024 | 52 | 5 |

BRUVVERS – See Joe BROWN and the BRUVVERS

Dora BRYAN ☺ UK, female vocalist — 6 wks

| 5 Dec 63 | ALL I WANT FOR CHRISTMAS IS A BEATLE Fontana TF 427 | 20 | 6 |

Anita BRYANT US, female vocalist — 6 wks

26 May 60	PAPER ROSES London HLL 9144	49	1
30 Jun 60	PAPER ROSES (re-entry) London HLL 9144	45	1
14 Jul 60	PAPER ROSES (2nd re-entry) London HLL 9144	24	2
6 Oct 60	MY LITTLE CORNER OF THE WORLD London HLL 9171	48	2

Peabo BRYSON 🖋 US, male vocalist — 35 wks

20 Aug 83	● TONIGHT I CELEBRATE MY LOVE Capitol CL 302 [1]	2	13
16 May 92	● BEAUTY AND THE BEAST Epic 6576607 [2]	9	7
17 Jul 93	BY THE TIME THIS NIGHT IS OVER Arista 74321157142 [3]	56	3
11 Dec 93	A WHOLE NEW WORLD (ALADDIN'S THEME) Columbia 6599002 [4] ▲	12	12

[1] Peabo Bryson and Roberta Flack [2] Celine Dion and Peabo Bryson [3] Kenny G with Peabo Bryson [4] Regina Belle and Peabo Bryson

BT ☺ US, male producer – Brian Transeau — 21 wks

18 Mar 95	EMBRACING THE SUNSHINE East West YZ 895CD	34	2
16 Sep 95	LOVING YOU MORE Perfecto PERF 110CD [1]	28	2
10 Feb 96	LOVING YOU MORE (re-mix) Perfecto PERF 117CD [1]	14	3
9 Nov 96	BLUE SKIES Perfecto PERF 130CD1	26	2
19 Jul 97	FLAMING JUNE Perfecto PERF 145CD1	19	4
29 Nov 97	LOVE, PEACE & GREASE Perfecto PERF 153CD1	41	1
10 Jan 98	FLAMING JUNE (re-mix) Perfecto PERF 157CD1	28	4
18 Apr 98	REMEMBER Perfecto PERF 160CD1	27	2
21 Nov 98	GODSPEED Renaissance RENCD 002	54	1

[1] BT featuring Vincent Covello [2] BT featuring Tori Amos

BT EXPRESS US, male instrumental/vocal group — 11 wks

29 Mar 75	EXPRESS Pye International 7N 25674	34	6
26 Jul 80	DOES IT FEEL GOOD/GIVE UP THE FUNK (LET'S DANCE) Calibre CAB 503	52	4
23 Apr 94	EXPRESS (re-mix) PWL International PWCD 285	67	1

BUBBLEROCK – See Jonathan KING

Catherine BUCHANAN – See JELLYBEAN

Roy BUCHANAN US, male instrumentalist – guitar — 3 wks

| 31 Mar 73 | SWEET DREAMS Polydor 2066 307 | 40 | 3 |

BUCKETHEADS ☺ US, male producer – Kenny Gonzalez — 16 wks

| 4 Mar 95 | ● THE BOMB! (THESE SOUNDS FALL INTO MY MIND) Positiva CDTIV 33 | 5 | 13 |
| 20 Jan 96 | GOT MYSELF TOGETHER Positiva CDTIV 48 | 12 | 3 |

Lindsey BUCKINGHAM US, male vocalist — 7 wks

| 16 Jan 82 | TROUBLE Mercury MER 85 | 31 | 7 |

Jeff BUCKLEY US, male vocalist — 3 wks

| 27 May 95 | LAST GOODBYE Columbia 6620422 | 54 | 2 |
| 6 Jun 98 | EVERYBODY HERE WANTS YOU Columbia 6657912 | 43 | 1 |

BUCKS FIZZ ☺ Chart-topping mixed quartet: Cheryl Baker, Mike Nolan, Jay Aston, Bobby G (Gubby). Formed for the 1981 Eurovision Song Contest, they were the last UK winners for 16 years. Despite little critical acclaim, the act had three UK No 1 singles — 150 wks

28 Mar 81	★ MAKING YOUR MIND UP RCA 56	1	12
6 Jun 81	PIECE OF THE ACTION RCA 88	12	9
15 Aug 81	ONE OF THOSE NIGHTS RCA 114	20	10
28 Nov 81	★ THE LAND OF MAKE BELIEVE RCA 163	1	16
27 Mar 82	★ MY CAMERA NEVER LIES RCA 202	1	8
19 Jun 82	● NOW THOSE DAYS ARE GONE RCA 241	8	9
27 Nov 82	● IF YOU CAN'T STAND THE HEAT RCA 300	10	11
12 Mar 83	RUN FOR YOUR LIFE RCA FIZ 1	14	7
18 Jun 83	● WHEN WE WERE YOUNG RCA 342	10	8
1 Oct 83	LONDON TOWN RCA 363	34	6
17 Dec 83	RULES OF THE GAME RCA 380	57	6
25 Aug 84	TALKING IN YOUR SLEEP RCA FIZ 2	15	9
27 Oct 84	GOLDEN DAYS RCA FIZ 3	42	4
29 Dec 84	I HEAR TALK RCA FIZ 4	34	8
22 Jun 85	YOU AND YOUR HEART SO BLUE RCA PB 40233	43	4
14 Sep 85	MAGICAL RCA PB 40367	57	3
7 Jun 86	● NEW BEGINNING (MAMBA SEYRA) Polydor POSP 794	8	10
30 Aug 86	LOVE THE ONE YOU'RE WITH Polydor POSP 813	47	3
15 Nov 86	KEEP EACH OTHER WARM Polydor POSP 835	45	4
5 Nov 88	HEART OF STONE RCA PB 42035	50	3

BUCKSHOT LEFONQUE US, male vocal/instrumental group — 1 wk

| 6 Dec 97 | ANOTHER DAY Columbia 6653762 | 65 | 1 |

BUDGIE UK, male vocal/instrumental group — 2 wks

| 3 Oct 81 | KEEPING A RENDEZVOUS RCA BUDGIE 3 | 71 | 2 |

BUG KANN and the PLASTIC JAM UK, male/female vocal/instrumental group — 2 wks

| 31 Aug 91 | MADE IN TWO MINUTES Optimum Dance BKPJ 1S [1] | 70 | 1 |
| 26 Feb 94 | MADE IN 2 MINUTES (re-mix) PWL International PWCD 286 | 64 | 1 |

[1] Bug Kann and Plastic Jam featuring Patti Low and Doogie

BUGGLES ☺ UK, male vocal/instrumental duo — 28 wks

22 Sep 79	★ VIDEO KILLED THE RADIO STAR Island WIP 6524	1	11
26 Jan 80	THE PLASTIC AGE Island WIP 6540	16	8
5 Apr 80	CLEAN CLEAN Island WIP 6584	38	5
8 Nov 80	ELSTREE Island WIP 6624	55	4

Silvah BULLET – See Jonny L

B. BUMBLE and the STINGERS ☺ US, male instrumental group — 26 wks

| 19 Apr 62 | ★ NUT ROCKER Top Rank JAR 611 | 1 | 15 |
| 3 Jun 72 | NUT ROCKER (re-issue) Stateside SS 2203 | 19 | 11 |

BUMP UK, male instrumental/production duo — 5 wks

| 4 Jul 92 | I'M RUSHING Good Boy EDGE7 1 | 40 | 4 |
| 11 Nov 95 | I'M RUSHING (re-mix) Deconstruction 74321320692 | 45 | 1 |

BUMP & FLEX UK, male/female vocal/production duo — 1 wk

| 23 May 98 | LONG TIME COMING Heat Recordings HEATCD 014 | 73 | 1 |

BUNKER KRU – See HARLEQUIN 4s / BUNKER KRU

BUNNYMEN – See ECHO and the BUNNYMEN

Eric BURDON – See ANIMALS

UK No 1 ★   UK Top 10 ●   UK million seller ◆   UK entry at No 1 ■   US No 1 ▲

Geoffrey BURGON UK, orchestra — 4 wks

26 Dec 81	BRIDESHEAD THEME *Chrysalis CHS 2562*	48	4

Keni BURKE US, male vocalist — 4 wks

27 Jun 81	LET SOMEBODY LOVE YOU *RCA 93*	59	3
18 Apr 92	RISIN' TO THE TOP *RCA PB 49103*	70	1

Hank C. BURNETTE Sweden, male multi-instrumentalist — 8 wks

30 Oct 76	SPINNING ROCK BOOGIE *Sonet SON 2094*	21	8

Johnny BURNETTE ◉ US, male vocalist — 48 wks

29 Sep 60 ●	DREAMIN' *London HLG 9172*	5	16
12 Jan 61 ●	YOU'RE SIXTEEN *London HLG 9254*	3	12
13 Apr 61	LITTLE BOY SAD *London HLG 9315*	12	12
10 Aug 61	GIRLS *London HLG 9388*	37	5
17 May 62	CLOWN SHOES *Liberty LIB 55416*	35	3

Rocky BURNETTE US, male vocalist — 7 wks

17 Nov 79	TIRED OF TOEIN' THE LINE *EMI 2992*	58	7

Jerry BURNS UK, female vocalist — 1 wk

25 Apr 92	PALE RED *Columbia 6579467*	64	1

Ray BURNS ℂ UK, male vocalist — 19 wks

11 Feb 55 ●	MOBILE *Columbia DB 3563*	4	13
26 Aug 55	THAT'S HOW A LOVE SONG WAS BORN *Columbia DB 3640* [1]	14	6

[1] Ray Burns with the Coronets

Malandra BURROWS ◉ ℂ UK, female vocalist — 10 wks

1 Dec 90	JUST THIS SIDE OF LOVE *Yorkshire Television DALE 1*	11	8
18 Oct 97	CARNIVAL IN HEAVEN *Warner.esp WESP 001CD*	49	1
29 Aug 98	DON'T LEAVE ME *Warner.esp WESP 004CD*	54	1

Jenny BURTON US, female vocalist — 2 wks

30 Mar 85	BAD HABITS *Atlantic A 9583*	68	2

BURUNDI STEIPHENSON BLACK Burundi, drummers and chanters with orchestral additions by Mike Steiphenson of Fran — 14 wks

13 Nov 71	BURUNDI BLACK *Barclay BAR 3*	31	14

BUS 75 – See WHALE

BUS STOP ◉ 🔊 UK / Canada, male production group — 15 wks

23 May 98 ●	KUNG FU FIGHTING (re-mix) *All Around The World CDGLOBE 173* [1]	8	11
24 Oct 98	YOU AIN'T SEEN NOTHIN' YET *All Around The World CDGLOBE 187* [2]	22	4

[1] Bus Stop featuring Carl Douglas [2] Bus Stop featuring Randy Bachman

Lou BUSCH ℂ US, orchestra and chorus — 17 wks

27 Jan 56 ●	ZAMBESI *Capitol CL 14504*	2	17

See also Joe 'Fingers' CARR

BUSH ◉ 🎸 UK, male vocal/instrumental group — 10 wks

8 Jun 96	MACHINEHEAD *Interscope IND 95505*	48	2
1 Mar 97 ●	SWALLOWED *Interscope IND 95528*	7	5
7 Jun 97	GREEDY FLY *Interscope IND 95536*	22	2
1 Nov 97	BONE DRIVEN *Interscope IND 95553*	49	1

Kate BUSH ◉ 🎸 Unmistakable singer/songwriter with operatic vocal ability, b. 30 July, 1958, Kent. Discovered by Dave Gilmour of Pink Floyd. First British female to top the singles chart with a self-composed song and the first to have a UK No 1 album — 168 wks

11 Feb 78 ★	WUTHERING HEIGHTS *EMI 2719*	1	12
13 May 78	WUTHERING HEIGHTS (re-entry) *EMI 2719*	75	1
10 Jun 78 ●	MAN WITH THE CHILD IN HIS EYES *EMI 2806*	6	11
11 Nov 78	HAMMER HORROR *EMI 2887*	44	6
17 Mar 79	WOW *EMI 2911*	14	10
15 Sep 79	KATE BUSH ON STAGE (EP) *EMI MIEP 2991*	10	9
26 Apr 80	BREATHING *EMI 5058*	16	7
5 Jul 80 ●	BABOOSHKA *EMI 5085*	5	10
4 Oct 80	ARMY DREAMERS *EMI 5106*	16	9
6 Dec 80	DECEMBER WILL BE MAGIC AGAIN *EMI 5121*	29	7
11 Jul 81	SAT IN YOUR LAP *EMI 5201*	11	7
7 Aug 82	THE DREAMING *EMI 5296*	48	3
17 Aug 85 ●	RUNNING UP THAT HILL *EMI KB 1*	3	11
26 Oct 85	CLOUDBUSTING *EMI KB 2*	20	6
1 Mar 86	HOUNDS OF LOVE *EMI KB 3*	18	5
10 May 86	THE BIG SKY *EMI KB 4*	37	3
1 Nov 86 ●	DON'T GIVE UP *Virgin PGS 2* [1]	9	11
8 Nov 86	EXPERIMENT IV *EMI KB 5*	23	4
30 Sep 89	THE SENSUAL WORLD *EMI EM 102*	12	5
2 Dec 89	THIS WOMAN'S WORK *EMI EM 119*	25	5
10 Mar 90	LOVE AND ANGER *EMI EM 134*	38	3
7 Dec 91	ROCKET MAN (I THINK IT'S GOING TO BE A LONG LONG TIME) *Mercury TRIBO 2*	12	8
18 Sep 93	RUBBERBAND GIRL *EMI CDEM 280*	12	5
27 Nov 93	MOMENTS OF PLEASURE *EMI CDEM 297*	26	3
16 Apr 94	THE RED SHOES *EMI CDEMS 316*	21	3
30 Jul 94	THE MAN I LOVE *Mercury MERCD 408* [2]	27	2
19 Nov 94	AND SO IS LOVE *EMI CDEMS 355*	26	2

[1] Peter Gabriel and Kate Bush [2] Kate Bush and Larry Adler

Tracks on On Stage (EP): Them Heavy People / Don't Push Your Foot on the Heartbrake / James and the Cold Gun / L'Amour Looks Something Like You

BUSTER UK, male vocal/instrumental group — 1 wk

19 Jun 76	SUNDAY *RCA 2678*	49	1

Bernard BUTLER ☹ ◉ UK, male vocal/instrumentalist — 19 wks

27 May 95 ●	YES *Hut HUTCD 53* [1]	8	8
4 Nov 95	YOU DO *Hut HUTDG 57* [1]	17	4
17 Jan 98	STAY *Creation CRESCD 281*	12	4
28 Mar 98	NOT ALONE *Creation CRESCD 289*	27	3

[1] McAlmont and Butler

See also David McALMONT

Jonathan BUTLER ◉ 🎸 South Africa, male vocalist/instrumentalist – guitar — 18 wks

25 Jan 86	IF YOU'RE READY (COME GO WITH ME) *Jive JIVE 109* [1]	30	7
8 Aug 87	LIES *Jive JIVE 141*	18	11

[1] Ruby Turner featuring Jonathan Butler

BUTTERSCOTCH ◉ UK, male vocal group — 11 wks

2 May 70	DON'T YOU KNOW *RCA 1937*	17	11

BUTTHOLE SURFERS US, male vocal/instrumental group — 1 wk

5 Oct 96	PEPPER *Capitol CDCL 778*	59	1

BUZZCOCKS ✏ UK, male vocal/instrumental group — 53 wks

18 Feb 78	WHAT DO I GET *United Artists UP 36348*	37	3
13 May 78	I DON'T MIND *United Artists UP 36386*	55	2
15 Jul 78	LOVE YOU MORE *United Artists UP 36433*	34	6
23 Sep 78	EVER FALLEN IN LOVE (WITH SOMEONE YOU SHOULDN'T'VE) *United Artists UP 36455*	12	11
25 Nov 78	PROMISES *United Artists UP 36471*	20	10
10 Mar 79	EVERYBODY'S HAPPY NOWADAYS *United Artists UP 36499*	29	6
21 Jul 79	HARMONY IN MY HEAD *United Artists UP 36541*	32	6
25 Aug 79	SPIRAL SCRATCH EP *New Hormones ORG 1*	31	6
6 Sep 80	ARE EVERYTHING/WHY SHE'S A GIRL FROM THE CHAINSTORE *United Artists BP 365*	61	3

UK No 1 ★ UK Top 10 ● UK million seller ◆ UK entry at No 1 ■ US No 1 ▲

Tracks on Spiral Scratch (EP): Breakdown / Time's Up / Boredom / Friends of Mine
Sleeve of EP (not the label) credits 'Buzzcocks with Howard Devoto'
'Why She's a Girl From the Chainstore' listed from 13 Sep, 1980

BUZZY BUNCH – *See Celi BEE and the BUZZY BUNCH*

BVSMP ○ ⬅ *US, male vocal group*   12 wks
| 23 Jul 88 | ● I NEED YOU *Debut DEBT 3044* ....3 12 |

BY ALL MEANS *US, male vocal group*   2 wks
| 18 Jun 88 | I SURRENDER TO YOUR LOVE |
| | *Fourth & Broadway BRW 102* ....65 2 |

Max BYGRAVES © *One of Britain's best-loved entertainers,*
b. 16 October, 1922, London. The comedian/singer/songwriter was
the only British male on the first ever UK album chart. He had five
Top 20 'sing-a-long' hit albums in just 15 months of the 1970s   131 wks
14 Nov 52	● COWPUNCHER'S CANTATA *HMV B 10250* 11 1
2 Jan 53	● COWPUNCHER'S CANTATA (re-entry) *HMV B 10250* 8 1
23 Jan 53	● COWPUNCHER'S CANTATA (2nd re-entry) *HMV B 10250* 6 5
6 Mar 53	● COWPUNCHER'S CANTATA (3rd re-entry) *HMV B 10250* 10 1
14 May 54	● HEART OF MY HEART *HMV B 10654* 7 8
10 Sep 54	● GILLY GILLY OSSENFEFFER KATZENELLEN BOGEN BY THE SEA *HMV B 10734* 7 7
5 Nov 54	● GILLY GILLY OSSENFEFFER KATZENELLEN BOGEN BY THE SEA (re-entry) *HMV B 10734* 20 1
21 Jan 55	MR. SANDMAN *HMV B 10801* 16 1
18 Nov 55	● MEET ME ON THE CORNER *HMV POP 116* 2 11
17 Feb 56	BALLAD OF DAVY CROCKETT *HMV POP 153* 20 1
25 May 56	OUT OF TOWN *HMV POP 164* 18 7
5 Apr 57	HEART *HMV B 10862* 14 8
2 May 58	● YOU NEED HANDS/TULIPS FROM AMSTERDAM *Decca F 11004* 3 25
22 Aug 58	LITTLE TRAIN/GOTTA HAVE RAIN *Decca F 11046* 28 2
2 Jan 59	MY UKELELE *Decca F 11077* 19 4
18 Dec 59	● JINGLE BELL ROCK *Decca F 11176* 7 4
10 Mar 60	● FINGS AIN'T WOT THEY USED T'BE *Decca F 11214* 5 15
28 Jul 60	CONSIDER YOURSELF *Decca F 11251* 50 1
1 Jun 61	BELLS OF AVIGNON *Decca F 11350* 36 5
19 Feb 69	YOU'RE MY EVERYTHING *Pye 7N 17705* 50 1
5 Mar 69	YOU'RE MY EVERYTHING (re-entry) *Pye 7N 17705* 34 3
6 Oct 73	DECK OF CARDS *Pye 7N 45276* 13 15
9 Dec 89	WHITE CHRISTMAS *Parkfield PMS 5012* 71 4

Cowpuncher's Cantata is a medley with the following songs: Cry of the Wild Goose /
Riders in the Sky / Mule Train / Jezebel. 'You Need Hands' was listed by itself on
2 May, 1958. 'Tulips From Amsterdam' was listed beginning 9 May, 1958
See also VARIOUS ARTISTS (EPs & LPs) – All Star Hit Parade No 2

BYKER GROOOVE! *UK, female vocal group*   3 wks
| 24 Dec 94 | LOVE YOUR SEXY . . .!! *Groove GROVD 01* ....48 3 |

Charlie BYRD – *See Stan GETZ*

Debra BYRD – *See Barry MANILOW*

Donald BYRD
US, male vocalist/instrumentalist – trumpet   6 wks
| 26 Sep 81 | LOVING YOU/LOVE HAS COME AROUND |
| | *Elektra K 12559* ....41 6 |

Gary BYRD and the GB EXPERIENCE ⬅
US, male vocalist and male/female instrumental group   9 wks
| 23 Jul 83 | ● THE CROWN *Motown TMGT 1312* ....6 9 |

BYRDS ✎ *US, male vocal/instrumental group*   52 wks
17 Jun 65	★ MR. TAMBOURINE MAN *CBS 201765* ▲ 1 14
12 Aug 65	● ALL I REALLY WANT TO DO *CBS 201796* 4 10
11 Nov 65	TURN! TURN! TURN! *CBS 202008* ▲ 26 8
5 May 66	EIGHT MILES HIGH *CBS 202067* 24 9

| 5 Jun 68 | YOU AIN'T GOIN' NOWHERE *CBS 3411* ....45 3 |
| 13 Feb 71 | CHESTNUT MARE *CBS 5322* ....19 8 |

Edward BYRNES – *See Connie STEVENS*

BYSTANDERS *UK, male vocal/instrumental group*   1 wk
| 9 Feb 67 | 98.6 *Piccadilly 7N 35363* ....45 1 |

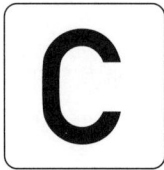

Roy C R&B ✎ *US, male vocalist*   24 wks
| 21 Apr 66 | ● SHOTGUN WEDDING *Island WI 273* ....6 11 |
| 25 Nov 72 | ● SHOTGUN WEDDING (re-issue) *UK 19* ....8 13 |

C & C MUSIC FACTORY / CLIVILLES & COLE ☺
US, male/female vocal/instrumental group   53 wks
15 Dec 90	● GONNA MAKE YOU SWEAT (EVERYBODY DANCE NOW) *CBS 6564540* [1] ▲ 3 12
30 Mar 91	HERE WE GO *Columbia 6567557* [1] 20 7
6 Jul 91	● THINGS THAT MAKE YOU GO HMMM... *Columbia 6566907* [1] 4 11
23 Nov 91	JUST A TOUCH OF LOVE (EVERYDAY) *Columbia 6575247* [2] 31 3
18 Jan 92	PRIDE (IN THE NAME OF LOVE) *Columbia 6577017* [3] 15 5
14 Mar 92	A DEEPER LOVE *Columbia 6578497* [3] 15 5
3 Oct 92	KEEP IT COMIN' (DANCE TILL YOU CAN'T DANCE NO MORE) *Columbia 6584307* [4] 34 3
27 Aug 94	DO YOU WANNA GET FUNKY *Columbia 6607622* [5] 27 3
18 Feb 95	I FOUND LOVE/TAKE A TOKE *Columbia 6612112* [6] 26 2
11 Nov 95	I'LL ALWAYS BE AROUND *MCA MCSTD 40001* [5] 42 2

[1] C & C Music Factory (featuring Freedom Williams) [2] C & C Music Factory featuring Zelma Davis [3] Clivilles and Cole [4] C & C Music Factory featuring Q Unique and Deborah Cooper [5] C & C Music Factory [6] C & C Music Factory / C & C Music Factory featuring Martha Wash

ÇA VA ÇA VA *UK, male vocal/instrumental group*   8 wks
| 18 Sep 82 | WHERE'S ROMEO *Regard RG 103* ....49 5 |
| 19 Feb 83 | BROTHER BRIGHT *Regard RG 105* ....65 3 |

Montserrat CABALLE – *See Freddie MERCURY*

CABANA *Brazil, male/female vocal/instrumental duo*   1 wk
| 15 Jul 95 | BAILANDO CON LOBOS *Hi-Life 5792512* ....65 1 |

CABARET VOLTAIRE *UK, male vocal/instrumental group*   8 wks
18 Jul 87	DON'T ARGUE *Parlophone R 6157* 69 2
4 Nov 89	HYPNOTISED *Parlophone R 6227* 66 2
12 May 90	KEEP ON *Parlophone R 6250* 55 2
18 Aug 90	EASY LIFE *Parlophone R 6261* 61 2

CABLE *UK, male vocal/instrumental group*   2 wks
| 14 Jun 97 | FREEZE THE ATLANTIC *Infectious INFECT 38CD* ....44 2 |

CACIQUE *UK, male/female vocal/instrumental group*   1 wk
| 1 Jun 85 | DEVOTED TO YOU *Diamond Duel DISC 1* ....69 1 |

CACTUS WORLD NEWS *Ireland, male vocal/instrumental group*   **7 wks**

8 Feb 86	**YEARS LATER** *MCA MCA 1024*	59	3
26 Apr 86	**WORLDS APART** *MCA MCA 1040*	58	3
20 Sep 86	**THE BRIDGE** *MCA MCA 1080*	74	1

CADETS with Eileen READ *Ireland, male/female vocal group*   **1 wk**

3 Jun 65	**JEALOUS HEART** *Pye 7N 15852*	42	1

Susan CADOGAN ⌄ *UK, female vocalist*   **19 wks**

5 Apr 75 ●	**HURT SO GOOD** *Magnet MAG 23*	4	12
19 Jul 75	**LOVE ME BABY** *Magnet MAG 36*	22	7

Athena CAGE – *See Keith SWEAT*

Al CAIOLA *US, orchestra*   **6 wks**

15 Jun 61	**THE MAGNIFICENT SEVEN** *HMV POP 889*	34	6

CAKE *US, male vocal / instrumental group*   **6 wks**

22 Mar 97	**THE DISTANCE** *Capricorn 5742212*	22	3
31 May 97	**I WILL SURVIVE** *Capricorn 5744712*	29	3

CALIBRE CUTS – *See VARIOUS ARTISTS (MONTAGES)*

CALIFORNIA SUNSHINE *Israel / Italy, male/female DJ / production group*   **1 wk**

16 Aug 97	**SUMMER '89** *Perfecto PERF 143CD*	56	1

CALL *US, male vocal/instrumental group*   **6 wks**

30 Sep 89	**LET THE DAY BEGIN** *MCA MCA 1362*	42	6

Terry CALLIER *US, male vocalist*   **1 wk**

23 May 98	**LOVE THEME FROM SPARTACUS** *Talkin Loud TLCD 32*	57	1

Eddie CALVERT ℂ *UK, male instrumentalist – trumpet*   **80 wks**

18 Dec 53 ★	**OH MEIN PAPA** *Columbia DB 3337*	1	21
8 Apr 55 ★	**CHERRY PINK AND APPLE BLOSSOM WHITE** *Columbia DB 3581*	1	21
13 May 55	**STRANGER IN PARADISE** *Columbia DB 3594*	14	4
29 Jul 55 ●	**JOHN AND JULIE** *Columbia DB 3624*	6	11
9 Mar 56	**ZAMBESI** *Columbia DB 3747*	18	1
23 Mar 56	**ZAMBESI (re-entry)** *Columbia DB 3747*	13	6
7 Feb 58 ●	**MANDY** *Columbia DB 3956*	9	14
20 Jun 58	**LITTLE SERENADE** *Columbia DB 4105*	28	2

Donnie CALVIN – *See ROCKER'S REVENGE*

CAM'RON ◄ *US, male rapper*   **4 wks**

19 Sep 98	**HORSE & CARRIAGE** *Epic 6662612* [1]	12	4

[1] Cam'ron featuring Mase

CAMEO ♀ *US, male vocal/instrumental group*   **66 wks**

31 Mar 84	**SHE'S STRANGE** *Club JAB 2*	37	8
13 Jul 85	**ATTACK ME WITH YOUR LOVE** *Club JAB 16*	65	2
14 Sep 85	**SINGLE LIFE** *Club JAB 21*	15	10
7 Dec 85	**SHE'S STRANGE (re-issue)** *Club JAB 25*	22	8
22 Mar 86	**A GOODBYE** *Club JAB 28*	65	2
30 Aug 86 ●	**WORD UP** *Club JAB 38*	3	13
29 Nov 86	**CANDY** *Club JAB 43*	27	9
25 Apr 87	**BACK AND FORTH** *Club JAB 49*	11	9
17 Oct 87	**SHE'S MINE** *Club JAB 57*	35	4
29 Oct 88	**YOU MAKE ME WORK** *Club JAB 70*	74	1

Andy CAMERON ◐ *UK, male vocalist*   **8 wks**

4 Mar 78 ●	**ALLY'S TARTAN ARMY** *Klub 03*	6	8

Tony CAMILLO'S BAZUKA *US, male instrumental/vocal group*   **5 wks**

31 May 75	**DYNOMITE (PART 1)** *A & M AMS 7168*	28	5

CAMISRA ☺ *UK, male DJ / producer – 'Tall Paul' Newman*   **10 wks**

21 Feb 98 ●	**LET ME SHOW YOU** *VC Recordings VCRD 31*	5	8
11 Jul 98	**FEEL THE BEAT** *VC Recordings VCRD 39*	32	2

CAMOUFLAGE featuring MYSTI
UK, male/female vocal/instrumental group   **3 wks**

24 Sep 77	**BEE STING** *State STAT 58*	48	3

CAMP LO *US, male rap duo*   **1 wk**

16 Aug 97	**LUCHINI AKA (THIS IT IT)** *ffrr FCD 305*	74	1

Ali CAMPBELL ◐ *UK, male vocalist*   **18 wks**

20 May 95 ●	**THAT LOOK IN YOUR EYE** *Kuff KUFFDG 1*	5	10
26 Aug 95	**LET YOUR YEAH BE YEAH** *Kuff KUFFD 2*	25	4
9 Dec 95	**SOMETHIN' STUPID** *Kuff KUFFDG 5* [1]	30	4

[1] Ali and Kibibi Campbell

See also Pato BANTON

Danny CAMPBELL – *See SASHA*

Don CAMPBELL – *See GENERAL SAINT*

Ethna CAMPBELL *UK, female vocalist*   **11 wks**

27 Dec 75	**THE OLD RUGGED CROSS** *Philips 6006 475*	33	11

Ian CAMPBELL FOLK GROUP
UK, male vocal/instrumental group   **5 wks**

11 Mar 65	**THE TIMES THEY ARE A-CHANGIN'** *Transatlantic SP 5*	42	2
1 Apr 65	**THE TIMES THEY ARE A-CHANGIN' (re-entry)** *Transatlantic SP 5*	47	1
15 Apr 65	**THE TIMES THEY ARE A-CHANGIN' (2nd re-entry)** *Transatlantic SP 5*	46	2

Glen CAMPBELL ℂ ⬳ *US, male vocalist*   **98 wks**

29 Jan 69 ●	**WICHITA LINEMAN** *Ember EMBS 261*	7	13
7 May 69	**GALVESTON** *Ember EMBS 263*	14	10
6 Dec 69 ●	**ALL I HAVE TO DO IS DREAM** *Capitol CL 15619* [1]	3	14
7 Feb 70	**TRY A LITTLE KINDNESS** *Capitol CL 15622*	45	2
9 May 70 ●	**HONEY COME BACK** *Capitol CL 15638*	4	19
26 Sep 70	**EVERYTHING A MAN COULD EVER NEED** *Capitol CL 15653*	32	5
21 Nov 70 ●	**IT'S ONLY MAKE BELIEVE** *Capitol CL 15663*	4	14
27 Mar 71	**DREAM BABY** *Capitol CL 15674*	39	3
4 Oct 75 ●	**RHINESTONE COWBOY** *Capitol CL 15824* ▲	4	12
26 Mar 77	**SOUTHERN NIGHTS** *Capitol CL 15907* ▲	28	6

[1] Bobbie Gentry and Glen Campbell

Jo Ann CAMPBELL *US, female vocalist*   **3 wks**

8 Jun 61	**MOTORCYCLE MICHAEL** *HMV POP 873*	41	3

Junior CAMPBELL ◐ *UK, male vocalist*   **18 wks**

14 Oct 72 ●	**HALLELUJAH FREEDOM** *Deram DM 364*	10	9
2 Jun 73	**SWEET ILLUSION** *Deram DM 387*	15	9

Kibibi CAMPBELL – *See Ali CAMPBELL*

Naomi CAMPBELL *UK, female vocalist*   **3 wks**

24 Sep 94	**LOVE AND TEARS** *Epic 6608352*	40	3

Pat CAMPBELL *Ireland, male vocalist*   **5 wks**

15 Nov 69	**THE DEAL** *Major Minor MM 648*	31	5

What: *Imagine*   **21**
Who: John Lennon
When: 1975 (6), 1980 (1), 1988 (45)
Which: Returned to top the charts soon after the ex-Beatle's death. It went to No 1 two weeks after his '(Just Like) Starting Over' and was replaced by his 'Woman'

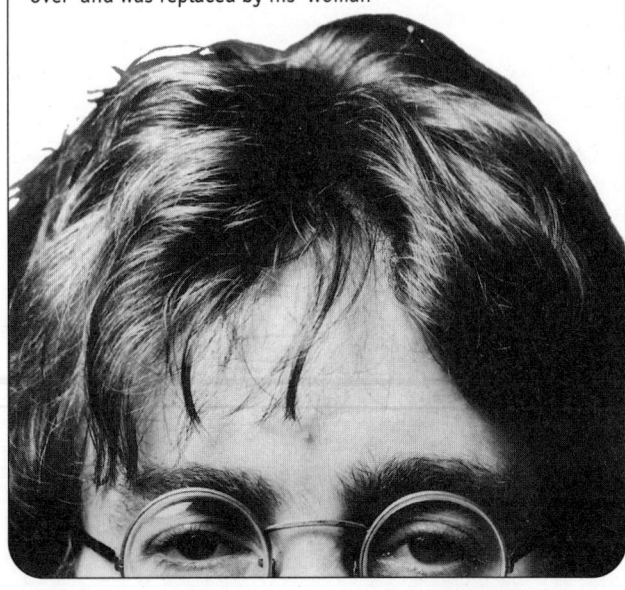

What: *You to Me Are Everything*   **22**
Who: Real Thing
When: 1976 (1), 1986 (5 – remix)
Which: Had two Top 10 runs, ten years apart. Top club DJs Froggy and Simon Harris helped to remix the song, which was penned by the group's producers, Ken Gold and Micky Denne

What: *Space Oddity*   **23**
Who: David Bowie
When: 1969 (5), 1975 (1)
Which: Gave him his first No 1 – six years after its initial release – and in 1973 became Bowie's first US Top 20 entry. His sequel, 'Ashes to Ashes', reached the No 1 spot in 1980

What: *Tainted Love*   **24**
Who: Soft Cell
When: 1981 (1), 1982 (50), 1985 (43), 1991 (5 – remix)
Which: Revived an old Northern Soul classic, previously recorded by Marc Bolan's partner Gloria Jones. This electro-rock favourite was the biggest UK hit of 1981 and broke the longevity record for the US Top 100

Stan CAMPBELL *UK, male vocalist* — 3 wks

6 Jun 87	YEARS GO BY *WEA YZ 127*	65	3

Tevin CAMPBELL *US, male vocalist* — 2 wks

18 Apr 92	TELL ME WHAT YOU WANT ME TO DO *Qwest W 0102*	63	2

CAN *Germany, male vocal/instrumental group* — 10 wks

28 Aug 76	I WANT MORE *Virgin VS 153*	26	10

CANDIDO *US, male multi-instrumentalist* — 3 wks

18 Jul 81	JINGO *Excalibur EXC 102*	55	3

CANDLEWICK GREEN *UK, male vocal/instrumental duo* — 8 wks

23 Feb 74	WHO DO YOU THINK YOU ARE *Decca F 13480*	21	8

CANDY FLIP ☻ *UK, male vocal/instrumental duo* — 14 wks

17 Mar 90	●	STRAWBERRY FIELDS FOREVER *Debut DEBT 3092*	3	10
14 Jul 90		THIS CAN BE REAL *Debut DEBT 3099*	60	4

CANDY GIRLS ☺ *UK, male/female instrumental/production duo* — 10 wks

30 Sep 95	FEE FI FO FUM *VC VCRD 1* [1]	23	4
24 Feb 96	WHAM BAM *VC VCRD 6* [1]	20	4
7 Dec 96	I WANT CANDY *Feverpitch CDFVR 1013* [2]	30	2

[1] Candy Girls featuring Sweet Pussy Pauline [2] Candy Girls featuring Valerie Malcolm

CANDYLAND *UK, male vocal/instrumental group* — 1 wk

9 Mar 91	FOUNTAIN O' YOUTH *Non Fiction YES 4*	72	1

CANDYSKINS *UK, male vocal/instrumental group* — 4 wks

19 Oct 96	MRS HOOVER *Ultimate TOPP 051CD*	65	1
8 Feb 97	MONDAY MORNING *Ultimate TOPP 055CD*	34	2
3 May 97	HANG MYSELF ON YOU *Ultimate TOPP 059CD*	65	1

CANIBUS *US, male rapper* — 3 wks

27 Jun 98	SECOND ROUND K.O. *Universal UND 56198*	35	2
10 Oct 98	HOW COME *Interscope IND 95598* [1]	52	1

[1] Youssou N'dour and Canibus

CANNED HEAT ✍ *US, male vocal/instrumental group* — 41 wks

24 Jul 68	●	ON THE ROAD AGAIN *Liberty LBS 15090*	8	15
1 Jan 69		GOING UP THE COUNTRY *Liberty LBF 15169*	19	10
17 Jan 70	●	LET'S WORK TOGETHER *Liberty LBF 15302*	2	15
11 Jul 70		SUGAR BEE *Liberty LBF 15350*	49	1

Freddy CANNON ♪ *US, male vocalist* — 51 wks

14 Aug 59		TALLAHASSEE LASSIE *Top Rank JAR 135*	17	8
1 Jan 60	●	WAY DOWN YONDER IN NEW ORLEANS *Top Rank JAR 247*	3	16
10 Mar 60		CALIFORNIA HERE I COME *Top Rank JAR 309*	33	1
17 Mar 60		INDIANA *Top Rank JAR 309*	42	1
24 Mar 60		CALIFORNIA HERE I COME (re-entry) *Top Rank JAR 309*	46	1
19 May 60		THE URGE *Top Rank JAR 369*	18	10
20 Apr 61		MUSKRAT RAMBLE *Top Rank JAR 548*	32	5
28 Jun 62		PALISADES PARK *Stateside SS 101*	20	9

Jim CAPALDI ✍ *UK, male vocalist* — 17 wks

27 Jul 74		IT'S ALL UP TO YOU *Island WIP 6198*	27	6
25 Oct 75	●	LOVE HURTS *Island WIP 6246*	4	11

CAPERCAILLIE *UK, male/female vocal/instrumental group* — 3 wks

23 May 92	A PRINCE AMONG ISLANDS EP *Survival ZB 45393*	39	2
17 Jun 95	DARK ALAN (AILEIN DUINN) *Survival SURCD 55*	65	1

Tracks on A Prince Among Islands (EP): Coisich a Ruin (Walk My Beloved)/Fagail

Bhearnaraid (Leaving Bernaray)/The Lorn Theme/Gun Teann Mi Ris Na Ruinn Tha Seo (Remembrance)

CAPPADONNA – See WU-TANG CLAN

CAPPELLA ☺ ☻ *Italy, male producer – Gianfranco Bortolotti* — 68 wks

9 Apr 88		PUSH THE BEAT/BAUHAUS *Fast Globe FGL 1*	60	2
6 May 89		HELYOM HALIB *Music Man MMPS 7004*	11	9
23 Sep 89		HOUSE ENERGY REVENGE *Music Man MMPS 7009*	73	1
27 Apr 91		EVERYBODY *ffrr F158*	66	1
18 Jan 92		TAKE ME AWAY *PWL Continental PWL 210* [1]	25	5
3 Apr 93	●	U GOT 2 KNOW *Internal Dance IDC 1*	6	11
14 Aug 93		U GOT 2 KNOW REVISITED (re-mix) *Internal Dance IDCR 2*	43	1
23 Oct 93		U GOT 2 LET THE MUSIC *Internal Dance IDC 3*	2	12
19 Feb 94	●	MOVE ON BABY *Internal Dance IDC 4*	7	7
18 Jun 94	●	U & ME *Internal Dance IDCC 6*	10	7
15 Oct 94		MOVE IT UP/BIG BEAT *Internal Dance IDC 7*	16	6
16 Sep 95		TELL ME THE WAY *Systematic SYSCD 17*	17	3
6 Sep 97		BE MY BABY *Nukleuz PSNC 0072*	53	1

[1] Cappella featuring Loleatta Holloway

Act was fronted by a UK, male/female vocal duo from U Got 2 Let The Music. See also 49ers

CAPRICORN *Belgium, male DJ* — 1 wks

29 Nov 97	20 HZ (NEW FREQUENCIES) *R&S RS 97126CD*	73	1

Tony CAPSTICK and the CARLTON MAIN / FRICKLEY COLLIERY BAND ℂ *UK, male vocalist and male instrumental band* — 8 wks

21 Mar 81	●	THE SHEFFIELD GRINDER/CAPSTICK COMES HOME *Dingles SID 27*	3	8

CAPTAIN BEAKY – See Keith MICHELL

CAPTAIN HOLLYWOOD PROJECT ☺ ☻
US/Germany, male/female vocal/instrumental group — 31 wks

22 Sep 90	●	I CAN'T STAND IT *BCM BCMR 395* [1]	7	10
24 Nov 90		ARE YOU DREAMING *BCM BCM 07504* [1]	17	10
27 Mar 93		ONLY WITH YOU *Pulse 8 CDLOSE 40*	67	1
6 Nov 93		MORE AND MORE *Pulse 8 CDLOSE 50*	23	5
5 Feb 94		IMPOSSIBLE *Pulse 8 CDLOSE 54*	29	3
11 Jun 94		ONLY WITH YOU (re-issue) *Pulse 8 CDLOSE 62*	61	1
1 Apr 95		FLYING HIGH *Pulse 8 CDLOSE 82*	58	1

[1] Twenty 4 Seven featuring Captain Hollywood

CAPTAIN SENSIBLE ☻ *UK, male vocalist* — 31 wks

26 Jun 82	★	HAPPY TALK *A & M CAP 1*	1	8
14 Aug 82		WOT *A & M CAP 2*	26	7
24 Mar 84		GLAD IT'S ALL OVER/DAMNED ON 45 *A & M CAP 6*	6	10
28 Jul 84		THERE ARE MORE SNAKES THAN LADDERS *A & M CAP 7*	57	5
10 Dec 94		THE HOKEY COKEY *Have A Nice Day CDHOKEY 1*	71	1

CAPTAIN and TENNILLE ☻
US, male instrumentalist – keyboards – and female vocalist — 24 wks

2 Aug 75		LOVE WILL KEEP US TOGETHER *A & M AMS 7165* ▲	32	5
24 Jan 76		THE WAY I WANT TO TOUCH YOU *A & M AMS 7203*	28	6
4 Nov 78		YOU NEVER DONE IT LIKE THAT *A & M AMS 7384*	63	3
16 Feb 80	●	DO THAT TO ME ONE MORE TIME *Casablanca CAN 175* ▲	7	10

Irene CARA ☻ *US, female vocalist* — 33 wks

3 Jul 82	★	FAME *RSO 90*	1	16
4 Sep 82		OUT HERE ON MY OWN *RSO 66*	58	3
4 Jun 83	●	FLASHDANCE . . . WHAT A FEELING *Casablanca CAN 1016* ▲	2	14

CARAMBA *Sweden, male vocalist/multi-instrumentalist dog impersonator – Michael Tretow* — 6 wks

12 Nov 83	FEDORA (I'LL BE YOUR DAWG) *Billco BILL 101*	56	6

CARAVELLES 😊 *UK, female vocal duo*   **13 wks**

| 8 Aug 63 ● | YOU DON'T HAVE TO BE A BABY TO CRY *Decca F 11697* ....6 | 13 |

CARDIGANS ☹ 😊
Sweden, male/female vocal/instrumental group   **39wks**

17 Jun 95		CARNIVAL *Trampolene PZCD 345* 72	1
30 Sep 95		SICK AND TIRED *Stockholm 5773112* 34	3
2 Dec 95		CARNIVAL (re-entry) *Trampolene PZCD 345* 35	2
17 Feb 96		RISE AND SHINE *Trampolene 5778252* 29	2
21 Sep 96		LOVEFOOL *Stockholm 5752952* 21	4
7 Dec 96	●	BEEN IT *Stockholm 5759672* 56	1
3 May 97		LOVEFOOL *Stockholm 5710502* 2	13
6 Sep 97		YOUR NEW COCKOO *Stockholm 5716632* 35	2
17 Oct 98		MY FAVOURITE GAME *Stockholm 5679912* ....14†	11

CARE *UK, male vocal/instrumental duo*   **4 wks**

| 12 Nov 83 | | FLAMING SWORD *Arista KBIRD 2* ....48 | 4 |

Mariah CAREY 😊 *Record-shattering vocalist/songwriter, b. 27 March, 1970, New York. Since her 1990 chart debut, she has broken countless records. She has sold more than 90 million albums worldwide and has topped the US singles chart 13 times – only Elvis Presley and The Beatles have spent longer at the top*   **193 wks**

4 Aug 90	●	VISION OF LOVE *CBS 6559320* ▲ 9	12
10 Nov 90		LOVE TAKES TIME *CBS 6563647* ▲ 37	8
26 Jan 91		SOMEDAY *Columbia 6565837* ▲ 38	5
1 Jun 91		THERE'S GOT TO BE A WAY *Columbia 6569317* 54	3
5 Oct 91		EMOTIONS *Columbia 6574037* ▲ 17	9
11 Jan 92		CAN'T LET GO *Columbia 6576627* 20	7
18 Apr 92		MAKE IT HAPPEN *Columbia 6579417* 17	5
27 Jun 92	●	I'LL BE THERE *Columbia 6581377* ▲ 2	9
21 Aug 93	●	DREAMLOVER *Columbia 6594445* ▲ 9	10
6 Nov 93	●	HERO *Columbia 6598122* ▲ 7	15
19 Feb 94	★	WITHOUT YOU *Columbia 6599192* 1	14
18 Jun 94	●	ANYTIME YOU NEED A FRIEND *Columbia 6603542* 8	10
17 Sep 94	●	ENDLESS LOVE *Epic 6608062* [1] 3	10
10 Dec 94	●	ALL I WANT FOR CHRISTMAS IS YOU *Columbia 6610702* 2	7
7 Jan 95		ENDLESS LOVE (re-entry) *Epic 6608062* [1] 70	2
4 Feb 95		ENDLESS LOVE (2nd re-entry) *Epic 6608062* [1] 55	4
11 Mar 95		ALL I WANT FOR CHRISTMAS IS YOU (re-entry) *Columbia 6610702* 59	1
23 Sep 95	●	FANTASY *Columbia 6624952* ▲ 4	11
9 Dec 95	●	ONE SWEET DAY *Columbia 6626035* [2] ▲ 6	11
17 Feb 96	●	OPEN ARMS *Columbia 6629772* 4	6
22 Jun 96	●	ALWAYS BE MY BABY *Columbia 6633345* ▲ 3	10
6 Sep 97	●	HONEY *Columbia 6650192* ▲ 3	8
13 Dec 97		BUTTERFLY *Columbia 6653365* 22	6
13 Jun 98	●	MY ALL *Columbia 6660592* ▲ 4	8
19 Dec 98	●	WHEN YOU BELIEVE *Columbia 6667522* [3] ....4†	2

[1] Luther Vandross and Mariah Carey [2] Mariah Carey and Boyz II Men
[3] Mariah Carey and Whitney Houston

Although he is uncredited, 'I'll Be There' is a duet with Trey Lorenz

CARL – *See CLUBHOUSE*

Belinda CARLISLE 😊 *Lead vocalist of the first really successful all-girl rock group, The Go-Gos; b. 17 August, 1958, Hollywood. She married the son of British-born film star James Mason in 1992 and her career fared even better in the UK than in her homeland*   **144 wks**

12 Dec 87	★	HEAVEN IS A PLACE ON EARTH *Virgin VS 1036* ▲ 1	14
27 Feb 88	●	I GET WEAK *Virgin VS 1046* 10	9
7 May 88	●	CIRCLE IN THE SAND *Virgin VS 1074* 4	11
6 Aug 88		MAD ABOUT YOU *IRS IRM 118* 67	3
10 Sep 88		WORLD WITHOUT YOU *Virgin VS 1114* 34	6
10 Dec 88		LOVE NEVER DIES . . . *Virgin VS 1150* 54	5
7 Oct 89	●	LEAVE A LIGHT ON *Virgin VS 1210* 4	10
9 Dec 89		LA LUNA *Virgin VS 1230* 38	6
24 Feb 90		RUNAWAY HORSES *Virgin VS 1244* 40	5

26 May 90		VISION OF YOU *Virgin VS 1264* 41	4
13 Oct 90	●	(WE WANT) THE SAME THING *Virgin VS 1219* 6	10
22 Dec 90		SUMMER RAIN *Virgin VS 1323* 23	10
20 Apr 91		VISION OF YOU (re-entry) *Virgin VS 1264* 71	1
28 Sep 91		LIVE YOUR LIFE BE FREE *Virgin VS 1370* 12	7
16 Nov 91		DO YOU FEEL LIKE I FEEL *Virgin VS 1383* 29	4
11 Jan 92		HALF THE WORLD *Virgin VS 1388* 35	4
29 Aug 92		LITTLE BLACK BOOK *Virgin VS 1428* 28	5
25 Sep 93		BIG SCARY ANIMAL *Virgin VSCDT 1472* 12	6
27 Nov 93		LAY DOWN YOUR ARMS *Virgin VSCDG 1476* 27	6
13 Jul 96	●	IN TOO DEEP *Chrysalis CDCHS 5033* 6	7
21 Sep 96	●	ALWAYS BREAKING MY HEART *Chrysalis CDCHS 5037* 8	6
30 Nov 96		LOVE IN THE KEY OF C *Chrysalis CDCHS 5044* 20	3
1 Mar 97		CALIFORNIA *Chrysalis CDCHSS 5047* 31	2

Bob CARLISLE *US, male vocalist*   **2 wks**

| 30 Aug 97 | | BUTTERFLY KISSES *Jive JIVECD 249* ....56 | 2 |

Sara CARLSON – *See MANIC MCs featuring Sara CARLSON*

CARLTON *UK, male vocalist*   **3 wks**

| 16 Feb 91 | | LOVE AND PAIN *Smith & Mighty SNM 4* ....56 | 2 |
| 1 Apr 95 | | 1 TO 1 RELIGION *Stoned Heights BRCDX 313* [1] ....53 | 1 |

[1] Bomb The Bass featuring Carlton

Carl CARLTON *US, male vocalist*   **8 wks**

| 18 Jul 81 | | SHE'S A BAD MAMA JAMA (SHE'S BUILT, SHE'S STACKED) *20th Century TC 2488* ....34 | 8 |

Larry CARLTON – *See Mike POST*

CARLTON MAIN / FRICKLEY COLLIERY BAND – *See Tony CAPSTICK and the CARLTON MAIN / FRICKLEY COLLIERY BAND*

CARMEL 😊 ✏ *UK, female/male vocal/instrumental group*   **19 wks**

6 Aug 83		BAD DAY *London LON 29* 15	9
11 Feb 84		MORE, MORE, MORE *London LON 44* 23	7
14 Jun 86		SALLY *London LON 90* 60	3

Eric CARMEN 😊 *US, male vocalist*   **7 wks**

| 10 Apr 76 | | ALL BY MYSELF *Arista 42* ....12 | 7 |

Jean CARN – *See Bobby M featuring Jean CARN*

Kim CARNEGIE *UK, female vocalist*   **1 wk**

| 19 Jan 91 | | JAZZ RAP *Best ZB 44085* ....73 | 1 |

Kim CARNES 😊 *US, female vocalist*   **15 wks**

9 May 81	●	BETTE DAVIS EYES *EMI America EA 121* ▲ 10	9
8 Aug 81		DRAW OF THE CARDS *EMI America EA 125* 49	4
9 Oct 82		VOYEUR *EMI America EA 143* 68	2

CARNIVAL featuring RIP vs RED RAT
UK, male production duo, and Jamaica, male vocalist   **1 wk**

| 12 Sep 98 | | ALL OF THE GIRLS (ALL AI-DI GIRL DEM) *Pepper 0530072* ....51 | 1 |

Renato CAROSONE and his SEXTET
Italy, male vocalist and instrumental backing group   **1 wk**

| 4 Jul 58 | | TORERO – CHA CHA CHA *Parlophone R 4433* ....25 | 1 |

Mary-Chapin CARPENTER *US, female vocalist*   **6 wks**

20 Nov 93		HE THINKS HE'LL KEEP HER *Columbia 6598632* 71	1
7 Jan 95		ONE COOL REMOVE *Columbia 6611342* [1] 40	3
3 Jun 95		SHUT UP AND KISS ME *Columbia 6613675* 35	2

[1] Shawn Colvin with Mary Chapin Carpenter

UK No 1 ★   UK Top 10 ●   UK million seller ◆   UK entry at No 1 ■   US No 1 ▲

CARPENTERS © All-time biggest-selling brother/sister duo: Karen Carpenter (v/d) (d. 1983), Richard Carpenter (k/v). This Connecticut couple were among the world's most popular pop/MOR acts of the 1970s, collecting an impressive catalogue of gold and platinum records before Karen's anorexia-associated death — **173 wks**

Date	Title	Pos	Wks
5 Sep 70 ●	(THEY LONG TO BE) CLOSE TO YOU *A & M AMS 800* ▲	6	18
9 Jan 71	WE'VE ONLY JUST BEGUN *A & M AMS 813*	28	7
18 Sep 71	SUPERSTAR/FOR ALL WE KNOW *A & M AMS 864*	18	13
1 Jan 72	MERRY CHRISTMAS DARLING *A & M AME 601*	45	1
23 Sep 72 ●	I WON'T LAST A DAY WITHOUT YOU/GOODBYE TO LOVE *A & M AMS 7023*	9	16
7 Jul 73 ●	YESTERDAY ONCE MORE *A & M AMS 7073*	2	17
20 Oct 73 ●	TOP OF THE WORLD *A & M AMS 7086* ▲	5	18
2 Mar 74	JAMBALAYA (ON THE BAYOU)/MR. GUDER *A & M AMS 7098*	12	11
8 Jun 74	I WON'T LAST A DAY WITHOUT YOU (re-issue) *A & M AMS 7111*	32	5
18 Jan 75 ●	PLEASE MR. POSTMAN *A & M AMS 7141* ▲	2	12
19 Apr 75 ●	ONLY YESTERDAY *A & M AMS 7159*	7	10
30 Aug 75	SOLITAIRE *A & M AMS 7187*	32	5
20 Dec 75	SANTA CLAUS IS COMIN' TO TOWN *A & M AMS 7144*	37	4
27 Mar 76	THERE'S A KIND OF HUSH (ALL OVER THE WORLD) *A & M AMS 7219*	22	6
3 Jul 76	I NEED TO BE IN LOVE *A & M AMS 7238*	36	5
8 Oct 77 ●	CALLING OCCUPANTS OF INTERPLANETARY CRAFT (THE RECOGNISED ANTHEM OF WORLD CONTACT DAY) *A & M AMS 7318*	9	9
11 Feb 78	SWEET SWEET SMILE *A & M AMS 7327*	40	4
22 Oct 83	MAKE BELIEVE IT'S YOUR FIRST TIME *A & M AM 147*	60	3
8 Dec 90	MERRY CHRISTMAS DARLING/(THEY LONG TO BE) CLOSE TO YOU (re-issue) *A & M AM 716*	25	5
13 Feb 93	RAINY DAYS AND MONDAYS *A & M AMCD 0180*	63	2
24 Dec 94	TRYIN' TO GET THE FEELING AGAIN *A & M 5807612*	44	2

'I Won't Last a Day Without You' AMS 703 listed by itself 23 Sep, 1972 at No 49. 'Goodbye to Love', the other side, listed by itself from 30 Sep, 1972, until the end of the record's chart run. 'Mr Guder' listed with 'Jambalaya' from 16 Mar, 1974, until the end of the record's chart run

Joe 'Fingers' CARR ©
US, male instrumentalist – piano, Lou Busch under a false name — **5 wks**

Date	Title	Pos	Wks
29 Jun 56	PORTUGUESE WASHERWOMAN *Capitol CL 14587*	20	5

See also Lou BUSCH

Linda CARR ◢ US, female vocalist — **12 wks**

Date	Title	Pos	Wks
12 Jul 75	HIGHWIRE *Chelsea 2005 025* [1]	15	8
5 Jun 76	SOLD MY ROCK 'N' ROLL (GAVE IT FOR FUNKY SOUL) *Spark SRL 1139* [2]	36	4

[1] Linda Carr and the Love Squad [2] Linda and the Funky Boys

Pearl CARR and Teddy JOHNSON ©
UK, female/male vocal duo — **19 wks**

Date	Title	Pos	Wks
20 Mar 59	SING LITTLE BIRDIE *Columbia DB 4275*	12	8
6 Apr 61	HOW WONDERFUL TO KNOW *Columbia DB 4603*	23	11

Suzi CARR US, female vocalist — **1 wk**

Date	Title	Pos	Wks
8 Oct 94	ALL OVER ME *Cowboy RODEO 947CD*	45	1

Valerie CARR US, female vocalist — **2 wks**

Date	Title	Pos	Wks
4 Jul 58	WHEN THE BOYS TALK ABOUT THE GIRLS *Columbia DB 4131*	29	1
18 Jul 58	WHEN THE BOYS TALK ABOUT THE GIRLS (re-entry) *Columbia DB 4131*	30	1

Vikki CARR © US, female vocalist — **26 wks**

Date	Title	Pos	Wks
1 Jun 67 ●	IT MUST BE HIM (SEUL SUR SON ETOILE) *Liberty LIB 55917*	2	20
30 Aug 67	THERE I GO *Liberty LBF 15022*	50	1
12 Mar 69	WITH PEN IN HAND *Liberty LBF 15166*	43	1
26 Mar 69	WITH PEN IN HAND (re-entry) *Liberty LBF 15166*	39	2
30 Apr 69	WITH PEN IN HAND (2nd re-entry) *Liberty LBF 15166*	40	2

Raffaella CARRA ◉ Italy, female vocalist — **12 wks**

Date	Title	Pos	Wks
15 Apr 78 ●	DO IT DO IT AGAIN *Epic EPC 6094*	9	12

Paul CARRACK UK, male vocalist — **18 wks**

Date	Title	Pos	Wks
16 May 87	WHEN YOU WALK IN THE ROOM *Chrysalis CHS 3109*	48	5
18 Mar 89	DON'T SHED A TEAR *Chrysalis CHS 3164*	60	3
6 Jan 96	EYES OF BLUE *IRS CDEIRS 192*	40	4
6 Apr 96	HOW LONG *IRS CDEIRS 193*	32	5
24 Aug 96	EYES OF BLUE (re-mix) *IRS CDEIRS 194*	45	1

José CARRERAS ♪ Spain, male vocalist — **19 wks**

Date	Title	Pos	Wks
11 Jul 92	AMIGOS PARA SIEMPRE (FRIENDS FOR LIFE) *Really Useful RUR 10* [1]	11	11
30 Jul 94	LIBIAMO/LA DONNA E MOBILE *Teldec YZ 843CD* [2]	21	4
25 Jul 98	YOU'LL NEVER WALK ALONE *Decca 4607982* [2]	21	4

[1] José Carreras and Sarah Brightman [2] José Carreras, Placido Domingo and Luciano Pavarotti

Tia CARRERE US, female vocalist — **6 wks**

Date	Title	Pos	Wks
30 May 92	BALLROOM BLITZ *Reprise W 0105*	26	6

Jim CARREY US, male vocalist — **3 wks**

Date	Title	Pos	Wks
21 Jan 95	CUBAN PETE *Columbia 6606625*	31	3

CARRIE US/UK, male vocal/instrumental group — **2 wks**

Date	Title	Pos	Wks
14 Mar 98	MOLLY *Island CID 687*	56	1
9 May 98	CALIFORNIA SCREAMIN' *Island CID 694*	55	1

Dina CARROLL ☺ ◉ ♪ UK, female vocalist — **90 wks**

Date	Title	Pos	Wks
2 Feb 91 ●	IT'S TOO LATE *Mercury ITM 3* [1]	8	14
15 Jun 91	NAKED LOVE (JUST SAY YOU WANT ME) *Mercury ITM 4* [2]	39	3
11 Jul 92	AIN'T NO MAN *A & M AM 0001*	16	8
10 Oct 92	SPECIAL KIND OF LOVE *A & M AM 0088*	16	5
5 Dec 92	SO CLOSE *A & M AM 0101*	20	8
27 Feb 93	THIS TIME *A & M AMCD 0184*	23	6
15 May 93	EXPRESS *A & M 5802632*	12	6
16 Oct 93 ●	DON'T BE A STRANGER *A & M 5803892*	3	13
11 Dec 93 ●	THE PERFECT YEAR *A & M 5804812*	5	11
28 Sep 96 ●	ESCAPING *Mercury DCCD 1*	3	8
21 Dec 96	ONLY HUMAN *Mercury DCCD 2*	33	4
24 Oct 98	ONE, TWO, THREE *1st Avenue MERCD 514*	16	4

[1] Quartz introducing Dina Carroll [2] Quartz and Dina Carroll

Ronnie CARROLL © UK, male vocalist — **50 wks**

Date	Title	Pos	Wks
27 Jul 56	WALK HAND IN HAND *Philips PB 605*	13	8
29 Mar 57	THE WISDOM OF A FOOL *Philips PB 667*	20	2
31 Mar 60	FOOTSTEPS *Philips PB 1004*	36	3
22 Feb 62	RING A DING GIRL *Philips PB 1222*	46	3
2 Aug 62 ●	ROSES ARE RED *Philips 326532 BF*	3	16
15 Nov 62	IF ONLY TOMORROW *Philips 326550 BF*	33	4
7 Mar 63 ●	SAY WONDERFUL THINGS *Philips 326574 BF*	6	14

Jasper CARROTT ◉ UK, male vocalist — **15 wks**

Date	Title	Pos	Wks
16 Aug 75 ●	FUNKY MOPED/MAGIC ROUNDABOUT *DJM DJS 388*	5	15

CARS ✦ US, male vocal/instrumental group — **51 wks**

Date	Title	Pos	Wks
11 Nov 78 ●	MY BEST FRIEND'S GIRL *Elektra K 12301*	3	10
17 Feb 79	JUST WHAT I NEEDED *Elektra K 12312*	17	10
28 Jul 79	LET'S GO *Elektra K 12371*	51	4
5 Jun 82	SINCE YOU'RE GONE *Elektra K 13177*	37	4
29 Sep 84 ●	DRIVE *Elektra E 9706*	5	11
3 Aug 85 ●	DRIVE (re-entry) *Elektra E 9706*	4	12

CARTER – THE UNSTOPPABLE SEX MACHINE ☹

UK, male vocal/instrumental duo　　　　　　　　**46 wks**

26 Jan 91	BLOODSPORTS FOR ALL *Rough Trade R 20112687*	48	2
22 Jun 91	SHERIFF FATMAN *Big Cat USM 1*	23	7
26 Oct 91	AFTER THE WATERSHED *Big Cat USM 2*	11	5
11 Jan 92	RUBBISH *Big Cat USM 3*	14	5
25 Apr 92 ●	THE ONLY LIVING BOY IN NEW CROSS *Big Cat USM 4*	7	5
4 Jul 92	DO RE ME SO FAR SO GOOD *Chrysalis USM 5*	22	3
28 Nov 92	THE IMPOSSIBLE DREAM *Chrysalis USM 6*	21	3
4 Sep 93	LEAN ON ME I WON'T FALL OVER *Chrysalis CDUSM 7*	16	3
16 Oct 93	LENNY AND TERENCE *Chrysalis CDUSM 8*	40	3
12 Mar 94	GLAM ROCK COPS *Chrysalis CDUSMS 10*	24	3
19 Nov 94	LET'S GET TATTOOS *Chrysalis CDUSMS 30*	30	3
4 Feb 95	THE YOUNG OFFENDER'S MUM *Chrysalis CDUSMS 12*	34	3
30 Sep 95	BORN ON THE 5TH OF NOVEMBER *Chrysalis CDUSM 13*	35	2

Aaron CARTER ◎ *US, male vocalist*　　　　**23 wks**

29 Nov 97 ●	CRUSH ON YOU *Ultra Pop 0099605 ULT*	9	8
7 Feb 98 ●	CRAZY LITTLE PARTY GIRL *Ultra Pop 0099645 ULT*	7	6
28 Mar 98	I'M GONNA MISS YOU FOREVER *Ultra Pop 0099725 ULT*	24	5
4 Jul 98	SURFIN' USA *Ultra Pop 0099805 ULT*	18	4

Clarence CARTER ✏ *US, male vocalist*　　**13 wks**

10 Oct 70 ●	PATCHES *Atlantic 2091 030*	2	13

CARTER TWINS *Ireland, male vocal duo*　　**1 wk**

8 Mar 97	THE TWELFTH OF NEVER/TOO RIGHT TO BE *RCA 74321453082*	61	1

Sam CARTWRIGHT – See VOLCANO

CARVELLS *UK, male vocalist/instrumentalist – Alan Carvell*　　**4 wks**

26 Nov 77	THE L.A. RUN *Creole CR 143*	31	4

CASCADES ◎ *US, male vocal group*　　**16 wks**

28 Feb 63 ●	RHYTHM OF THE RAIN *Warner Bros. WB 88*	5	16

CASE – See Foxy BROWN

Natalie CASEY *UK, female vocalist*　　**1 wk**

7 Jan 84	CHICK CHICK CHICKEN *Polydor CHICK 1*	72	1

Johnny CASH ☙ *US, male vocalist*　　**59 wks**

3 Jun 65	IT AIN'T ME BABE *CBS 201760*	28	8
6 Sep 69 ●	A BOY NAMED SUE *CBS 4460*	4	19
23 May 70	WHAT IS TRUTH *CBS 4934*	21	11
15 Apr 72 ●	A THING CALLED LOVE *CBS 7797* [1]	4	13
22 Jul 72	A THING CALLED LOVE (re-entry) *CBS 7797* [1]	48	1
3 Jul 76	ONE PIECE AT A TIME *CBS 4287* [2]	32	7

[1] Johnny Cash with the Evangel Temple Choir [2] Johnny Cash with the Tennessee Three

Pat CASH – See John McENROE and Pat CASH with the FULL METAL RACKETS

CA$HFLOW ♪ *US, male vocal/instrumental group*　　**8 wks**

24 May 86	MINE ALL MINE/PARTY FREAK *Club JAB 30*	15	8

CASHMERE *US, male vocal/instrumental group*　　**11 wks**

19 Jan 85	CAN I *Fourth & Broadway BRW 19*	29	8
23 Mar 85	WE NEED LOVE *Fourth & Broadway BRW 22*	52	3

CASINO *UK, male vocal / production group*　　**1 wk**

17 May 97	SOUND OF EDEN *Worx WORXCD 005*	52	1

CASINOS *US, male vocal group*　　**7 wks**

23 Feb 67	THEN YOU CAN TELL ME GOODBYE *President PT 123*	28	7

David CASSIDY ◎ *Top teen idol of 1970s, b. 12 April, 1950, New York. This photogenic singer/actor first found fame via the TV series The Partridge Family. His UK chart career took off as his US sales slowed down*　　**109 wks**

8 Apr 72 ●	COULD IT BE FOREVER/CHERISH *Bell 1224*	2	17
16 Sep 72 ★	HOW CAN I BE SURE *Bell 1258*	1	11
25 Nov 72	ROCK ME BABY *Bell 1268*	11	9
24 Mar 73	I'M A CLOWN/SOME KIND OF A SUMMER *Bell MABEL 4*	3	12
13 Oct 73 ★	DAYDREAMER/THE PUPPY SONG *Bell 1334*	1	15
11 May 74	IF I DIDN'T CARE *Bell 1350*	9	8
27 Jul 74	PLEASE PLEASE ME *Bell 1371*	16	6
5 Jul 75	I WRITE THE SONGS/GET IT UP FOR LOVE *RCA 2571*	11	8
25 Oct 75	DARLIN' *RCA 2622*	16	8
23 Feb 85	THE LAST KISS *Arista ARIST 589*	6	9
11 May 85	ROMANCE (LET YOUR HEART GO) *Arista ARIST 620*	54	6

See also PARTRIDGE FAMILY

CAST ☹ ◎ *UK, male vocal/instrumental group*　　**45 wks**

15 Jul 95	FINETIME *Polydor 5795072*	17	4
30 Sep 95	ALRIGHT *Polydor 5799272*	13	4
20 Jan 96 ●	SANDSTORM *Polydor 5778732*	8	5
30 Mar 96	WALKAWAY *Polydor 5762852*	9	7
26 Oct 96 ●	FLYING *Polydor 5754772*	4	5
5 Apr 97 ●	FREE ME *Polydor 5736512*	7	6
28 Jun 97 ●	GUIDING STAR *Polydor 5711732*	9	6
13 Sep 97 ●	LIVE THE DREAM *Polydor 5716852*	7	5
15 Nov 97	I'M SO LONELY *Polydor 5690592*	14	3

CAST FROM CASUALTY ◎ *UK, male/female vocal group*　　**6 wks**

14 Mar 98 ●	EVERLASTING LOVE *Warner.esp WESP 003CD*	5	6

CAST OF THE NEW ROCKY HORROR SHOW

UK, male / female vocal group　　**1 wk**

12 Dec 98	THE TIMEWARP *Damn It Janet DAMJAN 1CD*	57	1

Roy CASTLE *UK, male vocalist*　　**3 wks**

22 Dec 60	LITTLE WHITE BERRY *Philips PB 1087*	40	3

CASUALS ◎ *UK, male vocal/instrumental group*　　**26 wks**

14 Aug 68 ●	JESAMINE *Decca F 22784*	2	18
4 Dec 68	TOY *Decca F 22852*	30	8

CAT ◎ *UK, male vocalist*　　**4 wks**

23 Oct 93	TONGUE TIED *EMI CDEM 286*	17	4

CATATONIA ☹ ◎ *UK, male/female vocal/instrumental group*　　**41 wks**

3 Feb 96	SWEET CATATONIA *Blanco Y Negro NEG 85CD*	61	1
4 May 96	LOST CAT *Blanco Y Negro NEG 88CD1*	41	1
7 Sep 96	YOU'VE GOT A LOT TO ANSWER FOR *Blanco Y Negro NEG 93CD1*	35	2
30 Nov 96	BLEED *Blanco Y Negro NEG 97CD1*	46	1
18 Oct 97	I AM THE MOB *Blanco Y Negro NEG 107CD*	37	2
31 Jan 98 ●	MULDER AND SCULLY *Blanco Y Negro NEG 109CD*	3	10
7 Mar 98 ●	THE BALLAD OF TOM JONES *Gut CDGUT 18* [1]	4	8
2 May 98 ●	ROAD RAGE *Blanco Y Negro NEG 112CD*	5	8
1 Aug 98	STRANGE GLUE *Blanco Y Negro NEG 113CD*	11	6
7 Nov 98	GAME ON *WEA NEG 114CD*	33	2

[1] Space with Cerys of Catatonia

CATCH *UK, male vocal/instrumental group*　　**1 wk**

17 Nov 90	FREE (C'MON) *ffrr F 147*	70	1

CATCH UK, male vocal/instrumental group — 6 wks

| 11 Oct 97 | BINGO *Virgin VSCDT 1656* | 23 | 4 |
| 21 Feb 98 | DIVE IN *Virgin VSCDT 1665* | 44 | 2 |

CATHERINE WHEEL UK, male vocal/instrumental group — 12 wks

23 Nov 91	BLACK METALLIC (EP) *Fontana CW 1*	68	1
8 Feb 92	BALLOON *Fontana CW 2*	59	1
18 Apr 92	I WANT TO TOUCH YOU *Fontana CW 3*	35	2
9 Jan 93	30 CENTURY MAN *Fontana CWCD 4*	47	2
10 Jul 93	CRANK *Fontana CWCD 5*	66	1
16 Oct 93	SHOW ME MARY *Fontana CWCDA 6*	62	1
5 Aug 95	WAYDOWN *Fontana CWCD 7*	67	1
13 Dec 97	DELICIOUS *Chrysalis CDCHS 5071*	53	1
28 Feb 98	MA SOLITUDA *Chrysalis CDCHS 5077*	53	1
2 May 98	BROKEN NOSE *Chrysalis CDCHS 5086*	48	1

Tracks on Black Metallic (EP): Black Metallic / Crawling Over Me / Let Me Down Again / Saccharine

Lorraine CATO UK, female vocalist — 3 wks

| 6 Feb 93 | HOW CAN YOU TELL ME IT'S OVER *Columbia 6587662* | 46 | 2 |
| 3 Aug 96 | I WAS MADE TO LOVE YOU *MCA MCSTD 40055* | 41 | 1 |

CATS UK, male instrumental group — 2 wks

| 9 Apr 69 | SWAN LAKE *BAF 1* | 48 | 1 |
| 21 May 69 | SWAN LAKE (re-entry) *BAF 1* | 50 | 1 |

CATS UK, female vocal group — 8 wks

| 6 Oct 79 | LUTON AIRPORT *WEA K 18075* | 22 | 8 |

Nick CAVE and the BAD SEEDS 🎸 ☹
Australia/Germany, male vocal/instrumental group — 10 wks

11 Apr 92	STRAIGHT TO YOU / JACK THE RIPPER *Mute MUTE 140*	68	1
12 Dec 92	WHAT A WONDERFUL WORLD *Mute MUTE 151* [1]	72	1
9 Apr 94	DO YOU LOVE ME *Mute CDMUTE 160*	68	1
14 Oct 95	WHERE THE WILD ROSES GROW *Mute CDMUTE 185* [2]	11	4
9 Mar 96	HENRY LEE *Mute CDMUTE 189* [3]	36	1
22 Feb 97	INTO MY ARMS *Mute CDMUTE 192*	53	1
31 May 97	(ARE YOU) THE ONE THAT I'VE BEEN… *Mute CDMUTE 206*	67	1

[1] Nick Cave and Shane McGowan [2] Nick Cave and Kylie Minogue [3] Nick Cave and the Bad Seeds and PJ Harvey

CAVEMAN UK, male rap group — 2 wks

| 9 Mar 91 | I'M READY *Profile PROF 330* | 65 | 2 |

CCS 🎸 UK, male vocal/instrumental group — 55 wks

31 Oct 70	WHOLE LOTTA LOVE *RAK 104*	13	13
27 Feb 71	● WALKIN' *RAK 109*	7	16
4 Sep 71	● TAP TURNS ON THE WATER *RAK 119*	5	13
4 Mar 72	BROTHER *RAK 126*	25	8
4 Aug 73	BAND PLAYED THE BOOGIE *RAK 154*	36	5

CECIL UK, male vocal/instrumental group — 2 wks

| 25 Oct 97 | HOSTAGE IN A FROCK *Parlophone CDRS 6471* | 68 | 1 |
| 28 Mar 98 | THE MOST TIRING DAY *Parlophone CDR 6490* | 69 | 1 |

CELETIA UK, female vocalist/songwriter — 3 wks

| 11 Apr 98 | REWIND *Big Life BLRD 142* | 29 | 2 |
| 8 Aug 98 | RUNAWAY SKIES *Big Life BLRD 144* | 66 | 1 |

CENTORY US, male rapper — 1 wk

| 17 Dec 94 | POINT OF NO RETURN *EMI CDEM 354* | 67 | 1 |

CENTRAL LINE UK, male vocal/instrumental group — 30 wks

31 Jan 81	(YOU KNOW) YOU CAN DO IT *Mercury LINE 7*	67	3
15 Aug 81	WALKING INTO SUNSHINE *Mercury MER 78*	42	10
30 Jan 82	DON'T TELL ME *Mercury MER 90*	55	3
20 Nov 82	YOU'VE SAID ENOUGH *Mercury MER 117*	58	3
22 Jan 83	NATURE BOY *Mercury MER 131*	21	8
11 Jun 83	SURPRISE SURPRISE *Mercury MER 133*	48	3

CERRONE 🎵 France, male producer/multi-instrumentalist — 21 wks

5 Mar 77	LOVE IN C MINOR *Atlantic K 10895*	31	4
29 Jul 78	● SUPERNATURE *Atlantic K 11089*	8	12
13 Jan 79	JE SUIS MUSIC *CBS 6918*	39	4
10 Aug 96	SUPERNATURE (re-mix) *Encore CDCOR 013*	66	1

A CERTAIN RATIO UK, male vocal/instrumental group — 3 wks

| 16 Jun 90 | WON'T STOP LOVING YOU *A & M ACR 540* | 55 | 3 |

Peter CETERA ✪ US, male vocalist — 13 wks

| 2 Aug 86 | ● GLORY OF LOVE *Full Moon W 8662* ▲ | 3 | 13 |

CEVIN FISHER's BIG BREAK
US, male instrumentalist/producer — 2 wks

| 3 Oct 98 | THE FREAKS COME OUT *Ministry of Sound MOSCDS 127* | 34 | 2 |

Frank CHACKSFIELD ☾ UK, orchestra — 41 wks

3 Apr 53	● LITTLE RED MONKEY *Parlophone R 3658* [1]	10	3
22 May 53	● TERRY'S THEME FROM 'LIMELIGHT' *Decca F 10106*	2	24
12 Feb 54	● EBB TIDE *Decca F 10122*	9	2
24 Feb 56	IN OLD LISBON *Decca F 10689*	15	4
18 May 56	PORT AU PRINCE *Decca F 10727* [2]	18	6
31 Aug 56	DONKEY CART *Decca F 10743*	26	2

[1] Frank Chacksfield's Tunesmiths, featuring Jack Jordan – clavioline
[2] Winifred Atwell and Frank Chacksfield

CHAIRMEN OF THE BOARD 🎤 US, male vocal group — 77 wks

22 Aug 70	● GIVE ME JUST A LITTLE MORE TIME *Invictus INV 501*	3	13
14 Nov 70	● YOU'VE GOT ME DANGLING ON A STRING *Invictus INV 504*	5	13
20 Feb 71	EVERYTHING'S TUESDAY *Invictus INV 507*	12	9
15 May 71	PAY TO THE PIPER *Invictus INV 511*	34	7
4 Sep 71	CHAIRMAN OF THE BOARD *Invictus INV 516*	48	2
15 Jul 72	WORKING ON A BUILDING OF LOVE *Invictus INV 519*	20	8
7 Oct 72	ELMO JAMES *Invictus INV 524*	21	7
16 Dec 72	I'M ON MY WAY TO A BETTER PLACE *Invictus INV 527*	38	1
6 Jan 73	I'M ON MY WAY TO A BETTER PLACE (re-entry) *Invictus INV 527*	30	5
23 Jun 73	FINDERS KEEPERS *Invictus INV 530*	21	9
13 Sep 86	LOVERBOY *EMI EMI 5585* [1]	56	3

[1] Chairmen of the Board featuring General Johnson

CHAKACHAS Belgium, male/female vocal/instrumental group — 8 wks

| 11 Jan 62 | TWIST TWIST *RCA 1264* | 48 | 1 |
| 27 May 72 | JUNGLE FEVER *Polydor 2121 064* | 29 | 7 |

George CHAKIRIS US, male vocalist — 1 wk

| 2 Jun 60 | HEART OF A TEENAGE GIRL *Triumph RGM 1010* | 49 | 1 |

CHAKKA BOOM BANG
Holland, male instrumental/production group — 1 wk

| 20 Jan 96 | TOSSING AND TURNING *Hooj Choons HOOJCD 39* | 57 | 1 |

CHAKRA UK, male/female vocal/instrumental group — 3 wks

| 18 Jan 97 | I AM *WEA WEA 091CD* | 24 | 2 |
| 23 Aug 97 | HOME *WEA WEA 116CD2* | 46 | 1 |

Sue CHALONER *UK, female vocalist*   **1 wk**

| 22 May 93 | MOVE ON UP *Pulse 8 CDLOSE 41* | .64 | 1 |

Richard CHAMBERLAIN ☾ *US, male vocalist*   **36 wks**

7 Jun 62	THEME FROM 'DR. KILDARE' (THREE STARS WILL SHINE TONIGHT) *MGM 1160*	.12	10
1 Nov 62	LOVE ME TENDER *MGM 1173*	.15	11
21 Feb 63	HI-LILI HI-LO *MGM 1189*	.20	9
18 Jul 63	TRUE LOVE *MGM 1205*	.30	6

CHAMELEON *UK, male vocal/instrumental group*   **2 wks**

| 18 May 96 | THE WAY IT IS *Stress CDSTR 65* | .34 | 2 |

CHAMELEONS – *See LORI and the CHAMELEONS*

CHAMPAIGN 🎸
US, male/female vocal/instrumental group   **13 wks**

| 9 May 81 | ● HOW 'BOUT US *CBS A 1046* | .5 | 13 |

CHAMPIONSHIP LEGEND – *See RAZE*

CHAMPS 🎷 *US, male instrumental group*   **10 wks**

| 4 Apr 58 | ● TEQUILA *London HLU 8580* ▲ | .5 | 9 |
| 17 Mar 60 | TOO MUCH TEQUILA *London HLH 9052* | .49 | 1 |

CHAMPS BOYS *France, male instrumental group*   **6 wks**

| 19 Jun 76 | TUBULAR BELLS *Philips 6006 519* | .41 | 6 |

Gene CHANDLER 🎸 ✈ *US, male vocalist*   **29 wks**

5 Jun 68	NOTHING CAN STOP ME *Soul City SC 102*	.41	4
3 Feb 79	GET DOWN *20th Century BTC 1040*	.11	11
1 Sep 79	WHEN YOU'RE NUMBER 1 *20th Century TC 2411*	.43	4
28 Jun 80	DOES SHE HAVE A FRIEND *20th Century TC 2451*	.28	9

CHANELLE ☺ *US, female vocalist*   **9 wks**

| 11 Mar 89 | ONE MAN *Cooltempo COOL 183* | .16 | 8 |
| 10 Dec 94 | ONE MAN (re-mix) *Deep Distraxion OILYCD 031* | .50 | 1 |

CHANGE ☺ ✈ *US, male/female vocal/instrumental group*   **43 wks**

28 Jun 80	A LOVER'S HOLIDAY/GLOW OF LOVE *WEA K 79141*	.14	8
6 Sep 80	SEARCHING *WEA K 79156*	.11	10
2 Jun 84	CHANGE OF HEART *WEA YZ 7*	.17	10
11 Aug 84	YOU ARE MY MELODY *WEA YZ 14*	.48	4
16 Mar 85	LET'S GO TOGETHER *Cooltempo COOL 107*	.37	7
25 May 85	OH WHAT A FEELING *Cooltempo COOL 109*	.56	2
13 Jul 85	MUTUAL ATTRACTION *Cooltempo COOL 111*	.60	2

CHANGING FACES [R&B] *US, female vocal duo*   **12 wks**

24 Sep 94	STROKE YOU UP *Big Beat A 8251CD*	.43	3
26 Jul 97	● G.H.E.T.T.O.U.T. *Atlantic AT 0003CD*	.10	5
1 Nov 97	I GOT SOMEBODY ELSE *Atlantic AT 0014CD*	.42	1
4 Apr 98	TIME AFTER TIME *Atlantic AT 0027CD*	.35	2
1 Aug 98	SAME TEMPO *A&M 5826952*	.53	1

Bruce CHANNEL ❂ *US, male vocalist*   **28 wks**

| 22 Mar 62 | ● HEY! BABY *Mercury AMT 1171* ▲ | .2 | 12 |
| 26 Jun 68 | KEEP ON *Bell 1010* | .12 | 16 |

CHANNEL X *Belgium, male/female vocal/instrumental group*   **1 wk**

| 14 Dec 91 | GROOVE TO MOVE *PWL Continental PWL 209* | .67 | 1 |

CHANSON *US, male/female vocal group*   **7 wks**

| 13 Jan 79 | DON'T HOLD BACK *Ariola ARO 140* | .33 | 7 |

CHANTAYS ❂ *US, male instrumental group*   **14 wks**

| 18 Apr 63 | PIPELINE *London HLD 9696* | .16 | 14 |

CHANTER SISTERS *UK, female vocal group*   **5 wks**

| 17 Jul 76 | SIDE SHOW *Polydor 2058 735* | .43 | 5 |

CHAOS *UK, male vocal group*   **2 wks**

| 3 Oct 92 | FAREWELL MY SUMMER LOVE *Arista 74321116397* | .55 | 2 |

Harry CHAPIN *US, male vocalist*   **5 wks**

| 11 May 74 | W.O.L.D. *Elektra K 12133* | .34 | 5 |

Simone CHAPMAN – *See ILLEGAL MOTION featuring Simone CHAPMAN*

Tracy CHAPMAN ❂ 🎸 *US, female vocalist*   **15 wks**

| 11 Jun 88 | ● FAST CAR *Elektra EKR 73* | .5 | 12 |
| 30 Sep 89 | CROSSROADS *Elektra EKR 95* | .61 | 3 |

CHAPTERHOUSE *UK, male vocal/instrumental group*   **3 wks**

| 30 Mar 91 | PEARL *Dedicated STONE 003* | .67 | 1 |
| 12 Oct 91 | MESMERISE *Dedicated HOUSE 001* | .60 | 2 |

CHAQUITO *UK, male arranger/conductor – Johnny Gregory*   **1 wk**

| 27 Oct 60 | NEVER ON SUNDAY *Fontana H 265* | .50 | 1 |

CHARLATANS ☹ *UK, male vocal/instrumental group*   **61 wks**

2 Jun 90	● THE ONLY ONE I KNOW *Situation Two SIT 70T*	.9	9
22 Sep 90	THEN *Situation Two SIT 74T*	.12	5
9 Mar 91	OVER RISING *Situation Two SIT 76*	.15	5
17 Aug 91	INDIAN ROPE *Dead Dead Good GOOD 1T*	.57	1
9 Nov 91	ME. IN TIME *Situation Two SIT 84*	.28	3
7 Mar 92	WEIRDO *Situation Two SIT 88*	.19	4
18 Jul 92	TREMELO SONG (EP) *Situation Two SIT 97T*	.44	2
5 Feb 94	CAN'T GET OUT OF BED *Beggars Banquet BBQ 27CD*	.24	3
19 Mar 94	I NEVER WANT AN EASY LIFE IF ME AND HE WERE EVER TO GET THERE *Beggars Banquet BBQ 31CD*	.38	1
2 Jul 94	JESUS HAIRDO *Beggars Banquet BBQ 32CD1*	.48	2
7 Jan 95	CRASHIN' IN *Beggars Banquet BBQ 44CD*	.31	2
27 May 95	JUST LOOKIN'/BULLET COMES *Beggars Banquet BBQ 55CD*	.32	3
26 Aug 95	JUST WHEN YOU'RE THINKIN' THINGS OVER *Beggars Banquet BBQ 60CD*	.12	3
7 Sep 96	● ONE TO ANOTHER *Beggars Banquet BBQ 301CD*	.3	6
5 Apr 97	● NORTH COUNTRY BOY *Beggars Banquet BBQ 309CD*	.4	5
21 Jun 97	● HOW HIGH *Beggars Banquet BBQ 312CD*	.6	4
1 Nov 97	TELLIN' STORIES *Beggars Banquet BBQ 318CD*	.16	3

Tracks on Tremelo Song (EP): Tremelo Song / Happen to Die / Normality Swing

CHARLENE ❂ *US, female vocalist*   **12 wks**

| 15 May 82 | ★ I'VE NEVER BEEN TO ME *Motown TMG 1260* | .1 | 12 |

Don CHARLES *UK, male vocalist*   **5 wks**

| 22 Feb 62 | WALK WITH ME MY ANGEL *Decca F 11424* | .39 | 5 |

Ray CHARLES 🎸 ♫ *Rock era's first 'genius', b. Ray Charles Robinson, 23 September, 1930, Georgia. This blind singer/songwriter/pianist and band leader had a US chart career spanning six decades. In 1994 he received a prestigious National Medal of Arts from President Clinton*   **130 wks**

1 Dec 60	GEORGIA ON MY MIND *HMV POP 792* ▲	.47	1
15 Dec 60	GEORGIA ON MY MIND (re-entry) *HMV POP 792*	.24	7
19 Oct 61	● HIT THE ROAD JACK *HMV POP 935* ▲	.6	12
14 Jun 62	★ I CAN'T STOP LOVING YOU *HMV POP 1034* ▲	.1	17
13 Sep 62	● YOU DON'T KNOW ME *HMV POP 1064*	.9	13
13 Dec 62	YOUR CHEATING HEART *HMV POP 1099*	.13	8
28 Mar 63	DON'T SET ME FREE *HMV POP 1133*	.37	3
16 May 63	● TAKE THESE CHAINS FROM MY HEART *HMV POP 1161*	.5	20

12 Sep 63	NO ONE *HMV POP 1202*	.35	7
31 Oct 63	BUSTED *HMV POP 1221*	.21	10
24 Sep 64	NO ONE TO CRY TO *HMV POP 1333*	.38	3
21 Jan 65	MAKIN' WHOOPEE *HMV POP 1383*	.42	4
10 Feb 66	CRYIN' TIME *HMV POP 1502*	.50	1
21 Apr 66	TOGETHER AGAIN *HMV POP 1519*	.48	1
5 Jul 67	HERE WE GO AGAIN *HMV POP 1595*	.38	1
19 Jul 67	HERE WE GO AGAIN (re-entry) *HMV POP 1595*	.45	2
20 Dec 67	YESTERDAY *Stateside SS 2071*	.44	4
31 Jul 68	ELEANOR RIGBY *Stateside SS 2120*	.36	9
13 Jan 90	I'LL BE GOOD TO YOU *Qwest W 9992* [1]	.21	7

[1] Quincy Jones featuring Ray Charles and Chaka Khan

See also INXS

Suzette CHARLES *US, female vocalist* — 2 wks

21 Aug 93	FREE TO LOVE AGAIN *RCA 74321158372*	.58	2

Tina CHARLES ◢ *UK, female vocalist* — 63 wks

7 Feb 76 ★	I LOVE TO LOVE (BUT MY BABY LOVES TO DANCE) *CBS 3937*	.1	12
1 May 76	LOVE ME LIKE A LOVER *CBS 4237*	.31	7
21 Aug 76 ●	DANCE LITTLE LADY DANCE *CBS 4480*	.6	13
4 Dec 76 ●	DR. LOVE *CBS 4779*	.4	10
14 May 77	RENDEZVOUS *CBS 5174*	.27	6
29 Oct 77	LOVE BUG – SWEETS FOR MY SWEET (MEDLEY) *CBS 5680*	.26	4
11 Mar 78	I'LL GO WHERE YOUR MUSIC TAKES ME *CBS 6062*	.27	8
30 Aug 86	I LOVE TO LOVE (re-mix) *DMC DECK 1*	.67	3

CHARLES and EDDIE ☺ ♪ *US, male vocal duo* — 30 wks

31 Oct 92 ★	WOULD I LIE TO YOU *Capitol CL 673*	.1	17
20 Feb 93	N.Y.C. (CAN YOU BELIEVE THIS CITY) *Capitol CDCL 681*	.33	5
22 May 93	HOUSE IS NOT A HOME *Capitol CDCLS 688*	.29	4
13 May 95	24-7-365 *Capitol CDCLS 747*	.38	4

Dick CHARLESWORTH and his CITY GENTS
UK, male jazz band group, Dick Charlesworth – clarinet — 1 wk

4 May 61	BILLY BOY *Top Rank JAR 558*	.43	1

CHARLOTTE *UK, female vocalist* — 2 wks

12 Mar 94	QUEEN OF HEARTS *Big Life BLRD 106*	.54	1
2 May 98	BE MINE *Parlophone Rhythm CDRHYTHM 10*	.59	1

CHARME *US, male/female vocal group* — 2 wks

17 Nov 84	GEORGY PORGY *RCA 464*	.68	2

CHARO and the SALSOUL ORCHESTRA
US, female vocalist and orchestra — 4 wks

29 Apr 78	DANCE A LITTLE BIT CLOSER *Salsoul SSOL 101*	.44	4

CHARVONI – See BROTHERS IN RHYTHM

CHAS and DAVE ☺ *UK, male vocal/instrumental duo* — 66 wks

11 Nov 78	STRUMMIN' *EMI 2874* [1]	.52	3
26 May 79	GERTCHA *EMI 2947*	.20	8
1 Sep 79	THE SIDEBOARD SONG (GOT MY BEER IN THE SIDEBOARD HERE) *EMI 2986*	.55	3
29 Nov 80 ●	RABBIT *Rockney 9*	.8	11
12 Dec 81	STARS OVER 45 *Rockney KOR 12*	.21	8
13 Mar 82 ●	AIN'T NO PLEASING YOU *Rockney KOR 14*	.2	11
17 Jul 82	MARGATE *Rockney KOR 15*	.46	4
19 Mar 83	LONDON GIRLS *Rockney KOR 17*	.63	3
3 Dec 83	MY MELANCHOLY BABY *Rockney KOR 21*	.51	6
3 May 86 ●	SNOOKER LOOPY *Rockney POT 147* [2]	.6	9

[1] Chas and Dave with Rockney [2] Matchroom Mob with Chas and Dave

See also TOTTENHAM HOTSPUR FA CUP FINAL SQUAD

CHEAP TRICK *US, male vocal/instrumental group* — 14 wks

5 May 79	I WANT YOU TO WANT ME *Epic EPC 7258*	.29	9
2 Feb 80	WAY OF THE WORLD *Epic EPC 8114*	.73	2
31 Jul 82	IF YOU WANT MY LOVE *Epic EPC A 2406*	.57	3

Oliver CHEATHAM *US, male vocalist* — 5 wks

2 Jul 83	GET DOWN SATURDAY NIGHT *MCA 828*	.38	5

CHECK 1-2 – See Craig McLACHLAN

Chubby CHECKER ☺ *The 'King of the Twist', b. Ernest Evans, 3 October, 1941, South Carolina. This rotund vocalist helped to make the twist the most popular dance of the rock era. 'The Twist' was the only single to top the US chart on two separate occasions* — 112 wks

22 Sep 60	THE TWIST *Columbia DB 4503* ▲	.49	1
6 Oct 60	THE TWIST (re-entry) *Columbia DB 4503* ▲	.44	1
30 Mar 61	PONY TIME *Columbia DB 4591* ▲	.27	6
17 Aug 61	LET'S TWIST AGAIN *Columbia DB 4691*	.37	3
28 Dec 61 ●	LET'S TWIST AGAIN (re-entry) *Columbia DB 4691*	.2	27
11 Jan 62	THE TWIST (2nd re-entry) *Columbia DB 4503* ▲	.14	10
5 Apr 62	SLOW TWISTIN' *Columbia DB 4808*	.23	8
19 Apr 62	TEACH ME TO TWIST *Columbia DB 4802* [1]	.45	1
9 Aug 62	DANCIN' PARTY *Columbia DB 4876*	.19	13
23 Aug 62	LET'S TWIST AGAIN (2nd re-entry) *Columbia DB 4691*	.46	1
13 Sep 62	LET'S TWIST AGAIN (3rd re-entry) *Columbia DB 4691*	.49	3
1 Nov 62	LIMBO ROCK *Cameo Parkway P 849*	.32	10
20 Dec 62	JINGLE BELL ROCK *Cameo Parkway C 205* [1]	.40	3
31 Oct 63	WHAT DO YA SAY *Cameo Parkway P 806*	.37	4
29 Nov 75 ●	LET'S TWIST AGAIN/THE TWIST (re-issue) *London HL 10512*	.5	10
18 Jun 88 ●	THE TWIST (YO, TWIST) *Urban URB 20* [2]	.2	11

[1] Chubby Checker and Bobby Rydell [2] Fat Boys and Chubby Checker

CHECKMATES – See Emile FORD and the CHECKMATES

CHECKMATES LTD. *US, male vocal/instrumental group* — 8 wks

15 Nov 69	PROUD MARY *A & M AMS 769*	.30	8

Judy CHEEKS ☺ ♪ *US, female vocalist* — 15 wks

13 Nov 93	SO IN LOVE (THE REAL DEAL) *Positiva CDTIV 6*	.27	3
7 May 94	REACH *Positiva CDTIV 12*	.17	4
4 Mar 95	THIS TIME/RESPECT *Positiva CDTIV 28*	.23	2
17 Jun 95	YOU'RE THE STORY OF MY LIFE/AS LONG AS YOU'RE GOOD TO ME *Positiva CDTIV 34*	.30	3
13 Jan 96	REACH (re-mix) *Positiva CDTIV 42*	.22	3

CHEETAHS *UK, male vocal/instrumental group* — 6 wks

1 Oct 64	MECCA *Philips BF 1362*	.36	3
21 Jan 65	SOLDIER BOY *Philips BF 1383*	.39	3

CHEF ⓇⓀ ☺ *US, male vocalist – Isaac Hayes* — 1 wk

26 Dec 98 ●	CHOCOLATE SALTY BALLS (PS I LOVE YOU) *Columbia 6667985*	.2†	1

See also Isaac HAYES

CHELSEA F.C. ☺ *UK, male football team vocalists* — 20 wks

26 Feb 72 ●	BLUE IS THE COLOUR *Penny Farthing PEN 782*	.5	12
14 May 94	NO ONE CAN STOP US NOW *RCA 74321210452*	.23	3
17 May 97	BLUE DAY *WEA WEA 112CD* [1]	.22	5

[1] Suggs & Co featuring Chelsea Team

CHEMICAL BROTHERS ☺
UK, male instrumental/production duo — 25 wks

17 Jun 95	LEAVE HOME *Junior Boy's Own CHEMSD 1*	.17	4
9 Sep 95	LIFE IS SWEET *Junior Boy's Own CHEMSD 2*	.25	3
27 Jan 96	LOOPS OF FURY (EP) *Junior Boy's Own CHEMSD 3*	.13	1

12 Oct 96	★ SETTING SUN Junior Boy's Own CHEMSD 4 ■	1	7
5 Apr 97	★ BLOCK ROCKIN' BEATS Virgin CHEMSD 5 ■	1	6
20 Sep 97	ELEKTROBANK Virgin CHEMSD 6	17	4

Tracks on Loops of Fury (EP): Loops of Fury / (The Best Part of) Breaking Up /
Get on Up Like This / Chemical Beats
Uncredited vocal on 'Setting Sun' by Noel Gallagher

CHEQUERS UK, male vocal/instrumental group   10 wks
| 18 Oct 75 | ROCK ON BROTHER Creole CR 111 | ....21 | 5 |
| 28 Feb 76 | HEY MISS PAYNE Creole CR 116 | ....32 | 5 |

CHER ☺ Perennially popular vocalist, b. Cherilyn LaPierre, 20 May, 1946,
California. She was half of the most successful husband/wife duo ever,
Sonny and Cher, and had an equally stunning run of solo smashes. Her
No 1s now span a record 33 years, and at the age of 52 she is the
oldest female solo singer to top the chart   180 wks
19 Aug 65	● ALL I REALLY WANT TO DO Liberty LIB 66114	9	10
31 Mar 66	● BANG BANG (MY BABY SHOT ME DOWN) Liberty LIB 66160	3	12
4 Aug 66	I FEEL SOMETHING IN THE AIR Liberty LIB 12034	43	2
22 Sep 66	SUNNY Liberty LIB 12083	32	5
6 Nov 71	● GYPSIES TRAMPS AND THIEVES MCA MU 1142 ▲	4	13
16 Feb 74	DARK LADY MCA 101 ▲	36	3
16 Mar 74	DARK LADY (re-entry) MCA 101	45	1
19 Dec 87	● I FOUND SOMEONE Geffen GEF 31	5	10
2 Apr 88	WE ALL SLEEP ALONE Geffen GEF 35	47	5
2 Sep 89	● IF I COULD TURN BACK TIME Geffen GEF 59	6	14
13 Jan 90	JUST LIKE JESSE JAMES Geffen GEF 69	11	11
7 Apr 90	HEART OF STONE Geffen GEF 75	43	5
11 Aug 90	YOU WOULDN'T KNOW LOVE Geffen GEF 77	55	3
13 Apr 91	★ THE SHOOP SHOOP SONG (IT'S IN HIS KISS) Epic 6566737	1	15
13 Jul 91	● LOVE AND UNDERSTANDING Geffen GFS 5	10	8
12 Oct 91	SAVE UP ALL YOUR TEARS Geffen GFS 11	37	5
7 Dec 91	LOVE HURTS Geffen GFS 16	43	5
18 Apr 92	COULD'VE BEEN YOU Geffen GFS 19	31	4
14 Nov 92	OH NO NOT MY BABY Geffen GFS 29	33	4
16 Jan 93	MANY RIVERS TO CROSS Geffen GFSTD 31	37	3
6 Mar 93	WHENEVER YOU'RE NEAR Geffen GFSTD 32	72	1
15 Jan 94	I GOT YOU BABE Geffen GFSTD 64 [1]	35	3
18 Mar 95	★ LOVE CAN BUILD A BRIDGE London COCD 1 [2]	1	8
28 Oct 95	WALKING IN MEMPHIS WEA WEA 021CD1	11	7
20 Jan 96	ONE BY ONE WEA WEA 032CD	7	9
27 Apr 96	NOT ENOUGH LOVE IN THE WORLD WEA WEA 052CD	31	2
17 Aug 96	THE SUN AIN'T GONNA SHINE ANYMORE WEA WEA 071CD	26	3
31 Oct 98	★ BELIEVE WEA WEA 175CD ■	.....................1†	9

[1] Cher with Beavis and Butt-Head [2] Cher, Chrissie Hynde and Neneh Cherry with
Eric Clapton

See also SONNY and CHER; MEAT LOAF

CHERELLE US, female vocalist   25 wks
28 Dec 85	● SATURDAY LOVE Tabu A 6829 [1]	6	11
1 Mar 86	WILL YOU SATISFY? Tabu A 6927	57	3
6 Feb 88	NEVER KNEW LOVE LIKE THIS Tabu 6513827 [2]	26	7
6 May 89	AFFAIR Tabu 654673 7	67	2
24 Mar 90	SATURDAY LOVE (re-mix) Tabu 6558007 [1]	55	1

[1] Cherelle with Alexander O'Neal [2] Alexander O'Neal featuring Cherelle

CHERI ☺ ☺ Canada, female vocal duo   9 wks
| 19 Jun 82 | MURPHY'S LAW Polydor POSP 459 | ....13 | 9 |

CHEROKEES UK, male vocal/instrumental group   5 wks
| 3 Sep 64 | SEVEN DAFFODILS Columbia DB 7341 | ....33 | 5 |

Don CHERRY ☺ US, male vocalist   11 wks
| 10 Feb 56 | ● BAND OF GOLD Philips PB 549 | ....6 | 11 |

Eagle-Eye CHERRY ☺ Sweden, male vocalist   20 wks
| 4 Jul 98 | ● SAVE TONIGHT Polydor 5695952 | ....6 | 13 |
| 14 Nov 98 | ● FALLING IN LOVE AGAIN Polydor 5630252 | ....8† | 7 |

Neneh CHERRY ☺ ◀ US, female vocalist   91 wks
10 Dec 88	● BUFFALO STANCE Circa YR 21	3	13
20 May 89	● MANCHILD Circa YR 30	5	10
12 Aug 89	KISSES ON THE WIND Circa YR 33	20	6
23 Dec 89	INNA CITY MAMMA Circa YR 42	31	7
29 Sep 90	I'VE GOT YOU UNDER MY SKIN Circa YR 53	25	5
3 Oct 92	MONEY LOVE Circa YR 83	23	4
16 Jan 93	BUDDY X Circa YRCD 98	35	3
25 Jun 94	● 7 SECONDS Columbia 6605082 [1]	3	21
24 Dec 94	7 SECONDS (re-entry) Columbia 6605082 [1]	54	4
18 Mar 95	★ LOVE CAN BUILD A BRIDGE London COCD 1 [2]	1	8
3 Aug 96	● WOMAN Hut HUTCD 70	9	7
14 Dec 96	KOOTCHI Hut HUTDG 75	38	2
22 Feb 97	FEEL IT Hut HUTCD 79	68	1

[1] Youssou N'Dour (featuring Neneh Cherry) [2] Cher, Chrissie Hynde and Neneh
Cherry with Eric Clapton

CHI-LITES ♪ US, male vocal group   89 wks
28 Aug 71	(FOR GOD'S SAKE) GIVE MORE POWER TO THE PEOPLE MCA MU 1138	32	6
15 Jan 72	● HAVE YOU SEEN HER MCA MU 1146	3	12
27 May 72	● OH GIRL MCA MU 1156 ▲	14	9
23 Mar 74	● HOMELY GIRL Brunswick BR 9	5	13
20 Jul 74	I FOUND SUNSHINE Brunswick BR 12	35	5
2 Nov 74	● TOO GOOD TO BE FORGOTTEN Brunswick BR 13	10	11
21 Jun 75	● HAVE YOU SEEN HER/OH GIRL (re-issue) Brunswick BR 20	5	9
13 Sep 75	IT'S TIME FOR LOVE Brunswick BR 25	5	10
31 Jul 76	YOU DON'T HAVE TO GO Brunswick BR 34	3	11
13 Aug 83	CHANGING FOR YOU R & B RBS 215	61	3

CHIC ▲ US, male/female vocal/instrumental group   90 wks
26 Nov 77	● DANCE DANCE DANCE (YOWSAH YOWSAH YOWSAH) Atlantic K 11038	6	12
1 Apr 78	● EVERYBODY DANCE Atlantic K 11097	9	11
18 Nov 78	● LE FREAK Atlantic K 11209 ▲	7	16
24 Feb 79	● I WANT YOUR LOVE Atlantic LV 16	4	11
30 Jun 79	● GOOD TIMES Atlantic K 11310 ▲	5	11
13 Oct 79	MY FORBIDDEN LOVER Atlantic K 11385	15	8
8 Dec 79	MY FEET KEEP DANCING Atlantic K 11415	21	9
12 Mar 83	HANGIN' Atlantic A 9898	64	1
19 Sep 87	JACK LE FREAK Atlantic A 9198	19	6
14 Jul 90	MEGACHIC – CHIC MEDLEY East West A 7949	58	2
15 Feb 92	CHIC MYSTIQUE Warner Bros. W 0083	48	3

CHICAGO ✍ US, male vocal/instrumental group   81 wks
10 Jan 70	● I'M A MAN CBS 4715	8	11
18 Jul 70	● 25 OR 6 TO 4 CBS 5076	7	13
9 Oct 76	★ IF YOU LEAVE ME NOW CBS 4603 ▲	1	16
5 Nov 77	BABY WHAT A BIG SURPRISE CBS 5672	41	3
21 Aug 82	● HARD TO SAY I'M SORRY Full Moon K 79301 ▲	4	15
27 Oct 84	● HARD HABIT TO BREAK Full Moon W 9214	8	13
26 Jan 85	YOU'RE THE INSPIRATION Warner Bros. W 9126	14	10

CHICANE ☺ UK, male instrumental duo   19 wks
21 Dec 96	OFFSHORE Xtravaganza 0091005	14	7
14 Jun 97	SUNSTROKE Xtravaganza 0091125	21	3
13 Sep 97	OFFSHORE '97 (re-mix) Xtravaganza 0091255 EXT [1]	17	4
20 Dec 97	LOST YOU SOMEWHERE Xtravaganza 0091415	35	3
10 Oct 98	STRONG IN LOVE Xtravaganza 0091675EXT [2]	32	2

[1] Chicane with Power Circle [2] Chicane featuring Mason

Chicane are Disco Citizens under another name
See also DISCO CITIZENS

CHICKEN SHACK ✎
UK, male/female vocal/instrumental group   **19 wks**

7 May 69	I'D RATHER GO BLIND *Blue Horizon 57-3153*	14	13
6 Sep 69	TEARS IN THE WIND *Blue Horizon 57-3160*	29	6

CHICKEN SHED THEATRE ◐ ©
UK, theatre company   **6 wks**

27 Dec 98	I AM IN LOVE WITH THE WORLD *Columbia 6654172*	15	6

CHICORY TIP ◐
UK, male vocal/instrumental group   **34 wks**

29 Jan 72 ★	SON OF MY FATHER *CBS 7737*	1	13
20 May 72	WHAT'S YOUR NAME *CBS 8021*	13	8
31 Mar 73	GOOD GRIEF CHRISTINA *CBS 1258*	17	13

CHIEFTAINS – See Van MORRISON

CHIFFONS ♪
US, female vocal group   **40 wks**

11 Apr 63	HE'S SO FINE *Stateside SS 172* ▲	16	12
18 Jul 63	ONE FINE DAY *Stateside SS 202*	29	6
26 May 66	SWEET TALKIN' GUY *Stateside SS 512*	31	8
18 Mar 72 ●	SWEET TALKIN' GUY (re-issue) *London HL 10271*	4	14

CHILD ◐
UK, male vocal/instrumental group   **22 wks**

29 Apr 78	WHEN YOU WALK IN THE ROOM *Ariola Hansa AHA 511*	38	5
22 Jul 78 ●	IT'S ONLY MAKE BELIEVE *Ariola Hansa AHA 522*	10	12
28 Apr 79	ONLY YOU (AND YOU ALONE) *Ariola Hansa AHA 536*	33	5

Jane CHILD *Canada, female vocalist*   **8 wks**

12 May 90	DON'T WANNA FALL IN LOVE *Warner Bros. W 9817*	22	8

CHILDLINERS ◐
UK/Australia, male/female vocal group   **6 wks**

16 Dec 95 ●	THE GIFT OF CHRISTMAS *London LONCD 376*	9	6

CHILDREN FOR RWANDA *UK, male/female choir*   **2 wks**

10 Sep 94	LOVE CAN BUILD A BRIDGE *East West YZ 849CD*	57	2

CHILDREN OF THE NIGHT *UK, male vocalist/producer*   **2 wks**

26 Nov 88	IT'S A TRIP (TUNE IN, TURN ON, DROP OUT) *Jive JIVE 189*	52	2

CHILDREN OF THE REVOLUTION – See KLF

Toni CHILDS *US, female vocalist*   **4 wks**

25 Mar 89	DON'T WALK AWAY *A & M AM 462*	53	4

CHILL FAC-TORR *US, male vocal/instrumental group*   **8 wks**

2 Apr 83	TWIST (ROUND 'N' ROUND) *Phillyworld PWS 109*	37	8

CHILLI featuring CARRAPICHIO
US/Ghana/Brazil male/female vocal/instrumental group   **1 wk**

20 Sep 97	TIC, TIC TAC *Arista 74321511332*	59	1

CHIMES ♪ (R&B)
UK, male/female vocal/instrumental group   **28 wks**

19 Aug 89	1-2-3 *CBS 655166 7*	60	3
2 Dec 89	HEAVEN *CBS 655432 7*	66	2
6 Jan 90	HEAVEN (re-entry) *CBS 655432 7*	69	3
19 May 90 ●	I STILL HAVEN'T FOUND WHAT I'M LOOKING FOR *CBS CHIM 1*	6	9
28 Jul 90	TRUE LOVE *CBS CHIM 2*	48	3
29 Sep 90	HEAVEN (re-issue) *CBS CHIM 3*	24	6
1 Dec 90	LOVE COMES TO MIND *CBS CHIM 4*	49	2

CHIMIRA *South Africa, female vocalist*   **1 wk**

6 Dec 97	SHOW ME HEAVEN *Neoteric NRDCD 11*	70	1

CHINA BLACK ◐ ✝ *UK, male vocal/instrumental duo*   **35 wks**

16 Jul 94 ●	SEARCHING *Wild Card CARDD 7*	4	16
29 Oct 94	STARS *Wild Card CARDD 9*	19	7
17 Dec 94	SEARCHING (re-entry) *Wild Card CARDD 7*	54	4
11 Feb 95	ALMOST SEE YOU (SOMEWHERE) *Wild Card CARDW 15*	31	2
3 Jun 95	SWING LOW SWEET CHARIOT *PolyGram TV SWLOW 2* [1]	15	6

[1] Ladysmith Black Mambazo featuring China Black

CHINA CRISIS ◐ *UK, male vocal/instrumental group*   **66 wks**

7 Aug 82	AFRICAN AND WHITE *Inevitable INEV 011*	45	5
22 Jan 83	CHRISTIAN *Virgin VS 562*	12	9
21 May 83	TRAGEDY AND MYSTERY *Virgin VS 587*	46	6
15 Oct 83	WORKING WITH FIRE AND STEEL *Virgin VS 620*	48	5
14 Jan 84 ●	WISHFUL THINKING *Virgin VS 647*	9	8
10 Mar 84	HANNA HANNA *Virgin VS 665*	44	3
30 Mar 85	BLACK MAN RAY *Virgin VS 752*	14	9
1 Jun 85	KING IN A CATHOLIC STYLE (WAKE UP) *Virgin VS 765*	19	9
7 Sep 85	YOU DID CUT ME *Virgin VS 799*	54	3
8 Nov 86	ARIZONA SKY *Virgin VS 898*	47	4
24 Jan 87	BEST KEPT SECRET *Virgin VS 926*	36	5

CHINA DRUM *UK, male vocal/instrumental group*   **4 wks**

2 Mar 96	CAN'T STOP THESE THINGS *Mantra MNT 8CD*	65	1
20 Apr 96	LAST CHANCE *Mantra MNT 10CD*	60	1
9 Aug 97	FICTION OF LIFE *Mantra MNT 21CD*	65	1
27 Sep 97	SOMEWHERE ELSE *Mantra MNT 022CD1*	74	1

Jonny CHINGAS *US, male instrumentalist*   **6 wks**

19 Feb 83	PHONE HOME *CBS A 3121*	43	6

CHIPMUNKS ◐ *US, chipmunk vocal trio*   **12 wks**

24 Jul 59	RAGTIME COWBOY JOE *London HLU 8916* [1]	11	8
19 Dec 92	ACHY BREAKY HEART *Epic 6588837* [2]	53	3
14 Dec 96	MACARENA *Sony Wonder 6639981* [3]	65	1

[1] David Seville and the Chipmunks [2] Alvin and the Chipmunks featuring Billy Ray Cyrus [3] Los Del Chipmunks

The Chipmunk characters were created by David Seville, who died in 1972. His son resurrected the act in 1980. See also David SEVILLE

CHIPPENDALES *UK/US, male vocal group*   **4 wks**

31 Oct 92	GIVE ME YOUR BODY *XSrhythm XSR 3*	28	4

CHOPS-EMC + EXTENSIVE
UK, male instrumental group and rapper   **1 wk**

8 Aug 92	ME' ISRAELITES *Faze 2 FAZE 6*	60	1

CHORDETTES ◐ *US, female vocal group*   **25 wks**

17 Dec 54	MR. SANDMAN *Columbia DB 3553* ▲	11	8
31 Aug 56 ●	BORN TO BE WITH YOU *London HLA 8302*	8	9
18 Apr 58 ●	LOLLIPOP *London HLD 8584*	6	8

CHORDS *UK, male vocal/instrumental group*   **17 wks**

6 Oct 79	NOW IT'S GONE *Polydor 2059 141*	63	2
2 Feb 80	MAYBE TOMORROW *Polydor POSP 101*	40	5
26 Apr 80	SOMETHING'S MISSING *Polydor POSP 146*	55	3
12 Jul 80	THE BRITISH WAY OF LIFE *Polydor 2059 258*	54	3
18 Oct 80	IN MY STREET *Polydor POSP 185*	50	4

CHRIS and JAMES *UK, male instrumental/production duo*   **3 wks**

17 Sep 94	CALM DOWN (BASS KEEPS PUMPIN') *Stress 12STR 38*	74	1
4 Nov 95	FOX FORCE FIVE *Stress CDSTR 61*	71	1
7 Nov 98	CLUB FOR LIFE '98 *Stress CDSTR 85*	66	1

Neil CHRISTIAN ⊗ *UK, male vocalist* — **10 wks**

7 Apr 66	THAT'S NICE *Strike JH 301*	14	10

Roger CHRISTIAN *UK, male vocalist* — **3 wks**

30 Sep 89	TAKE IT FROM ME *Island IS 427*	63	3

CHRISTIANS ⊗ *UK, male vocal/instrumental group* — **84 wks**

31 Jan 87	FORGOTTEN TOWN *Island IS 291*	22	11
13 Jun 87	HOOVERVILLE (THEY PROMISED US THE WORLD) *Island IS 326*	21	10
26 Sep 87	WHEN THE FINGERS POINT *Island IS 335*	34	7
5 Dec 87	IDEAL WORLD *Island IS 347*	14	13
23 Apr 88	BORN AGAIN *Island IS 365*	25	7
15 Oct 88 ●	HARVEST FOR THE WORLD *Island IS 395*	8	7
20 May 89 ★	FERRY 'CROSS THE MERSEY *PWL PWL 41* 1 ■	1	7
23 Dec 89	WORDS *Island IS 450*	18	8
7 Apr 90	I FOUND OUT *Island IS 453*	56	2
15 Sep 90	GREENBANK DRIVE *Island IS 466*	63	2
5 Sep 92	WHAT'S IN A WORD *Island IS 536*	33	5
14 Nov 92	FATHER *Island IS 543*	55	2
6 Mar 93	THE BOTTLE *Island CID 549*	39	3

1 Christians, Holly Johnson, Paul McCartney, Gerry Marsden and Stock Aitken Waterman

CHRISTIE ⊗ *UK, male vocal/instrumental group* — **37 wks**

2 May 70 ★	YELLOW RIVER *CBS 4911*	1	22
10 Oct 70	SAN BERNADINO *CBS 5169*	49	1
24 Oct 70 ●	SAN BERNADINO (re-entry) *CBS 5169*	7	13
25 Mar 72	IRON HORSE *CBS 7747*	47	1

David CHRISTIE ⊗ *France, male vocalist* — **12 wks**

14 Aug 82 ●	SADDLE UP *KR KR 9*	9	12

John CHRISTIE *Australia, male vocalist* — **6 wks**

25 Dec 76	HERE'S TO LOVE (AULD LANG SYNE) *EMI 2554*	24	6

Lou CHRISTIE ⊗ *US, male vocalist* — **35 wks**

24 Feb 66	LIGHTNIN' STRIKES *MGM 1297* ▲	11	8
28 Apr 66	RHAPSODY IN THE RAIN *MGM 1308*	37	2
13 Sep 69 ●	I'M GONNA MAKE YOU MINE *Buddah 201 057*	2	17
27 Dec 69	SHE SOLD ME MAGIC *Buddah 201 073*	25	8

Tony CHRISTIE ℂ *UK, male vocalist* — **47 wks**

9 Jan 71	LAS VEGAS *MCA MK 5058*	21	9
8 May 71 ●	I DID WHAT I DID FOR MARIA *MCA MK 5064*	2	17
20 Nov 71	IS THIS THE WAY TO AMARILLO *MCA MKS 5073*	18	13
10 Feb 73	AVENUES AND ALLEYWAYS *MCA MKS 5101*	37	4
17 Jan 76	DRIVE SAFELY DARLIN' *MCA 219*	35	4

Shawn CHRISTOPHER *US, female vocalist* — **10 wks**

4 May 91	ANOTHER SLEEPLESS NIGHT *Arista 114186*	50	4
21 Mar 92	DON'T LOSE THE MAGIC *Arista 115097*	30	5
2 Jul 94	MAKE MY LOVE *BTB BTBCD 502*	57	1

CHUBBY CHUNKS VOLUME II *UK, male instrumental duo* — **1 wk**

4 Jun 94	TESTAMENT 4 *Cleveland City CLECD 13017*	52	1

CHUCKS *UK, male/female vocal group* — **7 wks**

24 Jan 63	LOO-BE-LOO *Decca F 11569*	22	7

CHUMBAWAMBA ☹
UK, male/female vocal/instrumental group — **31 wks**

18 Sep 93	ENOUGH IS ENOUGH *One Little Indian 79 TP7CD* 1	56	2
4 Dec 93	TIMEBOMB *One Little Indian 89 TP7CD*	59	1
23 Aug 97 ●	TUBTHUMPING *EMI CDEM 486*	2	20
31 Jan 98 ●	AMNESIA *EMI CDEM 498*	10	5
13 Jun 98	TOP OF THE WORLD (OLE, OLE, OLE) *EMI CDEM 511*	21	3

1 Chumbawamba and Credit to the Nation

CHUPITO *Spain, male vocalist* — **2 wks**

23 Sep 95	AMERICAN PIE *Eternal WEA 018CD*	54	2

CHYNA – See INCOGNITO

CICERO ⊗ ☺ *UK, male vocalist* — **12 wks**

18 Jan 92	LOVE IS EVERYWHERE *Spaghetti CIAO 3*	19	8
18 Apr 92	THAT LOVING FEELING *Spaghetti CIAO 4*	46	3
1 Aug 92	HEAVEN MUST HAVE SENT YOU BACK *Spaghetti CIAO 5*	70	1

CINDERELLA *US, male vocal/instrumental group* — **7 wks**

6 Aug 88	GYPSY ROAD *Vertigo VER 40*	54	2
4 Mar 89	DON'T KNOW WHAT YOU GOT *Vertigo VER 43*	54	2
17 Nov 90	SHELTER ME *Vertigo VER 51*	55	2
27 Apr 91	HEARTBREAK STATION *Vertigo VER 53*	63	1

CINDY and the SAFFRONS *UK, female vocal group* — **3 wks**

15 Jan 83	PAST, PRESENT AND FUTURE *Stiletto STL 9*	56	3

CINERAMA *UK, male/female vocal/instrumental duo* — **1 wk**

18 Jul 98	KERRY KERRY *Cooking Vinyl FRYCD 072*	71	1

Gigliola CINQUETTI ⊗ *Italy, female vocalist* — **27 wks**

23 Apr 64	NON HO L'ETA PER AMARTI *Decca F 21882*	17	17
4 May 74 ●	GO (BEFORE YOU BREAK MY HEART) *CBS 2294*	8	10

CIRCUIT *UK, male/female vocal/instrumental group* — **3 wks**

20 Jul 91	SHELTER ME *Cooltempo COOL 237*	44	2
1 Apr 95	SHELTER ME (re-issue) *Pukka CDPUKA 2*	50	1

CIRRUS *UK, male vocal group* — **1 wk**

30 Sep 78	ROLLIN' ON *Jet 123*	62	1

CITY BOY ✎ *UK, male vocal/instrumental group* — **20 wks**

8 Jul 78 ●	5-7-0-5 *Vertigo 6059 207*	8	12
28 Oct 78	WHAT A NIGHT *Vertigo 6059 211*	39	5
15 Sep 79	THE DAY THE EARTH CAUGHT FIRE *Vertigo 6059 238*	67	3

CITY GENTS – See Dick CHARLESWORTH and his CITY GENTS

C.J. & CO. *US, male vocal/instrumental group* — **2 wks**

30 Jul 77	DEVIL'S GUN *Atlantic K 10956*	43	2

Gary CLAIL ON-U SOUND SYSTEM ☺
UK, male vocal/instrumental group — **19 wks**

14 Jul 90	BEEF *RCA PB 49265* 1	64	2
30 Mar 91 ●	HUMAN NATURE *Perfecto PB 44401*	10	9
8 Jun 91	ESCAPE *Perfecto PB 44563*	44	3
14 Nov 92	WHO PAYS THE PIPER *Perfecto 74321117017*	31	3
22 May 93	THESE THINGS ARE WORTH FIGHTING FOR *Perfecto 74321147222*	45	2

1 Gary Clail

See also VARIOUS ARTISTS (EPs & LPs) – Gimme Shelter (EP); PRIMAL SCREAM

CLAIRE and FRIENDS ⊗
UK, female vocalist and young male/female friends — **11 wks**

7 Jun 86	IT'S 'ORRIBLE BEING IN LOVE (WHEN YOU'RE 8 1/2) *BBC RESL 189*	13	11

CLANNAD ♂ 🌐 *Ireland, male/female vocal group* — **29 wks**

6 Nov 82 ●	THEME FROM HARRY'S GAME *RCA 292*	5 10
2 Jul 83	NEW GRANGE *RCA 340*	65 1
12 May 84	ROBIN (THE HOODED MAN) *RCA HOOD 1*	42 5
25 Jan 86	IN A LIFETIME *RCA PB 40535* [1]	20 5
10 Jun 89	IN A LIFETIME (re-issue) *RCA PB 42873* [1]	17 7
10 Aug 91	BOTH SIDES NOW *MCA MCS 1546* [2]	74 1

[1] Clannad featuring Bono [2] Clannad and Paul Young

Jimmy CLANTON *US, male vocalist* — **1 wk**

21 Jul 60	ANOTHER SLEEPLESS NIGHT *Top Rank JAR 382*	50 1

Eric CLAPTON 🎸 *Generally considered the No 1 rock guitar player, b. Eric Clapp, 30 March, 1945, Surrey. Prior to long and lucrative solo career recorded with hitmakers like The Yardbirds, Cream, Blind Faith and Derek and The Dominoes. Multi-Grammy-winning singer/guitarist is among world's top-grossing live performers* — **148 wks**

20 Dec 69	COMIN' HOME *Atlantic 584 308* [1]	16 9
12 Aug 72 ●	LAYLA *Polydor 2058 130* [2]	7 11
27 Jul 74 ●	I SHOT THE SHERIFF *RSO 2090 132*	9 9
10 May 75	SWING LOW SWEET CHARIOT *RSO 2090 158*	19 9
16 Aug 75	KNOCKIN' ON HEAVEN'S DOOR *RSO 2090 166*	38 4
24 Dec 77	LAY DOWN SALLY *RSO 2090 264*	39 6
21 Oct 78	PROMISES *RSO 21*	37 7
6 Mar 82 ●	LAYLA (re-issue) *RSO 87* [2]	4 10
5 Jun 82	I SHOT THE SHERIFF (re-issue) *RSO 88* ▲	64 2
23 Apr 83	THE SHAPE YOU'RE IN *Duck W 9701*	75 1
16 Mar 85	FOREVER MAN *Warner Bros. W 9069*	51 4
4 Jan 86	EDGE OF DARKNESS *BBC RESL 178* [3]	65 3
17 Jan 87	BEHIND THE MASK *Duck W 8461*	15 11
20 Jun 87	TEARING US APART *Duck W 8299* [4]	56 3
27 Jan 90	BAD LOVE *Duck W 2644*	25 7
14 Apr 90	NO ALIBIS *Duck W 9981*	53 3
16 Nov 91	WONDERFUL TONIGHT (LIVE) *Duck W 0069*	30 7
8 Feb 92	TEARS IN HEAVEN *Reprise W 0081*	50 1
7 Mar 92 ●	TEARS IN HEAVEN (re-entry) *Reprise W 0081*	5 9
1 Aug 92	RUNAWAY TRAIN *Rocket EJS 29* [5]	31 4
29 Aug 92	IT'S PROBABLY ME *A & M AM 883* [6]	30 5
3 Oct 92	LAYLA (ACOUSTIC) *Duck W 0134*	45 3
15 Oct 94	MOTHERLESS CHILD *Duck W 0271CD*	63 1
18 Mar 95 ■	LOVE CAN BUILD A BRIDGE *London COCD 1* [7]	1 8
20 Jul 96	CHANGE THE WORLD *Reprise W 0358CD*	18 5
4 Apr 98	MY FATHER'S EYES *Duck W 0443CD*	33 2
4 Jul 98	CIRCUS *Duck W 0447CD*	39 2

[1] Delaney and Bonnie and Friends featuring Eric Clapton [2] Derek and the Dominoes [3] Eric Clapton featuring Michael Kamen [4] Eric Clapton and Tina Turner [5] Elton John and Eric Clapton [6] Sting with Eric Clapton [7] Cher, Chrissie Hynde and Neneh Cherry with Eric Clapton

'Layla (Acoustic)' is, as its title suggests, a re-recording of 'Layla'

Dee CLARK 🎤 *US, male vocalist* — **9 wks**

2 Oct 59	JUST KEEP IT UP *London HL 8915*	26 1
11 Oct 75	RIDE A WILD HORSE *Chelsea 2005 037*	16 8

Gary CLARK *UK, male vocalist* — **8 wks**

30 Jan 93	WE SAIL ON THE STORMY WATERS *Circa YRCDX 93*	34 4
3 Apr 93	FREEFLOATING *Circa YRCDX 94*	50 3
19 Jun 93	MAKE A FAMILY *Circa YRCDX 105*	70 1

Loni CLARK *US, female vocalist* — **6 wks**

5 Jun 93	RUSHING *A & M 5802862*	37 2
22 Jan 94	U *A & M 5804752*	28 3
17 Dec 94	LOVE'S GOT ME ON A TRIP SO HIGH *A & M 5808872*	59 1

Petula CLARK 🌐 ℭ *Britain's most consistently successful female vocalist, b. 15 November, 1931, Surrey. As a child prodigy, she was the star of the original V-E Day celebrations (1945) and has spent six decades in the spotlight. She was the first British female to win a Grammy Award* — **247 wks**

11 Jun 54	THE LITTLE SHOEMAKER *Polygon P 1117*	12 1
25 Jun 54 ●	THE LITTLE SHOEMAKER (re-entry) *Polygon P 1117*	7 9
18 Feb 55	MAJORCA *Polygon P 1146*	12 4
25 Mar 55	MAJORCA (re-entry) *Polygon P 1146*	18 1
25 Nov 55 ●	SUDDENLY THERE'S A VALLEY *Pye Nixa N 15013*	7 10
26 Jul 57 ●	WITH ALL MY HEART *Pye Nixa N 15096*	4 18
15 Nov 57 ●	ALONE *Pye Nixa N 15112*	8 12
28 Feb 58	BABY LOVER *Pye Nixa N 15126*	12 7
26 Jan 61 ★	SAILOR *Pye 7N 15324*	1 15
13 Apr 61	SOMETHING MISSING *Pye 7N 15337*	44 1
13 Jul 61	ROMEO *Pye 7N 15361*	3 15
16 Nov 61	MY FRIEND THE SEA *Pye 7N 15389*	7 13
8 Feb 62	I'M COUNTING ON YOU *Pye 7N 15407*	41 2
28 Jun 62	YA YA TWIST *Pye 7N 15448*	14 11
20 Sep 62	YA YA TWIST (re-entry) *Pye 7N 15448*	45 2
2 May 63	CASANOVA / CHARIOT *Pye 7N 15522*	39 7
12 Nov 64 ●	DOWNTOWN *Pye 7N 15722* ▲	2 15
11 Mar 65	I KNOW A PLACE *Pye 7N 15772*	17 8
12 Aug 65	YOU BETTER COME HOME *Pye 7N 15864*	44 3
14 Oct 65	ROUND EVERY CORNER *Pye 7N 15945*	43 3
4 Nov 65	YOU'RE THE ONE *Pye 7N 15991*	23 9
10 Feb 66 ●	MY LOVE *Pye 7N 17038* ▲	4 9
21 Apr 66	A SIGN OF THE TIMES *Pye 7N 17071*	49 1
30 Jun 66	I COULDN'T LIVE WITHOUT YOUR LOVE *Pye 7N 17133*	6 11
2 Feb 67 ★	THIS IS MY SONG *Pye 7N 17258*	1 14
25 May 67	DON'T SLEEP IN THE SUBWAY *Pye 7N 17325*	12 11
13 Dec 67	THE OTHER MAN'S GRASS *Pye 7N 17416*	20 9
6 Mar 68	KISS ME GOODBYE *Pye 7N 17466*	50 1
30 Jan 71	THE SONG OF MY LIFE *Pye 7N 45026*	41 1
13 Feb 71	THE SONG OF MY LIFE (re-entry) *Pye 7N 45026*	32 11
15 Jan 72	I DON'T KNOW HOW TO LOVE HIM *Pye 7N 45112*	47 1
29 Jan 72	I DON'T KNOW HOW TO LOVE HIM (re-entry) *Pye 7N 45112*	49 1
19 Nov 88 ●	DOWNTOWN (re-mix) *PRT PYS 19*	10 11

Dave CLARK FIVE 🌐 *Beat Boom superstars from Tottenham, London: Dave Clark (d), Mike Smith (v/k), Lenny Davidson (g), Denis Payton (s), Rick Huxley (g). In the first years of the 'British Invasion', this foot-stomping quintet were second only to The Beatles in the USA* — **174 wks**

3 Oct 63	DO YOU LOVE ME *Columbia DB 7112*	30 6
21 Nov 63 ★	GLAD ALL OVER *Columbia DB 7154*	1 19
20 Feb 64 ●	BITS AND PIECES *Columbia DB 7210*	2 11
28 May 64 ●	CAN'T YOU SEE THAT SHE'S MINE *Columbia DB 7291*	10 11
13 Aug 64	THINKING OF YOU BABY *Columbia DB 7335*	26 4
22 Oct 64	ANYWAY YOU WANT IT *Columbia DB 7377*	25 5
14 Jan 65	EVERYBODY KNOWS *Columbia DB 7453*	37 4
11 Mar 65	REELIN' AND ROCKIN' *Columbia DB 7503*	24 8
27 May 65	COME HOME *Columbia DB 7580*	16 8
15 Jul 65 ●	CATCH US IF YOU CAN *Columbia DB 7625*	5 11
11 Nov 65	OVER AND OVER *Columbia DB 7744* ▲	45 4
19 May 66	LOOK BEFORE YOU LEAP *Columbia DB 7909*	50 1
16 Mar 67	YOU GOT WHAT IT TAKES *Columbia DB 8152*	28 8
1 Nov 67 ●	EVERYBODY KNOWS *Columbia DB 8286*	2 14
28 Feb 68	NO ONE CAN BREAK A HEART LIKE YOU *Columbia DB 8342*	28 7
18 Sep 68 ●	RED BALLOON *Columbia DB 8465*	7 11
27 Nov 68	LIVE IN THE SKY *Columbia DB 8505*	39 6
25 Oct 69	PUT A LITTLE LOVE IN YOUR HEART *Columbia DB 8624*	31 4
6 Dec 69 ●	GOOD OLD ROCK 'N' ROLL *Columbia DB 8638*	7 12
7 Mar 70 ●	EVERYBODY GET TOGETHER *Columbia DB 8660*	8 8
4 Jul 70	HERE COMES SUMMER *Columbia DB 8689*	44 3
7 Nov 70	MORE GOOD OLD ROCK 'N' ROLL *Columbia DB 8724*	34 6
1 May 93	GLAD ALL OVER (re-issue) *EMI CDEMCT 8*	37 3

'Everybody Knows' on DB 7453 and 'Everybody Knows' on DB 8286 are two different songs. The two Rock'n'Roll titles are medleys as follows: Good Old Rock'n'Roll/Sweet Little Sixteen/Long Tall Sally/Whole Lotta Shakin' Goin' On/

UK No 1 ★   UK Top 10 ●   UK million seller ◆   UK entry at No 1 ■   US No 1 ▲

Blue Suede Shoes / Lucille / Reelin' And Rockin' / Memphis Tennessee. More Good Old Rock'n'Roll: *Rock'n'Roll Music / Blueberry Hill / Good Golly Miss Molly / My Blue Heaven / Keep a Knockin' / Loving You / One Night / Lawdy Miss Clawdy*

Dave CLARKE *UK, male producer*   6 wks

30 Sep 95	RED THREE: THUNDER/STORM *Deconstruction 74321306992*	45	2
3 Feb 96	SOUTHSIDE *Bush 74321335382*	34	2
15 Jun 96	NO ONE'S DRIVING *Bush 74321380162*	37	2

John Cooper CLARKE *UK, male vocalist*   3 wks

| 10 Mar 79 | GIMMIX! PLAY LOUD *Epic EPC 7009* | 39 | 3 |

Rick CLARKE *UK, male vocalist*   2 wks

| 30 Apr 88 | I'LL SEE YOU ALONG THE WAY *WA WA 1* | 63 | 2 |

Sharon Dee CLARKE – See FPI PROJECT; SERIOUS ROPE

Julian CLARY – See JOAN COLLINS FAN CLUB

CLASH 🖉 *Leading lights of the UK punk-rock explosion: Joe Strummer (b. John Mellors) (v/g), Mick Jones (g/v), Paul Simonon (b), Topper Headon (d). Their third LP,* London Calling *(first released 1979), was voted Best Album of the 1980s by* Rolling Stone *magazine*   135 wks

2 Apr 77	WHITE RIOT *CBS 5058*	38	3
8 Oct 77	COMPLETE CONTROL *CBS 5664*	28	2
4 Mar 78	CLASH CITY ROCKERS *CBS 5834*	35	4
24 Jun 78	(WHITE MAN) IN HAMMERSMITH PALAIS *CBS 6383*	32	7
2 Dec 78	TOMMY GUN *CBS 6788*	19	10
3 Mar 79	ENGLISH CIVIL WAR (JOHNNY COMES MARCHING HOME) *CBS 7082*	25	6
19 May 79	THE COST OF LIVING EP *CBS 7324*	22	8
15 Dec 79	LONDON CALLING *CBS 8087*	11	10
9 Aug 80	BANKROBBER *CBS 8323*	12	10
6 Dec 80	THE CALL UP *CBS 9339*	40	6
24 Jan 81	HITSVILLE UK *CBS 9480*	56	4
25 Apr 81	THE MAGNIFICENT SEVEN *CBS 1133*	34	5
28 Nov 81	THIS IS RADIO CLASH *CBS A 1797*	47	6
1 May 82	KNOW YOUR RIGHTS *CBS A 2309*	43	3
26 Jun 82	ROCK THE CASBAH *CBS A 2429*	30	10
25 Sep 82	SHOULD I STAY OR SHOULD I GO/STRAIGHT TO HELL *CBS A 2646*	17	9
12 Oct 85	THIS IS ENGLAND *CBS A 6122*	24	5
12 Mar 88	I FOUGHT THE LAW *CBS CLASH 1*	29	5
7 May 88	LONDON CALLING (re-issue) *CBS CLASH 2*	46	3
21 Jul 90	RETURN TO BRIXTON *CBS 656072 7*	57	2
2 Mar 91 ★	SHOULD I STAY OR SHOULD I GO (re-issue) *Columbia 6566677*	1	9
13 Apr 91	ROCK THE CASBAH (re-issue) *Columbia 6568147*	15	6
8 Jun 91	LONDON CALLING (re-issue) *Columbia 6569467*	64	2

Tracks on The Cost of Living (EP): *I Fought the Law / Groovy Times / Gates of the West / Capital Radio.* CBS CLASH 1 is a re-issue of a track from The Cost of Living (EP)

CLASS ACTION featuring Chris WILTSHIRE
US, female vocal group   3 wks

| 7 May 83 | WEEKEND *Jive JIVE 35* | 49 | 3 |

CLASSICS IV *US, male vocal/instrumental group*   1 wk

| 28 Feb 68 | SPOOKY *Liberty LBS 15051* | 46 | 1 |

CLASSIX NOUVEAUX ⓢ *UK, male vocal/instrumental group*   34 wks

28 Feb 81	GUILTY *Liberty BP 388*	43	7
16 May 81	TOKYO *Liberty BP 397*	67	3
8 Aug 81	INSIDE OUTSIDE *Liberty BP 403*	45	5
7 Nov 81	NEVER AGAIN (THE DAYS TIME ERASED) *Liberty BP 406*	44	4
13 Mar 82	IS IT A DREAM *Liberty BP 409*	11	9
29 May 82	BECAUSE YOU'RE YOUNG *Liberty BP 411*	43	4
30 Oct 82	THE END ... OR THE BEGINNING *Liberty BP 414*	60	2

CLAWFINGER *Norway/Sweden, male vocal/instrumental group*   1 wk

| 19 Mar 94 | WARFAIR *East West YZ 804CD1* | 54 | 1 |

Judy CLAY – See William BELL

Adam CLAYTON and Larry MULLEN 🎸 ☺
Ireland, male instrumental duo   12 wks

| 15 Jun 96 ● | THEME FROM MISSION: IMPOSSIBLE *Mother MUMCD 75* | 7 | 12 |

See also U2

Merry CLAYTON *US, female vocalist*   1 wk

| 21 May 88 | YES *RCA PB 49563* | 70 | 1 |

CLAYTOWN TROUPE *UK, male vocal/instrumental group*   3 wks

| 16 Jun 90 | WAYS OF LOVE *Island IS 464* | 57 | 2 |
| 14 Mar 92 | WANTED IT ALL *EMI USA MT 102* | 74 | 1 |

Johnny CLEGG and SAVUKA
UK/South Africa, male vocal/instrumental group   1 wk

| 16 May 87 | SCATTERLINGS OF AFRICA *EMI EMI 5605* | 75 | 1 |

CLEOPATRA ⓢ [R&B] *UK, female vocal group*   24 wks

14 Feb 98 ●	CLEOPATRA'S THEME *WEA WEA 133CD*	3	10
16 May 98 ●	LIFE AIN'T EASY *WEA WEA 159CD1*	4	7
22 Aug 98 ●	I WANT YOU BACK *WEA WEA 172CD1*	4	7

CLICK *US, male rap group*   1 wk

| 29 Jun 96 | SCANDALOUS *Jive JIVECD 393* | 54 | 1 |

Jimmy CLIFF 🖖 *Jamaica, male vocalist*   33 wks

25 Oct 69 ●	WONDERFUL WORLD BEAUTIFUL PEOPLE *Trojan TR 690*	6	13
14 Feb 70	VIETNAM *Trojan TR 7722*	47	1
28 Feb 70	VIETNAM (re-entry) *Trojan TR 7722*	46	2
8 Aug 70 ●	WILD WORLD *Island WIP 6087*	8	12
19 Mar 94	I CAN SEE CLEARLY NOW *Columbia 6601982*	23	5

Buzz CLIFFORD ⓢ *US, male vocalist*   13 wks

| 2 Mar 61 | BABY SITTIN' BOOGIE *Fontana H 297* | 17 | 13 |

Linda CLIFFORD *US, female vocalist*   12 wks

| 10 Jun 78 | IF MY FRIENDS COULD SEE ME NOW *Curtom K 17163* | 50 | 5 |
| 5 May 79 | BRIDGE OVER TROUBLED WATER *RSO 30* | 28 | 7 |

CLIMAX BLUES BAND 🎸 *UK, male vocal/instrumental group*   9 wks

| 9 Oct 76 ● | COULDN'T GET IT RIGHT *BTM SBT 105* | 10 | 9 |

Simon CLIMIE *UK, male vocalist*   2 wks

| 19 Sep 92 | SOUL INSPIRATION *Epic 6582837* | 60 | 2 |

CLIMIE FISHER ⓢ *UK, male vocal/instrumental duo*   44 wks

5 Sep 87	LOVE CHANGES (EVERYTHING) *EMI EM 15*	67	2
12 Dec 87 ●	RISE TO THE OCCASION *EMI EM 33*	10	11
12 Mar 88 ●	LOVE CHANGES (EVERYTHING) (re-mix) *EMI EM 47*	2	12
21 May 88	THIS IS ME *EMI EM 58*	22	5
20 Aug 88	I WON'T BLEED FOR YOU *EMI EM 66*	35	4
24 Dec 88	LOVE LIKE A RIVER *EMI EM 81*	22	7
23 Sep 89	FACTS OF LOVE *EMI EM 103*	50	3

Patsy CLINE 🎵 *US, female vocalist*   17 wks

26 Apr 62	SHE'S GOT YOU *Brunswick 05866*	43	1
29 Nov 62	HEARTACHES *Brunswick 05878*	31	5
8 Dec 90	CRAZY *MCA MCA 1465*	14	11

George CLINTON US, male vocalist — 10 wks

4 Dec 82	LOOPZILLA *Capitol CL 271*	57	5
26 Apr 86	DO FRIES GO WITH THAT SHAKE *Capitol CL 402*	57	2
27 Aug 94	BOP GUN (ONE NATION) *Fourth & Broadway BRCD 308* [1]	22	3

[1] Ice Cube featuring George Clinton

CLIVILLES & COLE – See C & C MUSIC FACTORY

CLOCK ☺ ◉ UK, male/female vocal/instrumental group — 69 wks

30 Oct 93	HOLDING ON *Media MRLCD 007*	66	1
21 May 94	THE RHYTHM *Media MCSTD 1971*	28	2
10 Sep 94	KEEP THE FIRES BURNING *Media MCSTD 1998*	36	3
4 Mar 95 ●	AXEL F/KEEP PUSHIN' *Media MCSTD 2041*	7	9
1 Jul 95 ●	WHOOMPH! (THERE IT IS) *Media MCSTD 2059*	4	9
26 Aug 95 ●	EVERYBODY *Media MCSTD 2077*	6	5
18 Nov 95	IN THE HOUSE *Media MCSTD 40005*	23	3
24 Feb 96	HOLDING ON 4 U (re-mix) *Media MCSTD 40019*	27	2
7 Sep 96	OH WHAT A NIGHT *Power Station MCSTD 40057*	13	10
22 Mar 97 ●	IT'S OVER *Media MCSTD 40100*	10	5
18 Oct 97	U SEXY THING *Media MCSTD 40138*	11	9
17 Jan 98	THAT'S THE WAY (I LIKE IT) *Media MCSTD 40148*	11	4
11 Jul 98	ROCK YOUR BODY *Media MCSTD 40160*	30	3
28 Nov 98	BLAME IT ON THE BOOGIE *Media MCSTD 40191*	16	4

Rosemary CLOONEY ◖ US, female vocalist — 81 wks

14 Nov 52 ●	HALF AS MUCH *Columbia DB 3129*	3	9
5 Feb 54 ●	MAN *Philips PB 220*	7	5
8 Oct 54 ★	THIS OLE HOUSE *Philips PB 336* ▲	1	18
17 Dec 54 ★	MAMBO ITALIANO *Philips PB 382*	1	16
20 May 55 ●	WHERE WILL THE DIMPLE BE? *Philips PB 428*	6	13
30 Sep 55 ●	HEY THERE *Philips PB 494* ▲	4	11
29 Mar 57	MANGOS *Philips PB 671*	25	2
26 Apr 57	MANGOS (re-entry) *Philips PB 671*	17	7

From 19 Feb, 1954, other side of 'Man, Woman' by José Ferrer, was also credited

CLOUD UK, male instrumental group — 1 wk

| 31 Jan 81 | ALL NIGHT LONG/TAKE IT TO THE TOP *UK Champagne FUNK 1* | 72 | 1 |

CLOUT ◉ South Africa, female vocal/instrumental group — 15 wks

| 17 Jun 78 ● | SUBSTITUTE *Carrere EMI 2788* | 2 | 15 |

CLS US, male vocal / production duo — 1 wk

| 30 May 98 | CAN YOU FEEL IT *Satellite 74321580162* | 46 | 1 |

CLUB NOUVEAU [R&B]
US, male/female vocal/instrumental group — 12 wks

| 21 Mar 87 ● | LEAN ON ME *King Jay W 8430* ▲ | 3 | 12 |

CLUB 69 Austria/US, male/female vocal/instrumental duo — 6 wks

| 5 Dec 92 | LET ME BE YOUR UNDERWEAR *ffrr F 204* | 33 | 5 |
| 14 Nov 98 | ALRIGHT *Twisted UK TWCD 10039* [1] | 70 | 1 |

[1] Club 69 featuring Suzanne Palmer

CLUBHOUSE ◉ ☺ Italy, male vocal/instrumental group — 40 wks

23 Jul 83	DO IT AGAIN – BILLIE JEAN (MEDLEY) *Island IS 132*	11	6
3 Dec 83	SUPERSTITION – GOOD TIMES (MEDLEY) *Island IS 147*	59	3
1 Jul 89	I'M A MAN – YE KE YE KE (MEDLEY) *Music Man MMPS 7003*	69	3
20 Apr 91	DEEP IN MY HEART *ffrr F 157*	59	2
22 Jun 91	DEEP IN MY HEART (re-entry) *ffrr F 157*	55	2
4 Sep 93	LIGHT MY FIRE *PWL Continental PWCD 272* [1]	59	1
13 Nov 93	LIGHT MY FIRE (re-entry) *PWL Continental PWCD 272* [1]	45	5
25 Dec 93	LIGHT MY FIRE (2nd re-entry) *PWL Continental PWCD 272* [1]	53	6
30 Apr 94 ●	LIGHT MY FIRE (re-mix) *PWL Continental PWCD 288* [1]	7	8
23 Jul 94	LIVING IN THE SUNSHINE *PWL Continental PWCD 309* [1]	21	3
11 Mar 95	NOWHERE LAND *PWL International PWCD 318* [1]	56	1

[1] Clubhouse featuring Carl

CLUBZONE UK/Germany, male vocal/instrumental group — 1 wk

| 19 Nov 94 | HANDS UP *Logic 74321236982* | 50 | 1 |

CLUELESS US, male / female vocal / production group — 1 wk

| 5 Apr 97 | DON'T SPEAK *ZYX ZYX 660738* | 61 | 1 |

Jeremy CLYDE – See Chad STUART and Jeremy CLYDE

CLYDE VALLEY STOMPERS UK, male instrumental group — 8 wks

| 9 Aug 62 | PETER AND THE WOLF *Parlophone R 4928* | 25 | 8 |

CO-CO ◉ UK, male/female vocal/instrumental group — 7 wks

| 22 Apr 78 | BAD OLD DAYS *Ariola Hansa AHA 513* | 13 | 7 |

CO-OPERATION CHOIR – See Peter E BENNETT with the CO-OPERATION CHOIR

COAST TO COAST ◉ UK, male vocal/instrumental group — 22 wks

| 31 Jan 81 ● | (DO) THE HUCKLEBUCK *Polydor POSP 214* | 5 | 15 |
| 23 May 81 | LET'S JUMP THE BROOMSTICK *Polydor POSP 249* | 28 | 7 |

COASTERS ♪ US, male vocal group — 32 wks

27 Sep 57	SEARCHIN' *London HLE 8450*	30	1
15 Aug 58	YAKETY YAK *London HLE 8665*	12	8
27 Mar 59 ●	CHARLIE BROWN *London HLE 8819*	6	12
30 Oct 59	POISON IVY *London HLE 8938*	15	7
9 Apr 94	SORRY BUT I'M GONNA HAVE TO PASS *Rhino A 4519CD*	41	4

Odia COATES – See Paul ANKA

Luis COBOS – See Placido DOMINGO

Eddie COCHRAN ♪ US, male vocalist — 90 wks

7 Nov 58	SUMMERTIME BLUES *London HLU 8702*	18	6
13 Mar 59 ●	C'MON EVERYBODY *London HLU 8792*	6	13
16 Oct 59	SOMETHIN' ELSE *London HLU 8944*	22	3
22 Jan 60	HALLELUJAH I LOVE HER SO *London HLW 9022*	28	1
5 Feb 60	HALLELUJAH I LOVE HER SO (re-entry) *London HLW 9022*	22	3
12 May 60 ★	THREE STEPS TO HEAVEN *London HLG 9115*	1	15
6 Oct 60	SWEETIE PIE *London HLG 9196*	38	3
3 Nov 60	LONELY *London HLG 9196*	41	1
15 Jun 61	WEEKEND *London HLG 9362*	15	16
30 Nov 61	JEANNIE, JEANNIE, JEANNIE *London HLG 9460*	31	4
25 Apr 63	MY WAY *Liberty LIB 10088*	23	10
24 Apr 68	SUMMERTIME BLUES (re-issue) *Liberty LBF 15071*	34	8
13 Feb 88	C'MON EVERYBODY (re-issue) *Liberty EDDIE 501*	14	7

Tom COCHRANE Canada, male vocalist — 2 wks

| 27 Jun 92 | LIFE IS A HIGHWAY *Capitol CL 660* | 62 | 2 |

COCK ROBIN US, male/female vocal/instrumental group — 12 wks

| 31 May 86 | THE PROMISE YOU MADE *CBS A 6764* | 28 | 12 |

Joe COCKER ♪ UK, male vocalist — 89 wks

22 May 68	MARJORINE *Regal-Zonophone RZ 3006*	48	1
2 Oct 68 ★	WITH A LITTLE HELP FROM MY FRIENDS *Regal-Zonophone RZ 3013*	1	13
27 Sep 69 ●	DELTA LADY *Regal-Zonophone RZ 3024*	10	11
4 Jul 70	THE LETTER *Regal-Zonophone RZ 3027*	39	6
26 Sep 81	I'M SO GLAD I'M STANDING HERE TODAY *MCA 741* [1]	61	3
15 Jan 83 ●	UP WHERE WE BELONG *Island WIP 6830* [2] ▲	7	13
14 Nov 87	UNCHAIN MY HEART *Capitol CL 465*	46	4

UK No 1 ★   UK Top 10 ●   UK million seller ◆   UK entry at No 1 ▦   US No 1 ▲

13 Jan 90	WHEN THE NIGHT COMES *Capitol CL 535*	65	2
7 Mar 92	(ALL I KNOW) FEELS LIKE FOREVER *Capitol CL 645*	25	5
9 May 92	NOW THAT THE MAGIC HAS GONE *Capitol CL 657*	28	6
4 Jul 92	UNCHAIN MY HEART (re-issue) *Capitol CL 664*	17	6
21 Nov 92	WHEN THE NIGHT COMES (re-issue) *Capitol CL 674*	61	3
13 Aug 94	THE SIMPLE THINGS *Capitol CDCLS 722*	17	5
22 Oct 94	TAKE ME HOME *Capitol CDCLS 729*	41	5
17 Dec 94	LET THE HEALING BEGIN *Capitol CDCLS 727*	32	5
23 Sep 95	HAVE A LITTLE FAITH *Capitol CDCLS 744*	67	2
12 Oct 96	DON'T LET ME BE MISUNDERSTOOD *Parlophone CDCLS 779*	53	1

[1] Crusaders, featured vocalist Joe Cocker [2] Joe Cocker and Jennifer Warnes
[3] Joe Cocker featuring Bekka Bramlett

COCKEREL CHORUS ◐ *UK, male vocal group* — 12 wks

24 Feb 73	NICE ONE CYRIL *Youngblood YB 1017*	14	12

COCKNEY REBEL – See Steve HARLEY

COCKNEY REJECTS *UK, male vocal/instrumental group* — 22 wks

1 Dec 79	I'M NOT A FOOL *EMI 5008*	65	2
16 Feb 80	BADMAN *EMI 5035*	65	3
26 Apr 80	THE GREATEST COCKNEY RIPOFF *EMI Z 2*	21	7
17 May 80	I'M FOREVER BLOWING BUBBLES *EMI Z 4*	35	5
12 Jul 80	WE CAN DO ANYTHING *EMI Z 6*	65	2
25 Oct 80	WE ARE THE FIRM *EMI Z 10*	54	3

COCO ◑ *UK, female vocalist* — 2 wks

8 Nov 97	I NEED A MIRACLE *Positiva CDTIV 81*	39	2

El COCO *US, male vocal/instrumental group* — 4 wks

14 Jan 78	COCOMOTION *Pye International 7N 25761*	31	4

COCONUTS *US, female vocal group* — 3 wks

11 Jun 83	DID YOU HAVE TO LOVE ME LIKE YOU DID *EMI America EA 156*	60	3

See also Kid CREOLE and the COCONUTS

COCTEAU TWINS *UK, male/female vocal/instrumental group* — 25 wks

28 Apr 84	PEARLY-DEWDROPS' DROPS *4AD 405*	29	5
30 Mar 85	AIKEA-GUINEA *4AD AD 501*	41	3
23 Nov 85	TINY DYNAMINE EP *4AD BAD 510*	52	2
7 Dec 85	ECHOES IN A SHALLOW BAY EP *4AD BAD 511*	65	1
25 Oct 86	LOVE'S EASY TEARS *4AD AD 610*	53	1
8 Sep 90	ICEBLINK LUCK *4AD AD 0011*	38	3
2 Oct 93	EVANGELINE *Fontana CTCD 1*	34	2
18 Dec 93	WINTER WONDERLAND/FROSTY THE SNOWMAN *Fontana COCCD 1*	58	1
26 Feb 94	BLUEBEARD *Fontana CTCD 2*	33	2
7 Oct 95	TWINLIGHTS EP *Fontana CTCD 3*	59	1
4 Nov 95	OTHERNESS EP *Fontana CTCD 4*	59	1
30 Mar 96	TISHBITE *Fontana CTCD 5*	34	2
20 Jul 96	VIOLAINE *Fontana CTCD 6*	56	1

Tracks on Tiny Dynamine EP: Pink Orange Red/Ribbed and Veined/Plain Tiger/
Sultitan Itan. Tracks on Echoes in a Shallow Bay EP: Great Spangled Fritillary/
Melonella/Pale Clouded White/Eggs and Their Shells.
Tracks on Twinlights EP: Golden-Vein/Half-Gifts/Pink Orange Red/Rilkean Heart.
Tracks on Otherness EP: Cherry Coloured Funk/Feet Like Fins/Seekers Who Are
Lovers/Violane

C.O.D *US, male vocal/instrumental group* — 2 wks

14 May 83	IN THE BOTTLE *Streetwave WAVE 2*	54	2

CODE RED *UK, male vocal group* — 7 wks

6 Jul 96	I GAVE YOU EVERYTHING *Polydor 5763992*	50	1
16 Nov 96	THIS IS OUR SONG *Polydor 5756332*	59	1
14 Jun 97	CAN WE TALK... *Polydor 5710992*	29	2

9 Aug 97	IS THERE SOMEONE OUT THERE? *Polydor 5714652*	34	2
4 Jul 98	WHAT WOULD YOU DO IF...? *Polydor 569932*	55	1

COFFEE ♫ *US, female vocal group* — 13 wks

27 Sep 80	CASANOVA *De-Lite MER 38*	13	10
6 Dec 80	SLIP AND DIP/I WANNA BE WITH YOU *De-Lite DE 1*	57	3

Alma COGAN ℂ *Very popular and 1950s radio, TV and record star, b. 19 May, 1932, d. 26 October, 1966. This singer, who was renowned for her glamour and was known as the 'gal with the giggle in her voice', was the only British female to top the chart in the 1950s* — 110 wks

19 Mar 54 ●	BELL BOTTOM BLUES *HMV B 10653*	4	9
27 Aug 54	LITTLE THINGS MEAN A LOT *HMV B 10717*	11	2
8 Oct 54	LITTLE THINGS MEAN A LOT (re-entry) *HMV B 10717*	19	1
22 Oct 54	LITTLE THINGS MEAN A LOT (2nd re-entry) *HMV B 10717*	18	2
3 Dec 54 ●	I CAN'T TELL A WALTZ FROM A TANGO *HMV B 10786*	6	11
27 May 55 ★	DREAMBOAT *HMV B 10872*	1	16
23 Sep 55	BANJO'S BACK IN TOWN *HMV B 10917*	17	1
14 Oct 55	GO ON BY *HMV B 10917*	16	4
16 Dec 55	TWENTY TINY FINGERS *HMV POP 129*	17	1
23 Dec 55 ●	NEVER DO A TANGO WITH AN ESKIMO *HMV POP 129*	6	5
30 Mar 56	WILLIE CAN *HMV POP 187* [1]	13	8
13 Jul 56	THE BIRDS AND THE BEES *HMV POP 223*	25	4
10 Aug 56	WHY DO FOOLS FALL IN LOVE *HMV POP 223*	22	3
2 Nov 56	IN THE MIDDLE OF THE HOUSE *HMV POP 261*	26	1
23 Nov 56	IN THE MIDDLE OF THE HOUSE (re-entry) *HMV POP 261*	20	3
18 Jan 57	YOU ME AND US *HMV POP 284*	18	6
29 Mar 57	WHATEVER LOLA WANTS *HMV POP 317*	26	2
31 Jan 58	THE STORY OF MY LIFE *HMV POP 433*	25	2
14 Feb 58	SUGARTIME *HMV POP 450*	16	10
2 May 58	SUGARTIME (re-entry) *HMV POP 450*	30	1
23 Jan 59	LAST NIGHT ON THE BACK PORCH *HMV POP 573*	27	2
18 Dec 59	WE GOT LOVE *HMV POP 670*	26	4
12 May 60	DREAM TALK *HMV POP 728*	48	1
11 Aug 60	TRAIN OF LOVE *HMV POP 760*	27	5
20 Apr 61	COWBOY JIMMY JOE *Columbia DB 4607*	37	6

[1] Alma Cogan with Desmond Lane – penny whistle

Shaye COGAN *US, female vocalist* — 1 wk

24 Mar 60	MEAN TO ME *MGM 1063*	40	1

Izhar COHEN and ALPHABETA ◐ *Israel, male/female vocal group* — 7 wks

13 May 78	A BA NI BI *Polydor 2001 781*	20	7

Marc COHN *US, male vocalist* — 15 wks

25 May 91	WALKING IN MEMPHIS *Atlantic A 7747*	66	4
10 Aug 91	SILVER THUNDERBIRD *Atlantic A 7657*	54	3
12 Oct 91	WALKING IN MEMPHIS (re-issue) *Atlantic A 7585*	22	5
29 May 93	WALK THROUGH THE WORLD *Atlantic A 7340CD*	37	3

COLA BOY ☺ *UK, male/female vocal/instrumental duo* — 7 wks

6 Jul 91 ●	7 WAYS TO LOVE *Arista 114526*	8	7

COLD JAM featuring GRACE *US, male/female vocal/instrumental group* — 2 wks

28 Jul 90	LAST NIGHT A DJ SAVED MY LIFE *Big Wave BWR 39*	64	2

COLDCUT ☺ *UK, male production duo* — 38 wks

20 Feb 88 ●	DOCTORIN' THE HOUSE *Ahead Of Our Time CCUT 27* [1]	6	9
10 Sep 88	STOP THIS CRAZY THING *Ahead Of Our Time CCUT 4* [2]	21	7
25 Mar 89	PEOPLE HOLD ON *Ahead Of Our Time CCUT 5* [3]	11	9
3 Jun 89	MY TELEPHONE *Ahead Of Our Time CCUT 6*	52	2
16 Dec 89	COLDCUT'S CHRISTMAS BREAK *Ahead Of Our Time CCUT 7*	67	3
26 May 90	FIND A WAY *Ahead Of Our Time CCUT 8* [4]	52	2
4 Sep 93	DREAMER *Arista 74321156642*	54	2

22 Jan 94	AUTUMN LEAVES *Arista 74321171052*	50	2
16 Aug 97	MORE BEATS & PIECES *Ninja Tune ZENCDS 58*	37	2

[1] Coldcut featuring Yazz and the Plastic Population [2] Coldcut featuring Junior Reid and the Ahead Of Our Time Orchestra [3] Coldcut featuring Lisa Stansfield [4] Coldcut featuring Queen Latifah

Cozy COLE *US, male instrumentalist – drums*   **1 wk**
5 Dec 58	TOPSY (PARTS 1 AND 2) *London HL 8750*	29	1

George COLE – *See Dennis WATERMAN*

Lloyd COLE ◎ ✔ *UK, male vocalist*   **62 wks**
26 May 84	PERFECT SKIN *Polydor COLE 1* [1]	71	1
9 Jun 84	PERFECT SKIN (re-entry) *Polydor COLE 1* [1]	26	8
25 Aug 84	FOREST FIRE *Polydor COLE 2* [1]	41	6
17 Nov 84	RATTLESNAKES *Polydor COLE 3* [1]	65	2
14 Sep 85	BRAND NEW FRIEND *Polydor COLE 4* [1]	19	8
9 Nov 85	LOST WEEKEND *Polydor COLE 5* [1]	17	7
18 Jan 86	CUT ME DOWN *Polydor COLE 6* [1]	38	4
3 Oct 87	MY BAG *Polydor COLE 7* [1]	46	4
9 Jan 88	JENNIFER SHE SAID *Polydor COLE 8* [1]	31	5
23 Apr 88	FROM THE HIP EP *Polydor COLE 9* [1]	59	2
3 Feb 90	NO BLUE SKIES *Polydor COLE 11*	42	4
7 Apr 90	DON'T LOOK BACK *Polydor COLE 12*	59	3
31 Aug 91	SHE'S A GIRL AND I'M A MAN *Polydor COLE 14*	55	2
25 Sep 93	SO YOU'D LIKE TO SAVE THE WORLD *Fontana VIBE D1*	72	2
16 Sep 95	LIKE LOVERS DO *Fontana LCDD 1*	24	3
2 Dec 95	SENTIMENTAL FOOL *Fontana LCDD 2*	73	1

[1] Lloyd Cole and the Commotions

Tracks on From the Hip (EP): *From the Hip / Please / Lonely Mile / Love Your Wife*

MJ COLE *UK, male producer – Matt Coleman*   **2 wks**
23 May 98	SINCERE *AM:PM 5826912*	38	2

Nat 'King' COLE ℂ *One of the century's most distinctive song stylists, b. 17 March, 1917, Alabama, d. 15 February, 1965. His 41-year chart span is proof that the highly regarded vocalist's recordings are timeless*   **237 wks**
14 Nov 52 ●	SOMEWHERE ALONG THE WAY *Capitol CL 13774*	3	7
19 Dec 52 ●	BECAUSE YOU'RE MINE *Capitol CL 13811*	6	2
2 Jan 53	FAITH CAN MOVE MOUNTAINS *Capitol CL 13811*	11	1
16 Jan 53	FAITH CAN MOVE MOUNTAINS (re-entry) *Capitol CL 13811*	12	2
23 Jan 53 ●	BECAUSE YOU'RE MINE (re-entry) *Capitol CL 13811*	10	1
6 Feb 53 ●	FAITH CAN MOVE MOUNTAINS (2nd re-entry) *Capitol CL 13811*	10	1
13 Feb 53	BECAUSE YOU'RE MINE (2nd re-entry) *Capitol CL 13811*	11	1
24 Apr 53 ●	PRETEND *Capitol CL 13878*	2	18
14 Aug 53 ●	CAN'T I? *Capitol CL 13937*	9	3
18 Sep 53 ●	CAN'T I? (re-entry) *Capitol CL 13937*	6	4
18 Sep 53 ●	MOTHER NATURE AND FATHER TIME *Capitol CL 13912*	7	7
30 Oct 53 ●	CAN'T I? (2nd re-entry) *Capitol CL 13937*	10	1
16 Apr 54 ●	TENDERLY *Capitol CL 14061*	10	1
10 Sep 54 ●	SMILE *Capitol CL 14149*	2	14
8 Oct 54	MAKE HER MINE *Capitol CL 14149*	11	2
25 Feb 55 ●	A BLOSSOM FELL *Capitol CL 14235*	3	10
26 Aug 55	MY ONE SIN *Capitol CL 14327*	18	1
16 Sep 55	MY ONE SIN (re-entry) *Capitol CL 14327*	17	1
27 Jan 56 ●	DREAMS CAN TELL A LIE *Capitol CL 14513*	10	9
11 May 56 ●	TOO YOUNG TO GO STEADY *Capitol CL 14573*	8	14
14 Sep 56	LOVE ME AS THOUGH THERE WERE NO TOMORROW *Capitol CL 14621*	24	2
5 Oct 56	LOVE ME AS IF THERE WERE NO TOMORROW (re-entry) *Capitol CL 14621*	11	13
19 Apr 57 ●	WHEN I FALL IN LOVE *Capitol CL 14709*	2	20
5 Jul 57	WHEN ROCK 'N ROLL CAME TO TRINIDAD *Capitol CL 14733*	28	1
18 Oct 57	MY PERSONAL POSSESSION *Capitol CL 14765*	21	2
25 Oct 57	STARDUST *Capitol CL 14787*	24	2
29 May 59	YOU MADE ME LOVE YOU *Capitol CL 15017*	22	1
4 Sep 59	MIDNIGHT FLYER *Capitol CL 15056*	27	1
18 Sep 59	MIDNIGHT FLYER (re-entry) *Capitol CL 15056*	23	3
12 Feb 60	TIME AND THE RIVER *Capitol CL 15111*	29	1
26 Feb 60	TIME AND THE RIVER (re-entry) *Capitol CL 15111*	23	2
31 Mar 60	TIME AND THE RIVER (2nd re-entry) *Capitol CL 15111*	47	1
26 May 60 ●	THAT'S YOU *Capitol CL 15129*	10	8
10 Nov 60	JUST AS MUCH AS EVER *Capitol CL 15163*	18	10
2 Feb 61	THE WORLD IN MY ARMS *Capitol CL 15178*	36	10
16 Nov 61	LET TRUE LOVE BEGIN *Capitol CL 15224*	29	10
22 Mar 62	BRAZILIAN LOVE SONG *Capitol CL 15241*	34	4
31 May 62	THE RIGHT THING TO SAY *Capitol CL 15250*	42	4
19 Jul 62	LET THERE BE LOVE *Capitol CL 15257* [1]	11	14
27 Sep 62 ●	RAMBLIN' ROSE *Capitol CL 15270*	5	14
20 Dec 62	DEAR LONELY HEARTS *Capitol CL 15280*	37	3
12 Dec 87 ●	WHEN I FALL IN LOVE (re-issue) *Capitol CL 15975*	4	7
14 Dec 91	THE CHRISTMAS SONG *Capitol CL 641*	69	2
19 Mar 94	LET'S FACE THE MUSIC AND DANCE *EMI CDEM 312*	30	3

[1] Nat 'King' Cole with George Shearing

See also Natalie COLE

Natalie COLE ✎ *US, female vocalist*   **87 wks**
11 Oct 75	THIS WILL BE *Capitol CL 15834*	32	5
8 Aug 87	JUMP START *Manhattan MT 22*	44	8
26 Mar 88 ●	PINK CADILLAC *Manhattan MT 35*	5	12
25 Jun 88	EVERLASTING *Manhattan MT 46*	28	6
20 Aug 88	JUMP START (re-issue) *Manhattan MT 50*	36	5
26 Nov 88	I LIVE FOR YOUR LOVE *Manhattan MT 57*	23	14
15 Apr 89 ●	MISS YOU LIKE CRAZY *EMI-USA MT 63*	2	15
22 Jul 89	REST OF THE NIGHT *EMI-USA MT 69*	56	2
16 Dec 89	STARTING OVER AGAIN *EMI-USA MT 77*	56	4
21 Apr 90	WILD WOMEN DO *EMI-USA MT 81*	16	7
22 Jun 91	UNFORGETTABLE *Elektra EKR 128*	19	8
16 May 92	THE VERY THOUGHT OF YOU *Elektra EKR 147*	71	1

'Unforgettable' features the uncredited vocals of Nat 'King' Cole

Paula COLE ◎ *US, female vocalist*   **9 wks**
28 Jun 97	WHERE HAVE ALL THE COWBOYS GONE? *Warner Bros. W 0406CD*	15	8
1 Aug 98	I DON'T WANT TO WAIT *Warner Bros. W 0422CD*	43	1

COLETTE – *See SISTER BLISS with COLETTE*

John Ford COLEY – *See ENGLAND DAN and John Ford COLEY*

COLLAGE
US/Canada/Philippines, male vocal/instrumental group   **5 wks**
21 Sep 85	ROMEO WHERE'S JULIET? *MCA MCA 1006*	46	5

COLLAPSED LUNG ☺ *UK, male vocal/instrumental group*   **8 wks**
22 Jun 96	LONDON TONIGHT/EAT MY GOAL *Deceptive BLUFF 029CD*	31	3
30 May 98	EAT MY GOAL *Deceptive BLUFF 060CD*	18	5

Dave and Ansil COLLINS ✌
Jamaica, male vocal/instrumental duo   **27 wks**
27 Mar 71 ★	DOUBLE BARREL *Technique TE 901*	1	15
26 Jun 71 ●	MONKEY SPANNER *Technique TE 914*	7	12

Edwyn COLLINS ◎ ✔ *UK, male vocalist*   **25 wks**
11 Aug 84	PALE BLUE EYES *Swamplands SWP 1* [1]	72	2
12 Nov 94	A GIRL LIKE YOU *Setanta ZOP 001CD1*	42	3
17 Jun 95 ●	A GIRL LIKE YOU (re-issue) *Setanta ZOP 003CD*	4	14
2 Mar 96	KEEP ON BURNING *Setanta ZOP 004CD1*	45	2
2 Aug 97	THE MAGIC PIPER (OF LOVE) *Setanta SETCDA 041*	32	3
18 Oct 97	ADIDAS WORLD *Setanta SETCDB 045*	71	1

[1] Paul Quinn and Edwyn Collins

'A Girl Like You' in 1994 was the only track available on all formats of the Expressly EP

What: *All Right Now* **25**
Who: Free
When: 1970 (2), 1973 (15), 1991 (8 – remix)
Which: Had its third Top 20 run after it was used in a Wrigley's Chewing Gum advert. This rock classic was also included on the *Free* (EP), which reached No 11 in 1978

What: *Secret Love* **26**
Who: Doris Day
When: 1954 (1)
Which: Came from the celluloid smash, *Calamity Jane*, and won an Oscar for Best Film Song. This ballad topped the chart for nine weeks – a record for a female artist, and not bettered until 1993

What: *Cars* **27**
Who: Gary Numan
When: 1979 (1), 1987 (16 – remix), 1993 (53 – 2nd remix), 1996 (17 – remix)
Which: Drove the ex-leader of the chart-topping band Tubeway Army into the chart on four separate occasions and gave this distinctive singer/songwriter/producer his only US hit

What: *I Heard It Through the Grapevine* **28**
Who: Marvin Gaye
When: 1969 (1), 1986 (8)
Which: Topped the UK/US charts, despite the fact that the Gladys Knight and the Pips version (surprisingly recorded after Marvin's) had become a million-seller one year previously

Felicia COLLINS – See LUKK featuring Felicia COLLINS

Jeff COLLINS UK, male vocalist — 8 wks
18 Nov 72	ONLY YOU *Polydor 2058 287*	40	8

Judy COLLINS ♂ US, female vocalist — 86 wks
17 Jan 70	BOTH SIDES NOW *Elektra EKSN 45043*	14	11
5 Dec 70 ●	AMAZING GRACE *Elektra 2101 020*	5	32
24 Jul 71	AMAZING GRACE (re-entry) *Elektra 2101 020*	48	1
4 Sep 71	AMAZING GRACE (2nd re-entry) *Elektra 2101 020*	40	7
20 Nov 71	AMAZING GRACE (3rd re-entry) *Elektra 2101 020*	50	1
18 Dec 71	AMAZING GRACE (4th re-entry) *Elektra 2101 020*	48	2
22 Apr 72	AMAZING GRACE (5th re-entry) *Elektra 2101 020*	20	19
9 Sep 72	AMAZING GRACE (6th re-entry) *Elektra 2101 020*	46	2
23 Dec 72	AMAZING GRACE (7th re-entry) *Elektra 2101 020*	49	3
17 May 75 ●	SEND IN THE CLOWNS *Elektra K 12177*	6	8

Phil COLLINS ☻ Continually popular singer/songwriter (b. 31 January, 1951, London) who simultaneously fronted Genesis (until 1996) and managed a successful solo career. Only members of The Beatles have appeared on more UK No 1 albums — 218 wks
17 Jan 81 ●	IN THE AIR TONIGHT *Virgin VSK 102*	2	10
7 Mar 81	I MISSED AGAIN *Virgin VS 402*	14	8
30 May 81	IF LEAVING ME IS EASY *Virgin VS 423*	17	8
23 Oct 82	THRU' THESE WALLS *Virgin VS 524*	56	2
4 Dec 82 ★	YOU CAN'T HURRY LOVE *Virgin VS 531*	1	16
19 Mar 83	DON'T LET HIM STEAL YOUR HEART AWAY *Virgin VS 572*	45	5
7 Apr 84 ●	AGAINST ALL ODDS (TAKE A LOOK AT ME NOW) *Virgin VS 674* ▲	2	14
26 Jan 85	SUSSUDIO *Virgin VS 736* ▲	12	9
9 Mar 85 ★	EASY LOVER *CBS A 4915* 1	1	12
13 Apr 85 ●	ONE MORE NIGHT *Virgin VS 755* ▲	4	9
27 Jul 85	TAKE ME HOME *Virgin VS 777*	19	9
23 Nov 85 ●	SEPARATE LIVES *Virgin VS 818* ▲ 2	4	13
18 Jun 88 ●	IN THE AIR TONIGHT (re-mix) *Virgin VS 102*	4	9
3 Sep 88 ★	A GROOVY KIND OF LOVE *Virgin VS 1117* ▲	1	13
26 Nov 88 ●	TWO HEARTS *Virgin VS 1141* ▲	6	11
4 Nov 89 ●	ANOTHER DAY IN PARADISE *Virgin VS 1234* ▲	2	11
27 Jan 90 ●	I WISH IT WOULD RAIN DOWN *Virgin VS 1240*	7	9
28 Apr 90	SOMETHING HAPPENED ON THE WAY TO HEAVEN *Virgin VS 1251*	15	7
28 Jul 90	THAT'S JUST THE WAY IT IS *Virgin VS 1277*	26	5
6 Oct 90	HANG IN LONG ENOUGH *Virgin VS 1300*	34	3
8 Dec 90	DO YOU REMEMBER (LIVE) *Virgin VS 1305*	57	5
15 May 93	HERO *Atlantic A 7360* 3	56	3
30 Oct 93 ●	BOTH SIDES OF THE STORY *Virgin VSCDT 1500*	7	9
1 Jan 94	BOTH SIDES OF THE STORY (re-entry) *Virgin VSCDT 1500*	61	1
15 Jan 94	EVERYDAY *Virgin VSCDT 1505*	15	5
7 Mar 94	WE WAIT AND WE WONDER *Virgin VSCDT 1510*	45	2
5 Oct 96 ●	DANCE INTO THE LIGHT *Face Value EW 066CD*	9	6
14 Dec 96	IT'S IN YOUR EYES *Face Value EW 076CD1*	30	3
12 Jul 97	WEAR MY HAT *Face Value EW 113CD*	43	1
7 Nov 98	TRUE COLORS *Virgin VSCDT 1715*	26	4

1 Philip Bailey (duet with Phil Collins) 2 Phil Collins and Marilyn Martin 3 David Crosby featuring Phil Collins

Rodger COLLINS US, male vocalist — 6 wks
3 Apr 76	YOU SEXY SUGAR PLUM (BUT I LIKE IT) *Fantasy FTC 132*	22	6

Willie COLLINS US, male vocalist — 4 wks
28 Jun 86	WHERE YOU GONNA BE TONIGHT? *Capitol CL 410*	46	4

Willie COLON US, male vocalist — 7 wks
28 Jun 86	SET FIRE TO ME *A & M AM 330*	41	7

COLOR ME BADD ☻ R&B US, male vocal group — 31 wks
18 May 91 ★	I WANNA SEX YOU UP *Giant W 0036*	1	14
3 Aug 91 ●	ALL 4 LOVE *Giant W 0053* ▲	5	10
12 Oct 91	I ADORE MI AMOR *Giant W 0067* ▲	44	2
9 Nov 91	I ADORE MI AMOR (re-issue) *Giant W 0076*	59	2
22 Feb 92	HEARTBREAKER *Giant W 0078*	58	1
20 Nov 93	TIME AND CHANCE *Giant 74321168992*	62	1
16 Apr 94	CHOOSE *Giant 74321199432*	65	1

COLORADO UK, female vocal group — 3 wks
21 Oct 78	CALIFORNIA DREAMIN' *Pinnacle PIN 67*	45	3

COLOUR FIELD ☻ UK, male vocal/instrumental group — 18 wks
21 Jan 84	THE COLOUR FIELD *Chrysalis COLF 1*	43	4
28 Jul 84	TAKE *Chrysalis COLF 2*	70	1
26 Jan 85	THINKING OF YOU *Chrysalis COLF 3*	12	10
13 Apr 85	CASTLES IN THE AIR *Chrysalis COLF 4*	51	3

Shawn COLVIN US, female vocalist — 11 wks
27 Nov 93	I DON'T KNOW WHY *Columbia 6598272*	62	1
12 Feb 94	ROUND OF BLUES *Columbia 6594282*	73	1
3 Sep 94	EVERY LITTLE THING HE DOES IS MAGIC *Columbia 6607742*	65	1
7 Jan 95	ONE COOL REMOVE *Columbia 6611342* 1	40	3
12 Aug 95	I DON'T KNOW WHY (re-issue) *Columbia 6622725*	52	1
15 Mar 97	GET OUT OF THIS HOUSE *Columbia 6638522*	70	1
30 May 98	SUNNY CAME HOME *Columbia 6648022*	29	3

1 Shawn Colvin with Mary Chapin Carpenter

COMETS – See Bill HALEY and his COMETS

COMING OUT CREW US, male/female vocal duo — 1 wk
18 Mar 95	FREE, GAY AND HAPPY *Out On Vinyl CDOOV 002*	50	1

COMMENTATORS ☻ UK, male impressionist – Rory Bremner — 7 wks
22 Jun 85	N-N-NINETEEN NOT OUT *Oval 100*	13	7

COMMITMENTS Ireland, male/female vocal/instrumental group — 1 wk
30 Nov 91	MUSTANG SALLY *MCA MCS 1598*	63	1

COMMODORES ♪ Top-notch US R&B combo: Lionel Richie (v/k), William King (t), Thomas McClary (g), Milan Williams (var), Ronald LaPread (b), Walter Orange (d). They were among the 1970s' biggest-selling groups, but lost ground when singer/songwriter Richie went solo in 1982 — 121 wks
24 Aug 74	MACHINE GUN *Tamla Motown TMG 902*	20	11
23 Nov 74	THE ZOO (THE HUMAN ZOO) *Tamla Motown TMG 924*	44	2
2 Jul 77 ●	EASY *Motown TMG 1073*	9	10
8 Oct 77	SWEET LOVE/BRICK HOUSE *Motown TMG 1086*	32	6
11 Mar 78	TOO HOT TO TROT/ZOOM *Motown TMG 1096*	38	4
24 Jun 78	FLYING HIGH *Motown TMG 1111*	37	7
5 Aug 78 ★	THREE TIMES A LADY *Motown TMG 1113* ▲	1	14
25 Nov 78	JUST TO BE CLOSE TO YOU *Motown TMG 1127*	62	4
25 Aug 79 ●	SAIL ON *Motown TMG 1155*	8	10
3 Nov 79	STILL *Motown TMG 1166* ▲	4	11
19 Jan 80	WONDERLAND *Motown TMG 1172*	40	4
1 Aug 81	LADY (YOU BRING ME UP) *Motown TMG 1238*	56	5
21 Nov 81	OH NO *Motown TMG 1245*	44	3
26 Jan 85 ●	NIGHTSHIFT *Motown TMG 1371*	3	14
11 May 85	ANIMAL INSTINCT *Motown ZB 40097*	74	1
25 Oct 86	GOIN' TO THE BANK *Polydor POSPA 826*	43	4
13 Aug 88	EASY (re-issue) *Motown ZB 41793*	15	11

Group was US/UK for 1985 and 1986 hits

COMMON – See Chantay SAVAGE

COMMOTIONS – See Lloyd COLE

COMMUNARDS ◐ UK, male vocal/instrumental duo   76 wks

12 Oct 85	YOU ARE MY WORLD London LON 77	30	8
24 May 86	DISENCHANTED London LON 89	29	5
23 Aug 86	★ DON'T LEAVE ME THIS WAY London LON 103 [1]	1	14
29 Nov 86	● SO COLD THE NIGHT London LON 110	8	10
21 Feb 87	YOU ARE MY WORLD ('87) (re-mix) London LON 123	21	6
12 Sep 87	TOMORROW London LON 143	23	7
7 Nov 87	● NEVER CAN SAY GOODBYE London LON 158	4	11
20 Feb 88	FOR A FRIEND London LON 166	28	7
11 Jun 88	THERE'S MORE TO LOVE London LON 173	20	8

[1] Communards with Sarah Jane Morris

Perry COMO ℭ One of the century's most enduring entertainers, b. 18 May, 1912, Pennsylvania. This easy-on-the-ear relaxed balladeer launched his career in 1933, collected 150 US chart entries, hosted an Emmy-winning TV series, and continued to score hits past the age of 60   294 wks

16 Jan 53	★ DON'T LET THE STARS GET IN YOUR EYES HMV B 10400 ▲	1	15
4 Jun 54	● WANTED HMV B 10691 ▲	4	14
25 Jun 54	● IDLE GOSSIP HMV B 10667	3	15
1 Oct 54	WANTED (re-entry) HMV B 10691	18	1
10 Dec 54	PAPA LOVES MAMBO HMV B 10776	16	1
30 Dec 55	TINA MARIE HMV POP 103	24	1
27 Apr 56	JUKE BOX BABY HMV POP 191	22	6
25 May 56	● HOT DIGGITY HMV POP 221	4	13
21 Sep 56	● MORE HMV POP 240	10	11
28 Sep 56	GLENDORA HMV POP 240	18	6
14 Dec 56	MORE (re-entry) HMV POP 240	29	1
7 Feb 58	★ MAGIC MOMENTS RCA 1036	1	17
7 Mar 58	● CATCH A FALLING STAR RCA 1036	9	10
9 May 58	● KEWPIE DOLL RCA 1055	9	7
30 May 58	I MAY NEVER PASS THIS WAY AGAIN RCA 1062	15	8
5 Sep 58	MOON TALK RCA 1071	17	11
7 Nov 58	● LOVE MAKES THE WORLD GO ROUND RCA 1086	6	14
21 Nov 58	MANDOLINS IN THE MOONLIGHT RCA 1086	13	12
27 Feb 59	● TOMBOY RCA 1111	10	12
10 Jul 59	I KNOW RCA 1126	13	16
26 Feb 60	● DELAWARE RCA 1170	3	13
10 May 62	CATERINA RCA 1283	37	4
14 Jun 62	CATERINA (re-entry) RCA 1283	45	2
30 Jan 71	● IT'S IMPOSSIBLE RCA 2043	4	23
15 May 71	I THINK OF YOU RCA 2075	14	11
21 Apr 73	● AND I LOVE YOU SO RCA 2346	3	31
25 Aug 73	● FOR THE GOOD TIMES RCA 2402	7	27
8 Dec 73	WALK RIGHT BACK RCA 2432	33	10
12 Jan 74	AND I LOVE YOU SO (re-entry) RCA 2346	40	4
25 May 74	I WANT TO GIVE RCA LPBO 7518	31	6

COMPAGNONS DE LA CHANSON France, male vocal group   3 wks

9 Oct 59	THE THREE BELLS (THE JIMMY BROWN SONG) Columbia DB 4358	27	1
23 Oct 59	THE THREE BELLS (THE JIMMY BROWN SONG) (re-entry) Columbia DB 4358	21	2

COMSAT ANGELS UK, male vocal/instrumental group   2 wks

21 Jan 84	INDEPENDENCE DAY Jive JIVE 54	75	1
4 Feb 84	INDEPENDENCE DAY (re-entry) Jive JIVE 54	71	1

CON FUNK SHUN US, male vocal/instrumental group   2 wks

19 Jul 86	BURNIN' LOVE Club JAB 32	68	2

CONCEPT US, male vocalist/instrumentalist – keyboards   6 wks

14 Dec 85	M. DJ Fourth & Broadway BRW 40	27	6

CONFEDERATES – See Elvis COSTELLO

CONGREGATION ◐ UK, male/female choir   14 wks

27 Nov 71	● SOFTLY WHISPERING I LOVE YOU Columbia DB 8830	4	14

CONGRESS UK, male/female vocal/instrumental group   4 wks

26 Oct 91	40 MILES Inner Rhythm 7HEART 01	26	4

Arthur CONLEY 🎤 US, male vocalist   15 wks

27 Apr 67	● SWEET SOUL MUSIC Atlantic 584 083	7	14
10 Apr 68	FUNKY STREET Atlantic 583 175	46	1

CONNELLS ◐ 🎸 US, male vocal/instrumental group   11 wks

12 Aug 95	'74-'75 TVT LONCD 369	14	8
16 Mar 96	'74-'75 (re-entry) TVT LONCD 413	21	3

Harry CONNICK Jr. US, male vocalist   11 wks

25 May 91	RECIPE FOR LOVE/IT HAD TO BE YOU Columbia 6568907	32	6
3 Aug 91	WE ARE IN LOVE Columbia 6572847	62	2
23 Nov 91	BLUE LIGHT RED LIGHT (SOMEONE'S THERE) Columbia 6575367	54	3

Billy CONNOLLY ◐ UK, male vocalist   31 wks

1 Nov 75	★ D.I.V.O.R.C.E. Polydor 2058 652	1	10
17 Jul 76	NO CHANCE (NO CHARGE) Polydor 2058 748	24	5
25 Aug 79	IN THE BROWNIES Polydor 2059 160	38	7
9 Mar 85	SUPER GRAN Stiff BUY 218	32	9

CONQUERING LION UK, male vocal group   1 wk

8 Oct 94	CODE RED Mango CIDM 821	53	1

Leena CONQUEST and HIP HOP FINGER US, female vocalist   1 wk

18 Jun 94	BOUNDARIES Naturalresponse 74321208522	67	1

Jess CONRAD ◐ UK, male vocalist   13 wks

30 Jun 60	CHERRY PIE Decca F 11236	39	1
26 Jan 61	MYSTERY GIRL Decca F 11315	44	1
9 Feb 61	MYSTERY GIRL (re-entry) Decca F 11315	18	9
11 Oct 62	PRETTY JENNY Decca F 11511	50	2

CONSORTIUM UK, male vocal group   9 wks

12 Feb 69	ALL THE LOVE IN THE WORLD Pye 7N 17635	22	9

Ann CONSUELO – See SUBTERRANIA featuring Ann CONSUELO

CONTOURS US, male vocal group   6 wks

24 Jan 70	JUST A LITTLE MISUNDERSTANDING Tamla Motown TMG 723	31	6

CONTRABAND
Germany/US, male/female vocal/instrumental group   2 wks

20 Jul 91	ALL THE WAY FROM MEMPHIS Impact American EM 195	65	2

CONTROL ☺ UK, male/female vocal/instrumental group   5 wks

2 Nov 91	DANCE WITH ME All Around The World GLOBE 105	17	5

CONVERT Belgium, male instrumental/production duo   7 wks

11 Jan 92	NIGHTBIRD A & M AM 845	39	4
29 May 93	ROCKIN' TO THE RHYTHM A & M 5802532	42	2
31 Jan 98	NIGHTBIRD (re-issue) Wonderboy WBOYD 008	45	1

CONWAY BROTHERS ☺ US, male vocal group   10 wks

22 Jun 85	TURN IT UP 10 TEN 57	11	10

Russ CONWAY ℭ Popular pianist and composer, b. Trevor Stanford, 2 September, 1927, Bristol. Against the trends of the day this MOR piano-player was the UK's top-selling artist in 1959   178 wks

29 Nov 57	PARTY POPS Columbia DB 4031	24	5
29 Aug 58	GOT A MATCH Columbia DB 4166	30	1

8 Nov 58 ●	MORE PARTY POPS *Columbia DB 4204*	10	7
23 Jan 59	THE WORLD OUTSIDE *Columbia DB 4234*	24	1
20 Feb 59 ★	SIDE SADDLE *Columbia DB 4256*	1	30
6 Mar 59	THE WORLD OUTSIDE (re-entry) *Columbia DB 4234*	24	3
15 May 59 ★	ROULETTE *Columbia DB 4298*	1	19
21 Aug 59 ●	CHINA TEA *Columbia DB 4337*	5	13
13 Nov 59	SNOW COACH *Columbia DB 4368*	7	9
20 Nov 59 ●	MORE AND MORE PARTY POPS *Columbia DB 4373*	5	8
10 Mar 60	ROYAL EVENT *Columbia DB 4418*	15	7
21 Apr 60	FINGS AIN'T WOT THEY USED T'BE *Columbia DB 4422*	47	1
19 May 60	LUCKY FIVE *Columbia DB 4457*	14	9
29 Sep 60	PASSING BREEZE *Columbia DB 4508*	16	10
24 Nov 60	EVEN MORE PARTY POPS *Columbia DB 4535*	27	9
19 Jan 61	PEPE *Columbia DB 4564*	19	9
25 May 61	PABLO *Columbia DB 4649*	45	2
24 Aug 61	SAY IT WITH FLOWERS *Columbia DB 4665* [1]	23	10
30 Nov 61 ●	TOY BALLOONS *Columbia DB 4738*	7	11
22 Feb 62	LESSON ONE *Columbia DB 4784*	21	7
29 Nov 62	ALWAYS YOU AND ME *Columbia DB 4934*	33	4
3 Jan 63	ALWAYS YOU AND ME (re-entry) *Columbia DB 4934*	35	3

[1] Dorothy Squires and Russ Conway

'Always You and Me' featured Russ Conway talking as well as playing piano. Several of the discs were medleys as follows: Party Pops: When You're Smiling / I'm Looking Over a Four-Leafed Clover / When You Wore a Tulip / Row Row Row / For Me and My Girl / Shine on Harvest Moon / By the Light of the Silvery Moon / Side by Side. More Party Pops: Music Music Music / If You Were the Only Girl in the World / Nobody's Sweetheart / Yes Sir That's My Baby / Some of These Days / Honeysuckle and the Bee / Hello Hello Who's Your Lady Friend / Shanty in Old Shanty Town. More and More Party Pops: Sheik of Araby / Who Were You With Last Night / Any Old Iron / Tiptoe Through the Tulips / If You Were the Only Girl in the World / When I Leave the World Behind. Even More Party Pops: Ain't She Sweet / I Can't Give You Anything But Love / Yes We Have No Bananas / I May Be Wrong / Happy Days and Lonely Nights / Glad Rag Doll. He really did feature 'If You Were the Only Girl in the World' on two different hits

Martin COOK – *See Richard DENTON and Martin COOK*

Norman COOK ○ *UK, male producer/multi-instrumentalist* — 10 wks

8 Jul 89	WON'T TALK ABOUT IT / BLAME IT ON THE BASSLINE *Go.Beat GOD 33* [1]	29	6
21 Oct 89	FOR SPACIOUS LIES *Go.Beat GOD 37* [2]	48	4

[1] Norman Cook featuring Billy Bragg / Norman Cook featuring MC Wildski
[2] Norman Cook featuring Lester

Norman Cook has also recorded under: Beats International, Fatboy Slim, Feelgood Factor, Freakpower, MC Wildski, Mighty Dub Katz and Pizzaman
See also BEATS INTERNATIONAL; FATBOY SLIM; FREAKPOWER; MC WILDSKI; MIGHTY DUB KATZ; PIZZAMAN

Peter COOK ○ *UK, male vocalist* — 15 wks

17 Jun 65	GOODBYE-EE *Decca F 12158* [1]	18	10
15 Jul 65	THE BALLAD OF SPOTTY MULDOON *Decca F 12182*	34	5

[1] Peter Cook and Dudley Moore

Brandon COOKE – *See Roxanne SHANTE*

Sam COOKE ♪ *US, male vocalist* — 82 wks

17 Jan 58	YOU SEND ME *London HLU 8506* ▲	29	1
14 Aug 59	ONLY SIXTEEN *HMV POP 642*	23	4
7 Jul 60	WONDERFUL WORLD *HMV POP 754*	27	8
29 Sep 60 ●	CHAIN GANG *RCA 1202*	9	11
27 Jul 61 ●	CUPID *RCA 1242*	7	14
8 Mar 62 ●	TWISTIN' THE NIGHT AWAY *RCA 1277*	6	14
16 May 63	ANOTHER SATURDAY NIGHT *RCA 1341*	23	12
5 Sep 63	FRANKIE AND JOHNNY *RCA 1361*	30	6
22 Mar 86 ●	WONDERFUL WORLD (re-issue) *RCA PB 49871*	2	11
10 May 86	ANOTHER SATURDAY NIGHT (re-issue) *RCA PB 49849*	75	1

COOKIE CREW ⌨ *UK, female rap duo* — 31 wks

9 Jan 88 ●	ROK DA HOUSE *Rhythm King LEFT 11* [1]	5	11

7 Jan 89	BORN THIS WAY (LET'S DANCE) *ffrr FFR 19*	23	5
1 Apr 89	GOT TO KEEP ON *ffrr FFR 25*	17	9
15 Jul 89	COME AND GET SOME *ffrr F 110*	42	3
27 Jul 91	SECRETS (OF SUCCESS) *ffrr F159* [2]	53	3

[1] Beatmasters featuring the Cookie Crew [2] Cookie Crew featuring Danny D

COOKIES *US, female vocal group* — 1 wk

10 Jan 63	CHAINS *London HLU 9634*	50	1

COOL DOWN ZONE *UK, male/female vocal/instrumental group* — 4 wks

30 Jun 90	HEAVEN KNOWS *10 TEN 309*	52	4

COOL JACK *Italy, male instrumental/production duo* — 1 wk

9 Nov 96	JUS' COME *AM:PM 5819892*	44	1

COOL, the FAB, and the GROOVY
UK, male production duo and US, male band — 1 wk

1 Aug 98	SOUL BOSSA NOVA *Manifesto FESCD 48* [1]	47	1

[1] Cool, the Fab, and the Groovy present Quincy Jones

Rita COOLIDGE ○ ♪ *US, female vocalist* — 24 wks

25 Jun 77 ●	WE'RE ALL ALONE *A & M AMS 7295*	6	13
15 Oct 77	(YOUR LOVE HAS LIFTED ME) HIGHER AND HIGHER *A & M AMS 7315*	49	1
29 Oct 77	(YOUR LOVE HAS LIFTED ME) HIGHER AND HIGHER (re-entry) *A & M AMS 7315*	48	1
4 Feb 78	WORDS *A & M AMS 7330*	25	1
25 Jun 83	ALL TIME HIGH *A & M AM 007*	75	1

COOLIO ⌨ *US, male rapper* — 62 wks

23 Jul 94	FANTASTIC VOYAGE *Tommy Boy TB 0617CD*	41	2
15 Oct 94	I REMEMBER *Tommy Boy TBXCD 635*	73	1
28 Oct 95 ★	GANGSTA'S PARADISE *Tommy Boy MCSTD 2104* [1] ◆ ■ ▲	1	20
20 Jan 96	TOO HOT *Tommy Boy TBCD 718*	9	6
6 Apr 96	1234 (SUMPIN' NEW) *Tommy Boy TBCD 7721*	13	7
17 Aug 96	IT'S ALL THE WAY LIVE (NOW) *Tommy Boy TBCD 7731*	34	2
5 Apr 97	HIT 'EM HIGH (THE MONSTARS' ANTHEM) *Atlantic A 5449CD* [2]	8	6
7 Jun 97	THE WINNER *Atlantic A 5433CD*	53	1
19 Jul 97 ●	C U WHEN U GET THERE *Tommy Boy TBCD 785* [3]	3	12
11 Oct 97	OOH LA LA *Tommy Boy TBCD 799*	14	5

[1] Coolio featuring LV [2] B Real / Busta Rhymes / Coolio / L L Cool J / Method Man
[3] Coolio featuring 40 Thevz

COOLNOTES ☺ ♪ *UK, male/female vocal/instrumental group* — 28 wks

18 Aug 84	YOU'RE NEVER TOO YOUNG *Abstract Dance AD 1*	42	5
17 Nov 84	I FORGOT *Abstract Dance AD 2*	63	2
23 Mar 85	SPEND THE NIGHT *Abstract Dance AD 3*	11	9
13 Jul 85	IN YOUR CAR *Abstract Dance AD 4*	13	9
19 Oct 85	HAVE A GOOD FOREVER *Abstract Dance AD 5*	73	1
17 May 86	INTO THE MOTION *Abstract Dance AD 8*	66	2

Alice COOPER ♪ *The alter ego of shock-rock vocalist Vincent Furnier, b. 4 February, 1948, Detroit. Transatlantic chart-topper, whose group was voted World's Top Band in 1972 in UK. Renowned for onstage theatrics, it was the only US rock group to top chart in early 1970s* — 104 wks

15 Jul 72 ★	SCHOOL'S OUT *Warner Bros. K 16188*	1	12
7 Oct 72 ●	ELECTED *Warner Bros. K 16214*	4	10
10 Feb 73 ●	HELLO HURRAY *Warner Bros. K 16248*	6	12
21 Apr 73 ●	NO MORE MR. NICE GUY *Warner Bros. K 16262*	10	10
19 Jan 74	TEENAGE LAMENT '74 *Warner Bros. K 16345*	12	7
21 May 77	(NO MORE) LOVE AT YOUR CONVENIENCE *Warner Bros. K 16935*	44	2
23 Dec 78	HOW YOU GONNA SEE ME NOW *Warner Bros. K 17270*	61	6
6 Mar 82	SEVEN AND SEVEN IS (LIVE VERSION) *Warner Bros. K 17924*	62	3
8 May 82	FOR BRITAIN ONLY / UNDER MY WHEELS *Warner Bros. K 17940*	66	2

UK No 1 ★   UK Top 10 ●   UK million seller ◆   UK entry at No 1 ■   US No 1 ▲

149

18 Oct 86	HE'S BACK (THE MAN BEHIND THE MASK) *MCA MCA 1090*	61	2
9 Apr 88	FREEDOM *MCA MCA 1241*	50	3
29 Jul 89 ●	POISON *Epic 655061 7*	2	11
7 Oct 89	BED OF NAILS *Epic ALICE 3*	38	5
2 Dec 89	HOUSE OF FIRE *Epic ALICE 4*	65	2
22 Jun 91	HEY STOOPID *Epic 6569837*	21	6
5 Oct 91	LOVE'S A LOADED GUN *Epic 6574387*	38	3
6 Jun 92	FEED MY FRANKENSTEIN *Epic 6580927*	27	3
28 May 94	LOST IN AMERICA *Epic 6603472*	22	3
23 Jul 94	IT'S ME *Epic 6605632*	34	2

For the first five hits, 'Alice Cooper' was the name of the entire group, not just of the lead vocalist

Deborah COOPER – See C & C MUSIC FACTORY / CLIVILLES & COLE

Tommy COOPER *UK, male vocalist*   3 wks

29 Jun 61	DON'T JUMP OFF THE ROOF DAD *Palette PG 9019*	40	2
20 Jul 61	DON'T JUMP OFF THE ROOF DAD (re-entry) *Palette PG 9019*	50	1

Julian COPE ○ ✓ *UK, male vocalist*   59 wks

19 Nov 83	SUNSHINE PLAYROOM *Mercury COPE 1*	64	1
31 Mar 84	THE GREATNESS AND PERFECTION OF LOVE *Mercury MER 155*	52	5
27 Sep 86	WORLD SHUT YOUR MOUTH *Island IS 290*	19	8
17 Jan 87	TRAMPOLENE *Island IS 305*	31	6
11 Apr 87	EVE'S VOLCANO (COVERED IN SIN) *Island IS 318*	41	5
24 Sep 88	CHARLOTTE ANNE *Island IS 380*	35	6
21 Jan 89	5 O'CLOCK WORLD *Island IS 399*	42	4
24 Jun 89	CHINA DOLL *Island IS 406*	53	2
9 Feb 91	BEAUTIFUL LOVE *Island IS 483*	32	6
20 Apr 91	EAST EASY RIDER *Island IS 492*	51	3
3 Aug 91	HEAD *Island IS 497*	57	2
8 Aug 92	WORLD SHUT YOUR MOUTH (re-issue) *Island IS 534*	44	3
17 Oct 92	FEAR LOVES THIS PLACE *Island IS 545*	42	2
12 Aug 95	TRY TRY TRY *Echo ECSCD 11*	24	3
27 Jul 96	I COME FROM ANOTHER PLANET BABY *Echo ECSCD 22*	34	2
5 Oct 96	PLANETARY SIT-IN (EVERY GIRL HAS YOUR NAME) *Echo ECSCD 25*	34	1

Imani COPPOLA *UK, female vocalist/instrumentalist*   3 wks

28 Feb 98	LEGEND OF A COWGIRL *Columbia 6656015*	32	3

Harry H CORBETT – See Wilfrid BRAMBELL and Harry H CORBETT

Frank CORDELL *UK, orchestra*   4 wks

24 Aug 56	SADIE'S SHAWL *HMV POP 229*	29	2
16 Feb 61	BLACK BEAR *HMV POP 824*	44	2

Louise CORDET ○ *UK, female vocalist*   13 wks

5 Jul 62	I'M JUST A BABY *Decca F 11476*	13	13

Don CORNELL ☾ *US, male vocalist*   23 wks

3 Sep 54 ★	HOLD MY HAND *Vogue Q 2013*	1	21
22 Apr 55	STRANGER IN PARADISE *Vogue Q 72073*	19	2

Lynn CORNELL *UK, female vocalist*   9 wks

20 Oct 60	NEVER ON SUNDAY *Decca F 11277*	30	9

CORNERSHOP ☹ ☺ *UK, male vocal/instrumental duo*   16 wks

30 Aug 97	BRIMFUL OF ASHA *Wiiija WIJ 75CD*	60	1
28 Feb 98 ★	BRIMFUL OF ASHA (re-mix) *Wiiija WIJ 81CD* ■	1	12
16 May 98	SLEEP ON THE LEFT SIDE *Wiiija WIJ 80CD*	23	3

Charlotte CORNWELL – See Julie COVINGTON, Rula LENSKA, Charlotte CORNWELL and Sue JONES-DAVIES

Hugh CORNWELL *UK, male vocalist/instrumentalist – guitar*   3 wks

24 Jan 87	FACTS + FIGURES *Virgin VS 922*	61	2
7 May 88	ANOTHER KIND OF LOVE *Virgin VS 945*	71	1

CORO featuring TARLISA
Germany, male/female vocal/production group   1 wk

12 Dec 92	BECAUSE THE NIGHT *ZYX ZYX 68227*	61	1

CORONA ☺ ☻ *Brazil, female vocalist*   44 wks

10 Sep 94 ●	THE RHYTHM OF THE NIGHT *WEA YZ 837CD1*	2	14
31 Dec 94	THE RHYTHM OF THE NIGHT (re-entry) *WEA YZ 837CD1*	55	4
8 Apr 95 ●	BABY BABY *Eternal YZ 919CD*	5	8
22 Jul 95	TRY ME OUT *Eternal YZ 955CD*	6	10
23 Dec 95	I DON'T WANNA BE A STAR *Eternal WEA 029CD*	22	6
22 Feb 97	MEGAMIX *Eternal WEA 092CD*	36	2

CORONATION STREET CAST featuring Bill WADDINGTON
UK, male/female vocal group   3 wks

16 Dec 95	ALWAYS LOOK ON THE BRIGHT SIDE OF LIFE *EMI Premier CDEMS 411*	35	3

The listed flip side of 'Always Look on the Bright Side of Life' was 'Something Stupid' by Amanda Barrie and Johnny Briggs

CORONETS ☾ *UK, male/female vocal group*   7 wks

26 Aug 55	THAT'S HOW A LOVE SONG WAS BORN *Columbia DB 3640* [1]	14	6
25 Nov 55	TWENTY TINY FINGERS *Columbia DB 3671*	20	1

[1] Ray Burns with the Coronets

Briana CORRIGAN *UK, female vocalist*   2 wks

11 May 96	LOVE ME NOW *East West EW 041CD1*	48	2

CORRS ○ ♂ *Ireland, female/male vocal/instrumental group*   34 wks

17 Feb 96	RUNAWAY *Atlantic A 5727CD*	49	2
7 Dec 96	RUNAWAY (re-entry) *Atlantic A 5727CD*	60	1
1 Feb 97	LOVE TO LOVE YOU/RUNAWAY *Atlantic A 5621CD*	62	1
25 Oct 97	ONLY WHEN I SLEEP *Atlantic AT00 15CD*	58	1
20 Dec 97	I NEVER LOVED YOU ANYWAY *Atlantic AT 0018CD*	43	2
28 Mar 98	WHAT CAN I DO *Atlantic AT 0029CD*	53	1
16 May 98 ●	DREAMS *Atlantic AT 0032CD*	6	10
29 Aug 98	WHAT CAN I DO (remix) *Atlantic AT 004CD*	3	11
28 Nov 98 ●	SO YOUNG *Atlantic AT 0057CD1*	6†	5

Vladimir COSMA *Hungary, orchestra*   1 wk

14 Jul 79	DAVID'S SONG (MAIN THEME FROM 'KIDNAPPED') *Decca FR 13841*	64	1

COSMIC BABY *Germany, male producer*   1 wk

26 Feb 94	LOOPS OF INFINITY *Logic 74321191432*	70	1

Don COSTA *US, orchestra*   10 wks

13 Oct 60	NEVER ON SUNDAY *London HLT 9195*	27	9
22 Dec 60	NEVER ON SUNDAY (re-entry) *London HLT 9195*	41	1

Elvis COSTELLO ✎ ✓ *Acclaimed singer/songwriter, b. Declan McManus, 25 August, 1954, Liverpool. He emerged during punk explosion of 1976, but was soon accepted as a mainstream artist. Has most UK hits without a No 1, and has clocked up 12 US Top 40 albums*   168 wks

5 Nov 77	WATCHING THE DETECTIVES *Stiff BUY 20*	15	11
11 Mar 78	(I DON'T WANNA GO TO) CHELSEA *Radar ADA 3* [1]	16	10
13 May 78	PUMP IT UP *Radar ADA 10* [1]	24	10
28 Oct 78	RADIO RADIO *Radar ADA 24* [1]	29	7
10 Feb 79	OLIVER'S ARMY *Radar ADA 31* [1]	2	12
12 May 79	ACCIDENTS WILL HAPPEN *Radar ADA 35* [1]	28	8
16 Feb 80	I CAN'T STAND UP FOR FALLING DOWN *F. Beat XX 1*	4	8
12 Apr 80	HI FIDELITY *F. Beat XX 3*	30	5
7 Jun 80	NEW AMSTERDAM *F. Beat XX 5*	36	6

Date	Title	Pos	Wks
20 Dec 80	CLUBLAND *F. Beat XX 12* [1]	60	4
3 Oct 81 ●	A GOOD YEAR FOR THE ROSES *F. Beat XX 17*	6	11
12 Dec 81	SWEET DREAMS *F. Beat XX 19*	42	8
10 Apr 82	I'M YOUR TOY *F. Beat XX 21* [2]	51	3
19 Jun 82	YOU LITTLE FOOL *F. Beat XX 26*	52	3
31 Jul 82	MAN OUT OF TIME *F. Beat XX 28*	58	2
25 Sep 82	FROM HEAD TO TOE *F. Beat XX 30*	43	4
11 Dec 82	PARTY PARTY *A & M AMS 8267* [3]	48	6
11 Jun 83	PILLS AND SOAP *Imp IMP 001* [4]	16	4
9 Jul 83	EVERYDAY I WRITE THE BOOK *F. Beat XX 32*	28	8
17 Sep 83	LET THEM ALL TALK *F. Beat XX 33*	59	2
28 Apr 84	PEACE IN OUR TIME *Imposter TRUCE 1* [4]	48	3
16 Jun 84	I WANNA BE LOVED/TURNING THE TOWN RED *F. Beat XX 35*	25	6
25 Aug 84	THE ONLY FLAME IN TOWN *F. Beat XX 37*	71	2
4 May 85	GREEN SHIRT *F. Beat ZB 40085*	71	1
18 May 85	GREEN SHIRT (re-entry) *F. Beat ZB 40085*	68	1
1 Feb 86	DON'T LET ME BE MISUNDERSTOOD *F. Beat ZB 40555* [5]	33	4
30 Aug 86	TOKYO STORM WARNING *Imp IMP 007*	73	1
4 Mar 89	VERONICA *Warner Bros. W 7558*	31	6
20 May 89	BABY PLAYS AROUND (EP) *Warner Bros. W 2949*	65	1
4 May 91	THE OTHER SIDE OF SUMMER *Warner Bros. W 0025*	43	4
5 Mar 94	SULKY GIRL *Warner Bros. W 0234CD* [1]	22	3
30 Apr 94	13 STEPS LEAD DOWN *Warner Bros. W 0245CD* [1]	59	1
26 Nov 94	LONDON'S BRILLIANT PARADE *Warner Bros. W 0270CD1* [1]	48	2
11 May 96	IT'S TIME *Warner Bros. W 0348CD* [1]	58	1

[1] Elvis Costello and the Attractions [2] Elvis Costello and the Attractions with the Royal Philharmonic Orchestra [3] Elvis Costello and the Attractions with the Royal Horn Guards [4] Imposter [5] Costello Show featuring the Confederates

Tracks on Baby Plays Around (EP): Baby Plays Around / Poisoned Rose / Almost Blue / My Funny Valentine

COTTAGERS – *See Tony REES and the COTTAGERS*

Billy COTTON and his BAND ℂ
UK, male bandleader / vocalist, with band and chorus **25 wks**

Date	Title	Pos	Wks
1 May 53 ●	IN A GOLDEN COACH *Decca F 10058* [1]	3	10
18 Dec 53	I SAW MOMMY KISSING SANTA CLAUS *Decca F 10206* [2]	11	3
30 Apr 54	FRIENDS AND NEIGHBOURS *Decca F 10299* [3]	12	1
14 May 54 ●	FRIENDS AND NEIGHBOURS (re-entry) *Decca F 10299* [3]	3	11

[1] Billy Cotton and his Band, vocals by Doreen Stephens [2] Billy Cotton and his Band, vocals by the Mill Girls and the Bandits [3] Billy Cotton and his Band, vocals by the Bandits

See also VARIOUS ARTISTS (EPs & LPs) – All Star Hit Parade No 2

Mike COTTON'S JAZZMEN
UK, male instrumental band – Mike Cotton – trumpet **4 wks**

Date	Title	Pos	Wks
20 Jun 63	SWING THAT HAMMER *Columbia DB 7029*	36	4

John COUGAR – *See John Cougar MELLENCAMP*

COUGARS *UK, male instrumental group* **8 wks**

Date	Title	Pos	Wks
28 Feb 63	SATURDAY NITE AT THE DUCK-POND *Parlophone R 4989*	33	8

COUNCIL COLLECTIVE
UK/US, male/female vocal/instrumental group **6 wks**

Date	Title	Pos	Wks
22 Dec 84	SOUL DEEP (PART 1) *Polydor MINE 1*	24	6

COUNT INDIGO *UK, male vocalist* **1 wk**

Date	Title	Pos	Wks
9 Mar 96	MY UNKNOWN LOVE *Cowboy RODEO 952CD*	59	1

COUNTING CROWS *US, male vocal/instrumental group* **10 wks**

Date	Title	Pos	Wks
30 Apr 94	MR. JONES *Geffen GFSTD 69*	28	2
9 Jul 94	ROUND HERE *Geffen GFSTD 74*	70	1
15 Oct 94	RAIN KING *Geffen GFSTD 82*	49	3
19 Oct 96	ANGELS OF THE SILENCES *Geffen GFSTD 22182*	41	1
14 Dec 96	A LONG DECEMBER *Geffen GFSTD 22190*	62	1
31 May 97	DAYLIGHT FADING *Geffen GFSTD 22247*	54	1
20 Dec 97	A LONG DECEMBER (re-entry) *Geffen GFSTD 22190*	68	1

COUNTRYMEN *UK, male vocal group* **2 wks**

Date	Title	Pos	Wks
3 May 62	I KNOW WHERE I'M GOING *Piccadilly 7N 35029*	45	2

COURSE ☺ ⊗ *Holland, male / female vocal / DJ / production* **15 wks**

Date	Title	Pos	Wks
19 Apr 97 ●	READY OR NOT *The Brothers CDBRUV 2*	5	7
5 Jul 97 ●	AIN'T NOBODY *The Brothers CDBRUV 3*	8	6
20 Dec 97 ●	BEST LOVE *The Brothers CDBRUV 6*	51	2

Tina COUSINS ☺ ⊗ *UK, female vocalist* **15 wks**

Date	Title	Pos	Wks
15 Aug 98	MYSTERIOUS TIMES *Multiply CDMULTY 40* [1]	2	12
21 Nov 98	PRAY *Jive 0519162*	20	3

[1] Sash! featuring Tina Cousins

Don COVAY *US, male vocalist* **6 wks**

Date	Title	Pos	Wks
7 Sep 74	IT'S BETTER TO HAVE (AND DON'T NEED) *Mercury 6052 634*	29	6

Vincent COVELLO – *See BT*

COVENTRY CITY CUP FINAL SQUAD
UK, male football team vocalists **2 wks**

Date	Title	Pos	Wks
23 May 87	GO FOR IT! *Sky Blue SKB 1*	61	2

COVER GIRLS *US, female vocal group* **4 wks**

Date	Title	Pos	Wks
1 Aug 92	WISHING ON A STAR *Epic 6581437*	38	4

David COVERDALE *UK, male vocalist* **1 wk**

Date	Title	Pos	Wks
7 Jun 97	TOO MANY TEARS *EMI CDEM 471* [1]	46	1

[1] David Coverdale and Whitesnake

COVERDALE PAGE *UK, male vocal/instrumental duo* **3 wks**

Date	Title	Pos	Wks
3 Jul 93	TAKE ME FOR A LITTLE WHILE *EMI CDEM 270*	29	2
23 Oct 93	TAKE A LOOK AT YOURSELF *EMI CDEM 279*	43	1

Julie COVINGTON ⊗ *UK, female vocalist* **29 wks**

Date	Title	Pos	Wks
25 Dec 76 ★	DON'T CRY FOR ME ARGENTINA *MCA 260*	1	15
3 Dec 77	ONLY WOMEN BLEED *Virgin VS 196*	12	11
15 Jul 78	DON'T CRY FOR ME ARGENTINA (re-entry) *MCA 260*	63	3

See also Julie COVINGTON, Rula LENSKA, Charlotte CORNWELL and Sue JONES-DAVIES

Warren COVINGTON – *See Tommy DORSEY ORCHESTRA starring Warren COVINGTON*

Julie COVINGTON, Rula LENSKA, Charlotte CORNWELL and Sue JONES-DAVIES ⊗ *UK, female vocal group* **6 wks**

Date	Title	Pos	Wks
21 May 77 ●	O.K? *Polydor 2001 714*	10	6

See also Julie COVINGTON

Patrick COWLEY – *See SYLVESTER*

Carl COX *UK, male producer* **17 wks**

Date	Title	Pos	Wks
28 Sep 91	I WANT YOU (FOREVER) *Perfecto PB 44885* [1]	23	7
8 Aug 92	DOES IT FEEL GOOD TO YOU *Perfecto PB 74321102877* [1]	35	3
6 Nov 93	THE PLANET OF LOVE *Perfecto 74321102877*	44	2
9 Mar 96	TWO PAINTINGS AND A DRUM (EP) *Edel 0090715COX*	24	2
8 Jun 96	SENSUAL SOPHIS-TI-CAT/THE PLAYER *Ultimatum 0090875COX*	25	2
12 Dec 98	THE LATIN THEME *Edel 0091685 COX*	52	1

[1] DJ Carl Cox

Tracks on Two Paintings and a Drum (EP): Phoebus Apollo / Yum Yum / Siberian Snow Storm

Deborah COX *US, female vocalist* — 6 wks

| 11 Nov 95 | SENTIMENTAL *Arista 74321324962* | 34 | 3 |
| 24 Feb 96 | WHO DO U LOVE *Arista 74321337942* | 31 | 3 |

Michael COX ◐ *UK, male vocalist* — 15 wks

| 9 Jun 60 ● | ANGELA JONES *Triumph RGM 1011* | 7 | 13 |
| 20 Oct 60 | ALONG CAME CAROLINE *HMV POP 789* | 41 | 2 |

Peter COX *UK, male vocalist* — 6 wks

2 Aug 97	AIN'T GONNA CRY AGAIN *Chrysalis CDCHS 5056*	37	2
15 Nov 97	IF YOU WALK AWAY *Chrysalis CDCHSS 5069*	24	2
20 Jun 98	WHAT A FOOL BELIEVES *Chrysalis CDCHS 5089*	39	2

See also GO WEST

CRACKER *US, male vocal/instrumental group* — 9 wks

28 May 94	LOW *Virgin America VUSDG 80*	43	4
23 Jul 94	GET OFF THIS *Virgin America VUSCD 83*	41	3
3 Dec 94	LOW (re-entry) *Virgin America VUSDG 80*	54	2

Sarah CRACKNELL *UK, female vocalist* — 1 wk

| 14 Sep 96 | ANYMORE *Gut CDGUT 3* | 39 | 1 |

See also ST ETIENNE

Floyd CRAMER ✎ *US, male instrumentalist - piano* — 24 wks

13 Apr 61 ★	ON THE REBOUND *RCA 1231*	1	14
20 Jul 61	SAN ANTONIO ROSE *RCA 1241*	36	8
23 Aug 62	HOT PEPPER *RCA 1301*	46	2

CRAMPS *US, male/female vocal/instrumental group* — 4 wks

| 9 Nov 85 | CAN YOUR PUSSY DO THE DOG? *Big Beat NS 110* | 68 | 1 |
| 10 Feb 90 | BIKINI GIRLS WITH MACHINE GUNS *Enigma ENV 17* | 35 | 3 |

CRANBERRIES ◐ ✎
Ireland, male/female vocal/instrumental group — 45 wks

27 Feb 93	LINGER *Island CID 556*	74	1
12 Feb 94	LINGER (re-issue) *Island CID 559*	14	11
7 May 94	DREAMS *Island CIDX 594*	27	5
1 Oct 94	ZOMBIE *Island CID 600*	14	6
3 Dec 94	ODE TO MY FAMILY *Island CIDX 601*	38	6
11 Mar 95	I CAN'T BE WITH YOU *Island CID 605*	23	5
12 Aug 95	RIDICULOUS THOUGHTS *Island CID 616*	20	3
20 Apr 96	SALVATION *Island CID 633*	13	5
13 Jul 96	FREE TO DECIDE *Island CID 637*	33	3

Les CRANE © *US, male vocalist* — 14 wks

| 19 Feb 72 ● | DESIDERATA *Warner Bros. K 16119* | 7 | 14 |

Whitfield CRANE – *See ICE-T ; MOTORHEAD*

CRANES *UK, male/female vocal/instrumental group* — 2 wks

| 25 Sep 93 | JEWEL *Dedicated CRANE 007CD* | 29 | 1 |
| 3 Sep 94 | SHINING ROAD *Dedicated CRANE 8CD1* | 57 | 1 |

CRASH TEST DUMMIES ◐ ✎
Canada, male/female vocal/instrumental group — 20 wks

23 Apr 94 ●	MMM MMM MMM MMM *RCA 74321201512*	2	11
16 Jul 94	AFTERNOONS & COFFEESPOONS *RCA 74321219622*	23	5
15 Apr 95	THE BALLAD OF PETER PUMPKINHEAD *RCA 74321276772* [1]	30	4

[1] Crash Test Dummies featuring Ellen Reid

Beverley CRAVEN ◐ *UK, female vocalist* — 33 wks

20 Apr 91 ●	PROMISE ME *Epic 6559437*	3	13
20 Jul 91	HOLDING ON *Epic 6565507*	32	7
5 Oct 91	WOMAN TO WOMAN *Epic 6574647*	40	5
7 Dec 91	MEMORIES *Epic 6576617*	68	2

| 25 Sep 93 | LOVE SCENES *Epic 6595952* | 34 | 4 |
| 20 Nov 93 | MOLLIE'S SONG *Epic 6598132* | 61 | 2 |

Billy CRAWFORD *US, male vocalist* — 2 wks

| 10 Oct 98 | URGENTLY IN LOVE *V2 WR 5003063* | 48 | 2 |

Jimmy CRAWFORD ◐ *UK, male vocalist* — 11 wks

| 8 Jun 61 | LOVE OR MONEY *Columbia DB 4633* | 49 | 1 |
| 16 Nov 61 | I LOVE HOW YOU LOVE ME *Columbia DB 4717* | 18 | 10 |

Michael CRAWFORD © *UK, male vocalist* — 14 wks

| 10 Jan 87 ● | THE MUSIC OF THE NIGHT *Polydor POSP 803* | 7 | 11 |
| 15 Jan 94 | THE MUSIC OF THE NIGHT *Columbia 6597382* [1] | 54 | 3 |

[1] Barbra Streisand (duet with Michael Crawford)

The flip side of 'The Music of the Night' – 'Wishing You Were Somehow Here Again' by Sarah Brightman – was also listed

Randy CRAWFORD ✎ *US, female vocalist* — 75 wks

21 Jun 80	LAST NIGHT AT DANCELAND *Warner Bros. K 17631*	61	2
30 Aug 80 ●	ONE DAY I'LL FLY AWAY *Warner Bros. K 17680*	2	11
30 May 81	YOU MIGHT NEED SOMEBODY *Warner Bros. K 17803*	11	13
8 Aug 81	RAINY NIGHT IN GEORGIA *Warner Bros. K 17840*	18	9
31 Oct 81	SECRET COMBINATION *Warner Bros. K 17872*	48	3
30 Jan 82	IMAGINE *Warner Bros. K 17906*	60	1
13 Feb 82	IMAGINE (re-entry) *Warner Bros. K 17906*	75	1
5 Jun 82	ONE HELLO *Warner Bros. K 17948*	48	4
19 Feb 83	HE REMINDS ME *Warner Bros. K 17970*	65	2
8 Oct 83	NIGHT LINE *Warner Bros. W 9530*	51	4
29 Nov 86 ●	ALMAZ *Warner Bros. W 8583*	4	17
18 Jan 92	DIAMANTE *London LON 313* [1]	44	7
15 Nov 97	GIVE ME THE NIGHT *WEA WEA 142CD*	60	1

[1] Zucchero with Randy Crawford

See also CRUSADERS

Robert CRAY BAND *US, male vocal/instrumental group* — 5 wks

| 20 Jun 87 | RIGHT NEXT DOOR (BECAUSE OF ME) *Mercury CRAY 3* | 50 | 4 |
| 20 Apr 96 | BABY LEE *Silvertone ORECD 81* [1] | 65 | 1 |

[1] John Lee Hooker with Robert Cray

CRAZY ELEPHANT ◐ *US, male vocal group* — 13 wks

| 21 May 69 | GIMME GIMME GOOD LOVIN' *Major Minor MM 609* | 12 | 13 |

CRAZYHEAD *UK, male vocal/instrumental group* — 4 wks

| 16 Jul 88 | TIME HAS TAKEN ITS TOLL ON YOU *Food FOOD 12* | 65 | 2 |
| 25 Feb 89 | HAVE LOVE, WILL TRAVEL (EP) *Food SGE 2025* | 68 | 2 |

Tracks on Have Love, Will Travel (EP): Have Love Will Travel / Out on a Limb (Live) / Baby Turpentine (Live) / Snake Eyes (Live)
See also VARIOUS ARTISTS (EPs & LPs) – The Food Christmas (EP)

CREAM ✎ *UK, male vocal/instrumental group* — 59 wks

20 Oct 66	WRAPPING PAPER *Reaction 591 007*	34	6
15 Dec 66	I FEEL FREE *Reaction 591 011*	11	12
8 Jun 67	STRANGE BREW *Reaction 591 015*	17	9
5 Jun 68	ANYONE FOR TENNIS (THE SAVAGE SEVEN THEME) *Polydor 56 258*	40	3
9 Oct 68	SUNSHINE OF YOUR LOVE *Polydor 56 286*	25	7
15 Jan 69	WHITE ROOM *Polydor 56 300*	28	8
9 Apr 69	BADGE *Polydor 56 315*	18	10
28 Oct 72	BADGE (re-issue) *Polydor 2058 285*	42	4

CREATION *UK, male vocal/instrumental group* — 3 wks

| 7 Jul 66 | MAKING TIME *Planet PLF 116* | 49 | 1 |
| 3 Nov 66 | PAINTER MAN *Planet PLF 119* | 36 | 2 |

CREATURES ✎ ☹ *UK, male/female vocal/instrumental group* — 26 wks

| 3 Oct 81 | MAD EYED SCREAMER *Polydor POSPD 354* | 24 | 7 |

23 Apr 83	MISS THE GIRL *Wonderland SHE 1*	21	7
16 Jul 83	RIGHT NOW *Wonderland SHE 2*	14	10
14 Oct 89	STANDING THERE *Wonderland SHE 17*	53	2

CREDIT TO THE NATION *UK, male rap group* — 11 wks

22 May 93	CALL IT WHAT YOU WANT *One Little Indian 94 TP7CD*	57	3
18 Sep 93	ENOUGH IS ENOUGH *One Little Indian 79 TP7CD* [1]	56	2
12 Mar 94	TEENAGE SENSATION *One Little Indian 124 TP7DC*	24	3
14 May 94	SOWING THE SEEDS OF HATRED		
	One Little Indian 134 TP7CD	72	1
22 Jul 95	LIAR LIAR *One Little Indian 144 TP7CD*	60	1
12 Sep 98	TACKY LOVE SONG *Chrysalis CDCHS 5097*	60	1

[1] Chumbawamba and Credit to the Nation

CREEDENCE CLEARWATER REVIVAL 🎸
US, male vocal/instrumental group — 94 wks

28 May 69 ●	PROUD MARY *Liberty LBF 15223*	8	13
16 Aug 69 ★	BAD MOON RISING *Liberty LBF 15230*	1	15
15 Nov 69	GREEN RIVER *Liberty LBF 15250*	19	11
14 Feb 70	DOWN ON THE CORNER *Liberty LBF 15283*	31	6
4 Apr 70 ●	TRAVELLIN' BAND *Liberty LBF 15310*	8	12
20 Jun 70 ●	UP AROUND THE BEND *Liberty LBF 15354*	3	12
4 Jul 70	TRAVELLIN' BAND (re-entry) *Liberty LBF 15310*	46	1
5 Sep 70	LONG AS I CAN SEE THE LIGHT *Liberty LBF 15384*	20	9
20 Mar 71	HAVE YOU EVER SEEN THE RAIN *Liberty LBF 15440*	36	6
24 Jul 71	SWEET HITCH-HIKER *United Artists UP 35261*	36	8
2 May 92	BAD MOON RISING (re-issue) *Epic 6580047*	71	1

Kid CREOLE and the COCONUTS ◎ ☺
US, male vocalist and female vocal group — 58 wks

13 Jun 81	ME NO POP I *Ze WIP 6711* [1]	32	7
15 May 82 ●	I'M A WONDERFUL THING, BABY *Ze WIP 6756*	4	11
24 Jul 82 ●	STOOL PIGEON *Ze WIP 6793*	7	9
9 Oct 82 ●	ANNIE I'M NOT YOUR DADDY *Ze WIP 6801*	2	8
11 Dec 82	DEAR DADDY *Ze WIP 6840*	29	7
10 Sep 83	THERE'S SOMETHING WRONG IN PARADISE *Island IS 130*	35	5
19 Nov 83	THE LIFEBOAT PARTY *Island IS 142*	49	4
14 Apr 90	THE SEX OF IT *CBS 655698 7*	29	5
10 Apr 93	I'M A WONDERFUL THING BABY (re-mix) *Island CID 551*	60	2

[1] Kid Creole and the Coconuts present Coati Mundi

See also COCONUTS

CRESCENDO ☺ *UK/US, male/female vocal/instrumental duo* — 5 wks

23 Dec 95	ARE YOU OUT THERE *ffrr FCD 270*	20	5

CREW CUTS ◎ ℂ *Canada, male vocal group* — 29 wks

1 Oct 54	SH-BOOM *Mercury MB 3140* ▲	12	9
15 Apr 55 ●	EARTH ANGEL *Mercury MB 3202*	4	20

Bernard CRIBBINS ◎ *UK, male vocalist* — 29 wks

15 Feb 62 ●	HOLE IN THE GROUND *Parlophone R 4869*	9	13
5 Jul 62 ●	RIGHT SAID FRED *Parlophone R 4923*	10	10
13 Dec 62	GOSSIP CALYPSO *Parlophone R 4961*	25	6

CRICKETS ♪ *US, male vocal/instrumental group* — 97 wks

27 Sep 57 ★	THAT'LL BE THE DAY *Vogue Coral Q 72279* ▲	1	14
27 Dec 57 ●	OH BOY *Coral Q 72298*	3	15
10 Jan 58	THAT'LL BE THE DAY (re-entry) *Vogue Coral Q 72279*	29	1
14 Mar 58 ●	MAYBE BABY *Coral Q 72307*	4	10
25 Jul 58	THINK IT OVER *Coral Q 72329*	11	7
24 Apr 59	LOVE'S MADE A FOOL OF YOU *Coral Q 72365*	26	1
8 May 59	LOVE'S MADE A FOOL OF YOU (re-entry) *Coral Q 72365*	30	1
15 Jan 60	WHEN YOU ASK ABOUT LOVE *Coral Q 72382*	27	1
12 May 60	MORE THAN I CAN SAY *Coral Q 72395*	42	1
26 May 60	BABY MY HEART *Coral Q 72395*	33	4
21 Jun 62 ●	DON'T EVER CHANGE *Liberty LIB 55441*	5	13
24 Jan 63	MY LITTLE GIRL *Liberty LIB 10067*	17	9
6 Jun 63	DON'T TRY TO CHANGE ME *Liberty LIB 10092*	37	4
14 May 64	YOU'VE GOT LOVE *Coral Q 72472* [1]	40	6

---

2 Jul 64	(THEY CALL HER) LA BAMBA *Liberty LIB 55696*	21	10

[1] Buddy Holly and the Crickets

Although not credited on the records, Buddy Holly was featured on the first four hits

CRIMINAL ELEMENT ORCHESTRA – See Wally JUMP Jr and the CRIMINAL ELEMENT

CRISPY AND COMPANY *US, male vocal/instrumental group* — 11 wks

16 Aug 75	BRAZIL *Creole CR 109*	26	5
27 Dec 75	GET IT TOGETHER *Creole CR 114*	21	6

CRITTERS *US, male vocal/instrumental group* — 5 wks

30 Jun 66	YOUNGER GIRL *London HL 10047*	38	5

Tony CROMBIE and his ROCKETS
UK, male vocal/instrumental group, Tony Crombie – drums — 2 wks

19 Oct 56	TEACH YOU TO ROCK/SHORT'NIN' BREAD *Columbia DB 3822*	25	2

Bing CROSBY ℂ *US, male vocalist* — 95 wks

14 Nov 52 ●	ISLE OF INNISFREE *Brunswick 04900*	3	12
5 Dec 52 ●	ZING A LITTLE ZONG *Brunswick 04981* [1]	10	2
19 Dec 52 ●	SILENT NIGHT *Brunswick 03929*	8	2
19 Mar 54 ●	CHANGING PARTNERS *Brunswick 05244*	10	1
2 Apr 54 ●	CHANGING PARTNERS (re-entry) *Brunswick 05244*	9	1
23 Apr 54	CHANGING PARTNERS (2nd re-entry) *Brunswick 05244*	11	1
7 Jan 55	COUNT YOUR BLESSINGS *Brunswick 05339*	18	1
21 Jan 55	COUNT YOUR BLESSINGS (re-entry) *Brunswick 05339*	11	2
29 Apr 55	STRANGER IN PARADISE *Brunswick 05410*	17	2
27 Apr 56	IN A LITTLE SPANISH TOWN *Brunswick 05543*	22	3
23 Nov 56 ●	TRUE LOVE *Capitol CL 14645* [2]	4	27
24 May 57 ●	AROUND THE WORLD *Brunswick 05674*	5	15
9 Aug 75	THAT'S WHAT LIFE IS ALL ABOUT *United Artists UP 35852*	41	4
3 Dec 77 ●	WHITE CHRISTMAS *MCA 111* ◆	5	7
27 Nov 82 ●	PEACE ON EARTH – LITTLE DRUMMER BOY		
	RCA BOW 12 [3]	3	8
17 Dec 83	TRUE LOVE (re-issue) *Capitol CL 315* [2]	70	3
21 Dec 85	WHITE CHRISTMAS (re-issue) *MCA BING 1*	69	1
19 Dec 98	WHITE CHRISTMAS (re-issue) *MCA MCSRD 48105*	29†	2

[1] Bing Crosby and Jane Wyman [2] Bing Crosby and Grace Kelly [3] David Bowie and Bing Crosby

David CROSBY – See Phil COLLINS; CROSBY, STILLS, NASH and YOUNG

CROSBY, STILLS, NASH and YOUNG 🎸
US/UK/Canada, male vocal/instrumental group — 12 wks

16 Aug 69	MARRAKESH EXPRESS *Atlantic 584 283* [1]	17	9
21 Jan 89	AMERICAN DREAM *Atlantic A 9003*	55	3

[1] Crosby, Stills and Nash

See also Stephen STILLS ; Neil YOUNG

CROSS *UK/US, male vocal/instrumental group* — 1 wk

17 Oct 87	COWBOYS AND INDIANS *Virgin VS 1007*	74	1

Christopher CROSS ◎ *US, male vocalist* — 27 wks

19 Apr 80	RIDE LIKE THE WIND *Warner Bros. K 17582*	69	1
14 Feb 81	SAILING *Warner Bros. K 17695* ▲	48	6
17 Oct 81	ARTHUR'S THEME (BEST THAT YOU CAN DO)		
	Warner Bros. K 17847 ▲	56	4
9 Jan 82 ●	ARTHUR'S THEME (BEST THAT YOU CAN DO)		
	(re-entry) *Warner Bros. K 17847*	7	11
5 Feb 83	ALL RIGHT *Warner Bros. W 9843*	51	5

Sheryl CROW ◎ 🎸 *US, female vocalist* — 67 wks

18 Jun 94	LEAVING LAS VEGAS *A & M 5806472*	66	1
5 Nov 94 ●	ALL I WANNA DO *A & M 5808452*	4	13
11 Feb 95	STRONG ENOUGH *A & M 5809212*	33	4
27 May 95	CAN'T CRY ANYMORE *A & M 5810552*	33	3
29 Jul 95	RUN BABY RUN *A & M 5811492*	24	4

11 Nov 95		WHAT I CAN DO FOR YOU *A & M 5812292*	43	1
21 Sep 96	●	IF IT MAKES YOU HAPPY *A & M 5819032*	9	6
30 Nov 96		EVERYDAY IS A WINDING ROAD *A & M 5820232*	12	6
29 Mar 97		HARD TO MAKE A STAND *A & M 5821492*	22	3
12 Jul 97	●	A CHANGE WOULD DO YOU GOOD *A & M 5822092*	8	5
18 Oct 97		HOME *A & M 0440312*	25	2
13 Dec 97		TOMORROW NEVER DIES *A & M 5824572*	12	9
12 Sep 98		MY FAVOURITE MISTAKE *Polydor 5827632*	9	6
5 Dec 98		THERE GOES THE NEIGHBORHOOD *A&M 5828092*	19†	4

CROWD ☻
International, male/female vocal/instrumental charity assembly   **11 wks**

| 1 Jun 85 | ★ | YOU'LL NEVER WALK ALONE *Spartan BRAD 1* | 1 | 11 |

CROWDED HOUSE ☻
New Zealand / Australia, male vocal / instrumental group   **64 wks**

6 Jun 87		DON'T DREAM IT'S OVER *Capitol CL 438*	27	8
22 Jun 91		CHOCOLATE CAKE *Capitol CL 618*	69	2
2 Nov 91		FALL AT YOUR FEET *Capitol CL 626*	17	7
29 Feb 92	●	WEATHER WITH YOU *Capitol CL 643*	7	9
20 Jun 92		FOUR SEASONS IN ONE DAY *Capitol CL 655*	26	5
26 Sep 92		IT'S ONLY NATURAL *Capitol CL 661*	24	4
2 Oct 93		DISTANT SUN *Capitol CDCLS 697*	19	6
20 Nov 93		NAILS IN MY FEET *Capitol CDCLS 701*	22	4
19 Feb 94		LOCKED OUT *Capitol CDCLS 707*	12	4
11 Jun 94		FINGERS OF LOVE *Capitol CDCLS 715*	25	3
24 Sep 94		PINEAPPLE HEAD *Capitol CDCLS 723*	27	3
22 Jun 96		INSTINCT *Capitol CDCLS 774*	12	4
17 Aug 96		NOT THE GIRL YOU THINK YOU ARE *Capitol CDCLS 776*	20	3
9 Nov 96		DON'T DREAM IT'S OVER (re-issue) *Capitol CDCL 780*	25	2

See also FINN; Neil FINN; Tim FINN

CROWN HEIGHTS AFFAIR ♀ ◢
US, male vocal/instrumental group   **34 wks**

19 Aug 78		GALAXY OF LOVE *Mercury 6168 801*	24	10
11 Nov 78		I'M GONNA LOVE YOU FOREVER *Mercury 6168 803*	47	4
14 Apr 79		DANCE LADY DANCE *Mercury 6168 804*	44	4
3 May 80	●	YOU GAVE ME LOVE *De-Lite MER 9*	10	12
9 Aug 80		YOU'VE BEEN GONE *De-Lite MER 28*	44	4

Julee CRUISE ☻ *US, female vocalist*   **13 wks**

| 10 Nov 90 | ● | FALLING *Warner Bros. W 9544* | 7 | 11 |
| 2 Mar 91 | | ROCKIN' BACK INSIDE MY HEART *Warner Bros. W 0004* | 66 | 2 |

CRUISERS – *See Dave BERRY*

CRUSADERS ✐ ♀ *US, male vocal/instrumental group*   **16 wks**

18 Aug 79	●	STREET LIFE *MCA 513*	5	11
26 Sep 81		I'M SO GLAD I'M STANDING HERE TODAY *MCA 741* [1]	61	3
7 Apr 84		NIGHT LADIES *MCA MCA 853*	55	2

[1] Crusaders, featured vocalist Joe Cocker

Vocalist on 'Street Life' was Randy Crawford, though uncredited

CRUSH *UK, female vocal duo*   **3 wks**

| 24 Feb 96 | | JELLYHEAD *Telstar CDSTAS 2809* | 50 | 2 |
| 3 Aug 96 | | LUV'D UP *Telstar CDSTAS 2833* | 45 | 1 |

Bobby CRUSH *UK, male instrumentalist – piano*   **4 wks**

| 4 Nov 72 | | BORSALINO *Philips 6006 248* | 37 | 4 |

CRY BEFORE DAWN *Ireland, male vocal/instrumental group*   **2 wks**

| 17 Jun 89 | | WITNESS FOR THE WORLD *Epic GONE 3* | 67 | 2 |

CRY OF LOVE *US, male/female vocal/instrumental group*   **1 wk**

| 15 Jan 94 | | BAD THING *Columbia 6600462* | 60 | 1 |

CRY SISCO! *UK, male producer – Barry Blue*   **9 wks**

| 2 Sep 89 | | AFRO DIZZI ACT *Escape AWOL 1* | 42 | 8 |
| 20 Jan 90 | | AFRO DIZZI ACT (re-entry) *Escape AWOL 1* | 70 | 1 |

CRYIN' SHAMES *UK, male vocal/instrumental group*   **7 wks**

| 31 Mar 66 | | PLEASE STAY *Decca F 12340* | 26 | 7 |

CRYPT-KICKERS – *See Bobby 'Boris' PICKETT and the CRYPT-KICKERS*

CRYSTAL METHOD *US, male instrumental duo*   **4 wks**

11 Oct 97		(CAN YOU) TRIP LIKE I DO *Epic 6650862* [1]	39	2
7 Mar 98		KEEP HOPE ALIVE *Sony S2 CM 3CD*	71	1
8 Aug 98		COMIN' BACK *Sony S2 CM 4CD*	73	1

[1] Filter and The Crystal Method

CRYSTAL PALACE *UK, male football team vocalists*   **2 wks**

| 12 May 90 | | GLAD ALL OVER/WHERE EAGLES FLY *Parkfield PMS 5019* | 50 | 2 |

CRYSTALS ☻ ♀ *US, female vocal group*   **54 wks**

22 Nov 62		HE'S A REBEL *London HLU 9611* ▲	19	13
20 Jun 63	●	DA DOO RON RON *London HLU 9732*	5	16
19 Sep 63	●	THEN HE KISSED ME *London HLU 9773*	2	14
5 Mar 64		I WONDER *London HLU 9852*	36	3
19 Oct 74		DA DOO RON RON (re-issue) *Warner Spector K 19010*	15	8

CSILLA *Hungary, female vocalist*   **1 wk**

| 13 Jul 96 | | MAN IN THE MOON *Worx WORXCD 001* | 69 | 1 |

CUBIC 22 ☺ *Belgium, male instrumental/production duo*   **7 wks**

| 22 Jun 91 | | NIGHT IN MOTION *XL XLS 20* | 15 | 7 |

CUD *UK, male vocal/instrumental group*   **16 wks**

19 Oct 91		OH NO WON'T DO (EP) *A & M AMB 829*	49	2
28 Mar 92		THROUGH THE ROOF *A & M AM 857*	44	2
30 May 92		RICH AND STRANGE *A & M AM 871*	24	3
15 Aug 92		PURPLE LOVE BALLOON *A & M AM 0024*	27	3
10 Oct 92		ONCE AGAIN *A & M AM 0081*	45	1
12 Feb 94		NEUROTICA *A & M 5805172*	37	2
2 Apr 94		STICKS AND STONES *A & M 5805472*	68	1
3 Sep 94		ONE GIANT LOVE *A & M 5807292*	52	2

Tracks on Oh No Won't Do (EP): Oh No Won't Do / Profession / Ariel / Price of Love
See also VARIOUS ARTISTS (EPs & LPs) – Gimme Shelter (EP)

CUFFLINKS ☻ *US, male vocal group*   **30 wks**

| 29 Nov 69 | ● | TRACY *MCA MU 1101* | 4 | 16 |
| 14 Mar 70 | ● | WHEN JULIE COMES AROUND *MCA MU 1112* | 10 | 14 |

CULT ☹ ✐ *UK, male vocal/instrumental group*   **80 wks**

22 Dec 84		RESURRECTION JOE *Beggars Banquet BEG 122*	74	2
25 May 85		SHE SELLS SANCTUARY *Beggars Banquet BEG 135*	15	17
28 Sep 85		SHE SELLS SANCTUARY (re-entry) *Beggars Banquet BEG 135*	61	2
5 Oct 85		RAIN *Beggars Banquet BEG 147*	17	8
30 Nov 85		REVOLUTION *Beggars Banquet BEG 152*	30	7
28 Feb 87		LOVE REMOVAL MACHINE *Beggars Banquet BEG 182*	18	7
2 May 87		LIL' DEVIL *Beggars Banquet BEG 188*	11	7
22 Aug 87		WILD FLOWER (DOUBLE SINGLE) *Beggars Banquet BEG 195D*	24	2
29 Aug 87		WILD FLOWER *Beggars Banquet BEG 195*	30	4
1 Apr 89		FIRE WOMAN *Beggars Banquet BEG 228*	15	4
8 Jul 89		EDIE (CIAO BABY) *Beggars Banquet BEG 230*	32	5
18 Nov 89		SUN KING/EDIE (CIAO BABY) (re-issue) *Beggars Banquet BEG 235*	39	2
10 Mar 90		SWEET SOUL SISTER *Beggars Banquet BEG 241*	42	4
14 Sep 91		WILD HEARTED SON *Beggars Banquet BEG 255*	40	2
29 Feb 92		HEART OF SOUL *Beggars Banquet BEG 260*	51	1

30 Jan 93		SHE SELLS SANCTUARY (re-mix)		
		Beggars Banquet BEG 253CD	15	4
8 Oct 94		COMING DOWN Beggars Banquet BBQ 40CD	50	1
7 Jan 95		STAR Beggars Banquet BBQ 45CD	65	1

Tracks on double single: Wild Flower / Love Trooper / Outlaw / Horse Nation

CULT JAM – *See LISA LISA*

CULTURE BEAT ☻ ☺
UK/US/Germany, male/female vocal/instrumental group **46 wks**

3 Feb 90		CHERRY LIPS (DER ERDBEERMUND) Epic 655637	55	3
7 Aug 93	★	MR VAIN Epic 6594682	1	15
6 Nov 93	●	GOT TO GET IT Epic 6597212	4	11
15 Jan 94	●	ANYTHING Epic 6600252	5	8
2 Apr 94		WORLD IN YOUR HANDS Epic 6602292	20	4
27 Jan 96		INSIDE OUT Epic 6626562	32	2
15 Jun 96		CRYING IN THE RAIN Epic 6633582	29	2
28 Sep 96		TAKE ME AWAY Epic 6637552	52	1

CULTURE CLUB ☻
Internationally successful London-based quartet, whose flamboyant lead singer, Boy George (b. George O'Dowd, 14 June, 1961, Kent), attracted considerable media attention. In 1984, they won both BRIT (Best Group) and Grammy Awards (Best New Artist). Original members re-formed for world tour in 1998 **112 wks**

18 Sep 82	★	DO YOU REALLY WANT TO HURT ME Virgin VS 518	1	18
27 Nov 82	●	TIME (CLOCK OF THE HEART) Virgin VS 558	3	12
9 Apr 83	●	CHURCH OF THE POISON MIND Virgin VS 571	2	9
17 Sep 83	★	KARMA CHAMELEON Virgin VS 612 ◆ ▲	1	20
10 Dec 83	●	VICTIMS Virgin VS 641	3	10
24 Mar 84	●	IT'S A MIRACLE Virgin VS 662	4	9
6 Oct 84	●	THE WAR SONG Virgin VS 694	2	8
1 Dec 84		THE MEDAL SONG Virgin VS 730	32	4
5 Jan 85		THE MEDAL SONG (re-entry) Virgin VS 730	74	1
15 Mar 86		MOVE AWAY Virgin VS 845	7	7
31 May 86		GOD THANK YOU WOMAN Virgin VS 861	31	5
31 Oct 98	●	I JUST WANNA BE LOVED Virgin VSCDT 1710	4	9

See also BOY GEORGE

Smiley CULTURE 🌴 *UK, male vocalist* **13 wks**

15 Dec 84		POLICE OFFICER Fashion FAD 7012	12	10
6 Apr 85		COCKNEY TRANSLATION Fashion FAD 7028	71	1
13 Sep 86		SCHOOLTIME CHRONICLE Polydor POSP 815	59	2

LARRY CUNNINGHAM AND THE MIGHTY AVONS
Ireland, male vocal/instrumental group **11 wks**

10 Dec 64		TRIBUTE TO JIM REEVES King KG 1016	40	8
25 Feb 65		TRIBUTE TO JIM REEVES (re-entry) King KG 1016	46	3

CUPID'S INSPIRATION ☻ *UK, male vocal/instrumental group* **19 wks**

19 Jun 68	●	YESTERDAY HAS GONE Nems 56 3500	4	11
2 Oct 68		MY WORLD Nems 56 3702	33	8

CURE ☹ 🎸
Goth rock giants: Robert Smith (v/g), Lol Tolhurst (k), Simon Gallup (b), Porl Thompson (g), Boris Williams (d), who went from UK cult heroes to stadium-packing supergroup. Voted Best Group at 1991 BRIT Awards, and have had impressive run of UK/US hit albums **144 wks**

12 Apr 80		A FOREST Fiction FICS 10	31	8
4 Apr 81		PRIMARY Fiction FICS 12	43	6
17 Oct 81		CHARLOTTE SOMETIMES Fiction FICS 14	44	4
24 Jul 82		HANGING GARDEN Fiction FICS 15	34	4
27 Nov 82		LET'S GO TO BED Fiction FICS 17	44	4
8 Jan 83		LET'S GO TO BED (re-entry) Fiction FICS 17	75	1
9 Jul 83		THE WALK Fiction FICS 18	12	8
29 Oct 83	●	THE LOVE CATS Fiction FICS 19	7	11
7 Apr 84		THE CATERPILLAR Fiction FICS 20	14	7
27 Jul 85		IN BETWEEN DAYS Fiction FICS 22	15	10
21 Sep 85		CLOSE TO ME Fiction FICS 23	24	8
3 May 86		BOYS DON'T CRY Fiction FICS 24	22	6
18 Apr 87		WHY CAN'T I BE YOU Fiction FICS 25	21	5

4 Jul 87		CATCH Fiction FICS 26	27	6
17 Oct 87		JUST LIKE HEAVEN Fiction FICS 27	29	5
20 Feb 88		HOT HOT HOT!!! Fiction FICSX 28	45	3
22 Apr 89	●	LULLABY Fiction FICS 29	5	6
2 Sep 89		LOVESONG Fiction FICS 30	18	7
31 Mar 90		PICTURES OF YOU Fiction FICS 34	24	6
29 Sep 90		NEVER ENOUGH Fiction FICS 35	13	5
3 Nov 90		CLOSE TO ME (re-mix) Fiction FICS 36	13	5
28 Mar 92	●	HIGH Fiction FICS 39	8	3
11 Apr 92		HIGH (re-mix) Fiction FICXS 41	44	1
23 May 92		FRIDAY I'M IN LOVE Fiction FICS 42	6	7
17 Oct 92		A LETTER TO ELISE Fiction FICS 46	28	2
4 May 96		THE 13TH Fiction 5764692	15	2
29 Jun 96		MINT CAR Fiction FISCD 52	31	2
14 Dec 96		GONE Fiction FICD 53	60	1
29 Nov 97		WRONG NUMBER Fiction FICD 54	62	1

CURIOSITY ☻ *UK, male vocal/instrumental group* **58 wks**

13 Dec 86	●	DOWN TO EARTH Mercury CAT 2 [1]	3	18
4 Apr 87		ORDINARY DAY Mercury CAT 3 [1]	11	7
20 Jun 87	●	MISFIT Mercury CAT 4 [1]	7	9
19 Sep 87		FREE Mercury CAT 5 [1]	56	2
16 Sep 89		NAME AND NUMBER Mercury CAT 6	14	9
25 Apr 92	●	HANG ON IN THERE BABY RCA PB 45377	3	10
29 Aug 92		I NEED YOUR LOVIN' RCA 74321111377	47	2
30 Oct 93		GIMME THE SUNSHINE RCA 74321168602	73	1

[1] Curiosity Killed the Cat

CURLS – *See Paul EVANS*

Chantal CURTIS *France, female vocalist* **3 wks**

14 Jul 79		GET ANOTHER LOVE Pye 7P 5003	51	3

T.C. CURTIS *Jamaica, male vocalist/instrumentalist* **4 wks**

23 Feb 85		YOU SHOULD HAVE KNOWN BETTER Hot Melt VS 754	50	4

CURVE *UK, male/female vocal/instrumental duo* **14 wks**

16 Mar 91		THE BLINDFOLD (EP) Anxious ANX 27	68	1
25 May 91		COAST IS CLEAR Anxious ANX 30	34	3
9 Nov 91		CLIPPED Anxious ANX 35	36	2
7 Mar 92		FAIT ACCOMPLI Anxious ANXT 36	22	3
18 Jul 92		HORROR HEAD (EP) Anxious ANXT 38	31	2
4 Sep 93		BLACKERTHREETRACKER EP Anxious ANXCD 42	39	2
16 May 98		COMING UP ROSES Universal UND 80489	51	1

Tracks on The Blindfold (EP): Ten Little Girls / I Speak Your Every Word / Blindfold / No Escape from Heaven. Tracks on Horror Head (EP): Horror Head / Falling Free / Mission from God / Today Is Not the Day. Only track available on all formats of Blackerthreetracker (EP): Missing Link

CURVED AIR 🎸 *UK, male/female vocal/instrumental group* **12 wks**

7 Aug 71	●	BACK STREET LUV Warner Bros. K 16092	4	12

CUT 'N' MOVE *Denmark, male/female vocal/instrumental group* **4 wks**

2 Oct 93		GIVE IT UP EMI CDEM 273	61	2
9 Sep 95		I'M ALIVE EMI CDEM 375	49	2

Frankie CUTLASS *US, male rapper* **1 wk**

5 Apr 97		THE CYPHER: PART 3 Epic 6641445	59	1

Adge CUTLER – *See WURZELS*

CUTTING CREW ☻
UK/Canada, male vocal/instrumental group **37 wks**

16 Aug 86	●	(I JUST) DIED IN YOUR ARMS Siren SIREN 21 ▲	4	12
25 Oct 86		I'VE BEEN IN LOVE BEFORE Siren SIREN 29	31	9
10 Jan 87		I'VE BEEN IN LOVE BEFORE (re-entry)		
		Siren SIREN 29	70	1
7 Mar 87		ONE FOR THE MOCKINGBIRD Siren SIREN 40	52	5

UK No 1 ★   UK Top 10 ●   UK million seller ◆   UK entry at No 1 ■   US No 1 ▲

21 Nov 87	I'VE BEEN IN LOVE BEFORE (re-mix) *Siren SRN 29*	24	8
22 Jul 89	(BETWEEN A) ROCK AND A HARD PLACE *Siren SRN 108*	66	2

CYBERSONIK US, male sampling group
1 wk

10 Nov 90	TECHNARCHY *Champion CHAMP 264*	73	1

Johnny CYMBAL Canada, male vocalist
10 wks

14 Mar 63	MR BASS MAN *London HLR 9682*	24	10

CYPRESS HILL US, male rap group
29 wks

31 Jul 93	INSANE IN THE BRAIN *Ruff House 6595332*	32	4
2 Oct 93	WHEN THE SH.. GOES DOWN *Ruff House 6596702*	19	4
11 Dec 93	I AIN'T GOIN' OUT LIKE THAT *Ruff House 6596902*	15	7
26 Feb 94	INSANE IN THE BRAIN (re-issue) *Ruff House 6601762*	21	4
7 May 94	LICK A SHOT *Ruff House 6603192*	20	3
7 Oct 95	THROW YOUR SET IN THE AIR *Ruff House 6623542*	15	3
17 Feb 96	ILLUSIONS *Columbia 6629052*	23	2
10 Oct 98	TEQUILA SUNRISE *Columbia 6664935*	23	2

Billy Ray CYRUS US, male vocalist
18 wks

25 Jul 92 ●	ACHY BREAKY HEART *Mercury MER 373*	3	10
10 Oct 92	COULD'VE BEEN ME *Mercury MER 378*	24	4
28 Nov 92	THESE BOOTS ARE MADE FOR WALKIN' *Mercury MER 384*	63	1
19 Dec 92	ACHY BREAKY HEART *Epic 6588837* [1]	53	3

[1] Alvin and the Chipmunks featuring Billy Ray Cyrus

D BO GENERAL – See URBAN SHAKEDOWN

Chuck D US, male rapper
6 wks

6 Jul 91	BRING THE NOISE *Island IS 490* [1]	14	5
26 Oct 96	NO *Mercury MERCD 476*	55	1

[1] Anthrax featuring Chuck D

Dimples D US, female rapper
10 wks

17 Nov 90	SUCKER DJ *FBI FBI 11*	17	10

Longsy D UK, male vocalist
7 wks

4 Mar 89	THIS IS SKA *Big One BIG 13*	56	7

Nikki D US, female rapper
6 wks

6 May 89	MY LOVE IS SO RAW *Def Jam 6548987* [1]	34	5
30 Mar 91	DADDY'S LITTLE GIRL *Def Jam 6567347*	75	1

[1] Alyson Williams featuring Nikki D

Vicky D US, female vocalist
6 wks

13 Mar 82	THIS BEAT IS MINE *Virgin VS 486*	42	6

Bobby D'AMBROSIO US, male DJ
3 wks

2 Aug 97	MOMENT OF MY LIFE *Ministry Of Sound MOSCDS 1* [1]	23	3

[1] Bobby D'Ambrosio featuring Michelle Weeks

D'BORA US, female vocalist
4 wks

14 Sep 91	DREAM ABOUT YOU *Polydor PO 161*	75	1
1 Jul 95	GOING ROUND *Vibe MCSTD 2055*	40	2
30 Mar 96	GOOD LOVE REAL LOVE *Music Plant MCSTD 40023*	58	1

D-INFLUENCE UK, male/female vocal/instrumental group
10 wks

20 Jun 92	GOOD LOVER *East West A 8573*	46	2
27 Mar 93	GOOD LOVER (re-mix) *East West America A 8439CD*	61	1
24 Jun 95	MIDNITE *East West A 4418CD*	58	1
16 Aug 97	HYPNOTIZE *Echo ECSCD 41*	33	2
11 Oct 97	MAGIC *Echo ECSCD 45*	45	1
5 Sep 98	ROCK WITH YOU *Echo ECSCD 56*	30	3

D'LUX UK, male/female vocal/instrumental group
1 wk

22 Jun 96	LOVE RESURRECTION *Logic 74321371012*	58	1

D'MENACE ☺ UK, male production duo
3 wks

8 Aug 98	DEEP MENACE *Inferno CDFERN 8*	20	3

D MOB ☺ UK, male producer – Danny D
48 wks

15 Oct 88 ●	WE CALL IT ACIEED *ffrr FFR 13* [1]	3	12
3 Jun 89	IT IS TIME TO GET FUNKY *ffrr F 107* [2]	9	10
21 Oct 89	C'MON AND GET MY LOVE *ffrr F 117* [3]	15	10
6 Jan 90 ●	PUT YOUR HANDS TOGETHER *ffrr F 124* [4]	7	8
7 Apr 90	THAT'S THE WAY OF THE WORLD *ffrr F 132* [3]	48	3
12 Feb 94	WHY *ffrr FCD 227* [3]	23	3
3 Sep 94	ONE DAY *ffrr FCDP 239*	41	2

[1] D Mob featuring Gary Haisman [2] D Mob featuring LRS [3] D Mob with Cathy Dennis [4] D Mob featuring Nuff Juice

D*NOTE UK, male producer – Matt Winn
2 wks

12 Jul 97	WAITING HOPEFULLY *A & M 5822792*	51	1
15 Nov 97	LOST AND FOUND *VC VCRD 25*	59	1

D:REAM ☻ ☺ UK, male vocal/instrumental duo
74 wks

4 Jul 92	U R THE BEST THING *FXU FXU 3*	72	1
30 Jan 93	THINGS CAN ONLY GET BETTER *Magnet MAG 1010CD*	24	5
24 Apr 93	U R THE BEST THING (re-mix) *Magnet MAG 1011CD*	19	8
31 Jul 93	UNFORGIVEN *Magnet MAG 1016CD*	29	3
2 Oct 93	STAR/I LIKE IT *Magnet MAG 1019CD*	26	4
8 Jan 94 ★	THINGS CAN ONLY GET BETTER (re-mix) *Magnet MAG 1020CD*	1	16
26 Mar 94 ●	U R THE BEST THING (2nd re-mix) *Magnet MAG 1021CD*	4	10
18 Jun 94	TAKE ME AWAY *Magnet MAG 1025CD*	18	5
10 Sep 94	BLAME IT ON ME *Magnet MAG 1027CD*	25	5
8 Jul 95 ●	SHOOT ME WITH YOUR LOVE *Magnet MAG 1034CD*	7	7
9 Sep 95	PARTY UP THE WORLD *Magnet MAG 1037CD*	20	6
11 Nov 95	THE POWER (OF ALL THE LOVE IN THE WORLD) *Magnet MAG 1039CD*	40	1
3 May 97	THINGS CAN ONLY GET BETTER (re-issue) *Magnet MAG 1050CD*	19	3

D-SHAKE ☺ Holland, male instrumental/production duo
8 wks

2 Jun 90	YAAAH/TECHNO TRANCE *Cooltempo COOL 213*	20	6
2 Feb 91	MY HEART THE BEAT *Cooltempo COOL 228*	42	2

D-TEK UK, male instrumental/production group
1 wk

6 Nov 93	DROP THE ROCK (EP) *Positiva 12TIV 5*	70	1

Tracks on Drop the Rock (EP): *Drop the Rock / Chunkafunk / Drop the Rock (re-mix) / Don't Breathe*

D TRAIN ☺ 🎵 US, male vocal/instrumental duo
36 wks

6 Feb 82	YOU'RE THE ONE FOR ME *Epic EPC A 2016*	30	8
8 May 82	WALK ON BY *Epic EPC A 2298*	44	6
7 May 83	MUSIC PART 1 *Prelude A 3332*	23	7
16 Jul 83	KEEP GIVING ME LOVE *Prelude A 3497*	65	2

27 Jul 85	YOU'RE THE ONE FOR ME (re-mix) *Prelude ZB 40302*	15 11
12 Oct 85	MUSIC *Prelude ZB 40431*	62 2

DA BRAT *US, female rapper* — 1 wk

22 Oct 94	FUNKDAFIED *Columbia 6609212*	65 1

Ricardo DA FORCE ○ ◁ *UK, male rapper* — 10 wks

18 Mar 95	PUMP UP THE VOLUME *Stress CDSTR 49* [1]	51 2
16 Sep 95 ●	STAYIN' ALIVE *All Around The World CDGLOBE 131* [2]	2 7
31 Aug 96	WHY *ffrr FCD 280*	58 1

[1] Greed featuring Ricardo Da Force [2] N-Trance featuring Ricardo Da Force

DA HOOL ☺ *Germany, male rapper* — 7 wks

14 Feb 98	MEET HER AT THE LOVE PARADE *Manifesto FESCD 39*	15 4
22 Aug 98	BORA BORA *Manifesto FESCD 47*	35 3

DA LENCH MOB *US, male rap group* — 2 wks

20 Mar 93	FREEDOM GOT AN A.K. *East west America A 8431CD*	51 2

DA MOB *US, male/female vocal/instrumental group* — 2 wks

2 May 98	FUN *INCcredible INCRL 2CD* [1]	33 2

[1] Da Mob featuring Jocelyn Brown

DA TECHNO BOHEMIAN *Holland, male production trio* — 1 wk

25 Jan 97	BANGIN' BASS *Hi-Life 5731772*	63 1

Paul DA VINCI ○ *UK, male vocalist* — 8 wks

20 Jul 74	YOUR BABY AIN'T YOUR BABY ANYMORE *Penny Farthing PEN 843*	20 8

Terry DACTYL and the DINOSAURS ○
UK, male vocal/instrumental group — 16 wks

15 Jul 72 ●	SEASIDE SHUFFLE *UK 5*	2 12
13 Jan 73	ON A SATURDAY NIGHT *UK 21*	45 4

Terry Dactyl is Jona Lewie

DADA *US, male vocal/instrumental group* — 1 wk

4 Dec 93	DOG *IRS CDEIRSS 185*	71 1

DADDY FREDDY – See Simon HARRIS

DADDY'S FAVOURITE *UK, male DJ/producer* — 2 wks

21 Nov 98	I FEEL GOOD THINGS FOR YOU *Go. Beat GONCD 12*	44 2

DAFFY DUCK featuring the GROOVE GANG
Germany, male instrumental/production group — 3 wks

6 Jul 91	PARTY ZONE *East West YZ 592*	58 3

DAFT PUNK ☺ *France, male instrumental/production duo* — 13 wks

22 Feb 97 ●	DA FUNK/MUSIQUE *Virgin VSCDT 1625*	7 5
26 Apr 97 ●	AROUND THE WORLD *Virgin VSCDT 1633*	5 5
4 Oct 97	BURNIN' *Virgin VSCDT 1649*	30 2
28 Feb 98	REVOLUTION 909 *Virgin VSCDT 1682*	47 1

Etienne DAHO – See SAINT ETIENNE

DAINTEES – See Martin STEPHENSON and the DAINTEES

DAISY CHAINSAW *UK, male/female vocal/instrumental group* — 6 wks

18 Jan 92	LOVE YOUR MONEY *Deva DEVA 001*	26 5
28 Mar 92	PINK FLOWER/ROOM ELEVEN *Deva 82 TP7*	65 1

DAKEYNE – See James BROWN; TINMAN

DAKOTAS ○ *UK, male instrumental group* — 13 wks

11 Jul 63	THE CRUEL SEA *Parlophone R 5044*	18 13

See also Billy J KRAMER and the DAKOTAS

DALE and GRACE *US, male/female vocal duo* — 2 wks

9 Jan 64	I'M LEAVING IT UP TO YOU *London HL 9807*	42 2

Jim DALE ○ *UK, male vocalist* — 22 wks

11 Oct 57 ●	BE MY GIRL *Parlophone R 4343*	2 16
10 Jan 58	JUST BORN *Parlophone R 4376*	27 1
17 Jan 58	CRAZY DREAM *Parlophone R 4376*	24 1
7 Mar 58	SUGARTIME *Parlophone R 4402*	25 3

DALE SISTERS *US, female vocal group* — 6 wks

23 Nov 61	MY SUNDAY BABY *Ember S 140*	36 6

DALI'S CAR *UK, male vocal/instrumental duo* — 2 wks

3 Nov 84	THE JUDGEMENT IS THE MIRROR *Paradox DOX 1*	66 2

Roger DALTREY ○ *UK, male vocalist* — 46 wks

14 Apr 73 ●	GIVING IT ALL AWAY *Track 2094 110*	5 11
4 Aug 73	I'M FREE *Ode ODS 66302*	13 10
14 May 77	WRITTEN ON THE WIND *Polydor 2121 319*	46 2
2 Aug 80	FREE ME *Polydor 2001 980*	39 6
11 Oct 80	WITHOUT YOUR LOVE *Polydor POSP 181*	55 4
3 Mar 84	WALKING IN MY SLEEP *WEA U 9686*	56 3
5 Oct 85	AFTER THE FIRE *10 TEN 69*	50 4
8 Mar 86	UNDER A RAGING MOON *10 TEN 81*	43 5

DAMAGE ○ (R&B) *UK, male vocal group* — 32 wks

20 Jul 96	ANYTHING *Big Life BLRD 129*	68 1
12 Oct 96	LOVE II LOVE *Big Life BLRD 131*	12 6
14 Dec 96	FOREVER *Big Life BLRD 132*	6 9
22 Mar 97 ●	LOVE GUARANTEED *Big Life BLRDA 133*	7 6
17 May 97 ●	WONDERFUL TONIGHT *Big Life BLRDA 134*	3 8
9 Aug 97	LOVE LADY *Big Life BLRDB 137*	33 2

Carolina DAMAS – See SUENO LATINO featuring Carolina DAMAS

DAMIAN ○ *UK, male vocalist* — 26 wks

26 Dec 87	THE TIME WARP 2 *Jive JIVE 160*	51 6
27 Aug 88	THE TIME WARP 2 (re-issue) *Jive JIVE 182*	64 3
19 Aug 89 ●	THE TIME WARP (re-mix) *Jive JIVE 209*	7 13
16 Dec 89	WIG WAM BAM *Jive JIVE 236*	49 4

'The Time Warp' is a re-mix of 'The Time Warp 2'

DAMNED ✐ *UK, male vocal/instrumental group* — 77 wks

5 May 79	LOVE SONG *Chiswick CHIS 112*	20 8
20 Oct 79	SMASH IT UP *Chiswick CHIS 116*	35 5
1 Dec 79	I JUST CAN'T BE HAPPY TODAY *Chiswick CHIS 120*	46 5
4 Oct 80	HISTORY OF THE WORLD (PART 1) *Chiswick CHIS 135*	51 4
28 Nov 81	FRIDAY 13TH (EP) *Stale One TRY 1*	50 4
10 Jul 82	LOVELY MONEY *Bronze BRO 149*	42 4
9 Jun 84	THANKS FOR THE NIGHT *Damned DAMNED 1*	43 4
30 Mar 85	GRIMLY FIENDISH *MCA GRIM 1*	21 7
22 Jun 85	THE SHADOW OF LOVE *MCA GRIM 2*	25 8
21 Sep 85	IS IT A DREAM *MCA GRIM 3*	34 4
8 Feb 86 ●	ELOISE *MCA GRIM 4*	3 9
19 Apr 86	ELOISE (re-entry) *MCA GRIM 4*	72 1
22 Nov 86	ANYTHING *MCA GRIM 5*	32 4
7 Feb 87	GIGOLO *MCA GRIM 6*	29 3
25 Apr 87	ALONE AGAIN OR *MCA GRIM 7*	27 6
28 Nov 87	IN DULCE DECORUM *MCA GRIM 8*	72 1

Tracks on Friday 13th (EP): Disco Man / Limit Club / Billy Bad Breaks / Citadel

Kenny DAMON *US, male vocalist* — 1 wk

19 May 66	WHILE I LIVE *Mercury MF 907*	48 1

Vic DAMONE © *US, male vocalist* — 22 wks

6 Dec 57	AN AFFAIR TO REMEMBER *Philips PB 745*	29	1
31 Jan 58	AN AFFAIR TO REMEMBER (re-entry) *Philips PB 745*	30	1
9 May 58	★ ON THE STREET WHERE YOU LIVE *Philips PB 819*	1	17
1 Aug 58	THE ONLY MAN ON THE ISLAND *Philips PB 837*	24	3

DAN-I *UK, male vocalist* — 9 wks

10 Nov 79	MONKEY CHOP *Island WIP 6520*	30	9

DANA ☻ *UK, female vocalist* — 75 wks

4 Apr 70	★ ALL KINDS OF EVERYTHING *Rex R 11054*	1	15
25 Jul 70	ALL KINDS OF EVERYTHING (re-entry) *Rex R 11054*	47	1
13 Feb 71	WHO PUT THE LIGHTS OUT *Rex R 11062*	14	11
25 Jan 75	● PLEASE TELL HIM THAT I SAID HELLO *GTO GT 6*	8	14
13 Dec 75	● IT'S GONNA BE A COLD COLD CHRISTMAS *GTO GT 45*	4	6
6 Mar 76	NEVER GONNA FALL IN LOVE AGAIN *GTO GT 55*	31	4
16 Oct 76	FAIRYTALE *GTO GT 66*	13	16
31 Mar 79	SOMETHING'S COOKIN' IN THE KITCHEN *GTO GT 243*	44	5
15 May 82	I FEEL LOVE COMIN' ON *Creole CR 32*	66	3

DANA INTERNATIONAL ☻ *Israel, female vocalist* — 4 wks

27 Jun 98	DIVA *Dance Pool DANA 1CD*	11	4

DANCE 2 TRANCE *Germany, male instrumental/production duo* — 8 wks

24 Apr 93	P.OWER OF A.MERICAN N.ATIVES *Logic 74321139582*	25	4
24 Jul 93	TAKE A FREE FALL *Logic 74321153602*	36	3
4 Feb 95	WARRIOR *Logic 74321257722*	56	1

DANCE CONSPIRACY *UK, male instrumental/production duo* — 1 wk

3 Oct 92	DUB WAR *XL XLT 34*	72	1

DANCE FLOOR VIRUS *Italy, male vocal/instrumental group* — 2 wks

21 Oct 95	MESSAGE IN A BOTTLE *Epic 6623742*	49	2

Evan DANDO – See Kirsty MacCOLL

DANDY WARHOLS ☹ *US, male/female vocal/instrumental group* — 8 wks

28 Feb 98	EVERY DAY SHOULD BE A HOLIDAY *Capitol CDCL 797*	29	2
2 May 98	NOT IF YOU WERE THE LAST JUNKIE ON EARTH *Capitol CDCL 800*	13	4
8 Aug 98	BOYS BETTER *Capitol CDCLS 805*	36	2

DANDYS *UK, male vocal/instrumental group* — 2 wks

14 Mar 98	YOU MAKE ME WANT TO SCREAM *Artificial ATFCD 3*	71	1
30 May 98	ENGLISH COUNTRY GARDEN *Artificial ATFCD 4*	57	1

D'ANGELO *US, male vocalist* — 9 wks

28 Oct 95	BROWN SUGAR *Cooltempo CDCOOL 307*	24	3
2 Mar 96	CRUISIN' *Cooltempo CDCOOL 316*	31	2
2 Mar 96	COLD WORLD *Geffen GFSTD 22114* [1]	40	2
15 Jun 96	LADY *Cooltempo CDCOOLS 323*	21	2

[1] Genius / GZA featuring D'Angelo

DANGER DANGER *US, male vocal/instrumental group* — 5 wks

8 Feb 92	MONKEY BUSINESS *Epic 6577517*	42	2
28 Mar 92	I STILL THINK ABOUT YOU *Epic 6578387*	46	2
13 Jun 92	COMIN' HOME *Epic 6581337*	75	1

Harvey DANGER *US, male vocal/instrumental group* — 1 wk

1 Aug 98	FLAGPOLE SITTA *Slash LASCD 64*	57	1

Charlie DANIELS BAND ⚓ *US, male vocal/instrumental group* — 10 wks

22 Sep 79	THE DEVIL WENT DOWN TO GEORGIA *Epic EPC 7737*	14	10

Johnny DANKWORTH ✒ *UK, male orchestral/group leader/instrumentalist – alto sax* — 33 wks

22 Jun 56	● EXPERIMENTS WITH MICE *Parlophone R 4185*	7	12
23 Feb 61	● AFRICAN WALTZ *Columbia DB 4590*	9	21

DANNY and the JUNIORS ♪ *US, male vocal group* — 19 wks

17 Jan 58	● AT THE HOP *HMV POP 436* ▲	3	14
10 Jul 76	AT THE HOP (re-issue) *ABC 4123*	39	5

DANNY WILSON ☻ *UK, male vocal/instrumental group* — 28 wks

22 Aug 87	MARY'S PRAYER *Virgin VS 934*	42	7
2 Apr 88	● MARY'S PRAYER (re-entry) *Virgin VS 934*	3	11
17 Jun 89	THE SECOND SUMMER OF LOVE *Virgin VS 1186*	23	9
16 Sep 89	NEVER GONNA BE THE SAME *Virgin VS 1203*	69	1

DANSE SOCIETY *UK, male vocal/instrumental group* — 5 wks

27 Aug 83	WAKE UP *Society SOC 5*	61	3
5 Nov 83	HEAVEN IS WAITING *Society SOC 6*	60	2

Steven DANTE ☺ *UK, male vocalist* — 16 wks

26 Sep 87	THE REAL THING *Chrysalis CHS 3167* [1]	13	10
9 Jul 88	I'M TOO SCARED *Cooltempo DANTE 1*	34	6

[1] Jellybean featuring Steven Dante

Tonja DANTZLER *US, female vocalist* — 1 wk

17 Dec 94	IN AND OUT OF MY LIFE *ffrr FCD 246*	66	1

DANY – See DOUBLE DEE featuring DANY

DANZIG *US, male vocal/instrumental group* — 1 wk

14 May 94	MOTHER *American MOMDD 1*	62	1

DAPHNE *US, female vocalist* — 1 wk

9 Dec 95	CHANGE *Stress CDSTR 54*	71	1

Terence Trent D'ARBY ☻ 🎤 *US, male vocalist* — 77 wks

14 Mar 87	● IF YOU LET ME STAY *CBS TRENT 1*	7	13
20 Jun 87	● WISHING WELL *CBS TRENT 2* ▲	4	11
10 Oct 87	DANCE LITTLE SISTER (PART ONE) *CBS TRENT 3*	20	7
9 Jan 88	● SIGN YOUR NAME *CBS TRENT 4*	2	10
20 Jan 90	TO KNOW SOMEONE DEEPLY IS TO KNOW SOMEONE SOFTLY *CBS TRENT 6*	55	3
17 Apr 93	DO YOU LOVE ME LIKE YOU SAY *Columbia 6590732*	14	6
19 Jun 93	DELICATE *Columbia 6593312* [1]	14	6
28 Aug 93	SHE KISSED ME *Columbia 6595922*	16	7
20 Nov 93	LET HER DOWN EASY *Columbia 6598642*	18	7
8 Apr 95	HOLDING ON TO YOU *Columbia 6614235*	20	6
5 Aug 95	VIBRATOR *Columbia 6622585*	57	1

[1] Terence Trent D'Arby featuring Des'ree

Richard DARBYSHIRE *UK, male vocalist* — 7 wks

20 Aug 88	COMING BACK FOR MORE *Chrysalis JEL 4* [1]	41	3
24 Jul 93	THIS I SWEAR *Dome CDDOME 1003*	50	3
12 Feb 94	WHEN ONLY LOVE WILL DO *Dome CDDOME 1008*	54	1

[1] Jellybean featuring Richard Darbyshire

DARE *UK, male vocal/instrumental group* — 7 wks

29 Apr 89	THE RAINDANCE *A & M AM 483*	62	2
29 Jul 89	ABANDON *A & M AM 519*	71	2
10 Aug 91	WE DON'T NEED A REASON *A & M AM 755*	52	2
5 Oct 91	REAL LOVE *A & M AM 824*	67	1

Bobby DARIN ○ ℂ Singer/songwriter/actor and multi-instrumentalist who had pop, rock, R&B, country and MOR hits, b. Walden Robert Cassotto, 14 May, 1936, New York, d. 20 December, 1973. This Grammy winner was posthumously inducted into Rock and Roll Hall of Fame in 1990 — 161 wks

1 Aug 58	SPLISH SPLASH London HLE 8666	28	1
15 Aug 58	SPLISH SPLASH (re-entry) London HLE 8666	18	6
9 Jan 59	QUEEN OF THE HOP London HLE 8737	24	2
29 May 59 ★	DREAM LOVER London HLE 8867	1	19
25 Sep 59 ★	MACK THE KNIFE London HLK 8939 ▲	1	16
22 Jan 60	MACK THE KNIFE (re-entry) London HLK 8939	30	1
29 Jan 60 ●	LA MER (BEYOND THE SEA) London HLK 9034	8	10
10 Mar 60	MACK THE KNIFE (2nd re-entry) London HLE 8939	50	1
31 Mar 60 ●	CLEMENTINE London HLK 9086	8	12
21 Apr 60	LA MER (BEYOND THE SEA) (re-entry) London HLE 9034	40	2
30 Jun 60	BILL BAILEY London HLK 9142	36	1
14 Jul 60	BILL BAILEY (re-entry) London HLK 9142	34	1
16 Mar 61 ●	LAZY RIVER London HLK 9303	2	13
6 Jul 61	NATURE BOY London HLK 9375	24	7
12 Oct 61 ●	YOU MUST HAVE BEEN A BEAUTIFUL BABY London HLK 9429	10	11
26 Oct 61	COME SEPTEMBER London HLK 9407 [1]	50	1
21 Dec 61 ●	MULTIPLICATION London HLK 9474	5	13
19 Jul 62 ●	THINGS London HLK 9575	2	17
4 Oct 62	IF A MAN ANSWERS Capitol CL 15272	24	6
29 Nov 62	BABY FACE London HLK 9624	40	4
25 Jul 63	EIGHTEEN YELLOW ROSES Capitol CL 15306	37	4
13 Oct 66 ●	IF I WERE A CARPENTER Atlantic 584 051	9	12
14 Apr 79	DREAM LOVER (RE-ISSUE)/MACK THE KNIFE (re-issue) Lightning LIG 9017	64	1

[1] Bobby Darin Orchestra

DARKMAN UK, male rapper — 7 wks

14 May 94	YABBA DABBA DOO Wild Card CARDD 6	49	2
20 Aug 94	WHO'S THE DARKMAN Wild Card CARDD 8	46	2
3 Dec 94	YABBA DABBA DOO (re-issue) Wild Card CARDD 11	37	2
21 Oct 95	BRAND NEW DAY Wild Card 5771892	74	1

DARLING BUDS UK, male/female vocal/instrumental group — 20 wks

8 Oct 88	BURST Epic BLOND 1	50	5
7 Jan 89	HIT THE GROUND CBS BLOND 2	27	5
25 Mar 89	LET'S GO ROUND THERE CBS BLOND 3	49	4
22 Jul 89	YOU'VE GOT TO CHOOSE CBS BLOND 4	45	3
2 Jun 90	TINY MACHINE CBS BLOND 5	60	2
12 Sep 92	SURE THING Epic 6582157	71	1

Guy DARRELL ○ UK, male vocalist — 13 wks

18 Aug 73	I'VE BEEN HURT Santa Ponsa PNS 4	12	13

James DARREN US, male vocalist — 25 wks

11 Aug 60	BECAUSE THEY'RE YOUNG Pye International 7N 25059	29	7
14 Dec 61	GOODBYE CRUEL WORLD Pye International 7N 25116	28	9
29 Mar 62	HER ROYAL MAJESTY Pye International 7N 25125	36	3
21 Jun 62	CONSCIENCE Pye International 7N 25138	30	6

DARTS ○ Britain's best-known doo-wop vocal group; line-up included Den Haggarty, Griff Fender, Rita Ray and Bob Fish. The popular London-based eight-piece band had three successive No 2 hits with revivals of early US rock'n'roll and R&B songs — 117 wks

5 Nov 77 ●	DADDY COOL/THE GIRL CAN'T HELP IT Magnet MAG 100	6	13
28 Jan 78 ●	COME BACK MY LOVE Magnet MAG 110	2	12
6 May 78 ●	BOY FROM NEW YORK CITY Magnet MAG 116	2	13
5 Aug 78 ●	IT'S RAINING Magnet MAG 126	2	11
11 Nov 78	DON'T LET IT FADE AWAY Magnet MAG 134	18	11
10 Feb 79 ●	GET IT Magnet MAG 140	10	9
21 Jul 79 ●	DUKE OF EARL Magnet MAG 147	6	11
20 Oct 79	CAN'T GET ENOUGH OF YOUR LOVE Magnet MAG 156	43	4
1 Dec 79	REET PETITE Magnet MAG 160	51	7
31 May 80	LET'S HANG ON Magnet MAG 174	11	14
6 Sep 80	PEACHES Magnet MAG 179	66	3

29 Nov 80	WHITE CHRISTMAS/SH-BOOM (LIFE COULD BE A DREAM) Magnet MAG 184	48	7

DAS EFX US, male production/rap duo — 5 wks

7 Aug 93	CHECK YO SELF Fourth & Broadway BRCD 283 [2]	36	4
25 Apr 98	RAP SCHOLAR East West E 3853CD [1]	42	1

[1] Das EFX featuring Red Man [2] Ice Cube featuring Das EFX

N'dea DAVENPORT US, female vocalist — 1 wk

20 Jun 98	BRING IT ON Gee Street VVR5002033	52	1

See also BRAND NEW HEAVIES; GURU

Anne-Marie DAVID ○ France, female vocalist — 9 wks

28 Apr 73	WONDERFUL DREAM Epic EPC 1446	13	9

F.R. DAVID ○ France, male vocalist — 13 wks

2 Apr 83 ●	WORDS Carrere CAR 248	2	12
18 Jun 83	MUSIC Carrere CAR 282	71	1

DAVID DEVANT AND HIS SPIRIT WIFE UK, male vocal/instrumental group — 2 wks

5 Apr 97	GINGER Rhythm King KIND 4CD	54	1
21 Jun 97	THIS IS FOR REAL Rhythm King KIND 5CD	61	1

DAVID and JONATHAN ○ UK, male vocal duo — 22 wks

13 Jan 66	MICHELLE Columbia DB 7800	11	6
7 Jul 66 ●	LOVERS OF THE WORLD UNITE Columbia DB 7950	7	16

Jim DAVIDSON UK, male vocalist — 4 wks

27 Dec 80	WHITE CHRISTMAS/TOO RISKY Scratch SCR 001	52	4

Paul DAVIDSON ꙮ Jamaica, male vocalist — 10 wks

27 Dec 75 ●	MIDNIGHT RIDER Tropical ALO 56	10	10

Dave DAVIES ○ UK, male vocalist — 17 wks

19 Jul 67 ●	DEATH OF A CLOWN Pye 7N 17356	3	10
6 Dec 67	SUSANNAH'S STILL ALIVE Pye 7N 17429	20	7

Windsor DAVIES and Don ESTELLE ℂ UK, male vocal duo — 16 wks

17 May 75 ★	WHISPERING GRASS EMI 2290	1	12
25 Oct 75	PAPER DOLL EMI 2361	41	4

Billie DAVIS ○ UK, female vocalist — 33 wks

30 Aug 62	WILL I WHAT Parlophone R 4932 [1]	18	10
7 Feb 63 ●	TELL HIM Decca F 11572	10	12
30 May 63	HE'S THE ONE Decca F 11658	40	3
9 Oct 68	I WANT YOU TO BE MY BABY Decca F 12823	33	8

[1] Mike Sarne with Billie Davis

Billy DAVIS Jr – See Marilyn McCOO and Billy DAVIS Jr

Darlene DAVIS US, female vocalist — 5 wks

7 Feb 87	I FOUND LOVE Serious 7OUS 1	55	5

John DAVIS and the MONSTER ORCHESTRA US, male vocal/instrumental group — 2 wks

10 Feb 79	AIN'T THAT ENOUGH FOR YOU Miracle M 2	70	2

Mac DAVIS US, male vocalist — 22 wks

4 Nov 72	BABY DON'T GET HOOKED ON ME CBS 8250 ▲	29	6
15 Nov 80	IT'S HARD TO BE HUMBLE Casablanca CAN 210	27	16

Richie DAVIS – See SHUT UP AND DANCE

Roy DAVIS Jr. featuring Peven EVERET
US, male producer, male vocalist — **4 wks**

1 Nov 97	**GABRIEL** *XL XLS 88CD*	22	4

Ruth DAVIS – *See Bo KIRKLAND and Ruth DAVIS*

Sammy DAVIS Jr. Ⓒ *US, male vocalist* — **37 wks**

29 Jul 55	**SOMETHING'S GOTTA GIVE** *Brunswick 05428*	19	2
19 Aug 55	**SOMETHING'S GOTTA GIVE (re-entry)** *Brunswick 05428*	11	5
9 Sep 55 ●	**LOVE ME OR LEAVE ME** *Brunswick 05428*	8	6
30 Sep 55	**THAT OLD BLACK MAGIC** *Brunswick 05450*	16	1
7 Oct 55	**HEY THERE** *Brunswick 05469*	19	1
4 Nov 55	**LOVE ME OR LEAVE ME (re-entry)** *Brunswick 05428*	18	2
20 Apr 56	**IN A PERSIAN MARKET** *Brunswick 05518*	28	1
28 Dec 56	**ALL OF YOU** *Brunswick 05629*	28	1
16 Jun 60	**HAPPY TO MAKE YOUR ACQUAINTANCE** *Brunswick 05830* [1]	46	1
22 Mar 62	**WHAT KIND OF FOOL AM I?/GONNA BUILD A MOUNTAIN** *Reprise R 20048*	26	8
13 Dec 62	**ME AND MY SHADOW** *Reprise R 20128* [2]	20	7
7 Feb 63	**ME AND MY SHADOW (re-entry)** *Reprise R 20128* [2]	47	2

[1] Sammy Davis Jr. and Carmen McRae [2] Frank Sinatra and Sammy Davis Jr.

Skeeter DAVIS ⏺ *US, female vocalist* — **13 wks**

14 Mar 63	**END OF THE WORLD** *RCA 1328*	18	13

T. J. DAVIS – *See FULL MONTY ALLSTARS featuring T. J. DAVIS*

Zelma DAVIS – *See C & C MUSIC FACTORY / CLIVILLES & COLE*

DAVIS PINCKNEY PROJECT – *See GO GO LORENZO and the DAVIS PINCKNEY PROJECT*

Spencer DAVIS GROUP ✎
UK, male vocal/instrumental group — **71 wks**

5 Nov 64	**I CAN'T STAND IT** *Fontana TF 499*	47	3
25 Feb 65	**EVERY LITTLE BIT HURTS** *Fontana TF 530*	43	2
18 Mar 65	**EVERY LITTLE BIT HURTS (re-entry)** *Fontana TF 530*	41	1
10 Jun 65	**STRONG LOVE** *Fontana TF 571*	50	1
24 Jun 65	**STRONG LOVE (re-entry)** *Fontana TF 571*	44	3
2 Dec 65 ★	**KEEP ON RUNNING** *Fontana TF 632*	1	14
24 Mar 66 ★	**SOMEBODY HELP ME** *Fontana TF 679*	1	10
1 Sep 66	**WHEN I COME HOME** *Fontana TF 739*	12	9
3 Nov 66 ●	**GIMME SOME LOVING** *Fontana TF 762*	2	12
26 Jan 67 ●	**I'M A MAN** *Fontana TF 785*	9	7
9 Aug 67	**TIME SELLER** *Fontana TF 854*	30	5
10 Jan 68	**MR. SECOND CLASS** *United Artists UP 1203*	35	4

DAWN ◑ *Top-notch vocal trio fronted by one-time teenage hitmaker Tony Orlando (b. Michael Cassavitis, 3 April, 1944, New York) and including Telma Hopkins and Joyce Vincent. Their 'Tie a Yellow Ribbon' was the Top Single of 1973 in both the UK and the USA* — **109 wks**

16 Jan 71 ●	**CANDIDA** *Bell 1118*	9	11
10 Apr 71 ★	**KNOCK THREE TIMES** *Bell 1146*	1	27
31 Jul 71 ●	**WHAT ARE YOU DOING SUNDAY** *Bell 1169* [1]	3	12
10 Mar 73 ★	**TIE A YELLOW RIBBON ROUND THE OLD OAK TREE** *Bell 1287* [1]	1	39
4 Aug 73 ●	**SAY, HAS ANYBODY SEEN MY SWEET GYPSY ROSE** *Bell 1322* [1]	12	15
5 Jan 74	**TIE A YELLOW RIBBON ROUND THE OLD OAK TREE (re-entry)** *Bell 1287* [1]	41	1
9 Mar 74	**WHO'S IN THE STRAWBERRY PATCH WITH SALLY** *Bell 1343* [2] 37	37	4

[1] Dawn featuring Tony Orlando [2] Tony Orlando and Dawn

Julie DAWN – *See Cyril STAPLETON*

Liz DAWN – *See Joe LONGTHORNE*

DAWN OF THE REPLICANTS
UK, male vocal/instrumental group — **2 wks**

7 Feb 98	**CANDLEFIRE** *East West EW 147CD1*	52	1
4 Apr 98	**HOGWASH FARM (THE DIESEL HANDS EP)** *East West EW 157CD.*	65	1

Dana DAWSON Ⓡ&Ⓑ *US, female vocalist* — **14 wks**

15 Jul 95 ●	**3 IS FAMILY** *EMI CDEM 378*	9	8
28 Oct 95	**GOT TO GIVE ME LOVE** *EMI CDEM 392*	27	2
4 May 96	**SHOW ME** *EMI CDEMS 423*	28	3
20 Jul 96	**HOW I WANNA BE LOVED** *EMI CDEMS 432*	42	1

Bobby DAY *US, male vocalist* — **2 wks**

7 Nov 58	**ROCKIN' ROBIN** *London HL 8726*	29	2

Darren DAY ◑ Ⓒ *UK, male vocalist* — **7 wks**

8 Oct 94	**YOUNG GIRL** *Bell 74321231082*	42	2
8 Jun 96	**SUMMER HOLIDAY MEDLEY** *RCA 74321384472*	17	4
9 May 98	**HOW CAN I BE SURE** *Eastcoast DDCD 001*	71	1

Doris DAY Ⓒ *The fifties' favourite singer/actress, b. Doris Kappelhoff, 3 April, 1922, Cincinnati. The No 1 female movie star of that era, she also had numerous British hits (not to mention 25 US best sellers) before the UK chart first started* — **146 wks**

14 Nov 52 ●	**SUGARBUSH** *Columbia DB 3123* [1]	8	2
21 Nov 52 ●	**MY LOVE AND DEVOTION** *Columbia DB 3157*	10	2
5 Dec 52 ●	**SUGARBUSH (re-entry)** *Columbia DB 3123* [1]	8	6
3 Apr 53	**MA SAYS PA SAYS** *Columbia DB 3242* [2]	12	1
17 Apr 53	**FULL TIME JOB** *Columbia DB 3242* [2]	11	1
24 Jul 53 ●	**LET'S WALK THAT-A-WAY** *Philips PB 157* [2]	4	14
2 Apr 54 ★	**SECRET LOVE** *Philips PB 230* ▲	1	29
27 Aug 54 ●	**THE BLACK HILLS OF DAKOTA** *Philips PB 287*	7	8
1 Oct 54 ●	**IF I GIVE MY HEART TO YOU** *Philips PB 325*	4	11
8 Apr 55 ●	**READY WILLING AND ABLE** *Philips PB 402*	7	9
9 Sep 55	**LOVE ME OR LEAVE ME** *Philips PB 479*	20	1
21 Oct 55	**I'LL NEVER STOP LOVING YOU** *Philips PB 497*	17	2
25 Nov 55	**I'LL NEVER STOP LOVING YOU (re-entry)** *Philips PB 497*	19	1
29 Jun 56 ★	**WHATEVER WILL BE WILL BE** *Philips PB 586*	1	22
13 Jun 58	**A VERY PRECIOUS LOVE** *Philips PB 799*	16	11
15 Aug 58	**EVERYBODY LOVES A LOVER** *Philips PB 843*	25	3
26 Sep 58	**EVERYBODY LOVES A LOVER (re-entry)** *Philips PB 843*	27	1
12 Mar 64 ●	**MOVE OVER DARLING** *CBS AAG 183*	8	16
18 Apr 87	**MOVE OVER DARLING (re-issue)** *CBS LEGS 1*	45	6

[1] Doris Day and Frankie Laine [2] Doris Day and Johnnie Ray

Patti DAY *US, female vocalist* — **1 wk**

9 Dec 89	**RIGHT BEFORE MY EYES** *Debut DEBT 3080*	69	1

Taylor DAYNE ◑ ☺ *US, female vocalist* — **54 wks**

23 Jan 88 ●	**TELL IT TO MY HEART** *Arista 109616*	3	13
19 Mar 88 ●	**PROVE YOUR LOVE** *Arista 109830*	8	10
11 Jun 88	**I'LL ALWAYS LOVE YOU** *Arista 111536*	41	7
18 Nov 89	**WITH EVERY BEAT OF MY HEART** *Arista 112760*	53	2
14 Apr 90	**I'LL BE YOUR SHELTER** *Arista 112996*	43	5
4 Aug 90	**LOVE WILL LEAD YOU BACK** *Arista 113277* ▲	69	1
3 Jul 93	**CAN'T GET ENOUGH OF YOUR LOVE** *Arista 74321147852*	14	8
16 Apr 94	**I'LL WAIT** *Arista 74321203472*	29	3
4 Feb 95	**ORIGINAL SIN (THEME FROM THE SHADOW)** *Arista 74321223462*	63	1
18 Nov 95	**SAY A PRAYER** *Arista 74321324292*	58	1
13 Jan 96	**TELL IT TO MY HEART (re-mix)** *Arista 74321335962*	23	3

DAYTON *US, male vocalist* — **1 wk**

10 Dec 83	**THE SOUND OF MUSIC** *Capitol CL 318*	75	1

DAZZ BAND ♪ *US, male vocal/instrumental group* — **12 wks**

3 Nov 84	**LET IT ALL BLOW** *Motown TMG 1361*	12	12

DBM *Germany, male/female vocal/instrumental group* **3 wks**

| 12 Nov 77 | DISCO BEATLEMANIA *Atlantic K 11027* | .....45 | 3 |

D, B, M and T *UK, male vocal/instrumental group* **8 wks**

| 1 Aug 70 | MR. PRESIDENT *Fontana 6007 022* | .....33 | 8 |

See also Dave DEE, DOZY, BEAKY, MICK and TICH

Nino DE ANGELO *Germany, male vocalist* **5 wks**

| 21 Jul 84 | GUARDIAN ANGEL *Carrere CAR 335* | .....57 | 5 |

DE BOS *Holland, male DJ/producer* **1 wk**

| 25 Oct 97 | ON THE RUN *Jive JIVECD 433* | .....51 | 1 |

Chris DE BURGH ☉ *Ireland, male vocalist* **70 wks**

23 Oct 82	DON'T PAY THE FERRYMAN *A & M AMS 8256*	48	5
12 May 84	HIGH ON EMOTION *A & M AM 190*	44	5
12 Jul 86 ★	THE LADY IN RED *A & M AM 331*	1	14
20 Sep 86	FATAL HESITATION *A & M AM 346*	44	4
13 Dec 86	A SPACEMAN CAME TRAVELLING/THE BALLROOM OF ROMANCE *A & M AM 365*	40	5
21 Feb 87	THE LADY IN RED (re-entry) *A & M AM 331*	74	1
12 Dec 87	THE SIMPLE TRUTH (A CHILD IS BORN) *A & M AM 427*	69	2
2 Jan 88	THE SIMPLE TRUTH (A CHILD IS BORN) (re-entry) *A & M AM 427*	55	1
29 Oct 88 ●	MISSING YOU *A & M AM 474*	3	12
7 Jan 89	TENDER HANDS *A & M AM 486*	43	6
14 Oct 89	THIS WAITING HEART *A & M AM 528*	59	3
25 May 91	THE SIMPLE TRUTH (A CHILD IS BORN) (re-issue) *A & M RELF 1*	36	2
11 Apr 92	SEPARATE TABLES *A & M AM 863*	30	4
21 May 94	BLONDE HAIR BLUE JEANS *A & M 5805932*	51	1
9 Dec 95	THE SNOWS OF NEW YORK *A & M 5813132*	60	1
27 Sep 97	SO BEAUTIFUL *A & M 5823932*	29	4

Etienne DE CRECY *France, male DJ/producer* **1 wk**

| 28 Mar 98 | PRIX CHOC – REMIXES *Different DIF 007CD* | .....60 | 1 |

DE CASTRO SISTERS *Cuba, female vocal group* **1 wk**

| 11 Feb 55 | TEACH ME TONIGHT *London HL 8104* | .....20 | 1 |

DE-CODE featuring Beverli SKEETE
UK, male/female vocal/instrumental group **1 wk**

| 18 May 96 | WONDERWALL/SOME MIGHT SAY *Neoteric NRCD 2* | .....69 | 1 |

DE LA SOUL 🗢 *US, male rap/sampling group* **57 wks**

8 Apr 89	ME MYSELF AND I *Big Life BLR 7*	22	8
8 Jul 89	SAY NO GO *Big Life BLR 10*	18	7
21 Oct 89	EYE KNOW *Big Life BLR 13*	14	7
23 Dec 89 ●	THE MAGIC NUMBER/BUDDY *Big Life BLR 14*	7	8
24 Mar 90	MAMA GAVE BIRTH TO THE SOUL CHILDREN *Gee Street GEE 26* [1]	14	7
27 Apr 91 ●	RING RING RING (HA HA HEY) *Big Life BLR 42*	10	7
3 Aug 91	A ROLLER SKATING JAM NAMED 'SATURDAYS' *Big Life BLR 55*	22	5
23 Nov 91	KEEPIN' THE FAITH *Big Life BLR 64*	50	2
18 Sep 93	BREAKADAWN *Big Life BLRD 103*	39	3
2 Apr 94	FALLIN' *Epic 6602622* [2]	59	1
29 Jun 96	STAKES IS HIGH *Tommy Boy TBCD 7730*	55	1
8 Mar 97	4 MORE *Tommy Boy TBCD 7779A* [3]	52	1

[1] Queen Latifah + De La Soul [2] Teenage Fanclub and De La Soul [3] De La Soul featuring Zhané

'Buddy' only listed for first three weeks, peaking at No 8
See also JUNGLE BROTHERS

Donna DE LORY *US, female vocalist* **1 wk**

| 24 Jul 93 | JUST A DREAM *MCA MCSTD 1750* | .....71 | 1 |

Vincent DE MOOR *Holland, male producer* **1 wk**

| 16 Aug 97 | FLOWTATION *XL XLS 89CD* | .....54 | 1 |

Lynsey DE PAUL ☉ *UK, female vocalist* **54 wks**

19 Aug 72 ●	SUGAR ME *MAM 81*	5	11
2 Dec 72	GETTING A DRAG *MAM 88*	18	8
27 Oct 73	WON'T SOMEBODY DANCE WITH ME *MAM 109*	14	7
8 Jun 74	OOH I DO *Warner Bros. K 16401*	25	6
2 Nov 74 ●	NO HONESTLY *Jet 747*	7	11
22 Mar 75	MY MAN AND ME *Jet 750*	40	4
26 Mar 77	ROCK BOTTOM *Polydor 2058 859* [1]	19	7

[1] Lynsey De Paul and Mike Moran

Tullio DE PISCOPO *Italy, male vocalist* **4 wks**

| 28 Feb 87 | STOP BAJON . . . PRIMAVERA *Greyhound GREY 9* | .....58 | 4 |

Rebecca DE RUVO *Sweden, female vocalist* **1 wk**

| 1 Oct 94 | I CAUGHT YOU OUT *Arista 74321230782* | .....72 | 1 |

Teri DE SARIO *US, female vocalist* **5 wks**

| 2 Sep 78 | AIN'T NOTHIN' (GONNA KEEP ME FROM YOU) *Casablanca CAN 128* | .....52 | 5 |

Stephanie DE SYKES ☉ *UK, female vocalist* **17 wks**

| 20 Jul 74 ● | BORN WITH A SMILE ON MY FACE *Bradley's BRAD 7409* [1] | .....2 | 10 |
| 19 Apr 75 | WE'LL FIND OUR DAY *Bradley's BRAD 7509* | .....17 | 7 |

[1] Stephanie De Sykes with Rain

DE VANTE – See *VARIOUS ARTISTS (EPs & LPs)* – The Dangerous Minds (EP)

William DE VAUGHN *US, male vocalist* **10 wks**

| 6 Jul 74 | BE THANKFUL FOR WHAT YOU'VE GOT *Chelsea 2005 002* | .....31 | 5 |
| 20 Sep 80 | BE THANKFUL FOR WHAT YOU'VE GOT *EMI 5101* | .....44 | 5 |

EMI version of hit is a new recording

Tony DE VIT *UK, male producer* **9 wks**

4 Mar 95	BURNING UP *Icon ICONCD 001*	25	3
12 Aug 95	HOOKED *Labello Dance LAD 18CD* [1]	28	2
9 Sep 95	TO THE LIMIT *X:Plode BANG 1CD*	44	2
30 May 96	I'LL BE THERE *Labello Dance LAD 25CD1* [1]	37	2

[1] 99th Floor Elevators featuring Tony De Vit

DE'LACY ☺ *US, male/female vocal/instrumental group* **16 wks**

2 Sep 95 ●	HIDEAWAY *Slip 'N' Slide 74321310472*	9	10
31 Aug 96	THAT LOOK *Slip 'N' Slide 74321398322*	19	4
14 Feb 98	HIDEAWAY 1998 *Slip 'N'Slide 74321561052*	21	2

DEACON BLUE ☉ *Scottish sextet with fervent following, led by singer/songwriter Ricky Ross (v) and featuring his wife Lorraine McIntosh (v). Named after the Steely Dan song, they achieved five Top 5 albums, including the million-selling When the World Knows Your Name* **111 wks**

23 Jan 88	DIGNITY *CBS DEAC 4*	31	8
9 Apr 88	WHEN WILL YOU MAKE MY TELEPHONE RING *CBS DEAC 5*	34	7
16 Jul 88	CHOCOLATE GIRL *CBS DEAC 6*	43	7
15 Oct 88 ●	REAL GONE KID *CBS DEAC 7*	8	13
4 Mar 89	WAGES DAY *CBS DEAC 8*	18	6
20 May 89	FERGUS SINGS THE BLUES *CBS DEAC 9*	14	6
16 Sep 89	LOVE AND REGRET *CBS DEAC 10*	28	5
6 Jan 90	QUEEN OF THE NEW YEAR *CBS DEAC 11*	21	5
25 Aug 90 ●	FOUR BACHARACH AND DAVID SONGS (EP) *CBS DEAC 12*	2	9
25 May 91	YOUR SWAYING ARMS *Columbia 6568937*	23	4
27 Jul 91 ●	TWIST AND SHOUT *Columbia 6573027*	10	9
12 Oct 91	CLOSING TIME *Columbia 6575027*	42	3
14 Dec 91	COVER FROM THE SKY *Columbia 6576737*	31	4
28 Nov 92	YOUR TOWN *Columbia 6587867*	14	8

What: *Two Tribes*　　**29**
Who: Frankie Goes to Hollywood
When: 1984 (1), 1994 (16)
Which: Made them the first act to achieve sales of one million with their first two releases in the UK. At times, this definitive dance track and the group's 'Relax' held the top two chart places

What: *Rivers of Babylon / Brown Girl in the Ring*　　**30**
Who: Boney M
When: 1978 (1)
Which: Sold an almost unprecedented two million copies in the UK, with both sides proving equally popular. Spent 40 weeks on the chart and was the band's only US Top 40 entry

What: *Young at Heart*　　**31**
Who: Bluebells
When: 1984 (8), 1993 (1)
Which: Took the Scottish group to the top at the second try, after being used in a £2.5-million advertising campaign by Volkswagen. Co-written by Bananarama's Siobhan Fahey

What: *Think Twice*　　**32**
Who: Celine Dion
When: 1994 (1)
Which: Took an unprecedented 16 weeks to top UK charts. Despite faring poorly Stateside, this British composition became the first of her two UK million sellers – a record for a female soloist

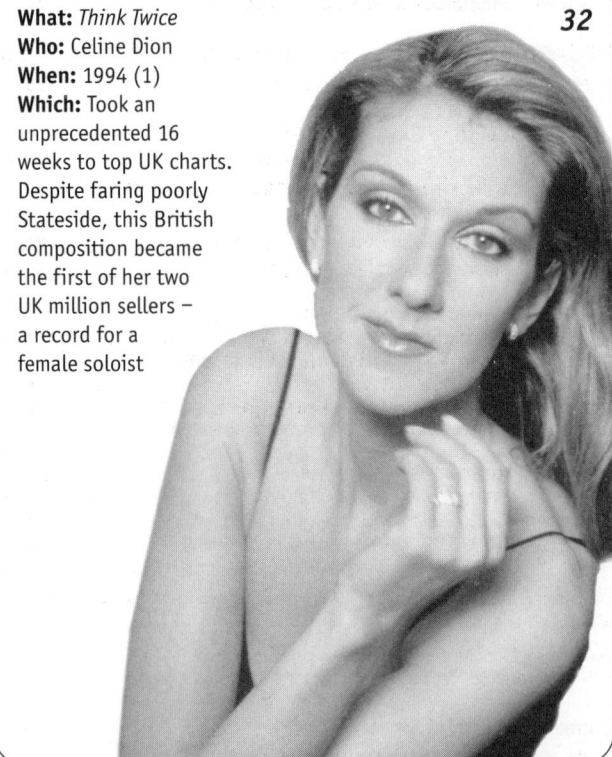

13 Feb 93		WILL WE BE LOVERS *Columbia 6589732*	31	4
24 Apr 93		ONLY TENDER LOVE *Columbia 6591842*	22	4
17 Jul 93		HANG YOUR HEAD *Columbia 6594602*	21	3
2 Apr 94		I WAS RIGHT AND YOU WERE WRONG *Columbia 6602222*	32	3
28 May 94		DIGNITY *Columbia 6604485*	20	3

Tracks on Four Bacharach and David Songs (EP): I'll Never Fall in Love Again / The Look of Love / Message to Michael / Are You There (With Another Girl). 'Dignity' in 1994 was the original recording of the song first issued in 1987 but never before a hit

DEAD DRED *UK, male instrumental/production duo* — 2 wks

5 Nov 94		DRED BASS *Moving Shadow SHADOW 50CD*	60	2

DEAD END KIDS ☺ *UK, male vocal/instrumental group* — 10 wks

26 Mar 77	●	HAVE I THE RIGHT *CBS 4972*	6	10

DEAD KENNEDYS *US, male vocal/instrumental group* — 9 wks

1 Nov 80		KILL THE POOR *Cherry Red CHERRY 16*	49	3
30 May 81		TOO DRUNK TO FUCK *Cherry Red CHERRY 24*	36	6

DEAD OR ALIVE ☺ ☺ *UK, male vocal/instrumental group* — 70 wks

24 Mar 84		THAT'S THE WAY (I LIKE IT) *Epic A 4271*	22	9
9 Mar 85	★	YOU SPIN ME ROUND (LIKE A RECORD) *Epic A 4861*	1	23
20 Apr 85		LOVER COME BACK TO ME *Epic A 6086*	11	8
29 Jun 85		IN TOO DEEP *Epic A 6360*	14	8
21 Sep 85		MY HEART GOES BANG (GET ME TO THE DOCTOR) *Epic A 6571*	23	6
20 Sep 86		BRAND NEW LOVER *Epic A 650075 7*	31	4
10 Jan 87		SOMETHING IN MY HOUSE *Epic BURNS 1*	12	7
4 Apr 87		HOOKED ON LOVE *Epic BURNS 2*	69	2
3 Sep 88		TURN ROUND AND COUNT 2 TEN *Epic BURNS 4*	70	1
22 Jul 89		COME HOME WITH ME BABY *Epic BURNS 5*	62	2

DEADLY SINS *UK/Italy, male vocal/instrumental duo* — 2 wks

30 Apr 94		WE ARE GOING ON DOWN *Ffrreedom TABCD 220*	45	2

Hazell DEAN ☺ ☺ *UK, female vocalist* — 71 wks

18 Feb 84		EVERGREEN / JEALOUS LOVE *Proto ENA 114*	63	3
21 Apr 84	●	SEARCHIN' (I GOTTA FIND A MAN) *Proto ENA 109*	6	15
28 Jul 84	●	WHATEVER I DO (WHEREVER I GO) *Proto ENA 119*	4	11
3 Nov 84		BACK IN MY ARMS (ONCE AGAIN) *Proto ENA 122*	41	4
2 Mar 85		NO FOOL (FOR LOVE) *Proto ENA 123*	41	5
12 Oct 85		THEY SAY IT'S GONNA RAIN *Parlophone R 6107*	58	4
2 Apr 88	●	WHO'S LEAVING WHO *EMI EM 45*	4	11
25 Jun 88		MAYBE (WE SHOULD CALL IT A DAY) *EMI EM 62*	15	6
24 Sep 88		TURN IT INTO LOVE *EMI EM 71*	21	7
26 Aug 89		LOVE PAINS *Lisson DOLE 12*	48	4
23 Mar 91		BETTER OFF WITHOUT YOU *Lisson DOLE 19*	72	1

Jimmy DEAN ☙ *US, male vocalist* — 17 wks

26 Oct 61	●	BIG BAD JOHN *Philips PB 1187* ▲	2	13
8 Nov 62		LITTLE BLACK BOOK *CBS AAG 122*	33	4

Letitia DEAN and Paul MEDFORD ☺
UK, female/male vocal duo — 7 wks

25 Oct 86		SOMETHING OUTA NOTHING *BBC RESL 203*	12	7

DEAR JON *UK, female/male vocal/instrumental group* — 1 wk

22 Apr 95		ONE GIFT OF LOVE *MDMC DEVCS 2*	68	1

DEATH IN VEGAS *UK, male instrumental / production duo* — 2 wks

2 Aug 97		DIRT *Concrete HARD 27CD*	61	1
1 Nov 97		ROCCO *Concrete HARD 29CDX*	51	1

DeBARGE ☺ ♪ *US, male/female vocal group* — 17 wks

6 Apr 85	●	RHYTHM OF THE NIGHT *Gordy TMG 1376*	4	14
21 Sep 85		YOU WEAR IT WELL *Gordy ZB 40345* [1]	54	3

[1] El DeBarge with DeBarge

See also El DeBARGE; Chico DeBARGE

Chico DeBARGE *US, male vocalist* — 1 wk

14 Mar 98		IGGIN' ME *Universal UND 56170*	50	1

See also DeBARGE

El DeBARGE *US, male vocalist* — 3 wks

28 Jun 86		WHO'S JOHNNY ('SHORT CIRCUIT' THEME) *Gordy ELD 1*	60	2
31 Mar 90		SECRET GARDEN *Qwest W 9992* [1]	67	1

[1] Quincy Jones featuring Al B Sure!, James Ingram, El DeBarge and Barry White

See also DeBARGE

Diana DECKER ☾ *US, female vocalist* — 10 wks

23 Oct 53	●	POPPA PICCOLINO *Columbia DB 3325*	2	8
8 Jan 54	●	POPPA PICCOLINO (re-entry) *Columbia DB 3325*	5	2

Dave DEE *UK, male vocalist* — 4 wks

14 Mar 70		MY WOMAN'S MAN *Fontana TF 1074*	42	4

See also Dave DEE, DOZY, BEAKY, MICK and TICH

Dave DEE, DOZY, BEAKY, MICK and TICH ☺ *Quirkily named UK quintet were very popular in late 1960s: Dave Dee (David Harman) (v), Dozy (Trevor Davies) (b), Beaky (John Dymond) (g), Mick (Michael Wilson) (d), Tich (Ian Amey) (g). Catchy productions and ultra-commercial songs (penned by managers Howard and Blaikley) ensured string of hits* — 141 wks

23 Dec 65		YOU MAKE IT MOVE *Fontana TF 630*	26	8
3 Mar 66	●	HOLD TIGHT *Fontana TF 671*	4	17
9 Jun 66	●	HIDEAWAY *Fontana TF 711*	10	11
15 Sep 66	●	BEND IT *Fontana TF 746*	2	12
8 Dec 66	●	SAVE ME *Fontana TF 775*	3	10
9 Mar 67		TOUCH ME TOUCH ME *Fontana TF 798*	13	9
18 May 67	●	OKAY! *Fontana TF 830*	4	11
11 Oct 67	●	ZABADAK! *Fontana TF 873*	3	14
14 Feb 68	★	LEGEND OF XANADU *Fontana TF 903*	1	12
3 Jul 68	●	LAST NIGHT IN SOHO *Fontana TF 953*	8	11
2 Oct 68		WRECK OF THE ANTOINETTE *Fontana TF 971*	14	9
5 Mar 69		DON JUAN *Fontana TF 1000*	23	9
14 May 69		SNAKE IN THE GRASS *Fontana TF 1020*	23	8

Jazzy DEE *US, male rapper / instrumentalist* — 5 wks

5 Mar 83		GET ON UP *Laurie LRS 101*	53	5

Joey DEE and the STARLITERS
US, male vocal/instrumental group — 8 wks

8 Feb 62		PEPPERMINT TWIST *Columbia DB 4758* ▲	33	8

Kiki DEE ☺ *UK, female vocalist* — 79 wks

10 Nov 73		AMOUREUSE *Rocket PIG 4*	13	13
7 Sep 74		I GOT THE MUSIC IN ME *Rocket PIG 12* [1]	19	8
12 Apr 75		(YOU DONT KNOW) HOW GLAD I AM *Rocket PIG 16* [1]	33	4
3 Jul 76	★	DON'T GO BREAKING MY HEART *Rocket ROKN 512* [2] ▲	1	14
11 Sep 76		LOVING AND FREE / AMOUREUSE (re-issue) *Rocket ROKN 515*	13	8
19 Feb 77		FIRST THING IN THE MORNING *Rocket ROKN 520*	32	5
11 Jun 77		CHICAGO *Rocket ROKN 526*	28	4
21 Feb 81		STAR *Ariola ARO 251*	13	10
23 May 81		PERFECT TIMING *Ariola ARO 257*	66	3
20 Nov 93	●	TRUE LOVE *Rocket EJSCX 32* [2]	2	10

[1] Kiki Dee Band [2] Elton John and Kiki Dee

On 18 Sep, 25 Sep and 2 Oct, 1976, 'Loving and Free' was listed by itself. 'Chicago' was one side of a double-sided chart entry, the other being 'Bite Your Lip (Get Up and Dance)' by Elton John

Nancy DEE – See BENELUX and Nancy DEE

DEEE-LITE ☺
US/Russia/Japan, male/female vocal/instrumental group **30 wks**

18 Aug 90 ●	GROOVE IS IN THE HEART/WHAT IS LOVE *Elektra EKR 114*	...2	13
24 Nov 90	POWER OF LOVE/DEEE-LITE THEME *Elektra EKR 117*	...25	7
23 Feb 91	HOW DO YOU SAY . . . LOVE/GROOVE IS IN THE HEART (re-mix) *Elektra EKR 118*	...52	2
27 Apr 91	GOOD BEAT/RIDING ON THROUGH *Elektra EKR 122*	...53	3
13 Jun 92	RUNAWAY *Elektra EKR 148*	...45	3
30 Jul 94	PICNIC IN THE SUMMERTIME *Elektra EKR 186CD1*	...43	2

'What Is Love' only listed from 25 Aug, 1990

DEEJAY PUNK-ROC *US, male DJ/producer* **4 wks**

21 Mar 98	DEAD HUSBAND *Independiente ISOM 9MS*	...71	1
9 May 98	MY BEATBOX *Independiente ISOM 12MS*	...43	1
8 Aug 98	FAR OUT *Independiente ISOM 17MS*	...43	2

DEEJAY SVEN – See MC Miker 'G' and Deejay SVEN

Carol DEENE *UK, female vocalist* **25 wks**

26 Oct 61	SAD MOVIES *HMV POP 922*	...44	3
25 Jan 62	NORMAN *HMV POP 973*	...24	8
5 Jul 62	JOHNNY GET ANGRY *HMV POP 1027*	...32	4
23 Aug 62	SOME PEOPLE *HMV POP 1058*	...25	10

Scotti DEEP *US, male producer / instrumentalist* **1 wk**

15 Mar 97	BROOKLYN BEATS *Xtravaganza 0090095*	...67	1

DEEP BLUE *UK, male producer – Sean O'Keefe* **2 wks**

16 Apr 94	HELICOPTER TUNE *Moving Shadow SHADOW 41CD*	...68	2

DEEP BLUE SOMETHING ❂
US, male vocal/instrumental group **17 wks**

6 Jul 96	BREAKFAST AT TIFFANY'S *Interscope IND 80032*	...55	2
21 Sep 96 ★	BREAKFAST AT TIFFANY'S (re-entry) *Interscope IND 80032*	...1	12
7 Dec 96	JOSEY *Interscope IND 95518*	...27	3

DEEP C *UK, male/female vocal/instrumental group* **3 wks**

19 Jan 91	AFRICAN REIGN *M & G MAGS 4*	...75	1
8 Jun 91	CHILL TO THE PANIC *M & G MAGS 10*	...73	2

DEEP CREED '94 *US, male producer – Armand van Helden* **1 wk**

7 May 94	CAN U FEEL IT *Eastern Bloc BLOCCD 005*	...59	1

DEEP DISH *US, male instrumental/production duo* **4 wks**

26 Oct 96	STAY GOLD *Deconstruction 74321418222*	...41	1
1 Nov 97	STRANDED *Deconstruction 74321512232*	...60	1
3 Oct 98	THE FUTURE OF THE FUTURE (STAY GOLD) *Deconstruction 74321616252* [1]	...31	2

[1] Deep Dish with Everything but the Girl

DEEP FEELING *UK, male vocal/instrumental group* **5 wks**

25 Apr 70	DO YOU LOVE ME *Page One POF 165*	...45	1
9 May 70	DO YOU LOVE ME (re-entry) *Page One POF 165*	...34	4

DEEP FOREST ⊛ ☺ *France, male instrumental duo* **14 wks**

5 Feb 94 ●	SWEET LULLABY *Columbia 6599242*	...10	6
21 May 94	DEEP FOREST *Columbia 6604115*	...20	4
23 Jul 94	SAVANNA DANCE *Columbia 6606355*	...28	2
24 Jun 95	MARTA'S SONG *Columbia 6621402*	...26	2

DEEP PURPLE ⤮ *UK, male vocal/instrumental group* **85 wks**

15 Aug 70 ●	BLACK NIGHT *Harvest HAR 5020*	...2	21
27 Feb 71 ●	STRANGE KIND OF WOMAN *Harvest HAR 5033*	...8	12
13 Nov 71	FIREBALL *Harvest HAR 5045*	...15	13
1 Apr 72	NEVER BEFORE *Purple PUR 102*	...35	6
16 Apr 77	SMOKE ON THE WATER *Purple PUR 132*	...21	7

15 Oct 77	NEW LIVE AND RARE (EP) *Purple PUR 135*	...31	4
7 Oct 78	NEW LIVE AND RARE II (EP) *Purple PUR 137*	...45	3
2 Aug 80	BLACK NIGHT (re-issue) *Harvest HAR 5210*	...43	6
1 Nov 80	NEW LIVE AND RARE VOLUME 3 EP *Harvest SHEP 101*	...48	3
26 Jan 85	PERFECT STRANGERS *Polydor POSP 719*	...48	3
15 Jun 85	KNOCKING AT YOUR BACK DOOR/PERFECT STRANGERS *Polydor POSP 749*	...68	1
18 Jun 88	HUSH *Polydor PO 4*	...62	2
20 Oct 90	KING OF DREAMS *RCA PB 49247*	...70	1
2 Mar 91	LOVE CONQUERS ALL *RCA PB 49225*	...57	2
24 Jun 95	BLACK NIGHT (re-mix) *EMI CDEM 382*	...66	1

Tracks on New Live and Rare (EP): Black Night (Live)/Painted Horse/When a Blind Man Cries. New Live and Rare II (EP): Burn (Edited Version)/Coronarias Redig/ Mistreated (Live)/Interpolating Rock Me Baby. New Live and Rare Volume 3 (EP): Smoke on the Water/Bird Has Flown/Grabsplatter

DEEP RIVER BOYS *US, male vocal group* **1 wk**

7 Dec 56	THAT'S RIGHT *HMV POP 263*	...29	1

Rick DEES and his CAST OF IDIOTS ⊙
US, male vocalist with male/female vocal/instrumental group **9 wks**

18 Sep 76 ●	DISCO DUCK (PART ONE) *RSO 2090 204* ▲	...6	9

DEETAH ⬅ *Chile/Sweden, female vocalist* **8 wks**

26 Sep 98	RELAX *ffrr FCDP 345*	...11	8

DEF LEPPARD ⤮ *Mainstream UK rock stalwarts who wooed USA before their homeland: Joe Elliott (v), Phil Collen (g – from 1983), Steve Clark (g) (d. 1991), Rick Savage (b), Rick Allen (d). In USA achieved unique feat of two consecutive albums selling more than eight million* **110 wks**

17 Nov 79	WASTED *Vertigo 6059 247*	...61	3
23 Feb 80	HELLO AMERICA *Vertigo LEPP 1*	...45	4
5 Feb 83	PHOTOGRAPH *Vertigo VER 5*	...66	3
27 Aug 83	ROCK OF AGES *Vertigo VER 6*	...41	4
1 Aug 87 ●	ANIMAL *Bludgeon Riffola LEP 1*	...6	9
19 Sep 87	POUR SOME SUGAR ON ME *Bludgeon Riffola LEP 2*	...18	6
28 Nov 87	HYSTERIA *Bludgeon Riffola LEP 3*	...26	5
9 Jan 88	HYSTERIA (re-entry) *Bludgeon Riffola LEP 3*	...74	1
9 Apr 88	ARMAGEDDON IT *Bludgeon Riffola LEP 4*	...20	5
16 Jul 88	LOVE BITES *Bludgeon Riffola LEP 5* ▲	...11	8
11 Feb 89	ROCKET *Bludgeon Riffola LEP 6*	...15	7
28 Mar 92 ●	LET'S GET ROCKED *Bludgeon Riffola DEF 7*	...2	7
27 Jun 92	MAKE LOVE LIKE A MAN *Bludgeon Riffola LEP 7*	...12	5
12 Sep 92	HAVE YOU EVER NEEDED SOMEONE SO BAD *Bludgeon Riffola LEP 8*	...16	5
30 Jan 93	HEAVEN IS *Bludgeon Riffola LEPCD 9*	...13	5
1 May 93	TONIGHT *Bludgeon Riffola LEPCD 10*	...34	3
18 Sep 93	TWO STEPS BEHIND *Bludgeon Riffola LEPCD 12*	...32	4
15 Jan 94	ACTION *Bludgeon Riffola LEPCD 13*	...14	5
14 Oct 95 ●	WHEN LOVE AND HATE COLLIDE *Bludgeon Riffola LEPCD 14*	...2	10
4 May 96	SLANG *Bludgeon Riffola LEPCD 15*	...17	5
13 Jul 96	WORK IT OUT *Bludgeon Riffola LEPCD 16*	...22	3
28 Sep 96	ALL I WANT IS EVERYTHING *Bludgeon Riffola LEPCD 17*	...38	2
30 Nov 96	BREATHE A SIGH *Bludgeon Riffola LEPCD 18*	...43	1

DEFINITION OF SOUND ⬅ ☺ *UK, male rap duo* **25 wks**

9 Mar 91	WEAR YOUR LOVE LIKE HEAVEN *Circa YR 61*	...17	9
1 Jun 91	NOW IS TOMORROW *Circa YR 66*	...46	4
8 Feb 92	MOIRA JANE'S CAFE *Circa YR 80*	...34	4
19 Sep 92	WHAT ARE YOU UNDER *Circa YR 95*	...68	1
14 Nov 92	CAN I GET OVER *Circa YR 97*	...61	2
20 May 95	BOOM BOOM *Fontana DOSCD 1*	...59	1
2 Dec 95	PASS THE VIBES *Fontana DOSCD 2*	...23	3
24 Feb 96	CHILD *Fontana DOSCD 3*	...48	1

DEFTONES *US, male vocal/instrumental group* **3 wks**

21 Mar 98	MY OWN SUMMER (SHOVE IT) *Maverick W 0432CD*	...29	2
11 Jul 98	BE QUIET AND DRIVE (FAR AWAY) *Maverick W 0445CD*	...50	1

UK No 1 ★   UK Top 10 ●   UK million seller ◆   UK entry at No 1 ■   US No 1 ▲

DEGREES OF MOTION featuring BITI ☺ ⬤
US, female vocal group   **21 wks**

25 Apr 92	DO YOU WANT IT RIGHT NOW *ffrr F 184*	31	5
18 Jul 92	SHINE ON *ffrr F 192* [1]	43	3
7 Nov 92	SOUL FREEDOM – FREE YOUR SOUL *ffrr FX 201*	64	1
19 Mar 94 ⬤	SHINE ON (re-mix) *ffrr FCD 229*	8	8
25 Jun 94	DO YOU WANT IT RIGHT NOW (re-mix) *ffrr FCD 236*	26	4

[1] Degrees of Motion featuring Biti with Kit West

DEJA *US, male / female vocal duo*   **1 wk**

29 Aug 87	SERIOUS *10 TEN 132*	75	1

See also AURRA

DEJA VU *UK, male vocal / instrumental duo*   **1 wk**

5 Feb 94	WHY WHY WHY *Cowboy RODEO 941CD*	57	1

Desmond DEKKER and the ACES 🌴
Jamaica, male vocal/instrumental group   **71 wks**

12 Jul 67	007 *Pyramid PYR 6004*	14	11
19 Mar 69 ★	ISRAELITES *Pyramid PYR 6058*	1	14
25 Jun 69 ⬤	IT MIEK *Pyramid PYR 6068*	7	11
2 Jul 69	ISRAELITES (re-entry) *Pyramid PYR 6058*	45	1
10 Jan 70	PICKNEY GAL *Pyramid PYR 6078*	42	3
22 Aug 70 ⬤	YOU CAN GET IT IF YOU REALLY WANT *Trojan TR 7777* [1]	2	15
10 May 75 ⬤	ISRAELITES (re-issue) *Cactus CT 57* [1]	10	9
30 Aug 75	SING A LITTLE SONG *Cactus CT 73* [1]	16	7

[1] Desmond Dekker

DEL AMITRI ⬤ ✓ *UK, male vocal/instrumental group*   **69 wks**

19 Aug 89	KISS THIS THING GOODBYE *A & M AM 515*	59	2
13 Jan 90	NOTHING EVER HAPPENS *A & M AM 536*	11	9
24 Mar 90	KISS THIS THING GOODBYE (re-issue) *A & M AM 551*	43	4
16 Jun 90	MOVE AWAY JIMMY BLUE *A & M AM 555*	36	6
3 Nov 90	SPIT IN THE RAIN *A & M AM 589*	21	6
9 May 92	ALWAYS THE LAST TO KNOW *A & M AM 870*	13	7
11 Jul 92	BE MY DOWNFALL *A & M AM 884*	30	4
12 Sep 92	JUST LIKE A MAN *A & M AM 0057*	25	4
23 Jan 93	WHEN YOU WERE YOUNG *A & M AMCD 0132*	20	3
18 Feb 95	HERE AND NOW *A & M 5809692*	21	4
29 Apr 95	DRIVING WITH THE BRAKES ON *A & M 5810072*	18	4
8 Jul 95	ROLL TO ME *A & M 5811312*	22	4
28 Oct 95	TELL HER THIS *A & M 5812172*	32	2
21 Jun 97	NOT WHERE IT'S AT *A & M 5822532*	21	3
6 Dec 97	SOME OTHER SUCKER'S PARADE *A&M 5824352*	46	1
13 Jun 98	DON'T COME HOME TOO SOON *A&M 5827052*	15	4
5 Sep 98	CRY TO BE FOUND *A&M MERCD 513*	40	2

DELAGE *UK, female vocal group*   **2 wks**

15 Dec 90	ROCK THE BOAT *PWL / Polydor PO 113*	63	2

DELAKOTA *UK, male vocal/instrumental duo*   **2 wks**

18 Jul 98	THE ROCK *Go.Beat GOBCD 10*	60	1
19 Sep 98	C'MON CINCINNATI *Go.Beat GOBCD 11* [1]	55	1

[1] Delakota featuring Rose Smith

DELANEY and BONNIE and FRIENDS featuring Eric CLAPTON –
See Eric CLAPTON

DELEGATION *UK, male vocal/instrumental group*   **7 wks**

23 Apr 77	WHERE IS THE LOVE (WE USED TO KNOW) *State STAT 40*	22	6
20 Aug 77	YOU'VE BEEN DOING ME WRONG *State STAT 55*	49	1

DELFONICS ✓ *US, male vocal group*   **23 wks**

10 Apr 71	DIDN'T I (BLOW YOUR MIND THIS TIME) *Bell 1099*	43	1
24 Apr 71	DIDN'T I (BLOW YOUR MIND THIS TIME) (re-entry) *Bell 1099*	22	8

10 Jul 71	LA-LA MEANS I LOVE YOU *Bell 1165*	19	10
16 Oct 71	READY OR NOT HERE I COME *Bell 1175*	41	4

DELGADOS *UK, male / female vocal / instrumental group*   **1 wk**

23 May 98	PULL THE WIRES FROM THE WALL *Chemikal CHEM 023CD*	69	1

DELIRIOUS? ⬤ *UK, male vocal/instrumental group*   **9 wks**

1 Mar 97	WHITE RIBBON DAY *Furious? CDFURY 1*	41	2
17 May 97	DEEPER *Furious? CDFURY 2*	20	3
26 Jul 97	PROMISE *Furious? CDFURY 3*	20	2
15 Nov 97	DEEPER (re-entry) *Furious? CXFURY 4*	36	2

'DELIVERANCE' SOUNDTRACK 🎵 *US, male instrumental duo –*
Eric Weissberg on banjo and Steve Mandell on guitar   **7 wks**

31 Mar 73	DUELLING BANJOS *Warner Bros. K 16223*	17	7

DELLS 🎵 *US, male vocal group*   **9 wks**

16 Jul 69	I CAN SING A RAINBOW – LOVE IS BLUE (MEDLEY) *Chess CRS 8099*	15	9

DELRONS – See REPARATA and the DELRONS

DELTA – See David MORALES; Crystal WATERS

DELUXE *US, female vocalist*   **1 wk**

18 Mar 89	JUST A LITTLE MORE *Unyque UNQ 5*	74	1

DEM 2 *UK, male production duo*   **2 wks**

24 Oct 98	DESTINY *Locked On LOX 101CD*	58	2

DEMOLITION MAN – See PRIZNA featuring DEMOLITION MAN

Chaka DEMUS and PLIERS 🌴 *Jamaica, male vocal duo*   **55 wks**

12 Jun 93 ⬤	TEASE ME *Mango CIDM 806*	3	15
18 Sep 93 ⬤	SHE DON'T LET NOBODY *Mango CIDM 810*	4	10
18 Dec 93 ★	TWIST AND SHOUT *Mango CIDM 814* [1]	1	13
12 Mar 94	MURDER SHE WROTE *Mango CIDM 812*	27	4
18 Jun 94	I WANNA BE YOUR MAN *Mango CIDM 817*	19	6
27 Aug 94	GAL WINE *Mango CIDM 818*	20	4
1 Apr 95	TWIST AND SHOUT (re-entry) *Mango CIDM 814* [1]	67	1
31 Aug 96	EVERY KINDA PEOPLE *Island Jamaica IJCD 2005*	47	1
30 Aug 97	EVERY LITTLE THING SHE DOES IS MAGIC *Virgin VSCDT 1654*	51	1

[1] Chaka Demus and Pliers featuring Jack Radics and Taxi Gang

Terry DENE ⬤ *UK, male vocalist*   **20 wks**

7 Jun 57	A WHITE SPORT COAT *Decca F 10895*	18	6
19 Jul 57	START MOVIN' *Decca F 10914*	15	8
26 Jul 57	A WHITE SPORT COAT (re-entry) *Decca F 10895*	30	1
16 May 58	STAIRWAY OF LOVE *Decca F 11016*	16	5

DENISE and JOHNNY ⬤ *UK, male/female vocal duo*   **1 wk**

26 Dec 98 ⬤	ESPECIALLY FOR YOU *RCA 74321644722*	3†	1

Cathy DENNIS ☺ *UK, female vocalist*   **68 wks**

21 Oct 89	C'MON AND GET MY LOVE *ffrr F 117* [1]	15	10
7 Apr 90	THAT'S THE WAY OF THE WORLD *ffrr F 132* [1]	48	3
4 May 91 ⬤	TOUCH ME (ALL NIGHT LONG) *Polydor CATH 3*	5	10
20 Jul 91	JUST ANOTHER DREAM *Polydor CATH 2*	13	7
5 Oct 91	TOO MANY WALLS *Polydor CATH 4*	17	7
7 Dec 91	EVERYBODY MOVE *Polydor Cath 5*	25	8
29 Aug 92	YOU LIED TO ME *Polydor CATH 6*	34	4
21 Nov 92	IRRESISTIBLE *Polydor CATH 7*	24	6
6 Feb 93	FALLING *Polydor CATHD 8*	32	2
12 Feb 94	WHY *ffrr FCD 227* [1]	23	3
10 Aug 96	WEST END PAD *Polydor 5752812*	25	2

1 Mar 97	WATERLOO SUNSET *Polydor 5759612*	11	5
21 Jun 97	WHEN DREAMS TURN TO DUST *Polydor 5711852*	43	1

[1] D Mob with Cathy Dennis

Jackie DENNIS ⓞ *UK, male vocalist* — 10 wks

14 Mar 58 ●	LA DEE DAH *Decca F 10992*	4	9
27 Jun 58	PURPLE PEOPLE EATER *Decca F 11033*	29	1

Stefan DENNIS ⓞ *Australia, male vocalist* — 8 wks

6 May 89	DON'T IT MAKE YOU FEEL GOOD *Sublime LIME 105*	16	7
7 Oct 89	THIS LOVE AFFAIR *Sublime LIME 113*	67	1

DENNISONS *UK, male vocal/instrumental group* — 13 wks

15 Aug 63	BE MY GIRL *Decca F 11691*	46	6
7 May 64	WALKIN' THE DOG *Decca F 11880*	36	7

Richard DENTON and Martin COOK *UK, male orchestra leaders – instrumental duo, guitar and keyboards* — 7 wks

15 Apr 78	THEME FROM 'THE HONG KONG BEAT' *BBC RESL 52*	25	7

John DENVER ⓒ *US, male vocalist* — 22 wks

17 Aug 74 ★	ANNIE'S SONG *RCA APBO 0295* ▲	1	13
12 Dec 81	PERHAPS LOVE *CBS A 1905* [1]	46	9

[1] Placido Domingo with John Denver

Karl DENVER ⓞ *Versatile Scottish singer with multi-octave vocal range, b. Angus McKenzie, 16 December, 1934, Glasgow (d. 21 Dec 1998). This unique artist, whose yodel-laced style added colour and contrast to the charts, reached the Top 20 with his first five singles* — 127 wks

22 Jun 61 ●	MARCHETA *Decca F 11360*	8	20
19 Oct 61 ●	MEXICALI ROSE *Decca F 11395*	8	11
25 Jan 62 ●	WIMOWEH *Decca F 11420*	4	17
22 Feb 62 ●	NEVER GOODBYE *Decca F 11431*	9	18
7 Jun 62	A LITTLE LOVE A LITTLE KISS *Decca F 11470*	19	10
20 Sep 62	BLUE WEEKEND *Decca F 11505*	33	5
21 Mar 63	CAN YOU FORGIVE ME *Decca F 11608*	32	8
13 Jun 63	INDIAN LOVE CALL *Decca F 11674*	32	8
22 Aug 63	STILL *Decca F 11720*	13	15
5 Mar 64	MY WORLD OF BLUE *Decca F 11828*	29	6
4 Jun 64	LOVE ME WITH ALL YOUR HEART *Decca F 11905*	37	6
9 Jun 90	LAZYITIS – ONE ARMED BOXER *Factory FAC 2227* [1]	46	3

[1] Happy Mondays and Karl Denver

DEODATO ✏ 🎵 *US, male multi-instrumentalist* — 9 wks

5 May 73 ●	ALSO SPRACH ZARATHUSTRA (2001) *Creed Taylor CTI 4000*	7	9

DEPARTMENT S *UK, male vocal/instrumental group* — 13 wks

4 Apr 81	IS VIC THERE? *Demon D 1003*	22	10
11 Jul 81	GOING LEFT RIGHT *Stiff BUY 118*	55	3

DEPECHE MODE ☺ 🎵 *Consistently successful synth-led Essex band: Dave Gahan (v), Martin Gore (syn), Andy Fletcher (b, syn), Vince Clarke (syn – replaced 1982 by Alan Wilder). One of the world's best-selling groups, who reached the Top 10 UK albums with first dozen releases* — 225 wks

4 Apr 81	DREAMING OF ME *Mute MUTE 013*	57	4
13 Jun 81	NEW LIFE *Mute MUTE 014*	11	15
19 Sep 81 ●	JUST CAN'T GET ENOUGH *Mute MUTE 016*	8	10
13 Feb 82 ●	SEE YOU *Mute MUTE 018*	6	10
8 May 82	THE MEANING OF LOVE *Mute MUTE 022*	12	8
28 Aug 82	LEAVE IN SILENCE *Mute BONG 1*	18	10
12 Feb 83	GET THE BALANCE RIGHT *Mute 7BONG 2*	13	8
23 Jul 83 ●	EVERYTHING COUNTS *Mute 7BONG 3*	6	11
1 Oct 83	LOVE IN ITSELF *Mute 7BONG 4*	21	7
24 Mar 84 ●	PEOPLE ARE PEOPLE *Mute 7BONG 5*	4	10
1 Sep 84 ●	MASTER AND SERVANT *Mute 7BONG 6*	9	9
10 Nov 84	SOMEBODY/BLASPHEMOUS RUMOURS *Mute 7BONG 7*	16	6
11 May 85	SHAKE THE DISEASE *Mute BONG 8*	18	9

28 Sep 85	IT'S CALLED A HEART *Mute BONG 9*	18	4
22 Feb 86	STRIPPED *Mute BONG 10*	15	5
26 Apr 86	A QUESTION OF LUST *Mute BONG 11*	28	5
23 Aug 86	A QUESTION OF TIME *Mute BONG 12*	17	6
9 May 87	STRANGELOVE *Mute BONG 13*	16	5
5 Sep 87	NEVER LET ME DOWN AGAIN *Mute BONG 14*	22	4
9 Jan 88	BEHIND THE WHEEL *Mute BONG 15*	21	5
28 May 88	LITTLE 15 (IMPORT) *Mute LITTLE 15*	60	2
25 Feb 89	EVERYTHING COUNTS *Mute BONG 16*	22	7
9 Sep 89	PERSONAL JESUS *Mute BONG 17*	13	8
17 Feb 90 ●	ENJOY THE SILENCE *Mute BONG 18*	6	9
19 May 90	POLICY OF TRUTH *Mute BONG 19*	16	6
29 Sep 90	WORLD IN MY EYES *Mute BONG 20*	17	6
27 Feb 93 ●	I FEEL YOU *Mute CDBONG 21*	8	7
8 May 93	WALKING IN MY SHOES *Mute CDBONG 22*	14	4
25 Sep 93 ●	CONDEMNATION *Mute CDBONG 23*	9	4
22 Jan 94 ●	IN YOUR ROOM *Mute CDBONG 24*	8	4
15 Feb 97 ●	BARREL OF A GUN *Mute CDBONG 25*	4	4
12 Apr 97 ●	IT'S NO GOOD *Mute CDBONG 26*	5	5
28 Jun 97	HOME *Mute CDBONG 27*	23	3
1 Nov 97	USELESS *Mute CDBONG 28*	28	2
19 Sep 98	ONLY WHEN I LOSE MYSELF *Mute CDBONG 29*	17	3

'BONG 16' is a live version of 'BONG 3'

DEPTH CHARGE *UK, male producer – Jonathan Kane* — 1 wk

29 Jul 95	LEGEND OF THE GOLDEN SNAKE *DC DC 01CD*	75	1

DEREK and the DOMINOES – See Eric CLAPTON

Kevin DESIMONE – See Barry MANILOW

DESIRELESS ⓞ ☺ *France, female vocalist* — 19 wks

31 Oct 87	VOYAGE VOYAGE *CBS DESI 1*	53	6
14 May 88 ●	VOYAGE VOYAGE (re-mix) *CBS DESI 2*	5	13

DESIYA featuring Melissa YIANNAKOU *UK, male/female vocal/instrumental duo* — 1 wk

1 Feb 92	COMIN' ON STRONG *Black Market 12MKT 2*	74	1

DESKEE *UK, male instrumentalist* — 3 wks

3 Feb 90	LET THERE BE HOUSE *Big One VBIG 19*	52	2
8 Sep 90	DANCE, DANCE *Big One VBIG 22*	74	1

DES'REE ⓞ 🎤 *UK, female vocalist* — 61 wks

31 Aug 91	FEEL SO HIGH *Dusted Sound 6573667*	51	5
11 Jan 92	FEEL SO HIGH (re-issue) *Dusted Sound 6576897*	13	7
21 Mar 92	MIND ADVENTURES *Dusted Sound 6578637*	43	3
27 Jun 92	WHY SHOULD I LOVE YOU *Dusted Sound 6580917*	44	3
19 Jun 93	DELICATE *Columbia 6593312* [1]	14	6
9 Apr 94	YOU GOTTA BE *Dusted Sound 6601342*	20	7
18 Jun 94	I AIN'T MOVIN' *Dusted Sound 6604672*	44	3
3 Sep 94	LITTLE CHILD *Dusted Sound 6604515*	69	1
11 Mar 95	YOU GOTTA BE (re-mix) *Dusted Sound 6613215*	14	8
20 Jun 98 ●	LIFE *Sony S2 6659302*	8	15
7 Nov 98	WHAT'S YOUR SIGN? *Sony S2 6665162*	19	3

[1] Terence Trent D'Arby featuring Des'ree

DESTINY'S CHILD 🆁🅰🅱 *US, female vocal trio* — 14 wks

28 Mar 98 ●	NO, NO, NO *Columbia 6656592*	5	8
11 Jul 98	WITH ME *Columbia 6661472*	19	3
7 Nov 98	SHE'S GONE *Columbia 6664915* [1]	24	3

[1] Matthew Marsden featuring Destiny's Child

DESTRY – See ZOO EXPERIENCE featuring DESTRY

Marcella DETROIT ⓞ *US, female vocalist* — 16 wks

12 Mar 94	I BELIEVE *London LONCD 347*	11	8
14 May 94	AIN'T NOTHING LIKE THE REAL THING *London LONCD 350* [1]	24	4

| 16 Jul 94 | I'M NO ANGEL London LOCDP 351 | 33 | 4 |

[1] Marcella Detroit and Elton John

DETROIT EMERALDS ✎ US, male vocal group — 44 wks

10 Feb 73 ●	FEEL THE NEED IN ME Janus 6146 020	4	15
5 May 73	YOU WANT IT YOU GOT IT Westbound 6146 103	12	9
11 Aug 73	I THINK OF YOU Westbound 6146 104	27	9
18 Jun 77	FEEL THE NEED Atlantic K 10945	12	11

'Feel the Need' in 1977 was a re-recording

DETROIT SPINNERS ✎ US, male vocal group — 93 wks

14 Nov 70	IT'S A SHAME Tamla Motown TMG 755 [1]	20	11
21 Apr 73	COULD IT BE I'M FALLING IN LOVE Atlantic K 10283	11	11
29 Sep 73 ●	GHETTO CHILD Atlantic K 10359	7	10
19 Oct 74	THEN CAME YOU Atlantic K 10495 [2] ▲	29	6
11 Sep 76	THE RUBBERBAND MAN Atlantic K 10807	16	11
29 Jan 77	WAKE UP SUSAN Atlantic K 10799	29	6
7 May 77	COULD IT BE I'M FALLING IN LOVE (EP) Atlantic K 10935	32	3
23 Feb 80 ★	WORKING MY WAY BACK TO YOU – FORGIVE ME GIRL – (MEDLEY) Atlantic K 11432	1	14
10 May 80	BODY LANGUAGE Atlantic K 11392	40	7
28 Jun 80 ●	CUPID – I'VE LOVED YOU FOR A LONG TIME (MEDLEY) Atlantic K 11498	4	10
24 Jun 95	I'LL BE AROUND Cooltempo CDCOOL 306 [3]	30	4

[1] Motown Spinners [2] Dionne Warwick and the Detroit Spinners [3] Rappin' 4-Tay featuring the Spinners

Group was known simply as the Spinners in the USA
Tracks on Could It Be I'm Falling in Love (EP): Could It Be I'm Falling in Love / You're Throwing a Good Love Away / Games People Play / Lazy Susan

DETROIT WHEELS – See Mitch RYDER and the DETROIT WHEELS

DEUCE ☺ UK, male/female vocal group — 23 wks

21 Jan 95	CALL IT LOVE London LONCD 355	11	10
22 Apr 95 ●	I NEED YOU London LONCD 365	10	5
19 Aug 95	ON THE BIBLE London LONCD 368	13	6
29 Jun 96	NO SURRENDER Love This LUVTHISCD 10	29	2

dEUS Belgium, male vocal/instrumental group — 5 wks

11 Feb 95	HOTEL LOUNGE (BE THE DEATH OF ME) Island CID 603	55	1
13 Jul 96	THEME FROM TURNPIKE (EP) Island CID 630	68	1
19 Oct 96	LITTLE ARITHMETICS Island CID 643	44	2
15 Mar 97	ROSES Island CID 645	56	1

Tracks on Theme from Turnpike EP: Theme from Turnpike / Worried About Satan / Overflow / My Little Contessa

Sidney DEVINE UK, male vocalist — 1 wk

| 1 Apr 78 | SCOTLAND FOREVER Philips SCOT 1 | 48 | 1 |

DEVO US, male vocal/instrumental group — 23 wks

22 Apr 78	(I CAN'T ME GET NO) SATISFACTION Stiff BOY 1	41	8
13 May 78	JOCKO HOMO Stiff DEV 1	62	3
12 Aug 78	BE STIFF Stiff BOY 2	71	1
2 Sep 78	COME BACK JONEE Virgin VS 223	60	4
22 Nov 80	WHIP IT Virgin VS 383	51	7

Sheila B DEVOTION ◢ France, female vocalist — 33 wks

11 Mar 78	SINGIN' IN THE RAIN PART 1 Carrere EMI 2751	11	13
22 Jul 78	YOU LIGHT MY FIRE Carrere EMI 2828	44	6
24 Nov 79	SPACER Carrere CAR 128	18	14

DEVOTIONS – See BELLE and the DEVOTIONS

Howard DEVOTO – See BUZZCOCKS

DEXY'S MIDNIGHT RUNNERS ☺ ✎ UK, male vocal/instrumental group — 93 wks

19 Jan 80	DANCE STANCE Oddball Productions R 6028	40	6
22 Mar 80 ★	GENO Late Night Feelings R 6033	1	14
12 Jul 80 ●	THERE THERE MY DEAR Late Night Feelings R 6038	7	9
21 Mar 81	PLAN B Parlophone R 6046	58	2
11 Jul 81	SHOW ME Mercury DEXYS 6	16	9
20 Mar 82	THE CELTIC SOUL BROTHERS Mercury DEXYS 8 [1]	45	4
3 Jul 82 ★	COME ON EILEEN Mercury DEXYS 9 [1] ◆ ▲	1	17
2 Oct 82 ●	JACKIE WILSON SAID (I'M IN HEAVEN WHEN YOU SMILE) Mercury DEXYS 10 [2]	5	7
4 Dec 82	LET'S GET THIS STRAIGHT (FROM THE START)/OLD Mercury DEXYS 11 [2]	17	9
2 Apr 83	THE CELTIC SOUL BROTHERS Mercury DEXYS 12 [2]	20	6
22 Nov 86	BECAUSE OF YOU Mercury BRUSH 1	13	10

[1] Dexy's Midnight Runners with the Emerald Express [2] Kevin Rowland and Dexy's Midnight Runners

DEXYS 12 is a different version from DEXYS 8

Tony DI BART ☺ ☺ UK, male vocalist — 19 wks

9 Apr 94 ★	THE REAL THING Cleveland City Blues CCBCD 15001	1	12
20 Aug 94	DO IT Cleveland City Blues CCBCD 15003	21	4
20 May 95	WHY DID YA Cleveland City Blues CCBCD 15004	46	1
2 Mar 96	TURN YOUR LOVE AROUND Cleveland City Blues CCBCD 15006	66	1
17 Oct 98	THE REAL THING Cleveland City CLECD 13050	51	1

Jim DIAMOND ☺ UK, male vocalist — 30 wks

3 Nov 84 ★	I SHOULD HAVE KNOWN BETTER A & M AM 220	1	13
2 Feb 85	I SLEEP ALONE AT NIGHT A & M AM 229	72	1
18 May 85	REMEMBER I LOVE YOU A & M AM 247	42	5
22 Feb 86 ●	HI HO SILVER A & M AM 296	5	11

Neil DIAMOND ℂ World-renowned singer/guitarist/songwriter, b. Noah Kaminsky, 24 January, 1941, Brooklyn. First found international fame as writer of 'I'm a Believer' (Monkees), before going on to become one of world's most popular live artists and biggest-selling album acts — 121 wks

7 Nov 70 ●	CRACKLIN' ROSIE Uni UN 529 ▲	3	17
20 Feb 71 ●	SWEET CAROLINE Uni UN 531	8	11
8 May 71 ●	I AM . . . I SAID Uni UN 532	4	12
13 May 72	SONG SUNG BLUE Uni UN 538 ▲	14	13
14 Aug 76	IF YOU KNOW WHAT I MEAN CBS 4398	35	4
23 Oct 76	BEAUTIFUL NOISE CBS 4601	13	9
24 Dec 77	DESIREE CBS 5869	39	6
25 Nov 78 ●	YOU DON'T BRING ME FLOWERS CBS 6803 [1] ▲	5	12
3 Mar 79	FOREVER IN BLUE JEANS CBS 7047	16	12
15 Nov 80	LOVE ON THE ROCKS Capitol CL 16173	17	12
14 Feb 81	HELLO AGAIN Capitol CL 16176	51	4
20 Nov 82	HEARTLIGHT CBS A 2814	47	7
21 Nov 92	MORNING HAS BROKEN Columbia 6588267	36	2

[1] Barbra and Neil

Barbra was Barbra Streisand

Gregg DIAMOND BIONIC BOOGIE US, male/female vocal group — 3 wks

| 20 Jan 79 | CREAM (ALWAYS RISES TO THE TOP) Polydor POSP 18 | 61 | 3 |

DIAMOND HEAD UK, male vocal/instrumental group — 2 wks

| 11 Sep 82 | IN THE HEAT OF THE NIGHT MCA DHM 102 | 67 | 2 |

DIAMONDS ☺ Canada/US, male vocal group — 17 wks

| 31 May 57 ● | LITTLE DARLIN' Mercury MT 148 | 3 | 17 |

DIANA – See Diana ROSS

DICK and DEEDEE US, male/female vocal duo — 3 wks

| 26 Oct 61 | THE MOUNTAIN'S HIGH London HLG 9408 | 37 | 3 |

UK No 1 ★   UK Top 10 ●   UK million seller ◆   UK entry at No 1 ■   US No 1 ▲

Charles DICKENS *UK, male vocalist*　　8 wks

1 Jul 65	THAT'S THE WAY LOVE GOES *Pye 7N 15887*	37	8

Gwen DICKEY ☺ 🎤 *US, female vocalist*　　13 wks

27 Jan 90	CAR WASH *Swanyard SYR 7*	72	2
2 Jul 94	AIN'T NOBODY (LOVES ME BETTER) *X-clusive XCLU 010CD* [1]	21	4
14 Feb 98	WISHING ON A STAR *Northwestside 74321554632* [2]	13	4
31 Oct 98	CAR WASH *MCA MCSTD 48096* [3]	18	3

[1] KWS and Gwen Dickey [2] Jay-Z featuring Gwen Dickey [3] Rose Royce featuring Gwen Dickey

'Car Wash' 1998 is a re-recording of the original hit

Neville DICKIE *UK, male instrumentalist – piano*　　10 wks

25 Oct 69	ROBIN'S RETURN *Major Minor MM 644*	33	7
20 Dec 69	ROBIN'S RETURN (re-entry) *Major Minor MM 644*	43	3

DICKIES ✎ *US, male vocal/instrumental group*　　28 wks

16 Dec 78	SILENT NIGHT *A & M AMS 7403*	47	4
21 Apr 79 ●	BANANA SPLITS (TRA LA LA SONG) *A & M AMS 7431*	7	8
21 Jul 79	PARANOID *A & M AMS 7368*	45	6
15 Sep 79	NIGHTS IN WHITE SATIN *A & M AMS 7469*	39	5
16 Feb 80	FAN MAIL *A & M AMS 7504*	57	3
19 Jul 80	GIGANTOR *A & M AMS 7544*	72	2

Bruce DICKINSON ✎ *UK, male vocalist*　　23 wks

28 Apr 90	TATTOOED MILLIONAIRE *EMI EM 138*	18	5
23 Jun 90	ALL THE YOUNG DUDES *EMI EM 142*	23	5
25 Aug 90	DIVE! DIVE! DIVE! *EMI EM 151*	45	2
4 Apr 92 ●	(I WANT TO BE) ELECTED *London LON 319* [1]	9	5
28 May 94	TEARS OF THE DRAGON *EMI CDEM 322*	28	2
8 Oct 94	SHOOT ALL THE CLOWNS *EMI CDEMS 341*	37	2
13 Apr 96	BACK FROM THE EDGE *Raw Power RAWX 1012*	68	1
3 May 97	ACCIDENT OF BIRTH *Raw Power RAWX 1042*	54	1

[1] Mr Bean and Smear Campaign featuring Bruce Dickinson

Barbara DICKSON ◐ *UK, female vocalist*　　49 wks

17 Jan 76 ●	ANSWER ME *RSO 2090 174*	9	7
26 Feb 77	ANOTHER SUITCASE IN ANOTHER HALL *MCA 266*	18	7
19 Jan 80	CARAVAN SONG *Epic EPC 8103*	41	7
15 Mar 80	JANUARY FEBRUARY *Epic EPC 8115*	11	10
14 Jun 80	IN THE NIGHT *Epic EPC 8593*	48	2
5 Jan 85 ★	I KNOW HIM SO WELL *RCA CHESS 3* [1]	1	16

[1] Elaine Paige and Barbara Dickson

DICTATORS *US, male vocal/instrumental group*　　2 wks

17 Sep 77	SEARCH AND DESTROY *Asylum K 13091*	49	1
1 Oct 77	SEARCH AND DESTROY (re-entry) *Asylum K 13091*	50	1

Bo DIDDLEY *US, male vocalist/instrumentalist – guitar*　　10 wks

10 Oct 63	PRETTY THING *Pye International 7N 25217*	34	6
18 Mar 65	HEY GOOD LOOKIN' *Chess 8000*	39	4

DIDDY *UK, male producer*　　2 wks

19 Feb 94	GIVE ME LOVE *Positiva CDTIV 8*	52	1
12 Jul 97	GIVE ME LOVE (re-mix) *Feverpitch CDFVR 19*	23	1

DIESEL PARK WEST *UK, male vocal/instrumental group*　　15 wks

4 Feb 89	ALL THE MYTHS ON SUNDAY *Food FOOD 17*	66	2
1 Apr 89	LIKE PRINCES DO *Food FOOD 19*	58	3
5 Aug 89	WHEN THE HOODOO COMES *Food FOOD 20*	62	2
18 Jan 92	FALL TO LOVE *Food FOOD 35*	48	3
21 Mar 92	BOY ON TOP OF THE NEWS *Food FOOD 36*	58	2
5 Sep 92	GOD ONLY KNOWS *Food FOOD 39*	57	3

See also VARIOUS ARTISTS (EPs & LPs) – The Food Christmas (EP)

DIFFORD and TILBROOK *UK, male vocal/instrumental duo*　　2 wks

30 Jun 84	LOVE'S CRASHING WAVES *A & M AM 193*	57	2

DIGABLE PLANETS *US, male/female vocal/instrumental group*　　2 wks

13 Feb 93	REBIRTH OF SLICK (COOL LIKE DAT) *Pendulum EKR 159CD*	67	2

DIGITAL DREAM BABY *UK, male vocalist – Peter Auty*　　4 wks

14 Dec 91	WALKING IN THE AIR *Columbia 6576067*	49	4

Hit is a dance re-mix of 'Walking in the Air' by Peter Auty

DIGITAL EXCITATION *Belgium, male producer – Frank de Wulf*　　2 wks

29 Feb 92	PURE PLEASURE *R&S RSUK 10*	37	2

DIGITAL ORGASM ☺

Belgium, male/female vocal/instrumental group　　14 wks

7 Dec 91	RUNNING OUT OF TIME *Dead Dead Good GOOD 009*	16	9
18 Apr 92	STARTOUCHERS *DDG International GOOD 13*	31	3
25 Jul 92	MOOG ERUPTION *DDG International GOOD 17*	62	2

DIGITAL UNDERGROUND *US, male rap group*　　4 wks

16 Mar 91	SAME SONG *Big Life BLR 40*	52	4

DILEMMA *Italy, male instrumental/production group*　　1 wk

6 Apr 96	IN SPIRIT *ffrr FCD 274*	42	1

Ricky DILLARD – See Farley 'Jackmaster' FUNK

Paolo DINI – See FPI PROJECT

Mark DINNING *US, male vocalist*　　4 wks

10 Mar 60	TEEN ANGEL *MGM 1053* ▲	37	3
7 Apr 60	TEEN ANGEL (re-entry) *MGM 1053*	42	1

DINOSAUR JR. ✎ ☹ *US, male vocal/instrumental group*　　13 wks

2 Feb 91	THE WAGON *Blanco Y Negro NEG 48*	49	2
14 Nov 92	GET ME *Blanco Y Negro NEG 60*	44	1
30 Jan 93	START CHOPPIN *Blanco Y Negro NEG 61CD*	20	3
12 Jun 93	OUT THERE *Blanco Y Negro NEG 63CD*	44	2
27 Aug 94	FEEL THE PAIN *Blanco Y Negro NEG 74CD*	25	3
11 Feb 95	I DON'T THINK SO *Blanco Y Negro NEG 77CD*	67	1
5 Apr 97	TAKE A RUN AT THE SUN *Blanco Y Negro NEG 103CD*	53	1

DINOSAURS – See Terry DACTYL and the DINOSAURS

DIO *UK/US, male vocal/instrumental group*　　22 wks

20 Aug 83	HOLY DIVER *Vertigo DIO 1*	72	2
29 Oct 83	RAINBOW IN THE DARK *Vertigo DIO 2*	46	3
11 Aug 84	WE ROCK *Vertigo DIO 3*	42	3
29 Sep 84	MYSTERY *Vertigo DIO 4*	34	4
10 Aug 85	ROCK 'N' ROLL CHILDREN *Vertigo DIO 5*	26	6
2 Nov 85	HUNGRY FOR HEAVEN *Vertigo DIO 6*	72	1
17 May 86	HUNGRY FOR HEAVEN (re-issue) *Vertigo DIO 7*	56	2
1 Aug 87	I COULD HAVE BEEN A DREAMER *Vertigo DIO 8*	69	1

DION ◐ *US, male vocalist*　　35 wks

26 Jun 59	A TEENAGER IN LOVE *London HLU 8874* [1]	28	2
19 Jan 61	LONELY TEENAGER *Top Rank JAR 521*	47	1
2 Nov 61	RUNAROUND SUE *Top Rank JAR 586* ▲	11	9
15 Feb 62 ●	THE WANDERER *HMV POP 971*	10	12
22 May 76	THE WANDERER (re-issue) *Philips 6146 700*	16	9
19 Aug 89	KING OF THE NEW YORK STREET *Arista 112556*	74	2

[1] Dion and the Belmonts

Celine DION ⓒ *French-Canadian vocalist who won the 1988 Eurovision Song Contest (for Switzerland), b. 30 March, 1968, Quebec. She sold more than 60 million albums between 1996-1998 (one every 1.2 seconds!) and is the only female with two UK million-selling singles* **201 wks**

16 May 92	● BEAUTY AND THE BEAST *Epic 6576607* [1]	9	7
4 Jul 92	IF YOU ASKED ME TO *Epic 6581927*	60	2
14 Nov 92	LOVE CAN MOVE MOUNTAINS *Epic 6587787*	46	2
26 Dec 92	IF YOU ASKED ME TO (re-entry) *Epic 6581927*	57	3
3 Apr 93	WHERE DOES MY HEART BEAT NOW *Epic 6563265*	72	1
29 Jan 94	● THE POWER OF LOVE *Epic 6597992* ▲	4	10
23 Apr 94	MISLED *Epic 6602922*	40	3
22 Oct 94	★ THINK TWICE *Epic 6606422* ◆	1	31
20 May 95	● ONLY ONE ROAD *Epic 6613535*	8	8
9 Sep 95	● TU M'AIMES ENCORE (TO LOVE ME AGAIN) *Epic 6624255*	7	9
2 Dec 95	MISLED (re-issue) *Epic 6626495*	15	6
2 Mar 96	● FALLING INTO YOU *Epic 6629795*	10	10
1 Jun 96	● BECAUSE YOU LOVED ME (THEME FROM UP CLOSE AND PERSONAL) *Epic 6632382* ▲	5	16
5 Oct 96	● IT'S ALL COMING BACK TO ME NOW *Epic 6637112*	3	14
21 Dec 96	● ALL BY MYSELF *Epic 6640622*	6	10
15 Mar 97	ALL BY MYSELF (re-entry) *Epic 6640622*	58	3
28 Jun 97	CALL THE MAN *Epic 6646922*	11	6
15 Nov 97	● TELL HIM *Epic 6653052* [2]	3	15
20 Dec 97	THE REASON *Epic 6653812*	11	8
21 Feb 98	★ MY HEART WILL GO ON *Epic 6655472* ◆ ■ ▲	1	20
18 Jul 98	● IMMORTALITY *Epic 6661662* [3]	5	12
28 Nov 98	● I'M YOUR ANGEL *Epic 6666282* [4] ▲	3†	5

[1] Celine Dion and Peabo Bryson [2] Barbra Streisand & Celine Dion [3] Celine Dion with Bee Gees [4] Celine Dion and R Kelly

DIONNE *Canada, female vocalist* **2 wks**

23 Sep 89	COME GET MY LOVIN' *Citybeat CBC 745*	69	2

Wasis DIOP – *See Lena FIAGBE*

DIRE STRAITS ✔ *Multi- BRIT- and Grammy-Award-winning group led by vocalist/lead guitarist/songwriter Mark Knopfler, b. 12 August, 1949, Glasgow. This London-based band, whose world tours attracted millions, are among the Top 5 album-selling acts in the UK* **119 wks**

10 Mar 79	● SULTANS OF SWING *Vertigo 6059 206*	8	11
28 Jul 79	LADY WRITER *Vertigo 6059 230*	51	6
17 Jan 81	● ROMEO AND JULIET *Vertigo MOVIE 1*	8	11
4 Apr 81	SKATEAWAY *Vertigo MOVIE 2*	37	5
10 Oct 81	TUNNEL OF LOVE *Vertigo MUSIC 3*	54	3
4 Sep 82	● PRIVATE INVESTIGATIONS *Vertigo DSTR 1*	2	8
22 Jan 83	TWISTING BY THE POOL *Vertigo DSTR 2*	14	7
18 Feb 84	LOVE OVER GOLD (LIVE)/SOLID ROCK (LIVE) *Vertigo DSTR 6*	50	3
20 Apr 85	SO FAR AWAY *Vertigo DSTR 9*	20	6
6 Jul 85	● MONEY FOR NOTHING *Vertigo DSTR 10* ▲	4	16
26 Oct 85	BROTHERS IN ARMS *Vertigo DSTR 11*	16	13
11 Jan 86	● WALK OF LIFE *Vertigo DSTR 12*	2	11
3 May 86	YOUR LATEST TRICK *Vertigo DSTR 13*	26	6
5 Nov 88	SULTANS OF SWING (re-issue) *Vertigo DSTR 15*	62	1
31 Aug 91	CALLING ELVIS *Vertigo DSTR 16*	21	4
2 Nov 91	HEAVY FUEL *Vertigo DSTR 17*	55	2
29 Feb 92	ON EVERY STREET *Vertigo DSTR 18*	42	2
27 Jun 92	THE BUG *Vertigo DSTR 19*	67	1
22 May 93	ENCORES EP *Vertigo DSCD 20*	31	3

Tracks on Encores (EP): Your Latest Trick / The Bug / Solid Rock / Local Hero-Wild Theme

DIRECKT *UK, male instrumental/production duo* **2 wks**

13 Aug 94	TWO FATT GUITARS (REVISITED) *UFG UFG 7CD*	36	2

DIRECT DRIVE *UK, male/female vocal/instrumental group* **3 wks**

26 Jan 85	ANYTHING *Polydor POSP 728*	67	2
4 May 85	A.B.C. (FALLING IN LOVE'S NOT EASY) *Boiling Point POSP 742*	75	1

DIRTY ROTTEN SCOUNDRELS – *See Lisa STANSFIELD*

DISCHARGE *UK, male vocal/instrumental group* **3 wks**

24 Oct 81	NEVER AGAIN *Clay CLAY 6*	64	3

DISCO ANTHEM *Holland, male producer – Lex van Coeverden* **2 wks**

18 Jun 94	SCREAM *Sweat MCSTD 1977*	47	2

DISCO CITIZENS *UK, male instrumental/producer* **5 wks**

22 Jul 95	RIGHT HERE RIGHT NOW *Deconstruction 74321293872*	40	2
12 Apr 97	FOOTPRINT *Xtravaganza 0091115*	34	2
4 Jul 98	NAGASAKI BADGER *Xtravaganza 0091595 EXT*	56	1

See also CHICANE

DISCO EVANGELISTS *UK, male instrumental/production group* **2 wks**

8 May 93	DE NIRO *Positiva CDTIV 2*	59	2

DISCO TEX and the SEX-O-LETTES ♫ *US, male vocalist/female vocal group* **22 wks**

23 Nov 74	● GET DANCING *Chelsea 2005 013*	8	12
26 Apr 75	● I WANNA DANCE WIT CHOO *Chelsea 2005 024* [1]	6	10

[1] Disco Tex and the Sex-O-Lettes featuring Sir Monti Rock III

DISPOSABLE HEROES OF HIPHOPRISY
US, male rap/instrumental duo **7 wks**

4 Apr 92	TELEVISION THE DRUG OF THE NATION *Fourth & Broadway BRW 241*	57	2
30 May 92	LANGUAGE OF VIOLENCE *Fourth & Broadway 12BRW 248*	68	1
19 Dec 92	TELEVISION THE DRUG OF THE NATION (re-entry) *Fourth & Broadway BRW 241*	44	4

Sacha DISTEL ⓒ *France, male vocalist* **27 wks**

10 Jan 70	RAINDROPS KEEP FALLING ON MY HEAD *Warner Bros. WB 7345*	50	1
24 Jan 70	● RAINDROPS KEEP FALLING ON MY HEAD (re-entry) *Warner Bros. WB 7345*	10	20
27 Jun 70	RAINDROPS KEEP FALLING ON MY HEAD (2nd re-entry) *Warner Bros. WB 7345*	43	4
1 Aug 70	RAINDROPS KEEP FALLING ON MY HEAD (3rd re-entry) *Warner Bros. WB 7345*	47	1
15 Aug 70	RAINDROPS KEEP FALLING ON MY HEAD (4th re-entry) *Warner Bros. WB 7345*	44	1

DIVA *Norway, female vocal duo* **2 wks**

7 Oct 95	THE SUN ALWAYS SHINES ON TV *East West YZ 947CD*	53	1
20 Jul 96	EVERYBODY (MOVE YOUR BODY) *East West EW 035CD*	44	1

DIVA SURPRISE
US, Spain, male production duo and US, female vocalist **2 wks**

14 Nov 98	ON TOP OF THE WORLD *Positiva CDTIV 100* [1]	29	2

[1] Diva Surprise featuring Georgia Jones

DIVE *UK, male production duo – Sacha Collisson, Simon Greenaway* **1 wk**

21 Feb 98	BOOGIE *WEA WEA 147CD1*	35	1

Hit featured vocalist Nasreen Shah

DIVERSIONS *UK, male/female vocal/instrumental group* **3 wks**

20 Sep 75	FATTIE BUM BUM *Gull GULS 18*	34	3

DIVINE ⓒ ☺ *US, male vocalist* **24 wks**

15 Oct 83	LOVE REACTION *Design Communication DES 4*	65	2
14 Jul 84	YOU THINK YOU'RE A MAN *Proto ENA 118*	16	10
20 Oct 84	I'M SO BEAUTIFUL *Proto ENA 121*	52	2
27 Apr 85	WALK LIKE A MAN *Proto ENA 125*	23	7
20 Jul 85	TWISTIN' THE NIGHT AWAY *Proto ENA 127*	47	3

DIVINE COMEDY ☺ ☹
UK, male vocalist/multi-instrumentalist – Neil Hannon **20 wks**

29 Jun 96	SOMETHING FOR THE WEEKEND		
	Setanta SETCD 26	14	5
24 Aug 96	BECOMING MORE LIKE ALFIE *Setanta SETCD 27*	27	2
16 Nov 96	THE FROG PRINCESS *Setanta SETCD 32*	15	2
22 Mar 97	EVERYBODY KNOWS (EXCEPT YOU)		
	Setanta SETCDA 038	14	4
11 Apr 98	SOMEDAY I'LL FIND YOU/I'VE BEEN TO A MARVELLOUS		
	PARTY *EMI CDTCB 001* [1]	28	3
26 Sep 98	GENERATION SEX *Setanta SETCDA 050*	19	3
28 Nov 98	THE CERTAINTY OF CHANCE *Setanta SETCDA 067*	49	1

[1] Shola Ama and Craig Armstrong / Divine Comedy

DIVINYLS ☹ *Australia, male/female vocal/instrumental duo* **12 wks**

| 18 May 91 ● | I TOUCH MYSELF *Virgin America VUS 36* | 10 | 12 |

DIXIE CUPS *US, female vocal group* **16 wks**

| 18 Jun 64 | CHAPEL OF LOVE *Pye International 7N 25245* ▲ | 22 | 8 |
| 13 May 65 | IKO IKO *Red Bird RB 10024* | 23 | 8 |

DIZZY HEIGHTS *UK, male vocal/instrumental group* **4 wks**

| 18 Dec 82 | CHRISTMAS RAPPING *Polydor WRAP 1* | 49 | 4 |

DJ BOBO *Switzerland, male vocalist – Rene Baumann* **4 wks**

| 24 Sep 94 | EVERYBODY *PWL Continental PWCD 312* | 47 | 2 |
| 17 Jun 95 | LOVE IS ALL AROUND *Avex UK AXEXCD 7* | 49 | 2 |

DJ DADO ☹ ☺ *Italy, male producer* **8 wks**

6 Apr 96 ●	X-FILES *ZYX ZYX 8065R8*	8	6
14 Mar 98	COMING BACK *ffrr TABCD 247*	63	1
11 Jul 98	GIVE ME LOVE *VC Recordings VCRD 37* [1]	59	1

[1] DJ Dado vs Michelle Weeks

DJ DISCIPLE *US, male vocalist* **1 wk**

| 12 Nov 94 | ON THE DANCEFLOOR *Mother MUMCD 55* | 67 | 1 |

DJ DUKE ☺ *US, male producer* **7 wks**

| 8 Jan 94 | BLOW YOUR WHISTLE *ffrr FCD 228* | 15 | 5 |
| 16 Jul 94 | TURN IT UP (SAY YEAH) *ffrr FCD 235* | 31 | 2 |

DJ E-Z ROCK – *See Rob BASE and DJ E-Z ROCK*

DJ 'FAST' EDDIE *US, male producer* **15 wks**

11 Apr 87	CAN U DANCE *Champion CHAMP 41* [1]	71	2
14 Nov 87	CAN U DANCE (re-entry) *Champion CHAMP 41* [1]	67	2
21 Jan 89	HIP HOUSE/I CAN DANCE *DJ International DJIN 5*	47	4
11 Mar 89	YO YO GET FUNKY *DJ International DJIN 7*	54	3
28 Oct 89	GIT ON UP *DJ International 655366 7* [2]	49	4

[1] Kenny 'Jammin' Jason and 'Fast' Eddie Smith [2] DJ 'Fast' Eddie featuring Sundance

DJ FLAVOURS ☺ *UK, male producer* **4 wks**

| 11 Oct 97 | YOUR CARESS (ALL I NEED) *All Around the World* | | |
| | *CDGLOBE 160* | 19 | 4 |

DJ HYPE *UK, male producer* **1 wk**

| 20 Mar 93 | SHOT IN THE DARK *Suburban Base SUBBASE 20CD* | 63 | 1 |

See also VARIOUS ARTISTS (EPs & LPs) – Subplates Volume 1

DJ JAZZY JEFF and the FRESH PRINCE – *See JAZZY JEFF and the FRESH PRINCE*

DJ KOOL ◀ *US, male rapper/DJ/producer* **7 wks**

| 22 Feb 97 ● | LET ME CLEAR MY THROAT *American 74321452092* | 8 | 7 |

DJ KRUSH *Japan, male producer* **2 wks**

| 16 Mar 96 | MEISO *Mo Wax MW 042CD* | 52 | 1 |
| 12 Oct 96 | ONLY THE STRONG SURVIVE *Mo Wax MW 060CD* | 71 | 1 |

DJ MIKO ☹ ☺ *Italy, male producer* **10 wks**

| 13 Aug 94 ● | WHAT'S UP *Systematic SYSCD 2* | 6 | 10 |

DJ MILANO *Italy, male DJ/producer* **2 wks**

| 28 Mar 98 | SANTA MARIA *All Around The World CDGLOBE 163* [1] | 31 | 2 |

[1] DJ Milano featuring Samantha Fox

DJ MISJAH and DJ TIM ☺
Holland, male instrumental/production duo **3 wks**

| 23 Mar 96 | ACCESS *Ffrreedom TABCD 240* | 16 | 3 |

DJ POWER *Italy, male producer – Steve Gambaroli* **2 wks**

| 7 Mar 92 | EVERYBODY PUMP *Cooltempo COOL 252* | 46 | 2 |

DJ PROFESSOR *Italy, male producer* **6 wks**

10 Aug 91	WE GOTTA DO IT *Fourth & Broadway BRW 225* [1]	57	2
28 Mar 92	ROCK ME STEADY *PWL Continental PWL 219*	49	2
8 Oct 94	ROCKIN' ME *Citra CITRA 1CD* [2]	56	1
1 Mar 97	WALKIN' ON UP *Nukleuz MCSTD 40098* [3]	64	1

[1] DJ Professor featuring Francesco Zappala [2] Professor [3] DJ PROF-X-OR

DJ Quik – *See TONY TONI TONE*

DJ QUICKSILVER ☺ ☹ *Turkey, male DJ/producer* **28 wks**

5 Apr 97 ●	BELISSIMA *Positiva CDTIV 72*	4	16
6 Sep 97 ●	FREE *Positiva CDTIVS 77*	7	7
21 Feb 98	PLANET LOVE *Positiva CDTIV 88*	12	5

DJ RAP *UK, female vocalist/DJ/producer* **4 wks**

| 4 Jul 98 | BAD GIRL *Higher Ground HIGHS 8CD* | 32 | 2 |
| 17 Oct 98 | GOOD TO BE ALIVE *Higher Ground HIGHS 14CD* | 36 | 2 |

DJ SCOT PROJECT *Germany, male DJ/producer* **2 wks**

| 27 Jul 96 | U (I GOT THE FEELING) *Positiva CDTIV 55* | 66 | 1 |
| 14 Feb 98 | Y (HOW DEEP IS YOUR LOVE) *Perfecto PERF 158CD1* | 57 | 1 |

DJ SCOTT *Scotland, male DJ* **5 wks**

| 28 Jan 95 | DO YOU WANNA PARTY *Steppin' Out SPONCD 2* [1] | 36 | 3 |
| 1 Apr 95 | SWEET DREAMS *Steppin' Out SPONCD 3* [1] | 37 | 2 |

[1] DJ Scott featuring Lorna B

DJ Doc SCOTT *UK, male producer* **2 wks**

| 1 Feb 92 | NHS EP *Absolute 2 ABS 001DJ* | 64 | 2 |

Tracks on NHS (EP): Surgery / Night Nurse

DJ SEDUCTION *UK, male producer – John Kallum* **8 wks**

| 22 Feb 92 | HARDCORE HEAVEN/YOU AND ME *Ffrreedom TAB 103* | 26 | 5 |
| 11 Jul 92 | COME ON *Ffrreedom TAB 111* | 37 | 3 |

DJ SHADOW *US, male producer* **7 wks**

25 Mar 95	WHAT DOES YOUR SOUL LOOK LIKE *Mo Wax MW 027CD*	59	1
14 Sep 96	MIDNIGHT IN A PERFECT WORLD *Mo Wax MW 057CD*	54	1
9 Nov 96	STEM *Mo Wax MW 058CD*	74	1
11 Oct 97	HIGH NOON *Mo Wax MW 063CD*	22	2
20 Dec 97	CAMEL BOBSLED RACE *Mo Wax MW 084CD*	62	1
24 Jan 98	WHAT DOES YOUR SOUL LOOK LIKE (PART 1)		
	Mo Wax MW 087CD	54	1

DJ SUPREME *UK, male producer – Nick Destri* **7 wks**

| 5 Oct 96 | THA WILD STYLE *Distinctive DISNCD 19* | 39 | 2 |

3 May 97		THA WILD STYLE (re-issue) *Distinctive DISNCD 29*	24	2
6 Dec 97		ENTER THE SCENE *Distinctive DISNCD 40* [1]	49	1
21 Feb 98		THA HORNS OF JERICHO		
		All Around the World CDGLOBE 164	29	2

[1] DJ Supreme vs Rhythm Masters

DJ TIM – See DJ MISJAH and DJ TIM

DJ's RULE *Canada, male instrumental/production duo* 2 wks

2 Mar 96		GET INTO THE MUSIC *Distinctive DISNCD 9*	72	1
5 Apr 97		GET INTO THE MUSIC (re-issue)		
		Distinctive DISNCDD27 [1]	65	1

[1] DJ's Rule featuring Karen Brown

DJAIMIN *Switzerland, male producer* 2 wks

19 Sep 92		GIVE YOU *Cooltempo COOL 262*	45	2

DJH featuring STEFY ☺ ◐
Italy, male instrumental/production group 14 wks

16 Feb 91		THINK ABOUT . . . *RCA PB 44385*	22	6
13 Jul 91		I LIKE IT *RCA PB 44741*	16	7
19 Oct 91		MOVE YOUR LOVE *RCA PB 44965*	73	1

DJPC *Belgium, male producer* 5 wks

26 Oct 91		INSSOMNIAK *Hype 7PUM 005*	62	4
29 Feb 92		INSSOMNIAK (re-issue) *Hype PUMR 005*	64	1

DJUM DJUM – See LEFTFIELD

Boris DLUGOSCH presents BOOM
Germany/US, male/female instrumental/vocal duo 4 wks

7 Dec 96		KEEP PUSHIN' *Manifesto FESCD 17*	41	2
13 Sep 97		HOLD YOUR HEAD UP HIGH *Positiva CDTIV 79*	23	2

DNA ◐ ☺ *UK, male production duo* 29 wks

28 Jul 90	●	TOM'S DINER *A & M AM 592* [1]	2	10
18 Aug 90		LA SERENISSIMA *Raw Bass RBASS 006*	34	8
3 Aug 91		REBEL WOMAN *DNA 7DNA 001* [2]	42	4
1 Feb 92		CAN YOU HANDLE IT *EMI EM 219* [3]	17	5
9 May 92		BLUE LOVE (CALL MY NAME) *EMI EM 226* [4]	66	2

[1] DNA featuring Suzanne Vega [2] DNA, rap performed by Jazzi P [3] DNA featuring Sharon Redd [4] DNA featuring Joe Nye

Carl DOBKINS Jr. *US, male vocalist* 1 wk

31 Mar 60		LUCKY DEVIL *Brunswick 05817*	44	1

Anita DOBSON ◐ *UK, female vocalist* 13 wks

9 Aug 86	●	ANYONE CAN FALL IN LOVE *BBC RESL 191* [1]	4	9
18 Jul 87		TALKING OF LOVE *Parlophone R 6159*	43	4

[1] Anita Dobson featuring the Simon May Orchestra

DR. ALBAN ◐ ☺ *Nigeria, male vocalist/producer* 28 wks

5 Sep 92	●	IT'S MY LIFE *Logic 7432115330*	2	12
14 Nov 92		ONE LOVE *Logic 74321108727*	45	2
10 Apr 93		SING HALLELUJAH! *Logic 74321136202*	16	8
26 Mar 94		LOOK WHO'S TALKING *Logic 74321195342*	55	3
13 Aug 94		AWAY FROM HOME *Logic 74321222682*	42	2
29 Apr 95		SWEET DREAMS *Logic 74321251552* [1]	59	1

[1] Swing featuring Dr Alban

DR. DRE ⏪ *US, male rapper* 29 wks

22 Jan 94		NUTHIN' BUT A 'G' THANG/LET ME RIDE		
		Death Row A 8328CD	31	3
3 Sep 94		DRE DAY *Death Row A 8292CD*	59	2
15 Apr 95		NATURAL BORN KILLAZ *Death Row A 8197CD* [1]	45	2
10 Jun 95		KEEP THEIR HEADS RINGIN' *Priority PTYCD 103*	25	4

13 Apr 96	●	CALIFORNIA LOVE *Death Row DRWCD 3* [2] ▲	6	8
19 Oct 96	●	NO DIGGITY *Interscope IND 95003* [3] ▲	9	7
11 Jul 98	●	ZOOM *Interscope IND 95594* [4]	15	3

[1] Dr Dre and Ice Cube [2] 2Pac featuring Dr Dre [3] Blackstreet featuring Dr Dre [4] Dr Dre and L L Cool J

DR. FEELGOOD ⏪ *UK, male vocal/instrumental group* 29 wks

11 Jun 77		SNEAKIN' SUSPICION *United Artists UP 36255*	47	3
24 Sep 77		SHE'S A WIND UP *United Artists UP 36304*	34	5
30 Sep 78		DOWN AT THE DOCTOR'S *United Artists UP 36444*	48	5
20 Jan 79	●	MILK AND ALCOHOL *United Artists UP 36468*	9	9
5 May 79		AS LONG AS THE PRICE IS RIGHT		
		United Artists YUP 36506	40	6
8 Dec 79		PUT HIM OUT OF YOUR MIND *United Artists BP 306*	73	1

DR. HOOK ⏪ ⏪ *Distinctive group fronted by vocalists Dennis Locorriere and Ray Sawyer; had eight years of regular UK/US hits. Early recordings often featured humorous anarchic Shel Silverstein songs, but this good-time New Jersey act had greater success with later gentler material* 104 wks

24 Jun 72	●	SYLVIA'S MOTHER *CBS 7929* [1]	2	13
26 Jun 76	●	A LITTLE BIT MORE *Capitol CL 15871*	2	14
30 Oct 76	●	IF NOT YOU *Capitol CL 15885*	5	10
25 Mar 78		MORE LIKE THE MOVIES *Capitol CL 15967*	14	10
22 Sep 79	★	WHEN YOU'RE IN LOVE WITH A BEAUTIFUL WOMAN		
		Capitol CL 16039	1	17
5 Jan 80	●	BETTER LOVE NEXT TIME *Capitol CL 16112*	8	8
29 Mar 80	●	SEXY EYES *Capitol CL 16127*	4	9
23 Aug 80		YEARS FROM NOW *Capitol CL 16154*	47	6
8 Nov 80		SHARING THE NIGHT TOGETHER *Capitol CL 16171*	43	4
22 Nov 80		GIRLS CAN GET IT *Mercury MER 51*	40	5
1 Feb 92		WHEN YOU'RE IN LOVE WITH A BEAUTIFUL WOMAN (re-issue)		
		Capitol EMCT 4	44	4
6 Jun 92		A LITTLE BIT MORE (re-issue) *EMI EMCT 6*	47	4

[1] Dr Hook and the Medicine Show

DR. OCTAGON *US, male producer – Keith Thornton* 1 wk

7 Sep 96		BLUE FLOWERS *Mo Wax MW 055CD*	66	1

DOCTOR and the MEDICS ◐
UK, male/female vocal/instrumental group 25 wks

10 May 86	★	SPIRIT IN THE SKY *IRS IRM 113*	1	15
9 Aug 86		BURN *IRS IRM 116*	29	6
22 Nov 86		WATERLOO *IRS IRM 125* [1]	45	4

[1] Doctor and the Medics featuring Roy Wood

DOCTOR SPIN ◐ ☺ *UK, male instrumental/production duo* 8 wks

3 Oct 92	●	TETRIS *Carpet CRPT 4*	6	8

Ken DODD Ⓒ *Seasoned stand-up comedian-cum-balladeer, b. 8 November, 1929, Liverpool. The tickling-stick-wielding troubadour was one of the most successful Merseyside acts in the mid-1960s, at times enjoying two Top 10 singles simultaneously* 233 wks

7 Jul 60		LOVE IS LIKE A VIOLIN *Decca F 11248*	8	18
15 Jun 61		ONCE IN EVERY LIFETIME *Decca F 11355*	28	7
10 Aug 61		ONCE IN EVERY LIFETIME (re-entry) *Decca F 11355*	47	1
24 Aug 61		ONCE IN EVERY LIFETIME (2nd re-entry) *Decca F 11355*	31	10
1 Feb 62		PIANISSIMO *Decca F 11422*	21	15
29 Aug 63		STILL *Columbia DB 7094*	35	10
6 Feb 64		EIGHT BY TEN *Columbia DB 7191*	22	11
23 Jul 64		HAPPINESS *Columbia DB 7325*	31	13
26 Nov 64		SO DEEP IS THE NIGHT *Columbia DB 7398*	31	7
2 Sep 65	★	TEARS *Columbia DB 7659* ◆	1	24
18 Nov 65	●	THE RIVER (LE COLLINE SONO IN FIORO) *Columbia DB 7750*	3	14
12 May 66	●	PROMISES *Columbia DB 7914*	6	14
4 Aug 66		MORE THAN LOVE *Columbia DB 7976*	14	11
27 Oct 66		IT'S LOVE *Columbia DB 8031*	36	7
19 Jan 67		LET ME CRY ON YOUR SHOULDER *Columbia DB 8101*	11	10
30 Jul 69		TEARS WON'T WASH AWAY THESE HEARTACHES		
		Columbia DB 8600	22	11

5 Dec 70	BROKEN HEARTED Columbia DB 8725	15	9
13 Feb 71	BROKEN HEARTED (re-entry) Columbia DB 8725	38	1
10 Jul 71	WHEN LOVE COMES ROUND AGAIN (L'ARCA DI NOE) Columbia DB 8796	19	16
18 Nov 72	JUST OUT OF REACH (OF MY TWO EMPTY ARMS) Columbia DB 8947	29	11
29 Nov 75	(THINK OF ME) WHEREVER YOU ARE EMI 2342	21	8
26 Dec 81	HOLD MY HAND Images IMGS 0002	44	5

Rory DODD – See Jim STEINMAN

DODGY ☻ ☹ UK, male vocal/instrumental group   41 wks

8 May 93	LOVEBIRDS A & M AMCD 0177	65	2
3 Jul 93	I NEED ANOTHER (EP) A & M 5803172	67	2
6 Aug 94	THE MELOD-EP Bostin 5806772	53	1
1 Oct 94	STAYING OUT FOR THE SUMMER Bostin 5807972	38	2
7 Jan 95	SO LET ME GO FAR Bostin 5809032	30	3
11 Mar 95	MAKING THE MOST OF Bostin 5809892 [1]	22	3
10 Jun 95	STAYING OUT FOR THE SUMMER (re-mix) Bostin 5810952	19	5
8 Jun 96	IN A ROOM A & M 5816252	12	6
10 Aug 96 ●	GOOD ENOUGH A & M 5818152	4	8
16 Nov 96	IF YOU'RE THINKING OF ME A & M 5819992	11	4
15 Mar 97	FOUND YOU A & M 5821332	19	3
26 Sep 98	EVERY SINGLE DAY A&M MERCD 512	32	2

[1] Dodgy with the Kick Horns

Tracks on I Need Another (EP): I Need Another / If I Fall / Hendre DDU. Tracks on The Melod-EP: Melodies Haunt You / The Snake / Don't Go / Summer Fayre

Tim DOG US, male rapper   3 wks

29 Oct 94	BITCH WITH A PERM Dis-stress DISCD 1	49	1
11 Feb 95	MAKE WAY FOR THE INDIAN Island CID 586 [1]	29	2

[1] Apache Indian and Tim Dog

DOG EAT DOG ✔ US, male vocal/instrumental group   7 wks

19 Aug 95	NO FRONTS Roadrunner RR 23312	64	1
3 Feb 96 ●	NO FRONTS (re-entry) Roadrunner RR 23312	9	5
13 Jul 96	ISMS Roadrunner RR 23083	43	1

Nate DOGG – See Warren G

DOGS D'AMOUR UK, male vocal/instrumental group   15 wks

4 Feb 89	HOW COME IT NEVER RAINS China CHINA 13	44	3
5 Aug 89	SATELLITE KID China CHINA 17	26	3
14 Oct 89	TRAIL OF TEARS China CHINA 20	47	3
23 Jun 90	VICTIMS OF SUCCESS China CHINA 24	36	3
15 Sep 90	EMPTY WORLD China CHINA 27	61	2
19 Jun 93	ALL OR NOTHING China WOKCD 2033	53	1

Ken DOH ☺ UK, male producer – Michael Devlin   7 wks

30 Mar 96 ●	I NEED A LOVER TONIGHT ffrr FCD 272	7	7

Joe DOLAN © Ireland, male vocalist   40 wks

25 Jun 69 ●	MAKE ME AN ISLAND Pye 7N 17738	3	18
1 Nov 69	TERESA Pye 7N 17833	20	7
8 Nov 69	MAKE ME AN ISLAND (re-entry) Pye 7N 17738	48	1
28 Feb 70	YOU'RE SUCH A GOOD LOOKING WOMAN Pye 7N 17891	17	13
17 Sep 77	I NEED YOU Pye 7N 45702	43	1

Thomas DOLBY ☻ ☹ UK, male vocalist/multi-instrumentalist   51 wks

3 Oct 81	EUROPA AND THE PIRATE TWINS Parlophone R 6051	48	3
14 Aug 82	WINDPOWER Venice In Peril VIPS 103	31	8
6 Nov 82	SHE BLINDED ME WITH SCIENCE Venice In Peril VIPS 104	49	4
16 Jul 83	SHE BLINDED ME WITH SCIENCE (re-issue) Venice In Peril VIP 105	56	4
21 Jan 84	HYPERACTIVE Parlophone Odeon R 6065	17	9
31 Mar 84	I SCARE MYSELF Parlophone Odeon R 6067	46	5

16 Apr 88	AIRHEAD Manhattan MT 38	53	3
9 May 92	CLOSE BUT NO CIGAR Virgin VS 1410	22	5
11 Jul 92	I LOVE YOU GOODBYE Virgin VS 1417	36	4
26 Sep 92	SILK PYJAMAS Virgin VS 1430	62	2
22 Jan 94	HYPERACTIVE! (re-mix) Parlophone CDEMCTS 10	23	4

Joe DOLCE MUSIC THEATRE ☻ US, male vocalist   10 wks

7 Feb 81 ★	SHADDAP YOU FACE Epic EPC 9518	1	10

DOLL UK, male/female vocal/instrumental group   8 wks

13 Jan 79	DESIRE ME Beggars Banquet BEG 11	28	8

DOLLAR ☻ Photogenic teen-targeted UK vocal duo, who were originally one third of Guys and Dolls: David Van Day, Thereze Bazaar. Their Top 10 hits came from writers as diverse as John Lennon/Paul McCartney, Trevor Horn, Erasure and themselves   128 wks

11 Nov 78	SHOOTING STAR Carrere 2871	14	12
19 May 79	WHO WERE YOU WITH IN THE MOONLIGHT Carrere CAR 110	14	12
18 Aug 79	LOVE'S GOTTA HOLD ON ME Carrere CAR 122	4	13
24 Nov 79	I WANNA HOLD YOUR HAND Carrere CAR 131	9	14
25 Oct 80	TAKIN' A CHANCE ON YOU WEA K 18353	62	3
15 Aug 81	HAND HELD IN BLACK AND WHITE WEA BUCK 1	19	12
14 Nov 81 ●	MIRROR MIRROR (MON AMOUR) WEA BUCK 2	4	17
20 Mar 82	RING RING Carrere CAR 225	61	2
27 Mar 82	GIVE ME BACK MY HEART WEA BUCK 3	4	9
19 Jun 82	VIDEOTHEQUE WEA BUCK 4	17	10
18 Sep 82	GIVE ME SOME KINDA MAGIC WEA BUCK 5	34	6
16 Aug 86	WE WALKED IN LOVE Arista DIME 1	61	4
26 Dec 87 ●	O L'AMOUR London LON 146	7	11
16 Jul 88	IT'S NATURE'S WAY (NO PROBLEM) London LON 179	58	3

Placido DOMINGO Spain, male vocalist   28 wks

12 Dec 81	PERHAPS LOVE CBS A 1905 [1]	46	9
27 May 89	TILL I LOVED YOU CBS 654843 7 [2]	24	9
16 Jun 90	NESSUN DORMA FROM 'TURANDOT' Epic 656005 7	59	2
30 Jul 94	LIBIAMO/LA DONNA E MOBILE Teldec YZ 843CD [4]	21	4
25 Jul 98	YOU'LL NEVER WALK ALONE Decca 4607982 [4]	35	4

[1] Placido Domingo with John Denver [2] Placido Domingo and Jennifer Rush [3] Luis Cobos featuring Placido Domingo [4] José Carreras, Placido Domingo and Luciano Pavarotti

DOMINO US, male rapper/vocalist   6 wks

22 Jan 94	GETTO JAM Chaos 6600402	33	4
14 May 94	SWEET POTATOE PIE Chaos 6603292	42	2

Fats DOMINO ♪ Pioneering rock'n'roll singer/songwriter and pianist, b. 26 February, 1928, New Orleans. Sold millions of rockin' records in pre-Haley/-Presley years and is still among the biggest-selling artists and most successful composers of the rock era   109 wks

27 Jul 56	I'M IN LOVE AGAIN London HLU 8280	28	1
17 Aug 56	I'M IN LOVE AGAIN (re-entry) London HLU 8280	12	13
30 Nov 56	BLUEBERRY HILL London HLU 8330	26	1
21 Dec 56 ●	BLUEBERRY HILL (re-entry) London HLU 8330	6	14
25 Jan 57	AIN'T THAT A SHAME London HLU 8173	23	2
1 Feb 57	HONEY CHILE London HLU 8356	29	1
29 Mar 57	BLUE MONDAY London HLP 8377	23	1
19 Apr 57	BLUE MONDAY (re-entry) London HLP 8377	30	1
19 Apr 57	I'M WALKIN' London HLP 8407	19	7
19 Jul 57	VALLEY OF TEARS London HLP 8449	25	1
28 Mar 58	THE BIG BEAT London HLP 8575	20	4
4 Jul 58	SICK AND TIRED London HLP 8628	26	1
22 May 59	MARGIE London HLP 8865	18	5
16 Oct 59	I WANT TO WALK YOU HOME London HLP 8942	14	5
18 Dec 59	BE MY GUEST London HLP 9005	11	8
19 Feb 60	BE MY GUEST (re-entry) London HLP 9005	19	3
17 Mar 60	COUNTRY BOY London HLP 9073	19	11
21 Jul 60	WALKING TO NEW ORLEANS London HLP 9163	19	10
10 Nov 60	THREE NIGHTS A WEEK London HLP 9198	45	2

5 Jan 61	MY GIRL JOSEPHINE *London HLP 9244*	32	4
27 Jul 61	IT KEEPS RAININ' *London HLP 9374*	49	1
30 Nov 61	WHAT A PARTY *London HLP 9456*	43	1
29 Mar 62	JAMBALAYA *London HLP 9520*	41	1
31 Oct 63	RED SAILS IN THE SUNSET *HMV POP 1219*	34	6
24 Apr 76	BLUEBERRY HILL (re-issue) *United Artists UP 35797*	41	5

DON PABLO'S ANIMALS ● ☺ *Italy, male instrumental group*   10 wks

19 May 90 ●	VENUS *Rumour RUMA 18*	4	10

DON-E R&B ● *UK, male vocalist*   8 wks

9 May 92	LOVE MAKES THE WORLD GO ROUND *Fourth & Broadway BRW 242*	18	6
25 Jul 92	PEACE IN THE WORLD *Fourth & Broadway BRW 256*	41	1
28 Feb 98	DELICIOUS *Mushroom MUSH 20CD* [1]	52	1

[1] Deni Hines featuring Don-E

Lonnie DONEGAN ● ♪ *The 'King of Skiffle', b. 29 April, 1931, Glasgow, Scotland. Britain's most successful and influential recording artist before The Beatles. Chalked up 28 successive Top 30 entries, and was first UK male to score two US Top 10s*   321 wks

6 Jan 56 ●	ROCK ISLAND LINE *Decca F 10647*	8	13
13 Apr 56	ROCK ISLAND LINE (re-entry) *Decca F 10647*	16	3
20 Apr 56	STEWBALL *Pye Nixa N 15036*	27	1
27 Apr 56 ●	LOST JOHN/STEWBALL *Pye Nixa N 15036*	2	17
11 May 56	ROCK ISLAND LINE (2nd re-entry) *Decca F 10647*	19	6
6 Jul 56	SKIFFLE SESSION EP *Pye Nixa NJE 1017*	20	2
7 Sep 56 ●	BRING A LITTLE WATER SYLVIE/DEAD OR ALIVE *Pye Nixa N 15071*	7	12
21 Dec 56	LONNIE DONEGAN SHOWCASE LP *Pye Nixa NPT 19012*	26	3
11 Jan 57	BRING A LITTLE WATER SYLVIE/DEAD OR ALIVE (re-entry) *Pye Nixa N 15071*	30	1
18 Jan 57 ●	DON'T YOU ROCK ME DADDY-O *Pye Nixa N 15080*	4	17
5 Apr 57 ★	CUMBERLAND GAP *Pye Nixa N 15087*	1	12
7 Jun 57 ★	GAMBLIN' MAN/PUTTING ON THE STYLE *Pye Nixa N 15093*	1	19
11 Oct 57 ●	MY DIXIE DARLING *Pye Nixa N 15108*	10	15
20 Dec 57	JACK O' DIAMONDS *Pye Nixa 7N 15116*	14	7
11 Apr 58 ●	GRAND COOLIE DAM *Pye Nixa 7N 15129*	6	15
11 Jul 58	SALLY DON'T YOU GRIEVE/BETTY BETTY BETTY *Pye Nixa 7N 15148*	11	7
26 Sep 58	LONESOME TRAVELLER *Pye Nixa 7N 15158*	28	1
14 Nov 58	LONNIE'S SKIFFLE PARTY *Pye Nixa 7N 15165*	23	5
21 Nov 58 ●	TOM DOOLEY *Pye Nixa 7N 15172*	3	14
6 Feb 59 ●	DOES YOUR CHEWING GUM LOSE ITS FLAVOUR *Pye Nixa 7N 15181*	3	12
8 May 59	FORT WORTH JAIL *Pye Nixa 7N 15198*	14	5
26 Jun 59 ●	BATTLE OF NEW ORLEANS *Pye 7N 15206*	2	16
11 Sep 59	SAL'S GOT A SUGAR LIP *Pye 7N 15223*	13	4
4 Dec 59	SAN MIGUEL *Pye 7N 15237*	19	4
24 Mar 60 ★	MY OLD MAN'S A DUSTMAN *Pye 7N 15256* ■	1	13
26 May 60 ●	I WANNA GO HOME *Pye 7N 15267*	5	17
25 Aug 60 ●	LORELEI *Pye 7N 15275*	10	8
24 Nov 60	LIVELY *Pye 7N 15312*	13	9
8 Dec 60	VIRGIN MARY *Pye 7N 15315*	27	5
11 May 61 ●	HAVE A DRINK ON ME *Pye 7N 15354*	8	15
31 Aug 61	MICHAEL ROW THE BOAT/LUMBERED *Pye 7N 15371*	6	11
18 Jan 62	THE COMANCHEROS *Pye 7N 15410*	14	10
5 Apr 62 ●	THE PARTY'S OVER *Pye 7N 15424*	9	12
16 Aug 62	PICK A BALE OF COTTON *Pye 7N 15455*	11	10

'Stewball' had one week on the chart by itself on 20 Apr, 1956. 'Lost John', the other side, replaced it on 27 Apr, 1956, but 'Stewball' was given co-billing with 'Lost John' for the weeks of 11, 18 and 25 May, 1956, only peaking at No 7. 'Dead or Alive' was not listed with 'Bring a Little Water Sylvie' for the week 7 Sep, 1956. 'Putting on the Style' was not listed with 'Gamblin' Man' for the weeks of 7 and 14 Jun, 1956. Tracks on Skiffle Session (EP): Railroad Bill / Stockalee / Ballad of Jesse James / Ol' Riley. Tracks on Lonnie Donegan Showcase (LP): Wabash Cannonball / How Long / How Long Blues / Nobody's Child / I Shall Not Be Moved / I'm Alabammy Bound / I'm a Rambling Man / Wreck of the Old '97 / Frankie and Johnny

Tanya DONELLY *US, female vocalist / instrumentalist*   4 wks

30 Aug 97	PRETTY DEEP *4AD BAD 7007CD*	55	1
6 Dec 97	THE BRIGHT LIGHT *4AD BAD 7012CD*	64	3

Ral DONNER *US, male vocalist*   10 wks

21 Sep 61	YOU DON'T KNOW WHAT YOU'VE GOT (UNTIL YOU LOSE IT) *Parlophone R 4820*	25	10

DONOVAN ♂ ✒ *Acclaimed Celtic singer/songwriter, b. Donovan Leitch, 10 February, 1946, Glasgow. Initially dubbed British version of Bob Dylan, he enjoyed massive fame on both sides of the Atlantic in the 'flower power' years of the late 1960s*   100 wks

25 Mar 65 ●	CATCH THE WIND *Pye 7N 15801*	4	13
3 Jun 65 ●	COLOURS *Pye 7N 15866*	4	12
11 Nov 65	TURQUOISE *Pye 7N 15984*	30	6
8 Dec 66 ●	SUNSHINE SUPERMAN *Pye 7N 17241* ▲	2	11
9 Feb 67 ●	MELLOW YELLOW *Pye 7N 17267*	8	8
25 Oct 67 ●	THERE IS A MOUNTAIN *Pye 7N 17403*	8	11
21 Feb 68 ●	JENNIFER JUNIPER *Pye 7N 17457*	5	11
29 May 68 ●	HURDY GURDY MAN *Pye 7N 17537*	4	10
4 Dec 68	ATLANTIS *Pye 7N 17660*	23	8
9 Jul 69	GOO GOO BARABAJAGAL (LOVE IS HOT) *Pye 7N 17778* [1]	12	9
1 Dec 90	JENNIFER JUNIPER *Fontana SYP 1* [2]	68	1

[1] Donovan with the Jeff Beck Group [2] Singing Corner meets Donovan

Jason DONOVAN ● *The top teen idol of the late 1980s, b. 1 June, 1968, Melbourne. Australian actor-turned-singer, who had impressive array of UK hits after leaving TV soap, Neighbours. His debut LP, Ten Good Reasons, was the UK's top-selling album of 1989*   137 wks

10 Sep 88 ●	NOTHING CAN DIVIDE US *PWL PWL 17*	5	12
10 Dec 88 ★	ESPECIALLY FOR YOU *PWL PWL 24* [1]	1	14
4 Mar 89 ★	TOO MANY BROKEN HEARTS *PWL PWL 32*	1	13
10 Jun 89 ★	SEALED WITH A KISS *PWL PWL 39* ■	1	10
9 Sep 89 ●	EVERY DAY (I LOVE YOU MORE) *PWL PWL 43*	2	9
9 Dec 89 ●	WHEN YOU COME BACK TO ME *PWL PWL 46*	2	11
7 Apr 90 ●	HANG ON TO YOUR LOVE *PWL PWL 51*	8	7
30 Jun 90	ANOTHER NIGHT *PWL PWL 58*	18	5
1 Sep 90	RHYTHM OF THE RAIN *PWL PWL 60*	9	6
27 Oct 90	I'M DOING FINE *PWL PWL 69*	22	6
18 May 91	RSVP *PWL PWL 80*	17	5
22 Jun 91 ★	ANY DREAM WILL DO *Really Useful RUR 7*	1	12
24 Aug 91 ●	HAPPY TOGETHER *PWL PWL 203*	10	6
7 Dec 91	JOSEPH MEGA REMIX *Really Useful RUR 9* [2]	13	8
18 Jul 92	MISSION OF LOVE *Polydor PO 222*	26	4
28 Nov 92	AS TIME GOES BY *Polydor PO 245*	26	6
7 Aug 93	ALL AROUND THE WORLD *Polydor PZCD 278*	41	3

[1] Kylie Minogue and Jason Donovan [2] Jason Donovan and Original London Cast featuring Linzi Hately, David Easter and Johnny Amobi

DOOBIE BROTHERS ✒ *US, male vocal/instrumental group*   45 wks

9 Mar 74	LISTEN TO THE MUSIC *Warner Bros. K 16208*	29	7
7 Jun 75	TAKE ME IN YOUR ARMS *Warner Bros. K 16559*	29	5
17 Feb 79	WHAT A FOOL BELIEVES *Warner Bros. K 17314* ▲	31	10
5 May 79	WHAT A FOOL BELIEVES (re-entry) *Warner Bros. K 17314*	72	1
14 Jul 79	MINUTE BY MINUTE *Warner Bros. K 17411*	47	4
24 Jan 87	WHAT A FOOL BELIEVES (re-issue) *Warner Bros. W 8451* [1]	57	3
29 Jul 89	THE DOCTOR *Capitol CL 536*	73	2
27 Nov 93 ●	LONG TRAIN RUNNIN' *Warner Bros. W 0217CD*	7	10
14 May 94	LISTEN TO THE MUSIC (re-mix) *Warner Bros. W 0228CD*	37	3

[1] Doobie Brothers featuring Michael McDonald

DOOGIE – See BUG KANN and PLASTIC JAM

DOOLALLY ☺ *UK, male production duo*   6 wks

14 Nov 98	STRAIGHT FROM THE HEART *Locked On LOX 104CD*	20	6

DOOLEYS ☺ *UK, male/female vocal/instrumental group* — **83 wks**

13 Aug 77	THINK I'M GONNA FALL IN LOVE WITH YOU *GTO GT 95*	13	10
12 Nov 77 ●	LOVE OF MY LIFE *GTO GT 110*	9	11
13 May 78	DON'T TAKE IT LYIN' DOWN *GTO GT 220*	60	3
2 Sep 78	A ROSE HAS TO DIE *GTO GT 229*	11	11
10 Feb 79	HONEY I'M LOST *GTO GT 242*	24	9
16 Jun 79 ●	WANTED *GTO GT 249*	3	14
22 Sep 79 ●	THE CHOSEN FEW *GTO GT 258*	7	11
8 Mar 80	LOVE PATROL *GTO GT 260*	29	7
6 Sep 80	BODY LANGUAGE *GTO GT 276*	46	4
10 Oct 81	AND I WISH *GTO GT 300*	52	3

Val DOONICAN ℂ *Popular balladeer and TV host, b. 3 February, 1928, Waterford, Ireland. This relaxed crooner, who was known for his rocking chair and multi-coloured jumpers, had five successive Top 10 albums in the swinging sixties* — **143 wks**

15 Oct 64 ●	WALK TALL *Decca F 11982*	3	21
21 Jan 65 ●	THE SPECIAL YEARS *Decca F 12049*	7	12
8 Apr 65	I'M GONNA GET THERE SOMEHOW *Decca F 12118*	25	5
22 Apr 65	THE SPECIAL YEARS (re-entry) *Decca F 12049*	49	1
17 Mar 66 ●	ELUSIVE BUTTERFLY *Decca F 12358*	5	12
3 Nov 66	WHAT WOULD I BE *Decca F 12505*	2	17
23 Feb 67	MEMORIES ARE MADE OF THIS *Decca F 12566*	11	12
25 May 67	TWO STREETS *Decca F 12608*	39	4
18 Oct 67 ●	IF THE WHOLE WORLD STOPPED LOVING *Pye 7N 17396*	3	19
21 Feb 68	YOU'RE THE ONLY ONE *Pye 7N 17465*	37	4
12 Jun 68	NOW *Pye 7N 17534*	43	2
23 Oct 68	IF I KNEW THEN WHAT I KNOW NOW *Pye 7N 17616*	14	13
23 Apr 69	RING OF BRIGHT WATER *Pye 7N 17713*	48	1
4 Dec 71	MORNING *Philips 6006 177*	12	13
10 Mar 73	HEAVEN IS MY WOMAN'S LOVE *Philips 6028 031*	34	6
28 Apr 73	HEAVEN IS MY WOMAN'S LOVE (re-entry) *Philips 6028 031*	47	1

DOOP ☺ *Holland, male instrumental duo* — **12 wks**

12 Mar 94 ★	DOOP *Citybeat CBE 774CD*	1	12

DOORS ✎ *US, male vocal/instrumental group* — **42 wks**

16 Aug 67	LIGHT MY FIRE *Elektra EKSN 45014* ▲	49	1
28 Aug 68	HELLO I LOVE YOU *Elektra EKSN 45037* ▲	15	12
16 Oct 71	RIDERS ON THE STORM *Elektra K 12021*	50	1
30 Oct 71	RIDERS ON THE STORM (re-entry) *Elektra K 12021*	22	10
20 Mar 76	RIDERS ON THE STORM (re-issue) *Elektra K 12203*	33	5
3 Feb 79	HELLO I LOVE YOU (re-issue) *Elektra K 12215*	71	2
27 Apr 91	BREAK ON THROUGH *Elektra EKR 121*	64	2
1 Jun 91 ●	LIGHT MY FIRE (re-issue) *Elektra EKR 125*	7	8
10 Aug 91	RIDERS ON THE STORM (re-issue) *Elektra EKR 131*	68	1

D.O.P. *UK, male instrumental/production duo* — **2 wks**

3 Feb 96	STOP STARTING TO START STOPPING (EP) *Hi-Life 5779472*	58	1
13 Jul 96	GROOVY BEAT *Hi-Life 5750652*	54	1

Tracks on Stop Starting to Stop Stopping (EP): *Gusta / Dance to the House / Can You Feel It / How Do Y'All Feel*

DOPE SMUGGLAZ *UK, male DJ/production duo* — **1 wk**

5 Dec 98	THE WORD *Mushroom PERFCDS 1*	62	1

Charlie DORE *UK, female vocalist* — **2 wks**

17 Nov 79	PILOT OF THE AIRWAVES *Island WIP 6526*	66	2

DOROTHY *UK, male instrumental duo* — **5 wks**

9 Dec 95	WHAT'S THAT TUNE (DOO DOO DOO DOO DOO-DOO-DOO-DOO-DOO-DOO) *RCA 74321330912*	31	5

Lee DORSEY ✎ *US, male vocalist* — **36 wks**

3 Feb 66	GET OUT OF MY LIFE WOMAN *Stateside SS 485*	22	7
5 May 66	CONFUSION *Stateside SS 506*	38	6
11 Aug 66 ●	WORKING IN THE COALMINE *Stateside SS 528*	8	11
27 Oct 66 ●	HOLY COW *Stateside SS 552*	6	12

Tommy DORSEY ORCHESTRA starring Warren COVINGTON ℂ
US, orchestra – Warren Covington, male instrumentalist – trombone — **19 wks**

17 Oct 58 ●	TEA FOR TWO CHA CHA *Brunswick 05757*	3	19

D.O.S.E. – See Mark E SMITH

DOUBLE ☺ *Switzerland, male vocal/instrumental duo* — **10 wks**

25 Jan 86 ●	THE CAPTAIN OF HER HEART *Polydor POSP 779*	8	9
5 Dec 87	DEVIL'S BALL *Polydor POSP 888*	71	1

DOUBLE DEE featuring DANY
Italy, male vocal/instrumental duo — **4 wks**

1 Dec 90	FOUND LOVE *Epic 6563766*	63	2
25 Nov 95	FOUND LOVE (re-mix) *Sony S3 DANUCD 1*	33	2

DOUBLE 99 ☺ *UK, male instrumental / production duo* — **9 wks**

31 May 97	RIPGROOVE *Satellite 74321485132*	31	3
1 Nov 97	RIPGROOVE (re-mix) *Satellite 74321529322*	14	6

'Ripgroove' re-mix features an uncredited rap by Em Cat
See also RIP PRODUCTIONS

DOUBLE SIX *UK, male vocal / instrumental group* — **1 wk**

19 Sep 98	REAL GOOD *Multiply CDMULTY 39*	66	1

DOUBLE TROUBLE ☺ 👜 — **35 wks**
UK, male instrumental/production duo

27 May 89	JUST KEEP ROCKIN' *Desire WANT 9* [1]	11	12
7 Oct 89 ●	STREET TUFF *Desire WANT 18* [1]	3	14
12 May 90	TALK BACK *Desire WANT 27* [2]	71	1
30 Jun 90	LOVE DON'T LIVE HERE ANYMORE *Desire WANT 32* [3]	21	6
15 Jun 91	RUB-A-DUB *Desire WANT 41*	66	2

[1] Double Trouble and the Rebel MC [2] Double Trouble featuring Janette Sewell
[3] Double Trouble featuring Janette Sewell and Carl Brown

DOUBLE YOU? *Italy, male vocalist – Willie Morales* — **3 wks**

2 May 92	PLEASE DON'T GO *ZYX ZYX 67487*	41	3

Rob DOUGAN
UK, male vocalist/instrumentalist/songwriter/producer — **1 wk**

4 Apr 98	FURIOUS ANGELS *Cheeky CHEKCD 025*	62	1

Carl DOUGLAS ☺ *Jamaica, male vocalist* — **39 wks**

17 Aug 74 ★	KUNG FU FIGHTING *Pye 7N 45377* ▲	1	13
30 Nov 74	DANCE THE KUNG FU *Pye 7N 45418*	35	5
3 Dec 77	RUN BACK *Pye 7N 46018*	25	10
23 May 98 ●	KUNG FU FIGHTING (re-mix) *All Around the World CDGLOBE 173* [1]	8	11

[1] Bus Stop featuring Carl Douglas

Carol DOUGLAS *US, female vocalist* — **4 wks**

22 Jul 78	NIGHT FEVER *Gull GULS 61*	66	4

Craig DOUGLAS ☺ *Clean-cut early sixties teen idol, b. Terence Perkins, 12 August, 1941, Isle of Wight. Voted Best New Singer of 1959; had eight cover versions among his nine Top 20 entries. He topped the bill on The Beatles' first major stage show* — **112 wks**

12 Jun 59	A TEENAGER IN LOVE *Top Rank JAR 133*	13	11
7 Aug 59 ★	ONLY SIXTEEN *Top Rank JAR 159*	1	15
22 Jan 60	PRETTY BLUE EYES *Top Rank JAR 268*	4	14
28 Apr 60 ●	THE HEART OF A TEENAGE GIRL *Top Rank JAR 340*	10	9
11 Aug 60	OH! WHAT A DAY *Top Rank JAR 406*	43	1

UK No 1 ★   UK Top 10 ●   UK million seller ◆   UK entry at No 1 ■   US No 1 ▲

20 Apr 61	● A HUNDRED POUNDS OF CLAY *Top Rank JAR 555*	9	9
29 Jun 61	● TIME *Top Rank JAR 569*	9	14
22 Mar 62	● WHEN MY LITTLE GIRL IS SMILING *Top Rank JAR 610*	9	13
28 Jun 62	● OUR FAVOURITE MELODIES *Columbia DB 4854*	9	10
18 Oct 62	OH LONESOME ME *Decca F 11523*	15	12
28 Feb 63	TOWN CRIER *Decca F 11575*	36	4

DOWLANDS *UK, male vocal duo* — 7 wks

9 Jan 64	ALL MY LOVING *Oriole CB 1897*	33	7

Robert DOWNEY Jr. *US, male vocalist* — 1 wk

30 Jan 93	SMILE *Epic 6589052*	68	1

Don DOWNING *US, male vocalist* — 10 wks

10 Nov 73	LONELY DAYS, LONELY NIGHTS *People PEO 102*	32	10

Will DOWNING ♪ *US, male vocalist* — 35 wks

2 Apr 88	A LOVE SUPREME *Fourth & Broadway BRW 90*	14	10
25 Jun 88	IN MY DREAMS *Fourth & Broadway BRW 104*	34	6
1 Oct 88	FREE *Fourth & Broadway BRW 112*	58	5
21 Jan 89	WHERE IS THE LOVE *Fourth & Broadway BRW 122* [1]	19	7
28 Oct 89	TEST OF TIME *Fourth & Broadway BRW 146*	67	2
24 Nov 90	COME TOGETHER AS ONE *Fourth & Broadway BRW 159*	48	4
18 Sep 93	THERE'S NO LIVING WITHOUT YOU *Fourth & Broadway BRCD 278*	67	1

[1] Mica Paris and Will Downing

Lamont DOZIER – See HOLLAND-DOZIER featuring Lamont DOZIER

Charlie DRAKE ☺ *UK, male vocalist* — 37 wks

8 Aug 58	● SPLISH SPLASH *Parlophone R 4461*	7	11
24 Oct 58	VOLARE *Parlophone R 4478*	28	2
27 Oct 60	MR. CUSTER *Parlophone R 4701*	12	12
5 Oct 61	MY BOOMERANG WON'T COME BACK *Parlophone R 4824*	14	11
1 Jan 72	PUCKWUDGIE *Columbia DB 8829*	47	1

DRAMATIS *UK, male vocal/instrumental group* — 8 wks

5 Dec 81	LOVE NEEDS NO DISGUISE *Beggars Banquet BEG 68* [1]	33	7
13 Nov 82	I CAN SEE HER NOW *Rocket XPRES 83*	57	1

[1] Gary Numan and Dramatis

Rusty DRAPER *US, male vocalist* — 4 wks

11 Aug 60	MULE SKINNER BLUES *Mercury AMT 1101*	39	4

DREAD ZEPPELIN *US, male vocal/instrumental group* — 3 wks

1 Dec 90	YOUR TIME IS GONNA COME *IRS DREAD 1*	59	1
13 Jul 91	STAIRWAY TO HEAVEN *IRS DREAD 2*	62	2

DREADZONE ☺ *UK, male instrumental group* — 15 wks

6 May 95	ZION YOUTH *Virgin VSCDG 1537*	49	2
29 Jul 95	CAPTAIN DREAD *Virgin VSCDG 1541*	49	2
23 Sep 95	MAXIMUM EP *Virgin VSCDT 1555*	56	2
6 Jan 96	LITTLE BRITAIN *Virgin VSCDG 1565*	20	6
30 Mar 96	LIFE LOVE AND UNITY *Virgin VSCDT 1583*	56	1
10 May 97	EARTH ANGEL *Virgin VSCDT 1593*	51	1
26 Jul 97	MOVING ON *Virgin VSCDT 1635*	58	1

Tracks on Maximum EP : Maximum / Fight the Power 95 / One Way

DREAM ACADEMY ☺
UK, male/female vocal/instrumental group — 10 wks

30 Mar 85	LIFE IN A NORTHERN TOWN *Blanco Y Negro NEG 10*	15	8
14 Sep 85	THE LOVE PARADE *Blanco Y Negro NEG 16*	68	2

DREAM FREQUENCY *UK, male producer – Ian Bland* — 12 wks

12 Jan 91	LOVE PEACE AND HARMONY *Citybeat CBE 756*	71	2
25 Jan 92	FEEL SO REAL *Citybeat CBE 763* [1]	23	5
25 Apr 92	TAKE ME *Citybeat CBE 768*	39	3
21 May 94	GOOD TIMES/THE DREAM *Citybeat CBE 773CD*	67	1
10 Sep 94	YOU MAKE ME FEEL MIGHTY REAL *Citybeat CBE 775CD*	65	1

[1] Dream Frequency featuring Debbie Sharp

DREAM WARRIORS ◀ *Canada, male rap group* — 19 wks

14 Jul 90	WASH YOUR FACE IN MY SINK *Fourth & Broadway BRW 183*	16	8
24 Nov 90	MY DEFINITION OF A BOOMBASTIC JAZZ STYLE *Fourth & Broadway BRW 197*	13	8
25 Apr 92	LUDI *Fourth & Broadway BRW 206*	39	3

DREAMERS – See FREDDIE and the DREAMERS

DREAMHOUSE *UK, male vocal/instrumental group* — 2 wks

3 Jun 95	STAY *Chase CDPALACE 1*	62	2

DREAMWEAVERS ☾ *US, male/female vocal group* — 18 wks

10 Feb 56	★ IT'S ALMOST TOMORROW *Brunswick 05515*	1	18

DREEM TEEM *UK, male production group* — 4 wks

13 Dec 97	THE THEME *4 Liberty 74321542032*	34	4

DRELLS – See Archie BELL and the DRELLS

Eddie DRENNON and B.B.S. UNLIMITED ◢
US, male vocal/instrumental group — 6 wks

28 Feb 76	LET'S DO THE LATIN HUSTLE *Pye International 7N 25702*	20	6

Alan DREW *UK, male vocalist* — 2 wks

26 Sep 63	ALWAYS THE LONELY ONE *Columbia DB 7090*	48	2

DRIFTERS ♪ *Ever-changing, ever-popular US group, founded in 1953 by Clyde McPhatter (d. 1972) and still active today, with erstwhile members including Ben E King, Johnny Moore (d. 1998) and Rudy Lewis (d. 1964). Inducted into Rock and Roll Hall of Fame in 1988* — 176 wks

8 Jan 60	DANCE WITH ME *London HLE 8988*	17	4
10 Mar 60	DANCE WITH ME (re-entry) *London HLE 8988*	35	1
3 Nov 60	● SAVE THE LAST DANCE FOR ME *London HLK 9201* ▲	2	18
16 Mar 61	I COUNT THE TEARS *London HLK 9287*	28	6
5 Apr 62	WHEN MY LITTLE GIRL IS SMILING *London HLK 9522*	31	3
10 Oct 63	I'LL TAKE YOU HOME *London HLK 9785*	37	5
24 Sep 64	UNDER THE BOARDWALK *Atlantic AT 4001*	45	4
8 Apr 65	AT THE CLUB *Atlantic AT 4019*	35	7
29 Apr 65	COME ON OVER TO MY PLACE *Atlantic AT 4023*	40	5
2 Feb 67	BABY WHAT I MEAN *Atlantic 584 065*	49	1
25 Mar 72	AT THE CLUB (re-issue) *Atlantic K 10148*	39	1
8 Apr 72	● AT THE CLUB/SATURDAY NIGHT AT THE MOVIES (re-entry of re-issue) *Atlantic K 10148*	3	19
26 Aug 72	● COME ON OVER TO MY PLACE (re-issue) *Atlantic K 10216*	9	11
4 Aug 73	● LIKE SISTER AND BROTHER *Bell 1313*	7	12
15 Jun 74	● KISSIN' IN THE BACK ROW OF THE MOVIES *Bell 1358*	2	13
12 Oct 74	● DOWN ON THE BEACH TONIGHT *Bell 1381*	7	9
8 Feb 75	LOVE GAMES *Bell 1396*	33	6
6 Sep 75	● THERE GOES MY FIRST LOVE *Bell 1433*	3	12
29 Nov 75	● CAN I TAKE YOU HOME LITTLE GIRL *Bell 1462*	10	10
13 Mar 76	HELLO HAPPINESS *Bell 1469*	12	8
11 Sep 76	EVERY NITE'S A SATURDAY NIGHT WITH YOU *Bell 1491*	29	7
18 Dec 76	● YOU'RE MORE THAN A NUMBER IN MY LITTLE RED BOOK *Arista 78*	5	12
14 Apr 79	SAVE THE LAST DANCE FOR ME/WHEN MY LITTLE GIRL IS SMILING (re-issue) *Lightning LIG 9014*	69	2

'Saturday Night at the Movies' only received chart credit with 'At the Club' after the re-issue's return to the chart on 8 Apr, 1972

UK No 1 ★   UK Top 10 ●   UK million seller ◆   UK entry at No 1 ■   US No 1 ▲

Julie DRISCOLL, Brian AUGER and the TRINITY ✔

UK, female vocalist/male instrumental group   **16 wks**

17 Apr 68 ● THIS WHEEL'S ON FIRE Marmalade 598 006 ....5 16

DRIVER 67 ❂ UK, male vocalist – Paul Phillips   **12 wks**

23 Dec 78 ● CAR 67 Logo GO 336 ....7 12

DRIZABONE R&B UK, male instrumental/production duo   **18 wks**

22 Jun 91	REAL LOVE Fourth & Broadway BRW 223 16	8
26 Oct 91	CATCH THE FIRE Fourth & Broadway BRW 232............54	2
23 Apr 94	PRESSURE Fourth & Broadway BRCD 264 33	2
4 Mar 95	REAL LOVE Fourth & Broadway BRCD 311 24	4
15 Oct 96	BRIGHTEST STAR Fourth & Broadway BRCD 293 45	2

'Real Love' in 1995 is a re-recording

Frank D'RONE US, male vocalist   **6 wks**

22 Dec 60   STRAWBERRY BLONDE Mercury AMT 1123................24 6

DRU HILL R&B US, male vocal group   **19 wks**

15 Feb 97	TELL ME Fourth & Broadway BRCD 342.................30	3
10 May 97	IN MY BED Fourth & Broadway BRCD 353 16	3
11 Oct 97	BIG BAD MAMMA Def Jam 5749792 [1] 12	3
6 Dec 97	5 STEPS Island Black Music CID 675 22	3
24 Oct 98	● HOW DEEP IS YOUR LOVE Island CID 725 9	7

[1] Foxy Brown featuring Dru Hill

DRUGSTORE ✔

UK/US/Brazil, male/female vocal/instrumental group   **5 wks**

10 Jun 95	FADER Honey HONCD 7 72	1
2 May 98	EL PRESIDENT Roadrunner RR 22369 20	3
4 Jul 98	SOBER Roadrunner RR22303 68	1

DRUM CLUB UK, male instrumental/production duo   **1 wk**

6 Nov 93   SOUND SYSTEM Butterfly BFLD 10 ....62 1

DRUM THEATRE UK, male vocal/instrumental group   **8 wks**

15 Feb 86	LIVING IN THE PAST Epic A 6798 67	2
17 Jan 87	ELDORADO Epic EMU 1................................44	6

DRUPI ❂ Italy, male vocalist   **12 wks**

1 Dec 73   VADO VIA A & M AMS 7083............................17 12

DSK UK, male/female vocal/instrumental/production group   **4 wks**

31 Aug 91	WHAT WOULD WE DO/READ MY LIPS Boy's Own BOI 6.........46	3
22 Nov 97	WHAT WOULD WE DO Fresh FRSHD 63 55	1

DSM US, male rap group   **4 wks**

7 Dec 85   WARRIOR GROOVE 10 DAZZ 45-7 ....68 4

DTI US, male vocal/instrumental group   **1 wk**

16 Apr 88   KEEP THIS FREQUENCY CLEAR/KEEP IT CLEAR
             Premiere UK ERE 501..................................73 1

DTOX UK, male/female vocal/instrumental group   **1 wk**

21 Nov 92   SHATTERED GLASS Vitality VITal 1 ....75 1

John DU CANN UK, male vocalist   **6 wks**

22 Sep 79   DON'T BE A DUMMY Vertigo 6059 241 ....33 6

John DU PREZ – See MODERN ROMANCE

DUB PISTOLS UK, male vocal / instrumental/production group **1 wk**

10 Oct 98   CYCLONE Deconstruction HARD 36CD 63 1

DUB WAR UK, male vocal/instrumental group   **5 wks**

3 Jun 95	STRIKE IT Earache MOSH 138CD......................70	1
27 Jan 96	ENEMY MAKER Earache MOSH 147CD..................41	2
24 Aug 96	CRY DIGNITY Earache MOSH 163CDD.................59	1
29 Mar 97	MILLION DOLLAR LOVE Earache MOSH 170CD1 73	1

DUBLINERS ♂ Ireland, male vocal/instrumental group   **45 wks**

30 Mar 67	● SEVEN DRUNKEN NIGHTS Major Minor MM 506 7	17
30 Aug 67	BLACK VELVET BAND Major Minor MM 530 15	15
20 Dec 67	MAIDS WHEN YOU'RE YOUNG NEVER WED AN OLD MAN	
	Major Minor MM 551 43	3
28 Mar 87	● THE IRISH ROVER Stiff BUY 258 [1] 8	8
16 Jun 90	JACK'S HEROES/WHISKEY IN THE JAR	
	Pogue Mahone YZ 500 [1] 63	2

[1] Pogues and the Dubliners

DUBSTAR ☹ ❂ UK, male/female vocal/instrumental group   **25 wks**

8 Jul 95	STARS Food CDFOOD 61..............................40	3
30 Sep 95	ANYWHERE Food CDFOOD 67 37	3
6 Jan 96	NOT SO MANIC NOW Food CDFOOD 71 18	5
30 Mar 96	STARS (re-issue) Food CDFOODS 75 15	6
3 Aug 96	ELEVATOR SONG Food CDFOOD 80 25	2
19 Jul 97	NO MORE TALK Food CDFOOD 96 20	3
20 Sep 97	CATHEDRAL PARK Food CDFOOD 104 41	1
7 Feb 98	I WILL BE YOUR GIRLFRIEND Food CDFOODS 108........28	2

Mary DUFF – See Daniel O'DONNELL

DUFFO Australia, male vocalist   **2 wks**

24 Mar 79   GIVE ME BACK ME BRAIN Beggars Banquet BEG 15 ....60 2

Stephen 'Tin Tin' DUFFY ❂ UK, male vocalist   **24 wks**

9 Jul 83	HOLD IT Curve X 9763 [1] 55	4
2 Mar 85	● KISS ME 10 TIN 2.................................4	11
18 May 85	ICING ON THE CAKE 10 TIN 3........................14	9

[1] Tin Tin

DUKE UK, male vocalist   **5 wks**

25 May 96	SO IN LOVE WITH YOU Encore CDCOR 009..............66	1
26 Oct 96	SO IN LOVE WITH YOU (re-issue) Pukka CDPUKKA 11 22	4

George DUKE US, male vocalist/instrumentalist   **6 wks**

12 Jul 80   BRAZILIAN LOVE AFFAIR Epic EPC 8751 ....36 6

DUKES UK, male vocal duo   **13 wks**

17 Oct 81	MYSTERY GIRL WEA K 18867...........................47	7
1 May 82	THANK YOU FOR THE PARTY WEA K 19136................53	6

Candy DULFER ❂ ✔

Holland, female instrumentalist – saxophone   **14 wks**

24 Feb 90	● LILY WAS HERE RCA ZB 43045 [1] 6	12
4 Aug 90	SAXUALITY RCA PB 43769 60	2

[1] David A Stewart featuring Candy Dulfer

Thuli DUMAKUDE South Africa, male vocalist   **1 wk**

2 Jan 88   THE FUNERAL (SEPTEMBER 25, 1977) MCA MCA 1228 ....75 1

The listed flip side of 'The Funeral' was 'Cry Freedom' by George Fenton
and Jonas Gwangwa

John DUMMER and Helen APRIL UK, male/female vocal duo   **3 wks**

28 Aug 82   BLUE SKIES Speed SPEED 8 ....54 3

DUNBLANE ❂ UK, male/female vocal/instrumental group   **15 wks**

21 Dec 96 ★ KNOCKIN' ON HEAVEN'S DOOR / THROW THESE GUNS AWAY
             BMG 74321442182 ■ 1 15

Johnny DUNCAN and the BLUE GRASS BOYS ☺
US, male vocal/instrumental group　　　　　　　　**20 wks**

26 Jul 57 ●	LAST TRAIN TO SAN FERNANDO *Columbia DB 3959*	2	17
25 Oct 57	BLUE BLUE HEARTACHES *Columbia DB 3996*	27	1
29 Nov 57	FOOTPRINTS IN THE SNOW *Columbia DB 4029*	27	1
3 Jan 58	FOOTPRINTS IN THE SNOW (re-entry) *Columbia DB 4029*	28	1

David DUNDAS ☺ *UK, male vocalist*　　　　　　　　**14 wks**

24 Jul 76 ●	JEANS ON *Air CHS 2094*	3	9
9 Apr 77	ANOTHER FUNNY HONEYMOON *Air CHS 2136*	29	5

Erroll DUNKLEY 🎵 *Jamaica, male vocalist*　　　　　　**14 wks**

22 Sep 79	O.K. FRED *Scope SC 6*	11	11
2 Feb 80	SIT DOWN AND CRY *Scope SC 11*	52	3

Clive DUNN ☺ *UK, male vocalist*　　　　　　　　**28 wks**

28 Nov 70 ★	GRANDAD *Columbia DB 8726*	1	27
26 Jun 71	GRANDAD (re-entry) *Columbia D8 8726*	50	1

Simon DUPREE and the BIG SOUND ☺
UK, male vocal/instrumental group　　　　　　　　**16 wks**

22 Nov 67 ●	KITES *Parlophone R 5646*	9	13
3 Apr 68	FOR WHOM THE BELL TOLLS *Parlophone R 5670*	43	3

DURAN DURAN ☺ *New-romantics-turned-teen-idols: Simon Le Bon (v), Nick Rhodes (k), John Taylor (b), Andy Taylor (g), Roger Taylor (d). The Birmingham band's ten successive Top 10 hits included 'A View to a Kill' – the best-selling James Bond theme ever in the UK and the USA. The three Taylors were unrelated*　　　　　　　　**218 wks**

21 Feb 81	PLANET EARTH *EMI 5137*	12	11
9 May 81	CARELESS MEMORIES *EMI 5168*	37	7
25 Jul 81 ●	GIRLS ON FILM *EMI 5206*	5	11
28 Nov 81	MY OWN WAY *EMI 5254*	14	11
15 May 82 ●	HUNGRY LIKE THE WOLF *EMI 5295*	5	12
21 Aug 82 ●	SAVE A PRAYER *EMI 5327*	2	9
13 Nov 82 ●	RIO *EMI 5346*	9	11
26 Mar 83 ★	IS THERE SOMETHING I SHOULD KNOW *EMI 5371* ■	1	9
29 Oct 83 ●	UNION OF THE SNAKE *EMI 5429*	3	7
24 Dec 83	UNION OF THE SNAKE (re-entry) *EMI 5429*	66	4
4 Feb 84 ●	NEW MOON ON MONDAY *EMI DURAN 1*	9	7
28 Apr 84 ★	THE REFLEX *EMI DURAN 2* ▲	1	14
3 Nov 84 ●	WILD BOYS *Parlophone DURAN 3*	2	14
18 May 85 ●	A VIEW TO A KILL *Parlophone DURAN 007* ▲	2	16
1 Nov 86 ●	NOTORIOUS *EMI DDN 45*	7	6
3 Jan 87	NOTORIOUS (re-entry) *EMI DDN 45*	73	1
21 Feb 87	SKIN TRADE *EMI TRADE 1*	22	6
25 Apr 87	MEET EL PRESIDENTE *EMI TOUR 1*	24	5
1 Oct 88	I DON'T WANT YOUR LOVE *EMI YOUR 1*	14	5
7 Jan 89 ●	ALL SHE WANTS IS *EMI DD 11*	9	5
22 Apr 89	DO YOU BELIEVE IN SHAME *EMI DD 12*	30	4
16 Dec 89	BURNING THE GROUND *EMI DD 13*	31	5
4 Aug 90	VIOLENCE OF SUMMER (LOVE'S TAKING OVER) *Parlophone DD 14*	20	4
17 Nov 90	SERIOUS *Parlophone DD 15*	48	2
30 Jan 93 ●	ORDINARY WORLD *Parlophone CDDDS 16*	6	9
10 Apr 93	COME UNDONE *Parlophone CDDDS 17*	13	8
4 Sep 93	TOO MUCH INFORMATION *Parlophone CDDDS 18*	35	3
25 Mar 95	PERFECT DAY *Parlophone CDDDS 20*	28	4
17 Jun 95	WHITE LINES (DON'T DO IT) *Parlophone CDDD 19*	17	5
24 May 97	OUT OF MY MIND *Virgin VSCDT 1639*	21	2

Group was UK/US from 'Burning the Ground'

Jimmy DURANTE *US, male vocalist*　　　　　　　　**1 wk**

14 Dec 96	MAKE SOMEONE HAPPY *Warner Bros. W 0385CD*	69	1

Judith DURHAM *Australia, female vocalist*　　　　　**5 wks**

15 Jun 67	OLIVE TREE *Columbia DB 8207*	33	5

Ian DURY and the BLOCKHEADS ✔
UK, male vocal/instrumental group　　　　　　　　**55 wks**

29 Apr 78 ●	WHAT A WASTE *Stiff BUY 27*	9	12
9 Dec 78 ★	HIT ME WITH YOUR RHYTHM STICK *Stiff BUY 38* [1]	1	15
4 Aug 79 ●	REASONS TO BE CHEERFUL (PT. 3) *Stiff BUY 50*	3	8
30 Aug 80	I WANT TO BE STRAIGHT *Stiff BUY 90*	22	7
15 Nov 80	SUEPERMAN'S BIG SISTER *Stiff BUY 100*	51	3
25 May 85	HIT ME WITH YOUR RHYTHM STICK (re-mix) *Stiff BUY 214*	55	4
26 Oct 85	PROFOUNDLY IN LOVE WITH PANDORA *EMI EMI 5534* [2]	45	5
27 Jul 91	HIT ME WITH YOUR RHYTHM STICK (2nd re-mix) *Flying FLYR 1*	73	1

[1] Ian and the Blockheads　[2] Ian Dury

DUST JUNKYS *UK, male vocal/instrumental group*　　**5 wks**

15 Nov 97	(NONSTOPOPERATION) *Polydor 5719732*	47	2
28 Feb 98	WHAT TIME IS IT? *Polydor 5694912*	39	2
16 May 98	NOTHIN' PERSONAL *Polydor 5699092*	62	1

Slim DUSTY 🎵 *Australia, male vocalist*　　　　　　**15 wks**

30 Jan 59 ●	A PUB WITH NO BEER *Columbia DB 4212*	3	15

Ondrea DUVERN – *See HUSTLERS CONVENTION featuring Dave LAUDAT and Ondrea DUVERN*

DWEEB *UK, male/female vocal/instrumental trio*　　**2 wks**

22 Feb 97	SCOOBY DOO *Blanco Y Negro NEG 100CD*	63	1
7 Jun 97	OH YEAH, BABY *Blanco Y Negro NEG 102CD1*	70	1

Bob DYLAN ♂ ✔ *The most influential folk/rock vocalist/guitarist ever, b. Robert Zimmerman, 24 May, 1941, Minnesota. The legendary performer, who led the 1960s folk-music movement, redefined the term and, indeed, image of the singer/songwriter. He remains one of the biggest-selling album acts of the rock era*　　　　　　　　**136 wks**

25 Mar 65 ●	TIMES THEY ARE A-CHANGIN' *CBS 201751*	9	11
29 Apr 65 ●	SUBTERRANEAN HOMESICK BLUES *CBS 201753*	9	9
17 Jun 65	MAGGIE'S FARM *CBS 201781*	22	8
19 Aug 65 ●	LIKE A ROLLING STONE *CBS 201811*	4	12
28 Oct 65 ●	POSITIVELY FOURTH STREET *CBS 201824*	8	12
27 Jan 66	CAN YOU PLEASE CRAWL OUT YOUR WINDOW *CBS 201900*	17	5
14 Apr 66	ONE OF US MUST KNOW (SOONER OR LATER) *CBS 202053*	33	5
12 May 66 ●	RAINY DAY WOMEN NOS. 12 & 35 *CBS 202307*	7	8
21 Jul 66	I WANT YOU *CBS 202258*	16	9
14 May 69	I THREW IT ALL AWAY *CBS 4219*	30	6
13 Sep 69 ●	LAY LADY LAY *CBS 4434*	5	12
10 Jul 71	WATCHING THE RIVER FLOW *CBS 7329*	24	9
6 Oct 73	KNOCKIN' ON HEAVEN'S DOOR *CBS 1762*	14	9
7 Feb 76	HURRICANE *CBS 3878*	43	4
29 Jul 78	BABY STOP CRYING *CBS 6499*	13	11
28 Oct 78	IS YOUR LOVE IN VAIN *CBS 6718*	56	3
20 May 95	DIGNITY *Columbia 6620762*	33	2
11 Jul 98	LOVE SICK *Columbia 6659972*	64	1

DYNAMIX II featuring TOO TOUGH TEE
US, male vocal/instrumental group　　　　　　　　**4 wks**

8 Aug 87	JUST GIVE THE DJ A BREAK *Cooltempo COOL 151*	50	4

DYNASTY 🎵 *US, male/female vocal/instrumental group*　**20 wks**

13 Oct 79	I DON'T WANT TO BE A FREAK (BUT I CAN'T HELP MYSELF) *Solar FB 1694*	20	13
9 Aug 80	I'VE JUST BEGUN TO LOVE YOU *Solar SO 10*	51	4
21 May 83	DOES THAT RING A BELL *Solar E 9911*	53	3

DYNASTY OF TWO featuring ROWETTA – *See VARIOUS ARTISTS (EPs & LPs) – The Further Adventures of North (EP)*

Ronnie DYSON *US, male vocalist*　　　　　　　　**6 wks**

4 Dec 71	WHEN YOU GET RIGHT DOWN TO IT *CBS 7449*	34	6

What: *Crazy for You*
Who: Madonna
When: 1985 (2), 1991 (2 – remix)
Which: Gave Ms Ciccone her first ballad hit and was the first of her two singles to visit the Top 5 twice (see 'Holiday'). Both records were produced by hitmaker John 'Jellybean' Benitez

33

What: *Tears*
Who: Ken Dodd
When: 1965 (1)
Which: Was sung by the comedian/entertainer voted Top Show Business Personality of 1965, and became the year's biggest chart hit. The song had originally been made popular by Rudy Vallee in 1931

34

What: *I Will Always Love You*
Who: Whitney Houston
When: 1992 (1), 1993 (25)
Which: Singer initially considered song "too country". It is the biggest-selling single in the UK by a female artist and also a Grammy award winner. Previously topped US country chart twice (a record) by writer Dolly Parton

35

36

What: *I Feel Love*
Who: Donna Summer
When: 1977 (1), 1982 (21 – remix), 1995 (9 – remix)
Which: Transported the Queen of Disco to the top in many countries, and produced her only UK No 1 single. This song helped to change the direction of dance music

E

Katherine E *US, female vocalist*   **7 wks**

6 Apr 91	I'M ALRIGHT *Dead Dead Good GOOD 2*	41	5
18 Jan 92	THEN I FEEL GOOD *PWL Continental PWL 13*	56	2

Lizz E – *See FRESH 4 featuring Lizz E*

Sheila E ☺ *US, female vocalist/instrumentalist – percussion*   **9 wks**

23 Feb 85	THE BELLE OF ST MARK *Warner Bros. W 9180*	18	9

E-LUSTRIOUS *UK, male instrumental/production duo*   **2 wks**

15 Feb 92	DANCE NO MORE *MOS MOS 001T* [1]	58	1
2 Jul 94	IN YOUR DANCE *UFG UFG 6CD*	69	1

[1] E-Lustrious featuring Deborah French

E-MALE *UK, male vocal/instrumental group*   **1 wk**

31 Jan 98	WE ARE E-MALE *East West EW 137CD*	44	1

E-MOTION ☺ *UK, male vocal/instrumental duo*   **7 wks**

3 Feb 96	THE NAUGHTY NORTH AND THE SEXY SOUTH *Soundproof MCSTD 40017*	20	3
17 Aug 96	I STAND ALONE *Soundproof MCSTD 40061*	60	1
26 Oct 96	THE NAUGHTY NORTH AND THE SEXY SOUTH (re-mix) *Soundproof MCSTD 40076*	17	3

E-ROTIC *Germany/US, male/female vocal/instrumental group*   **2 wks**

3 Jun 95	MAX DON'T HAVE SEX WITH YOUR EX *Stip CDSTIP 2*	45	2

E-SMOOVE featuring Latanza Waters
UK, male production team, and US female vocalist   **1 wk**

15 Aug 98	DEJA VU *AM:PM 5827671*	63	1

E-TYPE *Sweden, male vocalist*   **1 wk**

23 Sep 95	THIS IS THE WAY *Ffrreedom TABCD 237*	53	1

E-ZEE POSSEE ☺ *UK, male/female vocal/instrumental group*   **16 wks**

26 Aug 89	EVERYTHING STARTS WITH AN 'E' *More Protein PROT 1*	69	1
20 Jan 90	LOVE ON LOVE *More Protein PROT 3*	59	3
17 Mar 90	EVERYTHING STARTS WITH AN 'E' (re-entry) *More Protein PROT 1*	15	8
30 Jun 90	THE SUN MACHINE *More Protein PROT 4*	62	3
21 Sep 91	BREATHING IS E-ZEE *More Protein PROT 12* [1]	72	1

[1] E-Zee Possee featuring Tara Newley

EAGLES ✎ *US, male vocal/instrumental group*   **51 wks**

9 Aug 75	ONE OF THESE NIGHTS *Asylum AYM 543* ▲	23	7
1 Nov 75	LYIN' EYES *Asylum AYM 548*	23	7
6 Mar 76	TAKE IT TO THE LIMIT *Asylum K 13029*	12	7
15 Jan 77	NEW KID IN TOWN *Asylum K 13069* ▲	20	7
16 Apr 77	● HOTEL CALIFORNIA *Asylum K 13079* ▲	8	10
16 Dec 78	PLEASE COME HOME FOR CHRISTMAS *Asylum K 13145*	30	5
13 Oct 79	HEARTACHE TONIGHT *Asylum K 12394* ▲	40	5
1 Dec 79	THE LONG RUN *Elektra K 12404*	66	2
13 Jul 96	LOVE WILL KEEP US ALIVE *Geffen GFSTD 21980*	52	1

Robert EARL ☾ *UK, male vocalist*   **27 wks**

25 Apr 58	I MAY NEVER PASS THIS WAY AGAIN *Philips PB 805*	14	13
24 Oct 58	MORE THAN EVER (COME PRIMA) *Philips PB 867*	26	2
21 Nov 58	MORE THAN EVER (COME PRIMA) (re-entry) *Philips PB 867*	28	2
13 Feb 59	WONDERFUL SECRET OF LOVE *Philips PB 891*	17	10

Charles EARLAND *US, male instrumentalist – keyboards*   **5 wks**

19 Aug 78	LET THE MUSIC PLAY *Mercury 6167 703*	46	5

Steve EARLE *US, male vocalist/instrumentalist – guitar*   **7 wks**

15 Oct 88	COPPERHEAD ROAD *MCA MCA 1280*	45	6
31 Dec 88	JOHNNY COME LATELY *MCA MCA 1301*	75	1

EARLY MUSIC CONSORT directed by David MUNROW
UK, male/female instrumental group   **1 wk**

3 Apr 71	HENRY VIII SUITE (EP) *BBC RESL 1*	49	1

Tracks on Henry VIII Suite (EP): Fanfare Passomezo Du Roy, Gaillard De Escosse / Pavane, Mille Ducats / Larocque Gaillarde / Allemande / Wedding March, La Morisque / If Love Now Reigned / Ronde, Pourquoi

EARTH WIND AND FIRE ♪ *Colourful, mystical, Los Angeles-based group noted for flamboyant stage performances. Formed by Maurice White (d/v) and included Philip Bailey (v), Ronnie Laws (s/fl) and Verdine White (b). Few R&B acts outsold them in the late 1970s, when they achieved eight successive US Top 10 albums*   **125 wks**

12 Feb 77	SATURDAY NITE *CBS 4835*	17	9
11 Feb 78	FANTASY *CBS 6056*	14	10
13 May 78	JUPITER *CBS 6267*	41	5
29 Jul 78	MAGIC MIND *CBS 6490*	75	1
12 Aug 78	MAGIC MIND (re-entry) *CBS 6490*	54	4
7 Oct 78	GOT TO GET YOU INTO MY LIFE *CBS 6553*	33	7
9 Dec 78	● SEPTEMBER *CBS 6922*	3	13
12 May 79	● BOOGIE WONDERLAND *CBS 7292* [1]	4	13
28 Jul 79	● AFTER THE LOVE HAS GONE *CBS 7721*	4	10
6 Oct 79	STAR *CBS 7902*	16	8
15 Dec 79	CAN'T LET GO *CBS 8077*	46	7
8 Mar 80	IN THE STONE *CBS 8252*	53	3
11 Oct 80	LET ME TALK *CBS 8982*	29	5
20 Dec 80	BACK ON THE ROAD *CBS 9377*	63	4
7 Nov 81	● LET'S GROOVE *CBS A 1679*	3	13
6 Feb 82	I'VE HAD ENOUGH *CBS A 1959*	29	6
5 Feb 83	FALL IN LOVE WITH ME *CBS A 2927*	47	4
7 Nov 87	SYSTEM OF SURVIVAL *CBS EWF 1*	54	3

[1] Earth Wind and Fire with the Emotions

EARTHLING *UK, male vocal/instrumental duo*   **2 wks**

14 Oct 95	ECHO ON MY MIND PART II *Cooltempo CDCOOL 312*	61	1
1 Jun 96	BLOOD MUSIC EP *Cooltempo CDCOOL 319*	69	1

Tracks on Blood Music (EP): First Transmission / Because the Night / Soup or No Soup / Infinite M

EAST 57TH STREET *UK, male production*   **3 wks**

11 Oct 97	SATURDAY *AM:PM 5823752* [1]	29	3

[1] East 57th Street featuring Donna Allen

EAST OF EDEN ✎ *UK, male instrumental group*   **12 wks**

17 Apr 71	● JIG A JIG *Deram DM 297*	7	12

EAST 17 ☯ *London-based singing, rapping and dancing lads with international teen appeal: Tony Mortimer (v/k), Brian Harvey (v), John Hendy (v), Terry Coldwell (v). Bad press and personal problems resulted in main songwriter Mortimer quitting, and a name change for their 1998 comeback*   **162 wks**

29 Aug 92	● HOUSE OF LOVE *London LON 325*	10	9
14 Nov 92	GOLD *London LON 331*	28	4
19 Dec 92	GOLD (re-entry) *London LON 331*	64	4

UK No 1 ★   UK Top 10 ●   UK million seller ◆   UK entry at No 1 ■   US No 1 ▲

30 Jan 93 ●	DEEP *London LOCDP 334*......		5	10
10 Apr 93	SLOW IT DOWN *London LONCD 339*......		13	7
26 Jun 93	WEST END GIRLS *London LONCD 344*......		11	7
4 Dec 93 ●	IT'S ALRIGHT *London LONCD 345*......		3	14
14 May 94 ●	AROUND THE WORLD *London LONCD 349*......		3	13
1 Oct 94 ●	STEAM *London LONCD 353*......		7	8
3 Dec 94 ★	STAY ANOTHER DAY *London LONCD 354*......		1	15
25 Mar 95 ●	LET IT RAIN *London LONCD 363*......		10	7
6 May 95	STAY ANOTHER DAY (re-entry) *London LONCD 354*......		64	1
17 Jun 95	HOLD MY BODY TIGHT *London LONCD 367*......		12	7
4 Nov 95 ●	THUNDER *London LONCD 373*......		4	14
10 Feb 96 ●	DO U STILL *London LONCD 379*......		7	7
10 Aug 96	SOMEONE TO LOVE *London LONCD 385*......		16	8
2 Nov 96 ●	IF YOU EVER *London LONCD 388* [1]......		2	15
18 Jan 97 ●	HEY CHILD *London LONCD 390*......		3	5
14 Nov 98 ●	EACH TIME *Telstar CDSTAS 3017* [2]......		2†	7

[1] East 17 featuring Gabrielle [2] E-17 since Tony Mortimer quit

EAST SIDE BEAT ⊗ ☺ *Italy, male vocal/instrumental duo* 18 wks

30 Nov 91 ●	RIDE LIKE THE WIND *ffrr F 176*......		3	11
19 Dec 92	ALIVE AND KICKING *ffrr F 206*......		26	6
29 May 93	YOU'RE MY EVERYTHING *ffrr FCD 207*......		65	1

Sheena EASTON ⊗ *Scotland's most successful act Stateside, b. Sheena Orr, 27 April, 1959, Glasgow. This vocalist was first seen in TV documentary* The Big Time. *Reached the big time on both sides of the Atlantic and won the Grammy for Best New Artist of 1981* 103 wks

5 Apr 80	MODERN GIRL *EMI 5042*......		56	3
19 Jul 80	9 TO 5 *EMI 5066* ▲......		3	15
9 Aug 80 ●	MODERN GIRL (re-entry) *EMI 5042*......		8	12
25 Oct 80	ONE MAN WOMAN *EMI 5114*......		14	6
14 Feb 81	TAKE MY TIME *EMI 5135*......		44	5
2 May 81	WHEN HE SHINES *EMI 5166*......		12	8
27 Jun 81 ●	FOR YOUR EYES ONLY *EMI 5195*......		8	13
12 Sep 81	JUST ANOTHER BROKEN HEART *EMI 5232*......		33	8
5 Dec 81	YOU COULD HAVE BEEN WITH ME *EMI 5252*......		54	3
31 Jul 82	MACHINERY *EMI 5326*......		38	5
12 Feb 83	WE'VE GOT TONIGHT *Liberty UP 658* [1]......		28	7
21 Jan 89	THE LOVER IN ME *MCA MCA 1289*......		15	8
18 Mar 89	DAYS LIKE THIS *MCA MCA 1325*......		43	3
15 Jul 89	101 *MCA MCA 1348*......		54	2
18 Nov 89	THE ARMS OF ORION *Warner Bros. W 2757* [2]......		27	5

[1] Kenny Rogers and Sheena Easton [2] Prince with Sheena Easton

See also PRINCE

EASTSIDE CONNECTION *US, disco aggregation* 3 wks

8 Apr 78	YOU'RE SO RIGHT FOR ME *Creole CR 149*......		44	3

Clint EASTWOOD ℂ *US, male vocalist* 10 wks

7 Feb 70	I TALK TO THE TREES *Paramount PARA 3004*......		18	2
29 Sep 84	LAST PLANE (ONE WAY TICKET) *MCA MCA 910* [1]......		51	3
2 Apr 94	OH CAROL! *Copasetic COPCD 0009* [1]......		54	5

[1] Clint Eastwood and General Saint

This is the flip of 'Wand'rin Star' by Lee Marvin and was listed with Marvin's A-side for two weeks only

EASYBEATS ⊗ *Australia, male vocal/instrumental group* 24 wks

27 Oct 66 ●	FRIDAY ON MY MIND *United Artists UP 1157*......		6	15
10 Apr 68	HELLO HOW ARE YOU *United Artists UP 2209*......		20	9

EAT *UK/US, male/female vocal/instrumental group* 1 wk

12 Jun 93	BLEED ME WHITE *Fiction FICCD 48*......		73	1

EAT STATIC *UK, male production duo* 3 wks

22 Feb 97	HYBRID *Planet Dog BARK 024CD*......		41	1
27 Sep 97	INTERCEPTOR *Planet Dog BARK 030CD*......		44	1
27 Jun 98	CONTACT... *Planet Dog BARK 033CD*......		67	1

Cleveland EATON *US, male instrumentalist – keyboards* 6 wks

23 Sep 78	BAMA BOOGIE WOOGIE *Gull GULS 63*......		35	6

EAV *Austria, male vocal/instrumental group* 4 wks

27 Sep 86	BA-BA-BANKROBBERY (ENGLISH VERSION) *Columbia DB 9139*......		63	4

EAV is short for Erste Allgemeine Verunsicherung

EAZY-E *US, male rapper* 3 wks

6 Jan 96	JUST TAH LET YOU KNOW *Epic 6628162*......		30	3

EBTG – *see DEEP DISH; EVERYTHING BUT THE GIRL*

ECHO and the BUNNYMEN ☹ ✎ *UK, male vocal/instrumental group* 82 wks

17 May 80	RESCUE *Korova KOW 1*......		62	1
18 Apr 81	CROCODILES *Korova ECHO 1*......		37	4
18 Jul 81	A PROMISE *Korova KOW 15*......		49	4
29 May 82	THE BACK OF LOVE *Korova KOW 24*......		19	7
22 Jan 83 ●	THE CUTTER *Korova KOW 26*......		8	8
16 Jul 83	NEVER STOP *Korova KOW 28*......		15	7
28 Jan 84 ●	THE KILLING MOON *Korova KOW 32*......		9	6
21 Apr 84	SILVER *Korova KOW 34*......		30	5
14 Jul 84	SEVEN SEAS *Korova KOW 35*......		16	7
19 Oct 85	BRING ON THE DANCING HORSES *Korova KOW 43*......		21	7
13 Jun 87	THE GAME *WEA YZ 134*......		28	4
1 Aug 87	LIPS LIKE SUGAR *WEA YZ 144*......		36	4
20 Feb 88	PEOPLE ARE STRANGE *WEA YZ 175*......		29	5
2 Mar 91	PEOPLE ARE STRANGE (re-issue) *East West YZ 567*......		34	4
28 Jun 97 ●	NOTHING LASTS FOREVER *London LOCDP 396*......		8	6
13 Sep 97	I WANT TO BE THERE WHEN YOU COME *London LONCD 399*......		30	2
8 Nov 97	DON'T LET IT GET YOU DOWN *London LOCDP 406*......		50	1

ECHOBEATZ ☺ *UK, male DJ/production duo* 5 wks

25 Jul 98 ●	MAS QUE NADA *Eternal WEA 176CD*......		10	5

ECHOBELLY ☹ ⊗

UK/Sweden, male/female vocal/instrumental group 16 wks

2 Apr 94	INSOMNIAC *Fauve FAUV 1CD*......		47	1
2 Jul 94	I CAN'T IMAGINE THE WORLD WITHOUT ME *Fauve FAUV 2CD*......		39	2
5 Nov 94	CLOSE...BUT *Fauve FAUV 4CD*......		59	1
2 Sep 95	GREAT THINGS *Fauve FAUV 5CD*......		13	3
4 Nov 95	KING OF THE KERB *Fauve FAUV 7CD*......		25	3
2 Mar 96	DARK THERAPY *Fauve FAUV 8CD*......		20	3
23 Aug 97	THE WORLD IS FLAT *Epic 6648152*......		31	2
8 Nov 97	HERE COMES THE BIG RUSH *Epic 6652452*......		56	1

Billy ECKSTINE ℂ *US, male vocalist* 48 wks

12 Nov 54 ●	NO ONE BUT YOU *MGM 763*......		3	17
27 Sep 57	PASSING STRANGERS *Mercury MT 164* [1]......		22	2
13 Feb 59 ●	GIGI *Mercury AMT 1018*......		8	14
12 Mar 69	PASSING STRANGERS (re-issue) *Mercury MF 1082* [1]......		20	15

[1] Billy Eckstine and Sarah Vaughan

EDDIE and the HOTRODS ✎ *UK, male vocal/instrumental group* 26 wks

11 Sep 76	LIVE AT THE MARQUEE EP *Island IEP 2*......		43	5
13 Nov 76	TEENAGE DEPRESSION *Island WIP 6354*......		35	4
23 Apr 77	I MIGHT BE LYING *Island WIP 6388*......		44	3
13 Aug 77 ●	DO ANYTHING YOU WANNA DO *Island WIP 6401* [1]......		9	10
21 Jan 78	QUIT THIS TOWN *Island WIP 6411*......		36	4

[1] Rods

Tracks on Live at the Marquee (EP): 96 Tears/Get out of Denver/Medley/Gloria/Satisfaction

EDDY *UK, female vocalist*   **2 wks**

9 Jul 94	**SOMEDAY** *Positiva CDTIV 14*	.49	2

Duane EDDY and the REBELS 🎸 *Twangy guitar legend, b. 26 April, 1938, New York. Early rock's No 1 solo instrumentalist assembled a long string of UK and US hit singles and was one of the first rock acts to score on the album charts*   **196 wks**

5 Sep 58	**REBEL ROUSER** *London HL 8669*	.19	10
2 Jan 59	**CANNONBALL** *London HL 8764*	.22	4
19 Jun 59 ●	**PETER GUNN THEME** *London HLW 8879*	..6	10
24 Jul 59	**YEP** *London HLW 8879*	.17	5
4 Sep 59	**FORTY MILES OF BAD ROAD** *London HLW 8929*	.11	9
11 Sep 59	**PETER GUNN THEME (re-entry)** *London HLW 8879*	.27	1
18 Dec 59	**SOME KINDA EARTHQUAKE** *London HLW 9007*	.12	5
19 Feb 60	**BONNIE CAME BACK** *London HLW 9050*	.13	10
28 Apr 60 ●	**SHAZAM!** *London HLW 9104*	..4	13
21 Jul 60 ●	**BECAUSE THEY'RE YOUNG** *London HLW 9162*	..2	18
10 Nov 60	**KOMMOTION** *London HLW 9225*	.13	10
12 Jan 61	**PEPE** *London HLW 9257*	..2	14
20 Apr 61	**THEME FROM DIXIE** *London HLW 9324*	..7	10
22 Jun 61	**RING OF FIRE** *London HLW 9370*	.17	10
14 Sep 61	**DRIVIN' HOME** *London HLW 9406*	.30	4
5 Oct 61	**CARAVAN** *Parlophone R 4826* [1]	.42	3
24 May 62	**DEEP IN THE HEART OF TEXAS** *RCA 1288* [1]	.19	8
23 Aug 62 ●	**BALLAD OF PALADIN** *RCA 1300* [1]	.10	10
8 Nov 62 ●	**DANCE WITH THE GUITAR MAN** *RCA 1316* [2]	..4	16
14 Feb 63	**BOSS GUITAR** *RCA 1329* [2]	.27	8
30 May 63	**LONELY BOY LONELY GUITAR** *RCA 1344* [2]	.35	4
29 Aug 63	**YOUR BABY'S GONE SURFIN'** *RCA 1357* [2]	.49	1
8 Mar 75 ●	**PLAY ME LIKE YOU PLAY YOUR GUITAR** *GTO GT 11* [2]	..9	9
22 Mar 86 ●	**PETER GUNN** *China WOK 6* [3]	..8	9

[1] Duane Eddy [2] Duane Eddy and the Rebelettes [3] Art of Noise featuring Duane Eddy

EDDY and the SOUL BAND ☺ *US, male vocal/instrumental group*   **7 wks**

23 Feb 85	**THE THEME FROM 'SHAFT'** *Club JAB 11*	.13	7

Randy EDELMAN ● *US, male vocalist / pianist*   **18 wks**

6 Mar 76	**CONCRETE AND CLAY** *20th Century BTC 2261*	.11	7
18 Sep 76	**UPTOWN UPTEMPO WOMAN** *20th Century BTC 2225*	.25	7
15 Jan 77	**YOU** *20th Century BTC 2253*	.49	2
17 Jul 82	**NOBODY MADE ME** *Rocket XPRES 81*	.60	2

EDELWEISS ● *Austria, male/female vocal/instrumental group*   **10 wks**

29 Apr 89 ●	**BRING ME EDELWEISS** *WEA YZ 353*	..5	10

EDEN *UK/Australia, male/female vocal/instrumental group*   **2 wks**

6 Mar 93	**DO U FEEL 4 ME** *Logic 74321135422*	.51	2

Lyn EDEN – *See SMOKIN' BEATS featuring Lyn EDEN*

EDISON LIGHTHOUSE ● *UK, male vocal/instrumental group*   **13 wks**

24 Jan 70 ★	**LOVE GROWS (WHERE MY ROSEMARY GOES)** *Bell 1091*	..1	12
30 Jan 71	**IT'S UP TO YOU PETULA** *Bell 1136*	.49	1

Dave EDMUNDS ● 🎸 *UK, male vocalist/multi-instrumentalist*   **93 wks**

21 Nov 70 ★	**I HEAR YOU KNOCKING** *MAM 1*	..1	14
20 Jan 73 ●	**BABY I LOVE YOU** *Rockfield ROC 1*	..8	13
9 Jun 73 ●	**BORN TO BE WITH YOU** *Rockfield ROC 2*	..5	12
2 Jul 77	**I KNEW THE BRIDE** *Swansong SSK 19411*	.26	8
30 Jun 79 ●	**GIRLS TALK** *Swansong SSK 19418*	..4	11
22 Sep 79	**QUEEN OF HEARTS** *Swansong SSK 19419*	.11	9
24 Nov 79	**CRAWLING FROM THE WRECKAGE** *Swansong SSK 19420*	.59	4
9 Feb 80	**SINGING THE BLUES** *Swansong SSK 19422*	.28	8
28 Mar 81	**ALMOST SATURDAY NIGHT** *Swansong SSK 19424*	.58	3
20 Jun 81	**THE RACE IS ON** *Swansong SSK 19425* [1]	.34	6

26 Mar 83	**SLIPPING AWAY** *Arista ARIST 522*	.60	4
7 Apr 90	**KING OF LOVE** *Capitol CL 568*	.68	1

[1] Dave Edmunds and the Stray Cats

Alton EDWARDS ✎ ◑ *Zimbabwe, male vocalist*   **9 wks**

9 Jan 82	**I JUST WANNA (SPEND SOME TIME WITH YOU)** *Streetwave STRA 1897*	.20	9

Dennis EDWARDS featuring Siedah GARRETT ✎ *US, male/female vocal duo*   **10 wks**

24 Mar 84	**DON'T LOOK ANY FURTHER** *Gordy TMG 1334*	.45	5
20 Jun 87	**DON'T LOOK ANY FURTHER (re-entry)** *Gordy TMG 1334*	.55	5

See also Michael JACKSON

Rupie EDWARDS 🌴 *Jamaica, male vocalist*   **16 wks**

23 Nov 74 ●	**IRE FEELINGS (SKANGA)** *Cactus CT 38*	..9	10
8 Feb 75	**LEGO SKANGA** *Cactus CT 51*	.32	6

Tommy EDWARDS ℂ *US, male vocalist*   **18 wks**

3 Oct 58 ★	**IT'S ALL IN THE GAME** *MGM 989* ▲	..1	17
7 Aug 59	**MY MELANCHOLY BABY** *MGM 1020*	.29	1

EELS 🎸 *US, male vocal/instrumental group*   **16 wks**

15 Feb 97 ●	**NOVOCAINE FOR THE SOUL** *Dreamworks DRMCD 22174*	.10	5
17 May 97 ●	**SUSAN'S HOUSE** *Dreamworks DRMCD 22238*	..9	5
13 Sep 97	**YOUR LUCKY DAY IN HELL** *Dreamworks DRMCD 22277*	.35	2
26 Sep 98	**LAST STOP: THIS TOWN** *Dreamworks DRMCD 22346*	.23	3
12 Dec 98	**CANCER FOR THE CURE** *Dreamworks DRMCD 22373*	.60	1

EFUA *UK, female vocalist*   **5 wks**

3 Jul 93	**SOMEWHERE** *Virgin VSCDT 1463*	.42	5

EGGS ON LEGS *UK, male vocalist*   **1 wk**

23 Sep 95	**COCK A DOODLE DO IT** *Avex UK AVEXCD 18*	.42	1

EGYPTIAN EMPIRE *UK, male producer – Tim Taylor*   **2 wks**

24 Oct 92	**THE HORN TRACK** *Ffrreedom TAB 115*	.61	2

18 WHEELER *UK, male vocal/instrumental group*   **1 wk**

15 Mar 97	**STAY** *Creation CRESCD 249*	.59	1

EIGHTH WONDER ◑ *UK, male/female vocal/instrumental group*   **25 wks**

2 Nov 85	**STAY WITH ME** *CBS A 6594*	.65	2
20 Feb 88 ●	**I'M NOT SCARED** *CBS SCARE 1*	..7	13
25 Jun 88	**CROSS MY HEART** *CBS 651552 7*	.13	8
1 Oct 88	**BABY BABY** *CBS BABE 1*	.65	2

808 STATE ☺ *UK, male instrumental group*   **69 wks**

18 Nov 89 ●	**PACIFIC STATE** *ZTT ZANG 1*	.10	9
31 Mar 90	**THE EXTENDED PLEASURE OF DANCE EP** *ZTT 2T*	.56	1
2 Jun 90 ●	**THE ONLY RHYME THAT BITES** *ZTT ZANG 3* [1]	.10	10
15 Sep 90	**TUNES SPLITS THE ATOM** *ZTT ZANG 6* [1]	.18	7
10 Nov 90 ●	**CUBIK/OLYMPIC** *ZTT ZANG 5*	.10	10
16 Feb 91 ●	**IN YER FACE** *ZTT ZANG 14*	..9	6
27 Apr 91	**OOOPS** *ZTT ZANG 19* [2]	.42	3
17 Aug 91	**LIFT/OPEN YOUR MIND** *ZTT ZANG 20*	.38	4
29 Aug 92	**TIME BOMB/NIMBUS** *ZTT ZANG 33*	.59	1
12 Dec 92	**ONE IN TEN** *ZTT ZANG 39* [3]	.17	8
30 Jan 93	**PLAN 9** *ZTT ZANG 38CD*	.50	2
26 Jun 93	**10 X 10** *ZTT ZANG 42CD*	.67	1
13 Aug 94	**BOMBADIN** *ZTT ZANG 54CD*	.67	1
29 Jun 96	**BOND** *ZTT ZANG 80CD*	.57	1
8 Feb 97	**LOPEZ** *ZTT ZANG 87CD*	.20	2
16 May 98	**PACIFIC/CUBIK** *ZTT ZTT 98CD1*	.21	3

[1] MC Tunes versus 808 State [2] 808 State featuring Bjork [3] 808 State vs UB40

UK No 1 ★   UK Top 10 ●   UK million seller ◆   UK entry at No 1 ■   US No 1 ▲

Tracks on The Extended Pleasure of Dance (EP): Ancodia / Cubik / Cuba Bora.
'Cubik' is a re-issue of one of the tracks from The Extended Pleasure of Dance (EP).
'Lopez' features the uncredited vocals of James Dean Bradfield, lead singer of the
Manic Street Preachers.
See also VARIOUS ARTISTS (EPs & LPs) – Gimme Shelter (EP)

88.3 – *See Lisa MAY*

EINSTEIN *UK, male rapper*   **6 wks**

18 Nov 89	**ANOTHER MONSTERJAM** *ffrr F 116* 1	65	1
15 Dec 90	**TURN IT UP** *Swanyard SYD 9* 2	42	4
24 Aug 96	**THE POWER** *Arista 74321398672* 3	42	1

1 Simon Harris featuring Einstein 2 Technotronic featuring Melissa and Einstein
3 Snap featuring Einstein

See also AMBASSADORS OF FUNK featuring MC MARIO

EL MARIACHI *US, male producer – Roger Sanchez*   **2 wks**

9 Nov 96	**CUBA** *ffrr FCD 286*	38	2

See also FUNK JUNKEEZ

ELASTICA ☹ *UK, female/male vocal/instrumental group*   **11 wks**

12 Feb 94	**LINE UP** *Deceptive BLUFF 004CD*	20	3
22 Oct 94	**CONNECTION** *Deceptive BLUFF 010CD*	17	4
25 Feb 95	**WAKING UP** *Deceptive BLUFF 011CD*	13	4

ELATE *UK, male / female vocal / instrumental trio*   **2 wks**

26 Jul 97	**SOMEBODY LIKE YOU** *VC VCRD 22*	38	2

Donnie ELBERT 🎤 *US, male vocalist*   **29 wks**

8 Jan 72	● **WHERE DID OUR LOVE GO?** *London HL 10352*	8	10
26 Feb 72	**I CAN'T HELP MYSELF** *Avco 6105 009*	11	10
29 Apr 72	**LITTLE PIECE OF LEATHER** *London HL 10370*	27	9

ELECTRA *UK, male vocal/instrumental group*   **7 wks**

6 Aug 88	**JIBARO** *ffrr FFR 9*	54	3
30 Dec 89	**IT'S YOUR DESTINY/AUTUMN LOVE** *London F 121*	51	4

ELECTRAFIXION *UK, male vocal/instrumental group*   **6 wks**

19 Nov 94	**ZEPHYR** *WEA YZ 865CD*	47	2
9 Sep 95	**LOWDOWN** *WEA YZ 977CD*	54	2
4 Nov 95	**NEVER** *Spacejunk WEA 022CD*	58	1
16 Mar 96	**SISTER PAIN** *Spacejunk WEA 037CD1*	27	1

ELECTRASY ☹ 🎸 *UK, male vocal / instrumental group*   **7 wks**

13 Jun 98	**LOST IN SPACE** *MCA MCSTD 40171*	60	1
5 Sep 98	**MORNING AFTERGLOW** *MCA MCSTD 40184*	19	4
28 Nov 98	**BEST FRIEND'S GIRL** *MCA MCSXD 40195*	41	2

ELECTRIBE 101
UK/Germany, male/female vocal/instrumental group   **15 wks**

28 Oct 89	**TELL ME WHEN THE FEVER ENDED** *Mercury MER 310*	32	5
24 Feb 90	**TALKING WITH MYSELF** *Mercury MER 316*	23	5
22 Sep 90	**YOU'RE WALKING** *Mercury MER 328*	50	3
10 Oct 98	**TALKING WITH MYSELF '98 (re-mix)** *Manifesto FESDD 49*	39	2

ELECTRIC LIGHT ORCHESTRA 🎸 *Groundbreaking and innovative UK group, fronted by multi-talented Jeff Lynne (v/g) from Birmingham and originally included Roy Wood (The Move). Their unique sound, which featured an orchestral string section, helped them achieve numerous transatlantic hits*   **255 wks**

29 Jul 72	● **10538 OVERTURE** *Harvest HAR 5053*	9	8
27 Jan 73	● **ROLL OVER BEETHOVEN** *Harvest HAR 5063*	6	10
6 Oct 73	**SHOWDOWN** *Harvest HAR 5077*	12	10
9 Mar 74	**MA-MA-MA-BELLE** *Warner Bros. K 16349*	22	8
10 Jan 76	● **EVIL WOMAN** *Jet 764*	10	8
3 Jul 76	**STRANGE MAGIC** *Jet 779*	38	3
13 Nov 76	● **LIVIN' THING** *Jet UP 36184*	4	12
19 Feb 77	● **ROCKARIA!** *Jet UP 36209*	9	9
21 May 77	● **TELEPHONE LINE** *Jet UP 36254*	8	10
29 Oct 77	**TURN TO STONE** *Jet UP 36313*	18	12
28 Jan 78	**MR. BLUE SKY** *Jet UP 36342*	6	11
10 Jun 78	● **WILD WEST HERO** *Jet JET 109*	6	14
7 Oct 78	● **SWEET TALKIN' WOMAN** *Jet 121*	6	9
9 Dec 78	**ELO EP** *Jet ELO 1*	34	8
19 May 79	● **SHINE A LITTLE LOVE** *Jet 144*	6	10
21 Jul 79	● **THE DIARY OF HORACE WIMP** *Jet 150*	8	9
1 Sep 79	● **DON'T BRING ME DOWN** *Jet 153*	3	9
17 Nov 79	● **CONFUSION/LAST TRAIN TO LONDON** *Jet 166*	8	10
24 May 80	**I'M ALIVE** *Jet 179*	20	9
21 Jun 80	★ **XANADU** *Jet 185* 1	1	11
2 Aug 80	**ALL OVER THE WORLD** *Jet 195*	11	8
22 Nov 80	**DON'T WALK AWAY** *Jet 7004*	21	10
1 Aug 81	● **HOLD ON TIGHT** *Jet 7011*	4	12
24 Oct 81	**TWILIGHT** *Jet 7015*	30	7
9 Jan 82	**TICKET TO THE MOON/HERE IS THE NEWS** *Jet 7018*	24	8
18 Jun 83	**ROCK 'N' ROLL IS KING** *Jet A 3500*	13	9
3 Sep 83	**SECRET MESSAGES** *Jet A 3720*	48	3
1 Mar 86	**CALLING AMERICA** *Epic A 6844*	28	7
11 May 91	**HONEST MEN** *Telstar ELO 100* 2	60	1

1 Olivia Newton-John and Electric Light Orchestra 2 Electric Light Orchestra Part 2
'Here Is the News' listed from 16 Jan, 1982
Tracks on ELO (EP): Out of My Head / Strange Magic / Ma-Ma-Ma-Belle / Evil Woman

ELECTRIC PRUNES *US, male vocal/instrumental group*   **5 wks**

9 Feb 67	**I HAD TOO MUCH TO DREAM LAST NIGHT** *Reprise RS 20532*	49	1
11 May 67	**GET ME TO THE WORLD ON TIME** *Reprise RS 20564*	42	4

ELECTRONIC ❂ ☺ *UK, male vocal/instrumental group*   **33 wks**

16 Dec 89	**GETTING AWAY WITH IT** *Factory FAC 2577*	12	9
27 Apr 91	● **GET THE MESSAGE** *Factory FAC 2877*	8	7
21 Sep 91	**FEEL EVERY BEAT** *Factory FAC 3287*	39	4
4 Jul 92	● **DISAPPOINTED** *Parlophone R 6311*	6	5
6 Jul 96	**FORBIDDEN CITY** *Parlophone CDR 6436*	14	4
28 Sep 96	**FOR YOU** *Parlophone CDR 6445*	16	2
15 Feb 97	**SECOND NATURE** *Parlophone CDR 6455*	35	2

ELECTRONICAS *Holland, male instrumental group*   **8 wks**

19 Sep 81	**ORIGINAL BIRD DANCE** *Polydor POSP 360*	22	8

ELECTROSET *UK, male instrumental production group*   **4 wks**

21 Nov 92	**HOW DOES IT FEEL** *ffrr F 203*	27	3
15 Jul 95	**SENSATION** *Ffrreedom TABCD 231*	69	1

ELEGANTS *US, male vocal group*   **2 wks**

26 Sep 58	**LITTLE STAR** *HMV POP 520* ▲	25	2

ELEVATION *UK, male instrumental/production duo*   **1 wk**

23 May 92	**CAN YOU FEEL IT** *Nova Mute 12NOMU 3*	62	1

ELEVATORMAN *UK, male instrumental/production group*   **4 wks**

14 Jan 95	**FUNK AND DRIVE** *Wired WIRED 211*	37	3
1 Jul 95	**FIRED UP** *Wired WIRED 216*	44	1

ELGINS 🎤 *US, male/female vocal group*   **20 wks**

1 May 71	● **HEAVEN MUST HAVE SENT YOU** *Tamla Motown TMG 771*	3	13
9 Oct 71	**PUT YOURSELF IN MY PLACE** *Tamla Motown TMG 787*	28	7

ELIAS and his ZIGZAG JIVE FLUTES 🎷
South Africa, male instrumental group   **14 wks**

25 Apr 58	● **TOM HARK** *Columbia DB 4109*	2	14

Yvonne ELLIMAN ❂ *US, female vocalist*   **44 wks**

29 Jan 72	**I DON'T KNOW HOW TO LOVE HIM** *MCA MMKS 5077*	47	1
6 Nov 76	● **LOVE ME** *RSO 2090 205*	6	13

UK No 1 ★   UK Top 10 ●   UK million seller ◆   UK entry at No 1 ■   US No 1 ▲

7 May 77	HELLO STRANGER *RSO 2090 236*	26	5
13 Aug 77	I CAN'T GET YOU OUT OF MY MIND *RSO 2090 251*	17	13
6 May 78 ●	IF I CAN'T HAVE YOU *RSO 2090 266* ▲	4	12

'I Don't Know How to Love Him' was one of four tracks on a Maxi-Single, two of which were credited during the disc's one week on the chart. The other track credited was 'Superstar' by Murray Head

Duke ELLINGTON 🎻 *US, orchestra*   4 wks
| 5 Mar 54 ● | SKIN DEEP *Philips PB 243* | 7 | 4 |

Lance ELLINGTON *UK, male vocalist*   1 wk
| 21 Aug 93 | LONELY (HAVE WE LOST OUR LOVE) *RCA 74321158332* | 57 | 1 |

Ray ELLINGTON *UK, orchestra*   4 wks
| 15 Nov 62 | THE MADISON *Ember S 102* | 41 | 2 |
| 20 Dec 62 | THE MADISON (re-entry) *Ember S 102* | 36 | 2 |

Bern ELLIOTT and the FENMEN 🔊
UK, male vocal/instrumental group   22 wks
| 21 Nov 63 | MONEY *Decca F 11770* | 14 | 13 |
| 19 Mar 64 | NEW ORLEANS *Decca F 11852* | 24 | 9 |

Joe ELLIOTT – *See Mick RONSON with Joe ELLIOTT*

Missy 'Misdemeanour' ELLIOT R&B 👟
US, female rapper   25 wks
30 Aug 97	THE RAIN (SUPA DUPA FLY) *East West E 3919*	16	3
29 Nov 97	SOCK IT 2 ME *East West E 3890CD*	33	2
22 Aug 98	HIT 'EM WITH DA HEE *East West E3824 CD1* [1]	25	3
22 Aug 98	MAKE IT HOT *East West E 3821 CD* [2]	22	4
25 Apr 98	BEEP ME 911 *East West E 3859CD*	14	3
26 Sep 98 ★	I WANT YOU BACK *Virgin VSCDT 1716* [3] ■	1	9
21 Nov 99	5 MINUTES *Elektra E 3803CD* [4]	72	1

[1] Missy 'Misdemeanour' Elliott featuring Lil' Kim [2] Nicole featuring Missy 'Misdemeanour' Elliott and Mocha [3] Melanie B featuring Missy 'Misdemeanour' Elliott [4] Lil' Mo featuring Missy 'Misdemeanour' Elliott

Greg ELLIS – *See Reva RICE and Greg ELLIS*

Joey B ELLIS 🔊 🎻 *US, male rapper*   10 wks
| 16 Feb 91 | GO FOR IT (HEART AND FIRE) *Capitol CL 601* [1] | 20 | 8 |
| 18 May 91 | THOUGHT U WERE THE ONE FOR ME *Capitol CL 614* | 58 | 2 |

[1] Rocky V featuring Joey B Ellis and Tynetta Hare

Shirley ELLIS 🎺 *US, female vocalist*   17 wks
| 6 May 65 ● | THE CLAPPING SONG *London HLR 9961* | 6 | 13 |
| 8 Jul 78 | THE CLAPPING SONG (EP) *MCA MCEP 1* | 59 | 4 |

Tracks on The Clapping Song (EP): The Clapping Song / Ever See a Diver Kiss His Wife While the Bubbles Bounce Above the Water / The Name Game / The Nitty Gritty. 'The Clapping Song' itself qualifies as a re-issue

ELLIS, BEGGS and HOWARD
UK, male vocal/instrumental group   8 wks
| 2 Jul 88 | BIG BUBBLES, NO TROUBLES *RCA PB 42089* | 59 | 3 |
| 11 Mar 89 | BIG BUBBLES, NO TROUBLES (re-entry) *RCA PB 42089* | 41 | 5 |

EMBRACE ☺ 🎻 *UK, male vocal/instrumental group*   21 wks
17 May 97	FIREWORKS EP *Hut HUTCD 84*	34	2
19 Jul 97	ONE BIG FAMILY EP *Hut HUTCD 86*	21	3
8 Nov 97 ●	ALL YOU GOOD GOOD PEOPLE EP *Hut HUTCD 90*	8	4
6 Jun 98 ●	COME BACK TO WHAT YOU KNOW *Hut HUTCD 93*	6	8
29 Aug 98 ●	MY WEAKNESS IS NONE OF YOUR BUSINESS *Hut HUTCD 103*	9	4

Tracks on Fireworks EP: The Last Gas / Now You're Nobody / Blind / Fireworks
Tracks on One Big Family EP: One Big Family / Dry Kids / You've Only Got to Stop to Get Better / Butter Wouldn't Melt

Tracks on All You Good Good People EP: All You Good Good People (Radio Edit) / One Big Family (Perfecto Mix) / All You Good Good People (Fierce Panda Version) / All You Good Good People (Orchestral Mix)

Keith EMERSON *UK, male instrumentalist – piano*   5 wks
| 10 Apr 76 | HONKY TONK TRAIN BLUES *Manticore K 13513* | 21 | 5 |

See also EMERSON, LAKE and PALMER

EMERSON, LAKE and PALMER 🎻
UK, male instrumental group   13 wks
| 4 Jun 77 ● | FANFARE FOR THE COMMON MAN *Atlantic K 10946* | 2 | 13 |

See also Keith EMERSON; Greg LAKE

Dick EMERY *UK, male vocalist*   8 wks
| 26 Feb 69 | IF YOU LOVE HER *Pye 7N 17644* | 32 | 4 |
| 13 Jan 73 | YOU ARE AWFUL *Pye 7N 45202* | 43 | 4 |

EMF 🔊 ☺ *UK, male vocal/instrumental group*   50 wks
3 Nov 90 ●	UNBELIEVABLE *Parlophone R 6273* ▲	3	13
2 Feb 91 ●	I BELIEVE *Parlophone R 6279*	6	7
27 Apr 91	CHILDREN *Parlophone R 6288*	19	5
31 Aug 91	LIES *Parlophone R 6295*	28	3
2 May 92	UNEXPLAINED EP *Parlophone SGE 2026*	18	4
19 Sep 92	THEY'RE HERE *Parlophone R 6321*	29	3
21 Nov 92	IT'S YOU *Parlophone R 6327*	23	3
25 Feb 95	PERFECT DAY *Parlophone CDRS 6401*	27	3
8 Jul 95 ●	I'M A BELIEVER *Parlophone CDR 6412* [1]	3	8
28 Oct 95	AFRO KING *Parlophone CDRS 6416*	51	1

[1] EMF and Reeves and Mortimer

Tracks on Unexplained (EP): Getting Through / Far From Me / The Same / Search and Destroy

EMILIA 🔊 *Sweden, female vocalist*   3 wks
| 12 Dec 98 ● | BIG BIG WORLD *Universal UMD 87190* | 5† | 3 |

EMMA *UK, female vocalist*   6 wks
| 28 Apr 90 | GIVE A LITTLE LOVE BACK TO THE WORLD *Big Wave BWR 33* | 33 | 6 |

AN EMOTIONAL FISH *Ireland, male vocal/instrumental group*   5 wks
| 23 Jun 90 | CELEBRATE *East West YZ 489* | 46 | 5 |

EMOTIONS 🎵 *US, female vocal group*   28 wks
10 Sep 77 ●	BEST OF MY LOVE *CBS 5555* ▲	4	10
24 Dec 77	I DON'T WANNA LOSE YOUR LOVE *CBS 5819*	40	5
12 May 79 ●	BOOGIE WONDERLAND *CBS 7292* [1]	4	13

[1] Earth Wind and Fire with the Emotions

EMPIRION *UK, male instrumental/production group*   2 wks
| 6 Jul 96 | NARCOTIC INFLUENCE *XL XLS 72CD* | 64 | 1 |
| 21 Jun 97 | BETA *XL XLS 77CD* | 75 | 1 |

EN VOGUE R&B 🎵 *US, female vocal group*   81 wks
5 May 90 ●	HOLD ON *East West America 7908*	5	11
21 Jul 90	LIES *East West America 7893*	44	4
4 Apr 92	MY LOVIN' *East West America A 8578*	69	3
9 May 92 ●	MY LOVIN' (re-entry) *East West America A 8578*	4	9
15 Aug 92	GIVING HIM SOMETHING HE CAN FEEL *East West America A 8524*	44	3
7 Nov 92	GIVING HIM SOMETHING HE CAN FEEL (re-issue) / FREE YOUR MIND (re-issue) *East West America A 8524*	16	8
16 Jan 93	GIVE IT UP TURN IT LOOSE *East West America A 8445CD*	22	4
10 Apr 93	LOVE DON'T LOVE YOU *East West America A 8424CD*	64	1
9 Oct 93	RUNAWAY LOVE *East West America A 8359CD*	36	3
19 Mar 94 ●	WHATTA MAN *ffrr FCD 222* [1]	7	10
11 Jan 97 ●	DON'T LET GO (LOVE) *East West A 3976CD*	5	5

UK No 1 ★   UK Top 10 ●   UK million seller ◆   UK entry at No 1 ■   US No 1 ▲

14 Jun 97	WHATEVER *East West E 3642CD*	14	5
6 Sep 97	TOO GONE, TOO LONG *East West E 3908CD*	20	3
28 Nov 98	HOLD ON (re-mix) *East West E 3796 CD*	53	1

1 Salt-N-Pepa with En Vogue

ENCORE ☺ *France, female vocalist*   **4 wks**
14 Feb 98	LE DISC JOCKEY *Sum CDSUM 2*	12	4

ENERGISE *UK, male vocal/instrumental group*   **1 wk**
16 Feb 91	REPORT TO THE DANCEFLOOR *Network NWKT 16*	69	1

ENERGY 52 ☺ *Germany, male DJ/producer*   **7 wks**
8 Mar 97	CAFE DEL MAR *Hooj Choons HOOJCD 51*	51	1
25 Jul 98	CAFE DEL MAR '98 (re-mix) *Hooj Choons HOOJ 64CD*	12	6

ENERGY ORCHARD *Ireland, male vocal/instrumental group*   **6 wks**
27 Jan 90	BELFAST *MCA MCA 1392*	52	4
7 Apr 90	SAILORTOWN *MCA MCA 1402*	73	2

Harry ENFIELD ⊘ *UK, male vocalist*   **7 wks**
7 May 88 ●	LOADSAMONEY (DOIN' UP THE HOUSE) *Mercury DOSH 1*	4	7

ENGLAND DAN and John Ford COLEY *US, male vocal duo*   **12 wks**
25 Sep 76	I'D REALLY LOVE TO SEE YOU TONIGHT *Atlantic K 10810*	26	7
23 Jun 79	LOVE IS THE ANSWER *Big Tree K 11296*	45	5

ENGLAND RUGBY WORLD CUP SQUAD – See UNION featuring the ENGLAND RUGBY WORLD CUP SQUAD

ENGLAND SISTERS *UK, female vocal group*   **1 wk**
17 Mar 60	HEARTBEAT *HMV POP 710*	33	1

ENGLAND SUPPORTERS' BAND *UK, male instrumental group*   **2 wks**
27 Jun 98	THE GREAT ESCAPE *V2 VVR 5002163*	46	2

ENGLAND UNITED ⊘ *UK, male/female vocal/instrumental group*   **9 wks**
13 Jun 98 ●	(HOW DOES IT FEEL TO BE) ON TOP OF THE WORLD *London LONCD 414*	9	9

ENGLAND WORLD CUP SQUAD ⊘
UK, male football team vocalists   **46 wks**
18 Apr 70 ★	BACK HOME *Pye 7N 17920*	1	16
15 Aug 70	BACK HOME (re-entry) *Pye 7N 17920*	46	1
10 Apr 82 ●	THIS TIME (WE'LL GET IT RIGHT)/ENGLAND WE'LL FLY THE FLAG *England ER 1*	2	13
19 Apr 86	WE'VE GOT THE WHOLE WORLD AT OUR FEET/WHEN WE ARE FAR FROM HOME *Columbia DB 9128*	66	2
21 May 88	ALL THE WAY *MCA GOAL 1* 1	64	2
2 Jun 90 ★	WORLD IN MOTION . . . *Factory/MCA FAC 2937* 2	1	12

1 England Football Team and the 'sound' of Stock, Aitken and Waterman
2 Englandneworder

Kim ENGLISH *US, female vocalist*   **7 wks**
23 Jul 94	NITE LIFE *Hi-Life PZCD 323*	35	2
4 Mar 95	TIME FOR LOVE *Hi-Life HICD 8*	48	1
9 Sep 95	I KNOW A PLACE *Hi-Life 5798072*	52	1
30 Nov 96	NITE LIFE (re-mix) *Hi-Life 5755332*	35	2
26 Apr 97	SUPERNATURAL *Hi-Life 5736972*	50	1

Scott ENGLISH ⊘ *US, male vocalist*   **10 wks**
9 Oct 71	BRANDY *Horse HOSS 7*	12	10

ENIGMA ⊘ ⏴ *UK, male/female vocal/instrumental group*   **15 wks**
23 May 81	AIN'T NO STOPPING *Creole CR 9*	11	8
8 Aug 81	I LOVE MUSIC *Creole CR 14*	25	7

ENIGMA ☺ ⊘ ⏴ *Germany/Romania, male/female vocal/instrumental duo*   **47 wks**
15 Dec 90 ★	SADNESS PART 1 *Virgin International DINS 101*	1	12
30 Mar 91	MEA CULPA PART II *Virgin International DINS 104*	55	3
10 Aug 91	PRINCIPLES OF LUST *Virgin International DINS 110*	59	2
11 Jan 92	THE RIVERS OF BELIEF *Virgin International DINS 112*	68	2
29 Jan 94 ●	RETURN TO INNOCENCE *Virgin International DINSD 123*	3	14
14 May 94	THE EYES OF TRUTH *Virgin International DINSD 126*	21	4
20 Aug 94	AGE OF LONELINESS *Virgin International DINSD 135*	21	5
25 Jan 97	BEYOND THE INVISIBLE *Virgin International DINSD 155*	26	2
19 Apr 97	TNT FOR THE BRAIN *Virgin International DINSD 161*	60	1
13 Dec 97	ONLY IF . . . *WEA 143 CD*	43	2

ENYA ⏴ *Ireland, female vocalist*   **59 wks**
15 Oct 88 ★	ORINOCO FLOW *WEA YZ 312*	1	13
24 Dec 88	EVENING FALLS . . . *WEA YZ 356*	20	4
10 Jun 89	STORMS IN AFRICA (PART II) *WEA YZ 368*	41	4
19 Oct 91	CARIBBEAN BLUE *WEA YZ 604*	13	7
7 Dec 91	HOW CAN I KEEP FROM SINGING *WEA YZ 365*	32	5
1 Aug 92 ●	BOOK OF DAYS *WEA YZ 640*	10	6
14 Nov 92	THE CELTS *WEA YZ 705*	29	4
18 Nov 95 ●	ANYWHERE IS *WEA WEA 023CD*	7	12
7 Dec 96	ON MY WAY HOME *WEA WEA 047CD*	26	2
13 Dec 97	ONLY IF... *WEA WEA 143CD*	43	2

EON *UK, male producer – Ian Bela*   **1 wk**
17 Aug 91	FEAR: THE MINDKILLER *Vinyl Solution STORM 33*	63	1

EPMD *US, male vocal / production group*   **1 wk**
15 Aug 98	STRICTLY BUSINESS *Parlophone CDR 6502* 1	43	1

1 Mantronik versus EPMD

EQUALS ⌄* *UK/Guyana, male vocal/instrumental group*   **69 wks**
21 Feb 68	I GET SO EXCITED *President PT 180*	44	4
1 May 68	BABY COME BACK *President PT 135*	50	1
15 May 68	BABY COME BACK (re-entry) *President PT 135*	1	17
21 Aug 68	LAUREL AND HARDY *President PT 200*	35	5
27 Nov 68	SOFTLY SOFTLY *President PT 222*	48	3
2 Apr 69	MICHAEL AND THE SLIPPER TREE *President PT 240*	24	7
30 Jul 69 ●	VIVA BOBBY JOE *President PT 260*	6	14
27 Dec 69	RUB A DUB DUB *President PT 275*	34	7
19 Dec 70 ●	BLACK SKIN BLUE EYED BOYS *President PT 325*	9	11

ERASURE ⊘ ☺ *Award-winning UK duo formed by Vince Clarke (k) and Andy Bell (v). After hits with Depeche Mode, Yazoo and The Assembly, Clarke achieved greatest success, scoring 15 Top 10 singles and having five albums enter at No 1*   **201 wks**
5 Oct 85	WHO NEEDS LOVE LIKE THAT *Mute MUTE 40*	55	2
25 Oct 86 ●	SOMETIMES *Mute MUTE 51*	2	17
28 Feb 87	IT DOESN'T HAVE TO BE *Mute MUTE 56*	12	9
30 May 87 ●	VICTIM OF LOVE *Mute MUTE 61*	7	9
3 Oct 87 ●	THE CIRCUS *Mute MUTE 66*	6	10
5 Mar 88 ●	SHIP OF FOOLS *Mute MUTE 74*	6	8
11 Jun 88	CHAINS OF LOVE *Mute MUTE 83*	11	7
1 Oct 88 ●	A LITTLE RESPECT *Mute MUTE 85*	4	10
10 Dec 88 ●	CRACKERS INTERNATIONAL EP *Mute MUTE 93*	2	13
30 Sep 89 ●	DRAMA! *Mute MUTE 89*	4	8
9 Dec 89	YOU SURROUND ME *Mute MUTE 99*	15	9
10 Mar 90 ●	BLUE SAVANNAH *Mute MUTE 109*	3	10
2 Jun 90	STAR *Mute MUTE 111*	11	7
29 Jun 91 ●	CHORUS *Mute MUTE 125*	3	9
21 Sep 91 ●	LOVE TO HATE YOU *Mute MUTE 131*	4	9
7 Dec 91	AM I RIGHT EP *Mute MUTE 134*	15	6
11 Jan 92	AM I RIGHT EP (re-mix) *Mute L12MUTE 134*	22	3
28 Mar 92 ●	BREATH OF LIFE *Mute MUTE 142*	8	6
13 Jun 92 ★	ABBA-ESQUE EP *Mute MUTE 144* ■	1	12
7 Nov 92 ●	WHO NEEDS LOVE (LIKE THAT) (re-mix) *Mute MUTE 150*	10	4
23 Apr 94 ●	ALWAYS *Mute CDMUTE 152*	4	9
30 Jul 94 ●	RUN TO THE SUN *Mute CDMUTE 153*	6	5
3 Dec 94	I LOVE SATURDAY *Mute CDMUTE 166*	20	6

23 Sep 95	STAY WITH ME *Mute CDMUTE 174*	15 4
9 Dec 95	FINGERS AND THUMBS (COLD SUMMER'S DAY) *Mute CDMUTE 178*	20 3
18 Jan 97	IN MY ARMS *Mute CDMUTE 190*	13 4
8 Mar 97	DON'T SAY YOUR LOVE IS KILLING ME *Mute CDMUTE 195*	23 2

Tracks on Crackers International (EP): Stop / The Hardest Part / Knocking On Your Door / She Won't Be Home. Tracks on Am I Right (EP): Am I Right / Carry On Clangers / Let It Flow / Waiting for Sex. Tracks on Am I Right (Re-mix EP): Am I Right / Chorus / Love to Hate You / Perfect Stranger. Tracks on Abba-esque (EP): Lay All Your Love On Me / SOS / Take a Chance On Me / Voulez-Vous
'Take a Chance On Me' credits MC Kinky
See also KINKY

ERIC and the GOOD GOOD FEELING
UK, male/female vocal/instrumental group **1 wk**

3 Jun 89	GOOD GOOD FEELING *Equinox EQN 1*	73 1

ERIK *UK, female vocalist* **5 wks**

10 Apr 93	LOOKS LIKE I'M IN LOVE AGAIN *PWL Sanctuary PWCD 252* [1]	46 2
29 Jan 94	GOT TO BE REAL *PWL International PWCD 278*	42 2
1 Oct 94	WE GOT THE LOVE *PWL International PWCD 305*	55 1

[1] Key West featuring Erik

ERIN – See SHUT UP AND DANCE; BBG

EROTIC DRUM BAND
Canada, male/female vocal/instrumental group **3 wks**

9 Jun 79	LOVE DISCO STYLE *Scope SC 1*	47 3

ERUPTION 🎤 📻 *US, male/female vocal/instrumental group* **21 wks**

18 Feb 78 ●	I CAN'T STAND THE RAIN *Atlantic K 11068* [1]	5 11
21 Apr 79 ●	ONE WAY TICKET *Atlantic/Hansa K 11266*	9 10

[1] Eruption featuring Precious Wilson

ESCORTS *UK, male vocal/instrumental group* **2 wks**

2 Jul 64	THE ONE TO CRY *Fontana TF 474*	49 2

ESCRIMA *UK, male producer – Paul Newman* **4 wks**

11 Feb 95	TRAIN OF THOUGHT *Ffrreedom TABCD 225*	36 2
7 Oct 95	DEEPER *Hooj Choons TABCD 236*	27 2

ESKIMOS & EGYPT *UK, male vocal/instrumental group* **4 wks**

13 Feb 93	FALL FROM GRACE *One Little Indian EEF 96CD*	51 2
29 May 93	UK-USA *One Little Indian 99 TP7CD*	52 2

ESPIRITU ☺ *UK/France, male/female vocal/instrumental duo* **10 wks**

6 Mar 93	CONQUISTADOR *Heavenly HVN 28CD*	47 2
7 Aug 93	LOS AMERICANOS *Heavenly HVN 33CD*	45 2
20 Aug 94	BONITA MANANA *Columbia 6606925*	50 1
25 Mar 95	ALWAYS SOMETHING THERE TO REMIND ME *WEA YZ 911CD* [1]	14 5

[1] Tin Tin Out featuring Espiritu

ESSENCE *UK, male production group and UK, female vocalist* **2 wks**

21 Mar 98	THE PROMISE *Innocent SINCD 1*	27 2

ESSEX *US, male/female vocal group* **5 wks**

8 Aug 63	EASIER SAID THAN DONE *Columbia DB 7077* ▲	41 5

David ESSEX 🌐 *Actor/teeny-bop star turned popular entertainer, b. David Cook, 23 July, 1947, London. This singer/songwriter was voted No 1 British Male Vocalist (1974); was a teen idol for more than a decade. Later starred in the stage show Godspell and graduated successfully to films* **199 wks**

18 Aug 73 ●	ROCK ON *CBS 1693*	3 11
10 Nov 73 ●	LAMPLIGHT *CBS 1902*	7 15
11 May 74	AMERICA *CBS 2176*	32 5
12 Oct 74 ★	GONNA MAKE YOU A STAR *CBS 2492*	1 17
14 Dec 74 ●	STARDUST *CBS 2828*	7 10
5 Jul 75 ●	ROLLING STONE *CBS 3425*	5 7
13 Sep 75 ★	HOLD ME CLOSE *CBS 3572*	1 10
6 Dec 75	IF I COULD *CBS 3776*	13 8
20 Mar 76	CITY LIGHTS *CBS 4050*	24 4
16 Oct 76	COMING HOME *CBS 4486*	24 6
17 Sep 77	COOL OUT TONIGHT *CBS 5495*	23 6
11 Mar 78	STAY WITH ME BABY *CBS 6063*	45 5
19 Aug 78 ●	OH WHAT A CIRCUS *Mercury 6007 185*	3 11
21 Oct 78	BRAVE NEW WORLD *CBS 6705*	55 3
3 Mar 79	IMPERIAL WIZARD *Mercury 6007 202*	32 8
5 Apr 80 ●	SILVER DREAM MACHINE (PART 1) *Mercury BIKE 1*	4 11
14 Jun 80	HOT LOVE *Mercury HOT 11*	57 4
26 Jun 82	ME AND MY GIRL (NIGHT-CLUBBING) *Mercury MER 107*	13 10
11 Dec 82 ●	A WINTER'S TALE *Mercury MER 127*	2 10
4 Jun 83	THE SMILE *Mercury ESSEX 1*	52 4
27 Aug 83 ●	TAHITI (FROM 'MUTINY ON THE BOUNTY') *Mercury BOUNT 1*	8 11
26 Nov 83	YOU'RE IN MY HEART *Mercury ESSEX 2*	67 2
17 Dec 83	YOU'RE IN MY HEART (re-entry) *Mercury ESSEX 2*	59 4
23 Feb 85	FALLING ANGELS RIDING (MUTINY!) *Mercury ESSEX 5*	29 7
18 Apr 87	MYFANWY *Arista RIS 11*	41 7
26 Nov 94	TRUE LOVE WAYS *PolyGram TV TLWCD 2* [1]	38 3

[1] David Essex and Catherine Zeta Jones

Gloria ESTEFAN 🌐 ☺ *Latin music's leading lady, b. Gloria Fajardo, 1 December, 1957, Cuba. Successes in the dance and MOR fields have pushed her world sales to more than 35 million, with two of the vocalist's albums passing the one-million sales mark in the UK* **202 wks**

11 Aug 84 ●	DR BEAT *Epic A 4614* [1]	6 14
17 May 86	BAD BOY *Epic A 6537* [1]	16 11
16 Jul 88 ●	ANYTHING FOR YOU *Epic 651673 7* [2]	10 16
22 Oct 88	1-2-3 *Epic 652958 7* [2]	9 9
17 Dec 88	RHYTHM IS GONNA GET YOU *Epic 654514 7* [2]	16 9
31 Dec 88	1-2-3 (re-entry) *Epic 652958 7* [2]	72 1
11 Feb 89 ●	CAN'T STAY AWAY FROM YOU *Epic 651444 7* [2]	7 12
15 Jul 89 ●	DON'T WANNA LOSE YOU *Epic 655054 0* ▲	6 10
16 Sep 89	OYE MI CANTO (HEAR MY VOICE) *Epic 655287 7*	16 8
25 Nov 89	GET ON YOUR FEET *Epic 655450 7*	23 7
3 Mar 90	HERE WE ARE *Epic 655473 9*	23 6
26 May 90	CUTS BOTH WAYS *Epic 655982 7*	49 5
26 Jan 91	COMING OUT OF THE DARK *Epic 6565747* ▲	25 5
6 Apr 91	SEAL OUR FATE *Epic 6567737*	24 7
8 Jun 91	REMEMBER ME WITH LOVE *Epic 6569687*	22 6
21 Sep 91	LIVE FOR LOVING YOU *Epic 6573827*	33 5
24 Oct 92	ALWAYS TOMORROW *Epic 6583977*	24 4
12 Dec 92 ●	MIAMI HIT MIX/CHRISTMAS THROUGH YOUR EYES *Epic 6588377*	8 9
13 Feb 93	I SEE YOUR SMILE *Epic 6589612*	48 2
3 Apr 93	GO AWAY *Epic 6590952*	13 6
3 Jul 93	MI TIERRA *Epic 6593512*	36 3
14 Aug 93	IF WE WERE LOVERS/CON LOS ANOS QUE ME QUEDIN *Epic 6595702*	40 3
18 Dec 93	MONTUNO *Epic 6599972*	55 2
15 Oct 94	TURN THE BEAT AROUND *Epic 6606822*	21 6
3 Dec 94	HOLD ME THRILL ME KISS ME *Epic 6610802*	11 10
18 Feb 95	EVERLASTING LOVE *Epic 6611595*	19 5
18 Mar 95	HOLD ME THRILL ME KISS ME (re-entry) *Epic 6610802*	68 1
25 May 96	REACH *Epic 6632642*	15 6
3 Aug 96	REACH (re-entry) *Epic 6632642*	68 1
17 Aug 96	REACH (2nd re-entry) *Epic 6632642*	55 1
24 Aug 96	YOU'LL BE MINE (PARTY TIME) *Epic 6636505*	18 3
14 Dec 96	I'M NOT GIVING YOU UP *Epic 6640222*	28† 3
6 Jun 98 ●	HEAVEN'S WHAT I FEEL *Epic 6660042*	4 4
10 Oct 98	OYE *Epic 6664645*	33 2

[1] Miami Sound Machine [2] Gloria Estefan and Miami Sound Machine

'Christmas Through Your Eyes' was only listed from 19 Dec, 1992

Don ESTELLE – See Windsor DAVIES and Don ESTELLE

UK No 1 ★ UK Top 10 ● UK million seller ◆ UK entry at No 1 ■ US No 1 ▲

Deon ESTUS US, male vocalist/instrumentalist – bass — 7 wks

Date	Title	Pos	Wks
25 Jan 86	MY GUY – MY GIRL (MEDLEY) *Sedition EDIT 3310* [1]	63	3
29 Apr 89	HEAVEN HELP ME *Mika MIKA 2*	41	4

[1] Amii Stewart and Deon Estus

ETA Denmark, male instrumental group — 5 wks

Date	Title	Pos	Wks
28 Jun 97	CASUAL SUB (BURNING SPEAR) *East West EW 110CD*	28	3
31 Jan 98	CASUAL SUB (BURNING SPEAR) (re-mix) *East West Dance EW 145CD*	28	2

ETERNAL (R&B) ◉ London-based vocal group with across-the-board appeal: sisters Easther and Vernett Bennett, Kelle Bryan, Louise Nurding. First all-female act to shift more than one million copies of an album in the UK. Louise left for a successful solo career (1995) — 130 wks

Date	Title	Pos	Wks
2 Oct 93	● STAY *EMI CDEM 283*	4	9
15 Jan 94	● SAVE OUR LOVE *EMI CDEM 296*	8	7
30 Apr 94	● JUST A STEP FROM HEAVEN *EMI CDEM 311*	8	10
20 Aug 94	SO GOOD *EMI CDEMS 339*	13	7
5 Nov 94	OH BABY I . . . *EMI CDEM 353*	4	13
24 Dec 94	CRAZY *EMI CDEMX 364*	15	7
21 Oct 95	● POWER OF A WOMAN *EMI CDEM 396*	5	8
9 Dec 95	I AM BLESSED *EMI CDEMS 408*	7	12
9 Mar 96	● GOOD THING *EMI CDEM 419*	8	6
17 Aug 96	SOMEDAY *EMI CDEMS 439*	4	9
7 Dec 96	● SECRETS *EMI CDEM 459*	9	7
8 Mar 97	● DON'T YOU LOVE ME *EMI CDEMS 465*	3	7
31 May 97	★ I WANNA BE THE ONLY ONE *EMI CDEM 472* [1] ■	1	15
11 Oct 97	● ANGEL OF MINE *EMI CDEM 493*	4	13

[1] Eternal featuring BeBe Winans

ETHER UK, male vocal/instrumental group — 1 wk

Date	Title	Pos	Wks
28 Mar 98	WATCHING YOU *Parlophone CDR 6491*	74	1

ETHICS ☺ Holland, male producer – Patrick Prinz — 5 wks

Date	Title	Pos	Wks
25 Nov 95	TO THE BEAT OF THE DRUM (LA LUNA) *VC VCRD 5*	13	5

See also ARTEMESIA; MOVIN' MELODIES; SUBLIMINAL CUTS

ETHIOPIANS Jamaica, male vocal/instrumental group — 6 wks

Date	Title	Pos	Wks
13 Sep 67	TRAIN TO SKAVILLE *Rio RIO 130*	40	6

Tony ETORIA UK, male vocalist — 8 wks

Date	Title	Pos	Wks
4 Jun 77	I CAN PROVE IT *GTO GT 89*	21	8

E.U. – See SALT-N-PEPA

EUROGROOVE UK, male/female vocal group — 7 wks

Date	Title	Pos	Wks
20 May 95	MOVE YOUR BODY *Avex UK AVEXCD 4*	29	2
5 Aug 95	DIVE TO PARADISE *Avex UK AVEXCD 10*	31	2
21 Oct 95	IT'S ON YOU (SCAN ME) *Avex UK AVEXCD 17*	25	2
3 Feb 96	MOVE YOUR BODY (re-mix) *Avex UK AVEXCD 22*	44	1

EUROPE ✍ ◉ Sweden, male vocal/instrumental group — 46 wks

Date	Title	Pos	Wks
1 Nov 86	★ THE FINAL COUNTDOWN *Epic A 7127*	1	15
31 Jan 87	ROCK THE NIGHT *Epic EUR 1*	12	9
18 Apr 87	CARRIE *Epic EUR 2*	22	8
20 Aug 88	SUPERSTITIOUS *Epic EUR 3*	34	5
1 Feb 92	I'LL CRY FOR YOU *Epic 6576977*	28	5
21 Mar 92	HALFWAY TO HEAVEN *Epic 6578517*	42	4

EURYTHMICS ◉ Innovative and internationally popular duo formed by BRIT-Award-winning Scottish vocalist Annie Lennox and multi-instrumentalist/songwriter/producer Dave Stewart. The most charted male/female duo in the UK, whose Greatest Hits album sold more than two million copies in the UK and in Europe — 198 wks

Date	Title	Pos	Wks
4 Jul 81	NEVER GONNA CRY AGAIN *RCA 68*	63	3
92	LOVE IS A STRANGER *RCA DA 1*	54	5
12 Feb 83	● SWEET DREAMS (ARE MADE OF THIS) *RCA DA 2* ▲	2	14
9 Apr 83	● LOVE IS A STRANGER (re-entry) *RCA DA 1*	6	8
9 Jul 83	● WHO'S THAT GIRL? *RCA DA 3*	3	10
5 Nov 83	● RIGHT BY YOUR SIDE *RCA DA 4*	10	11
21 Jan 84	● HERE COMES THE RAIN AGAIN *RCA DA 5*	8	8
3 Nov 84	● SEXCRIME (NINETEEN EIGHTY FOUR) *Virgin VS 728*	4	13
19 Jan 85	JULIA *Virgin VS 734*	44	4
20 Apr 85	● WOULD I LIE TO YOU? *RCA PB 40101*	17	8
6 Jul 85	★ THERE MUST BE AN ANGEL (PLAYING WITH MY HEART) *RCA PB 40247*	1	13
2 Nov 85	● SISTERS ARE DOIN' IT FOR THEMSELVES *RCA PB 40339* [1]	9	11
11 Jan 86	● IT'S ALRIGHT (BABY'S COMING BACK) *RCA PB 40375*	12	8
14 Jun 86	WHEN TOMORROW COMES *RCA DA 7*	30	6
6 Sep 86	● THORN IN MY SIDE *RCA DA 8*	5	11
29 Nov 86	THE MIRACLE OF LOVE *RCA DA 9*	23	9
28 Feb 87	MISSIONARY MAN *RCA DA 10*	31	4
24 Oct 87	BEETHOVEN (I LOVE TO LISTEN TO) *RCA DA 11*	25	5
26 Dec 87	SHAME *RCA DA 14*	41	6
9 Apr 88	I NEED A MAN *RCA DA 15*	26	5
11 Jun 88	YOU HAVE PLACED A CHILL IN MY HEART *RCA DA 16*	16	8
26 Aug 89	REVIVAL *RCA DA 17*	26	6
4 Nov 89	DON'T ASK ME WHY *RCA DA 19*	25	6
3 Feb 90	THE KING AND QUEEN OF AMERICA *RCA DA 20*	29	5
12 May 90	ANGEL *RCA DA 21*	23	6
9 Mar 91	LOVE IS A STRANGER (re-issue) *RCA PB 44265*	46	3
16 Nov 91	SWEET DREAMS (ARE MADE OF THIS) (re-mix) *RCA PB 45031*	48	2

[1] Eurythmics and Aretha Franklin

EUSEBE UK, male/female vocal group — 3 wks

Date	Title	Pos	Wks
26 Aug 95	SUMMERTIME HEALING *Mama's Yard CDMAMA 4*	32	3

EVANGEL TEMPLE CHOIR – See Johnny CASH

Faith EVANS (R&B) US, female vocalist — 29 wks

Date	Title	Pos	Wks
14 Oct 95	YOU USED TO LOVE ME *Puff Daddy 74321299812*	42	2
23 Nov 96	STRESSED OUT *Jive JIVECD 404* [1]	33	2
28 Jun 97	★ I'LL BE MISSING YOU *Puff Daddy 74321499102* [2] ▲ ■ ◆	1	21
14 Nov 98	LOVE LIKE THIS *Puff Daddy 74321625592*	24	4

[1] A Tribe Called Quest featuring Faith Evans and Raphael Saadiq [2] Puff Daddy and Faith Evans

Maureen EVANS ☾ UK, female vocalist — 37 wks

Date	Title	Pos	Wks
22 Jan 60	THE BIG HURT *Oriole CB 1533*	26	2
17 Mar 60	LOVE KISSES AND HEARTACHES *Oriole CB 1540*	44	1
2 Jun 60	PAPER ROSES *Oriole CB 1550*	40	5
29 Nov 62	● LIKE I DO *Oriole CB 1760*	3	18
27 Feb 64	I LOVE HOW YOU LOVE ME *Oriole CB 1906*	34	10
14 May 64	I LOVE HOW YOU LOVE ME (re-entry) *Oriole CB 1906*	50	1

Paul EVANS ◉ US, male vocalist — 14 wks

Date	Title	Pos	Wks
27 Nov 59	SEVEN LITTLE GIRLS SITTING IN THE BACK SEAT *London HLL 8968* [1]	25	1
31 Mar 60	MIDNITE SPECIAL *London HLL 9045*	41	1
16 Dec 78	● HELLO THIS IS JOANIE (THE TELEPHONE ANSWERING MACHINE SONG) *Spring 2066 932*	6	12

[1] Paul Evans and the Curls

EVASIONS ◉ 📻 UK, male/female vocal/instrumental group — 8 wks

Date	Title	Pos	Wks
13 Jun 81	WIKKA WRAP *Groove GP 107*	20	8

E.V.E. UK/US, female vocal group — 5 wks

Date	Title	Pos	Wks
1 Oct 94	GROOVE OF LOVE *Gasoline Alley MCSTD 2007*	30	3
28 Jan 95	GOOD LIFE *Gasoline Alley MCSTD 2038*	39	2

Alison EVELYN – See BROTHERS LIKE OUTLAW featuring Alison EVELYN

EVERCLEAR US, male vocal/instrumental group — 5 wks

Date	Title	Pos	Wks
1 Jun 96	HEARTSPARK DOLLARSIGN *Capitol CDCLS 773*	48	2

31 Aug 96	SANTA MONICA (WATCH THE WORLD DIE)		
	Capitol CDCL 775	40	2
9 May 98	EVERYTHING TO EVERYONE Capitol CDCL 799	41	1

Betty EVERETT US, female vocalist — 14 wks

14 Jan 65	GETTING MIGHTY CROWDED Fontana TF 520	29	7
30 Oct 68	IT'S IN HIS KISS President PT 215	34	7

Kenny EVERETT ○ UK, male vocalist — 12 wks

12 Nov 77	CAPTAIN KREMMEN (RETRIBUTION) DJM DJS 10810 [1]	32	4
26 Mar 83 ●	SNOT RAP RCA KEN 1	9	8

[1] Kenny Everett and Mike Vickers

Peven EVERETT – See Roy DAVIS Jr

Phil EVERLY ○ US, male vocalist — 24 wks

6 Nov 82	LOUISE Capitol CL 266	47	6
19 Feb 83 ●	SHE MEANS NOTHING TO ME Capitol CL 276 [1]	9	9
10 Dec 94	ALL I HAVE TO DO IS DREAM EMI CDEMS 359 [2]	14	6
25 Feb 95	ALL I HAVE TO DO IS DREAM (re-entry)		
	EMI CDEMS 359 [2]	58	3

[1] Phil Everly and Cliff Richard [2] Cliff Richard and Phil Everly

'All I Have to Do Is Dream' was listed with its flip side 'Miss You Nights'
by Cliff Richard.
See also EVERLY BROTHERS

EVERLY BROTHERS 🎵 Award-winning and extremely influential
US brothers Don (g/v) and Phil (g/v) Everly. Achieved long string of
transatlantic hits and were among the first acts inducted into the
Rock and Roll Hall of Fame in 1986 — 344 wks

12 Jul 57 ●	BYE BYE LOVE London HLA 8440	6	16
8 Nov 57 ●	WAKE UP LITTLE SUSIE London HLA 8498 ▲	2	13
23 May 58 ★	ALL I HAVE TO DO IS DREAM/CLAUDETTE		
	London HLA 8618 ▲	1	21
12 Sep 58 ●	BIRD DOG London HLA 8685	2	16
23 Jan 59 ●	PROBLEMS London HLA 8781	6	12
22 May 59	TAKE A MESSAGE TO MARY London HLA 8863	29	1
29 May 59	POOR JENNY London HLA 8863	14	11
19 Jun 59	TAKE A MESSAGE TO MARY (re-entry) London HLA 8863	27	1
3 Jul 59	TAKE A MESSAGE TO MARY (2nd re-entry)		
	London HLA 8863	20	8
11 Sep 59 ●	('TIL) I KISSED YOU London HLA 8934	2	15
12 Feb 60	LET IT BE ME London HLA 9039	13	5
31 Mar 60	LET IT BE ME (re-entry) London HLA 9039	26	4
14 Apr 60 ★	CATHY'S CLOWN Warner Bros. WB 1 ▲	1	18
14 Jul 60 ●	WHEN WILL I BE LOVED London HLA 9157	4	16
22 Sep 60 ●	LUCILLE/SO SAD (TO WATCH GOOD LOVE GO BAD)		
	Warner Bros. WB 19	4	15
15 Dec 60	LIKE STRANGERS London HLA 9250	11	10
9 Feb 61 ★	WALK RIGHT BACK/EBONY EYES Warner Bros. WB 33	1	16
15 Jun 61 ★	TEMPTATION Warner Bros. WB 42	1	15
5 Oct 61	MUSKRAT/DON'T BLAME ME Warner Bros. WB 50	20	6
18 Jan 62 ●	CRYIN' IN THE RAIN Warner Bros. WB 56	6	15
17 May 62	HOW CAN I MEET HER Warner Bros. WB 67	12	10
25 Oct 62	NO ONE CAN MAKE MY SUNSHINE SMILE		
	Warner Bros. WB 79	11	11
21 Mar 63	SO IT WILL ALWAYS BE Warner Bros. WB 94	23	11
13 Jun 63	IT'S BEEN NICE Warner Bros. WB 99	26	5
17 Oct 63	THE GIRL SANG THE BLUES Warner Bros. WB 109	25	9
16 Jul 64	FERRIS WHEEL Warner Bros. WB 135	22	10
3 Dec 64	GONE GONE GONE Warner Bros. WB 146	36	7
6 May 65	THAT'LL BE THE DAY Warner Bros. WB 158	30	4
20 May 65 ●	THE PRICE OF LOVE Warner Bros. WB 161	2	14
26 Aug 65	I'LL NEVER GET OVER YOU Warner Bros. WB 5639	35	5
21 Oct 65	LOVE IS STRANGE Warner Bros. WB 5649	11	9
8 May 68	IT'S MY TIME Warner Bros. WB 7192	39	6
22 Sep 84	ON THE WINGS OF A NIGHTINGALE Mercury MER 170	41	9

'All I Have to Do Is Dream' was listed without Claudette for its first week on
the chart, but from 30 May, 1958, both sides were charted for 20 more weeks.
See also Phil EVERLY

EVERTON FOOTBALL CLUB ○ UK, male football team vocalists — 8 wks

11 May 85	HERE WE GO Columbia DB 9106 [1]	14	5
20 May 95	ALL TOGETHER NOW MDMC DEVCS 3	24	3

[1] Everton 1985

EVERYTHING BUT THE GIRL ○ ☺
UK, male/female vocal/instrumental duo — 88 wks

12 May 84	EACH AND EVERYONE Blanco Y Negro NEG 1	28	7
21 Jul 84	MINE Blanco Y Negro NEG 3	58	2
6 Oct 84	NATIVE LAND Blanco Y Negro NEG 6	73	2
2 Aug 86	COME ON HOME Blanco Y Negro NEG 21	44	7
11 Oct 86	DON'T LEAVE ME BEHIND Blanco Y Negro NEG 23	72	2
13 Feb 88	THESE EARLY DAYS Blanco Y Negro NEG 30	75	1
9 Jul 88 ●	I DON'T WANT TO TALK ABOUT IT Blanco Y Negro NEG 34	3	9
27 Jan 90	DRIVING Blanco Y Negro NEG 40	54	2
22 Feb 92	COVERS (EP) Blanco Y Negro NEG 54	13	6
24 Apr 93	THE ONLY LIVING BOY IN NEW YORK (EP)		
	Blanco Y Negro NEG 62CD	42	5
19 Jun 93	I DIDN'T KNOW I WAS LOOKING FOR LOVE (EP)		
	Blanco Y Negro NEG 64CD	72	1
4 Jun 94	ROLLERCOASTER (EP) Blanco Y Negro NEG 69CD	65	1
20 Aug 94	MISSING Blanco Y Negro NEG 71CD1	69	1
28 Oct 95 ●	MISSING (re-mix) Blanco Y Negro NEG 84CD	3	22
20 Apr 96 ●	WALKING WOUNDED Virgin VSCDT 1577	6	6
29 Jun 96 ●	WRONG Virgin VSCDT 1589	8	7
5 Oct 96	SINGLE Virgin VSCDT 1600	20	3
7 Dec 96	DRIVING (re-mix) Blanco Y Negro NEG 99CD1	36	2
1 Mar 97	BEFORE TODAY Virgin VSCDT 1624	25	2

Tracks on Covers (EP): Love Is Strange / Tougher Than the Rest / Time After Time /
Alison. Tracks on The Only Living Boy in New York (EP): The Only Living Boy in New
York / Birds / Gabriel / Horses in the Room. Tracks on I Didn't Know I Was Looking
For Love (EP): I Didn't Know I Was Looking For Love / My Head Is My Only House
Unless It Rains / Political Science / A Piece of My Mind. Tracks on Rollercoaster (EP):
Rollercoaster / Straight Back to You / Lights of Te Towan / I Didn't Know I Was
Looking For Love

E'VOKE UK, female vocal duo — 6 wks

25 Nov 95	RUNAWAY Ffrreedom TABCD 238	30	3
24 Aug 96	ARMS OF LOREN Manifesto FESCD 10	25	3

EVOLUTION ☺ ○ UK, male/female vocal/instrumental group — 12 wks

20 Mar 93	LOVE THING Deconstruction 74321134272	32	2
3 Jul 93	EVERYBODY DANCE Deconstruction 74321152012	19	5
8 Jan 94	EVOLUTIONDANCE PART 1 (EP)		
	Deconstruction 74321171912	52	3
4 Nov 95	LOOK UP TO THE LIGHT Deconstruction 74321318042	55	1
19 Oct 96	YOUR LOVE IS CALLING Deconstruction 74321422872	60	1

Tracks on Evolutiondance Part 1 (EP): Escape 2 Alcatraz / Everybody /
Don't Stop the Rain

EX PISTOLS UK, male vocal/instrumental group — 2 wks

2 Feb 85	LAND OF HOPE AND GLORY Virginia PISTOL 76	69	2

EXCITERS US, male/female vocal group — 7 wks

21 Feb 63	TELL HIM United Artists UP 1011	46	1
4 Oct 75	REACHING FOR THE BEST 20th Century BTC 1005	31	6

EXETER BRAMDEAN BOYS' CHOIR UK, male choir — 3 wks

18 Dec 93	REMEMBERING CHRISTMAS Golden Sounds DSCC 1	46	3

EXILE ○ US, male vocal/instrumental group — 18 wks

19 Aug 78 ●	KISS YOU ALL OVER RAK 279 ▲	6	12
12 May 79	HOW COULD THIS GO WRONG RAK 293	67	2
12 Sep 81	HEART AND SOUL RAK 333	54	4

EXOTERIX UK, male producer – Duncan Millar — 2 wks

24 Apr 93	VOID Positiva CDTIV 1	58	1
5 Feb 94	SATISFY MY LOVE Union UCRCD 26	62	1

UK No 1 ★   UK Top 10 ●   UK million seller ◆   UK entry at No 1 ■   US No 1 ▲

Adam FAITH ☺ *Teen-idol-vocalist turned top actor, b. Terence Nelhams, 23 June, 1940, London. One of the most charted acts of the 1960s; became the first UK artist to lodge initial seven hits in the Top 5* **251 wks**

20 Nov 59	★ WHAT DO YOU WANT *Parlophone R 4591*	1	19
22 Jan 60	★ POOR ME *Parlophone R 4623*	1	17
14 Apr 60	● SOMEONE ELSE'S BABY *Parlophone R 4643*	2	13
30 Jun 60	● WHEN JOHNNY COMES MARCHING HOME/MADE YOU *Parlophone R 4665*	5	13
15 Sep 60	● HOW ABOUT THAT *Parlophone R 4689*	4	14
17 Nov 60	● LONELY PUP (IN A CHRISTMAS SHOP) *Parlophone R 4708*	4	11
9 Feb 61	● WHO AM I/THIS IS IT! *Parlophone R 4735*	5	14
27 Apr 61	EASY GOING ME *Parlophone R 4766*	12	10
20 Jul 61	DON'T YOU KNOW IT *Parlophone R 4807*	12	10
26 Oct 61	● THE TIME HAS COME *Parlophone R 4837*	4	14
18 Jan 62	LONESOME *Parlophone R 4864*	12	9
3 May 62	● AS YOU LIKE IT *Parlophone R 4896*	5	15
30 Aug 62	● DON'T THAT BEAT ALL *Parlophone R 4930*	8	11
13 Dec 62	BABY TAKE A BOW *Parlophone R 4964*	22	6
31 Jan 63	WHAT NOW *Parlophone R 4990* 1	31	5
11 Jul 63	WALKIN' TALL *Parlophone R 5039*	23	6
19 Sep 63	● THE FIRST TIME *Parlophone R 5061* 2	5	13
12 Dec 63	WE ARE IN LOVE *Parlophone R 5091* 2	11	12
12 Mar 64	IF HE TELLS YOU *Parlophone R 5109* 2	25	9
28 May 64	I LOVE BEING IN LOVE WITH YOU *Parlophone R 5138* 2	33	6
26 Nov 64	MESSAGE TO MARTHA (KENTUCKY BLUEBIRD) *Parlophone R 5201*	12	11
11 Feb 65	STOP FEELING SORRY FOR YOURSELF *Parlophone R 5235*	23	6
17 Jun 65	SOMEONE'S TAKEN MARIA AWAY *Parlophone R 5289*	34	5
20 Oct 66	CHERYL'S GOIN' HOME *Parlophone R 5516*	46	2

1 Adam Faith with Johnny Keating and his Orchestra
2 Adam Faith and the Roulettes

Horace FAITH ⚐ *Jamaica, male vocalist* **10 wks**

12 Sep 70	BLACK PEARL *Trojan TR 7790*	13	10

Percy FAITH ℂ *Canada, orchestra* **30 wks**

10 Mar 60	● THE THEME FROM 'A SUMMER PLACE' *Philips PB 989* ▲	2	30

FAITH BROTHERS *UK, male vocal/instrumental group* **6 wks**

13 Apr 85	THE COUNTRY OF THE BLIND *Siren SIREN 2*	63	3
6 Jul 85	A STRANGER ON HOME GROUND *Siren SIREN 4*	69	3

FAITH, HOPE AND CHARITY *US, male/female vocal group* **4 wks**

31 Jan 76	JUST ONE LOOK *RCA 2632*	38	4

FAITH, HOPE AND CHARITY *UK, female vocal group* **3 wks**

23 Jun 90	BATTLE OF THE SEXES *WEA YZ 480*	53	3

FAITH NO MORE ✐ *US, male vocal/instrumental group* **63 wks**

6 Feb 88	WE CARE A LOT *Slash LASH 17*	53	3
10 Feb 90	EPIC *Slash LASH 21*	37	4
14 Apr 90	FROM OUT OF NOWHERE *Slash LASH 24*	23	6
14 Jul 90	FALLING TO PIECES *Slash LASH 25*	41	3
8 Sep 90	EPIC (re-issue) *Slash LASH 26*	25	5
6 Jun 92	● MIDLIFE CRISIS *Slash LASH 37*	10	5
15 Aug 92	A SMALL VICTORY *Slash LASH 39*	29	5
12 Sep 92	A SMALL VICTORY (re-mix) *Slash LASHX 40*	55	1
21 Nov 92	EVERYTHING'S RUINED *Slash LASH 43*	28	3
16 Jan 93	● I'M EASY/BE AGGRESSIVE *Slash LACDP 44*	3	7
13 Mar 93	I'M EASY/BE AGGRESSIVE (re-entry) *Slash LACDP 44*	75	1
6 Nov 93	ANOTHER BODY MURDERED *Epic 6597942* 1	26	3
11 Mar 95	DIGGING THE GRAVE *Slash LASCD 51*	16	4
27 May 95	RICOCHET *Slash LASCD 53*	27	2
29 Jul 95	EVIDENCE *Slash LASCD 54*	32	3
31 May 97	ASHES TO ASHES *Slash LASCD 61*	15	3
16 Aug 97	LAST CUP OF SORROW *Slash LASCD 62*	51	1
17 Jan 98	ASHES TO ASHES (re-issue) *Slash LACDP 63*	29	3
7 Nov 98	I STARTED A JOKE *Slash LASCD 65*	49	1

1 Faith No More & Boo-Yaa T.R.I.B.E.

Marianne FAITHFULL ☺ *UK, female vocalist* **59 wks**

13 Aug 64	● AS TEARS GO BY *Decca F 11923*	9	13
18 Feb 65	● COME AND STAY WITH ME *Decca F 12075*	4	13
6 May 65	● THIS LITTLE BIRD *Decca F 12162*	6	11
22 Jul 65	● SUMMER NIGHTS *Decca F 12193*	10	10
4 Nov 65	YESTERDAY *Decca F 12268*	36	4
9 Mar 67	IS THIS WHAT I GET FOR LOVING YOU *Decca F 22524*	43	2
24 Nov 79	THE BALLAD OF LUCY JORDAN *Island WIP 6491*	48	6

FAITHLESS ☺ *UK, male/female vocal/instrumental group* **43 wks**

5 Aug 95	SALVA MEA (SAVE ME) *Cheeky CHEKCD 008*	30	2
9 Dec 95	INSOMNIA *Cheeky CHEKCD 010*	27	2
23 Mar 96	DON'T LEAVE *Cheeky CHEKCD 012*	34	2
26 Oct 96	● INSOMNIA (re-mix) *Cheeky CHEKCD 017*	3	13
21 Dec 96	● SALVA MEA (re-issue) *Cheeky CHEKCD 018*	9	7
26 Apr 97	● REVERENCE *Cheeky CHEKCD 019*	10	3
15 Nov 97	DON'T LEAVE *Cheeky CHEKXCD 024*	21	2
5 Sep 98	GOD IS A DJ *Cheeky CHEKCD 028*	6	8
5 Dec 98	TAKE THE LONG WAY HOME *Cheeky CHEKCD 031*	15†	4

FALCO ☺ *Austria, male vocalist* **26 wks**

22 Mar 86	★ ROCK ME AMADEUS *A & M AM 278* ▲	1	15
31 May 86	● VIENNA CALLING *A & M AM 318*	10	8
2 Aug 86	JEANNY *A & M AM 333*	68	1
27 Sep 86	THE SOUND OF MUSIK *WEA U 8591*	61	2

FALL *UK, male vocalist/multi-instrumentalist – Mark E Smith* **25 wks**

13 Sep 86	MR. PHARMACIST *Beggars Banquet BEG 168*	75	1
20 Dec 86	HEY! LUCIANI *Beggars Banquet BEG 176*	59	1
9 May 87	THERE'S A GHOST IN MY HOUSE *Beggars Banquet BEG 187*	30	4
31 Oct 87	HIT THE NORTH *Beggars Banquet BEG 200*	57	5
30 Jan 88	VICTORIA *Beggars Banquet BEG 206*	35	3
26 Nov 88	BIG NEW PRINZ/JERUSALEM (DOUBLE SINGLE) *Beggars Banquet FALL 2/3*	59	2
27 Jan 90	TELEPHONE THING *Cog Sinister SIN 4*	58	1
8 Sep 90	WHITE LIGHTNING *Cog Sinister SIN 6*	56	2
14 Mar 92	FREE RANGE *Cog Sinister SINS 8*	40	1
17 Apr 93	WHY ARE PEOPLE GRUDGEFUL *Permanent CDSPERM 9*	43	1
25 Dec 93	BEHIND THE COUNTER *Permanent CDSPERM 13*	75	1
30 Apr 94	15 WAYS *Permanent CDSPERM 14*	65	1
17 Feb 96	THE CHISELERS *Jet JETSCD 500*	60	1
21 Feb 98	MASQUERADE *Artful CDARTFUL 1*	69	1

Tracks on 'Big New Prinz/Jerusalem' double single: Big New Prinz/Wrong Place Right Time Number Two/Jerusalem/Acid Priest 2088
See also MARK E SMITH

Harold FALTERMEYER ☺ ☺
Germany, male instrumentalist – keyboards **23 wks**

23 Mar 85	AXEL F *MCA MCA 949*	62	4
1 Jun 85	● AXEL F (re-entry) *MCA MCA 949*	2	18
24 Aug 85	FLETCH THEME *MCA MCA 991*	74	1

Agnetha FALTSKOG *Sweden, female vocalist* **12 wks**

28 May 83	THE HEAT IS ON *Epic A 3436*	35	6
13 Aug 83	WRAP YOUR ARMS AROUND ME *Epic A 3622*	44	5
22 Oct 83	CAN'T SHAKE LOOSE *Epic A 3812*	63	1

See also ABBA

Georgie FAME ☺ ♪ *Critically acclaimed R&B/jazz vocalist/keyboard player, b. Clive Powell, 26 June, 1943, Lancashire. The one-time rock'n'roll tour musician, who had a string of sixties' hits, is still a popular performer, often working with contemporaries such as Van Morrison* **115 wks**

17 Dec 64	★ YEH YEH *Columbia DB 7428* 1	1	12
4 Mar 65	IN THE MEANTIME *Columbia DB 7494* 1	22	8
29 Jul 65	LIKE WE USED TO BE *Columbia DB 7633* 1	33	7
28 Oct 65	SOMETHING *Columbia DB 7727* 1	23	7
23 Jun 66	★ GET AWAY *Columbia DB 7946* 1	1	11
22 Sep 66	SUNNY *Columbia DB 8015*	13	8

22 Dec 66	SITTING IN THE PARK *Columbia DB 8096* [1]	12	10
23 Mar 67	BECAUSE I LOVE YOU *CBS 202587*	15	8
13 Sep 67	TRY MY WORLD *CBS 2945*	37	5
13 Dec 67 ★	BALLAD OF BONNIE AND CLYDE *CBS 3124*	1	13
9 Jul 69	PEACEFUL *CBS 4295*	16	9
13 Dec 69	SEVENTH SON *CBS 4659*	25	7
10 Apr 71	ROSETTA *CBS 7108* [2]	11	10

[1] Georgie Fame and the Blue Flames [2] Fame and Price Together

FAMILY ✒ *UK, male vocal/instrumental group* — 44 wks

1 Nov 69	NO MULE'S FOOL *Reprise RS 27001*	29	7
22 Aug 70	STRANGE BAND *Reprise RS 27009*	11	12
17 Jul 71 ●	IN MY OWN TIME *Reprise K 14090*	4	13
23 Sep 72	BURLESQUE *Reprise K 14196*	13	12

FAMILY CAT *UK, male vocal/instrumental group* — 4 wks

28 Aug 93	AIRPLANE GARDENS/ATMOSPHERIC ROAD *Dedicated FCUK 003CD*	69	1
21 May 94	WONDERFUL EXCUSE *Dedicated 74321208432*	48	1
30 Jul 94	GOLDENBOOK *Dedicated 74321220072*	42	2

FAMILY COOKIN' – See LIMMIE and the FAMILY COOKIN'

FAMILY DOGG ☺ *UK, male/female vocal group* — 14 wks

28 May 69 ●	WAY OF LIFE *Bell 1055*	6	14

FAMILY FOUNDATION
UK, male/female vocal/instrumental group — 4 wks

13 Jun 92	XPRESS YOURSELF *380 PEW 1*	42	4

FAMILY STAND [R&B]
US, male/female vocal/instrumental group — 13 wks

31 Mar 90 ●	GHETTO HEAVEN *East West A 7997*	10	11
17 Jan 98	GHETTO HEAVEN (re-mix) *Perfecto PERF 156CD1*	30	2

FAMILY STONE – See SLY and the FAMILY STONE

FAMOUS FLAMES – See James BROWN

FANTASTIC FOUR *US, male vocal group* — 4 wks

24 Feb 79	B.Y.O.F. (BRING YOUR OWN FUNK) *Atlantic LV 14*	62	4

FANTASTICS ✎ *US, male vocal group* — 12 wks

27 Mar 71 ●	SOMETHING OLD, SOMETHING NEW *Bell 1141*	9	12

FANTASY UFO *UK, male instrumental group* — 6 wks

29 Sep 90	FANTASY *XL XLT 15*	56	3
10 Aug 91	MIND BODY SOUL *Strictly Underground YZ 591* [1]	50	3

[1] Fantasy UFO featuring Jay Groove

FAR CORPORATION ☺ ✒
UK/US/Germany/Switzerland, male vocal/instrumental group — 11 wks

26 Oct 85 ●	STAIRWAY TO HEAVEN *Arista ARIST 639*	8	11

Don FARDON ☺ *UK, male vocalist* — 22 wks

18 Apr 70	BELFAST BOY *Young Blood YB 1010*	32	5
10 Oct 70 ●	INDIAN RESERVATION *Young Blood YB 1015*	3	17

FARGETTA *Italy/UK, male/female vocal/instrumental duo* — 3 wks

23 Jan 93	MUSIC *Synthetic CDR 6334* [1]	34	2
10 Aug 96	THE MUSIC IS MOVING *Arista 74321381572*	74	1

[1] Fargetta and Anne-Marie Smith

Chris FARLOWE ✒ *UK, male vocalist* — 36 wks

27 Jan 66	THINK *Immediate IM 023*	49	1

10 Feb 66	THINK (re-entry) *Immediate IM 023*	37	2
23 Jun 66 ★	OUT OF TIME *Immediate IM 035*	1	13
27 Oct 66	RIDE ON BABY *Immediate IM 038*	31	7
16 Feb 67	MY WAY OF GIVING IN *Immediate IM 041*	48	1
29 Jun 67	MOANIN' *Immediate IM 056*	46	2
13 Dec 67	HANDBAGS AND GLADRAGS *Immediate IM 065*	33	6
27 Sep 75	OUT OF TIME (re-issue) *Immediate IMS 101*	44	4

FARM ☹ ☺ *UK, male vocal/instrumental group* — 54 wks

5 May 90	STEPPING STONE/FAMILY OF MAN *Produce MILK 101*	58	4
1 Sep 90 ●	GROOVY TRAIN *Produce MILK 102*	6	10
8 Dec 90 ●	ALL TOGETHER NOW *Produce MILK 103*	4	12
13 Apr 91	SINFUL! *Siren SRN 138* [1]	28	5
4 May 91	DON'T LET ME DOWN *Produce MILK 104*	36	3
24 Aug 91	MIND *Produce MILK 105*	31	4
14 Dec 91	LOVE SEE NO COLOUR *Produce MILK 106*	58	4
4 Jul 92	RISING SUN *End Product 6581737*	48	3
17 Oct 92	DON'T YOU WANT ME *End Product 6584687*	18	5
2 Jan 93	LOVE SEE NO COLOUR (re-issue) *End Product 6588682*	35	4

[1] Pete Wylie with the Farm

FARMERS BOYS *UK, male vocal/instrumental group* — 17 wks

9 Apr 83	MUCK IT OUT *EMI 5380*	48	6
30 Jul 83	FOR YOU *EMI 5401*	66	3
4 Aug 84	IN THE COUNTRY *EMI FAB 2*	44	5
3 Nov 84	PHEW WOW *EMI FAB 3*	59	3

John FARNHAM ☺ *Australia, male vocalist* — 17 wks

25 Apr 87 ●	YOU'RE THE VOICE *Wheatley PB 41093*	6	17

Joanne FARRELL *US, female vocalist* — 2 wks

24 Jun 95	ALL I WANNA DO *Big Beat A 8194CD*	40	2

Joe FARRELL *US, male instrumentalist – saxophone* — 4 wks

16 Dec 78	NIGHT DANCING *Warner Bros. LV 2*	57	4

Dionne FARRIS *US, female vocalist* — 6 wks

18 Mar 95	I KNOW *Columbia 6613542*	47	2
27 May 95	I KNOW (re-entry) *Columbia 6613542*	41	3
7 Jun 97	HOPELESS *Columbia 6645165*	42	1

Gene FARROW and G. F. BAND
UK, male vocal/instrumental group — 8 wks

1 Apr 78	MOVE YOUR BODY *Magnet MAG 109*	33	5
13 May 78	MOVE YOUR BODY (re-entry) *Magnet MAG 109*	67	1
5 Aug 78	DON'T STOP NOW *Magnet MAG 125*	71	1
19 Aug 78	DON'T STOP NOW (re-entry) *Magnet MAG 125*	74	1

FASCINATIONS *US, female vocal group* — 6 wks

3 Jul 71	GIRLS ARE OUT TO GET YOU *Mojo 2092 004*	32	6

FASHION *UK, male vocal/instrumental group* — 12 wks

3 Apr 82	STREETPLAYER (MECHANIK) *Arista ARIST 456*	46	5
21 Aug 82	LOVE SHADOW *Arista ARIST 483*	51	5
18 Feb 84	EYE TALK *De Stijl A 4106*	69	2

Susan FASSBENDER *UK, female vocalist* — 8 wks

17 Jan 81	TWILIGHT CAFE *CBS 9468*	21	8

FASTBALL *US, male vocal/instrumental trio* — 5 wks

3 Oct 98	THE WAY *Polydor 5699472*	21	5

FASTWAY *UK, male vocal/instrumental group* — 1 wk

2 Apr 83	EASY LIVIN' *CBS A 3196*	74	1

UK No 1 ★ UK Top 10 ● UK million seller ◆ UK entry at No 1 ■ US No 1 ▲

FAT BOYS 👟 US, male vocal rap group — 29 wks

Date	Title	Pos	Wks
4 May 85	JAIL HOUSE RAP Sultra U 9123	63	2
22 Aug 87 ●	WIPEOUT Urban URB 5 [1]	2	12
18 Jun 88 ●	THE TWIST (YO, TWIST) Urban URB 20 [2]	2	11
5 Nov 88	LOUIE LOUIE Urban URB 26	46	4

[1] Fat Boys and the Beach Boys [2] Fat Boys and Chubby Checker

FAT LADY SINGS Ireland, male vocal/instrumental group — 2 wks

Date	Title	Pos	Wks
17 Jul 93	DRUNKARD LOGIC East West YZ 756CD	56	2

FAT LARRY'S BAND 🎺 US, male vocal/instrumental group — 26 wks

Date	Title	Pos	Wks
2 Jul 77	CENTER CITY Atlantic K 10951	31	5
10 Mar 79	BOOGIE TOWN Fantasy FTC 168 [1]	46	4
18 Aug 79	LOOKING FOR LOVE TONIGHT Fantasy FTC 179	46	6
18 Sep 82 ●	ZOOM Virgin VS 546	2	11

[1] F.L.B.

FAT LES ☺ UK, male/female vocal group — 14 wks

Date	Title	Pos	Wks
20 Jun 98 ●	VINDALOO Telstar CDSTAS 2982	2	12
19 Dec 98	NAUGHTY CHRISTMAS (GOBLIN IN THE OFFICE) Turtleneck NECKCD 001	21†	2

FATBACK BAND 🎺 US, male vocal/instrumental group — 67 wks

Date	Title	Pos	Wks
6 Sep 75	YUM YUM (GIMME SOME) Polydor 2066 590	40	6
6 Dec 75	(ARE YOU READY) DO THE BUS STOP Polydor 2066 637	18	10
21 Feb 76 ●	(DO THE) SPANISH HUSTLE Polydor 2066 656	10	7
29 May 76	PARTY TIME Polydor 2066 682	41	4
14 Aug 76	NIGHT FEVER Spring 2066 706	38	4
12 Mar 77	DOUBLE DUTCH Spring 2066 777	31	4
9 Aug 80	BACKSTROKIN' Spring POSP 149 [1]	41	9
23 Jun 84	I FOUND LOVIN' Master Mix CHE 8401	49	4
4 May 85	GIRLS ON MY MIND Atlantic/Cotillion FBACK 1 [1]	69	2
6 Sep 86	I FOUND LOVIN' (re-mix) Important TAN 10	55	5
5 Sep 87 ●	I FOUND LOVIN' (re-entry) Master Mix CHE 8401	7	12

[1] Fatback

FATBOY SLIM ☺ ☺ UK, male producer – Norman Cook — 21 wks

Date	Title	Pos	Wks
3 May 97	GOING OUT OF MY HEAD Skint SKINT 19CD	57	1
1 Nov 97	EVERYBODY NEEDS A 303 Skint SKINT 31CD	34	2
20 Jun 98 ●	THE ROCKAFELLER SKANK Skint SKINT 35CD	6	10
17 Oct 98 ●	GANGSTER TRIPPIN' Skint SKINT 39CD	3	8

See also Norman COOK

FATHER ABRAHAM – See SMURFS

FATHER ABRAPHART and the SMURPS – See Jonathan KING

FATIMA MANSIONS 🎸 Ireland, male vocal/instrumental group — 11 wks

Date	Title	Pos	Wks
23 May 92	EVIL MAN Radioactive SKX 56	59	1
1 Aug 92	1000% Radioactive SKX 59	61	3
19 Sep 92 ●	(EVERYTHING I DO) I DO IT FOR YOU Columbia 6583827	7	6
6 Aug 94	THE LOYALISER Kitchenware SKCD 67	58	1

'(Everything I Do) I Do It For You' was listed with 'Theme From M.A.S.H. (Suicide Is Painless)' by Manic Street Preachers

FBI – See REDHEAD KINGPIN and the FBI

Phil FEARON ☺ 🎤 UK, male vocalist — 63 wks

Date	Title	Pos	Wks
23 Apr 83 ●	DANCING TIGHT Ensign ENY 501 [1]	4	11
30 Jul 83	WAIT UNTIL TONIGHT (MY LOVE) Ensign ENY 503 [1]	20	8
22 Oct 83	FANTASY REAL Ensign ENY 507 [2]	41	6
10 Mar 84 ●	WHAT DO I DO Ensign ENY 510 [2]	5	10
14 Jul 84 ●	EVERYBODY'S LAUGHING Ensign ENY 514 [2]	10	10
15 Jun 85	YOU DON'T NEED A REASON Ensign ENY 517 [2]	42	4
27 Jul 85	THIS KIND OF LOVE Ensign ENY 521 [3]	70	3
2 Aug 86 ●	I CAN PROVE IT Ensign PF 1	8	9
15 Nov 86	AIN'T NOTHING BUT A HOUSEPARTY Ensign PF 2	60	2

[1] Galaxy featuring Phil Fearon [2] Phil Fearon and Galaxy
[3] Phil Fearon and Galaxy featuring Dee Galdes

FEEDER UK, male vocal/instrumental group — 6 wks

Date	Title	Pos	Wks
8 Mar 97	TANGERINE Echo ECSCD 32	60	1
10 May 97	CEMENT Echo ECSCX 36	53	1
23 Aug 97	CRASH Echo ECSCD 42	48	1
18 Oct 97	HIGH Echo ECSCD 44	24	2
28 Feb 98	SUFFOCATE Echo ECSCX 52	37	1

Wilton FELDER US, male instrumentalist – tenor sax — 7 wks

Date	Title	Pos	Wks
1 Nov 80	INHERIT THE WIND MCA 646	39	5
16 Feb 85	(NO MATTER HOW HIGH I GET) I'LL STILL BE LOOKIN' UP TO YOU MCA MCA 919	63	2

Bobby Womack is the uncredited lead vocalist on both hits. Alltrina Grayson co-vocalises on MCA 919

José FELICIANO ♂ 🎸 US, male vocalist/instrumentalist – guitar — 23 wks

Date	Title	Pos	Wks
18 Sep 68 ●	LIGHT MY FIRE RCA 1715	6	16
18 Oct 69	AND THE SUN WILL SHINE RCA 1871	25	7

FELIX ☺ UK, male producer — 29 wks

Date	Title	Pos	Wks
8 Aug 92 ●	DON'T YOU WANT ME Deconstruction 74321110507	6	11
24 Oct 92	IT WILL MAKE ME CRAZY Deconstruction 74321118137	11	6
22 May 93	STARS Deconstruction 74321147102	29	3
12 Aug 95 ●	DON'T YOU WANT ME (re-mix) Deconstruction 74321293972	10	5
19 Oct 96	DON'T YOU WANT ME (2nd re-mix) Deconstruction 74321418142	17	4

Julie FELIX ♂ ☺ US, female vocalist — 19 wks

Date	Title	Pos	Wks
18 Apr 70	IF I COULD (EL CONDOR PASA) RAK 101	19	11
17 Oct 70	HEAVEN IS HERE RAK 105	22	8

FELLY – See TECHNOTRONIC

FEMME FATALE US, male/female vocal/instrumental group — 2 wks

Date	Title	Pos	Wks
11 Feb 89	FALLING IN AND OUT OF LOVE MCA MCA 1309	69	2

FENDERMEN US, male vocal/instrumental duo – guitars — 9 wks

Date	Title	Pos	Wks
18 Aug 60	MULE SKINNER BLUES Top Rank JAR 395	50	1
1 Sep 60	MULE SKINNER BLUES (re-entry) Top Rank JAR 395	37	2
29 Sep 60	MULE SKINNER BLUES (2nd re-entry) Top Rank JAR 395	32	6

FENMEN – See Bern ELLIOTT and the FENMEN

George FENTON and Jonas GWANGWA UK/South Africa, male instrumental production duo — 1 wk

Date	Title	Pos	Wks
2 Jan 88	CRY FREEDOM MCA MCA 1228	75	1

The listed flip side of 'Cry Freedom' was 'The Funeral' by Thuli Dumakude

Peter FENTON UK, male vocalist — 3 wks

Date	Title	Pos	Wks
10 Nov 66	MARBLE BREAKS IRON BENDS Fontana TF 748	46	3

Shane FENTON and the FENTONES ☺ UK, male vocal/instrumental group — 28 wks

Date	Title	Pos	Wks
26 Oct 61	I'M A MOODY GUY Parlophone R 4827	22	8
1 Feb 62	WALK AWAY Parlophone R 4866	38	5
5 Apr 62	IT'S ALL OVER NOW Parlophone R 4883	29	7
12 Jul 62	CINDY'S BIRTHDAY Parlophone R 4921	19	8

Fenton later became Alvin Stardust

FENTONES UK, male instrumental group — 4 wks

Date	Title	Pos	Wks
19 Apr 62	THE MEXICAN Parlophone R 4899	41	3
27 Sep 62	THE BREEZE AND I Parlophone R 4937	48	1

Sheila FERGUSON US, female vocalist — 1 wk

Date	Title	Pos	Wks
5 Feb 94	WHEN WILL I SEE YOU AGAIN *XSrhythm CDSTAS 2711*	60	1

FERKO STRING BAND (C) US, male instrumental group — 2 wks

Date	Title	Pos	Wks
12 Aug 55	ALABAMA JUBILEE *London HL 8140*	20	2

Luisa FERNANDEZ Spain, female vocalist — 8 wks

Date	Title	Pos	Wks
11 Nov 78	LAY LOVE ON YOU *Warner Bros. K 17061*	31	8

Pamela FERNANDEZ US, female vocalist — 3 wks

Date	Title	Pos	Wks
17 Sep 94	KICKIN' IN THE BEAT *Ore AG 5CD*	43	2
3 Jun 95	LET'S START OVER/KICKIN' IN THE BEAT (re-mix) *Ore AG 9CD*	59	1

FERRANTE and TEICHER (C)
US, male instrumental duo – pianos — 18 wks

Date	Title	Pos	Wks
18 Aug 60	THEME FROM 'THE APARTMENT' *London HLT 9164*	44	1
9 Mar 61 ●	EXODUS (THEME FROM 'EXODUS') *London HLT 9298 and HMV POP 881*	6	17

Exodus (Theme From 'Exodus') available first on London, then on HMV when the US label, United Artists, changed its UK outlet

José FERRER (C) US, male vocalist — 3 wks

Date	Title	Pos	Wks
19 Feb 54 ●	WOMAN *Philips PB 220*	7	3

'Woman' coupled with 'Man' by Rosemary Clooney

Tony FERRINO UK, male vocalist – comedian Steve Coogan — 2 wks

Date	Title	Pos	Wks
23 Nov 96	HELP YOURSELF/BIGAMY AT CHRISTMAS *RCA 74321430302*	42	2

FERRY AID (S) International, male/female charity ensemble — 7 wks

Date	Title	Pos	Wks
4 Apr 87 ★	LET IT BE *The Sun AID 1* ■	1	7

Bryan FERRY 🖉 Stylish UK vocalist/songwriter, b. 26 September, 1945, Tyne and Wear. Sophisticated singer who split his time between solo career and fronting the fashionable and successful group Roxy Music — 133 wks

Date	Title	Pos	Wks
29 Sep 73 ●	A HARD RAIN'S GONNA FALL *Island WIP 6170*	10	9
25 May 74	THE IN CROWD *Island WIP 6196*	13	6
31 Aug 74	SMOKE GETS IN YOUR EYES *Island WIP 6205*	17	8
5 Jul 75	YOU GO TO MY HEAD *Island WIP 6234*	33	3
12 Jun 76 ●	LET'S STICK TOGETHER (LET'S WORK TOGETHER) *Island WIP 6307*	4	10
7 Aug 76 ●	EXTENDED PLAY EP *Island IEP 1*	7	9
5 Feb 77 ●	THIS IS TOMORROW *Polydor 2001 704*	9	9
14 May 77	TOKYO JOE *Polydor 2001 711*	15	7
13 May 78	WHAT GOES ON *Polydor POSP 3*	67	2
5 Aug 78	SIGN OF THE TIMES *Polydor 2001 798*	37	8
11 May 85 ●	SLAVE TO LOVE *EG FERRY 1*	10	9
31 Aug 85	DON'T STOP THE DANCE *EG FERRY 2*	21	7
7 Dec 85	WINDSWEPT *EG FERRY 3*	46	3
29 Mar 86	IS YOUR LOVE STRONG ENOUGH? *EG FERRY 4*	22	7
10 Oct 87	THE RIGHT STUFF *Virgin VS 940*	37	6
13 Feb 88	KISS AND TELL *Virgin VS 1034*	41	5
29 Oct 88	LET'S STICK TOGETHER (re-mix) *EG EGO 44*	12	7
11 Feb 89	THE PRICE OF LOVE (re-mix) *EG EGO 46*	49	3
22 Apr 89	HE'LL HAVE TO GO *EG EGO 48*	63	1
6 Mar 93	I PUT A SPELL ON YOU *Virgin VSCDG 1400*	18	5
29 May 93	WILL YOU LOVE ME TOMORROW *Virgin VSCDG 1455*	23	5
4 Sep 93	GIRL OF MY BEST FRIEND *Virgin VSCDG 1488*	57	2
29 Oct 94	YOUR PAINTED SMILE *Virgin VSCDG 1508*	52	1
11 Feb 95	MAMOUNA *Virgin VSCDG 1528*	57	1

Tracks on Extended Play (EP): Price of Love/Shame Shame Shame/Heart on My Sleeve/It's Only Love

FEVER – See Tippa IRIE

Lena FIAGBE 🖉 ☺ UK, female vocalist — 13 wks

Date	Title	Pos	Wks
24 Jul 93	YOU COME FROM EARTH *Mother MUMCD 42* [1]	69	1
23 Oct 93	GOTTA GET IT RIGHT *Mother MUMCD 44*	20	5
16 Apr 94	WHAT'S IT LIKE TO BE BEAUTIFUL *Mother MUMCD 49*	52	3
25 Jun 94	VISIONS *Mother MUMCD 53*	48	2
10 Feb 96	AFRICAN DREAM *Mercury MERCD 453* [2]	44	2

[1] Lena [2] Wasis Diop featuring Lena Fiagbe

Karel FIALKA (S) UK, male vocalist/multi-instrumentalist — 12 wks

Date	Title	Pos	Wks
17 May 80	THE EYES HAVE IT *Blueprint BLU 2005*	52	4
5 Sep 87 ●	HEY MATTHEW *IRS IRM 140*	9	8

FIAT LUX UK, male vocal/instrumental group — 4 wks

Date	Title	Pos	Wks
28 Jan 84	SECRETS *Polydor FIAT 2*	65	3
17 Mar 84	BLUE EMOTION *Polydor FIAT 3*	59	1

FICTION FACTORY (S) UK, male vocal/instrumental group — 11 wks

Date	Title	Pos	Wks
14 Jan 84 ●	(FEELS LIKE) HEAVEN *CBS A 3996*	6	9
17 Mar 84	GHOST OF LOVE *CBS A 3819*	64	2

FIDDLER'S DRAM ♂ (S)
UK, male/female vocal/instrumental group — 9 wks

Date	Title	Pos	Wks
15 Dec 79 ●	DAY TRIP TO BANGOR (DIDN'T WE HAVE A LOVELY TIME) *Dingles SID 211*	3	9

FIDELFATTI featuring RONNETTE
Italy, male producer and female vocalist — 1 wk

Date	Title	Pos	Wks
27 Jan 90	JUST WANNA TOUCH ME *Urban URB 46*	65	1

Billy FIELD Australia, male vocalist — 3 wks

Date	Title	Pos	Wks
12 Jun 82	YOU WEREN'T IN LOVE WITH ME *CBS A 2344*	67	3

Ernie FIELDS 🎺 US, orchestra — 8 wks

Date	Title	Pos	Wks
25 Dec 59	IN THE MOOD *London HL 8985*	13	8

Gracie FIELDS (C) UK, female vocalist — 15 wks

Date	Title	Pos	Wks
31 May 57 ●	AROUND THE WORLD *Columbia DB 3953*	8	8
2 Aug 57	AROUND THE WORLD (re-entry) *Columbia DB 3953*	24	1
6 Nov 59	LITTLE DONKEY *Columbia DB 4360*	30	1
20 Nov 59	LITTLE DONKEY (re-entry) *Columbia DB 4360*	20	5

Richard 'Dimples' FIELDS US, male vocalist — 4 wks

Date	Title	Pos	Wks
20 Feb 82	I'VE GOT TO LEARN TO SAY NO *Epic EPC A 1918*	56	4

FIELDS OF THE NEPHILIM UK, male vocal/instrumental group — 9 wks

Date	Title	Pos	Wks
24 Oct 87	BLUE WATER *Situation Two SIT 48*	75	1
4 Jun 88	MOONCHILD *Situation Two SIT 52*	28	3
27 May 89	PSYCHONAUT *Situation Two ST 57*	35	3
4 Aug 90	FOR HER LIGHT *Beggars Banquet BEG 244T*	54	1
24 Nov 90	SUMERLAND (DREAMED) *Beggars Banquet BEG 250*	37	1

FIFTH DIMENSION (S) US, male/female vocal group — 21 wks

Date	Title	Pos	Wks
16 Apr 69	AQUARIUS/LET THE SUNSHINE IN (MEDLEY) *Liberty LBF 15193* ▲	11	12
17 Jan 70	WEDDING BELL BLUES *Liberty LBF 15288* ▲	16	9

52ND STREET UK, male/female vocal/instrumental group — 13 wks

Date	Title	Pos	Wks
2 Nov 85	TELL ME (HOW IT FEELS) *10 TEN 74*	54	5
11 Jan 86	YOU'RE MY LAST CHANCE *10 TEN 89*	49	4
8 Mar 86	I CAN'T LET YOU GO *10 TEN 114*	57	4

53RD and THIRD – See Jonathan KING

FILTER US, male vocal/instrumental group — 2 wks

| 11 Oct 97 | | (CAN YOU) TRIP LIKE I DO *Epic 6650862* [1] | 39 | 2 |

[1] Filter and The Crystal Method

FINAL CUT – See TRUE FAITH with FINAL CUT

FINE YOUNG CANNIBALS ☺
UK, male vocal/instrumental group — 81 wks

8 Jun 85	●	JOHNNY COME HOME *London LON 68*	8	13
9 Nov 85		BLUE *London LON 79*	41	6
11 Jan 86	●	SUSPICIOUS MINDS *London LON 82*	8	9
12 Apr 86		FUNNY HOW LOVE IS *London LON 88*	58	4
21 Mar 87	●	EVER FALLEN IN LOVE *London LON 121*	9	10
7 Jan 89	●	SHE DRIVES ME CRAZY *London LON 199* ▲	5	11
15 Apr 89	●	GOOD THING *London LON 218* ▲	7	8
19 Aug 89		DON'T LOOK BACK *London LON 220*	34	4
18 Nov 89		I'M NOT THE MAN I USED TO BE *London LON 244*	20	8
24 Feb 90		I'M NOT SATISFIED *London LON 252*	46	3
16 Nov 96		THE FLAME *ffrr LONCD 389*	17	3
11 Jan 97		SHE DRIVES ME CRAZY (re-mix) *ffrr LONCD 391*	36	2

FINITRIBE UK, male instrumental/production group — 2 wks

| 11 Jul 92 | | FOREVERGREEN *One Little Indian 74 TP12F* | 51 | 1 |
| 19 Nov 94 | | BRAND NEW *ffrr FCD 247* | 69 | 1 |

FINK BROTHERS UK, male vocal/instrumental duo — 4 wks

| 9 Feb 85 | | MUTANTS IN MEGA CITY ONE *Zarjazz JAZZ 2* | 50 | 4 |

FINN New Zealand, male vocal/instrumental duo — 5 wks

| 14 Oct 95 | | SUFFER NEVER *Parlophone CDRS 6417* | 29 | 3 |
| 9 Dec 95 | | ANGEL'S HEAP *Parlophone CDRS 6421* | 41 | 2 |

See also CROWDED HOUSE; Neil FINN; Tim FINN

Micky FINN – See URBAN SHAKEDOWN featuring Micky FINN

Neil FINN New Zealand, male vocalist/instrumentalist — 3 wks

| 13 Jun 98 | | SHE WILL HAVE HER WAY *Parlophone CDR 6495* | 26 | 2 |
| 17 Oct 98 | | SINNER *Parlophone CDR 6505* | 39 | 1 |

See also CROWDED HOUSE; FINN

Tim FINN New Zealand, male vocalist — 6 wks

| 26 Jun 93 | | PERSUASION *Capitol 6592482* | 43 | 3 |
| 18 Sep 93 | | HIT THE GROUND RUNNING *Capitol CDCLS 694* | 50 | 3 |

See also CROWDED HOUSE; FINN

Elisa FIORILLO ☺ US, female vocalist — 14 wks

| 28 Nov 87 | ● | WHO FOUND WHO *Chrysalis CHS JEL 1* [1] | 10 | 10 |
| 13 Feb 88 | | HOW CAN I FORGET YOU *Chrysalis ELISA 1* | 50 | 4 |

[1] Jellybean featuring Elisa Fiorillo

FIRE INC. – See Jim STEINMAN

FIRE ISLAND UK, male instrumental/production group — 7 wks

8 Aug 92		IN YOUR BONES/FIRE ISLAND *Boy's Own BOIX 11*	66	1
12 Mar 94		THERE BUT FOR THE GRACE OF GOD *Junior Boy's Own JBO 18CD* [1]	32	3
4 Mar 95		IF YOU SHOULD NEED A FRIEND *Junior Boy's Own JBO 26CDS* [2]	51	1
11 Apr 98		SHOUT TO THE TOP *JBO JNR 5001573* [3]	23	2

[1] Fire Island featuring Love Nelson [2] Fire Island featuring Mark Anthoni
[3] Fire Island featuring Loleatta Holloway

See also HELLER and FARLEY PROJECT

FIREBALLS US, male vocal/instrumental group — 17 wks

27 Jul 61		QUITE A PARTY *Pye International 7N 25092*	29	9
14 Nov 63		SUGAR SHACK *London HLD 9789* [1]	45	4
19 Dec 63		SUGAR SHACK (re-entry) *London HLD 9789* [1]	46	4

[1] Jimmy Gilmer and the Fireballs

FIREHOUSE US, male vocal/instrumental group — 2 wks

| 13 Jul 91 | | DON'T TREAT ME BAD *Epic 6567807* | 71 | 1 |
| 19 Dec 92 | | WHEN I LOOK INTO YOUR EYES *Epic 6588347* | 65 | 1 |

FIRM ☺ UK, male vocal/instrumental group — 21 wks

| 17 Jul 82 | | ARTHUR DALEY ('E'S ALRIGHT) *Bark HID 1* | 14 | 9 |
| 6 Jun 87 | ★ | STAR TREKKIN' *Bark TREK 1* | 1 | 12 |

FIRM featuring Dawn ROBINSON [R&B] ☺
US, male rap group, and US, female vocalist — 3 wks

| 29 Nov 97 | | FIRM BIZZ *Columbia 6651612* | 18 | 3 |

FIRST CHOICE ◢ US, female vocal group — 21 wks

| 19 May 73 | | ARMED AND EXTREMELY DANGEROUS *Bell 1297* | 16 | 10 |
| 4 Aug 73 | ● | SMARTY PANTS *Bell 1324* | 9 | 11 |

FIRST CLASS ☺ UK, male vocal group — 10 wks

| 15 Jun 74 | | BEACH BABY *UK 66* | 13 | 10 |

FIRST EDITION – See Kenny ROGERS

FIRST LIGHT UK, male vocal/instrumental duo — 5 wks

| 21 May 83 | | EXPLAIN THE REASONS *London LON 26* | 65 | 3 |
| 28 Jan 84 | | WISH YOU WERE HERE *London LON 43* | 71 | 2 |

FISCHER-Z UK, male vocal/instrumental group — 7 wks

| 26 May 79 | | THE WORKER *United Artists UP 36509* | 53 | 5 |
| 3 May 80 | | SO LONG *United Artists BP 342* | 72 | 2 |

FISH UK, male vocalist — 20 wks

18 Oct 86		SHORT CUT TO SOMEWHERE *Charisma CB 426* [1]	75	1
28 Oct 89		STATE OF MIND *EMI EM 109*	32	3
6 Jan 90		BIG WEDGE *EMI EM 125*	25	4
17 Mar 90		A GENTLEMAN'S EXCUSE ME *EMI EM 135*	30	3
28 Sep 91		INTERNAL EXILE *Polydor FISHY 1*	37	2
11 Jan 92		CREDO *Polydor FISHY 2*	38	2
4 Jul 92		SOMETHING IN THE AIR *Polydor FISHY 3*	51	2
16 Apr 94		LADY LET IT LIE *Dick Bros. DDICK 3CD1*	46	1
1 Oct 94		FORTUNES OF WAR *Dick Bros. DDICK 008CD1*	67	1
26 Aug 95		JUST GOOD FRIENDS *Dick Bros. DDICK 014CD1* [2]	63	1

[1] Fish and Tony Banks [2] Fish and Sam Brown

FISHBONE US, male vocal/instrumental group — 3 wks

| 1 Aug 92 | | EVERYDAY SUNSHINE/FIGHT THE YOUTH *Columbia 6581937* | 60 | 2 |
| 28 Aug 93 | | SWIM *Columbia 6596252* | 54 | 1 |

Eddie FISHER ℂ Leading 1950s heartthrob, b. 10 August, 1929, Philadelphia. The USA's most successful male singer between 1950-1954; accumulated many more UK hits in the pre-chart years. Married Elizabeth Taylor, Debbie Reynolds and Connie Stevens and is father of actress Carrie Fisher — 105 wks

2 Jan 53	★	OUTSIDE OF HEAVEN *HMV B 10362*	1	16
23 Jan 53		EVERYTHING I HAVE IS YOURS *HMV B 10398*	12	1
6 Feb 53	●	EVERYTHING I HAVE IS YOURS (re-entry) *HMV B 10398*	8	4
1 May 53	●	DOWNHEARTED *HMV B 10450*	3	15
1 May 53		OUTSIDE OF HEAVEN (re-entry) *HMV B 10362*	12	1
22 May 53	★	I'M WALKING BEHIND YOU *HMV B 10489* [1] ▲	1	18
6 Nov 53		WISH YOU WERE HERE *HMV B 10564*	8	9
22 Jan 54		OH MY PAPA *HMV B 10614* ▲	9	1
5 Feb 54		OH MY PAPA (re-entry) *HMV B 10614*	11	1
26 Feb 54	●	OH MY PAPA (2nd re-entry) *HMV B 10614*	10	1
12 Mar 54		OH MY PAPA (3rd re-entry) *HMV B 10614*	11	1
29 Oct 54		I NEED YOU NOW *HMV B 10755* ▲	16	2

What: *A Whiter Shade of Pale*   37
Who: Procol Harum
When: 1967 (1), 1972 (13)
Which: Is remembered as a classic single from the 'Summer of Love'. This haunting, surreal song based on a Bach air sold more than six million copies around the globe

What: *Let's Twist Again*   38
Who: Chubby Checker
When: 1961 (37) 1961 (2), 1975 (5)
Which: Was the sequel to his US chart-topper, 'The Twist'. However, unlike its predecessor, this party favourite was an international hit and started the world twisting

What: *Leader of the Pack*   39
Who: Shangri-Las
When: 1965 (11), 1972 (3), 1976 (7)
Which: Motored into the Top 20 on three separate occasions and is *the* biker anthem. Rumour has it that the piano-man on the track is a 15-year-old Billy Joel

What: *When a Man Loves a Woman*   40
Who: Percy Sledge
When: 1966 (4), 1987 (2)
Which: Epitomised the sixties' southern soul sound. It topped the US chart in 1966, and reached its UK peak almost 21 years later after it was used in a Levi's jeans advert

19 Nov 54	I NEED YOU NOW (re-entry) *HMV B 10755*	13	7
21 Jan 55	I NEED YOU NOW (2nd re-entry) *HMV B 10755*	19	1
18 Mar 55 ●	(I'M ALWAYS HEARING) WEDDING BELLS *HMV B 10839*	5	11
23 Nov 56 ●	CINDY OH CINDY *HMV POP 273*	5	16

[1] Eddie Fisher with Sally Sweetland (soprano)

Mark FISHER featuring Dotty GREEN
UK, male instrumentalist – keyboards and female vocalist **2 wks**

29 Jun 85	LOVE SITUATION *Total Control TOCO 3*	59	2

Toni FISHER *US, female vocalist* **1 wk**

12 Feb 60	THE BIG HURT *Top Rank JAR 261*	30	1

FITS OF GLOOM *UK/Italy, male vocal duo* **4 wks**

4 Jun 94	HEAVEN *Media MCSTD 1981*	47	2
5 Nov 94	THE POWER OF LOVE *Media MCSTD 2016* [1]	49	2

[1] Fits of Gloom featuring Lizzy Mack

Ella FITZGERALD *US, female vocalist* **29 wks**

23 May 58	SWINGIN' SHEPHERD BLUES *HMV POP 486*	15	5
16 Oct 59	BUT NOT FOR ME *HMV POP 657*	25	2
25 Dec 59	BUT NOT FOR ME (re-entry) *HMV POP 657*	29	1
21 Apr 60	MACK THE KNIFE *HMV POP 736*	19	9
6 Oct 60	HOW HIGH THE MOON *HMV POP 782*	46	1
22 Nov 62	DESAFINADO *Verve VS 502*	38	4
27 Dec 62	DESAFINADO (re-entry) *Verve VS 502*	41	2
30 Apr 64	CAN'T BUY ME LOVE *Verve VS 519*	34	5

Scott FITZGERALD *UK, male vocalist* **12 wks**

14 Jan 78 ●	IF I HAD WORDS *Pepper UP 36333* [1]	3	10
7 May 88	GO *PRT PYS 10*	52	2

[1] Scott Fitzgerald and Yvonne Keeley and the St Thomas More School Choir

5IVE *UK, male vocal group* **48 wks**

13 Dec 97 ●	SLAM DUNK (DA FUNK) *RCA 74321537352*	10	9
14 Mar 98 ●	WHEN THE LIGHTS GO OUT *RCA 74321562312*	4	9
20 Jun 98 ●	GOT THE FEELIN' *RCA 74321584892*	3	13
12 Sep 98 ●	EVERYBODY GET UP *RCA 74321613752*	2	12
28 Nov 98 ●	UNTIL THE TIME IS THROUGH *RCA 74321632602*	2†	5

FIVE SMITH BROTHERS *UK, male vocal group* **1 wk**

22 Jul 55	I'M IN FAVOUR OF FRIENDSHIP *Decca F 10527*	20	1

FIVE STAR ● ☺ ✏ *Britain's best known black family act: Deniece, Doris, Stedman, Lorraine and Delroy Pearson. The Essex-based group became youngest act to top LP chart with UK million seller. Silk and Steel. In 1987 were voted Top British Group in Smash Hits and at BRIT Awards* **140 wks**

4 May 85	ALL FALL DOWN *Tent PB 40039*	15	12
20 Jul 85	LET ME BE THE ONE *Tent PB 40193*	18	9
14 Sep 85	LOVE TAKE OVER *Tent PB 40353*	25	9
16 Nov 85	R.S.V.P. *Tent PB 40445*	45	5
11 Jan 86 ●	SYSTEM ADDICT *Tent PB 40515*	3	11
12 Apr 86 ●	CAN'T WAIT ANOTHER MINUTE *Tent PB 40697*	7	10
26 Jul 86 ●	FIND THE TIME *Tent PB 40799*	7	10
13 Sep 86 ●	RAIN OR SHINE *Tent PB 40901*	2	11
22 Nov 86	IF I SAY YES *Tent PB 40981*	15	9
7 Feb 87 ●	STAY OUT OF MY LIFE *Tent PB 41131*	9	8
18 Apr 87 ●	THE SLIGHTEST TOUCH *Tent PB 41265*	4	9
22 Aug 87	WHENEVER YOU'RE READY *Tent PB 41477*	11	6
10 Oct 87	STRONG AS STEEL *Tent PB 41565*	16	7
5 Dec 87	SOMEWHERE SOMEBODY *Tent PB 41661*	23	6
4 Jun 88	ANOTHER WEEKEND *Tent PB 42081*	18	4
6 Aug 88	ROCK MY WORLD *Tent PB 42145*	28	4
17 Sep 88	THERE'S A BRAND NEW WORLD *Tent PB 42235*	61	2
19 Nov 88	LET ME BE YOURS *Tent PB 42343*	51	3
8 Apr 89	WITH EVERY HEARTBEAT *Tent PB 42693*	49	2
10 Mar 90	TREAT ME LIKE A LADY *Tent FIVE 1*	54	2
7 Jul 90	HOT LOVE *Tent FIVE 2*	68	1

FIVE THIRTY *UK, male vocal/instrumental group* **4 wks**

4 Aug 90	ABSTAIN *East West YZ 530*	75	1
25 May 91	13TH DISCIPLE *East West YZ 577*	67	1
3 Aug 91	SUPERNOVA *East West YZ 594*	75	1
2 Nov 91	YOU EP *East West YZ 624*	72	1

Tracks on You (EP): You / Cuddly Drug / Slow Train into the Ocean

5000 VOLTS ⚐ ⊗ *UK, male/female vocal/instrumental group* **18 wks**

6 Sep 75 ●	I'M ON FIRE *Philips 6006 464*	4	9
24 Jul 76 ●	DR KISS KISS *Philips 6006 533*	8	9

FIXX *UK, male vocal/instrumental group* **8 wks**

24 Apr 82	STAND OR FALL *MCA FIXX 2*	54	4
17 Jul 82	RED SKIES *MCA FIXX 3*	57	4

FKW *UK, male vocal/instrumental group* **8 wks**

2 Oct 93	NEVER GONNA (GIVE YOU UP) *PWL International PWCD 273*	48	2
11 Dec 93	SEIZE THE DAY *PWL International PWCD 279*	45	2
5 Mar 94	JINGO *PWL International PWCD 283*	30	3
4 Jun 94	THIS IS THE WAY *PWL International PWCD 307*	63	1

Roberta FLACK ✎ *US, female vocalist* **79 wks**

27 May 72	THE FIRST TIME EVER I SAW YOUR FACE *Atlantic K 10161* ▲	14	14
5 Aug 72	WHERE IS THE LOVE *Atlantic K 10202* [1]	29	7
17 Feb 73 ●	KILLING ME SOFTLY WITH HIS SONG *Atlantic K 10282* ▲	6	14
24 Aug 74	FEEL LIKE MAKING LOVE *Atlantic K 10467* ▲	34	7
6 May 78	THE CLOSER I GET TO YOU *Atlantic K 11099* [1]	42	4
17 May 80 ●	BACK TOGETHER AGAIN *Atlantic K 11481* [1]	3	11
30 Aug 80	DON'T MAKE ME WAIT TOO LONG *Atlantic K 11555*	44	7
20 Aug 83 ●	TONIGHT I CELEBRATE MY LOVE *Capitol CL 302* [2]	2	13
29 Jul 89	UH-UH OOH OOH LOOK OUT (HERE IT COMES) *Atlantic A 8941*	72	2

[1] Roberta Flack and Donny Hathaway [2] Peabo Bryson and Roberta Flack

FLAJ – See GETO BOYS featuring FLAJ

FLAMING LIPS *US, male vocal/instrumental group* **1 wk**

9 Mar 96	THIS HERE GIRAFFE *Warner Bros. W 0335CD*	72	1

FLAMINGOS *US, male vocal group* **5 wks**

4 Jun 69	BOOGALOO PARTY *Philips BF 1786*	26	5

Michael FLANDERS *UK, male vocalist* **3 wks**

27 Feb 59	LITTLE DRUMMER BOY *Parlophone R 4528*	20	2
17 Apr 59	LITTLE DRUMMER BOY (re-entry) *Parlophone R 4528*	24	1

FLASH and the PAN ⊗
Australia, male vocal/instrumental group **15 wks**

23 Sep 78	AND THE BAND PLAYED ON (DOWN AMONG THE DEAD MEN) *Ensign ENY 15*	54	4
21 May 83 ●	WAITING FOR A TRAIN *Easybeat EASY 1*	7	11

Lester FLATT and Earl SCRUGGS
US, male instrumental duo – banjos **6 wks**

15 Nov 67	FOGGY MOUNTAIN BREAKDOWN *CBS 3038 and Mercury MF 1007*	39	6

The versions on the two labels were not the same cuts; CBS had a 1965 recording, Mercury a 1949 recording. The chart did not differentiate and listed both together

Fogwell FLAX and the ANKLEBITERS from FREEHOLD JUNIOR SCHOOL *UK, male vocalist and school choir* **2 wks**

26 Dec 81	ONE NINE FOR SANTA *EMI 5255*	68	2

F L B – See FAT LARRY'S BAND

UK No 1 ★   UK Top 10 ●   UK million seller ◆   UK entry at No 1 ■   US No 1 ▲

FLEE-REKKERS *UK, male instrumental group* **13 wks**

| 19 May 60 | GREEN JEANS *Triumph RGM 1008* | 23 | 13 |

FLEETWOOD MAC 🎸 *Record-breaking Anglo-American act. Members included: Mick Fleetwood (d), John McVie (b), Peter Green (g), Christine McVie (k/v), Lindsey Buckingham (g/v), Stevie Nicks (v). Grammy-winning album* Rumours *sold more than 18 million copies in the USA alone and spent more than eight years on the UK chart* **223 wks**

10 Apr 68	BLACK MAGIC WOMAN *Blue Horizon 57 3138*	37	7
17 Jul 68	NEED YOUR LOVE SO BAD *Blue Horizon 57 3139*	31	13
4 Dec 68 ★	ALBATROSS *Blue Horizon 57 3145*	1	20
16 Apr 69 ●	MAN OF THE WORLD *Immediate IM 080*	2	14
23 Jul 69	NEED YOUR LOVE SO BAD (re-issue) *Blue Horizon 57 3157*	32	6
13 Sep 69	NEED YOUR LOVE SO BAD (re-entry of re-issue) *Blue Horizon 57 3157*	42	3
4 Oct 69 ●	OH WELL *Reprise RS 27000*	2	16
23 May 70 ●	THE GREEN MANALISHI (WITH THE TWO-PRONG CROWN) *Reprise RS 27007*	10	12
12 May 73 ●	ALBATROSS (re-issue) *CBS 8306*	2	15
13 Nov 76	SAY YOU LOVE ME *Reprise K 14447*	40	4
19 Feb 77	GO YOUR OWN WAY *Warner Bros. K 16872*	38	4
30 Apr 77	DON'T STOP *Warner Bros. K 16930*	32	5
9 Jul 77	DREAMS *Warner Bros. K 16969* ▲	24	9
22 Oct 77	YOU MAKE LOVING FUN *Warner Bros. K 17013*	45	2
11 Mar 78	RHIANNON *Reprise K 14430*	46	3
6 Oct 79 ●	TUSK *Warner Bros. K 17468*	6	10
22 Dec 79	SARA *Warner Bros. K 17533*	37	8
25 Sep 82	GYPSY *Warner Bros. K 17997*	46	3
18 Dec 82 ●	OH DIANE *Warner Bros. FLEET 1*	9	15
4 Apr 87 ●	BIG LOVE *Warner Bros. W 8398*	9	12
11 Jul 87	SEVEN WONDERS *Warner Bros. W 8317*	56	4
26 Sep 87 ●	LITTLE LIES *Warner Bros. W 8291*	5	12
26 Dec 87	FAMILY MAN *Warner Bros. W 8114*	54	5
2 Apr 88 ●	EVERYWHERE *Warner Bros. W 8143*	4	10
18 Jun 88	ISN'T IT MIDNIGHT *Warner Bros. W 7860*	60	2
17 Dec 88	AS LONG AS YOU FOLLOW *Warner Bros. W 7644*	66	3
5 May 90	SAVE ME *Warner Bros. W 9866*	53	3
25 Aug 90	IN THE BACK OF MY MIND *Warner Bros. W 9739*	58	3

Group was UK and male-only up to and including the re-issue of 'Albatross'

FLEETWOODS 🌐 *US, male/female vocal group* **8 wks**

| 24 Apr 59 ● | COME SOFTLY TO ME *London HLU 8841* ▲ | 6 | 8 |

La FLEUR *Holland, male/female vocal/instrumental group* **4 wks**

| 30 Jul 83 | BOOGIE NIGHTS *Proto ENA 111* | 51 | 4 |

K.C. FLIGHTT *US, male rapper* **4 wks**

| 1 Apr 89 | PLANET E *RCA PT 49404* | 48 | 4 |

Dread FLIMSTONE and the NEW TONE AGE FAMILY *US, male vocal/instrumental group* **1 wk**

| 30 Nov 91 | FROM THE GHETTO *Urban URB 87* | 66 | 1 |

Berni FLINT 🌐 *UK, male vocalist* **11 wks**

| 19 Mar 77 ● | I DON'T WANT TO PUT A HOLD ON YOU *EMI 2599* | 3 | 10 |
| 23 Jul 77 | SOUTHERN COMFORT *EMI 2621* | 48 | 1 |

FLINTLOCK *UK, male vocal/instrumental group* **5 wks**

| 29 May 76 | DAWN *Pinnacle P 8419* | 30 | 5 |

FLIPMODE SQUAD *US, male/female production/rap group* **1 wk**

| 31 Oct 98 | CHA CHA CHA *Elektra E 3810CD* | 54 | 1 |

F.L.O. – *See Rahni HARRIS and F.L.O.*

FLOATERS 🎵 *US, male vocal group* **11 wks**

| 23 Jul 77 ★ | FLOAT ON *ABC 4187* | 1 | 11 |

A FLOCK OF SEAGULLS 🌐 *UK, male vocal/instrumental group* **46 wks**

27 Mar 82	I RAN *Jive JIVE 14*	43	6
12 Jun 82	SPACE AGE LOVE SONG *Jive JIVE 17*	34	6
6 Nov 82 ●	WISHING (IF I HAD A PHOTOGRAPH OF YOU) *Jive JIVE 25*	10	12
23 Apr 83	NIGHTMARES *Jive JIVE 33*	53	3
25 Jun 83	TRANSFER AFFECTION *Jive JIVE 41*	38	5
14 Jul 84	THE MORE YOU LIVE, THE MORE YOU LOVE *Jive JIVE 62*	26	11
19 Oct 85	WHO'S THAT GIRL (SHE'S GOT IT) *Jive JIVE 106*	66	3

FLOORPLAY *UK, male instrumental/production duo* **1 wk**

| 27 Jan 96 | AUTOMATIC *Perfecto PERF 115CD* | 50 | 1 |

FLOWERED UP ☹ ☺ *UK, male vocal/instrumental group* **17 wks**

28 Jul 90	IT'S ON *Heavenly HVN 3*	54	4
24 Nov 90	PHOBIA *Heavenly HVN 7*	75	1
11 May 91	TAKE IT *London FUP 1*	34	4
17 Aug 91	IT'S ON/EGG RUSH (re-issue) *London FUP 2*	38	3
2 May 92	WEEKENDER *Heavenly HVN 16*	20	5

See also VARIOUS ARTISTS (EPs & LPs) – The Fred EP

FLOWERPOT MEN 🌐 *UK, male vocal group* **12 wks**

| 23 Aug 67 ● | LET'S GO TO SAN FRANCISCO *Deram DM 142* | 4 | 12 |

Mike FLOWERS POPS 🌐 *UK, male/female vocal/instrumental group* **14 wks**

30 Dec 95 ●	WONDERWALL *London LONCD 378*	2	7
13 Apr 96	WONDERWALL (re-entry) *London LONCD 378*	52	2
8 Jun 96	LIGHT MY FIRE/PLEASE RELEASE ME *London LONCD 384*	39	2
28 Dec 96	DON'T CRY FOR ME ARGENTINA *Love This LUVTHIS 16*	30	3

Eddie FLOYD 🎺 *US, male vocalist* **29 wks**

2 Feb 67	KNOCK ON WOOD *Atlantic 584 041*	50	1
2 Mar 67	KNOCK ON WOOD (re-entry) *Atlantic 584 041*	19	17
16 Mar 67	RAISE YOUR HAND *Stax 601 001*	42	3
9 Aug 67	THINGS GET BETTER *Stax 601 016*	31	8

FLUFFY *UK, female vocal/instrumental group* **2 wks**

| 17 Feb 96 | HUSBAND *Parkway PARK 006CD* | 58 | 1 |
| 5 Oct 96 | NOTHING *Virgin VSCDT 1614* | 52 | 1 |

FLUKE ☺ *UK, male instrumental/production group* **19 wks**

20 Mar 93	SLID *Circa YRCD 103*	59	1
19 Jun 93	ELECTRIC GUITAR *Circa YRCD 104*	58	2
11 Sep 93	GROOVY FEELING *Circa YRCD 106*	45	3
23 Apr 94	BUBBLE *Circa YRCD 110*	37	2
29 Jul 95	BULLET *Circa YRCD 121*	23	3
16 Dec 95	TOSH *Circa YRCD 122*	32	3
16 Nov 96	ATOM BOMB *Circa YRCD 125*	20	3
31 May 97	ABSURD *Virgin YRCD 126*	25	1
27 Sep 97	SQUIRT *Circa YRCD 127*	46	1

See also LUCKY MONKEYS

FLUSH – *see SLADE*

FLYING LIZARDS 🎸 ✏ *UK, male/female vocal/instrumental group* **16 wks**

| 4 Aug 79 ● | MONEY *Virgin VS 276* | 5 | 10 |
| 9 Feb 80 | T.V. *Virgin VS 325* | 43 | 6 |

FLYING PICKETS 🌐 *UK, male vocal group* **20 wks**

26 Nov 83 ★	ONLY YOU *10 TEN 14*	1	11
21 Apr 84 ●	WHEN YOU'RE YOUNG AND IN LOVE *10 TEN 20*	7	8
8 Dec 84	WHO'S THAT GIRL *10 GIRL 1*	71	1

Jerome FLYNN – *See ROBSON AND JEROME*

UK No 1 ★   UK Top 10 ●   UK million seller ◆   UK entry at No 1 ■   US No 1 ▲

FM UK, male vocal/instrumental group		**11 wks**
31 Jan 87	FROZEN HEART Portrait DIDGE 1	.64 2
20 Jun 87	LET LOVE BE THE LEADER Portrait MERV 1	.71 2
5 Aug 89	BAD LUCK Epic 655031 7	.54 4
7 Oct 89	SOMEDAY (YOU'LL COME RUNNING) CBS DINK 1	.64 2
10 Feb 90	EVERYTIME I THINK OF YOU Epic DINK 2	.73 1

FOCUS ✔ Holland, male instrumental group		**21 wks**
20 Jan 73	HOCUS POCUS Polydor 2001 211	.20 10
27 Jan 73 ●	SYLVIA Polydor 2001 422	.4 11

FOG US, male DJ / producer		**4 wks**
19 Feb 94	BEEN A LONG TIME Columbia 6601212	.44 2
6 Jun 98	BEEN A LONG TIME (re-mix) Pukka CDPUKKA 16	.27 2

Dan FOGELBERG US, male vocalist		**4 wks**
15 Mar 80	LONGER Epic EPC 8230	.59 4

Ben FOLDS FIVE US, male vocal/instrumental group		**10 wks**
14 Sep 96	UNDERGROUND Caroline CDCAR 008	.37 2
1 Mar 97	BATTLE OF WHO COULD CARE LESS Epic 6642302	.26 3
7 Jun 97	KATE Epic 6645365	.39 2
18 Apr 98	BRICK Epic 6656612	.26 3

FOLK IMPLOSION US, male vocal/instrumental duo		**1 wk**
15 Jun 96	NATURAL ONE London LONCD 382	.45 1

Claudia FONTAINE – See BEATMASTERS

Wayne FONTANA ◎ UK, male vocalist		**31 wks**
9 Dec 65	IT WAS EASIER TO HURT HER Fontana TF 642	.36 6
21 Apr 66	COME ON HOME Fontana TF 684	.16 12
25 Aug 66	GOODBYE BLUEBIRD Fontana TF 737	.49 1
8 Dec 66	PAMELA PAMELA Fontana TF 770	.11 12

See also Wayne FONTANA and the MINDBENDERS

Wayne FONTANA and the MINDBENDERS ◎		
UK, male vocalist, male vocal/instrumental backing group		**45 wks**
11 Jul 63	HELLO JOSEPHINE Fontana TF 404	.46 2
28 May 64	STOP LOOK AND LISTEN Fontana TF 451	.37 4
8 Oct 64 ●	UM UM UM UM UM UM Fontana TF 497	.5 15
4 Feb 65 ●	GAME OF LOVE Fontana TF 535 ▲	.2 11
17 Jun 65	JUST A LITTLE BIT TOO LATE Fontana TF 579	.20 7
30 Sep 65	SHE NEEDS LOVE Fontana TF 611	.32 6

See also Wayne FONTANA; MINDBENDERS

FOO FIGHTERS ✔ US, male vocal/instrumental group		**24 wks**
1 Jul 95 ●	THIS IS A CALL Roswell CDCL 753	.5 4
16 Sep 95	I'LL STICK AROUND Roswell CDCL 757	.18 3
2 Dec 95	FOR ALL THE COWS Roswell CDCL 762	.28 2
6 Apr 96	BIG ME Roswell CDCL 768	.19 3
10 May 97	MONKEY WRENCH Roswell CDCLS 788	.12 4
30 Aug 97	EVERLONG Roswell CDCL 792	.18 3
31 Jan 98	MY HERO Roswell CDCL 796	.21 2
29 Aug 98	WALKING AFTER YOU; BEACON LIGHT	
	Elektra E 4100CD [1]	.20 3

[1] Foo Fighters: Ween

FOOL'S GARDEN Germany, male vocal/instrumental group		**4 wks**
25 May 96	LEMON TREE Encore CDCOR 014	.61 1
3 Aug 96	LEMON TREE (re-issue) Encore CDCOR 018	.26 3

FOR REAL US, female vocal group		**2 wks**
1 Jul 95	YOU DON'T KNOW NOTHIN' A & M 5811232	.54 1
12 Jul 97	LIKE I DO Rowdy 74321486582	.45 1

Bill FORBES UK, male vocalist		**1 wk**
15 Jan 60	TOO YOUNG Columbia DB 4386	.29 1

FORBIDDEN – See Jet BRONX and the FORBIDDEN

FORCE and STYLES UK, male DJ duo		**1 wk**
25 July 98	HEART OF GOLD Diverse VERSE 2CD [1]	.55 1

[1] Force and Styles featuring Kelly Llorenna

FORCE MDs US, male vocal group		**9 wks**
12 Apr 86	TENDER LOVE Tommy Boy IS 269	.23 9

Baby FORD UK, male instrumentalist – keyboards		**16 wks**
10 Sep 88	OOCHY KOOCHY Rhythm King 7BFORD 1	.58 6
24 Dec 88	CHIKKI CHIKKI AHH AHH Rhythm King 7BFORD 2	.75 1
7 Jan 89	CHIKKI CHIKKI AHH AHH (re-entry)	
	Rhythm King 7BFORD 2	.54 3
17 Jun 89	CHILDREN OF THE REVOLUTION	
	Rhythm King 7BFORD 4	.53 4
17 Feb 90	BEACH BUMP Rhythm King 7BFORD 6	.68 2

Clinton FORD UK, male vocalist		**25 wks**
23 Oct 59	OLD SHEP Oriole CB 1500	.27 1
17 Aug 61	TOO MANY BEAUTIFUL GIRLS Oriole CB 1623	.48 1
8 Mar 62	FANLIGHT FANNY Oriole CB 1706	.22 10
5 Jan 67	RUN TO THE DOOR Piccadilly 7N 35361	.25 13

Emile FORD and the CHECKMATES ◎		
Bahamas/UK, male vocal/instrumental group		**87 wks**
30 Oct 59 ★	WHAT DO YOU WANT TO MAKE THOSE EYES AT ME FOR	
	Pye 7N 15225	.1 25
5 Feb 60 ●	ON A SLOW BOAT TO CHINA Pye 7N 15245	.3 14
26 May 60	YOU'LL NEVER KNOW WHAT YOU'RE MISSING ('TIL YOU TRY)	
	Pye 7N 15268	.12 9
1 Sep 60	THEM THERE EYES Pye 7N 15282 [1]	.18 16
8 Dec 60 ●	COUNTING TEARDROPS Pye 7N 15314	.4 12
2 Mar 61	WHAT AM I GONNA DO Pye 7N 15331	.33 6
18 May 61	HALF OF MY HEART Piccadilly 7N 35003 [1]	.50 1
22 Jun 61	HALF OF MY HEART (re-entry) Piccadilly 7N 35003 [1]	.42 3
8 Mar 62	I WONDER WHO'S KISSING HER NOW Piccadilly 7N 35033	.43 1

[1] Emile Ford

Lita FORD UK, female vocalist		**7 wks**
17 Dec 88	KISS ME DEADLY RCA PB 49575	.75 1
20 May 89	CLOSE MY EYES FOREVER Dreamland PB 49409 [1]	.47 3
11 Jan 92	SHOT OF POISON RCA PB 49145	.63 3

[1] Lita Ford duet with Ozzy Osbourne

Martyn FORD UK, orchestra		**3 wks**
14 May 77	LET YOUR BODY GO DOWNTOWN Mountain TOP 26	.38 3

Mary FORD – See Les PAUL and Mary FORD

Penny FORD US, female vocalist		**7 wks**
4 May 85	DANGEROUS Total Experience FB 49975 [1]	.43 5
29 May 93	DAYDREAMING Columbia 6590592	.43 2

[1] Pennye Ford

Tennessee Ernie FORD ☙ ℂ US, male vocalist		**42 wks**
21 Jan 55 ★	GIVE ME YOUR WORD Capitol CL 14005	.1 24
6 Jan 56 ★	SIXTEEN TONS Capitol CL 14500 ▲	.1 11
13 Jan 56 ●	THE BALLAD OF DAVY CROCKETT Capitol CL 14506	.3 7

Julia FORDHAM ◎ UK, female vocalist		**32 wks**
2 Jul 88	HAPPY EVER AFTER Circa YR 15	.27 9
25 Feb 89	WHERE DOES THE TIME GO Circa YR 23	.41 5

UK No 1 ★   UK Top 10 ●   UK million seller ◆   UK entry at No 1 ■   US No 1 ▲

31 Aug 91	I THOUGHT IT WAS YOU *Circa YR 69*	64	2
18 Jan 92	LOVE MOVES (IN MYSTERIOUS WAYS) *Circa YR 73*	19	9
30 May 92	I THOUGHT IT WAS YOU (re-mix) *Circa YR 90*	45	3
30 Apr 94	DIFFERENT TIME DIFFERENT PLACE *Circa YRCD 111*	41	3
23 Jul 94	I CAN'T HELP MYSELF *Circa YRCD 116*	62	1

FOREIGNER ➹ *UK/US, male vocal/instrumental group* 78 wks

6 May 78	FEELS LIKE THE FIRST TIME *Atlantic K 11086*	39	6
15 Jul 78	COLD AS ICE *Atlantic K 10986*	24	10
28 Oct 78	HOT BLOODED *Atlantic K 11167*	42	3
24 Feb 79	BLUE MORNING BLUE DAY *Atlantic K 11236*	45	4
29 Aug 81	URGENT *Atlantic K 11665*	54	4
10 Oct 81	JUKE BOX HERO *Atlantic K 11678*	48	4
12 Dec 81 ●	WAITING FOR A GIRL LIKE YOU *Atlantic K 11696*	8	13
8 May 82	URGENT (re-issue) *Atlantic K 11728*	45	5
8 Dec 84 ★	I WANT TO KNOW WHAT LOVE IS *Atlantic A 9596* ▲	1	16
6 Apr 85	THAT WAS YESTERDAY *Atlantic A 9571*	28	6
22 Jun 85	COLD AS ICE (re-mix) *Atlantic A 9539*	64	2
19 Dec 87	SAY YOU WILL *Atlantic A 9169*	71	4
22 Oct 94	WHITE LIE *Arista 74321232862*	58	1

FORMATIONS *US, male vocal group* 11 wks

| 31 Jul 71 | AT THE TOP OF THE STAIRS *Mojo 2027 001* | 50 | 1 |
| 14 Aug 71 | AT THE TOP OF THE STAIRS (re-entry) *Mojo 2027 001* | 28 | 10 |

George FORMBY *UK, male vocalist/instrumentalist – ukelele* 3 wks

| 21 Jul 60 | HAPPY GO LUCKY ME/BANJO BOY *Pye 7N 15269* | 40 | 3 |

See also 2 IN A TENT

FORREST ◀ © *US, male vocalist* 20 wks

26 Feb 83 ●	ROCK THE BOAT *CBS A 3121*	4	10
14 May 83	FEEL THE NEED IN ME *CBS A 3411*	17	8
17 Sep 83	ONE LOVER (DON'T STOP THE SHOW) *CBS A 3734*	67	2

Sharon FORRESTER *Jamaica, female vocalist* 1 wk

| 11 Feb 95 | LOVE INSIDE *ffrr FCD 253* | 50 | 1 |

Lance FORTUNE ☺ *UK, male vocalist* 17 wks

| 19 Feb 60 ● | BE MINE *Pye 7N 15240* | 4 | 12 |
| 5 May 60 | THIS LOVE I HAVE FOR YOU *Pye 7N 15260* | 26 | 5 |

FORTUNES ☺ *UK, male vocal/instrumental group* 65 wks

8 Jul 65 ●	YOU'VE GOT YOUR TROUBLES *Decca F 12173*	2	14
7 Oct 65 ●	HERE IT COMES AGAIN *Decca F 12243*	4	14
3 Feb 66	THIS GOLDEN RING *Decca F 12321*	15	9
11 Sep 71 ●	FREEDOM COME FREEDOM GO *Capitol CL 15693*	6	17
29 Jan 72 ●	STORM IN A TEACUP *Capitol CL 15707*	7	11

40 THEVZ – *see COOLIO*

45 KING *US, male producer – Mark James* 6 wks

| 28 Oct 89 | THE KING IS HERE/THE 900 NUMBER *Dance Trax DRX 9* | 60 | 5 |
| 11 Aug 90 | THE KING IS HERE/THE 900 NUMBER (re-entry) *Dance Trax DRX 9* | 73 | 1 |

49ers ☺ *Italy, male producer – Gianfranco Bortolotti* 27 wks

16 Dec 89 ●	TOUCH ME *Fourth & Broadway BRW 157*	3	13
17 Mar 90 ●	DON'T YOU LOVE ME *Fourth & Broadway BRW 167*	12	6
9 Jun 90	GIRL TO GIRL *Fourth & Broadway BRW 174*	31	3
6 Jun 92	GOT TO BE FREE *Fourth & Broadway BRW 255*	46	2
29 Aug 92	THE MESSAGE *Fourth & Broadway BRW 257*	68	1
18 Mar 95	ROCKIN' MY BODY *Media MCSTD 2021* [1]	31	2

[1] 49ers featuring Ann-Marie Smith

See also CAPPELLA

FOSTER and ALLEN ♂ © *Ireland, male vocal duo* 47 wks

| 27 Feb 82 | A BUNCH OF THYME *Ritz RITZ 5* | 18 | 11 |

30 Oct 82	OLD FLAMES *Ritz RITZ 028*	51	8
19 Feb 83	MAGGIE *Ritz RITZ 025*	27	9
29 Oct 83	I WILL LOVE YOU ALL MY LIFE *Ritz RITZ 056*	49	6
30 Jun 84	JUST FOR OLD TIME'S SAKE *Ritz RITZ 066*	47	6
29 Mar 86	AFTER ALL THESE YEARS *Ritz RITZ 106*	43	7

Itsy FOSTER – *See EXOTICA featuring Itsy FOSTER*

FOUNDATIONS ☺ ✐

West Indies/UK/Sri Lanka, male vocal/instrumental group 57 wks

27 Sep 67 ★	BABY NOW THAT I'VE FOUND YOU *Pye 7N 17366*	1	16
24 Jan 68	BACK ON MY FEET AGAIN *Pye 7N 17417*	18	10
1 May 68	ANY OLD TIME *Pye 7N 17503*	48	1
15 May 68	ANY OLD TIME (re-entry) *Pye 7N 17503*	50	1
20 Nov 68 ●	BUILD ME UP BUTTERCUP *Pye 7N 17636*	2	15
12 Mar 69 ●	IN THE BAD BAD OLD DAYS *Pye 7N 17702*	8	10
13 Sep 69	BORN TO LIVE AND BORN TO DIE *Pye 7N 17809*	46	3
12 Dec 98	BUILD ME UP BUTTERCUP (re-entry) *Castle NEEX 1001*	71	1

FOUNTAINS OF WAYNE *US, male vocal/instrumental group* 6 wks

22 Mar 97	RADIATION VIBE *Atlantic 7567956262*	32	2
10 May 97	SINK TO THE BOTTOM *Atlantic A 5612CD*	42	1
26 Jul 97	SURVIVAL CAR *Atlantic AT 0004CD*	53	1
27 Dec 97	I WANT AN ALIEN FOR CHRISTMAS *Atlantic AT 0020CD*	36	2

FOUR ACES © *US, male vocal group* 40 wks

30 Jul 54 ●	THREE COINS IN THE FOUNTAIN *Brunswick 05308* [1]	5	5
22 Oct 54	THREE COINS IN THE FOUNTAIN (re-entry) *Brunswick 05308* [1]	17	1
7 Jan 55 ●	MR. SANDMAN *Brunswick 05355* [1]	9	5
20 May 55 ●	STRANGER IN PARADISE *Brunswick 05418*	6	6
18 Nov 55 ●	LOVE IS A MANY SPLENDOURED THING *Brunswick 05480* [1] ▲	2	13
19 Oct 56	WOMAN IN LOVE *Brunswick 05589* [1]	19	3
4 Jan 57	FRIENDLY PERSUASION *Brunswick 05623* [1]	29	1
23 Jan 59	THE WORLD OUTSIDE *Brunswick 05773*	18	6

[1] Four Aces featuring Al Roberts

FOUR BUCKETEERS *UK, male/female vocal group* 6 wks

| 3 May 80 | THE BUCKET OF WATER SONG *CBS 8393* | 26 | 6 |

4 THE CAUSE ☺ (R&B) *US, male/female vocal group* 9 wks

| 10 Oct 98 | STAND BY ME *RCA 74321622442* | 12 | 9 |

FOUR ESQUIRES *US, male vocal group* 2 wks

| 31 Jan 58 | LOVE ME FOREVER *London HLO 8533* | 23 | 2 |

4 HERO *UK, male instrumental group* 5 wks

24 Nov 90	MR. KIRK'S NIGHTMARE *Reinforced RIVET 1203*	73	2
9 May 92	COOKIN' UP YAH BRAIN *Reinforced RIVET 1216*	59	2
15 Aug 98	STAR CHASERS *Talkin' Loud TLCD 36*	41	1

400 BLOWS *UK, male vocal/instrumental duo* 4 wks

| 29 Jun 85 | MOVIN' *Illuminated ILL 61* | 54 | 4 |

FOUR KNIGHTS © *US, male vocal group* 11 wks

| 4 Jun 54 ● | I GET SO LONELY *Capitol CL 14076* | 5 | 7 |
| 30 Jul 54 ● | I GET SO LONELY (re-entry) *Capitol CL 14076* | 10 | 4 |

FOUR LADS © *Canada, male vocal group* 23 wks

19 Dec 52 ●	FAITH CAN MOVE MOUNTAINS *Columbia DB 3154* [1]	7	2
9 Jan 53 ●	FAITH CAN MOVE MOUNTAINS (re-entry) *Columbia DB 3154* [1]	9	1
22 Oct 54 ●	RAIN RAIN RAIN *Philips PB 311* [2]	8	16
28 Apr 60	STANDING ON THE CORNER *Philips PB 1000*	34	4

[1] Johnnie Ray and the Four Lads [2] Frankie Laine and the Four Lads

UK No 1 ★ UK Top 10 ● UK million seller ◆ UK entry at No 1 ■ US No 1 ▲

4 NON BLONDES 🎸 ⊘
US, female/male vocal/instrumental group — **19 wks**

| 19 Jun 93 ● | WHAT'S UP Interscope A 8412CD | ...2 | 17 |
| 16 Oct 93 | SPACEMAN Interscope A 8349CD | ...53 | 2 |

FOUR PENNIES ⊘ UK, male vocal/instrumental group — **56 wks**

16 Jan 64	DO YOU WANT ME TO Philips BF 1296	...47	1
6 Feb 64	DO YOU WANT ME TO (re-entry) Philips BF 1296	...49	1
2 Apr 64 ★	JULIET Philips BF 1322	...1	15
16 Jul 64	I FOUND OUT THE HARD WAY Philips BF 1349	...14	11
29 Oct 64	BLACK GIRL Philips BF 1366	...20	12
7 Oct 65	UNTIL IT'S TIME FOR YOU TO GO Philips BF 1435	...19	11
17 Feb 66	TROUBLE IS MY MIDDLE NAME Philips BF 1469	...32	5

FOUR PREPS ⊘ US, male vocal group — **23 wks**

13 Jun 58 ●	BIG MAN Capitol CL 14873	...2	13
19 Sep 58	BIG MAN (re-entry) Capitol CL 14873	...22	1
26 May 60	GOT A GIRL Capitol CL 15128	...28	6
14 Jul 60	GOT A GIRL (re-entry) Capitol CL 15128	...47	1
2 Nov 61	MORE MONEY FOR YOU AND ME (MEDLEY) Capitol CL 15217	...39	2

Tracks on medley: Mr Blue / Alley Oop / Smoke Gets in Your Eyes / In This Whole Wide World / A Worried Man / Tom Dooley / A Teenager in Love – all songs feature new lyrics

FOUR SEASONS ⊘ No 1 US group of the early 1960s: Frankie Valli (v), Bob Gaudio (k/v), Nick Massi (b/v), Tommy DeVito (g/v). Falsetto-voiced Valli's quartet, the first group to score three US No 1s in succession, have a chart span there of more than 38 years — **151 wks**

4 Oct 62 ●	SHERRY Stateside SS 122 ▲	...8	16
17 Jan 63	BIG GIRLS DON'T CRY Stateside SS 145 ▲	...13	10
28 Mar 63	WALK LIKE A MAN Stateside SS 169 ▲	...12	12
27 Jun 63	AIN'T THAT A SHAME Stateside SS 194	...38	3
27 Aug 64 ●	RAG DOLL Philips BF 1347 [1] ▲	...2	13
18 Nov 65 ●	LET'S HANG ON Philips BF 1439 [1]	...4	16
31 Mar 66	WORKIN' MY WAY BACK TO YOU Philips BF 1474 [2]	...50	3
2 Jun 66	OPUS 17 (DON'T YOU WORRY 'BOUT ME) Philips BF 1493 [2]	...20	9
29 Sep 66	I'VE GOT YOU UNDER MY SKIN Philips BF 1511 [2]	...12	11
12 Jan 67	TELL IT TO THE RAIN Philips BF 1538 [2]	...37	5
19 Apr 75 ●	NIGHT Mowest MW 3024 [3]	...7	9
20 Sep 75	WHO LOVES YOU Warner Bros. K 16602	...6	9
31 Jan 76 ★	DECEMBER '63 (OH WHAT A NIGHT) Warner Bros. K 16688 ▲	...1	10
24 Apr 76 ●	SILVER STAR Warner Bros. K 16742	...3	9
27 Nov 76	WE CAN WORK IT OUT Warner Bros. K 16845	...34	4
18 Jun 77	RHAPSODY Warner Bros. K 16932	...37	3
20 Aug 77	DOWN THE HALL Warner Bros. K 16982	...34	5
29 Oct 88	DECEMBER '63 (OH WHAT A NIGHT) (re-mix) BR 45277 [3]	...49	4

[1] Four Seasons with the sound of Frankie Valli [2] Four Seasons with Frankie Valli
[3] Frankie Valli and the Four Seasons

FOUR TOPS 🎵 Unmistakable R&B vocal group from Detroit: Levi Stubbs, Renaldo Benson, Lawrence Payton (d. 1997), Abdul Fakir. Legendary Motown act, who performed together for a record 44 years (to Payton's death) and were inducted into the Rock and Roll Hall of Fame in 1990 — **318 wks**

1 Jul 65	I CAN'T HELP MYSELF Tamla Motown TMG 515 ▲	...23	9
2 Sep 65	IT'S THE SAME OLD SONG Tamla Motown TMG 528	...34	8
21 Jul 66	LOVING YOU IS SWEETER THAN EVER Tamla Motown TMG 568	...21	12
13 Oct 66 ★	REACH OUT I'LL BE THERE Tamla Motown TMG 579 ▲	...1	16
12 Jan 67 ●	STANDING IN THE SHADOWS OF LOVE Tamla Motown TMG 589	...6	8
30 Mar 67 ●	BERNADETTE Tamla Motown TMG 601	...8	10
15 Jun 67	SEVEN ROOMS OF GLOOM Tamla Motown TMG 612	...12	9
11 Oct 67	YOU KEEP RUNNING AWAY Tamla Motown TMG 623	...26	7
13 Dec 67	WALK AWAY RENEE Tamla Motown TMG 634	...3	11
13 Mar 68 ●	IF I WERE A CARPENTER Tamla Motown TMG 647	...7	11
21 Aug 68	YESTERDAY'S DREAMS Tamla Motown TMG 665	...23	15
13 Nov 68	I'M IN A DIFFERENT WORLD Tamla Motown TMG 675	...27	13
28 May 69	WHAT IS A MAN Tamla Motown TMG 698	...16	11
27 Sep 69	DO WHAT YOU GOTTA DO Tamla Motown TMG 710	...11	11
21 Mar 70	I CAN'T HELP MYSELF (re-issue) Tamla Motown TMG 732	...10	11
30 May 70 ●	IT'S ALL IN THE GAME Tamla Motown TMG 736	...5	14
12 Sep 70	IT'S ALL IN THE GAME (re-entry) Tamla Motown TMG 736	...48	2
3 Oct 70	STILL WATER (LOVE) Tamla Motown TMG 752	...10	10
19 Dec 70	STILL WATER (LOVE) (re-entry) Tamla Motown TMG 752	...44	2
1 May 71	JUST SEVEN NUMBERS (CAN STRAIGHTEN OUT MY LIFE) Tamla Motown TMG 770	...36	5
26 Jun 71	RIVER DEEP MOUNTAIN HIGH Tamla Motown TMG 777 [1]	...11	10
25 Sep 71	SIMPLE GAME Tamla Motown TMG 785	...3	11
20 Nov 71	YOU GOTTA HAVE LOVE IN YOUR HEART Tamla Motown TMG 793 [1]	...25	10
11 Mar 72	BERNADETTE (re-issue) Tamla Motown TMG 803	...23	7
5 Aug 72	WALK WITH ME TALK WITH ME DARLING Tamla Motown TMG 823	...32	6
18 Nov 72	KEEPER OF THE CASTLE Probe PRO 575	...18	9
10 Nov 73	SWEET UNDERSTANDING LOVE Probe PRO 604	...29	10
17 Oct 81 ●	WHEN SHE WAS MY GIRL Casablanca CAN 1005	...3	10
19 Dec 81	DON'T WALK AWAY Casablanca CAN 1006	...16	11
6 Mar 82	TONIGHT I'M GONNA LOVE YOU ALL OVER Casablanca CAN 1008	...43	4
26 Jun 82	BACK TO SCHOOL AGAIN RSO 89	...62	2
23 Jul 88	REACH OUT I'LL BE THERE (re-mix) Motown ZB 41943	...11	9
17 Sep 88	INDESTRUCTIBLE Arista 111717	...55	4
3 Dec 88	LOCO IN ACAPULCO Arista 111850	...7	13
25 Feb 89	INDESTRUCTIBLE Arista 112074 [2]	...30	7

[1] Supremes and the Four Tops [2] Four Tops featuring Smokey Robinson

The original US recording of 'Indestructible' was not issued until after the chart run of the UK-only mix

4 OF US Ireland, male vocal/instrumental group — **6 wks**

| 27 Feb 93 | SHE HITS ME Columbia 6589192 | ...35 | 4 |
| 1 May 93 | I MISS YOU Columbia 6591722 | ...62 | 2 |

4MANDU UK, male vocal group — **6 wks**

29 Jul 95	THIS IS IT Final Vinyl 74321291222	...45	3
17 Feb 96	DO IT FOR LOVE Arista 74321343902	...45	2
15 Jun 96	BABY DON'T GO Arista 74321375914	...47	1

FOURMOST ⊘ UK, male vocal/instrumental group — **64 wks**

12 Sep 63 ●	HELLO LITTLE GIRL Parlophone R 5056	...9	17
26 Dec 63	I'M IN LOVE Parlophone R 5078	...17	12
23 Apr 64 ●	A LITTLE LOVING Parlophone R 5128	...6	13
13 Aug 64	HOW CAN I TELL HER Parlophone R 5157	...33	4
26 Nov 64	BABY I NEED YOUR LOVIN' Parlophone R 5194	...24	12
9 Dec 65	GIRLS GIRLS GIRLS Parlophone R 5379	...33	4

14-18 UK, male vocalist – Peter Waterman — **4 wks**

| 1 Nov 75 | GOODBYE-EE Magnet MAG 48 | ...33 | 4 |

Bernard FOWLER – See BOMB THE BASS

FOX ⊘ UK/US, male/female vocal/instrumental group — **29 wks**

15 Feb 75 ●	ONLY YOU CAN GTO GT 8	...3	11
10 May 75	IMAGINE ME IMAGINE YOU GTO GT 21	...15	8
10 Apr 76 ●	S-S-S-SINGLE BED GTO GT 57	...4	10

Noosha FOX UK, female vocalist — **6 wks**

| 12 Nov 77 | GEORGINA BAILEY GTO GT 106 | ...31 | 6 |

Samantha FOX ⊘ UK, female vocalist — **73 wks**

22 Mar 86 ●	TOUCH ME (I WANT YOUR BODY) Jive FOXY 1	...3	10
28 Jun 86	DO YA DO YA (WANNA PLEASE ME) Jive FOXY 2	...10	7
6 Sep 86	HOLD ON TIGHT Jive FOXY 3	...25	5
13 Dec 86	I'M ALL YOU NEED Jive FOXY 4	...41	6
30 May 87 ●	NOTHING'S GONNA STOP ME NOW Jive FOXY 5	...8	9
25 Jul 87	I SURRENDER (TO THE SPIRIT OF THE NIGHT) Jive FOXY 6	...25	7
17 Oct 87	I PROMISE YOU (GET READY) Jive FOXY 7	...58	3

UK No 1 ★ UK Top 10 ● UK million seller ◆ UK entry at No 1 ■ US No 1 ▲

19 Dec 87	TRUE DEVOTION *Jive FOXY 8*	62	3
21 May 88	NAUGHTY GIRLS *Jive FOXY 9* [1]	31	5
19 Nov 88	LOVE HOUSE *Jive FOXY 10*	32	6
28 Jan 89	I ONLY WANNA BE WITH YOU *Jive FOXY 11*	16	8
17 Jun 89	I WANNA HAVE SOME FUN *Jive FOXY 12*	63	2
28 Mar 98	SANTA MARIA *All Around The World CDGLOBE 163* [2]	31	2

[1] Samantha Fox featuring Full Force [2] DJ Milano featuring Samantha Fox

Bruce FOXTON *UK, male vocalist* — 9 wks

30 Jul 83	FREAK *Arista BFOX 1*	23	5
29 Oct 83	THIS IS THE WAY *Arista BFOX 2*	56	3
21 Apr 84	IT MAKES ME WONDER *Arista BFOX 3*	74	1

Inez FOXX *US, female vocalist* — 8 wks

23 Jul 64	HURT BY LOVE *Sue WI 323*	40	3
19 Feb 69	MOCKINGBIRD *United Artists UP 2269* [1]	36	2
19 Mar 69	MOCKINGBIRD (re-entry) *United Artists UP 2269* [1]	33	3

[1] Inez and Charlie Foxx

John FOXX *UK, male vocalist* — 31 wks

26 Jan 80	UNDERPASS *Virgin VS 318*	31	8
29 Mar 80	NO-ONE DRIVING (DOUBLE SINGLE) *Virgin VS 338*	32	4
19 Jul 80	BURNING CAR *Virgin VS 360*	35	7
8 Nov 80	MILES AWAY *Virgin VS 382*	51	3
29 Aug 81	EUROPE (AFTER THE RAIN) *Virgin VS 393*	40	5
2 Jul 83	ENDLESSLY *Virgin VS 543*	66	3
17 Sep 83	YOUR DRESS *Virgin VS 615*	61	1

Tracks on double single: No-one Driving / Glimmer / Mr No / This City

FPI PROJECT ☺ *Italy, male instrumental/production group* — 16 wks

9 Dec 89	● GOING BACK TO MY ROOTS / RICH IN PARADISE *Rumour RUMAT 9*	9	12
9 Mar 91	EVERYBODY (ALL OVER THE WORLD) *Rumour RUMA 29*	65	3
7 Aug 93	COME ON (AND DO IT) *Synthetic SYNTH 006CD*	59	1

'Going Back to My Roots' was a vocal track available in two formats and featured either Paolo Dini or Sharon D Clarke

FRAGGLES *UK/US, puppets from TV series* — 8 wks

| 18 Feb 84 | 'FRAGGLE ROCK' THEME *RCA 389* | 33 | 8 |

Roddy FRAME *UK, male vocalist / instrumentalist* — 2 wks

| 19 Sep 98 | REASON FOR LIVING *Independiente ISOM 18MS* | 45 | 2 |

See also AZTEC CAMERA

Peter FRAMPTON ✎ *UK, male vocalist* — 24 wks

1 May 76	● SHOW ME THE WAY *A & M AMS 7218*	10	12
11 Sep 76	BABY I LOVE YOUR WAY *A & M AMS 7246*	43	5
6 Nov 76	DO YOU FEEL LIKE WE DO *A & M AMS 7260*	39	4
23 Jul 77	I'M IN YOU *A & M AMS 7298*	41	3

Connie FRANCIS ● *The original Italian-American queen of pop, b. Concetta Franconero, 12 December, 1938, New Jersey. The most successful international female vocalist of the 1950s and 1960s, who was often voted World's Top Female Singer* — 244 wks

4 Apr 58	★ WHO'S SORRY NOW *MGM 975*	1	25
27 Jun 58	I'M SORRY I MADE YOU CRY *MGM 982*	11	10
22 Aug 58	★ CAROLINA MOON / STUPID CUPID *MGM 985*	1	19
31 Oct 58	I'LL GET BY *MGM 993*	19	6
21 Nov 58	FALLIN' *MGM 993*	20	5
26 Dec 58	YOU ALWAYS HURT THE ONE YOU LOVE *MGM 998*	13	7
13 Feb 59	● MY HAPPINESS *MGM 1001*	4	14
29 May 59	MY HAPPINESS (re-entry) *MGM 1001*	30	1
3 Jul 59	● LIPSTICK ON YOUR COLLAR *MGM 1036*	3	16
11 Sep 59	PLENTY GOOD LOVIN' *MGM 1036*	18	6
4 Dec 59	AMONG MY SOUVENIRS *MGM 1046*	11	10
17 Mar 60	VALENTINO *MGM 1060*	27	8
19 May 60	● MAMA / ROBOT MAN *MGM 1076*	2	19

18 Aug 60	● EVERYBODY'S SOMEBODY'S FOOL *MGM 1086* ▲	5	13
3 Nov 60	● MY HEART HAS A MIND OF ITS OWN *MGM 1100* ▲	3	15
12 Jan 61	MANY TEARS AGO *MGM 1111*	12	9
16 Mar 61	● WHERE THE BOYS ARE / BABY ROO *MGM 1121*	5	14
15 Jun 61	BREAKIN' IN A BRAND NEW BROKEN HEART *MGM 1136*	12	11
14 Sep 61	● TOGETHER *MGM 1138*	6	11
14 Dec 61	BABY'S FIRST CHRISTMAS *MGM 1145*	30	4
26 Apr 62	DON'T BREAK THE HEART THAT LOVES YOU *MGM 1157* ▲	39	3
2 Aug 62	VACATION *MGM 1165*	10	9
20 Dec 62	I'M GONNA BE WARM THIS WINTER *MGM 1185*	48	1
10 Jun 65	MY CHILD *MGM 1271*	26	6
20 Jan 66	JEALOUS HEART *MGM 1293*	44	2

Baby Roo listed with 'Where the Boys Are' for first eight weeks only

Jill FRANCIS *UK, female vocalist* — 1 wk

| 3 Jul 93 | MAKE LOVE TO ME *Glady Wax GW 003CD* | 70 | 1 |

Claude FRANCOIS *France, male vocalist* — 4 wks

| 10 Jan 76 | TEARS ON THE TELEPHONE *Bradley's BRAD 7528* | 35 | 4 |

Joe FRANK – See HAMILTON, Joe FRANK and REYNOLDS

FRANK AND WALTERS ☹ ◐ *Ireland, male vocal / instrumental group* — 13 wks

21 Mar 92	HAPPY BUSMAN *Setanta HOO 2*	49	2
12 Sep 92	THIS IS NOT A SONG *Setanta HOO 3*	46	3
9 Jan 93	AFTER ALL *Setanta HOCD 4*	11	5
17 Apr 93	FASHION CRISIS HITS NEW YORK *Setanta HOOCD 5*	42	3

FRANKE *UK, male vocalist – Franke Pharoah* — 3 wks

| 7 Nov 92 | UNDERSTAND THIS GROOVE *China WOK 2028* | 60 | 2 |
| 21 May 94 | LOVE COME HOME *Triangle BLUESCD 001* [1] | 73 | 1 |

[1] Our Tribe with Franke Pharoah and Kristine W

FRANKIE GOES TO HOLLYWOOD ◐ *Fiercely-marketed and controversial Merseyside-based quintet fronted by Holly Johnson (b. 9 February, 1960, Sudan). First act since Gerry and The Pacemakers to hit No 1 with initial three releases. During July 1984, 'Two Tribes' and 'Relax' held top two places in the chart* — 137 wks

26 Nov 83	★ RELAX *ZTT ZTAS 1* ◆	1	48
16 Jun 84	★ TWO TRIBES *ZTT ZTAS 3* ◆ ■	1	20
10 Nov 84	TWO TRIBES (re-entry) *ZTT ZTAS 3*	73	1
1 Dec 84	★ THE POWER OF LOVE *ZTT ZTAS 5*	1	11
16 Feb 85	RELAX (re-entry) *ZTT ZTAS 1*	58	4
23 Feb 85	THE POWER OF LOVE (re-entry) *ZTT ZTAS 5*	64	1
30 Mar 85	WELCOME TO THE PLEASURE DOME *ZTT ZTAS 7*	2	11
6 Sep 86	RAGE HARD *ZTT ZTAS 22*	4	7
22 Nov 86	WARRIORS (OF THE WASTELAND) *ZTT ZTAS 25*	19	8
7 Mar 87	WATCHING THE WILDLIFE *ZTT ZTAS 26*	28	6
2 Oct 93	● RELAX (re-issue) *ZTT FGTH 1CD*	5	7
20 Nov 93	WELCOME TO THE PLEASURE DOME (re-mix) *ZTT FGTH 2CD*	18	3
18 Dec 93	● THE POWER OF LOVE (re-issue) *ZTT FGTH 3CD*	10	7
26 Feb 94	TWO TRIBES (re-mix) *ZTT FGTH 4CD*	16	3

Aretha FRANKLIN ✎ ♪ *The 'Queen of Soul Music', b. 25 March, 1942, Tennessee. With five decades of recording behind her, this unmistakable gospel-influenced vocalist has won countless awards and amassed more pop and R & B hits than any other female in her homeland* — 182 wks

8 Jun 67	● RESPECT *Atlantic 584 115* ▲	10	14
23 Aug 67	BABY I LOVE YOU *Atlantic 584 127*	39	4
20 Dec 67	CHAIN OF FOOLS / SATISFACTION *Atlantic 584 157*	43	2
10 Jan 68	SATISFACTION (re-entry) *Atlantic 584 157*	37	5
13 Mar 68	SINCE YOU'VE BEEN GONE *Atlantic 584 172*	47	1
22 May 68	THINK *Atlantic 584 186*	26	9
7 Aug 68	I SAY A LITTLE PRAYER *Atlantic 584 206*	4	14
22 Aug 70	DON'T PLAY THAT SONG *Atlantic 2091 027*	13	11
2 Oct 71	SPANISH HARLEM *Atlantic 2091 138*	14	9

UK No 1 ★ UK Top 10 ● UK million seller ◆ UK entry at No 1 ■ US No 1 ▲

8 Sep 73	ANGEL *Atlantic K 10346*	37	5
16 Feb 74	UNTIL YOU COME BACK TO ME (THAT'S WHAT I'M GONNA DO) *Atlantic K 10399*	26	8
6 Dec 80	WHAT A FOOL BELIEVES *Arista ARIST 377*	46	7
19 Sep 81	LOVE ALL THE HURT AWAY *Arista ARIST 428* [1]	49	3
4 Sep 82	JUMP TO IT *Arista ARIST 479*	42	5
23 Jul 83	GET IT RIGHT *Arista ARIST 537*	74	2
13 Jul 85	FREEWAY OF LOVE *Arista ARIST 624*	68	3
2 Nov 85	● SISTERS ARE DOIN' IT FOR THEMSELVES *RCA PB 40339* [2]	9	11
23 Nov 85	WHO'S ZOOMIN' WHO *Arista ARIST 633*	11	14
22 Feb 86	ANOTHER NIGHT *Arista ARIST 657*	54	6
10 May 86	FREEWAY OF LOVE (re-entry) *Arista ARIST 624*	51	3
25 Oct 86	JUMPIN' JACK FLASH *Arista ARIST 678*	58	3
31 Jan 87	★ I KNEW YOU WERE WAITING (FOR ME) *Epic DUET 1* [3] ▲	1	9
14 Mar 87	JIMMY LEE *Arista RIS 6*	46	4
6 May 89	THROUGH THE STORM *Arista 112185* [4]	41	3
9 Sep 89	IT ISN'T, IT WASN'T, IT AIN'T NEVER GONNA BE *Arista 112545* [5]	29	5
7 Apr 90	THINK *East West A 7951*	31	2
27 Jul 91	EVERYDAY PEOPLE *Arista 114420*	69	1
12 Feb 94	● A DEEPER LOVE *Arista 74321187022*	5	7
25 Jun 94	WILLING TO FORGIVE *Arista 74321213342*	17	7
9 May 98	A ROSE IS STILL A ROSE *Arista 74321569742*	22	4
26 Sep 98	HERE WE GO AGAIN *Arista 74321612742*	68	1

[1] Aretha Franklin and George Benson [2] Eurythmics and Aretha Franklin
[3] Aretha Franklin and George Michael [4] Aretha Franklin and Elton John
[5] Aretha Franklin and Whitney Houston

'Think' on East West is a re-recording. It was the flip side of 'Everybody Needs Somebody to Love' by Blues Brothers and was listed for the first two weeks of that record's run

Erma FRANKLIN ♪ *US, female vocalist*   10 wks

10 Oct 92	● (TAKE A LITTLE) PIECE OF MY HEART *Epic 6583847*	9	10

Rodney FRANKLIN ♫ *US, male instrumentalist – piano*   9 wks

19 Apr 80	● THE GROOVE *CBS 8529*	7	9

Chevelle FRANKLYN / BEENIE MAN
Jamaica, female vocalist and Jamaica, male rapper / DJ   1 wk

20 Sep 97	DANCEHALL QUEEN *Island Jamaica IJCD 2018*	70	1

See also Beenie Man

FRANTIC FIVE – See Don LANG

FRANTIQUE ♪ *US, female vocal group*   12 wks

11 Aug 79	● STRUT YOUR FUNKY STUFF *Philadelphia Int. PIR 7728*	10	12

Elizabeth FRASER – See COCTEAU TWINS; MASSIVE ATTACK; Ian McCULLOCH

Wendy FRASER – See Patrick SWAYZE featuring Wendy FRASER

FRASH *UK, male vocal/instrumental group*   1 wk

18 Feb 95	HERE I GO AGAIN *PWL International FLIPCD 1*	69	1

FRAZIER CHORUS *UK, male/female vocal/instrumental group* 14 wks

4 Feb 89	DREAM KITCHEN *Virgin VS 1145*	57	3
15 Apr 89	TYPICAL! *Virgin VS 1174*	53	2
15 Jul 89	SLOPPY HEART *Virgin VS 1192*	73	1
9 Jun 90	CLOUD 8 *Virgin VS 1252*	52	3
25 Aug 90	NOTHING *Virgin VS 1284*	51	3
16 Feb 91	WALKING ON AIR *Virgin VS 1330*	60	2

FREAKPOWER ☺ *UK/Canada, male vocal/instrumental group*   20 wks

16 Oct 93	TURN ON TUNE IN COP OUT *Fourth & Broadway BRCD 284*	29	5
26 Feb 94	RUSH *Fourth & Broadway BRCD 291*	62	2
18 Mar 95	● TURN ON TUNE IN COP OUT (re-issue) *Fourth & Broadway BRCD 317*	3	9

8 Jun 96	NEW DIRECTION *Fourth & Broadway BRCD 331*	60	1
9 May 98	NO WAY *Deconstruction 74321578572*	29	3

FREAKY REALISTIC
UK/Japan, male/female vocal/instrumental group   3 wks

3 Apr 93	KOOCHIE RYDER *Frealism FRECD 2*	52	2
3 Jul 93	LEONARD NIMOY *Frealism FRECD 3*	71	1

FREAKYMAN *Holland, male producer – Andre Van Den Bosch*   1 wk

27 Sep 97	DISCOBUG '97 *Xtravaganza 0091285 EXT*	68	1

Stan FREBERG ℂ *US, male vocalist*   5 wks

19 Nov 54	SH-BOOM *Capitol CL 14187* [1]	15	2
27 Jul 56	ROCK ISLAND LINE/HEARTBREAK HOTEL *Capitol CL 14608*	24	1
10 Aug 56	ROCK ISLAND LINE/HEARTBREAK HOTEL (re-entry) *Capitol CL 14608*	29	1
12 May 60	THE OLD PAYOLA ROLL BLUES *Capitol CL 15122*	40	1

[1] Stan Freberg with the Toads

John FRED and the PLAYBOY BAND ◉
US, male vocal/instrumental group   12 wks

3 Jan 68	● JUDY IN DISGUISE (WITH GLASSES) *Pye International 7N 25442* ▲	3	12

FREDDIE and the DREAMERS ◉
UK, male vocal/instrumental group   85 wks

9 May 63	● IF YOU GOTTA MAKE A FOOL OF SOMEBODY *Columbia DB 7032*	3	14
8 Aug 63	● I'M TELLING YOU NOW *Columbia DB 7086* ▲	2	11
7 Nov 63	● YOU WERE MADE FOR ME *Columbia DB 7147*	3	15
20 Feb 64	OVER YOU *Columbia DB 7214*	13	11
14 May 64	I LOVE YOU BABY *Columbia DB 7286*	16	8
16 Jul 64	JUST FOR YOU *Columbia DB 7322*	41	3
5 Nov 64	I UNDERSTAND *Columbia DB 7381*	5	15
22 Apr 65	A LITTLE YOU *Columbia DB 7526*	26	5
4 Nov 65	THOU SHALT NOT STEAL *Columbia DB 7720*	44	3

FREDERICK – See NINA and FREDERICK

Dee FREDRIX *UK, female vocalist*   5 wks

27 Feb 93	AND SO I WILL WAIT FOR YOU *East West YZ 725CD*	56	4
3 Jul 93	DIRTY MONEY *East West YZ 750CD*	74	1

FREE ✦ *UK, male vocal/instrumental group*   75 wks

6 Jun 70	● ALL RIGHT NOW *Island WIP 6082*	2	16
1 May 71	● MY BROTHER JAKE *Island WIP 6100*	4	11
27 May 72	LITTLE BIT OF LOVE *Island WIP 6129*	13	10
13 Jan 73	● WISHING WELL *Island WIP 6146*	7	10
21 Jul 73	ALL RIGHT NOW (re-entry) *Island WIP 6082*	15	9
18 Feb 78	FREE EP *Island IEP 6*	11	7
23 Oct 82	FREE EP (re-entry) *Island IEP 6*	57	3
9 Feb 91	● ALL RIGHT NOW (re-mix) *Island IS 486*	8	9

Tracks on Free EP: All Right Now / My Brother Jake / Wishing Well

FREE – See QUEEN; Wyclef JEAN; Pras MICHEL; Queen LATIFAH

FREE SPIRIT *UK, male/female vocal duo*   1 wk

13 May 95	NO MORE RAINY DAYS *Columbia 6612822*	68	1

FREEEZ ☺ ◉ *UK, male vocal/instrumental group*   48 wks

7 Jun 80	KEEP IN TOUCH *Calibre CAB 103*	49	3
7 Feb 81	● SOUTHERN FREEEZ *Beggars Banquet BEG 51* [1]	8	11
18 Apr 81	FLYING HIGH *Beggars Banquet BEG 55*	35	5
18 Jun 83	I.O.U. *Beggars Banquet BEG 96*	2	15
1 Oct 83	POP GOES MY LOVE *Beggars Banquet BEG 98*	26	6
17 Jan 87	I.O.U. (re-mix) *Citybeat CBE 709* [2]	23	6

30 May 87 SOUTHERN FREEEZ (re-mix) *Total Control TOCO 14* [1] 63 2

[1] Freeez featuring Ingrid Mansfield Allman [2] Freeez featuring John Rocca

FREEFALL *UK/US, male instrumental/production group*　　2 wks

27 Jul 91 **FEEL SURREAL** *ffrr FX 160* [1] 63 1
28 Nov 98 **SKYDIVE** *Stress CDSTR 89* [2] 75 1

[1] Freefall featuring Psychotropic [2] Freefall featuring Jan Johnston

FREEHOLD JUNIOR SCHOOL – *See Fogwell FLAX and the ANKLEBITERS
from FREEHOLD JUNIOR SCHOOL*

FREESTYLERS *UK, male instrumental/vocal group*　　4 wks

7 Feb 98 **B-BOY STANCE** *Freskanova FND 7* [1] 23 3
14 Nov 98 **WARNING** *Freskanova FND 14* [2] 68 1

[1] Freestylers featuring Tenor Fly [2] Freestylers featuring Navigator

FREIHEIT ☉ *Germany, male vocal/instrumental group*　　9 wks

17 Dec 88 **KEEPING THE DREAM ALIVE** *CBS 652989 7* 14 9

Deborah FRENCH – *See E-LUSTRIOUS featuring Deborah FRENCH*

Nicki FRENCH ☉ ☺ *UK, female vocalist*　　16 wks

15 Oct 94 **TOTAL ECLIPSE OF THE HEART** *Bags Of Fun BAGSCD 1* 54 1
14 Jan 95 ● **TOTAL ECLIPSE OF THE HEART (re-entry)**
　　　　　　Bags Of Fun BAGSCD 1 ....5 12
22 Apr 95 **FOR ALL WE KNOW** *Bags Of Fun BAGSCD 4* 42 2
15 Jul 95 **DID YOU EVER REALLY LOVE ME**
　　　　　　Love This LUVTHISCD 2 ....55 1

FREQUENCY 9 – *See VARIOUS ARTISTS (EPs & LPs)* – The Further Adventures
of North (EP)

FRESH 4 featuring Lizz E (R&B) 👟
UK, male scratch group and female vocal group　　9 wks

7 Oct 89 ● **WISHING ON A STAR** *10 TEN 287* 10 9

Doug E. FRESH and the GET FRESH CREW 👟
US, male rapper/scratch group　　11 wks

9 Nov 85 ● **THE SHOW** *Cooltempo COOL 116* 7 11

FRESH PRINCE – *See JAZZY JEFF and FRESH PRINCE*

FRESHIES *UK, male vocal/instrumental group*　　3 wks

14 Feb 81 **I'M IN LOVE WITH THE GIRL ON A CERTAIN MANCHESTER
　　　　　　MEGASTORE CHECKOUT DESK** *MCA 670* 54 3

Matt FRETTON *UK, male vocalist*　　5 wks

11 Jun 83 **IT'S SO HIGH** *Chrysalis MATT 1* 50 5

FREUR *UK, male vocal/instrumental group*　　4 wks

23 Apr 83 **DOOT DOOT** *CBS A 3141* 59 4

Glenn FREY ☉ *US, male vocalist*　　20 wks

2 Mar 85 **THE HEAT IS ON** *MCA MCA 941* 12 12
22 Jun 85 **SMUGGLER'S BLUES** *BBC RESL 170* 22 8

FRIDA *Norway, female vocalist*　　12 wks

21 Aug 82 **I KNOW THERE'S SOMETHING GOING ON** *Epic EPC A2603* 43 7
17 Dec 83 **TIME** *Epic A 3983* [1] 45 5

[1] Frida and B.A. Robertson

Gavin FRIDAY – *See BONO*

Dean FRIEDMAN ☉ *US, male vocalist*　　22 wks

3 Jun 78 **WOMAN OF MINE** *Lifesong LS 401* 52 5

---

23 Sep 78 ● **LUCKY STARS** *Lifesong LS 402* 3 10
18 Nov 78 **LYDIA** *Lifesong LS 403* 31 7

FRIENDS AGAIN *UK, male vocal/instrumental group*　　3 wks

4 Aug 84 **THE FRIENDS AGAIN EP** *Mercury FA 1* 59 3

*Tracks on The Friends Again EP: Lullaby On Board/Wand You Wave/Thank You
for Being an Angel*

FRIJID PINK ↗ *US, male vocal/instrumental group*　　16 wks

28 Mar 70 ● **HOUSE OF THE RISING SUN** *Deram DM 288* 4 16

Robert FRIPP – *See David SYLVIAN*

Jane FROMAN ℂ *US, female vocalist*　　4 wks

17 Jun 55 **I WONDER** *Capitol CL 14254* 14 4

FRONT 242 *Belgium/US, male vocal/instrumental group*　　1 wk

1 May 93 **RELIGION** *RRE RRE 106CD* 46 1

Christian FRY *UK, male vocalist*　　2 wks

14 Nov 98 **YOU GOT ME** *Mushroom MUSH 33CDS* 45 2

FUGEES (REFUGEE CAMP) (R&B) 👟
US, male/female vocal/instrumental group　　65 wks

6 Apr 96 **FU-GEE-LA** *Columbia 6630662* 21 5
8 Jun 96 ★ **KILLING ME SOFTLY** *Columbia 6633435* ◆ ■ 1 20
14 Sep 96 ★ **READY OR NOT** *Columbia 6637215* 1 12
30 Nov 96 ● **NO WOMAN NO CRY** *Columbia 6639925* 2 9
15 Mar 97 ● **RUMBLE IN THE JUNGLE** *Mercury 5740692* 3 8
28 Jun 97 **WE TRYING TO STAY ALIVE** *Columbia 6648815* [1] 13 5
6 Sep 97 **THE SWEETEST THING** *Columbia 6649785* [2] 18 4
27 Sep 97 **GUANTANAMERA** *Columbia 6650852* [1] 25 4

[1] Wyclef Jean and The Refugee Allstars [2] Refugee Camp Allstars featuring
Lauryn Hill

See also Lauryn HILL; Wyclef JEAN; Pras MICHEL

FULL CIRCLE *US, male vocal group*　　5 wks

7 Mar 87 **WORKIN' UP A SWEAT** *EMI America EA 229* 41 5

FULL FORCE ☺ 👟 *US, male vocal/instrumental group*　　37 wks

4 May 85 **I WONDER IF I TAKE YOU HOME** *CBS A 6057* [1] 53 6
3 Aug 85 **I WONDER IF I TAKE YOU HOME (re-entry)**
　　　　　　CBS A 6057 [1] 12 11
21 Dec 85 ● **ALICE I WANT YOU JUST FOR ME** *CBS A 6640* 9 11
21 May 88 **NAUGHTY GIRLS** *Jive FOXY 9* [2] 31 5
4 Jun 88 **I'M REAL** *Scotti Brothers JSB 1* [3] 31 4

[1] Lisa Lisa and Cult Jam with Full Force [2] Samantha Fox featuring Full Force
[3] James Brown featuring Full Force

FULL INTENTION *UK, male instrumental/production group*　　7 wks

6 Apr 96 **AMERICA (I LOVE AMERICA)** *Stress CDSTR 56* 32 2
10 Aug 96 **UPTOWN DOWNTOWN** *Stress CDSTR 67* 61 1
26 Jul 97 **SHAKE YOUR BODY (DOWN TO THE GROUND)**
　　　　　　Sugar Daddy CDSTR 82 ....34 2
22 Nov 97 **AMERICA (I LOVE AMERICA)** *Sugar Daddy CDSTR 56* 56 1
6 Jun 98 **YOU ARE SOMEBODY** *Sugar Daddy CDSD 001* 75 1

See also HUSTLERS CONVENTION; SEX-O-SONIQUE

FULL METAL RACKETS – *See John McENROE and Pat CASH with the
FULL METAL RACKETS*

FULL MONTY ALLSTARS featuring T. J. DAVIS
UK, male vocal/instrumental group　　1 wk

27 Jul 96 **BRILLIANT FEELING** *Arista 74321380902* 72 1

Bobby FULLER FOUR US, male vocal/instrumental group — 4 wks

14 Apr 66	I FOUGHT THE LAW London HL 10030	33	4

FUN BOY THREE ☺ UK, male vocal/instrumental group — 70 wks

7 Nov 81	THE LUNATICS (HAVE TAKEN OVER THE ASYLUM) Chrysalis CHS 2563	20	12
13 Feb 82 ●	IT AIN'T WHAT YOU DO IT'S THE WAY THAT YOU DO IT Chrysalis CHS 2570 [1]	4	10
10 Apr 82 ●	REALLY SAYING SOMETHING Deram NANA 1 [2]	5	10
8 May 82	THE TELEPHONE ALWAYS RINGS Chrysalis CHS 2609	17	9
31 Jul 82	SUMMERTIME Chrysalis CHS 2629	18	8
15 Jan 83	THE MORE I SEE (THE LESS I BELIEVE) Chrysalis CHS 2664	68	1
5 Feb 83 ●	TUNNEL OF LOVE Chrysalis CHS 2678	10	10
30 Apr 83 ●	OUR LIPS ARE SEALED Chrysalis FUNB 1	7	10

[1] Fun Boy Three and Bananarama [2] Bananarama with Fun Boy Three

FUN LOVIN' CRIMINALS 🔊 ☺
US, male vocal/instrumental group — 21 wks

8 Jun 96	THE GRAVE AND THE CONSTANT Chrysalis CDCHS 5031	72	1
17 Aug 96	SCOOBY SNACKS Chrysalis CDCHS 5034	22	3
16 Nov 96	THE FUN LOVIN' CRIMINAL Chrysalis CDCHS 5040	28	3
29 Mar 97	KING OF NEW YORK Chrysalis CDCHS 5049	28	3
5 Jul 97	I'M NOT IN LOVE/SCOOBY SNACKS Chrysalis CDCHS 5060	12	5
15 Aug 98	LOVE UNLIMITED Chrysalis CDCHS 5096	18	4
17 Oct 98	BIG NIGHT OUT Chrysalis CDCHSS 5101	29	2

Farley 'Jackmaster' FUNK ☺ US, male producer — 16 wks

23 Aug 86 ●	LOVE CAN'T TURN AROUND DJ International LON 105	10	12
11 Feb 89	AS ALWAYS Champion CHAMP 90	49	2
14 Dec 96	LOVE CAN'T TURN AROUND (re-mix) 4 Liberty LIBTCD 27 [2]	40	2

[1] Farley 'Jackmaster' Funk featuring Ricky Dillard [2] Farley 'Jackmaster' Funk with Darryl Pandy.

'Love Can't Turn Around' in 1996 is a re-recording

FUNK JUNKEEZ US, male DJ/producer – Roger Sanches — 1 wk

21 Feb 98	GOT FUNK Evocative EVOKE 1CDS	57	1

See also EL MARIACHI

FUNK MASTERS ♪ UK, male/female vocal/instrumental group — 12 wks

18 Jun 83 ●	IT'S OVER Master Funk Records 7MP 004	8	12

FUNKADELIC ♪ US, male vocal/instrumental group — 12 wks

9 Dec 78 ●	ONE NATION UNDER A GROOVE (PART 1) Warner Bros. K 17246	9	12

FUNKAPOLITAN UK, male vocal/instrumental group — 7 wks

22 Aug 81	AS TIME GOES BY London LON 001	41	7

FUNKDOOBIEST US, male rap group — 6 wks

11 Dec 93	WOPBABALUBOP Immortal 6597112	37	4
5 Mar 94	BOW WOW WOW Immortal 6594052	34	2

FUNKY BOYS – See Linda CARR

FUNKY BUNCH – See MARKY MARK and the FUNKY BUNCH

FUNKY CHOAD featuring Nick SKITZ
Australia/Italy, male production duo, and Australia, male vocalist — 1 wk

29 Aug 98	THE ULTIMATE ffrr FCD 341	51	1

FUNKY GREEN DOGS ☺
US, male/female vocal/production group — 5 wks

12 Apr 97	FIRED UP! Twisted UK TWCD 10016	17	3

28 Jun 97	THE WAY Twisted UK TWCD 10026	43	1
20 Jun 98	UNTIL THE DAY Twisted UK TWCD 10034	75	1

FUNKY POETS US, male vocal group — 1 wk

7 May 94	BORN IN THE GHETTO Epic 6603522	72	1

FUNKY WORM ☺ UK, male/female vocal/instrumental group — 14 wks

30 Jul 88	HUSTLE! (TO THE MUSIC . . .) Fon FON 15	13	8
26 Nov 88	THE SPELL! Fon FON 16	61	3
20 May 89	U + ME = LOVE Fon FON 19	46	3

FUREYS ♂ Ireland, male vocal group — 14 wks

10 Oct 81	WHEN YOU WERE SWEET SIXTEEN Ritz RITZ 003 [1]	14	11
3 Apr 82	I WILL LOVE YOU (EV'RY TIME WHEN WE ARE GONE) Ritz RITZ 012	54	3

[1] Fureys with Davey Arthur

FURIOUS FIVE – See GRANDMASTER FLASH, Melle MEL and the FURIOUS FIVE

FURNITURE UK, male/female vocal/instrumental group — 10 wks

14 Jun 86	BRILLIANT MIND Stiff BUY 251	21	10

Billy FURY ♪ Early British rock'n'roll star, b. Ronald Wycherley, 17 April, 1941, Liverpool, d. 28 January, 1983. Scored more hits in the 1960s than fellow Liverpudlians, The Beatles, and spent 281 weeks on chart, but without ever without reaching No 1 — 281 wks

27 Feb 59	MAYBE TOMORROW Decca F 11102	22	3
27 Mar 59	MAYBE TOMORROW (re-entry) Decca F 11102	18	6
26 Jun 59	MARGO Decca F 11128	28	1
10 Mar 60 ●	COLETTE Decca F 11200	9	10
26 May 60	THAT'S LOVE Decca F 11237	19	11
22 Sep 60	WONDROUS PLACE Decca F 11267	25	9
19 Jan 61	A THOUSAND STARS Decca F 11311	14	10
27 Apr 61	DON'T WORRY Decca F 11334	40	2
11 May 61 ●	HALFWAY TO PARADISE Decca F 11349	3	23
7 Sep 61 ●	JEALOUSY Decca F 11384	2	12
14 Dec 61 ●	I'D NEVER FIND ANOTHER YOU Decca F 11409	5	15
15 Mar 62	LETTER FULL OF TEARS Decca F 11437	32	4
3 May 62 ●	LAST NIGHT WAS MADE FOR LOVE Decca F 11458	4	16
19 Jul 62 ●	ONCE UPON A DREAM Decca F 11485	7	13
25 Oct 62	BECAUSE OF LOVE Decca F 11508	18	14
14 Feb 63 ●	LIKE I'VE NEVER BEEN GONE Decca F11582	3	15
16 May 63 ●	WHEN WILL YOU SAY I LOVE YOU Decca F 11655	3	12
25 Jul 63 ●	IN SUMMER Decca F 11701	5	11
3 Oct 63	SOMEBODY ELSE'S GIRL Decca F 11744	18	7
2 Jan 64	DO YOU REALLY LOVE ME TOO Decca F 11792	13	10
30 Apr 64	I WILL Decca F 11888	14	12
23 Jul 64 ●	IT'S ONLY MAKE BELIEVE Decca F 11939	10	10
14 Jan 65	I'M LOST WITHOUT YOU Decca F 12048	16	10
22 Jul 65 ●	IN THOUGHTS OF YOU Decca F 12178	9	11
16 Sep 65	RUN TO MY LOVIN' ARMS Decca F 12230	25	7
10 Feb 66	I'LL NEVER QUITE GET OVER YOU Decca F 12325	35	5
4 Aug 66	GIVE ME YOUR WORD Decca F 12459	27	7
4 Sep 82	LOVE OR MONEY Polydor POSP 488	57	5
13 Nov 82	DEVIL OR ANGEL Polydor POSP 528	58	4
4 Jun 83	FORGET HIM Polydor POSP 558	59	4

FUTURE BREEZE Germany, male production duo – Markus Boehme and Martin Hensing — 1 wk

6 Sep 97	WHY DON'T YOU DANCE WITH ME AM:PM 5823312	50	1

FUTURE FORCE UK/US, male/female vocal/instrumental duo — 1 wk

17 Aug 96	WHAT YOU WANT AM:PM 5816592	47	1

FUTURE SOUND OF LONDON ☺
UK, male instrumental/production duo — 22 wks

23 May 92	PAPUA NEW GUINEA Jumpin' & Pumpin' TOT 17	22	6
6 Nov 93	CASCADE Virgin VSCDT 1478	27	3

UK No 1 ★   UK Top 10 ●   UK million seller ◆   UK entry at No 1 ■   US No 1 ▲

30 Jul 94	EXPANDER *Jumpin' & Pumpin' CDSTOT 37*......	72	1
13 Aug 94	LIFEFORMS *Virgin VSCD 1484*......	14	3
27 May 95	FAR-OUT SON OF LUNG AND THE RAMBLINGS OF A MADMAN *Virgin VSCDT 1540*......	22	3
26 Oct 96	MY KINGDOM *Virgin VSCDT 1605*......	13	3
12 Apr 97	WE HAVE EXPLOSIVE *Virgin VSCDX 1616*......	12	3

FUZZBOX – See WE'VE GOT A FUZZBOX AND WE'RE GONNA USE IT

Leslie FYSON – See Michael MEDWIN, Bernard BRESSLAW, Alfie BASS and Leslie FYSON

Bobby G *UK, male vocalist* — **12 wks**

1 Dec 84	BIG DEAL *BBC RESL 151*......	75	1
15 Dec 84	BIG DEAL (re-entry) *BBC RESL 151*......	65	5
19 Oct 85	BIG DEAL (2nd re-entry) *BBC RESL 151*......	46	6

Dario G ☺ *UK, male DJ / production trio* — **31 wks**

27 Sep 97 ●	SUNCHYME *Eternal WEA 130CD*......	2	18
20 Jun 98 ●	CARNAVAL DE PARIS *Eternal WEA 162CD*......	5	9
12 Sep 98	SUNMACHINE *Eternal WEA 173CD*......	17	4

Gina G ☺ *Australia, female vocalist* — **51 wks**

6 Apr 96 ★	OOH AAH...JUST A LITTLE BIT *Eternal WEA 041CD*......	1	23
21 Sep 96	OOH AAH...JUST A LITTLE BIT (re-entry) *Eternal WEA 041CD*......	62	1
5 Oct 96	OOH AAH...JUST A LITTLE BIT (2nd re-entry) *Eternal WEA 041CD*......	64	1
9 Nov 96 ●	I BELONG TO YOU *Eternal WEA 081CD*......	6	11
22 Mar 97 ●	FRESH! *Eternal WEA 095CD*......	6	7
7 Jun 97	TI AMO *Eternal WEA 107CD1*......	11	5
6 Sep 97	GIMME SOME LOVE *Eternal WEA 101CD1*......	25	2
15 Nov 97	EVERY TIME I FALL *Eternal WEA 134CD*......	52	1

Kenny G *US, male instrumentalist – saxophone* — **22 wks**

21 Apr 84	HI! HOW YA DOIN'? *Arista ARIST 561*......	70	3
30 Aug 86	WHAT DOES IT TAKE (TO WIN YOUR LOVE) *Arista ARIST 672*......	64	2
4 Jul 87	SONGBIRD *Arista RIS 18*......	22	7
9 May 92	MISSING YOU NOW *Columbia 6579917* [1]......	28	4
24 Apr 93	FOREVER IN LOVE *Arista 74321145552*......	47	3
17 Jul 93	BY THE TIME THIS NIGHT IS OVER *Arista 74321157142* [2]......	56	3

[1] Michael Bolton featuring Kenny G [2] Kenny G with Peabo Bryson

Warren G 🎧 *US, male rapper* — **58 wks**

23 Jul 94 ●	REGULATE *Death Row A 8290CD* [1]......	5	14
12 Nov 94	THIS DJ *RAL RALCD 1*......	12	5
31 Dec 94	THIS DJ (re-entry) *RAL RALCD 1*......	68	2
25 Mar 95	DO YOU SEE *RAL RALCD 3*......	29	2
23 Nov 96 ●	WHAT'S LOVE GOT TO DO WITH IT *Interscope IND 97008* [2]......	2	11
22 Feb 97 ●	I SHOT THE SHERIFF *Mercury DEFCD 31*......	2	8
31 May 97	SMOKIN' ME OUT *Def Jam 5744432* [3]......	14	5
10 Jan 98	PRINCE IGOR *Def Jam 5749652* [4]......	15	7

24 Jan 98	ALL NIGHT ALL RIGHT *Mushroom MUSH 21CD* [5]......	16	4

[1] Warren G and Nate Dogg [2] Warren G featuring Adina Howard [3] Warren G featuring Ron Isley [4] Warren G featuring SisselPeter [5] Andre featuring Warren G

G NATION featuring ROSIE
UK, male production duo – Jake Moses and Mark Smith – and UK, female vocalist — **1 wk**

9 Aug 97	FEEL THE NEED *Cooltempo CDCOOL 327*......	58	1

Andy G's STARSKY AND HUTCH ALL STARS
UK, male producer — **1 wk**

3 Oct 98	STARSKY AND HUTCH - THEME *Virgin VSCDT 1708*......	51	1

Eric GABLE *US, male vocalist* — **1 wk**

19 Mar 94	PROCESS OF ELIMINATION *Epic 6602282*......	63	1

Peter GABRIEL 🎸 *Award-winning singer/songwriter, b. 13 February, 1950, Surrey. Fronted Genesis until 1975, when replaced by Phil Collins. He broke through internationally with 'Sledgehammer', which also made him a video innovator. He is the driving force behind the WOMAD festival and is a tireless Amnesty International supporter* — **112 wks**

9 Apr 77	SOLSBURY HILL *Charisma CB 301*......	13	9
9 Feb 80 ●	GAMES WITHOUT FRONTIERS *Charisma CB 354*......	4	11
10 May 80	NO SELF CONTROL *Charisma CB 360*......	33	6
23 Aug 80	BIKO *Charisma CB 370*......	38	3
25 Sep 82	SHOCK THE MONKEY *Charisma SHOCK 1*......	58	5
9 Jul 83	I DON'T REMEMBER *Charisma GAB 1*......	62	3
2 Jun 84	WALK THROUGH THE FIRE *Virgin VS 689*......	69	3
26 Apr 86 ●	SLEDGEHAMMER *Virgin PGS 1* ▲......	4	16
1 Nov 86 ●	DON'T GIVE UP *Virgin PGS 2* [1]......	9	11
28 Mar 87	BIG TIME *Charisma PGS 3*......	13	7
11 Jul 87	RED RAIN *Charisma PGS 4*......	46	3
21 Nov 87	BIKO (LIVE) *Charisma PGS 6*......	49	6
3 Jun 89	SHAKING THE TREE *Virgin VS 1167* [2]......	61	3
22 Dec 90	SOLSBURY HILL/SHAKING THE TREE (re-issue) *Virgin VS 1322* [3]......	57	4
19 Sep 92	DIGGING IN THE DIRT *Realworld PGS 7*......	24	4
16 Jan 93 ●	STEAM *Realworld PGSDG 8*......	10	7
3 Apr 93	BLOOD OF EDEN *Realworld PGSDG 9*......	43	4
25 Sep 93	KISS THAT FROG *Realworld PGSDG 10*......	46	3
25 Jun 94	LOVETOWN *Epic 6604802*......	49	2
3 Sep 94	SW LIVE EP *Realworld PGSCD 11*......	39	2

[1] Peter Gabriel and Kate Bush [2] Youssou N'Dour and Peter Gabriel [3] Peter Gabriel/Youssou N'Dour and Peter Gabriel

Tracks available on all formats of SW Live EP: Red Rain / San Jacinto. 'Red Rain' is a live version of his 1987 hit

GABRIELLE ☺ 🎤 *UK, female vocalist* — **83 wks**

19 Jun 93 ★	DREAMS *Go.Beat GODCD 99*......	1	15
2 Oct 93 ●	GOING NOWHERE *Go.Beat GODCD 106*......	9	7
11 Dec 93	I WISH *Go.Beat GODCD 108*......	26	5
26 Feb 94	BECAUSE OF YOU *Go.Beat GODCD 109*......	24	5
24 Feb 96 ●	GIVE ME A LITTLE MORE TIME *Go.Beat GODCD 139*......	5	18
22 Jun 96	FORGET ABOUT THE WORLD *Go.Beat GODCD 146*......	23	5
5 Oct 96	IF YOU REALLY CARED *Go.Beat GODCD 153*......	15	5
2 Nov 96 ●	IF YOU EVER *London LONCD 388* [1]......	2	15
1 Feb 97 ●	WALK ON BY *Go.Beat GODCD 159*......	7	8

[1] East 17 featuring Gabrielle

Yvonne GAGE *US, female vocalist* — **4 wks**

16 Jun 84	DOIN' IT IN A HAUNTED HOUSE *Epic A 4519*......	45	4

Danni'elle GAHA *Australia, female vocalist* — **7 wks**

1 Aug 92	STUCK IN THE MIDDLE *Epic 6581247*......	68	2
27 Feb 93	DO IT FOR LOVE *Epic 6584612*......	52	2
12 Jun 93	SECRET LOVE *Epic 6592212*......	41	3

Billy and Sarah GAINES *US, male/female vocal duo* 1 wk

14 Jun 97	**I FOUND SOMEONE** *Expansion CDEXP 27*	48	1

Rosie GAINES ☺ 🎤 *US, female vocalist* 15 wks

11 Nov 95	**I WANT U** *Motown 8604852*	70	1
31 May 97 ●	**CLOSER THAN CLOSE** *Big Bang CDBBANG 1*	4	12
29 Nov 97	**I SURRENDER** *Big Bang CDBBANG 2*	39	2

Serge GAINSBOURG – *See Jane BIRKIN and Serge GAINSBOURG*

GALA ◐ ☺ *Italy, female vocalist* 24 wks

19 Jul 97 ●	**FREED FROM DESIRE** *Big Life BLRD 135*	3	14
6 Dec 97	**LET A BOY CRY** *Big Life BLRD 140*	11	8
22 Aug 98	**COME INTO MY LIFE** *Big Life BLRD 147*	38	2

GALAXY – *See Phil FEARON*

Dee GALDES – *See Phil FEARON*

Eve GALLAGHER *UK, female vocalist* 8 wks

1 Dec 90	**LOVE COME DOWN** *More Protein PROT 6*	61	3
29 Dec 90	**LOVE COME DOWN (re-entry)** *More Protein PROT 6*	68	1
15 Apr 95	**YOU CAN HAVE IT ALL** *Cleveland City CLECD 13023*	43	2
28 Oct 95	**LOVE COME DOWN** *Cleveland City CLECD 13028*	57	1
6 Jul 96	**HEARTBREAK** *React CDREACT 78* [1]	44	1

[1] Mrs Wood featuring Eve Gallagher

'Love Come Down' in 1995 is a re-recording

GALLAGHER and LYLE ◐ *UK, male vocal/instrumental duo* 27 wks

28 Feb 76 ●	**I WANNA STAY WITH YOU** *A & M AMS 7211*	6	9
22 May 76 ●	**HEART ON MY SLEEVE** *A & M AMS 7227*	6	10
11 Sep 76	**BREAKAWAY** *A & M AMS 7245*	35	4
29 Jan 77	**EVERY LITTLE TEARDROP** *A & M AMS 7274*	32	4

Patsy GALLANT ◢ *Canada, female vocalist* 9 wks

10 Sep 77 ●	**FROM NEW YORK TO L.A.** *EMI 2620*	6	9

GALLIANO ☺ ◣ *UK, male/female vocal/instrumental group* 14 wks

30 May 92	**SKUNK FUNK** *Talkin Loud TLK 23*	41	2
1 Aug 92	**PRINCE OF PEACE** *Talkin Loud TLK 24*	47	3
10 Oct 92	**JUS' REACH (RECYCLED)** *Talkin Loud TLK 29*	66	2
28 May 94	**LONG TIME GONE** *Talkin Loud TLKCD 48*	15	3
30 Jul 94	**TWYFORD DOWN** *Talkin Loud TLKCD 49*	37	2
27 Jul 96	**EASE YOUR MIND** *Talkin Loud TLCD 10*	45	2

James GALWAY ◖ *UK, male instrumentalist – flute* 13 wks

27 May 78 ●	**ANNIE'S SONG** *RCA Red Seal RB 5085*	3	13

GAMBAFREAKS featuring PACO RIVAZ
Italy, male production duo 1 wk

12 Sep 98	**INSTANT REPLAY** *Evocative EVOKE 7CDS*	57	1

GANG OF FOUR *UK, male vocal/instrumental group* 5 wks

16 Jun 79	**AT HOME HE'S A TOURIST** *EMI 2956*	58	3
22 May 82	**I LOVE A MAN IN UNIFORM** *EMI 5299*	65	2

GANG STARR *US, male rap group* 8 wks

13 Oct 90	**JAZZ THING** *CBS 356377 7*	66	2
23 Feb 91	**TAKE A REST** *Cooltempo COOL 230*	63	1
25 May 91	**LOVESICK** *Cooltempo COOL 234*	50	3
13 Jun 92	**2 DEEP** *Cooltempo COOL 256*	67	2

GANT *UK, production duo – Julian Jonah and Danny Harrison* 1 wk

27 Dec 97	**SOUND BWOY BURIAL / ALL NIGHT LONG** *Positiva CDTIV 85*	67	1

GAP BAND ♩ *US, male vocal/instrumental group* 82 wks

12 Jul 80 ●	**OOPS UP SIDE YOUR HEAD** *Mercury MER 22*	6	14
27 Sep 80	**PARTY LIGHTS** *Mercury MER 37*	30	8
27 Dec 80	**BURN RUBBER ON ME (WHY YOU WANNA HURT ME)** *Mercury MER 52*	22	11
11 Apr 81	**HUMPIN'** *Mercury MER 63*	36	6
27 Jun 81	**YEARNING FOR YOUR LOVE** *Mercury MER 73*	47	4
5 Jun 82	**EARLY IN THE MORNING** *Mercury MER 97*	55	3
19 Feb 83	**OUTSTANDING** *Total Experience TE 001*	68	7
31 Mar 84	**SOMEDAY** *Total Experience TE 5*	17	8
23 Jun 84	**JAMMIN' IN AMERICA** *Total Experience TE 6*	64	2
13 Dec 86 ●	**BIG FUN** *Total Experience FB 49779*	4	12
14 Mar 87	**HOW MUSIC CAME ABOUT (BOP B DA B DA DA)** *Total Experience FB 49755*	61	2
11 Jul 87	**OOPS UPSIDE YOUR HEAD (re-mix)** *Club JAB 54*	20	8
18 Feb 89	**I'M GONNA GIT YOU SUCKA** *Arista 112016*	63	2

GARBAGE 🎸 ☺ *US/UK, male/female vocal/instrumental group* 36 wks

19 Aug 95	**SUBHUMAN** *Mushroom D 1138*	50	1
30 Sep 95	**ONLY HAPPY WHEN IT RAINS** *Mushroom D 1199*	29	3
2 Dec 95	**QUEER** *Mushroom D 1237*	13	4
23 Mar 96 ●	**STUPID GIRL** *Mushroom D 1271*	4	7
23 Nov 96 ●	**MILK** *Mushroom D 1494* [1]	10	6
18 Jan 97	**MILK (re-entry)** *Mushroom D 1494* [1]	74	1
9 May 98 ●	**PUSH IT** *Mushroom MUSH 28CDS*	9	5
18 Jul 98 ●	**I THINK I'M PARANOID** *Mushroom MUSH 35CDS*	9	5
17 Oct 98	**SPECIAL** *Mushroom MUSH 39CDS*	15	4

[1] Garbage featuring Tricky

Adam GARCIA ◐ *Australia, male vocalist* 5 wks

16 May 98	**NIGHT FEVER** *Polydor 5697972*	15	5

Scott GARCIA featuring MC STYLES
UK, male producer and UK, male rapper 3 wks

1 Nov 97	**A LONDON THING** *Connected CDCONNECT 1*	29	3

Boris GARDINER ◥ *Jamaica, male vocalist/instrumentalist* 38 wks

17 Jan 70	**ELIZABETHAN REGGAE** *Duke DU 39*	48	1
31 Jan 70	**ELIZABETHAN REGGAE (re-entry)** *Duke DU 39*	14	13
26 Jul 86 ★	**I WANT TO WAKE UP WITH YOU** *Revue REV 733*	1	15
4 Oct 86	**YOU'RE EVERYTHING TO ME** *Revue REV 735*	11	8
27 Dec 86	**THE MEANING OF CHRISTMAS** *Revue REV 740*	69	1

The first copies of 'Elizabethan Reggae', an instrumental, were printed with the label incorrectly crediting Byron Lee as the performer. The charts for the first entry, and the first four weeks of the re-entry, all reprinted this error. All charts and discs printed after 28 Feb, 1970 gave Boris Gardiner the credit he deserved

Paul GARDINER *UK, male instrumentalist – bass* 4 wks

25 Jul 81	**STORMTROOPER IN DRAG** *Beggars Banquet BEG 61*	49	4

Uncredited vocalist is Gary Numan

Art GARFUNKEL ◐ *US, male vocalist* 37 wks

13 Sep 75 ★	**I ONLY HAVE EYES FOR YOU** *CBS 3575*	1	11
3 Mar 79 ★	**BRIGHT EYES** *CBS 6947* ◆	1	19
7 Jul 79	**SINCE I DON'T HAVE YOU** *CBS 7371*	38	7

Judy GARLAND ◖ *US, female vocalist* 2 wks

10 Jun 55	**THE MAN THAT GOT AWAY** *Philips PB 366*	18	2

Laurent GARNIER *France, male DJ / producer* 1 wk

15 Feb 97	**CRISPY BACON** *F Communications F 055CD*	60	1

Lee GARRETT 🎤 *US, male vocalist* 7 wks

29 May 76	**YOU'RE MY EVERYTHING** *Chrysalis CHS 2087*	15	7

Leif GARRETT ☺ *US, male vocalist* — 14 wks

20 Jan 79	● I WAS MADE FOR DANCIN' *Scotti Brothers K 11202*	4	10
21 Apr 79	FEEL THE NEED *Scotti Brothers K 11274*	38	4

Lesley GARRETT and Amanda THOMPSON ♪
UK, female vocal/instrumental duo — 10 wks

6 Nov 93	AVE MARIA *Internal Affairs KGBD 012*	16	10

Siedah GARRETT – See BRAND NEW HEAVIES; Dennis EDWARDS; Michael JACKSON

David GARRICK *UK, male vocalist* — 16 wks

9 Jun 66	LADY JANE *Piccadilly 7N 35317*	28	7
22 Sep 66	DEAR MRS APPLEBEE *Piccadilly 7N 35335*	22	9

GARY'S GANG ◢ *US, male vocal/instrumental group* — 18 wks

24 Feb 79	● KEEP ON DANCIN' *CBS 7109*	8	10
2 Jun 79	LET'S LOVE DANCE TONIGHT *CBS 7328*	49	4
6 Nov 82	KNOCK ME OUT *Arista ARIST 499*	45	4

Barbara GASKIN – See Dave STEWART

GAT DECOR ☺ *UK, male instrumental/production group* — 10 wks

16 May 92	PASSION *Effective EFFS 1*	29	4
9 Mar 96	● PASSION (re-mix) *Way Of Life WAYDA 1*	6	6

David GATES *US, male vocalist* — 2 wks

22 Jul 78	TOOK THE LAST TRAIN *Elektra K 12307*	50	2

GAY GORDON and the MINCE PIES
UK, male/female vocal/instrumental group — 5 wks

6 Dec 86	THE ESSENTIAL WALLY PARTY MEDLEY *Lifestyle XY 2*	60	5

GAYE BYKERS ON ACID *UK, male vocal/instrumental group* — 2 wks

31 Oct 87	GIT DOWN (SHAKE YOUR THANG) *Purple Fluid VS 1008*	54	2

Marvin GAYE ♪ *One of soul's most innovative and successful singer/songwriters, b. 2 April, 1939, Washington DC, d. 1 April, 1984. He went from doo-wop group member and session drummer to superstar. Posthumously awarded a Lifetime Achievement Grammy Award in 1996* — 200 wks

30 Jul 64	ONCE UPON A TIME *Stateside SS 316* [1]	50	1
10 Dec 64	HOW SWEET IT IS *Stateside SS 360*	49	1
29 Sep 66	LITTLE DARLIN' *Tamla Motown TMG 574*	50	1
26 Jan 67	IT TAKES TWO *Tamla Motown TMG 590* [2]	16	11
17 Jan 68	IF I COULD BUILD MY WHOLE WORLD AROUND YOU *Tamla Motown TMG 635* [3]	41	7
12 Jun 68	AIN'T NOTHIN' LIKE THE REAL THING *Tamla Motown TMG 655* [3]	34	7
2 Oct 68	YOU'RE ALL I NEED TO GET BY *Tamla Motown TMG 668* [3]	19	19
22 Jan 69	YOU AIN'T LIVIN' TILL YOU'RE LOVIN' *Tamla Motown TMG 681* [3]	21	8
12 Feb 69	★ I HEARD IT THROUGH THE GRAPEVINE *Tamla Motown TMG 686* ▲	1	15
4 Jun 69	GOOD LOVIN' AIN'T EASY TO COME BY *Tamla Motown TMG 697* [3]	26	7
23 Jul 69	● TOO BUSY THINKING 'BOUT MY BABY *Tamla Motown TMG 705*	5	16
30 Jul 69	GOOD LOVIN' AIN'T EASY TO COME BY (re-entry) *Tamla Motown TMG 697* [3]	48	1
15 Nov 69	● ONION SONG *Tamla Motown TMG 715* [3]	9	12
9 May 70	● ABRAHAM MARTIN AND JOHN *Tamla Motown TMG 734*	9	14
11 Dec 71	SAVE THE CHILDREN *Tamla Motown TMG 796*	41	6
22 Sep 73	LET'S GET IT ON *Tamla Motown TMG 868* ▲	31	7
23 Mar 74	● YOU ARE EVERYTHING *Tamla Motown TMG 890* [4]	5	12
20 Jul 74	STOP LOOK LISTEN (TO YOUR HEART) *Tamla Motown TMG 906* [4]	25	8
7 May 77	● GOT TO GIVE IT UP *Motown TMG 1069* ▲	7	10
24 Feb 79	POPS WE LOVE YOU *Motown TMG 1136* [5]	66	5
30 Oct 82	● (SEXUAL) HEALING *CBS A 2855*	4	14
8 Jan 83	MY LOVE IS WAITING *CBS A 3048*	34	5
18 May 85	SANCTIFIED LADY *CBS A 4894*	51	4
26 Apr 86	● I HEARD IT THRU THE GRAPEVINE (re-issue) *Tamla Motown ZB 40701*	8	8
14 May 94	LUCKY LUCKY ME *Motown TMGCD 1426*	67	1

[1] Marvin Gaye and Mary Wells [2] Marvin Gaye and Kim Weston [3] Marvin Gaye and Tammi Terrell [4] Diana Ross and Marvin Gaye [5] Diana Ross, Marvin Gaye, Smokey Robinson and Stevie Wonder

Crystal GAYLE ☚ *US, female vocalist* — 28 wks

12 Nov 77	● DON'T IT MAKE MY BROWN EYES BLUE *United Artists UP 36307*	5	14
26 Aug 78	TALKING IN YOUR SLEEP *United Artists UP 36422*	11	14

Michelle GAYLE ☺ (R&B) *UK, female vocalist* — 52 wks

7 Aug 93	LOOKING UP *RCA 743214154532*	11	6
24 Sep 94	SWEETNESS *RCA 74321230192*	4	16
17 Dec 94	I'LL FIND YOU *RCA 74321247762*	26	7
27 May 95	FREEDOM *RCA 74321284692*	16	6
26 Aug 95	HAPPY JUST TO BE WITH YOU *RCA 74321302692*	11	7
8 Feb 97	● DO YOU KNOW *RCA 74321419282*	6	6
26 Apr 97	SENSATIONAL *RCA 74321419302*	14	4

Roy GAYLE – See MIRAGE

GAYLE & GILLIAN *Australia, female vocal duo* — 2 wks

3 Jul 93	MAD IF YA DON'T *Mushroom CDMUSH 1*	75	1
19 Mar 94	WANNA BE YOUR LOVER *Mushroom D 11598*	62	1

Gloria GAYNOR ◢ *US, female vocalist* — 72 wks

7 Dec 74	● NEVER CAN SAY GOODBYE *MGM 2006 463*	2	13
8 Mar 75	REACH OUT I'LL BE THERE *MGM 2006 499*	14	8
9 Aug 75	ALL I NEED IS YOUR SWEET LOVIN' *MGM 2006 531*	44	3
17 Jan 76	HOW HIGH THE MOON *MGM 2006 558*	33	4
3 Feb 79	★ I WILL SURVIVE *Polydor 2095 017* ▲	1	15
6 Oct 79	LET ME KNOW (I HAVE A RIGHT) *Polydor STEP 5*	32	7
24 Dec 83	I AM WHAT I AM (FROM 'LA CAGE AUX FOLLES') *Chrysalis CHS 2765*	13	12
26 Jun 93	● I WILL SURVIVE (re-mix) *Polydor PZCD 270*	5	10

GAZ *US, male vocal/instrumental group* — 4 wks

24 Feb 79	SING SING *Salsoul SSOL 116*	60	4

GAZZA ☺ *UK, male vocalist – Paul Gascoigne* — 14 wks

10 Nov 90	● FOG ON THE TYNE (REVISITED) *Best ZB 44083* [1]	2	9
22 Dec 90	GEORDIE BOYS (GAZZA RAP) *Best ZB 44229*	31	5

[1] Gazza and Lindisfarne

GBH *UK, male vocal/instrumental group* — 5 wks

6 Feb 82	NO SURVIVORS *Clay CLAY 8*	63	2
20 Nov 82	GIVE ME FIRE *Clay CLAY 16*	69	3

G-CLEFS ♪ *US, male vocal group* — 12 wks

30 Nov 61	I UNDERSTAND *London HLU 9433*	17	12

J GEILS BAND ✎ *US, male vocal/instrumental group* — 20 wks

9 Jun 79	ONE LAST KISS *EMI America AM 507*	74	1
13 Feb 82	● CENTERFOLD *EMI America EA 135* ▲	3	9
10 Apr 82	FREEZE-FRAME *EMI America EA 134*	27	7
26 Jun 82	ANGEL IN BLUE *EMI America EA 138*	55	3

Bob GELDOF ☺ *Ireland, male vocalist* — 15 wks

1 Nov 86	THIS IS THE WORLD CALLING *Mercury BOB 101*	25	5
21 Feb 87	LOVE LIKE A ROCKET *Mercury BOB 102*	61	3
23 Jun 90	THE GREAT SONG OF INDIFFERENCE *Mercury BOB 104*	15	6
7 May 94	CRAZY *Vertigo VERCX 85*	65	1

GEM – See OUR TRIBE/ONE TRIBE

GEMINI *UK, male vocal duo* — 7 wks

30 Sep 95	EVEN THOUGH YOU BROKE MY HEART		
	EMI CDEMS 391	40	3
10 Feb 96	STEAL YOUR LOVE AWAY *EMI CDEMS 407*	37	2
29 Jun 96	COULD IT BE FOREVER *EMI CDEMS 426*	38	2

GEMS FOR JEM *UK, male instrumental/production duo* — 2 wks

| 6 May 95 | LIFTING ME HIGHER *Box 21 CDSBOKS 3* | 28 | 2 |

GENE ☹ ◐ *UK, male vocal/instrumental group* — 21 wks

13 Aug 94	BE MY LIGHT BE MY GUIDE		
	Costermonger COST 002CD	54	1
12 Nov 94	SLEEP WELL TONIGHT *Costermonger COST 003CD*	36	2
4 Mar 95	HAUNTED BY YOU *Costermonger COST 004CD*	32	2
22 Jul 95	OLYMPIAN *Costermonger COST 005CD*	18	2
13 Jan 96	FOR THE DEAD *Costermonger COST 006CD*	14	3
2 Nov 96	FIGHTING FIT *Costermonger COST 009CD*	22	2
1 Feb 97	WE WOULD BE KINGS *Polydor COSCD 10*	17	2
10 May 97	WHERE ARE THEY NOW? *Polydor COSCD 11*	22	2
9 Aug 97	SPEAK TO ME SOMEONE *Polydor COSCD 12*	30	2

GENE AND JIM ARE INTO SHAKES
UK, male vocal/instrumental duo — 2 wks

| 19 Mar 88 | SHAKE! (HOW ABOUT A SAMPLING GENE) | | |
| | *Rough Trade RT 216* | 68 | 2 |

GENE LOVES JEZEBEL *UK, male vocal/instrumental group* — 7 wks

29 Mar 86	SWEETEST THING *Beggars Banquet BEG 156*	75	1
14 Jun 86	HEARTACHE *Beggars Banquet BEG 161*	71	2
5 Sep 87	THE MOTION OF LOVE *Beggars Banquet BEG 192*	56	3
5 Dec 87	GORGEOUS *Beggars Banquet BEG 202*	68	1

GENERAL LEVY ⅃ *UK, male vocalist* — 13 wks

4 Sep 93	MONKEY MAN *ffrr FCD 214*	75	1
18 Jun 94	INCREDIBLE *Renk RENKT 42CD* [1]	39	3
10 Sep 94 ●	INCREDIBLE (re-mix) *Renk CDRENK 45* [1]	8	9

[1] M-Beat featuring General Levy

GENERAL PUBLIC *UK, male vocal/instrumental group* — 4 wks

| 10 Mar 84 | GENERAL PUBLIC *Virgin VS 659* | 60 | 3 |
| 2 Jul 94 | I'LL TAKE YOU THERE *Epic 6605532* | 73 | 1 |

GENERAL SAINT *UK, male vocalist* — 9 wks

29 Sep 84	LAST PLANE (ONE WAY TICKET) *MCA MCA 910* [1]	51	3
2 Apr 94	OH CAROL! *Copasetic COPCD 0009* [1]	54	5
6 Aug 94	SAVE THE LAST DANCE FOR ME *Copasetic COPCD 12* [2]	75	1

[1] Clint Eastwood and General Saint [2] General Saint featuring Don Campbell

GENERATION X ✎ *UK, male vocal/instrumental group* — 31 wks

17 Sep 77	YOUR GENERATION *Chrysalis CHS 2165*	36	4
11 Mar 78	READY STEADY GO *Chrysalis CHS 2207*	47	3
20 Jan 79	KING ROCKER *Chrysalis CHS 2261*	11	9
7 Apr 79	VALLEY OF THE DOLLS *Chrysalis CHS 2310*	23	7
30 Jun 79	FRIDAY'S ANGELS *Chrysalis CHS 2330*	62	2
18 Oct 80	DANCING WITH MYSELF *Chrysalis CHS 2444* [1]	62	2
24 Jan 81	DANCING WITH MYSELF (EP) *Chrysalis CHS 2488* [1]	60	4

[1] Gen X

Tracks on Dancing With Myself (EP): Dancing With Myself / Untouchables / Rock On / King Rocker

GENESIS ✍ Perennially popular UK group. Ever-present members are Tony Banks (k) and Mike Rutherford (g); others included Peter Gabriel (v), Phil Collins (v/d), Steve Hackett (g). These progressive 1970s rockers became a major act in the 1980s and had ten consecutive Top 3 albums — 187 wks

| 6 Apr 74 | I KNOW WHAT I LIKE (IN YOUR WARDROBE) | | |
| | *Charisma CB 224* | 21 | 7 |

26 Feb 77	YOUR OWN SPECIAL WAY *Charisma CB 300*	43	3
28 May 77	SPOT THE PIGEON (EP) *Charisma GEN 001*	14	7
11 Mar 78 ●	FOLLOW YOU FOLLOW ME *Charisma CB 309*	7	13
8 Jul 78	MANY TOO MANY *Charisma CB 315*	43	5
15 Mar 80 ●	TURN IT ON AGAIN *Charisma CB 356*	8	10
17 May 80	DUCHESS *Charisma CB 363*	46	5
13 Sep 80	MISUNDERSTANDING *Charisma CB 369*	42	5
22 Aug 81 ●	ABACAB *Charisma CB 388*	9	8
31 Oct 81	KEEP IT DARK *Charisma CB 391*	33	4
13 Mar 82	MAN ON THE CORNER *Charisma CB 393*	41	5
22 May 82	3 X 3 EP *Charisma GEN 1*	10	8
3 Sep 83 ●	MAMA *Virgin/Charisma MAMA 1*	4	10
12 Nov 83	THAT'S ALL *Charisma/Virgin TATA 1*	16	11
11 Feb 84	ILLEGAL ALIEN *Charisma/Virgin AL1*	46	3
10 Mar 84	ILLEGAL ALIEN (re-entry) *Charisma/Virgin AL1*	70	1
31 May 86	INVISIBLE TOUCH *Virgin GENS 1* ▲	15	8
30 Aug 86	IN TOO DEEP *Virgin GENS 2*	19	9
22 Nov 86	LAND OF CONFUSION *Virgin GENS 3*	14	12
14 Mar 87	TONIGHT TONIGHT TONIGHT *Virgin GENS 4*	18	6
20 Jun 87	THROWING IT ALL AWAY *Virgin GENS 5*	22	8
2 Nov 91 ●	NO SON OF MINE *Virgin GENS 6*	6	6
4 Jan 92	NO SON OF MINE (re-entry) *Virgin GENS 6*	70	1
11 Jan 92 ●	I CAN'T DANCE *Virgin GENS 7*	7	9
18 Apr 92	HOLD ON MY HEART *Virgin GENS 8*	16	5
25 Jul 92	JESUS HE KNOWS ME *Virgin GENS 9*	20	7
21 Nov 92 ●	INVISIBLE TOUCH (LIVE) *Virgin GENS 10*	7	4
20 Feb 93	TELL ME WHY *Virgin GENDG 11*	40	3
27 Sep 97	CONGO *Virgin GENSD 12*	29	2
13 Dec 97	SHIPWRECKED *Virgin GENDX14*	54	1
7 Mar 98	NOT ABOUT US *Virgin GENSD 15*	66	1

Tracks on Spot the Pigeon (EP): Match of the Day / Pigeons / Inside and Out.
Tracks on 3 x 3 (EP): Paperlate / You Might Recall / Me and Virgil

GENEVA *UK, male vocal/instrumental group* — 7 wks

26 Oct 96	NO ONE SPEAKS *Nude NUD 22CD*	32	2
8 Feb 97	INTO THE BLUE *Nude NUD 25CD*	26	2
31 May 97	TRANQUILIZER *Nude NUD 8CD1*	24	2
16 Aug 97	BEST REGRETS *Nude NUD 31CD1*	38	1

GENEVIEVE *France, female vocalist* — 1 wk

| 5 May 66 | ONCE *CBS 202061* | 43 | 1 |

GENIUS/GZA – See D'ANGELO

Bobbie GENTRY ◐ *US, female vocalist* — 48 wks

13 Sep 67	ODE TO BILLY JOE *Capitol CL 15511* ▲	13	11
30 Aug 69 ★	I'LL NEVER FALL IN LOVE AGAIN *Capitol CL 15606*	1	19
6 Dec 69 ●	ALL I HAVE TO DO IS DREAM *Capitol CL 15619* [1]	3	14
21 Feb 70	RAINDROPS KEEP FALLIN' ON MY HEAD *Capitol CL 15626*	40	4

[1] Bobbie Gentry and Glen Campbell

GEORDIE ◐ *UK, male vocal/instrumental group* — 35 wks

2 Dec 72	DON'T DO THAT *Regal Zonophone RZ 3067*	32	7
17 Mar 73 ●	ALL BECAUSE OF YOU *EMI 2008*	6	13
16 Jun 73	CAN YOU DO IT *EMI 2031*	13	9
25 Aug 73	ELECTRIC LADY *EMI 2048*	32	6

Robin GEORGE *UK, male vocalist/instrumentalist – guitar* — 2 wks

| 27 Apr 85 | HEARTLINE *Bronze BRO 191* | 68 | 2 |

Sophia GEORGE ⅃ *Jamaica, female vocalist* — 11 wks

| 7 Dec 85 ● | GIRLIE GIRLIE *Winner WIN 01* | 7 | 11 |

GEORGIA SATELLITES *US, male vocal/instrumental group* — 8 wks

7 Feb 87	KEEP YOUR HANDS TO YOURSELF		
	Elektra EKR 50	69	1
16 May 87	BATTLESHIP CHAINS *Elektra EKR 58*	44	4
21 Jan 89	HIPPY HIPPY SHAKE *Elektra EKR 86*	63	3

GEORGIE PORGIE US, male producer — 2 wks

| 12 Aug 95 | EVERYBODY MUST PARTY *Vibe MCSTD 2068* | 61 | 1 |
| 4 May 96 | TAKE ME HIGHER *Music Plant MCSTD 40031* | 61 | 1 |

GEORGIO US, male vocalist — 3 wks

| 20 Feb 88 | LOVER'S LANE *Motown ZB 41611* | 54 | 3 |

Danyel GERARD ◎ France, male vocalist — 12 wks

| 18 Sep 71 | BUTTERFLY *CBS 7454* | 11 | 12 |

GERIDEAU – See PROJECT featuring GERIDEAU

GERRY and the PACEMAKERS ◎ Record-breaking Merseybeat band:
Gerry Marsden (v/g), Les Chadwick (b), Les McGuire (p), Freddie Marsden (d).
Second Liverpool group to chart (after The Beatles), but first to reach No 1
and first act ever to top UK chart with their initial three singles — 114 wks

14 Mar 63	★ HOW DO YOU DO IT? *Columbia DB 4987*	1	18
30 May 63	★ I LIKE IT *Columbia DB 7041*	1	15
10 Oct 63	★ YOU'LL NEVER WALK ALONE *Columbia DB 7126*	1	19
16 Jan 64	● I'M THE ONE *Columbia DB 7189*	2	15
16 Apr 64	● DON'T LET THE SUN CATCH YOU CRYING *Columbia DB 7268*	6	11
3 Sep 64	IT'S GONNA BE ALL RIGHT *Columbia DB 7353*	24	7
17 Dec 64	● FERRY ACROSS THE MERSEY *Columbia DB 7437*	8	13
25 Mar 65	I'LL BE THERE *Columbia DB 7504*	15	9
18 Nov 65	WALK HAND IN HAND *Columbia DB 7738*	29	7

GET FRESH CREW – See Doug E FRESH and the GET FRESH CREW

GET READY UK, male vocal group — 1 wk

| 3 Jun 95 | WILD WILD WEST *Mega GACXCD 2698* | 65 | 1 |

GETO BOYS featuring FLAJ US, male rap group — 1 wk

| 11 May 96 | THE WORLD IS A GHETTO *Virgin America VUSCD 104* | 49 | 1 |

Stan GETZ ✐ US, male instrumentalist – tenor sax — 29 wks

8 Nov 62	DESAFINADO *HMV POP 1061* [1]	11	13
23 Jul 64	THE GIRL FROM IPANEMA (GAROTA DE IPANEMA) *Verve VS 520* [2]	29	10
25 Aug 84	THE GIRL FROM IPANEMA (re-issue) *Verve IPA 1* [3]	55	6

[1] Stan Getz and Charlie Byrd [2] Stan Getz and Joao Gilberto [3] Astrud Gilberto

*The re-issue of 'The Girl From Ipanema' was credited only to Astrud Gilberto,
the vocalist, even though it was exactly the same recording as the original hit*

GHOST DANCE UK, male vocal/instrumental group — 2 wks

| 17 Jun 89 | DOWN TO THE WIRE *Chrysalis CHS 3376* | 66 | 2 |

GHOSTFACE KILLAH ◄ US, male rapper — 4 wks

| 12 Jul 97 | ALL THAT I GOT IS YOU *Epic 6646842* | 11 | 4 |

Andy GIBB ◎ UK, male vocalist — 30 wks

25 Jun 77	I JUST WANNA BE YOUR EVERYTHING *RSO 2090 237* ▲	26	7
13 May 78	SHADOW DANCING *RSO 001* ▲	42	6
12 Aug 78	● AN EVERLASTING LOVE *RSO 015*	10	10
27 Jan 79	(OUR LOVE) DON'T THROW IT ALL AWAY *RSO 26*	32	7

See also BEE GEES

Barry GIBB – See BEE GEES; Barbra STREISAND

Robin GIBB ◎ UK, male vocalist — 21 wks

9 Jul 69	● SAVED BY THE BELL *Polydor 56-337*	2	16
15 Nov 69	SAVED BY THE BELL (re-entry) *Polydor 56-337*	49	1
7 Feb 70	AUGUST OCTOBER *Polydor 56-371*	45	3
11 Feb 84	ANOTHER LONELY NIGHT IN NEW YORK *Polydor POSP 668*	71	1

See also BEE GEES

Steve GIBBONS BAND ✐ UK, male vocal/instrumental group — 14 wks

| 6 Aug 77 | TULANE *Polydor 2058 889* | 12 | 10 |
| 13 May 78 | EDDY VORTEX *Polydor 2059 017* | 56 | 4 |

Georgia GIBBS € US, female vocalist — 2 wks

| 22 Apr 55 | TWEEDLE DEE *Mercury MB 3196* | 20 | 1 |
| 13 Jul 56 | KISS ME ANOTHER *Mercury MT 110* | 24 | 1 |

Debbie GIBSON ◎ US, female vocalist — 70 wks

26 Sep 87	ONLY IN MY DREAMS *Atlantic A 9322*	54	5
23 Jan 88	● SHAKE YOUR LOVE *Atlantic A 9187*	7	8
19 Mar 88	ONLY IN MY DREAMS (re-entry) *Atlantic A 9322*	11	7
7 May 88	OUT OF THE BLUE *Atlantic A 9091*	19	7
9 Jul 88	● FOOLISH BEAT *Atlantic A 9059* ▲	9	9
15 Oct 88	STAYING TOGETHER *Atlantic A 9020*	53	2
28 Jan 89	LOST IN YOUR EYES *Atlantic A 8970* ▲	34	7
29 Apr 89	ELECTRIC YOUTH *Atlantic A 8919*	14	8
19 Aug 89	WE COULD BE TOGETHER *Atlantic A 8896*	22	8
9 Mar 91	ANYTHING IS POSSIBLE *Atlantic A 7735*	51	2
3 Apr 93	SHOCK YOUR MAMA *Atlantic A 7386CD*	74	1
24 Jul 93	YOU'RE THE ONE THAT I WANT *Epic 6595222* [1]	13	6

[1] Craig McLachlan and Debbie Gibson

Don GIBSON ☛ US, male vocalist — 16 wks

| 31 Aug 61 | SEA OF HEARTBREAK *RCA 1243* | 14 | 13 |
| 1 Feb 62 | LONESOME NUMBER ONE *RCA 1272* | 47 | 3 |

Wayne GIBSON ◎ UK, male vocalist — 13 wks

| 3 Sep 64 | KELLY *Pye 7N 15680* | 48 | 2 |
| 23 Nov 74 | UNDER MY THUMB *Pye Disco Demand DDS 2001* | 17 | 11 |

GIBSON BROTHERS ◢
Martinique, male vocal/instrumental group — 54 wks

10 Mar 79	CUBA *Island WIP 6483*	41	9
21 Jul 79	● OOH! WHAT A LIFE *Island WIP 6503*	10	12
17 Nov 79	● QUE SERA MI VIDA (IF YOU SHOULD GO) *Island WIP 6525*	5	11
23 Feb 80	CUBA/BETTER DO IT SALSA (re-issue) *Island WIP 6561*	12	9
12 Jul 80	MARIANA *Island WIP 6617*	11	10
9 Jul 83	MY HEART'S BEATING WILD (TIC TAC TIC TAC) *Stiff BUY 184*	56	3

GIDEA PARK ◎ UK, male vocal/instrumentalist – Adrian Baker — 19 wks

| 4 Jul 81 | BEACHBOY GOLD *Stone SON 2162* | 11 | 13 |
| 12 Sep 81 | SEASONS OF GOLD *Polo POLO 14* | 28 | 6 |

GIFTED UK, male instrumentalist — 1 wk

| 23 Aug 97 | DO I *Perfecto PERF 140CD* | 60 | 1 |

GIGOLO AUNTS US, male vocal/instrumental group — 4 wks

| 23 Apr 94 | MRS WASHINGTON *Fire BLAZE 68CD* | 74 | 1 |
| 13 May 95 | WHERE I FIND MY HEAVEN *Fire BLAZE 87CD* | 29 | 3 |

Astrud GILBERTO – See Stan GETZ

Joao GILBERTO – See Stan GETZ

Donna GILES US, female vocalist — 4 wks

| 13 Aug 94 | AND I'M TELLING YOU I'M NOT GOING *Ore AG 4CD* | 43 | 2 |
| 10 Feb 96 | AND I'M TELLING YOU I'M NOT GOING (re-issue) *Ore AGR 4CD* | 27 | 2 |

Johnny GILL ⟨R&B⟩ US, male vocalist — 12 wks

23 Feb 91	WRAP MY BODY TIGHT *Motown ZB 44271*	57	2
28 Nov 92	SLOW AND SEXY *Epic 6587727* [1]	17	7
17 Jul 93	THE FLOOR *Motown TMGCD 1416*	53	1
29 Jan 94	A CUTE SWEET LOVE ADDICTION *Motown TMGCD 1420*	46	2

[1] Shabba Ranks featuring Johnny Gill

UK No 1 ★ UK Top 10 ● UK million seller ◆ UK entry at No 1 ■ US No 1 ▲

Vince GILL – See Amy GRANT

GILLAN ⌁ *UK, male vocal/instrumental group* — 46 wks

14 Jun 80	SLEEPIN' ON THE JOB *Virgin VS 355*	55	3
4 Oct 80	TROUBLE *Virgin VS 377*	14	6
14 Feb 81	MUTUALLY ASSURED DESTRUCTION *Virgin VS 103*	32	5
21 Mar 81	NEW ORLEANS *Virgin VS 406*	17	10
20 Jun 81	NO LAUGHING IN HEAVEN *Virgin VS 425*	31	6
10 Oct 81	NIGHTMARE *Virgin VS 441*	36	6
23 Jan 82	RESTLESS *Virgin VS 465*	25	7
4 Sep 82	LIVING FOR THE CITY *Virgin VS 519*	50	3

GILLETTE – See 20 FINGERS

Stuart GILLIES € *UK, male vocalist* — 10 wks

31 Mar 73	AMANDA *Philips 6006 293*	13	10

Jimmy GILMER – See FIREBALLS

James GILREATH *US, male vocalist* — 10 wks

2 May 63	LITTLE BAND OF GOLD *Pye International 7N 25190*	29	10

Jim GILSTRAP ◢ ♪ *US, male vocalist* — 11 wks

15 Mar 75 ●	SWING YOUR DADDY *Chelsea 2005 021*	4	11

Gordon GILTRAP *UK, male instrumentalist – guitar* — 10 wks

14 Jan 78	HEARTSONG *Electric WOT 19*	21	7
28 Apr 79	FEAR OF THE DARK *Electric WOT 29* [1]	58	3

[1] Gordon Giltrap Band

GIN BLOSSOMS *US, male vocal/instrumental group* — 12 wks

5 Feb 94	HEY JEALOUSY *Fontana GINCD 3*	24	5
16 Apr 94	FOUND OUT ABOUT YOU *Fontana GINCD 4*	40	3
10 Feb 96	TIL I HEAR IT FROM YOU *A & M 5812272*	39	2
27 Apr 96	FOLLOW YOU DOWN *A & M 5815512*	30	2

GINGERBREADS – See GOLDIE and the GINGERBREADS

GINUWINE ⓡ&ⓑ *US, male rapper* — 18 wks

25 Jan 97	PONY *Epic 6641282*	16	6
24 May 97	TELL ME DO U WANNA *Epic 6645272*	16	3
6 Sep 97 ●	WHEN DOVES CRY *Epic 6649245*	10	5
14 Mar 98	HOLLER *Epic 6653372*	13	4

GIPSY KINGS *France, male vocal/instrumental group* — 2 wks

3 Sep 94	HITS MEDLEY *Columbia 6606022*	53	2

Martine GIRAULT *UK, female vocalist* — 7 wks

29 Aug 92	REVIVAL *ffrr FX 195*	53	2
30 Jan 93	REVIVAL (re-issue) *ffrr FCD 205*	37	3
28 Oct 95	BEEN THINKING ABOUT YOU *RCA 74321316142*	63	1
1 Feb 97	REVIVAL (re-mix) *RCA 74321432162*	61	1

GIRL *UK, male vocal/instrumental group* — 3 wks

12 Apr 80	HOLLYWOOD TEASE *Jet 176*	50	3

GIRLFRIEND *Australia, female vocal group* — 6 wks

30 Jan 93	TAKE IT FROM ME *Arista 74321114252*	47	4
15 May 93	GIRL'S LIFE *Arista 74321138452*	68	2

GIRLSCHOOL ⌁ *UK, female vocal/instrumental group* — 25 wks

2 Aug 80	RACE WITH THE DEVIL *Bronze BRO 100*	49	6
21 Feb 81 ●	ST. VALENTINE'S DAY MASSACRE EP *Bronze BRO 116* [1]	5	8
11 Apr 81	HIT AND RUN *Bronze BRO 118*	32	6
11 Jul 81	C'MON LET'S GO *Bronze BRO 126*	42	3

3 Apr 82	WILDLIFE EP *Bronze BRO 144*	58	2

[1] Motorhead and Girlschool (also known as Headgirl)

Tracks on St. Valentine's Day Massacre (EP): Please Don't Touch / Emergency / Bomber. Tracks on Wildlife (EP): Don't Call It Love / Wildlife / Don't Stop

Junior GISCOMBE – See JUNIOR

GLADIATORS – See NERO and the GLADIATORS

GLADIATORS *UK, male/female vocal group* — 1 wk

30 Nov 96	THE BOYS ARE BACK IN TOWN *RCA 74321417002*	70	1

GLAM *Italy, male instrumental/production group* — 2 wks

1 May 93	HELL'S PARTY *Six6 SIXCD 001*	42	2

GLAM METAL DETECTIVES *UK, male/female vocal group* — 2 wks

11 Mar 95	EVERYBODY UP! *ZTT ZANG 62CD*	29	2

GLAMMA KID *UK, male vocalist/rapper* — 1 wk

21 Nov 98	FASHION '98 *WEA WEA 179CD*	49	1

GLASS TIGER *Canada, male vocal/instrumental group* — 18 wks

18 Oct 86	DON'T FORGET ME (WHEN I'M GONE) *Manhattan MT 13*	29	9
31 Jan 87	SOMEDAY *Manhattan MT 17*	66	2
26 Oct 91	MY TOWN *EMI EM 212*	33	7

'My Town' features the uncredited vocals of Rod Stewart

Mayson GLEN ORCHESTRA – See Paul HENRY and the Mayson GLEN ORCHESTRA

GLENN and CHRIS ◐ *UK, male vocal duo* — 8 wks

18 Apr 87	DIAMOND LIGHTS *Record Shack KICK 1*	12	8

Gary GLITTER ◐ *Glitter rock giant, b. Paul Gadd, 8 May, 1940, Oxfordshire. Started recording in 1960 (as Paul Raven), and was first act to put first 11 hits into the Top 10. This singer/songwriter remained a popular live performer after the hits stopped* — 170 wks

10 Jun 72 ●	ROCK AND ROLL (PARTS 1 & 2) *Bell 1216*	2	15
23 Sep 72 ●	I DIDN'T KNOW I LOVED YOU (TILL I SAW YOU ROCK 'N' ROLL) *Bell 1259*	4	11
20 Jan 73 ●	DO YOU WANNA TOUCH ME? (OH YEAH) *Bell 1280*	2	11
7 Apr 73 ●	HELLO HELLO I'M BACK AGAIN *Bell 1299*	2	14
21 Jul 73 ★	I'M THE LEADER OF THE GANG (I AM) *Bell 1321*	1	12
17 Nov 73 ★	I LOVE YOU LOVE ME LOVE *Bell 1337* ◆ ■	1	14
30 Mar 74 ●	REMEMBER ME THIS WAY *Bell 1349*	3	8
15 Jun 74 ★	ALWAYS YOURS *Bell 1359*	1	9
23 Nov 74 ●	OH YES! YOU'RE BEAUTIFUL *Bell 1391*	2	10
3 May 75 ●	LOVE LIKE YOU AND ME *Bell 1423*	10	6
21 Jun 75 ●	DOING ALRIGHT WITH THE BOYS *Bell 1429*	6	7
8 Nov 75	PAPA OOM MOW MOW *Bell 1451*	38	5
13 Mar 76	YOU BELONG TO ME *Bell 1473*	40	5
22 Jan 77	IT TAKES ALL NIGHT LONG *Arista 85*	25	6
16 Jul 77	A LITTLE BOOGIE WOOGIE IN THE BACK OF MY MIND *Arista 112*	31	5
20 Sep 80	GARY GLITTER EP *GTO GT 282*	57	3
10 Oct 81	AND THEN SHE KISSED ME *Bell BELL 1497*	39	5
5 Dec 81	ALL THAT GLITTERS *Bell BELL 1498*	48	5
23 Jun 84	DANCE ME UP *Arista ARIST 570*	25	5
1 Dec 84 ●	ANOTHER ROCK AND ROLL CHRISTMAS *Arista ARIST 592*	7	7
10 Oct 92	AND THE LEADER ROCKS ON *EMI EM 252*	58	2
21 Nov 92	THROUGH THE YEARS *EMI EM 256*	49	3
16 Dec 95	HELLO HELLO I'M BACK AGAIN (AGAIN!) *Carlton Sounds 3036000192*	50	2

'Rock and Roll Part 1' not listed with 'Part 2' for weeks of 10 and 17 Jun, 1972. Tracks on Gary Glitter (EP): I'm the Leader of the Gang (I Am) / Rock and Roll (Part 2) / Hello Hello I'm Back Again / Do You Wanna Touch Me? (Oh Yeah). All were re-issues. 'Hello Hello I'm Back Again (Again!)' in 1995 is a re-recording

What: *When I Fall in Love*   **41**
Who: Nat 'King' Cole
When: 1957 (3), 1987 (4)
Which: Despite no US chart success, twice visited the UK Top 5. It returned 23 years after his death, and just before his daughter, Natalie, took this standout ballad into US chart

What: *Cara Mia*   **42**
Who: David Whitfield
When: 1954 (1)
Which: Earned this big-voiced British balladeer a US gold disc – a rare feat in the 1950s. This song, which topped the chart for ten weeks, was co-written by Mantovani, whose orchestra backed him on the single

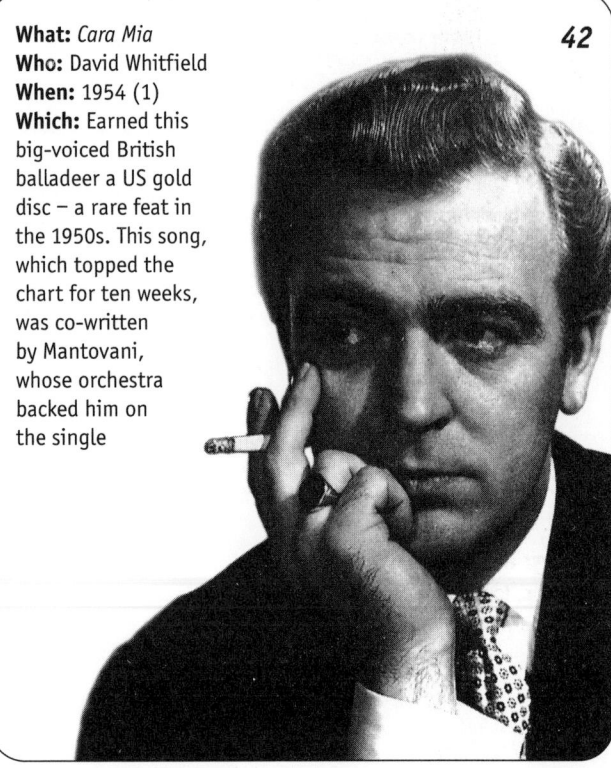

What: *The Last Waltz*   **43**
Who: Engelbert Humperdinck
When: 1967 (1)
Which: Aptly became the standard closing number in dance halls and ballrooms all over the country. It is the Vegas veteran's top seller and his biggest worldwide success

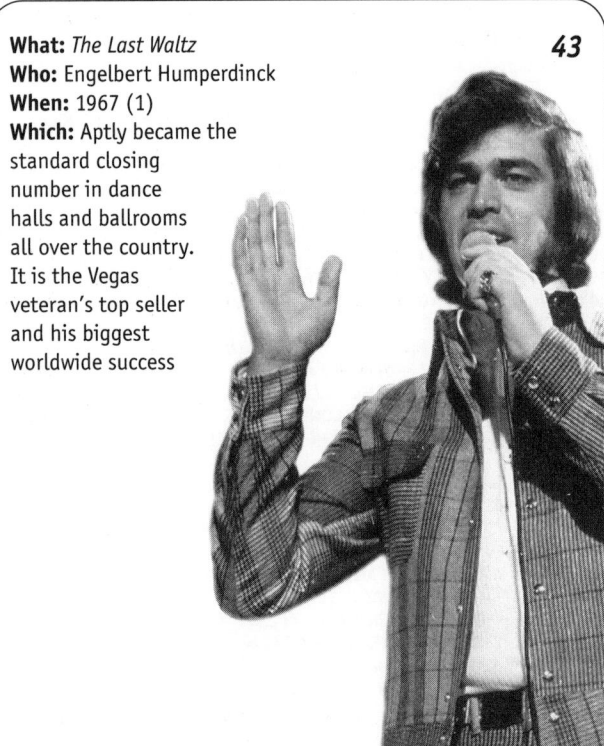

What: *Reach Out I'll Be There*   **44**
Who: Four Tops
When: 1966 (1), 1988 (11 – remix)
Which: Is considered the epitome of the Motown Sound. The famed foursome's only UK No 1, like many Motown hits of the time, was produced and written by Holland, Dozier and Holland

GLITTER BAND ☉ *UK, male vocal/instrumental group*   60 wks

23 Mar 74	●	ANGEL FACE *Bell 1348*	....4 10
3 Aug 74	●	JUST FOR YOU *Bell 1368*	....10 8
19 Oct 74	●	LET'S GET TOGETHER AGAIN *Bell 1383*	....8 8
18 Jan 75	●	GOODBYE MY LOVE *Bell 1395*	....2 9
12 Apr 75	●	THE TEARS I CRIED *Bell 1416*	....8 8
9 Aug 75		LOVE IN THE SUN *Bell 1437*	....15 8
28 Feb 76	●	PEOPLE LIKE YOU AND PEOPLE LIKE ME *Bell 1471*	....5 9

GLOBAL COMMUNICATION
UK, male instrumental/production duo   1 wk

11 Jan 97	THE WAY/THE DEEP *Dedicated GLOBA 002CD*	....51 1

GLOVE *UK, male vocal/instrumental group*   3 wks

20 Aug 83	LIKE AN ANIMAL *Wonderland SHE 3*	....52 3

GLOWORM ☺ *UK/US, male vocal/instrumental group*   17 wks

6 Feb 93		I LIFT MY CUP *Pulse 8 CDLOSE 37*	....20 4
14 May 94	●	CARRY ME HOME *Go.Beat GODCD 112*	....9 11
6 Aug 94		I LIFT MY CUP (re-issue) *Pulse 8 CDLOSE 67*	....46 2

GO GO LORENZO and the DAVIS PINCKNEY PROJECT
US, male vocal/instrumental group   8 wks

6 Dec 86	YOU CAN DANCE (IF YOU WANT TO) *Boiling Point POSP 836*	....46 8

GO-GOs *US, female vocal/instrumental group*   10 wks

15 May 82	OUR LIPS ARE SEALED *IRS GDN 102*	....47 6
26 Jan 91	COOL JERK *IRS AM 712*	....60 1
18 Feb 95	THE WHOLE WORLD LOST ITS HEAD *IRS CDEIRS 190*	....29 3

GO WEST ☉ *UK, male vocal/instrumental duo*   85 wks

23 Feb 85	●	WE CLOSE OUR EYES *Chrysalis CHS 2850*	....5 14
11 May 85		CALL ME *Chrysalis GOW 1*	....12 10
3 Aug 85		GOODBYE GIRL *Chrysalis GOW 2*	....25 7
23 Nov 85		DON'T LOOK DOWN – THE SEQUEL *Chrysalis GOW 3*	....13 10
29 Nov 86		TRUE COLOURS *Chrysalis GOW 4*	....48 7
9 May 87		I WANT TO HEAR IT FROM YOU *Chrysalis GOW 5*	....43 3
12 Sep 87		THE KING IS DEAD *Chrysalis GOW 6*	....67 2
28 Jul 90		THE KING OF WISHFUL THINKING *Chrysalis GOW 8*	....18 10
17 Oct 92		FAITHFUL *Chrysalis GOW 9*	....13 6
16 Jan 93		WHAT YOU WON'T DO FOR LOVE *Chrysalis CDGOWS 10*	....15 5
27 Mar 93		STILL IN LOVE *Chrysalis CDGOWS 11*	....43 3
2 Oct 93		TRACKS OF MY TEARS *Chrysalis CDGOWS 12*	....16 5
4 Dec 93		WE CLOSE OUR EYES (re-mix) *Chrysalis CDGOWS 13*	....40 3

See also Peter COX

GOATS *US, male rap group*   2 wks

29 May 93	AAAH D YAAA/TYPICAL AMERICAN *Ruff House 6593032*	....53 2

'Typical American' only listed from 5 Jun, 1993, peaking at No 65

GOD MACHINE *US, male vocal/instrumental group*   2 wks

30 Jan 93	HOME *Fiction FICCD 47*	....65 2

GODIEGO *Japan/US, male vocal/instrumental group*   11 wks

15 Oct 77	THE WATER MARGIN *BBC RESL 50*	....37 4
16 Feb 80	GANDHARA *BBC RESL 66*	....56 7

'The Water Margin' is the English version of the song, which shared chart credit with the Japanese language version by Pete Mac Jr

GODLEY and CREME ☉ *UK, male vocal/instrumental duo*   36 wks

12 Sep 81	●	UNDER YOUR THUMB *Polydor POSP 322*	....3 11
21 Nov 81	●	WEDDING BELLS *Polydor POSP 369*	....7 11
30 Mar 85		CRY *Polydor POSP 732*	....19 11
16 Aug 86		CRY (re-entry) *Polydor POSP 732*	....66 3

GOD'S PROPERTY *US, male/female gospel choir*   1 wk

22 Nov 97	STOMP *B-rite Music IND 95559*	....60 1

Andrew GOLD ☉ *US, male vocalist/instrumentalist – piano*   36 wks

2 Apr 77		LONELY BOY *Asylum K 13076*	....11 9
25 Mar 78	●	NEVER LET HER SLIP AWAY *Asylum K 13112*	....5 13
24 Jun 78		HOW CAN THIS BE LOVE *Asylum K 13126*	....19 10
14 Oct 78		THANK YOU FOR BEING A FRIEND *Asylum K 13135*	....42 4

GOLD BLADE *UK, male vocal / instrumental group*   1 wk

22 Mar 97	STRICTLY HARDCORE *Ultimate TOPP 056CD*	....64 1

Brian and Tony GOLD – *See RED DRAGON with Brian and Tony GOLD*

GOLDBUG ☺ *UK, male/female vocal/instrumental group*   5 wks

27 Jan 96	●	WHOLE LOTTA LOVE *Acid Jazz JAZID 125CD*	....3 5

GOLDEN EARRING ✒ *Holland, male vocal/instrumental group*   16 wks

8 Dec 73	●	RADAR LOVE *Track 2094 116*	....7 13
8 Oct 77		RADAR LOVE *Polydor 2121 335*	....44 3

These are two different recordings of the same song

GOLDEN GIRLS *UK, male producer / instrumentalist*   2 wks

3 Oct 98	KINETIC *Distinctive DISNCD 46*	....38 2

GOLDIE ☉ *UK, male vocal/instrumental group*   11 wks

27 May 78	●	MAKING UP AGAIN *Bronze BRO 50*	....7 11

GOLDIE ☺ *UK, male producer*   16 wks

3 Dec 94	INNER CITY LIFE *ffrr FCD 251*	[1]	....49 2
9 Sep 95	ANGEL *ffrr FCD 266*		....41 3
11 Nov 95	INNER CITY LIFE (re-mix) *ffrr FCD 267*		....39 2
1 Nov 97	DIGITAL *ffrr FCD 316*	[2]	....13 3
24 Jan 98	TEMPERTEMPER *ffrr FCD 325*	[2]	....13 4
18 Apr 98	BELIEVE *ffrr FCD 332*		....36 2

[1] Goldie presents Metalheads [2] Goldie featuring KRS One

GOLDIE and the GINGERBREADS
US, female vocal/instrumental group   5 wks

25 Feb 65	CAN'T YOU HEAR MY HEART BEAT? *Decca F 12070*	....25 5

Bobby GOLDSBORO ☉ *US, male vocalist*   47 wks

17 Apr 68	●	HONEY *United Artists UP2215* ▲	....2 15
4 Aug 73	●	SUMMER (THE FIRST TIME) *United Artists UP35558*	....9 10
3 Aug 74		HELLO SUMMERTIME *United Artists UP35705*	....14 10
29 Mar 75	●	HONEY (re-issue) *United Artists UP35633*	....2 12

Glen GOLDSMITH ☺ ✒ *UK, male vocalist*   24 wks

7 Nov 87	I WON'T CRY *Reproduction PB 41493*	....34 7
12 Mar 88	DREAMING *Reproduction PB 41711*	....12 11
11 Jun 88	WHAT YOU SEE IS WHAT YOU GET *Reproduction PB 42075*	....33 5
3 Sep 88	SAVE A LITTLE BIT *Reproduction PB 42147*	....73 1

GOMEZ *UK, male vocal / instrumental group*   5 wks

11 Apr 98	78 STONE WOBBLE *Hut HUTCD 95*	....44 1
13 Jun 98	GET MYSELF ARRESTED *Hut HUTCD 97*	....45 1
12 Sep 98	WHIPPIN' PICCADILLY *Hut HUTCD 105*	....35 3

Leroy GOMEZ – *See SANTA ESMERALDA and Leroy GOMEZ*

GOMPIE ☉ *Holland, male vocal/instrumental group*   12 wks

20 May 95	ALICE (WHO THE X IS ALICE) (LIVING NEXT DOOR TO ALICE) *Habana HABSCD 5*	....34 5
2 Sep 95	ALICE (WHO THE X IS ALICE) (LIVING NEXT DOOR TO ALICE) (re-entry) *Habana HABSCD 5*	....17 7

GONZALEZ ♪ UK/US, male vocal/instrumental group — 11 wks
31 Mar 79	HAVEN'T STOPPED DANCING YET Sidewalk SID 102	15	11

GOO GOO DOLLS US, male vocal/instrumental trio — 1 wk
1 Aug 98	IRIS Reprise W 0449CD	50	1

GOOD GIRLS US, female vocal group — 1 wk
24 Jul 93	JUST CALL ME Motown TMGCD 1417	75	1

GOODBYE MR. MACKENZIE
UK, male/female vocal/instrumental group — 13 wks
20 Aug 88	GOODBYE MR MACKENZIE Capitol CL 501	62	2
11 Mar 89	THE RATTLER Capitol CL 522	37	6
29 Jul 89	GOODWILL CITY/I'M SICK OF YOU Capitol CL 538	49	2
21 Apr 90	LOVE CHILD Parlophone R 6247	52	2
23 Jun 90	BLACKER THAN BLACK Parlophone R 6257	61	1

GOODFELLAZ US, male vocal trio — 2 wks
10 May 97	SUGAR HONEY ICE TEA Wild Card 5736132	25	2

GOODIES ☺ UK, male vocal group — 38 wks
7 Dec 74 ●	THE IN BETWEENIES/FATHER CHRISTMAS DO NOT TOUCH ME Bradley's BRAD 7421	7	9
15 Mar 75 ●	FUNKY GIBBON/SICK MAN BLUES Bradley's BRAD 7504	4	10
21 Jun 75	BLACK PUDDING BERTHA (THE QUEEN OF NORTHERN SOUL) Bradley's BRAD 7517	19	7
27 Sep 75	NAPPY LOVE/WILD THING Bradley's BRAD 7524	21	6
13 Dec 75	MAKE A DAFT NOISE FOR CHRISTMAS Bradley's BRAD 7533	20	6

Cuba GOODING US, male vocalist — 2 wks
19 Nov 83	HAPPINESS IS JUST AROUND THE BEND London LON 41	72	2

GOODMEN ☺ Holland, male instrumental/production duo — 19 wks
7 Aug 93	GIVE IT UP Fresh Fruit TABCD 118	23	5
9 Oct 93 ●	GIVE IT UP (re-entry) Fresh Fruit TABCD 118	5	14

Ron GOODWIN ℭ UK, orchestra — 24 wks
15 May 53 ●	TERRY'S THEME FROM 'LIMELIGHT' Parlophone R 3686	3	23
28 Oct 55	BLUE STAR (THE MEDIC THEME) Parlophone R 4074	20	1

See also Eamonn ANDREWS

GOODY GOODY US, female vocal duo — 5 wks
2 Dec 78	NUMBER ONE DEE JAY Atlantic LV 3	55	5

GOOMBAY DANCE BAND ☺
Germany/Montserrat, male/female vocal/instrumental group — 16 wks
27 Feb 82 ★	SEVEN TEARS Epic EPC A 1242	1	12
15 May 82	SUN OF JAMAICA Epic EPC A 2345	50	4

GOONS ☺ UK, male vocal group — 30 wks
29 Jun 56 ●	I'M WALKING BACKWARDS FOR CHRISTMAS/ BLUEBOTTLE BLUES Decca F 10756	4	10
14 Sep 56 ●	BLOODNOK'S ROCK 'N' ROLL CALL/YING TONG SONG Decca E 10780	3	10
21 Jul 73 ●	YING TONG SONG (re-issue) Decca F 13414	9	10

'Bluebottle Blues' only listed from 13 Jul, 1956. It peaked at No 5

Lonnie GORDON ☺ ☺ US, female vocalist — 23 wks
24 Jun 89	(I'VE GOT YOUR) PLEASURE CONTROL ffrr F 106 [1]	60	3
27 Jan 90 ●	HAPPENIN' ALL OVER AGAIN Supreme SUPE 159	4	10
11 Aug 90	BEYOND YOUR WILDEST DREAMS Supreme SUPE 167	48	2
17 Nov 90	IF I HAVE TO STAND ALONE Supreme SUPE 181	68	1
4 May 91	GONNA CATCH YOU Supreme SUPE 185	32	5

7 Oct 95	LOVE EVICTION X:Plode BANG 2CD [2]	32	2

[1] Simon Harris featuring Lonnie Gordon [2] Quartz Lock featuring Lonnie Gordon

Lesley GORE ☺ US, female vocalist — 20 wks
20 Jun 63 ●	IT'S MY PARTY Mercury AMT 1205 ▲	9	12
24 Sep 64	MAYBE I KNOW Mercury MF 829	20	8

GORKY'S ZYGOTIC MYNCI
UK, male/female vocal/instrumental group — 5 wks
9 Nov 96	PATIO SONG Fontana GZMCD 1	41	1
29 Mar 97	DIAMOND DEW Fontana GZMCD 2	42	1
21 Jun 97	YOUNG GIRLS & HAPPY ENDINGS/DARK NIGHT Fontana GZMCD 3	49	1
6 Jun 98	SWEET JOHNNY Fontana GZMCD 4	60	1
29 Aug 98	LETS GET TOGETHER (IN OUR MINDS) Fontana GZMCD 5	43	1

Eydie GORME ℭ US, female vocalist — 33 wks
24 Jan 58	LOVE ME FOREVER HMV POP 432	21	5
21 Jun 62 ●	YES MY DARLING DAUGHTER CBS AAG 105	10	9
31 Jan 63	BLAME IT ON THE BOSSA NOVA CBS AAG 131	32	6
22 Aug 63	I WANT TO STAY HERE CBS AAG 163 [1]	3	13

[1] Steve and Eydie

G.O.S.H. UK, male/female charity ensemble — 11 wks
28 Nov 87	THE WISHING WELL MBS GOSH 1	22	11

Luke GOSS and the BAND OF THIEVES
UK, male vocal/instrumental group — 3 wks
12 Jun 93	SWEETER THAN THE MIDNIGHT RAIN Sabre CDSAB 1	52	2
21 Aug 93	GIVE ME ONE MORE CHANCE Sabre CDSAB 2	68	1

Matt GOSS UK, male vocalist — 5 wks
26 Aug 95	THE KEY Atlas 5811532	40	2
27 Apr 96	IF YOU WERE HERE TONIGHT Atlas 5762932	23	3

Nigel GOULDING – See Abigail MEAD and Nigel GOULDING

Graham GOULDMAN UK, male vocalist — 4 wks
23 Jun 79	SUNBURN Mercury SUNNY 1	52	4

GQ US, male vocal/instrumental group — 6 wks
10 Mar 79	DISCO NIGHTS (ROCK FREAK) Arista ARIST 245	42	6

GRACE ☺ UK, female vocalist — 20 wks
8 Apr 95 ●	NOT OVER YET Perfecto PERF 104CD	6	8
23 Sep 95	I WANT TO LIVE Perfecto PERF 109CD	30	2
24 Feb 96	SKIN ON SKIN Perfecto PERF 116CD	21	3
1 Jun 96	DOWN TO EARTH Perfecto PERF 120CD	20	2
28 Sep 96	IF I COULD FLY Perfecto PERF 127CD	29	2
3 May 97	HAND IN HAND Perfecto PERF 129CD	38	1
26 Jul 97	DOWN TO EARTH Perfecto PERF 142CD1	29	2

GRACE BROTHERS UK, male instrumental duo — 1 wk
20 Apr 96	ARE YOU BEING SERVED EMI Premier PRESCD 1	51	1

Charlie GRACIE ♪ US, male vocalist — 41 wks
19 Apr 57	BUTTERFLY Parlophone R 4290	12	8
14 Jun 57 ●	FABULOUS Parlophone R 4313	8	16
23 Aug 57	I LOVE YOU SO MUCH IT HURTS/WANDERIN' EYES London HLU 8467	14	2
6 Sep 57 ●	WANDERIN' EYES London HLU 8467	6	12
6 Sep 57	I LOVE YOU SO MUCH IT HURTS London HLU 8467	20	2
10 Jan 58	COOL BABY London HLU 8521	26	1

'I Love You So Much It Hurts' and 'Wanderin' Eyes' were listed together for two weeks, then listed separately for a further two and 12 weeks respectively

UK No 1 ★ UK Top 10 ● UK million seller ◆ UK entry at No 1 ■ US No 1 ▲

UK No 1 ★   UK Top 10 ●   UK million seller ◆   UK entry at No 1 ■   US No 1 ▲

GRAVEDIGGAZ 🎤 US, male rap group — 6 wks

11 Mar 95	SIX FEET DEEP EP Gee Street GESCD 62	64	1
5 Aug 95	THE HELL EP Fourth & Broadway BRCD 326 [1]	12	3
24 Jan 98	THE NIGHT THE EARTH CRIED Gee Street GEE 5001013	44	1
25 Apr 98	UNEXPLAINED Gee Street GEE 5001623	48	1

[1] Tricky vs the Gravediggaz

Tracks on Six Feet Deep (EP): Bang Your Head / Mommy / Suicide.
Tracks on The Hell (EP): Hell Is Round the Corner / Hell Is Round the
Corner (remix) / Psychosis / Tonite Is a Special Nite

Dobie GRAY US, male vocalist — 11 wks

| 25 Feb 65 | THE IN CROWD London HL 9953 | 25 | 7 |
| 27 Sep 75 | OUT ON THE FLOOR Black Magic BM 107 | 42 | 4 |

Dorian GRAY UK, male vocalist — 7 wks

| 27 Mar 68 | I'VE GOT YOU ON MY MIND Parlophone R 5667 | 36 | 7 |

Les GRAY UK, male vocalist — 5 wks

| 26 Feb 77 | A GROOVY KIND OF LOVE Warner Bros. K 16883 | 32 | 5 |

Barry GRAY ORCHESTRA UK, orchestra — 8 wks

| 11 Jul 81 | THUNDERBIRDS PRT 7P 216 | 61 | 2 |
| 14 Jun 86 | JOE 90 / CAPTAIN SCARLET THEME PRT 7PX 345 [1] | 53 | 6 |

[1] Barry Gray Orchestra with Peter Beckett – keyboards

Alltrina GRAYSON – See Wilton FELDER

GREAT WHITE US, male vocal/instrumental group — 5 wks

24 Feb 90	HOUSE OF BROKEN LOVE Capitol CL 562	44	2
16 Feb 91	CONGO SQUARE Capitol CL 605	62	1
7 Sep 91	CALL IT ROCK 'N' ROLL Capitol CL 625	67	2

Buddy GRECO US, male vocalist — 8 wks

| 7 Jul 60 | LADY IS A TRAMP Fontana H 225 | 26 | 8 |

GREED – See Ricardo DA FORCE

GREEDIES Ireland/UK/US, male vocal/instrumental group — 5 wks

| 15 Dec 79 | A MERRY JINGLE Vertigo GREED 1 | 28 | 5 |

Al GREEN 🎤 US, male vocalist — 68 wks

9 Oct 71	● TIRED OF BEING ALONE London HL 10337	4	13
8 Jan 72	● LET'S STAY TOGETHER London HL 10348 ▲	7	12
20 May 72	LOOK WHAT YOU DONE FOR ME London HL 10369	44	4
19 Aug 72	I'M STILL IN LOVE WITH YOU London HL 10382	35	5
16 Nov 74	SHA-LA-LA (MAKE ME HAPPY) London HL 10470	20	11
15 Mar 75	L. O. V. E. London HL 10482	24	8
3 Dec 88	PUT A LITTLE LOVE IN YOUR HEART A & M AM 484 [1]	28	8
21 Oct 89	THE MESSAGE IS LOVE Breakout USA 668 [2]	38	5
2 Oct 93	LOVE IS A BEAUTIFUL THING Arista 74321162692	56	2

[1] Annie Lennox and Al Green [2] Arthur Baker and the Backbeat Disciples featuring Al Green

Dotty GREEN – See Mark FISHER featuring Dotty GREEN

Jesse GREEN 🎤 Jamaica, male vocalist — 26 wks

7 Aug 76	NICE AND SLOW EMI 2492	17	12
18 Dec 76	FLIP EMI 2564	26	8
11 Jun 77	COME WITH ME EMI 2615	29	6

Robson GREEN and Jerome FLYNN – See ROBSON and JEROME

GREEN DAY 🎸 US, male vocal/instrumental group — 34 wks

20 Aug 94	BASKET CASE Reprise W 0257CD	55	2
29 Oct 94	WELCOME TO PARADISE Reprise W 0269CDX	20	3
28 Jan 95	● BASKET CASE (re-issue) Reprise W 0279CD	7	6
18 Mar 95	LONGVIEW Reprise W 0278CD	30	3
20 May 95	WHEN I COME AROUND Reprise W 0294CD	27	3
7 Oct 95	GEEK STINK BREATH Reprise W 0320CD	16	3
6 Jan 96	STUCK WITH ME Reprise W 0327CD	24	3
6 Jul 96	BRAIN STEW / JADED Reprise W 0339CD	28	2
11 Oct 97	HITCHIN' A RIDE Reprise W 0424CD	25	2
31 Jan 98	TIME OF YOUR LIFE (GOOD RIDDANCE) Reprise W 0430CD1	11	5
9 May 98	REDUNDANT Reprise W 0438CD1	27	2

GREEN JELLY 🎸 US, male vocal/instrumental group — 15 wks

5 Jun 93	● THREE LITTLE PIGS Zoo 74321151422	5	8
14 Aug 93	ANARCHY IN THE UK Zoo 74321159052	27	3
25 Dec 93	I'M THE LEADER OF THE GANG Arista 74321174892 [1]	25	4

[1] Hulk Hogan with Green Jelly

Norman GREENBAUM 🌀 US, male vocalist — 20 wks

| 21 Mar 70 | ★ SPIRIT IN THE SKY Reprise RS 20885 | 1 | 20 |

Lorne GREENE Canada, male vocalist — 8 wks

| 17 Dec 64 | RINGO RCA 1428 ▲ | 22 | 8 |

Lee GREENWOOD US, male vocalist — 6 wks

| 19 May 84 | THE WIND BENEATH MY WINGS MCA 877 | 49 | 6 |

Iain GREGORY UK, male vocalist — 2 wks

| 4 Jan 62 | CAN'T YOU HEAR THE BEAT OF A BROKEN HEART Pye 7N 15397 | 39 | 2 |

Johnny GREGORY – See CHAQUITO

Band of the GRENADIER GUARDS – See ST. JOHN'S COLLEGE SCHOOL CHOIR and the Band of the GRENADIER GUARDS

GREYHOUND 🌴 Jamaica, male vocal/instrumental group — 33 wks

26 Jun 71	● BLACK AND WHITE Trojan TR 7820	6	13
8 Jan 72	MOON RIVER Trojan TR 7848	12	11
25 Mar 72	I AM WHAT I AM Trojan TR 7853	20	9

GRID ☺ UK, male instrumental/production duo — 47 wks

7 Jul 90	FLOATATION East West YZ 475	60	2
29 Sep 90	A BEAT CALLED LOVE East West YZ 498	64	4
25 Jul 92	FIGURE OF 8 Virgin VSTG 1421	50	3
3 Oct 92	HEARTBEAT Virgin VST 1427	72	2
13 Mar 93	CRYSTAL CLEAR Virgin VSCDT 1442	27	4
30 Oct 93	TEXAS COWBOYS Deconstruction 74321167762	21	3
4 Jun 94	● SWAMP THING Deconstruction 74321205842	3	17
17 Sep 94	ROLLERCOASTER Deconstruction 74321230772	19	4
3 Dec 94	TEXAS COWBOYS (re-issue) Deconstruction 74321244032	17	6
23 Sep 95	DIABLO Deconstruction 74321308402	32	2

Zaine GRIFF New Zealand, male vocalist — 6 wks

| 16 Feb 80 | TONIGHT Automatic K 17547 | 54 | 3 |
| 31 May 80 | ASHES AND DIAMONDS Automatic K 17610 | 68 | 3 |

Billy GRIFFIN 🎤 US, male vocalist — 12 wks

| 8 Jan 83 | HOLD ME TIGHTER IN THE RAIN CBS A 2935 | 17 | 9 |
| 14 Jan 84 | SERIOUS CBS A 4053 | 64 | 3 |

Clive GRIFFIN UK, male vocalist — 5 wks

| 24 Jun 89 | HEAD ABOVE WATER Mercury STEP 4 | 60 | 2 |
| 11 May 91 | I'LL BE WAITING Mercury STEP 6 | 56 | 3 |

Roni GRIFFITH US, female vocalist — 4 wks

| 30 Jun 84 | (THE BEST PART OF) BREAKING UP Making Waves SURF 101 | 63 | 4 |

GRIMETHORPE COLLIERY BAND – See Peter SKELLERN

GROOVE CONNEKTION 2 *UK, male producer / instrumentalist*   **1 wk**

11 Apr 98	CLUB LONELY *XL Recordings XLT 94CD*	.54	1

GROOVE CORPORATION
UK/Italy, male/female vocal/instrumental group   **1 wk**

16 Apr 94	RAIN *Six6 SIXCD 109*	.71	1

GROOVE GANG – See DAFFY DUCK featuring the GROOVE GANG

GROOVE GENERATION *UK, male production group*   **3 wks**

8 Aug 98	YOU MAKE ME FEEL LIKE DANCING *Brothers Org. CDBRUV 8* [1]	.32	3

[1] Groove Generation featuring Leo Sayer

Jay GROOVE – See FANTASY UFO

GROOVE THEORY *UK, male vocal/instrumental duo*   **3 wks**

18 Nov 95	TELL ME *Epic 6623882*	.31	3

GROOVERIDER *UK, male DJ/producer*   **2 wks**

26 Sep 98	RAINBOWS OF COLOUR *Higher Ground HIGHS 13CD*	.40	2

Scott GROOVES *US, male DJ/producer*   **2 wks**

16 May 98	EXPANSIONS *Soma Recordings SOMA 65CDS* [1]	.68	1
28 Nov 98	MOTHERSHIP RECONNECTION *Soma Recordings SOMA 71CDS*	.55	1

[1] Scott Grooves featuring Roy Ayers

Henry GROSS *US, male vocalist*   **4 wks**

28 Aug 76	SHANNON *Life Song ELS 45002*	.32	4

GROUND LEVEL *Australia, male instrumental/production group*   **2 wks**

30 Jan 93	DREAMS OF HEAVEN *Faze 2 CDFAZE 14*	.54	2

GROUP THERAPY *US, male rap group*   **1 wk**

30 Nov 96	EAST COAST/WEST COAST KILLAS *Interscope IND 95516*	.51	1

Boring Bob GROVER – See PIRANHAS

GSP *UK, male instrumental/production duo*   **3 wks**

3 Oct 92	THE BANANA SONG *Yoyo YOYO 1*	.37	3

GTO *UK, male/female instrumental/production duo*   **7 wks**

4 Aug 90	PURE *Cooltempo COOL 218*	.57	3
7 Sep 91	LISTEN TO THE RHYTHM FLOW/BULLFROG *React REACT 7001*	.72	2
2 May 92	ELEVATION *React REACT 4*	.59	2

GTO are also Tricky Disco and Technohead
See also TRICKY DISCO; TECHNOHEAD

GUESS WHO *Canada, male vocal/instrumental group*   **14 wks**

16 Feb 67	HIS GIRL *King KG 1044*	.45	1
9 May 70	AMERICAN WOMAN ▲ *RCA 1943*	.45	2
30 May 70	AMERICAN WOMAN (re-entry) *RCA 1943*	.19	11

GUN *UK, male vocal/instrumental group*   **11 wks**

20 Nov 68	● RACE WITH THE DEVIL *CBS 3734*	.8	11

GUN ◐ *UK, male vocal/instrumental group*   **46 wks**

1 Jul 89	BETTER DAYS *A & M AM 505*	.33	9
16 Sep 89	MONEY (EVERYBODY LOVES HER) *A & M AM 520*	.73	2

11 Nov 89	INSIDE OUT *A & M AM 531*	.57	2
10 Feb 90	TAKING ON THE WORLD *A & M AM 541*	.50	3
14 Jul 90	SHAME ON YOU *A & M AM 573*	.33	4
14 Mar 92	STEAL YOUR FIRE *A & M AM 851*	.24	4
2 May 92	HIGHER GROUND *A & M AM 869*	.48	2
4 Jul 92	WELCOME TO THE REAL WORLD *A & M AM 885*	.43	2
9 Jul 94	● WORD UP *A & M 5806672*	.8	7
24 Sep 94	DON'T SAY IT'S OVER *A & M 5807572*	.19	3
25 Feb 95	THE ONLY ONE *A & M 5809552*	.29	3
15 Apr 95	SOMETHING WORTHWHILE *A & M 5810452*	.39	2
26 Apr 97	CRAZY YOU *A & M 5821932*	.21	2
12 Jul 97	MY SWEET JANE *A & M 5822792*	.51	1

GUNS 'N' ROSES
Often controversial Los Angeles-based band: W Axl Rose (b. William Bailey) (v), Slash (b. Saul Hudson) (g), Izzy Stradlin (b. Jeffrey Isbell) (g). It is the only act to hold the top two album spots in both the UK and the USA on the week of releasing both records: Use Your Illusion 1 and 2 in 1991   **107 wks**

3 Oct 87	WELCOME TO THE JUNGLE *Geffen GEF 30*	.67	2
20 Aug 88	SWEET CHILD O' MINE *Geffen GEF 43* ▲	.24	8
29 Oct 88	WELCOME TO THE JUNGLE/NIGHTRAIN (re-issue) *Geffen GEF 47*	.24	5
18 Mar 89	● PARADISE CITY *Geffen GEF 50*	.6	9
3 Jun 89	● SWEET CHILD O' MINE (re-mix) *Geffen GEF 55*	.6	9
1 Jul 89	● PATIENCE *Geffen GEF 56*	.10	7
2 Sep 89	NIGHTRAIN (re-issue) *Geffen GEF 60*	.17	5
13 Jul 91	● YOU COULD BE MINE *Geffen GFS 6*	.3	10
21 Sep 91	● DON'T CRY *Geffen GFS 9*	.8	4
21 Dec 91	● LIVE AND LET DIE *Geffen GFS 17*	.5	7
7 Mar 92	● NOVEMBER RAIN *Geffen GFS 18*	.4	5
23 May 92	● KNOCKIN' ON HEAVEN'S DOOR *Geffen GFS 21*	.2	9
21 Nov 92	● YESTERDAYS/NOVEMBER RAIN (re-issue) *Geffen GFS 27*	.8	9
29 May 93	THE CIVIL WAR EP *Geffen GEFSTD 43*	.11	3
20 Nov 93	● AIN'T IT FUN *Geffen GFSTD 62*	.9	3
4 Jun 94	● SINCE I DON'T HAVE YOU *Geffen GFSTD 70*	.10	6
14 Jan 95	● SYMPATHY FOR THE DEVIL *Geffen GFSTD 86*	.9	6

The re-issue of 'November Rain' was only listed from 28 Nov, 1992.
Tracks on The Civil War (EP): Civil War/Garden of Eden/Dead Horse/Interview

GURU *US, male instrumentalist*   **11 wks**

11 Sep 93	TRUST ME *Cooltempo CDCOOL 278* [1]	.34	2
13 Nov 93	NO TIME TO PLAY *Cooltempo CDCOOL 282* [2]	.25	3
19 Aug 95	WATCH WHAT YOU SAY *Cooltempo CDCOOL 308* [3]	.28	3
18 Nov 95	FEEL THE MUSIC *Cooltempo CDCOOLS 313*	.34	2
13 Jul 96	LIVIN' IN THIS WORLD/LIFESAVER *Cooltempo CDCOOL 320*	.61	1

[1] Guru featuring N'Dea Davenport   [2] Guru featuring D C Lee
[3] Guru featuring Chaka Khan

GURU JOSH ☺ *UK, male instrumental group*   **14 wks**

24 Feb 90	● INFINITY *Deconstruction PB 43475*	.5	10
16 Jun 90	WHOSE LAW (IS IT ANYWAY) *Deconstruction PB 43647*	.26	4

Adrian GURVITZ ◐ *UK, male vocalist*   **16 wks**

30 Jan 82	● CLASSIC *RAK 339*	.8	13
12 Jun 82	YOUR DREAM *RAK 343*	.61	3

GUS GUS *Iceland, male/female vocal/instrumental group*   **1 wk**

21 Feb 98	POLYESTERDAY *4AD BAD 8002CD*	.55	1

GUSTO ☺ *US, male producer – Edward Green*   **8 wks**

2 Mar 96	● DISCO'S REVENGE *Manifesto FESCD 6*	.9	5
7 Sep 96	LET'S ALL CHANT *Manifesto FESCD 13*	.21	3

Gwen GUTHRIE ♪ ☺ *US, female vocalist*   **25 wks**

19 Jul 86	● AIN'T NOTHING GOIN' ON BUT THE RENT *Boiling Point POSP 807*	.5	12
11 Oct 86	(THEY LONG TO BE) CLOSE TO YOU *Boiling Point POSP 822*	.25	7

14 Feb 87	GOOD TO GO LOVER/OUTSIDE IN THE RAIN		
	Boiling Point POSP 841........................	37	4
4 Sep 93	AIN'T NOTHIN' GOIN' ON BUT THE RENT (re-mix)		
	Polydor PZCD 276........................	42	2

GUY US, male vocal group — 4 wks
4 May 91	HER *MCA MCS 1575*........................	58	4

See also VARIOUS ARTISTS (EPs & LPs) – The New York Undercover (EP)

A GUY CALLED GERALD ☺
UK, male producer – Gerald Simpson — 23 wks
8 Apr 89	VOODOO RAY *Rham! RS 804*........................	55	8
24 Jun 89	VOODOO RAY (re-entry) *Rham! RS 804*........................	12	10
16 Dec 89	FX/EYES OF SORROW *Subscape AGCG 1*........................	52	5

GUYS and DOLLS ☺ UK, male/female vocal group — 33 wks
1 Mar 75	● THERE'S A WHOLE LOT OF LOVING *Magnet MAG 20*........................	2	11
17 May 75	HERE I GO AGAIN *Magnet MAG 30*........................	33	5
21 Feb 76	● YOU DON'T HAVE TO SAY YOU LOVE ME *Magnet MAG 50*	5	8
6 Nov 76	STONEY GROUND *Magnet MAG 76*........................	38	4
13 May 78	ONLY LOVIN' DOES IT *Magnet MAG 115*........................	42	5

Jonas GWANGWA – See George FENTON and Jonas GWANGWA

GYRES UK, male vocal/instrumental group — 2 wks
13 Apr 96	POP COP *Sugar SUGA 9CD*........................	71	1
6 Jul 96	ARE YOU READY *Sugar SUGA 11CD*........................	71	1

H

HABIT UK, male vocal/instrumental group — 2 wks
30 Apr 88	LUCY *Virgin VS 1063*........................	56	2

Steve HACKETT UK, male vocalist/instrumentalist – guitar — 2 wks
2 Apr 83	CELL 151 *Charisma CELL 1*........................	66	2

HADDAWAY ☺ Trinidad & Tobago, male vocalist — 52 wks
5 Jun 93	● WHAT IS LOVE *Logic 74321148502*........................	2	15
25 Sep 93	LIFE *Logic 74321164212*........................	6	9
18 Dec 93	I MISS YOU *Logic 74321181522*........................	9	14
2 Apr 94	● ROCK MY HEART *Logic 74321194122*........................	9	9
24 Jun 95	FLY AWAY *Logic 74321286942*........................	20	3
23 Sep 95	CATCH A FIRE *Logic 74321306652*........................	39	2

Tony HADLEY UK, male vocalist — 9 wks
7 Mar 92	LOST IN YOUR LOVE *EMI EM 222*........................	42	4
29 Aug 92	FOR YOUR BLUE EYES ONLY *EMI EM 234*........................	67	2
16 Jan 93	GAME OF LOVE *EMI CDEM 254*........................	72	1
10 May 97	DANCE WITH ME *VC VCRD 17* [1]........................	35	2

[1] Tin Tin Out featuring Tony Hadley

Sammy HAGAR US, male vocalist/instrumentalist – guitar — 15 wks
15 Dec 79	THIS PLANET'S ON FIRE/SPACE STATION NO. 5		
	Capitol CL 16114........................	52	5

16 Feb 80	I'VE DONE EVERYTHING FOR YOU *Capitol CL 16120*........................	36	5
24 May 80	HEARTBEAT/LOVE OR MONEY *Capitol RED 1*........................	67	2
16 Jan 82	PIECE OF MY HEART *Geffen GEFA 1884*........................	67	1
30 Jan 82	PIECE OF MY HEART (re-entry) *Geffen GEFA 1884*........................	67	2

Paul HAIG UK, male vocalist — 3 wks
28 May 83	HEAVEN SENT *Island IS 111*........................	74	3

HAIRCUT 100 ☺ UK, male vocal/instrumental group — 47 wks
24 Oct 81	● FAVOURITE SHIRTS (BOY MEETS GIRL) *Arista CLIP 1*........................	4	14
30 Jan 82	● LOVE PLUS ONE *Arista CLIP 2*........................	3	12
10 Apr 82	● FANTASTIC DAY *Arista CLIP 3*........................	9	9
21 Aug 82	● NOBODY'S FOOL *Arista CLIP 4*........................	9	7
6 Aug 83	PRIME TIME *Polydor HC 1*........................	46	5

Curtis HAIRSTON ☺ 🎤 US, male vocalist — 16 wks
15 Oct 83	I WANT YOU (ALL TONIGHT) *RCA 368*........................	44	5
27 Apr 85	I WANT YOUR LOVIN' (JUST A LITTLE BIT) *London LON 66*	13	7
6 Dec 86	CHILLIN' OUT *Atlantic A 9335*........................	57	4

Gary HAISMAN – See D MOB

HAL featuring Gillian ANDERSON
UK, male producers and US, female vocalist — 3 wks
24 May 97	EXTREMIS *Virgin VSCDT 1636*........................	23	3

HALE and PACE and the STONKERS ☺
UK, male comedy duo and backing group — 7 wks
9 Mar 91	★ THE STONK *London LON 296*........................	1	7

Bill HALEY and his COMETS 🎸
Original 'King of Rock 'n' Roll', b. 6 July, 1925, Detroit, d. 9 February, 1981. He introduced rock to the world via a string of mid-1950s smashes, including the No 1 all-time hit, 'Rock Around the Clock'. At one time he had five singles simultaneously in the UK Top 20 — 199 wks
17 Dec 54	● SHAKE RATTLE AND ROLL *Brunswick 05338*........................	4	14
7 Jan 55	ROCK AROUND THE CLOCK *Brunswick 05317*........................	17	2
15 Apr 55	MAMBO ROCK *Brunswick 05405*........................	14	2
14 Oct 55	★ ROCK AROUND THE CLOCK (re-entry) *Brunswick 05317* ◆ ▲	1	17
30 Dec 55	● ROCK-A-BEATIN' BOOGIE *Brunswick 05509*........................	4	9
9 Mar 56	● SEE YOU LATER ALLIGATOR *Brunswick 05530*........................	7	13
25 May 56	● THE SAINTS ROCK 'N ROLL *Brunswick 05565*........................	5	24
17 Aug 56	● ROCKIN' THROUGH THE RYE *Brunswick 05582*........................	3	18
14 Sep 56	RAZZLE DAZZLE *Brunswick 05453*........................	13	8
21 Sep 56	● ROCK AROUND THE CLOCK (2nd re-entry) *Brunswick 05317*	5	11
21 Sep 56	SEE YOU LATER ALLIGATOR (re-entry) *Brunswick 05530*........................	12	8
9 Nov 56	● RIP IT UP *Brunswick 05615*........................	4	18
9 Nov 56	ROCK 'N ROLL STAGE SHOW LP *Brunswick LAT 8139*........................	30	1
23 Nov 56	RUDY'S ROCK *Brunswick 05616*........................	30	1
14 Dec 56	ROCK AROUND THE CLOCK (3rd re-entry)		
	Brunswick 05317........................	24	2
14 Dec 56	RUDY'S ROCK (re-entry) *Brunswick 05616*........................	26	4
4 Jan 57	ROCK AROUND THE CLOCK (4th re-entry)		
	Brunswick 05317........................	25	2
4 Jan 57	ROCKIN' THROUGH THE RYE (re-entry) *Brunswick 05582*........................	19	5
25 Jan 57	ROCK AROUND THE CLOCK (5th re-entry)		
	Brunswick 05317........................	22	2
1 Feb 57	ROCK THE JOINT *London HLF 8371*........................	20	4
8 Feb 57	● DON'T KNOCK THE ROCK *Brunswick 05640*........................	7	8
3 Apr 68	ROCK AROUND THE CLOCK (re-issue) *MCA MU 1013*........................	20	11
16 Mar 74	ROCK AROUND THE CLOCK (2nd re-issue) *MCA 128*........................	12	10
25 Apr 81	HALEY'S GOLDEN MEDLEY *MCA 694*........................	50	5

Tracks on Rock 'n' Roll Stage Show (LP): Calling All Comets / Rockin' Through the Rye / A Rockin' Little Tune / Hide and Seek / Hey There Now / Goofin' Around / Hook Line and Sinker / Rudy's Rock / Choo Choo Ch'Boogie / Blue Comets Rock / Hot Dog Buddy Buddy / Tonight's the Night. Occasionally, some of the 'Rock Around the Clock' labels billed the song as '(We're Gonna) Rock Around the Clock'

Aaron HALL US, male vocalist — 3 wks
13 Jun 92	DON'T BE AFRAID *MCA MCS 1632*........................	56	2

| 23 Oct 93 | GET A LITTLE FREAKY WITH ME *MCA MCSTD 1936* | 66 | 1 |

See also VARIOUS ARTISTS (EPs & LPs) – The Dangerous Minds (EP)

Audrey HALL ⌐ *Jamaica, female vocalist* — 20 wks

| 25 Jan 86 | ONE DANCE WON'T DO *Germain DG7-1985* | 20 | 11 |
| 5 Jul 86 | SMILE *Germain DG 15* | 14 | 9 |

Daryl HALL *US, male vocalist* — 26 wks

2 Aug 86	DREAMTIME *RCA HALL 1*	28	8
25 Sep 93	I'M IN A PHILLY MOOD *Epic 6595555*	59	2
8 Jan 94	STOP LOVING ME STOP LOVING YOU *Epic 6599982*	30	6
26 Mar 94	I'M IN A PHILLY MOOD (re-entry) *Epic 6595555*	52	2
14 May 94	HELP ME FIND A WAY TO YOUR HEART *Epic 6604102*	70	1
2 Jul 94	GLORYLAND *Mercury MERCD 404* [1]	36	4
10 Jun 95	WHEREVER WOULD I BE *Columbia 6620592* [2]	44	3

[1] Daryl Hall and the Sounds Of Blackness [2] Dusty Springfield and Daryl Hall

See also Daryl HALL and John OATES

Daryl HALL and John OATES ◑ ✐
US, male vocal/instrumental duo — 84 wks

16 Oct 76	SHE'S GONE *Atlantic K 10828*	42	4
14 Jun 80	RUNNING FROM PARADISE *RCA RUN 1*	41	6
20 Sep 80	YOU'VE LOST THAT LOVIN' FEELIN' *RCA 1*	55	3
15 Nov 80	KISS ON MY LIST *RCA 15* ▲	33	8
23 Jan 82 ●	I CAN'T GO FOR THAT (NO CAN DO) *RCA 172* ▲	8	10
10 Apr 82	PRIVATE EYES *RCA 134* ▲	32	7
30 Oct 82 ●	MANEATER *RCA 290* ▲	6	11
22 Jan 83	ONE ON ONE *RCA 305*	63	3
30 Apr 83	FAMILY MAN *RCA 323*	15	7
12 Nov 83	SAY IT ISN'T SO *RCA 375*	69	3
10 Mar 84	ADULT EDUCATION *RCA 396*	63	2
20 Oct 84	OUT OF TOUCH *RCA 449* ▲	48	5
9 Feb 85	METHOD OF MODERN LOVE *RCA RCA 472*	21	8
22 Jun 85	OUT OF TOUCH (re-mix) *RCA PB 4 9967*	62	3
21 Sep 85	A NIGHT AT THE APOLLO LIVE! *RCA PB 49935* [1]	58	2
29 Sep 90	SO CLOSE *Arista 113600* [2]	69	1
26 Jan 91	EVERYWHERE I LOOK *Arista 113980*	74	1

[1] Daryl Hall and John Oates featuring David Ruffin and Eddie Kendrick
[2] Hall and Oates

'A Night at the Apollo Live!' is a medley of 'The Way You Do the Things You Do' and 'My Girl'.
See also Daryl HALL

Lynden David HALL (R&B) *UK, male vocal/instrumentalist* — 8 wks

25 Oct 97	SEXY CINDERELLA *Cooltempo CDCOOL 328*	45	2
14 Mar 98	DO I QUALIFY? *Cooltempo CDCOOLS 331*	26	2
4 Jul 98	CRESCENT MOON *Cooltempo CDCOOL 333*	45	1
31 Oct 98	SEXY CINDERELLA (re-entry) *Cooltempo CDCOOLS 340*	17	3

Pam HALL *Jamaica, female vocalist* — 4 wks

| 16 Aug 86 | DEAR BOOPSIE *Bluemountain BM 027* | 54 | 4 |

Terry HALL *UK, male vocalist* — 6 wks

11 Nov 89	MISSING *Chrysalis CHS 3381*	75	1
27 Aug 94	FOREVER J *Anxious ANX 1024CDX*	67	1
12 Nov 94	SENSE *Anxious ANX 1027CD*	54	2
28 Oct 95	CHASING A RAINBOW *Anxious ANX 1033CD1*	62	1
14 Jun 97	BALLAD OF A LANDLORD *Southsea Bubble CDBUBBLE 1*	50	1

The sleeve, not the label, of 'Missing' credits Terry, Blair and Anouchka

Toni HALLIDAY – See LEFTFIELD; Paul VAN DYK

HALO JAMES ◑ *UK, male vocal/instrumental group* — 24 wks

7 Oct 89	WANTED *Epic HALO 1*	45	5
23 Dec 89 ●	COULD HAVE TOLD YOU SO *Epic HALO 2*	6	12
17 Mar 90	BABY *Epic HALO 3*	43	4
19 May 90	MAGIC HOUR *Epic HALO 4*	59	3

HAMILTON, Joe FRANK and REYNOLDS
US, male vocal group — 6 wks

| 13 Sep 75 | FALLIN' IN LOVE *Pye International 7N 25690* | 33 | 6 |

George HAMILTON IV *US, male vocalist* — 13 wks

7 Mar 58	WHY DON'T THEY UNDERSTAND *HMV POP 429*	22	9
18 Jul 58	I KNOW WHERE I'M GOING *HMV POP 505*	29	1
8 Aug 58	I KNOW WHERE I'M GOING (re-entry) *HMV POP 505*	23	3

Lynne HAMILTON ◑ *Australia, female vocalist* — 11 wks

| 29 Apr 89 ● | ON THE INSIDE (THEME FROM 'PRISONER CELL BLOCK H') *A1 A1 311* | 3 | 11 |

Russ HAMILTON ◑ *UK, male vocalist* — 26 wks

| 24 May 57 ● | WE WILL MAKE LOVE *Oriole CB 1359* | 2 | 20 |
| 27 Sep 57 | WEDDING RING *Oriole CB 1388* | 20 | 6 |

Marvin HAMLISCH *US, male instrumentalist – piano* — 13 wks

| 30 Mar 74 | THE ENTERTAINER *MCA 121* | 25 | 13 |

HAMMER ⌐ *US, male rapper* — 68 wks

9 Jun 90 ●	U CAN'T TOUCH THIS *Capitol CL 578* [1]	3	16
6 Oct 90 ●	HAVE YOU SEEN HER *Capitol CL 590* [1]	8	7
8 Dec 90 ●	PRAY *Capitol CL 599* [1]	8	10
23 Feb 91	HERE COMES THE HAMMER *Capitol CL 610* [1]	15	5
1 Jun 91	YO!! SWEETNESS *Capitol CL 616* [1]	16	5
20 Jul 91	(HAMMER HAMMER) THEY PUT ME IN THE MIX *Capitol CL 607* [1]	20	4
26 Oct 91	2 LEGIT 2 QUIT *Capitol CL 636*	60	2
21 Dec 91 ●	ADDAMS GROOVE *Capitol CL 642*	4	9
21 Mar 92	DO NOT PASS ME BY *Capitol CL 650*	14	6
12 Mar 94	IT'S ALL GOOD *RCA 74321188612*	52	2
13 Aug 94	DON'T STOP *RCA 74321220012*	72	1
3 Jun 95	STRAIGHT TO MY FEET *Priority PTYCD 102* [2]	57	1

[1] MC Hammer [2] Hammer featuring Deion Saunders

Jan HAMMER ◑
Czechoslovakia, male instrumentalist – keyboards — 26 wks

12 Oct 85 ●	MIAMI VICE THEME *MCA MCA 1000* ▲	5	8
19 Sep 87 ●	CROCKETT'S THEME *MCA MCA 1193*	2	12
1 Jun 91	CROCKETT'S THEME (re-issue) *MCA MCS 1541*	47	6

Albert HAMMOND ◑ *UK, male vocalist* — 11 wks

| 30 Jun 73 | FREE ELECTRIC BAND *Mums 1494* | 19 | 11 |

Beres HAMMOND – See Maxi PRIEST

Herbie HANCOCK ✐ 🎙
US, male vocalist/instrumentalist – keyboards — 41 wks

26 Aug 78	I THOUGHT IT WAS YOU *CBS 6530*	15	9
3 Feb 79	YOU BET YOUR LOVE *CBS 7010*	18	10
30 Jul 83 ●	ROCKIT *CBS A 3577*	8	8
8 Oct 83	AUTO DRIVE *CBS A 3802*	33	4
21 Jan 84	FUTURE SHOCK *CBS A 4075*	54	3
4 Aug 84	HARDROCK *CBS A 4616*	65	3

HANDBAGGERS *UK, male/female vocal/instrumental group* — 1 wk

| 15 Jun 96 | U FOUND OUT *Tidy Trax TIDY 104CD* | 55 | 1 |

HANDLEY FAMILY *UK, male/female vocal group* — 7 wks

| 7 Apr 73 | WAM BAM *GL 100* | 30 | 7 |

Jayn HANNA *UK, female vocalist* — 2 wks

| 13 Apr 96 | LOVELIGHT (RIDE ON A LOVE TRAIN) *VC VCRD 10* | 42 | 1 |
| 1 Feb 97 | LOST WITHOUT YOU *VC VCRD 16* | 44 | 1 |

HANNAH – See MAN WITH NO NAME

HANNAH and her SISTERS – See Hannah JONES

HANOI ROCKS *Finland/UK, male vocal/instrumental group*   **2 wks**

7 Jul 84	UP AROUND THE BEND *CBS A 4513*	61	2

HANSON ☺ *US, male vocal/instrumental group*   **42 wks**

06 Jul 97 ★	MMMBOP *Mercury 5745012* ▲	1	13
13 Sep 97 ●	WHERE'S THE LOVE *Mercury 5749032*	4	9
22 Nov 97 ●	I WILL COME TO YOU *Mercury 5680672*	5	9
28 Mar 98	WEIRD *Mercury 5685412*	19	5
4 Jul 98	THINKING OF YOU *Mercury 5688132*	23	6

HAPPENINGS *US, male vocal group*   **14 wks**

18 May 67	I GOT RHYTHM *Stateside SS 2013*	28	9
16 Aug 67	MY MAMMY *Pye Int 7N 25501 and B.T. Puppy BTS 45530*	34	5

Pye gave the US B.T. Puppy label its own identification halfway through the success of 'My Mammy'

HAPPY CLAPPERS ☺
UK, male/female vocal/instrumental group   **19 wks**

3 Jun 95	I BELIEVE *Shindig SHIN 4CD*	21	3
26 Aug 95	HOLD ON *Shindig SHIN 7CD*	27	2
18 Nov 95 ●	I BELIEVE (re-issue) *Shindig SHIN 9CD*	7	8
15 Jun 96	CAN'T HELP IT *Coliseum TOGA 004CD*	18	3
21 Dec 96	NEVER AGAIN *Coliseum TOGA 012CD*	49	1
22 Nov 97	I BELIEVE 97 *Coalition COLA 027CD*	28	2

HAPPY MONDAYS ☹ ☺ *UK, male vocal/instrumental group*   **51 wks**

30 Sep 89	WFL *Factory FAC 2327*	68	2
25 Nov 89	MADCHESTER RAVE ON EP *Factory FAC 2427*	19	14
7 Apr 90 ●	STEP ON *Factory FAC 2727*	5	11
9 Jun 90	LAZYITIS – ONE ARMED BOXER *Factory FAC 2227* 1	46	3
20 Oct 90 ●	KINKY AFRO *Factory FAC 3027*	5	7
9 Mar 91	LOOSE FIT *Factory FAC 3127*	17	7
30 Nov 91	JUDGE FUDGE *Factory FAC 3327*	24	3
19 Sep 92	STINKIN THINKIN *Factory FAC 3627*	31	3
21 Nov 92	SUNSHINE AND LOVE *Factory FAC 3727*	62	1

1 Happy Mondays and Karl Denver

Tracks on Madchester Rave on (EP): Hallelujah / Holy Ghost / Clap Your Hands / Rave on

Paul HARDCASTLE ☺ ☻ *UK, male producer*   **66 wks**

7 Apr 84	YOU'RE THE ONE FOR ME – DAYBREAK – A.M. *Total Control TOCO 1*	41	4
28 Jul 84	GUILTY *Total Control TOCO 2*	55	3
22 Sep 84	RAIN FOREST *Bluebird BR 8*	41	5
17 Nov 84	EAT YOUR HEART OUT *Cooltempo COOL 102*	59	4
4 May 85 ★	NINETEEN *Chrysalis CHS 2860*	1	16
15 Jun 85	RAIN FOREST (re-issue) *Bluebird 10 BR 15*	53	4
9 Nov 85	JUST FOR MONEY *Chrysalis CASH 1*	19	5
1 Feb 86 ●	DON'T WASTE MY TIME *Chrysalis PAUL 1* 1	8	11
21 Jun 86	FOOLIN' YOURSELF *Chrysalis PAUL 2*	51	3
11 Oct 86	THE WIZARD *Chrysalis PAUL 3*	15	6
9 Apr 88	WALK IN THE NIGHT *Chrysalis PAUL 4*	54	3
4 Jun 88	40 YEARS *Chrysalis PAUL 5*	53	2

1 Paul Hardcastle featuring Carol Kenyon

'Just for Money' features the voices of Laurence Olivier, Bob Hoskins, Ed O'Ross and Alan Talbot, who are credited on the sleeve only.
See also SILENT UNDERDOG

HARDCORE RHYTHM TEAM *UK, male vocal/production group*   **1 wk**

14 Mar 92	HARDCORE – THE FINAL CONFLICT *Furious FRUT 001*	69	1

HARDFLOOR *Germany, male instrumental/production group*   **6 wks**

26 Dec 92	HARDTRANCE ACPERIENCE *Harthouse UK HARTUK 1*	56	4

10 Apr 93	TRANCESCRIPT *Harthouse UK HARTUK 5CD*	72	1
25 Oct 97	ACPERIENCE *Eye-q EYEUK 018CD1*	60	1

Tim HARDIN *US, male vocalist*   **1 wk**

5 Jan 67	HANG ON TO A DREAM *Verve VS 1504*	50	1

Mike HARDING *UK, male vocalist*   **8 wks**

2 Aug 75	ROCHDALE COWBOY *Rubber ADUB 3*	22	8

Françoise HARDY ☻ *France, female vocalist*   **26 wks**

25 Jun 64	TOUS LES GARCONS ET LES FILLES *Pye 7N 15653*	36	7
7 Jan 65	ET MEME *Pye 7N 15740*	31	4
25 Mar 65	ALL OVER THE WORLD *Pye 7N 15802*	16	15

Tynetta HARE – See Joey B ELLIS

Morten HARKET *Norway, male vocalist*   **1 wk**

19 Aug 95	A KIND OF CHRISTMAS CARD *Warner Bros. W 0304CD*	53	1

HARLEM COMMUNITY CHOIR – See John LENNON

HARLEQUIN 4s / BUNKER KRU *US, male/female vocal/instrumental group with UK, male production duo*   **4 wks**

19 Mar 88	SET IT OFF *Champion CHAMP 64*	55	4

HARLEY QUINNE ☻ *UK, male vocal group*   **8 wks**

14 Oct 72	NEW ORLEANS *Bell 1255*	19	8

Steve HARLEY and COCKNEY REBEL ☻
UK, male vocalist and male vocal/instrumental backing group   **69 wks**

11 May 74 ●	JUDY TEEN *EMI 2128* 1	5	11
10 Aug 74 ●	MR. SOFT *EMI 2191* 1	8	9
8 Feb 75 ★	MAKE ME SMILE (COME UP AND SEE ME) *EMI 2263*	1	9
7 Jun 75	MR. RAFFLES (MAN IT WAS MEAN) *EMI 2299*	13	6
31 Jul 76 ●	HERE COMES THE SUN *EMI 2505* 2	10	7
6 Nov 76	LOVE'S A PRIMA DONNA *EMI 2539* 2	41	4
20 Oct 79	FREEDOM'S PRISONER *EMI 2994* 2	58	3
13 Aug 83	BALLERINA (PRIMA DONNA) *Stiletto STL 14* 2	51	5
11 Jan 86 ●	THE PHANTOM OF THE OPERA *Polydor POSP 800* 3	7	10
25 Apr 92	MAKE ME SMILE (COME UP AND SEE ME) (re-issue) *EMI EMCT 5* 2	46	2
30 Dec 95	MAKE ME SMILE (COME UP AND SEE ME) (2nd re-issue) *EMI CDHARLEY 1*	33	3

1 Cockney Rebel 2 Steve Harley 3 Sarah Brightman and Steve Harley

HARMONIX *UK, male producer – Hamish Brown*   **2 wks**

30 Mar 96	LANDSLIDE *Deconstruction 74321330762*	28	2

HARMONY GRASS *UK, male vocal/instrumental group*   **7 wks**

29 Jan 69	MOVE IN A LITTLE CLOSER *RCA 1772*	24	7

Ben HARPER *US, male vocalist/instrumentalist*   **1 wk**

4 Apr 98	FADED *Virgin VUSCD 134*	54	1

Charlie HARPER *UK, male vocalist*   **1 wk**

19 Jul 80	BARMY LONDON ARMY *Gem GEMS 35*	68	1

HARPERS BIZARRE *US, male vocal group*   **13 wks**

30 Mar 67	59TH STREET BRIDGE SONG (FEELING GROOVY) *Warner Bros. WB 5890*	34	7
4 Oct 67	ANYTHING GOES *Warner Bros. WB 7063*	33	6

HARPO *Sweden, male vocalist*   **6 wks**

17 Apr 76	MOVIE STAR *DJM DJS 400*	24	6

T. HARRINGTON – See Rahni HARRIS and F.L.O.

Anita HARRIS ☺ UK, female vocalist — 50 wks

29 Jun 67	● JUST LOVING YOU CBS 2724	6	30
11 Oct 67	PLAYGROUND CBS 2991	46	3
24 Jan 68	ANNIVERSARY WALTZ CBS 3211	21	9
14 Aug 68	DREAM A LITTLE DREAM OF ME CBS 3637	33	8

Emmylou HARRIS US, female vocalist — 6 wks

6 Mar 76	HERE THERE AND EVERYWHERE Reprise K 14415	30	6

Jet HARRIS ☺ UK, male instrumentalist – bass — 18 wks

24 May 62	BESAME MUCHO Decca F 11466	22	7
16 Aug 62	MAIN TITLE THEME FROM 'MAN WITH THE GOLDEN ARM' Decca F 11488	12	11

See also Jet HARRIS and Tony MEEHAN

Jet HARRIS and Tony MEEHAN ☺
UK, male instrumental duo – bass and drums — 39 wks

10 Jan 63	★ DIAMONDS Decca F 11563	1	13
25 Apr 63	● SCARLETT O'HARA Decca F 11644	2	13
5 Sep 63	● APPLEJACK Decca F 11710	4	13

See also Jet HARRIS; Tony MEEHAN

Keith HARRIS and ORVILLE ☺
UK, male ventriloquist vocalist with feathered dummy — 20 wks

18 Dec 82	● ORVILLE'S SONG BBC RESL 124	4	11
24 Dec 83	COME TO MY PARTY BBC RESL 138 [1]	44	4
14 Dec 85	WHITE CHRISTMAS Columbia DB 9121	40	5

[1] Keith Harris and Orville with Dippy

Major HARRIS US, male vocalist — 9 wks

9 Aug 75	LOVE WON'T LET ME WAIT Atlantic K 10585	37	7
5 Nov 83	ALL MY LIFE London LON 37	61	2

Max HARRIS ℂ UK, orchestra — 10 wks

1 Dec 60	GURNEY SLADE Fontana H 282	11	10

Rahni HARRIS and F.L.O. US, male instrumental group — 7 wks

16 Dec 78	SIX MILLION STEPS (WEST RUNS SOUTH) Mercury 6007 198	43	7

Hit has credit 'vocals by T Harrington and O Rasbury'

Richard HARRIS ☺ Ireland, male vocalist — 18 wks

26 Jun 68	● MACARTHUR PARK RCA 1699	4	12
8 Jul 72	MACARTHUR PARK (re-issue) Probe GFF 101	38	6

Rochelle HARRIS – See ANGELHEART featuring Rochelle HARRIS

Rolf HARRIS ℂ Australia, male vocalist — 74 wks

21 Jul 60	● TIE ME KANGAROO DOWN SPORT Columbia DB 4483	9	13
25 Oct 62	● SUN ARISE Columbia DB 4888	3	16
28 Feb 63	JOHNNY DAY Columbia DB 4979	44	2
16 Apr 69	BLUER THAN BLUE Columbia DB 8553	30	8
22 Nov 69	★ TWO LITTLE BOYS Columbia DB 8630	1	24
20 Jun 70	TWO LITTLE BOYS (re-entry) Columbia DB 8630	50	1
13 Feb 93	● STAIRWAY TO HEAVEN Vertigo VERCD 73	7	6
1 Jun 96	BOHEMIAN RHAPSODY Living Beat LBECD 41	50	1
25 Oct 97	SUN ARISE (re-recording) EMI CDR 0000 1	26	3

Ronnie HARRIS ℂ UK, male vocalist — 3 wks

24 Sep 54	STORY OF TINA Columbia DB 3499	12	3

Sam HARRIS US, male vocalist — 2 wks

9 Feb 85	HEARTS ON FIRE/OVER THE RAINBOW Motown TMG 1370	67	2

Simon HARRIS ⬛ ☺ UK, male producer — 17 wks

19 Mar 88	BASS (HOW LOW CAN YOU GO) ffrr FFR 4	12	6
29 Oct 88	HERE COMES THAT SOUND ffrr FFR 12	38	4
24 Jun 89	(I'VE GOT YOUR) PLEASURE CONTROL ffrr F 106 [1]	60	3
18 Nov 89	ANOTHER MONSTERJAM ffrr F 116 [2]	65	1
10 Mar 90	RAGGA HOUSE (ALL NIGHT LONG) Living Beat 7SMASH 9 [3]	56	3

[1] Simon Harris featuring Lonnie Gordon [2] Simon Harris featuring Einstein
[3] Simon Harris featuring Daddy Freddy

George HARRISON ☺ ✎ UK, male vocalist — 82 wks

23 Jan 71	★ MY SWEET LORD Apple R 5884 ▲	1	17
14 Aug 71	● BANGLA DESH Apple R 5912	10	9
2 Jun 73	● GIVE ME LOVE (GIVE ME PEACE ON EARTH) Apple R 5988 ▲	8	10
21 Dec 74	DING DONG Apple R 6002	38	5
11 Oct 75	YOU Apple R 6007	38	5
10 Mar 79	BLOW AWAY Dark Horse K 17327	51	5
23 May 81	ALL THOSE YEARS AGO Dark Horse K 17807	13	7
24 Oct 87	● GOT MY MIND SET ON YOU Dark Horse W 8178 ▲	2	14
6 Feb 88	WHEN WE WAS FAB Dark Horse W 8131	25	7
25 Jun 88	THIS IS LOVE Dark Horse W 7913	55	3

Noel HARRISON ☺ UK, male vocalist — 14 wks

26 Feb 69	● WINDMILLS OF YOUR MIND Reprise RS 20758	8	14

Deborah HARRY ☺ US, female vocalist — 52 wks

1 Aug 81	BACKFIRED Chrysalis CHS 2526 [1]	32	6
15 Nov 86	● FRENCH KISSIN' IN THE USA Chrysalis CHS 3066 [1]	8	10
28 Feb 87	FREE TO FALL Chrysalis CHS 3093 [1]	46	4
9 May 87	IN LOVE WITH LOVE Chrysalis CHS 3128 [1]	45	5
7 Oct 89	I WANT THAT MAN Chrysalis CHS 3369	13	10
2 Dec 89	BRITE SIDE Chrysalis CHS 3452	59	4
31 Mar 90	SWEET AND LOW Chrysalis CHS 3491	57	3
5 Jan 91	WELL DID YOU EVAH! Chrysalis CHS 3646 [2]	42	4
3 Jul 93	I CAN SEE CLEARLY NOW Chrysalis CDCHSS 4900	23	4
18 Sep 93	STRIKE ME PINK Chrysalis CDCHSS 5000	46	2

[1] Debbie Harry [2] Deborah Harry and Iggy Pop

See also BLONDIE

HARRY J. ALL STARS ⬩ Jamaica, male instrumental group — 25 wks

25 Oct 69	● LIQUIDATOR Trojan TR 675	9	20
29 Mar 80	LIQUIDATOR (re-issue) Trojan TRO 9063	42	5

Re-issue of 'Liquidator' coupled with re-issue of 'Long Shot Kick De Bucket'
by the Pioneers

Richard HARTLEY/Michael REED ORCHESTRA ℂ
UK, male instrumentalist – synthesizer, orchestra — 10 wks

25 Feb 84	● THE MUSIC OF TORVILL AND DEAN EP Safari SKATE 1	9	10

Tracks on EP: Bolero/Capriccio Espagnole Opus 34 (Nos 4 and 5) by Richard Hartley;
Barnum on Ice/Discoskate by the Michael Reed Orchestra

Dan HARTMAN ⬥ ☺ US, male vocalist — 34 wks

21 Oct 78	● INSTANT REPLAY Sky 6706	8	15
13 Jan 79	THIS IS IT Blue Sky SKY 6999	17	8
18 May 85	SECOND NATURE MCA MCA 957	66	2
24 Aug 85	I CAN DREAM ABOUT YOU MCA MCA 988	12	8
1 Apr 95	KEEP THE FIRE BURNIN' Columbia 6611552 [1]	49	1

[1] Dan Hartman starring Loleatta Holloway

Sensational Alex HARVEY BAND ✎
UK, male vocal/instrumental group — 25 wks

26 Jul 75	● DELILAH Vertigo ALEX 001	7	7
22 Nov 75	GAMBLIN' BAR ROOM BLUES Vertigo ALEX 002	38	8
19 Jun 76	THE BOSTON TEA PARTY Mountain TOP 12	13	10

P J HARVEY UK, female vocalist — 15 wks

29 Feb 92	SHEELA-NA-GIG Too Pure PURE 008	69	1
1 May 93	50 FT QUEENIE Island CID 538	27	2
17 Jul 93	MAN-SIZE Island CID 569	42	2
18 Feb 95	DOWN BY THE WATER Island CID 607	38	2
22 Jul 95	C'MON BILLY Island CID 614	29	2
28 Oct 95	SEND HIS LOVE TO ME Island CID 610	34	2
9 Mar 96	HENRY LEE Mute CDMUTE 189 [1]	36	1
23 Nov 96	THAT WAS MY VEIL Island CID 648 [2]	75	1
26 Sep 98	A PERFECT DAY ELISE Island CID 718	25	2

[1] Nick Cave and the Bad Seeds and P J Harvey
[2] John Parish and Polly Jean Harvey

For the first three hits P J Harvey was the name of the entire group, not just the lead singer

Steve HARVEY UK, male vocalist — 6 wks

28 May 83	SOMETHING SPECIAL London LON 25	46	4
29 Oct 83	TONIGHT London LON 36	63	2

David HASSELHOFF US, male vocalist — 2 wks

13 Nov 93	IF I COULD ONLY SAY GOODBYE Arista 74321172262	35	2

Tony HATCH UK, orchestra — 1 wk

4 Oct 62	OUT OF THIS WORLD Pye 7N 15460	50	1

Juliana HATFIELD US, female vocalist — 2 wks

11 Sep 93	MY SISTER Mammoth YZ 767CD [1]	71	1
18 Mar 95	UNIVERSAL HEART-BEAT East West YZ 916CD	65	1

[1] Juliana Hatfield Three

Donny HATHAWAY – See Roberta FLACK

Lalah HATHAWAY US, female vocalist — 10 wks

1 Sep 90	HEAVEN KNOWS Virgin America VUS 28	66	2
2 Feb 91	BABY DON'T CRY Virgin America VUS 35	54	3
27 Jul 91	FAMILY AFFAIR Ten TEN 369 [1]	37	5

[1] BEF featuring Lalah Hathaway

HAVANA UK, male instrumental/production group — 1 wk

6 Mar 93	ETHNIC PRAYER Limbo LIMBO 007CD	71	1

Nic HAVERSON UK, male vocalist — 3 wks

30 Jan 93	HEAD OVER HEELS Telstar CDHOH 1	48	3

Chesney HAWKES ☻ UK, male vocalist — 25 wks

23 Feb 91	★ THE ONE AND ONLY Chrysalis CHS 3627	1	16
22 Jun 91	I'M A MAN NOT A BOY Chrysalis CHS 3708	27	5
28 Sep 91	SECRETS OF THE HEART Chrysalis CHS 3681	57	3
29 May 93	WHAT'S WRONG WITH THIS PICTURE Chrysalis CDCHS 3969	63	1

Screamin' Jay HAWKINS US, male vocalist — 3 wks

3 Apr 93	HEART ATTACK AND VINE Columbia 6591092	42	3

Edwin HAWKINS SINGERS featuring
Dorothy Combs MORRISON ♀ US, male/female vocal group — 13 wks

21 May 69	● OH HAPPY DAY Buddah 201 048	2	12
23 Aug 69	OH HAPPY DAY (re-entry) Buddah 201 048	43	1

Sophie B HAWKINS ☻ ✎ US, female vocalist — 37 wks

4 Jul 92	DAMN I WISH I WAS YOUR LOVER Columbia 6581077	14	9
12 Sep 92	CALIFORNIA HERE I COME Columbia 6583177	53	3
6 Feb 93	I WANT YOU Columbia 6587772	49	2
13 Aug 94	RIGHT BESIDE YOU Columbia 6606915	13	12

26 Nov 94	DON'T DON'T TELL ME NO Columbia 6610152	36	5
11 Mar 95	AS I LAY ME DOWN Columbia 6612125	24	6

HAWKWIND ✈
UK, male vocal/instrumental group with female dancer — 28 wks

1 Jul 72	● SILVER MACHINE United Artists UP 35381	3	15
11 Aug 73	URBAN GUERRILLA United Artists UP 35566	39	3
21 Oct 78	SILVER MACHINE (re-entry) United Artists UP 35381	34	5
19 Jul 80	SHOT DOWN IN THE NIGHT Bronze BRO 98	59	3
15 Jan 83	SILVER MACHINE (2nd re-entry) United Artists UP 35381	67	2

See also VARIOUS ARTISTS (EPs & LPs) – Gimme Shelter (EP)

Bill HAYES ℭ US, male vocalist — 9 wks

6 Jan 56	● BALLAD OF DAVY CROCKETT London HLA 8220 ▲	2	9

Isaac HAYES ✎ US, male vocalist/multi-instrumentalist — 22 wks

4 Dec 71	● THEME FROM 'SHAFT' Stax 2025 069 ▲	4	12
3 Apr 76	● DISCO CONNECTION ABC 4100 [1]	10	9
26 Dec 98	● CHOCOLATE SALTY BALLS (PS I LOVE YOU) Columbia 6667985 [2]	2†	1

[1] Isaac Hayes Movement [2] Chef

See also CHEF

HAYSI FANTAYZEE ✆ UK, male/female vocal duo — 25 wks

24 Jul 82	JOHN WAYNE IS BIG LEGGY Regard RG 100	11	10
13 Nov 82	HOLY JOE Regard RG 104	51	3
22 Jan 83	SHINY SHINY Regard RG 106	16	10
25 Jun 83	SISTER FRICTION Regard RG 108	62	2

Justin HAYWARD ✎ UK, male vocalist — 20 wks

25 Oct 75	● BLUE GUITAR Threshold TH 21 [1]	8	7
8 Jul 78	● FOREVER AUTUMN CBS 6368	5	13

[1] Justin Hayward and John Lodge

Leon HAYWOOD ♀ US, male vocalist — 11 wks

15 Mar 80	DON'T PUSH IT, DON'T FORCE IT 20th Century Fox TC 2443	12	11

HAYWOODE ☺ ✎ UK, female vocalist — 31 wks

17 Sep 83	A TIME LIKE THIS CBS A 3651	48	7
29 Sep 84	I CAN'T LET YOU GO CBS A 4664	63	4
13 Apr 85	ROSES CBS A 6069	65	3
5 Oct 85	GETTING CLOSER CBS A 6582	67	2
21 Jun 86	ROSES (re-issue) CBS A 7224	11	11
13 Sep 86	I CAN'T LET YOU GO (re-issue) CBS 650076 7	50	4

Ofra HAZA ✆☺ Israel, female vocalist — 8 wks

30 Apr 88	IM NIN'ALU WEA YZ 190	15	8

Lee HAZLEWOOD – See Nancy SINATRA

Murray HEAD ☻ UK, male vocalist — 15 wks

29 Jan 72	SUPERSTAR MCA MMKS 5077	47	1
10 Nov 84	ONE NIGHT IN BANGKOK RCA CHESS 1	12	13
16 Feb 85	ONE NIGHT IN BANGKOK (re-entry) RCA CHESS 1	74	1

'Superstar' was one of four tracks on a maxi single, two of which were credited during the disc's one week on the chart. The other track credited was 'I Don't Know How to Love Him' by Yvonne Elliman

Roy HEAD US, male vocalist — 5 wks

4 Nov 65	TREAT HER RIGHT Vocalion V-P 9248	30	5

HEADBANGERS UK, male vocal/instrumental group — 3 wks

10 Oct 81	STATUS ROCK Magnet MAG 206	60	3

HEADBOYS UK, male vocal/instrumental group — 8 wks

22 Sep 79	THE SHAPE OF THINGS TO COME RSO 40	45	8

HEADGIRL – See MOTORHEAD; GIRLSCHOOL

Max HEADROOM – See ART OF NOISE

HEADS UK, male instrumental group — 4 wks

21 Jun 86	AZTEC LIGHTNING (THEME FROM BBC WORLD CUP GRANDSTAND) BBC RESL 184	45	4

HEADS with Shaun RYDER
US/UK, male/female vocal/instrumental group — 1 wk

9 Nov 96	DON'T TAKE MY KINDNESS FOR WEAKNESS Radioactive MCSTD 48024	60	1

Heads are Talking Heads minus lead singer David Byrne.
See also TALKING HEADS

HEADSWIM UK, male vocal/instrumental group — 5 wks

25 Feb 98	CRAWL Epic 6612252	64	1
14 Feb 98	TOURNIQUET Epic 6650442	30	3
16 May 98	BETTER MADE Epic 6658402	42	1

Jeremy HEALY – See AMOS

HEAR 'N' AID International, male/female vocal/instrumental
charity assembly — 6 wks

19 Apr 86	STARS Vertigo HEAR 1	26	6

HEART ✍ ◉ US, female/male vocal/instrumental group — 76 wks

29 Mar 86	THESE DREAMS Capitol CL 394 ▲	62	4
13 Jun 87 ●	ALONE Capitol CL 448 ▲	3	16
19 Sep 87	WHO WILL YOU RUN TO Capitol CL 457	30	7
12 Dec 87	THERE'S THE GIRL Capitol CL 473	34	7
5 Mar 88 ●	NEVER/THESE DREAMS (re-issue) Capitol CL 482	8	9
14 May 88	WHAT ABOUT LOVE Capitol CL 487	14	6
22 Oct 88	NOTHIN' AT ALL Capitol CL 507	38	3
24 Mar 90 ●	ALL I WANNA DO IS MAKE LOVE TO YOU Capitol CL 569	8	13
28 Jul 90	I DIDN'T WANT TO NEED YOU Capitol CL 580	47	3
17 Nov 90	STRANDED Capitol CL 595	60	2
14 Sep 91	YOU'RE THE VOICE Capitol CLS 624	56	2
20 Nov 93	WILL YOU BE THERE (IN THE MORNING) Capitol CDCLS 700	19	4

HEARTBEAT UK, male/female vocal/instrumental group — 5 wks

24 Oct 87	TEARS FROM HEAVEN Priority P 17	32	4
23 Apr 88	THE WINNER Priority P 19	70	1

HEARTBEAT COUNTRY UK, male vocalist – Bill Maynard — 1 wk

31 Dec 94	HEARTBEAT MMM MMM 01CD	75	1

HEARTBREAKERS – See Tom PETTY and the HEARTBREAKERS; Stevie NICKS

HEARTISTS Italy, male DJ/production trio — 5 wks

9 Aug 97	BELO HORIZONTI VC VCRD 23	42	3
31 Jan 98	BELO HORIZONTI (re-mix) VC VCRD 28	40	2

Ted HEATH ◖ UK, orchestra — 56 wks

16 Jan 53	VANESSA Decca F 9983	11	1
3 Jul 53 ●	HOT TODDY Decca F 10093	6	11
23 Oct 53	DRAGNET Decca F 10176	12	1
27 Nov 53 ●	DRAGNET (re-entry) Decca F 10176	9	1
11 Dec 53	DRAGNET (2nd re-entry) Decca F 10176	11	1
15 Jan 54	DRAGNET (3rd re-entry) Decca F 10176	11	1
5 Feb 54	DRAGNET (4th re-entry) Decca F 10176	12	1
12 Feb 54 ●	SKIN DEEP Decca F 10246	9	3
6 Jul 56	THE FAITHFUL HUSSAR Decca F 10746	18	9

14 Mar 58 ●	SWINGIN' SHEPHERD BLUES Decca F 11000	3	14
11 Apr 58	TEQUILA Decca F 11003	21	6
4 Jul 58	TOM HARK Decca F 11025	24	2
5 Oct 61	SUCU SUCU Decca F 11392	36	4
9 Nov 61	SUCU SUCU (re-entry) Decca F 11392	47	1

HEATWAVE ♪ UK/US, male vocal/instrumental group — 80 wks

22 Jan 77 ●	BOOGIE NIGHTS GTO GT 77	2	14
7 May 77	TOO HOT TO HANDLE/SLIP YOUR DISC TO THIS GTO GT 91	15	11
14 Jan 78	THE GROOVE LINE GTO GT 115	12	8
3 Jun 78	MIND BLOWING DECISIONS GTO GT 226	12	11
4 Nov 78 ●	ALWAYS AND FOREVER/MIND BLOWING DECISIONS (re-mix) GTO GT 236	9	14
26 May 79	RAZZLE DAZZLE GTO GT 248	43	5
17 Jan 81	GANGSTERS OF THE GROOVE GTO GT 285	19	8
21 Mar 81	JITTERBUGGIN' GTO GT 290	34	7
1 Sep 90	MIND BLOWING DECISIONS (re-mix) Brothers Organisation HW 1	65	2

HEAVEN 17 ❂ ☺ UK, male vocal/instrumental group — 87 wks

21 Mar 81	(WE DON'T NEED THIS) FASCIST GROOVE THANG Virgin VS 400	45	5
5 Sep 81	PLAY TO WIN Virgin VS 433	46	7
14 Nov 81	PENTHOUSE AND PAVEMENT Virgin VS 455	57	3
30 Oct 82	LET ME GO Virgin VS 532	41	6
16 Apr 83 ●	TEMPTATION Virgin VS 570	2	13
25 Jun 83 ●	COME LIVE WITH ME Virgin VS 607	5	11
10 Sep 83	CRUSHED BY THE WHEELS OF INDUSTRY Virgin VS 628	17	7
1 Sep 84	SUNSET NOW Virgin VS 708	24	6
27 Oct 84	THIS IS MINE Virgin VS 722	23	7
19 Jan 85	. . . (AND THAT'S NO LIE) Virgin VS 740	52	5
17 Jan 87	TROUBLE Virgin VS 920	51	3
21 Nov 92 ●	TEMPTATION (re-mix) Virgin VS 1446	4	11
27 Feb 93	(WE DON'T NEED THIS) FASCIST GROOVE THANG Virgin VSCDT 1451	40	2
10 Apr 93	PENTHOUSE AND PAVEMENT (re-mix) Virgin VSCDT 1457	54	1

Carol Kenyon is the uncredited vocalist on 'Temptation'.
'Fascist Groove Thang' in 1993 is a re-recording.
See also VARIOUS ARTISTS (EPs & LPs) – Gimme Shelter (EP)

HEAVY D. and the BOYZ ⬛ Jamaica/US, male rap/vocal duo — 28 wks

6 Dec 86	MR. BIG STUFF MCA MCA 1106	61	8
15 Jul 89	WE GOT OUR OWN THANG MCA MCA 23942	69	2
6 Jul 91 ●	NOW THAT WE FOUND LOVE MCA MCS 1550	2	12
28 Sep 91	IS IT GOOD TO YOU MCA MCS 1564	46	3
8 Oct 94	THIS IS YOUR NIGHT MCA MCSTD 2010	30	3

HEAVY PETTIN' UK, male vocal/instrumental group — 2 wks

17 Mar 84	LOVE TIMES LOVE Polydor HEP 3	69	2

HEAVY STEREO UK, male vocal/instrumental group — 4 wks

22 Jul 95	SLEEP FREAK Creation CRESCD 203	46	1
28 Oct 95	SMILER Creation CRESCD 213	46	1
10 Feb 96	CHINESE BURN Creation CRESCD 218	45	1
24 Aug 96	MOUSE IN A HOLE Creation CRESCD 230	53	1

HEAVY WEATHER US, male vocalist – Peter Lee — 1 wk

29 Jun 96	LOVE CAN'T TURN AROUND Pukka CDPUKKA 6	56	1

Bobby HEBB ♪ US, male vocalist — 15 wks

8 Sep 66	SUNNY Philips BF 1503	12	9
19 Aug 72	LOVE LOVE LOVE Philips 6051 023	32	6

HED BOYS UK, male instrumental/production duo — 6 wks

6 Aug 94	GIRLS + BOYS Deconstruction 74321223322	21	4
4 Nov 95	GIRLS + BOYS (re-mix) Deconstruction 74321322032	36	2

UK No 1 ★ UK Top 10 ● UK million seller ◆ UK entry at No 1 ■ US No 1 ▲

What: *Y M C A*   **45**
Who: Village People
When: 1978 (10), 1993 (12 – remix)
Which: Started life as a gay anthem and established itself as a must-play for most parties. It is one of the few records to pass the one-million sales mark in the USA, the UK and Germany

What: *Unchained Melody*   **46**
Who: Righteous Brothers
When: 1965 (14), 1990 (1)
Which: After being heard in the movie *Ghost*, returned to top the chart 25 years after first entering. Five years later Robson and Jerome's closely cloned cover version also reached No 1

What: *Hey Jude*   **47**
Who: Beatles
When: 1968 (1), 1976 (12), 1988 (52)
Which: Was the first release on Apple and the longest single (seven minutes and eleven seconds) to reach No 1 at the time. It spent nine weeks at the top in the USA – a record for the group

What: *Sugar Sugar*   **48**
Who: The Archies (cartoon characters)
When: 1969 (1)
Which: Outsold every single in the world in 1969. Session singer Ron Dante and noted composer Toni Wine handled the vocals on this song, which had earlier been rejected by The Monkees

HEDGEHOPPERS ANONYMOUS ◎
UK, male vocal/instrumental group **12 wks**

30 Sep 65	●	IT'S GOOD NEWS WEEK *Decca F 12241* 5 12	

Neal HEFTI *US, male orchestra* **4 wks**

9 Apr 88	BATMAN THEME *RCA PB 49571* 55 4

Den HEGARTY *UK, male vocalist* **2 wks**

31 Mar 79	VOODOO VOODOO *Magnet MAG 143* 73 2

Anita HEGERLAND – *See Mike OLDFIELD*

HEINZ ◎ *UK, male vocalist* **35 wks**

8 Aug 63	●	JUST LIKE EDDIE *Decca F 11693* 5 15
28 Nov 63		COUNTRY BOY *Decca F 11768* 26 9
27 Feb 64		YOU WERE THERE *Decca F 11831* 26 8
15 Oct 64		QUESTIONS I CAN'T ANSWER *Columbia DB 7374*.............39 2
18 Mar 65		DIGGIN' MY POTATOES *Columbia DB 7482* [1] 49 1

[1] Heinz and the Wild Boys

HELICOPTER *UK, male instrumental/production duo* **4 wks**

27 Aug 94	ON YA WAY *Helicopter TIG 007CD* 32 2
22 Jun 96	ON YA WAY (re-mix) *Systematic SYSCD 27* 37 2

HELIOCENTRIC WORLD
UK, male/female vocal/instrumental group **2 wks**

14 Jan 95	WHERE'S YOUR LOVE BEEN *Talkin Loud TLKCD 51*............71 2

HELLER and FARLEY PROJECT
UK, male instrumental/production duo **7 wks**

24 Feb 96	ULTRA FLAVA *AM:PM 5814372* 22 3
28 Dec 96	ULTRA FLAVA (re-mix) *AM:PM 5820552* 32 4

Duo also known as Fire Island.
See also FIRE ISLAND

HELLO ◎ *UK, male vocal/instrumental group* **21 wks**

9 Nov 74	●	TELL HIM *Bell 1377* 6 12
18 Oct 75	●	NEW YORK GROOVE *Bell 1438* 9 9

HELLOWEEN *US, male vocal/instrumental group* **7 wks**

27 Aug 88	DR STEIN *Noise International 7HELLO 1* 57 3
12 Nov 88	I WANT OUT *Noise International 7HELLO 2* 69 2
2 Mar 91	KIDS OF THE CENTURY *EMI EM 178* 56 2

Bobby HELMS ⬧ *US, male vocalist* **7 wks**

29 Nov 57	MY SPECIAL ANGEL *Brunswick 05721* 22 3
21 Feb 58	NO OTHER BABY *Brunswick 05730* 30 1
1 Aug 58	JACQUELINE *Brunswick 05748* 20 3

Jimmy HELMS ✎ *US, male vocalist* **10 wks**

24 Feb 73	●	GONNA MAKE YOU AN OFFER YOU CAN'T REFUSE *Cube BUG 27* 8 10

HELTAH SKELTAH and ORIGINOO GUNN CLAPPAZ
as the FABULOUS FIVE *US, male vocal/instrumental duo* **1 wk**

1 Jun 96	BLAH *Priority PTYCD 117* 60 1

Eddie HENDERSON *US, male vocalist/instrumentalist – trumpet* **6 wks**

28 Oct 78	PRANCE ON *Capitol CL 16015* 44 6

Joe 'Mr. Piano' HENDERSON ℭ
UK, male instrumentalist – piano **23 wks**

3 Jun 55	SING IT WITH JOE *Polygon P 1167* 14 4
2 Sep 55	SING IT AGAIN WITH JOE *Polygon P 1184* 18 3

25 Jul 58	TRUDIE *Pye Nixa N 15147*........................14 12
24 Oct 58	TRUDIE (re-entry) *Pye Nixa N 15147*.........23 2
23 Oct 59	TREBLE CHANCE *Pye 7N 15224*............28 1
24 Mar 60	OOH LA LA *Pye 7N 15257*....................46 1

*First two hits are medleys as follows: Sing It With Joe: Margie/I'm Nobody's
Sweetheart/Somebody Stole My Gal/Moonlight Bay/By the Light of the Silvery
Moon/Cuddle Up a Little Closer. Sing It Again With Joe: Put Your Arms Around Me
Honey/Ain't She Sweet/When You're Smiling/Shine on Harvest Moon/My Blue
Heaven/Show Me the Way to Go Home*

Wayne HENDERSON – *See Roy AYERS*

Billy HENDRIX *Germany, male producer – Sharan Jay* **2 wks**

12 Sep 98	THE BODY SHINE EP *Hooj Choons HOOJ 65CD* 55 2

*Tracks on The Body Shine (EP): The Body Shine / Funky Shine / Colour Systems Inc.'s
Amber Dub / Timewriter re-mix*

Jimi HENDRIX EXPERIENCE ✔ *US/UK, male*
vocal/instrumental group, Jimi Hendrix – vocals and guitar **87 wks**

5 Jan 67	●	HEY JOE *Polydor 56 139* 6 10
23 Mar 67	●	PURPLE HAZE *Track 604 001*..............3 14
11 May 67	●	THE WIND CRIES MARY *Track 604 004* 6 11
30 Aug 67		BURNING OF THE MIDNIGHT LAMP *Track 604 007*...........18 9
23 Oct 68	●	ALL ALONG THE WATCHTOWER *Track 604 025* 5 11
16 Apr 69		CROSSTOWN TRAFFIC *Track 604 029*............37 3
7 Nov 70	★	VOODOO CHILE *Track 2095 001* 1 13
30 Oct 71		GYPSY EYES/REMEMBER *Track 2094 010*.........35 5
12 Feb 72		JOHNNY B. GOODE *Polydor 2001 277* [1] 35 5
21 Apr 90		CROSSTOWN TRAFFIC (re-issue) *Polydor PO 71* [1] 61 3
20 Oct 90		ALL ALONG THE WATCHTOWER (EP) *Polydor PO 100* [1] 52 3

[1] Jimi Hendrix

*Tracks on All Along the Watchtower (EP): All Along the Watchtower /
Voodoo Chile / Hey Joe*

Nona HENDRYX *US, female vocalist* **2 wks**

16 May 87	WHY SHOULD I CRY *EMI America EA 234* 60 2

Don HENLEY ◎ *US, male vocalist* **30 wks**

12 Feb 83	DIRTY LAUNDRY *Asylum E 9894* 59 3
9 Feb 85	THE BOYS OF SUMMER *Geffen A 4945* 12 10
29 Jul 89	THE END OF THE INNOCENCE *Geffen GEF 57*............48 5
3 Oct 92	SOMETIMES LOVE JUST AIN'T ENOUGH *MCA MCS 1692* [1] 22 6
18 Jul 98	BOYS OF SUMMER *Geffen GFSTD 22350* 12 6

[1] Patty Smyth with Don Henley

Clarence 'Frogman' HENRY ⬧ *US, male vocalist* **35 wks**

4 May 61	●	BUT I DO *Pye International 7N 25078* 3 19
13 Jul 61	●	YOU ALWAYS HURT THE ONE YOU LOVE *Pye International 7N 25089* 6 12
21 Sep 61		LONELY STREET/WHY CAN'T YOU *Pye International 7N 25108* 42 2
17 Jul 93		(I DON'T KNOW WHY) BUT I DO (re-issue) *MCA MCSTD 1797* 65 2

Kevin HENRY – *See L A MIX*

Paul HENRY and the Mayson GLEN ORCHESTRA
UK, male vocalist/orchestra **2 wks**

14 Jan 78	BENNY'S THEME *Pye 7N 46027*.................39 2

Pauline HENRY ✎ ◎ *UK, female vocalist* **21 wks**

18 Sep 93	TOO MANY PEOPLE *Sony S2 6595942*.............38 2
6 Nov 93	FEEL LIKE MAKING LOVE *Sony S2 6597972* 12 7
29 Jan 94	CAN'T TAKE YOUR LOVE *Sony S2 6599902* 30 3
21 May 94	WATCH THE MIRACLE START *Sony S2 6602772* 54 1
30 Sep 95	SUGAR FREE *Sony S2 6624362* 57 2
23 Dec 95	LOVE HANGOVER *Sony S2 6626132* 37 3

UK No 1 ★   UK Top 10 ●   UK million seller ◆   UK entry at No 1 ■   US No 1 ▲

24 Feb 96	NEVER KNEW LOVE LIKE THIS *Sony S2 6629382* [1]	.....40 2
1 Jun 96	HAPPY *Sony S2 6630692*	.....46 1

[1] Pauline Henry featuring Wayne Marshall

Pierre HENRY *France, male instrumentalist* — 1 wk
4 Oct 97	PSYCHE ROCK *Hi-Life 4620312*	.....58 1

HERD ☉ *UK, male vocal/instrumental group* — 35 wks
13 Sep 67 ●	FROM THE UNDERWORLD *Fontana TF 856*	.....6 13
20 Dec 67	PARADISE LOST *Fontana TF 887*	.....15 9
10 Apr 68 ●	I DON'T WANT OUR LOVING TO DIE *Fontana TF 925*	.....5 13

HERMAN'S HERMITS ☉ *Manchester quintet fronted by teenage vocalist Peter Noone, b. 5 November, 1947, whose US popularity in the mid-1960s rivalled The Beatles. This band sold more than 40 million records and at times had three singles simultaneously in the US Top 20* — 211 wks
20 Aug 64 ★	I'M INTO SOMETHING GOOD *Columbia DB 7338*	.....1 15
19 Nov 64	SHOW ME GIRL *Columbia DB 7408*	.....19 9
18 Feb 65 ●	SILHOUETTES *Columbia DB 7475*	.....3 12
29 Apr 65 ●	WONDERFUL WORLD *Columbia DB 7546*	.....7 9
2 Sep 65	JUST A LITTLE BIT BETTER *Columbia DB 7670*	.....15 9
23 Dec 65 ●	A MUST TO AVOID *Columbia DB 7791*	.....6 11
24 Mar 66	YOU WON'T BE LEAVING *Columbia DB 7861*	.....20 7
23 Jun 66	THIS DOOR SWINGS BOTH WAYS *Columbia DB 7947*	.....18 7
6 Oct 66 ●	NO MILK TODAY *Columbia DB 8012*	.....7 11
1 Dec 66	EAST WEST *Columbia DB 8076*	.....37 7
9 Feb 67 ●	THERE'S A KIND OF HUSH *Columbia DB 8123*	.....7 11
17 Jan 68	I CAN TAKE OR LEAVE YOUR LOVING *Columbia DB 8327*	.....11 9
1 May 68	SLEEPY JOE *Columbia DB 8404*	.....12 10
17 Jul 68 ●	SUNSHINE GIRL *Columbia DB 8446*	.....8 14
18 Dec 68 ●	SOMETHING'S HAPPENING *Columbia DB 8504*	.....6 15
23 Apr 69 ●	MY SENTIMENTAL FRIEND *Columbia DB 8563*	.....2 12
8 Nov 69	HERE COMES THE STAR *Columbia DB 8626*	.....33 9
7 Feb 70 ●	YEARS MAY COME, YEARS MAY GO *Columbia DB 8656*	.....7 11
2 May 70	YEARS MAY COME, YEARS MAY GO (re-entry) *Columbia DB 8656*	.....45 1
23 May 70	BET YER LIFE I DO *RAK 102*	.....22 10
14 Nov 70	LADY BARBARA *RAK 106* [1]	.....13 12

[1] Peter Noone and Herman's Hermits

See also Peter NOONE

HERNANDEZ *UK, male vocalist* — 3 wks
15 Apr 89	ALL MY LOVE *Epic HER 1*	.....58 3

Patrick HERNANDEZ ◢ *Guadeloupe, male vocalist* — 14 wks
16 Jun 79 ●	BORN TO BE ALIVE *Gem GEM 4*	.....10 14

HERREYS *Sweden, male vocal group* — 3 wks
26 May 84	DIGGI LOO-DIGGI LEY *Panther PAN 5*	.....46 3

Kristin HERSH *US, female vocalist* — 3 wks
22 Jan 94	YOUR GHOST *4AD BAD 4001CD*	.....45 2
16 Apr 94	STRINGS *4AD BAD 4006CD*	.....60 1

Nick HEYWARD ☉ *UK, male vocalist* — 65 wks
19 Mar 83	WHISTLE DOWN THE WIND *Arista HEY 1*	.....13 8
4 Jun 83	TAKE THAT SITUATION *Arista HEY 2*	.....11 10
24 Sep 83	BLUE HAT FOR A BLUE DAY *Arista HEY 3*	.....14 8
3 Dec 83	ON A SUNDAY *Arista HEY 4*	.....52 5
2 Jun 84	LOVE ALL DAY *Arista HEY 5*	.....31 6
3 Nov 84	WARNING SIGN *Arista HEY 6*	.....25 8
5 Jan 85	WARNING SIGN (re-entry) *Arista HEY 6*	.....72 1
8 Jun 85	LAURA *Arista HEY 8*	.....45 4
10 May 86	OVER THE WEEKEND *Arista HEY 9*	.....43 5
10 Sep 88	YOU'RE MY WORLD *Warner Bros. W 7758*	.....67 2
21 Aug 93	KITE *Epic 6594882*	.....44 2

16 Oct 93	HE DOESN'T LOVE YOU LIKE I DO *Epic 6597282*	.....58 2
30 Sep 95	THE WORLD *Epic 6623845*	.....47 2
13 Jan 96	ROLLERBLADE *Epic 6627912*	.....37 2

HHC *UK, male DJ/production duo* — 1 wk
19 Apr 97	WE'RE NOT ALONE *Perfecto PERF 138CD*	.....44 1

HI-FIVE *US, male vocal group* — 8 wks
1 Jun 91	I LIKE THE WAY (THE KISSING GAME) *Jive JIVE 271* ▲	.....43 6
24 Oct 92	SHE'S PLAYING HARD TO GET *Jive JIVE 316*	.....55 2

HI GLOSS ◢ *US, disco aggregation* — 13 wks
8 Aug 81	YOU'LL NEVER KNOW *Epic EPC A 1387*	.....12 13

HI-LUX *UK, male instrumental/production duo* — 3 wks
18 Feb 95	FEEL IT *Cheeky CHEKCD 006*	.....41 2
2 Sep 95	NEVER FELT THIS WAY/FEEL IT *Champion CHAMPCD 319*	.....58 1

HI POWER *Germany, male rap group* — 1 wk
1 Sep 90	CULT OF SNAP/SIMBA GROOVE *Rumour RUMAT 24*	.....73 1

HI-TEK 3 featuring YA KID K ☉ ☺ *Belgium, male/female vocal/instrumental group* — 10 wks
3 Feb 90	SPIN THAT WHEEL *Brothers Organisation BORG 1*	.....69 3
29 Sep 90	SPIN THAT WHEEL (TURTLES GET REAL) (re-issue) *Brothers Organisation BORG 16*	.....15 7

See also TECHNOTRONIC

HI TENSION ♪ *UK, male vocal/instrumental group* — 23 wks
6 May 78	HI TENSION *Island WIP 6422*	.....13 12
12 Aug 78 ●	BRITISH HUSTLE/PEACE ON EARTH *Island WIP 6446*	.....8 11

'Peace on Earth' credited with 'British Hustle' from 2 Sep, 1978 to end of record's chart run

Al HIBBLER ℂ *US, male vocalist* — 17 wks
13 May 55 ●	UNCHAINED MELODY *Brunswick 05420*	.....2 17

Hinda HICKS R&B *UK, female vocalist* — 14 wks
7 Mar 98	IF YOU WANT ME *Island CID 689*	.....25 3
16 May 98	YOU THINK YOU OWN ME *Island*	.....19 4
15 Aug 98	I WANNA BE YOUR LADY *Island CID 709*	.....14 5
24 Oct 98	TRULY *Island CID 721*	.....31 2

Bertie HIGGINS *US, male vocalist* — 4 wks
5 Jun 82	KEY LARGO *Epic EPC A 2168*	.....60 4

HIGH *UK, male vocal group* — 11 wks
25 Aug 90	UP AND DOWN *London LON 272*	.....53 4
27 Oct 90	TAKE YOUR TIME *London LON 280*	.....56 2
12 Jan 91	BOX SET GO *London LONG 286*	.....28 3
6 Apr 91	MORE . . . *London LON 297*	.....67 2

HIGH FIDELITY *UK, male vocal/instrumental group* — 1 wk
25 Jul 98	LUV DUP *Plastique FAKE 03CDS*	.....70 1

HIGH NUMBERS *UK, male vocal/instrumental group* — 4 wks
5 Apr 80	I'M THE FACE *Back Door DOOR 4*	.....49 4

The High Numbers were an early version of the Who
See also the WHO

HIGH SOCIETY *UK, male vocal/instrumental group* — 4 wks
15 Nov 80	I NEVER GO OUT IN THE RAIN *Eagle ERS 002*	.....53 4

HIGHLY LIKELY UK, male vocal/instrumental group — 4 wks

| 21 Apr 73 | WHATEVER HAPPENED TO YOU ('LIKELY LADS' THEME) BBC RESL 10 | 35 | 4 |

HIGHWAYMEN ♂ ◐ US, male vocal group — 18 wks

7 Sep 61	★ MICHAEL HMV POP 910 ▲	1	14
7 Dec 61	GYPSY ROVER HMV POP 948	41	3
11 Jan 62	GYPSY ROVER (re-entry) HMV POP 948	43	1

HIJACK UK, male producer — 3 wks

| 6 Jan 90 | THE BADMAN IS ROBBIN' Rhyme Syndicate 655517 7 | 56 | 3 |

Benny HILL ◐ UK, male vocalist — 43 wks

16 Feb 61	GATHER IN THE MUSHROOMS Pye 7N 15327	12	8
1 Jun 61	TRANSISTOR RADIO Pye 7N 15359	24	6
16 May 63	HARVEST OF LOVE Pye 7N 15520	20	8
13 Nov 71	★ ERNIE (THE FASTEST MILKMAN IN THE WEST) Columbia DB 8833	1	17
30 May 92	ERNIE (THE FASTEST MILKMAN IN THE WEST) (re-issue) EMI ERN 1	29	4

Chris HILL ◐ UK, male vocalist/DJ/producer — 14 wks

| 6 Dec 75 | ● RENTA SANTA Philips 6006 491 | 10 | 7 |
| 4 Dec 76 | ● BIONIC SANTA Philips 6006 551 | 10 | 7 |

Dan HILL ◐ Canada, male vocalist — 13 wks

| 18 Feb 78 | SOMETIMES WHEN WE TOUCH 20th Century BTC 2355 | 46 | 1 |
| 4 Mar 78 | SOMETIMES WHEN WE TOUCH (re-entry) 20th Century BTC 2355 | 13 | 12 |

Faith HILL ➷ US, female vocalist — 7 wks

| 14 Nov 98 | THIS KISS Warner Brothers W463CD | 13† | 7 |

Lauryn HILL ♪ US, female vocalist — 8 wks

| 27 Dec 97 | ALL MY TIME World Entertainment OWEDC 2 [1] | 57 | 1 |
| 3 Oct 98 | DOO WOP (THAT THING) Ruffhouse 6665152 | 3 | 7 |

[1] Paid and Live featuring Lauryn Hill

See also FUGEES

Lonnie HILL US, male vocalist — 4 wks

| 22 Mar 86 | GALVESTON BAY 10 TEN 111 | 51 | 4 |

Roni HILL US, female vocalist — 4 wks

| 7 May 77 | YOU KEEP ME HANGIN' ON – STOP IN THE NAME OF LOVE (MEDLEY) Creole CR 138 | 36 | 4 |

Vince HILL ◖ UK, male vocalist — 91 wks

7 Jun 62	THE RIVER'S RUN DRY Piccadilly 7N 35043	49	1
28 Jun 62	THE RIVER'S RUN DRY (re-entry) Piccadilly 7N 35043	41	1
6 Jan 66	TAKE ME TO YOUR HEART AGAIN Columbia DB 7781	13	11
17 Mar 66	HEARTACHES Columbia DB 7852	28	5
2 Jun 66	MERCI CHERI Columbia DB 7924	36	6
9 Feb 67	● EDELWEISS Columbia DB 8127	2	17
11 May 67	ROSES OF PICARDY Columbia DB 8185	13	11
27 Sep 67	LOVE LETTERS IN THE SAND Columbia DB 8268	23	9
26 Jun 68	IMPORTANCE OF YOUR LOVE Columbia DB 8414	32	12
12 Feb 69	DOESN'T ANYBODY KNOW MY NAME? Columbia DB 8515	50	1
25 Oct 69	LITTLE BLUE BIRD Columbia DB 8616	42	1
25 Sep 71	LOOK AROUND Columbia DB 8804	12	16

HILLMAN MINX
UK/France, male/female vocal/instrumental group — 1 wk

| 5 Sep 98 | I'VE HAD ENOUGH Mercury MERCD 509 | 72 | 1 |

HILLTOPPERS ◖ US, male vocal group — 30 wks

27 Jan 56	● ONLY YOU London HLD 8221	3	22
10 Aug 56	ONLY YOU (re-entry) London HLD 8221	24	1
14 Sep 56	TRYIN' London HLD 8298	30	1
5 Apr 57	MARIANNE London HLD 8381	20	2
26 Apr 57	MARIANNE (re-entry) London HLD 8381	23	4

Ronnie HILTON ◖ Favourite 1950s balladeer, b. Adrian Hill, 26 January, 1926, Hull. Despite the rise of rock'n'roll, he amassed a formidable selection of best sellers, albeit mainly with cover versions (the customary UK practice in the 1950s) — 128 wks

26 Nov 54	● I STILL BELIEVE HMV B 10785	3	14
10 Dec 54	VENI VIDI VICI HMV B 10785	12	8
11 Mar 55	● A BLOSSOM FELL HMV B 10808	10	5
26 Aug 55	STARS SHINE IN YOUR EYES HMV B 10901	13	7
11 Nov 55	YELLOW ROSE OF TEXAS HMV B 10924	15	2
10 Feb 56	YOUNG AND FOOLISH HMV POP 154	17	1
24 Feb 56	YOUNG AND FOOLISH (re-entry) HMV POP 154	20	1
9 Mar 56	YOUNG AND FOOLISH (2nd re-entry) HMV POP 154	19	1
20 Apr 56	★ NO OTHER LOVE HMV POP 198	1	14
29 Jun 56	● WHO ARE WE HMV POP 221	6	12
21 Sep 56	WOMAN IN LOVE HMV POP 248	30	1
9 Nov 56	TWO DIFFERENT WORLDS HMV POP 274	13	13
24 May 57	● AROUND THE WORLD HMV POP 338	4	18
2 Aug 57	WONDERFUL WONDERFUL HMV POP 364	27	2
21 Feb 58	MAGIC MOMENTS HMV POP 446	22	2
18 Apr 58	I MAY NEVER PASS THIS WAY AGAIN HMV POP 468 [1]	30	1
2 May 58	I MAY NEVER PASS THIS WAY AGAIN (re-entry) HMV POP 468 [1]	30	1
6 Jun 58	I MAY NEVER PASS THIS WAY AGAIN (2nd re-entry) HMV POP 468 [1]	27	1
9 Jan 59	THE WORLD OUTSIDE HMV POP 559 [1]	18	6
21 Aug 59	THE WONDER OF YOU HMV POP 638	22	3
21 May 64	DON'T LET THE RAIN COME DOWN HMV POP 1291	21	10
11 Feb 65	A WINDMILL IN OLD AMSTERDAM HMV POP 1378	23	13

[1] Ronnie Hilton with the Michael Sammes Singers

HINDSIGHT UK, male vocal/instrumental group — 3 wks

| 5 Sep 87 | LOWDOWN Circa YR 5 | 62 | 3 |

Deni HINES Australia, female vocalist — 6 wks

14 Jun 97	IT'S ALRIGHT Mushroom D 1593	35	2
20 Sep 97	I LIKE THE WAY Mushroom MUSH 7CDX	37	2
28 Feb 98	DELICIOUS Mushroom MUSH 20CD [1]	52	1
23 May 98	JOY Mushroom MUSH 30CDS	49	1

[1] Deni Hines featuring Don-E

Gregory HINES – See Luther VANDROSS

HIPSWAY ◐ UK, male vocal/instrumental group — 21 wks

13 Jul 85	THE BROKEN YEARS Mercury MER 193	72	3
14 Sep 85	ASK THE LORD Mercury MER 195	72	1
22 Feb 86	THE HONEYTHIEF Mercury MER 212	17	9
10 May 86	ASK THE LORD Mercury LORD 1	50	5
20 Sep 86	LONG WHITE CAR Mercury MER 230	55	2
1 Apr 89	YOUR LOVE Mercury MER 279	66	1

LORD 1 was a re-recording of MER 195

HISTORY – See Q-TEE

Carol HITCHCOCK Australia, female vocalist — 5 wks

| 30 May 87 | GET READY A & M AM 391 | 56 | 5 |

HITHOUSE ◐ ☺ Holland, male producer – Peter Slaghuis — 13 wks

| 5 Nov 88 | JACK TO THE SOUND OF THE UNDERGROUND Supreme SUPE 137 | 14 | 12 |
| 19 Aug 89 | MOVE YOUR FEET TO THE RHYTHM OF THE BEAT Supreme SUPE 149 | 69 | 1 |

HITMAN HOWIE TEE – *See REAL ROXANNE*

Edmund HOCKRIDGE Ⓒ *Canada, male vocalist*   **18 wks**

17 Feb 56	●	YOUNG AND FOOLISH *Nixa N 15039*	10 7
13 Apr 56		YOUNG AND FOOLISH (re-entry) *Nixa N 15039*	28 1
4 May 56		YOUNG AND FOOLISH (2nd re-entry) *Nixa N 15039*	26 1
11 May 56		NO OTHER LOVE *Nixa N 15048*	24 2
1 Jun 56		NO OTHER LOVE (re-entry) *Nixa N 15048*	29 1
15 Jun 56		NO OTHER LOVE (2nd re-entry) *Nixa N 15048*	30 1
31 Aug 56		BY THE FOUNTAINS OF ROME *Pye Nixa N 15063*	17 5

Eddie HODGES *US, male vocalist*   **10 wks**

28 Sep 61	I'M GONNA KNOCK ON YOUR DOOR *London HLA 9369*	37 6
9 Aug 62	MADE TO LOVE (GIRLS GIRLS GIRLS) *London HLA 9576*	37 4

Roger HODGSON – *See SUPERTRAMP*

Susanna HOFFS *US, female vocalist*   **8 wks**

2 Mar 91	MY SIDE OF THE BED *Columbia 6565547*	44 4
11 May 91	UNCONDITIONAL LOVE *Columbia 6567827*	65 2
19 Oct 96	ALL I WANT *London LONCD 387*	32 2

Hulk HOGAN – *See GREEN JELLY*

HOLE ✍ ☹ *US, female/male vocal/instrumental group*   **11 wks**

17 Apr 93	BEAUTIFUL SON *City Slang EFA 0491603*	54 1
9 Apr 94	MISS WORLD *City Slang EFA 049362*	64 1
15 Apr 95	DOLL PARTS *Geffen GFSTD 91*	16 3
29 Jul 95	VIOLET *Geffen GFSTD 94*	17 2
12 Sep 98	CELEBRITY SKIN *Geffen GFSTD 22345*	19 4

HOLE IN ONE *Holland, male DJ / producer*   **2 wks**

15 Feb 97	LIFE'S TOO SHORT *Manifesto FESCD 21*	36 2

HOLLAND-DOZIER featuring Lamont DOZIER
US, male vocal duo   **5 wks**

28 Oct 72	WHY CAN'T WE BE LOVERS *Invictus INV 525*	29 5

Jennifer HOLLIDAY *US, female vocalist*   **6 wks**

4 Sep 82	AND I'M TELLING YOU I'M NOT GOING *Geffen GEF A 2644*	32 6

Michael HOLLIDAY Ⓒ *UK, male vocalist*   **65 wks**

30 Mar 56		NOTHIN' TO DO *Columbia DB 3746*	20 1
27 Apr 56		NOTHIN' TO DO (re-entry) *Columbia DB 3746*	23 2
15 Jun 56		GAL WITH THE YALLER SHOES *Columbia DB 3783*	13 3
22 Jun 56		HOT DIGGITY (DOG ZIGGITY BOOM) *Columbia DB 3783*	14 5
3 Aug 56		HOT DIGGITY (DOG ZIGGITY BOOM)/	
		GAL WITH THE YALLER SHOES (re-entry)	
		Columbia DB 3783	17 3
5 Oct 56		TEN THOUSAND MILES *Columbia DB 3813*	24 3
17 Jan 58	★	THE STORY OF MY LIFE *Columbia DB 4058*	1 15
14 Mar 58		IN LOVE *Columbia DB 4087*	26 3
16 May 58		STAIRWAY OF LOVE *Columbia DB 4121*	3 13
11 Jul 58		I'LL ALWAYS BE IN LOVE WITH YOU *Columbia DB 4155*	27 1
1 Jan 60	★	STARRY EYED *Columbia DB 4378*	1 12
14 Apr 60		SKYLARK *Columbia DB 4437*	39 3
1 Sep 60		LITTLE BOY LOST *Columbia DB 4475*	50 1

*When 'Hot Diggity (Dog Ziggity Boom) / Gal With the Yaller Shoes' re-entered
the chart on 3 Aug, 1956, 'Hot Diggity (Dog Ziggity Boom)' was listed by itself
on 3 Aug and 10 Aug. Both sides were listed on 17 Aug – 'Gal With the Yaller
Shoes' peaking at No 25*

HOLLIES ☺ *Distinctive, influential and well-respected Manchester group:*
*Allan Clarke (v), Graham Nash (g), Tony Hicks (g), Eric Haydock (b),
Bobby Elliott (d). They were among the most regular chart visitors
of the 1960s, and their No 1s span 23 years*   **318 wks**

30 May 63	(AIN'T THAT) JUST LIKE ME *Parlophone R 5030*	25 10
29 Aug 63	SEARCHIN' *Parlophone R 5052*	12 14

21 Nov 63	●	STAY *Parlophone R 5077*	8 16
27 Feb 64	●	JUST ONE LOOK *Parlophone R 5104*	2 13
21 May 64	●	HERE I GO AGAIN *Parlophone R 5137*	4 12
17 Sep 64	●	WE'RE THROUGH *Parlophone R 5178*	7 11
28 Jan 65	●	YES I WILL *Parlophone R 5232*	9 13
27 May 65	★	I'M ALIVE *Parlophone R 5287*	1 14
2 Sep 65	●	LOOK THROUGH ANY WINDOW *Parlophone R 5322*	4 11
9 Dec 65		IF I NEEDED SOMEONE *Parlophone R 5392*	20 9
24 Feb 66	●	I CAN'T LET GO *Parlophone R 5409*	2 10
23 Jun 66	●	BUS STOP *Parlophone R 5469*	5 9
13 Oct 66	●	STOP STOP STOP *Parlophone R 5508*	2 12
16 Feb 67	●	ON A CAROUSEL *Parlophone R 5562*	4 11
1 Jun 67	●	CARRIE-ANNE *Parlophone R 5602*	3 11
27 Sep 67		KING MIDAS IN REVERSE *Parlophone R 5637*	18 8
27 Mar 68	●	JENNIFER ECCLES *Parlophone R 5680*	7 11
2 Oct 68		LISTEN TO ME *Parlophone R 5733*	11 11
5 Mar 69	●	SORRY SUZANNE *Parlophone R 5765*	3 12
4 Oct 69	●	HE AIN'T HEAVY, HE'S MY BROTHER *Parlophone R 5806*	3 15
18 Apr 70	●	I CAN'T TELL THE BOTTOM FROM THE TOP	
		Parlophone R 5837	7 10
3 Oct 70		GASOLINE ALLEY BRED *Parlophone R 5862*	14 7
22 May 71		HEY WILLY *Parlophone R 5905*	22 7
26 Feb 72		THE BABY *Polydor 2058 199*	26 6
2 Sep 72		LONG COOL WOMAN IN A BLACK DRESS	
		Parlophone R 5939	32 8
13 Oct 73		THE DAY THAT CURLY BILLY SHOT DOWN CRAZY	
		SAM McGHEE *Polydor 2058 403*	24 6
9 Feb 74	●	THE AIR THAT I BREATHE *Polydor 2058 435*	2 13
14 Jun 80		SOLDIER'S SONG *Polydor 2059 246*	58 3
29 Aug 81		HOLLIEDAZE (MEDLEY) *EMI 5229*	28 7
3 Sep 88	★	HE AIN'T HEAVY, HE'S MY BROTHER (re-issue) *EMI EM 74*	1 11
3 Dec 88		THE AIR THAT I BREATHE (re-issue) *EMI EM 80*	60 5
20 Mar 93		THE WOMAN I LOVE *EMI CDEM 264*	42 2

Loleatta HOLLOWAY ♪ ☺ *US, female vocalist*   **16 wks**

31 Aug 91	GOOD VIBRATIONS *Interscope A 8764* [1]	14 7
18 Jan 92	TAKE ME AWAY *PWL Continental PWL 210* [2]	25 5
26 Mar 94	STAND UP *Six6 SIXCD 111*	68 1
1 Apr 95	KEEP THE FIRE BURNIN' *Columbia 6611552* [3]	49 1
11 Apr 98	SHOUT TO THE TOP *JBO JNR 5001573* [4]	23 2

[1] Marky Mark and the Funky Bunch featuring Loleatta Holloway [2] Cappella
featuring Loleatta Holloway [3] Dan Hartman starring Loleatta Holloway [4] Fire
Island featuring Loleatta Holloway

Buddy HOLLY ♪ *Highly respected and exceptionally influential singer/
songwriter, b. Charles Hardin Holley, 7 September, 1936, Texas, d. 3 February,
1959 (aka 'The day the music died'). Despite a relatively brief career,
his records and songs are still frequently heard around the globe*   **190 wks**

6 Dec 57	●	PEGGY SUE *Coral Q 72293*	6 17
14 Mar 58		LISTEN TO ME *Coral Q 72288*	16 2
20 Jun 58	●	RAVE ON *Coral Q 72325*	5 14
29 Aug 58		EARLY IN THE MORNING *Coral Q 72333*	17 4
16 Jan 59		HEARTBEAT *Coral Q 72346*	30 1
27 Feb 59	★	IT DOESN'T MATTER ANYMORE *Coral Q 72360*	1 21
31 Jul 59		MIDNIGHT SHIFT *Brunswick 05800*	26 3
11 Sep 59		PEGGY SUE GOT MARRIED *Coral Q 72376*	13 10
28 Apr 60		HEARTBEAT (re-issue) *Coral Q 72392*	30 3
26 May 60		TRUE LOVE WAYS *Coral Q 72397*	25 7
20 Oct 60		LEARNIN' THE GAME *Coral Q 72411*	36 3
26 Jan 61		WHAT TO DO *Coral Q 72419*	34 6
6 Jul 61		BABY I DON'T CARE/VALLEY OF TEARS *Coral Q 72432*	12 14
15 Mar 62		LISTEN TO ME (re-issue) *Coral Q 72449*	48 1
13 Sep 62		REMINISCING *Coral Q 72455*	17 11
14 Mar 63	●	BROWN-EYED HANDSOME MAN *Coral Q 72459*	3 17
6 Jun 63	●	BO DIDDLEY *Coral Q 72463*	4 12
5 Sep 63		WISHING *Coral Q 72466*	10 11
19 Dec 63		WHAT TO DO *Coral Q 72469*	27 8
14 May 64		YOU'VE GOT LOVE *Coral Q 72472* [1]	40 6
10 Sep 64		LOVE'S MADE A FOOL OF YOU *Coral Q 72475*	39 6
3 Apr 68		PEGGY SUE/RAVE ON (re-issue) *MCA MU 1012*	32 9
10 Dec 88		TRUE LOVE WAYS (re-issue) *MCA MCA 1302*	65 4

[1] Buddy Holly and the Crickets

Buddy Holly's version of 'Love's Made a Fool of You' is not the same version as the Crickets' hit of 1959, on which Holly did not appear. 'Valley of Tears' was not listed together with 'Baby I Don't Care' until 13 Jul, 1961. 'What to Do' on Q 72469 was a re-recording

HOLLY and the IVYS UK, male/female vocal/instrumental group · 4 wks

19 Dec 81	CHRISTMAS ON 45 Decca SANTA 1	40	4

HOLLYWOOD ARGYLES US, male vocal group · 10 wks

21 Jul 60	ALLEY OOP London HLU 9146 ▲	24	10

HOLLYWOOD BEYOND ⊙ UK, male group · 14 wks

12 Jul 86 ●	WHAT'S THE COLOUR OF MONEY? WEA YZ 76	7	10
20 Sep 86	NO MORE TEARS WEA YZ 81	47	4

Eddie HOLMAN 🎤 US, male vocalist · 13 wks

19 Oct 74 ●	(HEY THERE) LONELY GIRL ABC 4012	4	13

David HOLMES UK, male producer · 7 wks

6 Apr 96	GONE Go! Discs GODCD 140	75	1
23 Aug 97	GRITTY SHAKER Go. Beat GOBCD 2	53	1
10 Jan 98	DON'T DIE JUST YET Go. Beat GOLCD 6	33	3
4 Apr 98	MY MATE PAUL Go. Beat GOBCD 8	39	2

Rupert HOLMES US, male vocalist · 14 wks

12 Jan 80	ESCAPE (THE PINA COLADA SONG) Infinity INF 120 ▲	23	7
22 Mar 80	HIM MCA 565	31	7

John HOLT 👑 Jamaica, male vocalist · 14 wks

14 Dec 74 ●	HELP ME MAKE IT THROUGH THE NIGHT Trojan TR 7909	6	14

A HOMEBOY, A HIPPIE and A FUNKI DREDD
UK, male vocal/instrumental group · 9 wks

13 Oct 90	TOTAL CONFUSION Tam Tam 7TTT 031	56	3
29 Dec 90	FREEDOM Tam Tam 7TTT 039	68	4
8 Jan 94	HERE WE GO AGAIN Polydor PZCD 302	57	2

HONDY Italy, female vocalist · 2 wks

12 Apr 97	HONDY (NO ACCESS) Manifesto FESCD 20	26	2

HONEYBUS ⊙ UK, male vocal/instrumental group · 12 wks

20 Mar 68 ●	I CAN'T LET MAGGIE GO Deram DM 182	8	12

HONEYCOMBS ⊙ UK, male/female vocal/instrumental group · 39 wks

23 Jul 64 ★	HAVE I THE RIGHT Pye 7N 15664	1	15
22 Oct 64	IS IT BECAUSE Pye 7N 15705	38	6
29 Apr 65	SOMETHING BETTER BEGINNING Pye 7N 15827	39	4
5 Aug 65	THAT'S THE WAY Pye 7N 15890	12	14

HONEYCRACK UK, male vocal/instrumental group · 9 wks

4 Nov 95	SITTING AT HOME Epic 6625382	42	2
24 Feb 96	GO AWAY Epic 6628642	41	2
11 May 96	KING OF MISERY Epic 6631472	32	2
20 Jul 96	SITTING AT HOME (re-issue) Epic 6635032	32	2
16 Nov 96	ANYWAY EG EGO 52A	67	1

HONEYDRIPPERS UK/US, male vocal/instrumental group · 3 wks

2 Feb 85	SEA OF LOVE Es Paranza YZ 33	56	3

HONEYZ ℝ&𝔹 ⊙ UK, female vocal trio · 14 wks

5 Sep 98 ●	FINALLY FOUND 1st Avenue HNZCD 1	4	12
19 Dec 98 ●	END OF THE LINE 1st Avenue HNZCD 2	5†	2

HONKY UK, male vocal/instrumental group · 5 wks

30 Oct 93	THE HONKY DOODLE DAY EP ZTT ZANG 45CD	61	1
19 Feb 94	THE WHISTLER ZTT ZANG 48CD	41	2
20 Apr 96	HIP HOP DON'T YA DROP Higher Ground HIGHS 1CD	70	1
10 Aug 96	WHAT'S GOIN DOWN Higher Ground HIGHS 2CD	49	1

Tracks on The Honky Doodle Day EP: KKK (Boom Boom Tra La La La)/ Honky Doodle Dub/Chains

HONKY UK, male vocal/instrumental group · 5 wks

28 May 77	JOIN THE PARTY Creole CR 137	28	5

Frank HOOKER and POSITIVE PEOPLE
US, male vocal/instrumental group · 4 wks

5 Jul 80	THIS FEELIN' DJM DJS 10947	48	4

John Lee HOOKER 🎤 US, male vocalist · 23 wks

11 Jun 64	DIMPLES Stateside SS 297	23	10
24 Oct 92	BOOM BOOM Pointblank POB 3	16	5
16 Jan 93	BOOGIE AT RUSSIAN HILL Pointblank POBDX 4	53	2
15 May 93	GLORIA Exile VANCD 11 [1]	31	3
11 Feb 95	CHILL OUT (THINGS GONNA CHANGE) Pointblank POBD 10	45	2
20 Apr 96	BABY LEE Silvertone ORECD 81 [2]	65	1

[1] Van Morrison and John Lee Hooker [2] John Lee Hooker with Robert Cray

HOOTERS US, male vocal/instrumental group · 9 wks

21 Nov 87	SATELLITE CBS 651168 7	22	9

HOOTIE AND THE BLOWFISH
US, male vocal/instrumental group · 6 wks

25 Feb 95	HOLD MY HAND Atlantic A 7230CD	50	3
27 May 95	LET HER CRY Atlantic A 7188CD	75	1
4 May 96	OLD MAN AND ME (WHEN I GET TO HEAVEN) Atlantic A 5513CD	57	1
7 Nov 98	I WILL WAIT Atlantic AT 0048CD	57	1

HOPE A.D. UK, male producer – David Hope · 1 wk

4 Jun 94	TREE FROG Sun-Up SUN 003CD	73	1

See also MIND OF KANE

Mary HOPKIN ⊙ UK, female vocalist · 74 wks

4 Sep 68 ★	THOSE WERE THE DAYS Apple 2	1	21
2 Apr 69 ●	GOODBYE Apple 10	2	14
31 Jan 70 ●	TEMMA HARBOUR Apple 22	6	11
28 Mar 70 ●	KNOCK KNOCK WHO'S THERE Apple 26	2	14
31 Oct 70	THINK ABOUT YOUR CHILDREN Apple 30	19	7
2 Jan 71	THINK ABOUT YOUR CHILDREN (re-entry) Apple 30	46	2
31 Jul 71	LET MY NAME BE SORROW Apple 34	46	1
20 Mar 76	IF YOU LOVE ME Good Earth GD 2	32	4

See also VARIOUS ARTISTS (EPs & LPs) – The Apple EP

Anthony HOPKINS UK, male vocalist · 1 wk

27 Dec 86	DISTANT STAR Juice AA 5	75	1

Nick HORNBY – *See PRETENDERS/Chrissie HYNDE*

Bruce HORNSBY and the RANGE ⊙ 🎤
US, male vocal/instrumental group · 15 wks

2 Aug 86	THE WAY IT IS RCA PB 49805 ▲	15	10
25 Apr 87	MANDOLIN RAIN RCA PB 49769	70	1
28 May 88	THE VALLEY ROAD RCA PB 49561	44	4

HORSE UK, female/male vocal/instrumental group · 10 wks

24 Nov 90	CAREFUL Capitol CL 587	52	3
21 Aug 93	SHAKE THIS MOUNTAIN Oxygen GASPD 7	52	2
23 Oct 93	GOD'S HOME MOVIE Oxygen GASXD 10	56	1
15 Jan 94	CELEBRATE Oxygen GASPD 11	49	2
5 Apr 97	CAREFUL Stress CDSTRX 79	44	2

Johnny HORTON 🎵 US, male vocalist — 15 wks

26 Jun 59	BATTLE OF NEW ORLEANS Philips PB 932 ▲	16 4
19 Jan 61	NORTH TO ALASKA Philips PB 1062	23 11

HOT BLOOD France, male instrumental group — 5 wks

9 Oct 76	SOUL DRACULA Creole CR 132	32 5

HOT BUTTER ◒ US, male instrumental group — 19 wks

22 Jul 72 ●	POPCORN Pye International 7N 25583	5 16
23 Dec 72	POPCORN (re-entry) Pye International 7N 25583	50 3

HOT CHOCOLATE ◒ London-based band who were chart regulars throughout the 1970s and 1980s. Group founders were West Indian-born Erroll Brown (v) and Tony Wilson (b/v). This act had at least one hit every year between 1970-1984 — 283 wks

15 Aug 70 ●	LOVE IS LIFE RAK 103	6 12
6 Mar 71	YOU COULD HAVE BEEN A LADY RAK 110	22 9
28 Aug 71 ●	I BELIEVE (IN LOVE) RAK 118	8 11
28 Oct 72	YOU'LL ALWAYS BE A FRIEND RAK 139	23 8
14 Apr 73 ●	BROTHER LOUIE RAK 149	7 10
18 Aug 73	RUMOURS RAK 157	44 3
16 Mar 74 ●	EMMA RAK 168	3 10
30 Nov 74	CHERI BABE RAK 188	31 9
24 May 75	DISCO QUEEN RAK 202	11 7
9 Aug 75 ●	A CHILD'S PRAYER RAK 212	7 10
8 Nov 75 ●	YOU SEXY THING RAK 221	2 12
20 Mar 76	DON'T STOP IT NOW RAK 230	11 8
26 Jun 76	MAN TO MAN RAK 238	14 8
21 Aug 76	HEAVEN IS IN THE BACK SEAT OF MY CADILLAC RAK 240	25 8
18 Jun 77 ★	SO YOU WIN AGAIN RAK 259	1 11
26 Nov 77 ●	PUT YOUR LOVE IN ME RAK 266	10 9
4 Mar 78	EVERY 1'S A WINNER RAK 270	12 11
2 Dec 78	I'LL PUT YOU TOGETHER AGAIN RAK 286	13 11
19 May 79	MINDLESS BOOGIE RAK 292	46 5
28 Jul 79	GOING THROUGH THE MOTIONS RAK 296	53 4
3 May 80 ●	NO DOUBT ABOUT IT RAK 310	2 11
19 Jul 80	ARE YOU GETTING ENOUGH OF WHAT MAKES YOU HAPPY RAK 318	17 7
13 Dec 80	LOVE ME TO SLEEP RAK 324	50 5
30 May 81	YOU'LL NEVER BE SO WRONG RAK 331	52 4
17 Apr 82 ●	GIRL CRAZY RAK 341	7 11
10 Jul 82 ●	IT STARTED WITH A KISS RAK 344	5 12
25 Sep 82	CHANCES RAK 350	32 5
7 May 83 ●	WHAT KINDA BOY YOU LOOKING FOR (GIRL) RAK 357	10 9
17 Sep 83	TEARS ON THE TELEPHONE RAK 363	37 5
4 Feb 84	I GAVE YOU MY HEART (DIDN'T I) RAK 369	13 10
17 Jan 87	YOU SEXY THING (re-mix) EMI 5592	10 10
4 Apr 87	EVERY 1'S A WINNER (re-mix) EMI 5607	69 2
6 Mar 93	IT STARTED WITH A KISS (re-issue) EMI CDEMCTS 7	31 5
22 Nov 97 ●	YOU SEXY THING (re-issue) EMI CDHOT 100	6 8
14 Feb 98	IT STARTED WITH A KISS (2nd re-issue) EMI CDHOT 101 [1]	18 3

[1] Hot Chocolate featuring Errol Brown

HOT GOSSIP – See Sarah BRIGHTMAN

HOT HOUSE UK, male/female vocal/instrumental group — 3 wks

14 Feb 87	DON'T COME TO STAY Deconstruction CHEZ 1	74 1
24 Sep 88	DON'T COME TO STAY (re-issue) Deconstruction PB 42233	70 2

HOT 'N' JUICY – See Mousse T vs HOT 'N' JUICY

HOT STREAK ☺ US, male vocal/instrumental group — 8 wks

10 Sep 83	BODY WORK Polydor POSP 642	19 8

HOTHOUSE FLOWERS ◒ ✎
Ireland, male vocal/instrumental group — 36 wks

14 May 88	DON'T GO London LON 174	11 8

23 Jul 88	I'M SORRY London LON 187	53 3
12 May 90	GIVE IT UP London LON 258	30 5
28 Jul 90	I CAN SEE CLEARLY NOW London LON 269	23 7
20 Oct 90	MOVIES London LON 276	68 2
13 Feb 93	EMOTIONAL TIME London LONCD 335	38 4
8 May 93	ONE TONGUE London LOCDP 340	45 3
19 Jun 93	ISN'T IT AMAZING London LOCDP 343	46 2
27 Nov 93	THIS IS IT (YOUR SOUL) London LONCD 346	67 1
16 May 98	YOU CAN LOVE ME NOW London LONCD 410	65 1

HOTLEGS ◒ UK, male vocal/instrumental group — 14 wks

4 Jul 70 ●	NEANDERTHAL MAN Fontana 6007 019	2 14

HOTRODS – See EDDIE and the HOTRODS

HOTSHOTS 🎵 UK, male vocal group — 15 wks

2 Jun 73 ●	SNOOPY VS. THE RED BARON Mooncrest MOON 5	4 15

Steven HOUGHTON ◒ UK, male vocalist — 20 wks

29 Nov 97 ●	WIND BENEATH MY WINGS RCA 74321529272	3 15
7 Mar 98	TRULY RCA 74321558552	23 5

A HOUSE Ireland, male vocal/instrumental group — 8 wks

13 Jun 92	ENDLESS ART Setanta AHOU 1	46 3
8 Aug 92	TAKE IT EASY ON ME Setanta AHOU 2	55 2
25 Jun 94	WHY ME Setanta CDAHOU 4	52 1
1 Oct 94	HERE COME THE GOOD TIMES Setanta CDAHOUS 5	37 2

HOUSE ENGINEERS UK, male vocal/instrumental duo — 2 wks

5 Dec 87	GHOST HOUSE Syncopate SY 8	69 2

HOUSE OF LOVE ☹ ◒ UK, male vocal/instrumental group — 21 wks

22 Apr 89	NEVER Fontana HOL 1	41 2
18 Nov 89	I DON'T KNOW WHY I LOVE YOU Fontana HOL 2	41 3
3 Feb 90	SHINE ON Fontana HOL 3	20 4
7 Apr 90	BEATLES AND THE STONES Fontana HOL 4	36 4
26 Oct 91	THE GIRL WITH THE LONELIEST EYES Fontana HOL 5	58 1
2 May 92	FEEL Fontana HOL 6	45 3
27 Jun 92	YOU DON'T UNDERSTAND Fontana HOL 7	46 3
5 Dec 92	CRUSH ME Fontana HOL 810	67 1

HOUSE OF PAIN 🎵 US, male rap group — 24 wks

10 Oct 92	JUMP AROUND Ruffness XLS 32	32 4
22 May 93 ●	JUMP AROUND (RE-ISSUE)/TOP O' THE MORNING TO YA (re-issue) Ruffness XL 43CD	8 7
23 Oct 93	SHAMROCKS AND SHENANIGANS/WHO'S THE MAN Ruffness XLS 46CD	23 4
16 Jul 94	ON POINT Ruffness XLS 52CD	19 3
12 Nov 94	IT AIN'T A CRIME Ruffness XLS 55CD1	37 2
1 Jul 95	OVER THERE (I DON'T CARE) Ruffness XLS 61CD1	20 3
5 Oct 96	FED UP Tommy Boy TBCD 7744	68 1

HOUSE TRAFFIC Italy / UK, male / female vocal / production duo — 3 wks

4 Oct 97	EVERY DAY OF MY LIFE Logic 74321249442	24 3

HOUSE OF VIRGINISM Sweden, male vocal/instrumental group — 6 wks

20 Nov 93	I'LL BE THERE FOR YOU (DOYA DODODO DOYA) ffrr FCD 221	29 3
30 Jul 94	REACHIN ffrr FCD 238	35 2
17 Feb 96	EXCLUSIVE Logic 74321324102 [1]	67 1

[1] Apollo presents House of Virginism

HOUSE OF ZEKKARIYAS – See WOMACK and WOMACK

HOUSEMARTINS ◒ ☹ UK, male vocal/instrumental group — 59 wks

8 Mar 86	SHEEP Go! Discs GOD 9	54 3
5 Apr 86	SHEEP (re-entry) Go! Discs GOD 9	71 1
7 Jun 86 ●	HAPPY HOUR Go! Discs GOD 11	3 13

UK No 1 ★   UK Top 10 ●   UK million seller ◆   UK entry at No 1 ■   US No 1 ▲

4 Oct 86		THINK FOR A MINUTE *Go! Discs GOD 13*	18	8
6 Dec 86 ★		CARAVAN OF LOVE *Go! Discs GOD 16*	1	11
23 May 87		FIVE GET OVER EXCITED *Go! Discs GOD 18*	11	6
5 Sep 87		ME AND THE FARMER *Go! Discs GOD 19*	15	5
21 Nov 87		BUILD *Go! Discs GOD 21*	15	8
23 Apr 88		THERE IS ALWAYS SOMETHING THERE TO REMIND ME *Go! Discs GOD 22*	35	4

HOUSEMASTER BOYZ and the RUDE BOY OF HOUSE ☺
US, male vocal/instrumental group — **14 wks**

9 May 87		HOUSE NATION *Magnetic Dance MAGD 1*	48	6
12 Sep 87 ●		HOUSE NATION (re-entry) *Magnetic Dance MAGD 1*	8	8

Thelma HOUSTON 🎤 *US, female vocalist* — **22 wks**

5 Feb 77		DON'T LEAVE ME THIS WAY *Motown TMG 1060* ▲	13	8
27 Jun 81		IF YOU FEEL IT *RCA 77*	48	4
1 Dec 84		YOU USED TO HOLD ME SO TIGHT *MCA MCA 932*	49	8
21 Jan 95		DON'T LEAVE ME THIS WAY *Dynamo DYND 001*	35	2

'Don't Leave Me This Way' in 1995 is a re-recording

Whitney HOUSTON ❂ 🎤 *Multi-award-winning, record-shattering vocalist*
b. 9 August, 1963, New Jersey. She recorded the second biggest-selling UK single by a female, and scored a record seven successive No 1s in the USA. Her UK album sales amount to more than seven million and worldwide exceed 100 million — **238 wks**

16 Nov 85 ★		SAVING ALL MY LOVE FOR YOU *Arista ARIST 640* ▲	1	16
25 Jan 86 ●		HOW WILL I KNOW *Arista ARIST 656* ▲	5	12
25 Jan 86		HOLD ME *Asylum EKR 32* [1]	44	5
12 Apr 86 ●		GREATEST LOVE OF ALL *Arista ARIST 658* ▲	8	11
23 May 87 ★		I WANNA DANCE WITH SOMEBODY (WHO LOVES ME) *Arista RIS 1* ▲	1	16
22 Aug 87		DIDN'T WE ALMOST HAVE IT ALL *Arista RIS 31* ▲	14	8
14 Nov 87 ●		SO EMOTIONAL *Arista RIS 43* ▲	5	11
12 Mar 88		WHERE DO BROKEN HEARTS GO *Arista 109793* ▲	14	8
28 May 88 ●		LOVE WILL SAVE THE DAY *Arista 111516*	10	7
24 Sep 88 ★		ONE MOMENT IN TIME *Arista 111613*	1	12
9 Sep 89		IT ISN'T, IT WASN'T, IT AIN'T NEVER GONNA BE *Arista 112545* [2]	29	5
20 Oct 90 ●		I'M YOUR BABY TONIGHT *Arista 113594* ▲	5	9
22 Dec 90 ●		ALL THE MAN THAT I NEED *Arista 114000* ▲	13	10
29 Dec 90		I'M YOUR BABY TONIGHT (re-entry) *Arista 113594*	69	1
6 Jul 91		MY NAME IS NOT SUSAN *Arista 114510*	29	5
28 Sep 91		I BELONG TO YOU *Arista 114727*	54	2
14 Nov 92 ★		I WILL ALWAYS LOVE YOU *Arista 74321120657* ◆ ▲	1	23
20 Feb 93 ●		I'M EVERY WOMAN *Arista 74321131502*	4	11
24 Apr 93 ●		I HAVE NOTHING *Arista 74321146142*	3	10
31 Jul 93		RUN TO YOU *Arista 74321153332*	15	6
6 Nov 93		QUEEN OF THE NIGHT *Arista 74321169302*	14	5
18 Dec 93		I WILL ALWAYS LOVE YOU (re-entry) *Arista 74321120652*	25	5
22 Jan 94		SOMETHING IN COMMON *MCA MCSTD 1957* [3]	16	5
18 Nov 95		EXHALE (SHOOP SHOOP) *Arista 74321332472*	11	9
24 Feb 96		COUNT ON ME *Arista 74321345842* [4]	12	6
21 Dec 96		STEP BY STEP *Arista 74321449332*	17	12
29 Mar 97		I BELIEVE IN YOU AND ME *Arista 74321468602*	16	5
19 Dec 98 ●		WHEN YOU BELIEVE *Columbia 6667522* [5]	4†	2

[1] Teddy Pendergrass with Whitney Houston [2] Aretha Franklin and Whitney Houston [3] Bobby Brown and Whitney Houston [4] Whitney Houston and Ce Ce Winans [5] Mariah Carey and Whitney Houston

Adina HOWARD R&B *US, female vocalist* — **10 wks**

4 Mar 95		FREAK LIKE ME *East West A 4473CD*	67	1
6 May 95		FREAK LIKE ME (re-entry) *East West A 4473CD*	33	3
23 Nov 96 ●		WHAT'S LOVE GOT TO DO WITH IT *Interscope IND 97008* [1]	2	6

[1] Warren G featuring Adina Howard

Billy HOWARD ❂ *UK, male vocalist* — **12 wks**

13 Dec 75 ●		KING OF THE COPS *Penny Farthing PEN 892*	6	12

Miki HOWARD *US, female vocalist* — **2 wks**

26 May 90		UNTIL YOU COME BACK (THAT'S WHAT I'M GONNA DO) *East West 7935*	67	2

Nick HOWARD *Australia, male vocalist* — **1 wk**

21 Jan 95		EVERYBODY NEEDS SOMEBODY *Bell 74321220942*	64	1

Robert HOWARD – *See Kym MAZELLE*

HOWLIN' WOLF *US, male vocalist* — **5 wks**

4 Jun 64		SMOKESTACK LIGHTNIN' *Pye International 7N 25244*	42	5

H20 ☺ *US/Switzerland, male/female vocal/instrumental group* — **4 wks**

14 Sep 96		NOBODY'S BUSINESS *AM:PM 5818832* [1]	19	3
30 Aug 97		SATISFIED (TAKE ME HIGHER) *AM:PM 5823252*	66	1

[1] H20 featuring Billie

H₂O ❂ *UK, male vocal/instrumental group* — **16 wks**

21 May 83		DREAM TO SLEEP *RCA 330*	17	10
13 Aug 83		JUST OUTSIDE OF HEAVEN *RCA 349*	38	6

Al HUDSON 🎤 *US, male vocalist* — **22 wks**

9 Sep 78		DANCE, GET DOWN (FEEL THE GROOVE)/HOW DO YOU DO *ABC 4229*	57	4
15 Sep 79		YOU CAN DO IT *MCA 511* [1]	15	10
8 Dec 79		MUSIC *MCA 542* [2]	56	6
29 Jun 85		LET'S TALK *MCA 972* [2]	64	2

[1] Al Hudson and the Partners [2] One Way featuring Al Hudson

Lavine HUDSON *UK, female vocalist* — **3 wks**

21 May 88		INTERVENTION *Virgin VS 1067*	57	3

HUDSON-FORD ❂ *UK, male vocal/instrumental duo* — **20 wks**

18 Aug 73 ●		PICK UP THE PIECES *A & M AMS 7078*	8	9
16 Feb 74		BURN BABY BURN *A & M AMS 7096*	15	9
29 Jun 74		FLOATING IN THE WIND *A & M AMS 7116*	35	2

See also MONKS

HUE AND CRY ❂ *UK, male vocal/instrumental duo* — **59 wks**

13 Jun 87 ●		LABOUR OF LOVE *Circa YR 4*	6	16
19 Sep 87		STRENGTH TO STRENGTH *Circa YR 6*	46	5
30 Jan 88		I REFUSE *Circa YR 8*	47	3
22 Oct 88		ORDINARY ANGEL *Circa YR 18*	42	6
28 Jan 89		LOOKING FOR LINDA *Circa YR 24*	15	9
6 May 89		VIOLENTLY EP *Circa YR 29*	21	6
30 Sep 89		SWEET INVISIBILITY *Circa YR 37*	55	3
25 May 91		MY SALT HEART *Circa YR 64*	47	3
3 Aug 91		LONG TERM LOVERS OF PAIN (EP) *Circa YR 71*	48	3
11 Jul 92		PROFOUNDLY YOURS *Fidelity FIDEL 1*	74	1
13 Mar 93		LABOUR OF LOVE (re-mix) *Circa HUESCD 1*	25	4

Tracks on Violently (EP): Violently/The Man With the Child In His Eyes/Calamity John. Tracks on Long Term Lovers of Pain (EP): Long Term Lovers of Pain/Heart of Saturday Night/Remember and Gold/Stars Crash Down

HUES CORPORATION ☺ *US, male/female vocal group* — **16 wks**

27 Jul 74 ●		ROCK THE BOAT *RCA APBO 0232* ▲	6	10
19 Oct 74		ROCKIN' SOUL *RCA PB 10066*	24	6

HUFF and HERB *UK, male DJ/production duo* — **4 wks**

6 Dec 97		FEELING GOOD *Planet 3 GXY 2018CD*	31	3
7 Nov 98		FEELING GOOD '98 (re-mix) *Planet 3 GXY 2020CD*	69	1

HUFF and PUFF *UK, male instrumental/production duo* — **4 wks**

2 Nov 96		HELP ME MAKE IT *Skyway SKYWCD 4*	31	2
21 Jun 97		HELP ME MAKE IT (re-issue) *Skyway SKYWCD 8*	37	2

David HUGHES *UK, male vocalist* **1 wk**

21 Sep 56		BY THE FOUNTAINS OF ROME *Philips PB 606*	27 1

HUGO and LUIGI *US, orchestra and chorus* **2 wks**

24 Jul 59		LA PLUME DE MA TANTE *RCA 1127*	29 2

HUMAN LEAGUE ✪ ☺ *Early-1980s UK pop sensation. Fronted by Phil Oakey (b. 2 October, 1955, Sheffield) (v/syn) and joined in 1980 by vocalists Joanne Catherall and Susanne Sulley. The group, which also topped the US chart, won Best Newcomers at the 1982 BRIT Awards* **155 wks**

3 May 80		HOLIDAY 80 (DOUBLE SINGLE) *Virgin SV 105*	56 5
21 Jun 80		EMPIRE STATE HUMAN *Virgin VS 351*	62 2
28 Feb 81		BOYS AND GIRLS *Virgin VS 395*	48 4
2 May 81		THE SOUND OF THE CROWD *Virgin VS 416*	12 10
8 Aug 81	●	LOVE ACTION (I BELIEVE IN LOVE) *Virgin VS 435*	3 13
10 Oct 81	●	OPEN YOUR HEART *Virgin VS 453*	6 9
5 Dec 81	★	DON'T YOU WANT ME *Virgin VS 466* ◆ ▲	1 13
9 Jan 82	●	BEING BOILED *EMI FAST 4*	6 9
6 Feb 82		HOLIDAY 80 (DOUBLE SINGLE) (re-entry) *Virgin SV 105*	46 5
20 Nov 82	●	MIRROR MAN *Virgin VS 522*	2 10
23 Apr 83	●	(KEEP FEELING) FASCINATION *Virgin VS 569*	2 9
5 May 84		THE LEBANON *Virgin VS 672*	11 6
23 Jun 84		THE LEBANON (re-entry) *Virgin VS 672*	75 1
30 Jun 84		LIFE ON YOUR OWN *Virgin VS 688*	16 6
17 Nov 84		LOUISE *Virgin VS 723*	13 10
23 Aug 86	●	HUMAN *Virgin VS 880* ▲	8 8
22 Nov 86		I NEED YOUR LOVING *Virgin VS 900*	72 1
15 Oct 88		LOVE IS ALL THAT MATTERS *Virgin VS 1025*	41 5
18 Aug 90		HEART LIKE A WHEEL *Virgin VS 1262*	29 5
7 Jan 95	●	TELL ME WHEN *East West YZ 882CD1*	6 9
18 Mar 95		ONE MAN IN MY HEART *East West YZ 904CD1*	13 8
17 Jun 95		FILLING UP WITH HEAVEN *East West YZ 944CD1*	36 2
28 Oct 95		DON'T YOU WANT ME (re-mix) *Virgin VSCDT 1557*	16 3
20 Jan 96		STAY WITH ME TONIGHT *East West EW 020CD*	40 2

Tracks on double single: Being Boiled / Marianne / Rock and Roll – Nightclubbing / Dancevision

HUMAN NATURE *Australia, male vocal group* **2 wks**

10 May 97		WISHES *Epic 6644485*	44 1
30 Aug 97		WHISPER YOUR NAME *Epic 6649465*	53 1

HUMAN RESOURCE ☺ *Holland, male instrumental / production group* **14 wks**

14 Sep 91		DOMINATOR *R&S RSUK 4*	36 7
21 Dec 91		THE COMPLETE DOMINATOR (re-mix) *R&S RSUK 4X*	18 7

HUMANOID ☺ *UK, male producer* **13 wks**

26 Nov 88		STAKKER HUMANOID *Westside WSR 12*	17 8
22 Apr 89		SLAM *Westside WSR 14*	54 2
8 Aug 92		STAKKER HUMANOID (re-issue) *Jumpin' + Pumpin' TOT 27*	40 3

HUMBLE PIE ⚞ *UK, male vocal / instrumental group* **10 wks**

23 Aug 69	●	NATURAL BORN BUGIE *Immediate IM 082*	4 10

Engelbert HUMPERDINCK ☾ *Internationally popular cabaret entertainer and easy-on-the-ear vocalist, b. Arnold Dorsey, 2 May, 1936, Madras, India. After a slow career start, an unlikely name change helped him to become one of the biggest-earning performers of the 1960s. This Vegas veteran was the UK's biggest-selling artist of 1967* **235 wks**

26 Jan 67	★	RELEASE ME *Decca F 12541* ◆	1 56
25 May 67	●	THERE GOES MY EVERYTHING *Decca F 12610*	2 29
23 Aug 67	★	THE LAST WALTZ *Decca F 12655* ◆	1 27
10 Jan 68	●	AM I THAT EASY TO FORGET *Decca F 12722*	3 13
24 Apr 68	●	A MAN WITHOUT LOVE *Decca F 12770*	2 15
25 Sep 68	●	LES BICYCLETTES DE BELSIZE *Decca F 12834*	5 15

5 Feb 69	●	THE WAY IT USED TO BE *Decca F 12879*	3 14
9 Aug 69		I'M A BETTER MAN (FOR HAVING LOVED YOU) *Decca F 12957*	15 13
15 Nov 69	●	WINTER WORLD OF LOVE *Decca F 12980*	7 13
30 May 70		MY MARIE *Decca F 13032*	31 7
12 Sep 70		SWEETHEART *Decca F 13068*	22 6
31 Oct 70		SWEETHEART (re-entry) *Decca F 13068*	50 1
11 Sep 71		ANOTHER TIME ANOTHER PLACE *Decca F 13212*	13 12
4 Mar 72		TOO BEAUTIFUL TO LAST *Decca F 13281*	14 10
20 Oct 73		LOVE IS ALL *Decca F 13443*	44 3
17 Nov 73		LOVE IS ALL (re-entry) *Decca F 13443*	45 1

Peter HUNNIGALE – See ARSENAL F C First Team Squad

Geraldine HUNT *Canada, female vocalist* **5 wks**

25 Oct 80		CAN'T FAKE THE FEELING *Champagne FIZZ 501*	44 5

Lisa HUNT – See LOVESTATION

Marsha HUNT *US, female vocalist* **3 wks**

21 May 69		WALK ON GILDED SPLINTERS *Track 604 030*	46 2
2 May 70		KEEP THE CUSTOMER SATISFIED *Track 604 037*	41 1

Tommy HUNT *US, male vocalist* **17 wks**

11 Oct 75		CRACKIN' UP *Spark SRL 1132*	39 5
21 Aug 76		LOVING ON THE LOSING SIDE *Spark SRL 1146*	28 9
4 Dec 76		ONE FINE MORNING *Spark SRL 1148*	44 3

HUNTER – See Ruby TURNER

Alfonzo HUNTER *US, male rap / instrumentalist* **2 wks**

22 Feb 97		JUST THE WAY *Cooltempo CDCOOL 326*	38 2

Ian HUNTER ⚞ *UK, male vocalist* **10 wks**

3 May 75		ONCE BITTEN TWICE SHY *CBS 3194*	14 10

Tab HUNTER ✪ *US, male vocalist* **30 wks**

8 Feb 57	★	YOUNG LOVE *London HLD 8380* ▲	1 18
12 Apr 57	●	99 WAYS *London HLD 8410*	5 11
5 Jul 57		99 WAYS (re-entry) *London HLD 8410*	29 1

Terry HUNTER *US, male DJ / producer* **1 wk**

26 Jul 97		HARVEST FOR THE WORLD *Delirious DELICD 4*	48 1

Steve 'Silk' HURLEY ☺ *US, male producer* **9 wks**

10 Jan 87	★	JACK YOUR BODY *DJ International LON 117*	1 9

HURRICANE # 1 ☹ ⚞ *UK, male vocal / instrumental group* **16 wks**

10 May 97		STEP INTO MY WORLD *Creation CRESCD 253*	29 2
5 Jul 97		JUST ANOTHER ILLUSION *Creation CRESCD 264*	35 2
6 Sep 97		CHAIN REACTION *Creation CRESCD 271*	30 2
1 Nov 97		STEP INTO MY WORLD *Creation CRESCD 276*	19 3
21 Feb 98		ONLY THE STRONGEST WILL SURVIVE *Creation CRERSCD 285*	19 6
24 Oct 98		RISING SIGN *Creation CRESCD 303*	47 1

HURRICANES – See JOHNNY and the HURRICANES

Phil HURTT *US, male vocalist* **5 wks**

11 Nov 78		GIVING IT BACK *Fantasy FTC 161*	36 5

HUSTLERS CONVENTION featuring Dave LAUDAT and Ondrea DUVERNEY *UK, male instrumental / production duo* **1 wk**

20 May 95		DANCE TO THE MUSIC *Stress CDSTR 53*	71 1

See also SEX-O-SONIQUE; FULL INTENTION

UK No 1 ★ UK Top 10 ● UK million seller ◆ UK entry at No 1 ■ US No 1 ▲

Willie HUTCH *US, male vocalist* **8 wks**

4 Dec 82	IN AND OUT *Motown TMG 1285*	51	7
6 Jul 85	KEEP ON JAMMIN' *Motown ZB 40173*	73	1

June HUTTON and Axel STORDAHL
with the BOYS NEXT DOOR ℂ
US, female vocalist and male orchestra with male vocal group **7 wks**

7 Aug 53 ●	SAY YOU'RE MINE AGAIN *Capitol CL 13918*	10	3
4 Sep 53 ●	SAY YOU'RE MINE AGAIN (re-entry)		
	Capitol CL 13918	6	4

HWA featuring SONIC THE HEDGEHOG
UK, male producer – Jeremy Healy **6 wks**

5 Dec 92	SUPERSONIC *Internal Affairs KGB 008*	33	6

Brian HYLAND ◎ *US, male vocalist* **72 wks**

7 Jul 60 ●	ITSY BITSY TEENY WEENY YELLOW POLKA DOT BIKINI		
	London HLR 9161 ▲	8	13
20 Oct 60	FOUR LITTLE HEELS *London HLR 9203*	29	6
10 May 62 ●	GINNY COME LATELY *HMV POP 1013*	5	15
2 Aug 62 ●	SEALED WITH A KISS *HMV POP 1051*	3	15
8 Nov 62	WARMED OVER KISSES *HMV POP 1079*	28	6
27 Mar 71	GYPSY WOMAN *Uni UN 530*	45	1
10 Apr 71	GYPSY WOMAN (re-entry) *Uni UN 530*	42	5
28 Jun 75 ●	SEALED WITH A KISS (re-issue) *ABC 4059*	7	11

Sheila HYLTON *Jamaica, female vocalist* **12 wks**

15 Sep 79	BREAKFAST IN BED *United Artists BP 304*	57	5
17 Jan 81	THE BED'S TOO BIG WITHOUT YOU *Island WIP 6671*	35	7

Phyllis HYMAN *US, female vocalist* **9 wks**

16 Feb 80	YOU KNOW HOW TO LOVE ME *Arista ARIST 323*	47	6
12 Sep 81	YOU SURE LOOK GOOD TO ME *Arista ARIST 424*	56	3

Dick HYMAN TRIO ℂ
US, male instrumentalist – Dick Hyman, keyboards **10 wks**

16 Mar 56 ●	THEME FROM 'THE THREEPENNY OPERA' *MGM 890*	9	10

Chrissie HYNDE – See PRETENDERS / Chrissie HYNDE

HYPER GO GO *UK, male instrumental/production duo* **15 wks**

22 Aug 92	HIGH *Deconstruction 74321110497*	30	5
31 Jul 93	NEVER LET GO *Positiva CDTIV 3*	45	3
5 Feb 94	RAISE *Positiva CDTIV 9*	36	2
26 Nov 94	IT'S ALRIGHT *Positiva CDTIV 20*	49	1
6 Apr 96	DO WATCHA DO *Avex UK AVEXCD 24* ▫1	54	1
12 Oct 96	HIGH (re-mix) *Distinctive DISNCD 24*	32	2
12 Apr 97	DO WATCHA DO (re-mix) *Distinctive DISNCD 28* ▫1	60	1

▫1 Hyper Go Go and Adeva

HYPERLOGIC *UK, male instrumental/production duo* **3 wks**

29 Jul 95	ONLY ME *Systematic SYSCD 15*	35	2
9 May 98	ONLY ME (re-mix) *Tidy Trax TIDY 113CD1*	48	1

HYPERSTATE *UK, male/female vocal/instrumental duo* **1 wk**

6 Feb 93	TIME AFTER TIME *M & G MAGCD 34*	71	1

HYPNOTIST *UK, male producer – Caspar Pound* **5 wks**

28 Sep 91	THE HOUSE IS MINE *Rising High RSN 4*	65	2
21 Dec 91	THE HARDCORE EP *Rising High RSN 13*	68	3

Tracks on The Hardcore EP: Hardcore U Know the Score / The Ride / Night of the Livin' E Heads / God of the Universe

HYSTERIC EGO *UK, male producer – Rob White* **7 wks**

31 Aug 96	WANT LOVE *WEA WEA 070CD*	28	4

21 Jun 97	MINISTRY OF LOVE *WEA WEA 094CD*	39	2
28 Feb 98	WANT LOVE – THE REMIXES *WEA WEA 150CD*	46	1

HYSTERICS *UK, male vocal/instrumental group* **5 wks**

12 Dec 81	JINGLE BELLS LAUGHING ALL THE WAY		
	Record Delivery KA 5	44	5

HYSTERIX *UK, male/female vocal/instrumental group* **4 wks**

7 May 94	MUST BE THE MUSIC *Deconstruction 74321207362*	40	3
18 Feb 95	EVERYTHING *Deconstruction 74321236882*	65	1

Janis IAN *US, female vocalist* **10 wks**

17 Nov 79	FLY TOO HIGH *CBS 7936*	44	7
28 Jun 80	THE OTHER SIDE OF THE SUN *CBS 8611*	44	3

ICE CUBE *US, male rapper* **23 wks**

27 Mar 93	IT WAS A GOOD DAY *Fourth & Broadway BRCD 270*	27	4
7 Aug 93	CHECK YO SELF *Fourth & Broadway BRCD 283* ▫1	36	4
11 Sep 93	WICKED *Fourth & Broadway BRCD 282*	62	1
18 Dec 93	REALLY DOE *Fourth & Broadway BRCD 302*	66	1
26 Mar 94	YOU KNOW HOW WE DO IT *Fourth & Broadway BRCD 303*	41	3
27 Aug 94	BOP GUN (ONE NATION)		
	Fourth & Broadway BRCD 308 ▫2	22	3
24 Dec 94	YOU KNOW HOW WE DO IT (re-entry)		
	Fourth & Broadway BRCD 303	46	2
11 Mar 95	HAND OF THE DEAD BODY *Virgin America VUSCD 88* ▫3	41	2
15 Apr 95	NATURAL BORN KILLAZ *Death Row A 8197CD* ▫4	45	2
22 Mar 97	WORLD IS MINE *Jive JIVECD 419*	60	1

▫1 Ice Cube featuring Das EFX ▫2 Ice Cube featuring George Clinton ▫3 Scarface featuring Ice Cube ▫4 Dr Dre and Ice Cube

ICE MC *UK, male rapper* **5 wks**

6 Aug 94	THINK ABOUT THE WAY (BOM DIGI DIGI BOM...)		
	WEA YZ 829CD	42	2
8 Apr 95	IT'S A RAINY DAY *Eternal YZ 902CD*	73	1
14 Sep 96	BOM DIGI BOM (THINK ABOUT THE WAY) (re-issue)		
	Eternal WEA 073CD	38	2

ICE-T 🔊 *US, male rapper* **28 wks**

18 Mar 89	HIGH ROLLERS *Sire W 7574*	63	2
17 Feb 90	YOU PLAYED YOURSELF *Sire W 9994*	64	2
29 Sep 90	SUPERFLY 1990 *Capitol CL 586* ▫1	48	3
8 May 93	I AIN'T NEW TA THIS *Rhyme Syndicate SYNDD 1*	62	2
18 Dec 93	THAT'S HOW I'M LIVIN' *Rhyme Syndicate SYNDD 2*	21	6
9 Apr 94	GOTTA LOTTA LOVE *Rhyme Syndicate SYNDD 3*	24	4
10 Dec 94	BORN TO RAISE HELL *Fox 74321230152* ▫2	47	2
1 Jun 96	I MUST STAND *Rhyme Syndicate SYNDD 5*	23	3
7 Dec 96	THE LANE *Rhyme Syndicate SYNDD 6*	18	4

▫1 Curtis Mayfield and Ice-T ▫2 Motorhead / Ice-T / Whitfield Crane

ICEHOUSE ◎ *New Zealand, male vocal/instrumental group* **28 wks**

5 Feb 83	HEY LITTLE GIRL *Chrysalis CHS 2670*	17	10
23 Apr 83	STREET CAFE *Chrysalis COOL 1*	62	4

3 May 86	NO PROMISES *Chrysalis CHS 2978*	72	1
29 Aug 87	CRAZY *Chrysalis CHS 3156*	74	1
13 Feb 88	CRAZY (re-entry) *Chrysalis CHS 3156*	38	8
14 May 88	ELECTRIC BLUE *Chrysalis CHS 3239*	53	4

ICICLE WORKS ☻ *UK, male vocal/instrumental group* — 28 wks

24 Dec 83	LOVE IS A WONDERFUL COLOUR *Beggars Banquet BEG 99*	15	8
10 Mar 84	BIRDS FLY (WHISPER TO A SCREAM)/ IN THE CAULDRON OF LOVE *Beggars Banquet BEG 108*	53	4
26 Jul 86	UNDERSTANDING JANE *Beggars Banquet BEG 160*	52	3
4 Oct 86	WHO DO YOU WANT FOR YOUR LOVE *Beggars Banquet BEG 172*	54	4
14 Feb 87	EVANGELINE *Beggars Banquet BEG 181*	53	4
30 Apr 88	LITTLE GIRL LOST *Beggars Banquet BEG 215*	59	4
17 Mar 90	MOTORCYCLE RIDER *Epic WORKS 100*	73	1

ICON *UK, male/female vocal/instrumental duo* — 1 wk

15 Jun 96	TAINTED LOVE *Eternal WEA 057CD*	51	1

IDEAL LIFE *UK, male producer – Jon Da Silva* — 2 wks

6 Aug 94	HOT *Cleveland City CLECD 13019*	49	2

IDES OF MARCH *US, male vocal/instrumental group* — 9 wks

6 Jun 70	VEHICLE *Warner Bros. WB 7378*	31	9

Eric IDLE featuring Richard WILSON *UK, male vocal duo* — 3 wks

17 Dec 94	ONE FOOT IN THE GRAVE *Victa CDVICTA 1*	50	3

IDLEWILD *UK, male vocal/instrumental group* — 3 wks

9 May 98	A FILM FOR THE FUTURE *Food CDFOOD 111*	53	1
25 Jul 98	EVERYONE SAYS YOU'RE SO FRAGILE *Food CDFOOD 113*	47	1
24 Oct 98	I'M A MESSAGE *Food CDFOOD 114*	41	1

Billy IDOL ☻ *Snarling rock'n'roll rebel of the 1980s. Former vocalist of punk-rock hitmakers Generation X, b. William Broad, 30 November, 1955, Middlesex. He had his greatest success in the USA, where four singles reached the Top 5 and 'Mony Mony' reached No 1* — 106 wks

11 Sep 82	HOT IN THE CITY *Chrysalis CHS 2625*	58	4
24 Mar 84	REBEL YELL *Chrysalis IDOL 2*	62	2
30 Jun 84	EYES WITHOUT A FACE *Chrysalis IDOL 3*	18	11
29 Sep 84	FLESH FOR FANTASY *Chrysalis IDOL 4*	54	3
13 Jul 85 ●	WHITE WEDDING *Chrysalis IDOL 5*	6	15
14 Sep 85 ●	REBEL YELL (re-issue) *Chrysalis IDOL 6*	6	12
4 Oct 86	TO BE A LOVER *Chrysalis IDOL 8*	22	8
7 Mar 87	DON'T NEED A GUN *Chrysalis IDOL 9*	26	5
13 Jun 87	SWEET SIXTEEN *Chrysalis IDOL 10*	17	9
3 Oct 87 ●	MONY MONY *Chrysalis IDOL 11* ▲	7	10
16 Jan 88	HOT IN THE CITY (re-mix) *Chrysalis IDOL 12*	13	9
13 Aug 88	CATCH MY FALL *Chrysalis IDOL 13*	63	3
28 Apr 90	CRADLE OF LOVE *Chrysalis IDOL 14*	34	4
11 Aug 90	L.A. WOMAN *Chrysalis IDOL 15*	70	2
22 Dec 90	PRODIGAL BLUES *Chrysalis IDOL 16*	47	4
26 Jun 93	SHOCK TO THE SYSTEM *Chrysalis CDCHS 3994*	30	3
10 Sep 94	SPEED *Fox 74321223472*	47	2

Frank IFIELD ☾ *Early sixties superstar, b. 30 November, 1937, Coventry, and raised in Australia. This pop vocalist / yodeller had four No 1s in 12 months with revivals of US standards. Unlike many of his early 1960s UK contemporaries, his records also did well internationally* — 162 wks

19 Feb 60	LUCKY DEVIL *Columbia DB 4399*	22	5
7 Apr 60	LUCKY DEVIL (re-entry) *Columbia DB 4399*	33	2
29 Sep 60	GOTTA GET A DATE *Columbia DB 4496*	49	1
5 Jul 62 ★	I REMEMBER YOU *Columbia DB 4856* ◆	1	28
25 Oct 62 ★	LOVESICK BLUES *Columbia DB 4913*	1	17
24 Jan 63 ★	WAYWARD WIND *Columbia DB 4960*	1	13
11 Apr 63 ●	NOBODY'S DARLIN' BUT MINE *Columbia DB 7007*	4	16
27 Jun 63 ★	CONFESSIN' *Columbia DB 7062*	1	16
17 Oct 63	MULE TRAIN *Columbia DB 7131*	22	6

9 Jan 64 ●	DON'T BLAME ME *Columbia DB 7184*	8	13
23 Apr 64	ANGRY AT THE BIG OAK TREE *Columbia DB 7263*	25	8
23 Jul 64	I SHOULD CARE *Columbia DB 7319*	33	3
1 Oct 64	SUMMER IS OVER *Columbia DB 7355*	25	6
19 Aug 65	PARADISE *Columbia DB 7655*	26	9
23 Jun 66	NO ONE WILL EVER KNOW *Columbia DB 7940*	25	4
8 Dec 66	CALL HER YOUR SWEETHEART *Columbia DB 8078*	24	11
7 Dec 91	THE YODELLING SONG *EMI 7YODEL 1* [1]	40	4

[1] Frank Ifield featuring the Backroom Boys

Julio IGLESIAS ☾ *Spain, male vocalist* — 75 wks

24 Oct 81 ★	BEGIN THE BEGUINE (VOLVER A EMPEZAR) *CBS A 1612*	1	14
6 Mar 82 ●	QUIEREME MUCHO (YOURS) *CBS A 1939*	3	9
9 Oct 82	AMOR *CBS A 2801*	32	7
9 Apr 83	HEY! *CBS JULIO 1*	31	7
7 Apr 84	TO ALL THE GIRLS I'VE LOVED BEFORE *CBS A 4252* [1]	17	10
7 Jul 84	ALL OF YOU *CBS A 4522* [2]	43	8
6 Aug 88 ●	MY LOVE *CBS JULIO 2* [3]	5	11
4 Jun 94	CRAZY *Columbia 6603695*	43	3
27 Aug 94	CRAZY (re-entry) *Columbia 6603695*	50	2
26 Nov 94	FRAGILE *Columbia 6610192*	53	2
31 Dec 94	FRAGILE (re-entry) *Columbia 6610192*	66	2

[1] Julio Iglesias and Willie Nelson [2] Julio Iglesias and Diana Ross [3] Julio Iglesias featuring Stevie Wonder

IGNORANTS *UK, male vocal duo* — 3 wks

25 Dec 93	PHAT GIRLS *Spaghetti CIOCD 8*	59	3

I-LEVEL *UK, male vocal/instrumental group* — 9 wks

16 Apr 83	MINEFIELD *Virgin VS 563*	52	6
18 Jun 83	TEACHER *Virgin VS 595*	56	3

ILLEGAL MOTION featuring Simone CHAPMAN
UK, male/female vocal/instrumental duo — 1 wk

9 Oct 93	SATURDAY LOVE *Arista 74321163032*	67	1

IMAANI ☻ ☺ *UK, female vocalist* — 7 wks

9 May 98	WHERE ARE YOU *EMI CDEM 510*	15	7

IMAGINATION ☻ ♪ ☺ *Distinctive London-based trio, who created a unique blend of soul and dance music: Lee John (v), Ashley Ingram (k), Errol Kennedy (d). One of the most original British acts of the early 1980s, they were fronted by a charismatic and flamboyant lead singer* — 105 wks

16 May 81 ●	BODY TALK *R & B RBS 201*	4	18
5 Sep 81	IN AND OUT OF LOVE *R & B RBS 202*	16	9
14 Nov 81	FLASHBACK *R & B RBS 206*	16	13
6 Mar 82 ●	JUST AN ILLUSION *R & B RBS 208*	2	11
26 Jun 82	MUSIC AND LIGHTS *R & B RBS 210*	5	9
25 Sep 82	IN THE HEAT OF THE NIGHT *R & B RBS 211*	22	8
11 Dec 82	CHANGES *R & B RBS 213*	31	8
4 Jun 83	LOOKING AT MIDNIGHT *R & B RBS 214*	29	7
5 Nov 83	NEW DIMENSIONS *R & B RBS 216*	56	3
26 May 84	STATE OF LOVE *R & B RBS 218*	67	2
24 Nov 84	THANK YOU MY LOVE *R & B RBS 219*	22	15
16 Jan 88	INSTINCTUAL *RCA PB 41697*	62	2

IMAJIN *US, male vocal group* — 3 wks

27 Jun 98	SHORTY (YOU KEEP PLAYING WITH MY MIND) *Jive 0521212* [1]	22	3

[1] Imajin featuring Keith Murray

Natalie IMBRUGLIA ☻ *Australia, female vocalist* — 39 wks

8 Nov 97	TORN *RCA 74321527982*	2	17
14 Mar 98	BIG MISTAKE *RCA 74321566782*	2	10
6 Jun 98	WISHING I WAS THERE *RCA 74321585062*	19	5
17 Oct 98 ●	SMOKE *RCA 74321621942*	5	7

IMMACULATE FOOLS *UK, male vocal/instrumental group*   **4 wks**

26 Jan 85	IMMACULATE FOOLS *A & M AM 227*	51	4

IMMATURE – See SMOOTH

IMPALAS *US, male vocal group*   **1 wk**

21 Aug 59	SORRY (I RAN ALL THE WAY HOME) *MGM 1015*	28	1

IMPEDANCE *UK, male producer – Daniel Haydon*   **4 wks**

11 Nov 89	TAINTED LOVE *Jumpin' & Pumpin' TOT 4*	54	4

IMPERIAL DRAG *UK, male vocal/instrumental group*   **1 wk**

12 Oct 96	BOY OR A GIRL *Columbia 6632992*	54	1

IMPERIAL TEEN *US, male/female vocal/instrumental group*   **1 wk**

7 Sep 96	YOU'RE ONE *Slash LASCD 57*	69	1

IMPERIALS *US, male vocal group*   **9 wks**

24 Dec 77	WHO'S GONNA LOVE ME *Power Exchange PX 266*	17	9

IMPOSTER – See Elvis COSTELLO

IMPRESSIONS *US, male vocal group*   **10 wks**

22 Nov 75	FIRST IMPRESSIONS *Curtom K 16638*	16	10

IN CROWD *UK, male vocal/instrumental group*   **1 wk**

20 May 65	THAT'S HOW STRONG MY LOVE IS *Parlophone R 5276*	48	1

IN TUA NUA *Ireland, male/female vocal/instrumental group*   **2 wks**

14 May 88	ALL I WANTED *Virgin VS 1072*	69	2

INAURA *UK, male vocal/instrumental group*   **1 wk**

18 May 96	COMA AROMA *EMI CDEM 421*	57	1

INCANTATION *UK, male instrumental group*   **12 wks**

4 Dec 82	CACHARPAYA (ANDES PUMPSA DAESI) *Beggars Banquet BEG 84*	12	12

INCOGNITO *UK, male/female vocal/instrumental group*   **37 wks**

15 Nov 80	PARISIENNE GIRL *Ensign ENY 44*	73	2
29 Jun 91 ●	ALWAYS THERE *Talkin Loud TLK 10* [1]	6	9
14 Sep 91	CRAZY FOR YOU *Talkin Loud TLK 14* [2]	59	2
6 Jun 92	DON'T YOU WORRY 'BOUT A THING *Talkin Loud TLK 21*	19	6
15 Aug 92	CHANGE *Talkin Loud TLK 26*	52	2
21 Aug 93	STILL A FRIEND OF MINE *Talkin Loud TLKCD 42*	47	2
20 Nov 93	GIVIN' IT UP *Talkin Loud TLKCD 44*	43	2
12 Mar 94	PIECES OF A DREAM *Talkin Loud TLKCD 46*	35	2
27 May 95	EVERYDAY *Talkin Loud TLKCD 55*	23	3
5 Aug 95	I HEAR YOUR NAME *Talkin Loud TLKCD 56*	42	3
11 May 96	JUMP TO MY LOVE/ALWAYS THERE *Talkin Loud TLCD 7*	29	3
26 Oct 96	OUT OF THE STORM *Talkin Loud TLCD 14*	57	1

[1] Incognito featuring Jocelyn Brown [2] Incognito featuring Chyna

'Always There' in 1996 is a re-recording

INDEEP *US, male/female vocal/rap duo*   **11 wks**

22 Jan 83	LAST NIGHT A DJ SAVED MY LIFE *Sound Of New York SNY 1*	13	9
14 May 83	WHEN BOYS TALK *Sound Of New York SNY 3*	67	2

INDIA *US, female vocalist*   **10 wks**

26 Feb 94	LOVE AND HAPPINESS (YEMAYA Y OCHUN) *Cooltempo CDCOOL 287* [1]	50	2
5 Aug 95	I CAN'T GET NO SLEEP *A & M 5811412* [2]	44	2
16 Mar 96	OYE COMO VA *Media MCSTD 40013* [3]	36	2
8 Feb 97	RUNAWAY *Talkin Loud TLCD20* [4]	24	4

[1] River Ocean featuring India [2] Masters at Work present India [3] Tito Puente Jr and the Latin Rhythm featuring Tito Puente, India and Cali Aleman [4] Nuyorican Soul featuring India

INDIAN VIBES *UK, male vocal/instrumental group*   **2 wks**

24 Sep 94	MATHAR *Virgin International DINSD 136*	68	1
2 May 98	MATHAR (re-issue) *VC Recordings VCRD 32*	52	1

INDO *US, female vocal duo*   **3 wks**

18 Apr 98	R U SLEEPING *Satellite 74321568212*	31	3

INDUSTRY STANDARD *UK, male DJ/production duo*   **3 wks**

10 Jan 98	VOLUME 1 (WHAT YOU WANT WHAT YOU NEED) *Satellite 74321543742*	34	3

INFINITI – See GRAND PUBA

INGRAM *US, male vocal/instrumental group*   **2 wks**

11 Jun 83	SMOOTHIN' GROOVIN' *Streetwave WAVE 3*	56	2

James INGRAM *US, male vocalist*   **42 wks**

12 Feb 83	BABY COME TO ME *Qwest K 15005* [1] ▲	11	10
18 Feb 84	YAH MO B THERE *Qwest W 9394* [2]	44	5
7 Apr 84	YAH MO B THERE (re-entry) *Qwest W 9394* [2]	69	3
12 Jan 85	YAH MO B THERE (re-mix) *Qwest W 9394* [2]	12	8
11 Jul 87	SOMEWHERE OUT THERE *MCA MCA 1132* [3]	8	13
31 Mar 90	SECRET GARDEN *Qwest W 9992* [4]	67	1
16 Apr 94	THE DAY I FALL IN LOVE *Columbia 6600282* [5]	64	2

[1] Patti Austin and James Ingram [2] James Ingram with Michael McDonald [3] Linda Ronstadt and James Ingram [4] Quincy Jones featuring Al B Sure!, James Ingram, El DeBarge and Barry White [5] Dolly Parton and James Ingram

INK SPOTS *US, male vocal group*   **4 wks**

29 Apr 55 ●	MELODY OF LOVE *Parlophone R 3977*	10	4

John INMAN *UK, male vocalist*   **6 wks**

25 Oct 75	ARE YOU BEING SERVED SIR *DJM DJS 602*	39	6

INMATES *UK, male vocal/instrumental group*   **9 wks**

8 Dec 79	THE WALK *Radar ADA 47*	36	9

INNER CIRCLE *Jamaica, male vocal/instrumental group*   **35 wks**

24 Feb 79	EVERYTHING IS GREAT *Island WIP 6472*	37	8
12 May 79	STOP BREAKING MY HEART *Island WIP 6488*	50	3
31 Oct 92	SWEAT (A LA LA LA LA LONG) *Magnet 9031776802*	43	5
1 May 93 ●	SWEAT (A LA LA LA LA LONG) (re-entry) *Magnet 9031776802*	3	14
31 Jul 93	BAD BOYS *Magnet MAG 1017CD*	52	3
10 Sep 94	GAMES PEOPLE PLAY *Magnet MAG 1026CD*	67	2

INNER CITY *US, male/female vocal/instrumental duo*   **74 wks**

3 Sep 88 ●	BIG FUN *10 TEN 240* [1]	8	14
10 Dec 88 ●	GOOD LIFE *10 TEN 249*	4	12
22 Apr 89 ●	AIN'T NOBODY BETTER *10 TEN 252*	10	7
29 Jul 89	DO YOU LOVE WHAT YOU FEEL *10 TEN 273*	16	7
18 Nov 89	WATCHA GONNA DO WITH MY LOVIN' *10 TEN 290*	12	9
13 Oct 90	THAT MAN (HE'S ALL MINE) *10 TEN 334*	42	4
23 Feb 91	TILL WE MEET AGAIN *Ten TEN 337*	47	2
7 Dec 91	LET IT REIGN *Ten TEN 392*	51	2
4 Apr 92	HALLELUJAH '92 *Ten TEN 398*	22	4
13 Jun 92	PENNIES FROM HEAVEN *Ten TEN 405*	24	4
12 Sep 92	PRAISE *Ten TENX 408*	59	2
27 Feb 93	TILL WE MEET AGAIN (re-mix) *Ten TENCD 414*	55	1
5 Feb 94	DO YA *Six6 SIXCD 107*	44	2
9 Jul 94	SHARE MY LIFE *Six6 SIXCD 114*	62	1

| 10 Feb 96 | YOUR LOVE *Six6 SIXCD 127* | 28 | 2 |
| 5 Oct 96 | DO ME RIGHT *Six6 SIXXCD 2* | 47 | 1 |

[1] Inner City featuring Kevin Saunderson

INNER SANCTUM *Canada, male/female dance group* — 1 wk

| 23 May 98 | HOW SOON IS NOW *Malarky MLKD 6* | 75 | 1 |

INNERZONE ORCHESTRA *US, male producer – Carl Craig* — 1 wk

| 28 Sep 96 | BUG IN THE BASSBIN *Mo Wax MW 049CD* | 68 | 1 |

INNOCENCE ☻ ✍ *UK, male/female vocal/instrumental group* — 33 wks

3 Mar 90	NATURAL THING *Cooltempo COOL 201*	16	7
21 Jul 90	SILENT VOICE *Cooltempo COOL 212*	37	5
13 Oct 90	LET'S PUSH IT *Cooltempo COOL 220*	25	6
8 Dec 90	A MATTER OF FACT *Cooltempo COOL 223*	37	7
30 Mar 91	REMEMBER THE DAY *Cooltempo COOL 226*	56	2
20 Jun 92	I'LL BE THERE *Cooltempo COOL 255*	26	3
3 Oct 92	ONE LOVE IN MY LIFETIME *Cooltempo COOL 263*	40	2
21 Nov 92	BUILD *Cooltempo COOL 267*	72	1

INSANE CLOWN POSSE *US, male rap duo* — 2 wks

| 17 Jan 98 | HALLS OF ILLUSION *Island CID 685* | 56 | 1 |
| 6 Jun 98 | HOKUS POKUS *Island CIDX 705* | 53 | 1 |

INSPIRAL CARPETS ☹ *UK, male vocal/instrumental group* — 50 wks

18 Nov 89	MOVE *Cow DUNG 6*	49	2
17 Mar 90	THIS IS HOW IT FEELS *Cow DUNG 7*	14	8
30 Jun 90	SHE COMES IN THE FALL *Cow DUNG 10*	27	6
17 Nov 90	ISLAND HEAD EP *Cow DUNG 11*	21	4
30 Mar 91	CARAVAN *Cow DUNG 13*	30	5
22 Jun 91	PLEASE BE CRUEL *Cow DUNG 15*	50	2
29 Feb 92	DRAGGING ME DOWN *Cow DUNG 16*	12	5
30 May 92	TWO WORLDS COLLIDE *Cow DUNG 17*	32	2
19 Sep 92	GENERATIONS *Cow DUNG 18T*	28	3
14 Nov 92	BITCHES BREW *Cow DUNG 20T*	36	2
5 Jun 93	HOW IT SHOULD BE *Cow DUNG 22CD*	49	1
22 Jan 94	SATURN 5 *Cow DUNG 23CD*	20	4
5 Mar 94	I WANT YOU *Cow DUNG 24CD* [1]	18	3
7 May 94	UNIFORM *Cow DUNG 26CD*	51	1
16 Sep 95	JOE *Cow DUNG 27CD*	37	2

[1] Inspiral Carpets featuring Mark E Smith

Tracks on Island Head EP: *Biggest Mountain / Gold Top / Weakness / I'll Keep It In Mind*

INSPIRATIONAL CHOIR *US, male/female choir* — 11 wks

| 22 Dec 84 | ABIDE WITH ME *Epic A 4997* | 44 | 5 |
| 14 Dec 85 | ABIDE WITH ME (re-issue) *Portrait A 4997* | 36 | 6 |

Label credits the Royal Choral Society

INSTANT FUNK *US, male vocal/instrumental group* — 5 wks

| 20 Jan 79 | GOT MY MIND MADE UP *Salsoul SSOL 114* | 46 | 5 |

INTASTELLA *UK, male/female vocal/instrumental group* — 6 wks

25 May 91	DREAM SOME PARADISE *MCA MCS 1520*	69	1
24 Aug 91	PEOPLE *MCA MCS 1559*	74	2
16 Nov 91	CENTURY *MCA MCS 1585*	70	2
23 Sep 95	THE NIGHT *Planet 3 GXY 2005CD*	60	1

INTELLIGENT HOODLUM *US, male rap group* — 3 wks

| 6 Oct 90 | BACK TO REALITY *A & M AM 598* | 55 | 3 |

INTERACTIVE *Germany, male instrumental/production group* — 4 wks

| 13 Apr 96 | FOREVER YOUNG *Ffrreedom TABCD 235* | 28 | 4 |

INTRUDERS ✍ *US, male vocal group* — 21 wks

| 13 Apr 74 | I'LL ALWAYS LOVE MY MAMA | | |
| | *Philadelphia International PIR 2159* | 32 | 7 |

6 Jul 74	(WIN PLACE OR SHOW) SHE'S A WINNER		
	Philadelphia International PIR 2212	14	9
22 Dec 84	WHO DO YOU LOVE? *Streetwave KHAN 34*	65	5

INVADERS OF THE HEART – *See Jah WOBBLE'S INVADERS OF THE HEART*

INVISIBLE GIRLS – *See Pauline MURRAY and the INVISIBLE GIRLS*

INXS ✍ *Stadium-packing rock sextet led by Australian Michael Hutchence (b. 22 January, 1962, Sydney; d. 23 November, 1997). Both Hutchence and group won BRIT Awards in 1991, and the video for their US chart-topper, 'Need You Tonight', won five MTV awards in 1988* — 121 wks

19 Apr 86	WHAT YOU NEED *Mercury INXS 5*	51	6
28 Jun 86	LISTEN LIKE THIEVES *Mercury INXS 6*	46	7
30 Aug 86	KISS THE DIRT (FALLING DOWN THE MOUNTAIN)		
	Mercury INXS 7	54	3
24 Oct 87	NEED YOU TONIGHT *Mercury INXS 8* ▲	58	3
9 Jan 88	NEW SENSATION *Mercury INXS 9*	25	6
12 Mar 88	DEVIL INSIDE *Mercury INXS 10*	47	5
25 Jun 88	NEVER TEAR US APART *Mecury INXS 11*	24	7
12 Nov 88 ●	NEED YOU TONIGHT (re-issue) *Mercury INXS 12*	2	11
8 Apr 89	MYSTIFY *Mercury INXS 13*	14	7
15 Sep 90	SUICIDE BLONDE *Mercury INXS 14*	11	6
8 Dec 90	DISAPPEAR *Mercury INXS 15*	21	8
26 Jan 91	GOOD TIMES *Atlantic A 7751* [1]	18	8
30 Mar 91	BY MY SIDE *Mercury INXS 16*	42	4
13 Jul 91	BITTER TEARS *Mercury INXS 17*	30	3
2 Nov 91	SHINING STAR (EP) *Mercury INXS 18*	27	3
18 Jul 92	HEAVEN SENT *Mercury INXS 19*	31	3
5 Sep 92	BABY DON'T CRY *Mercury INXS 20*	20	5
14 Nov 92	TASTE IT *Mercury INXS 23*	21	4
13 Feb 93	BEAUTIFUL GIRL *Mercury INXCD 24*	23	5
23 Oct 93	THE GIFT *Mercury INXCD 25*	11	4
11 Dec 93	PLEASE (YOU GOT THAT . . .) *Mercury INXCD 26*	50	3
22 Oct 94	THE STRANGEST PARTY (THESE ARE THE TIMES)		
	Mercury INXCD 27	15	5
22 Mar 97	ELEGANTLY WASTED *Mercury INXCD 28*	20	4
7 Jun 97	EVERYTHING *Mercury INXDD 29*	71	1

[1] Jimmy Barnes and INXS

Tracks on Shining Star (EP): *Shining Star / Send a Message (Live) / Faith In Each Other (Live) / Bitter Tears (Live). Although uncredited 'Please (You Got That...)' is a duet with Ray Charles*

Sweetie IRIE – *See ASWAD; SCRITTI POLITTI*

Tippa IRIE *UK, male vocalist* — 14 wks

22 Mar 86	HELLO DARLING *Greensleeves/UK Bubb TIPPA 4*	22	7
19 Jul 86	HEARTBEAT *Greensleeves/UK Bubb TIPPA 5*	59	3
15 May 93	SHOUTING FOR THE GUNNERS *London LONCD 342* [1]	34	3
8 Jul 95	STAYING ALIVE 95 *Telstar CDSTAS 2776* [2]	48	1

[1] Arsenal FA Cup Squad featuring Tippa Irie and Peter Hunnigale
[2] Fever featuring Tippa Irie

IRON MAIDEN ⌁ *Legendary London-based group named after a medieval torture device. Lead vocalists have included Paul Di'Anno and Blaze Bayley, but it was with front man Bruce Dickinson that they enjoyed a period as, arguably, the world's top metal band* — 147 wks

23 Feb 80	RUNNING FREE *EMI 5032*	34	5
7 Jun 80	SANCTUARY *EMI 5065*	29	5
8 Nov 80	WOMEN IN UNIFORM *EMI 5105*	35	4
14 Mar 81	TWILIGHT ZONE/WRATH CHILD *EMI 5145*	31	5
27 Jun 81	PURGATORY *EMI 5184*	52	3
26 Sep 81	MAIDEN JAPAN *EMI 5219*	43	4
20 Feb 82 ●	RUN TO THE HILLS *EMI 5263*	7	10
15 May 82	THE NUMBER OF THE BEAST *EMI 5287*	18	8
23 Apr 83	FLIGHT OF ICARUS *EMI 5378*	11	6
2 Jul 83	THE TROOPER *EMI 5397*	12	7
18 Aug 84	2 MINUTES TO MIDNIGHT *EMI 5849*	11	6
3 Nov 84	ACES HIGH *EMI 5502*	20	5
5 Oct 85	RUNNING FREE (LIVE) *EMI EMI 5532*	19	5
14 Dec 85	RUN TO THE HILLS (LIVE) *EMI 5542*	26	6

UK No 1 ★   UK Top 10 ●   UK million seller ◆   UK entry at No 1 ■   US No 1 ▲

Dee D JACKSON ♫ *UK, female vocalist* — **14 wks**

22 Apr 78	● AUTOMATIC LOVER *Mercury 6007 171*	4	9
2 Sep 78	METEOR MAN *Mercury 6007 182*	48	5

Freddie JACKSON ♫ *US, male vocalist* — **31 wks**

23 Nov 85	YOU ARE MY LADY *Capitol CL 379*	49	4
22 Feb 86	ROCK ME TONIGHT (FOR OLD TIME'S SAKE) *Capitol CL 358*	18	9
11 Oct 86	TASTY LOVE *Capitol CL 428*	73	1
7 Feb 87	HAVE YOU EVER LOVED SOMEBODY *Capitol CL 437*	33	6
9 Jul 88	NICE 'N' SLOW *Capitol CL 502*	56	2
15 Oct 88	CRAZY (FOR ME) *Capitol CL 510*	41	3
5 Sep 92	ME AND MRS JONES *Capitol CL 668*	32	5
15 Jan 94	MAKE LOVE EASY *RCA 74321179162*	70	1

Gisele JACKSON *US, female vocalist* — **1 wk**

30 Aug 97	LOVE COMMANDMENTS *Manifesto FESCD 28*	54	1

Janet JACKSON ☺ R&B *Multi-award-winning, record-breaking vocalist/performer, b. 16 May, 1966, Indiana. Although not an overnight sensation, the youngest of the talented Jackson family became one of the world's biggest-selling recording artists and has amassed a staggering collection of gold albums and singles* — **231 wks**

22 Mar 86	● WHAT HAVE YOU DONE FOR ME LATELY *A & M AM 308*	3	14
31 May 86	NASTY *A & M AM 316*	19	9
9 Aug 86	● WHEN I THINK OF YOU *A & M AM 337* ▲	10	10
1 Nov 86	CONTROL *A & M AM 359*	42	5
21 Mar 87	● LET'S WAIT AWHILE *Breakout USA 601*	3	10
13 Jun 87	PLEASURE PRINCIPLE *Breakout USA 604*	24	5
14 Nov 87	FUNNY HOW TIME FLIES (WHEN YOU'RE HAVING FUN) *Breakout USA 613*	59	2
2 Sep 89	MISS YOU MUCH *Breakout USA 663* ▲	22	7
4 Nov 89	RHYTHM NATION *Breakout USA 673*	23	5
27 Jan 90	COME BACK TO ME *Breakout USA 681*	20	7
31 Mar 90	ESCAPADE *Breakout USA 684* ▲	17	7
7 Jul 90	ALRIGHT *A & M USA 693*	20	5
8 Sep 90	BLACK CAT *A & M EM 587* ▲	15	6
27 Oct 90	LOVE WILL NEVER DO (WITHOUT YOU) *A & M EM 700* ▲	34	4
15 Aug 92	● THE BEST THINGS IN LIFE ARE FREE *Perspective PERSS 7400* [1]	2	13
8 May 93	● THAT'S THE WAY LOVE GOES *Virgin VSCDG 1460* ▲	2	10
31 Jul 93	IF *Virgin VSCDT 1474*	14	7
20 Nov 93	● AGAIN *Virgin VSCDG 1481* ▲	6	11
12 Mar 94	BECAUSE OF LOVE *Virgin VSCDG 1488*	19	4
18 Jun 94	ANY TIME ANY PLACE *Virgin VSCDT 1501*	13	5
26 Nov 94	YOU WANT THIS *Virgin VSCDT 1519*	14	3
18 Mar 95	● WHOOPS NOW/WHAT'LL I DO *Virgin VSCDT 1533*	9	8
10 Jun 95	● SCREAM *Epic 6620222* [2]	3	12
24 Jun 95	SCREAM (re-mix) *Epic 6621277* [2]	43	2
23 Sep 95	RUNAWAY *A & M 5811972*	6	7
2 Dec 95	SCREAM (re-entry) *Epic 6620222* [2]	72	1
16 Dec 95	● THE BEST THINGS IN LIFE ARE FREE (re-mix) *A & M 5813092* [3]	7	7
6 Apr 96	● TWENTY FOREPLAY *A & M 5815112*	22	4
4 Oct 97	● GOT 'TIL IT'S GONE *Virgin VSCDG 1666* [4]	6	9
13 Dec 97	● TOGETHER AGAIN *Virgin VSCDG 1670*	4	19
4 Apr 98	● I GET LONELY *Virgin VSCDT 1683*	5	7
27 Jun 98	GO DEEP *Virgin VSCDT 1680*	13	5
19 Dec 98	EVERY TIME *Virgin VSCDT 1720*	46	1

[1] Luther Vandross and Janet Jackson with special guests BBD and Ralph Tresvant [2] Michael Jackson and Janet Jackson [3] Luther Vandross and Janet Jackson [4] Janet featuring Q-Tip and Joni Mitchell

See also Herb ALPERT

Jermaine JACKSON ☺ ♫ *US, male vocalist* — **43 wks**

10 May 80	● LET'S GET SERIOUS *Motown TMG 1183*	8	11
26 Jul 80	BURNIN' HOT *Motown TMG 1194*	32	6
30 May 81	YOU LIKE ME DON'T YOU *Motown TMG 1222*	41	5
12 May 84	SWEETEST SWEETEST *Arista JJK 1*	52	4
27 Oct 84	WHEN THE RAIN BEGINS TO FALL *Arista ARIST 584* [1]	68	2

---

16 Feb 85	● DO WHAT YOU DO *Arista ARIST 609*	6	13
21 Oct 89	DON'T TAKE IT PERSONAL *Arista 112634*	69	2

[1] Jermaine Jackson and Pia Zadora

Joe JACKSON ♪ *UK, male vocalist* — **49 wks**

4 Aug 79	IS SHE REALLY GOING OUT WITH HIM? *A & M AMS 7459*	13	9
12 Jan 80	● IT'S DIFFERENT FOR GIRLS *A & M AMS 7493*	5	9
4 Jul 81	JUMPIN' JIVE *A & M AMS 8145* [1]	43	5
8 Jan 83	● STEPPIN' OUT *A & M AMS 8262*	6	8
12 Mar 83	BREAKING US IN TWO *A & M AM 101*	59	4
28 Apr 84	HAPPY ENDING *A & M AM 186*	58	3
7 Jul 84	BE MY NUMBER TWO *A & M AM 200*	70	2
7 Jun 86	LEFT OF CENTER *A & M AM 320* [2]	32	9

[1] Joe Jackson's Jumpin' Jive [2] Suzanne Vega featuring Joe Jackson

Michael JACKSON ♪ ◑ *The 'King of Pop', b. 29 August, 1958, Indiana. He was the youngest vocalist to top the US chart (aged 11) and was also the first artist to enter the US chart at No 1 (with 'You Are Not Alone'). His Thriller album is the world's biggest-selling record (45 million). This outstanding performer was briefly married to Lisa-Marie Presley* — **479 wks**

12 Feb 72	● GOT TO BE THERE *Tamla Motown TMG 797*	5	11
20 May 72	● ROCKIN' ROBIN *Tamla Motown TMG 816*	3	14
19 Aug 72	● AIN'T NO SUNSHINE *Tamla Motown TMG 826*	8	11
25 Nov 72	● BEN *Tamla Motown TMG 834* ▲	7	14
18 Nov 78	EASE ON DOWN THE ROAD *MCA 396* [1]	45	4
15 Sep 79	● DON'T STOP TILL YOU GET ENOUGH *Epic EPC 7763* ▲	3	12
24 Nov 79	● OFF THE WALL *Epic EPC 8045*	7	10
9 Feb 80	● ROCK WITH YOU *Epic EPC 8206* ▲	7	9
3 May 80	● SHE'S OUT OF MY LIFE *Epic EPC 8384*	3	9
26 Jul 80	GIRLFRIEND *Epic EPC 8782*	41	5
23 May 81	★ ONE DAY IN YOUR LIFE *Motown TMG 976*	1	14
1 Aug 81	WE'RE ALMOST THERE *Motown TMG 977*	46	4
6 Nov 82	● THE GIRL IS MINE *Epic EPC A 2729* [2]	8	9
15 Jan 83	THE GIRL IS MINE (re-entry) *Epic EPC A 2729* [2]	75	1
29 Jan 83	★ BILLIE JEAN *Epic EPC A 3084* ▲	1	15
9 Apr 83	● BEAT IT *Epic EPC A 3258* ▲	3	12
11 Jun 83	● WANNA BE STARTIN' SOMETHING *Epic A 3427*	8	9
23 Jul 83	HAPPY (LOVE THEME FROM 'LADY SINGS THE BLUES') *Tamla Motown TMG 986*	52	3
15 Oct 83	● SAY SAY SAY *Parlophone R 6062* [3] ▲	2	15
19 Nov 83	● THRILLER *Epic A 3643*	10	18
31 Mar 84	● P.Y.T. (PRETTY YOUNG THING) *Epic A 4136*	11	8
2 Jun 84	● FAREWELL MY SUMMER LOVE *Motown TMG 1342*	7	12
11 Aug 84	GIRL YOU'RE SO TOGETHER *Motown TMG 1355*	33	8
8 Aug 87	★ I JUST CAN'T STOP LOVING YOU *Epic 650202 7* ▲	1	9
26 Sep 87	● BAD *Epic 651155 7* ▲	3	11
5 Dec 87	● THE WAY YOU MAKE ME FEEL *Epic 651275 7* ▲	3	10
20 Feb 88	MAN IN THE MIRROR *Epic 651388 7* ▲	21	5
28 May 88	GET IT *Motown ZB 41883* [4]	37	4
16 Jul 88	● DIRTY DIANA *Epic 651546 7* ▲	4	8
10 Sep 88	ANOTHER PART OF ME *Epic 652844 7*	15	6
26 Nov 88	● SMOOTH CRIMINAL *Epic 653026 7*	8	10
25 Feb 89	● LEAVE ME ALONE *Epic 654672 7*	2	9
15 Jul 89	LIBERIAN GIRL *Epic 654947 0*	13	6
23 Nov 91	★ BLACK OR WHITE *Epic 6575987* ■ ▲	1	10
18 Jan 92	BLACK OR WHITE (re-mix) *Epic 6577316*	14	4
15 Feb 92	● REMEMBER THE TIME/COME TOGETHER *Epic 6577747*	3	8
2 May 92	● IN THE CLOSET *Epic 6580187*	8	6
25 Jul 92	● WHO IS IT *Epic 6581797*	10	7
12 Sep 92	JAM *Epic 6583607*	13	5
5 Dec 92	● HEAL THE WORLD *Epic 6584887*	2	15
27 Feb 93	● GIVE IN TO ME *Epic 6590692*	2	9
10 Jul 93	● WILL YOU BE THERE *Epic 6592222*	9	8
18 Dec 93	GONE TOO SOON *Epic 6599762*	33	5
10 Jun 95	● SCREAM *Epic 6620222* [5]	3	12
24 Jun 95	SCREAM (re-mix) *Epic 6621277* [5]	43	2
1 Sep 95	SCREAM (re-entry) *Epic 6620222* [5]	72	1
2 Dec 95	★ YOU ARE NOT ALONE *Epic 6623102* ▲	1	15
9 Dec 95	★ EARTH SONG *Epic 6626955* ◆ ■	1	17
20 Apr 96	● THEY DON'T CARE ABOUT US *Epic 6629502*	4	12
3 Aug 96	THEY DON'T CARE ABOUT US (re-entry) *Epic 6629502*	66	1
17 Aug 96	THEY DON'T CARE ABOUT US (2nd re-entry) *Epic 6629502*	66	1

UK No 1 ★   UK Top 10 ●   UK million seller ◆   UK entry at No 1 ■   US No 1 ▲

Date	Title	Pos	Wks
24 Aug 96	● WHY *Epic 6629502* [6]	2	9
16 Nov 96	● STRANGER IN MOSCOW *Epic 6637872*	4	10
3 May 97	★ BLOOD ON THE DANCEFLOOR *Epic 6644625* ■	1	9
19 Jul 97	● HISTORY/GHOSTS *Epic 6647962*	5	8

[1] Diana Ross and Michael Jackson [2] Michael Jackson and Paul McCartney
[3] Paul McCartney and Michael Jackson [4] Stevie Wonder and Michael Jackson
[5] Michael Jackson and Janet Jackson [6] 3T featuring Michael Jackson

The sleeve of 'I Just Can't Stop Loving You' credits Siedah Garrett but the label does not. 'Come Together' was only listed from 7 Mar, 1992. It peaked at No 10

Mick JACKSON ◢ *UK, male vocalist*   16 wks
30 Sep 78	BLAME IT ON THE BOOGIE *Atlantic K 11102*	15	8
3 Feb 79	WEEKEND *Atlantic K 11224*	38	8

Millie JACKSON *US, female vocalist*   8 wks
18 Nov 72	MY MAN A SWEET MAN *Mojo 2093 022*	50	1
10 Mar 84	I FEEL LIKE WALKIN' IN THE RAIN *Sire W 9348*	55	2
15 Jun 85	ACT OF WAR *Rocket EJS 8* [1]	32	5

[1] Elton John and Millie Jackson

JACKSON SISTERS *US, female vocal group*   2 wks
20 Jun 87	I BELIEVE IN MIRACLES *Urban URB 4*	72	2

Stonewall JACKSON *US, male vocalist*   2 wks
17 Jul 59	WATERLOO *Philips PB 941*	24	2

Tony JACKSON – *See Q*

Tony JACKSON and the VIBRATIONS
UK, male vocal/instrumental group   3 wks
8 Oct 64	BYE BYE BABY *Pye 7N 15685*	38	3

Wanda JACKSON *US, female vocalist*   11 wks
1 Sep 60	LET'S HAVE A PARTY *Capitol CL 15147*	32	8
26 Jan 61	MEAN MEAN MAN *Capitol CL 15176*	46	1
9 Feb 61	MEAN MEAN MAN (re-entry) *Capitol CL 15176*	40	2

JACKSONS ✍ ◎ *One of the world's biggest-selling and most popular groups: brothers Jackie, Tito, Jermaine, Marlon and later solo superstar, Michael Jackson. The Indiana quartet topped the US chart with their first four hits, and have reportedly sold more than 100 million records*   235 wks
31 Jan 70	● I WANT YOU BACK *Tamla Motown TMG 724* [1] ▲	2	13
16 May 70	● ABC *Tamla Motown TMG 738* [1] ▲	8	11
1 Aug 70	● THE LOVE YOU SAVE *Tamla Motown TMG 746* [1] ▲	7	9
21 Nov 70	● I'LL BE THERE *Tamla Motown TMG 758* [1] ▲	4	16
10 Apr 71	MAMA'S PEARL *Tamla Motown TMG 769* [1]	25	7
17 Jul 71	NEVER CAN SAY GOODBYE *Tamla Motown TMG 778* [1]	33	7
11 Nov 72	● LOOKIN' THROUGH THE WINDOWS *Tamla Motown TMG 833* [1]	9	11
23 Dec 72	SANTA CLAUS IS COMING TO TOWN *Tamla Motown TMG 837* [1]	43	3
17 Feb 73	● DOCTOR MY EYES *Tamla Motown TMG 842* [1]	9	10
9 Jun 73	HALLELUJAH DAY *Tamla Motown TMG 856* [1]	20	9
8 Sep 73	SKYWRITER *Tamla Motown TMG 865* [1]	25	8
9 Apr 77	ENJOY YOURSELF *Epic EPC 5063*	42	4
4 Jun 77	★ SHOW YOU THE WAY TO GO *Epic EPC 5266*	1	10
13 Aug 77	DREAMER *Epic EPC 5458*	22	9
5 Nov 77	GOIN' PLACES *Epic EPC 5732*	26	7
11 Feb 78	EVEN THOUGH YOU'VE GONE *Epic EPC 5919*	31	4
23 Sep 78	● BLAME IT ON THE BOOGIE *Epic EPC 6683*	8	12
3 Feb 79	DESTINY *Epic EPC 6983*	39	6
24 Mar 79	● SHAKE YOUR BODY (DOWN TO THE GROUND) *Epic EPC 7181*	4	12
25 Oct 80	LOVELY ONE *Epic EPC 9302*	29	6
13 Dec 80	HEARTBREAK HOTEL *Epic EPC 9391*	44	6
28 Feb 81	● CAN YOU FEEL IT *Epic EPC 9554*	6	15
4 Jul 81	● WALK RIGHT NOW *Epic EPC A 1294*	7	11
7 Jul 84	STATE OF SHOCK *Epic A 4431* [2]	14	8

8 Sep 84	TORTURE *Epic A 4675*	26	6
16 Apr 88	● I WANT YOU BACK (re-mix) *Motown ZB 41913* [3]	8	9
13 May 89	NOTHIN' (THAT COMPARES 2 U) *Epic 654808 7*	33	6

[1] Jackson Five [2] Jacksons, lead vocals Mick Jagger and Michael Jackson
[3] Michael Jackson with the Jackson Five

JACKY – *See Jackie LEE*

JACQUELINE – *See MACK VIBE featuring JACQUELINE*

JADE (R&B) *US, female vocal group*   28 wks
20 Mar 93	● DON'T WALK AWAY *Giant W 0160CD*	7	8
3 Jul 93	I WANNA LOVE YOU *Giant 74321151662*	13	7
18 Sep 93	ONE WOMAN *Giant 74321165122*	22	5
5 Feb 94	ALL THRU THE NITE *Giant 74321187552* [1]	32	3
11 Feb 95	EVERY DAY OF THE WEEK *Giant 74321260242*	19	5

[1] P.O.V. featuring Jade

JADE 4 U – *See Praga KHAN*

JAGGED EDGE *UK, male vocal/instrumental group*   2 wks
15 Sep 90	YOU DON'T LOVE ME *Polydor PO 97*	66	2

Mick JAGGER ✍ *UK, male vocalist*   42 wks
14 Nov 70	MEMO FROM TURNER *Decca F 13067*	32	5
7 Jul 84	STATE OF SHOCK *Epic A 4431* [1]	14	8
16 Feb 85	JUST ANOTHER NIGHT *CBS A 4722*	32	6
7 Sep 85	★ DANCING IN THE STREET *EMI America EA 204* [2] ■	1	12
12 Sep 87	LET'S WORK *CBS 651028 7*	31	7
6 Feb 93	SWEET THING *Atlantic A 7410CD*	24	4

[1] Jacksons, lead vocals Mick Jagger and Michael Jackson
[2] David Bowie and Mick Jagger

JAGS ✍ ✎ *UK, male vocal/instrumental group*   11 wks
8 Sep 79	BACK OF MY HAND *Island WIP 6501*	17	10
2 Feb 80	WOMAN'S WORLD *Island WIP 6531*	75	1

JALN BAND *UK/Jamaica, male vocal/instrumental group*   17 wks
11 Sep 76	DISCO MUSIC/I LIKE IT *Magnet MAG 73*	21	9
27 Aug 77	I GOT TO SING *Magnet MAG 97*	40	4
1 Jul 78	GET UP *Magnet MAG 118*	53	4

JAM ◎ ✎ *Influential and extremely popular punk-based mod trio from Surrey: Paul Weller (v/g), Bruce Foxton (b), Rick Buckler (d). It was the first act to enter the chart at No 1 with three singles, and hold the record for the most simultaneous Top 75 singles with 13 (all reactivated by their 1982 dissolution)*   205 wks
7 May 77	IN THE CITY *Polydor 2058 866*	40	6
23 Jul 77	ALL AROUND THE WORLD *Polydor 2058 903*	13	8
5 Nov 77	THE MODERN WORLD *Polydor 2058 945*	36	4
11 Mar 78	NEWS OF THE WORLD *Polydor 2058 995*	27	5
26 Aug 78	DAVID WATTS/'A' BOMB IN WARDOUR STREET *Polydor 2059 054*	25	8
21 Oct 78	DOWN IN THE TUBE STATION AT MIDNIGHT *Polydor POSP 8*	15	7
17 Mar 79	STRANGE TOWN *Polydor POSP 34*	15	9
25 Aug 79	WHEN YOU'RE YOUNG *Polydor POSP 69*	17	7
3 Nov 79	● THE ETON RIFLES *Polydor POSP 83*	3	12
22 Mar 80	★ GOING UNDERGROUND/DREAMS OF CHILDREN *Polydor POSP 113* ■	1	9
26 Apr 80	ALL AROUND THE WORLD (re-entry) *Polydor 2058 903*	43	3
26 Apr 80	DAVID WATTS/'A' BOMB IN WARDOUR STREET (re-entry) *Polydor 2059 054*	54	3
26 Apr 80	IN THE CITY (re-entry) *Polydor 2058 866*	40	4
26 Apr 80	NEWS OF THE WORLD (re-entry) *Polydor 2058 995*	53	3
26 Apr 80	STRANGE TOWN (re-entry) *Polydor POSP 34*	44	4
26 Apr 80	THE MODERN WORLD (re-entry) *Polydor 2058 945*	52	3
23 Aug 80	★ START *Polydor 2059 266*	1	8
7 Feb 81	THAT'S ENTERTAINMENT (IMPORT) *Metronome 0030 364*	21	7

UK No 1 ★   UK Top 10 ●   UK million seller ◆   UK entry at No 1 ■   US No 1 ▲

What: *Temptation*   **49**
Who: Heaven 17
When: 1983 (2), 1992 (4 – remix)
Which: Took the Human League spin-off group into the Top 5 twice in less than ten years. This electronic/soul fusion track includes an uncredited vocal by Carol Kenyon

What: *Good Vibrations*   **50**
Who: Beach Boys
When: 1966 (1), 1976 (18)
Which: At the time was the most expensive single ever recorded ($50 000). It was the group's only UK/US No 1, and is still considered by many to be the greatest pop single of all time

What: *Dancing Queen*   **51**
Who: Abba
When: 1976 (1), 1992 (16)
Which: Gave the group their third successive No 1 and returned to the Top 20 ten years after they had split up. This club favourite was also their only US chart-topper

What: *I'll Do Anything For Love (But I Won't Do That)*   **52**
Who: Meat Loaf
When: 1993 (1)
Which: At almost eight minutes in duration was the longest No 1 until 1998. It was his biggest hit and came 12 years after his previous Top 10 entry

6 Jun 81	● FUNERAL PYRE *Polydor POSP 257*	.....4 **6**
24 Oct 81	● ABSOLUTE BEGINNERS *Polydor POSP 350*	.....4 **6**
13 Feb 82	★ TOWN CALLED MALICE/PRECIOUS *Polydor POSP 400* ■	.....1 **8**
3 Jul 82	● JUST WHO IS THE FIVE O'CLOCK HERO *Polydor 2059 504*	.....8 **5**
18 Sep 82	● THE BITTEREST PILL (I EVER HAD TO SWALLOW) *Polydor POSP 505*	.....2 **7**
4 Dec 82	★ BEAT SURRENDER *Polydor POSP 540* ■	.....1 **9**
22 Jan 83	ALL AROUND THE WORLD (2nd re-entry) *Polydor 2058 903*	.....38 **4**
22 Jan 83	DAVID WATTS/'A' BOMB IN WARDOUR STREET (2nd re-entry) *Polydor 2059 054*	.....50 **4**
22 Jan 83	DOWN IN THE TUBE STATION AT MIDNIGHT (re-entry) *Polydor POSP 8*	.....30 **6**
22 Jan 83	GOING UNDERGROUND/DREAMS OF CHILDREN (re-entry) *Polydor POSP 113*	.....21 **6**
22 Jan 83	IN THE CITY (2nd re-entry) *Polydor 2058 866*	.....47 **4**
22 Jan 83	NEWS OF THE WORLD (2nd re-entry) *Polydor 2058 995*	.....39 **4**
22 Jan 83	STRANGE TOWN (2nd re-entry) *Polydor POSP 34*	.....42 **5**
22 Jan 83	THE MODERN WORLD (2nd re-entry) *Polydor 2058 945*	.....51 **4**
22 Jan 83	WHEN YOU'RE YOUNG (re-entry) *Polydor POSP 69*	.....53 **4**
29 Jan 83	THAT'S ENTERTAINMENT (re-issue) *Polydor POSP 482*	.....60 **3**
5 Feb 83	START (re-entry) *Polydor 2059 266*	.....62 **2**
5 Feb 83	THE ETON RIFLES (re-entry) *Polydor POSP 83*	.....54 **3**
5 Feb 83	TOWN CALLED MALICE/PRECIOUS (re-entry) *Polydor POSP 400*	.....73 **1**
29 Jun 91	THAT'S ENTERTAINMENT (2nd re-issue) *Polydor PO 155*	.....57 **2**
11 Oct 97	THE BITTEREST PILL (I EVER HAD TO SWALLOW) (re-issue) *Polydor 5715992*	.....30 **2**

JAM AND SPOON featuring PLAVKA ☺
Germany, male/female vocal/instrumental group **24 wks**

2 May 92	TALES FROM A DANCEOGRAPHIC OCEAN EP *R&S RSUK 14* 1	.....49 **1**
6 Jun 92	THE COMPLETE STELLA (re-mix) *R&S RSUK 14X* 1	.....66 **2**
26 Feb 94	RIGHT IN THE NIGHT (FALL IN LOVE WITH MUSIC) *Epic 6600822*	.....31 **4**
24 Sep 94	FIND ME (ODYSSEY TO ANYOONA) *Epic 6608082*	.....37 **3**
10 Jun 95	● RIGHT IN THE NIGHT (FALL IN LOVE WITH MUSIC) (re-issue) *Epic 6620182*	.....10 **8**
16 Sep 95	FIND ME (ODYSSEY TO ANYOONA) (re-issue) *Epic 6623242*	.....22 **3**
25 Nov 95	ANGEL (LADADI O-HEYO) *Epic 6626382*	.....26 **2**
30 Aug 97	KALEIDOSCOPE SKIES *Epic 6647614*	.....48 **1**

1 Jam and Spoon

Tracks on Tales From a Danceographic Ocean EP: Stella / Keep on Movin' / My First Fantastic FF. 'The Complete Stella' is a re-mix of a track from the EP
See also STORM; TOKYO GHETTO PUSSY

JAM MACHINE *Italy/US, male vocal/instrumental group* **1 wk**

23 Dec 89	EVERYDAY *Deconstruction PB 43299*	.....68 **1**

JAM ON THE MUTHA *UK, male vocal/instrumental group* **2 wks**

11 Aug 90	HOTEL CALIFORNIA *M & G MAGS 3*	.....62 **2**

JAM TRONIK ☯ ☺
Germany, male/female vocal/instrumental group **7 wks**

24 Mar 90	ANOTHER DAY IN PARADISE *Debut DEBT 3093*	.....19 **7**

JAMAICA UNITED *Jamaica, male vocal ensemble* **1 wk**

4 Jul 98	RISE UP *Columbia 6660522*	.....54 **1**

JAMES ☯ ✒ *UK, male vocal/instrumental group* **75 wks**

12 May 90	HOW WAS IT FOR YOU *Fontana JIM 5*	.....32 **3**
7 Jul 90	COME HOME *Fontana JIM 6*	.....32 **4**
8 Dec 90	LOSE CONTROL *Fontana JIM 7*	.....38 **5**
30 Mar 91	● SIT DOWN *Fontana JIM 8*	.....2 **10**
30 Nov 91	● SOUND *Fontana JIM 9*	.....9 **7**
1 Feb 92	BORN OF FRUSTRATION *Fontana JIM 10*	.....13 **6**
4 Apr 92	RING THE BELLS *Fontana JIM 11*	.....37 **2**
18 Jul 92	SEVEN EP *Fontana JIM 12*	.....46 **2**
11 Sep 93	SOMETIMES *Fontana JIMCD 13*	.....18 **4**
13 Nov 93	LAID *Fontana JIMCD 14*	.....25 **4**
2 Apr 94	JAM J / SAY SOMETHING *Fontana JIMCD 152*	.....24 **4**
22 Feb 97	SHE'S A STAR *Fontana JIMCD 16*	.....9 **5**
3 May 97	TOMORROW *Fontana JIMCD 17*	.....12 **3**
5 Jul 97	WALTZING ALONG *Fontana JIMCD 18*	.....23 **4**
21 Mar 98	DESTINY CALLING *Fontana JIMCD 19*	.....17 **4**
6 Jun 98	RUNAGROUND *Fontana JIMCD 20*	.....29 **2**
21 Nov 98	● SIT DOWN (re-mix) *Fontana JIMCD 21*	.....7† **6**

Tracks on Seven (EP): Seven / Goalie's Ball / William Burroughs / Still Alive.
'Say Something' only listed with 'Jam J' for first two weeks of record's run

JAMES – *See CHRIS and JAMES*

Dick JAMES ℂ *UK, male vocalist* **13 wks**

20 Jan 56	ROBIN HOOD *Parlophone R 4117*	.....14 **8**
18 May 56	ROBIN HOOD/BALLAD OF DAVY CROCKETT (re-entry) *Parlophone R 4117*	.....29 **1**
11 Jan 57	GARDEN OF EDEN *Parlophone R 4255*	.....18 **4**

'Robin Hood' is with Stephen James and his Chums

Etta JAMES ♀ *US, female vocalist* **7 wks**

10 Feb 96	● I JUST WANT TO MAKE LOVE TO YOU *MCA MCSTD 48003*	.....5 **7**

Freddie JAMES *Canada, male vocalist* **3 wks**

24 Nov 79	GET UP AND BOOGIE *Warner Bros. K 17478*	.....54 **3**

Jimmy JAMES and the VAGABONDS ☄
UK, male vocal/instrumental group **25 wks**

11 Sep 68	RED RED WINE *Pye 7N 17579*	.....36 **8**
24 Apr 76	I'LL GO WHERE YOUR MUSIC TAKES ME *Pye 7N 45585*	.....23 **8**
17 Jul 76	● NOW IS THE TIME *Pye 7N 45606*	.....5 **9**

Joni JAMES ℂ *US, female vocalist* **2 wks**

6 Mar 53	WHY DON'T YOU BELIEVE ME *MGM 582* ▲	.....11 **1**
30 Jan 59	THERE MUST BE A WAY *MGM 1002*	.....24 **1**

Rick JAMES *US, male vocalist* **30 wks**

8 Jul 78	YOU AND I *Motown TMG 1110*	.....46 **7**
7 Jul 79	I'M A SUCKER FOR YOUR LOVE *Motown TMG 1146* 1	.....43 **8**
6 Sep 80	BIG TIME *Motown TMG 1198*	.....41 **6**
4 Jul 81	GIVE IT TO ME BABY *Motown TMG 1229*	.....47 **3**
12 Jun 82	STANDING ON THE TOP (PART 1) *Motown TMG 1263* 2	.....53 **3**
3 Jul 82	DANCE WIT' ME *Motown TMG 1266*	.....53 **3**

1 Teena Marie, co-lead vocals Rick James 2 Temptations featuring Rick James

Sonny JAMES ☘ *US, male vocalist* **8 wks**

30 Nov 56	THE CAT CAME BACK *Capitol CL 14635*	.....30 **1**
8 Feb 57	YOUNG LOVE *Capitol CL 14683*	.....11 **7**

Tommy JAMES and the SHONDELLS ☯
US, male vocal/instrumental group **25 wks**

21 Jul 66	HANKY PANKY *Roulette RK 7000* ▲	.....38 **7**
5 Jun 68	★ MONY MONY *Major Minor MM 567*	.....1 **18**

Wendy JAMES *UK, female vocalist* **4 wks**

20 Feb 93	THE NAMELESS ONE *MCA MCSTD 1732*	.....34 **3**
17 Apr 93	LONDON'S BRILLIANT *MCA MCSTD 1763*	.....62 **1**

JAMES BOYS *UK, male vocal duo* **6 wks**

19 May 73	OVER AND OVER *Penny Farthing PEN 806*	.....39 **6**

JAMESTOWN – *See Jocelyn BROWN*

JAMIROQUAI ☯ ☺ *UK, male vocal/instrumental group* **86 wks**

31 Oct 92	WHEN YOU GONNA LEARN *Acid Jazz JAZID 46T*	.....52 **2**
20 Feb 93	WHEN YOU GONNA LEARN (re-entry) *Acid Jazz JAZID 46*	.....69 **1**

UK No 1 ★ UK Top 10 ● UK million seller ◆ UK entry at No 1 ■ US No 1 ▲

JB's ALL STARS UK, male/female vocal/instrumental group — 4 wks

11 Feb 84	BACKFIELD IN MOTION RCA Victor RCA 384	48	4

JC UK, male producer — 1 wk

7 Feb 98	SO HOT East West EW 146CD	74	1

J.C. 001 UK, male rapper — 4 wks

24 Apr 93	NEVER AGAIN Anxious ANX 1012CD	67	2
26 Jun 93	CUPID Anxious ANX 1014CD	56	2

JDS Italy / UK, male DJ / production duo – Julian Napolitano and Darren Pearce — 2 wks

27 Sep 97	NINE WAYS ffrr FCD 310	61	1
23 May 98	LONDON TOWN Jive 0530042	49	1

Wyclef JEAN ◀ [R&B] US, male vocalist/producer — 22 wks

28 Jun 97	WE TRYING TO STAY ALIVE Columbia 6646815 [1]	13	5
27 Sep 97	GUANTANAMERA Columbia 6650852 [1]	25	2
16 May 98 ●	GONE TILL NOVEMBER Columbia 6658712	3	9
14 Nov 98 ●	ANOTHER ONE BITES THE DUST Dreamworks DRMCD 22364 [2]	5	6

[1] Wyclef Jean and the Refugee Allstars
[2] Queen with Wyclef Jean featuring Pras Michel and Free

See also FUGEES

JEFFERSON UK, male vocalist — 8 wks

9 Apr 69	COLOUR OF MY LOVE Pye 7N 17706	22	8

JEFFERSON STARSHIP – See STARSHIP

Garland JEFFREYS US, male vocalist — 1 wk

8 Feb 92	HAIL HAIL ROCK 'N' ROLL RCA PB 49171	72	1

JELLYBEAN ☺ ● US, male producer — 47 wks

1 Feb 86	SIDEWALK TALK EMI America EA 210 [1]	47	4
26 Sep 87	THE REAL THING Chrysalis CHS 3167 [2]	13	10
28 Nov 87 ●	WHO FOUND WHO Chrysalis CHS JEL 1 [3]	10	10
12 Dec 87	JINGO Chrysalis JEL 2	12	10
12 Mar 88	JUST A MIRAGE Chrysalis JEL 3 [4]	13	10
20 Aug 88	COMING BACK FOR MORE Chrysalis JEL 4 [5]	41	3

[1] Jellybean featuring Catherine Buchanan [2] Jellybean featuring Steven Dante
[3] Jellybean featuring Elisa Fiorillo [4] Jellybean featuring Adele Bertei
[5] Jellybean featuring Richard Darbyshire

JELLYFISH US, male vocal/instrumental group — 20 wks

26 Jan 91	THE KING IS HALF UNDRESSED Charisma CUSS 1	39	6
27 Apr 91	BABY'S COMING BACK Charisma CUSS 2	51	4
3 Aug 91	THE SCARY-GO-ROUND EP Charisma CUSS 3	49	3
26 Oct 91	I WANNA STAY HOME Charisma CUSS 4	59	2
1 May 93	THE GHOST AT NUMBER ONE Charisma CUSDG 10	43	3
17 Jul 93	NEW MISTAKE Charisma CUSDG 11	55	2

Tracks on The Scary-Go-Round EP: Now She Knows She's Wrong / Bedspring Kiss / She Still Loves Him (Live) / Baby's Coming Back (Live)

JERU THE DAMAJA US, male rapper — 1 wk

7 Dec 96	YA PLAYIN YASELF ffrr FCD 289	67	1

JESUS AND MARY CHAIN ☹ ✎ UK, male vocal/instrumental group — 59 wks

2 Mar 85	NEVER UNDERSTAND Blanco Y Negro NEG 8	47	4
8 Jun 85	YOU TRIP ME UP Blanco Y Negro NEG 13	55	3
12 Oct 85	JUST LIKE HONEY Blanco Y Negro NEG 17	45	3
26 Jul 86	SOME CANDY TALKING Blanco Y Negro NEG 19	13	5
2 May 87 ●	APRIL SKIES Blanco Y Negro NEG 24	8	6
15 Aug 87	HAPPY WHEN IT RAINS Blanco Y Negro NEG 25	25	5

7 Nov 87	DARKLANDS Blanco Y Negro NEG 29	33	4
9 Apr 88	SIDEWALKING Blanco Y Negro NEG 32	30	3
23 Sep 89	BLUES FROM A GUN Blanco Y Negro NEG 41	32	2
18 Nov 89	HEAD ON Blanco Y Negro NEG 42	57	2
8 Sep 90	ROLLERCOASTER EP Blanco Y Negro NEG 45	46	2
15 Feb 92 ●	REVERENCE Blanco Y Negro NEG 55	10	4
14 Mar 92	FAR GONE AND OUT Blanco Y Negro NEG 56	23	3
4 Jul 92	ALMOST GOLD Blanco Y Negro NEG 57	41	2
10 Jul 93	SOUND OF SPEED EP Blanco Y Negro NEG 66CD	30	2
30 Jul 94	SOMETIMES ALWAYS Blanco Y Negro NEG 70CD	22	3
22 Oct 94	COME ON Blanco Y Negro NEG 73CD1	52	2
17 Jun 95	I HATE ROCK 'N' ROLL Blanco Y Negro NEG 81CD	61	1
18 Apr 98	CRACKING UP Creation CRESCD 292	35	2
30 May 98	ILOVEROCKNROLL Creation CRESCD 296	38	1

Tracks on Rollercoaster (EP): Rollercoaster / Silverblade / Lowlife / Tower of Song.
Tracks on Sound of Speed (EP): Snakedriver / Something I Can't Have / Write Record Release Blues / Little Red Rooster

JESUS JONES ● ☺ UK, male vocal/instrumental group — 52 wks

25 Feb 89	INFO-FREAKO Food FOOD 18	42	3
8 Jul 89	NEVER ENOUGH Food FOOD 21	42	3
23 Sep 89	BRING IT ON DOWN Food FOOD 22	46	3
7 Apr 90	REAL REAL REAL Food FOOD 24	19	8
6 Oct 90	RIGHT HERE RIGHT NOW Food FOOD 25	31	4
12 Jan 91 ●	INTERNATIONAL BRIGHT YOUNG THING Food FOOD 27	7	7
2 Mar 91	WHO WHERE WHY Food FOOD 28	21	7
20 Jul 91	RIGHT HERE RIGHT NOW (re-issue) Food FOOD 30	31	4
9 Jan 93 ●	THE DEVIL YOU KNOW Food CDPERV 1	10	5
10 Apr 93	THE RIGHT DECISION Food CDPERV 2	36	3
10 Jul 93	ZEROES & ONES Food CDFOODS 44	30	3
14 Jun 97	THE NEXT BIG THING Food CDFOOD 95	49	1
16 Aug 97	CHEMICAL #1 Food CDFOOD 102	71	1

See also VARIOUS ARTISTS (EPs & LPs) – The Food Christmas EP

JESUS LIZARD ✎ US, male vocal/instrumental group — 2 wks

6 Mar 93	PUSS Touch And Go TG 83CD	12	2

The listed flip side of 'Puss' was 'Oh, the Guilt' by Nirvana

JESUS LOVES YOU UK, male vocalist – Boy George — 18 wks

11 Nov 89	AFTER THE LOVE More Protein PROT 2	68	1
23 Feb 91	BOW DOWN MISTER More Protein PROT 8	27	8
8 Jun 91	GENERATIONS OF LOVE More Protein PROT 10	35	8
12 Dec 92	SWEET TOXIC LOVE Virgin VS 1449	65	1

JETHRO TULL ✎ UK, male vocal/instrumental group — 68 wks

1 Jan 69	LOVE STORY Island WIP 6048	29	8
14 May 69 ●	LIVING IN THE PAST Island WIP 6056	3	14
1 Nov 69 ●	SWEET DREAM Chrysalis WIP 6070	7	11
24 Jan 70 ●	TEACHER/THE WITCH'S PROMISE Chrysalis WIP 6077	4	9
18 Sep 71	LIFE IS A LONG SONG/UP THE POOL Chrysalis WIP 6106	11	8
11 Dec 76	RING OUT SOLSTICE BELLS EP Chrysalis CXP 2	28	6
15 Sep 84	LAP OF LUXURY Chrysalis TULL 1	70	2
16 Jan 88	SAID SHE WAS A DANCER Chrysalis TULL 4	55	4
21 Mar 92	ROCKS ON THE ROAD Chrysalis TULLX 7	47	3
22 May 93	LIVING IN THE (SLIGHTLY MORE RECENT) PAST Chrysalis CDCHSS 3970	32	3

Tracks on Ring Out Solstice Bells EP: Ring Out Solstice Bells / March the Mad Scientist / The Christmas Song / Pan Dance. 'Living in the (Slightly More Recent) Past' is a live version of the original

JETS UK, male vocal/instrumental group — 38 wks

22 Aug 81	SUGAR DOLL EMI 5211	55	3
31 Oct 81	YES TONIGHT JOSEPHINE EMI 5247	25	11
6 Feb 82	LOVE MAKES THE WORLD GO ROUND EMI 5262	21	9
24 Apr 82	THE HONEYDRIPPER EMI 5289	58	3
9 Oct 82	SOMEBODY TO LOVE EMI 5342	56	3
6 Aug 83	BLUE SKIES EMI 5405	53	3
17 Dec 83	ROCKIN' AROUND THE CHRISTMAS TREE PRT 7P 297	62	4
13 Oct 84	PARTY DOLL PRT JETS 2	72	2

JETS ☺ 🎤 US, male/female vocal/instrumental group — 19 wks

31 Jan 87	●	CRUSH ON YOU *MCA MCA 1048*	5 13
25 Apr 87		CURIOSITY *MCA MCA 1119*	41 4
28 May 88		ROCKET 2 U *MCA MCA 1226*	69 2

Joan JETT and the BLACKHEARTS ◎ 🎸
US, female vocalist with male vocal/instrumental group — 21 wks

24 Apr 82	●	I LOVE ROCK `N' ROLL *Epic EPC A 2087* ▲	4 10
10 Jul 82		CRIMSON AND CLOVER *Epic EPC A 2485*	60 3
20 Aug 88		I HATE MYSELF FOR LOVING YOU *London LON 195*	46 6
31 Mar 90		DIRTY DEEDS *Chrysalis CHS 3518* 1	69 1
19 Feb 94		I LOVE ROCK & ROLL (re-issue) *Reprise W 0232CD*	75 1

1 Joan Jett

JEWEL US, female vocalist/instrumentalist – guitar — 6 wks

14 Jun 97		WHO WILL SAVE YOUR SOUL *Atlantic A 8514CD*	52 1
9 Aug 97		YOU WERE MEANT FOR ME *Atlantic A 5463CD*	53 1
21 Nov 98		HANDS *Atlantic AT 0055CD*	41 2
22 Nov 97		YOU WERE MEANT FOR ME (re-entry) *Atlantic A 5463CD*	32 2

JEZ and CHOOPIE UK / Israel, male DJ / production duo — 2 wks

21 Mar 98		YIM *Multiply CDMULTY 31*	36 2

JHELISA US, female vocalist — 1 wk

1 Jul 95		FRIENDLY PRESSURE *Dorado DOR 040CD*	75 1

JIGSAW ◎ UK, male vocal/instrumental group — 16 wks

1 Nov 75	●	SKY HIGH *Splash CP1 1*	9 11
6 Aug 77		IF I HAVE TO GO AWAY *Splash CP 11*	36 5

JILTED JOHN ◎ UK, male vocalist — 12 wks

12 Aug 78	●	JILTED JOHN *EMI International INT 567*	4 12

JIMMY THE HOOVER ◎
UK, male/female vocal/instrumental group — 8 wks

25 Jun 83		TANTALISE (WO WO EE YEH YEH) *Innervision A 3406*	18 8

JINGLE BELLES US/UK, female vocal group — 4 wks

17 Dec 83		CHRISTMAS SPECTRE *Passion PASH 14*	37 4

JINNY ☺ ◎ Italy, female vocalist — 16 wks

29 Jun 91		KEEP WARM *Virgin VS 1356*	68 3
22 May 93		FEEL THE RHYTHM *Logic 401633001022*	74 1
15 Jul 95		KEEP WARM (re-mix) *Multiply CDMULTY 5*	11 8
16 Dec 95		WANNA BE WITH YOU *Multiply CDMULTY 8*	30 4

JIVE BUNNY and the MASTERMIXERS ◎
UK, male production/mixing group — 68 wks

15 Jul 89	★	SWING THE MOOD *Music Factory Dance MFD 001*	1 19
14 Oct 89	★	THAT'S WHAT I LIKE *Music Factory Dance MFD 002*	1 12
16 Dec 89	★	LET'S PARTY *Music Factory Dance MFD 003* ■	1 6
17 Mar 90	●	THAT SOUNDS GOOD TO ME *Music Factory Dance MFD 004*	4 6
25 Aug 90	●	CAN CAN YOU PARTY *Music Factory Dance MFD 007*	8 6
17 Nov 90		LET'S SWING AGAIN *Music Factory Dance MFD 009*	19 5
22 Dec 90		THE CRAZY PARTY MIXES *Music Factory Dance MFD 010*	13 5
23 Mar 91		OVER TO YOU JOHN (HERE WE GO AGAIN) *Music Factory Dance MFD 012*	28 5
20 Jul 91		HOT SUMMER SALSA *Music Factory Dance MFD 013*	43 2
23 Nov 91		ROCK 'N' ROLL DANCE PARTY *Music Factory Dance MFD 015*	48 2

See also Liz KERSHAW and Bruno BROOKES

JJ UK, male/female vocal/instumental duo — 3 wks

9 Feb 91		IF THIS IS LOVE *Columbia 6566097*	55 3

JKD BAND UK, male vocal/instrumental group — 4 wks

1 Jul 78		DRAGON POWER *Satril SAT 132*	58 4

JM SILK US, male vocal/instrumental duo — 6 wks

25 Oct 86		I CAN'T TURN AROUND *RCA PB 49793*	62 3
7 Mar 87		LET THE MUSIC TAKE CONTROL *RCA PB 49767*	47 3

JMD – See TYREE

JO BOXERS ◎ UK, male vocal/instrumental group — 33 wks

19 Feb 83	●	BOXER BEAT *RCA BOXX 1*	3 15
21 May 83	●	JUST GOT LUCKY *RCA BOXX 2*	7 9
13 Aug 83		JOHNNY FRIENDLY *RCA BOXX 3*	31 8
12 Nov 83		JEALOUS LOVE *RCA BOXX 4*	72 1

JO JO GUNNE 🎸 US, male vocal/instrumental group — 12 wks

25 Mar 72	●	RUN RUN RUN *Asylum AYM 501*	6 12

JOAN COLLINS FAN CLUB UK, male vocalist – Julian Clary — 3 wks

18 Jun 88		LEADER OF THE PACK *10 TEN 227*	60 3

John Paul JOANS UK, male vocalist — 7 wks

19 Dec 70		MAN FROM NAZARETH *RAK 107*	41 3
16 Jan 71		MAN FROM NAZARETH (re-entry) *RAK 107*	25 4

JOCASTA UK, male vocal/instrumental group — 2 wks

15 Feb 97		GO *Epic 6641415*	50 1
3 May 97		CHANGE ME *Epic 6643902*	60 1

JOCKMASTER B.A. – See MAD JOCKS featuring JOCKMASTER B.A.

JOCKO US, male rapper – DJ Jocko Henderson — 3 wks

23 Feb 80		RHYTHM TALK *Philadelphia Interna PIR 8222*	56 3

JODE UK, male / female vocal duo — 2 wks

19 Dec 98		WALK...(THE DOG) LIKE AN EGYPTIAN *Logic 74321640332* 1	48† 2

1 Jode featuring Yo-Hans

JODECI R&B US, male vocal group — 19 wks

16 Jan 93		CHERISH *Uptown MCSTD 1726*	56 2
11 Dec 93		CRY FOR YOU *Uptown MCSTD 1951*	56 1
16 Jul 94		FEENIN' *Uptown MCSTD 1984*	18 3
28 Jan 95		CRY FOR YOU (re-issue) *Uptown MCSTD 2039*	20 3
24 Jun 95		FREEK 'N YOU *Uptown MCSTD 2072*	17 5
9 Dec 95		LOVE U 4 LIFE *Uptown MCSTD 2105*	23 3
25 May 96		GET ON UP *MCA MCSTD 48010*	20 2

JODIE Australia, female vocalist — 1 wk

25 Feb 95		ANYTHING YOU WANT *Mercury MERCD 423*	47 1

JOE R&B US, male vocalist — 21 wks

22 Jan 94		I'M IN LUV *Mercury JOECD 1*	22 4
25 Jun 94		THE ONE FOR ME *Mercury JOECD 2*	34 2
22 Oct 94		ALL OR NOTHING *Mercury JOECD 3*	56 1
27 Apr 96		ALL THE THINGS (YOUR MAN WON'T DO) *Island CID 634*	34 3
14 Jun 97		DON'T WANNA BE A PLAYER *Jive JIVECD 410*	16 3
27 Sep 97		THE LOVE SCENE *Jive JIVECD 430*	22 2
10 Jan 98		GOOD GIRLS *Jive JIVECD 442*	29 3
22 Aug 98		NO ONE ELSE COMES CLOSE *Jive 0521682*	41 2
31 Oct 98		ALL THAT I AM *Jive 0518532*	52 1

JOE PUBLIC US, male rap group — 5 wks

11 Jul 92		LIVE AND LEARN *Columbia 6575267*	43 4
28 Nov 92		I'VE BEEN WATCHIN' *Columbia 6587657*	75 1

Billy JOEL ✪
Platinum-plated singer/songwriter/pianist, b. 9 May, 1949, Long Island. This relatively youthful Grammy Living Legend Award recipient was first artist to have five albums pass the seven million mark Stateside. The box-office record-breaking performer briefly quit pop music for the classics in 1997

146 wks

Date	Title	Pos	Wks
11 Feb 78	JUST THE WAY YOU ARE *CBS 5872*	19	9
24 Jun 78	MOVIN' OUT (ANTHONY'S SONG) *CBS 6412*	35	6
2 Dec 78	MY LIFE *CBS 6821*	12	15
28 Apr 79	UNTIL THE NIGHT *CBS 7242*	50	3
12 Apr 80	ALL FOR LEYNA *CBS 8325*	40	4
9 Aug 80	IT'S STILL ROCK AND ROLL TO ME *CBS 8753* ▲	14	11
15 Oct 83 ★	UPTOWN GIRL *CBS A 3775*	1	17
10 Dec 83 ●	TELL HER ABOUT IT *CBS A 3655* ▲	4	10
18 Feb 84 ●	AN INNOCENT MAN *CBS A 4142*	8	10
28 Apr 84	THE LONGEST TIME *CBS A 4280*	25	8
23 Jun 84	LEAVE A TENDER MOMENT ALONE/GOODNIGHT SAIGON *CBS A 4521*	29	7
22 Feb 86	SHE'S ALWAYS A WOMAN/JUST THE WAY YOU ARE (re-issue) *CBS A 6862*	53	1
20 Sep 86	A MATTER OF TRUST *CBS 650057 7*	52	4
30 Sep 89 ●	WE DIDN'T START THE FIRE *CBS JOEL 1* ▲	7	10
16 Dec 89	LENINGRAD *CBS JOEL 3*	53	4
10 Mar 90	I GO TO EXTREMES *CBS JOEL 2*	70	2
29 Aug 92	ALL SHOOK UP *Columbia 6583437*	27	4
31 Jul 93 ●	THE RIVER OF DREAMS *Columbia 6595432*	3	14
23 Oct 93	ALL ABOUT SOUL *Columbia 6597362*	32	4
26 Feb 94	NO MAN'S LAND *Columbia 6599202*	50	3

'Goodnight Saigon' only listed from 30 Jun, 1984

JOHANN
Germany, male producer – Johann Bley

1 wk

Date	Title	Pos	Wks
16 Mar 96	NEW KICKS *Perfecto PERF 118CD*	54	1

Elton JOHN ✪
World-renowned singer/songwriter/pianist, b. Reginald Dwight, 25 March, 1947, Middlesex, and was knighted in 1998. He was the biggest-selling pop act of the 1970s and the first artist to enter the US album chart at No 1. This often outrageously dressed performer has charted every year since 1971 in the UK and the USA, and has recorded the world's biggest-selling single, 'Candle in the Wind 1997'

558 wks

Date	Title	Pos	Wks
23 Jan 71 ●	YOUR SONG *DJM DJS 233*	7	12
22 Apr 72 ●	ROCKET MAN (I THINK IT'S GOING TO BE A LONG LONG TIME) *DJM DJX 501*	2	13
9 Sep 72	HONKY CAT *DJM DJS*	31	6
4 Nov 72 ●	CROCODILE ROCK *DJM DJS 271* ▲	5	14
20 Jan 73 ●	DANIEL *DJM DJS 275*	4	10
7 Jul 73	SATURDAY NIGHT'S ALRIGHT FOR FIGHTING *DJM DJX 502*	7	9
29 Sep 73 ●	GOODBYE YELLOW BRICK ROAD *DJM DJS 285*	6	16
8 Dec 73	STEP INTO CHRISTMAS *DJM DJS 290*	24	7
2 Mar 74	CANDLE IN THE WIND *DJM DJS 297*	11	9
1 Jun 74	DON'T LET THE SUN GO DOWN ON ME *DJM DJS 302*	16	8
14 Sep 74	THE BITCH IS BACK *DJM DJS 322*	15	7
23 Nov 74 ●	LUCY IN THE SKY WITH DIAMONDS *DJM DJS 340* ▲	10	10
8 Mar 75	PHILADELPHIA FREEDOM *DJM DJS 354* [1] ▲	12	9
28 Jun 75	SOMEONE SAVED MY LIFE TONIGHT *DJM DJS 385*	22	5
4 Oct 75	ISLAND GIRL *DJM DJS 610* ▲	14	8
20 Mar 76	PINBALL WIZARD *DJM DJS 652*	7	7
3 Jul 76 ★	DON'T GO BREAKING MY HEART *Rocket ROKN 512* [2] ▲	1	14
25 Sep 76	BENNIE AND THE JETS *DJM DJS 10705* ▲	37	5
13 Nov 76	SORRY SEEMS TO BE THE HARDEST WORD *Rocket ROKN 517*	11	10
26 Feb 77	CRAZY WATER *Rocket ROKN 521*	27	6
11 Jun 77	BITE YOUR LIP (GET UP AND DANCE) *Rocket ROKN 526*	28	4
15 Apr 78	EGO *Rocket ROKN 538*	34	6
21 Oct 78	PART TIME LOVE *Rocket XPRES 1*	15	13
16 Dec 78 ●	SONG FOR GUY *Rocket XPRES 5*	4	10
12 May 79	ARE YOU READY FOR LOVE *Rocket XPRES 13*	42	6
24 May 80	LITTLE JEANNIE *Rocket XPRES 32*	33	7
23 Aug 80	SARTORIAL ELOQUENCE *Rocket XPRES 41*	44	5
21 Mar 81	I SAW HER STANDING THERE *DJM DJS 10965* [3]	40	4
23 May 81	NOBODY WINS *Rocket XPRES 54*	42	5
27 Mar 82 ●	BLUE EYES *Rocket XPRES 71*	8	10
12 Jun 82	EMPTY GARDEN *Rocket XPRES 77*	51	4
30 Apr 83 ●	I GUESS THAT'S WHY THEY CALL IT THE BLUES *Rocket XPRES 91*	5	15
30 Jul 83 ●	I'M STILL STANDING *Rocket EJS 1*	4	11
15 Oct 83	KISS THE BRIDE *Rocket EJS 2*	20	7
10 Dec 83	COLD AS CHRISTMAS *Rocket EJS 3*	33	6
26 May 84 ●	SAD SONGS (SAY SO MUCH) *Rocket PH 7*	7	12
11 Aug 84 ●	PASSENGERS *Rocket EJS 5*	5	11
20 Oct 84	WHO WEARS THESE SHOES *Rocket EJS 6*	50	3
2 Mar 85	BREAKING HEARTS (AIN'T WHAT IT USED TO BE) *Rocket EJS 7*	59	3
15 Jun 85	ACT OF WAR *Rocket EJS 8* [4]	32	5
12 Oct 85 ●	NIKITA *Rocket EJS 9*	3	13
9 Nov 85	THAT'S WHAT FRIENDS ARE FOR *Arista ARIST 638* [5]	16	9
7 Dec 85	WRAP HER UP *Rocket EJS 10*	12	10
1 Mar 86	CRY TO HEAVEN *Rocket EJS 11*	47	4
4 Oct 86	HEARTACHE ALL OVER THE WORLD *Rocket EJS 12*	45	4
29 Nov 86	SLOW RIVERS *Rocket EJS 13* [6]	44	8
20 Jun 87	FLAMES OF PARADISE *CBS 6508657* [7]	59	3
16 Jan 88 ●	CANDLE IN THE WIND *Rocket EJS 15*	5	11
4 Jun 88	I DON'T WANNA GO ON WITH YOU LIKE THAT *Rocket EJS 16*	30	8
3 Sep 88	TOWN OF PLENTY *Rocket EJS 17*	74	1
6 May 89	THROUGH THE STORM *Arista 112185* [8]	41	3
26 Aug 89	HEALING HANDS *Rocket EJS 19*	45	5
4 Nov 89	SACRIFICE *Rocket EJS 20*	55	3
9 Jun 90 ★	SACRIFICE/HEALING HANDS (re-issue) *Rocket EJS 22*	1	15
18 Aug 90	CLUB AT THE END OF THE STREET/WHISPERS *Rocket EJS 23*	47	3
20 Oct 90	YOU GOTTA LOVE SOMEONE *Rocket EJS 24*	33	4
15 Dec 90	EASIER TO WALK AWAY *Rocket EJS 25*	67	1
29 Dec 90	EASIER TO WALK AWAY (re-entry) *Rocket EJS 25*	63	1
7 Dec 91 ★	DON'T LET THE SUN GO DOWN ON ME *Epic 6576467* [9] ▲ ■	1	10
6 Jun 92 ●	THE ONE *Rocket EJS 28*	10	8
1 Aug 92	RUNAWAY TRAIN *Rocket EJS 29* [10]	31	4
7 Nov 92	THE LAST SONG *Rocket EJS 30*	21	4
22 May 93	SIMPLE LIFE *Rocket EJSCD 31*	44	2
20 Nov 93 ●	TRUE LOVE *Rocket EJSCX 32* [2]	2	10
26 Feb 94 ●	DON'T GO BREAKING MY HEART *Rocket EJRCD 33* [11]	7	7
14 May 94	AIN'T NOTHING LIKE THE REAL THING *London LONCD 350* [12]	24	4
9 Jul 94	CAN YOU FEEL THE LOVE TONIGHT *Mercury EJCD 34*	14	9
8 Oct 94	CIRCLE OF LIFE *Rocket EJSCD 35*	11	12
4 Mar 95	BELIEVE *Rocket EJSCD 36*	15	7
20 May 95	MADE IN ENGLAND *Rocket EJSCD 37*	18	5
3 Feb 96	PLEASE *Rocket EJSCD 40*	33	3
14 Dec 96 ●	LIVE LIKE HORSES *Rocket LLHDD 1* [13]	9	6
20 Sep 97 ★	CANDLE IN THE WIND 1997 / SOMETHING IN THE WAY... *Rocket PTCD 1* ▲ ◆ ■	1	24
14 Feb 98	RECOVER YOUR SOUL *Rocket EJSCD 42*	16	3
13 Jun 98	IF THE RIVER CAN BEND *Rocket EJSDD 43*	32	2

[1] Elton John Band [2] Elton John and Kiki Dee [3] Elton John Band featuring John Lennon and the Muscle Shoals Horns [4] Elton John and Millie Jackson [5] Dionne Warwick and Friends featuring Elton John, Stevie Wonder and Gladys Knight [6] Elton John and Cliff Richard [7] Jennifer Rush and Elton John [8] Aretha Franklin and Elton John [9] George Michael and Elton John [10] Elton John and Eric Clapton [11] Elton John with RuPaul [12] Marcella Detroit and Elton John [13] Elton John and Luciano Pavarotti

'Bite Your Lip (Get Up and Dance)' was one side of a double-sided chart entry, the other being 'Chicago' by Kiki Dee. 'Wrap Her Up' features George Michael as uncredited co-vocalist. 'Candle in the Wind' 1988 was a live recording

Robert JOHN
US, male vocalist

13 wks

Date	Title	Pos	Wks
17 Jul 68	IF YOU DON'T WANT MY LOVE *CBS 3436*	42	5
20 Oct 79	SAD EYES *EMI American EA 101* ▲	31	8

JOHNNA
US, female vocalist

3 wks

Date	Title	Pos	Wks
10 Feb 96	DO WHAT YOU FEEL *PWL International PWL 323CD*	43	2
11 May 96	IN MY DREAMS *PWL International PWL 325CD*	66	1

UK No 1 ★   UK Top 10 ●   UK million seller ◆   UK entry at No 1 ■   US No 1 ▲

JOHNNY and CHARLEY *Spain, male vocal duo* — 1 wk

14 Oct 65		LA YENKA *Pye International 7N 25326*	49	1

JOHNNY and the HURRICANES 🎻
US, male instrumental group — 88 wks

9 Oct 59	●	RED RIVER ROCK *London HL 8948*	3	16
25 Dec 59		REVEILLE ROCK *London HL 9017*	14	5
17 Mar 60		BEATNIK FLY *London HLI 9072*	8	19
16 Jun 60		DOWN YONDER *London HLX 9134*	8	11
29 Sep 60	●	ROCKING GOOSE *London HLX 9190*	3	20
2 Mar 61		JA-DA *London HLX 9289*	14	9
6 Jul 61		OLD SMOKEY / HIGH VOLTAGE *London HLX 9378*	24	8

JOHNNY HATES JAZZ ◑ *UK, male vocal/instrumental group* — 45 wks

11 Apr 87	●	SHATTERED DREAMS *Virgin VS 948*	5	14
29 Aug 87		I DON'T WANT TO BE A HERO *Virgin VS 1000*	11	10
21 Nov 87		TURN BACK THE CLOCK *Virgin VS 1017*	12	11
27 Feb 88		HEART OF GOLD *Virgin VS 1045*	19	7
9 Jul 88		DON'T SAY IT'S LOVE *Virgin VS 1081*	48	3

Bryan JOHNSON ◖ *UK, male vocalist* — 11 wks

10 Mar 60		LOOKING HIGH HIGH HIGH *Decca F 11213*	20	11

Carey JOHNSON ⌁ *Australia, male vocalist* — 8 wks

25 Apr 87		REAL FASHION REGGAE STYLE *Oval TEN 170*	19	8

Denise JOHNSON *UK, female vocalist* — 4 wks

24 Aug 91		DON'T FIGHT IT FEEL IT *Creation CRE 110* [1]	41	2
14 May 94		RAYS OF THE RISING SUN *Magnet MAG 1022CD*	45	2

[1] Primal Scream featuring Denise Johnson

Don JOHNSON ◑ *US, male vocalist* — 12 wks

18 Oct 86		HEARTBEAT *Epic 650064 7*	46	5
5 Nov 88		TILL I LOVED YOU (LOVE THEME FROM 'GOYA') *CBS BARB 2* [1]	16	7

[1] Barbra Streisand and Don Johnson

General JOHNSON – See CHAIRMEN OF THE BOARD

Holly JOHNSON ◑ ☺ *UK, male vocalist* — 36 wks

14 Jan 89	●	LOVE TRAIN *MCA MCA 1306*	4	11
1 Apr 89	●	AMERICANOS *MCA MCA 1323*	4	11
20 May 89	★	FERRY 'CROSS THE MERSEY *PWL PWL 41* [1] ■	1	7
24 Jun 89		ATOMIC CITY *MCA MCA 1342*	18	4
30 Sep 89		HEAVEN'S HERE *MCA MCA 1365*	62	2
1 Dec 90		WHERE HAS LOVE GONE *MCA MCA 1460*	73	1

[1] Christians, Holly Johnson, Paul McCartney, Gerry Marsden and Stock Aitken Waterman

Howard JOHNSON *US, male vocalist* — 6 wks

4 Sep 82		KEEPIN' LOVE NEW / SO FINE *A & M USA 1221*	45	6

'Keepin' Love New' listed 4 Sep, 1982 only

Johnny JOHNSON and the BANDWAGON ⌁
US, male vocal group — 50 wks

16 Oct 68	●	BREAKIN' DOWN THE WALLS OF HEARTACHE *Direction 58-3670* [1]	4	15
5 Feb 69		YOU *Direction 58-3923* [1]	34	4
28 May 69		LET'S HANG ON *Direction 58-4180* [1]	36	6
25 Jul 70	●	SWEET INSPIRATION *Bell 1111*	10	12
24 Oct 70		SWEET INSPIRATION (re-entry) *Bell 1111*	46	1
28 Nov 70	●	BLAME IT ON THE PONY EXPRESS *Bell 1128*	7	12

[1] Bandwagon

Kevin JOHNSON *Australia, male vocalist* — 6 wks

11 Jan 75		ROCK 'N ROLL (I GAVE YOU THE BEST YEARS OF MY LIFE) *UK UKR 84*	23	6

LJ JOHNSON *US, male vocalist* — 6 wks

7 Feb 76		YOUR MAGIC PUT A SPELL ON ME *Philips 6006 492*	27	6

Laurie JOHNSON ◖ *UK, orchestra* — 14 wks

28 Sep 61	●	SUCU SUCU *Pye 7N 15383*	9	12
17 May 97		THEME FROM THE PROFESSIONALS *Virgin VSCDT 1643* [1]	36	2

[1] Laurie Johnson's London Big Band

Lou JOHNSON *US, male vocalist* — 2 wks

26 Nov 64		MESSAGE TO MARTHA *London HL 9929*	36	2

Marv JOHNSON ⌁ *US, male vocalist* — 39 wks

12 Feb 60	●	YOU GOT WHAT IT TAKES *London HLT 9013*	7	16
5 May 60		I LOVE THE WAY YOU LOVE *London HLT 9109*	35	3
11 Aug 60		AIN'T GONNA BE THAT WAY *London HLT 9165*	50	1
22 Jan 69		I'LL PICK A ROSE FOR MY ROSE *Tamla Motown TMG 680*	10	11
25 Oct 69		I MISS YOU BABY *Tamla Motown TMG 713*	25	8

Orlando JOHNSON – See SECCHI featuring Orlando JOHNSON

Paul JOHNSON *UK, male vocalist* — 7 wks

21 Feb 87		WHEN LOVE COMES CALLING *CBS PJOHN 1*	52	5
25 Feb 89		NO MORE TOMORROWS *CBS PJOHN 7*	67	2

Puff JOHNSON [R&B] *US, female vocalist* — 6 wks

18 Jan 97		OVER AND OVER *Columbia 6640345*	20	4
12 Apr 97		FOREVER MORE *Work 644075*	29	2

Teddy JOHNSON – See Pearl CARR and Teddy JOHNSON

Bruce JOHNSTON *US, male instrumentalist – keyboards* — 4 wks

27 Aug 77		PIPELINE *CBS 5514*	33	4

Jan JOHNSTON – see FREEFALL; SUBMERGE

Sabrina JOHNSTON ☺ ⌁ *US, female vocalist* — 19 wks

7 Sep 91	●	PEACE *East West YZ 616*	8	10
7 Dec 91		FRIENDSHIP *East West YZ 637*	58	4
11 Jul 92		I WANNA SING *East West YZ 661*	46	2
3 Oct 92		PEACE (re-mix) *Epic 6584377*	35	2
13 Aug 94		SATISFY MY LOVE *Champion CHAMPCD 311*	62	1

The listed flipside of 'Peace' (re-mix) was 'Gypsy Woman' (re-mix) by Crystal Waters

JOHNSTON BROTHERS ◖ *UK, male vocal group* — 33 wks

3 Apr 53	●	OH HAPPY DAY *Decca F 10071*	4	8
5 Nov 54		WAIT FOR ME DARLING *Decca F 10362* [1]	18	1
21 Jan 55		HAPPY DAYS AND LONELY NIGHTS *Decca F 10389* [2]	14	2
7 Oct 55	★	HERNANDO'S HIDEAWAY *Decca F 10608*	1	13
30 Dec 55	●	JOIN IN AND SING AGAIN *Decca F 10636*	9	1
13 Apr 56		NO OTHER LOVE *Decca F 10721*	22	1
30 Nov 56		IN THE MIDDLE OF THE HOUSE *Decca F 10781*	27	1
7 Dec 56		JOIN IN AND SING (NO. 3) *Decca F 10814*	30	1
28 Dec 56		JOIN IN AND SING (NO. 3) (re-entry) *Decca F 10814*	24	1
8 Feb 57		GIVE HER MY LOVE *Decca F 10828*	27	1
19 Apr 57		HEART *Decca F 10860*	23	3

[1] Joan Regan and the Johnston Brothers [2] Suzi Miller and the Johnston Brothers

The following two hits were medleys: Join in and Sing Again: Sheik of Araby / Yes Sir That's My Baby / California Here I Come / Some of These Days / Charleston / Margie. Join in and Sing (No 3): Coal Black Morning / When You're Smiling / Alexander's Ragtime Band / Sweet Sue Just You / When You Wore a Tulip / If You Were the Only Girl in the World.
See also VARIOUS ARTISTS (EPs & LPs) – All Star Hit Parade No 2

UK No 1 ★   UK Top 10 ●   UK million seller ◆   UK entry at No 1 ■   US No 1 ▲

James JOLIS – See Barry MANILOW

JOJO – See 2PAC

JOLLY BROTHERS *Jamaica, male vocal/instrumental group*　　**7 wks**

28 Jul 79	CONSCIOUS MAN *United Artists UP 36415*	46	7

JOLLY ROGER *UK, male instrumentalist/producer*　　**12 wks**

10 Sep 88	ACID MAN *10 TEN 236*	.23	12

JOMALSKI – See WILDCHILD

JOMANDA *US, female vocal group*　　**10 wks**

22 Apr 89	MAKE MY BODY ROCK *RCA PB 42749*	.44	3
29 Jun 91	GOT A LOVE FOR YOU *Giant W 0040*	.43	4
11 Sep 93	I LIKE IT *Big Beat A 8377CD*	.67	1
13 Nov 93	NEVER *Big Beat A 8347CD*	.40	2

JON and VANGELIS ☻ ✍
UK, male vocalist/Greece, male multi-instrumentalist　　**28 wks**

5 Jan 80	● I HEAR YOU NOW *Polydor POSP 96*	.8	11
12 Dec 81	● I'LL FIND MY WAY HOME *Polydor JV 1*	.6	13
30 Jul 83	HE IS SAILING *Polydor JV 4*	.61	2
18 Aug 84	STATE OF INDEPENDENCE *Polydor JV 5*	.67	2

See also VANGELIS

JON OF THE PLEASED WIMMIN *UK, male DJ*　　**5 wks**

18 Feb 95	PASSION *Perfecto YZ 884CD*	.27	3
6 Apr 96	GIVE ME STRENGTH *Perfecto PERF 119CD*	.30	2

Aled JONES ℂ *UK, male vocalist*　　**24 wks**

20 Jul 85	MEMORY *BBC RESL 175*	.42	4
30 Nov 85	● WALKING IN THE AIR *HMV ALED 1*	.5	11
14 Dec 85	PICTURES IN THE DARK *Virgin VS 836* [1]	.50	6
20 Dec 86	A WINTER STORY *HMV ALED 2*	.51	3

[1] Mike Oldfield featuring Aled Jones, Anita Hegerland and Barry Palmer

Barbara JONES *Jamaica, female vocalist*　　**7 wks**

31 Jan 81	JUST WHEN I NEEDED YOU MOST *Sonet SON 2221*	.31	7

Catherine Zeta JONES *UK, female vocalist*　　**9 wks**

19 Sep 92	FOR ALL TIME *Columbia 6583547*	.36	5
26 Nov 94	TRUE LOVE WAYS *PolyGram TV TLWCD 2* [1]	.38	3
1 Apr 95	IN THE ARMS OF LOVE *Wow! WOWCD 7101*	.72	1

[1] David Essex and Catherine Zeta Jones

Donell JONES *US, male vocalist*　　**1 wk**

15 Feb 97	KNOCKS ME OFF MY FEET *LaFace 74321458502*	.58	1

Georgia JONES – See PLUX featuring Georgia JONES

Grace JONES ☻ ☺ *US, female vocalist*　　**45 wks**

26 Jul 80	PRIVATE LIFE *Island WIP 6629*	.17	8
20 Jun 81	PULL UP TO THE BUMPER *Island WIP 6696*	.53	4
30 Oct 82	THE APPLE STRETCHING/NIPPLE TO THE BOTTLE		
	Island WIP 6779	.50	4
9 Apr 83	MY JAMAICAN GUY *Island IS 103*	.56	3
12 Oct 85	SLAVE TO THE RHYTHM *ZTT IS 206*	.12	8
18 Jan 86	PULL UP TO THE BUMPER (RE-ISSUE)/LA VIE EN ROSE		
	(re-issue) *Island IS 240*	.12	9
1 Mar 86	LOVE IS THE DRUG *Island IS 266*	.35	4
15 Nov 86	I'M NOT PERFECT (BUT I'M PERFECT FOR YOU)		
	Manhattan MT 15	.56	3
7 May 94	SLAVE TO THE RHYTHM (re-mix) *Zance ZANG 50CD1*	.28	2

'La Vie En Rose' was only listed from 1 Feb, 1986

Hannah JONES *US, female vocalist*　　**9 wks**

14 Sep 91	BRIDGE OVER TROUBLED WATER *Dance Pool 6565467* [1]	21	8
30 Jan 93	KEEP IT ON *TMRC CDTMRC 7*	.67	1

[1] PJB featuring Hannah and her Sisters

Howard JONES ☻ *Accomplished singer/songwriter, b. 23 February, 1955, Southampton, who was a regular chart visitor in the mid-1980s with his brand of synth-based pop. Jones, who was equally popular Stateside, appeared at Live Aid*　　**103 wks**

17 Sep 83	● NEW SONG *WEA HOW 1*	.3	12
26 Nov 83	● WHAT IS LOVE *WEA HOW 2*	.2	15
14 Jan 84	NEW SONG (re-entry) *WEA HOW 1*	.60	3
18 Feb 84	HIDE AND SEEK *WEA HOW 3*	.12	9
26 May 84	● PEARL IN THE SHELL *WEA HOW 4*	.7	10
11 Aug 84	● LIKE TO GET TO KNOW YOU WELL *WEA HOW 5*	.4	12
9 Feb 85	● THINGS CAN ONLY GET BETTER *WEA HOW 6*	.6	8
20 Apr 85	● LOOK MAMA *WEA HOW 7*	.10	6
29 Jun 85	LIFE IN ONE DAY *WEA HOW 8*	.14	7
15 Mar 86	NO ONE IS TO BLAME *WEA HOW 9*	.16	7
4 Oct 86	ALL I WANT *WEA HOW 10*	.35	4
29 Nov 86	YOU KNOW I LOVE YOU...DON'T YOU? *WEA HOW 11*	.43	3
21 Mar 87	A LITTLE BIT OF SNOW *WEA HOW 12*	.70	1
4 Mar 89	EVERLASTING LOVE *WEA HOW 13*	.62	3
11 Apr 92	LIFT ME UP *East West HOW 15*	.52	2

Janie JONES *UK, female vocalist*　　**3 wks**

27 Jan 66	WITCHES' BREW *HMV POP 1495*	.46	3

Jimmy JONES ♥ ☻ *US, male vocalist*　　**47 wks**

17 Mar 60	● HANDY MAN *MGM 1051*	.3	21
16 Jun 60	★ GOOD TIMIN' *MGM 1078*	.1	15
18 Aug 60	HANDY MAN (re-entry) *MGM 1051*	.32	3
8 Sep 60	I JUST GO FOR YOU *MGM 1091*	.35	4
17 Nov 60	READY FOR LOVE *MGM 1103*	.46	1
30 Mar 61	I TOLD YOU SO *MGM 1123*	.33	3

Juggy JONES *US, male multi-instrumentalist*　　**4 wks**

7 Feb 76	INSIDE AMERICA *Contempo CS 2080*	.39	4

Lavinia JONES *South Africa, female vocalist*　　**2 wks**

18 Feb 95	SING IT TO YOU (DEE-DOOB-DEE-DOO)		
	Virgin International DINDG 142	.45	2

Mick JONES – See AZTEC CAMERA

Oran 'Juice' JONES ✒ *US, male vocalist*　　**14 wks**

15 Nov 86	● THE RAIN *Def Jam A 7303*	.4	14

Paul JONES ☻ *UK, male vocalist*　　**34 wks**

6 Oct 66	● HIGH TIME *HMV POP 1554*	.4	15
19 Jan 67	● I'VE BEEN A BAD BAD BOY *HMV POP 1576*	.5	9
23 Aug 67	THINKIN' AIN'T FOR ME *HMV POP 1602*	.47	1
13 Sep 67	THINKIN' AIN'T FOR ME (re-entry) *HMV POP 1602*	.32	7
5 Feb 69	AQUARIUS *Columbia DB 8514*	.45	2

Quincy JONES ✒ ♥
US, male producer/instrumentalist – keyboards　　**42 wks**

29 Jul 78	STUFF LIKE THAT *A & M AMS 7367*	.34	9
11 Apr 81	AI NO CORRIDA (I-NO-KO-REE-DA) *A & M AMS 8109*	.14	10
20 Jun 81	RAZZAMATAZZ *A & M AMS 8140* [1]	.11	9
5 Sep 81	BETCHA' WOULDN'T HURT ME		
	A & M AMS 8157 [1]	.52	3
13 Jan 90	I'LL BE GOOD TO YOU *Qwest W 2697* [2]	.21	7
31 Mar 90	SECRET GARDEN *Qwest W 9992* [3]	.67	1
14 Sep 96	STOMP *Qwest W 0372CD* [4]	.28	2
1 Aug 98	SOUL BOSSA NOVA *Manifesto FESCD 48* [5]	.47	1

[1] Quincy Jones featuring Patti Austin [2] Quincy Jones featuring Ray Charles and Chaka Khan [3] Quincy Jones featuring Al B. Sure!, James Ingram, El DeBarge and

Barry White [4] Quincy Jones featuring Melle Mel, Coolio, Yo-Yo, Shaquille O'Neal, The Luniz [5] Cool, the Fab, and the Groovy present Quincy Jones

Uncredited vocals on 'Stuff Like That' were by Ashford and Simpson and Chaka Khan, and on 'Ai No Corrida' by Dune

Rickie Lee JONES ◉ *US, female vocalist*   9 wks

23 Jun 79	CHUCK E.'S IN LOVE *Warner Bros. K 17390*	18	9

Shirley JONES – *See PARTRIDGE FAMILY; VARIOUS ARTISTS (EPs & LPs) – Carousel LP*

Tammy JONES ◉ *UK, female vocalist*   10 wks

26 Apr 75 ●	LET ME TRY AGAIN *Epic EPC 3211*	5	10

Tom JONES ℭ *Continually popular vocalist who has remained an international headliner for four decades. B. Thomas Woodward, 7 June, 1940, South Wales. This long-time sex symbol was arguably the top British solo singer of the 1960s on both sides of Atlantic*   356 wks

11 Feb 65 ★	IT'S NOT UNUSUAL *Decca F 12062*	1	14
6 May 65	ONCE UPON A TIME *Decca F 12121*	32	4
8 Jul 65	WITH THESE HANDS *Decca F 12191*	13	11
12 Aug 65	WHAT'S NEW PUSSYCAT *Decca F 12203*	11	10
13 Jan 66	THUNDERBALL *Decca F 12292*	35	4
19 May 66	ONCE THERE WAS A TIME/NOT RESPONSIBLE *Decca F 12390*	18	9
18 Aug 66	THIS AND THAT *Decca F 12461*	44	3
10 Nov 66 ★	GREEN GREEN GRASS OF HOME *Decca F 22511* ◆	1	22
16 Feb 67 ●	DETROIT CITY *Decca F 22555*	8	10
13 Apr 67 ●	FUNNY FAMILIAR FORGOTTEN FEELINGS *Decca F 12599*	7	15
26 Jul 67 ●	I'LL NEVER FALL IN LOVE AGAIN *Decca F 12639*	2	25
22 Nov 67 ●	I'M COMING HOME *Decca F 12693*	2	16
28 Feb 68 ●	DELILAH *Decca F 12747*	2	17
17 Jul 68 ●	HELP YOURSELF *Decca F 12812*	5	26
27 Nov 68	A MINUTE OF YOUR TIME *Decca F 12854*	14	15
14 May 69	LOVE ME TONIGHT *Decca F 12924*	9	12
13 Dec 69	WITHOUT LOVE *Decca F 12990*	10	11
14 Mar 70	WITHOUT LOVE (re-entry) *Decca F 12990*	49	1
18 Apr 70 ●	DAUGHTER OF DARKNESS *Decca F 13013*	5	15
15 Aug 70	I (WHO HAVE NOTHING) *Decca F 13061*	16	8
17 Oct 70	I (WHO HAVE NOTHING) (re-entry) *Decca F 13061*	47	1
16 Jan 71	SHE'S A LADY *Decca F 13113*	13	9
27 Mar 71	SHE'S A LADY (re-entry) *Decca F 13113*	47	1
5 Jun 71	PUPPET MAN *Decca F 13183*	49	1
19 Jun 71	PUPPET MAN (re-entry) *Decca F 13183*	50	1
23 Oct 71 ●	TILL *Decca F 13236*	2	15
1 Apr 72 ●	THE YOUNG NEW MEXICAN PUPPETEER *Decca F 13298*	6	12
14 Apr 73	LETTER TO LUCILLE *Decca F 13393*	31	8
7 Sep 74	SOMETHING 'BOUT YOU BABY I LIKE *Decca F 13550*	36	5
16 Apr 77	SAY YOU'LL STAY UNTIL TOMORROW *EMI 2583*	40	3
18 Apr 87 ●	A BOY FROM NOWHERE *Epic OLE 1*	2	12
30 May 87	IT'S NOT UNUSUAL (re-issue) *Decca F 103*	17	8
2 Jan 88	I WAS BORN TO BE ME *Epic OLE 4*	61	1
29 Oct 88 ●	KISS *China CHINA 11* [1]	5	7
29 Apr 89	MOVE CLOSER *Jive JIVE 203*	49	3
26 Jan 91	COULDN'T SAY GOODBYE *Dover ROJ 10*	51	2
16 Mar 91	CARRYING A TORCH *Dover ROJ 12*	57	2
4 Jul 92	DELILAH (re-issue) *The Hit Label TOM 10*	68	2
6 Feb 93	ALL YOU NEED IS LOVE *Childline CHILDCD 93*	19	4
5 Nov 94	IF I ONLY KNEW *ZTT ZANG 59CD*	11	9

[1] Art of Noise featuring Tom Jones

See also VARIOUS ARTISTS (EPs & LPs) – Gimme Shelter (EP)

Sue JONES-DAVIES – *See Julie COVINGTON, Rula LENSKA, Charlotte CORNWELL and Sue JONES-DAVIES*

JONESTOWN *US, male vocal duo*   1 wk

13 Jun 98	SWEET THANG *Universal UMD 70376*	49	1

Alison JORDAN *UK, female vocalist*   4 wks

9 May 92	BOY FROM NEW YORK CITY *Arista 74321100427*	23	4

Dick JORDAN *UK, male vocalist*   4 wks

17 Mar 60	HALLELUJAH I LOVE HER SO *Oriole CB 1534*	47	1
9 Jun 60	LITTLE CHRISTINE *Oriole CB 1548*	39	3

Jack JORDAN – *See Frank CHACKSFIELD*

Montell JORDAN [R&B] *US, male vocalist*   17 wks

13 May 95	THIS IS HOW WE DO IT *Def Jam DEFCD 07* ▲	11	8
2 Sep 95	SOMETHIN' 4 DA HONEYZ *Def Jam DEFCD 10*	15	4
19 Oct 96	I LIKE *Def Jam DEFCD 19* [1]	24	3
23 May 98	LET'S RIDE *Def Jam 5686912*	25	2

[1] Montell Jordan featuring Slick Rick

Ronny JORDAN *UK, male instrumentalist – guitar*   7 wks

1 Feb 92	SO WHAT! *Antilles ANN 14*	32	4
25 Sep 93	UNDER YOUR SPELL *Island CID 565*	72	1
15 Jan 94	TINSEL TOWN *Island CID 566*	64	1
28 May 94	COME WITH ME *Island CID 584*	63	1

David JOSEPH ♫ ✍ *UK, male vocalist*   21 wks

26 Feb 83	YOU CAN'T HIDE (YOUR LOVE FROM ME) *Island IS 101*	13	9
28 May 83	LET'S LIVE IT UP (NITE PEOPLE) *Island IS 116*	26	5
18 Feb 84	JOYS OF LIFE *Island IS 153*	61	2
31 May 86	EXPANSIONS '86 (EXPAND YOUR MIND) *Fourth & Broadway BRW 48* [1]	58	5

[1] Chris Paul featuring David Joseph

Martyn JOSEPH *UK, male vocalist*   10 wks

20 Jun 92	DOLPHINS MAKE ME CRY *Epic 6581347*	34	4
12 Sep 92	WORKING MOTHER *Epic 6582937*	65	1
9 Jan 93	PLEASE SIR *Epic 6588552*	45	3
3 Jun 95	TALK ABOUT IT IN THE MORNING *Epic 6613342*	43	2

JOURNEY *US, male vocal/instrumental group*   9 wks

27 Feb 82	DON'T STOP BELIEVIN' *CBS A 1728*	62	4
11 Sep 82	WHO'S CRYING NOW *CBS A 2725*	46	5

Ruth JOY *UK, female vocalist*   3 wks

26 Aug 89	DON'T PUSH IT *MCA RJOY 1*	66	2
22 Feb 92	FEEL *MCA MCS 1574*	67	1

JOY DIVISION ☹ *UK, male vocal/instrumental group*   24 wks

28 Jun 80	LOVE WILL TEAR US APART *Factory FAC 23*	13	9
29 Oct 83	LOVE WILL TEAR US APART (re-entry) *Factory FAC 23*	19	7
18 Jun 88	ATMOSPHERE *Factory FAC 2137*	34	5
17 Jun 95	LOVE WILL TEAR US APART (re-mix) *London YOJCD 1*	19	3

JOY STRINGS *UK, male/female vocal/instrumental group*   11 wks

27 Feb 64	IT'S AN OPEN SECRET *Regal-Zonophone RZ 501*	32	7
17 Dec 64	A STARRY NIGHT *Regal-Zonophone RZ 504*	35	4

JOYRIDER *UK, male vocal/instrumental group*   4 wks

27 Jul 96	RUSH HOUR *Paradox PDOXD 012*	22	3
28 Sep 96	ALL GONE AWAY *A & M 5819552*	54	1

JT and the BIG FAMILY ◉ ☺
Italy, male/female vocal/instrumental group   8 wks

3 Mar 90 ●	MOMENTS IN SOUL *Champion CHAMP 237*	7	8

JT PLAYAZ *UK, male production team*   4 wks

5 Apr 97	JUST PLAYIN' *Pukka CDJTP 1*	30	3
2 May 98	LET'S GET DOWN *MCA MCSTD 40161*	64	1

JTQ UK, male instrumental group — 6 wks

Date	Title	Pos	Wks
3 Apr 93	LOVE THE LIFE *Big Life BLRD 93* [1]	34	3
3 Jul 93	SEE A BRIGHTER DAY *Big Life BLRDA 97* [1]	49	2
25 Feb 95	LOVE WILL KEEP US TOGETHER *Acid Jazz JAZID 112CD* [2]	63	1

[1] JTQ with Noel McKoy [2] JTQ featuring Alison Limerick

JUDAS PRIEST ⚡ UK, male vocal/instrumental group — 51 wks

Date	Title	Pos	Wks
20 Jan 79	TAKE ON THE WORLD *CBS 6915*	14	10
12 May 79	EVENING STAR *CBS 7312*	53	4
29 Mar 80	LIVING AFTER MIDNIGHT *CBS 8379*	12	7
7 Jun 80	BREAKING THE LAW *CBS 8644*	12	6
23 Aug 80	UNITED *CBS 8897*	26	8
21 Feb 81	DON'T GO *CBS 9520*	51	3
25 Apr 81	HOT ROCKIN' *CBS 1153*	60	3
21 Aug 82	YOU'VE GOT ANOTHER THING COMIN' *CBS A 2611*	66	2
21 Jan 84	FREEWHEEL BURNIN' *CBS A 4054*	42	3
23 Apr 88	JOHNNY B. GOODE *Atlantic A 9114*	64	2
15 Sep 90	PAINKILLER *CBS 656273 7*	74	1
23 Mar 91	A TOUCH OF EVIL *Columbia 6565897*	58	1
24 Apr 93	NIGHT CRAWLER *Columbia 6590972*	63	1

JUDGE DREAD 🌴 UK, male vocalist — 95 wks

Date	Title	Pos	Wks
26 Aug 72	BIG SIX *Big Shot BI 608*	11	27
9 Dec 72 ●	BIG SEVEN *Big Shot BI 613*	8	18
21 Apr 73	BIG EIGHT *Big Shot BI 619*	14	10
5 Jul 75 ●	JE T'AIME (MOI NON PLUS) *Cactus CT 65*	9	9
27 Sep 75	BIG TEN *Cactus CT 77*	14	7
6 Dec 75	CHRISTMAS IN DREADLAND/COME OUTSIDE *Cactus CT 80*	14	7
8 May 76	THE WINKLE MAN *Cactus CT 90*	35	4
28 Aug 76	Y VIVA SUSPENDERS *Cactus CT 99*	27	4
2 Apr 77	5TH ANNIVERSARY EP *Cactus CT 98*	31	4
14 Jan 78	UP WITH THE COCK/BIG PUNK *Cactus CT 110*	49	1
16 Dec 78	HOKEY COKEY/JINGLE BELLS *EMI 2881*	59	4

Tracks on 5th Anniversary EP: Jamaica Jerk (Off)/Bring Back the Skins/End of the World/Big Everything

JUICE Denmark, female vocal trio — 3 wks

Date	Title	Pos	Wks
18 Apr 98	BEST DAYS *Chrysalis CDCHS 5081*	28	2
22 Aug 98	I'LL COME RUNNIN' *Chrysalis CDCHS 5090*	48	1

JUICY US, male/female vocal duo — 5 wks

Date	Title	Pos	Wks
22 Feb 86	SUGAR FREE *Epic A 6917*	45	5

JUICY LUCY ✏ UK, male vocal/instrumental group — 17 wks

Date	Title	Pos	Wks
7 Mar 70	WHO DO YOU LOVE *Vertigo V 1*	14	12
10 Oct 70	PRETTY WOMAN *Vertigo 6059 015*	45	2
31 Oct 70	PRETTY WOMAN (re-entry) *Vertigo 6059 015*	44	3

Thomas JULES-STOCK UK, male vocalist — 1 wk

Date	Title	Pos	Wks
15 Aug 98	DIDN'T I TELL YOU TRUE *Mercury MERCD 501*	59	1

JULIA and COMPANY ☺ US, male/female vocal group — 10 wks

Date	Title	Pos	Wks
3 Mar 84	BREAKIN' DOWN (SUGAR SAMBA) *London LON 46*	15	8
23 Feb 85	I'M SO HAPPY *Next Plateau LON 61*	56	2

JULUKA UK/South Africa, male/female vocal/instrumental group — 4 wks

Date	Title	Pos	Wks
12 Feb 83	SCATTERLINGS OF AFRICA *Safari ZULU 1*	44	4

JUMP UK, male instrumental group — 1 wk

Date	Title	Pos	Wks
1 Mar 97	FUNKATARIUM *Heat Recordings HEATCD 005*	56	1

Wally JUMP Jr. and the CRIMINAL ELEMENT
US, male producer – Arthur Baker — 19 wks

Date	Title	Pos	Wks
28 Feb 87	TURN ME LOOSE *London LON 126*	60	2
5 Sep 87	PUT THE NEEDLE TO THE RECORD *Cooltempo COOL 150* [1]	63	3

Date	Title	Pos	Wks
12 Dec 87	TIGHTEN UP – I JUST CAN'T STOP DANCING *Breakout USA 621*	24	7
19 Mar 88	PRIVATE PARTY *Breakout USA 624*	57	3
6 Oct 90	EVERYBODY (RAP) *Deconstruction PB 44701* [2]	30	4

[1] Criminal Element Orchestra [2] Criminal Element Orchestra and Wendell Williams

JUMPING JACKS – See Danny PEPPERMINT and the JUMPING JACKS

Rosemary JUNE ◉ US, female vocalist — 9 wks

Date	Title	Pos	Wks
23 Jan 59	I'LL BE WITH YOU IN APPLE BLOSSOM TIME *Pye International 7N 25005*	14	9

JUNGLE BOOK ◉ US, male/female vocal group — 8 wks

Date	Title	Pos	Wks
8 May 93	THE JUNGLE BOOK GROOVE *Hollywood HWCD 128*	14	8

JUNGLE BROTHERS 🐢 US, male rap duo — 29 wks

Date	Title	Pos	Wks
22 Oct 88	I'LL HOUSE YOU *Gee Street GEE 003* [1]	22	5
18 Mar 89	BLACK IS BLACK/STRAIGHT OUT OF THE JUNGLE *Gee Street GEE 15*	72	1
31 Mar 90	WHAT 'U' WAITIN' '4' *Eternal W 9865*	35	5
21 Jul 90	DOIN' OUR OWN DANG *Eternal W 9754*	33	6
19 Jul 97	BRAIN *Gee Street GEE 5000388*	52	1
29 Nov 97	JUNGLE BROTHER *Gee Street GEE 5000493*	18	4
11 Jul 98	I'LL HOUSE YOU '98 (re-mix) *Gee Street FCD 338*	26	5
28 Nov 98	BECAUSE I GOT IT LIKE THAT *Gee Street GEE 5003593*	32	2

[1] Richie Rich meets the Jungle Brothers

'Doin' Our Own Dang' features the uncredited De La Soul and Monie Love

JUNGLE HIGH – See BLUE PEARL

JUNIOR 🎤 ☺ UK, male vocalist — 57 wks

Date	Title	Pos	Wks
24 Apr 82 ●	MAMA USED TO SAY *Mercury MER 98*	7	13
10 Jul 82	TOO LATE *Mercury MER 112*	20	9
25 Sep 82	LET ME KNOW/I CAN'T HELP IT *Mercury MER 116*	53	3
23 Apr 83	COMMUNICATION BREAKDOWN *Mercury MER 134*	57	3
8 Sep 84	SOMEBODY *London LON 50*	64	2
9 Feb 85	DO YOU REALLY (WANT MY LOVE) *London LON 60*	47	4
30 Nov 85	OH LOUISE *London LON 75*	74	3
4 Apr 87 ●	ANOTHER STEP (CLOSER TO YOU) *MCA KIM 5* [1]	6	11
25 Aug 90	STEP OFF *MCA MCA 1432* [2]	63	3
15 Aug 92	THEN CAME YOU *MCA MCS 1676* [2]	32	5
31 Oct 92	ALL OVER THE WORLD *MCA MCS 1691* [2]	74	1

[1] Kim Wilde and Junior [2] Junior Giscombe

JUNIOR M.A.F.I.A. US, male/female rap ensemble — 2 wks

Date	Title	Pos	Wks
3 Feb 96	I NEED YOU TONIGHT *Big Beat A 8130CD* [1]	66	1
19 Oct 96	GETTIN' MONEY *Big Beat A 5674CD*	63	1

[1] Junior M.A.F.I.A. featuring Aaliyah

JUNIORS – See DANNY and the JUNIORS

JUNO REACTOR UK/Germany, male production duo — 1 wk

Date	Title	Pos	Wks
8 Feb 97	JUNGLE HIGH *Perfecto PERF 133CD*	45	1

JURASSIC 5 US, male rap group — 4 wks

Date	Title	Pos	Wks
25 Jul 98	JAYOU *Pan PAN 018CD*	56	1
24 Oct 98	CONCRETE SCHOOLYARD *Pan PAN 020CD*	35	3

Christopher JUST Austria, male producer — 1 wk

Date	Title	Pos	Wks
13 Dec 97	I'M A DISCO DANCER *Slut Trax SLUT 001CD*	72	1

JUST LUIS Australia, male vocalist — 3 wks

Date	Title	Pos	Wks
14 Oct 95	AMERICAN PIE *Pro-Activ CDPTV 1*	31	2
17 Feb 96	AMERICAN PIE (re-entry) *Pro-Activ CDPTV 1*	70	1

UK No 1 ★   UK Top 10 ●   UK million seller ◆   UK entry at No 1 ■   US No 1 ▲

Jimmy JUSTICE ☻ UK, male vocalist — 35 wks

29 Mar 62	● WHEN MY LITTLE GIRL IS SMILING Pye 7N 15421	9	13
14 Jun 62	● AIN'T THAT FUNNY Pye 7N 15443	8	11
23 Aug 62	SPANISH HARLEM Pye 7N 15457	20	11

JUSTIFIED ANCIENTS OF MU MU
UK, male production duo — 6 wks

9 Nov 91	● IT'S GRIM UP NORTH KLF Communications JAMS 028	10	5
4 Jan 92	IT'S GRIM UP NORTH (re-entry)		
	KLF Communications JAMS 028	67	1

Justified Ancients of Mu Mu are The KLF under an assumed name
See also KLF

JUSTIN UK, male vocalist — 2 wks

| 22 Aug 98 | THIS BOY Virgin STCDT 1 | 34 | 2 |

Bill JUSTIS ♪ US, male instrumentalist – alto sax — 8 wks

| 10 Jan 58 | RAUNCHY London HLS 8517 | 24 | 2 |
| 31 Jan 58 | RAUNCHY (re-entry) London HLS 8517 | 11 | 6 |

Patrick JUVET ♪ France, male vocalist — 19 wks

| 2 Sep 78 | GOT A FEELING Casablanca CAN 127 | 34 | 7 |
| 4 Nov 78 | I LOVE AMERICA Casablanca CAN 132 | 12 | 12 |

JX ☺ UK, male producer – Jake Williams — 33 wks

2 Apr 94	SON OF A GUN Internal Dance IDC 5	13	6
1 Apr 95	YOU BELONG TO ME Ffrreedom TABCD 227	17	5
19 Aug 95	● SON OF A GUN (re-mix) Ffrreedom TABCD 233	6	6
18 May 96	● THERE'S NOTHING I WON'T DO		
	Ffrreedom TABCD 241	4	13
8 Mar 97	CLOSE TO YOUR HEART Ffrreedom TABCD 245	18	3

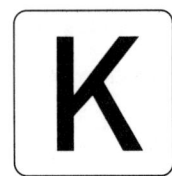

Frank K featuring Wiston OFFICE
Italy/US, male vocal/instrumental duo — 1 wk

| 26 Jan 91 | EVERYBODY LET'S SOMEBODY LOVE Urban URB 66 | 61 | 1 |

Leila K ☻ ☺ ⬛ Sweden, female vocalist — 22 wks

25 Nov 89	● GOT TO GET Arista 112696 [1]	8	14
17 Mar 90	ROK THE NATION Arista 112971 [1]	41	3
23 Jan 93	OPEN SESAME Polydor PQCD 1	23	4
3 Jul 93	CA PLANE POUR MOI Polydor PQCD 3	69	1

[1] Rob 'n' Raz featuring Leila K

K CREATIVE UK, male vocal/instrumental group — 2 wks

| 7 Mar 92 | THREE TIMES A MAYBE Talkin Loud TLK 17 | 58 | 2 |

The listed flipside of 'Three Times a Maybe' was 'Feed the Feeling' by Perception

Ernie K-DOE US, male vocalist — 7 wks

| 11 May 61 | MOTHER-IN-LAW London HLU 9330 ▲ | 29 | 7 |

K-CI & JOJO R&B US, male vocal duo — 16 wks

23 Aug 97	YOU BRING ME UP MCA MCSTD 48057	21	2
18 Apr 98	● ALL MY LIFE MCA MCSTD 48076 ▲	8	11
19 Sep 98	DON'T RUSH (TAKE LOVE SLOWLY) MCA MCSD 48090	16	3

K-KLASS ☺ UK, male/female vocal/instrumental group — 31 wks

4 May 91	RHYTHM IS A MYSTERY Deconstruction CREED 11	61	2
9 Nov 91	RHYTHM IS A MYSTERY (re-issue) Deconstruction R 6302	3	10
25 Apr 92	SO RIGHT Deconstruction R 6309	20	5
7 Nov 92	DON'T STOP Deconstruction R 6325	32	3
27 Nov 93	LET ME SHOW YOU Deconstruction CDR 6367	13	7
28 May 94	WHAT YOU'RE MISSING Deconstruction CDRS 6380	24	3
1 Aug 98	BURNIN' Parlophone CDK 2001	45	1

Joshua KADISON ☻ US, male vocalist — 19 wks

26 Feb 94	JESSIE SBK CDSBK 43	69	2
1 Oct 94	JESSIE (re-entry) SBK CDSBK 43	48	3
12 Nov 94	BEAUTIFUL IN MY EYES SBK CDSBK 50	65	1
29 Apr 95	JESSIE (re-issue) SBK CDSBK 53	15	10
12 Aug 95	BEAUTIFUL IN MY EYES (re-issue) SBK CDSBK 55	37	3

KADOC ☺ UK/Spain, male vocal/instrumental group — 11 wks

6 Apr 96	THE NIGHTTRAIN Positiva CDTIV 26	14	8
17 Aug 96	YOU GOT TO BE THERE Positiva CDTIV 58	45	1
23 Aug 97	ROCK THE BELLS Manifesto FESCD 30	34	2

Bert KAEMPFERT Germany, orchestra — 10 wks

| 23 Dec 65 | BYE BYE BLUES Polydor BM 56 504 | 24 | 10 |

KAJAGOOGOO ☻ UK, male vocal/instrumental group — 50 wks

22 Jan 83	★ TOO SHY EMI 5359	1	13
2 Apr 83	● OOH TO BE AH EMI 5383	7	8
4 Jun 83	HANG ON NOW EMI 5394	13	7
17 Sep 83	● BIG APPLE EMI 5423	8	8
3 Mar 84	THE LION'S MOUTH EMI 5449	25	7
5 May 84	TURN YOUR BACK ON ME EMI 5646	47	4
21 Sep 85	SHOULDN'T DO THAT Parlophone R 6106 [1]	63	3

[1] Kaja

KALEEF UK, male rap/vocal group — 12 wks

30 Mar 96	WALK LIKE A CHAMPION Payday KACD 5 [1]	23	3
7 Dec 96	GOLDEN BROWN Unity UNITY 010CD	22	4
14 Jun 97	TRIALS OF LIFE Unity UNITY 012CD	75	1
11 Oct 97	I LIKE THE WAY (THE KISSING GAME) Unity UNITY 015CD1	58	1
24 Jan 98	SANDS OF TIME Unity UNITY 016CD	26	3

[1] Kaliphz featuring Prince Naseem

KALIN TWINS ☻ US, male vocal duo — 18 wks

| 18 Jul 58 | ★ WHEN Brunswick 05751 | 1 | 18 |

Kitty KALLEN ☾ US, female vocalist — 23 wks

| 2 Jul 54 | ★ LITTLE THINGS MEAN A LOT Brunswick 05287 ▲ | 1 | 23 |

Gunter KALLMAN CHOIR Germany, male/female vocal group — 3 wks

| 24 Dec 64 | ELISABETH SERENADE Polydor NH 24678 | 45 | 3 |

KAMASUTRA Italy, male DJ / production duo — 1 wk

| 22 Nov 97 | HAPPINESS Sony S£ KAMCD 2 [1] | 45 | 1 |

[1] Kamasutra featuring Jocelyn Brown

Nick KAMEN ☻ UK, male vocalist — 33 wks

8 Nov 86	● EACH TIME YOU BREAK MY HEART WEA YZ 90	5	12
28 Feb 87	LOVING YOU IS SWEETER THAN EVER WEA YZ 106	16	9
16 May 87	NOBODY ELSE WEA YZ 122	47	3
28 May 88	TELL ME WEA YZ 184	40	5
28 Apr 90	I PROMISED MYSELF WEA YZ 454	50	4

Ini KAMOZE ✴ *Jamaica, male vocalist* · 15 wks

7 Jan 95 ●	HERE COMES THE HOTSTEPPER *Columbia 6610472* ▲	4	15

KANDIDATE ✎ *UK, male vocal/instrumental group* · 28 wks

19 Aug 78	DON'T WANNA SAY GOODNIGHT *RAK 280*	47	6
17 Mar 79	I DON'T WANNA LOSE YOU *RAK 289*	11	12
4 Aug 79	GIRLS GIRLS GIRLS *RAK 295*	34	7
22 Mar 80	LET ME ROCK YOU *RAK 306*	58	3

Eden KANE ◎ *UK, male vocalist* · 73 wks

1 Jun 61 ★	WELL I ASK YOU *Decca F 11353*	1	21
14 Sep 61 ●	GET LOST *Decca F 11381*	10	11
18 Jan 62 ●	FORGET ME NOT *Decca F 11418*	3	14
10 May 62 ●	I DON'T KNOW WHY *Decca F 11460*	7	13
30 Jan 64 ●	BOYS CRY *Fontana TF 438*	8	14

KANE GANG ◎ *UK, male vocal/instrumental group* · 37 wks

19 May 84	SMALL TOWN CREED *Kitchenware SK 11*	60	2
7 Jul 84	CLOSEST THING TO HEAVEN *Kitchenware SK 15*	12	11
10 Nov 84	RESPECT YOURSELF *Kitchenware SK 16*	21	10
26 Jan 85	RESPECT YOURSELF (re-entry) *Kitchenware SK 16*	75	1
9 Mar 85	GUN LAW *Kitchenware SK 20*	53	4
27 Jun 87	MOTORTOWN *Kitchenware SK 30*	45	5
16 Apr 88	DON'T LOOK ANY FURTHER *Kitchenware SK 33*	52	4

KANSAS *US, male vocal/instrumental group* · 7 wks

1 Jul 78	CARRY ON WAYWARD SON *Kirshner KIR 4932*	51	7

Mory KANTE *Guinea, male vocalist* · 14 wks

23 Jul 88	YEKE YEKE *London LON 171*	29	9
11 Mar 95	YEKE YEKE (re-mix) *Ffrreedom TABCD 226*	25	3
30 Nov 96	YEKE YEKE (2nd re-mix) *ffrr FCD 288*	28	2

KAOMA ◎ *France, male/female vocal/instrumental group* · 20 wks

21 Oct 89 ●	LAMBADA *CBS 655011 7*	4	18
27 Jan 90	DANCANDO LAMBADA *CBS 655235 7*	62	2

KAOTIC CHEMISTRY *UK, male instrumental/production group* · 1 wk

31 Oct 92	LSD EP *Moving Shadow SHADOW 20*	68	1

Tracks on LSD (EP): Space Cakes/LSD/Illegal Substances/Drumtrip II

KARIN – See UNIQUE 3

KARIYA *US, female vocalist* · 9 wks

8 Jul 89	LET ME LOVE YOU FOR TONIGHT *Sleeping Bag SBUK 4*	44	6
21 Oct 89	LET ME LOVE YOU FOR TONIGHT (re-entry) *Sleeping Bag SBUK 4*	57	3

Mick KARN *UK, male instrumentalist* · 6 wks

9 Jul 83	AFTER A FASHION *Musicfest FEST 1* [1]	39	4
17 Jan 87	BUOY *Virgin VS 910* [2]	63	2

[1] Midge Ure and Mick Karn [2] Mick Karn featuring David Sylvian

KARTOON KREW *US, rap/instrumental group* · 6 wks

7 Dec 85	INSPECTOR GADGET *Champion CHAMP 6*	58	6

KASENETZ-KATZ SINGING ORCHESTRAL CIRCUS ◎
US, male vocal/instrumental group · 15 wks

20 Nov 68	QUICK JOEY SMALL (RUN JOEY RUN) *Buddah 201 022*	19	15

KATRINA and the WAVES ◎
US/UK, female/male vocal/instrumental group · 33 wks

4 May 85 ●	WALKING ON SUNSHINE *Capitol CL 354*	8	12
5 Jul 86	SUN STREET *Capitol CL 407*	22	9

8 Jun 96	WALKING ON SUNSHINE (re-issue) *EMI Premier PRESCD 2*	53	1
10 May 97 ●	LOVE SHINE A LIGHT *Eternal WEA 106CD1*	3	11

KAVANA ◎ *UK, male vocalist* · 23 wks

11 May 96	CRAZY CHANCE *Nemesis NMSD 1*	35	3
24 Aug 96	WHERE ARE YOU *Nemesis NMSD 2*	26	2
11 Jan 97 ●	I CAN MAKE YOU FEEL GOOD *Nemesis NMSDX 3*	8	5
19 Apr 97 ●	MFEO *Nemesis NMSD 4*	8	4
13 Sep 97	CRAZY CHANCE 97 *Nemesis NMSD 5*	16	3
29 Aug 98	SPECIAL KIND OF SOMETHING *Virgin VSCDT 1704*	13	4
12 Dec 98	FUNKY LOVE *Virgin VSCDT 1711*	32	2

Niamh KAVANAGH *Ireland, female vocalist* · 5 wks

12 Jun 93	IN YOUR EYES *Arista 74321154152*	24	5

Janet KAY ✴ *UK, female vocalist* · 24 wks

9 Jun 79 ●	SILLY GAMES *Scope SC 2*	2	14
11 Aug 90	SILLY GAMES *Arista 113452* [1]	22	7
11 Aug 90	SILLY GAMES (re-mix) *Music Factory Dance MFD 006*	62	3

[1] Lindy Layton featuring Janet Kay

Danny KAYE ℂ *US, male vocalist* · 10 wks

27 Feb 53 ●	WONDERFUL COPENHAGEN *Brunswick 05023*	5	10

KAYE SISTERS ℂ *UK, female vocal group* · 45 wks

25 May 56	IVORY TOWER *HMV POP 209* [1]	20	5
1 Nov 57 ●	GOTTA HAVE SOMETHING IN THE BANK FRANK *Philips PB 751* [2]	8	11
3 Jan 58	SHAKE ME I RATTLE/ALONE *Philips PB 752*	27	1
1 May 59 ●	COME SOFTLY TO ME *Philips PB 913* [2]	9	9
7 Jul 60 ●	PAPER ROSES *Philips PB 1024*	7	19

[1] Three Kayes [2] Frankie Vaughan and The Kaye Sisters

KC – See 2PAC

KC and the SUNSHINE BAND ♫ ♥ *Red-hot disco act from Florida, fronted by KC (b. Harry Wayne Casey, 31 January, 1951, Florida) and including co-writer/producer Richard Finch (b.). Internationally successful group whose wall-to-wall late 1970s hits included five US No 1s* · 104 wks

17 Aug 74 ●	QUEEN OF CLUBS *Jayboy BOY 88*	7	12
23 Nov 74	SOUND YOUR FUNKY HORN *Jayboy BOY 83*	17	9
29 Mar 75	GET DOWN TONIGHT *Jayboy BOY 93* ▲	21	9
2 Aug 75 ●	THAT'S THE WAY (I LIKE IT) *Jayboy BOY 99* ▲	4	10
22 Nov 75	I'M SO CRAZY ('BOUT YOU) *Jayboy BOY 101*	34	3
17 Jul 76	(SHAKE SHAKE SHAKE) SHAKE YOUR BOOTY *Jayboy BOY 110* ▲	22	8
11 Dec 76	KEEP IT COMIN' LOVE *Jayboy BOY 112*	31	8
30 Apr 77	I'M YOUR BOOGIE MAN *TK XB 2167* ▲	41	4
6 May 78	BOOGIE SHOES *TK TKR 6025*	34	5
22 Jul 78	IT'S THE SAME OLD SONG *TK TKR 6037*	47	5
8 Dec 79 ●	PLEASE DON'T GO *TK TKR 7558* ▲	3	12
16 Jul 83 ★	GIVE IT UP *Epic EPC A 3017*	1	14
24 Sep 83	(YOU SAID) YOU'D GIMME SOME MORE *Epic A 2760*	41	3
11 May 91	THAT'S THE WAY I LIKE IT (re-mix) *Music Factory Dance M7FAC 2*	59	2

KE *US, male vocalist* · 1 wk

13 Apr 96	STRANGE WORLD *Venture 74321349412*	73	1

Johnny KEATING ℂ *UK, orchestra* · 14 wks

1 Mar 62 ●	THEME FROM 'Z CARS' *Piccadilly 7N 35032*	8	14

Kevin KEEGAN *UK, male vocalist* · 6 wks

9 Jun 79	HEAD OVER HEELS IN LOVE *EMI 2965*	31	6

Yvonne KEELEY – See Scott FITZGERALD

UK No 1 ★   UK Top 10 ●   UK million seller ◆   UK entry at No 1 ■   US No 1 ▲

Nelson KEENE *UK, male vocalist* **5 wks**

25 Aug 60	IMAGE OF A GIRL *HMV POP 771*	37	4
29 Sep 60	IMAGE OF A GIRL (re-entry) *HMV POP 771*	45	1

KEITH *US, male vocalist* **8 wks**

26 Jan 67	98.6 *Mercury MF 955*	24	7
16 Mar 67	TELL ME TO MY FACE *Mercury MF 968*	50	1

Jerry KELLER ○ *US, male vocalist* **14 wks**

28 Aug 59	★ HERE COMES SUMMER *London HLR 8890*	1	14

Frank KELLY *Ireland, male vocalist* **5 wks**

24 Dec 83	CHRISTMAS COUNTDOWN *Ritz RITZ 062*	26	4
29 Dec 84	CHRISTMAS COUNTDOWN (re-entry) *Ritz RITZ 062*	54	1

Frankie KELLY *US, male vocalist/instrumentalist* **2 wks**

2 Nov 85	AIN'T THAT THE TRUTH *10 TEN 87*	65	2

Grace KELLY – See Bing CROSBY

Keith KELLY *UK, male vocalist* **5 wks**

5 May 60	TEASE ME *Parlophone R 4640*	46	1
19 May 60	TEASE ME (re-entry) *Parlophone R 4640*	27	3
18 Aug 60	LISTEN LITTLE GIRL *Parlophone R 4676*	47	1

R KELLY R&B *US, male vocalist* **88 wks**

9 May 92	SHE'S GOT THAT VIBE *Jive JIVET 292* [1]	57	2
20 Nov 93	SEX ME *Jive JIVECD 346* [1]	75	1
14 May 94	YOUR BODY'S CALLIN' *Jive JIVECD 353*	19	4
3 Sep 94	SUMMER BUNNIES *Jive JIVECD 358*	23	3
22 Oct 94	● SHE'S GOT THAT VIBE (re-issue) *Jive JIVECD 364*	3	13
21 Jan 95	● BUMP 'N' GRIND *Jive JIVECD 368* ▲	8	9
6 May 95	THE 4 PLAY EPS *Jive JIVECD 376*	23	3
11 Nov 95	YOU REMIND ME OF SOMETHING *Jive JIVECD 388*	24	3
2 Mar 96	DOWN LOW (NOBODY HAS TO KNOW) *Jive JIVECD 392* [2]	23	3
22 Jun 96	THANK GOD IT'S FRIDAY *Jive JIVECD 395*	23	3
29 Mar 97	★ I BELIEVE I CAN FLY *Jive JIVECD 415*	1	16
19 Jul 97	● GOTHAM CITY *Jive JIVECD 428*	9	8
18 Jul 98	● BE CAREFUL *Jive 0521452* [3]	7	6
26 Sep 98	HALF ON A BABY *Jive 0521802*	16	4
14 Nov 98	HOME ALONE *Jive 0522392* [4]	17	5
28 Nov 98	● I'M YOUR ANGEL *Epic 6666282* ▲ [5]	3	5

[1] R Kelly and Public Announcement [2] R Kelly featuring Ronald Isley [3] Sparkle featuring R Kelly [4] R Kelly featuring Keith Murray [5] Celine Dion and R Kelly

The 4 Play EP was available on 2 CDs, each featuring 'Your Body's Callin' and three further tracks

Roberta KELLY *US, female vocalist* **3 wks**

21 Jan 78	ZODIACS *Oasis/Hansa 3*	48	1
4 Feb 78	ZODIACS (re-entry) *Oasis/Hansa 3*	44	2

KELLY FAMILY *Ireland, male/female vocal/instrumental group* **1 wk**

21 Oct 95	AN ANGEL *EMI CDEM 390*	69	1

Johnny KEMP *Barbados, male vocalist* **1 wk**

27 Aug 88	JUST GOT PAID *CBS 651470 7*	68	1

Tara KEMP *US, female vocalist* **2 wks**

20 Apr 91	HOLD YOU TIGHT *Giant W 0020*	69	2

Graham KENDRICK *UK, male vocalist* **4 wks**

9 Sep 89	LET THE FLAME BURN BRIGHTER *Power P 30*	55	4

Eddie KENDRICKS ♪ *US, male vocalist* **20 wks**

3 Nov 73	KEEP ON TRUCKIN' *Tamla Motown TMG 873* ▲	18	14
16 Mar 74	BOOGIE DOWN *Tamla Motown TMG 888*	39	4
21 Sep 85	A NIGHT AT THE APOLLO LIVE! *RCA PB 49935* [1]	58	2

[1] Daryl Hall and John Oates featuring David Ruffin and Eddie Kendrick

A Night at the Apollo Live! is a medley of 'The Way You Do The Things You Do' and 'My Girl'. Kendricks dropped the 's' from his name for last hit

KENICKIE *UK, female/male vocal/instrumental group* **13 wks**

14 Sep 96	PUNKA *Emidisc CDDISC 001*	43	2
16 Nov 96	MILLIONAIRE SWEEPER *Emidisc CDDISC 002*	60	1
11 Jan 97	IN YOUR CAR *Emidisc CDDISC 005*	24	3
3 May 97	NIGHTLIFE *Emidisc CDDISC 006*	27	2
5 Jul 97	PUNKA (re-issue) *Emidisc CDDISC 007*	38	2
6 Jun 98	I WOULD FIX YOU *EMI CDEM 513*	36	2
22 Aug 98	STAY IN THE SUN *EMI CDEMS 520*	43	1

Jane KENNAWAY and STRANGE BEHAVIOUR
UK, female vocalist, male instrumental group **3 wks**

24 Jan 81	I.O.U. *Deram DM 436*	65	3

Brian KENNEDY *Ireland, male vocalist* **8 wks**

22 Jun 96	A BETTER MAN *RCA 74321382642*	28	3
21 Sep 96	LIFE, LOVE AND HAPPINESS *RCA 74321409921*	27	3
5 Apr 97	PUT THE MESSAGE IN THE BOX *RCA 74321462272*	37	2

KENNY ○ *Ireland, male vocalist* **16 wks**

3 Mar 73	HEART OF STONE *RAK 144*	11	13
30 Jun 73	GIVE IT TO ME NOW *RAK 153*	38	3

KENNY ○ *UK, male vocal/instrumental group* **39 wks**

7 Dec 74	● THE BUMP *RAK 186*	3	15
8 Mar 75	● FANCY PANTS *RAK 196*	4	9
7 Jun 75	BABY I LOVE YOU OK *RAK 207*	12	7
16 Aug 75	● JULIE ANN *RAK 214*	10	8

Gerard KENNY *US, male vocalist* **21 wks**

9 Dec 78	NEW YORK, NEW YORK *RCA PB 5117*	43	8
21 Jun 80	FANTASY *RCA PB 5256*	65	1
5 Jul 80	FANTASY (re-entry) *RCA PB 5256*	34	5
18 Feb 84	THE OTHER WOMAN, THE OTHER MAN *Impression IMS 3*	69	4
4 May 85	NO MAN'S LAND *WEA YZ 38*	56	3

Klark KENT *US, male vocalist/multi-instrumentalist* **4 wks**

26 Aug 78	DON'T CARE *A & M AMS 7376*	48	4

Carol KENYON – See Paul HARDCASTLE; HEAVEN 17; RAPINATION

KERBDOG *Ireland, male vocal/instrumental group* **5 wks**

12 Mar 94	DRY RISER *Vertigo VERCC 83*	60	1
6 Aug 94	DUMMY CRUSHER *Vertigo VERCD 86*	37	2
12 Oct 96	SALLY *Fontana KERCD 2*	69	1
29 Mar 97	MEXICAN WAVE *Fontana KERCD 3*	49	1

KERRI and MICK *Australia, female/male vocal duo* **3 wks**

28 Apr 84	'SONS AND DAUGHTERS' THEME *A1 A1 286*	68	3

KERRI-ANN *Ireland, female vocalist* **1 wk**

8 Aug 98	DO YOU LOVE ME BOY? *Raglan Road 5671012*	58	1

Liz KERSHAW and Bruno BROOKES
UK, male/female vocal duo **3 wks**

2 Dec 89	IT TAKES TWO BABY *Spartan CIN 101* [1]	53	2
1 Dec 90	LET'S DANCE *Jive BRUNO 1* [2]	54	1

[1] Liz Kershaw, Bruno Brookes, Jive Bunny and Londonbeat
[2] Bruno and Liz and the Radio 1 DJ Posse

See also JIVE BUNNY and the MASTERMIXERS; LONDONBEAT

UK No 1 ★ UK Top 10 ● UK million seller ◆ UK entry at No 1 ■ US No 1 ▲

Nik KERSHAW ☺ UK, male vocalist — 87 wks

19 Nov 83	I WON'T LET THE SUN GO DOWN ON ME *MCA MCA 816*	47	5
28 Jan 84 ●	WOULDN'T IT BE GOOD *MCA NIK 2*	4	14
14 Apr 84	DANCING GIRLS *MCA NIK 3*	13	9
16 Jun 84 ●	I WON'T LET THE SUN GO DOWN ON ME (re-issue) *MCA NIK 4*	2	13
15 Sep 84	HUMAN RACING *MCA NIK 5*	19	7
17 Nov 84	THE RIDDLE *MCA NIK 6*	3	11
16 Mar 85 ●	WIDE BOY *MCA NIK 7*	9	8
3 Aug 85 ●	DON QUIXOTE *MCA NIK 8*	10	7
30 Nov 85	WHEN A HEART BEATS *MCA NIK 9*	27	7
11 Oct 86	NOBODY KNOWS *MCA NIK 10*	44	3
13 Dec 86	RADIO MUSICOLA *MCA NIK 11*	43	2
4 Feb 89	ONE STEP AHEAD *MCA NIK 12*	55	1

KEVIN THE GERBIL UK, male gerbil vocalist — 6 wks

4 Aug 84	SUMMER HOLIDAY *Magnet RAT 3*	50	6

KEY WEST – See ERIK

KEYNOTES – See Dave KING

Chaka KHAN 🎤 ✈ US, female vocalist — 94 wks

2 Dec 78	I'M EVERY WOMAN *Warner Bros. K 17269*	11	13
31 Mar 84 ●	AIN'T NOBODY *Warner Bros. RCK 1* [1]	8	12
20 Oct 84 ★	I FEEL FOR YOU *Warner Bros. W 9209*	1	16
19 Jan 85	THIS IS MY NIGHT *Warner Bros. W 9097*	14	6
20 Apr 85	EYE TO EYE *Warner Bros. W 9009*	16	7
12 Jul 86	LOVE OF A LIFETIME *Warner Bros. W 8671*	52	4
21 Jan 89	IT'S MY PARTY *Warner Bros. W 7678*	71	2
6 May 89 ●	I'M EVERY WOMAN (re-mix) *Warner Bros. W 2963*	8	8
8 Jul 89 ●	AIN'T NOBODY (re-mix) *Warner Bros. W 2880* [1]	6	9
7 Oct 89	I FEEL FOR YOU (re-mix) *Warner Bros. W 2764*	45	2
13 Jan 90	I'LL BE GOOD TO YOU *Qwest W 2697* [2]	21	7
28 Mar 92	LOVE YOU ALL MY LIFETIME *Warner Bros. W 0087*	49	3
17 Jul 93	DON'T LOOK AT ME THAT WAY *Warner Bros. W 0192CD*	73	1
19 Aug 95	WATCH WHAT YOU SAY *Cooltempo CDCOOL 308* [3]	28	3
1 Mar 97	NEVER MISS THE WATER *Reprise W 1393CD* [4]	59	1

[1] Rufus and Chaka Khan [2] Quincy Jones featuring Ray Charles and Chaka Khan
[3] Guru featuring Chaka Khan [4] Chaka Khan featuring Me'Shell Ndegeocello

See also Quincy JONES

Praga KHAN ☺ Belgium, male producer — 8 wks

4 Apr 92	FREE YOUR BODY/INJECTED WITH A POISON *Profile PROFT 347* [1]	16	6
11 Jul 92	RAVE ALERT *Profile PROF 369*	39	2

[1] Praga Khan featuring Jade 4 U

Mary KIANI ⊙ ☺ UK, female vocalist — 15 wks

12 Aug 95	WHEN I CALL YOUR NAME *Mercury MERCD 440*	18	4
23 Dec 95	I GIVE IT ALL TO YOU/I IMAGINE *Mercury MERCD 449*	35	4
27 Apr 96	LET THE MUSIC PLAY *Mercury MERCD 456*	19	3
18 Jan 97	100% *Mercury MERCD 469*	23	3
21 Jun 97	WITH OR WITHOUT YOU *Mercury MERCD 487*	46	1

KICK HORNS – See DODGY

KICK SQUAD UK/Germany, male vocal/instrumental group — 2 wks

10 Nov 90	SOUND CLASH (CHAMPION SOUND) *Kickin KICK 2*	59	2

KICKING BACK with TAXMAN
UK, male/female vocal/instrumental duo with male rapper — 8 wks

17 Mar 90	DEVOTION *10 TEN 297*	47	4
7 Jul 90	EVERYTHING *10 TEN 307*	54	4

KICKS LIKE A MULE ☺ UK, male instrumental/production duo — 6 wks

1 Feb 92 ●	THE BOUNCER *Tribal Bass TRIBE 3S*	7	6

K.I.D. Antilles, male/female vocal/instrumental group — 4 wks

28 Feb 81	DON'T STOP *EMI 5143*	49	4

KID 'N' PLAY US, male rap duo — 7 wks

18 Jul 87	LAST NIGHT *Cooltempo COOL 148*	71	1
26 Mar 88	DO THIS MY WAY *Cooltempo COOL 164*	48	3
17 Sep 88	GITTIN' FUNKY *Cooltempo COOL 168*	55	3

KID UNKNOWN UK, male producer – Paul Fitzpatrick — 1 wk

2 May 92	NIGHTMARE *Warp WAP 20CD*	64	1

Carol KIDD featuring Terry WAITE
UK, female/male vocal duo — 3 wks

17 Oct 92	WHEN I DREAM *The Hit Label HLS 1*	58	3

Johnny KIDD and the PIRATES ⊙ 🎻
UK, male vocal/instrumental group — 62 wks

12 Jun 59	PLEASE DON'T TOUCH *HMV POP 615* [1]	26	3
17 Jul 59	PLEASE DON'T TOUCH (re-entry) *HMV POP 615* [1]	25	2
12 Feb 60	YOU GOT WHAT IT TAKES *HMV POP 698*	25	3
16 Jun 60 ★	SHAKIN' ALL OVER *HMV POP 753*	1	19
6 Oct 60	RESTLESS *HMV POP 790*	22	7
13 Apr 61	LINDA LU *HMV POP 853*	47	1
10 Jan 63	SHOT OF RHYTHM AND BLUES *HMV POP 1088*	48	1
25 Jul 63 ●	I'LL NEVER GET OVER YOU *HMV POP 1173*	4	15
28 Nov 63	HUNGRY FOR LOVE *HMV POP 1228*	20	10
30 Apr 64	ALWAYS AND EVER *HMV POP 1269*	46	1

[1] Johnny Kidd

KIDS FROM 'FAME' ⊙ US, male/female vocal group — 36 wks

14 Aug 82 ●	HI-FIDELITY *RCA 254* [1]	5	10
2 Oct 82 ●	STARMAKER *RCA 280*	3	10
11 Dec 82	MANNEQUIN *RCA 299* [2]	50	6
9 Apr 83	FRIDAY NIGHT (LIVE VERSION) *RCA 320*	13	10

[1] Kids From Fame featuring Valerie Landsberg
[2] Kids From Fame featuring Gene Anthony Ray

Greg KIHN BAND US, male vocal/instrumental group — 2 wks

23 Apr 83	JEOPARDY *Beserkley E 9847*	63	2

KILLAH PRIEST US, male rapper — 1 wk

7 Feb 98	ONE STEP *Geffen GFSTD 22318*	45	1

KILLING JOKE ✏ 🎸 UK, male vocal/instrumental group — 48 wks

23 May 81	FOLLOW THE LEADERS *Malicious Damage EGMDS 101*	55	5
20 Mar 82	EMPIRE SONG *Malicious Damage EGO 4*	43	4
30 Oct 82	BIRDS OF A FEATHER *EG EGO 10*	64	2
25 Jun 83	LET'S ALL (GO TO THE FIRE DANCES) *EG EGO 11*	51	3
15 Oct 83	ME OR YOU? *EG EGO 14*	57	1
7 Apr 84	EIGHTIES *EG EGO 16*	60	5
21 Jul 84	A NEW DAY *EG EGO 17*	56	2
2 Feb 85	LOVE LIKE BLOOD *EG EGO 20*	16	9
30 Mar 85	KINGS AND QUEENS *EG EGO 21*	58	3
16 Aug 86	ADORATIONS *EG EGO 27*	42	6
18 Oct 86	SANITY *EG EGO 30*	70	1
7 May 88	MILLENNIUM *Butterfly BFLD 12*	34	2
16 Jul 94	PANDEMONIUM *Butterfly BFLD 17*	28	3
4 Feb 95	JANA *Butterfly BFLDA 21*	54	1
23 Mar 96	DEMOCRACY *Butterfly BFLDA 33*	39	1

Andy KIM ⊙ Canada, male vocalist — 12 wks

24 Aug 74 ●	ROCK ME GENTLY *Capitol CL 15787* ▲	2	12

KINANE Ireland, female vocalist — 4 wks

18 May 96	ALL THE LOVER I NEED *Coliseum TOGA 003CD* [1]	59	1
21 Sep 96	THE WOMAN IN ME *Coliseum TOGA 007CD* [1]	73	1

UK No 1 ★ UK Top 10 ● UK million seller ◆ UK entry at No 1 ■ US No 1 ▲

| 16 May 98 | | HEAVEN Coalition COLA 047CD | 49 | 1 |
| 22 Aug 98 | | SO FINE Coalition COLA 055CD1 | 63 | 1 |

[1] Bianca Kinane

KING ◉ UK/Ireland, male vocal/instrumental group　44 wks

12 Jan 85	●	LOVE AND PRIDE CBS A 4988	2	14
23 Mar 85		WON'T YOU HOLD MY HAND NOW CBS A 6094	24	8
17 Aug 85	●	ALONE WITHOUT YOU CBS A 6308	8	9
19 Oct 85		THE TASTE OF YOUR TEARS CBS A 6618	11	9
11 Jan 86		TORTURE CBS A 6761	23	4

See also Paul KING

Albert KING – See Gary MOORE

BB KING ♟ US, male vocalist/instrumentalist – guitar　10 wks

| 15 Apr 89 | ● | WHEN LOVE COMES TO TOWN Island IS 411 [1] | 6 | 7 |
| 18 Jul 92 | | SINCE I MET YOU BABY Virgin VS 1423 [2] | 59 | 3 |

[1] U2 with BB King [2] Gary Moore and BB King

Ben E KING ♪ US, male vocalist　35 wks

2 Feb 61		FIRST TASTE OF LOVE London HLK 9258	27	11
22 Jun 61		STAND BY ME London HLK 9358	50	1
6 Jul 61		STAND BY ME (re-entry) London HLK 9358	27	6
5 Oct 61		AMOR AMOR London HLK 9416	38	4
14 Feb 87	★	STAND BY ME (re-issue) Atlantic A 9361	1	11
4 Jul 87		SAVE THE LAST DANCE FOR ME Manhattan MT 25	69	2

Carole KING ◉ ✎ US, female vocalist　29 wks

20 Sep 62	●	IT MIGHT AS WELL RAIN UNTIL SEPTEMBER London HLU 9591	3	13
7 Aug 71	●	IT'S TOO LATE A & M AMS 849 ▲	6	12
28 Oct 72		IT MIGHT AS WELL RAIN UNTIL SEPTEMBER (re-issue) London HL 10391	43	4

Dave KING ◖ UK, male vocalist　29 wks

17 Feb 56	●	MEMORIES ARE MADE OF THIS Decca F 10684 [1]	5	15
13 Apr 56		YOU CAN'T BE TRUE TO TWO Decca F 10720 [1]	11	9
21 Dec 56		CHRISTMAS AND YOU Decca F 10791	23	2
24 Jan 58		THE STORY OF MY LIFE Decca F 10973	20	3

[1] Dave King featuring The Keynotes

See also VARIOUS ARTISTS (EPs & LPs) – All Star Hit Parade

Denis KING – See STUTZ BEARCATS and the Denis KING ORCHESTRA

Diana KING ⬥ Jamaica, female vocalist　22 wks

8 Jul 95	●	SHY GUY Columbia 6621682	2	13
28 Oct 95		AIN'T NOBODY Columbia 6625495	13	5
1 Nov 97		I SAY A LITTLE PRAYER Columbia 6651472	17	4

Evelyn 'Champagne' KING ✎ ◣ US, female vocalist　76 wks

13 May 78		SHAME RCA PC 1122	39	23
3 Feb 79		I DON'T KNOW IF IT'S RIGHT RCA PB 1386	67	2
27 Jun 81		I'M IN LOVE RCA 95 [1]	27	11
26 Sep 81		IF YOU WANT MY LOVIN' RCA 131 [1]	43	6
28 Aug 82	●	LOVE COME DOWN RCA 249 [1]	7	13
20 Nov 82		BACK TO LOVE RCA 287 [1]	40	4
19 Feb 83		GET LOOSE RCA 315 [1]	45	5
9 Nov 85		YOUR PERSONAL TOUCH RCA PB 49915	37	5
29 Mar 86		HIGH HORSE RCA PB 49891	55	3
23 Jul 88		HOLD ON TO WHAT YOU'VE GOT Manhattan MT 49	47	3
10 Oct 92		SHAME (re-mix) Network NWKTEN 56 [2]	74	1

[1] Evelyn King [2] Altern 8 vs Evelyn King

Jonathan KING ◉ King of pseudonym singers, b. 6 December, 1944, London. A multi-faceted pop maestro who masterminded numerous hits and helped Britain win the Eurovision Song Contest in 1997. He also helped guide the early careers of Genesis, Bay City Rollers and 10cc　128 wks

29 Jul 65	●	EVERYONE'S GONE TO THE MOON Decca F 12187	4	11
10 Jan 70		LET IT ALL HANG OUT Decca F 12988	26	7
16 Jan 71		IT'S THE SAME OLD SONG B & C CB 139 [1]	19	9
3 Apr 71		SUGAR SUGAR RCA 2064 [2]	12	14
29 May 71		LAZY BONES Decca F 13177	23	8
20 Nov 71		HOOKED ON A FEELING Decca F 13241	23	10
5 Feb 72		FLIRT Decca F 13276	22	9
14 Oct 72		LOOP DI LOVE UK 7 [3]	4	13
26 Jan 74		(I CAN'T GET NO) SATISFACTION UK 53 [4]	29	5
6 Sep 75		UNA PALOMA BLANCA UK 105	5	11
20 Sep 75		CHICK-A-BOOM (DON'T YA JES LOVE IT) UK 2012 002 [5]	36	4
7 Feb 76		IN THE MOOD UK 121 [6]	46	3
26 Jun 76	●	IT ONLY TAKES A MINUTE UK 135 [7]	9	9
7 Oct 78		ONE FOR YOU ONE FOR ME GTO GT 237	29	6
16 Dec 78		LICK A SMURP FOR CHRISTMAS (ALL FALL DOWN) Petrol GAS 1 [8]	58	4
16 Jun 79		YOU'RE THE GREATEST LOVER UK International INT 586	67	2
3 Nov 79		GLORIA Ariola ARO 198	65	3

[1] Weathermen [2] Sakkarin [3] Shag [4] Bubblerock [5] 53rd and 3rd featuring the Sound of Shag [6] Sound 9418 [7] One Hundred Ton and a Feather [8] Father Abraphart and the Smurps

Petrol GAS 1 transferred to Magnet MAG 139 after the first week on chart

Paul KING UK, male vocalist　3 wks

| 2 May 87 | | I KNOW CBS PKING 1 | 59 | 3 |

See also KING

Nosmo KING – See JAVELLS featuring Nosmo KING

Solomon KING ◖ US, male vocalist　28 wks

| 3 Jan 68 | ● | SHE WEARS MY RING Columbia DB 8325 | 3 | 18 |
| 1 May 68 | | WHEN WE WERE YOUNG Columbia DB 8402 | 21 | 10 |

Tony KING – See Kylie MINOGUE

KING BEE UK, male rapper　6 wks

| 26 Jan 91 | | MUST BEE THE MUSIC Columbia 6565827 | 44 | 4 |
| 23 Mar 91 | | BACK BY DOPE DEMAND First Bass 7RUFF 6X | 61 | 2 |

KING BROTHERS ◉ UK, male vocal/instrumental group　74 wks

31 May 57	●	A WHITE SPORT COAT Parlophone R 4310	6	14
9 Aug 57		IN THE MIDDLE OF AN ISLAND Parlophone R 4338	19	13
6 Dec 57		WAKE UP LITTLE SUSIE Parlophone R 4367	22	3
31 Jan 58		PUT A LIGHT IN THE WINDOW Parlophone R 4389	29	1
14 Feb 58		PUT A LIGHT IN THE WINDOW (re-entry) Parlophone R 4389	28	1
28 Feb 58		PUT A LIGHT IN THE WINDOW (2nd re-entry) Parlophone R 4389	25	2
14 Apr 60	●	STANDING ON THE CORNER Parlophone R 4639	4	11
28 Jul 60		MAIS OUI Parlophone R 4672	16	10
12 Jan 61		DOLL HOUSE Parlophone R 4715	21	8
2 Mar 61		76 TROMBONES Parlophone R 4737	19	11

KING KURT UK, male vocal/instrumental group　16 wks

15 Oct 83		DESTINATION ZULULAND Stiff BUY 189	36	6
28 Apr 84		MACK THE KNIFE Stiff BUY 199	55	4
4 Aug 84		BANANA BANANA Stiff BUY 206	54	4
15 Nov 86		AMERICA Polydor KURT 1	73	1
2 May 87		THE LAND OF RING DANG DO Polydor KURT 2	67	1

KING SUN-D'MOET US, male rap/scratch duo　3 wks

| 11 Jul 87 | | HEY LOVE Flame MELT 5 | 66 | 3 |

KING TRIGGER UK, male/female vocal/instrumental group — 4 wks

14 Aug 82	THE RIVER *Chrysalis CHS 2623*	57	4

KINGDOM COME US, male vocal/instrumental group — 2 wks

| 16 Apr 88 | GET IT ON *Polydor KCS 1* | 75 | 1 |
| 6 May 89 | DO YOU LIKE IT *Polydor KCS 3* | 73 | 1 |

KINGMAKER ○ ✔ UK, male vocal/instrumental group — 22 wks

18 Jan 92	IDIOTS AT THE WHEEL EP *Scorch SCORCH 3*	30	3
23 May 92	EAT YOURSELF WHOLE *Scorch SCORCHG 5*	15	3
31 Oct 92	ARMCHAIR ANARCHIST *Scorch SCORCHG 6*	47	2
8 May 93	10 YEARS ASLEEP *Scorch CDSCORCHS 8*	15	4
19 Jun 93	QUEEN JANE *Scorch CDSCORS 9*	29	4
30 Oct 93	SATURDAY'S NOT WHAT IT USED TO BE *Scorch CDSCORCH 10*	63	1
15 Apr 95	YOU AND I WILL NEVER SEE THINGS EYE TO EYE *Scorch CDSCORCHS 11*	33	3
3 Jun 95	IN THE BEST POSSIBLE TASTE (PART 2) *Scorch CDSCORCHS 12*	41	2

Tracks on Idiots at the Wheel EP: *Really Scrape the Sky / Revelation / Every Teenage Suicide / Strip Away*
See also VARIOUS ARTISTS (EPs & LPs) – Gimme Shelter (EP)

KINGS OF SWING ORCHESTRA Australia, orchestra — 5 wks

| 1 May 82 | SWITCHED ON SWING *Philips Swing 1* | 48 | 5 |

KINGSMEN US, male vocal/instrumental group — 7 wks

| 30 Jan 64 | LOUIE LOUIE *Pye International 7N 25231* | 26 | 7 |

KINGSTON TRIO ♂ US, male vocal/instrumental group — 15 wks

| 21 Nov 58 ● | TOM DOOLEY *Capitol CL 14951* ▲ | 5 | 14 |
| 4 Dec 59 | SAN MIGUEL *Capitol CL 15073* | 29 | 1 |

KINKS ✔

Well respected and innovative London band, who had few equals in the 1960s: Ray Davies (v/g), Dave Davies (g), Pete Quaife (b), Mick Avory (d). Ray Davies, regarded as one of rock's premier songwriters, remains active 35 years after the group's first hit — **215 wks**

13 Aug 64 ★	YOU REALLY GOT ME *Pye 7N 15673*	1	12
29 Oct 64 ●	ALL DAY AND ALL OF THE NIGHT *Pye 7N 15714*	2	14
21 Jan 65 ★	TIRED OF WAITING FOR YOU *Pye 7N 15759*	1	10
25 Mar 65	EVERYBODY'S GONNA BE HAPPY *Pye 7N 15813*	17	8
27 May 65 ●	SET ME FREE *Pye 7N 15854*	9	11
5 Aug 65 ●	SEE MY FRIEND *Pye 7N 15919*	10	9
2 Dec 65 ●	TILL THE END OF THE DAY *Pye 7N 15981*	8	12
3 Mar 66 ●	DEDICATED FOLLOWER OF FASHION *Pye 7N 17064*	4	11
9 Jun 66 ★	SUNNY AFTERNOON *Pye 7N 17125*	1	13
24 Nov 66 ●	DEAD END STREET *Pye 7N 17222*	5	11
11 May 67 ●	WATERLOO SUNSET *Pye 7N 17321*	2	11
18 Oct 67 ●	AUTUMN ALMANAC *Pye 7N 17400*	3	11
17 Apr 68	WONDERBOY *Pye 7N 17468*	36	5
17 Jul 68	DAYS *Pye 7N 17573*	12	10
16 Apr 69	PLASTIC MAN *Pye 7N 17724*	31	4
10 Jan 70	VICTORIA *Pye 7N 17865*	33	4
4 Jul 70 ●	LOLA *Pye 7N 17961*	2	14
12 Dec 70 ●	APEMAN *Pye 7N 45016*	5	14
27 May 72	SUPERSONIC ROCKET SHIP *RCA 2211*	16	8
27 Jun 81	BETTER THINGS *Arista ARIST 415*	46	5
6 Aug 83	COME DANCING *Arista ARIST 502*	12	9
15 Oct 83	DON'T FORGET TO DANCE *Arista ARIST 524*	58	3
15 Oct 83	YOU REALLY GOT ME (re-issue) *PRT KD1*	47	4
18 Jan 97	THE DAYS EP *When! WENX 1016*	35	2

Tracks on The Days EP: *Days / You Really Got Me / Dead End Street / Lola*

KINKY UK, female rapper — 1 wk

| 24 Aug 96 | EVERYBODY *Feverpitch CDFVR 1009* | 26 | 1 |

See also ERASURE

KINKY MACHINE UK, male vocal/instrumental group — 4 wks

6 Mar 93	SUPERNATURAL GIVER *Lemon LEMON 006CD*	70	1
29 May 93	SHOCKAHOLIC *Oxygen GASPD 5*	70	1
14 Aug 93	GOING OUT WITH GOD *Oxygen GASPD 9*	74	1
2 Jul 94	10 SECOND BIONIC MAN *Oxygen GASPD 14*	66	1

Fern KINNEY ✎ ◢ US, female vocalist — 11 wks

| 16 Feb 80 ★ | TOGETHER WE ARE BEAUTIFUL *WEA K 79111* | 1 | 11 |

KINSHASA BAND – See Johnny WAKELIN

Kathy KIRBY ☾ UK, female vocalist — 54 wks

15 Aug 63	DANCE ON *Decca F 11682*	11	13
7 Nov 63 ●	SECRET LOVE *Decca F 11759*	4	18
20 Feb 64 ●	LET ME GO LOVER *Decca F 11832*	10	11
7 May 64	YOU'RE THE ONE *Decca F 11892*	17	9
4 Mar 65	I BELONG *Decca F 12087*	36	3

Bo KIRKLAND and Ruth DAVIS ✎ US, male/female vocal duo — 9 wks

| 4 Jun 77 | YOU'RE GONNA GET NEXT TO ME *EMI International INT 532* | 12 | 9 |

KISS ⊺ US, male/female vocal/instrumental group — 57 wks

30 Jun 79	I WAS MADE FOR LOVIN' YOU *Casablanca CAN 152*	50	7
20 Feb 82	A WORLD WITHOUT HEROES *Casablanca KISS 002*	55	3
30 Apr 83	CREATURES OF THE NIGHT *Casablanca KISS 4*	34	4
29 Oct 83	LICK IT UP *Vertigo KISS 5*	31	5
8 Sep 84	HEAVEN'S ON FIRE *Vertigo VER 12*	43	3
9 Nov 85	TEARS ARE FALLING *Vertigo KISS 6*	57	2
3 Oct 87 ●	CRAZY CRAZY NIGHTS *Vertigo KISS 7*	4	9
5 Dec 87	REASON TO LIVE *Vertigo KISS 8*	33	7
10 Sep 88	TURN ON THE NIGHT *Vertigo KISS 9*	41	3
18 Nov 89	HIDE YOUR HEART *Vertigo KISS 10*	59	2
31 Mar 90	FOREVER *Vertigo KISS 11*	65	2
11 Jan 92 ●	GOD GAVE ROCK AND ROLL TO YOU II *Interscope A 8696*	4	8
9 May 92	UNHOLY *Mercury KISS 12*	26	2

KISS AMC UK, female rap duo — 5 wks

1 Jul 89	A BIT OF . . . *Syncopate SY 29*	58	2
19 Aug 89	A BIT OF U2 (re-entry) *Syncopate SY 29*	58	2
3 Feb 90	MY DOCS *Syncopate XAMC 1*	66	1

Before the re-entry of 'A Bit of U2', copyright problems meant that the disc was unable to be given its full title

KISSING THE PINK ○
UK, male/female vocal/instrumental group — 14 wks

| 5 Mar 83 | LAST FILM *Magnet KTP 3* | 19 | 14 |

Mac and Katie KISSOON ○ Trinidad/UK, male/female vocal duo — 33 wks

19 Jun 71	CHIRPY CHIRPY CHEEP CHEEP *Young Blood YB 1026*	41	1
18 Jan 75 ●	SUGAR CANDY KISSES *Polydor 2058 531*	3	10
3 May 75 ●	DON'T DO IT BABY *State STAT 4*	9	8
30 Aug 75	LIKE A BUTTERFLY *State STAT 9*	18	9
15 May 76	THE TWO OF US *State STAT 21*	46	5

Kevin KITCHEN UK, male vocalist — 3 wks

| 20 Apr 85 | PUT MY ARMS AROUND YOU *China WOK 1* | 64 | 3 |

Eartha KITT ☾ US, female vocalist — 34 wks

1 Apr 55 ●	UNDER THE BRIDGES OF PARIS *HMV B 10647*	7	9
10 Jun 55	UNDER THE BRIDGES OF PARIS (re-entry) *HMV B 10647*	20	1
3 Dec 83	WHERE IS MY MAN *Record Shack SOHO 11*	36	11
7 Jul 84	I LOVE MEN *Record Shack SOHO 21*	50	3
12 Apr 86	THIS IS MY LIFE *Record Shack SOHO 61*	73	1
1 Jul 89	CHA CHA HEELS *Arista 112331* [1]	32	7
5 Mar 94	IF I LOVE YA THEN I NEED YA IF I NEED YA THEN I WANT YA AROUND *RCA 74321190342*	43	2

[1] Eartha Kitt and Bronski Beat

What: *Chain Reaction*   **53**
Who: Diana Ross
When: 1986 (1), 1993 (20)
Which: Became the sixth chart-topper penned by the Gibb Brothers (Bee Gees) and the ex-Supreme's first No 1 for almost 15 years (a record gap at the time)

What: *In the Air Tonight*   **54**
Who: Phil Collins
When: 1981 (2), 1988 (4 – remix)
Which: Was the first solo single from the lead singer of Genesis and out-performed all of the group's hits. A remix did well when used in a Mercury Communications advert

What: *It's Not Unusual*   **55**
Who: Tom Jones
When: 1965 (1), 1987 (17)
Which: Launched the Welsh superstar's career and also features legendary rock guitarist Jimmy Page. The song was only offered to Jones after Sandie Shaw rejected it

What: *The Power of Love*   **56**
Who: Frankie Goes to Hollywood
When: 1984 (1), 1993 (10)
Which: Is their third entry in this Top 100 – equalling The Beatles. It was the band's third release, and their third No 1 – equalling a record set by yet another Liverpool group, Gerry and The Pacemakers

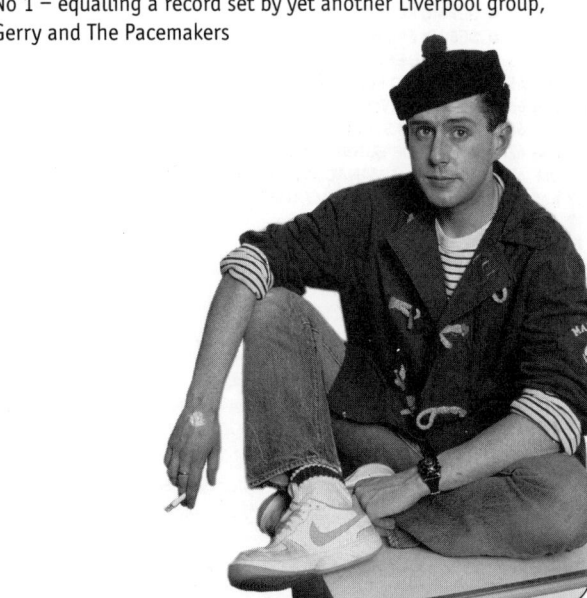

KLAXONS *Belgium, male vocal/instrumental group* **6 wks**

10 Dec 83	THE CLAP CLAP SOUND *PRT 7P 290*	45	6

KLEEER *US, male/female vocal/instrumental group* **10 wks**

17 Mar 79	KEEEP YOUR BODY WORKING *Atlantic LV 21*	51	6
14 Mar 81	GET TOUGH *Atlantic 11560*	49	4

KLESHAY *UK, female vocal trio* **2 wks**

19 Sep 98	REASONS *Epic KLE 1CD*	33	2

KLF ☺ ◐ *UK, male vocal/instrumental duo* **51 wks**

11 Aug 90 ●	WHAT TIME IS LOVE (LIVE AT TRANCENTRAL) *KLF Communications KLF 004* [1]	5	12
19 Jan 91 ★	3 AM ETERNAL *KLF Communications KLF 005* [1]	1	11
4 May 91 ●	LAST TRAIN TO TRANCENTRAL *KLF Communications KLF 008*	2	9
7 Dec 91 ●	JUSTIFIED AND ANCIENT *KLF Communications KLF 099* [2]	2	12
7 Mar 92 ●	AMERICA: WHAT TIME IS LOVE *KLF Communications KLFUSA 004*	4	7

[1] KLF featuring the Children of the Revolution
[2] KLF Guest vocals: Tammy Wynette

See also JUSTIFIED ANCIENTS OF MU MU; TIMELORDS

KLUBBHEADS ☺ *Holland, male instrumental/production duo* **10 wks**

11 May 96 ●	KLUBBHOPPING *AM:PM 5815572*	10	6
16 Aug 97	DISCOHOPPING *AM:PM 5823032*	35	2
15 Aug 98	KICKIN' HARD *Wonderboy WBOYD 011*	36	2

Duo also known as Itty Bitty Boozy Woozy
See also ITTY BITTY BOOZY WOOZY

KNACK ◐ *US, male vocal/instrumental group* **12 wks**

30 Jun 79 ●	MY SHARONA *Capitol CL 16087* ▲	6	10
13 Oct 79	GOOD GIRLS DON'T *Capitol CL 16097*	66	2

Beverley KNIGHT *UK, female vocalist* **11 wks**

8 Apr 95	FLAVOUR OF THE OLD SCHOOL *Dome CDDOME 101*	50	2
2 Sep 95	DOWN FOR THE ONE *Dome CDDOME 102*	55	1
21 Oct 95	FLAVOUR OF THE OLD SCHOOL (re-mix) *Dome CDDOME 105*	33	2
23 Mar 96	MOVING ON UP (ON THE RIGHT SIDE) *Dome CDDOME 107*	42	1
30 May 98	MADE IT BACK *Parlophone CDRHYTHM 11* [1]	21	3
22 Aug 98	REWIND (FIND A WAY) *Parlophone Rhythm CDRhyths 13*	40	2

[1] Beverley Knight featuring Redman

Frederick KNIGHT *US, male vocalist* **10 wks**

10 Jun 72	I'VE BEEN LONELY SO LONG *Stax 2025 098*	22	10

Gladys KNIGHT and the PIPS ✎ *One of soul music's foremost female singers for almost 40 years; b. 28 May, 1944, Georgia. The celebrated vocalist first appeared on US TV aged eight with her family quartet, The Pips. The group was inducted into the Rock and Roll Hall of Fame in 1996* **187 wks**

8 Jun 67	TAKE ME IN YOUR ARMS AND LOVE ME *Tamla Motown TMG 604*	13	15
27 Dec 67	I HEARD IT THROUGH THE GRAPEVINE *Tamla Motown TMG 629*	47	1
17 Jun 72	JUST WALK IN MY SHOES *Tamla Motown TMG 813*	35	8
25 Nov 72	HELP ME MAKE IT THROUGH THE NIGHT *Tamla Motown TMG 830*	11	17
3 Mar 73	LOOK OF LOVE *Tamla Motown TMG 844*	21	9
26 May 73	NEITHER ONE OF US *Tamla Motown TMG 855*	31	7
5 Apr 75 ●	THE WAY WE WERE – TRY TO REMEMBER *Buddah BDS 428*	4	15
2 Aug 75 ●	BEST THING THAT EVER HAPPENED TO ME *Buddah BDS 432*	7	10
15 Nov 75	PART TIME LOVE *Buddah BDS 438*	30	5
8 May 76 ●	MIDNIGHT TRAIN TO GEORGIA *Buddah BDS 444* ▲	10	9
21 Aug 76	MAKE YOURS A HAPPY HOME *Buddah BDS 447*	35	4
6 Nov 76	SO SAD THE SONG *Buddah BDS 448*	20	9
15 Jan 77	NOBODY BUT YOU *Buddah BDS 451*	34	2
28 May 77 ●	BABY DON'T CHANGE YOUR MIND *Buddah BDS 458*	4	12
24 Sep 77	HOME IS WHERE THE HEART IS *Buddah BDS 460*	35	4
8 Apr 78	THE ONE AND ONLY *Buddah BDS 470*	32	4
13 May 78	THE ONE AND ONLY (re-entry) *Buddah BDS 470*	66	1
24 Jun 78	COME BACK AND FINISH WHAT YOU STARTED *Buddah BDS 473*	15	13
30 Sep 78	IT'S A BETTER THAN GOOD TIME *Buddah BDS 478*	59	4
30 Aug 80	TASTE OF BITTER LOVE *CBS 8890*	35	6
8 Nov 80	BOURGIE BOURGIE *CBS 9081*	32	6
26 Dec 81	WHEN A CHILD IS BORN *CBS S 1758* [1]	74	2
9 Nov 85	THAT'S WHAT FRIENDS ARE FOR *Arista ARIST 638* [2]	16	9
16 Jan 88	LOVE OVERBOARD *MCA MCA 1223*	42	4
10 Jun 89 ●	LICENCE TO KILL *MCA MCA 1339* [3]	6	11

[1] Johnny Mathis and Gladys Knight [2] Dionne Warwick and Friends featuring Elton John, Stevie Wonder and Gladys Knight [3] Gladys Knight

Robert KNIGHT ✎ *US, male vocalist* **26 wks**

17 Jan 68	EVERLASTING LOVE *Monument MON 1008*	40	2
24 Nov 73 ●	LOVE ON A MOUNTAIN TOP *Monument MNT 1875*	10	16
9 Mar 74	EVERLASTING LOVE (re-issue) *Monument MNT 2106*	19	8

Mark KNOPFLER *UK, male vocalist/instrumentalist – guitar* **7 wks**

12 Mar 83	GOING HOME (THEME OF 'LOCAL HERO') *Vertigo DSTR 4*	56	3
16 Mar 96	DARLING PRETTY *Vertigo VERCD 88*	33	2
25 May 96	CANNIBALS *Vertigo VERCD 89*	42	2

KNOWLEDGE *Italy, male production duo* **1 wk**

8 Nov 97	AS (UNTIL THE DAY) *ffrr FCD 312*	70	1

Buddy KNOX *US, male vocalist* **5 wks**

10 May 57	PARTY DOLL *Columbia DB 3914* ▲	29	3
16 Aug 62	SHE'S GONE *Liberty LIB 55473*	45	2

Frankie KNUCKLES ☺ *US, male producer* **19 wks**

17 Jun 89	TEARS *ffrr F 108* [1]	50	3
21 Oct 89	YOUR LOVE *Trax TRAXT 3*	59	4
27 Jul 91	THE WHISTLE SONG *Virgin America VUS 47*	17	5
23 Nov 91	IT'S HARD SOMETIMES *Virgin America VUS 52*	67	1
6 Jun 92	RAIN FALLS *Virgin America VUST 60* [2]	48	2
27 May 95	TOO MANY FISH *Virgin America VUSCD 89* [3]	34	2
18 Nov 95	WHADDA U WANT (FROM ME) *Virgin America VUSCD 98* [3]	36	2

[1] Frankie Knuckles presents Satoshi Tomiie [2] Frankie Knuckles featuring Lisa Michaelis [3] Frankie Knuckles featuring Adeva

Moe KOFFMAN QUARTETTE
Canada, male instrumental group, Moe Koffman – flute **2 wks**

28 Mar 58	SWINGIN' SHEPHERD BLUES *London HLJ 8549*	23	2

Mike KOGLIN ☺ *Germany, male producer* **2 wks**

28 Nov 98	THE SILENCE *Multiply CDMULTY 44*	20	2

KOKOMO *US, male instrumentalist – piano* **7 wks**

13 Apr 61	ASIA MINOR *London HLU 9305*	35	7

KOKOMO *UK, male/female vocal/instrumental group* **3 wks**

29 May 82	A LITTLE BIT FURTHER AWAY *CBS A 2064*	45	3

KON KAN ◐ ☺ *Canada, male vocal/instrumental duo* **13 wks**

4 Mar 89 ●	I BEG YOUR PARDON *Atlantic A 8969*	5	13

John KONGOS ◉
South Africa, male vocalist/multi-instrumentalist   25 wks

22 May 71 ●	HE'S GONNA STEP ON YOU AGAIN *Fly BUG 8*	4	14
20 Nov 71 ●	TOKOLOSHE MAN *Fly BUG 14*	4	11

KOOL and the GANG 🎷 ♀ *One of the most consistently successful R&B acts, hailing from New Jersey and including Robert 'Kool' Bell (b) and James 'JT' Taylor (v). The band spent ten years as top US R&B stars before starting their impressive run of international hits*   207 wks

27 Oct 79 ●	LADIES NIGHT *Mercury KOOL 7*	9	12
19 Jan 80	TOO HOT *Mercury KOOL 8*	23	8
12 Jul 80	HANGIN' OUT *De-Lite KOOL 9*	52	4
1 Nov 80 ●	CELEBRATION *De-Lite KOOL 10* ▲	7	13
21 Feb 81	JONES VS JONES/SUMMER MADNESS *De-Lite KOOL 11*	17	11
30 May 81	TAKE IT TO THE TOP *De-Lite DE 2*	15	9
31 Oct 81	STEPPIN' OUT *De-Lite DE 4*	12	13
19 Dec 81 ●	GET DOWN ON IT *De-Lite DE 5*	3	12
6 Mar 82	TAKE MY HEART (YOU CAN HAVE IT IF YOU WANT IT) *De-Lite DE 6*	29	7
7 Aug 82	BIG FUN *De-Lite DE 7*	14	8
16 Oct 82 ●	OOH LA LA LA (LET'S GO DANCIN') *De-Lite DE 9*	6	9
4 Dec 82	HI DE HI, HI DE HO *De-Lite DE 14*	29	8
10 Dec 83	STRAIGHT AHEAD *De-Lite DE 15*	15	10
11 Feb 84 ●	JOANNA/TONIGHT *De-Lite DE 16*	2	11
14 Apr 84 ●	(WHEN YOU SAY YOU LOVE SOMEBODY) IN THE HEART *De-Lite DE 17*	7	8
24 Nov 84	FRESH *De-Lite DE 18*	11	12
9 Feb 85	MISLED *De-Lite DE 19*	28	5
11 May 85 ●	CHERISH *De-Lite DE 20*	4	22
2 Nov 85	EMERGENCY *De-Lite DE 21*	50	3
22 Nov 86	VICTORY *Club JAB 44*	67	2
20 Dec 86	VICTORY (re-entry) *Club JAB 44*	30	10
21 Mar 87	STONE LOVE *Club JAB 47*	45	4
31 Dec 88	CELEBRATION (re-mix) *Club JAB 78*	56	5
6 Jul 91	GET DOWN ON IT (re-mix) *Mercury MER 346*	69	1

'Funky Stuff' and 'Hollywood Swinging' only appeared on 12-inch and EP versions of 'Kool 11', although the chart listed all four songs

KOOLROCK STEADY – See TYREE

KOON + STEPHENSON – See WESTBAM

KORGIS ◉ *UK, male vocal/instrumental duo*   27 wks

23 Jun 79	IF I HAD YOU *Rialto TREB 103*	13	12
24 May 80 ●	EVERYBODY'S GOT TO LOVE SOMETIME *Rialto TREB 115*	5	12
30 Aug 80	IF IT'S ALRIGHT WITH YOU BABY *Rialto TREB 118*	56	3

KORN *US, male vocal/instrumental group*   8 wks

19 Oct 96	NO PLACE TO HIDE *Epic 6638452*	26	2
15 Feb 97	A.D.I.D.A.S. *Epic 6642042*	22	2
7 Jun 97	GOOD GOD *Epic 6646585*	25	2
22 Aug 98	GOT THE LIFE *Epic 6663912*	23	2

KP and ENVYI R&B ☺ *US, female vocal/rap duo*   4 wks

13 Jun 98	SWING MY WAY *East West E 3849 CD*	14	4

KRAFTWERK ☺ ⚓ *Germany, male instrumental/vocal group*   69 wks

10 May 75	AUTOBAHN *Vertigo 6147 012*	11	9
28 Oct 78	NEON LIGHTS *Capitol CL 15998*	53	3
9 May 81	POCKET CALCULATOR *EMI 5175*	39	6
11 Jul 81	COMPUTER LOVE/THE MODEL *EMI 5207*	36	8
26 Dec 81 ★	COMPUTER LOVE/THE MODEL (re-entry) *EMI 5207*	1	13
20 Feb 82	SHOWROOM DUMMIES *EMI 5272*	25	5
6 Aug 83	TOUR DE FRANCE *EMI 5413*	22	8
25 Aug 84	TOUR DE FRANCE (re-entry) *EMI 5413*	24	11
1 Jun 91	THE ROBOTS *EMI EM 192*	20	4
2 Nov 91	RADIOACTIVITY *EMI EM 201*	43	2

Billy J KRAMER and the DAKOTAS ◉
UK, male vocalist and male instrumental backing group   71 wks

2 May 63 ●	DO YOU WANT TO KNOW A SECRET? *Parlophone R 5023*	2	15
1 Aug 63 ★	BAD TO ME *Parlophone R 5049*	1	14
7 Nov 63 ●	I'LL KEEP YOU SATISFIED *Parlophone R 5073*	4	13
27 Feb 64 ●	LITTLE CHILDREN *Parlophone R 5105*	1	13
23 Jul 64	FROM A WINDOW *Parlophone R 5156*	10	8
20 May 65	TRAINS AND BOATS AND PLANES *Parlophone R 5285*	12	8

KRANKIES *UK, male/female vocal duo*   6 wks

7 Feb 81	FAN'DABI'DOZI *Monarch MON 21*	71	1
7 Mar 81	FAN'DABI'DOZI (re-entry) *Monarch MON 21*	46	5

Lenny KRAVITZ 🎸 ◉ R&B *US, male vocalist*   55 wks

2 Jun 90	MR. CABDRIVER *Virgin America VUS 20*	58	2
4 Aug 90	LET LOVE RULE *Virgin America VUS 26*	39	4
30 Mar 91	ALWAYS ON THE RUN *Virgin America VUS 34*	41	3
15 Jun 91	IT AIN'T OVER TIL IT'S OVER *Virgin America VUS 43*	11	8
14 Sep 91	STAND BY MY WOMAN *Virgin America VUS 45*	55	3
20 Feb 93 ●	ARE YOU GONNA GO MY WAY *Virgin America VUSDG 65*	4	11
22 May 93	BELIEVE *Virgin America VUSCD 72*	30	5
28 Aug 93	HEAVEN HELP *Virgin America VUSDG 73*	20	7
4 Dec 93	IS THERE ANY LOVE IN YOUR HEART *Virgin America VUSDG 76*	52	2
9 Sep 95	ROCK AND ROLL IS DEAD *Virgin America VUSCD 93*	22	3
23 Dec 95	CIRCUS *Virgin America VUSCD 96*	54	2
2 Mar 96	CAN'T GET YOU OFF MY MIND *Virgin America VUSCD 100*	54	2
16 May 98	IF YOU CAN'T SAY NO *Virgin America VUSCD 130*	48	2
10 Oct 98	I BELONG TO YOU *Virgin VUSCD 138*	75	1

KRAZE *US, male/female vocal/instrumental group*   6 wks

22 Oct 88	THE PARTY *MCA MCA 1288*	29	5
17 Jun 89	LET'S PLAY HOUSE *MCA MCA 1337*	71	1

KREUZ *UK, male vocal group*   1 wk

8 Jul 95	PARTY ALL NIGHT *Diesel DES 004C*	75	1

KREW-KATS *UK, male instrumental group*   10 wks

9 Mar 61	TRAMBONE *HMV POP 840*	33	9
18 May 61	TRAMBONE (re-entry) *HMV POP 840*	49	1

KRIS KROSS ◀ *US, male rap duo*   22 wks

30 May 92 ●	JUMP *Ruff House 6578547* ▲	2	8
25 Jul 92	WARM IT UP *Ruff House 6582187*	16	6
17 Oct 92	I MISSED THE BUS *Ruff House 6583927*	57	1
19 Dec 92	IT'S A SHAME *Ruff House 6588587*	31	5
11 Sep 93	ALRIGHT *Ruff House 6595652*	47	2

Marty KRISTIAN – See NEW SEEKERS

KROKUS *Switzerland/Argentina, male vocal/instrumental group*   2 wks

16 May 81	INDUSTRIAL STRENGTH EP *Ariola ARO 258*	62	2

Tracks on Industrial Strength EP: Bedside Radio/Easy Rocker/Celebration/Bye Bye Baby

KRS ONE ◀ *US, male rapper*   7 wks

8 Feb 97	WORD PERFECT *Jive JIVECD 418*	70	1
26 Apr 97	STEP INTO A WORLD (RAPTURE'S DELIGHT) *Jive JIVECD 411*	24	2
20 Sep 97	HEARTBEAT/A FRIEND *Jive JIVECD 431*	66	1
1 Nov 97	DIGITAL *ffrr FCD 316* [1]	13	3

[1] Goldie featuring KRS One

KRUSH ☺ ❷ *UK, male/female vocal/instrumental group*   **16 wks**

5 Dec 87	●	HOUSE ARREST *Club JAB 63*	3	15
14 Nov 92		WALKING ON SUNSHINE *Network NWK 55*	71	1

KRUSH PERSPECTIVE *US, female vocal group*   **2 wks**

16 Jan 93	LET'S GET TOGETHER (SO GROOVY NOW)		
	Perspective PERD 7416	61	2

K7 ❷ R&B *US, male vocal/rap group*   **22 wks**

11 Dec 93	●	COME BABY COME *Big Life BLRD 105*	3	16
2 Apr 94		HI DE HO *Big Life BLRD 108* [1]	17	5
25 Jun 94		ZUNGA ZENG *Big Life BLRD 111* [1]	63	1

[1] K7 and the Swing Kids

K3M *Italy, male/female vocal/instrumental duo*   **1 wk**

21 Mar 92	LISTEN TO THE RHYTHM *PWL Continental PWL 214*	71	1

KULA SHAKER ✍ *UK, male vocal/instrumental group*   **41 wks**

4 May 96		GRATEFUL WHEN YOU'RE DEAD – JERRY WAS THERE		
		Columbia KULACD 2	35	3
6 Jul 96	●	TATTVA *Columbia KULACD 3*	4	8
7 Sep 96	●	HEY DUDE *Columbia KULACD 4*	2	7
23 Nov 96	●	GOVINDA *Columbia KULACD 5*	7	8
8 Mar 97	●	HUSH *Columbia KULACD 6*	2	8
9 Aug 97		HUSH (re-entry) *Columbia KULACD 6*	70	1
2 May 98	●	SOUND OF DRUMS *Columbia KULA 21CD*	3	6

KULAY *Philippines, male/female vocal group*   **1 wk**

12 Sep 98	DELICIOUS *INCcredible INCRL 4CD*	73	1

Charlie KUNZ ℂ *US, male instrumentalist – piano*   **4 wks**

17 Dec 54	PIANO MEDLEY NO. 114 *Decca F 10419*	20	3
14 Jan 55	PIANO MEDLEY NO. 114 (re-entry) *Decca F 10419*	16	1

Medley titles: There Must Be a Reason / Hold My Hand / If I Give My Heart to You /
Little Things Mean a Lot / Make Her Mine / My Son My Son

KURSAAL FLYERS ❷ *UK, male vocal/instrumental group*   **10 wks**

20 Nov 76	LITTLE DOES SHE KNOW *CBS 4689*	14	10

KUT KLOSE *US, female vocal group*   **1 wk**

29 Apr 95	I LIKE *Elektra EKR 200CD*	72	1

Li KWAN *UK, male producer – Joey Negro*   **2 wks**

17 Dec 94	I NEED A MAN *Deconstruction 74321252192*	51	2

See also Joey NEGRO

KWS ❷ ☺ *UK, male vocal/instrumental group*   **36 wks**

25 Apr 92	★	PLEASE DON'T GO/GAME BOY *Network NWK 46*	1	16
22 Aug 92	●	ROCK YOUR BABY *Network NWK 54*	8	7
12 Dec 92		HOLD BACK THE NIGHT *Network NWK 65* [1]	30	5
5 Jun 93		CAN'T GET ENOUGH OF YOUR LOVE *Network NWKCD 72*	71	1
9 Apr 94		IT SEEMS TO HANG ON *X-clusive XCLU 006CD*	58	1
2 Jul 94		AIN'T NOBODY (LOVES ME BETTER)		
		X-clusive XCLU 010CD	21	4
19 Nov 94		THE MORE I GET THE MORE I WANT		
		X-clusive XCLU 011CD [3]	35	2

[1] KWS features guest vocal from the Trammps [2] KWS and Gwen Dickey
[3] KWS featuring Teddy Pendergrass

'Game Boy' was only listed from 9 May, 1992

KY-MANI – *see PM DAWN*

KYO – *See BEDROCK featuring KYO*

Jonny L *UK, male vocalist*   **2 wks**

28 Aug 93	OOH I LIKE IT *XL XLS 44CD*	73	1
31 Oct 98	20 DEGREES *XL Recordings XLS 103CD* [1]	66	1

[1] Jonny L featuring Silvah Bullet

LA GANZ *US, male vocal/instrumental group*   **1 wk**

9 Nov 96	LIKE A PLAYA *Jive JIVECD 405*	75	1

L.A. GUNS *US, male/female vocal/instrumental group*   **4 wks**

30 Nov 91	SOME LIE 4 LOVE *Mercury MER 358*	61	1
21 Dec 91	THE BALLAD OF JAYNE *Mercury MER 361*	53	3

L.A. MIX ☺ *UK, male/female vocal/instrumental duo*   **25 wks**

10 Oct 87		DON'T STOP (JAMMIN') *Breakout USA 615*	47	4
21 May 88	●	CHECK THIS OUT *Breakout USA 629*	6	7
8 Jul 89		GET LOOSE *Breakout USA 659* [1]	25	6
16 Sep 89		LOVE TOGETHER *Breakout USA 662* [2]	66	2
15 Sep 90		COMING BACK FOR MORE *A & M AM 579*	50	3
19 Jan 91		MYSTERIES OF LOVE *A & M AM 707*	46	2
23 Mar 91		WE SHOULDN'T HOLD HANDS IN THE DARK		
		A & M AM 755	69	1

[1] L.A. Mix performed by Jazzi P [2] L.A. Mix featuring Kevin Henry

LA NA NEE NEE NOO NOO – *See BANANARAMA*

Danny LA RUE *UK, male vocalist*   **9 wks**

18 Dec 68	ON MOTHER KELLY'S DOORSTEP *Page One POF 108*	33	9

Denise LA SALLE ✍ *US, female vocalist*   **13 wks**

15 Jun 85	●	MY TOOT TOOT *Epic A 6334*	6	13

LA TREC – *See SASH!*

LaBELLE ◢ ✍ *US, female vocal group*   **9 wks**

22 Mar 75	LADY MARMALADE		
	(VOULEZ-VOUS COUCHER AVEC MOI CE SOIR?)		
	Epic EPC 2852 ▲	17	9

See also Patti LaBELLE

Patti LaBELLE ✍ *US, female vocalist*   **21 wks**

3 May 86	●	ON MY OWN *MCA MCA 1045* [1] ▲	2	13
2 Aug 86		OH, PEOPLE *MCA MCA 1075*	26	6
3 Sep 94		THE RIGHT KINDA LOVER *MCA MCSTD 1995*	50	2

[1] Patti LaBelle and Michael McDonald

See also LaBELLE

LADIES CHOICE *UK, male vocal/instrumental group*   **4 wks**

25 Jan 86	FUNKY SENSATION *Sure Delight SD 01*	41	4

LADY J – *See RAZE*

LADY OF RAGE *US, female rapper*   **1 wk**

8 Oct 94	AFRO PUFFS *Interscope A 8288CD*	72	1

UK No 1 ★   UK Top 10 ●   UK million seller ◆   UK entry at No 1 ■   US No 1 ▲

LADYSMITH BLACK MAMBAZO ☺ ◉
South Africa, male vocal group   **15 wks**

3 Jun 95	SWING LOW SWEET CHARIOT *PolyGram TV SWLOW 2* [1]	15	6
3 Jun 95	WORLD IN UNION '95 *PolyGram TV RUGBY 2* [2]	47	5
15 Nov 97	INKANYEZI NEZAZI (THE STAR & THE WISEMAN) *A & M 5823892*	33	3
11 Jul 98	THE STAR AND THE WISEMAN *AM:PM 5825692*	63	1

[1] Ladysmith Black Mambazo featuring China Black [2] Ladysmith Black Mambazo featuring PJ Powers

LAGUNA *Italy, male DJ / production duo*   **2 wks**

1 Nov 97	SPILLER FROM RIO (DO IT EASY) *Positiva CDTIV 83*	40	2

LAID BACK *Norway, male vocal/instrumental duo*   **4 wks**

5 May 90	BAKERMAN *Arista 112356*	44	4

Cleo LAINE Ⓒ *UK, female vocalist*   **14 wks**

29 Dec 60	LET'S SLIP AWAY *Fontana H 269*	42	1
14 Sep 61 ●	YOU'LL ANSWER TO ME *Fontana H 326*	5	13

Frankie LAINE Ⓒ *Powerful-voiced No 1 hitmaker of the pre-rock years, b. Frank Lovecchio, 30 March, 1913, Chicago. He spent an unequalled 27 weeks at the top of the UK chart in 1953, and at one time had three singles in the Top 5*   **281 wks**

14 Nov 52 ●	HIGH NOON *Columbia DB 3113*	7	7
14 Nov 52 ●	SUGARBUSH *Columbia DB 3123* [1]	8	2
5 Dec 52 ●	SUGARBUSH (re-entry) *Columbia DB 3123* [1]	8	6
20 Mar 53	GIRL IN THE WOOD *Columbia DB 2907*	11	1
3 Apr 53 ★	I BELIEVE *Philips PB 117*	1	36
8 May 53 ●	TELL ME A STORY *Philips PB 126* [2]	5	15
4 Sep 53 ●	WHERE THE WINDS BLOW *Philips PB 167*	2	12
11 Sep 53	TELL ME A STORY (re-entry) *Philips PB 126* [2]	12	1
16 Oct 53 ●	HEY JOE *Philips PB 172*	1	8
30 Oct 53 ★	ANSWER ME *Philips PB 196*	1	17
8 Jan 54 ●	BLOWING WILD *Philips PB 207*	2	12
26 Mar 54 ●	GRANADA *Philips PB 242*	10	1
9 Apr 54 ●	GRANADA (re-entry) *Philips PB 242*	9	1
16 Apr 54 ●	THE KID'S LAST FIGHT *Philips PB 258*	3	10
13 Aug 54 ●	MY FRIEND *Philips PB 316*	3	15
8 Oct 54 ●	THERE MUST BE A REASON *Philips PB 306*	9	9
22 Oct 54 ●	RAIN RAIN RAIN *Philips PB 311* [3]	8	16
11 Mar 55	IN THE BEGINNING *Philips PB 404*	20	1
24 Jun 55 ●	COOL WATER *Philips PB 465*	2	22
15 Jul 55 ●	STRANGE LADY IN TOWN *Philips PB 478*	6	13
11 Nov 55	HUMMING BIRD *Philips PB 498*	16	1
25 Nov 55 ●	HAWKEYE *Philips PB 519*	7	8
20 Jan 56 ●	SIXTEEN TONS *Philips PB 539*	10	3
4 May 56	HELL HATH NO FURY *Philips PB 585*	28	1
7 Sep 56 ★	A WOMAN IN LOVE *Philips PB 617*	1	21
28 Dec 56	MOONLIGHT GAMBLER *Philips PB 638*	13	12
29 Mar 57	MOONLIGHT GAMBLER (re-entry) *Philips PB 638*	28	1
26 Apr 57	LOVE IS A GOLDEN RING *Philips PB 676*	19	5
4 Oct 57	GOOD EVENING FRIENDS/UP ABOVE MY HEAD I HEAR MUSIC IN THE AIR *Philips PB 708* [4]	25	4
13 Nov 59 ●	RAWHIDE *Philips PB 965*	6	17
31 Mar 60	RAWHIDE (re-entry) *Philips PB 965*	41	2
11 May 61	GUNSLINGER *Philips PB 1135*	50	1

[1] Doris Day and Frankie Laine [2] Frankie Laine and Jimmy Boyd
[3] Frankie Laine and the Four Lads [4] Frankie Laine and Johnnie Ray

Greg LAKE ◉ *UK, male vocalist*   **12 wks**

6 Dec 75 ●	I BELIEVE IN FATHER CHRISTMAS *Manticore K 13511*	2	7
25 Dec 82	I BELIEVE IN FATHER CHRISTMAS (re-entry) *Manticore K 13511*	72	3
24 Dec 83	I BELIEVE IN FATHER CHRISTMAS (2nd re-entry) *Manticore K 13511*	65	2

See also EMERSON, LAKE and PALMER

LAMB *UK, male/female vocal/production duo*   **2 wks**

29 Mar 97	GORECKI *Fontana LAMCD 4*	30	2

Annabel LAMB *UK, female vocalist*   **7 wks**

27 Aug 83	RIDERS ON THE STORM *A & M AM 131*	27	7

LAMBRETTAS ◉ *UK, male vocal/instrumental group*   **24 wks**

1 Mar 80 ●	POISON IVY *Rocket XPRESS 25*	7	12
24 May 80	D-A-A-ANCE *Rocket XPRESS 33*	12	8
23 Aug 80	ANOTHER DAY (ANOTHER GIRL) *Rocket XPRESS 36*	49	4

LANCASTRIANS *UK, male vocal/instrumental group*   **2 wks**

24 Dec 64	WE'LL SING IN THE SUNSHINE *Pye 7N 15732*	47	2

Major LANCE *US, male vocalist*   **2 wks**

13 Feb 64	UM UM UM UM UM UM *Columbia DB 7205*	40	2

Valerie LANDSBERG – See KIDS FROM FAME

LANDSCAPE ◉ ◢ *UK, male vocal/instrumental group*   **20 wks**

28 Feb 81 ●	EINSTEIN A GO-GO *RCA 22*	5	13
23 May 81	NORMAN BATES *RCA 60*	40	7

Desmond LANE – See Alma COGAN; Cyril STAPLETON

Ronnie LANE and SLIM CHANCE ✎ ♫
UK, male vocalist and male instrumental group   **12 wks**

12 Jan 74	HOW COME *GM GMS 011*	11	8
15 Jun 74	THE POACHER *GM GMS 024*	36	4

Don LANG ◉ *UK, male vocalist*   **18 wks**

4 Nov 55	CLOUDBURST *HMV POP 115*	16	2
2 Dec 55	CLOUDBURST (re-entry) *HMV POP 115*	18	1
13 Jan 56	CLOUDBURST (2nd re-entry) *HMV POP 115*	20	1
5 Jul 57	SCHOOL DAY *HMV POP 350* [1]	26	2
23 May 58 ●	WITCH DOCTOR *HMV POP 488* [1]	5	11
10 Mar 60	SINK THE BISMARCK *HMV POP 714*	43	1

[1] Don Lang and his Frantic Five

kd lang ◉ ✈ *Canada, female vocalist*   **25 wks**

16 May 92	CONSTANT CRAVING *Sire W 0100*	52	4
22 Aug 92	CRYING *Virgin America VUS 63* [1]	13	6
27 Feb 93	CONSTANT CRAVING (re-issue) *Sire W 0157CD*	15	8
1 May 93	THE MIND OF LOVE *Sire W 0170CD1*	72	1
26 Jun 93	MISS CHATELAINE *Sire W 0181CDX*	68	2
11 Dec 93	JUST KEEP ME MOVING *Sire W 0227CD*	59	1
30 Sep 95	IF I WERE YOU *Sire W 0319CD*	53	1
18 May 96	YOU'RE OK *Warner Bros. W 0332CD*	44	2

[1] Roy Orbison (duet with kd lang)

Thomas LANG *UK, male vocalist*   **3 wks**

30 Jan 88	THE HAPPY MAN *Epic VOW 4*	67	3

Mario LANZA Ⓒ *US, male vocalist*   **32 wks**

14 Nov 52 ●	BECAUSE YOU'RE MINE *HMV DA 2017*	3	24
4 Feb 55	DRINKING SONG *HMV DA 2065*	13	1
18 Feb 55	I'LL WALK WITH GOD *HMV DA 2062*	18	1
22 Apr 55	SERENADE *HMV DA 2065*	19	1
6 May 55	I'LL WALK WITH GOD (re-entry) *HMV DA 2062*	20	1
6 May 55	SERENADE (re-entry) *HMV DA 2065*	15	2
14 Sep 56	SERENADE *HMV DA 2085*	25	1
12 Oct 56	SERENADE (re-entry) *HMV DA 2085*	29	1

DA 2065 and DA 2085 are two different songs

Julius LAROSA Ⓒ *US, male vocalist*   **9 wks**

4 Jul 58	TORERO *RCA 1063*	15	9

LA's ☹ ◐ *UK, male vocal/instrumental group* — 19 wks

Date	Title	Pos	Wks
14 Jan 89	THERE SHE GOES *Go! Discs GOLAS 2*	59	4
15 Sep 90	TIMELESS MELODY *Go! Discs GOLAS 4*	57	2
3 Nov 90	THERE SHE GOES (re-issue) *Go! Discs GOLAS 5*	13	9
16 Feb 91	FEELIN' *Go! Discs GOLAS 6*	43	3
10 May 97	FEVER PITCH THE EP *Blancy Y Negro NEG 104CD* [1]	65	1

[1] Pretenders: La's: Orlando: Nick Hornby

James LAST BAND *Germany, male orchestra* — 4 wks

Date	Title	Pos	Wks
3 May 80	THE SEDUCTION (LOVE THEME) *Polydor PD 2071*	48	4

LAST RHYTHM *Italy, male instrumental/production group* — 1 wk

Date	Title	Pos	Wks
14 Sep 96	LAST RHYTHM *Stress CDSTR 76*	62	1

LATE SHOW *UK, male vocal/instrumental group* — 6 wks

Date	Title	Pos	Wks
3 Mar 79	BRISTOL STOMP *Decca F 13822*	40	6

LATIN QUARTER ◐
UK, male/female vocal/instrumental group — 10 wks

Date	Title	Pos	Wks
18 Jan 86	RADIO AFRICA *Rockin' Horse RH 102*	19	9
18 Apr 87	NOMZAMO (ONE PEOPLE ONE CAUSE) *Rockin' Horse RH 113*	73	1

LATIN RHYTHM – See Tito PUENTE JR and the LATIN RHYTHM featuring Tito PUENTE, INDIA and Cali ALEMAN

LATIN THING
Canada/Spain, male/female vocal/instrumental group — 1 wk

Date	Title	Pos	Wks
13 Jul 96	LATIN THING *Faze 2 CDFAZE 33*	41	1

Gino LATINO ☺ *Italy, male producer* — 7 wks

Date	Title	Pos	Wks
20 Jan 90	WELCOME *ffrr F 126*	17	7

LATINO RAVE – See VARIOUS ARTISTS (MONTAGES)

LATOUR ☺ *US, male vocalist/producer* — 7 wks

Date	Title	Pos	Wks
8 Jun 91	PEOPLE ARE STILL HAVING SEX *Polydor PO 147*	15	7

Stacy LATTISAW ✎ *US, female vocalist* — 14 wks

Date	Title	Pos	Wks
14 Jun 80	● JUMP TO THE BEAT *Atlantic/Cotillion K 11496*	3	11
30 Aug 80	DYNAMITE *Atlantic K 11554*	51	3

Dave LAUDAT – See HUSTLERS CONVENTION featuring Dave LAUDAT and Ondrea DUVERN

LAUNCHERS – See Ezz RECO and the LAUNCHERS with Boysie GRANT

Cyndi LAUPER ◐ *Flamboyant and versatile singer/songwriter, b. 20 June, 1953, New York. Her debut album,* She's So Unusual *(1983), spawned four Top 5 US singles, and she won Grammy for Best New Artist of 1984 (easily outpacing her major female rival, Madonna)* — 103 wks

Date	Title	Pos	Wks
14 Jan 84	● GIRLS JUST WANT TO HAVE FUN *Portrait A 3943*	2	12
24 Mar 84	TIME AFTER TIME *Portrait A 4290* ▲	54	4
16 Jun 84	● TIME AFTER TIME (re-entry) *Portrait A 4290*	3	13
1 Sep 84	SHE BOP *Portrait A 4620*	46	5
17 Nov 84	ALL THROUGH THE NIGHT *Portrait A 4849*	64	2
20 Sep 86	TRUE COLOURS *Portrait 650026 7* ▲	12	11
27 Dec 86	CHANGE OF HEART *Portrait CYNDI 1*	74	1
10 Jan 87	CHANGE OF HEART (re-entry) *Portrait CYNDI 1*	67	1
28 Mar 87	WHAT'S GOING ON *Portrait CYN 1*	57	3
20 May 89	● I DROVE ALL NIGHT *Epic CYN 4*	7	12
5 Aug 89	MY FIRST NIGHT WITHOUT YOU *Epic CYN 5*	53	4
30 Dec 89	HEADING WEST *Epic CYN 6*	68	1
6 Jun 92	THE WORLD IS STONE *Epic 6579707*	15	7
13 Nov 93	THAT'S WHAT I THINK *Epic 6598782*	31	4
8 Jan 94	WHO LET IN THE RAIN *Epic 6590392*	32	4
17 Sep 94	● HEY NOW (GIRLS JUST WANT TO HAVE FUN) *Epic 6608072*	4	13
11 Feb 95	I'M GONNA BE STRONG *Epic 6611962*	37	2
26 Aug 95	COME ON HOME *Epic 6614255*	39	2
1 Feb 97	YOU DON'T KNOW *Epic 6641845*	27	2

'Hey Now (Girls Just Want to Have Fun)' is a re-recording of her first hit

LAUREL and HARDY ℭ *UK, male vocal/instrumental duo* — 2 wks

Date	Title	Pos	Wks
2 Apr 83	CLUNK CLINK *CBS A 3213*	65	2

LAUREL and HARDY with the AVALON BOYS featuring Chill WILLS
UK/US, male vocal duo with US, male vocal group — 10 wks

Date	Title	Pos	Wks
22 Nov 75	● THE TRAIL OF THE LONESOME PINE *United Artists UP 36026*	2	10

LAURNEA *US, female vocalist* — 1 wk

Date	Title	Pos	Wks
12 Jul 97	DAYS OF YOUTH *Epic 6646932*	36	1

Joanna LAW ☺ *UK, female vocalist* — 8 wks

Date	Title	Pos	Wks
7 Jul 90	FIRST TIME EVER *Citybeat CBE 752*	67	3
14 Sep 96	THE GIFT *Deconstruction 74321401912* [1]	15	5

[1] Way Out West featuring Miss Joanna Law

Joanna's contribution to 'The Gift' is a sample from 'First Time Ever'

Joey LAWRENCE ◐ *US, male vocalist* — 15 wks

Date	Title	Pos	Wks
26 Jun 93	NOTHIN' MY LOVE CAN'T FIX *EMI CDEM 271*	13	7
28 Aug 93	I CAN'T HELP MYSELF *EMI CDEM 277*	24	4
30 Oct 93	STAY FOREVER *EMI CDEM 289*	41	3
19 Sep 98	NEVER GONNA CHANGE MY MIND *Curb CUBC 34*	49	1

Lee LAWRENCE ℭ *UK, male vocalist* — 10 wks

Date	Title	Pos	Wks
20 Nov 53	CRYING IN THE CHAPEL *Decca F 10177*	11	1
11 Dec 53	● CRYING IN THE CHAPEL (re-entry) *Decca F 10177*	7	5
2 Dec 55	SUDDENLY THERE'S A VALLEY *Columbia DB 3681*	19	1
16 Dec 55	SUDDENLY THERE'S A VALLEY (re-entry) *Columbia DB 3681*	14	3

Sophie LAWRENCE *UK, female vocalist* — 7 wks

Date	Title	Pos	Wks
3 Aug 91	LOVE'S UNKIND *IQ ZB 44821*	21	7

Steve LAWRENCE ℭ *US, male vocalist* — 27 wks

Date	Title	Pos	Wks
21 Apr 60	● FOOTSTEPS *HMV POP 726*	4	13
18 Aug 60	GIRLS GIRLS GIRLS *London HLT 9166*	49	1
22 Aug 63	● I WANT TO STAY HERE *CBS AAG 163* [1]	3	13

[1] Steve and Eydie

Lindy LAYTON *UK, female vocalist* — 15 wks

Date	Title	Pos	Wks
11 Aug 90	SILLY GAMES *Arista 113452* [1]	22	7
26 Jan 91	ECHO MY HEART *Arista 113845*	42	2
31 Aug 91	WITHOUT YOU (ONE AND ONE) *Arista 114636*	71	2
24 Apr 93	WE GOT THE LOVE *PWL International PWCD 250*	38	3
30 Oct 93	SHOW ME *PWL International PWCD 275*	47	1

[1] Lindy Layton featuring Janet Kay

See also BEATS INTERNATIONAL

Doug LAZY *US, male rapper* — 9 wks

Date	Title	Pos	Wks
15 Jul 89	LET IT ROLL *Atlantic A 8866* [1]	27	5
4 Nov 89	LET THE RHYTHM PUMP *Atlantic A 8784*	45	3
26 May 90	LET THE RHYTHM PUMP (re-mix) *East West A 7919*	63	1

[1] Raze presents Doug Lazy

LCD ◐ ☺ *UK, male production group* — 5 wks

Date	Title	Pos	Wks
27 Jun 98	ZORBA'S DANCE *Virgin VSCDT 1693*	20	5

Keith LE BLANC – See Malcolm X

UK No 1 ★ UK Top 10 ● UK million seller ◆ UK entry at No 1 ■ US No 1 ▲

LE CLICK *Sweden / US, male / female vocal duo* **2 wks**

| 30 Aug 97 | CALL ME *Logic 74321509672* | 38 | 2 |

Kele LE ROC [R&B] *UK, female vocalist* **7 wks**

| 31 Oct 98 ● | LITTLE BIT OF LOVIN' *1st Avenue 5672812* | 8 | 7 |

Vicky LEANDROS ℂ *Greece, female vocalist* **29 wks**

8 Apr 72 ●	COME WHAT MAY *Philips 6000 049*	2	16
23 Dec 72	THE LOVE IN YOUR EYES *Philips 6000 081*	48	3
20 Jan 73	THE LOVE IN YOUR EYES (re-entry) *Philips 6000 081*	40	4
7 Apr 73	THE LOVE IN YOUR EYES (2nd re-entry) *Philips 6000 081*	46	1
7 Jul 73	WHEN BOUZOUKIS PLAYED *Philips 6000 111*	44	2
28 Jul 73	WHEN BOUZOUKIS PLAYED (re-entry) *Philips 6000 111*	45	3

Denis LEARY *US, male vocalist* **2 wks**

| 13 Jan 96 | ASSHOLE *A & M 5813352* | 58 | 2 |

LED ZEPPELIN *UK, male vocal/instrumental group* **2 wks**

| 13 Sep 97 | WHOLE LOTTA LOVE *Atlantic ATT00 13CD* | 21 | 2 |

See also Robert PLANT

Brenda LEE ◐ *Biggest-selling teenage female vocalist of the early rock years; b. Brenda Tarpley, 11 December, 1944, Georgia. 'Little Miss Dynamite', who first recorded aged 11, had back-to-back UK/US hits in the early 1960s. She was inducted into the Country Music Hall of Fame in 1997* **210 wks**

17 Mar 60	SWEET NOTHIN'S *Brunswick 05819*	45	1
7 Apr 60 ●	SWEET NOTHIN'S (re-entry) *Brunswick 05819*	4	18
30 Jun 60	I'M SORRY *Brunswick 05833* ▲	12	16
20 Oct 60	I WANT TO BE WANTED *Brunswick 05839* ▲	31	6
19 Jan 61	LET'S JUMP THE BROOMSTICK *Brunswick 05823*	12	15
6 Apr 61	EMOTIONS *Brunswick 05847*	45	1
20 Jul 61	DUM DUM *Brunswick 05854*	22	8
16 Nov 61	FOOL NUMBER ONE *Brunswick 05860*	38	3
8 Feb 62	BREAK IT TO ME GENTLY *Brunswick 05864*	46	2
5 Apr 62	SPEAK TO ME PRETTY *Brunswick 05867*	3	12
21 Jun 62	HERE COMES THAT FEELING *Brunswick 05871*	5	12
13 Sep 62	IT STARTED ALL OVER AGAIN *Brunswick 05876*	15	11
29 Nov 62 ●	ROCKIN' AROUND THE CHRISTMAS TREE *Brunswick 05880*	6	7
17 Jan 63 ●	ALL ALONE AM I *Brunswick 05882*	7	17
28 Mar 63	LOSING YOU *Brunswick 05886*	10	16
18 Jul 63	I WONDER *Brunswick 05891*	14	9
31 Oct 63	SWEET IMPOSSIBLE YOU *Brunswick 05896*	28	6
9 Jan 64 ●	AS USUAL *Brunswick 05899*	5	15
9 Apr 64	THINK *Brunswick 05903*	26	8
10 Sep 64	IS IT TRUE *Brunswick 05915*	17	8
10 Dec 64	CHRISTMAS WILL BE JUST ANOTHER LONELY DAY *Brunswick 05921*	29	5
4 Feb 65	THANKS A LOT *Brunswick 05927*	41	2
29 Jul 65	TOO MANY RIVERS *Brunswick 05936*	22	12

Byron LEE – *See Boris GARDINER*

Curtis LEE *US, male vocalist* **2 wks**

| 31 Aug 61 | PRETTY LITTLE ANGEL EYES *London HLX 9397* | 47 | 1 |
| 14 Sep 61 | PRETTY LITTLE ANGEL EYES (re-entry) *London HLX 9397* | 48 | 1 |

D C LEE ◐ ♪ *UK, female vocalist* **20 wks**

9 Nov 85 ●	SEE THE DAY *CBS A 6570*	3	12
8 Mar 86	COME HELL OR WATERS HIGH *CBS A 6869*	46	5
13 Nov 93	NO TIME TO PLAY *Cooltempo CDCOOL 282* [1]	25	3

[1] Guru featuring D C Lee

Garry LEE and SHOWDOWN
Canada, male vocal/instrumental group **3 wks**

| 31 Jul 93 | THE RODEO SONG *Party Dish VCD 101* | 44 | 3 |

Jackie LEE ℂ *UK, female vocalist* **31 wks**

| 10 Apr 68 ● | WHITE HORSES *Philips BF 1674* [1] | 10 | 14 |
| 2 Jan 71 | RUPERT *Pye 7N 45003* | 14 | 17 |

[1] Jacky

Leapy LEE ◐ *UK, male vocalist* **28 wks**

21 Aug 68 ●	LITTLE ARROWS *MCA MU 1028*	2	21
20 Dec 69	GOOD MORNING *MCA MK 5021*	47	1
10 Jan 70	GOOD MORNING (re-entry) *MCA MK 5021*	29	6

Peggy LEE ℂ *US, female vocalist* **29 wks**

24 May 57 ●	MR. WONDERFUL *Brunswick 05671*	5	13
15 Aug 58 ●	FEVER *Capitol CL 14902*	5	11
23 Mar 61	TILL THERE WAS YOU *Capitol CL 15184*	40	1
6 Apr 61	TILL THERE WAS YOU (re-entry) *Capitol CL 15184*	30	3
22 Aug 92	FEVER (re-issue) *Capitol PEG 1*	75	1

Toney LEE *US, male vocalist* **4 wks**

| 29 Jan 83 | REACH UP *TMT TMT 2* | 64 | 4 |

Tracey LEE *US, male vocalist* **1 wk**

| 19 Jul 97 | THE THEME *Universal UND 56133* | 51 | 1 |

LEEDS UNITED FC ◐ *UK, male football team vocalists* **13 wks**

29 Apr 72 ●	LEEDS UNITED *Chapter One SCH 168*	10	10
25 Apr 92	LEEDS LEEDS LEEDS *Q Music LUFC 2*	61	1
9 May 92	LEEDS LEEDS LEEDS (re-entry) *Q Music LUFC 2*	54	2

Carol LEEMING – *See STAXX*

Raymond LEFEVRE *France, orchestra* **2 wks**

| 15 May 68 | SOUL COAXING *Major Minor MM 559* | 46 | 2 |

LEFTFIELD ☺ *UK, male instrumental/production duo* **15 wks**

12 Dec 92	SONG OF LIFE *Hard Hands HAND 002T*	59	1
13 Nov 93	OPEN UP *Hard Hands HAND 009CD* [1]	13	5
25 Mar 95	ORIGINAL *Hard Hands HAND 18CD* [2]	18	3
5 Aug 95	THE AFRO-LEFT EP *Hard Hands HAND 23CD* [3]	22	3
20 Jan 96	RELEASE THE PRESSURE *Hard Hands HAND 29CD*	13	3

[1] Leftfield Lydon [2] Leftfield Halliday [3] Leftfield featuring Djum Djum

Tracks on The Afro-Left (EP): Afro-Left / Afro Ride / Afro Central / Afro Sol

LEGEND B *Germany, male production* **1 wk**

| 22 Feb 97 | LOST IN LOVE *Perfecto PERF 132CD* | 45 | 1 |

Paul LEKAKIS *US, male vocalist* **4 wks**

| 30 May 87 | BOOM BOOM (LET'S GO BACK TO MY ROOM) *Champion CHAMP 43* | 60 | 4 |

LEMON PIPERS ◐ *US, male vocal/instrumental group* **16 wks**

| 7 Feb 68 ● | GREEN TAMBOURINE *Pye International 7N 25444* ▲ | 7 | 11 |
| 1 May 68 | RICE IS NICE *Pye International 7N 25454* | 41 | 5 |

LEMON TREES *UK, male vocal/instrumental group* **9 wks**

26 Sep 92	LOVE IS IN YOUR EYES *Oxygen GASP 1*	75	1
7 Nov 92	THE WAY I FEEL *Oxygen GASP 2*	62	2
13 Feb 93	LET IT LOOSE *Oxygen GASPD 3*	55	2
17 Apr 93	CHILD OF LOVE *Oxygen GASPD 4*	55	3
3 Jul 93	I CAN'T FACE THE WORLD *Oxygen GASPD 6*	52	1

LEMONHEADS ☹
US/Australia, male vocal/instrumental group **26 wks**

17 Oct 92	IT'S A SHAME ABOUT RAY *Atlantic A 7423*	70	1
5 Dec 92	MRS ROBINSON/BEIN' AROUND *Atlantic A 7401*	19	9
6 Feb 93	CONFETTI/MY DRUG BUDDY *Atlantic A 7430CD*	44	2

10 Apr 93	IT'S A SHAME ABOUT RAY (re-issue) *Atlantic A 5764CD*	31	3
16 Oct 93	INTO YOUR ARMS *Atlantic A 7302CD*	14	4
27 Nov 93	IT'S ABOUT TIME *Atlantic A 7296CD*	57	2
14 May 94	BIG GAY HEART *Atlantic A 7259CD*	55	2
28 Sep 96	IF I COULD TALK I'D TELL YOU *Atlantic A 5495CD*	39	2
14 Dec 96	IT'S ALL TRUE *Atlantic A 5635CD*	61	1

LENA – *See Lena FIAGBE*

John LENNON ◎ *One of the century's greatest musical talents, b. 9 October, 1990, Liverpool, d. 8 December, 1980. World-famous singer/songwriter who, together with Paul McCartney, fronted The Beatles and penned their hits. Three of his singles topped the UK chart in the two months after his murder in New York* **184 wks**

9 Jul 69 ●	GIVE PEACE A CHANCE *Apple 13* [1]	2	13
1 Nov 69	COLD TURKEY *Apple APPLES 1001* [1]	14	8
21 Feb 70 ●	INSTANT KARMA *Apple APPLES 1003* [2]	5	9
20 Mar 71 ●	POWER TO THE PEOPLE *Apple R 5892* [3]	7	9
9 Dec 72 ●	HAPPY XMAS (WAR IS OVER) *Apple R 5970* [4]	4	8
24 Nov 73	MIND GAMES *Apple R 5994*	26	9
19 Oct 74	WHATEVER GETS YOU THROUGH THE NIGHT *Apple R 5998* [5] ▲	36	4
4 Jan 75	HAPPY XMAS (WAR IS OVER) (re-entry) *Apple R 5970* [4]	48	1
8 Feb 75	NUMBER 9 DREAM *Apple R 6003*	23	8
3 May 75	STAND BY ME *Apple R 6005*	30	7
1 Nov 75 ●	IMAGINE *Apple R 6009* ◆	6	11
8 Nov 80 ★	(JUST LIKE) STARTING OVER *Geffen K 79186* ▲	1	15
20 Dec 80 ●	HAPPY XMAS (WAR IS OVER) (2nd re-entry) *Apple R 5970* [4]	2	9
27 Dec 80 ★	IMAGINE (re-entry) *Apple R 6009*	1	13
24 Jan 81 ★	WOMAN *Geffen K 79195*	1	11
24 Jan 81	GIVE PEACE A CHANCE (re-entry) *Apple 13*	33	5
21 Mar 81	I SAW HER STANDING THERE *DJM DJS 10965* [6]	40	4
4 Apr 81	WATCHING THE WHEELS *Geffen K 79207*	30	6
19 Dec 81	HAPPY XMAS (WAR IS OVER) (3rd re-entry) *Apple R 5970* [4]	28	5
20 Nov 82	LOVE *Parlophone R 6059*	41	7
25 Dec 82	HAPPY XMAS (WAR IS OVER) (4th re-entry) *Apple R 5970* [4]	56	3
21 Jan 84 ●	NOBODY TOLD ME *Ono Music/Polydor POSP 700*	6	6
17 Mar 84	BORROWED TIME *Polydor POSP 701*	32	6
30 Nov 85	JEALOUS GUY *Parlophone R 6117*	65	2
10 Dec 88	IMAGINE / JEALOUS GUY / HAPPY XMAS (WAR IS OVER) (re-issue) *Parlophone R 6199*	45	5

[1] Plastic Ono Band [2] Lennon, Ono and the Plastic Ono Band [3] The Elton John Band featuring Lennon and the Muscle Shoals Horns [4] John and Yoko and the Plastic Ono Band with the Harlem Community Choir [5] John Lennon with the Plastic Ono Nuclear Band [6] The Elton John Band featuring John Lennon and the Muscle Shoals Horns

Julian LENNON ◎ *UK, male vocalist* **47 wks**

6 Oct 84 ●	TOO LATE FOR GOODBYES *Charisma JL 1*	6	11
15 Dec 84	VALOTTE *Charisma JL 2*	55	6
9 Mar 85	SAY YOU'RE WRONG *Charisma JL 3*	75	1
7 Dec 85	BECAUSE *EMI 5538*	40	7
11 Mar 89	NOW YOU'RE IN HEAVEN *Virgin VS 1154*	59	3
24 Aug 91 ●	SALTWATER *Virgin VS 1361*	6	13
30 Nov 91	HELP YOURSELF *Virgin VS 1379*	53	2
25 Apr 92	GET A LIFE *Virgin VS 1398*	56	3
23 May 98	DAY AFTER DAY *Music From Another JULIAN 4CD*	66	1

Annie LENNOX ◎ *UK, female vocalist* **68 wks**

3 Dec 88	PUT A LITTLE LOVE IN YOUR HEART *A & M AM 484* [1]	28	8
28 Mar 92 ●	WHY *RCA PB 45317*	5	8
6 Jun 92	PRECIOUS *RCA 74321100257*	23	5
22 Aug 92 ●	WALKING ON BROKEN GLASS *RCA 74321107227*	8	8
31 Oct 92	COLD *RCA 74321116902*	26	4
13 Feb 93 ●	LITTLE BIRD / LOVE SONG FOR A VAMPIRE *RCA 743211233832*	3	12
18 Feb 95 ●	NO MORE 'I LOVE YOU'S *RCA 74321257162*	2	12
10 Jun 95	A WHITER SHADE OF PALE *RCA 74321284822*	16	6
30 Sep 95	WAITING IN VAIN *RCA 74321316132*	31	3
9 Dec 95	SOMETHING SO RIGHT *RCA 74321332392* [2]	44	2

[1] Annie Lennox and Al Green [2] Annie Lennox featuring Paul Simon

Rula LENSKA – *See Julie COVINGTON, Rula LENSKA, Charlotte CORNWELL and Sue JONES-DAVIES*

Phillip LEO *UK, male vocalist* **3 wks**

23 Jul 94	SECOND CHANCE *EMI CDEM 327*	57	2
25 Mar 95	THINKING ABOUT YOUR LOVE *EMI CDEM 358*	64	1

LES RYTHMES DIGITALES
France, male DJ / production project – Jacques Le Cont **1 wk**

25 Apr 98	MUSIC MAKES YOU LOSE CONTROL *Wall Of Sound WALLD 037*	69	1

LeSHAUN – *See LL Cool J*

LESTER – *See Norman COOK*

Ketty LESTER ℭ *US, female vocalist* **16 wks**

19 Apr 62 ●	LOVE LETTERS *London HLN 9527*	4	12
19 Jul 62	BUT NOT FOR ME *London HLN 9574*	45	4

LET LOOSE ◎ *UK, male vocal/instrumental group* **62 wks**

24 Apr 93	CRAZY FOR YOU *Vertigo VERCD 74*	44	3
9 Apr 94	SEVENTEEN *Mercury MERCD 400*	44	2
25 Jun 94 ●	CRAZY FOR YOU (re-issue) *Mercury MERCD 402*	2	20
22 Oct 94	SEVENTEEN (re-mix) *Mercury MERCD 406*	11	6
24 Dec 94	CRAZY FOR YOU (re-entry of re-issue) *Mercury MERCD 402*	46	4
7 Jan 95	SEVENTEEN (re-entry of re-mix) *Mercury MERCD 406*	47	3
28 Jan 95	ONE NIGHT STAND *Mercury MERCD 419*	12	6
29 Apr 95 ●	BEST IN ME *Mercury MERCD 428*	8	5
4 Nov 95	EVERYBODY SAY EVERYBODY DO *Mercury MERCD 446*	29	3
13 Jan 96	EVERYBODY SAY EVERYBODY DO (re-entry) *Mercury MERCD 446*	71	1
22 Jun 96 ●	MAKE IT WITH YOU *Mercury MERCD 464*	7	6
7 Sep 96	TAKE IT EASY *Mercury MERCD 472*	25	2
16 Nov 96	DARLING BE HOME SOON *Mercury MERCD 475*	65	1

Gerald LETHAN – *See WALL OF SOUND featuring Gerald LETHAN*

LETTERMEN *US, male vocal group* **3 wks**

23 Nov 61	THE WAY YOU LOOK TONIGHT *Capitol CL 15222*	36	3

LEVEL 42 ◢ ◎ *Critically acclaimed Manchester band: Mark King (v, b), Boon Gould (g), Mike Lindup (k/v), Phil Gould (d). Boasting a world-class bass player in King, they went from Brit-funk cult heroes to international stardom* **177 wks**

30 Aug 80	LOVE MEETING LOVE *Polydor POSP 170*	61	4
18 Apr 81	LOVE GAMES *Polydor POSP 234*	38	6
8 Aug 81	TURN IT ON *Polydor POSP 286*	57	6
14 Nov 81	STARCHILD *Polydor POSP 343*	47	4
8 May 82	ARE YOU HEARING (WHAT I HEAR)? *Polydor POSP 396*	49	5
2 Oct 82	WEAVE YOUR SPELL *Polydor POSP 500*	43	4
15 Jan 83	THE CHINESE WAY *Polydor POSP 538*	24	8
16 Apr 83	OUT OF SIGHT, OUT OF MIND *Polydor POSP 570*	41	4
30 Jul 83 ●	THE SUN GOES DOWN (LIVING IT UP) *Polydor POSP 622*	10	12
22 Oct 83	MICRO KID *Polydor POSP 643*	37	5
1 Sep 84	HOT WATER *Polydor POSP 697*	18	9
3 Nov 84	THE CHANT HAS BEGUN *Polydor POSP 710*	41	5
21 Sep 85	SOMETHING ABOUT YOU *Polydor POSP 759*	6	17
7 Dec 85	LEAVING ME NOW *Polydor POSP 776*	15	11
26 Apr 86 ●	LESSONS IN LOVE *Polydor POSP 790*	3	13
14 Feb 87 ●	RUNNING IN THE FAMILY *Polydor POSP 842*	6	10
25 Apr 87 ●	TO BE WITH YOU AGAIN *Polydor POSP 855*	10	7
12 Sep 87 ●	IT'S OVER *Polydor POSP 900*	10	8
12 Dec 87	CHILDREN SAY *Polydor POSP 911*	22	6
3 Sep 88	HEAVEN IN MY HANDS *Polydor PO 14*	12	5
29 Oct 88	TAKE A LOOK *Polydor PO 24*	32	4

UK No 1 ★ UK Top 10 ● UK million seller ◆ UK entry at No 1 ■ US No 1 ▲

21 Jan 89	TRACIE Polydor PO 34	25	5
28 Oct 89	TAKE CARE OF YOURSELF Polydor PO 58	39	3
17 Aug 91	GUARANTEED RCA PB 44745	17	4
19 Oct 91	OVERTIME RCA PB 44997	62	2
18 Apr 92	MY FATHER'S SHOES RCA PB 45271	55	1
26 Feb 94	FOREVER NOW RCA 74321190272	19	4
30 Apr 94	ALL OVER YOU RCA 74321205662	26	2
6 Aug 94	LOVE IN A PEACEFUL WORLD RCA 74321220332	31	3

LEVELLERS ☺ ♂ UK, male vocal/instrumental group — 53 wks

21 Sep 91	ONE WAY China WOK 2008	51	2
7 Dec 91	FAR FROM HOME China WOK 2010	71	1
23 May 92	15 YEARS EP China WOKX 2020	11	5
10 Jul 93	BELARUSE China WOKCD 2034	12	5
30 Oct 93	THIS GARDEN China WOKCD 2039	12	4
14 May 94	JULIE EP China WOKCD 2042	17	3
12 Aug 95	HOPE ST. China WOKCD 2059	12	5
14 Oct 95	FANTASY China WOKCD 2067	16	3
23 Dec 95	JUST THE ONE China WOKCD 2076 [1]	12	8
20 Jul 96	EXODUS – LIVE China WOKCD 2082	24	2
9 Aug 97	WHAT A BEAUTIFUL DAY China WOKCD 2088	13	5
18 Oct 97	CELEBRATE China WOKCD 2089	28	2
20 Dec 97	DOG TRAIN China WOKCD 2090	24	5
14 Mar 98	TOO REAL China WOKCD 2091	46	1
24 Oct 98	BOZOS China WOKCD 2096	44	2

[1] Levellers, special guest Joe Strummer

Tracks on 15 Years (EP): 15 Years / Dance Before the Storm / The River Flow (Live) / Plastic Jeezus. Tracks on Julie (EP): Julie / English Civil War / Lowlands of Holland / 100 Years

LEVERT [R&B] US, male vocal group — 10 wks

22 Aug 87	● CASANOVA Atlantic A 9217	9	10

See also LEVERT SWEAT GILL

LEVERT SWEAT GILL US, male production trio — 7 wks

14 Mar 98	MY BODY East West E 3857CD	21	3
6 Jun 98	CURIOUS East West E 3842CD	23	2
12 Sep 98	DOOR #1 East West E 3817CD	45	2

See also LEVERT

Hank LEVINE US, orchestra — 4 wks

21 Dec 61	IMAGE HMV POP 947	45	4

LEVITICUS UK, male vocalist — 1 wk

25 Mar 95	BURIAL ffrr FCD 255	66	1

Barrington LEVY ♈ Jamaica, male vocalist — 11 wks

2 Feb 85	HERE I COME London LON 62	41	4
15 Jun 91	TRIBAL BASE Desire WANT 44 [1]	20	6
24 Sep 94	WORK MCA MCSTD 2003	65	1

[1] Rebel MC featuring Tenor Fly and Barrington Levy

Jona LEWIE ✪ UK, male vocalist — 20 wks

10 May 80	YOU'LL ALWAYS FIND ME IN THE KITCHEN AT PARTIES Stiff BUY 73	16	9
29 Nov 80	● STOP THE CAVALRY Stiff BUY 104	3	11

On some copies first title was simply 'Kitchen at Parties'
See also Terry DACTYL and the DINOSAURS

CJ LEWIS ♈ UK, male vocalist — 32 wks

23 Apr 94	● SWEETS FOR MY SWEET Black Market BMITD 017	3	13
23 Jul 94	● EVERYTHING IS ALRIGHT (UPTIGHT) Black Market BMITD 019	10	7
8 Oct 94	BEST OF MY LOVE Black Market BMITD 021	13	6
17 Dec 94	DOLLARS Black Market BMITD 023	34	4
9 Sep 95	R TO THE A Black Market BMITD 030	34	2

Danny J LEWIS UK, male producer — 2 wks

20 Jun 98	SPEND THE NIGHT Locked On LOX 98CD	29	2

Darlene LEWIS ☺ US, female vocalist — 4 wks

16 Apr 94	LET THE MUSIC (LIFT YOU UP) KMS/Eastern Bloc KMSCD 10	16	4

All formats of 'Let the Music Lift You Up' featured versions by Loveland featuring Rachel McFarlane and also by Darlene Lewis

Dee LEWIS UK, female vocalist — 5 wks

18 Jun 88	BEST OF MY LOVE Mercury DEE 3	47	5

Donna LEWIS ✪ UK, female vocalist — 16 wks

7 Sep 96	● I LOVE YOU ALWAYS FOREVER Atlantic A 5495CD	5	14
8 Feb 97	WITHOUT LOVE Atlantic A 5468CD	39	2

Gary LEWIS and the PLAYBOYS
US, male vocal/instrumental group — 7 wks

8 Feb 75	MY HEART'S SYMPHONY United Artists UP 35780	36	7

Huey LEWIS and the NEWS ✪ ♪
US, male vocal/instrumental group — 66 wks

27 Oct 84	IF THIS IS IT Chrysalis CHS 2829	39	6
31 Aug 85	THE POWER OF LOVE Chrysalis HUEY 1 ▲	11	10
23 Nov 85	HEART AND SOUL EP Chrysalis HUEY 2	61	4
8 Feb 86	● THE POWER OF LOVE (RE-ISSUE) / DO YOU BELIEVE IN LOVE (re-issue) Chrysalis HUEY 3	9	12
10 May 86	THE HEART OF ROCK AND ROLL Chrysalis HUEY 4	49	3
23 Aug 86	STUCK WITH YOU Chrysalis HUEY 5 ▲	12	12
6 Dec 86	HIP TO BE SQUARE Chrysalis HUEY 6	41	8
21 Mar 87	SIMPLE AS THAT Chrysalis HUEY 7	47	5
16 Jul 88	PERFECT WORLD Chrysalis HUEY 10	48	6

Tracks on Heart and Soul EP: Heart and Soul / Hope You Love Me Like You Say You Do / Heart of Rock and Roll / Buzz Buzz Buzz. 'Do You Believe in Love' only listed from 15 Feb, 1986

Jerry LEWIS ☾ US, male vocalist — 8 wks

8 Feb 57	ROCK-A-BYE YOUR BABY (WITH A DIXIE MELODY) Brunswick 05636	12	7
5 Apr 57	ROCK-A-BYE YOUR BABY (WITH A DIXIE MELODY) (re-entry) Brunswick 05636	22	1

Jerry Lee LEWIS ♪ US, male vocalist/instrumentalist – piano — 68 wks

27 Sep 57	● WHOLE LOTTA SHAKIN' GOIN' ON London HLS 8457	8	10
20 Dec 57	★ GREAT BALLS OF FIRE London HLS 8529	1	12
27 Dec 57	WHOLE LOTTA SHAKIN' GOIN' ON (re-entry) London HLS 8457	26	1
11 Apr 58	● BREATHLESS London HLS 8592	8	7
23 Jan 59	HIGH SCHOOL CONFIDENTIAL London HLS 8780	12	6
1 May 59	LOVIN' UP A STORM London HLS 8840	28	2
9 Jun 60	BABY BABY BYE BYE London HLS 9131	47	1
4 May 61	● WHAT'D I SAY London HLS 9335	10	12
3 Aug 61	WHAT'D I SAY (re-entry) London HLS 9335	49	2
6 Sep 62	SWEET LITTLE SIXTEEN London HLS 9584	38	5
14 Mar 63	GOOD GOLLY MISS MOLLY London HLS 9688	31	6
6 May 72	CHANTILLY LACE Mercury 6052 141	33	5

Linda LEWIS ♪ ✪ UK, female vocalist — 30 wks

2 Jun 73	ROCK-A-DOODLE-DOO Raft RA 18502	15	11
12 Jul 75	● IT'S IN HIS KISS Arista 17	6	8
17 Apr 76	BABY I'M YOURS Arista 43	33	6
2 Jun 79	I'D BE SURPRISINGLY GOOD FOR YOU Ariola ARO 166	40	5

Ramsey LEWIS US, male instrumentalist – piano — 8 wks

15 Apr 72	WADE IN THE WATER Chess 6145 004	31	8

Shirley LEWIS – See Arthur BAKER

John LEYTON ⓞ *UK, male vocalist* — 70 wks

3 Aug 61 ★	JOHNNY REMEMBER ME *Top Rank JAR 577*	1	15
5 Oct 61 ●	WILD WIND *Top Rank JAR 585*	2	10
28 Dec 61	SON THIS IS SHE *HMV POP 956*	15	10
15 Mar 62	LONE RIDER *HMV POP 992*	40	5
3 May 62	LONELY CITY *HMV POP 1014*	14	11
23 Aug 62	DOWN THE RIVER NILE *HMV POP 1054*	42	3
21 Feb 63	CUPBOARD LOVE *HMV POP 1122*	22	12
18 Jul 63	I'LL CUT YOUR TAIL OFF *HMV POP 1175*	50	1
8 Aug 63	I'LL CUT YOUR TAIL OFF (re-entry) *HMV POP 1175*	36	2
20 Feb 64	MAKE LOVE TO ME *HMV POP 1264*	49	1

LEYTON BUZZARDS *UK, male vocal/instrumental group* — 5 wks

3 Mar 79	SATURDAY NIGHT (BENEATH THE PLASTIC PALM TREES) *Chrysalis CHS 2288*	53	5

LFO ☺ *UK, male instrumental group* — 15 wks

14 Jul 90	LFO *Warp WAP 5*	12	10
6 Jul 91	WE ARE BACK/NURTURE *Warp 7WAP 14*	47	3
1 Feb 92	WHAT IS HOUSE EP *Warp WAP 17*	62	2

Tracks on What Is House (EP): *Tan Ta Ra / Mashed Potato / What Is House / Syndrome*

LIBERACE Ⓒ *US, male instrumentalist – piano* — 2 wks

17 Jun 55	UNCHAINED MELODY *Philips PB 430*	20	1
19 Oct 56	I DON'T CARE *Columbia DB 3834*	28	1

'I Don't Care' featured Liberace as vocalist too

LIBERATION *UK, male instrumental/production duo* — 3 wks

24 Oct 92	LIBERATION *ZYX ZYX 68657*	28	3

LIBIDO *Norway, male vocal/instrumental group* — 1 wk

31 Jan 98	OVERTHROWN *Fire BLAZE 119CD*	53	1

LIBRA presents TAYLOR *UK, male vocal/instrumental group* — 1 wk

26 Oct 96	ANOMALY – CALLING YOUR NAME *Platipus PLATCD 24*	71	1

LICK THE TINS *UK, male/female vocal/instrumental group* — 8 wks

29 Mar 86	CAN'T HELP FALLING IN LOVE *Sedition EDIT 3308*	42	8

Ben LIEBRAND *Holland, male producer/multi-instrumentalist* — 2 wks

9 Jun 90	PULS(T)AR *Epic LIEB 1*	68	2

LIEUTENANT PIGEON ⓞ *UK, male/female instrumental group* — 29 wks

16 Sep 72 ★	MOULDY OLD DOUGH *Decca F 13278*	1	19
16 Dec 72	DESPERATE DAN *Decca F 13365*	17	10

LIGHT OF THE WORLD *UK, male vocal/instrumental group* — 25 wks

14 Apr 79	SWINGIN' *Ensign ENY 22*	45	5
14 Jul 79	MIDNIGHT GROOVIN' *Ensign ENY 29*	72	1
18 Oct 80	LONDON TOWN *Ensign ENY 43*	41	5
17 Jan 81	I SHOT THE SHERIFF *Ensign ENY 46*	40	5
28 Mar 81	I'M SO HAPPY / TIME *Ensign MER 64*	35	6
21 Nov 81	RIDE THE LOVE TRAIN *EMI 5242*	49	3

LIGHTER SHADE OF BROWN *US, male vocal duo* — 3 wks

9 Jul 94	HEY DJ *Mercury MERCD 401*	33	3

Gordon LIGHTFOOT *Canada, male vocalist* — 26 wks

19 Jun 71	IF YOU COULD READ MY MIND *Reprise RS 20974*	30	9
3 Aug 74	SUNDOWN *Reprise K 14327* ▲	33	7
15 Jan 77	THE WRECK OF THE EDMUND FITZGERALD *Reprise K 14451*	40	4
16 Sep 78	DAYLIGHT KATY *Warner Bros. K 17214*	41	6

Terry LIGHTFOOT and his NEW ORLEANS JAZZMEN

UK, vocalist/instrumentalist – clarinet – and male jazz band — 17 wks

7 Sep 61	TRUE LOVE *Columbia DB 4696*	33	4
23 Nov 61	KING KONG *Columbia SCD 2165*	29	12
3 May 62	TAVERN IN THE TOWN *Columbia DB 4822*	49	1

LIGHTHOUSE FAMILY ⓞ 🎤 *UK, male vocal/instrumental duo* — 69 wks

27 May 95	LIFTED *Wild Card CARDW 17*	61	2
14 Oct 95	OCEAN DRIVE *Wild Card 5797072*	34	3
10 Feb 96 ●	LIFTED (re-issue) *Wild Card 5779432*	4	10
1 Jun 96	OCEAN DRIVE (re-issue) *Wild Card 5766192*	11	8
21 Sep 96	GOODBYE HEARTBREAK *Wild Card 5753492*	14	6
21 Dec 96	LOVING EVERY MINUTE *Wild Card 5731012*	20	6
11 Oct 97 ●	RAINCLOUD *Wild Card 5717932*	6	7
10 Jan 98 ●	HIGH *Polydor 5691492*	4	14
27 Jul 98 ●	LOST IN SPACE *Polydor 5670592*	6	8
10 Oct 98	QUESTION OF FAITH *Wild Card 5673932*	21	5

LIGHTNING SEEDS ⓞ *UK, male vocal/instrumental group* — 93 wks

22 Jul 89	PURE *Ghetto GTG 4*	16	8
14 Mar 92	THE LIFE OF RILEY *Virgin VS 1402*	28	6
30 May 92	SENSE *Virgin VS 1414*	31	5
20 Aug 94	LUCKY YOU *Epic 6606282*	42	2
14 Jan 95	CHANGE *Epic 6609865*	13	6
15 Apr 95	MARVELLOUS *Epic 6614265*	24	5
22 Jul 95	PERFECT *Epic 6621792*	18	5
21 Oct 95	LUCKY YOU (re-issue) *Epic 6625182*	15	6
9 Mar 96	READY OR NOT *Epic 6629672*	20	4
1 Jun 96 ★	THREE LIONS (THE OFFICIAL SONG OF THE ENGLAND FOOTBALL TEAM) *Epic 6632732* [1] ■	1	15
2 Nov 96	WHAT IF... *Epic 6638635*	14	3
11 Jan 97	WHAT IF ... (re-entry) *Epic 6638635*	64	1
18 Jan 97	SUGAR COATED ICEBERG *Epic 6640432*	12	4
26 Apr 97 ●	YOU SHOWED ME *Epic 6643282*	8	5
13 Dec 97	WHAT YOU SAY *Epic 6653572*	41	5
20 Jun 98 ★	3 LIONS '98 *Epic 6660982* [1] ■	1	13

[1] Baddiel and Skinner and the Lightning Seeds

LIL' KIM ◀ (R&B) *US, female vocalist* — 14 wks

26 Apr 97	NO TIME *Atlantic A 5594CD* [1]	45	1
5 Jul 97	CRUSH ON YOU *Atlantic AT 0002CD*	36	5
16 Aug 97	NOT TONIGHT *Atlantic AT 0007CD*	11	5
22 Aug 98	HIT 'EM WIT DA HEE *East West E3824 CD1* [2]	25	3

[1] Lil' Kim featuring Puff Daddy [2] Missy 'Misdemeanor' Elliott featuring Lil' Kim

LIL' LOUIS ☺ *US, male producer* — 18 wks

29 Jul 89 ●	FRENCH KISS *ffrr FX 115*	2	11
13 Jan 90	I CALLED U *ffrr F 123*	16	6
26 Sep 92	SAVED MY LIFE *ffrr FX 197* [1]	74	1

[1] Lil' Louis and the World

See also BLACK MAGIC; LIL' MO' YIN YANG

LIL' MO *US, female vocalist* — 1 wk

21 Nov 98	5 MINUTES *Elektra E 3803CD* [1]	72	1

[1] Lil' Mo featuring Missy 'Misdemeanor' Elliott

LIL MO' YIN YANG *US, male instrumental/production duo* — 2 wks

9 Mar 96	REACH *Multiply CDMULTY 9*	28	2

One half of Lil Mo' Yin Yang is Lil' Louis
See also LIL' LOUIS

LILYS ✍ ⓞ *US, male vocal/instrumental group* — 4 wks

21 Feb 98	A NANNY IN MANHATTAN *Che CHE 77CD*	16	4

LIMAHL ⓞ *UK, male vocalist* — 25 wks

5 Nov 83	ONLY FOR LOVE *EMI LML 1*	16	7

UK No 1 ★   UK Top 10 ●   UK million seller ◆   UK entry at No 1 ■   US No 1 ▲

7 Jan 84	ONLY FOR LOVE (re-entry) *EMI LML 1*	75	1
2 Jun 84	TOO MUCH TROUBLE *EMI LML 2*	64	3
13 Oct 84 ●	NEVER ENDING STORY *EMI LML 3*	4	14

Alison LIMERICK ☺ *UK, female vocalist* — 39 wks

30 Mar 91	WHERE LOVE LIVES *Arista 144208*	27	8
12 Oct 91	COME BACK (FOR REAL LOVE) *Arista 114530*	53	2
21 Dec 91	MAGIC'S BACK (THEME FROM THE GHOSTS OF OXFORD STREET) *RCA PB 45223* [1]	42	4
29 Feb 92	MAKE IT ON MY OWN *Arista 114996*	16	6
18 Jul 92	GETTIN' IT RIGHT *Arista 74321102867*	57	2
28 Nov 92	HEAR MY CALL *Arista 115337*	73	1
8 Jan 94	TIME OF OUR LIVES *Arista 74321180332*	36	4
19 Mar 94	LOVE COME DOWN *Arista 74321191952*	36	2
25 Feb 95	LOVE WILL KEEP US TOGETHER *Acid Jazz JAZID 112CD* [2]	63	1
6 Jul 96 ●	WHERE LOVE LIVES (re-mix) *Arista 74321381592*	9	6
14 Sep 96	MAKE IT ON MY OWN (re-mix) *Arista 74321407812*	30	2
23 Aug 97	PUT YOUR FAITH IN ME *MBA XES 9001*	42	1

[1] Malcolm McLaren featuring Alison Limerick [2] JTQ featuring Alison Limerick

LIMIT ◢ *Holland, male vocal/instrumental duo* — 8 wks

5 Jan 85	SAY YEAH *Portrait A 4808*	17	8

LIMMIE and the FAMILY COOKIN' ♪
US, male/female vocal group — 28 wks

21 Jul 73 ●	YOU CAN DO MAGIC *Avco 6105 019*	3	13
20 Oct 73	DREAMBOAT *Avco 6105 025*	31	5
6 Apr 74 ●	A WALKIN' MIRACLE *Avco 6105 027*	6	10

Bob LIND ♂ ❸ *US, male vocalist* — 10 wks

10 Mar 66 ●	ELUSIVE BUTTERFLY *Fontana TF 670*	5	9
26 May 66	REMEMBER THE RAIN *Fontana TF 702*	46	1

LINDA and the FUNKY BOYS – See Linda CARR

LINDISFARNE ♂ ♪ *UK, male vocal/instrumental group* — 55 wks

26 Feb 72 ●	MEET ME ON THE CORNER *Charisma CB 173*	5	11
13 May 72 ●	LADY ELEANOR *Charisma CB 153*	3	11
23 Sep 72	ALL FALL DOWN *Charisma CB 191*	34	5
3 Jun 78 ●	RUN FOR HOME *Mercury 6007 177*	10	15
7 Oct 78	JUKE BOX GYPSY *Mercury 6007 187*	56	4
10 Nov 90 ●	FOG ON THE TYNE (REVISITED) *Best ZB 44083* [1]	2	9

[1] Gazza and Lindisfarne

LINER *UK, male vocal/instrumental group* — 6 wks

10 Mar 79	KEEP REACHING OUT FOR LOVE *Atlantic K 11235*	49	3
26 May 79	YOU AND ME *Atlantic K 11285*	44	3

Laurie LINGO and the DIPSTICKS ❸
UK, male vocal duo – DJs Dave Lee Travis and Paul Burnett — 7 wks

17 Apr 76 ●	CONVOY G. B. *State STAT 23*	4	7

LINK *US, male rapper* — 1 wk

7 Nov 98	WHATCHA GONE DO? *Relativity 6666055*	48	1

LINOLEUM *UK, male/female vocal/instrumental group* — 1 wk

12 Jul 97	MARQUIS *Lino Vinyl LINO 004CD1*	73	1

LINX ♪ ◢ *UK, male vocal/instrumental duo* — 45 wks

20 Sep 80	YOU'RE LYING *Chrysalis CHS 2461*	15	10
7 Mar 81 ●	INTUITION *Chrysalis CHS 2500*	7	11
13 Jun 81	THROW AWAY THE KEY *Chrysalis CHS 2519*	21	9
5 Sep 81	SO THIS IS ROMANCE *Chrysalis CHS 2546*	15	9
21 Nov 81	CAN'T HELP MYSELF *Chrysalis CHS 2565*	55	3
10 Jul 82	PLAYTHING *Chrysalis CHS 2621*	48	3

LIONROCK ☺ *UK, male producer – Justin Robertson* — 14 wks

5 Dec 92	LIONROCK *Deconstruction 74321124381*	63	1
8 May 93	PACKET OF PEACE *Deconstruction 74321144372*	32	3
23 Oct 93	CARNIVAL *Deconstruction 74321164862*	34	2
27 Aug 94	TRIPWIRE *Deconstruction 74321204702*	44	1
6 Apr 96	STRAIGHT AT YER HEAD *Deconstruction 74321342972*	33	2
27 Jul 96	FIRE UP THE SHOESAW *Deconstruction 74321382652*	43	1
14 Mar 98	RUDE BOY ROCK *Concrete HARD 31CD*	20	3
30 May 98	SCATTER & SWING *Concrete HARD 35CD*	54	1

LIPPS INC. ◢ *US, male/female vocal/instrumental group* — 13 wks

17 May 80 ●	FUNKYTOWN *Casablanca CAN 194* ▲	2	13

LIQUID ☺ *UK, male instrumental/production duo* — 19 wks

21 Mar 92	SWEET HARMONY *XL XLS 28*	15	6
5 Sep 92	THE FUTURE MUSIC EP *XL XLT 33*	59	2
20 Mar 93	TIME TO GET UP *XL XLS 40CD*	46	2
8 Jul 95	SWEET HARMONY/ONE LOVE FAMILY (re-mix) *XL XLS 65CD*	14	6
21 Oct 95	CLOSER *XL XLS 66CD*	47	2
25 Jul 98	STRONG *Higher Ground HIGHS 7CD*	59	1

Tracks on The Future Music EP: *Liquid Is Liquid/Music/House (Is a Feeling)/ The Year 3000*

LIQUID GOLD ❸ ◢ *UK, male/female vocal/instrumental group* — 46 wks

2 Dec 78	ANYWAY YOU DO IT *Creole CR 159*	41	7
23 Feb 80 ●	DANCE YOURSELF DIZZY *Polo POLO 1*	2	14
31 May 80 ●	SUBSTITUTE *Polo POLO 4*	8	9
1 Nov 80	THE NIGHT THE WINE AND THE ROSES *Polo 6*	32	7
28 Mar 81	DON'T PANIC *Polo POLO 8*	42	5
21 Aug 82	WHERE DID WE GO WRONG *Polo POLO 23*	56	4

LIQUID OXYGEN *US, male producer* — 2 wks

28 Apr 90	THE PLANET DANCE (MOVE YA BODY) *Champion CHAMP 242*	56	2

LISA LISA ☺ *US, female vocalist* — 32 wks

4 May 85	I WONDER IF I TAKE YOU HOME *CBS A 6057* [1]	53	6
3 Aug 85	I WONDER IF I TAKE YOU HOME (re-entry) *CBS A 6057* [1]	12	11
31 Oct 87	LOST IN EMOTION *CBS 651036 7* [2] ▲	58	4
13 Jul 91	LET THE BEAT HIT 'EM *Columbia 6572867* [2]	17	6
24 Aug 91	LET THE BEAT HIT 'EM PART 2 *Columbia 6573747* [2]	49	2
26 Mar 94	SKIP TO MY LU *Chrysalis CDCHS 5006*	34	3

[1] Lisa Lisa and Cult Jam with Full Force [2] Lisa Lisa and Cult Jam

LISA MARIE – See Malcolm McLAREN

LISA MARIE EXPERIENCE ☺
UK, male instrumental/production duo — 15 wks

27 Apr 96 ●	KEEP ON JUMPIN' *ffrr FCD 271*	7	10
20 Jul 96	KEEP ON JUMPIN' (re-entry) *ffrr FCD 271*	61	3
10 Aug 96	DO THAT TO ME *Positiva CDTIV 57*	33	2

LITHIAM and Sonya MADAN
US, male producer and UK, female vocalist — 2 wks

1 Mar 97	RIDE A ROCKET *ffrr FCD 293*	40	2

Sonya Madan is lead singer of Echobelly

De Etta LITTLE and Nelson PIGFORD
US, female/male vocal duo — 5 wks

13 Aug 77	YOU TAKE MY HEART AWAY *United Artists UP 36257*	35	5

LITTLE ANGELS ⬈ *UK, male vocal/instrumental group* — 41 wks

4 Mar 89	BIG BAD EP *Polydor LTLEP 2*	74	1
24 Feb 90	KICKING UP DUST *Polydor LTL 5*	46	4
12 May 90	RADICAL YOUR LOVER *Polydor LTL 6* [1]	34	4
4 Aug 90	SHE'S A LITTLE ANGEL *Polydor LTL 7*	21	3

2 Feb 91	BONEYARD *Polydor LTL 8*	33	4
30 Mar 91	PRODUCT OF THE WORKING CLASS *Polydor LTL 9*	40	2
1 Jun 91	YOUNG GODS *Polydor LTL 10*	34	2
20 Jul 91	I AIN'T GONNA CRY *Polydor LTL 11*	26	3
7 Nov 92	TOO MUCH TOO YOUNG *Polydor LTL 12*	22	3
9 Jan 93	WOMANKIND *Polydor LTL CD 13*	12	5
24 Apr 93	SOAPBOX *Polydor LTLCD 14*	33	4
25 Sep 93	SAIL AWAY *Polydor LTLCD 15*	45	3
9 Apr 94	TEN MILES HIGH *Polydor LTLCD 16*	18	3

1 Little Angels featuring the Big Bad Horns

*Tracks on Big Bad EP: She's a Little Angel / Don't Waste My Time /
Better Than the Rest / Sex in Cars
See also VARIOUS ARTISTS (EPs & LPs) – Gimme Shelter (EP)*

LITTLE ANTHONY and the IMPERIALS *US, male vocal group* 4 wks

31 Jul 76	BETTER USE YOUR HEAD *United Artists UP 36141*	42	4

LITTLE BENNY and the MASTERS *US, male rapper / instrumentalist – trumpet – and male instrumental group* 7 wks

2 Feb 85	WHO COMES TO BOOGIE *Bluebird 10 BR 13*	33	7

LITTLE CAESAR *UK, male vocalist* 3 wks

9 Jun 90	THE WHOLE OF THE MOON *A1 EAU 1*	68	3

LITTLE EVA ✪ *US, female vocalist* 45 wks

6 Sep 62 ●	THE LOCO-MOTION *London HL 9581* ▲	2	17
3 Jan 63	KEEP YOUR HANDS OFF MY BABY *London HLU 9633*	30	5
7 Mar 63	LET'S TURKEY TROT *London HLU 9687*	13	12
29 Jul 72	THE LOCO-MOTION (re-entry) *London HL 9581*	11	11

See also BIG DEE IRWIN

LITTLE RICHARD 🎸 *Frantic, no-holds-barred rock'n'roll singer / songwriter and piano-pounder, b. Richard Penniman, 5 December, 1932, Georgia. This legendary performer's wild vocals and unrestrained stage show influenced many later stars. Both The Beatles and the Rolling Stones supported him on tour* 116 wks

14 Dec 56	RIP IT UP *London HLO 8336*	30	1
8 Feb 57 ●	LONG TALL SALLY *London HLO 8366*	3	16
22 Feb 57	TUTTI FRUTTI *London HLO 8366*	29	1
8 Mar 57	SHE'S GOT IT *London HLO 8382*	15	7
15 Mar 57 ●	THE GIRL CAN'T HELP IT *London HLO 8382*	9	11
24 May 57	SHE'S GOT IT (re-entry) *London HLO 8382*	28	2
28 Jun 57 ●	LUCILLE *London HLO 8446*	10	9
13 Sep 57	JENNY JENNY *London HLO 8470*	11	5
29 Nov 57	KEEP A KNOCKIN' *London HLO 8509*	21	7
28 Feb 58 ●	GOOD GOLLY MISS MOLLY *London HLU 8560*	8	9
11 Jul 58	OOH MY SOUL *London HLO 8647*	30	1
25 Jul 58	OOH MY SOUL (re-entry) *London HLO 8647*	22	3
2 Jan 59 ●	BABY FACE *London HLU 8770*	2	15
3 Apr 59	BY THE LIGHT OF THE SILVERY MOON *London HLU 8831*	17	5
5 Jun 59	KANSAS CITY *London HLU 8868*	26	5
11 Oct 62	HE GOT WHAT HE WANTED *Mercury AMT 1189*	38	4
4 Jun 64	BAMA LAMA BAMA LOO *London HL 9896*	20	7
2 Jul 77	GOOD GOLLY MISS MOLLY / RIP IT UP *Creole CR 140*	37	4
14 Jun 86	GREAT GOSH A'MIGHTY (IT'S A MATTER OF TIME) *MCA MCA 1049*	62	2
25 Oct 86	OPERATOR *WEA YZ 89*	67	2

*The 1977 versions of 'Good Golly Miss Molly' and 'Rip It Up' on Creole
are re-recordings*

LITTLE STEVEN *US, male vocalist / instrumentalist – guitar* 3 wks

23 May 87	BITTER FRUIT *Manhattan MT 21*	66	3

LITTLE T *– See REBEL MC*

LITTLE TONY ✪ *Italy, male vocalist* 3 wks

15 Jan 60	TOO GOOD *Decca F 11190*	19	3

LIVE *US, male vocal / instrumental group* 12 wks

18 Feb 95	I ALONE *Radioactive RAXTD 13*	48	4
1 Jul 95	SELLING THE DRAMA *Radioactive RAXTD 17*	30	2
7 Oct 95	ALL OVER YOU *Radioactive RAXTD 20*	48	1
13 Jan 96	LIGHTNING CRASHES *Radioactive RAXTD 23*	33	2
13 May 97	LAKINI'S JUICE *Radioactive RAD 49023*	29	2
12 Jul 97	FREAKS *Radioactive RAXTD 29*	60	1

LIVE REPORT *UK, male vocal / instrumental group* 1 wk

20 May 89	WHY DO I ALWAYS GET IT WRONG *Brouhaha CUE 7*	73	1

LIVERPOOL EXPRESS ✪ *UK, male vocal / instrumental group* 26 wks

26 Jun 76	YOU ARE MY LOVE *Warner Bros. K 16743*	11	9
16 Oct 76	HOLD TIGHT *Warner Bros. K 16799*	46	2
18 Dec 76	EVERY MAN MUST HAVE A DREAM *Warner Bros. K 16854*	17	11
4 Jun 77	DREAMIN' *Warner Bros. K 16933*	40	4

LIVERPOOL FC ✪ *UK, male football team vocalists* 21 wks

28 May 77	WE CAN DO IT EP *State STAT 50*	15	4
23 Apr 83	LIVERPOOL (WE'RE NEVER GONNA...) / LIVERPOOL (ANTHEM) *Mean MEAN 102*	54	4
17 May 86	SITTING ON THE TOP OF THE WORLD *Columbia DB 9116*	50	2
14 May 88 ●	ANFIELD RAP (RED MACHINE IN FULL EFFECT) *Virgin LFC 1*	3	6
18 May 96 ●	PASS AND MOVE (IT'S THE LIVERPOOL GROOVE) *Telstar LFCCD 96* 1	4	5

1 Liverpool FC and the Boot Room Boyz

*Tracks on We Can Do It (EP): We Can Do It / Liverpool Lou / We Shall Not Be Moved /
You'll Never Walk Alone*

LIVIN' JOY ☺ *US / Italy, male / female vocal / instrumental group* 44 wks

3 Sep 94	DREAMER *Undiscovered MCSTD 1993*	18	6
13 May 95 ★	DREAMER (re-mix) *Undiscovered MCSTD 2056*	1	11
15 Jun 96 ●	DON'T STOP MOVIN' *Undiscovered MCSTD 40041*	5	14
2 Nov 96 ●	FOLLOW THE RULES *Undiscovered MCSTD 40081*	9	5
5 Apr 97	WHERE CAN I FIND LOVE *Undiscovered MCSTD 40108*	12	4
23 Aug 97	DEEP IN YOU *Universal MCSTD 40136*	17	4

LIVING IN A BOX ✪ ☺ *UK, male vocal / instrumental group* 62 wks

4 Apr 87 ●	LIVING IN A BOX *Chrysalis LIB 1*	5	13
13 Jun 87	SCALES OF JUSTICE *Chrysalis LIB 2*	30	6
26 Sep 87	SO THE STORY GOES *Chrysalis LIB 3* 1	34	8
30 Jan 88	LOVE IS THE ART *Chrysalis LIB 4*	45	4
18 Feb 89 ●	BLOW THE HOUSE DOWN *Chrysalis LIB 5*	10	9
10 Jun 89	GATECRASHING *Chrysalis LIB 6*	36	6
23 Sep 89 ●	ROOM IN YOUR HEART *Chrysalis LIB 7*	5	13
30 Dec 89	DIFFERENT AIR *Chrysalis LIB 8*	64	1
13 Jan 90	DIFFERENT AIR (re-entry) *Chrysalis LIB 8*	57	2

1 Living In a Box featuring Bobby Womack

LIVING COLOUR 🎸 ✪ *US, male vocal / instrumental group* 22 wks

27 Oct 90	TYPE *Epic LCL 7*	75	1
2 Feb 91	LOVE REARS ITS UGLY HEAD *Epic 6565937*	12	11
1 Jun 91	SOLACE OF YOU *Epic 6569087*	33	5
26 Oct 91	CULT OF PERSONALITY *Epic 6575357*	67	2
20 Feb 93	LEAVE IT ALONE *Epic 6589762*	34	2
17 Apr 93	AUSLANDER *Epic 6591732*	53	1

Dandy LIVINGSTONE 🏴 *Jamaica, male vocalist* 19 wks

2 Sep 72	SUZANNE BEWARE OF THE DEVIL *Horse HOSS 16*	14	11
13 Jan 73	BIG CITY / THINK ABOUT THAT *Horse HOSS 25*	26	8

LL COOL J 🎤 *US, male rapper* 76 wks

4 Jul 87	I'M BAD *Def Jam 650856 7*	71	1
12 Sep 87 ●	I NEED LOVE *Def Jam 651101 7*	8	10
21 Nov 87	GO CUT CREATOR GO *Def Jam LLCJ 1*	66	2
13 Feb 88	GOING BACK TO CALI / JACK THE RIPPER *Def Jam LLCJ 2*	37	4
10 Jun 89	I'M THAT TYPE OF GUY *Def Jam LLCJ 3*	43	5

1 Dec 90	AROUND THE WAY GIRL/MAMA SAID KNOCK YOU OUT *Def Jam 6564470*	41	4
9 Mar 91	AROUND THE WAY GIRL (re-issue) *Columbia 6564470*	36	4
10 Apr 93	HOW I'M COMIN' *Def Jam 6591692*	37	2
20 Jan 96	HEY LOVER *Def Jam DEFCD 14* [1]	17	4
1 Jun 96	DOIN' IT *Def Jam DEFCD 15* [2]	15	3
5 Oct 96	● LOUNGIN' *Def Jam DEFCD 30*	7	8
8 Feb 97	★ AIN'T NOBODY *Geffen GFSTD 22195* ■	1	9
5 Apr 97	● HIT 'EM HIGH (THE MONSTARS' ANTHEM) *Atlantic A 5449CD* [3]	8	6
1 Nov 97	● PHENOMENON *Def Jam 5681172*	9	5
28 Mar 98	● FATHER *Def Jam 5685292*	10	5
11 Jul 98	ZOOM *Interscope IND 95594* [4]	15	3
5 Dec 98	INCREDIBLE *Jive 0522102* [5]	52	1

[1] LL Cool J featuring Boyz II Men [2] LL Cool J, guest vocals by LeShaun
[3] B Real / Busta Rhymes / Coolio / LL Cool J / Method Man [4] Dr. Dre and LL Cool J
[5] Keith Murray featuring LL Cool J

'Jack the Ripper' only listed from 20 Feb, 1988

Kelly LLORENNA *UK, female vocalist*   7 wks

7 May 94	SET YOU FREE *All Around The World CDGLOBE 124* [1]	39	4
24 Feb 96	BRIGHTER DAY *Pukka CDPUKKA 5*	43	2
25 Jul 98	HEART OF GOLD *Diverse VERSE 2CD* [2]	55	1

[1] N-Trance featuring Kelly Llorenna [2] Force and Styles featuring Kelly Llorenna

See also N-TRANCE

David LLOYDIE – See SOUNDMAN and David LLOYDIE featuring Elizabeth TROY

LNR *US, male vocal/instrumental duo*   2 wks

3 Jun 89	WORK IT TO THE BONE *Kool Kat KOOL 501*	64	2

LO FIDELITY ALLSTARS *UK, male vocal/instrumental group*   5 wks

11 Oct 97	DISCO MACHINE GUN *Skint SKINT 30CD*	50	1
2 May 98	VISION INCISION *Skint SKINT 33CD*	30	2
28 Nov 98	BATTLEFLAG *Skint SKINT 38CD* [1]	36	2

[1] Lo Fidelity Allstars featuring Pigeonhead

LO-PRO – See X-PRESS 2

LOBO ◐ *US, male vocalist*   25 wks

19 Jun 71	● ME AND YOU AND A DOG NAMED BOO *Philips 6073 801*	4	14
8 Jun 74	● I'D LOVE YOU TO WANT ME *UK 68*	5	11

LOBO ◐ *Holland, male vocalist*   11 wks

25 Jul 81	● THE CARIBBEAN DISCO SHOW *Polydor POSP 302*	8	11

Tone LOC ◁ *US, male rapper*   19 wks

11 Feb 89	WILD THING/LOC'ED AFTER DARK *Fourth & Broadway BRW 121*	21	8
20 May 89	FUNKY COLD MEDINA/ON FIRE *Fourth & Broadway BRW 129*	13	9
5 Aug 89	I GOT IT GOIN' ON *Fourth & Broadway BRW 140*	55	2

Hank LOCKLIN ↙ *US, male vocalist*   41 wks

11 Aug 60	● PLEASE HELP ME I'M FALLING *RCA 1188*	9	19
15 Feb 62	FROM HERE TO THERE TO YOU *RCA 1273*	44	3
15 Nov 62	WE'RE GONNA GO FISHIN' *RCA 1305*	18	11
5 May 66	I FEEL A CRY COMING ON *RCA 1510*	29	8

LOCKSMITH *US, male vocal/instrumental group*   6 wks

23 Aug 80	UNLOCK THE FUNK *Arista ARIST 364*	42	6

LOCOMOTIVE *UK, male vocal/instrumental group*   8 wks

16 Oct 68	RUDI'S IN LOVE *Parlophone R 5718*	25	8

John LODGE – See Justin HAYWARD

LODGER *UK, male/female vocal/instrumental group*   2 wks

2 May 98	I'M LEAVING *Island CID 693*	40	2

Lisa LOEB and NINE STORIES ◐
US, female/male vocal/instrumental group   17 wks

3 Sep 94	● STAY (I MISSED YOU) *RCA 74321212522* ▲	6	15
16 Sep 95	DO YOU SLEEP *Geffen GFSTD 96*	45	2

Nils LOFGREN *US, male vocalist/instrumentalist – guitar*   3 wks

8 Jun 85	SECRETS IN THE STREET *Towerbell TOW 68*	53	3

Johnny LOGAN ◐ *Ireland, male vocalist*   24 wks

3 May 80	★ WHAT'S ANOTHER YEAR *Epic EPC 8572*	1	8
23 May 87	● HOLD ME NOW *Epic LOG 1*	2	11
22 Aug 87	I'M NOT IN LOVE *Epic LOG 2*	51	5

Kenny LOGGINS ◐ *US, male vocalist*   21 wks

28 Apr 84	● FOOTLOOSE *CBS A 4101* ▲	6	10
1 Nov 86	DANGER ZONE *CBS A 7188*	45	11

LOLA *US, female vocalist*   1 wk

28 Mar 87	WAX THE VAN *Syncopate SY 1*	65	1

Jackie LOMAX – See VARIOUS ARTISTS (EPs & LPs) – The Apple EP

Alain LOMBARD – See Mady MESPLE and Danielle MILLET with the PARIS OPERA-COMIQUE ORCHESTRA conducted by Alain LOMBARD

Julie LONDON *US, female vocalist*   3 wks

5 Apr 57	CRY ME A RIVER *London HLU 8240*	22	3

Laurie LONDON ◖ *UK, male vocalist*   12 wks

8 Nov 57	HE'S GOT THE WHOLE WORLD IN HIS HANDS *Parlophone R 4359*	12	12

LONDON BOYS ◐ ☺ *UK, male vocal duo*   46 wks

10 Dec 88	REQUIEM *WEA YZ 345*	59	6
1 Apr 89	● REQUIEM (re-entry) *WEA YZ 345*	4	15
1 Jul 89	● LONDON NIGHTS *WEA YZ 393*	2	9
16 Sep 89	HARLEM DESIRE *WEA YZ 415*	17	7
2 Dec 89	MY LOVE *WEA YZ 433*	46	6
16 Jun 90	CHAPEL OF LOVE *East West YZ 458*	75	1
19 Jan 91	FREEDOM *East West YZ 554*	54	2

LONDON COMMUNITY GOSPEL CHOIR – See Sal SOLO

LONDON PHILHARMONIC ORCHESTRA – See Cliff RICHARD

LONDON STRING CHORALE *UK, orchestra/choir*   13 wks

15 Dec 73	GALLOPING HOME *Polydor 2058 280*	49	3
19 Jan 74	GALLOPING HOME (re-entry) *Polydor 2058 280*	31	10

LONDON SYMPHONY ORCHESTRA *UK, orchestra*   5 wks

6 Jan 79	THEME FROM 'SUPERMAN' (MAIN TITLE) *Warner Bros. K 17292*	32	5

Orchestra conducted by John Williams

LONDONBEAT ◐ ♪ *UK/US, male vocal group*   45 wks

26 Nov 88	9 A.M. (THE COMFORT ZONE) *Anxious ANX 008*	19	10
18 Feb 89	FAILING IN LOVE AGAIN *Anxious ANX 007*	60	2
1 Sep 90	● I'VE BEEN THINKING ABOUT YOU *Anxious ANX 14* ▲	2	13
24 Nov 90	A BETTER LOVE *Anxious ANX 21*	52	5
2 Mar 91	NO WOMAN NO CRY *Anxious ANX 25*	64	2
20 Jul 91	A BETTER LOVE (re-issue) *Anxious ANX 32*	23	6
27 Jun 92	YOU BRING ON THE SUN *Anxious ANX 37*	32	4
24 Oct 92	THAT'S HOW I FEEL ABOUT YOU *Anxious ANX 40*	69	1

8 Apr 95	I'M JUST YOUR PUPPET ON A . . . (STRING)		
	Anxious 74321270982	55	1
20 May 95	COME BACK *Anxious 74321226682*	69	1

LONE JUSTICE *US, female/male vocal/instrumental group*   4 wks
7 Mar 87	I FOUND LOVE *Geffen GEF 18*	45	4

Shorty LONG *US, male vocalist*   7 wks
17 Jul 68	HERE COMES THE JUDGE *Tamla Motown TMG 663*	30	7

LONG AND THE SHORT *UK, male vocal/instrumental group*   8 wks
10 Sep 64	THE LETTER *Decca F 11964*	35	5
24 Dec 64	CHOC ICE *Decca F 12043*	49	3

LONG RYDERS *US, male vocal/instrumental group*   4 wks
5 Oct 85	LOOKING FOR LEWIS AND CLARK *Island IS 237*	59	4

LONGPIGS ✔ ❂ *UK, male vocal/instrumental group*   14 wks
22 Jul 95	SHE SAID *Mother MUMCD 66*	67	1
28 Oct 95	JESUS CHRIST *Mother MUMCD 68*	61	1
17 Feb 96	FAR *Mother MUMCD 71*	37	2
13 Apr 96	ON AND ON *Mother MUMCD 74*	16	5
22 Jun 96	SHE SAID (re-issue) *Mother MUMCD 77*	16	4
5 Oct 96	LOST MYSELF *Mother MUMCD 82*	22	3

Joe LONGTHORNE *UK, male vocalist*   6 wks
30 Apr 94	YOUNG GIRL *EMI CDEM 310*	61	2
10 Dec 94	PASSING STRANGERS *EMI CDEM 362* [1]	34	4

[1] Joe Longthorne and Liz Dawn

LOOK ❂ *UK, male vocal/instrumental group*   15 wks
20 Dec 80 ●	I AM THE BEAT *MCA 647*	6	12
29 Aug 81	FEEDING TIME *MCA 736*	50	3

LOOP DA LOOP *UK, male producer – Nick Dresti*   1 wk
7 Jun 97	GO WITH THE FLOW *Manifesto FESCD 24*	47	1

LOOSE ENDS ♪ ◣
UK, male/female vocal/instrumental group   76 wks
25 Feb 84	TELL ME WHAT YOU WANT *Virgin VS 658*	74	1
28 Apr 84	EMERGENCY (DIAL 999) *Virgin VS 677*	41	6
21 Jul 84	CHOOSE ME (RESCUE ME) *Virgin VS 697*	59	3
23 Feb 85	HANGIN' ON A STRING (CONTEMPLATING) *Virgin VS 748*	13	13
11 May 85	MAGIC TOUCH *Virgin VS 761*	16	7
27 Jul 85	GOLDEN YEARS *Virgin VS 795*	59	4
14 Jun 86	STAY A LITTLE WHILE, CHILD *Virgin VS 819*	52	5
20 Sep 86	SLOW DOWN *Virgin VS 884*	27	7
29 Nov 86	NIGHTS OF PLEASURE *Virgin VS 919*	42	7
4 Jun 88	MR BACHELOR *Virgin VS 1080*	50	4
25 Aug 90	DON'T BE A FOOL *10 TEN 312*	13	9
17 Nov 90	LOVE'S GOT ME *10 TEN 330*	40	4
20 Jun 92	HANGIN' ON A STRING (re-mix) *Ten TEN 406*	25	5
5 Sep 92	MAGIC TOUCH (re-mix) *Ten TEN 409*	75	1

Trini LOPEZ ❂ *US, male vocalist*   37 wks
12 Sep 63 ●	IF I HAD A HAMMER *Reprise R 20198*	4	17
12 Dec 63	KANSAS CITY *Reprise R 20236*	35	5
12 May 66	I'M COMING HOME CINDY *Reprise R 20455*	28	5
6 Apr 67	GONNA GET ALONG WITHOUT YA NOW *Reprise R 20547*	41	5
19 Dec 81	TRINI TRAX *RCA 154*	59	5

LORD ROCKINGHAM'S XI ❂
UK, male/female instrumental group   21 wks
24 Oct 58 ★	HOOTS MON *Decca F 11059*	1	17
6 Feb 59	WEE TOM *Decca F 11104*	16	3
25 Sep 93	HOOTS MON (re-issue) *Decca 8820982*	60	1

Both of the group's hits contain a little spoken Scottish

LORD TANAMO *Trinidad & Tobago, male vocalist*   2 wks
1 Dec 90	I'M IN THE MOOD FOR LOVE *Mooncrest MOON 1009*	58	2

LORD TARIQ and Peter GUNZ *US, male vocal/rap duo*   3 wks
2 May 98	DEJA VU (UPTOWN BABY) *Columbia 6658722*	21	3

Jerry LORDAN ❂ *UK, male vocalist*   15 wks
8 Jan 60	I'LL STAY SINGLE *Parlophone R 4588*	26	2
26 Feb 60	WHO COULD BE BLUER *Parlophone R 4627*	17	9
10 Mar 60	I'LL STAY SINGLE (re-entry) *Parlophone R 4588*	41	1
19 May 60	WHO COULD BE BLUER (re-entry) *Parlophone R 4627*	45	1
2 Jun 60	SING LIKE AN ANGEL *Parlophone R 4653*	36	2

Traci LORDS *US, female vocalist*   1 wk
7 Oct 95	FALLEN ANGEL *Radioactive RAXTD 18*	72	1

Sophia LOREN – See Peter SELLERS

Trey LORENZ *US, male vocalist*   5 wks
21 Nov 92	SOMEONE TO HOLD *Epic 6587857*	65	2
30 Jan 93	PHOTOGRAPH OF MARY *Epic 6589542*	38	3

See also Mariah CAREY

LORI and the CHAMELEONS
UK, female/male vocal/instrumental group   1 wk
8 Dec 79	TOUCH *Sire SIR 4025*	70	1

LORRAINE – See BOMB THE BASS

LOS BRAVOS ❂
Spain/Germany, male vocal/instrumental group   24 wks
30 Jun 66 ●	BLACK IS BLACK *Decca F 22419*	2	13
8 Sep 66	I DON'T CARE *Decca F 22484*	16	11

LOS DEL CHIPMUNKS – See CHIPMUNKS

LOS DEL MAR featuring Wil VELOZ
Cuba/Canada, male vocal/instrumental group   7 wks
8 Jun 96	MACARENA *Pulse 8 CDLOSE 101*	66	2
6 Jul 96	MACARENA (re-entry) *Pulse 8 CDLOSE 101*	43	5

LOS DEL RIO ❂ *Spain, male vocal/instrumental duo*   19 wks
1 Jun 96	MACARENA *RCA 74321345372* ▲	64	1
13 Jul 96 ●	MACARENA (re-entry) *RCA 74321345372*	2	18

LOS INDIOS TABAJARAS ❂❂
Brazil, male instrumental duo – guitars   17 wks
31 Oct 63 ●	MARIA ELENA *RCA 1365*	5	17

LOS LOBOS ✔ *US, male vocal/instrumental group*   24 wks
6 Apr 85	DON'T WORRY BABY/WILL THE WOLF SURVIVE		
	London LASH 4	57	4
18 Jul 87 ★	LA BAMBA *Slash LASH 13* ▲	1	11
26 Sep 87	COME ON LET'S GO *Slash LASH 14*	18	9

LOS UMERELLOS *Denmark, male/female vocal trio*   2 wks
3 Oct 98	NO TENGO DINERO *Virgin VUSCD 139*	33	2

Joe LOSS ♫ *UK, orchestra*   53 wks
29 Jun 61	WHEELS CHA CHA *HMV POP 880*	21	21
19 Oct 61	SUCU SUCU *HMV POP 937*	48	1
29 Mar 62	THE MAIGRET THEME *HMV POP 995*	20	10
1 Nov 62	MUST BE MADISON *HMV POP 1075*	20	13
5 Nov 64	MARCH OF THE MODS *HMV POP 1351*	35	4
24 Dec 64	MARCH OF THE MODS (re-entry) *HMV POP 1351*	31	4

LOST *UK, male/instrumental/production duo*　　　**1 wk**

| 22 Jun 91 | TECHNO FUNK *Perfecto PT 44560*............ | 75 | 1 |

LOST BOYZ *US, male rap group*　　　**2 wks**

| 2 Nov 96 | MUSIC MAKES ME HIGH *Universal MCSTD 48015*...... | 42 | 1 |
| 12 Jul 97 | LOVE, PEACE & NAPPINESS *Universal UND 56131* ...... | 57 | 1 |

See also VARIOUS ARTISTS (EPs and LPs) – The New York Undercover EP

LOTUS EATERS ◉ *UK, male vocal/instrumental duo*　　**16 wks**

| 2 Jul 83 | FIRST PICTURE OF YOU *Sylvan SYL 1*......... | 15 | 12 |
| 8 Oct 83 | YOU DON'T NEED SOMEONE NEW *Sylvan SYL 2*...... | 53 | 4 |

Bonnie LOU ⚓ *US, female vocalist*　　**10 wks**

| 5 Feb 54 | ● TENNESSEE WIG WALK *Parlophone R 3730* ...... | 4 | 10 |

Lippy LOU *UK, female rapper*　　**2 wks**

| 22 Apr 95 | LIBERATION *More Protein PROCD 105*...... | 57 | 2 |

Louchie LOU and Michie ONE ◉ ⚓ *UK, female vocal duo*　**36 wks**

29 May 93	● SHOUT *ffrr FCD 211*.........	7	8
14 Aug 93	SOMEBODY ELSE'S GUY *ffrr FCD 216*......	54	2
26 Aug 95	GET DOWN ON IT *China WOKCD 2054*......	58	1
13 Apr 96	● CECILIA *WEA WEA 042CD1* [1]......	4	17
15 Jun 96	GOOD SWEET LOVIN' *Indochina ID 050CD*......	34	2
24 Aug 96	CECILIA (re-entry) *WEA WEA 042CD1* [1]......	65	1
7 Sep 96	CECILIA (2nd re-entry) *WEA WEA 042CD1* [1]......	59	1
21 Sep 96	NO MORE ALCOHOL *WEA WEA 065CD1* [1]......	24	4

[1] Suggs featuring Louchie Lou and Michie One

LOUD *UK, male vocal/instrumental group*　　**2 wks**

| 28 Mar 92 | EASY *China WOK 2016* ...... | 67 | 2 |

John D. LOUDERMILK ◉ *US, male vocalist*　　**10 wks**

| 4 Jan 62 | THE LANGUAGE OF LOVE *RCA 1269*...... | 13 | 10 |

Louie LOUIE *US, male vocalist*　　**5 wks**

| 19 Dec 92 | THE THOUGHT OF IT *Hardback YZ 724* ...... | 34 | 5 |

LOUISE ◉ *UK, female vocalist*　　**56 wks**

7 Oct 95	● LIGHT OF MY LIFE *EMI CDEMS 397*......	8	8
16 Mar 96	IN WALKED LOVE *EMI CDEMS 413*......	17	6
8 Jun 96	● NAKED *EMI CDEM 431*......	5	8
31 Aug 96	● UNDIVIDED LOVE *EMI CDEM 441*......	5	6
30 Nov 96	● ONE KISS FROM HEAVEN *EMI CDEM 454*......	9	6
4 Oct 97	● ARMS AROUND THE WORLD *EMI CDEM 490*......	4	7
29 Nov 97	● LET'S GO ROUND AGAIN *EMI CDEM 500*......	10	9
4 Apr 98	ALL THAT MATTERS *1st Avenue CDEM 506*......	11	5
20 Jun 98	ALL THAT MATTERS (re-entry) *1st Avenue CDEM 506*......	73	1

Darlene LOVE *US, female vocalist*　　**5 wks**

| 19 Dec 92 | ALL ALONE ON CHRISTMAS *Arista 7432112476*...... | 31 | 4 |
| 1 Jan 94 | ALL ALONE ON CHRISTMAS (re-entry) *Arista 7432112476*...... | 72 | 1 |

Helen LOVE *UK, male/female vocal/instrumental group*　**2 wks**

| 20 Sep 97 | DOES YOUR HEART GO BOOM *Che CHE 72CD*...... | 71 | 1 |
| 19 Sep 98 | LONG LIVE THE UK MUSIC SCENE *Che CHE 82CD* ...... | 65 | 1 |

Geoff LOVE – *See MANUEL and his MUSIC OF THE MOUNTAINS*

Monie LOVE ⚓ *UK, female rapper*　　**49 wks**

4 Feb 89	I CAN DO THIS *Cooltempo COOL 177*......	37	4
24 Jun 89	GRANDPA'S PARTY *Cooltempo COOL 184*......	16	9
14 Jul 90	MONIE IN THE MIDDLE *Cooltempo COOL 210*	46	3
22 Sep 90	IT'S A SHAME (MY SISTER) *Cooltempo COOL 219* [1]......	12	8
1 Dec 90	DOWN TO EARTH *Cooltempo COOL 222*......	31	6
6 Apr 91	RING MY BELL *Cooltempo COOL 224* [2]......	20	5
25 Jul 92	FULL TERM LOVE *Cooltempo COOL 258*......	34	4
13 Mar 93	BORN 2 B.R.E.E.D. *Cooltempo CDCOOL 269*......	18	5
12 Jun 93	IN A WORD OR 2/THE POWER *Cooltempo CDCOOL 273*	33	3
21 Aug 93	NEVER GIVE UP *Cooltempo CDCOOL 276*......	41	2

[1] Monie Love featuring True Image　[2] Monie Love vs Adeva

Vikki LOVE – *See NUANCE featuring Vikki LOVE*

See also JUNGLE BROTHERS

LOVE AFFAIR ◉ *UK, male vocal/instrumental group*　**56 wks**

3 Jan 68	★ EVERLASTING LOVE *CBS 3125*	1	12
17 Apr 68	● RAINBOW VALLEY *CBS 3366*	5	13
11 Sep 68	● A DAY WITHOUT LOVE *CBS 3674*	6	12
19 Feb 69	ONE ROAD *CBS 3994*	16	9
16 Jul 69	● BRINGING ON BACK THE GOOD TIMES *CBS 4300*	9	10

LOVE AND MONEY *UK, male vocal/instrumental group*　**23 wks**

24 May 86	CANDYBAR EXPRESS *Mercury MONEY 1*......	56	4
25 Apr 87	LOVE AND MONEY *Mercury MONEY 4*......	68	4
17 Sep 88	HALLELUJAH MAN *Fontana MONEY 5*......	63	4
14 Jan 89	STRANGE KIND OF LOVE *Fontana MONEY 6*......	45	5
25 Mar 89	JOCELYN SQUARE *Fontana MONEY 7*......	51	4
16 Nov 91	WINTER *Fontana MONEY 9*......	52	2

LOVE CITY GROOVE ◉ ⚓
UK, male/female vocal/instrumental group　**11 wks**

| 8 Apr 95 | ● LOVE CITY GROOVE *Planet 3 GXY 2003CD* ...... | 7 | 11 |

LOVE DECADE ☺ *UK, male/female vocal/instrumental group*　**14 wks**

6 Jul 91	DREAM ON (IS THIS A DREAM) *All Around The World GLOBE 100*......	52	2
23 Nov 91	SO REAL *All Around The World GLOBE 106*	14	7
11 Apr 92	I FEEL YOU *All Around The World GLOBE 107*......	34	3
6 Feb 93	WHEN THE MORNING COMES *All Around The World CDGLOBE 114*	69	1
17 Feb 96	IS THIS A DREAM *All Around The World CDGLOBE 132*......	39	1

'Is This a Dream' in 1996 is a re-recording

LOVE DECREE *UK, male vocal/instrumental group*　**4 wks**

| 16 Sep 89 | SOMETHING SO REAL (CHINHEADS THEME) *Ariola 112642* ...... | 61 | 4 |

LOVE / HATE *US, male vocal/instrumental group*　**4 wks**

| 30 Nov 91 | EVIL TWIN *Columbia 6575967* ...... | 59 | 1 |
| 4 Apr 92 | WASTED IN AMERICA *Columbia 6578897*...... | 38 | 3 |

LOVE INC *UK, male vocal/production duo*　**3 wks**

| 9 Feb 91 | LOVE IS THE MESSAGE *Love EVOL 1* ...... | 59 | 3 |

LOVE TO INFINITY *UK, male/female vocal/instrumental group*　**4 wks**

24 Jun 95	KEEP LOVE TOGETHER *Mushroom D 00467*	38	2
18 Nov 95	SOMEDAY *Mushroom D 1143*......	75	1
3 Aug 96	PRAY FOR LOVE *Mushroom D 1213*	69	1

LOVE NELSON – *See FIRE ISLAND*

LOVE REACTION – *See ZODIAC MINDWARP and the LOVE REACTION*

LOVE SCULPTURE 🎸 *UK, instrumental group*　**14 wks**

| 27 Nov 68 | ● SABRE DANCE *Parlophone R 5744* ...... | 5 | 14 |

LOVE SQUAD – *See Linda CARR*

LOVE TRIBE *US, male/female vocal/instrumental duo*　**3 wks**

| 29 Jun 96 | STAND UP *AM:PM 5816272* ...... | 23 | 3 |

LOVE UNLIMITED 🎵 US, female vocal group — 19 wks

17 Jun 72	WALKIN' IN THE RAIN WITH THE ONE I LOVE *Uni UN 539*	14	10
25 Jan 75	IT MAY BE WINTER OUTSIDE		
	(BUT IN MY HEART IT'S SPRING) *20th Century BTC 2149*	11	9

LOVE UNLIMITED ORCHESTRA 🎵 US, orchestra — 10 wks

2 Feb 74	● LOVE'S THEME *Pye International 7N 25635* ▲	10	10

LOVEBUG STARSKI 🎵 US, male rapper — 9 wks

31 May 86	AMITYVILLE (THE HOUSE ON THE HILL) *Epic A 7182*	12	9

LOVEDEEJAY AKEMI – See YOSH presents LOVEDEEJAY AKEMI

LOVEHAPPY US/UK, male/female vocal/instrumental group — 3 wks

18 Feb 95	MESSAGE OF LOVE *MCA MCSTD 2040*	37	2
20 Jul 96	MESSAGE OF LOVE (re-mix) *MCA MCSTD 40052*	70	1

Bill LOVELADY 🎵 UK, male vocalist — 10 wks

18 Aug 79	REGGAE FOR IT NOW *Charisma CB 337*	12	10

LOVELAND featuring the voice of Rachel McFARLANE ☺
UK, male/female vocal/instrumental group — 15 wks

16 Apr 94	LET THE MUSIC (LIFT YOU UP)		
	KMS/Eastern Bloc KMSCD 10 [1]	16	4
5 Nov 94	(KEEP ON) SHINING/HOPE (NEVER GIVE UP)		
	Eastern Bloc BLOCCD 016	37	2
14 Jan 95	I NEED SOMEBODY *Eastern Bloc BLOCCD 019*	21	3
10 Jun 95	DON'T MAKE ME WAIT *Eastern Bloc BLOC 20CD*	22	3
2 Sep 95	THE WONDER OF LOVE *Eastern Bloc BLOC 22CD*	53	1
11 Nov 95	I NEED SOMEBODY (re-mix) *Eastern Bloc BLOC 23CD*	38	2

[1] Loveland featuring Rachel McFarlane vs Darlene Lewis

All formats of 'Let the Music (Lift You Up)' featured versions by Loveland featuring Rachel McFarlane and also by Darlene Lewis

LOVER SPEAKS UK, male vocal/instrumental duo — 5 wks

16 Aug 86	NO MORE 'I LOVE YOUS' *A & M AM 326*	58	5

Michael LOVESMITH US, male vocalist — 1 wk

5 Oct 85	AIN'T NOTHIN' LIKE IT *Motown ZB 40369*	75	1

LOVESTATION ☺ UK, male/female vocal/instrumental group — 14 wks

13 Mar 93	SHINE ON ME *RCA 743211337912* [1]	71	1
13 Nov 93	BEST OF MY LOVE *Fresh FRSHD 1*	73	1
18 Mar 95	LOVE COME RESCUE ME *Fresh FRSHD 22*	42	2
1 Aug 98	TEARDROPS *Fresh FRSHD 65*	14	6
5 Dec 98	SENSUALITY *Fresh FRSHD 71*	16†	4

[1] Lovestation featuring Lisa Hunt

Lene LOVICH 🎵 US, female vocalist — 38 wks

17 Feb 79	● LUCKY NUMBER *Stiff BUY 42*	3	11
12 May 79	SAY WHEN *Stiff BUY 46*	19	10
20 Oct 79	BIRD SONG *Stiff BUY 53*	39	7
29 Mar 80	WHAT WILL I DO WITHOUT YOU *Stiff BUY 69*	58	3
14 Mar 81	NEW TOY *Stiff BUY 97*	53	5
27 Nov 82	IT'S YOU ONLY YOU (MEIN SCHMERZ) *Stiff BUY 164*	68	2

LOVIN' SPOONFUL ⚙
US/Canada, male vocal/instrumental group — 33 wks

14 Apr 66	● DAYDREAM *Pye International 7N 25361*	2	13
14 Jul 66	● SUMMER IN THE CITY *Kama Sutra KAS 200* ▲	8	11
5 Jan 67	NASHVILLE CATS *Kama Sutra KAS 204*	26	7
9 Mar 67	DARLING BE HOME SOON *Kama Sutra KAS 207*	44	2

LOVINDEER Jamaica, male vocalist — 3 wks

27 Sep 86	MAN SHORTAGE *TSOJ TS 1*	69	3

Gary LOW Italy, male vocalist — 3 wks

8 Oct 83	I WANT YOU *Savoir Faire FAIS 004*	52	3

Patti LOW – See BUG KANN and the PLASTIC JAM

Jim LOWE ☕ US, male vocalist — 9 wks

26 Oct 56	● THE GREEN DOOR *London HLD 8317*	8	9

Nick LOWE 🎵 UK, male vocalist — 27 wks

11 Mar 78	● I LOVE THE SOUND OF BREAKING GLASS *Radar ADA*	7	8
9 Jun 79	CRACKIN' UP *Radar ADA 34*	34	5
25 Aug 79	CRUEL TO BE KIND *Radar ADA 43*	12	11
26 May 84	HALF A BOY HALF A MAN *F. Beat XX 34*	53	3

LOWRELL US, male vocalist — 9 wks

24 Nov 79	MELLOW MELLOW RIGHT ON *AVI AVIS 108*	37	9

LRS – See D MOB

L7 US, female vocal/instrumental group — 18 wks

4 Apr 92	PRETEND WE'RE DEAD *Slash LASH 34*	21	7
30 May 92	EVERGLADE *Slash LASH 36*	27	3
12 Sep 92	MONSTER *Slash LASH 38*	33	3
28 Nov 92	PRETEND WE'RE DEAD (re-issue) *Slash LASH 42*	50	3
9 Jul 94	ANDRES *Slash LASCD 48*	34	2

LSG Germany, male DJ/producer – Oliver Lieb — 1 wk

10 May 97	NETHERWORLD *Hooj Choons HOOJCD 52*	63	1

See also LEVERT SWEAT GILL

L.T.D. US, male vocal/instrumental group — 3 wks

9 Sep 78	HOLDING ON (WHEN LOVE IS GONE) *A & M AMS 7378*	70	3

LUCAS US, male vocalist — 4 wks

6 Aug 94	LUCAS WITH THE LID OFF *WEA YZ 832CD*	37	4

Carrie LUCAS US, female vocalist — 6 wks

16 Jun 79	DANCE WITH YOU *Solar FB 1482*	40	6

Tammy LUCAS – See Teddy RILEY

LUCIANA UK, female vocalist — 5 wks

23 Apr 94	GET IT UP FOR LOVE *Chrysalis CDCHS 5008*	55	2
6 Aug 94	IF YOU WANT *Chrysalis CDCHS 5009*	47	2
5 Nov 94	WHAT GOES AROUND/ONE MORE RIVER		
	Chrysalis CDCHS 5015	67	1

LUCID ☺ UK, male/female vocal/instrumental group — 8 wks

8 Aug 98	● I CAN'T HELP MYSELF *ffrr FCD 339*	7	8

LUCKY MONKEYS UK, male instrumental group — 1 wk

9 Nov 96	BJANGO *Hi-Life 5757132*	50	1

Lucky Monkeys is a pseudonym for Fluke
See also FLUKE

Robin LUKE US, male vocalist — 6 wks

17 Oct 58	SUSIE DARLIN' *London HLD 8676*	24	3
21 Nov 58	SUSIE DARLIN' (re-entry) *London HLD 8676*	23	1
5 Dec 58	SUSIE DARLIN' (2nd re-entry) *London HLD 8676*	23	2

LUKK featuring Felicia COLLINS
US, male/female vocal/instrumental group — 1 wk

28 Sep 85	ON THE ONE *Important TAN 6*	72	1

What: *Oh Mein Papa*   **57**
Who: Eddie Calvert
When: 1954 (1)
Which: Spent nine weeks at No 1, entered the US Top 10 (very rare for UK acts in the 1950s) and earned 'The Man With the Golden Trumpet' a gold disc

What: *Last Christmas / Everything She Wants*   **58**
Who: Wham!
When: 1984 (2), 1985 (6), 1986 (45)
Which: Is one of the most popular recent Christmas songs. It was only kept off the top by Band Aid's record-breaking release (which featured George Michael among its singers)

What: *Baby Love*   **59**
Who: Supremes
When: 1964 (1), 1974 (12)
Which: Was the first record by a girl group to head the UK chart and the last for another 25 years. It was the acclaimed act's only transatlantic No 1

What: *The Israelites*   **60**
Who: Desmond Dekker and The Aces
When: 1969 (1), 1975 (10)
Which: Was hugely successful, even though few people could fully understand its lyrics. It was the first reggae record to reach No 1 in the UK and was also a US Top 10 hit

LULU ☺ *Arguably, Scotland's best-known female vocalist, b. Marie Lawrie, 3 November, 1948, Strathclyde. She scored her first hit aged 15, had a US chart-topper ('To Sir With Love') aged 18, won the Eurovision Song Contest aged 20, and finally reached No 1 aged 44* **164 wks**

14 May 64	● SHOUT *Decca F 11884* [1]	7	13
12 Nov 64	HERE COMES THE NIGHT *Decca F 12017*	50	1
17 Jun 65	● LEAVE A LITTLE LOVE *Decca F 12169*	8	11
2 Sep 65	TRY TO UNDERSTAND *Decca F 12214*	25	8
13 Apr 67	● THE BOAT THAT I ROW *Columbia DB 8169*	6	11
29 Jun 67	LET'S PRETEND *Columbia DB 8221*	11	11
8 Nov 67	LOVE LOVES TO LOVE LOVE *Columbia DB 8295*	32	6
28 Feb 68	● ME THE PEACEFUL HEART *Columbia DB 8358*	9	9
5 Jun 68	BOY *Columbia DB 8425*	15	7
6 Nov 68	● I'M A TIGER *Columbia DB 8500*	9	13
12 Mar 69	● BOOM BANG-A-BANG *Columbia DB 8550*	2	13
22 Nov 69	OH ME OH MY (I'M A FOOL FOR YOU BABY) *Atco 226008*	47	2
26 Jan 74	● THE MAN WHO SOLD THE WORLD *Polydor 2001 490*	3	9
19 Apr 75	TAKE YOUR MAMA FOR A RIDE *Chelsea 2005 022*	37	4
12 Dec 81	I COULD NEVER MISS YOU (MORE THAN I DO) *Alfa ALFA 1700*	62	4
16 Jan 82	I COULD NEVER MISS YOU (MORE THAN I DO) (re-entry) *Alfa ALFA 1700*	63	1
19 Jul 86	● SHOUT *Jive LULU1/Decca SHOUT 1*	8	10
30 Jan 93	INDEPENDENCE *Dome CDDOME 1001*	11	5
3 Apr 93	I'M BACK FOR MORE *Dome CDDOME 1002* [2]	27	5
4 Sep 93	LET ME WAKE UP IN YOUR ARMS *Dome CDDOME 1005*	51	2
9 Oct 93	★ RELIGHT MY FIRE *RCA 74321167722* [3] ■	1	12
27 Nov 93	HOW 'BOUT US *Dome CDDOME 1007*	46	3
27 Aug 94	GOODBYE BABY AND AMEN *Dome CDDOME 1011*	40	2
26 Nov 94	EVERY WOMAN KNOWS *Dome CDDOME 1013*	44	2

[1] Lulu and the Luvvers [2] Lulu and Bobby Womack [3] Take That featuring Lulu

The newly recorded 'Shout' entered the chart on 19 Jul, 1986, and the next week the original Decca version by Lulu and the Luvvers also charted. For all subsequent weeks Gallup amalgamated both versions under one entry

Bob LUMAN ☺ *US, male vocalist* **21 wks**

8 Sep 60	● LET'S THINK ABOUT LIVING *Warner Bros. WB 18*	6	18
15 Dec 60	WHY WHY BYE BYE *Warner Bros. WB 28*	46	1
4 May 61	THE GREAT SNOWMAN *Warner Bros. WB 37*	49	2

LUNIZ 📟 *US, male rap duo* **18 wks**

17 Feb 96	I GOT 5 ON IT *Virgin America VUSCD 101*	3	13
11 May 96	PLAYA HATA *Virgin America VUSCD 103*	20	3
31 Oct 98	I GOT 5 ON IT (re-entry) *Virgin VCRD 41*	28	2

LURKERS *UK, male vocal/instrumental group* **11 wks**

3 Jun 78	AIN'T GOT A CLUE *Beggars Banquet BEG 6*	45	3
5 Aug 78	I DON'T NEED TO TELL HER *Beggars Banquet BEG 9*	49	4
3 Feb 79	JUST THIRTEEN *Beggars Banquet BEG 14*	66	2
9 Jun 79	OUT IN THE DARK/CYANIDE *Beggars Banquet BEG 19*	72	1
17 Nov 79	NEW GUITAR IN TOWN *Beggars Banquet BEG 28*	72	1

LUSCIOUS JACKSON *US, female vocal/instrumental group* **4 wks**

18 Mar 95	DEEP SHAG/CITYSONG *Capitol CDCL 739*	69	1
21 Oct 95	HERE *Capitol CDCL 758*	59	1
12 Apr 97	NAKED EYE *Capitol CDCL 786*	25	1

LUSH *UK, female/male vocal/instrumental group* **19 wks**

10 Mar 90	MAD LOVE (EP) *4AD BAD 003*	55	1
27 Oct 90	SWEETNESS AND LIGHT *4AD BAD 0013*	47	2
19 Oct 91	NOTHING NATURAL *4AD AD 1016*	43	2
11 Jan 92	FOR LOVE (EP) *4AD BAD 2001*	35	2
11 Jun 94	HYPOCRITE *4AD BAD 4008CD*	52	2
11 Jun 94	DESIRE LINES *4AD BAD 4010CD*	60	1
20 Jan 96	SINGLE GIRL *4AD BAD 6001CD*	21	3
9 Mar 96	LADYKILLERS *4AD BAD 6002CD*	22	3
27 Jul 96	500 (SHAKE BABY SHAKE) *4AD BAD 6009CD*	21	3

Tracks on Mad Love (EP): De-Luxe / Leaves Me Cold / Downer / Thoughtforms
Tracks on For Love (EP): For Love / Starlust / Outdoor Miner / Astronaut

LUSTRAL *UK, male DJ/production duo – Ricky Simmons and Steve Jones* **1 wk**

18 Oct 97	EVERYTIME *Hooj Choons HOOJCD 55*	60	1

LUVVERS – See LULU

LV *US, male vocalist* **24 wks**

28 Oct 95	★ GANGSTA'S PARADISE *Tommy Boy MCSTD 2104* [1] ▲	1	19
23 Dec 95	THROW YOUR HANDS UP/GANGSTA'S PARADISE *Tommy Boy TBCD 699*	24	4
4 May 96	● I AM LV *Tommy Boy TBCD 7724*	64	1

[1] Coolio featuring LV

The version of 'Gangsta's Paradise' coupled with 'Throw Your Hands Up' is a re-recorded version without Coolio's vocals

Annabella LWIN *Burma, female vocalist* **1 wk**

28 Jan 95	DO WHAT YOU DO *Sony S2 6611235*	61	1

LWS *Italy, male instrumental group* **1 wk**

29 Oct 94	GOSP *Transworld TRANNY 4CD*	65	1

John LYDON *UK, male vocalist* **1 wk**

2 Aug 97	● SUN *Virgin VUSCD 122*	42	1

See also PUBLIC IMAGE LTD

Frankie LYMON and the TEENAGERS 🎻
US, male vocal group **38 wks**

29 Jun 56	★ WHY DO FOOLS FALL IN LOVE *Columbia DB 3772* [1]	1	16
29 Mar 57	I'M NOT A JUVENILE DELINQUENT *Columbia DB 3878*	12	7
12 Apr 57	● BABY BABY *Columbia DB 3878*	4	12
20 Sep 57	● GOODY GOODY *Columbia DB 3983*	24	3

[1] Teenagers featuring Frankie Lymon

Des LYNAM *UK, male vocalist – TV presenter* **3 wks**

12 Dec 98	IF – READ TO FAURE'S 'PAVANE' *BBC Worldwide WMSS 60062* [1]	45†	3

[1] Des Lynam featuring Wimbledon Choral Society

Kenny LYNCH ☺ *UK, male vocalist* **59 wks**

30 Jun 60	MOUNTAIN OF LOVE *HMV POP 751*	33	3
13 Sep 62	PUFF *HMV POP 1057*	33	5
25 Oct 62	PUFF (re-entry) *HMV POP 1057*	46	1
6 Dec 62	● UP ON THE ROOF *HMV POP 1090*	10	12
20 Jun 63	● YOU CAN NEVER STOP ME LOVING YOU *HMV POP 1165*	10	14
16 Apr 64	STAND BY ME *HMV POP 1280*	39	7
27 Aug 64	WHAT AM I TO YOU *HMV POP 1321*	37	4
1 Oct 64	WHAT AM I TO YOU (re-entry) *HMV POP 1321*	44	2
17 Jun 65	I'LL STAY BY YOU *HMV POP 1430*	29	7
20 Aug 83	HALF THE DAY'S GONE AND WE HAVEN'T EARNT A PENNY *Satril SAT 510*	50	4

Cheryl LYNN *US, female vocalist* **2 wks**

8 Sep 84	ENCORE *Streetwave KHAN 23*	68	2

Patti LYNN *UK, female vocalist* **5 wks**

10 May 62	JOHNNY ANGEL *Fontana H 391*	37	5

Tami LYNN 🎤 *US, female vocalist* **20 wks**

22 May 71	● I'M GONNA RUN AWAY FROM YOU *Mojo 2092 001*	4	14
3 May 75	I'M GONNA RUN AWAY FROM YOU (re-issue) *Contempo Raries CS 9026*	36	6

Vera LYNN ℭ *UK, female vocalist* **46 wks**

14 Nov 52	● AUF WIEDERSEHEN *Decca F 9927* ▲	10	1
14 Nov 52	● FORGET ME NOT *Decca F 9985*	7	1

UK No 1 ★   UK Top 10 ●   UK million seller ◆   UK entry at No 1 ■   US No 1 ▲

14 Nov 52	●	HOMING WALTZ *Decca F 9959*	....	9	3
28 Nov 52	●	FORGET ME NOT (re-entry) *Decca F 9985*	....	5	5
5 Jun 53		WINDSOR WALTZ *Decca F 10092*	....	11	1
15 Oct 54	★	MY SON MY SON *Decca F 10372* [1]	....	1	14
8 Jun 56		WHO ARE WE *Decca F 10715*	....	30	1
26 Oct 56		A HOUSE WITH LOVE IN IT *Decca F 10799*	....	17	13
15 Mar 57		THE FAITHFUL HUSSAR (DON'T CRY MY LOVE) *Decca F 10846*	....	29	2
21 Jun 57		TRAVELLIN' HOME *Decca F 10903*	....	20	5

[1] Vera Lynn with Frank Weir, his saxophone, his Orchestra and Chorus

Jeff LYNNE *UK, male vocalist*   4 wks

| 30 Jun 90 | | EVERY LITTLE THING *Reprise W 9799* | .... | 59 | 4 |

Philip LYNOTT ✎ *Ireland, male vocalist*   36 wks

5 Apr 80		DEAR MISS LONELY HEARTS *Vertigo SOLO 1*	....	32	6
21 Jun 80		KING'S CALL *Vertigo SOLO 2*	....	35	6
21 Mar 81		YELLOW PEARL *Vertigo SOLO 3*	....	56	3
26 Dec 81		YELLOW PEARL (re-entry) *Vertigo SOLO 3*	....	14	9
18 May 85	●	OUT IN THE FIELDS *10 TEN 49* [1]	....	5	10
24 Jan 87		KING'S CALL (re-mix) *Vertigo LYN 1*	....	68	2

[1] Gary Moore and Phil Lynott

See also THIN LIZZY

LYNYRD SKYNYRD *US, male vocal/instrumental group*   21 wks

11 Sep 76		FREE BIRD EP *MCA 251*	....	31	4
22 Dec 79		FREE BIRD EP (re-entry) *MCA 251*	....	43	8
19 Jun 82		FREE BIRD EP (2nd re-entry) *MCA 251*	....	21	9

Tracks on Free Bird EP: Free Bird / Sweet Home Alabama / Double Trouble

Barbara LYON ℂ *US, female vocalist*   12 wks

| 24 Jun 55 | | STOWAWAY *Columbia DB 3619* | .... | 12 | 8 |
| 21 Dec 56 | | LETTER TO A SOLDIER *Columbia DB 3865* | .... | 27 | 4 |

Humphrey LYTTELTON BAND ✎
UK, male jazz band, Humphrey Lyttelton – trumpet   6 wks

| 13 Jul 56 | | BAD PENNY BLUES *Parlophone R 4184* | .... | 19 | 6 |

M ☺ *UK, male vocalist/multi-instrumentalist – Robin Scott*   39 wks

7 Apr 79	●	POP MUZIK *MCA 413* ▲	....	2	14
8 Dec 79		MOONLIGHT AND MUZAK *MCA 541*	....	33	9
15 Mar 80		THAT'S THE WAY THE MONEY GOES *MCA 570*	....	45	5
22 Nov 80		OFFICIAL SECRETS *MCA 650*	....	64	2
10 Jun 89		POP MUZIK (re-mix) *Freestyle FRS 1*	....	15	9

Bobby M featuring Jean CARN
US, male/female vocal/instrumental duo   3 wks

| 29 Jan 83 | | LET'S STAY TOGETHER *Gordy TMG 1288* | .... | 53 | 3 |

M-BEAT ☺ *UK, male producer*   24 wks

| 18 Jun 94 | | INCREDIBLE *Renk RENK 42CD* [1] | .... | 39 | 3 |
| 10 Sep 94 | ● | INCREDIBLE (re-mix) *Renk CDRENK 44* [1] | .... | 8 | 9 |

| 17 Dec 94 | | SWEET LOVE *Renk CDRENK 49* [2] | .... | 18 | 7 |
| 1 Jun 96 | | DO U KNOW WHERE YOU'RE COMING FROM *Renk CDRENK 63* [3] | .... | 12 | 5 |

[1] M-Beat featuring General Levy [2] M-Beat featuring Nazlyn [3] M-Beat featuring Jamiroquai

M-D-EMM *UK, male producer – Mark Ryder*   3 wks

| 22 Feb 92 | | GET DOWN *Strictly Underground 7STUR 13* | .... | 55 | 2 |
| 30 May 92 | | MOVE YOUR FEET *Strictly Underground STUR 15* | .... | 67 | 1 |

M + M *Canada, male/female vocal duo*   4 wks

| 28 Jul 84 | | BLACK STATIONS WHITE STATIONS *RCA 426* | .... | 46 | 4 |

See also MARTHA and the MUFFINS

M and O BAND ✎ *UK, male vocal/instrumental group*   6 wks

| 28 Feb 76 | | LET'S DO THE LATIN HUSTLE *Creole CR 120* | .... | 16 | 6 |

M PEOPLE ☺ ◑ ✎ *Clubland-favourites turned pop-soul-sophisticates: Heather Small (v), backed by Paul Heard and Mike Pickering (both k/prog). In 1994 this Manchester act were voted Best British Dance Act at the BRITS and won the Mercury Music Prize for their LP* Elegant Slumming   133 wks

26 Oct 91		HOW CAN I LOVE YOU MORE *Deconstruction PB 44855*	....	29	9
7 Mar 92		COLOUR MY LIFE *Deconstruction PB 45241*	....	35	4
18 Apr 92		SOMEDAY *Deconstruction PB 45369* [1]	....	38	3
10 Oct 92		EXCITED *Deconstruction 74321116337*	....	29	5
5 Feb 93	●	HOW CAN I LOVE YOU MORE (re-mix) *Deconstruction 74321130232*	....	8	8
26 Jun 93	●	ONE NIGHT IN HEAVEN *Deconstruction 74321151852*	....	6	11
25 Sep 93	●	MOVING ON UP *Deconstruction 74321166162*	....	2	11
4 Dec 93	●	DON'T LOOK ANY FURTHER *Deconstruction 74321177112*	....	9	10
12 Mar 94	●	RENAISSANCE *Deconstruction 74321194132*	....	5	7
17 Sep 94		ELEGANTLY AMERICAN: ONE NIGHT IN HEAVEN/ MOVING ON UP (RE-MIXES) (re-mix) *Deconstruction 74321231882*	....	31	2
19 Nov 94	●	SIGHT FOR SORE EYES *Deconstruction 74321245472*	....	6	9
4 Feb 95	●	OPEN YOUR HEART *Deconstruction 74321261532*	....	9	7
24 Jun 95	●	SEARCH FOR THE HERO *Deconstruction 74321287962*	....	9	7
14 Oct 95		LOVE RENDEZVOUS *Deconstruction 74321319282*	....	32	4
25 Nov 95		ITCHYCOO PARK *Deconstruction 74321330732*	....	11	8
4 Oct 97	●	JUST FOR YOU *BMG 74321523002*	....	8	7
6 Dec 97		FANTASY ISLAND *BMG 74321542932*	....	33	8
28 Feb 98		FANTASY ISLAND (re-entry) *BMG 74321542932*	....	69	1
28 Mar 98	●	ANGEL STREET *M People 74321564182*	....	8	6
7 Nov 98		TESTIFY *M People 74321621742*	....	12	6

[1] M People with Heather Small

Pete MAC Jr. *US, male vocalist*   4 wks

| 15 Oct 77 | | THE WATER MARGIN *BBC RESL 50* | .... | 37 | 4 |

This is the Japanese version of the song which shared chart credit with the English language version by Godiego
See also GODIEGO

MAC BAND featuring the McCAMPBELL BROTHERS ☺ ✎
US, male vocal group   17 wks

| 18 Jun 88 | ● | ROSES ARE RED *MCA MCA 1264* | .... | 8 | 13 |
| 10 Sep 88 | | STALEMATE *MCA MCA 1271* | .... | 40 | 4 |

'Stalemate' credits the McCampbell Brothers on the sleeve only, not on the label

Keith MAC PROJECT *UK, male/female vocal/instrumental group*   1 wk

| 25 Jun 94 | | DE DAH DAH (SPICE OF LIFE) *Public Demand PPDCD 3* | .... | 66 | 1 |

David McALMONT ◑ *UK, male vocalist*   17 wks

27 May 95	●	YES *Hut HUTCD 53* [1]	....	8	8
4 Nov 95		YOU DO *Hut HUTDG 57* [1]	....	17	4
27 Apr 96		HYMN *Blanco Y Negro NEG 87CD* [2]	....	65	1

| 9 Aug 97 | | LOOK AT YOURSELF *Hut HUTCD 87* | 40 | 2 |
| 22 Nov 97 | | DIAMONDS ARE FOREVER *East West EW 141CD* [3] | 39 | 2 |

[1] McAlmont and Butler [2] Ultramarine featuring David McAlmont
[3] David McAlmont/David Arnold

Neil MacARTHUR *UK, male vocalist* — 5 wks

| 5 Feb 69 | SHE'S NOT THERE *Deram DM 225* | 34 | 5 |

Neil MacArthur is Colin Blunstone under a pseudonym

David MacBETH ℭ *UK, male vocalist* — 4 wks

| 30 Oct 59 | MR. BLUE *Pye 7N 15231* | 18 | 4 |

Nicko McBRAIN *UK, male vocalist/instrumentalist – drums* — 1 wk

| 13 Jul 91 | RHYTHM OF THE BEAST *EMI NICK 01* | 72 | 1 |

Frankie McBRIDE *Ireland, male vocalist* — 15 wks

| 9 Aug 67 | FIVE LITTLE FINGERS *Emerald MD 1081* | 19 | 15 |

Dan McCAFFERTY *UK, male vocalist* — 3 wks

| 13 Sep 75 | OUT OF TIME *Mountain TOP 1* | 41 | 3 |

CW McCALL *US, male vocalist* — 10 wks

| 14 Feb 76 | ● CONVOY *MGM 2006 560* ▲ | 2 | 10 |

David McCALLUM *UK, male vocalist* — 4 wks

| 14 Apr 66 | COMMUNICATION *Capitol CL 15439* | 32 | 4 |

McCAMPBELL BROTHERS – See MAC BAND featuring the McCAMPBELL BROTHERS

Linda McCARTNEY *US, female vocalist* — 1 wk

| 21 Nov 98 | WIDE PRAIRIE *Parlophone CDR 6510* | 74 | 1 |

Paul McCARTNEY ✪ *Pop's most successful singer/songwriter, b. 18 June, 1942, Liverpool. The Guinness Book of World Records presented the ex-Beatle with a unique Rhodium record to honour outstanding sales achievements. He also received a Lifetime Achievement Grammy (1990) and a knighthood (1997)* — 405 wks

22 Feb 71	● ANOTHER DAY *Apple R 5889*	2	12
28 Aug 71	BACK SEAT OF MY CAR *Apple R 5914* [1]	39	5
26 Feb 72	GIVE IRELAND BACK TO THE IRISH *Apple R 5936* [2]	16	8
27 May 72	● MARY HAD A LITTLE LAMB *Apple R 5949* [2]	9	11
9 Dec 72	● HI HI HI / C MOON *Apple R 5973* [2]	5	13
7 Apr 73	● MY LOVE *Apple R 5985* [3] ▲	9	11
9 Jun 73	● LIVE AND LET DIE *Apple R 5987* [2]	9	13
15 Sep 73	LIVE AND LET DIE (re-entry) *Apple R 5987* [2]	49	1
3 Nov 73	HELEN WHEELS *Apple R 5993* [3]	12	12
2 Mar 74	● JET *Apple R 5996* [3]	7	9
6 Jul 74	BAND ON THE RUN *Apple R 5997* [3] ▲	3	11
9 Nov 74	JUNIOR'S FARM *Apple R 5999* [3]	16	10
31 May 75	● LISTEN TO WHAT THE MAN SAID *Capitol R 6006* [2] ▲	6	8
18 Oct 75	LETTING GO *Capitol R 6008* [2]	41	3
15 May 76	● SILLY LOVE SONGS *Parlophone R 6014* [2] ▲	2	11
7 Aug 76	● LET 'EM IN *Parlophone R 6015* [2]	2	10
19 Feb 77	MAYBE I'M AMAZED *Parlophone R 6017* [2]	28	5
19 Nov 77	MULL OF KINTYRE / GIRLS' SCHOOL *Capitol R 6018* [2]	1	17
1 Apr 78	● WITH A LITTLE LUCK *Parlophone R 6019* [2] ▲	5	9
1 Jul 78	I'VE HAD ENOUGH *Parlophone R 6020* [2]	42	7
9 Sep 78	LONDON TOWN *Parlophone R 6021* [2]	60	4
7 Apr 79	● GOODNIGHT TONIGHT *Parlophone R 6023* [2]	5	10
16 Jun 79	OLD SIAM SIR *MPL R 6026* [2]	35	6
1 Sep 79	GETTING CLOSER / BABY'S REQUEST *R 6027* [2]	60	3
1 Dec 79	● WONDERFUL CHRISTMASTIME *Parlophone R 6029*	6	8
19 Apr 80	● COMING UP *Parlophone R 6035*	2	9
21 Apr 80	WATERFALLS *Parlophone R 6037*	9	8
10 Apr 82	★ EBONY AND IVORY *Parlophone 6054* [4] ▲	1	10
3 Jul 82	TAKE IT AWAY *Parlophone R 6056*	15	10
9 Oct 82	TUG OF WAR *Parlophone R 6057*	53	3
6 Nov 82	● THE GIRL IS MINE *Epic EPC A 2729* [5]	8	9
15 Jan 83	THE GIRL IS MINE (re-entry) *Epic EPC A 2729* [5]	75	1
15 Oct 83	SAY SAY SAY *Parlophone R 6062* [6] ▲	2	15
17 Dec 83	PIPES OF PEACE *Parlophone R 6064*	1	12
6 Oct 84	● NO MORE LONELY NIGHTS (BALLAD) *Parlophone R 6080*	2	15
24 Nov 84	● WE ALL STAND TOGETHER *Parlophone R 6086*	3	13
30 Nov 85	SPIES LIKE US *Parlophone R 6118*	13	10
21 Dec 85	WE ALL STAND TOGETHER (re-entry) *Parlophone R 6086* [7]	32	5
26 Jul 86	PRESS *Parlophone R 6133*	25	8
13 Dec 86	ONLY LOVE REMAINS *Parlophone R 6148*	34	5
28 Nov 87	● ONCE UPON A LONG AGO *Parlophone R 6170*	10	7
20 May 89	★ FERRY 'CROSS THE MERSEY *PWL PWL 41* [8]	1	7
20 May 89	MY BRAVE FACE *Parlophone R 6213*	18	5
29 Jul 89	THIS ONE *Parlophone R 6223*	18	6
25 Nov 89	FIGURE OF EIGHT *Parlophone R 6235*	42	3
17 Feb 90	PUT IT THERE *Parlophone R 6246*	32	2
20 Oct 90	BIRTHDAY *Parlophone R 6271*	29	3
8 Dec 90	ALL MY TRIALS *Parlophone CDR 6330*	35	5
5 Feb 93	HOPE OF DELIVERANCE *Parlophone CDR 6330*	18	6
6 Mar 93	C'MON PEOPLE *Parlophone CDRS 6338*	41	3
10 May 97	YOUNG BOYS *Parlophone CDRS 6462*	19	3
26 Jul 97	THE WORLD TONIGHT *Parlophone CDR 6472*	23	1
27 Dec 97	BEAUTIFUL TONIGHT *Parlophone CDR 6489*	25	4

[1] Paul and Linda McCartney [2] Wings [3] Paul McCartney and Wings
[4] Paul McCartney with Stevie Wonder [5] Michael Jackson and Paul McCartney
[6] Paul McCartney and Michael Jackson [7] Paul McCartney and the Frog Chorus
[8] Christians, Holly Johnson, Paul McCartney, Gerry Marsden and Stock Aitken Waterman

R 6027 credits no label at all, although the number is a Parlophone one

Kirsty MacCOLL ✪ *UK, female vocalist* — 65 wks

13 Jun 81	THERE'S A GUY WORKS DOWN THE CHIPSHOP SWEARS HE'S ELVIS *Polydor POSP 250*	14	9
19 Jan 85	● A NEW ENGLAND *Stiff BUY 216*	7	10
15 Nov 86	GREETINGS TO THE NEW BRUNETTE *Go! Discs GOD 12* [1]	58	2
5 Dec 87	● FAIRYTALE OF NEW YORK *Pogue Mahone NY 7* [2]	2	9
8 Apr 89	FREE WORLD *Virgin KMA 1*	43	6
1 Jul 89	DAYS *Virgin KMA 2*	12	9
25 May 91	WALKING DOWN MADISON *Virgin VS 1348*	23	7
17 Aug 91	MY AFFAIR *Virgin VS 1354*	56	2
14 Dec 91	FAIRYTALE OF NEW YORK *PM YZ 628* [2]	36	5
4 Mar 95	CAROLINE *Virgin VSCDX 1517*	58	2
24 Jun 95	PERFECT DAY *Virgin VSCDT 1552* [3]	75	1
29 Jul 95	DAYS (re-issue) *Virgin VSCDT 1558*	42	3

[1] Billy Bragg with Johnny Marr and Kirsty MacColl
[2] Pogues featuring Kirsty MacColl [3] Kirsty MacColl and Evan Dando

Marilyn McCOO and Billy DAVIS Jr. ✪ ♪ *US, female/male vocal duo* — 9 wks

| 19 Mar 77 | ● YOU DON'T HAVE TO BE A STAR (TO BE IN MY SHOW) *ABC 4147* ▲ | 7 | 9 |

Van McCOY *US, orchestra* — 36 wks

31 May 75	● THE HUSTLE *Avco 6105 038* [1] ▲	3	12
1 Nov 75	CHANGE WITH THE TIMES *Avco 6105 042*	36	4
12 Feb 77	SOUL CHA CHA *H & L 6105 065*	34	6
9 Apr 77	● THE SHUFFLE *H & L 6105 076*	4	14

[1] Van McCoy with the Soul City Symphony

McCOYS ✪ *US, male vocal/instrumental group* — 18 wks

| 2 Sep 65 | ● HANG ON SLOOPY *Immediate IM 001* ▲ | 5 | 14 |
| 16 Dec 65 | FEVER *Immediate IM 021* | 44 | 4 |

George McCRAE ♪ *US, male vocalist* — 62 wks

29 Jun 74	★ ROCK YOUR BABY *Jayboy BOY 85* ▲	1	14
5 Oct 74	I CAN'T LEAVE YOU ALONE *Jayboy BOY 90*	9	9
14 Dec 74	YOU CAN HAVE IT ALL *Jayboy BOY 92*	23	9
22 Mar 75	SING A HAPPY SONG *Jayboy BOY 95*	38	4

19 Jul 75	● IT'S BEEN SO LONG *Jayboy BOY 100*	4	11
18 Oct 75	I AIN'T LYIN' *Jayboy BOY 105*	12	7
24 Jan 76	HONEY I *Jayboy BOY 107*	33	4
25 Feb 84	ONE STEP CLOSER (TO LOVE) *President PT 522*	57	4

Gwen McCRAE *US, female vocalist* — 5 wks

30 Apr 88	ALL THIS LOVE THAT I'M GIVING *Flame MELT 7*	63	2
13 Feb 93	ALL THIS LOVE I'M GIVING *KTDA CDKTDA 2* [1]	36	3

[1] Music and Mystery featuring Gwen McCrae

'All This Love I'm Giving' is a re-recording of her first hit

MacCRARYS *US, male/female vocal group* — 4 wks

31 Jul 82	LOVE ON A SUMMER NIGHT *Capitol CL 251*	52	4

Mindy McCREADY *US, female vocalist* — 3 wks

1 Aug 98	OH ROMEO *BNA 74321597242*	41	3

Ian McCULLOCH *UK, male vocalist* — 14 wks

15 Dec 84	SEPTEMBER SONG *Korova KOW 40*	51	5
2 Sep 89	PROUD TO FALL *WEA YZ 417*	51	4
12 May 90	CANDLELAND (THE SECOND COMING) *East West YZ 452* [1]	75	1
22 Feb 92	LOVER LOVER LOVER *East West YZ 643*	47	4

[1] Ian McCulloch featuring Elizabeth Fraser

Martine McCUTCHEON – See UNO CLIO featuring Martine McCUTCHEON

Gene McDANIELS *US, male vocalist* — 2 wks

16 Nov 61	TOWER OF STRENGTH *London HLG 9448*	49	1
30 Nov 61	TOWER OF STRENGTH (re-entry) *London HLG 9448*	49	1

Julie McDERMOTT – See THIRD DIMENSION featuring Julie McDERMOTT; AWESOME 3

Charles McDEVITT SKIFFLE GROUP featuring Nancy WHISKEY ☺ *UK, male/female vocal/instrumental group* — 20 wks

12 Apr 57	● FREIGHT TRAIN *Oriole CB 1352*	5	17
14 Jun 57	GREENBACK DOLLAR *Oriole CB 1371*	28	1
5 Jul 57	GREENBACK DOLLAR (re-entry) *Oriole CB 1371*	30	1
20 Sep 57	FREIGHT TRAIN (re-entry) *Oriole CB 1352*	27	1

Jane McDONALD ☺ ☾ *UK, female vocalist* — 1 wk

26 Dec 98	● CRUISE INTO CHRISTMAS MEDLEY *Focus Music Int CDFM 2*	10†	1

Michael McDONALD ☺ ✎ *US, male vocalist* — 45 wks

18 Feb 84	YAH MO B THERE *Qwest W 9394* [1]	44	5
7 Apr 84	YAH MO B THERE (re-entry) *Qwest W 9394* [1]	69	3
12 Jan 85	YAH MO B THERE (2nd re-entry) *Qwest W 9394* [1]	12	8
3 May 86	● ON MY OWN *MCA MCA 1045* [2] ▲	2	13
26 Jul 86	I KEEP FORGETTIN' *Warner Bros K 17992*	43	6
6 Sep 86	SWEET FREEDOM *MCA MCA 1073*	12	10

[1] James Ingram with Michael McDonald [2] Patti Labelle and Michael McDonald

The 1985 entry of 'Yah Mo B There' is a re-mix of the original hit with the same catalogue number
See also DOOBIE BROTHERS

Carrie McDOWELL *US, female vocalist* — 3 wks

26 Sep 87	UH UH NO NO CASUAL SEX *Motown ZV 41501*	68	3

John McENROE and Pat CASH with the FULL METAL RACKETS
US/Australia, male vocal/instrumental duo with UK backing group — 1 wk

13 Jul 91	ROCK 'N' ROLL *Music For Nations KUT 141*	66	1

McFADDEN and WHITEHEAD ✎ *US, male vocal duo* — 10 wks

19 May 79	● AIN'T NO STOPPIN' US NOW *Philadelphia Interna PIR 7365*	5	10

Rachel McFARLANE *UK, female vocalist* — 2 wks

1 Aug 98	LOVER *Multiply CDMULTY 37*	38	2

See also LOVELAND featuring the voice of Rachel McFARLANE

Bobby McFERRIN ♪ ✎ *US, male vocalist* — 15 wks

24 Sep 88	● DON'T WORRY BE HAPPY *Manhattan MT 56* ▲	2	11
17 Dec 88	THINKIN' ABOUT YOUR BODY *Manhattan BLUE 6*	46	4

McGANNS *UK, male vocal trio* — 1 wk

14 Nov 98	JUST MY IMAGINATION *Coalition COLA 062CD*	59	1

Mike McGEAR *UK, male vocalist* — 4 wks

5 Oct 74	LEAVE IT *Warner Bros. K 16446*	36	4

Maureen McGOVERN ☾ *US, female vocalist* — 8 wks

5 Jun 76	THE CONTINENTAL *20th Century BTC 2222*	16	8

Shane MacGOWAN *UK, male vocalist* — 9 wks

12 Dec 92	WHAT A WONDERFUL WORLD *Mute MUTE 151* [1]	72	1
3 Sep 94	THE CHURCH OF THE HOLY SPOOK *ZTT ZANG 57CD* [2]	74	1
15 Oct 94	THAT WOMAN'S GOT ME DRINKING *ZTT ZANG 57CD* [2]	34	3
29 Apr 95	HAUNTED *ZTT ZANG 65CD* [3]	30	2
20 Apr 96	MY WAY *ZTT ZANG 79CD*	29	2

[1] Nick Cave and Shane MacGowan [2] Shane MacGowan and the Popes
[3] Shane MacGowan and Sinead O'Connor

Ewan McGREGOR – See PF PROJECT

Freddie McGREGOR ⚘ *Jamaica, male vocalist* — 16 wks

27 Jun 87	● JUST DON'T WANT TO BE LONELY *Germain DG 24*	9	11
19 Sep 87	THAT GIRL (GROOVY SITUATION) *Polydor POSP 884*	47	5

Mary MacGREGOR ☺ *US, female vocalist* — 10 wks

19 Feb 77	● TORN BETWEEN TWO LOVERS *Ariola America AA 111* ▲	4	10

McGUINNESS FLINT ♂ ✎
UK, male vocal/instrumental group — 26 wks

21 Nov 70	● WHEN I'M DEAD AND GONE *Capitol CL 15662*	2	14
1 May 71	● MALT AND BARLEY BLUES *Capitol CL 15682*	5	12

Barry McGUIRE ♂ ✎ *US, male vocalist* — 13 wks

9 Sep 65	● EVE OF DESTRUCTION *RCA 1469* ▲	3	13

McGUIRE SISTERS ☾ *US, female vocal group* — 24 wks

1 Apr 55	NO MORE *Vogue Coral Q 72050*	20	1
15 Jul 55	SINCERELY *Vogue Coral Q 72050* ▲	14	4
1 Jun 56	DELILAH JONES *Vogue Coral Q 72161*	24	2
14 Feb 58	SUGARTIME *Coral Q 72305*	14	6
1 May 59	MAY YOU ALWAYS *Coral Q 72356*	15	10
17 Jul 59	MAY YOU ALWAYS (re-entry) *Coral Q 72356*	28	1

MACHEL *Trinidad, male vocal* — 2 wks

14 Sep 96	COME DIG IT *London LONCD 386*	56	2

MACHINE HEAD *UK, male vocal/instrumental group* — 3 wks

27 May 95	OLD *Roadrunner RR 23403*	43	2
6 Dec 97	TAKE MY SCARS *Roadrunner RR 22573*	73	1

Craig MACK *US, male rapper* — 5 wks

12 Nov 94	FLAVA IN YA EAR *Bad Boy 74321242582*	57	2
1 Apr 95	GET DOWN *Puff Daddy 74321263402*	54	1

7 Jun 97	**SPIRIT** *Perspective 5822312* [1]	35 2

[1] Sound of Blackness featuring Craig Mack

See also VARIOUS ARTISTS (EPs and LPs) – The Dangerous Minds EP

Lizzy MACK *UK, female vocalist* — 3 wks

5 Nov 94	**THE POWER OF LOVE** *Media MCSTD 2016* [1]	49 2
4 Nov 95	**DON'T GO** *Power Station MCSTD 40004*	52 1

[1] Fits of Gloom featuring Lizzy Mack

Lonnie MACK *US, male instrumentalist – guitar* — 3 wks

14 Apr 79	**MEMPHIS** *Lightning LIG 9011*	47 3

'Memphis' was coupled with 'Let's Dance' by Chris Montez as a double A-side

MACK VIBE featuring JACQUELINE
US, male/female vocal/instrumental duo — 1 wk

4 Feb 95	**I CAN'T LET YOU GO** *MCA MCSTD 20020*	53 1

Maria McKEE ☻ �@ *US, female vocalist* — 23 wks

15 Sep 90	★ **SHOW ME HEAVEN** *Epic 656303 7*	1 14
26 Jan 91	**BREATHE** *Geffen GFS 1*	59 1
1 Aug 92	**SWEETEST CHILD** *Geffen GFS 23*	45 4
22 May 93	**I'M GONNA SOOTHE YOU** *Geffen GFSTD 39*	35 3
18 Sep 93	**I CAN'T MAKE IT ALONE** *Geffen GFSTD 53*	74 1

Kenneth McKELLAR *UK, male vocalist* — 4 wks

10 Mar 66	**A MAN WITHOUT LOVE** *Decca F 12341*	30 4

Terence McKENNA – *See SHAMEN*

Gisele McKENZIE ℂ *Canada, female vocalist* — 6 wks

17 Jul 53	**SEVEN LONELY DAYS** *Capitol CL 13920*	12 1
31 Jul 53	**SEVEN LONELY DAYS (re-entry)** *Capitol CL 13920*	11 1
21 Aug 53	● **SEVEN LONELY DAYS (2nd re-entry)** *Capitol CL 13920*	6 4

Scott McKENZIE ☻ *US, male vocalist* — 18 wks

12 Jul 67	★ **SAN FRANCISCO (BE SURE TO WEAR SOME FLOWERS IN YOUR HAIR)** *CBS 2816*	1 17
1 Nov 67	**LIKE AN OLD TIME MOVIE** *CBS 3009* [1]	50 1

[1] The Voice of Scott McKenzie

Ken MACKINTOSH ℂ *UK, orchestra* — 9 wks

15 Jan 54	**THE CREEP** *HMV BD 1295*	12 1
29 Jan 54	● **THE CREEP (re-entry)** *HMV BD 1295*	10 1
7 Feb 58	**RAUNCHY** *HMV POP 426*	19 6
10 Mar 60	**NO HIDING PLACE** *HMV POP 713*	45 1

Brian McKNIGHT *US, male vocalist* — 4 wks

6 Jun 98	**ANYTIME** *Motown 8607752*	48 2
3 Oct 98	**YOU SHOULD BE MINE** *Motown 8608412*	36 2

Vivienne McKONE *UK, female vocalist* — 5 wks

25 Jul 92	**SING (OOH-EE-OOH)** *ffrr F 183*	47 4
31 Oct 92	**BEWARE** *ffrr F 202*	69 1

McKOY *UK, male/female vocal group* — 2 wks

6 Mar 93	**FIGHT** *Rightrack CDTUM 1*	54 2

Noel McKOY – *See JTQ; McKOY*

Craig McLACHLAN ☻ *Australia, male vocalist* — 40 wks

16 Jun 90	● **MONA** *Epic 655784 7* [1]	2 11
4 Aug 90	**AMANDA** *Epic 656170 7* [1]	19 6
10 Nov 90	**I ALMOST FELT LIKE CRYING** *Epic 656310 7* [1]	50 3
23 May 92	**ONE REASON WHY** *Epic 6580677*	29 6
14 Nov 92	**ON MY OWN** *Epic 6584677*	59 2
24 Jul 93	**YOU'RE THE ONE THAT I WANT** *Epic 6595222* [2]	13 6
25 Dec 93	**GREASE** *Epic 6600242*	44 4
8 Jul 95	**EVERYDAY** *MDMC DEVCS 6* [3]	65 2

[1] Craig McLachlan and Check 1-2 [2] Craig McLachlan and Debbie Gibson [3] Craig McLachlan and the Culprits

Sarah McLACHLAN ☻ ♂ *Canada, female vocalist/instrumentalist* — 5 wks

3 Oct 98	**ADIA** *Arista 74321613902*	18 5

Tommy McLAIN *US, male vocalist* — 1 wk

8 Sep 66	**SWEET DREAMS** *London HL 10065*	49 1

Malcolm McLAREN ☺ 🎸 *UK, male vocalist* — 65 wks

4 Dec 82	● **BUFFALO GALS** *Charisma MALC 1* [1]	9 12
26 Feb 83	**SOWETO** *Charisma MALC 2* [2]	32 5
2 Jul 83	● **DOUBLE DUTCH** *Charisma MALC 3*	3 13
17 Dec 83	**DUCK FOR THE OYSTER** *Charisma MALC 4*	54 5
1 Sep 84	**MADAM BUTTERFLY (UN BEL DI VEDREMO)** *Charisma MALC 5*	13 9
27 May 89	**WALTZ DARLING** *Epic WALTZ 2* [3]	31 8
19 Aug 89	**SOMETHING'S JUMPIN' IN YOUR SHIRT** *Epic WALTZ 3* [4]	29 7
25 Nov 89	**HOUSE OF THE BLUE DANUBE** *Epic WALTZ 4* [3]	73 1
21 Dec 91	**MAGIC'S BACK (THEME FROM THE GHOSTS OF OXFORD STREET)** *RCA PB 45223* [5]	42 4
3 Oct 98	**BUFFALO GAS STAMPEDE** *Virgin VSCDT 1717*	65 1

[1] Malcolm McLaren and the World's Famous Supreme Team [2] Malcolm McLaren and the McLarenettes [3] Malcolm McLaren and the Bootzilla Orchestra [4] Malcolm McLaren and the Bootzilla Orchestra featuring Lisa Marie [5] Malcolm McLaren featuring Alison Limerick

Bitty McLEAN 🏏 *UK, male vocalist* — 50 wks

31 Jul 93	● **IT KEEP RAININ' (TEARS FROM MY EYES)** *Brilliant CDBRIL 1*	2 15
30 Oct 93	**PASS IT ON** *Brilliant CDBRIL 2*	35 3
15 Jan 94	● **HERE I STAND** *Brilliant CDBRIL 3*	10 6
9 Apr 94	● **DEDICATED TO THE ONE I LOVE** *Brilliant CDBRIL 4*	6 10
6 Aug 94	**WHAT GOES AROUND** *Brilliant CDBRIL 5*	36 3
8 Apr 95	**OVER THE RIVER** *Brilliant CDBRIL 9*	27 4
17 Jun 95	**WE'VE ONLY JUST BEGUN** *Brilliant CDBRIL 10*	23 5
30 Sep 95	**NOTHING CAN CHANGE THIS LOVE** *Brilliant CDBRIL 11*	55 2
27 Jan 96	**NATURAL HIGH** *Brilliant CDBRIL 12*	63 1
5 Oct 96	**SHE'S ALRIGHT** *Kuff KUFFD 9*	53 1

Don McLEAN ♂ �@ *US, male vocalist* — 68 wks

22 Jan 72	● **AMERICAN PIE** *United Artists UP 35325* ▲	2 16
13 May 72	★ **VINCENT** *United Artists UP 35359*	1 15
14 Apr 73	**EVERYDAY** *United Artists UP 35519*	38 5
10 May 80	★ **CRYING** *EMI 5051*	1 14
17 Apr 82	**CASTLES IN THE AIR** *EMI 5258*	47 8
5 Oct 91	**AMERICAN PIE (re-issue)** *Liberty EMCT 3*	12 10

Jackie McLEAN *US, male instrumentalist – alto sax* — 4 wks

7 Jul 79	**DR. JACKYLL AND MISTER FUNK** *RCA PB 1575*	53 4

Phil McLEAN *US, male vocalist* — 4 wks

18 Jan 62	**SMALL SAD SAM** *Top Rank JAR 597*	34 4

Ian McNABB *UK, male vocalist* — 6 wks

23 Jan 93	**IF LOVE WAS LIKE GUITARS** *This Way Up WAY 233*	67 1
2 Jul 94	**YOU MUST BE PREPARED TO DREAM** *This Way Up WAY 3199* [1]	54 1
17 Sep 94	**GO INTO THE LIGHT** *This Way Up WAY 3699*	66 2
27 Apr 96	**DON'T PUT YOUR SPELL ON ME** *This Way Up WAY 5033*	72 1
6 Jul 96	**MERSEYBEAST** *This Way Up WAY 5266*	74 1

[1] Ian McNabb featuring Ralph Molina and Billy Talbot

UK No 1 ★   UK Top 10 ●   UK million seller ◆   UK entry at No 1 ■   US No 1 ▲

LUTRICIA McNEAL ◎ R&B US, female vocalist — 39 wks

29 Nov 97	● AIN'T THAT JUST THE WAY Wildstar CXSTAS 2907	6	18
23 May 98	● STRANDED Wildstar CXSTAS 2973	3	12
26 Sep 98	● SOMEONE LOVES YOU HONEY Wildstar CDWILD 9	9	7
19 Dec 98	THE GREATEST LOVE YOU'LL NEVER KNOW Wildstar CDWILD 11	17†	2

Patrick MacNEE and Honor BLACKMAN ◎
UK, male/female vocal duo — 7 wks

1 Dec 90	● KINKY BOOTS Deram KINKY 1	5	7

Rita MacNEIL ℂ Canada, female vocalist — 10 wks

6 Oct 90	WORKING MAN Polydor PO 98	11	10

Clyde McPHATTER US, male vocalist — 1 wk

24 Aug 56	TREASURE OF LOVE London HLE 8293	27	1

Carmen McRAE – See Sammy DAVIS Jr

Gordon MacRAE – See VARIOUS ARTISTS (EPs & LPs) – Carousel LP

Ralph McTELL ♂ UK, male vocalist — 18 wks

7 Dec 74	● STREETS OF LONDON Reprise K 14380	2	12
20 Dec 75	DREAMS OF YOU Warner Bros. K 16648	36	6

MAD COBRA featuring Ritchie STEPHENS
Jamaica/UK, male vocal duo — 2 wks

15 May 93	LEGACY Columbia 6592852	64	2

MAD JOCKS featuring JOCKMASTER B.A.
UK, male vocal/instrumental group — 9 wks

19 Dec 87	JOCK MIX 1 Debut DEBT 3037	46	5
18 Dec 93	PARTY FOUR EP SMP CDSSKM 24	57	4

Tracks on Party Four EP: No Lager / Here We Go Again / Jock Party Mix / Jock Jak Mix

MAD MOSES US, male DJ / producer – 'Mad' Mitch Moses — 1 wk

16 Aug 97	PANTHER PARTY Hi-Life 5744932	50	1

MAD STUNTMAN – See REEL 2 REAL

Sonya MADAN – See LITHIAM and Sonya MADAN

Danny MADDEN US, male vocalist — 2 wks

14 Jul 90	THE FACTS OF LIFE Eternal YZ 473	72	2

MADDER ROSE US, male/female vocal/instrumental group — 2 wks

26 Mar 94	PANIC ON Atlantic A 8301CD	65	1
16 Jul 94	CAR SONG Seed A 7256CD	68	1

MADDOG – See STRETCH 'N' VERN featuring MADDOG

MADNESS ◎ ♈ London-based band whose ska-rooted 'nutty' sound
earned them a huge haul of hits. This good-time septet fronted by
Graham 'Suggs' McPherson (b. 13 January, 1961) spent more weeks
on the chart in the 1980s than any other group — 258 wks

1 Sep 79	THE PRINCE 2 Tone TT 3	16	11
10 Nov 79	● ONE STEP BEYOND Stiff BUY 56	7	14
5 Jan 80	● MY GIRL Stiff BUY 62	3	10
5 Apr 80	● WORK REST AND PLAY EP Stiff BUY 71	6	8
13 Sep 80	● BAGGY TROUSERS Stiff BUY 84	3	20
22 Nov 80	● EMBARRASSMENT Stiff BUY 102	4	12
24 Jan 81	● THE RETURN OF THE LOS PALMAS SEVEN Stiff BUY 108	7	11
25 Apr 81	● GREY DAY Stiff BUY 112	4	10
26 Sep 81	● SHUT UP Stiff BUY 126	7	9
5 Dec 81	● IT MUST BE LOVE Stiff BUY 134	4	12
20 Feb 82	CARDIAC ARREST Stiff BUY 140	14	10
22 May 82	★ HOUSE OF FUN Stiff BUY 146	1	9
24 Jul 82	● DRIVING IN MY CAR Stiff BUY 153	4	8
27 Nov 82	● OUR HOUSE Stiff BUY 163	5	13
19 Feb 83	● TOMORROW'S (JUST ANOTHER DAY) / MADNESS (IS ALL IN THE MIND) Stiff BUY 169	8	9
20 Aug 83	● WINGS OF A DOVE Stiff BUY 181	2	10
5 Nov 83	● THE SUN AND THE RAIN Stiff BUY 192	5	10
11 Feb 84	MICHAEL CAINE Stiff BUY 196	11	8
2 Jun 84	ONE BETTER DAY Stiff BUY 201	17	7
31 Aug 85	YESTERDAY'S MEN Zarjazz JAZZ 5	18	7
26 Oct 85	UNCLE SAM Zarjazz JAZZ 7	21	11
1 Feb 86	SWEETEST GIRL Zarjazz JAZZ 8	35	6
8 Nov 86	(WAITING FOR) THE GHOST TRAIN Zarjazz JAZZ 9	18	7
3 Jan 87	(WAITING FOR) THE GHOST TRAIN (re-entry) Zarjazz JAZZ 9	74	1
19 Mar 88	I PRONOUNCE YOU Virgin VS 1054 [1]	44	4
15 Feb 92	● IT MUST BE LOVE (re-issue) Virgin VS 1405	6	9
25 Apr 92	HOUSE OF FUN (re-issue) Virgin VS 1413	40	3
8 Aug 92	MY GIRL (re-issue) Virgin VS 1425	27	4
28 Nov 92	THE HARDER THEY COME Go! Discs GOD 93	44	3
27 Feb 93	NIGHT BOAT TO CAIRO Virgin VSCDT 1447	56	2

[1] The Madness

Tracks on Work Rest and Play EP: Night Boat to Cairo / Deceives the Eye /
The Young and the Old / Don't Quote Me on That. 'Night Boat to Cairo'
in 1993 is a re-issue of a track from the Work Rest and Play EP.
See also VARIOUS ARTISTS (EPs & LPs) – The Two Tone EP

MADONNA ◎ The most successful female artist of all time with sales in
excess of 100 million. B. Madonna Ciccone, 16 August, 1958, Michigan.
Often controversial, she has amassed an unequalled 32 consecutive
Top 10 hits and has an overall chart track record bettered only by
Elvis Presley and The Beatles — 477 wks

14 Jan 84	● HOLIDAY Sire W 9405	6	11
17 Mar 84	LUCKY STAR Sire W 9522	14	9
2 Jun 84	BORDERLINE Sire W 9260	56	4
17 Nov 84	● LIKE A VIRGIN Sire W 9210 ▲	3	18
2 Mar 85	● MATERIAL GIRL Sire W 9083	3	10
8 Jun 85	● CRAZY FOR YOU Geffen A 6323 ▲	2	15
27 Jul 85	★ INTO THE GROOVE Sire W 8934	1	14
3 Aug 85	● HOLIDAY (re-entry) Sire W 9405	2	10
21 Sep 85	● ANGEL Sire W 8881	5	9
12 Oct 85	● GAMBLER Geffen A 6585	4	11
7 Dec 85	● DRESS YOU UP Sire W 8848	5	11
4 Jan 86	GAMBLER (re-entry) Geffen A 6585	61	1
25 Jan 86	● BORDERLINE (re-entry) Sire W 9260	2	9
26 Apr 86	● LIVE TO TELL Sire W 8717 ▲	2	12
28 Jun 86	★ PAPA DON'T PREACH Sire W 8636 ▲	1	14
4 Oct 86	● TRUE BLUE Sire W 8550	1	15
13 Dec 86	● OPEN YOUR HEART Sire W 8480 ▲	4	9
4 Apr 87	★ LA ISLA BONITA Sire W 8378	1	11
18 Jul 87	★ WHO'S THAT GIRL Sire W 8341 ▲	1	10
19 Sep 87	● CAUSING A COMMOTION Sire W 8224	4	9
12 Dec 87	● THE LOOK OF LOVE Sire W 8115	9	7
18 Mar 89	★ LIKE A PRAYER Sire W 7539 ▲	1	12
3 Jun 89	● EXPRESS YOURSELF Sire W 2948	5	10
16 Sep 89	● CHERISH Sire W 2883	3	8
16 Dec 89	● DEAR JESSIE Sire W 2668	5	9
7 Apr 90	★ VOGUE Sire W 9851 ▲	1	14
21 Jul 90	● HANKY PANKY Sire W 9789	2	9
8 Dec 90	● JUSTIFY MY LOVE Sire W 9000 ▲	2	10
2 Mar 91	● CRAZY FOR YOU (re-mix) Sire W 0008	2	8
13 Apr 91	● RESCUE ME Sire W 0024	3	8
8 Jun 91	● HOLIDAY (re-issue) Sire W 0037	5	7
25 Jul 92	● THIS USED TO BE MY PLAYGROUND Sire W 0122 ▲	3	9
17 Oct 92	● EROTICA Maverick W 0138	3	8
12 Dec 92	● DEEPER AND DEEPER Maverick W 0146	6	9
9 Jan 93	EROTICA (re-entry) Maverick W 0138	65	1
6 Mar 93	● BAD GIRL Maverick W 0145CD	10	7
3 Apr 93	● FEVER Maverick W 0168CD	6	6
31 Jul 93	● RAIN Maverick W 0190CD	7	8
2 Apr 94	● I'LL REMEMBER Maverick W 0240CD	7	8
8 Oct 94	● SECRET Maverick W 0268CD	5	9

17 Dec 94	TAKE A BOW *Maverick W 0278CD* ▲	16	9
25 Feb 95 ●	BEDTIME STORY *Maverick W 0285CD*	4	8
6 May 95	BEDTIME STORY (re-entry) *Maverick W 0285CD*	66	1
26 Aug 95 ●	HUMAN NATURE *Maverick W 0300CD*	8	5
4 Nov 95 ●	YOU'LL SEE *Maverick W 0324CD*	5	13
6 Jan 96	OH FATHER *Maverick W 0326CD*	16	6
23 Mar 96	ONE MORE CHANCE *Maverick W 0337CD*	11	4
2 Nov 96 ●	YOU MUST LOVE ME *Warner Bros. W 0378CD*	10	4
28 Dec 96 ●	DON'T CRY FOR ME ARGENTINA *Warner Bros. W 0384CD*	3	11
18 Jan 97	YOU MUST LOVE ME (re-entry) *Warner Bros. W 0378CD*	71	1
29 Mar 97 ●	ANOTHER SUITCASE IN ANOTHER HALL *Warner Bros. W 0388CD*	7	5
7 Mar 98 ★	FROZEN *Maverick W 0433CD* ■	1	13
9 May 98 ●	RAY OF LIGHT *Maverick W 0444CD*	2	9
5 Sep 98 ●	DROWNED WORLD (SUBSTITUTE FOR LOVE) *Maverick W 0453CD1*	10	5
5 Dec 98 ●	THE POWER OF GOODBYE / LITTLE STAR *Maverick W 459CD*	6†	4

MAGAZINE *UK, male vocal/instrumental group*   7 wks

11 Feb 78	SHOT BY BOTH SIDES *Virgin VS 200*	41	4
26 Jul 80	SWEET HEART CONTRACT *Virgin VS 368*	54	3

MAGIC AFFAIR ☺
US/Germany, male/female vocal/instrumental group   8 wks

4 Jun 94	OMEN III *EMI CDEM 317*	17	4
27 Aug 94	GIVE ME ALL YOUR LOVE *EMI CDEM 340*	30	2
5 Nov 94	IN THE MIDDLE OF THE NIGHT *EMI CDEM 349*	38	2

MAGIC LADY *US, female vocal duo*   3 wks

14 May 88	BETCHA CAN'T LOSE (WITH MY LOVE) *Motown ZB 42003*	58	3

MAGIC LANTERNS *UK, male vocal/instrumental group*   3 wks

7 Jul 66	EXCUSE ME BABY *CBS 202094*	46	1
28 Jul 66	EXCUSE ME BABY (re-entry) *CBS 202094*	44	1
11 Aug 66	EXCUSE ME BABY (2nd re-entry) *CBS 202094*	46	1

MAGNUM *UK, male vocal/instrumental group*   26 wks

22 Mar 80	MAGNUM (DOUBLE SINGLE) *Jet 175*	47	6
12 Jul 86	LONELY NIGHT *Polydor POSP 798*	70	2
19 Mar 88	DAYS OF NO TRUST *Polydor POSP 910*	32	4
7 May 88	START TALKING LOVE *Polydor POSP 920*	22	4
2 Jul 88	IT MUST HAVE BEEN LOVE *Polydor POSP 930*	33	4
23 Jun 90	ROCKIN' CHAIR *Polydor PO 88*	27	4
25 Aug 90	HEARTBROKE AND BUSTED *Polydor PO 94*	49	2

Tracks on double single: Invasion / Kingdom of Madness / All of My Life / Great Adventure

Sean MAGUIRE ☺ *UK, male vocalist*   34 wks

20 Aug 94	SOMEONE TO LOVE *Parlophone CDR 6390*	14	7
5 Nov 94	TAKE THIS TIME *Parlophone CDR 6395*	27	4
31 Dec 94	TAKE THIS TIME (re-entry) *Parlophone CDR 6395*	74	1
25 Mar 95	SUDDENLY *Parlophone CDR 6403*	18	5
24 Jun 95	NOW I'VE FOUND YOU *Parlophone CDLEEPYS 1*	22	3
18 Nov 95	YOU TO ME ARE EVERYTHING *Parlophone CDR 6420*	16	3
25 May 96	GOOD DAY *Parlophone CDR 6432*	12	4
3 Aug 96	DON'T PULL YOUR LOVE *Parlophone CDR 6440*	14	4
29 Mar 97	TODAY'S THE DAY *Parlophone CDR 6459*	27	3

Siobhan MAHER – See OCEANIC

MAHLATHINI and the MAHOTELLA QUEENS – See ART OF NOISE

MAI TAI ☺ ☺ *Guyana, female vocal group*   30 wks

25 May 85 ●	HISTORY *Virgin VS 773*	8	13
3 Aug 85 ●	BODY AND SOUL *Virgin VS 801*	9	13
15 Feb 86	FEMALE INTUITION *Virgin VS 844*	54	4

MAIN INGREDIENT *US, male vocal group*   7 wks

29 Jun 74	JUST DON'T WANT TO BE LONELY *RCA APBO 0205*	27	7

MAISONETTES ☺ *UK, male/female vocal group*   12 wks

11 Dec 82 ●	HEARTACHE AVENUE *Ready Steady Go! RSG 1*	7	12

Raven MAIZE *UK, male vocalist / producer – Dave Lee*   1 wk

5 Aug 89	FOREVER TOGETHER *Republic LIC 014*	67	1

See also Joey NEGRO

MAKADOPOULOS and his GREEK SERENADERS
Greece, male vocal/instrumental group   14 wks

20 Oct 60	NEVER ON SUNDAY *Palette PG 9005*	36	14

MAKAVELI ← *US, male rapper – 2Pac (Tupac Shakur)*   8 wks

12 Apr 97	TO LIVE & DIE IN LA *Interscope IND 95529*	10	4
9 Aug 97	TOSS IT UP *Interscope IND 95521*	15	3
14 Feb 98	HAIL MARY *Interscope IND 95575*	43	1

Jack E. MAKOSSA *Kenya, male producer*   5 wks

12 Sep 87	THE OPERA HOUSE *Champion CHAMP 50*	48	5

MALA – See BOWA featuring MALA

MALAIKA *US, female vocalist*   1 wk

31 Jul 93	GOTTA KNOW (YOUR NAME) *A & M 5802732*	68	1

Carl MALCOLM ⅄ *Jamaica, male vocalist*   8 wks

13 Sep 75 ●	FATTIE BUM BUM *UK 108*	8	8

Valerie MALCOLM – See CANDY GIRLS

Timmy MALLETT – See BOMBALURINA

MAMA CASS ☺ *US, female vocalist*   27 wks

14 Aug 68	DREAM A LITTLE DREAM OF ME *RCA 1726*	11	12
16 Aug 69 ●	IT'S GETTING BETTER *Stateside SS 8021*	8	15

See also MAMAS and the PAPAS

MAMAS and the PAPAS ♂ ← ☺
US, female/male vocal group   71 wks

28 Apr 66	CALIFORNIA DREAMIN' *RCA 1503*	23	9
12 May 66 ●	MONDAY MONDAY *RCA 1516* ▲	3	13
28 Jul 66	I SAW HER AGAIN *RCA 1533*	11	11
9 Feb 67	WORDS OF LOVE *RCA 1564*	47	3
6 Apr 67 ●	DEDICATED TO THE ONE I LOVE *RCA 1576*	2	17
26 Jul 67 ●	CREEQUE ALLEY *RCA 1613*	9	11
2 Aug 97 ●	CALIFORNIA DREAMIN' (re-entry) *MCA MCSTD 48058*	9	7

See also MAMA CASS

MAMBAS – See Marc ALMOND

A MAN CALLED ADAM
UK, male/female vocal/instrumental group   4 wks

29 Sep 90	BAREFOOT IN THE HEAD *Big Life BLR 28*	70	2
20 Oct 90	BAREFOOT IN THE HEAD (re-entry) *Big Life BLR 28*	60	2

MAN TO MAN ☺ *US, male vocal/instrumental duo*   19 wks

13 Sep 86	MALE STRIPPER *Bolts BOLTS 4* [1]	64	3
3 Jan 87	MALE STRIPPER (re-entry) *Bolts BOLTS 4* [1]	63	3
7 Feb 87 ●	MALE STRIPPER (2nd re-entry) *Bolts BOLTS 4* [1]	4	12
4 Jul 87	I NEED A MAN / ENERGY IS EUROBEAT *Bolts BOLTS 5*	43	3

[1] Man 2 Man meet Man Parrish

MAN WITH NO NAME *UK, male producer – Martin Freeland*   **6 wks**

30 Sep 95	FLOOR-ESSENCE *Perfecto PERF 108CD*	68	1
20 Jan 96	PAINT A PICTURE *Perfecto PERF 114CD* [1]	42	2
12 Oct 96	TELEPORT/SUGAR RUSH *Perfecto PERF 126CD*	55	1
2 May 98	VAVOOM! *Perfecto PERF 159CD1*	43	1
18 Jul 98	THE FIRST DAY (HORIZON) *Perfecto PERF 164CD*	72	1

[1] Man With No Name featuring Hannah

Melissa MANCHESTER – *See Al JARREAU*

MANCHESTER UNITED FOOTBALL CLUB ◉
UK, male football team vocalists   **49 wks**

8 May 76	MANCHESTER UNITED *Decca F 13633*	50	1
21 May 83	GLORY GLORY MAN. UNITED *EMI 5390*	13	5
18 May 85	● WE ALL FOLLOW MAN. UNITED *Columbia DB 9107*	10	5
19 Jun 93	UNITED (WE LOVE YOU) *Living Beat LBECD 026* [1]	37	2
30 Apr 94	★ COME ON YOU REDS *PolyGram TV MANU 2*	1	15
13 May 95	● WE'RE GONNA DO IT AGAIN *PolyGram TV MANU 952* [2]	6	6
4 May 96	● MOVE MOVE MOVE (THE RED TRIBE)		
	Music Collection MANUCD 1 [3]	6	11
3 Aug 96	MOVE MOVE MOVE (THE RED TRIBE) (re-entry)		
	Music Collection MANUCD 1 [3]	50	4

[1] Manchester United and the Champions [2] Manchester United Football Squad
featuring Stryker [3] 1996 Manchester United FA Cup Squad

See also REDS UNITED

Henry MANCINI © *US, orchestra/chorus*   **23 wks**

7 Dec 61	MOON RIVER *RCA 1256*	46	2
28 Dec 61	MOON RIVER (re-entry) *RCA 1256*	44	1
24 Sep 64	● HOW SOON *RCA 1414*	10	12
25 Mar 72	THEME FROM 'CADE'S COUNTY' *RCA 2182*	42	1
11 Feb 84	MAIN THEME FROM 'THE THORNBIRDS'		
	Warner Bros. 9677	23	7

Steve MANDELL – *See 'DELIVERANCE' SOUNDTRACK*

MANFRED MANN ◉ *One of the most regular chart entrants of the 1960s: Manfred Mann (k), Mike Vickers (g), Tom McGuinness (b), Mike Hugg (d), Paul Jones (v) – Jones was replaced by Mike D'Abo in 1966. They were the first group from the south of England to top the US charts during 1964's so-called 'British Invasion'*   **217 wks**

23 Jan 64	● 5-4-3-2-1 *HMV POP 1252*	5	13
16 Apr 64	HUBBLE BUBBLE TOIL AND TROUBLE *HMV POP 1282*	11	8
16 Jul 64	★ DO WAH DIDDY DIDDY *HMV POP 1320* ▲	1	14
15 Oct 64	● SHA LA LA *HMV POP 1346*	3	12
14 Jan 65	● COME TOMORROW *HMV POP 1381*	4	9
15 Apr 65	OH NO NOT MY BABY *HMV POP 1413*	11	10
16 Sep 65	● IF YOU GOTTA GO GO NOW *HMV POP 1466*	2	12
21 Apr 66	★ PRETTY FLAMINGO *HMV POP 1523*	1	12
7 Jul 66	YOU GAVE ME SOMEBODY TO LOVE *HMV POP 1541*	36	4
4 Aug 66	● JUST LIKE A WOMAN *Fontana TF 730*	10	10
27 Oct 66	● SEMI-DETACHED SUBURBAN MR. JAMES *Fontana TF 757*	2	12
30 Mar 67	● HA HA SAID THE CLOWN *Fontana TF 812*	4	11
25 May 67	SWEET PEA *Fontana TF 828*	36	4
24 Jan 68	★ MIGHTY QUINN *Fontana TF 897*	1	11
12 Jun 68	● MY NAME IS JACK *Fontana TF 943*	8	11
18 Dec 68	● FOX ON THE RUN *Fontana TF 985*	5	12
30 Apr 69	● RAGAMUFFIN MAN *Fontana TF 1013*	8	11
8 Sep 73	● JOYBRINGER *Vertigo 6059 083* [1]	9	10
28 Aug 76	● BLINDED BY THE LIGHT *Bronze BRO 29* [1] ▲	6	10
20 May 78	● DAVY'S ON THE ROAD AGAIN *Bronze BRO 52* [1]	6	12
17 Mar 79	YOU ANGEL YOU *Bronze BRO 68* [1]	54	5
7 Jul 79	DON'T KILL IT CAROL *Bronze BRO 77* [1]	45	4

[1] Manfred Mann's Earth Band

MANHATTAN TRANSFER © *US, male/female vocal group*   **72 wks**

7 Feb 76	TUXEDO JUNCTION *Atlantic K 10670*	24	6
5 Feb 77	★ CHANSON D'AMOUR *Atlantic K 10886*	1	13
28 May 77	DON'T LET GO *Atlantic K 10930*	32	6

18 Feb 78	WALK IN LOVE *Atlantic K 11075*	48	1
4 Mar 78	WALK IN LOVE (re-entry) *Atlantic K 11075*	12	11
20 May 78	ON A LITTLE STREET IN SINGAPORE *Atlantic K 11136*	20	9
16 Sep 78	WHERE DID OUR LOVE GO/ JE VOULAIS TE DIRE		
	(QUE J'ATTENDS) *Atlantic K 11182*	40	4
23 Dec 78	WHO WHAT WHEN WHERE WHY *Atlantic K 11233*	49	6
17 May 80	TWILIGHT ZONE – TWILIGHT TONE (MEDLEY)		
	Atlantic K 11476	25	8
21 Jan 84	SPICE OF LIFE *Atlantic A 9728*	19	8

MANHATTANS ♪ *US, male vocal group*   **31 wks**

19 Jun 76	● KISS AND SAY GOODBYE *CBS 4317* ▲	4	11
2 Oct 76	● HURT *CBS 4562*	4	11
23 Apr 77	IT'S YOU *CBS 5093*	43	3
26 Jul 80	SHINING STAR *CBS 8624*	45	4
6 Aug 83	CRAZY *CBS A 3578*	63	2

M.A.N.I.C. *UK, male vocal/production duo*   **1 wk**

18 Apr 92	I'M COMIN' HARDCORE *Union City UCRT 2*	60	1

MANIC MCs featuring Sara CARLSON
UK, male production duo and female vocalist   **5 wks**

12 Aug 89	MENTAL *RCA PB 43037*	30	5

MANIC STREET PREACHERS ✏ ◉
Best-selling Welsh act of the 1990s – James Dean Bradfield (v/g), Nicky Wire (b), Sean Moore (d) and Richey Edwards (v/g – missing and presumed dead since 1995). Won trophies for the Best British Pop Group and Best Album (Everything Must Go) at the 1997 BRIT Awards   **102 wks**

25 May 91	YOU LOVE US *Heavenly HVN 10*	62	2
10 Aug 91	STAY BEAUTIFUL *Columbia 6573377*	40	3
9 Nov 91	LOVE'S SWEET EXILE/REPEAT *Columbia 6575827*	26	3
1 Feb 92	YOU LOVE US (re-issue) *Columbia 6577247*	16	4
28 Mar 92	SLASH 'N' BURN *Columbia 6578737*	20	4
13 Jun 92	MOTORCYCLE EMPTINESS *Columbia 6580837*	17	6
19 Sep 92	● THEME FROM M.A.S.H. (SUICIDE IS PAINLESS)		
	Columbia 6583827	7	6
21 Nov 92	LITTLE BABY NOTHING *Columbia 6587967*	29	3
12 Jun 93	FROM DESPAIR TO WHERE *Columbia 6593372*	25	4
31 Jul 93	LA TRISTESSE DURERA (SCREAM TO A SIGH)		
	Columbia 6594772	22	5
2 Oct 93	ROSES IN THE HOSPITAL *Columbia 6597272*	15	3
12 Feb 94	LIFE BECOMING A LANDSLIDE *Columbia 6600702*	36	2
11 Jun 94	FASTER/PCP *Epic 6604472*	16	3
13 Aug 94	REVOL *Epic 6608862*	22	3
15 Oct 94	SHE IS SUFFERING *Epic 6608952*	25	3
27 Apr 96	● A DESIGN FOR LIFE *Epic 6630705*	2	10
27 Jul 96	A DESIGN FOR LIFE (re-entry) *Epic 6630705*	71	1
3 Aug 96	● EVERYTHING MUST GO *Epic 6634685*	5	6
12 Oct 96	● KEVIN CARTER *Epic 6637752*	9	4
14 Dec 96	● AUSTRALIA *Epic 6640442*	7	7
13 Sep 97	MOTORCYCLE EMPTINESS (re-issue)		
	Epic MANIC 5CD	41	2
13 Sep 97	● YOU LOVE US (2nd re-issue) *Epic MANIC 3CD*	0	1
13 Sep 97	LITTLE BABY NOTHING (re-issue) *Epic MANIC 6CD*	50	1
13 Sep 97	STAY BEAUTIFUL (re-issue) *Epic MANIC 1CD*	52	1
13 Sep 97	SLASH 'N' BURN (re-issue) *Epic MANIC 4CD*	54	1
13 Sep 97	LOVE'S SWEET EXILE (re-issue) *Epic MANIC 2CD*	55	1
5 Sep 98	● IF YOU TOLERATE THIS YOUR CHILDREN WILL BE NEXT		
	Epic 6663452 ■	1	10
12 Dec 98	THE EVERLASTING *Epic 6666862*	11†	3

The listed flipside of 'Theme From M.A.S.H. (Suicide Is Painless)' was with '(Everything I Do) I Do It For You' by Fatima Mansions

Barry MANILOW © *Middle-of-the-road superstar, b. Barry Pincus, 17 June, 1946, Brooklyn. This crowd-pulling singer/songwriter/pianist with a vast and loyal fan following on both sides of the Atlantic has sold in excess of 50 million albums*   **136 wks**

22 Feb 75	MANDY *Arista 1* ▲	11	9
6 May 78	CAN'T SMILE WITHOUT YOU *Arista 176*	43	7

29 Jul 78	SOMEWHERE IN THE NIGHT / COPACABANA		
	(AT THE COPA) *Arista 196*	42	10
23 Dec 78	COULD IT BE MAGIC *Arista ARIST 229*	25	10
8 Nov 80	LONELY TOGETHER *Arista ARIST 373*	21	13
7 Feb 81	I MADE IT THROUGH THE RAIN *Arista ARIST 384*	37	6
11 Apr 81	BERMUDA TRIANGLE *Arista ARIST 406*	15	9
26 Sep 81	LET'S HANG ON *Arista ARIST 429*	12	11
12 Dec 81	THE OLD SONGS *Arista ARIST 443*	48	8
20 Feb 82	IF I SHOULD LOVE AGAIN *Arista ARIST 453*	66	2
17 Apr 82	STAY *Arista ARIST 464* 1	23	8
16 Oct 82 ●	I WANNA DO IT WITH YOU *Arista ARIST 495*	8	8
4 Dec 82	I'M GONNA SIT RIGHT DOWN AND WRITE MYSELF A LETTER		
	Arista ARIST 503	36	7
25 Jun 83	SOME KIND OF FRIEND *Arista ARIST 516*	48	2
27 Aug 83	YOU'RE LOOKING HOT TONIGHT *Arista ARIST 542*	47	6
10 Dec 83	READ 'EM AND WEEP *Arista ARIST 551*	17	7
8 Apr 89	PLEASE DON'T BE SCARED *Arista 112186*	35	5
10 Apr 93	COPACABANA (AT THE COPA) (re-mix) *Arista 74321136912*	22	4
20 Nov 93	COULD IT BE MAGIC *Arista 74321174882*	36	3
6 Aug 94	LET ME BE YOUR WINGS *EMI CDEM 336* 2	73	1

1 Barry Manilow featuring Kevin Desimone and James Jolis
2 Barry Manilow and Debra Byrd

ARIST 464 was available as both a live and studio recording.
'Could It Be Magic' in 1993 is a re-recording

MANIX *UK, male/female vocal/instrumental group* 6 wks

23 Nov 91	MANIC MINDS *Reinforced RIVET 1209*	63	2
7 Mar 92	OBLIVION (HEAD IN THE CLOUDS) EP *Reinforced RIVET 1212*	43	3
8 Aug 92	RAINBOW PEOPLE *Reinforced RIVET 1221*	57	1

Tracks on Oblivion (Head in the Clouds) (EP): Oblivion (Head in the Clouds) /
Never Been to Belgium (Gotta Rush) / I Can't Stand It / You Held My Hand

MANKEY *UK, male producer – Andy Manston* 1 wk

| 16 Nov 96 | BELIEVE IN ME *Frisky DISKY 3* | 74 | 1 |

MANKIND *UK, male instrumental group* 12 wks

| 25 Nov 78 | DR. WHO *Pinnacle PIN 71* | 25 | 12 |

Aimee MANN *US, female vocalist* 9 wks

31 Oct 87	TIME STAND STILL *Vertigo RUSH 13*	42	3
28 Aug 93	I SHOULD'VE KNOWN *Imago 72787250432*	55	2
20 Nov 93	STUPID THING *Imago 72787250432*	47	2
5 Mar 94	I SHOULD'VE KNOWN (re-issue) *Imago 72787250602*	45	2

1 Rush with Aimee Mann

Johnny MANN SINGERS ℂ *US, male/female vocal group* 13 wks

| 12 Jul 67 ● | UP, UP AND AWAY *Liberty LIB 55972* | 6 | 13 |

MANSUN ☹ ✎ *UK, male vocal/instrumental group* 33 wks

6 Apr 96	ONE EP *Parlophone CDR 6430*	37	2
15 Jun 96	TWO EP *Parlophone CDR 6437*	32	2
21 Sep 96	STRIPPER VICAR *Parlophone CDR 6447*	19	3
17 Dec 96	WIDE OPEN SPACE *Parlophone CDR 6453*	15	4
15 Feb 97	SHE MAKES MY NOSE BLEED *Parlophone CDR 6453*	9	5
10 May 97	TAX LOSS *Parlophone CDRS 6465*	15	3
11 Jul 98 ●	LEGACY EP *Parlophone CDR 6497*	7	4
5 Sep 98	BEING A GIRL (PART ONE) EP *Parlophone CDR 6503*	13	4
7 Nov 98	NEGATIVE *Parlophone CDR 6508*	27	2

Tracks on One EP: Egg Shaped Fred / Ski Jump Nose / Lemonade Secret Drinker /
Thief. Tracks on Two EP: Take It Easy Chicken / Drastic Sturgeon / The Greatest Pain /
Moronica. Tracks on Legacy EP: Legacy / Railings / Check Under the Bed / Can't
Afford to Die. Tracks on Being a Girl (Part One) EP: I Care / Been Here Before /
Hide Out / Railing

MANTOVANI ℂ *UK, orchestra* 52 wks

19 Dec 52 ●	WHITE CHRISTMAS *Decca F 10017*	6	3
29 May 53 ★	MOULIN ROUGE *Decca F 10094*	1	21
23 Oct 53 ●	SWEDISH RHAPSODY *Decca F 10168*	2	17

13 Nov 53 ●	MOULIN ROUGE (re-entry) *Decca F 10094*	10	1
4 Dec 53	MOULIN ROUGE (2nd re-entry) *Decca F 10094*	12	1
26 Feb 54	SWEDISH RHAPSODY (re-entry) *Decca F 10168*	12	1
11 Feb 55	LONELY BALLERINA *Decca F 10395*	16	3
18 Mar 55	LONELY BALLERINA (re-entry) *Decca F 10395*	18	1
31 May 57	AROUND THE WORLD *Decca F 10888*	20	4

See also David WHITFIELD

MANTRONIK

US, male vocalist / instrumentalist / producer – Curtis Mantronik 1 wk

| 15 Aug 98 | STRICTLY BUSINESS *Parlophone CDR 6502* 1 | 43 | 1 |

1 Mantronik versus EPMD

MANTRONIX ⟵ *US /, male vocal/instrumental duo* 48 wks

22 Feb 86	LADIES *10 TEN 116*	55	4
17 May 86	BASSLINE *10 TEN 118*	34	6
7 Feb 87	WHO IS IT *10 TEN 137*	40	6
4 Jul 87	SCREAM (PRIMAL SCREAM) *10 TEN 169*	46	4
30 Jan 88	SING A SONG (BREAK IT DOWN) *10 TEN 206*	61	2
12 Mar 88	SIMPLE SIMON (YOU GOTTA REGARD) *10 TEN 217*	72	2
6 Jan 90 ●	GOT TO HAVE YOUR LOVE *Capitol CL 559* 1	4	11
12 May 90 ●	TAKE YOUR TIME *Capitol CL 573* 1	10	7
2 Mar 91	DON'T GO MESSIN' WITH MY HEART *Capitol CL 608*	22	5
22 Jun 91	STEP TO ME (DO ME) *Capitol CL 613*	59	1

1 Mantronix featuring Wondress

MANUEL and his MUSIC OF THE MOUNTAINS ℂ

UK, orchestra, leader Geoff Love 31 wks

28 Aug 59	THE HONEYMOON SONG *Columbia DB 4323*	29	2
25 Sep 59	THE HONEYMOON SONG (re-entry) *Columbia DB 4323*	22	5
6 Nov 59	THE HONEYMOON SONG (2nd re-entry) *Columbia DB 4323*	27	2
13 Oct 60	NEVER ON SUNDAY *Columbia DB 4515*	29	10
13 Oct 66	SOMEWHERE MY LOVE *Columbia DB 7969*	42	2
31 Jan 76 ●	RODRIGO'S GUITAR CONCERTO DE ARANJUEZ		
	(THEME FROM 2ND MOVEMENT) *EMI 2383*	3	10

MARATHON *Germany/UK, male vocal/instrumental group* 3 wks

| 25 Jan 92 | MOVIN' *Ten TEN 395* | 36 | 3 |

MARAUDERS *UK, male vocal/instrumental group* 4 wks

| 8 Aug 63 | THAT'S WHAT I WANT *Decca F 11695* | 48 | 1 |
| 22 Aug 63 | THAT'S WHAT I WANT (re-entry) *Decca F 11695* | 43 | 3 |

MARBLES ◯ *UK, male vocal duo* 18 wks

| 25 Sep 68 ● | ONLY ONE WOMAN *Polydor 56 272* | 5 | 12 |
| 26 Mar 69 | THE WALLS FELL DOWN *Polydor 56 310* | 28 | 6 |

MARC et CLAUDE *Germany, male DJ / production trio* 3 wks

| 21 Nov 98 | LA *Positiva CDTIV 104* | 28 | 3 |

MARC and the MAMBAS – *See Marc ALMOND*

MARCELS ♩ *US, male vocal group* 17 wks

| 13 Apr 61 ★ | BLUE MOON *Pye International 7N 25073* ▲ | 1 | 13 |
| 8 Jun 61 | SUMMERTIME *Pye International 7N 25083* | 46 | 4 |

Little Peggy MARCH *US, female vocalist* 7 wks

| 12 Sep 63 | HELLO HEARTACHE GOODBYE LOVE *RCA 1362* | 29 | 7 |

MARCY PLAYGROUND *US, male vocal/instrumental trio* 3 wks

| 18 Apr 98 | SEX AND CANDY *EMI CDEM 508* | 29 | 3 |

MARDI GRAS ◯ *UK, male vocal/instrumental group* 9 wks

| 5 Aug 72 | TOO BUSY THINKING 'BOUT MY BABY *Bell 1226* | 19 | 9 |

MARIA – *See Maria NAYLER*

UK No 1 ★ UK Top 10 ● UK million seller ◆ UK entry at No 1 ■ US No 1 ▲

Kelly MARIE 🌐 ◢ *UK, female vocalist* — 36 wks

2 Aug 80 ★	FEELS LIKE I'M IN LOVE *Calibre PLUS 1*	1 16
18 Oct 80	LOVING JUST FOR FUN *Calibre PLUS 4*	21 7
7 Feb 81	HOT LOVE *Calibre PLUS 5*	22 10
30 May 81	LOVE TRIAL *Calibre PLUS 7*	51 3

Teena MARIE 🎵 *US, female vocalist* — 28 wks

7 Jul 79	I'M A SUCKER FOR YOUR LOVE *Motown TMG 1146* [1]	43 8
31 May 80 ●	BEHIND THE GROOVE *Motown TMG 1185*	6 10
11 Oct 80	I NEED YOUR LOVIN' *Motown TMG 1203*	28 6
26 Mar 88	OOO LA LA LA *Epic 651423 7*	74 2
10 Nov 90	SINCE DAY ONE *Epic 656429 7*	69 2

[1] Teena Marie, co-lead vocals Rick James

MARILLION ✍ *Progressive rock group formed in Buckinghamshire and originally named after Tolkien's novel,* Silmarillion. *They reached their height of popularity between 1981 and 1988, when fronted by Scottish vocalist/songwriter Fish (b. Derek Dick, 15 April, 1958)* — 103 wks

20 Nov 82	MARKET SQUARE HEROES *EMI 5351*	60 2
12 Feb 83	HE KNOWS YOU KNOW *EMI 5362*	35 4
16 Apr 83	MARKET SQUARE HEROES (re-entry) *EMI 5351*	53 6
18 Jun 83	GARDEN PARTY *EMI 5393*	16 5
11 Feb 84	PUNCH AND JUDY *EMI MARIL 1*	29 4
12 May 84	ASSASSING *EMI MARIL 2*	22 5
18 May 85 ●	KAYLEIGH *EMI MARIL 3*	2 14
7 Sep 85 ●	LAVENDER *EMI MARIL 4*	5 9
30 Nov 85	HEART OF LOTHIAN *EMI MARIL 5*	29 6
23 May 87 ●	INCOMMUNICADO *EMI MARIL 6*	6 5
25 Jul 87	SUGAR MICE *EMI MARIL 7*	22 5
7 Nov 87	WARM WET CIRCLES *EMI MARIL 8*	22 4
26 Nov 88	FREAKS (LIVE) *EMI MARIL 9*	24 3
9 Sep 89	HOOKS IN YOU *Capitol MARIL 10*	30 3
9 Dec 89	UNINVITED GUEST *EMI MARIL 11*	53 2
14 Apr 90	EASTER *EMI MARIL 12*	34 2
8 Jun 91	COVER MY EYES (PAIN AND HEAVEN) *EMI MARIL 13*	34 4
3 Aug 91	NO ONE CAN *EMI MARIL 14*	33 4
5 Oct 91	DRY LAND *EMI MARIL 15*	34 2
23 May 92	SYMPATHY *EMI MARIL 16*	17 3
1 Aug 92	NO ONE CAN (re-issue) *EMI MARIL 17*	26 4
26 Mar 94	THE HOLLOW MAN *EMI CDEMS 307*	30 2
7 May 94	ALONE AGAIN IN THE LAP OF LUXURY *EMI CDEMS 318*	53 3
10 Jun 95	BEAUTIFUL *EMI CDMARILS 18*	29 2

MARILYN 🌐 *UK, male vocalist* — 26 wks

5 Nov 83 ●	CALLING YOUR NAME *Mercury MAZ 1*	4 12
11 Feb 84	CRY AND BE FREE *Mercury MAZ 2*	31 6
21 Apr 84	YOU DON'T LOVE ME *Mercury MAZ 3*	40 7
13 Apr 85	BABY U LEFT ME (IN THE COLD) *Mercury MAZ 4*	70 1

MARILYN MANSON ✓ *US, male vocal/instrumental group* — 8 wks

7 Jun 97	THE BEAUTIFUL PEOPLE *Interscope IND 95541*	18 3
20 Sep 97	TOURNIQUET *Interscope IND 95552*	28 2
21 Nov 98	THE DOPE SHOW *Interscope IND 95610*	12 3

Marino MARINI and his QUARTET ℂ *Italy, male vocalist and instrumental group* — 23 wks

3 Oct 58	VOLARE *Durium DC 16632*	13 7
10 Oct 58 ●	COME PRIMA *Durium DC 16632*	2 14
20 Mar 59	CIAO CIAO BAMBINA *Durium DC 16636*	25 1
3 Apr 59	CIAO CIAO BAMBINA (re-entry) *Durium DC 16636*	24 1

MARION ☺ ✍ *UK, male vocal/instrumental group* — 9 wks

25 Feb 95	SLEEP *London LONCD 360*	53 1
13 May 95	TOYS FOR BOYS *London LONCD 366*	57 1
21 Oct 95	LET'S ALL GO TOGETHER *London LONCD 371*	37 2
3 Feb 96	TIME *London LONCD 377*	29 2
30 Mar 96	SLEEP (re-mix) *London LONCD 381*	17 2
7 Mar 98	MIYAKO HIDEAWAY *London LONCD 403*	45 1

MARK 'OH *Germany, male producer – Marko Albrecht* — 3 wks

6 May 95	TEARS DON'T LIE *Systematic SYSCD 9*	24 3

Pigmeat MARKHAM 🎵 *US, male vocalist* — 8 wks

17 Jul 68	HERE COMES THE JUDGE *Chess CRS 8077*	19 8

Biz MARKIE *US, male rapper* — 2 wks

26 May 90	JUST A FRIEND *Cold Chillin' W 9823*	55 2

Yannis MARKOPOULOS ℂ *Greece, orchestra* — 8 wks

17 Dec 77	WHO PAYS THE FERRYMAN *BBC RESL 51*	11 8

Guy MARKS *US, male vocalist* — 8 wks

13 May 78	LOVING YOU HAS MADE ME BANANAS *ABC 4211*	25 8

MARKY MARK and the FUNKY BUNCH 🌐 ◢ *US, male/female vocal/instrumental group* — 14 wks

31 Aug 91	GOOD VIBRATIONS *Interscope A 8764* [1] ▲	14 7
2 Nov 91	WILDSIDE *Interscope A 8674*	42 3
12 Dec 92	YOU GOTTA BELIEVE *Interscope A 8480*	54 4

[1] Marky Mark and the Funky Bunch featuring Loleatta Holloway

Bob MARLEY and the WAILERS ✓ *Legendary, globally successful n group. Varying line-up included Bob Marley (v/g) (d. 1981), Peter Tosh (v/g) (d. 1987), Bunny Wailer (v/prc). Their compilation LP,* Legend, *is the biggest-selling reggae album in the UK and the USA with combined sales of more than 11 million* — 142 wks

27 Sep 75	NO WOMAN NO CRY *Island WIP 6244*	22 7
25 Jun 77	EXODUS *Island WIP 6390*	14 9
10 Sep 77	WAITING IN VAIN *Island WIP 6402*	27 6
10 Dec 77 ●	JAMMING/PUNKY REGGAE PARTY *Island WIP 6410*	9 12
25 Feb 78 ●	IS THIS LOVE *Island WIP 6420*	9 9
10 Jun 78	SATISFY MY SOUL *Island WIP 6440*	21 10
20 Oct 79	SO MUCH TROUBLE IN THE WORLD *Island WIP 6510*	56 4
21 Jun 80 ●	COULD YOU BE LOVED *Island WIP 6610*	5 12
13 Sep 80	THREE LITTLE BIRDS *Island WIP 6641*	17 9
13 Jun 81 ●	NO WOMAN NO CRY (re-entry) *Island WIP 6244*	8 11
7 May 83 ●	BUFFALO SOLDIER *Island/Tuff Gong IS 108*	4 12
21 Apr 84 ●	ONE LOVE – PEOPLE GET READY *Island IS 169*	5 11
23 Jun 84	WAITING IN VAIN (re-issue) *Island IS 180*	31 7
8 Dec 84	COULD YOU BE LOVED (re-issue) *Island IS 210*	71 2
18 May 91	ONE LOVE – PEOPLE GET READY (re-issue) *Tuff Gong TGX 1*	42 3
19 Sep 92 ●	IRON LION ZION *Tuff Gong TGX 2*	5 9
28 Nov 92	WHY SHOULD I/EXODUS *Tuff Gong TGX 3*	42 3
2 Jan 93	WHY SHOULD I/EXODUS (re-entry) *Tuff Gong TGX 3*	75 1
20 May 95	KEEP ON MOVING *Tuff Gong TGXCD 4*	17 4
8 Jun 96	WHAT GOES AROUND COMES AROUND *Anansi ANACS 002*	42 1

'Exodus' on Tuff Gong TGX 3 only listed with 'Why Should I' from 5 Dec, 1992, and is a different version from the Island hit. It peaked at No 53

Ziggy MARLEY and the MELODY MAKERS , *male/female vocal/instrumental group* — 11 wks

11 Jun 88	TOMORROW PEOPLE *Virgin VS 1049*	22 10
23 Sep 89	LOOK WHO'S DANCING *Virgin America VUS 5*	65 1

MARMALADE 🌐 *The first Scottish act to top the chart: included Dean Ford (v), Junior Campbell (g/p/v), Alan Whitehead (d). This pop quintet, who first recorded as Dean Ford and The Gaylords, had a large late-1960s teen following* — 130 wks

22 May 68 ●	LOVIN' THINGS *CBS 3412*	6 13
23 Oct 68	WAIT FOR ME MARIANNE *CBS 3708*	30 5
4 Dec 68 ★	OB-LA-DI OB-LA-DA *CBS 3892*	1 20
11 Jun 69 ●	BABY MAKE IT SOON *CBS 4287*	9 13
20 Dec 69 ●	REFLECTIONS OF MY LIFE *Decca F 12982*	3 12

UK No 1 ★ UK Top 10 ● UK million seller ◆ UK entry at No 1 ■ US No 1 ▲

18 Jul 70 ●	RAINBOW *Decca F 13035*	3	14
27 Mar 71	MY LITTLE ONE *Decca F 13135*	15	11
4 Sep 71 ●	COUSIN NORMAN *Decca F 13214*	6	11
27 Nov 71	BACK ON THE ROAD *Decca F 13251*	35	7
22 Jan 72	BACK ON THE ROAD (re-entry) *Decca F 13251*	50	1
1 Apr 72 ●	RADANCER *Decca F 13297*	6	12
21 Feb 76 ●	FALLING APART AT THE SEAMS *Target TGT 105*	9	11

MARMION *Spain/Holland, male instrumental/production duo* — 2 wks

18 May 96	SCHONEBERG *Hooj Choons HOOJCD 43*	53	1
14 Feb 98	SCHONEBERG (re-issue) *ffrr FCD 324*	56	1

Johnny MARR – See Billy BRAGG

MARRADONA *UK, male DJ / production group* — 5 wks

26 Feb 94	OUT OF MY HEAD *Peach PWCD 282*	38	3
26 Jul 97	OUT OF MY HEAD 97 (re-mix) *Soopa SPCD 1*	39	2

M/A/R/R/S *UK, male instrumental/scratch group* — 14 wks

5 Sep 87 ★	PUMP UP THE VOLUME/ANITINA (THE FIRST TIME I SEE SHE DANCE) *4AD AD 70*	1	14

The B-side of this record was listed on the chart at the record company's request without evidence of consumer interest

Gerry MARSDEN – See CHRISTIANS; Holly JOHNSON; Paul McCARTNEY; STOCK AITKEN WATERMAN; GERRY and the PACEMAKERS

Matthew MARSDEN ☻ *UK, male vocalist* — 10 wks

11 Jul 98	THE HEART'S LONE DESIRE *Columbia 6661152*	13	7
7 Nov 98	SHE'S GONE *Columbia 6664915* [1]	24	3

[1] Matthew Marsden featuring Destiny's Child

Stevie MARSH *UK, female vocalist* — 4 wks

4 Dec 59	THE ONLY BOY IN THE WORLD *Decca F 11181*	29	2
25 Dec 59	THE ONLY BOY IN THE WORLD (re-entry) *Decca F 11181*	24	2

MARSHA – See SHAGGY

Joy MARSHALL *UK, female vocalist* — 2 wks

23 Jun 66	THE MORE I SEE YOU *Decca F 12422*	34	2

Keith MARSHALL ☻ *UK, male vocalist* — 10 wks

4 Apr 81	ONLY CRYING *Arrival PIK 2*	12	10

Wayne MARSHALL *UK, male vocalist* — 7 wks

1 Oct 94	OOH AAH (G-SPOT) *Soultown SOULCDS 322*	29	3
3 Jun 95	SPIRIT *Soultown SOULCDS 00352*	58	1
24 Feb 96	NEVER KNEW LOVE LIKE THIS *Sony S2 6629382* [1]	40	2
7 Dec 96	G SPOT (re-mix) *MBA INTER 9006*	50	1

[1] Pauline Henry featuring Wayne Marshall

MARSHALL HAIN ☻ *UK, male/female vocal/instrumental duo* — 19 wks

3 Jun 78 ●	DANCING IN THE CITY *Harvest HAR 5157*	3	15
14 Oct 78	COMING HOME *Harvest HAR 5168*	39	4

Lena MARTELL ℂ *UK, female vocalist* — 18 wks

29 Sep 79 ★	ONE DAY AT A TIME *Pye 7N 46021*	1	18

MARTHA and the MUFFINS ☻ ✏
Canada, female/male vocal/instrumental group — 10 wks

1 Mar 80 ●	ECHO BEACH *Dindisc DIN 9*	10	10

See also M + M, who are Martha and a Muffin

MARTHA and the VANDELLAS – See Martha REEVES and the VANDELLAS

MARTIKA ☻ *US, female vocalist* — 57 wks

29 Jul 89 ●	TOY SOLDIERS *CBS 655049 7* ▲	5	11
14 Oct 89 ●	I FEEL THE EARTH MOVE *CBS 655294 7*	7	14
13 Jan 90	MORE THAN YOU KNOW *CBS 655526 7*	15	7
17 Mar 90	WATER *CBS 655731 7*	59	3
17 Aug 91 ●	LOVE . . . THY WILL BE DONE *Columbia 6573137*	9	9
30 Nov 91	MARTIKA'S KITCHEN *Columbia 6575687*	17	10
22 Feb 92	COLOURED KISSES *Columbia 6577097*	41	3

Billie Ray MARTIN ☺ *Germany, female vocalist* — 19 wks

19 Nov 94	YOUR LOVING ARMS *Magnet MAG 1028CD*	38	3
20 May 95 ●	YOUR LOVING ARMS (re-mix) *Magnet MAG 1031CD*	6	10
2 Sep 95	RUNNING AROUND TOWN *Magnet MAG 1035CD*	29	2
6 Jan 96	IMITATION OF LIFE *Magnet MAG 1040CD*	29	3
6 Apr 96	SPACE OASIS *Magnet MAG 1042CD*	66	1

Dean MARTIN ℂ
Acclaimed vocalist/entertainer/film actor and cabaret performer, b. Dino Crocetti, 7 June, 1917, Ohio, d. 25 December, 1995. He first found fame partnering Jerry Lewis (1946-56), and had a long and successful solo career. He was a member of Frank Sinatra's 'Rat Pack' and has an impressive 43-year chart span — 156 wks

18 Sep 53 ●	KISS *Capitol CL 13893*	9	1
2 Oct 53	KISS (re-entry) *Capitol CL 13893*	5	7
22 Jan 54	THAT'S AMORE *Capitol CL 14008*	2	11
1 Oct 54	SWAY *Capitol CL 14138*	6	7
22 Oct 54	HOW DO YOU SPEAK TO AN ANGEL *Capitol CL 14150*	15	2
19 Nov 54	HOW DO YOU SPEAK TO AN ANGEL (re-entry) *Capitol CL 14150*	17	4
28 Jan 55 ●	NAUGHTY LADY OF SHADY LANE *Capitol CL 14226*	5	10
4 Feb 55	MAMBO ITALIANO *Capitol CL 14227*	14	2
25 Feb 55 ●	LET ME GO LOVER *Capitol CL 14226*	3	9
1 Apr 55 ●	UNDER THE BRIDGES OF PARIS *Capitol CL 14255*	6	8
10 Feb 56 ★	MEMORIES ARE MADE OF THIS *Capitol CL 14523* ▲	1	16
2 Mar 56	YOUNG AND FOOLISH *Capitol CL 14519*	20	1
27 Apr 56	INNAMORATA *Capitol CL 14507*	21	3
22 Mar 57	THE MAN WHO PLAYS THE MANDOLINO *Capitol CL 14690*	21	2
13 Jun 58 ●	RETURN TO ME *Capitol CL 14844*	2	22
29 Aug 58 ●	VOLARE *Capitol CL 14910*	2	14
27 Aug 64	EVERYBODY LOVES SOMEBODY *Reprise R 20281* ▲	11	13
12 Nov 64	THE DOOR IS STILL OPEN TO MY HEART *Reprise R 20307*	42	4
5 Feb 69 ●	GENTLE ON MY MIND *Reprise RS 23343*	2	23
30 Aug 69	GENTLE ON MY MIND (re-entry) *Reprise RS 23343*	49	1
22 Jun 96	THAT'S AMORE (re-issue) *EMI Premier PRESCD 3*	43	2

Juan MARTIN ℂ *Spain, male instrumentalist – guitar* — 7 wks

28 Jan 84 ●	LOVE THEME FROM 'THE THORN BIRDS' *WEA X 9518*	10	7

Linda MARTIN *Ireland, female vocalist* — 2 wks

30 May 92	WHY ME *Columbia 6581317*	59	2

Marilyn MARTIN – See Phil COLLINS

Ray MARTIN ℂ *UK, orchestra* — 11 wks

14 Nov 52 ●	BLUE TANGO *Columbia DB 3051*	8	1
28 Nov 52 ●	BLUE TANGO (re-entry) *Columbia DB 3051*	10	3
4 Dec 53 ●	SWEDISH RHAPSODY *Columbia DB 3346*	10	1
18 Dec 53 ●	SWEDISH RHAPSODY (re-entry) *Columbia DB 3346*	4	3
15 Jun 56	CAROUSEL WALTZ *Columbia DB 3771*	28	1
3 Aug 56	CAROUSEL WALTZ (re-entry) *Columbia DB 3771*	24	2

Ricky MARTIN ☻ *Mexico, male vocalist* — 9 wks

20 Sep 97 ●	(UN, DOS, TRES) MARIA *Columbia 6649595*	6	6
11 Jul 98	THE CUP OF LIFE *Columbia 6661502*	29	3

Tony MARTIN ℂ *US, male vocalist* — 28 wks

22 Apr 55 ●	STRANGER IN PARADISE *HMV B 10849*	6	13
13 Jul 56 ●	WALK HAND IN HAND *HMV POP 222*	2	15

Vince MARTIN – See TARRIERS

Wink MARTINDALE ℂ *US, male vocalist* — 41 wks

Date	Title	Pos	Wks
4 Dec 59	DECK OF CARDS *London HLD 8962*	18	5
15 Jan 60	DECK OF CARDS (re-entry) *London HLD 8962*	28	2
31 Mar 60	DECK OF CARDS (2nd re-entry) *London HLD 8962*	45	1
18 Apr 63 ●	DECK OF CARDS (3rd re-entry) *London HLD 8962*	5	21
20 Oct 73	DECK OF CARDS (re-issue) *Dot DOT 109*	22	12

Al MARTINO ℂ *US, male vocalist* — 87 wks

Date	Title	Pos	Wks
14 Nov 52 ★	HERE IN MY HEART *Capitol CL 13779* ▲	1	18
21 Nov 52 ●	TAKE MY HEART *Capitol CL 13769*	9	1
30 Jan 53 ●	NOW *Capitol CL 13835*	3	12
10 Jul 53 ●	RACHEL *Capitol CL 13879*	10	4
11 Sep 53	RACHEL (re-entry) *Capitol CL 13879*	12	1
4 Jun 54	WANTED *Capitol CL 14128*	12	1
18 Jun 54 ●	WANTED (re-entry) *Capitol CL 14128*	4	14
1 Oct 54 ●	THE STORY OF TINA *Capitol CL 14163*	10	8
1 Oct 54	WANTED (2nd re-entry) *Capitol CL 14128*	17	1
23 Sep 55	THE MAN FROM LARAMIE *Capitol CL 14343*	19	2
28 Oct 55	THE MAN FROM LARAMIE (re-entry) *Capitol CL 14343*	20	1
31 Mar 60	SUMMERTIME *Top Rank JAR 312*	49	1
29 Aug 63	I LOVE YOU BECAUSE *Capitol CL 15300*	48	1
22 Aug 70	SPANISH EYES *Capitol CL 15430*	49	1
14 Jul 73 ●	SPANISH EYES (re-entry) *Capitol CL 15430*	5	21

MARVELETTES ✎ *US, female vocal group* — 10 wks

Date	Title	Pos	Wks
15 Jun 67	WHEN YOU'RE YOUNG AND IN LOVE *Tamla Motown TMG 609*	13	10

Hank MARVIN ◐ *UK, male vocalist/instrumentalist – guitar* — 36 wks

Date	Title	Pos	Wks
13 Sep 69 ●	THROW DOWN A LINE *Columbia DB 8615* [1]	7	9
21 Feb 70	JOY OF LIVING *Columbia DB 8657* [1]	25	8
6 Mar 82	DON'T TALK *Polydor POSP 420*	49	4
22 Mar 86 ★	LIVING DOLL *WEA YZ 65* [2]	1	11
7 Jan 89	LONDON KID *Polydor PO 32* [3]	52	3
17 Oct 92	WE ARE THE CHAMPIONS *PolyGram TV PO 229* [4]	66	1

[1] Cliff and Hank [2] Cliff Richard and the Young Ones featuring Hank B Marvin
[3] Jean-Michel Jarre featuring Hank Marvin [4] Hank Marvin featuring Brian May

Lee MARVIN ℂ *US, male vocalist* — 23 wks

Date	Title	Pos	Wks
7 Feb 70 ★	WAND'RIN' STAR *Paramount PARA 3004*	1	18
20 Jun 70	WAND'RIN' STAR (re-entry) *Paramount PARA 3004*	42	3
15 Aug 70	WAND'RIN' STAR (2nd re-entry) *Paramount PARA 3004*	47	2

'I Talk to the Trees' by Clint Eastwood, the flip side of 'Wand'rin' Star' was listed with 'Wand'rin' Star' for 7 Feb, 1970, and 14 Feb, 1970 only

MARVIN THE PARANOID ANDROID *UK, robot* — 4 wks

Date	Title	Pos	Wks
16 May 81	MARVIN *Polydor POSP 261*	53	4

Richard MARX ◐ ✐ *US, male vocalist* — 75 wks

Date	Title	Pos	Wks
27 Feb 88	SHOULD'VE KNOWN BETTER *Manhattan MT 32*	50	5
14 May 88	ENDLESS SUMMER NIGHTS *Manhattan MT 39*	50	3
17 Jun 89	SATISFIED *EMI-USA MT 64* ▲	52	4
2 Sep 89 ●	RIGHT HERE WAITING *EMI-USA MT 72* ▲	2	10
11 Nov 89	ANGELIA *EMI-USA MT 74*	45	4
24 Mar 90	TOO LATE TO SAY GOODBYE *EMI-USA MT 80*	38	3
7 Jul 90	CHILDREN OF THE NIGHT *EMI-USA MT 84*	54	2
1 Sep 90	ENDLESS SUMMER NIGHTS / HOLD ON TO THE NIGHTS (re-issue) *EMI-USA MT 89* ▲	60	2
19 Oct 91	KEEP COMING BACK *Capitol CL 634*	55	2
9 May 92 ●	HAZARD *Capitol CL 654*	3	15
29 Aug 92	TAKE THIS HEART *Capitol CL 667*	13	6
28 Nov 92	CHAINS AROUND MY HEART *Capitol CL 676*	29	6
29 Jan 94	NOW AND FOREVER *Capitol CDCLS 703*	13	6
30 Apr 94	SILENT SCREAM *Capitol CDCLS 714*	32	4
13 Aug 94	THE WAY SHE LOVES ME *Capitol CDCL 721*	38	3

MARXMAN *UK/Ireland, rap/instrumental group* — 5 wks

Date	Title	Pos	Wks
6 Mar 93	ALL ABOUT EVE *Talkin Loud TLKCD 35*	28	4
1 May 93	SHIP AHOY *Talkin Loud TLKCD 39*	64	1

Sinead O'Connor provides uncredited vocals on 'Ship Ahoy'

MARY JANE GIRLS ✐ ◀ *US, female vocal group* — 11 wks

Date	Title	Pos	Wks
25 Jun 83	ALL NIGHT LONG *Gordy TMG 1309*	13	9
8 Oct 83	BOYS *Gordy TMG 1315*	74	1
18 Feb 95	ALL NIGHT LONG (re-mix) *Motown TMGCD 1436*	51	1

Carolyne MAS *US, female vocalist* — 2 wks

Date	Title	Pos	Wks
2 Feb 80	QUOTE GOODBYE QUOTE *Mercury 6167 873*	71	2

MASE ◀ *US, male rapper* — 27 wks

Date	Title	Pos	Wks
29 Mar 97	CAN'T NOBODY HOLD ME DOWN *Arista 74321464552* [1] ▲	19	4
9 Aug 97 ●	MO MONEY MO PROBLEMS *Puff Daddy 74321492492* [2]	6	10
27 Dec 97	FEEL SO GOOD *Puff Daddy 74321526442*	10	8
18 Apr 98	WHAT YOU WANT *Puff Daddy 7432157877* [3]	15	5
19 Sep 98	HORSE AND CARRIAGE *Epic 6662612* [4]	12	4
10 Oct 98 ●	TOP OF THE WORLD *Atlantic AT00 46CD* [5]	2	8
12 Dec 98 ●	TAKE ME THERE *Interscope IND 95620* [6]	7†	3

[1] Puff Daddy featuring Mase [2] Notorious B.I.G. featuring Puff Daddy and Mase
[3] Mase featuring Total [4] Cam'ron featuring Mase [5] Brandy featuring Mase
[6] Blackstreet and Mya featuring Mase and Blinky Blink

MASH ◐ *US, male vocal/instrumental group* — 12 wks

Date	Title	Pos	Wks
10 May 80 ★	THEME FROM M*A*S*H* (SUICIDE IS PAINLESS) *CBS 8536*	1	12

MASH! *UK/US, male/female vocal group* — 3 wks

Date	Title	Pos	Wks
21 May 94	U DON'T HAVE TO SAY U LOVE ME *React CDREACT 37*	37	2
4 Feb 95	LET'S SPEND THE NIGHT TOGETHER *Playa CDXPLAYA 2*	66	1

MASON – See CHICANE featuring MASON

Barbara MASON *US, female vocalist* — 5 wks

Date	Title	Pos	Wks
21 Jan 84	ANOTHER MAN *Streetwave KHAN 3*	45	5

Glen MASON *UK, male vocalist* — 7 wks

Date	Title	Pos	Wks
28 Sep 56	GLENDORA *Parlophone R 4203*	28	2
16 Nov 56	GREEN DOOR *Parlophone R 4244*	24	5

Mary MASON *UK, female vocalist* — 6 wks

Date	Title	Pos	Wks
8 Oct 77	ANGEL OF THE MORNING – ANY WAY THAT YOU WANT ME (MEDLEY) *Epic EPC 5552*	27	6

MASQUERADE *UK, male/female vocal group* — 10 wks

Date	Title	Pos	Wks
11 Jan 86	ONE NATION *Streetwave KHAN 59*	54	6
5 Jul 86	(SOLUTION TO) THE PROBLEM *Streetwave KHAN 67*	65	2
26 Jul 86	(SOLUTION TO) THE PROBLEM (re-entry) *Streetwave KHAN 67*	64	2

MASS ORDER *US, male vocal/instrumental duo* — 5 wks

Date	Title	Pos	Wks
14 Mar 92	LIFT EVERY VOICE (TAKE ME AWAY) *Columbia 6577487*	35	3
23 May 92	LET'S GET HAPPY *Columbia 6580737*	45	2

MASS PRODUCTION *US, male vocal/instrumental group* — 7 wks

Date	Title	Pos	Wks
12 Mar 77	WELCOME TO OUR WORLD (OF MERRY MUSIC) *Atlantic K 10898*	44	3
17 May 80	SHANTE *Atlantic K 11475*	59	4

MASS SYNDICATE featuring Su Su BOBIEN
US, male producer, and US, female vocalist — 1 wk

Date	Title	Pos	Wks
24 Oct 98	YOU DON'T KNOW *ffrr FCD 347*	71	1

Zeitia MASSIAH UK, female vocalist — 2 wks

12 Mar 94	I SPECIALIZE IN LOVE *Union City UCRCD 27* [1]	74	1
24 Sep 94	THIS IS THE PLACE *Virgin VSCDT 1511*	62	1

[1] Arizona featuring Zeitia

MASSIEL Spain, female vocalist — 4 wks

24 Apr 68	LA LA LA *Philips BF 1667*	35	4

MASSIVE ATTACK ☺
UK, male/female vocal/instrumental group — 42 wks

23 Feb 91	UNFINISHED SYMPATHY *Wild Bunch WBRS 2* [1]	13	9
8 Jun 91	SAFE FROM HARM *Wild Bunch WBRS 3*	25	6
22 Feb 92	MASSIVE ATTACK EP *Wild Bunch WBRS 4*	27	4
29 Oct 94	SLY *Wild Bunch WBRDX 5*	24	4
21 Jan 95	PROTECTION *Wild Bunch WBRX 6* [2]	14	4
1 Apr 95	KARMACOMA *Wild Bunch WBRX 7*	28	4
19 Jul 97	RISINGSON *Circa WBRX 8*	11	3
9 May 98	TEARDROP *Virgin WBRX 9*	10	6
25 Jul 98	ANGEL *Virgin WBRX 10*	30	2

[1] Massive [2] Massive Attack featuring Tracey Thorn

Tracks on Massive Attack EP: Hymn of the Big Wheel / Home of the Whale / Be Thankful / Any Love

MASSIVO featuring TRACY
UK, male/female vocal/instrumental group — 11 wks

26 May 90	LOVING YOU *Debut DEBT 3097*	25	11

MASTER SINGERS UK, male vocal group — 7 wks

14 Apr 66	HIGHWAY CODE *Parlophone R 5428*	25	6
17 Nov 66	WEATHER FORECAST *Parlophone R 5523*	50	1

MASTERMIXERS – See JIVE BUNNY and the MASTERMIXERS

MASTERS AT WORK – See INDIA

Sammy MASTERS US, male vocalist — 5 wks

9 Jun 60	ROCKIN' RED WING *Warner Bros. WB 10*	36	5

MATCH UK, male vocal/instrumental group — 3 wks

16 Jun 79	BOOGIE MAN *Flamingo FM 2*	48	3

MATCHBOX ♪ ☺ UK, male vocal/instrumental group — 66 wks

3 Nov 79	ROCKABILLY REBEL *Magnet MAG 155*	18	12
19 Jan 80	BUZZ BUZZ A DIDDLE IT *Magnet MAG 157*	22	8
10 May 80	MIDNITE DYNAMOS *Magnet MAG 169*	14	12
27 Sep 80 ●	WHEN YOU ASK ABOUT LOVE *Magnet MAG 191*	4	12
29 Nov 80	OVER THE RAINBOW – YOU BELONG TO ME (MEDLEY) *Magnet MAG 192*	15	11
4 Apr 81	BABES IN THE WOOD *Magnet MAG 193*	46	6
1 Aug 81	LOVE'S MADE A FOOL OF YOU *Magnet MAG 194*	63	3
29 May 82	ONE MORE SATURDAY NIGHT *Magnet MAG 223*	63	2

MATCHBOX 20 US, male vocal/instrumental group — 3 wks

11 Apr 98	PUSH *Atlantic AT 0021CD*	38	2
4 Jul 98	3 AM *Atlantic AT 0034CD*	64	1

MATCHROOM MOB – See CHAS and DAVE

Mireille MATHIEU France, female vocalist — 7 wks

13 Dec 67	LA DERNIERE VALSE *Columbia DB 8323*	26	7

Johnny MATHIS ☾ *Legendary MOR vocal superstar, b. 30 September, 1935, San Francisco. Frank Sinatra and Elvis Presley are the only males with more hit albums in the USA, where his* Greatest Hits *album charted for almost ten years – a record for a solo performer* — 137 wks

23 May 58	TEACHER TEACHER *Fontana H 130*	27	5
26 Sep 58 ●	A CERTAIN SMILE *Fontana H 142*	4	16
19 Dec 58	WINTER WONDERLAND *Fontana H 165*	17	3
7 Aug 59 ●	SOMEONE *Fontana H 199*	6	15
27 Nov 59	THE BEST OF EVERYTHING *Fontana H 218*	30	1
29 Jan 60	MISTY *Fontana H 219*	12	9
24 Mar 60	YOU ARE BEAUTIFUL *Fontana H 234*	38	8
14 Apr 60	MISTY (re-entry) *Fontana H 219*	46	2
26 May 60	YOU ARE BEAUTIFUL (re-entry) *Fontana H 234*	46	1
28 Jul 60	STARBRIGHT *Fontana H 254*	47	2
6 Oct 60 ●	MY LOVE FOR YOU *Fontana H 267*	9	18
4 Apr 63	WHAT WILL MARY SAY *CBS AAG 135*	49	1
25 Jan 75 ●	I'M STONE IN LOVE WITH YOU *CBS 2653*	10	12
13 Nov 76 ★	WHEN A CHILD IS BORN (SOLEADO) *CBS 4599*	1	12
25 Mar 78 ●	TOO MUCH TOO LITTLE TOO LATE *CBS 6164* [1] ▲	3	14
29 Jul 78	YOU'RE ALL I NEED TO GET BY *CBS 6483* [1]	45	6
11 Aug 79	GONE GONE GONE *CBS 7730*	15	10
26 Dec 81	WHEN A CHILD IS BORN *CBS S 1758* [2]	74	2

[1] Johnny Mathis and Deniece Williams [2] Johnny Mathis and Gladys Knight

Ivan MATIAS US, male vocalist — 1 wk

6 Apr 96	SO GOOD (TO COME HOME TO)/I'VE HAD ENOUGH *Arista 74321345072*	69	1

Al MATTHEWS ♪ US, male vocalist — 8 wks

23 Aug 75	FOOL *CBS 3429*	16	8

John MATTHEWS – See UNDERCOVER

MATTHEWS SOUTHERN COMFORT ♂ 🎸
UK, male vocal/instrumental group — 18 wks

26 Sep 70 ★	WOODSTOCK *Uni UNS 526*	1	18

MATUMBI UK, male vocal/instrumental group — 7 wks

29 Sep 79	POINT OF VIEW *Matumbi RIC 101*	35	7

Susan MAUGHAN ☺ UK, female vocalist — 25 wks

11 Oct 62 ●	BOBBY'S GIRL *Philips 326544 BF*	3	19
14 Feb 63	HAND A HANDKERCHIEF TO HELEN *Philips 326562 BF*	41	3
9 May 63	SHE'S NEW TO YOU *Philips 326586 BF*	45	3

MAUREEN ☺ ☺ UK, female vocalist — 22 wks

26 Nov 88 ●	SAY A LITTLE PRAYER *Rhythm King DOOD 3* [1]	10	10
16 Jun 90	THINKING OF YOU *Urban URB 55*	11	9
12 Jan 91	WHERE HAS ALL THE LOVE GONE *Urban URB 65*	51	3

[1] Bomb The Bass featuring Maureen

Some copies of 'Thinking of You' are credited to the fuller name of Maureen Walsh

Paul MAURIAT ☾ France, orchestra — 14 wks

21 Feb 68	LOVE IS BLUE (L'AMOUR EST BLEU) *Philips BF 1637* ▲	12	14

MAVERICKS 🎸 US, male vocal/instrumental group — 22 wks

2 May 98	DANCE THE NIGHT AWAY *MCA Nashville MCSTD 48081*	4	18
26 Sep 98	I'VE GOT THIS FEELING *MCA Nashville MCSTD 48095*	27	4

MAX Q Australia, male vocal/instrumental duo — 3 wks

17 Feb 90	SOMETIMES *Mercury MXQ 2*	53	3

MAX WEBSTER Canada, male vocal/instrumental group — 3 wks

19 May 79	PARADISE SKIES *Capitol CL 16079*	43	3

MAXIMA featuring LILY
UK/Spain, male/female vocal/instrumental duo — 2 wks

14 Aug 93	IBIZA *Yo! Yo! CDLILY 1*	55	2

UK No 1 ★   UK Top 10 ●   UK million seller ◆   UK entry at No 1 ■   US No 1 ▲

MAXWELL US, male vocalist — 10 wks

Date	Title	Pos	Wks
11 May 96	...TIL THE COPS COME KNOCKIN' Columbia 6631792	63	1
24 Aug 96	ASCENSION NO ONE'S GONNA LOVE YOU SO DON'T EVER WONDER Columbia 6636265	39	3
1 Mar 97	SUMTHIN' SUMTHIN' THE MANTRA Columbia 6638642	27	3
24 May 97	ASCENSION DON'T EVER WONDER Columbia 6645952	28	3

MAXX ☻ ☺
UK/Sweden/Germany, male/female vocal/instrumental group — 24 wks

Date	Title	Pos	Wks
21 May 94	● GET-A-WAY Pulse 8 CDLOSE 59	4	12
6 Aug 94	● NO MORE (I CAN'T STAND IT) Pulse 8 CDLOSE 66	8	8
29 Oct 94	YOU CAN GET IT Pulse 8 CDLOSE 75	21	3
22 Jul 95	I CAN MAKE YOU FEEL LIKE Pulse 8 CDLOSE 88	56	1

Billy MAY ℂ US, orchestra — 10 wks

Date	Title	Pos	Wks
27 Apr 56	● MAIN TITLE THEME FROM 'MAN WITH THE GOLDEN ARM' Capitol CL 14551	9	10

Brian MAY 🎸 UK, male vocalist/instrumentalist – guitar — 33 wks

Date	Title	Pos	Wks
5 Nov 83	STAR FLEET EMI 5436 [1]	65	3
7 Dec 91	DRIVEN BY YOU Parlophone R 6304	6	9
5 Sep 92	● TOO MUCH LOVE WILL KILL YOU Parlophone R 6320	5	9
17 Oct 92	WE ARE THE CHAMPIONS PolyGram TV PO 229 [2]	66	1
21 Nov 92	BACK TO THE LIGHT Parlophone R 6329	19	4
19 Jun 93	RESURRECTION Parlophone CDRS 6351 [3]	23	3
18 Dec 93	LAST HORIZON Parlophone CDR 6371	51	2
6 Jun 98	THE BUSINESS Parlophone CD 6498	51	1
12 Sep 98	WHY DON'T WE TRY AGAIN Parlophone CD 6504	44	1

[1] Brian May and Friends [2] Hank Marvin featuring Brian May
[3] Brian May with Cozy Powell

Lisa MAY UK, female vocalist — 2 wks

Date	Title	Pos	Wks
15 Jul 95	WISHING ON A STAR Urban Gorilla UG 3CD [1]	16	1
14 Sep 96	THE CURSE OF VOODOO RAY Fontana VOOCD 1	64	1

[1] 88.3 featuring Lisa MAY

Mary MAY UK, female vocalist — 1 wk

Date	Title	Pos	Wks
27 Feb 64	ANYONE WHO HAD A HEART Fontana TF 440	49	1

Shernette MAY UK, female vocalist — 1 wk

Date	Title	Pos	Wks
6 Jun 98	ALL THE MAN THAT I NEED Virgin VSCDT 1691	50	1

Simon MAY ℂ UK, male vocalist — 21 wks

Date	Title	Pos	Wks
9 Oct 76	● SUMMER OF MY LIFE Pye 7N 45627	7	8
21 May 77	WE'LL GATHER LILACS – ALL MY LOVING (MEDLEY) Pye 7N 45688	49	1
4 Jun 77	WE'LL GATHER LILACS – ALL MY LOVING (MEDLEY) (re-entry) Pye 7N 45688	50	1
26 Oct 85	HOWARD'S WAY BBC RESL 174 [1]	21	11

[1] Simon May Orchestra

See also Anita DOBSON; Marti WEBB

MAYA – See TAMPERER featuring MAYA

Curtis MAYFIELD 🎸 US, male vocalist — 18 wks

Date	Title	Pos	Wks
31 Jul 71	MOVE ON UP Buddah 2011 080	12	10
2 Dec 78	NO GOODBYES Atlantic LV 1	65	3
30 May 87	(CELEBRATE) THE DAY AFTER YOU RCA MONK 6 [1]	52	2
29 Sep 90	SUPERFLY 1990 Capitol CL 586 [2]	48	3

[1] Blow Monkeys with Curtis Mayfield [2] Curtis Mayfield and Ice-T

MAYTALS Jamaica, male vocal/instrumental group — 4 wks

Date	Title	Pos	Wks
25 Apr 70	MONKEY MAN Trojan TR 7711	50	1
9 May 70	MONKEY MAN (re-entry) Trojan TR 7711	47	3

MAYTE US, female vocalist — 1 wk

Date	Title	Pos	Wks
18 Nov 95	IF EYE LOVE U 2 NIGHT NPG 0061635	67	1

MAZE featuring Frankie BEVERLY
US, male vocal/instrumental group — 14 wks

Date	Title	Pos	Wks
20 Jul 85	TOO MANY GAMES Capitol CL 363	36	7
23 Aug 86	I WANNA BE WITH YOU Capitol CL 421	55	3
27 May 89	JOY AND PAIN Capitol CL 531 [1]	57	4

[1] Maze

Kym MAZELLE ☺ 🎤 US, female vocalist — 65 wks

Date	Title	Pos	Wks
12 Nov 88	USELESS (I DON'T NEED YOU NOW) Syncopate SY 18	53	3
14 Jan 89	● WAIT RCA PB 42595 [1]	7	10
25 Mar 89	GOT TO GET YOU BACK Syncopate SY 25	29	4
7 Oct 89	LOVE STRAIN Syncopate SY 30	52	3
20 Jan 90	WAS THAT ALL IT WAS Syncopate SY 32	33	6
26 May 90	USELESS (I DON'T NEED YOU NOW) (re-mix) Syncopate SY 36	48	2
24 Nov 90	MISSING YOU Ten TEN 345 [2]	22	7
25 May 91	NO ONE CAN LOVE YOU MORE THAN ME Parlophone R 6287	62	2
26 Dec 92	LOVE ME THE RIGHT WAY Arista 74321128097 [3]	22	10
11 Jun 94	NO MORE TEARS (ENOUGH IS ENOUGH) Ding Dong 74321209032 [4]	13	7
8 Oct 94	GIMME ALL YOUR LOVIN' Ding Dong 74321231322 [4]	22	3
23 Dec 95	SEARCHING FOR THE GOLDEN EYE Eternal WEA 027CD [5]	40	3
28 Sep 96	LOVE ME THE RIGHT WAY (re-mix) Logic 74321404442 [3]	55	1
16 Aug 97	YOUNG HEARTS RUN FREE EMI CDEM 488	20	4

[1] Robert Howard and Kym Mazelle [2] Soul II Soul featuring Kym Mazelle
[3] Rapination and Kym Mazelle [4] Jocelyn Brown and Kym Mazelle
[5] Motiv 8 and Kym Mazelle

MAZZY STAR US, male/female vocal/instrumental duo — 3 wks

Date	Title	Pos	Wks
27 Aug 94	FADE INTO YOU Capitol CDCL 720	48	1
2 Nov 96	FLOWERS IN DECEMBER Capitol CDCL 781	40	2

MC DUKE UK, male rapper — 1 wk

Date	Title	Pos	Wks
11 Mar 89	I'M RIFFIN (ENGLISH RASTA) Music Of Life 7NOTE 25	75	1

MC ERIC – See TECHNOTRONIC

MC FIXX IT – See ANTICAPPELLA

MC Mikee FREEDOM – See NOMAD

MC HAMMER – See HAMMER

MC LETHAL UK, male producer — 1 wk

Date	Title	Pos	Wks
14 Nov 92	THE RAVE DIGGER Network NWKT 60	66	1

MC LYTE ☚ US, female rapper — 12 wks

Date	Title	Pos	Wks
15 Jan 94	RUFFNECK Atlantic A 8336CD	67	1
29 Jun 96	KEEP ON KEEPIN' ON East West A 4287CD [1]	39	2
18 Jan 97	COLD ROCK A PARTY East West A 3975CD	15	4
19 Apr 97	KEEP ON KEEPIN' ON East West A 3950CD1 [1]	27	2
5 Sep 98	I CAN'T MAKE A MISTAKE Elektra E 3813CD	46	1
19 Dec 98	IT'S ALL YOURS East West E 3789CD [2]	36†	2

[1] MC Lyte featuring Xscape [2] MC Lyte featuring Gina Thompson

MC MARIO – See AMBASSADORS OF FUNK featuring MC MARIO

MC MIKER 'G' and Deejay SVEN ☻ ☚
Holland, male vocal/instrumental rap duo — 7 wks

Date	Title	Pos	Wks
6 Sep 86	● HOLIDAY RAP Debut DEBT 3008	6	7

MC SAR – See REAL McCOY

MC SKAT KAT and the STRAY MOB
US, male cartoon feline rap/vocal group   **2 wks**

9 Nov 91	SKAT STRUT *Virgin America VUS 51*	64	2

MC SOLAAR – *See URBAN SPECIES*

MC SPY-D + FRIENDS
UK, male/female vocal/instrumental group   **2 wks**

11 Mar 95	THE AMAZING SPIDER-MAN *Parlophone CDR 6404*	37	2

MC TUNES ◄ *UK, male rapper*   **18 wks**

2 Jun 90 ●	THE ONLY RHYME THAT BITES *ZTT ZANG 3* [1]	10	10
15 Sep 90	TUNES SPLITS THE ATOM *ZTT ZANG 6* [1]	18	7
1 Dec 90	PRIMARY RHYMING *ZTT ZANG 10*	67	1

[1] MC Tunes versus 808 State

MC WILDSKI *UK, male rapper*   **10 wks**

8 Jul 89	BLAME IT ON THE BASSLINE *Go.Beat GOD 33* [1]	29	6
3 Mar 90	WARRIOR *Arista 112956*	49	4

[1] Norman Cook featuring MC Wildski

'Blame It on the Bassline' was listed with 'Won't Talk About It' by Norman Cook featuring Billy Bragg

ME AND YOU featuring WE THE PEOPLE BAND
Jamaica/UK, male/female vocal/instrumental group   **9 wks**

28 Jul 79	YOU NEVER KNOW WHAT YOU'VE GOT *Laser LAS 8*	31	9

ME ME ME ◐ ☹ *UK, male vocal/instrumental group*   **4 wks**

17 Aug 96	HANGING AROUND *Indolent DUFF 005CD*	19	4

Abigail MEAD and Nigel GOULDING ◐
UK/US, female/male producers   **10 wks**

26 Sep 87 ●	FULL METAL JACKET (I WANNA BE YOUR DRILL INSTRUCTOR) *Warner Bros. W 8187*	2	10

MEAT BEAT MANIFESTO *UK, male production duo*   **1 wk**

20 Feb 93	MINDSTREAM *Play It Again Sam BIAS 232CD*	55	1

MEAT LOAF ✔
Larger-than-life vocalist/actor; b. Marvin Lee Aday, 27 September, 1951, Dallas. His collaborations with producer/songwriter Jim Steinman resulted in some of rock's finest recordings. His album Bat Out of Hell sold more than 25 million copies and spent more than eight years in total on the UK chart   **142 wks**

20 May 78	YOU TOOK THE WORDS RIGHT OUT OF MY MOUTH *Epic EPC 5980*	33	8
19 Aug 78	TWO OUT OF THREE AIN'T BAD *Epic EPC 6281*	32	8
10 Feb 79	BAT OUT OF HELL *Epic EPC 7018*	15	7
26 Sep 81	I'M GONNA LOVE HER FOR BOTH OF US *Epic EPCA 1580*	62	3
28 Nov 81 ●	DEAD RINGER FOR LOVE *Epic EPCA 1697*	5	17
28 May 83	IF YOU REALLY WANT TO *Epic A 3357*	59	2
24 Sep 83	MIDNIGHT AT THE LOST AND FOUND *Epic A 3748*	17	8
14 Jan 84	RAZOR'S EDGE *Epic A 4080*	41	3
6 Oct 84	MODERN GIRL *Arista ARIST 585*	17	9
22 Dec 84	NOWHERE FAST *Arista ARIST 600*	67	4
23 Mar 85	PIECE OF THE ACTION *Arista ARIST 603*	47	5
30 Aug 86	ROCK 'N' ROLL MERCENARIES *Arista ARIST 666* [1]	31	6
22 Jun 91	DEAD RINGER FOR LOVE (re-issue) *Epic 6569827*	53	2
27 Jun 92	TWO OUT OF THREE AIN'T BAD (re-issue) *Epic 6574917*	69	1
9 Oct 93 ★	I'D DO ANYTHING FOR LOVE (BUT I WON'T DO THAT) *Virgin VSCDT 1443* ▲	1	19
18 Dec 93 ●	BAT OUT OF HELL (re-issue) *Epic 6600062*	8	9
19 Feb 94	ROCK AND ROLL DREAMS COME THROUGH *Virgin VSCDT 1479*	11	7
7 May 94	OBJECTS IN THE REAR VIEW MIRROR MAY APPEAR CLOSER THAN THEY ARE *Virgin VSCDT 1492*	26	4
28 Oct 95 ●	I'D LIE FOR YOU (AND THAT'S THE TRUTH) *Virgin VSCDT 1563*	2	11
27 Jan 96 ●	NOT A DRY EYE IN THE HOUSE *Virgin VSCDT 1567*	7	6
27 Apr 96	RUNNIN' FOR THE RED LIGHT (I GOTTA LIFE) *Virgin VSCDX 1582*	21	3

[1] Meat Loaf featuring John Parr

'Dead Ringer for Love' features Cher as uncredited co-vocalist

MECHANICS – *See MIKE and the MECHANICS*

MECO ◢ *US, orchestra*   **9 wks**

1 Oct 77 ●	STAR WARS THEME – CANTINA BAND *RCA XB 1028* ▲	7	9

Glenn MEDEIROS ◐ *US, male vocalist*   **26 wks**

18 Jun 88 ★	NOTHING'S GONNA CHANGE MY LOVE FOR YOU *London LON 184*	1	13
3 Sep 88	LONG AND LASTING LOVE (ONCE IN A LIFETIME) *London LON 202*	42	4
30 Jun 90	SHE AIN'T WORTH IT *London LON 265* [1] ▲	12	9

[1] Glenn Medeiros featuring Bobby Brown

Paul MEDFORD – *See Letitia DEAN and Paul MEDFORD*

MEDICINE HEAD ✔ *UK, male vocal/instrumental duo*   **37 wks**

26 Jun 71	(AND THE) PICTURES IN THE SKY *Dandelion DAN 7003*	22	8
5 May 73 ●	ONE AND ONE IS ONE *Polydor 2001 432*	3	13
4 Aug 73	RISING SUN *Polydor 2058 389*	11	9
9 Feb 74	SLIP AND SLIDE *Polydor 2058 436*	22	7

MEDICINE SHOW – *See DR HOOK*

Bill MEDLEY ◐ *US, male vocalist*   **29 wks**

31 Oct 87 ●	(I'VE HAD) THE TIME OF MY LIFE *RCA PB 49625* [1] ▲	6	12
27 Aug 88	HE AIN'T HEAVY, HE'S MY BROTHER *Scotti Brothers PO 10*	25	6
15 Dec 90 ●	(I'VE HAD) THE TIME OF MY LIFE (re-entry) *RCA PB 49625* [1]	8	11

[1] Bill Medley and Jennifer Warnes

Michael MEDWIN, Bernard BRESSLAW, Alfie BASS and Leslie FYSON ◐ *UK, male vocal group*   **9 wks**

30 May 58 ●	THE SIGNATURE TUNE OF 'THE ARMY GAME' *HMV POP 490*	5	9

See also Bernard BRESSLAW

MEECHIE *US, female vocalist*   **1 wk**

2 Sep 95	YOU BRING ME JOY *Vibe MCSTD 2069*	74	1

Tony MEEHAN COMBO ◐
UK, male instrumental group, Tony Meehan – drums   **4 wks**

16 Jan 64	SONG OF MEXICO *Decca F 11801*	39	4

See also Jet HARRIS and Tony MEEHAN

MEGA CITY FOUR *UK, male vocal/instrumental group*   **7 wks**

19 Oct 91	WORDS THAT SAY *Big Life MEGA 2*	66	1
8 Feb 92	STOP EP *Big Life MEGA 3*	36	2
16 May 92	SHIVERING SAND *Big Life MEGA 4*	35	2
1 May 93	IRON SKY *Big Life MEGAD 5*	48	1
17 Jul 93	WALLFLOWER *Big Life MEGAD 6*	69	1

Tracks on Stop (EP): Stop/Desert Song/Back to Zero/Overlap

MEGABASS – *See VARIOUS ARTISTS (MONTAGES)*

UK No 1 ★   UK Top 10 ●   UK million seller ◆   UK entry at No 1 ■   US No 1 ▲

What: *Green Green Grass of Home* **61**
Who: Tom Jones
When: 1966 (1)
Which: Became his most requested song, even though it is about a condemned man waiting for his execution. This worldwide smash had first been recorded by country singer Johnny Darrell

What: *Stay* **62**
Who: Shakespears Sister
When: 1992
Which: Holds the singles chart record for most weeks at the top by a female group or duo. The haunting song was produced at George Harrison's home studio

What: *Give Me Your Word* **63**
Who: Tennessee Ernie Ford
When: 1955 (1)
Which: A critic that said the British loved it because of the novelty of hearing "a cowboy singing a plush ballad." In the USA it was the overlooked B-side of pop flop *River of No Return*

What: *Candle in the Wind 1997 / Something About the Way You Look Tonight* **64**
Who: Elton John
When: 1997 (1)
Which: Sold a record-shattering 33 million copies worldwide in just three months. This tribute to Princess Diana was a No 1 in every corner of the globe – a truly unique feat. It is the biggest seller ever in many countries including the UK and the USA

MEGADETH ✈ US, male vocal/instrumental group — 32 wks

Date	Title	Pos	Wks
19 Dec 87	WAKE UP DEAD Capitol CL 476	65	2
27 Feb 88	ANARCHY IN THE UK Capitol CL 480	45	3
21 May 88	MARY JANE Capitol CL 489	46	2
13 Jan 90	NO MORE MR. NICE GUY SBK SBK 4	13	6
29 Sep 90	HOLY WARS . . . THE PUNISHMENT DUE Capitol CLP 588	24	3
16 Mar 91	HANGAR 18 Capitol CLS 604	26	4
27 Jun 92	SYMPHONY OF DESTRUCTION Capitol CLS 662	15	3
24 Oct 92	SKIN O' MY TEETH Capitol CLP 669	13	3
29 May 93	SWEATING BULLETS Capitol CDCL 682	26	3
7 Jan 95	TRAIN OF CONSEQUENCES Capitol CDCL 730	22	3

MEJA ⊕ Sweden, female vocalist — 5 wks

Date	Title	Pos	Wks
24 Oct 98	ALL 'BOUT THE MONEY Columbia 6665662	12	5

MEL and KIM – See Mel SMITH; Kim WILDE

MEL and KIM ⊕ ☺ UK, female vocal duo — 51 wks

Date	Title	Pos	Wks
20 Sep 86 ●	SHOWING OUT (GET FRESH AT THE WEEKEND) Supreme SUPE 107	3	19
7 Mar 87 ★	RESPECTABLE Supreme SUPE 111	1	15
11 Jul 87 ●	F.L.M. Supreme SUPE 113	7	10
27 Feb 88 ●	THAT'S THE WAY IT IS Supreme SUPE 117	10	7

See also Kim APPLEBY

Melle MEL – See GRANDMASTER FLASH, Melle MEL and the FURIOUS FIVE

George MELACHRINO ORCHESTRA © UK, orchestra — 9 wks

Date	Title	Pos	Wks
12 Oct 56	AUTUMN CONCERTO HMV B 10958	18	9

MELANIE ♂ US, female vocalist — 35 wks

Date	Title	Pos	Wks
26 Sep 70 ●	RUBY TUESDAY Buddah 2011 038	9	14
9 Jan 71	RUBY TUESDAY (re-entry) Buddah 2011 038	43	1
16 Jan 71	WHAT HAVE THEY DONE TO MY SONG MA Buddah 2011 038	39	1
1 Jan 72 ●	BRAND NEW KEY Buddah 2011 105 ▲	4	12
16 Feb 74	WILL YOU LOVE ME TOMORROW Neighbourhood NBH 9	37	5
24 Sep 83	EVERY BREATH OF THE WAY Neighbourhood HOOD NB1	70	2

John Cougar MELLENCAMP US, male vocalist — 18 wks

Date	Title	Pos	Wks
23 Oct 82	JACK AND DIANE Riva RIVA 37 [1] ▲	25	8
1 Feb 86	SMALL TOWN Riva JCM 5	53	4
10 May 86	R.O.C.K. IN THE U.S.A. Riva JCM 6	67	3
3 Sep 94	WILD NIGHT Mercury MERCD 409 [2]	34	3

[1] John Cougar [2] John Mellencamp featuring Me'Shell NdegeoCello

Will MELLOR ⊕ UK, male vocalist — 9 wks

Date	Title	Pos	Wks
28 Feb 98 ●	WHEN I NEED YOU Unity UNITY 017RCD	5	6
27 Jun 98	NO MATTER WHAT I DO Jive 0540012	23	3

MELODIANS Jamaica, male vocal/instrumental group — 1 wk

Date	Title	Pos	Wks
10 Jan 70	SWEET SENSATION Trojan TR 695	41	1

MELODY MAKERS – See Ziggy MARLEY and the MELODY MAKERS

MELTDOWN UK/US, male instrumental/production duo — 1 wk

Date	Title	Pos	Wks
27 Apr 96	MY LIFE IS IN YOUR HANDS Sony S3 DANU 7CD	44	1

Harold MELVIN and the BLUENOTES ✎ US, male vocal group — 52 wks

Date	Title	Pos	Wks
13 Jan 73 ●	IF YOU DON'T KNOW ME BY NOW CBS 8496	9	9
12 Jan 74	THE LOVE I LOST Philadelphia Interna PIR 1879	21	8
13 Apr 74	SATISFACTION GUARANTEED (OR TAKE YOUR LOVE BACK) Philadelphia Interna PIR 2187	32	6
31 May 75	GET OUT Route RT 06	35	5
28 Feb 76	WAKE UP EVERYBODY Philadelphia PIR 3866	23	7
22 Jan 77 ●	DON'T LEAVE ME THIS WAY Philadelphia Interna PIR 4909	5	10

Date	Title	Pos	Wks
2 Apr 77	REACHING FOR THE WORLD ABC 4161	48	1
28 Apr 84	DON'T GIVE ME UP London LON 47	59	4
4 Aug 84	TODAY'S YOUR LUCKY DAY London LON 52	66	2

MEMBERS ✐ UK, male vocal/instrumental group — 14 wks

Date	Title	Pos	Wks
3 Feb 79	THE SOUND OF THE SUBURBS Virgin VS 242	12	9
7 Apr 79	OFFSHORE BANKING BUSINESS Virgin VS 248	31	5

MEN AT WORK ⊕ ✐
Australia, male vocal/instrumental group — 39 wks

Date	Title	Pos	Wks
30 Oct 82	WHO CAN IT BE NOW? Epic EPC A 2392 ▲	45	5
8 Jan 83 ★	DOWN UNDER Epic EPC A 1980 ▲	1	12
9 Apr 83	OVERKILL Epic EPC A 3220	21	10
2 Jul 83	IT'S A MISTAKE Epic EPC A 3475	33	6
10 Sep 83	DR. HECKYLL AND MR. JIVE Epic EPC A 3668	31	6

MEN THEY COULDN'T HANG
UK, male vocal/instrumental group — 4 wks

Date	Title	Pos	Wks
2 Apr 88	THE COLOURS Magnet SELL 6	61	4

MEN WITHOUT HATS ⊕
Canada, male vocal/instrumental group — 11 wks

Date	Title	Pos	Wks
8 Oct 83 ●	THE SAFETY DANCE Statik TAK 1	6	11

Sergio MENDES Brazil, male conductor — 5 wks

Date	Title	Pos	Wks
9 Jul 83	NEVER GONNA LET YOU GO A & M AM 118	45	5

Uncredited vocals by Joe Pizzulo and Leza Miller

Andrea MENDEZ UK, female vocalist — 1 wk

Date	Title	Pos	Wks
3 Aug 96	BRING ME LOVE AM:PM 5817872	44	1

MENSWEAR ☹ ⊕ UK, male vocal/instrumental group — 18 wks

Date	Title	Pos	Wks
15 Apr 95	I'LL MANAGE SOMEHOW Laurel LAUCD 4	49	1
1 Jul 95	DAYDREAMER Laurel LAUCD 5	14	4
30 Sep 95	STARDUST Laurel LAUCD 6	16	3
16 Dec 95	SLEEPING IN Laurel LAUCD 7	24	3
23 Mar 96 ●	BEING BRAVE Laurel LAUCD 8	10	4
7 Sep 96	WE LOVE YOU Laurel LAUCD 11	22	3

MENTAL AS ANYTHING ⊕ ✐
Australia, male vocal/instrumental group — 13 wks

Date	Title	Pos	Wks
7 Feb 87 ●	LIVE IT UP Epic ANY 1	3	13

Freddie MERCURY ⊕ ✐ UK, male vocalist — 79 wks

Date	Title	Pos	Wks
22 Sep 84 ●	LOVE KILLS CBS A 4735	10	8
20 Apr 85	I WAS BORN TO LOVE YOU CBS A 6019	11	10
13 Jul 85	MADE IN HEAVEN CBS A 6413	57	4
21 Sep 85	LIVING ON MY OWN CBS A 6555	50	3
24 May 86	TIME EMI EMI 5559	32	5
7 Mar 87 ●	THE GREAT PRETENDER Parlophone R 6151	4	9
7 Nov 87 ●	BARCELONA Polydor POSP 887 [1]	8	9
8 Aug 92 ●	BARCELONA (re-issue) Polydor PO 221 [1]	2	8
12 Dec 92 ●	IN MY DEFENCE Parlophone R 6331	8	7
6 Feb 93	THE GREAT PRETENDER (re-issue) Parlophone CDR 6336	29	3
31 Jul 93 ★	LIVING ON MY OWN (re-mix) Parlophone CDR 6355	1	13

[1] Freddie Mercury and Montserrat Caballé

MERCURY REV US, male / female vocal / instrumental group — 1 wk

Date	Title	Pos	Wks
14 Nov 98	GODDESS ON A HIWAY V2 VVR 5003323	51	1

MERCY MERCY UK, male vocal/instrumental group — 2 wks

Date	Title	Pos	Wks
21 Sep 85	WHAT ARE WE GONNA DO ABOUT IT? Ensign ENY 522	59	2

Tony MERRICK UK, male vocalist — 1 wk

Date	Title	Pos	Wks
2 Jun 66	LADY JANE Columbia DB 7913	49	1

MERSEYBEATS ☺ UK, male vocal/instrumental group — 64 wks

Date	Title	Pos	Wks
12 Sep 63	IT'S LOVE THAT REALLY COUNTS *Fontana TF 412*	24	12
16 Jan 64 ●	I THINK OF YOU *Fontana TF 431*	5	17
16 Apr 64	DON'T TURN AROUND *Fontana TF 459*	13	11
9 Jul 64	WISHIN' AND HOPIN' *Fontana TF 482*	13	10
5 Nov 64	LAST NIGHT *Fontana TF 504*	40	3
14 Oct 65	I LOVE YOU, YES I DO *Fontana TF 607*	22	8
20 Jan 66	I STAND ACCUSED *Fontana TF 645*	38	3

MERSEYS ☺ UK, male vocal duo — 13 wks

Date	Title	Pos	Wks
28 Apr 66 ●	SORROW *Fontana TF 694*	4	13

MERTON PARKAS UK, male vocal/instrumental group — 6 wks

Date	Title	Pos	Wks
4 Aug 79	YOU NEED WHEELS *Beggars Banquet BEG 22*	40	6

Mady MESPLE and Danielle MILLET with the PARIS OPERA-COMIQUE ORCHESTRA conducted by Alain LOMBARD
France, female vocal duo and orchestra — 4 wks

Date	Title	Pos	Wks
6 Apr 85	FLOWER DUET (FROM LAKME) *EMI 5481*	47	4

MESSIAH ☺ UK, male instrumental/production group — 13 wks

Date	Title	Pos	Wks
20 Jun 92	TEMPLE OF DREAMS *Kickin KICK 12S*	20	5
26 Sep 92	I FEEL LOVE *Kickin KICK 22S* [1]	19	5
27 Nov 93	THUNDERDOME *WEA YZ 790CD1*	29	3

[1] Messiah featuring Precious Wilson

METAL GURUS UK, male vocal/instrumental group — 2 wks

Date	Title	Pos	Wks
8 Dec 90	MERRY XMAS EVERYBODY *Mercury GURU 1*	55	2

METALHEADS – See GOLDIE

METALLICA ✈ US/Denmark, male vocal/instrumental group — 54 wks

Date	Title	Pos	Wks
22 Aug 87	THE $5.98 EP – GARAGE DAYS REVISITED *Vertigo METAL 112*	27	4
3 Sep 88	HARVESTER OF SORROW *Vertigo METAL 212*	20	3
22 Apr 89	ONE *Vertigo METAL 5*	13	7
10 Aug 91 ●	ENTER SANDMAN *Vertigo METAL 7*	5	4
9 Nov 91	THE UNFORGIVEN *Vertigo METAL 8*	15	4
2 May 92 ●	NOTHING ELSE MATTERS *Vertigo METAL 10*	6	6
31 Oct 92	WHEREVER I MAY ROAM *Vertigo METAL 9*	25	4
20 Feb 93	SAD BUT TRUE *Vertigo METCD 11*	20	3
1 Jun 96 ●	UNTIL IT SLEEPS *Vertigo UKMETCD 12*	5	4
28 Sep 96	HERO OF THE DAY *Vertigo METCD 13*	17	4
7 Dec 96	MAMA SAID *Vertigo METCD 14*	19	2
22 Nov 97	THE MEMORY REMAINS *Vertigo METCD 15*	13	3
7 Mar 98	THE UNFORGIVEN II *Vertigo METDD 17*	15	4
4 Jul 98	FUEL *Vertigo METCD 16*	31	2

Tracks on The $5.98 EP: Garage Days Revisited/Helpless/Crash Course in Brain Surgery/The Small Hours/Last Caress/Green Hell

METEORS UK, male vocal/instrumental group — 2 wks

Date	Title	Pos	Wks
26 Feb 83	JOHNNY REMEMBER ME *ID EYE 1*	66	2

Pat METHENY GROUP – See David BOWIE

METHOD MAN ✒ US, male rapper — 12 wks

Date	Title	Pos	Wks
29 Apr 95	RELEASE YO' SELF *Def Jam DEFCD 6*	46	1
29 Jul 95 ●	I'LL BE THERE FOR YOU – YOU'RE ALL I NEED TO GET BY *Def Jam DEFCD 11* [1]	10	5
5 Apr 97 ●	HIT 'EM HIGH (THE MONSTARS' ANTHEM) *Atlantic A 5449CD* [2]	8	6

[1] Method Man featuring Mary J Blige [2] B Real / Busta Rhymes / Coolio / LL Cool J / Method Man

MEZZOFORTE ✒ (R&B) Iceland, male instrumental group — 10 wks

Date	Title	Pos	Wks
5 Mar 83	GARDEN PARTY *Steinar STE 705*	17	9
11 Jun 83	ROCKALL *Steinar STE 710*	75	1

MFSB US, orchestra — 18 wks

Date	Title	Pos	Wks
27 Apr 74	TSOP (THE SOUND OF PHILADELPHIA) *Philadelphia Interna PIR 2289* [1] ▲	22	9
26 Jul 75	SEXY *Philadelphia Interna PIR 3381*	37	5
31 Jan 81	MYSTERIES OF THE WORLD *Sound Of Philadelphi a PIR 9501*	41	4

[1] MFSB featuring the Three Degrees

MG's – See BOOKER T and the MG's

MIAMI SOUND MACHINE – See Gloria ESTEFAN

George MICHAEL ☺
Previously half of internationally celebrated duo Wham!, b. Georgios Panayiotou, 25 June, 1963, London. This multi-talented award-winning singer/songwriter/producer/arranger and instrumentalist has successfully made the difficult transition from teeny-bopper hero to world-renowned solo star — 220 wks

Date	Title	Pos	Wks
4 Aug 84 ★	CARELESS WHISPER *Epic A 4603* ◆ ▲	1	17
5 Apr 86 ★	A DIFFERENT CORNER *Epic A 7033*	1	10
31 Jan 87 ★	I KNEW YOU WERE WAITING (FOR ME) *Epic DUET 2* [1] ▲	1	9
13 Jun 87 ●	I WANT YOUR SEX *Epic LUST 1*	3	10
24 Oct 87 ●	FAITH *Epic EMU 3* ▲	2	12
9 Jan 88	FATHER FIGURE *Epic EMU 4* ▲	11	6
23 Apr 88 ●	ONE MORE TRY *Epic EMU 5* ▲	8	7
16 Jul 88	MONKEY *Epic EMU 6* ▲	13	6
3 Dec 88	KISSING A FOOL *Epic EMU 7*	18	6
25 Aug 90	PRAYING FOR TIME *Epic GEO 1* ▲	6	7
27 Oct 90	WAITING FOR THAT DAY *Epic GEO 2*	23	5
15 Dec 90	FREEDOM *Epic GEO 3*	28	6
16 Feb 91	HEAL THE PAIN *Epic 6566477*	31	4
30 Mar 91	COWBOYS AND ANGELS *Epic 6567747*	45	3
7 Dec 91 ★	DON'T LET THE SUN GO DOWN ON ME *Epic 6576467* [2] ■ ▲	1	10
13 Jun 92	TOOFUNKY *Epic 6580587*	4	9
1 May 93 ★	FIVE LIVE EP *Parlophone CDRS 6340* [3]	1	11
24 Jul 93	FIVE LIVE EP (re-entry) *Parlophone CDRS 6340* [3]	74	1
20 Jan 96 ★	JESUS TO A CHILD *Virgin VSCDG 1571* ■	1	10
20 Apr 96	JESUS TO A CHILD (re-entry) *Virgin VSCDG 1571*	68	1
4 May 96 ●	FASTLOVE *Virgin VSCDG 1579* ■	1	14
4 May 96	JESUS TO A CHILD (2nd re-entry) *Virgin VSCDG 1571*	65	2
31 Aug 96 ●	SPINNING THE WHEEL *Virgin VSCDG 1595*	2	12
1 Feb 97 ●	OLDER/I CAN MAKE YOU LOVE ME *Virgin VSCDG 1626*	3	8
10 May 97 ●	STAR PEOPLE '97 *Virgin VSCDG 1641*	2	9
7 Jun 97 ●	WALTZ AWAY DREAMING *Aegean AECD 01* [4]	10	4
19 Jul 97	STAR PEOPLE '97 (re-entry) *Virgin VSCDG 1641*	59	4
20 Sep 97 ●	YOU HAVE BEEN LOVED/THE STRANGEST THING '97 *Virgin VSCD 1663*	2	8
31 Oct 98 ●	OUTSIDE *Epic 6665625*	2†	9

[1] Aretha Franklin and George Michael [2] George Michael and Elton John [3] George Michael and Queen with Lisa Stansfield [4] Toby Bourke with George Michael

Tracks on Five Live EP: Somebody to Love/These Are the Days of Our Lives/Calling You/Papa Was a Rolling Stone – Killer (medley). The first track on the EP features Queen, the second Queen and Lisa Stansfield.
See also Elton JOHN; Lisa MOORISH

MICHAELA UK, female vocalist — 6 wks

Date	Title	Pos	Wks
2 Sep 89	H-A-P-P-Y RADIO *London H 1*	62	4
28 Apr 90	TAKE GOOD CARE OF MY HEART *London WAC 90*	66	2

Lisa MICHAELIS – See Frankie KNUCKLES

Pras MICHEL ✒ US, male rapper/producer — 31 wks

Date	Title	Pos	Wks
27 Jun 98 ●	GHETTO SUPASTAR THAT IS WHAT YOU ARE *Interscope IND 95593* [1]	2	17
7 Nov 98 ●	BLUE ANGELS *Ruffhouse 6666215* [2]	6†	8
14 Nov 98 ●	ANOTHER ONE BITES THE DUST *Dreamworks DRMCD 22364* [3]	5	6

[1] Pras Michel featuring Ol' Dirty Bastard introducing Mya [2] Pras [3] Queen with Wyclef Jean featuring Pras Michel and Free

UK No 1 ★　UK Top 10 ●　UK million seller ◆　UK entry at No 1 ■　US No 1 ▲

Keith MICHELL ℂ Australia, male vocalist   25 wks

27 Mar 71	I'LL GIVE YOU THE EARTH (TOUS LES BATEAUX, TOUS LES OISEAUX) Spark SRL 1046	43	1
17 Apr 71	I'LL GIVE YOU THE EARTH (TOUS LES BATEAUX, TOUS LES OISEAUX) (re-entry) Spark SRL 1046	30	10
26 Jan 80 ●	CAPTAIN BEAKY/WILFRED THE WEASEL Polydor POSP 106	5	10
29 Mar 80	THE TRIAL OF HISSING SID Polydor HISS 1 [1]	53	4

[1] Keith Michell, Captain Beaky and his Band

MICHELLE Trinidad, female vocalist   1 wk

8 Jun 96	STANDING HERE ALL ALONE Positiva CDTIV 54	69	1

Yvette MICHELLE US, female vocalist   3 wks

5 Apr 97	I'M NOT FEELING YOU Loud 74321465222	36	3

Lloyd MICHELS – See MISTURA featuring Lloyd MICHELS

MICK and PAT – See PAT and MICK

MICROBE UK, male vocalist   7 wks

14 May 69	GROOVY BABY CBS 4158	29	7

MICRODISNEY Ireland, male vocal/instrumental group   3 wks

21 Feb 87	TOWN TO TOWN Virgin VS 927	55	3

MIDDLE OF THE ROAD ⊛
UK, male/female vocal/instrumental group   76 wks

5 Jun 71 ★	CHIRPY CHIRPY CHEEP CHEEP RCA 2047	1	34
4 Sep 71 ●	TWEEDLE DEE TWEEDLE DUM RCA 2110	2	17
11 Dec 71 ●	SOLEY SOLEY RCA 2151	5	12
25 Mar 72	SACRAMENTO RCA 2184	49	1
8 Apr 72	SACRAMENTO (re-entry) RCA 2184	23	6
29 Jul 72	SAMSON AND DELILAH RCA 2237	26	6

MIDDLESBROUGH F.C. UK, male football team / vocal group   1 wk

24 May 97	LET'S DANCE Magnet EW 112CD	44	1

[1] Middlesbrough FC featuring Bob Mortimer and Chris Rea

MIDGET UK, male vocal/instrumental group   2 wks

31 Jan 98	ALL FALL DOWN Radarscope TINYCDS 6X	57	1
18 Apr 98	INVISIBLE BALLOON Radarscope TINYCDS 7	66	1

MIDI XPRESS UK, male vocal/instrumental duo   1 wk

11 May 96	CHASE Labello Dance LAD 26CD	73	1

Bette MIDLER ⊛ ℂ US, female vocalist   27 wks

17 Jun 89 ●	WIND BENEATH MY WINGS Atlantic A 8972 ▲	5	12
13 Oct 90	FROM A DISTANCE Atlantic A 7820	45	5
15 Jun 91 ●	FROM A DISTANCE (re-entry) Atlantic A 7820	6	9
5 Dec 98	MY ONE TRUE FRIEND Warner Brothers W 460CD	58	1

MIDNIGHT BAND – See Tony RALLO and the MIDNIGHT BAND

MIDNIGHT COWBOY SOUNDTRACK US, orchestra   4 wks

8 Nov 80	MIDNIGHT COWBOY United Artists UP 634	47	4

MIDNIGHT OIL ✎ Australia, male vocal/instrumental group   32 wks

23 Apr 88	BEDS ARE BURNING Sprint OIL 1	48	5
2 Jul 88	THE DEAD HEART Spring OIL 2	68	2
25 Mar 89 ●	BEDS ARE BURNING (re-issue) Sprint OIL 3	6	13
1 Jul 89	THE DEAD HEART (re-issue) Sprint OIL 4	62	4
10 Feb 90	BLUE SKY MINE CBS OIL 5	66	2
17 Apr 93	TRUGANINI Columbia 6590492	29	4
3 Jul 93	MY COUNTRY Columbia 6593702	66	1
6 Nov 93	IN THE VALLEY Columbia 6598492	60	1

MIDNIGHT STAR ✈ ♪ US, male/female vocal/instrumental group   26 wks

23 Feb 85	OPERATOR Solar MCA 942	66	2
28 Jun 86	HEADLINES Solar MCA 1065	16	8
4 Oct 86 ●	MIDAS TOUCH Solar MCA 1096	8	10
7 Feb 87	ENGINE NO.9 Solar MCA 1117	64	3
2 May 87	WET MY WHISTLE Solar MCA 1127	60	3

MIGHTY AVENGERS UK, male vocal/instrumental group   2 wks

26 Nov 64	SO MUCH IN LOVE Decca F 11962	46	2

MIGHTY AVONS – See Larry CUNNINGHAM and the MIGHTY AVONS

MIGHTY DIAMONDS – See VARIOUS ARTISTS – Gimme Shelter (EP)

MIGHTY DUB KATZ UK, male producer – Norman Cook   5 wks

7 Dec 96	JUST ANOTHER GROOVE ffrr FCD 287	43	1
2 Aug 97	MAGIC CARPET RIDE ffrr FCD 306	24	4

See also Norman COOK

MIGHTY LEMON DROPS UK, male vocal/instrumental group   7 wks

13 Sep 86	THE OTHER SIDE OF YOU Blue Guitar AZUR 1	67	2
18 Apr 87	OUT OF HAND Blue Guitar AZUR 4	66	3
23 Jan 88	INSIDE OUT Blue Guitar AZUR 6	74	2

MIGHTY MIGHTY BOSSTONES ⊛ ⋎
US, male vocal/instrumental group   6 wks

25 Apr 98	THE IMPRESSION THAT I GET Mercury 5748432	12	5
27 Jun 98	THE RASCAL KING Mercury 5661092	63	1

MIGHTY MORPH'N POWER RANGERS ⊛
US, male/female vocal group   13 wks

17 Dec 94 ●	POWER RANGERS RCA 74321253022	3	9
25 Feb 95	POWER RANGERS (re-entry) RCA 74321253022	57	2
25 Mar 95	POWER RANGERS (2nd re-entry) RCA 74321253022	65	1
8 Apr 95	POWER RANGERS (3rd re-entry) RCA 74321253022	74	1

MIGHTY WAH – See WAH!

MIGIL FIVE ⊛ ⋎ UK, male vocal/instrumental group   20 wks

19 Mar 64 ●	MOCKINGBIRD HILL Pye 7N 15597	10	13
4 Jun 64	NEAR YOU Pye 7N 15645	31	7

MIG29 Italy, male instrumental/production group   2 wks

22 Feb 92	MIG29 Champion CHAMP 292	62	2

MIKE UK male producer – Mark Jolley   2 wks

19 Nov 94	TWANGLING THREE FINGERS IN A BOX Pukka CDMIKE 100	40	2

MIKE and the MECHANICS ⊛
UK, male vocal/instrumental group   64 wks

15 Feb 86	SILENT RUNNING (ON DANGEROUS GROUND) WEA U 8908	21	9
31 May 86	ALL I NEED IS A MIRACLE WEA U 8765	53	4
14 Jan 89 ●	THE LIVING YEARS WEA U 7717 ▲	2	11
16 Mar 91	WORD OF MOUTH Virgin VS 1345	13	10
15 Jun 91	A TIME AND PLACE Virgin VS 1351	58	3
8 Feb 92	EVERYBODY GETS A SECOND CHANCE Virgin VS 1396	56	4
25 Feb 95	OVER MY SHOULDER Virgin VSCDT 1526	12	9
17 Jun 95	A BEGGAR ON A BEACH OF GOLD Virgin VSCDT 1535	33	5
2 Sep 95	ANOTHER CUP OF COFFEE Virgin VSCDT 1554	51	4
17 Feb 96	ALL I NEED IS A MIRACLE (re-mix) Virgin VSCDT 1576	27	4
1 Jun 96	SILENT RUNNING (re-issue) Virgin VSCDT 1585	61	1

MIKI and GRIFF ⊛ ✿ UK, female/male vocal duo   25 wks

2 Oct 59	HOLD BACK TOMORROW Pye 7N 15213	26	2
13 Oct 60	ROCKIN' ALONE Pye 7N 15296	44	3

1 Feb 62	LITTLE BITTY TEAR *Pye 7N 15412*	16	13
22 Aug 63	I WANNA STAY HERE *Pye 7N 15555*	23	7

John MILES ☺ *UK, male vocalist/multi-instrumentalist*   30 wks

18 Oct 75	HIGH FLY *Decca F 13595*	17	6
20 Mar 76 ●	MUSIC *Decca F 13627*	3	9
16 Oct 76	REMEMBER YESTERDAY *Decca F 13667*	32	5
18 Jun 77 ●	SLOW DOWN *Decca F 13709*	10	10

Robert MILES ☺ *Italy, male instrumentalist – keyboards*   47 wks

24 Feb 96 ●	CHILDREN *Deconstruction 74321348322*	2	18
8 Jun 96 ●	FABLE *Deconstruction 74321382622*	7	7
3 Aug 96	FABLE (re-entry) *Deconstruction 74321382622*	71	1
31 Aug 96	FABLE (2nd re-entry) *Deconstruction 74321382622*	69	1
16 Nov 96 ●	ONE AND ONE *Deconstruction 74321427692* [1]	3	16
29 Nov 97 ●	FREEDOM *Deconstruction 74321536952* [2]	15	4

[1] Robert Miles featuring Maria Nayler [2] Robert Miles featuring Kathy Sledge

June MILES-KINGSTON – See Jimmy SOMERVILLE

Paul MILES-KINGSTON – See Sarah BRIGHTMAN

MILK AND HONEY featuring Gali ATARI ☾
Israel, male/female vocal/instrumental group   8 wks

14 Apr 79 ●	HALLELUJAH *Polydor 2001 870*	5	8

MILK INCORPORATED
Belgium, male/female vocal / production group   3 wks

28 Feb 98	GOOD ENOUGH (LA VACHE) *Malarky MLKD 5*	23	3

MILL GIRLS – See Billy COTTON and his BAND

MILLA *US, female vocalist*   1 wk

18 Jun 94	GENTLEMAN WHO FELL *SBK CDSBK 49*	65	1

Frankie MILLER ✎ *UK, male vocalist*   32 wks

4 Jun 77	BE GOOD TO YOURSELF *Chrysalis CHS 2147*	27	6
14 Oct 78 ●	DARLIN' *Chrysalis CHS 2255*	6	15
20 Jan 79	WHEN I'M AWAY FROM YOU *Chrysalis CHS 2276*	42	5
21 Mar 92	CALEDONIA *MCS MCS 2001*	45	6

Gary MILLER ☾ *UK, male vocalist*   35 wks

21 Oct 55	YELLOW ROSE OF TEXAS *Nixa N 15004*	13	5
13 Jan 56 ●	ROBIN HOOD *Nixa N 15020*	10	6
11 Jan 57	GARDEN OF EDEN *Pye Nixa N 15070*	14	6
1 Mar 57	GARDEN OF EDEN (re-entry) *Pye Nixa N 15070*	27	1
19 Jul 57	WONDERFUL WONDERFUL *Pye Nixa N 15094*	29	1
17 Jan 58	STORY OF MY LIFE *Pye Nixa N 15120*	14	6
21 Dec 61	THERE GOES THAT SONG AGAIN/THE NIGHT IS YOUNG *Pye 7N 15404*	29	9
1 Mar 62	THERE GOES THAT SONG AGAIN (re-entry) *Pye 7N 15404*	48	1

'The Night Is Young' only listed with 'There Goes That Song Again' for weeks
21 and 28 Dec, 1961, and 4 Jan, 1962. It peaked at No 32

Glenn MILLER ☾ *US, orchestra, Glenn Miller – trombone*   9 wks

12 Mar 54	MOONLIGHT SERENADE *HMV BD 5942*	12	1
24 Jan 76	MOONLIGHT SERENADE/LITTLE BROWN JUG/IN THE MOOD (re-issue) *RCA 2644*	13	8

Jody MILLER *US, female vocalist*   1 wk

21 Oct 65	HOME OF THE BRAVE *Capitol CL 15415*	49	1

Leza MILLER – See Sergio MENDES

Mitch MILLER ☾ *US, orchestra and chorus*   13 wks

7 Oct 55 ●	YELLOW ROSE OF TEXAS *Philips PB 505* ▲	2	13

Ned MILLER ☚ *US, male vocalist*   22 wks

14 Feb 63 ●	FROM A JACK TO A KING *London HL 9658*	2	21
18 Feb 65	DO WHAT YOU DO DO WELL *London HL 9937*	48	1

Roger MILLER ☚ *US, male vocalist*   42 wks

18 Mar 65 ★	KING OF THE ROAD *Philips BF 1397*	1	15
3 Jun 65	ENGINE ENGINE NO. 9 *Philips BF 1416*	33	5
21 Oct 65	KANSAS CITY STAR *Philips BF 1437*	48	1
16 Dec 65	ENGLAND SWINGS *Philips BF 1456*	45	1
6 Jan 66	ENGLAND SWINGS (re-entry) *Philips BF 1456*	13	7
27 Mar 68	LITTLE GREEN APPLES *Mercury MF 1021*	19	10
2 Apr 69	LITTLE GREEN APPLES (re-entry) *Mercury MF 1021*	48	1
7 May 69	LITTLE GREEN APPLES (2nd re-entry) *Mercury MF 1021*	39	2

Suzi MILLER – See JOHNSTON BROTHERS

Steve MILLER BAND ☚ *US, male vocal/instrumental group*   36 wks

23 Oct 76	ROCK 'N ME *Mercury 6078 804* ▲	11	9
19 Jun 82 ●	ABRACADABRA *Mercury STEVE 3* ▲	2	11
4 Sep 82	KEEPS ME WONDERING WHY *Mercury STEVE 4*	52	3
11 Aug 90 ★	THE JOKER *Capitol CL 583* ▲	1	13

Lisa MILLETT – See SHEER BRONZE featuring Lisa MILLETT

MILLI VANILLI ☺ ☺ ☚ *France/Germany, male duo*   50 wks

1 Oct 88 ●	GIRL YOU KNOW IT'S TRUE *Cooltempo COOL 170*	3	13
17 Dec 88	BABY DON'T FORGET MY NUMBER *Cooltempo COOL 178* ▲	16	11
22 Jul 89	BLAME IT ON THE RAIN *Cooltempo COOL 180* ▲	53	5
30 Sep 89 ●	GIRL I'M GONNA MISS YOU *Cooltempo COOL 191* ▲	2	15
2 Dec 89	BLAME IT ON THE RAIN (re-entry) *Cooltempo COOL 180*	52	5
10 Mar 90	ALL OR NOTHING *Cooltempo COOL 199*	74	1

MILLICAN and NESBITT ☾ *UK, male vocal duo*   14 wks

1 Dec 73	VAYA CON DIOS *Pye 7N 45310*	20	11
18 May 74	FOR OLD TIME'S SAKE *Pye 7N 45357*	38	3

MILLIE ☂ *Jamaica, female vocalist*   33 wks

12 Mar 64 ●	MY BOY LOLLIPOP *Fontana TF 449*	2	18
25 Jun 64	SWEET WILLIAM *Fontana TF 479*	30	9
11 Nov 65	BLOODSHOT EYES *Fontana TF 617*	48	1
25 Jul 87	MY BOY LOLLIPOP (re-issue) *Island WIP 6574*	46	5

MILLIONAIRE HIPPIES *UK, male producer – Danny Rampling*   4 wks

18 Dec 93	I AM THE MUSIC HEAR ME! *Deconstruction 74321175432*	52	3
10 Sep 94	C'MON *Deconstruction 74321229372*	59	1

Garry MILLS ☺ *UK, male vocalist*   31 wks

7 Jul 60 ●	LOOK FOR A STAR *Top Rank JAR 336*	7	14
20 Oct 60	TOP TEEN BABY *Top Rank JAR 500*	24	12
22 Jun 61	I'LL STEP DOWN *Decca F 11358*	39	5

Hayley MILLS ☺ *UK, female vocalist*   11 wks

19 Oct 61	LET'S GET TOGETHER *Decca F 21396*	17	11

Stephanie MILLS ✎ ☚ *US, female vocalist*   33 wks

18 Oct 80 ●	NEVER KNEW LOVE LIKE THIS BEFORE *20th Century TC 2460*	4	14
23 May 81	TWO HEARTS *20th Century TC 2492* [1]	49	5
15 Sep 84	THE MEDICINE SONG *Club JAB 8*	29	9
5 Sep 87	(YOU'RE PUTTIN') A RUSH ON ME *MCA MCA 1187*	62	2
1 May 93	NEVER DO YOU WRONG *MCA MCSTD 1767*	57	2
10 Jul 93	ALL DAY ALL NIGHT *MCA MCSTD 1778*	68	1

[1] Stephanie Mills featuring Teddy Pendergrass

Warren MILLS *Zambia, male vocalist*   1 wk

28 Sep 85	SUNSHINE *Jive JIVE 99*	74	1

MILLS BROTHERS © *US, male vocal group* — 1 wk

9 Jan 53 ●	GLOW WORM *Brunswick 05007*	10	1

MILLTOWN BROTHERS *UK, male vocal/instrumental group* — 16 wks

2 Feb 91	WHICH WAY SHOULD I JUMP *A & M AM 711*	38	5
13 Apr 91	HERE I STAND *A & M AM 758*	41	4
6 Jul 91	APPLE GREEN *A & M AM 787*	43	4
22 May 93	TURN OFF *A & M 5802692*	55	1
17 Jul 93	IT'S ALL OVER NOW BABY BLUE *A & M 5803332*	48	2

CB MILTON *Holland, male vocalist* — 5 wks

21 May 94	IT'S A LOVING THING *Logic 74321208062*	49	2
25 Mar 95	IT'S A LOVING THING (re-mix) *Logic 74321267212*	34	2
19 Aug 95	HOLD ON *Logic 74321292112*	62	1

Garnet MIMMS and TRUCKIN' CO.
US, male vocalist and male instrumental group — 1 wk

25 Jun 77	WHAT IT IS *Arista 109*	44	1

MIND OF KANE *UK, male producer – David Hope* — 1 wk

27 Jul 91	STABBED IN THE BACK *Deja Vu DJV 007*	64	1

See also HOPE AD

MINDBENDERS © *UK, male vocal/instrumental group* — 34 wks

13 Jan 66 ●	A GROOVY KIND OF LOVE *Fontana TF 644*	2	14
5 May 66	CAN'T LIVE WITH YOU (CAN'T LIVE WITHOUT YOU) *Fontana TF 697*	28	7
25 Aug 66	ASHES TO ASHES *Fontana TF 731*	14	9
20 Sep 67	THE LETTER *Fontana TF 869*	42	4

See also Wayne FONTANA and the MINDBENDERS

MINDS OF MEN *UK, male/female vocal/instrumental group* — 1 wk

22 Jun 96	BRAND NEW DAY *Perfecto PERF 121CD*	41	1

Sal MINEO © *US, male vocalist* — 11 wks

12 Jul 57	START MOVIN' *Philips PB 707*	16	11

Marcello MINERBI © *Italy, orchestra* — 16 wks

22 Jul 65 ●	ZORBA'S DANCE *Durium DRS 54001*	6	16

MINI POPS *UK, male/female vocal group* — 2 wks

26 Dec 87	SONGS FOR CHRISTMAS '87 EP *Bright BULB 9*	39	2

Tracks on Songs for Christmas '87 EP: Thanks for Giving Us Christmas / The Man In Red / Christmas Time Around the World / Shine On

MINIMAL FUNK 2 *Italy, male production duo* — 1 wk

18 Jul 98	THE GROOVY THANG *Cleveland City CLECD 13046*	65	1

MINISTRY *US, male vocal/instrumental group* — 3 wks

8 Aug 92	NWO *Sire W 0125TE*	49	1
6 Jan 96	THE FALL *Warner Bros. W 0328CD*	53	2

MINK DE VILLE ✎ *US, male vocal/instrumental group* — 9 wks

6 Aug 77	SPANISH STROLL *Capitol CLX 103*	20	9

Liza MINNELLI © *US, female vocalist* — 15 wks

12 Aug 89 ●	LOSING MY MIND *Epic ZEE 1*	6	7
7 Oct 89	DON'T DROP BOMBS *Epic ZEE 2*	46	3
25 Nov 89	SO SORRY I SAID *Epic ZEE 3*	62	2
3 Mar 90	LOVE PAINS *Epic ZEE 4*	41	3

Dannii MINOGUE © *Australia, female vocalist* — 67 wks

30 Mar 91 ●	LOVE AND KISSES *MCA MCS 1529*	8	8
18 May 91	SUCCESS *MCA MCS 1538*	11	7

27 Jul 91 ●	JUMP TO THE BEAT *MCA MCS 1556*	8	6
19 Oct 91	BABY LOVE *MCA MCS 1580*	14	6
14 Dec 91	I DON'T WANNA TAKE THIS PAIN *MCA MCS 1600*	40	5
1 Aug 92	SHOW YOU THE WAY TO GO *MCA MCS 1671*	30	3
12 Dec 92	LOVE'S ON EVERY CORNER *MCA MCSR 1723*	44	4
17 Jul 93	THIS IS IT *MCA MCSTD 1790*	10	8
2 Oct 93	THIS IS THE WAY *MCA MCSTD 1935*	27	3
11 Jun 94	GET INTO YOU *Mushroom D 11751*	36	2
23 Aug 97 ●	ALL I WANNA DO *Eternal WEA 119CD*	4	8
1 Nov 97	EVERYTHING I WANTED *Eternal WEA 137CD* [1]	15	4
28 Mar 98	DISREMEMBRANCE *Eternal WEA 153CD* [1]	21	3

[1] Dannii

Kylie MINOGUE ☺ ☺ *Biggest-selling female vocalist of the late 1980s, b. 28 May, 1968, Melbourne. The Australian actress-turned-singer has had the best ever female chart career start with 13 successive Top 10 entries, and was also the youngest woman to top the album chart* — 217 wks

23 Jan 88 ★	I SHOULD BE SO LUCKY *PWL PWL 8*	1	16
14 May 88 ●	GOT TO BE CERTAIN *PWL PWL 12*	2	12
6 Aug 88 ●	THE LOCO-MOTION *PWL PWL 14*	2	11
22 Oct 88 ●	JE NE SAIS PAS POURQUOI *PWL PWL 21*	2	13
10 Dec 88 ★	ESPECIALLY FOR YOU *PWL PWL 24* [1]	1	14
6 May 89 ★	HAND ON YOUR HEART *PWL PWL 35*	1	11
5 Aug 89 ●	WOULDN'T CHANGE A THING *PWL PWL 42*	2	9
4 Nov 89 ●	NEVER TOO LATE *PWL PWL 45*	4	10
20 Jan 90 ★	TEARS ON MY PILLOW *PWL PWL 47*	1	8
12 May 90 ●	BETTER THE DEVIL YOU KNOW *PWL PWL 56*	2	10
3 Nov 90 ●	STEP BACK IN TIME *PWL PWL 64*	4	8
2 Feb 91 ●	WHAT DO I HAVE TO DO *PWL PWL 72*	6	8
1 Jun 91 ●	SHOCKED *PWL PWL 81*	6	7
7 Sep 91	WORD IS OUT *PWL PWL 204*	16	5
2 Nov 91 ●	IF YOU WERE WITH ME NOW *PWL PWL 208* [2]	4	7
30 Nov 91	KEEP ON PUMPIN' IT *PWL PWL 207* [3]	49	1
25 Jan 92 ●	GIVE ME JUST A LITTLE MORE TIME *PWL PWL 212*	2	8
25 Apr 92	FINER FEELINGS *PWL International PWL 227*	11	6
22 Aug 92	WHAT KIND OF FOOL (HEARD IT ALL BEFORE) *PWL International PWL 241*	14	5
28 Nov 92	CELEBRATION *PWL International PWL 257*	20	7
10 Sep 94 ●	CONFIDE IN ME *Deconstruction 74321227482*	2	9
26 Nov 94	PUT YOURSELF IN MY PLACE *Deconstruction 74321246572*	11	9
22 Jul 95	WHERE IS THE FEELING *Deconstruction 74321293612*	16	3
14 Oct 95	WHERE THE WILD ROSES GROW *Mute CDMUTE 185* [4]	11	4
20 Sep 97	SOME KIND OF BLISS *Deconstruction 74321517252*	22	5
6 Dec 97	DID IT AGAIN *Deconstruction 74321535702*	14	6
21 Mar 98	BREATHE *Deconstruction 74321570132*	14	4
31 Oct 98	GBI *Arthrob ART 021CD* [5]	63	1

[1] Kylie Minogue and Jason Donovan [2] Kylie Minogue and Keith Washington
[3] Visionmasters with Tony King featuring Kylie Minogue [4] Nick Cave and Kylie Minogue [5] Towa Tei featuring Kylie Minogue

Morris MINOR and the MAJORS ☺ *UK, male vocal group* — 11 wks

19 Dec 87 ●	STUTTER RAP (NO SLEEP 'TIL BEDTIME) *10 TEN 203*	4	11

Sugar MINOTT ✦ *Jamaica, male vocalist* — 16 wks

28 Mar 81 ●	GOOD THING GOING (WE'VE GOT A GOOD THING GOING) *RCA 58*	4	12
17 Oct 81	NEVER MY LOVE *RCA 138*	52	4

MINT CONDITION *US, male vocal group* — 3 wks

21 Jun 97	WHAT KIND OF MAN WOULD I BE *Wild Card 5710492*	38	2
4 Oct 97	LET ME BE THE ONE *Wild Card 5717132*	63	1

MINT JULEPS *UK, female vocal group* — 7 wks

22 Mar 86	ONLY LOVE CAN BREAK YOUR HEART *Stiff BUY 241*	62	2
30 May 87	EVERY KINDA PEOPLE *Stiff BUY 257*	58	5

MIRACLES ✎ *US, male vocal group* — 10 wks

10 Jan 76 ●	LOVE MACHINE *Tamla Motown TMG 1015* ▲	3	10

See also Smokey ROBINSON and the MIRACLES

MIRAGE ◐ ☺ *UK, male vocal/instrumental group* — 35 wks

14 Jan 84	GIVE ME THE NIGHT *Passion PASH 15* [1]	49	4
9 May 87 ●	JACK MIX II/III *Debut DEBT 3022*	4	11
25 Jul 87	SERIOUS MIX *Debut DEBT 3028*	42	4
7 Nov 87 ●	JACK MIX IV *Debut DEBT 3035*	8	10
27 Feb 88	JACK MIX VII *Debut DEBT 3042*	50	3
2 Jul 88	PUSH THE BEAT *Debut DEBT 3050*	67	2
11 Nov 89	LATINO HOUSE *Debut DEBT 3085*	70	1

[1] Mirage featuring Roy Gayle

'Jack Mix III' only listed with 'Jack Mix II' from 6 Jun, 1987

Danny MIRROR ◐ *Holland, male vocalist* — 9 wks

17 Sep 77 ●	I REMEMBER ELVIS PRESLEY (THE KING IS DEAD) *Sonet SON 2121*	4	9

MISS X *UK, female vocalist – Joyce Blair* — 6 wks

1 Aug 63	CHRISTINE *Ember S 175*	37	6

MISSION ☹ ✔ *UK, male vocal/instrumental group* — 58 wks

14 Jun 86	SERPENTS KISS *Chapter 22 CHAP 6*	70	3
26 Jul 86	GARDEN OF DELIGHT/LIKE A HURRICANE *Chapter 22 CHAP 7*	49	4
18 Oct 86	STAY WITH ME *Mercury MYTH 1*	30	4
17 Jan 87	WASTELAND *Mercury MYTH 2*	11	6
14 Mar 87	SEVERINA *Mercury MYTH 3*	25	5
13 Feb 88	TOWER OF STRENGTH *Mercury MYTH 4*	12	7
23 Apr 88	BEYOND THE PALE *Mercury MYTH 6*	32	4
13 Jan 90	BUTTERFLY ON A WHEEL *Mercury MYTH 8*	12	4
10 Mar 90	DELIVERANCE *Mercury MYTH 9*	27	4
2 Jun 90	INTO THE BLUE *Mercury MYTH 10*	32	3
17 Nov 90	HANDS ACROSS THE OCEAN *Mercury MYTH 11*	28	2
25 Apr 92	NEVER AGAIN *Mercury MYTH 12*	34	3
20 Jun 92	LIKE A CHILD AGAIN *Mercury MYTH 13*	30	2
17 Oct 92	SHADES OF GREEN *Vertigo MYTH 14*	49	2
8 Jan 94	TOWER OF STRENGTH (re-mix) *Vertigo MYTCD 15*	33	3
26 Mar 94	AFTERGLOW *Vertigo MYTCD 16*	53	1
4 Feb 95	SWOON *Neverland HOOKCD 002*	73	1

MISSJONES *US, female vocalist/songwriter* — 1 wk

10 Oct 98	2 WAY STREET *Motown 8608572*	49	1

MRS. MILLS ◐ ℭ *UK, female instrumentalist – piano* — 5 wks

14 Dec 61	MRS. MILLS' MEDLEY *Parlophone R 4856*	18	5

Mrs. Mills' Medley consisted of the following tunes: I Want to Be Happy/Sheik of Araby/Baby Face/Somebody Stole My Gal/Ma (He's Making Eyes At Me)/Swanee/Ain't She Sweet/California Here I Come

MRS. WOOD *UK, female producer* — 6 wks

16 Sep 95	JOANNA *React CDREACT 066*	40	2
6 Jul 96	HEARTBREAK *React CDREACT 78* [1]	44	1
4 Oct 97	JOANNA (re-mix) *React CDREACT 107*	34	2
15 Aug 98	1234 *React CDREACT 121*	54	1

[1] Mrs. Wood featuring Eve Gallagher

MISTA E *UK, male producer – Damon Rochefort* — 5 wks

10 Dec 88	DON'T BELIEVE THE HYPE *Urban URB 28*	41	5

MR. BEAN and SMEAR CAMPAIGN featuring Bruce DICKINSON ◐ *UK, male comedians and male vocalist* — 5 wks

4 Apr 92 ●	(I WANT TO BE) ELECTED *London LON 319*	9	5

MR. BIG ◐ *UK, male vocal/instrumental group* — 14 wks

12 Feb 77 ●	ROMEO *EMI 2567*	4	10
21 May 77	FEEL LIKE CALLING HOME *EMI 2610*	35	4

MR. BIG ◐ *US, male vocal/instrumental group* — 17 wks

7 Mar 92 ●	TO BE WITH YOU *Atlantic A 7514* ▲	3	11
23 May 92	JUST TAKE MY HEART *Atlantic A 7490*	26	4
8 Aug 92	GREEN TINTED SIXTIES MIND *Atlantic A 7468*	72	1
20 Nov 93	WILD WORLD *Atlantic A 7310CD*	59	1

MR. BLOBBY ◐ *UK, male pink, yellow spotted blob vocalist* — 16 wks

4 Dec 93 ★	MR. BLOBBY *Destiny Music CDDMUS 104*	1	12
16 Dec 95	CHRISTMAS IN BLOBBYLAND *Destiny DMUSCD 108*	36	4

MR. BLOE ◐ *UK, male instrumental group* — 18 wks

9 May 70 ●	GROOVIN' WITH MR. BLOE *DJM DJS 216*	2	18

MR. FINGERS *US, male producer – Larry Heard* — 5 wks

17 Mar 90	WHAT ABOUT THIS LOVE *ffrr F 131*	74	1
7 Mar 92	CLOSER *MCA MCS 1601*	50	3
23 May 92	ON MY WAY *MCA MCS 1630*	71	1

MR. FOOD *UK, male vocalist* — 3 wks

9 Jun 90	. . . AND THAT'S BEFORE ME TEA! *Tangible TGB 005*	62	3

MR. JACK *Belgium, male producer – Lucente Vito* — 2 wks

25 Jan 97	WIGGLY WORLD *Extravaganza 0090965*	32	2

MR. LEE *US, male producer – Leroy Haggard* — 6 wks

6 Aug 88	PUMP UP LONDON *Breakout USA 639*	64	2
11 Nov 89	GET BUSY *Jive JIVE 231*	71	1
24 Feb 90	GET BUSY (re-entry) *Jive JIVE 231*	41	3

MR. MISTER ◐ ✔ *US, male vocal/instrumental group* — 22 wks

21 Dec 85 ●	BROKEN WINGS *RCA PB 49945* ▲	4	13
1 Mar 86	KYRIE *RCA PB 49927* ▲	11	9

MR. PRESIDENT ◐ ☺ *Germany, male / female vocal group* — 13 wks

14 Jun 97 ●	COCO JAMBOO *WEA WEA 110CD*	8	11
20 Sep 97	I GIVE YOU MY HEART *WEA WEA 126CD*	52	1
25 Apr 98	JOJO ACTION *WEA WEA 156CD*	73	1

MR. ROY *UK, male instrumental/production group* — 6 wks

7 May 94	SOMETHING ABOUT YOU *Fresh FRSHD 11*	74	1
21 Jan 95	SAVED *Fresh FRSHD 21*	24	4
16 Dec 95	SOMETHING ABOUT U (CAN'T BE BEAT) (re-mix) *Fresh FRSHCD 33*	49	1

MR. and MRS. SMITH
UK, male/female instrumental/production group — 1 wk

12 Oct 96	GOTTA GET LOOSE *Hooj Choons HOOJCD 46*	70	1

MR. V *UK, male producer – Rob Villiers* — 2 wks

6 Aug 94	GIVE ME LIFE *Cheeky CHEKCD 005*	40	2

MR. VEGAS *Jamaica, male vocalist – Clifford Smith* — 1 wk

22 Aug 98	HEADS HIGH *Greensleeves GRECD 650*	71	1

MISTURA featuring Lloyd MICHELS
US, male instrumental group, Lloyd Michels – trumpet — 10 wks

15 May 76	THE FLASHER *Route RT 30*	23	10

Cameron MITCHELL – *See VARIOUS ARTISTS (EPs & LPs) – Carousel LP*

Guy MITCHELL ℭ *Extremely popular pre-rock vocalist, b. Al Cernik, 27 February, 1927, Detroit. He appeared on the first and last charts of the 1950s, and was one of most consistently successful singers and performers of that decade* — 163 wks

14 Nov 52 ●	FEET UP *Columbia DB 3151*	2	10

13 Feb 53 ★	SHE WEARS RED FEATHERS *Columbia DB 3238*	1	15
24 Apr 53 ●	PRETTY LITTLE BLACK-EYED SUSIE *Columbia DB 3255*	2	11
12 Jun 53	SHE WEARS RED FEATHERS (re-entry) *Columbia DB 3238*	12	1
28 Aug 53 ★	LOOK AT THAT GIRL *Philips PB 162*	1	14
6 Nov 53 ●	CHICKA BOOM *Philips PB 178*	5	9
18 Dec 53 ●	CLOUD LUCKY SEVEN *Philips PB 210*	2	16
15 Jan 54 ●	CHICKA BOOM (re-entry) *Philips PB 178*	4	6
19 Feb 54 ●	CUFF OF MY SHIRT *Philips PB 225*	9	1
26 Feb 54	SIPPIN' SODA *Philips PB 210*	11	1
19 Mar 54	CUFF OF MY SHIRT (re-entry) *Philips PB 225*	12	1
2 Apr 54	CUFF OF MY SHIRT (2nd re-entry) *Philips PB 225*	11	1
30 Apr 54 ●	DIME AND A DOLLAR *Philips PB 248*	8	1
14 May 54 ●	DIME AND A DOLLAR (re-entry) *Philips PB 248*	8	4
7 Dec 56 ★	SINGING THE BLUES *Philips PB 650* ▲	1	22
15 Feb 57 ●	KNEE DEEP IN THE BLUES *Philips PB 669*	3	12
26 Apr 57 ★	ROCK-A-BILLY *Philips PB 685*	1	14
26 Jul 57	IN THE MIDDLE OF A DARK DARK NIGHT/ SWEET STUFF *Philips PB 712*	27	2
23 Aug 57	IN THE MIDDLE OF A DARK DARK NIGHT/ SWEET STUFF (re-entry) *Philips PB 712*	25	1
11 Oct 57	CALL ROSIE ON THE PHONE *Philips PB 743*	17	6
27 Nov 59	HEARTACHES BY THE NUMBER *Philips PB 964* ▲	26	2
18 Dec 59 ●	HEARTACHES BY THE NUMBER (re-entry) *Philips PB 964*	5	13

Joni MITCHELL ♂ ℂ *Canada, female vocalist* — 24 wks

13 Jun 70	BIG YELLOW TAXI *Reprise RS 20906*	11	15
4 Oct 97 ●	GOT 'TIL IT'S GONE *Virgin VSCDG 1666* [1]	6	9

[1] Janet/Q-Tip/Joni Mitchell

VSCDG 1666 uses samples from RS 20906

Willie MITCHELL ☺ *US, male instrumentalist – guitar* — 3 wks

24 Apr 68	SOUL SERENADE *London HLU 10186*	43	1
11 Dec 76	THE CHAMPION *London HL 10545*	47	2

MIX FACTORY *UK, male/female vocal/instrumental group* — 2 wks

30 Jan 93	TAKE ME AWAY (PARADISE) *All Around The World CDGLOBE 120*	51	2

MIXMASTER ☺ *Italy, male producer – Daniele Davoli* — 10 wks

4 Nov 89 ●	GRAND PIANO *BCM BCM 344*	9	10

MIXTURES ☻ *Australia, male vocal/instrumental group* — 21 wks

16 Jan 71 ●	THE PUSHBIKE SONG *Polydor 2058 083*	2	21

Hank MIZELL ♪ *US, male vocalist* — 13 wks

20 Mar 76 ●	JUNGLE ROCK *Charly CS 1005*	3	13

MK *US, male producer – Mark Kinchen* — 3 wks

4 Feb 95	ALWAYS *Activ CDTV 3* [1]	69	1
27 May 95	BURNING *Activ CDTVR 6*	44	2

[1] MK featuring Alana

Alana appears on both hits, although she is only credited on the first

MN8 ♪ (R&B) *UK/Trinidad, male vocal group* — 47 wks

4 Feb 95 ●	I'VE GOT A LITTLE SOMETHING FOR YOU *Columbia 6608802*	2	13
29 Apr 95 ●	IF YOU ONLY LET ME IN *Columbia 6613252*	6	7
15 Jul 95 ●	HAPPY *Columbia 6622192*	8	7
4 Nov 95	BABY IT'S YOU *Columbia 6624522*	22	2
6 Jan 96	BABY IT'S YOU (re-entry) *Columbia 6624522*	59	1
24 Feb 96	PATHWAY TO THE MOON *Columbia 6629212*	25	2
31 Aug 96	TUFF ACT TO FOLLOW *Columbia 6635345*	15	3
26 Oct 96	DREAMING *Columbia 6638302*	21	3

MNO *Belgium, male instrumental/production group* — 2 wks

28 Sep 91	GOD OF ABRAHAM *A & M AM 820*	66	2

MOBILES ☻ *UK, male/female vocal/instrumental group* — 14 wks

9 Jan 82 ●	DROWNING IN BERLIN *Rialto RIA 3*	9	10
27 Mar 82	AMOUR AMOUR *Rialto RIA 5*	45	4

MOBO ALLSTARS
UK/US male/female vocal/instrumental group — 1 wk

26 Dec 98	AIN'T NO STOPPING US NOW *PolyGram TV 5632302*	52†	1

Artists featured include: Another Level, Shola Ama, Kelle Bryan, Celetia, Cleopatra, Damage, Des'ree, D'Influence, E17, Michelle Gayle, Glamma Kid, Lynden David Hall, Hinda Hicks, Honeyz, Kle'Shay, Kele Le Roc, Beverley Knight, Tony Momrelle, Nine Yards, Mica Paris, Karen Ramirez, Conner Reeves, Roachford, 7th Son, Byron Stingily, Truce, Soundproof, Ultimate Kaos

MOBY ☺ *US, male producer – Richard Hall* — 38 wks

27 Jul 91	GO *Outer Rhythm FOOT 15*	46	3
19 Oct 91 ●	GO (re-entry) *Outer Rhythm FOOT 15*	10	7
3 Jul 93	I FEEL IT *Equinox AXISCD 001*	38	3
11 Sep 93	MOVE *Mute CDMUTE 158*	21	5
28 May 94	HYMN *Mute CDMUTE 161*	31	2
29 Oct 94	FEELING SO REAL *Mute CDMUTE 173*	30	2
25 Feb 95	EVERY TIME YOU TOUCH ME *Mute CDMUTE 176*	28	3
1 Jul 95	INTO THE BLUE *Mute CDMUTE 179A*	50	1
7 Sep 96	THAT'S WHEN I REACH FOR MY REVOLVER *Mute CDMUTE 184*	33	2
15 Nov 97	JAMES BOND THEME *Mute CDMUTE 210*	8	7
10 Jan 98	JAMES BOND THEME (re-entry) *Mute CDMUTE 210*	74	1
5 Sep 98	HONEY *Mute CDMUTE 218*	33	2

MOCHA – *See Missy 'Misdemeanour' ELLIOT*

MOCK TURTLES ☹ ☻ *UK, male vocal/instrumental group* — 6 wks

5 Sep 98	HONEY *Mute CDMUTE 218*	18	2

MODERN LOVERS – *See Jonathan RICHMAN and the MODERN LOVERS*

MODERN ROMANCE ☻ *UK, male vocal/instrumental group* — 77 wks

15 Aug 81	EVERYBODY SALSA *WEA K 18815*	12	10
7 Nov 81 ●	AY AY AY AY MOOSEY *WEA K 18883*	10	12
30 Jan 82	QUEEN OF THE RAPPING SCENE (NOTHING EVER GOES THE WAY YOU PLAN) *WEA K 18928*	37	8
14 Aug 82	CHERRY PINK AND APPLE BLOSSOM WHITE *WEA K 19245* [1]	15	8
13 Nov 82 ●	BEST YEARS OF OUR LIVES *WEA ROM 1*	4	13
26 Feb 83 ●	HIGH LIFE *WEA ROM 2*	8	8
7 May 83	DON'T STOP THAT CRAZY RHYTHM *WEA ROM 3*	14	6
6 Aug 83 ●	WALKING IN THE RAIN *WEA X 9733*	7	12

[1] Modern Romance featuring John du Prez

MODERN TALKING ☻ *Germany, male vocal/instrumental duo* — 22 wks

15 Jun 85	YOU'RE MY HEART, YOU'RE MY SOUL *Magnet 277*	69	2
17 Aug 85	YOU'RE MY HEART, YOU'RE MY SOUL (re-entry) *Magnet MAG 277*	56	5
12 Oct 85	YOU CAN WIN IF YOU WANT *Magnet MAG 282*	70	2
16 Aug 86 ●	BROTHER LOUIE *RCA PB 40875*	4	10
4 Oct 86	ATLANTIS IS CALLING (S.O.S. FOR LOVE) *RCA PB 40969*	55	3

MODETTES *UK, female vocal/instrumental group* — 6 wks

12 Jul 80	PAINT IT BLACK *Deram DET-R 1*	42	5
18 Jul 81	TONIGHT *Deram DET 3*	68	1

Domenico MODUGNO ℂ *Italy, male vocalist* — 13 wks

5 Sep 58 ●	VOLARE *Oriole ICB 5000* ▲	10	12
27 Mar 59	CIAO CIAO BAMBINA *Oriole CB 1489*	29	1

MOGWAI *UK, male instrumental group* — 3 wks

4 Apr 98	SWEET LEAF: BLACK SABBATH *Fierce Panda NING 47CD* [1]	60	1

UK No 1 ★   UK Top 10 ●   UK million seller ◆   UK entry at No 1 ■   US No 1 ▲

293

11 Apr 98	FEAR SATAN – REMIXES *Eye-Q EYEUK 032CD*	57	1
11 Jul 98	NO EDUCATION NO FUTURE (F**K THE CURFEW) *Chemikal CHEM 026CD*	68	1

[1] Mogwai: Magoo

MOHAWKS *Jamaica, male vocal/instrumental group* — 2 wks

24 Jan 87	THE CHAMP *Pama PM 1*	58	2

Frank'o MOIRAGHI featuring AMNESIA
Italy, male/female vocal/instrumental duo — 4 wks

1 Jun 96	FEEL MY BODY *Multiply CDMULTY 10*	39	2
26 Oct 96	FEEL MY BODY (re-mix) *Multiply CDMULTY 15*	40	2

MOIST ✏ *Canada, male vocal/instrumental group* — 10 wks

12 Nov 94	PUSH *Chrysalis CDCHS 5016*	35	3
25 Feb 95	SILVER *Chrysalis CDCHS 5019*	50	2
29 Apr 95	FREAKY BE BEAUTIFUL *Chrysalis CDCHS 5022*	47	2
19 Aug 95	PUSH (re-issue) *Chrysalis CDCHS 5024*	20	3

MOJO ◯ *UK, male instrumental group* — 3 wks

22 Aug 81	DANCE ON *Creole CR 17*	70	3

MOJOS *UK, male vocal/instrumental group* — 26 wks

26 Mar 64 ●	EVERYTHING'S ALRIGHT *Decca F 11853*	9	11
11 Jun 64	WHY NOT TONIGHT *Decca F 11918*	25	10
10 Sep 64	SEVEN DAFFODILS *Decca F 11959*	30	5

MOKENSTEF *US, female vocal group* — 1 wk

23 Sep 95	HE'S MINE *Def Jam DEFCD 13*	70	1

MOLELLA – See OUTHERE BROTHERS

Ralph MOLINA – See Ian McNABB

Sam MOLLISON – See SASHA

MOLLY HALF HEAD *UK, male vocal/instrumental group* — 1 wk

3 Jun 95	SHINE *Columbia 6620732*	73	1

MOLOKO *Ireland/UK, male/female vocal/instrumental duo* — 4 wks

24 Feb 96	DOMINOID *Echo ECSCD 016*	65	1
25 May 96	FUN FOR ME *Echo ECSCD 20*	36	2
20 Jun 98	THE FLIPSIDE *Echo ECSCD 54*	53	1

MOMBASSA *UK, male production duo* — 1 wk

8 Mar 97	CRY FREEDOM *Soundproof SPCD 021*	63	1

MOMENTS ✏ *US, male vocal group* — 32 wks

8 Mar 75 ●	GIRLS *All Platinum 6146 302* [1]	3	10
19 Jul 75 ●	DOLLY MY LOVE *All Platinum 6146 306*	10	9
25 Oct 75	LOOK AT ME (I'M IN LOVE) *All Platinum 6146 309*	42	4
22 Jan 77 ●	JACK IN THE BOX *All Platinum 6146 318*	7	9

[1] Moments and Whatnauts

Tony MOMRELLE *UK, male vocalist* — 1 wk

15 Aug 98	LET ME SHOW YOU *Art & Soul ART 1CDS*	67	1

MONACO ☹ ◯ *UK, male vocal/instrumental duo* — 11 wks

5 Mar 97	WHAT DO YOU WANT FROM ME? *Polydor 5731912*	11	6
31 May 97	SWEET LIPS *Polydor 5710552*	18	4
20 Sep 97	SHINE (SOMEONE WHO NEEDS ME) *Polydor 5714182*	55	1

Jay MONDI and the LIVING BASS
US, male/female vocal/instrumental group — 3 wks

24 Mar 90	ALL NIGHT LONG *10 TEN 304*	63	3

MONDO KANE *UK, male vocal/instrumental group* — 2 wks

16 Aug 86	NEW YORK AFTERNOON *Lisson DOLE 2*	70	2

MONE *US, female vocalist* — 2 wks

12 Aug 95	WE CAN MAKE IT *A & M 5811592*	64	1
16 Mar 96	MOVIN' *AM:PM 5814392*	48	1

MONEY MARK *US, male vocal/instrumentalist* — 3 wks

28 Feb 98	HAND IN YOUR HEAD *Mo Wax MW 066CD*	40	2
6 Jun 98	MAYBE I'M DEAD *Mo Wax MW 089CD1*	45	1

Zoot MONEY and the BIG ROLL BAND
UK, male vocal/instrumental — 8 wks

18 Aug 66	BIG TIME OPERATOR *Columbia DB 7975*	25	8

MONICA R&B *US, female vocalist* — 36 wks

29 Jul 95	DON'T TAKE IT PERSONAL (JUST ONE OF DEM DAYS) *Arista 74321301452*	32	3
17 Feb 96	LIKE THIS AND LIKE THAT *Rowdy 74321344222*	33	2
8 Jun 96	BEFORE YOU WALK OUT OF MY LIFE *Rowdy 74321374042*	22	3
24 May 97	FOR YOU I WILL *Atlantic A 5437CD*	27	2
6 Jun 98 ●	THE BOY IS MINE *Atlantic AT 0036CD* [1]	2	20
17 Oct 98 ●	THE FIRST NIGHT *Rowdy 74321619342* ▲	6	6

[1] Brandy and Monica

MONIFAH – See VARIOUS ARTISTS (EPs & LPs) – The New York Undercover EP

TS MONK *US, male/female vocal/instrumental group* — 6 wks

7 Mar 81	BON BON VIE *Mirage K 11653*	63	2
25 Apr 81	CANDIDATE FOR LOVE *Mirage K 11648*	58	4

MONKEES ◯
The world's top act of 1967: Davy Jones (v/g), Mike Nesmith (v/g), Peter Tork (v/k), Mickey Dolenz (v/d). This Anglo-American quartet were hand-picked for a Beatles-style TV series, which helped to rocket them, albeit briefly, to the top — 101 wks

5 Jan 67 ★	I'M A BELIEVER *RCA 1560* ▲	1	17
26 Jan 67	LAST TRAIN TO CLARKSVILLE *RCA 1547* ▲	23	7
6 Apr 67 ●	A LITTLE BIT ME A LITTLE BIT YOU *RCA 1580*	3	12
22 Jun 67 ●	ALTERNATE TITLE *RCA 1604*	2	12
16 Aug 67	PLEASANT VALLEY SUNDAY *RC 1620*	11	8
15 Nov 67 ●	DAYDREAM BELIEVER *RCA 1645* ▲	5	17
27 Mar 68	VALLERI *RCA 1673*	12	8
26 Jun 68	D.W. WASHBURN *RCA 1706*	17	6
26 Mar 69	TEARDROP CITY *RCA 1802*	46	1
25 Jun 69	SOMEDAY MAN *RCA 1824*	47	1
15 Mar 80	THE MONKEES EP *Arista ARIST 326*	33	9
18 Oct 86	THAT WAS THEN, THIS IS NOW *Arista ARIST 673*	68	1
1 Apr 89	THE MONKEES EP *Arista 112157*	62	2

Tracks on Arista 326 EP: I'm a Believer / Daydream Believer / Last Train to Clarksville / A Little Bit Me a Little Bit You. Tracks on Arista 112157 EP: Daydream Believer / Monkees Theme / Last Train to Clarksville

MONKEY MAFIA
UK, male vocal/instrumental/DJ/production group — 3 wks

7 Jun 97	15 STEPS EP *Heavenly HVN 67CD*	67	1
10 Aug 96	WORK MI BODY *Heavenly HVN 53CD* [1]	75	1
2 May 98	LONG AS I CAN SEE THE LIGHT *Heavenly HVN 84CD*	51	1

Tracks on 15 Steps EP: Lion in the Hall / Krash the Decks: Slaughter the Vinyl / Metro Love / Beats in the Hall

[1] Monkey Mafia featuring Patra

MONKS ◯ *UK, male vocal/instrumental duo* — 9 wks

21 Apr 79	NICE LEGS SHAME ABOUT HER FACE *Carrere CAR 104*	19	9

The Monks were Hudson-Ford under a different name

MONO *UK, male/female vocal/instrumental duo*   **1 wk**

2 May 98	**LIFE IN MONO** *Echo ECSCD 64*	.....60 1

Matt MONRO Ⓒ *Superior British balladeer, b. Terence Parsons, 1 December, 1932, London, d. 7 February, 1985. This Sinatra-styled vocalist, who was re-named by hitmaker Winifred Atwell, had few MOR equals in the 1960s. In 1961, Billboard magazine named him Top International Act and Most Promising Male Singer*   **127 wks**

15 Dec 60 ●	**PORTRAIT OF MY LOVE** *Parlophone R 4714*	.....3 16
9 Mar 61 ●	**MY KIND OF GIRL** *Parlophone R 4755*	.....5 12
18 May 61	**WHY NOT NOW/CAN THIS BE LOVE** *Parlophone R 4775*	.....24 9
28 Sep 61	**GONNA BUILD A MOUNTAIN** *Parlophone R 4819*	.....44 3
8 Feb 62 ●	**SOFTLY AS I LEAVE YOU** *Parlophone R 4868*	.....10 18
14 Jun 62	**WHEN LOVE COMES ALONG** *Parlophone R 4911*	.....46 3
8 Nov 62	**MY LOVE AND DEVOTION** *Parlophone R 4954*	.....29 5
14 Nov 63	**FROM RUSSIA WITH LOVE** *Parlophone R 5068*	.....20 13
17 Sep 64 ●	**WALK AWAY** *Parlophone R 5171*	.....4 20
24 Dec 64	**FOR MAMA** *Parlophone R 5215*	.....36 4
25 Mar 65	**WITHOUT YOU** *Parlophone R 5251*	.....37 4
21 Oct 65 ●	**YESTERDAY** *Parlophone R 5348*	.....8 12
24 Nov 73	**AND YOU SMILED** *EMI 2091*	.....28 8

Gerry MONROE Ⓒ *UK, male vocalist*   **57 wks**

23 May 70 ●	**SALLY** *Chapter One CH 122*	.....4 20
19 Sep 70	**CRY** *Chapter One CH 128*	.....38 5
14 Nov 70 ●	**MY PRAYER** *Chapter One CH 132*	.....9 12
17 Apr 71	**IT'S A SIN TO TELL A LIE** *Chapter One CH 144*	.....13 12
21 Aug 71	**LITTLE DROPS OF SILVER** *Chapter One CH 152*	.....37 6
12 Feb 72	**GIRL OF MY DREAMS** *Chapter One CH 159*	.....43 2

MONSOON ⊚ Ⓞ *UK, male/female vocal/instrumental group*   **12 wks**

3 Apr 82	**EVER SO LONELY** *Mobile Suit Corp CORP 2*	.....12 9
5 Jun 82	**SHAKTI (THE MEANING OF WITHIN)** *Mobile Suit Corp CORP 4*	.....41 3

MONSTER MAGNET *US, male vocal/instrumental group*   **3 wks**

29 May 93	**TWIN EARTH** *A & M 5802812*	.....67 1
18 Mar 95	**NEGASONIC TEENAGE WARHEAD** *A & M 5809812*	.....49 1
6 May 95	**DOPES TO INFINITY** *A & M 5810332*	.....58 1

MONTAGE *UK, female vocal trio*   **1 wk**

15 Feb 97	**THERE AIN'T NOTHIN' LIKE THE LOVE** *Wildcard 5733172*	.....64 1

MONTANA SEXTET *US, male/female vocal/instrumental group*   **1 wk**

15 Jan 83	**HEAVY VIBES** *Virgin VS 560*	.....59 1

Hugo MONTENEGRO Ⓞ *US, orchestra*   **26 wks**

11 Sep 68 ★	**THE GOOD THE BAD AND THE UGLY** *RCA 1727*	.....1 24
8 Jan 69	**HANG 'EM HIGH** *RCA 1771*	.....50 1
19 Mar 69	**THE GOOD THE BAD AND THE UGLY (re-entry)** *RCA 1727*	.....48 1

Chris MONTEZ Ⓞ *US, male vocalist*   **61 wks**

4 Oct 62 ●	**LET'S DANCE** *London HLU 9596*	.....2 18
17 Jan 63 ●	**SOME KINDA FUN** *London HLU 9650*	.....10 9
30 Jun 66 ●	**THE MORE I SEE YOU** *Pye International 7N 25369*	.....3 13
22 Sep 66	**THERE WILL NEVER BE ANOTHER YOU** *Pye International 7N 25381*	.....37 4
14 Oct 72 ●	**LET'S DANCE (re-issue)** *London HLU 10205*	.....9 14
14 Apr 79	**LET'S DANCE (2nd re-issue)** *Lightning LIG 9011*	.....47 3

The second re-issue of 'Let's Dance' on Lightning was coupled with 'Memphis' by Lonnie Mack as a double A-side

MONTROSE *US, male vocal/instrumental group*   **2 wks**

28 Jun 80	**SPACE STATION NO. 5/GOOD ROCKIN' TONIGHT** *WB HM 9*	.....71 2

MONTROSE AVENUE *UK, male vocal/instrumental group*   **4 wks**

28 Mar 98	**WHERE DO I STAND?** *Columbia 6656072*	.....38 2

20 Jun 98	**SHINE** *Columbia 6660012*	.....58 1
17 Oct 98	**START AGAIN** *Columbia 6664255*	.....59 1

MONTY PYTHON Ⓞ *UK, male comedy group*   **9 wks**

5 Oct 91 ●	**ALWAYS LOOK ON THE BRIGHT SIDE OF LIFE** *Virgin PYTH 1*	.....3 9

MONYAKA ⅋ ◢ *US/Jamaica, male vocal/instrumental group*   **8 wks**

10 Sep 83	**GO DEH YAKA (GO TO THE TOP)** *Polydor POSP 641*	.....14 8

MOOD *UK, male vocal/instrumental group*   **10 wks**

6 Feb 82	**DON'T STOP** *RCA 171*	.....59 4
22 May 82	**PARIS IS ONE DAY AWAY** *RCA 211*	.....42 5
30 Oct 82	**PASSION IN DARK ROOMS** *RCA 276*	.....74 1

MOODSWINGS – *See PRETENDERS / Chrissie HYNDE*

MOODY BLUES ♪ *Long-lived and internationally popular cosmic rock quintet from Birmingham: line-up has included Denny Laine (v/g), Ray Thomas (fl/v), Mike Pinder, (k), Graeme Edge (d), Justin Hayward (v/g), John Lodge (b/v). This album-oriented act has sold more than 50 million records worldwide*   **114 wks**

10 Dec 64 ★	**GO NOW** *Decca F 12022*	.....1 14
4 Mar 65	**I DON'T WANT TO GO ON WITHOUT YOU** *Decca F 12095*	.....33 9
10 Jun 65	**FROM THE BOTTOM OF MY HEART** *Decca F 12166*	.....22 9
18 Nov 65	**EVERYDAY** *Decca F 12266*	.....44 2
27 Dec 67	**NIGHTS IN WHITE SATIN** *Deram DM 161*	.....19 11
7 Aug 68	**VOICES IN THE SKY** *Deram DM 196*	.....27 10
4 Dec 68	**RIDE MY SEE-SAW** *Deram DM 213*	.....42 1
2 May 70 ●	**QUESTION** *Threshold TH 4*	.....2 12
6 May 72	**ISN'T LIFE STRANGE** *Threshold TH 9*	.....13 10
2 Dec 72 ●	**NIGHTS IN WHITE SATIN (re-entry)** *Deram DM 161*	.....9 11
10 Feb 73	**I'M JUST A SINGER (IN A ROCK 'N' ROLL BAND)** *Threshold TH 13*	.....36 4
10 Nov 79	**NIGHTS IN WHITE SATIN (2nd re-entry)** *Deram DM 161*	.....14 12
20 Aug 83	**BLUE WORLD** *Threshold TH 30*	.....35 5
25 Jun 88	**I KNOW YOU'RE OUT THERE SOMEWHERE** *Polydor POSP 921*	.....52 4

MOONMAN *Holland, male DJ/producer*   **1 wk**

9 Aug 97	**DON'T BE AFRAID** *Heat Recordings HEATCD 009*	.....60 1

MOONTREKKERS *UK, male instrumental group*   **1 wk**

2 Nov 61	**NIGHT OF THE VAMPIRE** *Parlophone R 4814*	.....50 1

Chante MOORE *US, female vocalist*   **4 wks**

20 Mar 93	**LOVE'S TAKEN OVER** *MCA MCSTD 1744*	.....54 3
4 Mar 95	**FREE/SAIL ON** *MCA MCSTD 2042*	.....69 1

Dorothy MOORE 🎵 *US, female vocalist*   **24 wks**

19 Jun 76 ●	**MISTY BLUE** *Contempo CS 2087*	.....5 12
16 Oct 76	**FUNNY HOW TIME SLIPS AWAY** *Contempo CS 2092*	.....38 3
15 Oct 77	**I BELIEVE YOU** *Epic EPC 5573*	.....20 9

Dudley MOORE – *See Peter COOK*

Gary MOORE ♪ *Noted blues guitarist, b. 4 April, 1952, Belfast. Played in early 1970s Irish band Skid Row (with Phil Lynott) as well as Thin Lizzy and Colosseum II, before successfully launching his solo career*   **103 wks**

21 Apr 79 ●	**PARISIENNE WALKWAYS** *MCA 419*	.....8 11
21 Jan 84	**HOLD ON TO LOVE** *10 TEN 13*	.....65 3
11 Aug 84	**EMPTY ROOMS** *10 TEN 25*	.....51 5
18 May 85 ●	**OUT IN THE FIELDS** *10 TEN 49* [1]	.....5 10
27 Jul 85	**EMPTY ROOMS (re-issue)** *10 TEN 58*	.....23 8
20 Dec 86	**OVER THE HILLS AND FAR AWAY** *10 TEN 134*	.....20 8
28 Feb 87	**WILD FRONTIER** *10 TEN 159*	.....35 5
9 May 87	**FRIDAY ON MY MIND** *10 TEN 164*	.....26 6
29 Aug 87	**THE LONER** *10 TEN 178*	.....53 5
5 Dec 87	**TAKE A LITTLE TIME (DOUBLE SINGLE)** *10 TEN 190*	.....75 1

What: *Mull of Kintyre / Girls' School*
Who: Paul McCartney
When: 1977 (1)
Which: Not only gave the ex-Beatle his first solo No 1, but also became the first single to sell more than two million copies in Britain – a feat no Beatles' single has equalled

65

What: *Rhythm Is a Dancer*
Who: Snap
When: 1992 (1)
Which: Took the German-based dance act to the top in many countries. Vocalist Thea Austin and rapper Turbo B (pictured), who disliked this track, left the group when the record was released

66

What: *Never Ever*
Who: All Saints
When: 1998 (1)
Which: Passed the 750000 sales mark before it reached No 1 – a record never ever equalled. In total, the single, which also cracked the US Top 10, sold more than 1.25 million in Britain

67

What: *Happy Xmas (War Is Over)*
Who: John and Yoko & The Plastic Ono Band
When: 1972 (4), 1975 (48), 1980 (2), 1981 (28), 1982 (56)
Which: Also featured the Harlem Community Choir. It had five separate chart runs (a Beatles record) and reached its highest position soon after Lennon's death

68

14 Jan 89	AFTER THE WAR *Virgin GMS 1*	37	4
18 Mar 89	READY FOR LOVE *Virgin GMS 2*	56	2
24 Mar 90	OH PRETTY WOMAN *Virgin VS 1233* [2]	48	3
12 May 90	STILL GOT THE BLUES (FOR YOU) *Virgin VS 1267*	31	7
18 Aug 90	WALKING BY MYSELF *Virgin VS 1281*	48	5
15 Dec 90	TOO TIRED *Virgin VS 1306*	71	1
22 Feb 92	COLD DAY IN HELL *Virgin VS 1393*	24	5
9 May 92	STORY OF THE BLUES *Virgin VS 1412*	40	4
18 Jul 92	SINCE I MET YOU BABY *Virgin VS 1423* [3]	59	3
24 Oct 92	SEPARATE WAYS *Virgin VS 1437*	59	1
8 May 93	PARISIENNE WALKWAYS (re-mix) *Virgin VSCDX 1456*	32	4
17 Jun 95	NEED YOUR LOVE SO BAD *Virgin VSCDG 1546*	48	2

[1] Gary Moore and Phil Lynott [2] Gary Moore featuring Albert King
[3] Gary Moore and BB King

*'Parisienne Walkways' features uncredited vocals by Phil Lynott. Tracks on double
single: Take a Little Time / Out in the Fields / All Messed Up / Thunder Rising*

Jackie MOORE *US, female vocalist* 5 wks

15 Sep 79	THIS TIME BABY *CBS 7722*	49	5

Mark MOORE – *See S EXPRESS*

Melba MOORE 🎤 *US, female vocalist* 29 wks

15 May 76 ●	THIS IS IT *Buddah BDS 443*	9	8
26 May 79	PICK ME UP I'LL DANCE *Epic EPC 7234*	48	5
9 Oct 82	LOVE'S COMIN' AT YA *EMI America EA 146*	15	8
15 Jan 83	MIND UP TONIGHT *Capitol CL 272*	22	6
5 Mar 83	UNDERLOVE *Capitol CL 281*	60	2

Ray MOORE *UK, male vocalist* 9 wks

29 Nov 86	O' MY FATHER HAD A RABBIT *Play PLAY 213*	24	7
5 Dec 87	BOG EYED JOG *Play PLAY 224*	61	2

Sam MOORE – *See SAM and DAVE; Lou REED*

Tina MOORE ☺ 🎤 *US, female vocalist* 18 wks

30 Aug 97 ●	NEVER GONNA LET YOU GO *Delirious 74321511052*	7	15
25 Apr 98	NOBODY BETTER *RCA 74321571612*	20	3

Lisa MOORISH *UK, female vocalist* 11 wks

7 Jan 95	JUST THE WAY IT IS *Go.Beat GODCD 123*	42	3
19 Aug 95	I'M YOUR MAN *Go.Beat GODCD 128*	24	3
3 Feb 96	MR. FRIDAY NIGHT *Go.Beat GODCD 137*	24	3
18 May 96	LOVE FOR LIFE *Go.Beat GODCD 145*	37	2

'I'm Your Man' features the uncredited vocals of George Michael

Angel MORAES *US, male producer* 2 wks

16 Nov 96	HEAVEN KNOWS – DEEP DEEP DOWN *ffrr FCD 282*	72	1
17 May 97	I LIKE IT *AM:PM 5871792*	70	1

David MORALES ☺ *US, male DJ / producer* 14 wks

10 Jul 93	GIMME LUV (EENIE MEENIE MINY MO) *Mercury MERCD 390*	37	3
20 Nov 93	THE PROGRAM *Mercury MERCD 396*	66	1
24 Aug 96	IN DE GHETTO *Manifesto FESCD 12* [1]	35	2
15 Aug 98 ●	NEEDIN' U *Manifesto FESCD 46* [2]	8	8

[1] David Morales and the Bad Yard Club featuring Crystal Waters and Delta
[2] David Morales presents The Face

See also BOSS; PULSE featuring Antoinette ROBERSON

Mike MORAN – *See Lynsey DE PAUL*

MORCHEEBA *UK, male/female vocal/instrumental group* 9 wks

13 Jul 96	TAPE LOOP *Indochina ID 045CD*	42	1
5 Oct 96	TRIGGER HIPPIE *Indochina ID 052CD*	40	2
15 Feb 97	THE MUSIC THAT WE HEAR (MOOG ISLAND) *Indochina ID 054CD*	47	1
11 Oct 97	SHOULDER HOLSTER *Indochina ID 064CD*	53	1

11 Apr 98	BLINDFOLD (LIMITED EDITION) *Indochina ID 070CD*	56	1
20 Jun 98	LET ME SEE *Indochina ID 076CD*	46	1
29 Aug 98	PART OF THE PROCESS *China WOKCD 2097*	38	2

MORE *UK, male vocal/instrumental group* 2 wks

14 Mar 81	WE ARE THE BAND *Atlantic K 11561*	59	2

George MOREL featuring Heather WILDMAN
US, male/female vocal/instrumental duo 2 wks

26 Oct 96	LET'S GROOVE *Positiva CDTIV 62*	42	2

Derrick MORGAN *Jamaica, male vocalist* 1 wk

17 Jan 70	MOON HOP *Crab 32*	49	1

Jamie J MORGAN *US, male vocalist* 6 wks

10 Feb 90	WALK ON THE WILD SIDE *Tabu 655596 7*	27	6

Jane MORGAN Ⓒ *US, female vocalist* 22 wks

5 Dec 58 ★	THE DAY THE RAINS CAME *London HLR 8751*	1	16
22 May 59	IF ONLY I COULD LIVE MY LIFE AGAIN *London HLR 8810*	27	1
21 Jul 60	ROMANTICA *London HLR 9120*	39	5

Meli'sa MORGAN *US, female vocalist* 7 wks

9 Aug 86	FOOL'S PARADISE *Capitol CL 415*	41	5
25 Jun 88	GOOD LOVE *Capitol CL 483*	59	2

Ray MORGAN *UK, male vocalist* 6 wks

25 Jul 70	THE LONG AND WINDING ROAD *B & C CB 128*	32	6

Erick 'More' MORILLO presents RAW
US, male/female vocal/instrumental duo 1 wk

4 Feb 95	HIGHER (FEEL IT) *A & M 5809412*	74	1

Alanis MORISSETTE ⊘ 🎸 *Canada, female vocalist* 40 wks

5 Aug 95	YOU OUGHTA KNOW *Maverick W 0307CD*	22	7
28 Oct 95	HAND IN MY POCKET *Maverick W 0312CD*	26	3
24 Feb 96	YOU LEARN *Maverick W 0334CD*	24	4
20 Apr 96	IRONIC *Maverick W 0343CD*	11	9
3 Aug 96 ●	HEAD OVER FEET *Maverick W 0355CD*	7	7
7 Dec 96	ALL I REALLY WANT *Maverick W 0382CD*	59	1
31 Oct 98 ●	THANK U *Maverick W 0458CD*	5†	9

Giorgio MORODER ◢ ⊘
Italy, male instrumentalist – synthesizer 35 wks

24 Sep 77	FROM HERE TO ETERNITY *Oasis 1* [1]	16	10
17 Mar 79	CHASE *Casablanca CAN 144*	48	6
22 Sep 84 ●	TOGETHER IN ELECTRIC DREAMS *Virgin VS 713* [2]	3	13
29 Jun 85	GOODBYE BAD TIMES *Virgin VS 772* [2]	44	5
11 Jul 98	CARRY ON *Almighty CDALMY 120* [3]	65	1

[1] Giorgio [2] Giorgio Moroder and Phil Oakey
[3] Donna Summer and Giorgio Moroder

Ennio MORRICONE Ⓒ *Italy, orchestra* 12 wks

11 Apr 81 ●	CHI MAI (THEME FROM THE TV SERIES 'THE LIFE AND TIMES OF DAVID LLOYD GEORGE') *BBC RESL 92*	2	12

Sarah Jane MORRIS – *See COMMUNARDS*

Diana MORRISON – *See Michael BALL*

Dorothy Combs MORRISON – *See Edwin HAWKINS SINGERS featuring Dorothy Combs MORRISON*

Mark MORRISON R&B *UK, male vocalist* 64 wks

22 Apr 95	CRAZY *WEA YZ 907CD*	19	4
16 Sep 95	LET'S GET DOWN *WEA WEA 001CD*	39	2

---

16 Mar 96 ★	RETURN OF THE MACK *WEA WEA 040CD*	1	23
27 Jul 96 ●	CRAZY (re-mix) *WEA WEA 054CD1*	6	8
31 Aug 96	RETURN OF THE MACK (re-entry) *WEA WEA 040CD*	60	1
19 Oct 96	CRAZY (re-entry of re-mix) *WEA WEA 054CD1*	71	1
19 Oct 96 ●	TRIPPIN' *WEA WEA 079CD1*	8	6
21 Dec 96 ●	HORNY *WEA WEA 090CD1*	5	8
15 Mar 97 ●	MOAN & GROAN *WEA WEA 096CD1*	7	6
20 Sep 97	WHO'S THE MACK! *WEA WEA 128CD1*	13	5

Van MORRISON ✍ UK, male vocalist — 17 wks

20 Oct 79	BRIGHT SIDE OF THE ROAD *Mercury 6001 121*	63	3
1 Jul 89	HAVE I TOLD YOU LATELY *Polydor VANS 1*	74	1
9 Dec 89	WHENEVER GOD SHINES HIS LIGHT *Polydor VANS 2* [1]	20	6
15 May 93	GLORIA *Exile VANCD 11* [2]	31	3
18 Mar 95	HAVE I TOLD YOU LATELY THAT I LOVE YOU *RCA 74321271702* [3]	71	1
10 Jun 95	DAYS LIKE THIS *Exile VANCD 12*	65	1
2 Dec 95	NO RELIGION *Exile 5775792*	54	1
1 Mar 97	THE HEALING GAME *Exile 5733912*	46	1

[1] Van Morrison with Cliff Richard [2] Van Morrison and John Lee Hooker
[3] Chieftans with Van Morrison

'Have I Told You Lately That I Love You' is a re-recording of his second hit

MORRISSEY ☺ UK, male vocalist — 74 wks

27 Feb 88 ●	SUEDEHEAD *HMV POP 1618*	5	6
11 Jun 88 ●	EVERYDAY IS LIKE SUNDAY *HMV POP 1619*	9	6
11 Feb 89 ●	LAST OF THE FAMOUS INTERNATIONAL PLAYBOYS *HMV POP 1620*	6	5
29 Apr 89 ●	INTERESTING DRUG *HMV POP 1621*	9	4
25 Nov 89	OUIJA BOARD OUIJA BOARD *HMV POP 1622*	18	4
5 May 90	NOVEMBER SPAWNED A MONSTER *HMV POP 1623*	12	4
20 Oct 90	PICCADILLY PALARE *HMV POP 1624*	18	2
23 Feb 91	OUR FRANK *HMV POP 1625*	26	3
13 Apr 91	SING YOUR LIFE *HMV POP 1626*	33	2
27 Jul 91	PREGNANT FOR THE LAST TIME *HMV POP 1627*	25	4
12 Oct 91	MY LOVE LIFE *HMV POP 1628*	29	2
9 May 92	WE HATE IT WHEN OUR FRIENDS BECOME SUCCESSFUL *HMV POP 1629*	17	3
18 Jul 92	YOU'RE THE ONE FOR ME, FATTY *HMV POP 1630*	19	3
19 Dec 92	CERTAIN PEOPLE I KNOW *HMV POP 1631*	35	4
12 Mar 94 ●	THE MORE YOU IGNORE ME THE CLOSER I GET *Parlophone CDR 6372*	8	3
11 Jun 94	HOLD ON TO YOUR FRIENDS *Parlophone CDR 6383*	47	2
20 Aug 94	INTERLUDE *Parlophone CDR 6365* [1]	25	2
28 Jan 95	BOXERS *Parlophone CDR 6400*	23	3
2 Sep 95	DAGENHAM DAVE *RCA Victor 74321299802*	26	2
9 Dec 95	THE BOY RACER *RCA Victor 74321332952*	36	2
23 Dec 95	SUNNY *Parlophone CDR 6243*	42	2
2 Aug 97	ALMA MATTERS *Island CID 667*	16	3
18 Oct 97	ROY'S KEEN *Island CID 671*	42	1
10 Jan 98	SATAN REJECTED MY SOUL *Island CID 686*	39	2

[1] Morrissey and Siouxsie

MORRISTON ORPHEUS MALE VOICE CHOIR – See ALARM

Buddy MORROW ♩ US, orchestra — 1 wk

20 Mar 53	NIGHT TRAIN *HMV B 10347*	12	1

MORTIMER – See Vic REEVES; EMF

Bob MORTIMER ☺ UK, male vocalist — 9 wks

8 Jul 95 ●	I'M A BELIEVER *Parlophone CDR 6412* [1]	3	8
24 May 97	LET'S DANCE *Magnet EW 112CD* [2]	44	1

[1] EMF and Reeves and Mortimer
[2] Middlesborough FC featuring Bob Mortimer and Chris Rea

Mickie MOST UK, male vocalist — 1 wk

25 Jul 63	MISTER PORTER *Decca F 11664*	45	1

MOTELS US/UK, male/female vocal/instrumental group — 7 wks

11 Oct 80	WHOSE PROBLEM? *Capitol CL 16162*	42	4
10 Jan 81	DAYS ARE O.K. *Capitol CL 16149*	41	3

Wendy MOTEN ❍ ✍ US, female vocalist — 13 wks

5 Feb 94 ●	COME IN OUT OF THE RAIN *EMI-USA CDMT 105*	8	9
14 May 94	SO CLOSE TO LOVE *EMI-USA CDMTS 106*	35	4

MOTHER UK, male instrumental/production duo — 4 wks

12 Jun 93	ALL FUNKED UP *Bosting BYSNCD 101*	34	2
1 Oct 94	GET BACK *Six6 SIXT 119*	73	1
31 Aug 96	ALL FUNKED UP (re-mix) *Six6 SIXXCD 1*	66	1

MOTHER'S PRIDE UK, male DJ/production duo — 1 wk

21 Mar 98	FLORIBUNDA *Heat Recordings HEATCD 013*	42	1

MOTIV 8 ☺ UK, male producer – Steve Rodway — 10 wks

17 Jul 93	ROCKIN' FOR MYSELF *Nuff Respect NUFF 002CD* [1]	67	1
7 May 94	ROCKIN' FOR MYSELF (re-mix) *WEA YZ 814CD*	18	4
21 Oct 95	BREAK THE CHAIN *Eternal WEA 010CD*	31	2
23 Dec 95	SEARCHING FOR THE GOLDEN EYE *Eternal WEA 027CD* [2]	40	3

[1] Motiv 8 featuring Angie Brown [2] Motiv 8 featuring Kym Mazelle

MOTLEY CRUE US, male vocal/instrumental group — 28 wks

24 Aug 85	SMOKIN' IN THE BOYS ROOM *Elektra EKR 16*	71	2
8 Feb 86	HOME SWEET HOME/SMOKIN' IN THE BOYS ROOM (re-issue) *Elektra EKR 33*	51	3
1 Aug 87	GIRLS GIRLS GIRLS *Elektra EKR 59*	26	6
16 Jan 88	YOU'RE ALL I NEED/WILD SIDE *Elektra EKR 65*	23	4
4 Nov 89	DR. FEELGOOD *Elektra EKR 97*	50	3
12 May 90	WITHOUT YOU *Elektra EKR 109*	39	3
7 Sep 91	PRIMAL SCREAM *Elektra EKR 133*	32	2
11 Jan 92	HOME SWEET HOME (re-mix) *Elektra EKR 136*	37	2
5 Mar 94	HOOLIGAN'S HOLIDAY *Elektra EKR 180CDX*	36	2
19 Jul 97	AFRAID *Elektra E3936*	58	1

'Wild Side' only listed with 'You're All I Need' from 30 Jan, 1988.
It peaked at No 26

MOTORHEAD ⚡ UK, male vocal/instrumental group — 81 wks

16 Sep 78	LOUIE LOUIE *Bronze BRO 60*	75	1
30 Sep 78	LOUIE LOUIE (re-entry) *Bronze BRO 60*	68	1
10 Mar 79	OVERKILL *Bronze BRO 67*	39	4
14 Apr 79	OVERKILL (re-entry) *Bronze BRO 67*	57	3
30 Jun 79	NO CLASS *Bronze BRO 78*	61	4
1 Dec 79	BOMBER *Bronze BRO 85*	34	7
3 May 80 ●	THE GOLDEN YEARS EP *Bronze BRO 92*	8	7
1 Nov 80 ●	ACE OF SPADES *Bronze BRO 106*	15	12
22 Nov 80	BEER DRINKERS AND HELL RAISERS *Big Beat SWT 61*	43	4
21 Feb 81 ●	ST. VALENTINE'S DAY MASSACRE EP *Bronze BRO 116* [1]	5	8
11 Jul 81 ●	MOTORHEAD LIVE *Bronze BRO 124*	6	7
3 Apr 82	IRON FIST *Bronze BRO 146*	29	5
21 May 83	I GOT MINE *Bronze BRO 165*	46	2
30 Jul 83	SHINE *Bronze BRO 167*	59	2
1 Sep 84	KILLED BY DEATH *Bronze BRO 185*	51	2
5 Jul 86	DEAF FOREVER *GWR GWR 2*	67	1
5 Jan 91	THE ONE TO SING THE BLUES *Epic 6565787*	45	3
14 Nov 92	'92 TOUR EP *Epic 6588096*	63	1
11 Sep 93	ACE OF SPADES *WGAF CDWGAF 101*	23	5
10 Dec 94	BORN TO RAISE HELL *Fox 74321230152* [2]	47	2

[1] Motorhead and Girlschool (also known as Headgirl)
[2] Motorhead/Ice-T/Whitfield Crane

Tracks on The Golden Years EP: Dead Men Tell No Tales/Too Late Too Late/Leaving Here/Stone Dead Forever. Tracks on St. Valentine's Day Massacre EP: Please Don't Touch/Emergency/Bomber. Tracks on '92 Tour EP: Hellraiser/You Better Run/ Going to Brazil/Ramones

UK No 1 ★   UK Top 10 ●   UK million seller ◆   UK entry at No 1 ■   US No 1 ▲

MOTORS ⊕ ✏ UK, male vocal/instrumental group   29 wks

24 Sep 77	DANCING THE NIGHT AWAY *Virgin VS 186*	.42 4
10 Jun 78 ●	AIRPORT *Virgin VS 219*	.4 13
19 Aug 78	FORGET ABOUT YOU *Virgin VS 222*	.13 9
12 Apr 80	LOVE AND LONELINESS *Virgin VS 263*	.58 3

MOTOWN SPINNERS – *See DETROIT SPINNERS*

MOTT THE HOOPLE ✐ UK, male vocal/instrumental group   55 wks

12 Aug 72 ●	ALL THE YOUNG DUDES *CBS 8271*	.3 11
16 Jun 73	HONALOOCHIE BOOGIE *CBS 1530*	.12 9
8 Sep 73 ●	ALL THE WAY FROM MEMPHIS *CBS 1764*	.10 8
24 Nov 73 ●	ROLL AWAY THE STONE *CBS 1895*	.8 12
30 Mar 74	GOLDEN AGE OF ROCK AND ROLL *CBS 2177*	.16 7
22 Jun 74	FOXY FOXY *CBS 2439*	.33 5
2 Nov 74	SATURDAY GIG *CBS 2754*	.41 3

Nana MOUSKOURI ℂ Greece, female vocalist   11 wks

11 Jan 86 ●	ONLY LOVE *Philips PH 38*	.2 11

MOUTH and MACNEAL ⊕ Holland, male/female vocal duo   10 wks

4 May 74 ●	I SEE A STAR *Decca F 13504*	.8 10

MOVE ✐ Innovative and influential Birmingham band: included Carl Wayne (v), Roy Wood (v/g). They were the first group heard on BBC Radio 1 ('Flowers in the Rain'), and had eight consecutive Top 20 entries. Wood later moved on to a successful solo career, helped to form ELO and went on to front Wizzard   110 wks

5 Jan 67 ●	NIGHT OF FEAR *Deram DM 109*	.2 10
6 Apr 67 ●	I CAN HEAR THE GRASS GROW *Deram DM 117*	.5 10
6 Sep 67 ●	FLOWERS IN THE RAIN *Regal Zonophone RZ3001*	.2 13
7 Feb 68 ●	FIRE BRIGADE *Regal Zonophone RZ3005*	.3 11
25 Dec 68 ★	BLACKBERRY WAY *Regal Zonophone RZ3015*	.1 12
23 Jul 69	CURLY *Regal Zonophone RZ3021*	.12 12
25 Apr 70 ●	BRONTOSAURUS *Regal Zonophone RZ3026*	.7 10
3 Jul 71	TONIGHT *Harvest HAR 5038*	.11 10
23 Oct 71	CHINATOWN *Harvest HAR 5043*	.23 8
13 May 72 ●	CALIFORNIA MAN *Harvest HAR 5050*	.7 14

MOVEMENT US, male vocal/instrumental group   2 wks

24 Oct 92	JUMP! *Arista 74321116677*	.57 2

MOVEMENT 98 featuring Carroll THOMPSON
UK, male/female vocal/instrumental group   8 wks

19 May 90	JOY AND HEARTBREAK *Circa YR 45*	.27 5
15 Sep 90	SUNRISE *Circa YR 51*	.58 3

See also Courtney PINE

MOVIN' MELODIES Holland, male producer – Patrick Prinz   3 wks

22 Oct 94	LA LUNA *Effective EFFS 017CD*	.64 1
29 Jun 96	INDICA *Hooj Choons HOOJCD 44*	.62 1
26 Jul 97	ROLLERBLADE *Movin' Melodies 5822352*	.71 1

☐1 Movin' Melodies Production

See also ARTEMESIA; ETHICS; SUBLIMINAL CUTS

Alison MOYET ⊕ After five Top 20 hits with Yazoo, the distinctive, bluesy-voiced vocalist (b. 18 June, 1961, Essex), nicknamed Alf, enjoyed a string of solo successes. Her biggest hits included covers of songs made popular by Billie Holiday and Ketty Lester   107 wks

23 Jun 84 ●	LOVE RESURRECTION *CBS A 4497*	.10 11
13 Oct 84 ●	ALL CRIED OUT *CBS A 4757*	.8 11
1 Dec 84	INVISIBLE *CBS A 4930*	.21 10
16 Mar 85 ●	THAT OLE DEVIL CALLED LOVE *CBS A 6044*	.2 10
29 Nov 86 ●	IS THIS LOVE? *CBS MOYET 1*	.3 16
7 Mar 87 ●	WEAK IN THE PRESENCE OF BEAUTY *CBS MOYET 2*	.6 10
30 May 87	ORDINARY GIRL *CBS MOYET 3*	.43 4
28 Nov 87 ●	LOVE LETTERS *CBS MOYET 5*	.4 10
6 Apr 91	IT WON'T BE LONG *Columbia 6567577*	.50 4
1 Jun 91	WISHING YOU WERE HERE *Columbia 6569397*	.72 1
12 Oct 91	THIS HOUSE *Columbia 6575157*	.40 5
12 Mar 93	WHISPERING YOUR NAME *Columbia 6601622*	.18 7
16 Oct 93	FALLING *Columbia 6595962*	.42 3
28 May 94	GETTING INTO SOMETHING *Columbia 6603565*	.51 2
22 Oct 94	ODE TO BOY *Columbia 6607952*	.59 1
26 Aug 95	SOLID WOOD *Columbia 6623265*	.44 2

See also YAZOO

MOZAIC ☺ UK, female vocal group   7 wks

5 Aug 95	SING IT (THE HALLELUJAH SONG) *Perfecto PERF 106CD*	.14 4
10 Aug 96	RAYS OF THE RISING SUN *Perfecto PERF 123CD*	.32 2
30 Nov 96	MOVING UP MOVING ON *Perfecto PERF 131CD*	.62 1

MTUME US, male/female vocal/instrumental group   12 wks

14 May 83	JUICY FRUIT *Epic A 3424*	.34 9
22 Sep 84	PRIME TIME *Epic A 4720*	.57 3

MUD ⊕ Rock'n'roll-influenced seventies stars: Les Gray (v), Rob Davis (g/v), Ray Stiles (b/v), Dave Mount (d/v). After joining RAK Records and teaming with writer/producers Nicky Chinn and Mike Chapman, this good-time British band had a noteworthy run of hits, including three No 1s   139 wks

10 Mar 73	CRAZY *RAK 146*	.12 12
23 Jun 73	HYPNOSIS *RAK 152*	.16 13
27 Oct 73 ●	DYNA-MITE *RAK 159*	.4 12
19 Jan 74 ★	TIGER FEET *RAK 166*	.1 11
13 Apr 74 ●	THE CAT CREPT IN *RAK 170*	.2 9
27 Jul 74 ●	ROCKET *RAK 178*	.6 9
30 Nov 74 ★	LONELY THIS CHRISTMAS *RAK 187*	.1 10
15 Feb 75 ●	THE SECRETS THAT YOU KEEP *RAK 194*	.3 9
26 Apr 75 ★	OH BOY *RAK 201*	.1 9
21 Jun 75 ●	MOONSHINE SALLY *RAK 208*	.10 7
2 Aug 75	ONE NIGHT *RAK 213*	.32 4
4 Oct 75 ●	L-L-LUCY *Private Stock PVT 41*	.10 6
29 Nov 75 ●	SHOW ME YOU'RE A WOMAN *Private Stock PVT 45*	.8 8
15 May 76	SHAKE IT DOWN *Private Stock PVT 65*	.12 8
27 Nov 76 ●	LEAN ON ME *Private Stock PVT 85*	.7 9
21 Dec 85	LONELY THIS CHRISTMAS (re-entry) *RAK 187*	.61 3

MUDHONEY US, male vocal/instrumental group   2 wks

17 Aug 91	LET IT SLIDE *Subpop SP 15154*	.60 1
24 Oct 92	SUCK YOU DRY *Reprise W 0137*	.65 1

MUDLARKS ⊕ UK, male/female vocal group   19 wks

2 May 58 ●	LOLLIPOP *Columbia DB 4099*	.2 9
6 Jun 58 ●	BOOK OF LOVE *Columbia DB 4133*	.8 9
27 Feb 59	THE LOVE GAME *Columbia DB 4250*	.30 1

MUFFINS – *See MARTHA and the MUFFINS*

Idris MUHAMMAD US, male instrumentalist – drums   3 wks

17 Sep 77	COULD HEAVEN EVER BE LIKE THIS *Kudu 935*	.42 3

Vocal by Frank Floyd

MUKKAA UK, male instrumental/production duo   1 wk

27 Feb 93	BURUCHACCA *Limbo LIMBO 008*	.74 1

Maria MULDAUR US, female vocalist   8 wks

29 Jun 74	MIDNIGHT AT THE OASIS *Reprise K 14331*	.21 8

Arthur MULLARD – *See Hylda BAKER and Arthur MULLARD*

Larry MULLEN – *See Adam CLAYTON and Larry MULLEN*

UK No 1 ★   UK Top 10 ●   UK million seller ◆   UK entry at No 1 ■   US No 1 ▲

MULU *UK, male/female vocal/instrumental duo* — 1 wk

2 Aug 97	PUSSYCAT *Dedicated MULU 003CD1*	50	1

Coati MUNDI – *See Kid CREOLE and the COCONUTS*

MUNDY *Ireland, male vocalist* — 2 wks

3 Aug 96	TO YOU I BESTOW *Epic MUNDY 1CD*	60	1
5 Oct 96	LIFE'S A CINCH *Epic MUNDY 2CD*	75	1

MUNGO JERRY ☻ *UK, male vocal/instrumental group* — 87 wks

6 Jun 70 ★	IN THE SUMMERTIME *Dawn DNX 2502*	1	20
6 Feb 71	BABY JUMP *Dawn DNX 2505*	32	1
20 Feb 71 ★	BABY JUMP (re-entry) *Dawn DNX 2505*	1	12
29 May 71 ●	LADY ROSE *Dawn DNX 2510*	5	12
18 Sep 71	YOU DON'T HAVE TO BE IN THE ARMY TO FIGHT IN THE WAR *Dawn DNX 2513*	13	8
22 Apr 72	OPEN UP *Dawn DNX 2514*	21	8
7 Jul 73 ●	ALRIGHT ALRIGHT ALRIGHT *Dawn DNS 1037*	3	12
10 Nov 73	WILD LOVE *Dawn DNS 1051*	32	5
6 Apr 74	LONGLEGGED WOMAN DRESSED IN BLACK *Dawn DNS 1061*	13	9

MUNICH MACHINE *Germany, male instrumental group* — 8 wks

10 Dec 77	GET ON THE FUNK TRAIN *Oasis OASIS 2*	41	4
4 Nov 78	A WHITER SHADE OF PALE *Oasis OASIS 5* [1]	42	4

[1] Munich Machine introducing Chris Bennett

David MUNROW – *See EARLY MUSIC CONSORT directed by David MUNROW*

MUPPETS Ⓒ *US, puppets* — 15 wks

28 May 77 ●	HALFWAY DOWN THE STAIRS *Pye 7N 45698*	7	8
17 Dec 77	THE MUPPET SHOW MUSIC HALL EP *Pye 7NX 8004*	19	7

'Halfway Down the Stairs' is sung by Jerry Nelson as Kermit the Frog's nephew, Robin. Tracks on The Muppet Show Music Hall EP: Don't Dilly Dally On the Way/ Waiting at the Church/ The Boy in the Gallery/ Wotcher (Knocked 'Em in the Old Kent Road)

Lydia MURDOCK *US, female vocalist* — 9 wks

24 Sep 83	SUPERSTAR *Korova KOW 30*	14	9

Shirley MURDOCK *US, female vocalist* — 2 wks

12 Apr 86	TRUTH OR DARE *Elektra EKR 36*	60	2

Eddie MURPHY – *See Shabba RANKS*

Noel MURPHY *Ireland, male vocalist* — 4 wks

27 Jun 87	MURPHY AND THE BRICKS *Murphy's STACK 1*	57	4

Walter MURPHY and the BIG APPLE BAND *US, orchestra* — 9 wks

10 Jul 76	A FIFTH OF BEETHOVEN *Private Stock PVT 59* ▲	28	9

Anne MURRAY *Canada, female vocalist* — 40 wks

24 Oct 70	SNOWBIRD *Capitol CL 15654*	23	17
21 Oct 72	DESTINY *Capitol CL 15734*	41	4
9 Dec 78	YOU NEEDED ME *Capitol CL 16011* ▲	22	14
21 Apr 79	I JUST FALL IN LOVE AGAIN *Capitol CL 16069*	58	2
19 Apr 80	DAYDREAM BELIEVER *Capitol CL 16123*	61	3

Keith MURRAY *US, male rapper* — 10 wks

2 Nov 96	THE RHYME *Jive JIVECD 407*	59	1
27 Jun 98	SHORTY (YOU KEEP PLAYIN' WITH MY MIND) *Jive 0521212* [3]	22	3
14 Nov 98	HOME ALONE *Jive 0522392* [2]	17	5
5 Dec 98	INCREDIBLE *Jive 0522102* [1]	52	1

[1] Keith Murray featuring LL Cool J [2] R Kelly featuring Keith Murray
[3] Imajin featuring Keith Murray

Pauline MURRAY and the INVISIBLE GIRLS
UK, female vocalist with male (really) vocal/instrumental group — 2 wks

2 Aug 80	DREAM SEQUENCE (ONE) *Illusive IVE 1*	67	2

Ruby MURRAY Ⓒ *Britain's singing sensation of 1955, b. 29 March, 1935, Belfast, d. 17 December, 1996. This nasal-sounding 'girl-next-door' vocalist captivated UK audiences in the mid-1950s. She was the first artist to have five simultaneous Top 20 singles* — 110 wks

3 Dec 54 ●	HEARTBEAT *Columbia DB 3542*	3	16
28 Jan 55 ★	SOFTLY SOFTLY *Columbia DB 3558*	1	22
4 Feb 55 ●	HAPPY DAYS AND LONELY NIGHTS *Columbia DB 3577*	6	8
4 Mar 55 ●	LET ME GO LOVER *Columbia DB 3577*	5	7
18 Mar 55 ●	IF ANYONE FINDS THIS I LOVE YOU *Columbia DB 3580* [1]	4	11
1 Jul 55 ●	EVERMORE *Columbia DB 3617*	3	17
8 Jul 55	SOFTLY SOFTLY (re-entry) *Columbia DB 3558*	20	1
14 Oct 55 ●	I'LL COME WHEN YOU CALL *Columbia DB 3643*	6	7
31 Aug 56	YOU ARE MY FIRST LOVE *Columbia DB 3770*	16	4
5 Oct 56	YOU ARE MY FIRST LOVE (re-entry) *Columbia DB 3770*	21	1
12 Dec 58	REAL LOVE *Columbia DB 4192*	18	6
5 Jun 59 ●	GOODBYE JIMMY GOODBYE *Columbia DB 4305*	10	13
9 Oct 59	GOODBYE JIMMY GOODBYE (re-entry) *Columbia DB 4305*	26	1

[1] Ruby Murray with Anne Warren

Junior MURVIN *Jamaica, male vocalist* — 9 wks

3 May 80	POLICE AND THIEVES *Island WIP 6539*	23	9

MUSIC AND MYSTERY – *See Gwen McCRAE*

MUSIC RELIEF '94 *UK, male/female vocal/instrumental group* — 1 wk

5 Nov 94	WHAT'S GOING ON *Jive RWANDACD 1*	70	1

MUSICAL YOUTH ☻ ↑ *UK, male vocal/instrumental group* — 55 wks

25 Sep 82 ★	PASS THE DUTCHIE *MCA YOU 1*	1	12
20 Nov 82	YOUTH OF TODAY *MCA YOU 2*	13	9
8 Jan 83	PASS THE DUTCHIE (re-entry) *MCA YOU 1*	65	1
12 Feb 83 ●	NEVER GONNA GIVE YOU UP *MCA YOU 3*	6	10
16 Apr 83	HEARTBREAKER *MCA YOU 4*	44	3
9 Jul 83	TELL ME WHY *MCA YOU 5*	33	6
22 Oct 83	007 *MCA YOU 6*	26	6
14 Jan 84	SIXTEEN *MCA YOU 7*	23	8

See also Donna SUMMER

MUSIQUE ☺ *US, female vocal group* — 12 wks

18 Nov 78	IN THE BUSH *CBS 6791*	16	12

MUSTAFAS – *See STAIFFI and his MUSTAFAS*

MXM *Italy, male/female vocal/instrumental group* — 1 wk

2 Jun 90	NOTHING COMPARES 2 U *London LON 267*	68	1

MY BLOODY VALENTINE
UK, male/female vocal/instrumental group — 5 wks

5 May 90	SOON *Creation CRE 073*	41	3
16 Feb 91	TO HERE KNOWS WHEN *Creation CRE 085*	29	2

MY LIFE STORY *UK, male/female vocal/instrumental group* — 8 wks

17 Aug 96	12 REASONS WHY I LOVE HER *Parlophone CDR 6442*	32	2
9 Nov 96	SPARKLE *Parlophone CDR 6450*	34	2
1 Mar 97	THE KINGDOM OF KISSINGDOM *Parlophone CDRS 6457*	35	1
17 May 97	STRUMPET *Parlophone CDR 6464*	27	2
23 Aug 97	DUCHESS *Parlophone CDR 6474*	39	1

MYA – *See BLACKSTREET; MASE; Pras MICHEL*

Tim MYCROFT – *See SOUNDS NICE*

UK No 1 ★   UK Top 10 ●   UK million seller ◆   UK entry at No 1 ■   US No 1 ▲

Alicia MYERS *US, female vocalist*   **3 wks**

1 Sep 84	YOU GET THE BEST FROM ME (SAY SAY SAY) *MCA MCA 914*	58	3

Billie MYERS ☺ ✎ *UK, female vocalist*   **12 wks**

11 Apr 98 ●	KISS THE RAIN *Universal UND 56182*	4	9
25 Jul 98	TELL ME *Universal UND 56201*	28	3

Richard MYHILL ☺ *UK, male vocalist*   **9 wks**

1 Apr 78	IT TAKES TWO TO TANGO *Mercury 6007 167*	17	9

Alannah MYLES ☺ ✎ *Canada, female vocalist*   **17 wks**

17 Mar 90 ●	BLACK VELVET *East West A 8742* ▲	2	15
16 Jun 90	LOVE IS *East West A 8918*	61	2

Marie MYRIAM *France, female vocalist*   **4 wks**

28 May 77	L'OISEAU ET L'ENFANT *Polydor 2056 634*	42	4

MYRON *US male vocalist*   **1 wk**

22 Nov 97	WE CAN GET DOWN *Island Black Music CID 677*	74	1

MYSTERIANS – See ? (QUESTION MARK) and the MYSTERIANS

MYSTI – See CAMOUFLAGE featuring MYSTI

MYSTIC MERLIN 🔊 🎤
US, male vocal/instrumental and magic group   **9 wks**

26 Apr 80	JUST CAN'T GIVE YOU UP *Capitol CL 16133*	20	9

MYSTICA *Israel, male production trio*   **2 wks**

24 Jan 98	EVER REST *Perfecto PERF 152CD*	62	1
9 May 98	AFRICAN HORIZON *Perfecto PERF 161CD*	59	1

Youssou N'DOUR 🌐 *Senegal, male vocalist*   **35 wks**

3 Jun 89	SHAKING THE TREE *Virgin VS 1167* [1]	61	3
22 Dec 90	SHAKING THE TREE (re-issue) *Virgin VS 1322* [1]	57	4
25 Jun 94 ●	7 SECONDS *Columbia 6605082* [2]	3	21
24 Dec 94	7 SECONDS (re-entry) *Columbia 6605082* [2]	54	4
14 Jan 95	UNDECIDED *Columbia 6609712*	53	2
10 Oct 98	HOW COME *Interscope IND 95598* [3]	52	1

[1] Youssou N'Dour and Peter Gabriel [2] Youssou N'Dour (featuring Neneh Cherry)
[3] Youssou N'Dour and Canibus

*The re-issue of 'Shaking the Tree' was listed with its flip side, 'Solsbury Hill'
by Peter Gabriel*

N-JOI ☺ *UK, male instrumental/production group*   **28 wks**

27 Oct 90	ANTHEM *Deconstruction PB 44041*	45	5
2 Mar 91	ADRENALIN EP *Deconstruction PT 44344*	23	5
6 Apr 91 ●	ANTHEM (re-issue) *Deconstruction PB 44445*	8	8
22 Feb 92	LIVE IN MANCHESTER (PARTS 1 + 2) *Deconstruction PT 45252*	12	5

24 Jul 93	THE DRUMSTRUCK EP *Deconstruction 74321154832*	33	3
17 Dec 94	PAPILLON *Deconstruction 74321252132*	70	1
8 Jul 95	BAD THINGS *Deconstruction 74321277292*	57	1

*Tracks on Adrenalin (EP): Adrenalin / The Kraken / Rhythm Zone / Phoenix
Tracks on The Drumstruck (EP): The Void / Boom Bass / Drumstruck*

'N SYNC *US, male vocal group*   **3 wks**

13 Sep 97	TEARIN' UP MY HEART *Arista 74321505152*	40	2
22 Nov 97	I WANT YOU BACK *Arista 74321541122*	62	1

N-TRANCE ☺ ☺ *US male production duo*   **61 wks**

7 May 94	SET YOU FREE *All Around The World CDGLOBE 124* [1]	39	4
22 Oct 94	TURN UP THE POWER *All Around The World CDGLOBE 125*	23	3
14 Jan 95 ●	SET YOU FREE (re-mix) *All Around The World CDGLOBE 126*	2	15
16 Sep 95 ●	STAYIN' ALIVE *All Around The World CDGLOBE 131* [2]	2	11
24 Feb 96	ELECTRONIC PLEASURE *All Around The World CDGLOBE 135*	11	4
5 Apr 97	D.I.S.C.O. *All Around The World CDGLOBE 153*	11	6
23 Aug 97	THE MIND OF THE MACHINE *All Around The World CDGLOBE 159*	15	4
1 Nov 97 ●	DA YA THINK I'M SEXY? *All Around The World CDGLOBE 150* [3]	7	10
12 Sep 98	PARADISE CITY *All Around The World CDGLOBE 140*	28	3
19 Dec 98	TEARS IN THE RAIN *All Around The Globe CDGLOBE 185*	53	1

[1] N-Trance featuring Kelly Llorenna [2] N-Trance featuring Ricardo Da Force
[3] N-Trance featuring Rod Stewart

*Although she is the vocalist on both versions of 'Set You Free', Kelly Llorenna is
only credited on the former. Similarly, Ricardo da Force is the vocalist on both
'Stayin' Alive' and 'Electronic Pleasure'*

N-TYCE [R&B] *UK, female vocal group*   **15 wks**

5 Jul 97	HEY DJ! (PLAY THAT SONG) *Telstar CDSTAS 2885*	20	2
13 Sep 97	WE COME TO PARTY *Telstar CDSTAS 2915*	12	4
28 Feb 98	TELEFUNKIN' *Telstar CDSTAS 2944*	16	5
6 Jun 98	BOOM BOOM *Telstar CDSTAS 2971*	18	4

Jimmy NAIL ☺ *UK, male vocalist*   **72 wks**

27 Apr 85 ●	LOVE DON'T LIVE HERE ANYMORE *Virgin VS 764*	3	11
11 Jul 92 ★	AIN'T NO DOUBT *East West YZ 686*	1	12
3 Oct 92	LAURA *East West YZ 702*	58	2
26 Nov 94 ●	CROCODILE SHOES *East West YZ 867CD*	4	13
11 Feb 95	COWBOY DREAMS *East West YZ 878CD*	13	7
11 Mar 95	CROCODILE SHOES (re-entry) *East West YZ 867CD*	68	3
8 Apr 95	CROCODILE SHOES (2nd re-entry) *East West YZ 867CD*	56	4
6 May 95	CALLING OUT YOUR NAME *East West YZ 935CD*	65	1
28 Oct 95	BIG RIVER *East West EW 008CD*	18	5
23 Dec 95	LOVE *East West EW 018CD*	33	4
3 Feb 96	BIG RIVER (re-mix) *East West EW 024CD*	72	2
16 Nov 96	COUNTRY BOY *East West EW 070CD*	25	7
21 Nov 98	THE FLAME STILL BURNS *London LONCD 420* [1]	47	1

[1] Jimmy Nail with Strange Fruit

NAKATOMI *Scotland, male/female production group*   **2 wks**

7 Feb 98	CHILDREN OF THE NIGHT *Peach PCHCD 006*	47	2

NAKED EYES *UK, male vocal/instrumental duo*   **3 wks**

23 Jul 83	ALWAYS SOMETHING THERE TO REMIND ME *RCA 348*	59	3

NALIN & KANE ☺ *Germany, male DJ/production duo*   **6 wks**

1 Nov 97	BEACHBALL *ffrr FCD 318*	48	1
3 Oct 98	BEACHBALL (remix) *LONDON FCD349*	17	5

See also NALIN INC

NALIN INC *Germany, male vocalist*   **1 wk**

28 Mar 98	PLANET VIOLET *Logic 74321565702*	51	1

See also NALIN & KANE

NAPOLEON XIV ☺ US, male vocalist   10 wks

| 4 Aug 66 | ● THEY'RE COMING TO TAKE ME AWAY HA-HAAA! | | |
| | *Warner Bros. WB 5831* | 4 | 10 |

NARADA – See Narada Michael WALDEN

NAS ◄━ US, male rapper   15 wks

28 May 94	IT AIN'T HARD TO TELL *Columbia 6604702*	64	1
17 Aug 96	IF I RULED THE WORLD *Columbia 6634022*	12	7
25 Jan 97	STREET DREAMS *Columbia 6641302*	12	4
14 Jun 97	HEAD OVER HEALS *Epic 6645942* [1]	18	3

[1] Allure featuring NAS

Johnny NASH ⌇ 🎤 US singer/songwriter/actor and label co-owner,
b. 19 August, 1940, Texas. This versatile vocalist first charted in his
homeland in 1957. After recording in Jamaica in the late 1960s, he
helped to popularise reggae on both sides of the Atlantic and
introduced the public to Bob Marley's songs   106 wks

7 Aug 68	● HOLD ME TIGHT *Regal Zonophone RZ 3010*	5	16
8 Jan 69	YOU GOT SOUL *Major Minor MM 586*	6	12
2 Apr 69	CUPID *Major Minor MM 603*	6	11
25 Jun 69	CUPID (re-entry) *Major Minor MM 603*	50	1
1 Apr 72	STIR IT UP *CBS 7800*	13	12
24 Jun 72	● I CAN SEE CLEARLY NOW *CBS 8113* ▲	5	15
7 Oct 72	THERE ARE MORE QUESTIONS THAN ANSWERS *CBS 8351*	9	9
14 Jun 75	★ TEARS ON MY PILLOW *CBS 3220*	1	11
11 Oct 75	LET'S BE FRIENDS *CBS 3597*	42	3
12 Jun 76	(WHAT A) WONDERFUL WORLD *Epic EPC 4294*	25	7
9 Nov 85	ROCK ME BABY *2000 AD FED 19*	47	4
15 Apr 89	I CAN SEE CLEARLY NOW (re-mix) *Epic JN 1*	54	5

NASHVILLE TEENS ☺ UK, male vocal/instrumental group   37 wks

9 Jul 64	● TOBACCO ROAD *Decca F 11930*	6	13
22 Oct 64	● GOOGLE EYE *Decca F 12000*	10	11
4 Mar 65	FIND MY WAY BACK HOME *Decca F 12089*	34	6
20 May 65	THIS LITTLE BIRD *Decca F 12143*	38	4
3 Feb 66	THE HARD WAY *Decca F 12316*	45	2
24 Feb 66	THE HARD WAY (re-entry) *Decca F 12316*	48	1

NATASHA ☺ UK, female vocalist   16 wks

| 5 Jun 82 | IKO IKO *Towerbell TOW 22* | 10 | 11 |
| 4 Sep 82 | THE BOOM BOOM ROOM *Towerbell TOW 25* | 44 | 5 |

NATURAL BORN CHILLERS UK, male production duo   3 wks

| 1 Nov 97 | ROCK THE FUNKY BEAT *East West EW 138CD1* | 30 | 3 |

NATURAL BORN GROOVES Belgium, male DJ/production duo –
Burn Boon and Jaco van Rijsvijck   3 wks

| 2 Nov 96 | FORERUNNER *XL XLS 76CD* | 64 | 1 |
| 19 Apr 97 | GROOVEBIRD *Positiva CDTIV 75* | 21 | 2 |

NATURAL LIFE UK, male/female vocal/instrumental group   3 wks

| 7 Mar 92 | NATURAL LIFE *Tribe NLIFE 3* | 47 | 3 |

NATURAL SELECTION US, male vocal/instrumental duo   2 wks

| 9 Nov 91 | DO ANYTHING *East West A 8724* | 69 | 2 |

NATURALS UK, male vocal/instrumental group   9 wks

| 20 Aug 64 | I SHOULD HAVE KNOWN BETTER *Parlophone R 5165* | 24 | 9 |

David NAUGHTON US, male vocalist   6 wks

| 25 Aug 79 | MAKIN' IT *RSO 32* | 44 | 6 |

NAUGHTY BY NATURE ◄━ US, male rap group   16 wks

| 9 Nov 91 | O.P.P. *Big Life BLR 62* | 73 | 1 |
| 20 Jun 92 | O.P.P. (re-issue) *Big Life BLR 74* | 35 | 3 |

30 Jan 93	HIP HOP HOORAY *Big Life BLRD 89*	22	3
19 Jun 93	IT'S ON *Big Life BLRD 99*	48	2
27 Nov 93	HIP HOP HOORAY (re-mix) *Big Life BLRDA 104*	20	4
29 Apr 95	FEEL ME FLOW *Big Life BLRD 115*	23	3

NAVIGATOR – see FREESTYLERS

Maria NAYLER UK, female vocalist   14 wks

9 Mar 96	BE AS ONE *Deconstruction 74321342962* [1]	17	3
16 Nov 96	● ONE AND ONE *Deconstruction 74321427692* [2]	3	7
7 Mar 98	NAKED AND SACRED *Deconstruction 74321534242*	32	3
5 Sep 98	WILL YOU BE WITH ME/LOVE IS THE GOD		
	Deconstruction 74321591772	65	1

[1] Sasha and Maria   [2] Robert Miles featuring Maria Nayler

NAZARETH ✍ UK, male vocal/instrumental group   75 wks

5 May 73	● BROKEN DOWN ANGEL *Mooncrest MOON 1*	9	11
21 Jul 73	● BAD BAD BOY *Mooncrest MOON 9*	10	9
13 Oct 73	THIS FLIGHT TONIGHT *Mooncrest MOON 14*	11	13
23 Mar 74	SHANGHAI'D IN SHANGHAI *Mooncrest MOON 22*	41	4
14 Jun 75	MY WHITE BICYCLE *Mooncrest MOON 47*	14	8
15 Nov 75	HOLY ROLLER *Mountain TOP 3*	36	4
24 Sep 77	HOT TRACKS EP *Mountain NAZ 1*	15	11
18 Feb 78	GONE DEAD TRAIN *Mountain NAZ 002*	49	2
13 May 78	PLACE IN YOUR HEART *Mountain TOP 37*	70	1
27 May 78	PLACE IN YOUR HEART (re-entry) *Mountain TOP 37*	74	1
27 Jan 79	MAY THE SUN SHINE *Mountain NAZ 003*	22	8
28 Jul 79	STAR *Mountain TOP 45*	54	3

Tracks on Hot Tracks EP: Love Hurts/This Flight Tonight/Broken Down Angel/
Hair of the Dog

NAZLYN – See M-BEAT

Me'Shell NDEGEOCELLO
US, female vocalist/instrumentalist – bass   5 wks

12 Feb 94	IF THAT'S YOUR BOYFRIEND (HE WASN'T LAST NIGHT)		
	Maverick W 0223CD1	74	1
3 Sep 94	WILD NIGHT *Mercury MERCD 409* [1]	34	3
1 Mar 97	NEVER MISS THE WATER *Reprise W 0393CD* [2]	59	1

[1] John Mellencamp featuring Me'Shell NdegeoCello   [2] Chaka Khan featuring
Me'Shell Ndegeocello

NEARLY GOD UK, male/female vocal/instrumental group   2 wks

| 20 Apr 96 | POEMS *Durban Poison DPCD 3* | 28 | 2 |

Terry NEASON UK, female vocalist   1 wk

| 25 Jun 94 | LIFEBOAT *WEA YZ 830* | 72 | 1 |

NEBULA II UK, male instrumental/production group   3 wks

| 1 Feb 92 | SEANCE/ATHEAMA *Reinforced RIVET 1211* | 55 | 2 |
| 16 May 92 | FLATLINERS *J4M 12NEBULA 2* | 54 | 1 |

NED'S ATOMIC DUSTBIN ☹
UK, male vocal/instrumental group   24 wks

14 Jul 90	KILL YOUR TELEVISION *Chapter 22 CHAP 48*	53	2
27 Oct 90	UNTIL YOU FIND OUT *Chapter 22 CHAP 52*	51	2
9 Mar 91	HAPPY *Columbia 6566807*	16	4
21 Sep 91	TRUST *Furtive 6574627*	21	4
10 Oct 92	NOT SLEEPING AROUND *Furtive 6583866*	19	3
5 Dec 92	INTACT *Furtive 6588166*	36	6
25 Mar 95	ALL I ASK OF MYSELF IS THAT I HOLD TOGETHER		
	Furtive 6613565	33	2
15 Jul 95	STUCK *Furtive 6620562*	64	1

Joey NEGRO UK, male producer – Dave Lee   10 wks

18 Mar 89	REACHIN' *Republic LIC 006* [1]	70	1
16 Nov 91	DO WHAT YOU FEEL *Ten TEN 391*	36	3
21 Dec 91	REACHIN' (re-mix) *Republic LIC 160* [2]	70	1

18 Jul 92		ENTER YOUR FANTASY EP *Ten TEN 397*	35	3
25 Sep 93		WHAT HAPPENED TO THE MUSIC		
		Virgin VSCD 1466	51	2

[1] Phase II [2] Joey Negro presents Phase II

Tracks on Enter Your Fantasy EP: Love Fantasy / Get Up / Enter Your Mind / Everybody
See also LI KWAN

neil ☯ *UK, male vocalist*   **10 wks**

14 Jul 84	●	HOLE IN MY SHOE *WEA YZ 10*	2	10

Vince NEIL *US, male vocalist*   **1 wk**

3 Oct 92		YOU'RE INVITED (BUT YOUR FRIEND CAN'T COME)		
		Hollywood HWD 123	63	1

NEJA *Italy, female vocalist*   **1 wk**

26 Sep 98		RESTLESS (I KNOW YOU) *Panorama CDPAN 1*	47	1

NEK *Italy, male vocalist*   **1 wk**

29 Aug 98		LAURA *Coalition COLA 054CD*	59	1

NELSON *US, male vocal duo*   **3 wks**

27 Oct 90		(CAN'T LIVE WITHOUT YOUR) LOVE AND AFFECTION		
		DGC GEF 82 ▲	54	3

Bill NELSON
UK, male vocalist/instrumentalist – guitar and synthesizer   **12 wks**

24 Feb 79		FURNITURE MUSIC *Harvest HAR 5176* [1]	59	3
5 May 79		REVOLT INTO STYLE *Harvest HAR 5183* [1]	69	2
5 Jul 80		DO YOU DREAM IN COLOUR? *Cocteau COQ 1*	52	4
13 Jun 81		YOUTH OF NATION ON FIRE *Mercury WILL 2*	73	3

[1] Bill Nelson's Red Noise

Pete NELSON – *See WHITE PLAINS*

Phyllis NELSON ♪ *US, female vocalist*   **24 wks**

23 Feb 85	★	MOVE CLOSER *Carrerre CAR 337*	1	21
21 May 94		MOVE CLOSER (re-issue) *EMI CDEMCT 9*	34	3

Ricky NELSON ♪ *TV-star turned teen-idol and later singer/songwriter,*
b. 8 May, 1940, New Jersey, d. 31 December, 1985. He was virtually raised
on a US radio/TV family show. In the 1950s, he enjoyed sales on a par with
Elvis Presley and Pat Boone. Both his father and his two sons also
topped the US chart (1935 and 1990)   **137 wks**

21 Feb 58		STOOD UP *London HLP 8542*	27	1
7 Mar 58		STOOD UP (re-entry) *London HLP 8542*	29	1
22 Aug 58	●	POOR LITTLE FOOL *London HLP 8670* ▲	4	13
7 Nov 58	●	SOMEDAY *London HLP 8732*	9	13
21 Nov 58		I GOT A FEELING *London HLP 8732*	27	1
28 Nov 58		POOR LITTLE FOOL (re-entry)		
		London HLP 8670	28	1
17 Apr 59	●	IT'S LATE *London HLP 8817*	3	20
15 May 59		NEVER BE ANYONE ELSE BUT YOU		
		London HLP 8817	19	1
5 Jun 59		NEVER BE ANYONE ELSE BUT YOU (re-entry)		
		London HLP 8817	14	9
4 Sep 59		SWEETER THAN YOU *London HLP 8927*	19	3
11 Sep 59		JUST A LITTLE TOO MUCH *London HLP 8927*	11	8
15 Jan 60		I WANNA BE LOVED *London HLP 9021*	30	1
7 Jul 60		YOUNG EMOTIONS *London HLP 9121*	48	1
1 Jun 61	●	HELLO MARY LOU/TRAVELLIN' MAN		
		London HLP 9347 ▲	2	18
16 Nov 61		EVERLOVIN' *London HLP 9440* [1]	23	5
29 Mar 62		YOUNG WORLD *London HLP 9524*	19	13
30 Aug 62		TEENAGE IDOL *London HLP 9583* [1]	39	4
17 Jan 63		IT'S UP TO YOU *London HLP 9648* [1]	22	9
17 Oct 63		FOOLS RUSH IN *Brunswick 05895* [1]	12	9
30 Jan 64		FOR YOU *Brunswick 05900* [1]	14	10
21 Oct 72		GARDEN PARTY *MCA MU 1165* [1]	41	4

24 Aug 91		HELLO MARY LOU (GOODBYE HEART) (re-issue)		
		Liberty EMCT 2	45	5

[1] Rick Nelson

Sandy NELSON ♪ *US, male instrumentalist – drums*   **42 wks**

6 Nov 59	●	TEEN BEAT *Top Rank JAR 197*	9	11
5 Feb 60		TEEN BEAT (re-entry) *Top Rank JAR 197*	25	1
14 Dec 61	●	LET THERE BE DRUMS *London HLP 9466*	3	16
22 Mar 62		DRUMS ARE MY BEAT *London HLP 9521*	30	6
7 Jun 62		DRUMMIN' UP A STORM *London HLP 9558*	39	8

Shara NELSON ♪ ☺ *UK, female vocalist*   **23 wks**

24 Jul 93		DOWN THAT ROAD *Cooltempo CDCOOL 275*	19	6
18 Sep 93		ONE GOODBYE IN TEN *Cooltempo CDCOOL 279*	21	5
12 Feb 94		UPTIGHT *Cooltempo CDCOOL 286*	19	5
4 Jun 94		NOBODY *Cooltempo CDCOOL 290*	49	1
10 Sep 94		INSIDE OUT / DOWN THAT ROAD (re-mix)		
		Cooltempo CDCOOLX 295	34	3
16 Sep 95		ROUGH WITH THE SMOOTH *Cooltempo CDCOOL 311*	30	2
5 Dec 98		SENSE OF DANGER *Pagan PAGAN 024CDS* [1]	61	1

[1] Presence featuring Shara Nelson

Shelley NELSON – *See TIN TIN OUT*

Willie NELSON ☾ ✈ *US, male vocalist*   **13 wks**

31 Jul 82		ALWAYS ON MY MIND *CBS A 2511*	49	3
7 Apr 84		TO ALL THE GIRLS I'VE LOVED BEFORE *CBS A 4252* [1]	17	10

[1] Julio Iglesias and Willie Nelson

NENA ☯ *Germany, female/male vocal/instrumental group*   **14 wks**

4 Feb 84	★	99 RED BALLOONS *Epic A 4074*	1	12
5 May 84		JUST A DREAM *Epic H 3249*	70	2

Frances NERO ☺ *US, female vocalist*   **9 wks**

13 Apr 91		FOOTSTEPS FOLLOWING ME *Debut DEBT 3109*	17	9

NERO and the GLADIATORS *UK, male instrumental group*   **6 wks**

23 Mar 61		ENTRY OF THE GLADIATORS *Decca F 11329*	50	1
6 Apr 61		ENTRY OF THE GLADIATORS (re-entry) *Decca F 11329*	37	4
27 Jul 61		IN THE HALL OF THE MOUNTAIN KING *Decca F 11367*	48	1

Ann NESBY *US, female vocalist*   **3 wks**

21 Dec 96		WITNESS EP *AM:PM 5875612*	42	2
17 May 97		HOLD ON EP *AM:PM 5822332*	75	1

Tracks on Witness EP: Can I Get a Witness / (mix) / In the Spirit / I'm Still Wearing
Your Name. Tracks on Hold On EP: Hold On (Mousse T's Uplifting Garage Edit) /
Hold On (Mousse T's Hard Soul Remix) / Hold On (Klub Head Mix) / This Weekend
(Laidback Mix)

Michael NESMITH *US, male vocalist*   **6 wks**

26 Mar 77		RIO *Island WIP 6373*	28	6

NETWORK *UK, male vocal/instrumental group*   **4 wks**

12 Dec 92		BROKEN WINGS *Chrysalis CHS 3923*	46	4

NEVADA *UK, male/female vocal/instrumental group*   **1 wk**

8 Jan 83		IN THE BLEAK MID WINTER *Polydor POSP 203*	71	1

Robbie NEVIL ☯ *US, male vocalist*   **24 wks**

20 Dec 86	●	C'EST LA VIE *Manhattan MT 14*	3	11
2 May 87		DOMINOES *Manhattan MT 19*	26	6
11 Jul 87		WOT'S IT TO YA *Manhattan MT 24*	43	7

Aaron NEVILLE – *See Linda RONSTADT; NEVILLE BROTHERS*

UK No 1 ★   UK Top 10 ●   UK million seller ◆   UK entry at No 1 ■   US No 1 ▲

NEVILLE BROTHERS ♪ US, male vocal/instrumental group　7 wks

| 25 Nov 89 | WITH GOD ON OUR SIDE A & M AM 545 | 47 | 6 |
| 7 Jul 90 | BIRD ON A WIRE A & M AM 568 | 72 | 1 |

Jason NEVINS 📻 ☺ US, male DJ/producer　21 wks

21 Feb 98	IT'S LIKE THAT (IMPORT) Columbia 6652932 [1]	63	3
21 Mar 98 ★	IT'S LIKE THAT Smile Communications SM 90652 [1]	1	17
18 Apr 98	IT'S TRICKY (re-mix) Epidrome EPD 6656982 [1]	74	1

[1] Run-DMC vs Jason Nevins

NEW ATLANTIC ☺ UK, male instrumental/production duo　15 wks

29 Feb 92	I KNOW 3 Beat 3BT 1	12	7
3 Oct 92	INTO THE FUTURE 3 Beat 3BT 2 [1]	70	1
13 Feb 93	TAKE OFF SOME TIME 3 Beat 3BTCD 14	64	1
26 Nov 94	THE SUNSHINE AFTER THE RAIN Ffrreedom TABCD 223 [2]	26	6

[1] New Atlantic featuring Linda Wright [2] New Atlantic / U4EA featuring Berri

'The Sunshine After the Rain' was re-issued in 1995, credited simply to the vocalist Berri

NEW BOHEMIANS – See Edie BRICKELL and the NEW BOHEMIANS

NEW EDITION (R&B) ✪ US, male vocal group　36 wks

16 Apr 83 ★	CANDY GIRL London LON 21	1	13
13 Aug 83	POPCORN LOVE London LON 31	43	5
23 Feb 85	MR. TELEPHONE MAN MCA MCA 938	19	9
15 Apr 89	CRUCIAL MCA MCA 23934	70	1
10 Aug 96	HIT ME OFF MCA MCSTD 48014	20	4
7 Jun 97	SOMETHING ABOUT YOU MCA MCSTD 48032	16	4

NEW GENERATION UK, male vocal/instrumental group　5 wks

| 26 Jun 68 | SMOKEY BLUES AWAY Spark SRL 1007 | 38 | 5 |

NEW KIDS ON THE BLOCK ✪ US, male vocal group　90 wks

16 Sep 89	HANGIN' TOUGH CBS BLOCK 1 ▲	52	4
11 Nov 89 ★	YOU GOT IT (THE RIGHT STUFF) CBS BLOCK 2	1	13
6 Jan 90 ★	HANGIN' TOUGH (re-issue) CBS BLOCK 3	1	9
17 Mar 90 ●	I'LL BE LOVING YOU (FOREVER) CBS BLOCK 4 ▲	5	8
12 May 90 ●	COVER GIRL CBS BLOCK 5	4	8
16 Jun 90 ●	STEP BY STEP CBS BLOCK 6 ▲	2	7
4 Aug 90 ●	TONIGHT CBS BLOCK 7	3	10
13 Oct 90 ●	LET'S TRY AGAIN/DIDN'T I BLOW YOUR MIND CBS BLOCK 8	8	5
8 Dec 90 ●	THIS ONE'S FOR THE CHILDREN CBS BLOCK 9	9	7
9 Feb 91	GAMES CBS 6566267	14	4
18 May 91	CALL IT WHAT YOU WANT Columbia 6567857	12	5
14 Dec 91	IF YOU GO AWAY Columbia 6576667	9	5
19 Feb 94	DIRTY DAWG Columbia 6600362 [1]	27	3
26 Mar 94	NEVER LET YOU GO Columbia 6602072 [1]	42	2

[1] NKOTB

NEW MODEL ARMY UK, male vocal/instrumental group　33 wks

27 Apr 85	NO REST EMI NMA 1	28	5
3 Aug 85	BETTER THAN THEM/NO SENSE EMI NMA 2	49	2
30 Nov 85	BRAVE NEW WORLD EMI NMA 3	57	1
8 Nov 86	FIFTY-FIRST STATE EMI NMA 4	71	2
28 Feb 87	POISON STREET EMI NMA 5	64	1
26 Sep 87	WHITE COATS EP EMI NMA 6	50	3
21 Jan 89	STUPID QUESTION EMI NMA 7	31	3
11 Mar 89	VAGABONDS EMI NMA 8	37	3
10 Jun 89	GREEN AND GREY EMI NMA 9	37	3
8 Sep 90	GET ME OUT EMI NMA 10	34	3
3 Nov 90	PURITY EMI NMA 11	61	2
8 Jun 91	SPACE EMI NMA 12	39	2
20 Feb 93	HERE COMES THE WAR Epic 6589352	25	2
24 Jul 93	LIVING IN THE ROSE (THE BALLADS EP) Epic 6592492	51	1

Tracks on White Coats EP: The Charge / Chinese Whispers / My Country.
Tracks on Living in the Rose (The Ballads EP): Living in the Rose / Drummy B /
Marry the Sea, Sleepwalking
See also VARIOUS ARTISTS (EPs & LPs) – Gimme Shelter (EP)

NEW MUSIK ✪ UK, male vocal/instrumental group　27 wks

6 Oct 79	STRAIGHT LINES GTO GT 255	53	5
19 Jan 80	LIVING BY NUMBERS GTO GT 261	13	8
26 Apr 80	THIS WORLD OF WATER GTO GT 268	31	7
12 Jul 80	SANCTUARY GTO GT 275	31	7

NEW ORDER ☺ ☹ Innovative Mancunian group featuring three former members of critically acclaimed Joy Division: Bernard Sumner (v/g), Peter Hook (b), Stephen Morris (d), and augmented by Gillian Gilbert (k). 'Blue Monday' remains the UK's biggest-selling 12-inch single of all time　179 wks

14 Mar 81	CEREMONY Factory FAC 33	34	5
3 Oct 81	PROCESSION/EVERYTHING'S GONE GREEN Factory FAC 53	38	5
22 May 82	TEMPTATION Factory FAC 63	29	7
19 Mar 83	BLUE MONDAY Factory FAC 73	12	17
13 Aug 83 ●	BLUE MONDAY (re-entry) Factory FAC 73	9	17
3 Sep 83	CONFUSION Factory FAC 93	12	7
7 Jan 84	BLUE MONDAY (2nd re-entry) Factory FAC 73	52	4
28 Apr 84	THIEVES LIKE US Factory FAC 103	18	5
25 May 85	THE PERFECT KISS Factory FAC 123	46	4
9 Nov 85	SUB-CULTURE Factory FAC 133	63	4
29 Mar 86	SHELLSHOCK Factory FAC 143	28	5
27 Sep 86	STATE OF THE NATION Factory FAC 153	30	3
27 Sep 86	THE PEEL SESSIONS (1ST JUNE 1982) Strange Fruit SFPS 001	54	1
15 Nov 86	BIZARRE LOVE TRIANGLE Factory FAC 163	56	2
1 Aug 87 ●	TRUE FAITH Factory FAC 183/7	4	10
19 Dec 87	TOUCHED BY THE HAND OF GOD Factory FAC 1937	20	7
7 May 88 ●	BLUE MONDAY (re-mix) Factory FAC 737	3	11
10 Dec 88	FINE TIME Factory FAC 2237	11	8
11 Mar 89	ROUND AND ROUND Factory FAC 2637	21	7
9 Sep 89	RUN 2 Factory FAC 273	49	2
2 Jun 90 ★	WORLD IN MOTION . . . Factory/MCA FAC 2937 [1]	1	12
17 Apr 93 ●	REGRET Centredate Co. NUOCD 1	4	7
3 Jul 93	RUINED IN A DAY Centredate Co. NUOCD 2	22	4
4 Sep 93	WORLD (THE PRICE OF LOVE) Centredate Co. NUOCD 3	13	5
18 Dec 93	SPOOKY Centredate Co. NUOCD 4	22	4
19 Nov 94 ●	TRUE FAITH (re-mix) Centredate Co. NUOCD 5	9	8
21 Jan 95	NINETEEN63 London NUOCD 6	21	4
5 Aug 95	BLUE MONDAY (2nd re-mix) London NUOCD 7	17	4

[1] Englandneworder

Group was male only on first hit. 'Blue Monday' in 1988 is a re-mixed version of the original 1983 hit which was made available on 7-inch for the first time, hence the slight difference in catalogue number. Sales for the re-mix and the original were combined from 7 May, 1988, onwards when calculating its chart position

NEW ORLEANS JAZZMEN – See Terry LIGHTFOOT and his NEW ORLEANS JAZZMEN

NEW POWER GENERATION (R&B)
US, male/female vocal/instrumental group　13 wks

1 Apr 95	GET WILD NPG 0061045	19	4
19 Aug 95	THE GOOD LIFE NPG 0061515	29	3
5 Jul 97	THE GOOD LIFE NPG 0061515 NPG	15	5
21 Nov 98	COME ON RCA 74321634722	65	1

See also PRINCE

NEW SEEKERS ✪ Anglo-Australian vocal group formed by ex-Seeker Keith Potger with Eve Graham, Lyn Paul, Peter Doyle, Paul Layton, Marty Kristian. Hits included a Coca-Cola advertisement and a Eurovision entry. The group sold more than 25 million records worldwide and equalled the eight Top 20 entries by The Seekers　143 wks

17 Oct 70	WHAT HAVE THEY DONE TO MY SONG MA Philips 6006 027	48	1
31 Oct 70	WHAT HAVE THEY DONE TO MY SONG MA (re-entry) Philips 6006 027	44	1
10 Jul 71 ●	NEVER ENDING SONG OF LOVE Philips 6006 125	2	19
18 Dec 71 ★	I'D LIKE TO TEACH THE WORLD TO SING (IN PERFECT HARMONY) Polydor 2058 184	1	21
4 Mar 72 ●	BEG STEAL OR BORROW Polydor 2058 201	2	13
10 Jun 72 ●	CIRCLES Polydor 2058 242	4	16
2 Dec 72	COME SOFTLY TO ME Polydor 2058 315 [1]	20	11

24 Feb 73	PINBALL WIZARD – SEE ME FEEL ME (MEDLEY)		
	Polydor 2058 338	16	8
7 Apr 73	NEVERTHELESS Polydor 2068 340 [2]	34	5
16 Jun 73	GOODBYE IS JUST ANOTHER WORD Polydor 2058 368	36	5
24 Nov 73 ★	YOU WON'T FIND ANOTHER FOOL LIKE ME		
	Polydor 2058 421	1	16
9 Mar 74 ●	I GET A LITTLE SENTIMENTAL OVER YOU		
	Polydor 2058 439	5	9
14 Aug 76	IT'S SO NICE (TO HAVE YOU HOME) CBS 4391	44	4
29 Jan 77	I WANNA GO BACK CBS 4786	25	4
15 Jul 78	ANTHEM (ONE DAY IN EVERY WEEK) CBS 6413	21	10

[1] New Seekers featuring Marty Kristian [2] Eve Graham and the New Seekers

NEW TONE AGE FAMILY – See Dread FLIMSTONE and the NEW TONE AGE FAMILY

NEW VAUDEVILLE BAND ◉
UK, male vocal/instrumental group — **43 wks**

8 Sep 66 ●	WINCHESTER CATHEDRAL Fontana TF 741 ▲	4	19
26 Jan 67 ●	PEEK-A-BOO Fontana TF 784 [1]	7	11
11 May 67	FINCHLEY CENTRAL Fontana TF 824	11	9
2 Aug 67	GREEN STREET GREEN Fontana TF 853	37	4

[1] New Vaudeville Band featuring Tristram

NEW WORLD ◉ Australia, male vocal/instrumental group — **53 wks**

27 Feb 71	ROSE GARDEN RAK 111	15	11
3 Jul 71 ●	TOM TOM TURNAROUND RAK 117	6	15
4 Dec 71	KARA KARA RAK 123	17	13
13 May 72 ●	SISTER JANE RAK 130	9	13
12 May 73	ROOF TOP SINGING RAK 148	50	1

NEW YORK CITY ✎ US, male vocal group — **11 wks**

21 Jul 73	I'M DOING FINE NOW RCA 2351	20	11

NEW YORK SKYY US, male/female vocal/instrumental group — **2 wks**

16 Jan 82	LET'S CELEBRATE Epic EPC A 1898	71	1
30 Jan 82	LET'S CELEBRATE (re-entry) Epic EPC A 1898	67	1

NEWBEATS ◉ US, male vocal group — **22 wks**

10 Sep 64	BREAD AND BUTTER Hickory 1269	15	9
23 Oct 71 ●	RUN BABY RUN London HL 10341	10	13

Booker NEWBURY III ✎ ◢ US, male vocalist — **11 wks**

28 May 83 ●	LOVE TOWN Polydor POSP 613	6	8
8 Oct 83	TEDDY BEAR Polydor POSP 637	44	3

Mickey NEWBURY US, male vocalist — **5 wks**

1 Jul 72	AMERICAN TRILOGY Elektra K 12047	42	5

NEWCLEUS US, male vocal/instrumental group — **6 wks**

3 Sep 83	JAM ON REVENGE (THE WIKKI WIKKI SONG)		
	Beckett BKS 8	44	6

Anthony NEWLEY ◉ ♫ Acclaimed actor/singer and composer.
b. 24 September. 1931. London. He appeared in more than 20 films before his singing career started. He was among the most innovative UK acts of the early rock years, before moving into musicals and cabaret — **129 wks**

1 May 59 ●	I'VE WAITED SO LONG Decca F 11127	3	15
8 May 59	IDLE ON PARADE EP Decca DFE 6566	13	4
12 Jun 59 ●	PERSONALITY Decca F 11142	6	12
15 Jan 60 ★	WHY Decca F 11194	1	17
24 Mar 60 ★	DO YOU MIND Decca F 11220	1	15
14 Jul 60 ●	IF SHE SHOULD COME TO YOU Decca F 11254	4	15
24 Nov 60 ●	STRAWBERRY FAIR Decca F 11295	3	11
16 Mar 61 ●	AND THE HEAVENS CRIED Decca F 11331	6	12
15 Jun 61	POP GOES THE WEASEL/BEE BOM		
	Decca F 11362	12	9
3 Aug 61	WHAT KIND OF FOOL AM I? Decca F 11376	36	8
25 Jan 62	D-DARLING Decca F 11419	25	6

26 Jul 62	THAT NOISE Decca F 11486	34	5

'Bee Bom' only listed together with 'Pop Goes the Weasel' for weeks of 15 and 22 June, 1961. It peaked at No 15. Tracks on Idle On Parade EP: I've Waited So Long/ Idle Rock-a-Boogie/Idle on Parade/Saturday Night Rock-a-Boogie

Tara NEWLEY – See E-ZEE POSSEE

Alfred NEWMAN – See VARIOUS ARTISTS (EPs & LPs) – Carousel LP

Brad NEWMAN UK, male vocalist — **1 wk**

22 Feb 62	SOMEBODY TO LOVE Fontana H 357	47	1

Dave NEWMAN UK, male vocalist — **6 wks**

15 Apr 72	THE LION SLEEPS TONIGHT Pye 7N 45134	48	1
29 Apr 72	THE LION SLEEPS TONIGHT (re-entry) Pye 7N 45134	34	5

NEWS – See Huey LEWIS and the NEWS

NEWS UK, male vocal/instrumental group — **3 wks**

29 Aug 81	AUDIO VIDEO George GEORGE 1	52	3

NEWTON UK, male vocalist — **6 wks**

15 Jul 95	SKY HIGH Bags Of Fun BAGSCD 6	56	2
15 Feb 97	SOMETIMES WHEN WE TOUCH Dominion CDDMIN 202	32	3
16 Aug 97	DON'T WORRY Dominion CDDMIN 206	61	1

Juice NEWTON US, female vocalist — **6 wks**

2 May 81	ANGEL OF THE MORNING Capitol CL 16189	43	6

Olivia NEWTON-JOHN ◉ Top female vocalist in the USA in the 1970s,
b. 26 September. 1948. Cambridge. This photogenic Australian-raised singer/actress has won numerous pop and country awards and was the first female to score one dozen US Top 5 singles — **234 wks**

20 Mar 71 ●	IF NOT FOR YOU Pye International 7N 25543	7	11
23 Oct 71 ●	BANKS OF THE OHIO Pye International 7N 25568	6	17
11 Mar 72	WHAT IS LIFE Pye International 7N 25575	16	8
13 Jan 73	TAKE ME HOME COUNTRY ROADS		
	Pye International 7N 25599	15	13
16 Mar 74 ●	LONG LIVE LOVE Pye International 7N 25638	11	8
12 Oct 74 ●	I HONESTLY LOVE YOU EMI 2216 ▲	22	6
11 Jun 77 ●	SAM EMI 2616	6	9
20 May 78 ★	YOU'RE THE ONE THAT I WANT RSO 006 [1] ◆ ▲	1	26
16 Sep 78 ★	SUMMER NIGHTS RSO 18 [1] ◆	1	19
4 Nov 78 ●	HOPELESSLY DEVOTED TO YOU RSO 17	2	11
16 Dec 78 ●	A LITTLE MORE LOVE EMI 2879	4	12
30 Jun 79	DEEPER THAN THE NIGHT EMI 2954	64	3
21 Jun 80 ★	XANADU Jet 185 [2]	1	11
23 Aug 80	MAGIC Jet 196 ▲	32	7
25 Oct 80	SUDDENLY Jet 7002 [3]	15	7
10 Oct 81 ●	PHYSICAL EMI 5234 ▲	7	16
16 Jan 82	LANDSLIDE EMI 5257	18	9
17 Apr 82	MAKE A MOVE ON ME EMI 5291	43	3
23 Oct 82	HEART ATTACK EMI 5347	46	4
15 Jan 83	I HONESTLY LOVE YOU (re-issue) EMI 5360	52	4
12 Nov 83	TWIST OF FATE EMI 5438	57	2
22 Dec 90 ●	THE GREASE MEGAMIX Polydor PO 114 [1]	3	10
23 Mar 91	GREASE – THE DREAM MIX PWL/Polydor PO 136 [4]	47	2
4 Jul 92	I NEED LOVE Mercury MER 370	75	1
9 Dec 95	HAD TO BE EMI CDEMS 410 [5]	22	4
25 Jul 98 ●	YOU'RE THE ONE THAT I WANT (re-issue)		
	Polydor 0441332 [1]	4	9

[1] John Travolta and Olivia Newton-John [2] Olivia Newton-John and Electric Light Orchestra [3] Olivia Newton-John and Cliff Richard [4] Franki Valli, John Travolta and Olivia Newton-John [5] Cliff Richard and Olivia Newton-John

NEXT US, male vocal trio — **3 wks**

6 Jun 98	TOO CLOSE Arista 74321580672 ▲	24	3

NIAGRA UK, male / female vocal / DJ/production duo — 1 wk

27 Sep 97	CLOUDBURST *Freeflow FLOW CD2*	.65	1

NICE UK, male instrumental group — 15 wks

10 Jul 68	AMERICA *Immediate IM 068*	.21	15

Paul NICHOLAS ◎ UK, male vocalist — 31 wks

17 Apr 76	REGGAE LIKE IT USED TO BE *RSO 2090 185*	.17	8
9 Oct 76 ●	DANCING WITH THE CAPTAIN *RSO 2090 206*	.8	9
4 Dec 76 ●	GRANDMA'S PARTY *RSO 2090 216*	.9	11
9 Jul 77	HEAVEN ON THE 7TH FLOOR *RSO 2090 249*	.40	3

Sue NICHOLLS ◎ UK, female vocalist — 8 wks

3 Jul 68	WHERE WILL YOU BE *Pye 7N 17565*	.17	8

Stevie NICKS ◎ ✍ US, female vocalist — 30 wks

15 Aug 81	STOP DRAGGIN' MY HEART AROUND *WEA K 79231* [1]	.50	4
25 Jan 86	I CAN'T WAIT *Parlophone R 6110*	.54	4
29 Mar 86	TALK TO ME *Parlophone R 6124*	.68	2
6 May 89	ROOMS ON FIRE *EMI EM 90*	.16	7
12 Aug 89	LONG WAY TO GO *EMI EM 97*	.60	2
11 Nov 89	WHOLE LOTTA TROUBLE *EMI EM 114*	.62	2
24 Aug 91	SOMETIMES IT'S A BITCH *EMI EM 203*	.40	4
9 Nov 91	I CAN'T WAIT (re-issue) *EMI EM 214*	.47	2
2 Jul 94	MAYBE LOVE *EMI CDEMS 328*	.42	3

[1] Stevie Nicks with Tom Petty and the Heartbreakers

NICOLE – See Nicole RAY

NICOLE ◎ Germany, female vocalist — 14 wks

8 May 82 ★	A LITTLE PEACE *CBS A 2365*	.1	9
21 Aug 82	GIVE ME MORE TIME *CBS A 2467*	.75	1

NICOLE US, female vocalist — 9 wks

28 Dec 85	NEW YORK EYES *Portrait A 6805* [1]	.41	7
26 Dec 92	ROCK THE HOUSE *React 12REACT 12* [2]	.63	1
6 Jul 96	RUNNIN' AWAY *Ore AG 18CD*	.69	1

[1] Nicole with Timmy Thomas [2] Source featuring Nicole

NICOLETTE UK, female vocalist — 1 wk

23 Dec 95	NO GOVERNMENT *Talkin Loud TLCD 1*	.67	1

NIGHTCRAWLERS featuring John REID ☺
UK, male vocalist/multi-instrumentalist – John Reid — 35 wks

15 Oct 94	PUSH THE FEELING ON *ffrr FCD 245* [1]	.22	5
4 Mar 95 ●	PUSH THE FEELING ON (re-mix) *ffrr FCD 257*	.3	11
27 May 95 ●	SURRENDER YOUR LOVE *Final Vinyl 74321283982*	.7	7
9 Sep 95	DON'T LET THE FEELING GO *Final Vinyl 7432129882*	.13	4
20 Jan 96	LET'S PUSH IT *Final Vinyl 74321328142*	.23	4
20 Apr 96	SHOULD I EVER (FALL IN LOVE) *Arista 74321358072*	.34	2
27 Jul 96	KEEP ON PUSHING OUR LOVE *Arista 74321390422* [2]	.30	2

[1] Nightcrawlers [2] Nightcrawlers featuring John Reid and Alysha Warren

Maxine NIGHTINGALE ✈ ✍ UK, female vocalist — 16 wks

1 Nov 75 ●	RIGHT BACK WHERE WE STARTED FROM *United Artists UP 36015*	.8	8
12 Mar 77	LOVE HIT ME *United Artists UP 36215*	.11	8

NIGHTMARES ON WAX UK, male instrumental group — 5 wks

27 Oct 90	AFTERMATH/I'M FOR REAL *Warp WAP 6*	.38	5

NIGHTWRITERS US, male vocal/instrumental duo — 2 wks

23 May 92	LET THE MUSIC USE YOU *Ffrreedom TABX 112*	.51	2

NIKKE? NICOLE! US, female rapper — 1 wk

1 Jun 91	NIKKE DOES IT BETTER *Love EVOL 5*	.73	1

NILSSON ◎ US, male vocalist — 55 wks

27 Sep 69	EVERYBODY'S TALKIN' *RCA 1876*	.50	1
11 Oct 69	EVERYBODY'S TALKIN' (re-entry) *RCA 1876*	.23	9
14 Mar 70	EVERYBODY'S TALKIN' (2nd re-entry) *RCA 1876*	.39	5
5 Feb 72 ★	WITHOUT YOU *RCA 2165* ▲	.1	20
3 Jun 72	COCONUT *RCA 2214*	.42	5
16 Oct 76	WITHOUT YOU (re-issue) *RCA 2733*	.22	8
20 Aug 77	ALL I THINK ABOUT IS YOU *RCA PB 9104*	.43	3
19 Feb 94	WITHOUT YOU (re-issue) *RCA 74321193092*	.47	4

NINA and FREDERICK ☾ Denmark, female/male vocal duo — 29 wks

18 Dec 59	MARY'S BOY CHILD *Columbia DB 4375*	.26	1
10 Mar 60	LISTEN TO THE OCEAN *Columbia DB 4332*	.47	1
7 Apr 60	LISTEN TO THE OCEAN (re-entry) *Columbia DB 4332*	.46	1
17 Nov 60 ●	LITTLE DONKEY *Columbia DB 4536*	.3	10
28 Sep 61	LONGTIME BOY *Columbia DB 4703*	.43	3
5 Oct 61	SUCU SUCU *Columbia DB 4632*	.23	13

NINE INCH NAILS
US, male vocalist – Trent Reznor and backing musicians — 13 wks

14 Sep 91	HEAD LIKE A HOLE *TVT IS 484*	.45	4
16 Nov 91	SIN *TVT IS 508*	.35	2
9 Apr 94	MARCH OF THE PIGS *TVT CID 592*	.45	3
18 Jun 94	CLOSER *TVT CIDX 596*	.25	3
13 Sep 97	THE PERFECT DRUG *Interscope IND 95542*	.43	1

999 UK, male vocal/instrumental group — 13 wks

25 Nov 78	HOMICIDE *United Artists UP 36467*	.40	3
27 Oct 79	FOUND OUT TOO LATE *Radar ADA 46*	.69	2
16 May 81	OBSESSED *Albion ION 1011*	.71	1
18 Jul 81	LIL RED RIDING HOOD *Albion ION 1017*	.59	3
14 Nov 81	INDIAN RESERVATION *Albion ION 1023*	.51	4

911 ◎ UK, male vocal group — 69 wks

11 May 96	NIGHT TO REMEMBER *Ginga CDGINGA 1*	.38	2
10 Aug 96	LOVE SENSATION *Ginga CDGINGA 2*	.21	4
9 Nov 96 ●	DON'T MAKE ME WAIT *Ginga VSCDT 1618*	.10	6
4 Jan 97	DON'T MAKE ME WAIT (re-entry) *Ginga VSCDT 1618*	.63	2
22 Feb 97	THE DAY WE FIND LOVE *Virgin VSCDT 1619*	.4	8
3 May 97	BODYSHAKIN' *Virgin VSCDT 1634*	.3	7
12 Jul 97	THE JOURNEY *Virgin VSCDT 1645*	.3	7
1 Nov 97	PARTY PEOPLE...FRIDAY NIGHT *Virgin VSCDT 1658*	.5	7
3 Jan 98	PARTY PEOPLE...FRIDAY NIGHT (re-entry) *Ginga VSCDT 1658*	.60	3
4 Apr 98 ●	ALL I WANT IS YOU *Virgin VSCDT 1681*	.4	6
20 Jun 98	ALL I WANT IS YOU (re-entry) *Virgin VSCDT 1681*	.64	1
4 Jul 98 ●	HOW DO YOU WANT ME TO LOVE YOU? *Ginga VSCDT 1686*	.10	7
24 Oct 98 ●	MORE THAN A WOMAN *Virgin VSCDT 1707*	.2	9

NINE YARDS UK, male vocal group — 1 wk

21 Nov 98	LONELINESS IS GONE *Virgin VSCDT 1696*	.70	1

9.9 US, female/male vocal group — 3 wks

6 Jul 85	ALL OF ME FOR ALL OF YOU *RCA PB 49951*	.53	3

1910 FRUITGUM CO. ◎ US, male vocal/instrumental group — 16 wks

20 Mar 68 ●	SIMON SAYS *Pye International 7N 25447*	.2	16

1927 Australia, male vocal/instrumental group — 6 wks

22 Apr 89	THAT'S WHEN I THINK OF YOU *WEA YZ 351*	.46	6

98 DEGREES US, male vocal group — 2 wks

29 Nov 97	INVISIBLE MAN *Motown 8607092*	.66	1
31 Oct 98	TRUE TO YOUR HEART *Motown 8608832* [1]	.51	1

[1] 98 Degrees featuring Stevie Wonder

99TH FLOOR ELEVATORS – *See Tony DE VIT*

NIRVANA *UK/Ireland, male vocal/instrumental duo* — **6 wks**

Date	Title	Pos	Wks
15 May 68	RAINBOW CHASER *Island WIP 6029*	34	6

NIRVANA ✒ *US, male vocal/instrumental group* — **36 wks**

Date	Title	Pos	Wks
30 Nov 91 ●	SMELLS LIKE TEEN SPIRIT *DGC DGCS 5*	7	6
14 Mar 92 ●	COME AS YOU ARE *DGC DGCS 7*	9	5
25 Jul 92	LITHIUM *DGC DGCS 9*	11	6
12 Dec 92	IN BLOOM *Geffen GFS 34*	28	7
6 Mar 93	OH THE GUILT *Touch And Go TG 83CD*	12	2
11 Sep 93 ●	HEART-SHAPED BOX *Geffen GFSTD 54*	5	5
18 Dec 93	ALL APOLOGIES/RAPE ME *Geffen GFSTD 66*	32	5

The listed flip side of 'Oh the Guilt' was Puss by Jesus Lizard

NITRO DELUXE *US, male multi-instrumentalist – Lee Junior* — **16 wks**

Date	Title	Pos	Wks
14 Feb 87	THIS BRUTAL HOUSE *Cooltempo COOL 142*	47	7
13 Jun 87	THIS BRUTAL HOUSE (re-entry) *Cooltempo COOL 142*	62	4
6 Feb 88	LET'S GET BRUTAL *Cooltempo COOL 142*	24	5

'Let's Get Brutal' is a re-mixed version of 'This Brutal House'

NITZER EBB *UK, male vocal/instrumental group* — **3 wks**

Date	Title	Pos	Wks
11 Jan 92	GODHEAD *Mute 1MUTE 135T*	56	1
11 Apr 92	ASCEND *Mute 110MUTE 145*	52	1
4 Mar 95	KICK IT *Mute LCDMUTE 155*	75	1

N.K.O.T.B. – *See NEW KIDS ON THE BLOCK*

NO AUTHORITY *US, male vocal group* — **1 wk**

Date	Title	Pos	Wks
14 Mar 98	DON'T STOP *EPIC 6655592*	54	1

NO DICE *UK, male vocal/instrumental group* — **2 wks**

Date	Title	Pos	Wks
5 May 79	COME DANCING *EMI 2927*	65	2

NO DOUBT ◐ ✒ *US, male/female vocal/instrumental group* — **33 wks**

Date	Title	Pos	Wks
26 Oct 96	JUST A GIRL *Interscope IND 80034*	38	2
22 Feb 97 ★	DON'T SPEAK *Interscope IND 95515* ■	1	18
5 Jul 97 ●	JUST A GIRL (re-issue) *Interscope IND 95539*	3	7
4 Oct 97	SPIDERWEBS *Interscope IND 95551*	16	3
20 Dec 97	SUNDAY MORNING *Interscope IND 95566*	50	3

NO MERCY ◐ ☺ *US, male vocal/instrumental group* — **26 wks**

Date	Title	Pos	Wks
18 Jan 97 ●	WHERE DO YOU GO *Arista 74321401502*	2	15
24 May 97 ●	PLEASE DON'T GO *Arista 74321481372*	4	7
6 Sep 97	KISS YOU ALL OVER *Arista 7432151452*	16	4

NO SWEAT *Ireland, male vocal/instrumental group* — **5 wks**

Date	Title	Pos	Wks
13 Oct 90	HEART AND SOUL *London LON 274*	64	4
2 Feb 91	TEAR DOWN THE WALLS *London LON 288*	61	1

NO WAY JOSE *US, male instrumental group* — **6 wks**

Date	Title	Pos	Wks
3 Aug 85	TEQUILA *Fourth & Broadway BRW 28*	47	6

NO WAY SIS *UK, male vocal/instrumental group* — **3 wks**

Date	Title	Pos	Wks
21 Dec 96	I'D LIKE TO TEACH THE WORLD TO SING *EMI CDEM 461*	27	3

NOLANS ◐ *Ireland, female vocal group* — **90 wks**

Date	Title	Pos	Wks
6 Oct 79	SPIRIT BODY AND SOUL *Epic EPC 7796* [1]	34	6
22 Dec 79 ●	I'M IN THE MOOD FOR DANCING *Epic EPC 8068*	3	15
12 Apr 80	DON'T MAKE WAVES *Epic EPC 8349*	12	11
13 Sep 80 ●	GOTTA PULL MYSELF TOGETHER *Epic EPC 8878*	9	13
6 Dec 80	WHO'S GONNA ROCK YOU *Epic EPC 9325*	12	11
14 Mar 81 ●	ATTENTION TO ME *Epic EPC 9571*	9	13
15 Aug 81	CHEMISTRY *Epic EPC A1485*	15	8
20 Feb 82	DON'T LOVE ME TOO HARD *Epic EPC A 1927*	14	12

Date	Title	Pos	Wks
1 Apr 95	I'M IN THE MOOD FOR DANCING (re-mix) *Living Beat LBECD 31*	51	1

[1] Nolan Sisters

NOMAD ☺ *UK, male/female vocal/instrumental duo* — **22 wks**

Date	Title	Pos	Wks
2 Feb 91 ●	(I WANNA GIVE YOU) DEVOTION *Rumour RUMA 25* [1]	2	10
4 May 91	JUST A GROOVE *Rumour RUMA 33*	16	6
28 Sep 91	SOMETHING SPECIAL *Rumour RUMA 35*	73	1
25 Apr 92	YOUR LOVE IS LIFTING ME *Rumour RUMA 48*	60	2
7 Nov 92	24 HOURS A DAY *Rumour RUMA 60*	61	1
25 Nov 95	(I WANNA GIVE YOU) DEVOTION (re-mix) *Rumour RUMACD 75*	42	2

[1] Nomad featuring MC Mikee Freedom

NONCHALANT *US, female vocalist* — **1 wk**

Date	Title	Pos	Wks
29 Jun 96	5 O'CLOCK *MCA MCSTD 48011*	44	1

Peter NOONE ◐ *UK, male vocalist* — **9 wks**

Date	Title	Pos	Wks
22 May 71	OH YOU PRETTY THING *RAK 114*	12	9

See also Herman's HERMITS

NOOTROPIC *UK, male instrumental/production duo* — **1 wk**

Date	Title	Pos	Wks
16 Mar 96	I SEE ONLY YOU *Hi-Life 5779832*	42	1

Ken NORDENE – *See Billy VAUGHN*

Chris NORMAN – *See Suzi QUATRO*

NORTH AND SOUTH ◐ *UK, male vocal/instrumental group* — **16 wks**

Date	Title	Pos	Wks
17 May 97 ●	I'M A MAN NOT A BOY *RCA 74321461142*	7	5
9 Aug 97	TARANTINO'S NEW STAR *RCA 74321501242*	18	5
8 Nov 97	BREATHING *RCA 74321528422*	27	2
4 Apr 98	NO SWEAT '98 *RCA 74321562212*	29	4

NORTHERN UPROAR ☹ *UK, male vocal/instrumental group* — **11 wks**

Date	Title	Pos	Wks
21 Oct 95	ROLLERCOASTER/ROUGH BOYS *Heavenly HVN 047CD*	41	2
3 Feb 96	FROM A WINDOW/THIS MORNING *Heavenly HVN 051CD*	17	3
20 Apr 96	LIVIN' IT UP *Heavenly HVN 52CD*	24	2
22 Jun 96	TOWN *Heavenly HVN 54CD*	48	1
7 Jun 97	ANY WAY YOU LOOK *Heavenly HVN 70CD*	36	2
23 Aug 97	A GIRL I ONCE KNEW *Heavenly HVN 73CD*	63	1

NORTHSIDE *UK, male vocal/instrumental group* — **12 wks**

Date	Title	Pos	Wks
9 Jun 90	SHALL WE TAKE A TRIP/MOODY PLACES *Factory FAC 268*	50	5
3 Nov 90	MY RISING STAR *Factory FAC 2987*	32	3
1 Jun 91	TAKE 5 *Factory FAC 3087*	40	4

Freddie NOTES and the RUDIES
Jamaica, male vocal/instrumental group — **2 wks**

Date	Title	Pos	Wks
10 Oct 70	MONTEGO BAY *Trojan TR 7791*	45	2

NOTORIOUS B.I.G. ◄ *US, male rapper – Christopher Wallace* — **25 wks**

Date	Title	Pos	Wks
29 Oct 94	JUICY *Bad Boy 74321240102*	72	1
1 Apr 95	BIG POPPA *Puff Daddy 74321263412*	63	1
15 Jul 95	CAN'T YOU SEE *Tommy Boy TBCD 700* [1]	43	2
19 Aug 95	ONE MORE CHANCE / STAY WITH ME *Puff Daddy 74321300782*	34	2
3 May 97 ●	HYPNOTIZE *Arista 74321466412* ▲	10	4
9 Aug 97 ●	MO MONEY MO PROBLEMS *Puff Daddy 74321492492* [2] ▲	6	10
14 Feb 98	SKY'S THE LIMIT *Puff Daddy 74321561992* [3]	35	2
18 Jul 98	RUNNIN' *Black Jam BJAM 9005* [4]	15	3

[1] Total featuring the Notorious B.I.G. [2] Notorious B.I.G. featuring 112
[3] 2Pac and Notorious B.I.G. [4] Notorious B.I.G. featuring Puff Daddy and Mase

NOTTINGHAM FOREST F.C. – *See PAPER LACE*

UK No 1 ★   UK Top 10 ●   UK million seller ◆   UK entry at No 1 ■   US No 1 ▲

Heather NOVA *US, female vocalist*   **1 wk**
25 Feb 95   WALK THIS WORLD *Butterfly BFLD 19*...........................69   1

Nancy NOVA *UK, female vocalist*   **2 wks**
4 Sep 82   NO NO NO *EMI 5328* 63   2

NOVY vs ENIAC
Germany, male production duo   **3 wks**
2 May 98   SUPERSTAR *D:disco 74321569352* 32   3

NRG *UK, male DJ / production duo*   **2 wks**
29 Mar 97   NEVER LOST HIS HARDCORE *Top Banana TOPCD 04* 71   1
12 Dec 98   NEVER LOST HIS HARDCORE '98 (re-mix)
             Top Banana TOPCD 010 61   1

NT GANG *Germany, male vocal/instrumental group*   **1 wk**
2 Apr 88   WAM BAM *Cooltempo COOL 163* 71   1

NU-BIRTH *UK, male production duo*   **2 wks**
6 Sep 97   ANYTIME *XL XLS 85CD* 48   1
6 Jun 98   ANYTIME (re-entry) *Locked On LOX 97CD* 41   1

NU COLOURS *UK, male/female vocal/instrumental group*   **11 wks**
6 Jun 92   TEARS *Wild Card CARD 1* 55   2
10 Oct 92   POWER *Wild Card CARD 3* 64   1
5 Jun 93   WHAT IN THE WORLD *Wild Card CARDD 4* 57   2
27 Nov 93   POWER (re-issue) *Wild Card CARDD 5* 40   2
25 May 96   DESIRE *Wild Card 5763652* 31   2
24 Aug 96   SPECIAL KIND OF LOVER *Wild Card 5752012* 38   2

NU MATIC *UK, male instrumental/production duo*   **1 wk**
8 Aug 92   SPRING IN MY STEP *XL XLS 31* 58   1

NU SHOOZ ◐ ☺ *US, male/female vocal duo*   **17 wks**
24 May 86 ● I CAN'T WAIT *Atlantic A 9446* 2   14
26 Jul 86   POINT OF NO RETURN *Atlantic A 9392* 48   3

NU SOUL featuring Kelli RICH
US, male/female vocal/instrumental duo   **2 wks**
13 Jan 96   HIDE-A-WAY *ffrr FCD 269* 27   2

NUANCE featuring Vikki LOVE
US, male/female vocal/instrumental group   **3 wks**
19 Jan 85   LOVERIDE *Fourth & Broadway BRW 20* 59   3

NUBIAN PRINZ – See POWERCUT featuring NUBIAN PRINZ

NUFF JUICE – See D MOB

Gary NUMAN ◐ ✦ *The moody, synthesized sound of London-born*
Gary Webb (b. 8 March, 1958, London) first hit the charts in 1979 under
the group name Tubeway Army. This distinctive vocalist/music-maker
had more solo hits in the 1980s than any other artist   **164 wks**
19 May 79 ★ ARE 'FRIENDS' ELECTRIC *Beggars Banquet BEG 18* [1] 1   16
1 Sep 79 ★ CARS *Beggars Banquet BEG 23*.................................1   11
24 Nov 79 ● COMPLEX *Beggars Banquet BEG 29*.............................6   9
24 May 80 ● WE ARE GLASS *Beggars Banquet BEG 35*.......................5   7
30 Aug 80 ● I DIE: YOU DIE *Beggars Banquet BEG 46*......................6   7
20 Dec 80   THIS WRECKAGE *Beggars Banquet BEG 50*.....................20   7
29 Aug 81 ● SHE'S GOT CLAWS *Beggars Banquet BEG 62*.....................6   6
5 Dec 81   LOVE NEEDS NO DISGUISE *Beggars Banquet BEG 68* [2] 33   7
6 Mar 82   MUSIC FOR CHAMELEONS *Beggars Banquet BEG 70* 19   7
19 Jun 82 ● WE TAKE MYSTERY (TO BED) *Beggars Banquet BEG 77* 9   4
28 Aug 82   WHITE BOYS AND HEROES *Beggars Banquet BEG 81* 20   4
3 Sep 83   WARRIORS *Beggars Banquet BEG 95*..........................20   5
22 Oct 83   SISTER SURPRISE *Beggars Banquet BEG 101* 32   3
3 Nov 84   BERSERKER *Numa NU 4*......................................32   5

22 Dec 84   MY DYING MACHINE *Numa NU 6* 66   1
9 Feb 85   CHANGE YOUR MIND *Polydor POSP 722* [3] 17   8
25 May 85   THE LIVE EP *Numa NUM 7*..................................27   4
10 Aug 85   YOUR FASCINATION *Numa NU 9*..............................46   5
21 Sep 85   CALL OUT THE DOGS *Numa NU 11*............................49   2
16 Nov 85   MIRACLES *Numa NU 13*.....................................49   3
19 Apr 86   THIS IS LOVE *Numa NU 16*.................................28   3
28 Jun 86   I CAN'T STOP *Numa NU 17*.................................27   4
4 Oct 86   NEW THING FROM LONDON TOWN *Numa NU 19* [3].............52   3
6 Dec 86   I STILL REMEMBER *Numa NU 21*.............................74   1
28 Mar 87   RADIO HEART *GFM GFM 109* [4] 35   6
13 Jun 87   LONDON TIMES *GFM GFM 112* [4] 48   2
19 Sep 87   CARS (E REG MODEL)/ARE 'FRIENDS' ELECTRIC (re-mix)
             Beggars Banquet BEG 199.................................16   7
30 Jan 88   NO MORE LIES *Polydor POSP 894* [3] 34   3
1 Oct 88   NEW ANGER *Illegal ILS 1003*..............................46   2
3 Dec 88   AMERICA *Illegal ILS 1004*.................................49   1
3 Jun 89   I'M ON AUTOMATIC *Polydor PO 43* [3] 44   2
16 Mar 91   HEART *IRS NUMAN 1*.......................................43   2
21 Mar 92   THE SKIN GAME *Numa NU 23*................................68   1
1 Aug 92   MACHINE + SOUL *Numa NUM 124*.............................72   1
4 Sep 93   CARS (2nd re-mix) *Beggars Banquet BEG 264CD*.............53   1
16 Mar 96   CARS (re-issue of re-mix) *PolyGram TV PRMCD 1*...........17   4

[1] Tubeway Army [2] Gary Numan and Dramatis [3] Sharpe and Numan [4] Radio
Heart featuring Gary Numan

Tracks on The Live EP: Are 'Friends' Electric/Berserker/Cars/We Are Glass.
'Cars' in 1996 is a re-issue of the 1987 remix.
See also Paul GARDINER

NUMBER ONE CUP *US, male vocal/instrumental group*   **1 wk**
2 Mar 96   DIVEBOMB *Blue Rose BRRC 10032*............................61   1

José NUNEZ featuring OCTAHVIA
US, male DJ/producer, and US female vocalist   **1 wk**
5 Sep 98   IN MY LIFE *Ministry Of Sound MOSCDS 126*..................56   1

Bobby NUNN *US, male vocalist/multi-instrumentalist*   **3 wks**
4 Feb 84   DON'T KNOCK IT (UNTIL YOU TRY IT) *Motown TMG 1323*.......65   3

NUSH ☺ *UK, male instrumental/production duo*   **7 wks**
23 Jul 94   U GIRLS *Blunted Vinyl BLNCDX 006* 58   1
22 Apr 95   MOVE THAT BODY *Blunted Vinyl BLNCD 012*..................46   2
16 Sep 95   U GIRLS (LOOK SO SEXY) (re-mix) *Blunted Vinyl BLNCD 13*...15   4

NUT *UK, female vocalist*   **4 wks**
8 Jun 96   BRAINS *Epic NUTCD 2* 64   1
21 Sep 96   CRAZY *Epic NUTCD 5*......................................56   1
11 Jan 97   SCREAM *Epic NUTCD 6*.....................................43   2

NUTTIN' NYCE *US, female vocal group*   **2 wks**
10 Jun 95   DOWN 4 WHATEVA *Jive JIVECD 365*..........................62   1
12 Aug 95   FROGGY STYLE *Jive JIVECD 381*............................68   1

NUYORICAN SOUL *US, male DJ / production group*   **8 wks**
8 Feb 97   RUNAWAY *Talkin Loud TLCD20* [1] 24   4
10 May 97   IT'S ALRIGHT, I FEEL IT! *Talkin Loud TLCD 22* [2] 26   2
25 Oct 97   I AM THE BLACK GOLD OF THE SUN
             Talkin Loud TLCD 26 [2] 31   2

[1] Nuyorican Soul featuring India [2] Nuyorican Soul featuring Jocelyn Brown

NWA *US, male rap group*   **15 wks**
9 Sep 89   EXPRESS YOURSELF *Fourth & Broadway BRW 144*..............50   4
26 May 90   EXPRESS YOURSELF (re-entry)
             Fourth & Broadway BRW 144...............................26   5
1 Sep 90   GANGSTA, GANGSTA *Fourth & Broadway BRW 191*..............70   1
10 Nov 90   100 MILES AND RUNNIN' *Fourth & Broadway BRW 200* 38   3
23 Nov 91   ALWAYZ INTO SOMETHIN' *Fourth & Broadway BRW 238* 60   2

NYCC ☞ ☺ *German, male rap trio* **6 wks**

30 May 98	**FIGHT FOR YOUR RIGHT (TO PARTY)** *Control 0042645 CON* 14	5
19 Sep 98	**CAN YOU FEEL IT (ROCK DA HOUSE)** *Control 0042785 CON* 68	1

Joe NYE – *See DNA*

NYLON MOON *Italy, male instrumental duo* **2 wks**

13 Apr 96	**SKY PLUS** *Positiva CDTIV 50* 43	2

Michael NYMAN *UK, male instrumentalist – piano* **2 wks**

19 Mar 94	**THE HEART ASKS PLEASURE FIRST / THE PROMISE** *Virgin VEND 3* 60	2

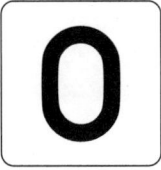

Phil OAKEY – *See HUMAN LEAGUE; Giorgio MORODER*

OASIS ✍ ☹ *Peerless Manchester-based, Beatles-influenced band: Liam (v) and Noel (g/v) Gallagher, Paul Arthurs (g), Paul McGuigan (b), Tony McCarroll (d). The often controversial Britpop group smashed many records including most weeks on the chart in one year (134 in 1996)* **273 wks**

23 Apr 94	**SUPERSONIC** *Creation CRESCD 176* 31	3
2 Jul 94	**SHAKERMAKER** *Creation CRESCD 182* 11	5
20 Aug 94 ●	**LIVE FOREVER** *Creation CRESCD 185* 10	5
22 Oct 94 ●	**CIGARETTES AND ALCOHOL** *Creation CRESCD 190* 7	6
31 Dec 94 ●	**WHATEVER** *Creation CRESCD 195* 3	10
31 Dec 94	**CIGARETTES AND ALCOHOL (re-entry)** *Creation CRESCD 190* 69	1
6 May 95 ★	**SOME MIGHT SAY** *Creation CRESCD 204* ■ 1	14
13 May 95	**SOME MIGHT SAY** *Creation CRE 204T* 71	1
24 Jun 95	**SUPERSONIC (re-entry)** *Creation CRESCD 176* 44	3
24 Jun 95	**WHATEVER (re-entry)** *Creation CRESCD 195* 48	3
24 Jun 95	**LIVE FOREVER (re-entry)** *Creation CRESCD 185* 50	3
24 Jun 95	**SHAKERMAKER (re-entry)** *Creation CRESCD 182* 52	3
24 Jun 95	**CIGARETTES AND ALCOHOL (2nd re-entry)** *Creation CRESCD 190* 53	3
26 Aug 95 ●	**ROLL WITH IT** *Creation CRESCD 212* 2	11
26 Aug 95	**SOME MIGHT SAY (re-entry)** *Creation CRESCD 204* 73	1
11 Nov 95 ●	**WONDERWALL** *Creation CRESCD 215* 2	20
25 Nov 95	**WIBBLING RIVALRY (INTERVIEWS WITH NOEL AND LIAM GALLAGHER)** *Fierce Panda NING 12CD* [1] 52	2
9 Dec 95	**WHATEVER (2nd re-entry)** *Creation CRESCD 195* 75	1
30 Dec 95	**CIGARETTES AND ALCOHOL (3rd re-entry)** *Creation CRESCD 190* 58	7
30 Dec 95	**WHATEVER (3rd re-entry)** *Creation CRESCD 195* 55	3
30 Dec 95	**SUPERSONIC (2nd re-entry)** *Creation CRESCD 176* 54	4
6 Jan 96	**SHAKERMAKER (2nd re-entry)** *Creation CRESCD 182* 61	2
6 Jan 96	**LIVE FOREVER (2nd re-entry)** *Creation CRESCD 185* 64	1
6 Jan 96	**SOME MIGHT SAY (2nd re-entry)** *Creation CRESCD 204* 59	3
6 Jan 96	**ROLL WITH IT (re-entry)** *Creation CRESCD 212* 65	3
20 Jan 96	**LIVE FOREVER (3rd re-entry)** *Creation CRESCD 185* 71	2
27 Jan 96	**WHATEVER (4th re-entry)** *Creation CRESCD 195* 61	3
24 Feb 96	**WHATEVER (5th re-entry)** *Creation CRESCD 195* 55	15
2 Mar 96 ★	**DON'T LOOK BACK IN ANGER** *Creation CRESCD 221* ■ 1	16
2 Mar 96	**CIGARETTES AND ALCOHOL (4th re-entry)** *Creation CRESCD 190* 62	4
2 Mar 96	**SUPERSONIC (3rd re-entry)** *Creation CRESCD 176* 71	1
2 Mar 96	**SHAKERMAKER (3rd re-entry)** *Creation CRESCD 182* 74	1

2 Mar 96	**LIVE FOREVER (4th re-entry)** *Creation CRESCD 185* 74	2
16 Mar 96	**SOME MIGHT SAY (3rd re-entry)** *Creation CRESCD 204* 75	1
13 Apr 96	**CIGARETTES AND ALCOHOL (5th re-entry)** *Creation CRESCD 190* 74	2
11 May 96	**CIGARETTES AND ALCOHOL (6th re-entry)** *Creation CRESCD 190* 72	3
17 Aug 96	**WHATEVER (6th re-entry)** *Creation CRESCD 195* 62	4
24 Aug 96	**WONDERWALL (re-entry)** *Creation CRESCD 215* 60	5
24 Aug 96	**SOME MIGHT SAY (4th re-entry)** *Creation CRESCD 204* 70	1
24 Aug 96	**CIGARETTES AND ALCOHOL (7th re-entry)** *Creation CRESCD 190* 72	1
21 Sep 96	**WHATEVER (7th re-entry)** *Creation CRESCD 195* 66	1
16 Nov 96	**WHATEVER (8th re-entry)** *Creation CRESCD 195* 34	10
16 Nov 96	**WONDERWALL (2nd re-entry)** *Creation CRESCD 215* 36	8
16 Nov 96	**CIGARETTES AND ALCOHOL (8th re-entry)** *Creation CRESCD 190* 38	5
16 Nov 96	**SOME MIGHT SAY (5th re-entry)** *Creation CRESCD 204* 40	4
16 Nov 96	**LIVE FOREVER (5th re-entry)** *Creation CRESCD 185* 42	2
16 Nov 96	**SUPERSONIC (4th re-entry)** *Creation CRESCD 176* 47	2
16 Nov 96	**SHAKERMAKER (3rd re-entry)** *Creation CRESCD 182* 48	2
16 Nov 96	**DON'T LOOK BACK IN ANGER (re-entry)** *Creation CRESCD 221* 53	5
16 Nov 96	**ROLL WITH IT (2nd re-entry)** *Creation CRESCD 212* 55	2
28 Dec 96	**DON'T LOOK BACK IN ANGER (2nd re-entry)** *Creation CRESCD 221* 67	2
28 Dec 96	**CIGARETTES AND ALCOHOL (9th re-entry)** *Creation CRESCD 190* 71	2
28 Dec 96	**SOME MIGHT SAY (6th re-entry)** *Creation CRESCD 204* 73	2
28 Dec 96	**LIVE FOREVER (6th re-entry)** *Creation CRESCD 185* 75	2
26 Jul 97 ★	**D'YOU KNOW WHAT I MEAN?** *Creation CRESCD 256* ■ 1	18
4 Oct 97 ●	**STAND BY ME** *Creation CRESCD 278* 2	18
24 Jan 98 ★	**ALL AROUND THE WORLD** *Creation CRESCD 282* ■ 1	9

[1] Oas*s

Chart rules allow for a maximum of three formats; the 12-inch of 'Some Might Say' – already available on CD, 7-inch and cassette – was therefore listed separately

John OATES – *See Daryl HALL and John OATES*

OBERNKIRCHEN CHILDREN'S CHOIR ℂ
Germany, children's choir **26 wks**

22 Jan 54 ●	**HAPPY WANDERER** *Parlophone R 3799* 2	23
9 Jul 54 ●	**HAPPY WANDERER (re-entry)** *Parlophone R 3799* 8	3

Dermot O'BRIEN *Ireland, male vocalist* **2 wks**

20 Oct 66	**THE MERRY PLOUGHBOY** *Envoy ENV 016* 46	1
3 Nov 66	**THE MERRY PLOUGHBOY (re-entry)** *Envoy ENV 016* 50	1

Billy OCEAN ♪ *Top British-based R&B singer/songwriter of the 1980s, b. Leslie Charles, 21 January, 1950, Trinidad. He waited seven years after scoring his first four UK Top 20 hits before accumulating an impressive run of transatlantic successes, which include three US No 1s* **153 wks**

21 Feb 76 ●	**LOVE REALLY HURTS WITHOUT YOU** *GTO GT 52* 2	10
10 Jul 76	**L.O.D. (LOVE ON DELIVERY)** *GTO GT 62* 19	8
13 Nov 76	**STOP ME (IF YOU'VE HEARD IT ALL BEFORE)** *GTO GT 72* 12	11
19 Mar 77 ●	**RED LIGHT SPELLS DANGER** *GTO GT 85* 2	10
1 Sep 79	**AMERICAN HEARTS** *GTO GT 244* 54	5
19 Jan 80	**ARE YOU READY** *GTO GT 259* 42	7
13 Oct 84 ●	**CARIBBEAN QUEEN (NO MORE LOVE ON THE RUN)** *Jive JIVE 77* ▲ 6	14
19 Jan 85	**LOVERBOY** *Jive JIVE 80* 15	10
11 May 85 ●	**SUDDENLY** *Jive JIVE 90* 4	14
17 Aug 85	**MYSTERY LADY** *Jive JIVE 98* 49	4
25 Jan 86 ★	**WHEN THE GOING GETS TOUGH, THE TOUGH GET GOING** *Jive JIVE 114* 1	13
12 Apr 86	**THERE'LL BE SAD SONGS (TO MAKE YOU CRY)** *Jive JIVE 117* ▲ 12	13
9 Aug 86	**LOVE ZONE** *Jive JIVE 124* 49	3
11 Oct 86	**BITTERSWEET** *Jive JIVE 133* 44	4
10 Jan 87	**LOVE IS FOREVER** *Jive JIVE 134* 34	7
6 Feb 88 ●	**GET OUTTA MY DREAMS GET INTO MY CAR** *Jive BOS 1* ▲ 3	11
7 May 88	**CALYPSO CRAZY** *Jive BOS 2* 35	4

UK No 1 ★   UK Top 10 ●   UK million seller ◆   UK entry at No 1 ■   US No 1 ▲

| 6 Aug 88 | THE COLOUR OF LOVE *Jive BOS 3* | 65 | 3 |
| 6 Feb 93 | PRESSURE *Jive BOSCD 6* | 55 | 2 |

OCEAN COLOUR SCENE ☻ ✎
UK, male vocal/instrumental group **48 wks**

23 Mar 91	YESTERDAY TODAY *!Phfft FIT 2*	49	1
17 Feb 96	THE RIVERBOAT SONG *MCA MCSTD 40021*	15	5
6 Apr 96 ●	YOU'VE GOT IT BAD *MCA MCSTD 40036*	7	4
15 Jun 96 ●	THE DAY WE CAUGHT THE TRAIN *MCA MCSTD 40046*	4	11
28 Sep 96 ●	THE CIRCLE *MCA MCSTD 40077*	6	6
28 Jun 97 ●	HUNDRED MILE HIGH CITY *MCA MCSTD 40133*	4	7
6 Sep 97 ●	TRAVELLERS TUNE *MCA MCSTD 40144*	5	5
22 Nov 97 ●	BETTER DAY *MCA MCSTD 40151*	9	5
28 Feb 98 ●	IT'S A BEAUTIFUL THING *MCA MCSTD 40157*	12	4

OCEANIC ☺ *UK, male/female vocal/instrumental group* **26 wks**

24 Aug 91 ●	INSANITY *Dead Dead Good GOOD 4*	3	15
30 Nov 91	WICKED LOVE *Dead Dead Good GOOD 5*	25	3
28 Dec 91	WICKED LOVE (re-entry) *Dead Dead Good GOOD 5*	65	2
13 Jun 92	CONTROLLING ME *Dead Dead Good GOOD 14*	14	5
14 Nov 92	IGNORANCE *Dead Dead Good GOOD 22* [1]	72	1

[1] Oceanic featuring Siobhan Maher

Des O'CONNOR ☾ *Very popular entertainer, comedian and MOR vocalist, b. 12 January, 1932. This London-based all-round entertainer toured with Buddy Holly and Lonnie Donegan in the 1950s and had a series of hits in the 1960s. He has been a top-rated TV star for 30 years* **117 wks**

1 Nov 67 ●	CARELESS HANDS *Columbia DB 8275*	6	17
8 May 68 ★	I PRETEND *Columbia DB 8397*	1	36
20 Nov 68 ●	1-2-3 O'LEARY *Columbia DB 8492*	4	11
7 May 69	DICK-A-DUM-DUM (KING'S ROAD) *Columbia DB 8566*	14	10
29 Nov 69	LONELINESS *Columbia DB 8632*	18	11
14 Mar 70	I'LL GO ON HOPING *Columbia DB 8661*	30	7
26 Sep 70	THE TIPS OF MY FINGERS *Columbia DB 8713*	15	15
8 Nov 86 ●	THE SKYE BOAT SONG *Tempo TML 119* [1]	10	10

[1] Roger Whittaker and Des O'Connor

Hazel O'CONNOR ☻ ✐ *UK, female vocalist* **46 wks**

16 Aug 80 ●	EIGHTH DAY *A & M AMS 7553*	5	11
25 Oct 80	GIVE ME AN INCH *A & M AMS 7569*	41	4
21 Mar 81 ●	D-DAYS *Albion ION 1009*	10	9
23 May 81 ●	WILL YOU *A & M AMS 8131*	8	10
1 Aug 81	(COVER PLUS) WE'RE ALL GROWN UP *Albion ION 1018*	41	6
3 Oct 81	HANGING AROUND *Albion ION 1022*	45	3
23 Jan 82	CALLS THE TUNE *A & M AMS 8203*	60	3

Sinead O'CONNOR ☻ ✎ *Ireland, female vocalist* **64 wks**

16 Jan 88	MANDINKA *Ensign ENY 611*	17	9
20 Jan 90 ★	NOTHING COMPARES 2 U *Ensign ENY 630* ▲	1	14
21 Jul 90	THE EMPEROR'S NEW CLOTHES *Ensign ENY 633*	31	5
20 Oct 90	THREE BABIES *Ensign ENY 635*	42	4
8 Jun 91	MY SPECIAL CHILD *Ensign ENY 646*	42	3
14 Dec 91	SILENT NIGHT *Ensign ENY 652*	60	4
12 Sep 92	SUCCESS HAS MADE A FAILURE OF OUR HOME *Ensign ENY 656*	18	4
12 Dec 92	DON'T CRY FOR ME ARGENTINA *Ensign ENY 657*	53	4
19 Feb 94	YOU MADE ME THE THIEF OF YOUR HEART *Island CID 588*	42	3
26 Nov 94	THANK YOU FOR HEARING ME *Ensign CDENYS 662*	13	7
29 Apr 95	HAUNTED *ZTT ZANG 65CD* [1]	30	2
26 Aug 95	FAMINE *Ensign CDENY 663*	51	1
17 May 97	GOSPEL OAK EP *Chrysalis CDCHS 5051*	28	3
6 Dec 97	THIS IS A REBEL SONG *Columbia 6652992*	60	1

[1] Shane MacGowan and Sinead O'Connor

Tracks on Gospel Oak EP: *This Is to Mother You / I Am Enough for Myself / Petit Poulet / 4 My Love*

See also Jah WOBBLE'S INVADERS OF THE HEART; MARXMAN

OCTOPUS *UK/France, male vocal/instrumental group* **5 wks**

| 22 Jun 96 | YOUR SMILE *Food CDFOOD 78* | 42 | 2 |

| 14 Sep 96 | SAVED *Food CDFOODS 84* | 40 | 2 |
| 23 Nov 96 | JEALOUSY *Food CDFOODS 87* | 59 | 1 |

Alan O'DAY *US, male vocalist* **3 wks**

| 2 Jul 77 | UNDERCOVER ANGEL *Atlantic K 10926* ▲ | 43 | 3 |

ODETTA – *See Harry BELAFONTE*

Daniel O'DONNELL ☾ ✈ *Ireland, male vocalist* **46 wks**

12 Sep 92	I JUST WANT TO DANCE WITH YOU *Ritz RITZ 250P*	20	7
2 Jan 93	THE THREE BELLS *Ritz RITZCD 239*	71	1
8 May 93	THE LOVE IN YOUR EYES *Ritz RITZCD 257*	47	3
7 Aug 93	WHAT EVER HAPPENED TO OLD FASHIONED LOVE *Ritz RITZCD 262*	21	5
16 Apr 94	SINGING THE BLUES *Ritz RITZCD 270*	23	3
26 Nov 94	THE GIFT *Ritz RITZCD 275*	46	3
10 Jun 95	SECRET LOVE *Ritz RITZCD 285* [1]	28	3
9 Mar 96	TIMELESS *Ritz RITZCD 293* [1]	32	3
28 Sep 96	FOOTSTEPS *Ritz RITZCD 300*	25	5
7 Jun 97	THE LOVE SONGS EP *Ritz RITZCD 306*	27	4
11 Apr 98 ●	GIVE A LITTLE LOVE *Ritz RITZCD 315*	7	5
17 Oct 98	THE MAGIC IS THERE *RITZ RZCD 320*	16	4

[1] Daniel O'Donnell and Mary Duff

Tracks on The Love Songs EP: *Save the Last Dance for Me / I Can't Stop Loving You / You're the Only Good Thing / Limerick You're a Lady*

ODYSSEY ✎ *US, male/female vocal group* **82 wks**

24 Dec 77 ●	NATIVE NEW YORKER *RCA PC 1129*	5	11
21 Jun 80 ★	USE IT UP AND WEAR IT OUT *RCA PB 1962*	1	12
13 Sep 80 ●	IF YOU'RE LOOKIN' FOR A WAY OUT *RCA 5*	6	15
17 Jan 81	HANG TOGETHER *RCA 23*	36	7
30 May 81 ●	GOING BACK TO MY ROOTS *RCA 85*	4	12
19 Sep 81	IT WILL BE ALRIGHT *RCA 128*	43	5
12 Jun 82 ●	INSIDE OUT *RCA 226*	3	11
11 Sep 82	MAGIC TOUCH *RCA 275*	41	5
17 Aug 85	(JOY) I KNOW IT *Mirror BUTCH 12*	51	4

Esther and Abi OFARIM ☾ *Israel, female/male vocal duo* **22 wks**

| 14 Feb 68 ★ | CINDERELLA ROCKEFELLA *Philips BF 1640* | 1 | 13 |
| 19 Jun 68 | ONE MORE DANCE *Philips BF 1678* | 13 | 9 |

OFF-SHORE ☺ *Germany, male instrumental/production duo* **12 wks**

| 22 Dec 90 ● | I CAN'T TAKE THE POWER *CBS 6565707* | 7 | 11 |
| 17 Aug 91 | I GOT A LITTLE SONG *Dance Pool 6568257* | 64 | 1 |

Wiston OFFICE – *See Frank K featuring Wiston OFFICE*

OFFSPRING *US, male vocal/instrumental group* **8 wks**

25 Feb 95	SELF ESTEEM *Golf CDSHOLE 001*	37	3
19 Aug 95	GOTTA GET AWAY *Out Of Step WOOS 2CDS*	43	2
1 Feb 97	ALL I WANT *Epitaph 64912*	31	2
26 Apr 97	GONE AWAY *Epitaph 64982*	42	1

OH WELL *Germany, male producer – Ackim Faulker* **7 wks**

| 14 Oct 89 | OH WELL *Parlophone R 6236* | 28 | 6 |
| 3 Mar 90 | RADAR LOVE *Parlophone R 6244* | 65 | 1 |

OHIO EXPRESS ☻ *US, male vocal/instrumental group* **15 wks**

| 5 Jun 68 ● | YUMMY YUMMY YUMMY *Pye International 7N 25459* | 5 | 15 |

OHIO PLAYERS *US, male vocal/instrumental group* **4 wks**

| 10 Jul 76 | WHO'D SHE COO *Mercury PLAY 001* | 43 | 4 |

O'JAYS ✎ *US, male vocal group* **72 wks**

23 Sep 72	BACK STABBERS *CBS 8270*	14	9
3 Mar 73 ●	LOVE TRAIN *CBS 1181* ▲	9	13
31 Jan 76	I LOVE MUSIC *Philadelphia Interna PIR 3879*	13	9

UK No 1 ★   UK Top 10 ●   UK million seller ◆   UK entry at No 1 ■   US No 1 ▲

12 Feb 77	DARLIN' DARLIN' BABY (SWEET, TENDER, LOVE)			
	Philadelphia Interna PIR 4834		24	6
8 Apr 78	I LOVE MUSIC (re-issue) *Philadelphia Interna PIR 6093*	36	3
17 Jun 78	USED TA BE MY GIRL *Philadelphia Interna PIR 6332*		12	12
30 Sep 78	BRANDY *Philadelphia Interna PIR 6658*		21	9
29 Sep 79	SING A HAPPY SONG *Philadelphia Interna PIR 7825*		39	4
30 Jul 83	PUT OUR HEADS TOGETHER *Philadelphia Interna A 3642*	45	5

John O'KANE *UK, male vocalist*   4 wks

9 May 92	STAY WITH ME *Circa YR 88*	41	4

OL' DIRTY BASTARD – See Pras MICHEL

Mike OLDFIELD 🎸 *Composer/producer/multi-instrumentalist, b. 15 May, 1953, Reading. His chart-topping 1973 debut album,* Tubular Bells, *spent five years on the chart, and the belated* Tubular Bells II *also reached UK No 1 (1992)*   112 wks

13 Jul 74	MIKE OLDFIELD'S SINGLE (THEME FROM TUBULAR BELLS)		
	Virgin VS 101	31	6
20 Dec 75 ●	IN DULCE JUBILO/ON HORSEBACK *Virgin VS 131*	4	10
27 Nov 76 ●	PORTSMOUTH *Virgin VS 163*	3	12
23 Dec 78	TAKE 4 EP *Virgin VS 238*	72	3
21 Apr 79	GUILTY *Virgin VS 245*	22	9
8 Dec 79	BLUE PETER *Virgin VS 317*	19	9
20 Mar 82	FIVE MILES OUT *Virgin VS 464* [1]	43	5
12 Jun 82	FAMILY MAN *Virgin VS 489* [1]	45	6
28 May 83 ●	MOONLIGHT SHADOW *Virgin VS 586* [1]	4	17
14 Jan 84	CRIME OF PASSION *Virgin VS 648* [1]	61	3
30 Jun 84	TO FRANCE *Virgin VS 686* [1]	48	7
14 Dec 85	PICTURES IN THE DARK *Virgin VS 836* [2]	50	6
3 Oct 92 ●	SENTINEL *WEA YZ 698*	10	6
19 Dec 92	TATTOO *WEA YZ 708*	33	5
17 Apr 93	THE BELL *WEA YZ 737CD*	50	2
9 Oct 93	MOONLIGHT SHADOW (re-issue) *Virgin VSCDT 1477*	52	2
17 Dec 94	HIBERNACULUM *WEA YZ 871CD*	47	3
2 Sep 95	LET THERE BE LIGHT *WEA YZ 880CD*	51	1
22 Nov 97	WOMEN OF IRELAND *WEA WEA 093CD*	70	1

[1] Mike Oldfield featuring Maggie Reilly [2] Mike Oldfield featuring Aled Jones, Anita Hegerland and Barry Palmer

Tracks on Take 4 EP: Portsmouth/In Dulce Jubilo/Wrekorder Wrondo/Sailors Hornpipe. 'The Bell' credits Viv Stanshall

Sally OLDFIELD 🌐 *UK, female vocalist*   13 wks

9 Dec 78	MIRRORS *Bronze BRO 66*	19	13

Misty OLDLAND *UK, female vocalist*   7 wks

16 Oct 93	GOT ME A FEELING *Columbia 6597872*	59	2
12 Mar 94	A FAIR AFFAIR (JE T'AIME) *Columbia 6601612*	49	4
9 Jul 94	I WROTE YOU A SONG *Columbia 6603732*	73	1

OLGA *Italy, female vocalist*   1 wk

1 Oct 94	I'M A BITCH *UMM UMM 144UKCD*	68	1

OLIVE 🌐 ☺ *UK, male/female vocal/instrumental group*   24 wks

7 Sep 96	YOU'RE NOT ALONE *RCA 74321406272*	42	4
15 Mar 97	MIRACLE *RCA 74321461242*	41	2
17 May 97 ★	YOU'RE NOT ALONE (re-issue) *RCA 74321473232* ■	1	13
16 Aug 97	OUTLAW *RCA 74321508372*	14	4
8 Nov 97	MIRACLE *RCA 74321530842*	41	1

OLIVER 🌐 *US, male vocalist*   18 wks

9 Aug 69 ●	GOOD MORNING STARSHINE *CBS 4435*	6	16
27 Dec 69	GOOD MORNING STARSHINE (re-entry) *CBS 4435*	39	2

Frankie OLIVER *UK, male vocalist*   1 wk

7 Jun 97	GIVE HER WHAT SHE WANTS		
	Island Jamaica IJCD 2011	58	1

OLLIE and JERRY ☺ 🎤 *US, male vocal duo*   14 wks

23 Jun 84 ●	BREAKIN'... THERE'S NO STOPPING US		
	Polydor POSP 690	5	11
9 Mar 85	ELECTRIC BOOGALOO *Polydor POSP 730*	57	3

OLYMPIC ORCHESTRA *UK, orchestra*   15 wks

1 Oct 83	REILLY *Red Bus RBUS 82*	26	15

OLYMPIC RUNNERS *UK, male vocal/instrumental group*   21 wks

13 May 78	WHATEVER IT TAKES *RCA PC 5078*	61	2
14 Oct 78	GET IT WHILE YOU CAN *Polydor RUN 7*	35	6
20 Jan 79	SIR DANCEALOT *Polydor POSP 17*	35	6
28 Jul 79	THE BITCH *Polydor POSP 63*	37	7

OLYMPICS 🎤 *US, male vocal group*   9 wks

3 Oct 58	WESTERN MOVIES *HMV POP 528*	12	8
19 Jan 61	I WISH I COULD SHIMMY LIKE MY SISTER KATE *Vogue V 9174*	40	1

OMAR R&B 🎤 *UK, male vocalist*   18 wks

22 Jun 91	THERE'S NOTHING LIKE THIS *Talkin Loud TLK 9*	14	7
23 May 92	YOUR LOSS MY GAIN *Talkin Loud TLK 22*	47	2
26 Sep 92	MUSIC *Talkin Loud TLK 28*	53	2
23 Jul 94	OUTSIDE/SATURDAY *RCA 74321213982*	43	2
15 Oct 94	KEEP STEPPIN' *RCA 74321233682*	57	1
2 Aug 97	SAY NOTHIN' *RCA 74321502872*	29	2
18 Oct 97	GOLDEN BROWN *RCA 74321525422*	37	2

OMC 🌐 *New Zealand, male vocalist*   17 wks

20 Jul 96 ●	HOW BIZARRE *Polydor 5776202*	5	16
18 Jan 97	ON THE RUN *Polydor 5732452*	56	1

OMD – See ORCHESTRAL MANOEUVRES IN THE DARK

ONE *UK, male vocal group*   2 wks

11 Jan 97	ONE MORE CHANCE *Mercury MERDD 478*	31	2

Michie ONE – See Louchie LOU and Michie ONE

ONE DOVE *UK, male/female vocal/instrumental group*   9 wks

7 Aug 93	WHITE LOVE *Boy's Own BOICD 14*	43	3
16 Oct 93	BREAKDOWN *Boy's Own BOICD 15*	24	3
15 Jan 94	WHY DON'T YOU TAKE ME *Boy's Own BOICD 16*	30	3

112 – See Notorious B.I.G.

187 LOCKDOWN ☺ *UK, male production duo – Danny Harrison, Julian Jonah*   15 wks

15 Nov 97	GUNMAN *East West EW 140CD*	16	4
25 Apr 98 ●	KUNG-FU *East West EW 155CD*	9	5
25 Jul 98	GUNMAN (re-mix) *East West EW 176CD*	17	4
3 Oct 98	THE DON *East West EW 180CD*	29	2

ONE HUNDRED TON AND A FEATHER – See Jonathan KING

ONE THE JUGGLER *UK, male vocal/instrumental group*   1 wk

19 Feb 83	PASSION KILLER *Regard RG 107*	71	1

ONE TRIBE – See OUR TRIBE/ONE TRIBE

ONE 2 MANY *Norway, male/female vocal/instrumental group*   11 wks

12 Nov 88	DOWNTOWN *A & M AM 476*	65	4
3 Jun 89	DOWNTOWN (re-issue) *A & M AM 456*	43	7

ONE WAY *US, male vocal/instrumental group*   8 wks

8 Dec 79	MUSIC *MCA 542* [1]	56	6
29 Jun 85	LET'S TALK *MCA 972* [1]	64	2

[1] One Way featuring Al Hudson

UK No 1 ★   UK Top 10 ●   UK million seller ◆   UK entry at No 1 ■   US No 1 ▲

Alexander O'NEAL 🎵 US, male vocalist — 104 wks

28 Dec 85 ●	SATURDAY LOVE *Tabu A 6829* [1]	.6 11
15 Feb 86	IF YOU WERE TONIGHT *Tabu A 6391*	.13 10
5 Apr 86	A BROKEN HEART CAN MEND *Tabu A 6244*	.53 4
6 Jun 87	FAKE *Tabu 650891 7*	.33 6
31 Oct 87 ●	CRITICIZE *Tabu 651211 7*	.4 14
6 Feb 88	NEVER KNEW LOVE LIKE THIS *Tabu 651382 7* [2]	.26 7
28 May 88	(WHAT CAN I SAY) TO MAKE YOU LOVE ME *Tabu 652852 7*	.27 5
24 Sep 88	FAKE '88 (re-mix) *Tabu 652949 7*	.16 7
10 Dec 88	CHRISTMAS SONG (CHESTNUTS ROASTING ON AN OPEN FIRE) / THANK YOU FOR A GOOD YEAR *Tabu 653182 7*	.30 5
25 Feb 88	HEARSAY '88 *Tabu 654466 7*	.56 2
2 Sep 89	SUNSHINE *Tabu 655191 7*	.72 1
9 Dec 89	HITMIX (OFFICIAL BOOTLEG MEGA-MIX) *Tabu 655504 7*	.19 7
24 Mar 90	SATURDAY LOVE (re-mix) *Tabu 655680 7* [1]	.55 2
12 Jan 91	ALL TRUE MAN *Tabu 6565717*	.18 6
23 Mar 91	WHAT IS THIS THING CALLED LOVE *Tabu 6567317*	.53 2
11 May 91	SHAME ON ME *Tabu 6568737*	.71 1
9 May 92	SENTIMENTAL *Tabu 6580147*	.53 2
30 Jan 93	LOVE MAKES NO SENSE *Tabu AMCD 7708*	.28 6
3 Jul 93	IN THE MIDDLE *Tabu 5877152*	.32 3
25 Sep 93	ALL THAT MATTERS TO ME *Tabu 6577232*	.67 1
2 Nov 96	LET'S GET TOGETHER *EMI Premier PRESCD 11*	.38 2
2 Aug 97	BABY COME TO ME *Rage RAGECDX 3*	.56 1
12 Dec 98	CRITICIZE '98 MIX *One World OWECD 3*	.51 1

[1] Cherelle with Alexander O'Neal [2] Alexander O'Neal featuring Cherelle

Shaquille O'NEAL US, male rapper — 4 wks

26 Mar 94	I'M OUTSTANDING *Jive JIVECD 349*	.70 1
1 Feb 97	YOU CAN'T STOP THE REIGN *Interscope IND 95522*	.40 2
17 Oct 98	THE WAY IT'S GOIN' DOWN (T.W.I.S.M. FOR LIFE) *A&M 5827932*	.62 1

ONLY ONES UK, male vocal/instrumental group — 2 wks

1 Feb 92	ANOTHER GIRL – ANOTHER PLANET *Columbia 6577507*	.57 2

Yoko ONO Japan, female vocalist — 5 wks

28 Feb 81	WALKING ON THIN ICE *Geffen K 79202*	.35 5

See also John LENNON

ONSLAUGHT UK, male vocal/instrumental group — 3 wks

6 May 89	LET THERE BE ROCK *London LON 224*	.50 3

ONYX US, male rap group — 7 wks

28 Aug 93	SLAM *Columbia 6596302*	.31 4
27 Nov 93	THROW YA GUNZ *Columbia 6598312*	.34 3

OO LA LA UK, male vocal/instrumental group — 2 wks

5 Sep 92	OO . . . AH . . . CANTONA *North Speed OOAH 1*	.64 2

OPEN ARMS featuring ROWETTA
UK, male/female vocal/instrumental group — 1 wk

15 Jun 96	HEY MR. DJ *All Around The World CDGLOBE 136*	.62 1

See also VARIOUS ARTISTS (EPs and LPs) – The Further Adventures of North EP

OPTIMYSTIC UK, male/female vocal group — 6 wks

17 Sep 94	CAUGHT UP IN MY HEART *WEA YZ 841CD*	.49 3
10 Dec 94	NOTHING BUT LOVE *WEA 864CD1*	.37 2
13 May 95	BEST THING IN THE WORLD *WEA YZ 920CD*	.70 1

OPUS ● Austria, male/instrumental group — 15 wks

15 Jun 85 ●	LIVE IS LIFE *Polydor POSP 743*	.6 15

OPUS III ● ☺ UK, male/female vocal/instrumental group — 10 wks

22 Feb 92 ●	IT'S A FINE DAY *PWL International PWL 215*	.5 8
27 Jun 92	I TALK TO THE WIND *PWL Continental PWL 235*	.52 1
11 Jun 94	WHEN YOU MADE THE MOUNTAIN *PWL International PWCD 302*	.71 1

ORANGE UK, male vocal/instrumental group — 1 wk

8 Oct 94	JUDY OVER THE RAINBOW *Chrysalis CDCHS 5012*	.73 1

ORANGE JUICE ● ☹ UK, male vocal/instrumental group — 34 wks

7 Nov 81	L.O.V.E . . . LOVE *Polydor POSP 357*	.65 2
30 Jan 82	FELICITY *Polydor POSP 386*	.63 3
21 Aug 82	TWO HEARTS TOGETHER/HOKOYO *Polydor POSP 470*	.60 2
23 Oct 82	I CAN'T HELP MYSELF *Polydor POSP 522*	.42 3
19 Feb 83 ●	RIP IT UP *Polydor POSP 547*	.8 11
4 Jun 83	FLESH OF MY FLESH *Polydor OJ 4*	.41 6
25 Feb 84	BRIDGE *Polydor OJ 5*	.67 2
12 May 84	WHAT PRESENCE? *Polydor OJ 6*	.47 4
27 Oct 84	LEAN PERIOD *Polydor OJ 7*	.74 1

ORB ☺ UK, male instrumental/production duo — 30 wks

15 Jun 91	PERPETUAL DAWN *Big Life BLR 46*	.61 1
20 Jun 92	BLUE ROOM *Big Life BLRT 75*	.8 6
17 Oct 92	ASSASSIN *Big Life BLRT 81*	.12 5
13 Nov 93 ●	LITTLE FLUFFY CLOUDS *Big Life BLRD 98*	.10 5
5 Feb 94	PERPETUAL DAWN (re-entry) *Big Life BLRD 46*	.18 5
27 May 95	OXBOW LAKES *Island CID 609*	.38 2
8 Feb 97	TOXYGENE *Island CID 652*	.4 4
24 May 97	ASYLUM *Island CID 657*	.20 2

Roy ORBISON ● Truly original singer/songwriter, b. 23 April, 1936, Texas, d. 6 December, 1988. He was the most popular US vocalist in Britain during the 1960s Beat Group period, and his trademark was his dark glasses. He has a hit span of more than 33 years — 345 wks

28 Jul 60	ONLY THE LONELY *London HLU 9149*	.36 1
11 Aug 60 ★	ONLY THE LONELY (re-entry) *London HLU 9149*	.1 23
27 Oct 60	BLUE ANGEL *London HLU 9207*	.11 16
25 May 61 ●	RUNNING SCARED *London HLU 9342* ▲	.9 15
21 Sep 61	CRYIN' *London HLU 9405*	.25 9
8 Mar 62 ●	DREAM BABY *London HLU 9511*	.2 14
28 Jun 62	THE CROWD *London HLU 9561*	.40 4
8 Nov 62	WORKIN' FOR THE MAN *London HLU 9607*	.50 1
28 Feb 63 ●	IN DREAMS *London HLU 9676*	.6 23
30 May 63 ●	FALLING *London HLU 9727*	.9 11
19 Sep 63 ●	BLUE BAYOU/MEAN WOMAN BLUES *London HLU 9777*	.3 19
20 Feb 64	BORNE ON THE WIND *London HLU 9845*	.15 10
30 Apr 64 ★	IT'S OVER *London HLU 9882*	.1 18
10 Sep 64 ★	OH PRETTY WOMAN *London HLU 9919* ▲	.1 18
19 Nov 64 ●	PRETTY PAPER *London HLU 9930*	.6 11
11 Feb 65	GOODNIGHT *London HLU 9951*	.14 9
22 Jul 65	(SAY) YOU'RE MY GIRL *London HLU 9978*	.23 8
9 Sep 65	RIDE AWAY *London HLU 9986*	.34 9
4 Nov 65	CRAWLIN' BACK *London HLU 10000*	.19 9
27 Jan 66	BREAKIN' UP IS BREAKIN' MY HEART *London HL 10015*	.22 6
7 Apr 66	TWINKLE TOES *London HLU 10034*	.29 5
16 Jun 66	LANA *London HL 10051*	.15 9
18 Aug 66	TOO SOON TO KNOW *London HLU 10067*	.3 17
1 Dec 66	THERE WON'T BE MANY COMING HOME *London HL 10096*	.12 9
23 Feb 67	SO GOOD *London HL 10113*	.32 6
24 Jul 68	WALK ON *London HLU 10206*	.39 10
25 Sep 68	HEARTACHE *London HLU 10222*	.44 4
30 Apr 69	MY FRIEND *London HL 10261*	.35 4
13 Sep 69	PENNY ARCADE *London HL 10285*	.40 3
11 Oct 69	PENNY ARCADE (re-entry) *London HL 10285*	.27 11
14 Jan 89	YOU GOT IT *Virgin VS 1166*	.3 10
1 Apr 89	SHE'S A MYSTERY TO ME *Virgin VS 1173*	.27 5
4 Jul 92 ●	I DROVE ALL NIGHT *MCA MCS 1652*	.7 10
22 Aug 92	CRYING *Virgin America VUS 63* [1]	.13 6
7 Nov 92	HEARTBREAK RADIO *Virgin America VUS 68*	.36 3

UK No 1 ★　UK Top 10 ●　UK million seller ◆　UK entry at No 1 ■　US No 1 ▲

| 13 Nov 93 | I DROVE ALL NIGHT (re-issue) *Virgin America VUSCD 79* | 47 | 2 |

[1] Roy Orbison (duet with kd lang)

William ORBIT *UK, male producer* — 1 wk

| 26 Jun 93 | WATER FROM A VINE LEAF *Guerilla VSCDT 1465* | 59 | 1 |

ORBITAL ☺ *UK, male instrumental duo* — 41 wks

24 Mar 90	CHIME *ffrr F B5*	17	7
22 Sep 90	OMEN *ffrr F 145*	46	3
19 Jan 91	SATAN *ffrr FX 149*	31	4
15 Feb 92	MUTATIONS EP *ffrr FCD 181*	24	3
26 Sep 92	RADICCIO EP *Internal LIARX 1*	37	2
21 Aug 93	LUSH *Internal LIECD 7*	43	2
24 Sep 94	ARE WE HERE *Internal LIECD 15*	33	2
27 May 95	BELFAST *Volume VOLCD 1*	53	1
27 Apr 96	THE BOX *Internal LIECD 30*	11	4
11 Jan 97 ●	SATAN *Internal LIECD 37*	3	6
19 Apr 97 ●	THE SAINT *ffrr FCD 296*	3	7

Tracks on Mutations EP: Chime Crime / Oolaa / Farenheit 3D 3 / Speed Freak.
Tracks on Radiccio EP: Halcyon / The Naked and the Dead / Sunday.
The listed flip side of 'Belfast' was 'Innocent X' by Therapy?

ORCHESTRA ON THE HALF SHELL
US, male vocal/instrumental group — 6 wks

| 15 Dec 90 | TURTLE RHAPSODY *SBK SBK 17* | 36 | 6 |

ORCHESTRAL MANOEUVRES IN THE DARK ☺ *One of the most regular chart visitors of the 1980s had a nucleus of Andy McCluskey (v/syn) and Paul Humphreys (syn), who left in 1989. This Liverpool-based synthesiser band had numerous international hits including 'Maid of Orleans', which was Germany's biggest seller in 1982* — 201 wks

9 Feb 80	RED FRAME WHITE LIGHT *Dindisc DIN 6*	67	2
10 May 80	MESSAGES *Dindisc DIN 15*	13	11
4 Oct 80 ●	ENOLA GAY *Dindisc DIN 22*	8	15
29 Aug 81 ●	SOUVENIR *Dindisc DIN 24*	3	12
24 Oct 81 ●	JOAN OF ARC *Dindisc DIN 36*	5	14
23 Jan 82 ●	MAID OF ORLEANS (THE WALTZ JOAN OF ARC) *Dindisc DIN 40*	4	10
19 Feb 83	GENETIC ENGINEERING *Virgin VS 527*	20	8
9 Apr 83	TELEGRAPH *Virgin VS 580*	42	4
14 Apr 84 ●	LOCOMOTION *Virgin VS 660*	5	11
16 Jun 84	TALKING LOUD AND CLEAR *Virgin VS 685*	11	10
8 Sep 84	TESLA GIRLS *Virgin VS 705*	21	8
10 Nov 84	NEVER TURN AWAY *Virgin VS 727*	70	2
25 May 85	SO IN LOVE *Virgin VS 766*	27	7
20 Jul 85	SECRET *Virgin VS 796*	34	7
26 Oct 85	LA FEMME ACCIDENT *Virgin VS 811*	42	4
3 May 86	IF YOU LEAVE *Virgin VS 843*	48	4
6 Sep 86	(FOREVER) LIVE AND DIE *Virgin VS 888*	11	10
15 Nov 86	WE LOVE YOU *Virgin VS 911*	54	5
2 May 87	SHAME *Virgin VS 938*	52	3
6 Feb 88	DREAMING *Virgin VS 987*	50	3
2 Jul 88	DREAMING (re-entry) *Virgin VS 987*	60	3
30 Mar 91 ●	SAILING ON THE SEVEN SEAS *Virgin VS 1310*	3	13
6 Jul 91 ●	PANDORA'S BOX *Virgin VS 1331*	7	10
14 Sep 91	THEN YOU TURN AWAY *Virgin VS 1368*	50	4
7 Dec 91	CALL MY NAME *Virgin VS 1380*	50	2
15 May 93	STAND ABOVE ME *Virgin VSCDG 1444*	21	4
17 Jul 93	DREAM OF ME (BASED ON LOVE'S THEME) *Virgin VSCDT 1461*	24	5
18 Sep 93	EVERYDAY *Virgin VSCDT 1471*	59	2
17 Aug 96	WALKING ON THE MILKY WAY *Virgin VSCDT 1599*	17	5
2 Nov 96	UNIVERSAL *Virgin VSCDT 1606*	55	1
26 Sep 98	THE OMD REMIXES *Virgin VSCDT*	35	2

Group often known as OMD

Raul ORELLANA *Italy, male producer* — 8 wks

| 30 Sep 89 | THE REAL WILD HOUSE *RCA BCM 322* | 29 | 8 |

O.R.G.A.N. *Spain, male DJ/producer* — 2 wks

| 16 May 98 | TO THE WORLD *Multiply CDMULTY 34* | 33 | 2 |

ORIGIN UNKNOWN *UK, male instrumental/production duo* — 1 wk

| 13 Jul 96 | VALLEY OF THE SHADOWS *Ram RAMM 16CD* | 60 | 1 |

ORIGINAL *US, male vocal/instrumental duo* — 14 wks

14 Jan 95	I LUV U BABY *Ore AG 8CD*	31	3
19 Aug 95 ●	I LUV U BABY (re-mix) *Ore AGR 8CD*	2	9
11 Nov 95	B 2 GETHER *Ore AG 12CD*	29	2

ORIGINOO GUNN CLAPPAZ – See HELTAH SKELTAH and ORIGINOO GUNN CLAPPAZ

ORLANDO – See PRETENDERS / Chrissie HYNDE

Tony ORLANDO ☺ *US, male vocalist* — 11 wks

| 5 Oct 61 ● | BLESS YOU *Fontana H 330* | 5 | 11 |

See also DAWN

ORLONS *US, female/male vocal group* — 3 wks

| 27 Dec 62 | DON'T HANG UP *Cameo Parkway C 231* | 50 | 1 |
| 10 Jan 63 | DON'T HANG UP (re-entry) *Cameo Parkway C 231* | 39 | 2 |

ORN *UK, male DJ/producer – Omio Nourizadeh* — 1 wk

| 1 Mar 97 | SNOW *Deconstruction 74321447612* | 61 | 1 |

Beth ORTON *UK, female vocalist* — 7 wks

1 Feb 97	TOUCH ME WITH YOUR LOVE *Heavenly HVN 64CD*	60	1
5 Apr 97	SOMEONE'S DAUGHTER *Heavenly HVN 65CD*	49	1
14 Jun 97	SHE CRIES YOUR NAME *Heavenly HVN 68CD*	40	2
13 Dec 97	BEST BIT EP *Heavenly HVN 72CD* [1]	36	3

[1] Beth Orton featuring Terry Callier

Tracks on Best Bit EP: Best Bit / Skimming Stone / Dolphins / Lean on Me

ORVILLE – See Keith HARRIS and ORVILLE

Jeffrey OSBORNE ♪ *US, male vocalist* — 38 wks

17 Sep 83	DON'T YOU GET SO MAD *A & M AM 140*	54	2
14 Apr 84	STAY WITH ME TONIGHT *A & M AM 188*	18	11
23 Jun 84	ON THE WINGS OF LOVE *A & M AM 198*	11	14
20 Oct 84	DON'T STOP *A & M AM 222*	61	2
26 Jul 86	SOWETO *A & M AM 334*	44	5
6 Sep 86	SOWETO (re-entry) *A & M AM 334*	75	1
15 Aug 87	LOVE POWER *Arista RIS 27* [1]	63	3

[1] Dionne Warwick and Jeffrey Osborne

Joan OSBORNE ☺ ✔ *US, female vocalist* — 13 wks

| 10 Feb 96 ● | ONE OF US *Blue Gorilla JOACD 1* | 6 | 10 |
| 8 Jun 96 | ST. TERESA *Blue Gorilla JOACD 3* | 33 | 3 |

Tony OSBORNE SOUND *UK, orchestra* — 3 wks

| 23 Feb 61 | MAN FROM MADRID *HMV POP 827* [1] | 50 | 1 |
| 3 Feb 73 | THE SHEPHERD'S SONG *Philips 6006 266* | 46 | 2 |

[1] Tony Osborne Sound featuring Joanne Brown

Ozzy OSBOURNE ✔ *UK, male vocalist* — 42 wks

13 Sep 80	CRAZY TRAIN *Jet 197* [1]	49	4
15 Nov 80	MR. CROWLEY *Jet 7003* [1]	46	3
26 Nov 83	BARK AT THE MOON *Epic A 3915*	21	8
2 Jun 84	SO TIRED *Epic A 4452*	20	9
1 Feb 86	SHOT IN THE DARK *Epic A 6859*	20	6
9 Aug 86	THE ULTIMATE SIN/LIGHTNING STRIKES *Epic A 7311*	72	1
20 May 89	CLOSE MY EYES FOREVER *Dreamland PB 49409* [2]	47	3
28 Sep 91	NO MORE TEARS *Epic 6574407*	32	3

What: *Merry Xmas Everybody*　　**69**
Who: Slade
When: 1973 (1), 1981 (32), 1982 (67), 1983 (20), 1984 (47), 1985 (48), 1986 (71)
Which: Is one of the most popular and biggest-selling Christmas records. Penned by group members Noddy Holder and Jim Lea, as were their five other No 1s

What: *I'll Be Missing You*　　**70**
Who: Puff Daddy (pictured) and Faith Evans
When: 1997 (1)
Which: Topped both the UK and the US charts, and is based on Sting's song 'Every Breath You Take'. This tribute raised more than $3 million for the children of murdered rapper Notorious B.I.G. (Christopher Wallace)

What: *Vienna*　　**71**
Who: Ultravox
When: 1981 (2), 1993 (13)
Which: Introduced influential synth-rock band to the Top 20. This haunting new-romantic anthem was the title track of their fourth album – the first to feature melodramatic vocalist Midge Ure

What: *Distant Drums*　　**72**
Who: Jim Reeves
When: 1966
Which: Reached the top of the charts two years after the singer's death in a plane crash. It was his biggest hit and the first song composed solely by a woman (Cindy Walker) to top the UK chart

30 Nov 91		MAMA I'M COMING HOME *Epic 6576177*	46	2
25 Nov 95		PERRY MASON *Epic 6626395*	23	2
31 Aug 96		I JUST WANT YOU *Epic 6635702*	43	1

[1] Ozzy Osbourne's Blizzard of Ozz [2] Lita Ford duet with Ozzy Osbourne

OSIBISA ♪ ⊕ *Ghana/Nigeria, male vocal/instrumental group* **12 wks**

17 Jan 76		SUNSHINE DAY *Bronze BRO 20*	17	6
5 Jun 76		DANCE THE BODY MUSIC *Bronze BRO 26*	31	6

OSMOND BOYS *US, male vocal group* **6 wks**

9 Nov 91		BOYS WILL BE BOYS *Curb 6573847*	65	2
11 Jan 92		SHOW ME THE WAY *Curb 6577227*	60	4

Donny OSMOND ⊕ *Teenage teen-idol vocalist, b. 9 December, 1957, Utah. The main focal point of the hitmaking family act The Osmonds, he was one of the most popular pin-ups of the 1970s, and had three solo No 1s before his 16th birthday* **118 wks**

17 Jun 72	★	PUPPY LOVE *MGM 2006 104*	1	17
16 Sep 72	●	TOO YOUNG *MGM 2006 113*	5	12
21 Oct 72		PUPPY LOVE (re-entry) *MGM 2006 104*	45	2
11 Nov 72	●	WHY *MGM 2006 119*	3	20
23 Dec 72		PUPPY LOVE (2nd re-entry) *MGM 2006 104*	46	3
23 Dec 72		TOO YOUNG (re-entry) *MGM 2006 113*	47	3
27 Jan 73		PUPPY LOVE (3rd re-entry) *MGM 2006 104*	48	1
10 Mar 73	★	THE TWELFTH OF NEVER *MGM 2006 199*	1	14
18 Aug 73	★	YOUNG LOVE *MGM 2006 300*	1	10
10 Nov 73	●	WHEN I FALL IN LOVE *MGM 2006 365*	4	13
9 Nov 74		WHERE DID ALL THE GOOD TIMES GO *MGM 2006 468*	18	10
26 Sep 87		I'M IN IT FOR LOVE *Virgin VS 994*	70	1
6 Aug 88		SOLDIER OF LOVE *Virgin VS 1094*	29	4
12 Nov 88		IF IT'S LOVE THAT YOU WANT *Virgin VS 1140*	70	2
9 Feb 91		MY LOVE IS A FIRE *Capitol CL 600*	64	2

See also Donny and Marie OSMOND; OSMONDS

Donny and Marie OSMOND ⊕ *US, male/female vocal duo* **37 wks**

3 Aug 74	●	I'M LEAVING IT (ALL) UP TO YOU *MGM 2006 446*	2	12
14 Dec 74	●	MORNING SIDE OF THE MOUNTAIN *MGM 2006 474*	5	12
21 Jun 75		MAKE THE WORLD GO AWAY *MGM 2006 523*	18	6
17 Jan 76		DEEP PURPLE *MGM 2006 561*	25	7

See also Donny OSMOND; Marie OSMOND

Little Jimmy OSMOND ⊕ *US, male vocalist* **50 wks**

25 Nov 72	★	LONG HAIRED LOVER FROM LIVERPOOL *MGM 2006 109*	1	24
31 Mar 73	●	TWEEDLE DEE *MGM 2006 175*	4	13
19 May 73		LONG HAIRED LOVER FROM LIVERPOOL (re-entry) *MGM 2006 109*	41	3
23 Mar 74		I'M GONNA KNOCK ON YOUR DOOR *MGM 2006 389*	11	10

See also Osmonds

Marie OSMOND ⊕ *US, female vocalist* **15 wks**

17 Nov 73	●	PAPER ROSES *MGM 2006 315*	2	15

See also Donny and Marie OSMOND; OSMONDS

OSMONDS ⊕ *US, male vocal/instrumental group* **92 wks**

25 Mar 72		DOWN BY THE LAZY RIVER *MGM 2006 096*	40	5
11 Nov 72	●	CRAZY HORSES *MGM 2006 142*	2	18
14 Jul 73	●	GOING HOME *MGM 2006 288*	4	10
27 Oct 73	●	LET ME IN *MGM 2006 321*	2	14
20 Apr 74		I CAN'T STOP *MCA 129*	12	10
24 Aug 74	●	LOVE ME FOR A REASON *MGM 2006 458*	1	9
1 Mar 75		HAVING A PARTY *MGM 2006 492*	28	8
24 May 75	●	THE PROUD ONE *MGM 2006 520*	5	8
15 Nov 75		I'M STILL GONNA NEED YOU *MGM 2006 551*	32	4
30 Oct 76		I CAN'T LIVE A DREAM *Polydor 2066 726*	37	5
23 Sep 95		CRAZY HORSES (re-mix) *Polydor 5793212*	50	1

See also Donny OSMOND; Donny and Marie OSMOND; Little Jimmy OSMOND; Marie OSMOND

Gilbert O'SULLIVAN ⊕ *Distinctive Irish singer/songwriter/pianist, b. Raymond O'Sullivan, 1 December, 1946, Waterford. His unusual image – short trousers, flat cap and pudding-basin haircut – helped to launch the successful international career of the performer voted No 1 UK Male Singer of 1972* **145 wks**

28 Nov 70	●	NOTHING RHYMED *MAM 3*	8	11
3 Apr 71		UNDERNEATH THE BLANKET GO *MAM 13*	40	1
17 Apr 71		UNDERNEATH THE BLANKET GO (re-entry) *MAM 13*	42	3
24 Jul 71		WE WILL *MAM 30*	16	11
27 Nov 71	●	NO MATTER HOW I TRY *MAM 53*	5	15
4 Mar 72	●	ALONE AGAIN (NATURALLY) *MAM 66* ▲	3	12
17 Jun 72	●	OOH-WAKKA-DOO-WAKKA-DAY *MAM 78*	8	11
21 Oct 72	★	CLAIR *MAM 84*	1	14
17 Mar 73	★	GET DOWN *MAM 96*	1	13
15 Sep 73		OOH BABY *MAM 107*	18	7
10 Nov 73	●	WHY OH WHY OH WHY *MAM 111*	6	14
9 Feb 74		HAPPINESS IS ME AND YOU *MAM 114*	19	7
24 Aug 74		A WOMAN'S PLACE *MAM 122*	42	3
14 Dec 74		CHRISTMAS SONG *MAM 124*	12	6
14 Jun 75		I DON'T LOVE YOU BUT I THINK I LIKE YOU *MAM 130*	14	6
27 Sep 80		WHAT'S IN A KISS? *CBS 8929*	19	9
24 Feb 90		SO WHAT *Dover ROJ 3*	70	2

O.T. QUARTET – *See OUR TRIBE*

OTHER TWO *UK, male/female vocal/instrumental duo* **5 wks**

9 Nov 91		TASTY FISH *Factory FAC 3297*	41	3
6 Nov 93		SELFISH *London TWOCD 1*	46	2

Johnny OTIS SHOW ⊕ *US, band* **22 wks**

22 Nov 57	●	MA HE'S MAKING EYES AT ME *Capitol CL 14794* [1]	2	15
10 Jan 58		BYE BYE BABY *Capitol CL 14817* [2]	20	7

[1] Johnny Otis and his orchestra with Marie Adams and the Three Tons of Joy
[2] Johnny Otis Show, vocals by Marie Adams and Johnny Otis

OTT ⊕ *Ireland, male vocal group* **18 wks**

1 Mar 97		LET ME IN *Epic 6642052*	12	5
17 May 97		FOREVER GIRL *Epic 6645082*	24	3
23 Aug 97		ALL OUT OF LOVE *Epic 6649152*	11	4
24 Jan 98		THE STORY OF LOVE *Epic OTT 1CD*	11	6

OTTAWAN ☺ ⊕ *France, male/female vocal duo* **45 wks**

13 Sep 80	●	D.I.S.C.O. *Carrere CAR 161*	2	18
13 Dec 80		YOU'RE O.K. *Carrere CAR 168*	56	6
29 Aug 81	●	HANDS UP (GIVE ME YOUR HEART) *Carrere CAR 183*	3	15
5 Dec 81		HELP, GET ME SOME HELP! *Carrere CAR 215*	49	6

John OTWAY and Wild Willy BARRETT
UK, male vocal/instrumental duo **12 wks**

3 Dec 77		REALLY FREE *Polydor 2058 951*	27	8
5 Jul 80		DK 50–80 *Polydor 2059 250* [1]	45	4

[1] Otway and Barrett

OUI 3 ⊕ 📀
UK/US/Switzerland, male/female vocal/instrumental group **21 wks**

20 Feb 93		FOR WHAT IT'S WORTH *MCA MCSTD 1736*	28	6
24 Apr 93		ARMS OF SOLITUDE *MCA MCSTD 1759*	54	2
17 Jul 93		BREAK FROM THE OLD ROUTINE *MCA MCSTD 1793*	17	6
23 Oct 93		FOR WHAT IT'S WORTH (re-mix) *MCA MCSTD 1941*	26	3
29 Jan 94		FACT OF LIFE *MCA MCSTD 1939*	38	2
27 May 95		JOY OF LIVING *MCA MCSTD 2057*	55	2

OUR DAUGHTER'S WEDDING
US, male vocal/instrumental group **6 wks**

1 Aug 81		LAWNCHAIRS *EMI America EA 124*	49	6

UK No 1 ★ UK Top 10 ● UK million seller ◆ UK entry at No 1 ■ US No 1 ▲

OUR HOUSE *Australia, male instrumental production duo* — 1 wk
31 Aug 96	FLOOR SPACE *Perfecto PERF 125CD*	52	1

OUR KID 🌑 *UK, male vocal group* — 11 wks
29 May 76 ●	YOU JUST MIGHT SEE ME CRY *Polydor 2058 729*	2	11

OUR TRIBE / ONE TRIBE
UK/US, male/female vocal/instrumental group — 12 wks
20 Jun 92	WHAT HAVE YOU DONE (IS THIS ALL) *Inner Rhythm HEART 03* 1	52	2
27 Mar 93	I BELIEVE IN YOU *Ffrreedom TABCD 117* 2	42	2
30 Apr 94	HOLD THAT SUCKER DOWN *Cheeky CHEKCD 004* 3	24	3
21 May 94 ●	LOVE COME HOME *Triangle BLUESCD 001* 4	73	1
13 May 95	HIGH AS A KITE *ffrr FCD 259* 5	55	1
30 Sep 95 ●	HOLD THAT SUCKER DOWN (re-mix) *Cheeky CHEKCD 009* 3	26	3

1 One Tribe featuring Gem 2 Our Tribe 3 OT Quartet 4 Our Tribe with Franke Pharoah and Kristne W 5 One Tribe featuring Roger

OUT OF MY HAIR *UK, male vocal/instrumental group* — 1 wk
1 Jul 95	MISTER JONES *RCA 74321267812*	73	1

OUTHERE BROTHERS 📀☺ *US, male vocal/instrumental duo* — 50 wks
18 Mar 95 ★	DON'T STOP (WIGGLE WIGGLE) *Eternal YZ 917CD*	1	15
17 Jun 95 ★	BOOM BOOM BOOM *Eternal YZ 938CD*	1	15
23 Sep 95 ●	LA LA LA HEY HEY *Eternal YZ 974CD*	7	7
16 Dec 95 ●	IF YOU WANNA PARTY *Eternal WEA 030CD* 1	9	10
25 Jan 97	LET ME HEAR YOU SAY 'OLE OLE' *WEA 089CD*	18	3

1 Molella featuring the Outhere Brothers

OUTLANDER *Belgium, male producer – Marcos Salon* — 3 wks
31 Aug 91	VAMP *R&S RSUK 1*	51	2
7 Feb 98	THE VAMP (REVAMPED) *R&S RS 97113CDX*	62	1

OUTLAWS *UK, male instrumental group* — 4 wks
13 Apr 61	SWINGIN' LOW *HMV POP 844*	46	2
8 Jun 61	AMBUSH *HMV POP 877*	43	2

See also Mike BERRY

OUTRAGE *US, male vocalist* — 2 wks
11 Mar 95	TALL 'N' HANDSOME *Effective ECFL 001CD*	57	1
23 Nov 96	TALL 'N' HANDSOME (re-mix) *Positiva CDTIV 64*	51	1

OVERLANDERS 🌑 *UK, male vocal/instrumental group* — 10 wks
13 Jan 66 ★	MICHELLE *Pye 7N 17034*	1	10

OVERWEIGHT POOCH – See Ce Ce PENISTON

Mark OWEN 🌑 *UK, male vocalist* — 22 wks
30 Nov 96 ●	CHILD *RCA 74321424422*	3	9
15 Feb 97 ●	CLEMENTINE *RCA 74321454982*	3	6
22 Feb 97	CHILD (re-entry) *RCA 74321424422*	45	4
23 Aug 97	I AM WHAT I AM *RCA 74321501222*	29	3

Reg OWEN ℂ *UK, orchestra* — 10 wks
27 Feb 59	MANHATTAN SPIRITUAL *Pye International 7N 25009*	20	8
27 Oct 60	OBSESSION *Palette PG 9004*	43	2

Sid OWEN and Patsy PALMER *UK, male/female vocal duo* — 1 wk
16 Dec 95	BETTER BELIEVE IT (CHILDREN IN NEED) *Trinity TDM 001CD*	60	1

Robert OWENS *US, male vocalist* — 4 wks
7 Dec 91	I'LL BE YOUR FRIEND *Perfecto PB 45161*	75	2
26 Apr 97	I'LL BE YOUR FRIEND (re-mix) *Perfecto PERF 137CD1*	25	2

See also VARIOUS ARTISTS (EPs & LPs) – Gimme Shelter (EP)

Jazzi P *UK, female rapper* — 12 wks
8 Jul 89	GET LOOSE *Breakout USA 659* 1	25	6
9 Jun 90	FEEL THE RHYTHM *A & M AMUSA 691*	51	2
3 Aug 91	REBEL WOMAN *DNA 7DNA 001* 2	42	4

1 L.A. Mix performed by Jazzi P 2 DNA performed by Jazzi P

Thom PACE 🌑 *US, male vocalist* — 15 wks
19 May 79	MAYBE *RSO 34*	14	15

PACEMAKERS – See GERRY and the PACEMAKERS

PACK featuring Nigel BENN
UK, male vocal/instrumental group — 2 wks
8 Dec 90	STAND AND FIGHT *IQ ZB 44237*	61	2

PACKABEATS *UK, male instrumental group* — 1 wk
23 Feb 61	GYPSY BEAT *Parlophone R 4729*	49	1

Jose PADILLA featuring Angela JOHN
Spain, male DJ, and UK, female vocalist — 1 wk
8 Aug 98	WHO DO YOU LOVE *Manifesto FESCD 45*	59	1

PAGANINI TRAXX *Italy, male DJ/producer* — 1 wk
1 Feb 97	ZOE *Sony S3 DANUCD 18X*	47	1

Jimmy PAGE – See Robert PLANT; PUFF DADDY

Patti PAGE ℂ *US, female vocalist* — 5 wks
27 Mar 53 ●	(HOW MUCH IS) THAT DOGGIE IN THE WINDOW *Oriole CB 1156* ▲	9	5

Tommy PAGE *US, male vocalist* — 3 wks
26 May 90	I'LL BE YOUR EVERYTHING *Sire W 9959* ▲	53	3

PAGLIARO *Canada, male vocalist* — 6 wks
19 Feb 72	LOVING YOU AIN'T EASY *Pye 7N 45111*	31	6

PAID AND LIVE *US, male production duo* — 1 wk
27 Dec 97	ALL MY TIME *World Entertainment OWEDC 2* 1	57	1

1 Paid and Live featuring Lauryn Hill

Elaine PAIGE ℂ *UK, female vocalist* — 41 wks
21 Oct 78	DON'T WALK AWAY TILL I TOUCH YOU *EMI 2862*	46	5
6 Jun 81 ●	MEMORY *Polydor POSP 279*	6	12
30 Jan 82	MEMORY (re-entry) *Polydor POSP 279*	67	3
14 Apr 84	SOMETIMES (THEME FROM 'CHAMPIONS') *Island IS 174*	72	1
5 Jan 85 ★	I KNOW HIM SO WELL *RCA CHESS 3* 1	1	16
21 Nov 87	THE SECOND TIME (THEME FROM 'BILITIS') *WEA YZ 163*	69	1
21 Jan 95	HYMNE A L'AMOUR (IF YOU LOVE ME) *WEA YZ 899CD*	68	1
24 Oct 98	MEMORY (re-recording) *WEA WEA 197CD*	36	2

1 Elaine Paige and Barbara Dickson

UK No 1 ★ UK Top 10 ● UK million seller ◆ UK entry at No 1 ■ US No 1 ▲

Hal PAIGE and the WHALERS
US, male vocal/instrumental group **1 wk**

25 Aug 60	GOING BACK TO MY HOME TOWN *Melodisc MEL 1553*	50	1

Jennifer PAIGE ❻ *US, female vocalist* **12 wks**

12 Sep 98	CRUSH *EAR 0039425*	4	12

Orchestre De Chambre Jean-Francois PAILLARD
France, male conductor and orchestra **3 wks**

20 Aug 88	THEME FROM 'VIETNAM' (CANON IN D) *Debut DEBT 3053*	61	3

PALE *Ireland, male vocal/instrumental group* **2 wks**

13 Jun 92	DOGS WITH NO TAILS *A & M AM 866*	51	2

PALE FOUNTAINS *UK, male vocal/instrumental group* **6 wks**

27 Nov 82	THANK YOU *Virgin VS 557*	48	6

PALE SAINTS *Australia, male/female vocal/instrumental group* **1 wk**

6 Jul 91	KINKY LOVE *4AD AD 1009*	72	1

Barry PALMER – See Mike OLDFIELD

Patsy PALMER – See Sid OWEN and Patsy PALMER

Robert PALMER ❻ ✍ *Grammy-winning UK rock-group veteran, b. 19 January, 1949, Yorkshire. This vocalist's hottest run of transatlantic hits came after he fronted short-lived Anglo-American supergroup Power Station in 1985. He benefited from some striking award-winning videos featuring an all-female backing band* **128 wks**

20 May 78	EVERY KINDA PEOPLE *Island WIP 6425*	53	4
7 Jul 79	BAD CASE OF LOVIN' YOU (DOCTOR DOCTOR) *Island WIP 6481*	61	2
6 Sep 80	JOHNNY AND MARY *Island WIP 6638*	44	8
22 Nov 80	LOOKING FOR CLUES *Island WIP 6651*	33	9
13 Feb 82	SOME GUYS HAVE ALL THE LUCK *Island WIP 6754*	16	8
2 Apr 83	YOU ARE IN MY SYSTEM *Island IS 104*	53	4
18 Jun 83	YOU CAN HAVE IT (TAKE MY HEART) *Island IS 121*	66	2
10 May 86 ●	ADDICTED TO LOVE *Island IS 270* ▲	5	15
19 Jul 86 ●	I DIDN'T MEAN TO TURN YOU ON *Island IS 283*	9	9
1 Nov 86	DISCIPLINE OF LOVE *Island IS 242*	68	1
26 Mar 88	SWEET LIES *Island IS 352*	58	3
11 Jun 88	SIMPLY IRRESISTIBLE *EMI EM 61*	44	4
15 Oct 88 ●	SHE MAKES MY DAY *EMI EM 65*	6	12
13 May 89	CHANGE HIS WAYS *EMI EM 85*	28	7
26 Aug 89	IT COULD HAPPEN TO YOU *EMI EM 99*	71	1
3 Nov 90 ●	I'LL BE YOUR BABY TONIGHT *EMI EM 167* [1]	6	10
5 Jan 91 ●	MERCY MERCY ME – I WANT YOU *EMI EM 173*	9	9
15 Jun 91	DREAMS TO REMEMBER *EMI EM 193*	68	1
7 Mar 92	EVERY KINDA PEOPLE (re-issue) *Island IS 498*	43	3
17 Oct 92	WITCHCRAFT *EMI EM 251*	50	3
9 Jul 94	GIRL U WANT *EMI CDEMS 331*	57	2
3 Sep 94	KNOW BY NOW *EMI CDEMS 343*	25	5
24 Dec 94	YOU BLOW ME AWAY *EMI CDEMS 350*	38	4
14 Oct 95	RESPECT YOURSELF *EMI CDEMS 399*	45	2

[1] Robert Palmer and UB40

Suzanne PALMER – See CLUB 69; ABSOLUTE

PAN POSITION
Italy/Venezuela, male instrumental/production group **1 wk**

18 Jun 94	ELEPHANT PAW (GET DOWN TO THE FUNK) *Positiva CDTIV 13*	55	1

PANDORA'S BOX *US, male/female vocal/instrumental group* **3 wks**

21 Oct 89	IT'S ALL COMING BACK TO ME NOW *Virgin VS 1216*	51	3

Darryl PANDY – See Farley 'Jackmaster' FUNK

Johnny PANIC and the BIBLE OF DREAMS
UK, male / female vocal / instrumental group **2 wks**

2 Feb 91	JOHNNY PANIC AND THE BIBLE OF DREAMS *Fontana PANIC 1*	70	2

See also TEARS FOR FEARS

PANTERA ⚡ *US, male vocal/instrumental group* **8 wks**

10 Oct 92	MOUTH FOR WAR *Atco A 5845T*	73	1
27 Feb 93	WALK *Atco B 6076CD*	35	2
19 Mar 94	I'M BROKEN *Atco B 5932CD1*	19	2
22 Oct 94	PLANET CARAVAN *East West A 5836CD1*	26	3

PAPER DOLLS ❻ *UK, female vocal group* **13 wks**

13 Mar 68	SOMETHING HERE IN MY HEART (KEEPS A-TELLIN' ME NO) *Pye 7N 17456*	11	13

PAPER LACE ❻ *UK, male vocal/instrumental group* **41 wks**

23 Feb 74 ★	BILLY DON'T BE A HERO *Bus Stop BUS 1014*	1	14
4 May 74 ●	THE NIGHT CHICAGO DIED *Bus Stop BUS 1016* ▲	3	11
24 Aug 74	THE BLACK EYED BOYS *Bus Stop BUS 1019*	11	10
4 Mar 78	WE'VE GOT THE WHOLE WORLD IN OUR HANDS *Warner Bros. K17110* [1]	24	6

[1] Nottingham forest FC with Paper Lace

PAPERDOLLS *UK, female vocal group* **1 wk**

12 Sep 98	GONNA MAKE YOU BLUSH *MCA MCSTD 40175*	65	1

PAPPA BEAR featuring VAN DER TOORN
Germany, male rapper, and Holland, male vocalist **1 wk**

16 May 98	CHERISH *Universal UMD 70316*	47	1

Vanessa PARADIS ❻ *France, female vocalist* **30 wks**

13 Feb 88 ●	JOE LE TAXI *FA Productions POSP 902*	3	10
10 Oct 92 ●	BE MY BABY *Remark PO 235*	6	15
27 Feb 93	SUNDAY MONDAYS *Remark PZCD 251*	49	4
24 Jul 93	JUST AS LONG AS YOU ARE THERE *Remark PZCD 272*	57	1

PARADISE *UK, male vocal/instrumental group* **4 wks**

10 Sep 83	ONE MIND, TWO HEARTS *Priority P 1*	42	4

PARADISE LOST *UK, male vocal/instrumental group* **3 wks**

20 May 95	THE LAST TIME *Music For Nations CDKUT 165*	60	1
7 Oct 95	FOREVER FAILURE *Music For Nations CDKUT 169*	66	1
28 Jun 97	SAY JUST WORDS *Music For Nations CDKUT 174*	53	1

PARADISE ORGANISATION
UK, male instrumental/production group **1 wk**

23 Jan 93	PRAYER TOWER *Cowboy RODEO 13*	70	1

PARADOX *UK, male instrumental duo* **2 wks**

24 Feb 90	JAILBREAK *Ronin 7R2*	66	2

Norrie PARAMOR *UK, orchestra* **8 wks**

17 Mar 60	THEME FROM 'A SUMMER PLACE' *Columbia DB 4419*	36	2
22 Mar 62	THEME FROM 'Z CARS' *Columbia DB 4789*	33	6

PARAMOUNT JAZZ BAND – See Mr Acker BILK and his PARAMOUNT JAZZ BAND

PARAMOUNTS *UK, male vocal/instrumental group* **7 wks**

16 Jan 64	POISON IVY *Parlophone R 5093*	35	7

PARCHMENT *UK, male/female vocal/instrumental group* **5 wks**

16 Sep 72	LIGHT UP THE FIRE *Pye 7N 45178*	31	5

UK No 1 ★   UK Top 10 ●   UK million seller ◆   UK entry at No 1 ■   US No 1 ▲

PARIS UK, male/female vocal group — 4 wks
19 Jun 82	NO GETTING OVER YOU *RCA 222*....................	49	4

PARIS US, male vocalist — 2 wks
21 Jan 95	GUERRILLA FUNK *Priority PTYCD 100*	38	2

Mica PARIS ♪ ☺ UK, female vocalist — 63 wks
7 May 88 ●	MY ONE TEMPTATION *Fourth & Broadway BRW 85*	7	11
30 Jul 88	LIKE DREAMERS DO *Fourth & Broadway BRW 108* [1] ...26	5
22 Oct 88	BREATHE LIFE INTO ME *Fourth & Broadway BRW 115* ...26	10
21 Jan 89	WHERE IS THE LOVE *Fourth & Broadway BRW 122* [2] 19	7
6 Oct 90	CONTRIBUTION *Fourth & Broadway BRW 188*................33	4
1 Dec 90	SOUTH OF THE RIVER *Fourth & Broadway BRW 199* 50	2
23 Feb 91	IF I LOVE U 2 NITE *Fourth & Broadway BRW 207* 43	3
31 Aug 91	YOUNG SOUL REBELS *Big Life BLR 57* 61	3
3 Apr 93	I NEVER FELT LIKE THIS BEFORE *Fourth & Broadway BRCD 263*.................15	5
5 Jun 93	I WANNA HOLD ON TO YOU *Fourth & Broadway BRCD 275*....27	3
7 Aug 93	TWO IN A MILLION *Fourth & Broadway BRCD 285* 51	2
4 Dec 93	WHISPER A PRAYER *Fourth & Broadway BRCD 287*..........65	1
8 Apr 95	ONE *Cooltempo CDCOOL 304* 29	4
16 May 98	STAY *Cooltempo CDCOOL 334* 40	2
14 Nov 98	BLACK ANGEL *Cooltempo CDCOOL 341*......................72	1

[1] Mica Paris featuring Courtney Pine [2] Mica Paris and Will Downing

Ryan PARIS ✪ France, male vocalist — 10 wks
3 Sep 83 ●	DOLCE VITA *Carrere CAR 289* 5	10

PARIS ANGELS UK, male/female vocal/instrumental group — 5 wks
3 Nov 90	SCOPE *Sheer Joy SHEER 0047* 75	1
20 Jul 91	PERFUME *Virgin VS 1360* 55	3
21 Sep 91	FADE *Virgin VS 1365* 70	1

PARIS RED US/Germany, male/female vocal/instrumental duo — 2 wks
29 Feb 92	GOOD FRIEND *Columbia 6569417* 61	1
15 May 93	PROMISES *Columbia 6592342* 59	1

John PARISH – See P J HARVEY

Simon PARK ☾ UK, orchestra — 24 wks
25 Nov 72	EYE LEVEL *Columbia DB 8946* ◆ 41	2
15 Sep 73 ★	EYE LEVEL (re-entry) *Columbia DB 8946* 1	22

Graham PARKER and the RUMOUR
UK, male vocal/instrumental group — 16 wks
19 Mar 77	THE PINK PARKER EP *Vertigo PARK 001* 24	5
22 Apr 78	HEY LORD DON'T ASK ME QUESTIONS *Vertigo PARK 002* 32	7
20 Mar 82	TEMPORARY BEAUTY *RCA PARK 100* [1] 50	4

[1] Graham Parker

Tracks on The Pink Parker EP: Hold Back the Night/(Let Me Get) Sweet on You/ White Honey/Soul Shoes

Ray PARKER Jr. ♪ US, male vocalist — 47 wks
25 Aug 84 ●	GHOSTBUSTERS *Arista ARIST 580* ▲ 2	31
18 Jan 86	GIRLS ARE MORE FUN *Arista ARIST 641* 46	4
3 Oct 87	I DON'T THINK THAT MAN SHOULD SLEEP ALONE *Geffen GEF 27* 13	10
30 Jan 88	OVER YOU *Geffen GEF 33* 65	2

See also RAYDIO

Robert PARKER US, male vocalist — 8 wks
4 Aug 66	BAREFOOTIN' *Island WI 286*......................24	8

Sara PARKER US, female vocalist — 2 wks
12 Apr 97	MY LOVE IS DEEP *Manifesto FESCD 22* 22	2

Jimmy PARKINSON ☾ Australia, male vocalist — 19 wks
2 Mar 56 ●	THE GREAT PRETENDER *Columbia DB 3729* ▲ 9	13
17 Aug 56	WALK HAND IN HAND *Columbia DB 3775*.................30	1
5 Oct 56	WALK HAND IN HAND (re-entry) *Columbia DB 3775*....................26	1
9 Nov 56	IN THE MIDDLE OF THE HOUSE *Columbia DB 3833* 26	2
30 Nov 56	IN THE MIDDLE OF THE HOUSE (re-entry) *Columbia DB 3833*....................20	2

John PARR ✪ ✒ UK, male vocalist — 22 wks
14 Sep 85 ●	ST ELMO'S FIRE (MAN IN MOTION) *London LON 73* ▲ 6	13
18 Jan 86	NAUGHTY NAUGHTY *London LON 80* 58	3
30 Aug 86	ROCK 'N' ROLL MERCENARIES *Arista ARIST 666* [1] 31	6

[1] Meat Loaf featuring John Parr

Dean PARRISH US, male vocalist — 5 wks
8 Feb 75	I'M ON MY WAY *UK USA 2* 38	5

Man PARRISH ☺ US, male mixer — 26 wks
26 Mar 83	HOP HOP, BE BOP (DON'T STOP) *Polydor POSP 575* 41	6
23 Mar 85	BOOGIE DOWN (BRONX) *Boiling Point POSP 731* 56	4
13 Sep 86	MALE STRIPPER *Bolts BOLTS 4* [1] 64	3
3 Jan 87	MALE STRIPPER (re-entry) *Bolts BOLTS 4* [1] 63	1
7 Feb 87 ●	MALE STRIPPER (2nd re-entry) *Bolts BOLTS 4* [1] 4	12

[1] Man 2 Man meet Man Parrish

Bill PARSONS US, male vocalist — 2 wks
10 Apr 59	ALL AMERICAN BOY *London HL 8798* 22	2

Record erroneously credited to Bill Parsons, actual vocalist is Bobby Bare

Alan PARSONS PROJECT UK, male vocal/instrumental group — 4 wks
15 Jan 83	OLD AND WISE *Arista ARIST 494* 74	1
10 Mar 84	DON'T ANSWER ME *Arista ARIST 553* 58	3

PARTIZAN UK, male DJ/production duo –
'Tall Paul' Newman and Craig Daniel-Yefet — 3 wks
8 Feb 97	DRIVE ME CRAZY *Multiply CDMULTY 17*...................36	2
6 Dec 97	KEEP YOUR LOVE *Multiply CDMULTY 29* [1] 53	1

[1] Partizan featuring Natalie Robb

PARTNERS – See Al HUDSON

PARTNERS IN KRYME ◀ US, male rap duo — 10 wks
21 Jul 90 ★	TURTLE POWER *SBK TURTLE 1* 1	10

David PARTON ✪ UK, male vocalist — 9 wks
15 Jan 77 ●	ISN'T SHE LOVELY *Pye 7N 45663* 4	9

Dolly PARTON ⬐ US, female vocalist — 33 wks
15 May 76 ●	JOLENE *RCA 2675*...................7	10
21 Feb 81	9 TO 5 *RCA 25* ▲ 47	5
12 Nov 83 ●	ISLANDS IN THE STREAM *RCA 378* [1] ▲ 7	15
7 Apr 84	HERE YOU COME AGAIN *RCA 395* 75	1
16 Apr 94	THE DAY I FALL IN LOVE *Columbia 6600282* [2] 64	2

[1] Kenny Rogers and Dolly Parton [2] Dolly Parton and James Ingram

Stella PARTON US, female vocalist — 4 wks
22 Oct 77	THE DANGER OF A STRANGER *Elektra K 12272*........................35	4

Don PARTRIDGE ✪ UK, male vocalist — 32 wks
7 Feb 68 ●	ROSIE *Columbia DB 8330* 4	12
29 May 68 ●	BLUE EYES *Columbia DB 8416* 3	13
19 Feb 69	BREAKFAST ON PLUTO *Columbia DB 8538*...................26	7

PARTRIDGE FAMILY ⊘ US, male/female vocal group — 53 wks

13 Feb 71	I THINK I LOVE YOU Bell 1130 [1] ▲	18	9
26 Feb 72	IT'S ONE OF THOSE NIGHTS (YES LOVE) Bell 1203 [1]	11	11
8 Jul 72 ●	BREAKING UP IS HARD TO DO Bell MABEL 1 [1]	3	13
3 Feb 73 ●	LOOKING THROUGH THE EYES OF LOVE Bell 1278 [2]	9	9
19 May 73 ●	WALKING IN THE RAIN Bell 1293 [2]	10	11

[1] Partridge Family starring Shirley Jones featuring David Cassidy
[2] Partridge Family starring David Cassidy

PARTY ANIMALS Holland, male instrumental/production duo — 3 wks

| 1 Jun 96 | HAVE YOU EVER BEEN MELLOW Mokum DB 17553 | 56 | 1 |
| 19 Oct 96 | HAVE YOU EVER BEEN MELLOW EP Mokum DB 17413 | 43 | 2 |

Tracks on Have You Ever Been Mellow (EP): Have You Ever Been Mellow/ Hava Nequilla/Aquarius

PARTY FAITHFUL UK, male/female vocal/instrumental group — 1 wk

| 22 Jul 95 | BRASS: LET THERE BE HOUSE Ore AG 10CD | 54 | 1 |

PASADENAS ⊘ 🎤 UK, male vocal group — 57 wks

28 May 88 ●	TRIBUTE (RIGHT ON) CBS PASA 1	5	14
17 Sep 88	RIDING ON A TRAIN CBS PASA 2	13	9
26 Nov 88	ENCHANTED LADY CBS PASA 3	31	6
12 May 90	LOVE THING CBS PASA 4	22	5
14 Jul 90	REELING CBS PASA 5	75	1
1 Feb 92 ●	I'M DOING FINE NOW Columbia 6577187	4	10
4 Apr 92	MAKE IT WITH YOU Columbia 6579257	20	4
6 Jun 92	I BELIEVE IN MIRACLES Columbia 6580567	34	3
29 Aug 92	MOVING IN THE RIGHT DIRECTION Columbia 6583417	49	2
21 Nov 92	LET'S STAY TOGETHER Columbia 6587747	22	3

PASSENGERS 🎸🎵 Ireland/UK/Italy, male vocal/instrumental group — 9 wks

| 2 Dec 95 ● | MISS SARAJEVO Island CID 625 | 6 | 9 |

PASSION UK, male vocal / rap group — 1 wk

| 25 Jan 97 | SHARE YOUR LOVE (NO DIGGITY MIX) Charm CRTCDS 269 | 62 | 1 |

PASSIONS UK, male/female vocal/instrumental group — 8 wks

| 31 Jan 81 | I'M IN LOVE WITH A GERMAN FILM STAR Polydor POSP 222 | 25 | 8 |

PAT and MICK ⊘ UK, male vocal duo — 27 wks

9 Apr 88	LET'S ALL CHANT/ON THE NIGHT PWL PWL 10 [1]	11	9
25 Mar 89 ●	I HAVEN'T STOPPED DANCING YET PWL PWL 33	9	8
14 Apr 90	USE IT UP AND WEAR IT OUT PWL PWL 55	22	6
23 Mar 91	GIMME SOME PWL PWL 75	53	2
15 May 93	HOT HOT HOT PWL International PARKCD 1	47	2

[1] Mick and Pat

'On the Night' only listed from 4 Jun, 1988. It peaked at No 70

PATIENCE and PRUDENCE US, female vocal duo — 8 wks

2 Nov 56	TONIGHT YOU BELONG TO ME London HLU 8321	28	3
1 Mar 57	GONNA GET ALONG WITHOUT YA NOW London HLU 8369	22	4
12 Apr 57	GONNA GET ALONG WITHOUT YA NOW (re-entry) London HLU 8369	24	1

PATRA 🎵 Jamaica, female vocalist — 11 wks

25 Dec 93	FAMILY AFFAIR Polydor PZCD 304 [1]	18	8
30 Sep 95	PULL UP TO THE BUMPER Epic 6623942	50	2
10 Aug 96	WORK MI BODY Heavenly HVN 53CD [2]	75	1

[1] Shabba Ranks featuring Patra and Terry & Monica
[2] Monkey Mafia featuring Patra

PATRIC UK, male vocalist — 2 wks

| 9 Jul 94 | LOVE ME Bell 7432125352 | 54 | 2 |

Kellee PATTERSON US, female vocalist — 7 wks

| 18 Feb 78 | IF IT DON'T FIT DON'T FORCE IT EMI International INT 544 | 44 | 7 |

Rahsaan PATTERSON US, male vocalist — 2 wks

| 26 Jul 97 | STOP BY MCA MCSTD 48055 | 50 | 1 |
| 21 Mar 98 | WHERE YOU ARE MCA MCSTD 48073 | 55 | 1 |

Billy PAUL 🎤 US, male vocalist — 44 wks

13 Jan 73	ME AND MRS JONES Epic EPC 1055 ▲	12	9
12 Jan 74	THANKS FOR SAVING MY LIFE Philadelphia Interna PIR 1928	33	6
22 May 76	LET'S MAKE A BABY Philadelphia Interna PIR 4144	30	5
30 Apr 77	LET 'EM IN Philadelphia Interna PIR 5143	26	5
16 Jul 77	YOUR SONG Philadelphia Interna PIR 5391	37	7
19 Nov 77	ONLY THE STRONG SURVIVE Philadelphia Interna PIR 5699	33	7
14 Jul 79	BRING THE FAMILY BACK Philadelphia Interna PIR 7456	51	5

Chris PAUL UK, male instrumentalist – guitar — 8 wks

31 May 86	EXPANSIONS '86 (EXPAND YOUR MIND) Fourth & Broadway BRW 48 [1]	58	5
21 Nov 87	BACK IN MY ARMS Syncopate SY 5	74	2
13 Aug 88	TURN THE MUSIC UP Syncopate SY 13	73	1

[1] Chris Paul featuring David Joseph

Frankie PAUL – See APACHE INDIAN

Les PAUL and Mary FORD Ⓒ

US, male instrumentalist – guitar, and female vocalist — 4 wks

| 20 Nov 53 ● | VAYA CON DIOS Capitol CL 13943 ▲ | 7 | 4 |

Lyn PAUL UK, female vocalist — 6 wks

| 28 Jun 75 | IT OUGHTA SELL A MILLION Polydor 2058 602 | 37 | 6 |

Owen PAUL ⊘ UK, male vocalist — 14 wks

| 31 May 86 ● | MY FAVOURITE WASTE OF TIME Epic A 7125 | 3 | 14 |

PAUL and PAULA ⊘ US, male/female vocal duo — 31 wks

14 Feb 63 ●	HEY PAULA Philips 304012 BF ▲	8	12
18 Apr 63 ●	YOUNG LOVERS Philips 304016 BF	9	14
16 May 63	HEY PAULA (re-entry) Philips 304012 BF	37	5

Luciano PAVAROTTI 🎵 Italy, male vocalist — 30 wks

16 Jun 90 ●	NESSUN DORMA Decca PAV 03	2	11
24 Oct 92	MISERERE London LON 329 [1]	15	5
30 Jul 94	LIBIAMO/LA DONNA E MOBILE Teldec YZ 843CD [2]	21	4
14 Dec 96 ●	LIVE LIKE HORSES Rocket LLHDD 1 [3]	9	6
25 Jul 98	YOU'LL NEVER WALK ALONE Decca 4607982 [4]	35	4

[1] Zucchero with Luciano Pavarotti [2] José Carreras, Placido Domingo and Luciano Pavarotti [3] Elton John and Luciano Pavarotti [4] José Carreras, Placido Domingo and Luciano Pavarotti

PAVEMENT US, male vocal/instrumental group — 4 wks

28 Nov 92	WATERY DOMESTIC EP Big Cat ABB 38T	58	1
12 Feb 94	CUT YOUR HAIR Big Cat ABB 55SCD	52	1
8 Feb 97	STEREO Domino RUG 51CD	48	1
3 May 97	SHADY LANE Domino RUG 53CD	40	1

Tracks on Watery Domestic EP: Brick Wall/Sick Profile/Annual Report/ Fear the Panzers

Rita PAVONE Italy, female vocalist — 19 wks

| 1 Dec 66 | HEART RCA 1553 | 27 | 12 |
| 19 Jan 67 | YOU ONLY YOU RCA 1561 | 21 | 7 |

Freda PAYNE ✨ US, female vocalist — 30 wks

5 Sep 70 ★	BAND OF GOLD *Invictus INV 502*	1	19
21 Nov 70	DEEPER AND DEEPER *Invictus INV 505*	33	9
27 Mar 71	CHERISH WHAT IS DEAR TO YOU *Invictus INV 509*	46	2

Tammy PAYNE UK, female vocalist — 2 wks

20 Jul 91	TAKE ME NOW *Talkin Loud TLK 12*	55	2

PEACE BY PIECE UK, male vocal group — 2 wks

21 Sep 96	SWEET SISTER *Blanco Y Negro NEG 94CD*	46	1
25 Apr 98	NOBODY'S BUSINESS *Blanco Y Negro NEG 110CD1*	50	1

PEACH UK / Belgium female/male vocal / production group — 1 wk

17 Jan 98	ON MY OWN *Mute CDMUTE 215*	69	1

PEACHES and HERB ✨ US, female/male vocal duo — 23 wks

20 Jan 79	SHAKE YOUR GROOVE THING *Polydor 2066 992*	26	10
21 Apr 79 ●	REUNITED *Polydor POSP 43* ▲	4	13

Mary PEARCE – See UP YER RONSON featuring Mary PEARCE

PEARL JAM ✔ US, male vocal/instrumental group — 37 wks

15 Feb 92	ALIVE *Epic 6575727*	16	6
18 Apr 92	EVEN FLOW *Epic 6578577*	27	3
26 Sep 92	JEREMY *Epic 6582587*	15	4
1 Jan 94	DAUGHTER *Epic 6600202*	18	5
28 May 94	DISSIDENT *Epic 6604415*	14	4
26 Nov 94 ●	SPIN THE BLACK CIRCLE *Epic 6610362*	10	3
25 Feb 95	NOT FOR YOU *Epic 6612032*	34	2
16 Dec 95	I GOT ID *Epic 6627162*	25	3
17 Aug 96	WHO YOU ARE *Epic 6635392*	18	2
31 Jan 98	GIVEN TO FLY *Epic 6653942*	12	3
23 May 98	WISHLIST *Epic 6657902*	30	2

PEARLS ◯ UK, female vocal duo — 24 wks

27 May 72	THIRD FINGER, LEFT HAND *Bell 1217*	31	6
23 Sep 72	YOU CAME YOU SAW YOU CONQUERED *Bell 1254*	32	5
24 Mar 73	YOU ARE EVERYTHING *Bell 1284*	41	3
1 Jun 74 ●	GUILTY *Bell 1352*	10	10

Johnny PEARSON ℂ
UK, orchestra, Johnny Pearson featured pianist — 15 wks

18 Dec 71 ●	SLEEPY SHORES *Penny Farthing PEN 778*	8	15

PEBBLES ✨ ☺ US, female vocalist — 17 wks

19 Mar 88 ●	GIRLFRIEND *MCA MCA 1233*	8	11
28 May 88	MERCEDES BOY *MCA MCA 1248*	42	4
27 Oct 90	GIVING YOU THE BENEFIT *MCA MCA 1448*	73	2

PEDDLERS ◯ ✔ UK, male vocal/instrumental group — 14 wks

7 Jan 65	LET THE SUNSHINE IN *Philips BF 1375*	50	1
23 Aug 69	BIRTH *CBS 4449*	17	9
31 Jan 70	GIRLIE *CBS 4720*	34	4

PEE BEE SQUAD UK, male vocalist – Paul Burnett — 3 wks

5 Oct 85	RUGGED AND MEAN, BUTCH AND ON SCREEN *Project PRO 3*	52	3

Ann PEEBLES US, female vocalist — 3 wks

20 Apr 74	I CAN'T STAND THE RAIN *London HL 10428*	50	1
4 May 74	I CAN'T STAND THE RAIN (re-entry) *London HL 10428*	41	2

PEECH BOYS US, male vocal/instrumental group — 3 wks

30 Oct 82	DON'T MAKE ME WAIT *TMT QTMT 7001*	49	3

Donald PEERS ℂ UK, male vocalist — 27 wks

18 Dec 68 ●	PLEASE DON'T GO *Columbia DB 8502*	3	18
30 Apr 69	PLEASE DON'T GO (re-entry) *Columbia DB 8502*	38	3
24 Jun 72	GIVE ME ONE MORE CHANCE *Decca F 13302*	36	6

PELE UK, male/female vocal/instrumental group — 3 wks

15 Feb 92	MEGALOMANIA *M & G MAGS 20*	73	1
13 Jun 92	FAIR BLOWS THE WIND FOR FRANCE *M & G MAGS 24*	62	1
31 Jul 93	FAT BLACK HEART *M & G MAGCD 43*	75	1

Debbie PENDER US, female vocalist — 1 wk

30 May 98	MOVIN' ON *AM:PM 5826492*	41	1

Teddy PENDERGRASS US, male vocalist — 24 wks

21 May 77	THE WHOLE TOWN'S LAUGHING AT ME *Philadelphia Interna PIR 5116*	44	3
28 Oct 78	ONLY YOU / CLOSE THE DOOR *Philadelphia Interna PIR 6713*	41	6
23 May 81	TWO HEARTS *20th Century TC 2492* [1]	49	5
25 Jan 86	HOLD ME *Asylum EKR 32* [2]	44	5
28 May 88	JOY *Elektra EKR 75*	58	3
19 Nov 94	THE MORE I GET THE MORE I WANT *X-clusive XCLU 011CD* [3]	35	2

[1] Stephanie Mills featuring Teddy Pendergrass
[2] Teddy Pendergrass with Whitney Houston [3] KWS featuring Teddy Pendergrass

Ce Ce PENISTON ☺ ✨ US, female vocalist — 53 wks

12 Oct 91	FINALLY *A & M AM 822*	29	7
11 Jan 92 ●	WE GOT A LOVE THANG *A & M AM 846*	6	8
18 Jan 92	I LIKE IT *A & M AM 847* [1]	58	2
21 Mar 92 ●	FINALLY (re-issue) *A & M AM 858*	2	8
23 May 92 ●	KEEP ON WALKIN' *A & M AM 878*	10	6
5 Sep 92	CRAZY LOVE *A & M AM 0060*	44	3
12 Dec 92	INSIDE THAT I CRIED *A & M AM 0121*	42	2
15 Jan 94	I'M IN THE MOOD *A & M 5804552*	16	4
2 Apr 94	KEEP GIVIN' ME YOUR LOVE *A & M 5805492*	36	2
6 Aug 94	HIT BY LOVE *A & M 5806932*	33	2
13 Sep 97	FINALLY *AM:PM 5823432*	26	5
7 Feb 98	SOMEBODY ELSE'S GUY *AM:PM 5825112*	13	4

[1] Overweight Pooch featuring Ce Ce Peniston

Dawn PENN ⚑ Jamaica, female vocalist — 12 wks

11 Jun 94 ●	YOU DON'T LOVE ME (NO, NO, NO) *Big Beat A 8295CD*	3	12

Barbara PENNINGTON US, female vocalist — 8 wks

27 Apr 85	FAN THE FLAME *Record Shack SOHO 37*	62	3
27 Jul 85	ON A CROWDED STREET *Record Shack SOHO 49*	57	5

Tricia PENROSE UK, female vocalist — 1 wk

7 Dec 96	WHERE DID OUR LOVE GO *RCA 74321428152*	71	1

PENTANGLE UK, male/female vocal/instrumental group — 4 wks

28 May 69	ONCE I HAD A SWEETHEART *Big T BIG 124*	46	1
14 Feb 70	LIGHT FLIGHT *Big T BIG 128*	43	1
28 Feb 70	LIGHT FLIGHT (re-entry) *Big T BIG 128*	45	2

PENTHOUSE 4 UK, male vocal/instrumental duo — 3 wks

23 Apr 88	BUST THIS HOUSE DOWN *Syncopate SY 10*	56	3

PEOPLES CHOICE US, male vocal/instrumental group — 9 wks

20 Sep 75	DO IT ANYWAY YOU WANNA *Philadelphia Interna PIR 3500*	36	5
21 Jan 78	JAM JAM JAM *Philadelphia Interna PIR 5891*	40	4

Danny PEPPERMINT and the JUMPING JACKS
US, male vocal/instrumental group — 8 wks

18 Jan 62	PEPPERMINT TWIST *London HLL 9478*	26	8

PEPPERS ☺ *France, male instrumental group*   **12 wks**

26 Oct 74 ●	PEPPER BOX *Spark SRL 1100*	6 12

PEPSI and SHIRLIE ☺ *UK, female vocal duo*   **24 wks**

17 Jan 87 ●	HEARTACHE *Polydor POSP 837*	2 12
30 May 87 ●	GOODBYE STRANGER *Polydor POSP 865*	9 7
26 Sep 87	CAN'T GIVE ME LOVE *Polydor POSP 885*	58 3
12 Dec 87	ALL RIGHT NOW *Polydor POSP 896*	50 2

PERCEPTION *UK, male vocal group*   **2 wks**

7 Mar 92	FEED THE FEELING *Talkin Loud TLK 17*	58 2

The listed flip side of 'Feed the Feeling' was 'Three Times a Maybe' by K-Creative

Lance PERCIVAL *UK, male vocalist*   **3 wks**

28 Oct 65	SHAME AND SCANDAL IN THE FAMILY *Parlophone R 5335*	37 3

PERFECT DAY *UK, male vocal/instrumental group*   **4 wks**

21 Jan 89	LIBERTY TOWN *London LON 214*	58 3
1 Apr 89	JANE *London LON 188*	68 1

PERFECTLY ORDINARY PEOPLE
UK, male vocal/instrumental group   **3 wks**

22 Oct 88	THEME FROM P.O.P. *Urban URB 25*	61 3

PERFECTO ALLSTARZ ☺
UK, male instrumental/production duo   **11 wks**

4 Feb 95 ●	REACH UP (PAPA'S GOT A BRAND NEW PIG BAG) *Perfecto YZ 892CD*	6 11

PERFUME *UK, male vocal/instrumental group*   **1 wk**

10 Feb 96	HAVEN'T SEEN YOU *Aromasound AROMA 005CDS*	71 1

Emilio PERICOLI *Italy, male vocalist*   **14 wks**

28 Jun 62	AL DI LA *Warner Bros. WB 69*	30 14

Carl PERKINS ♪ *US, male vocalist*   **8 wks**

18 May 56 ●	BLUE SUEDE SHOES *London HLU 8271*	10 8

PERPETUAL MOTION ☺
UK, male instrumental / production group   **5 wks**

2 May 98	KEEP ON DANCIN' (LET'S GO) *Positiva CDTIV 90*	12 5

Steve PERRY *UK, male vocalist*   **1 wk**

4 Aug 60	STEP BY STEP *HMV POP 745*	41 1

Jon PERTWEE *UK, male vocalist*   **7 wks**

1 Mar 80	WORZEL'S SONG *Decca F 13885*	33 7

PESHAY *UK, male DJ/producer*   **1 wk**

9 May 98	MILES FROM HOME *Mo Wax MW 092*	75 1

PET SHOP BOYS ☻ ☺ *Critically-acclaimed and quintessentially English duo: former assistant editor of* Smash Hits, *Neil Tennant (v), and Chris Lowe (k). No duo has amassed more chart entries than this act, whose first hit was voted Best British Single at the 1987 BRIT Awards*   **216 wks**

23 Nov 85 ★	WEST END GIRLS *Parlophone R 6115* ▲	1 15
8 Mar 86 ●	LOVE COMES QUICKLY *Parlophone R 6116*	19 9
31 May 86	OPPORTUNITIES (LET'S MAKE LOTS OF MONEY) *Parlophone R 6129*	11 8
4 Oct 86 ●	SUBURBIA *Parlophone R 6140*	8 9
27 Jun 87 ★	IT'S A SIN *Parlophone R 6158*	1 11
22 Aug 87 ●	WHAT HAVE I DONE TO DESERVE THIS *Parlophone R 6163* [1]	2 9
24 Oct 87 ●	RENT *Parlophone R 6168*	8 7

12 Dec 87 ★	ALWAYS ON MY MIND *Parlophone R 6171*	1 11
2 Apr 88 ★	HEART *Parlophone R 6177*	1 10
24 Sep 88 ●	DOMINO DANCING *Parlophone R 6190*	7 8
26 Nov 88 ●	LEFT TO MY OWN DEVICES *Parlophone R 6198* ..	4 8
8 Jul 89 ●	IT'S ALRIGHT *Parlophone R 6220*	5 8
6 Oct 90 ●	SO HARD *Parlophone R 6269*	4 6
24 Nov 90	BEING BORING *Parlophone R 6275*	20 8
23 Mar 91 ●	WHERE THE STREETS HAVE NO NAME – CAN'T TAKE MY EYES OFF YOU/HOW CAN YOU EXPECT TO BE TAKEN SERIOUSLY *Parlophone R 6285*	4 8
8 Jun 91	JEALOUSY *Parlophone R 6283*	12 5
26 Oct 91	DJ CULTURE *Parlophone R 6301*	13 3
23 Nov 91	DJ CULTURE (re-mix) *Parlophone 12RX 6301*	40 2
21 Dec 91	WAS IT WORTH IT *Parlophone R 6306*	24 4
12 Jun 93 ●	CAN YOU FORGIVE HER *Parlophone CDR 6348* ...	7 7
18 Sep 93 ●	GO WEST *Parlophone CDR 6356*	2 9
11 Dec 93	I WOULDN'T NORMALLY DO THIS KIND OF THING *Parlophone CDR 6370*	13 7
16 Apr 94	LIBERATION *Parlophone CDR 6377*	14 5
11 Jun 94 ●	ABSOLUTELY FABULOUS *Spaghetti CDR 6382* [2] ..	6 7
10 Sep 94	YESTERDAY WHEN I WAS MAD *Parlophone CDR 6386* ..	13 4
5 Aug 95	PANINARO *Parlophone CDR 6414*	15 4
4 May 96 ●	BEFORE *Parlophone CDR 6431*	7 5
24 Aug 96 ●	SE A VIDE E (THAT'S THE WAY LIFE IS) *Parlophone CDR 6443*	8 8
23 Nov 96	SINGLE *Parlophone CDR 6452*	14 3
29 Mar 97 ●	A RED LETTER DAY *Parlophone CDR 6460*	9 3
5 Jul 97 ●	SOMEWHERE *Parlophone CDR 6470*	9 5

[1] Pet Shop Boys and Dusty Springfield   [2] Absolutely Fabulous

PETER and GORDON ☻ *UK, male vocal duo*   **77 wks**

12 Mar 64 ★	A WORLD WITHOUT LOVE *Columbia DB 7225* ▲ ..	1 14
4 Jun 64 ●	NOBODY I KNOW *Columbia DB 7292*	10 11
8 Apr 65 ●	TRUE LOVE WAYS *Columbia DB 7524*	2 15
24 Jun 65 ●	TO KNOW YOU IS TO LOVE YOU *Columbia DB 7617* ..	5 10
21 Oct 65	BABY I'M YOURS *Columbia DB 7729*	19 9
24 Feb 66	WOMAN *Columbia DB 7834*	28 7
22 Sep 66	LADY GODIVA *Columbia DB 8003*	16 11

PETER, PAUL and MARY ♂ ☻
US, male/female vocal/instrumental group   **38 wks**

10 Oct 63	BLOWING IN THE WIND *Warner Bros. WB 104*	13 16
16 Apr 64	TELL IT ON THE MOUNTAIN *Warner Bros. WB 127* ..	33 4
15 Oct 64	THE TIMES THEY ARE A-CHANGIN' *Warner Bros. WB 142* ..	44 2
17 Jan 70 ●	LEAVIN' ON A JET PLANE *Warner Bros. WB 7340* ▲ ..	2 16

PETERS and LEE ℂ *UK, male/female vocal duo*   **57 wks**

26 May 73 ★	WELCOME HOME *Philips 6006 307*	1 24
3 Nov 73	BY YOUR SIDE *Philips 6006 339*	39 4
20 Apr 74 ●	DON'T STAY AWAY TOO LONG *Philips 6006 388* ..	3 15
17 Aug 74	RAINBOW *Philips 6006 406*	17 7
6 Mar 76	HEY MR. MUSIC MAN *Philips 6006 502*	16 7

Ray PETERSON *US, male vocalist*   **9 wks**

4 Sep 59	THE WONDER OF YOU *RCA 1131*	23 1
24 Mar 60	ANSWER ME *RCA 1175*	47 1
19 Jan 61	CORRINE, CORRINA *London HLX 9246*	48 1
2 Feb 61	CORRINE, CORRINA (re-entry) *London HLX 9246* ..	41 6

Tom PETTY and the HEARTBREAKERS
US, male vocal/instrumental group   **43 wks**

25 Jun 77	ANYTHING THAT'S ROCK 'N' ROLL *Shelter WIP 6396* ..	36 3
13 Aug 77	AMERICAN GIRL *Shelter WIP 6403*	40 5
15 Aug 81	STOP DRAGGIN' MY HEART AROUND *WEA K 79231* [1] ..	50 4
13 Apr 85	DON'T COME AROUND HERE NO MORE *MCA MCA 926* ..	50 4
13 May 89	I WON'T BACK DOWN *MCA MCA 1334* [2]	28 10
12 Aug 89	RUNNIN' DOWN A DREAM *MCA MCA 1359* [2] ...	55 4
25 Nov 89	FREE FALLIN' *MCA MCA 1381* [2]	64 2
29 Jun 91	LEARNING TO FLY *MCA MCS 1555*	46 4
4 Apr 92	TOO GOOD TO BE TRUE *MCA MCS 1616*	34 3

30 Oct 93	SOMETHING IN THE AIR *MCA MCSTD 1945* [2]	53 2
12 Mar 94	MARY JANE'S LAST DANCE *MCA MCSTD 1966*	52 2

[1] Stevie Nicks with Tom Petty and the Heartbreakers [2] Tom Petty

PF PROJECT ☺ *UK, male producers*   **11 wks**

15 Nov 97 ●	CHOOSE LIFE *Positiva CDTIV 84* [1]	6 11

[1] PF Project featuring Ewan McGregor

PHANTOMS – *See Johnny BRANDON*

PHARAO *Germany, male/female vocal/instrumental group*   **2 wks**

4 Mar 95	THERE IS A STAR *Epic 6611832*	43 2

PHARAOHS – *See SAM THE SHAM and the PHARAOHS*

PHARCYDE *US, male rap group*   **6 wks**

31 Jul 93	PASSIN' ME BY *Atlantic A 8360CD*	55 3
6 Apr 96	RUNNIN' *Go.Beat GODCD 142*	36 2
10 Aug 96	SHE SAID *Go.Beat GODCD 144*	51 1

Franke PHAROAH – *See FRANKE*

PHAT 'N' PHUNKY *UK, male production duo*   **1 wk**

14 Jun 97	LET'S GROOVE *Chase CDCHASE 8*	61 1

PhD ☺ *UK, male vocal/instrumental duo*   **14 wks**

3 Apr 82 ●	I WON'T LET YOU DOWN *WEA K 79209*	3 14

Barrington PHELOUNG *Australia, male composer*   **2 wks**

13 Mar 93	INSPECTOR MORSE THEME *Virgin VSCDT 1458*	61 2

PHILADELPHIA INTERNATIONAL ALL-STARS
US, amalgamation of various acts   **8 wks**

13 Aug 77	LET'S CLEAN UP THE GHETTO	
	Philadelphia Interna PIR 5451	34 8

PHILHARMONIA ORCHESTRA, conductor Lorin MAAZEL
UK, orchestra, US, male conductor   **7 wks**

30 Jul 69	THUS SPAKE ZARATHUSTRA *Columbia DB 8607*	33 7

Chynna PHILLIPS *US, female vocalist*   **1 wk**

3 Feb 96	NAKED AND SACRED *EMI CDEM 409*	62 1

Esther PHILLIPS ♪ *US, female vocalist*   **8 wks**

4 Oct 75 ●	WHAT A DIFFERENCE A DAY MADE *Kudu 925*	6 8

PHOEBE ONE *UK, female rapper*   **1 wk**

12 Dec 98	DOIN' OUR THING/ONE MAN'S B*TCH	
	Mecca Recordings MECX 1020	59 1

Paul PHOENIX *UK, male vocalist*   **4 wks**

3 Nov 79	NUNC DIMITTIS *Different HAVE 20*	56 4

Full artist credit on hit as follows: Paul Phoenix (treble) with Instrumental
Ensemble – James Watson (trumpet), John Scott (organ), conducted by Barry Rose

PHOTEK *UK, male jungle producer – Rupert Parkes*   **3 wks**

22 Mar 97	NI-TEN-ICHI-RYU *Science QEDCD 2*	37 2
28 Feb 98	MODUS OPERANDI *Virgin QEDCD 6*	66 1

PHOTOS *UK, male/female vocal/instrumental group*   **4 wks**

17 May 80	IRENE *Epic EPC 8517*	56 4

PHUNKY PHANTOM *UK, male producer*   **3 wks**

16 May 98	GET UP STAND UP *Club For Life DISNCD 44*	27 3

PHUTURE ASSASSINS *UK, male instrumental/production group*   **1 wk**

6 Jun 92	FUTURE SOUND EP *Suburban Base SUBBASE 010*	64 1

Tracks on Future Sound (EP): Future Sound / African Sanctus / Rydim Come Foward / Freedom Sound

PIA – *See Pia ZADORA*

Edith PIAF *France, female vocalist*   **15 wks**

12 May 60	MILORD *Columbia DC 754*	41 4
3 Nov 60	MILORD (re-entry) *Columbia DC 754*	24 11

PIANOHEADZ *US, male DJ/production duo*   **2 wks**

11 Jul 98	IT'S OVER (DISTORTION)	
	Incredible Music INCRL 3CD	39 2

PIANOMAN ☺ *UK, male producer – James Salmon*   **8 wks**

15 Jun 96 ●	BLURRED *Ffrreedom TABCD 243*	6 7
26 Apr 97	PARTY PEOPLE (LIVE YOUR LIFE BE FREE) *3 Beat 3 BTCD1*	43 1

See also Bass BOYZ

Bobby 'Boris' PICKETT and the CRYPT-KICKERS ☻
US, male vocalist, male vocal/instrumental backing group   **13 wks**

1 Sep 73 ●	MONSTER MASH *London HL 10320* ▲	3 13

Wilson PICKETT ♪ *US, male vocalist*   **61 wks**

23 Sep 65	IN THE MIDNIGHT HOUR *Atlantic AT 4036*	12 11
25 Nov 65	DON'T FIGHT IT *Atlantic AT 4052*	29 8
10 Mar 66	634-5789 *Atlantic AT 4072*	36 5
1 Sep 66	LAND OF 1000 DANCES *Atlantic 584-039*	22 9
15 Dec 66	MUSTANG SALLY *Atlantic 584-066*	28 7
27 Sep 67	FUNKY BROADWAY *Atlantic 584-130*	43 3
11 Sep 68	I'M A MIDNIGHT MOVER *Atlantic 584-203*	38 6
8 Jan 69	HEY JUDE *Atlantic 584-236*	16 9
21 Nov 87	IN THE MIDNIGHT HOUR *Motown ZB 41583*	62 3

'In the Midnight Hour' on Motown is a re-recording

PICKETTYWITCH ☻
UK, male/female vocal/instrumental group   **34 wks**

28 Feb 70 ●	THAT SAME OLD FEELING *Pye 7N 17887*	5 14
4 Jul 70	(IT'S LIKE A) SAD OLD KINDA MOVIE *Pye 7N 17951*	16 10
7 Nov 70	BABY I WON'T LET YOU DOWN *Pye 7N 45002*	27 10

PIGBAG ☹ ☺ *UK, male instrumental group*   **20 wks**

7 Nov 81	SUNNY DAY *Y Records Y 12*	53 3
27 Feb 82	GETTING UP *Y Records Y 16*	61 3
3 Apr 82 ●	PAPA'S GOT A BRAND NEW PIGBAG	
	Y Records Y 10	3 11
10 Jul 82	THE BIG BEAN *Y Records Y 24*	40 3

PIGEONHEAD – *See LO FIDELITY ALLSTARS*

Nelson PIGFORD – *See De Etta LITTLE and Nelson PIGFORD*

PIGLETS ☻ *UK, female vocal group*   **12 wks**

6 Nov 71 ●	JOHNNY REGGAE *Bell 1180*	3 12

Dick PIKE – *See Ruby WRIGHT*

P.I.L. – *See PUBLIC IMAGE LTD*

PILOT ☻ *UK, male vocal/instrumental group*   **29 wks**

2 Nov 74	MAGIC *EMI 2217*	11 11
18 Jan 75 ★	JANUARY *EMI 2255*	1 10
19 Apr 75	CALL ME ROUND *EMI 2287*	34 4
27 Sep 75	JUST A SMILE *EMI 2338*	31 4

PILTDOWN MEN ✪ US, male instrumental group   36 wks

8 Sep 60	MACDONALD'S CAVE *Capitol CL 15149*	14	18
12 Jan 61	PILTDOWN RIDES AGAIN *Capitol CL 15175*	14	10
9 Mar 61	GOODNIGHT MRS. FLINTSTONE *Capitol CL 15186*	18	8

Courtney PINE UK, male instrumentalist – saxophone   6 wks

30 Jul 88	LIKE DREAMERS DO *Fourth & Broadway BRW 108* [1]	26	5
7 Jul 90	I'M STILL WAITING *Mango MNG 749* [2]	66	1

[1] Mica Paris featuring Courtney Pine
[2] Courtney Pine featuring Carroll Thompson

See also MOVEMENT 98 featuring Carroll THOMPSON

PING PING and Al VERLAINE Belgium, male vocal duo   4 wks

28 Sep 61	SUCU SUCU *Oriole CB 1589*	41	4

PINK FLOYD ✔ UK, male vocal/instrumental group   55 wks

30 Mar 67	ARNOLD LAYNE *Columbia DB 8156*	20	8
22 Jun 67 ●	SEE EMILY PLAY *Columbia DB 8214*	6	12
1 Dec 79 ★	ANOTHER BRICK IN THE WALL (PART 2) *Harvest HAR 5194* ▲ ◆	1	12
7 Aug 82	WHEN THE TIGERS BROKE FREE *Harvest HAR 5222*	39	5
7 May 83	NOT NOW JOHN *Harvest HAR 5224*	30	4
19 Dec 87	ON THE TURNING AWAY *EMI EM 34*	55	4
25 Jun 88	ONE SLIP *EMI EM 52*	50	3
4 Jun 94	TAKE IT BACK *EMI CDEMS 309*	23	4
29 Oct 94	HIGH HOPES/KEEP TALKING *EMI CDEMS 342*	26	3

PINKEES ✪ UK, male vocal/instrumental group   9 wks

18 Sep 82 ●	DANGER GAMES *Creole CR 39*	8	9

PINKERTON'S ASSORTED COLOURS ✪
UK, male vocal/instrumental group   12 wks

13 Jan 66 ●	MIRROR MIRROR *Decca F 12307*	9	11
21 Apr 66	DON'T STOP LOVIN' ME BABY *Decca F 12377*	50	1

PINKY and PERKY UK, puppet duo   3 wks

29 May 93	REET PETITE *Telstar CDPIGGY 1*	47	3

PIONEERS ✔ Jamaica, male vocal/instrumental group   34 wks

18 Oct 69	LONG SHOT KICK DE BUCKET *Trojan TR 672*	21	10
10 Jan 70	LONG SHOT KICK DE BUCKET (re-entry) *Trojan TR 672*	40	1
31 Jul 71 ●	LET YOUR YEAH BE YEAH *Trojan TR 7825*	5	12
15 Jan 72	GIVE AND TAKE *Trojan TR 7846*	35	6
29 Mar 80	LONG SHOT KICK DE BUCKET (re-issue) *Trojan TRO 9063*	42	5

Re-issue of 'Long Shot Kick De Bucket' coupled with re-issue of Liquidator by Harry J All Star

PIPKINS ✪ UK, male vocal duo   10 wks

28 Mar 70 ●	GIMME DAT DING *Columbia DB 8662*	6	10

PIPS – See Gladys KNIGHT and the PIPS

PIRANHAS ✪ UK, male vocal/instrumental group   21 wks

2 Aug 80 ●	TOM HARK *Sire SIR 4044*	6	12
16 Oct 82	ZAMBESI *Dakota DAK 6* [1]	17	9

[1] Piranhas featuring Boring Bob Grover

PIRATES – See Johnny KIDD and the PIRATES

PITCH SHIFTER UK, male vocal / instrumental group   2 wks

28 Feb 98	GENIUS *Geffen GFSTD 22324*	71	1
26 Sep 98	MICROWAVED *Geffen GFSTD 22348*	54	1

Gene PITNEY ✪ Leading US performer in the 1960s, b. 17 February, 1941, Connecticut. This unmistakable vocalist and songwriter had a longer and more impressive track record in UK than in his homeland. Nonetheless, it took him 28 years to reach No 1   212 wks

23 Mar 61	(I WANNA) LOVE MY LIFE AWAY *London HL 9270*	26	11
8 Mar 62	TOWN WITHOUT PITY *HMV POP 952*	32	6
5 Dec 63 ●	TWENTY FOUR HOURS FROM TULSA *United Artists UP 1035*	5	19
5 Mar 64 ●	THAT GIRL BELONGS TO YESTERDAY *United Artists UP 1045*	7	12
15 Oct 64	IT HURTS TO BE IN LOVE *United Artists UP 1063*	36	4
12 Nov 64 ●	I'M GONNA BE STRONG *Stateside SS 358*	2	14
18 Feb 65 ●	I MUST BE SEEING THINGS *Stateside SS 390*	6	10
10 Jun 65 ●	LOOKING THROUGH THE EYES OF LOVE *Stateside SS 420*	3	12
4 Nov 65 ●	PRINCESS IN RAGS *Stateside SS 471*	9	12
17 Feb 66 ●	BACKSTAGE *Stateside SS 490*	4	10
9 Jun 66 ●	NOBODY NEEDS YOUR LOVE *Stateside SS 518*	2	13
10 Nov 66 ●	JUST ONE SMILE *Stateside SS 558*	8	12
23 Feb 67	(IN THE) COLD LIGHT OF DAY *Stateside SS 597*	38	6
15 Nov 67 ●	SOMETHING'S GOTTEN HOLD OF MY HEART *Stateside SS 2060*	5	13
3 Apr 68	SOMEWHERE IN THE COUNTRY *Stateside SS 2103*	19	9
27 Nov 68	YOURS UNTIL TOMORROW *Stateside SS 2131*	34	7
5 Mar 69	MARIA ELENA *Stateside SS 2142*	25	6
14 Mar 70	A STREET CALLED HOPE *Stateside SS 2164*	37	5
3 Oct 70	SHADY LADY *Stateside SS 2177*	29	8
28 Apr 73	24 SYCAMORE *Pye International 7N 25606*	34	7
2 Nov 74	BLUE ANGEL *Bronze BRO 11*	49	1
16 Nov 74	BLUE ANGEL (re-entry) *Bronze BRO 11*	39	3
14 Jan 89 ★	SOMETHING'S GOTTEN HOLD OF MY HEART *Parlophone R 6201* [1]	1	12

[1] Marc Almond featuring special guest star Gene Pitney

PIXIES US, male/female vocal/instrumental group   13 wks

1 Apr 89	MONKEY GONE TO HEAVEN *4AD AD 904*	60	3
1 Jul 89	HERE COMES YOUR MAN *4AD AD 909*	54	1
28 Jul 90	VELOURIA *4AD AD 0009*	28	3
10 Nov 90	DIG FOR FIRE *4AD AD 0014*	62	1
8 Jun 91	PLANET OF SOUND *4AD AD 1008*	27	3
4 Oct 97	DEBASER *4AD BAD 7010CD*	23	2

PIZZAMAN ☺ UK, male production group – Norman Cook   18 wks

27 Aug 94	TRIPPIN' ON SUNSHINE *Loaded CDLOAD 16*	33	2
10 Jun 95	SEX ON THE STREETS *Loaded CDLOAD 24*	24	4
18 Nov 95	HAPPINESS *Loaded CDLOAD 29*	19	4
6 Jan 96	SEX ON THE STREETS (re-entry) *Loaded CDLOAD 24*	23	4
1 Jun 96	TRIPPIN' ON SUNSHINE (re-issue) *Loaded CDLOAD 32*	18	3
14 Sep 96	HELLO HONKY TONKS (ROCK YOUR BODY) *Loaded CDLOAD 39*	41	1

PIZZICATO FIVE Japan, male/female vocal/instrumental group   1 wk

1 Nov 97	MON AMOUR TOKYO *Matador OLE 2902*	72	1

Joe PIZZULO – See Sergio MENDES

PJ Canada, male producer – Paul Jacobs   1 wk

20 Sep 97	HAPPY DAYS *Deconstruction 74321511822*	72	1

PJ and DUNCAN ✪ UK, male vocal duo   81 wks

18 Dec 93	TONIGHT I'M FREE *Telstar CDSTAS 2706*	62	3
23 Apr 94	WHY ME *Telstar CDSTAS 2719*	27	4
23 Jul 94 ●	LET'S GET READY TO RHUMBLE *XSrhythm CDANT 1*	9	11
8 Oct 94	IF I GIVE YOU MY NUMBER *XSrhythm CDANT 2*	15	7
3 Dec 94	ETERNAL LOVE *XSrhythm CDANT 3*	12	9
25 Feb 95	OUR RADIO ROCKS *XSrhythm CDANT 4*	15	5
29 Jul 95	STUCK ON U *XSrhythm CDANT 5*	12	5
14 Oct 95	U KRAZY KATZ *XSrhythm CDANT 6*	15	4
2 Dec 95	PERFECT *Telstar CDANT 7*	16	7
20 Mar 96	STEPPING STONE *Telstar CDANT 8*	11	5
24 Aug 96 ●	BETTER WATCH OUT *Telstar CDANT 9* [1]	10	4

23 Nov 96	WHEN I FALL IN LOVE *Telstar CDANT 10* [1]	12 8
15 Mar 97 ●	SHOUT *Telstar CDDEC 11* [1]	10 5
10 May 97	FALLING *Telstar CDDEC 12* [1]	14 4

[1] Ant and Dec

P J POWERS – See LADYSMITH BLACK MAMBAZO

P J B featuring HANNAH and her SISTERS – See Hannah JONES

PKA UK, male producer – Phil Kelsey   2 wks

20 Apr 91	TEMPERATURE RISING *Stress SS 4*	68 1
7 Mar 92	POWERGEN (ONLY YOUR LOVE) *Stress PKA 1*	70 1

PLACEBO ☹ ✎
US/Sweden, male instrumental/production group   23 wks

28 Sep 96	TEENAGE ANGST *Elevator Music FLOORCD 3*	30 3
1 Feb 97 ●	NANCY BOY *Elevator Music FLOORCD 4*	4 6
24 May 97	BRUISE PRISTINE *Elevator Music FLOORCD 5*	14 3
15 Aug 98 ●	PURE MORNING *Hut FLOORCD 6*	4 6
10 Oct 98 ●	YOU DON'T CARE ABOUT US *Hut FLOORCD 7*	5 5

PLANET PATROL US, male vocal/instrumental group   3 wks

17 Sep 83	CHEAP THRILLS *Polydor POSP 639*	64 3

PLANETS UK, male vocal/instrumental group   8 wks

18 Aug 79	LINES *Rialto TREB 104*	36 6
25 Oct 80	DON'T LOOK DOWN *Rialto TREB 116*	66 2

Robert PLANT ✎ UK, male vocalist   33 wks

9 Oct 82	BURNING DOWN ONE SIDE *Swansong SSK 19429*	73 1
16 Jul 83	BIG LOG *WEA B 9848*	11 10
30 Jan 88	HEAVEN KNOWS *Es Paranza A 9373*	33 5
28 Apr 90	HURTING KIND (I'VE GOT MY EYES ON YOU) *Es Paranza A 8985*	45 3
8 May 93	29 PALMS *Fontana FATEX 1*	21 5
3 Jul 93	I BELIEVE *Fontana FATEX 2*	64 2
25 Dec 93	IF I WERE A CARPENTER *Fontana FATEX 4*	63 2
17 Dec 94	GALLOWS POLE *Fontana PPCD 2* [1]	35 3
11 Apr 98	MOST HIGH *Mercury 5687512* [2]	26 2

[1] Jimmy Page and Robert Plant [2] Page and Plant

PLASMATICS US, female/male vocal/instrumental group   4 wks

26 Jul 80	BUTCHER BABY *Stiff BUY 76*	55 4

PLASTIC BERTRAND ☺ Belgium, male vocalist   17 wks

13 May 78 ●	CA PLANE POUR MOI *Sire 6078 616*	8 12
5 Aug 78	SHA LA LA LA LEE *Vertigo 6059 209*	39 5

PLASTIC JAM – See BUG KANN and PLASTIC JAM

PLASTIC ONO BAND – See John LENNON

PLASTIC PENNY ☺ UK, male vocal/instrumental group   10 wks

3 Jan 68 ●	EVERYTHING I AM *Page One POF 051*	6 10

PLASTIC POPULATION – See YAZZ

PLATINUM HOOK US, male vocal/instrumental group   1 wk

2 Sep 78	STANDING ON THE VERGE (OF GETTING IT ON) *Motown TMG 1115*	72 1

PLATTERS ✎ US, male/female vocal group   91 wks

7 Sep 56 ●	THE GREAT PRETENDER/ONLY YOU *Mercury MT 117*	5 12
2 Nov 56 ●	MY PRAYER *Mercury MT 120* ▲	4 10
7 Dec 56	THE GREAT PRETENDER/ONLY YOU (re-entry) *Mercury MT 117*	21 1
18 Jan 57	MY PRAYER (re-entry) *Mercury MT 120*	28 2
25 Jan 57	YOU'LL NEVER NEVER KNOW/IT ISN'T RIGHT *Mercury MT 130*	23 1
8 Feb 57	YOU'LL NEVER NEVER KNOW/IT ISN'T RIGHT (re-entry) *Mercury MT 130*	29 1
29 Mar 57	MY PRAYER (2nd re-entry) *Mercury MT 120*	22 1
29 Mar 57	ONLY YOU (2nd re-entry) *Mercury MT 117*	18 3
12 Apr 57	YOU'LL NEVER NEVER KNOW/IT ISN'T RIGHT (2nd re-entry) *Mercury MT 130*	29 1
17 May 57	I'M SORRY *Mercury MT 145*	18 6
5 Jul 57	I'M SORRY (re-entry) *Mercury MT 145*	23 1
19 Jul 57	I'M SORRY (2nd re-entry) *Mercury MT 145*	22 1
16 May 58 ●	TWILIGHT TIME *Mercury MT 214* ▲	3 18
16 Jan 59 ★	SMOKE GETS IN YOUR EYES *Mercury AMT 1016* ▲	1 20
28 Aug 59	REMEMBER WHEN *Mercury AMT 1053*	25 2
29 Jan 60	HARBOUR LIGHTS *Mercury AMT 1081*	11 11

PLAVKA – See JAM and SPOON featuring PLAVKA

PLAYBOY BAND – See John FRED and the PLAYBOY BAND

PLAYBOYS – See Gary LEWIS and the PLAYBOYS

PLAYER US/UK, male vocal/instrumental group   7 wks

25 Feb 78	BABY COME BACK *RSO 2090 254* ▲	32 7

PLAYERS ASSOCIATION ♪ US, male vocal/instrumental group   17 wks

10 Mar 79 ●	TURN THE MUSIC UP *Vanguard VS 5011*	8 9
5 May 79	RIDE THE GROOVE *Vanguard VS 5012*	42 5
9 Feb 80	WE GOT THE GROOVE *Vanguard VS 5016*	61 3

PLUS ONE featuring SIRRON
UK, male/female vocal/instrumental group   4 wks

19 May 90	IT'S HAPPENIN' *MCA MCA 1405*	40 4

PLUTO – See Pluto SHERVINGTON

PLUX featuring Georgia JONES
US, male/female vocal/instrumental group   2 wks

4 May 96	OVER AND OVER *ffrr FCD 277*	33 2

PM DAWN ◄ ☺ US, male vocal/instrumental/rap group   39 wks

8 Jun 91	A WATCHER'S POINT OF VIEW *Gee Street GEE 32*	36 5
17 Aug 91	SET ADRIFT ON MEMORY BLISS *Gee Street GEE 33*	3 8
19 Oct 91	PAPER DOLL *Gee Street GEE 35*	49 3
22 Feb 92	REALITY USED TO BE A FRIEND OF MINE *Gee Street GEE 37*	29 4
7 Nov 92	I'D DIE WITHOUT YOU *Gee Street GEE 39*	30 5
13 Mar 93	LOOKING THROUGH PATIENT EYES *Gee Street GESCD 47*	11 7
12 Jun 93	MORE THAN LIKELY *Gee Street GESCD 49* [1]	40 3
30 Sep 95	DOWNTOWN VENUS *Gee Street GESCD 63*	58 2
6 Apr 96	SOMETIMES I MISS YOU SO MUCH *Gee Street GESCD 65*	58 1
31 Oct 98	GOTTA BE...MOVIN' ON UP *Gee Street GEE 5003933* [2]	68 1

[1] PM Dawn featuring Boy George [2] PM Dawn featuring Ky-Mani

POETS UK, male vocal/instrumental group   5 wks

29 Oct 64	NOW WE'RE THRU *Decca F 11995*	31 5

POGUES ☺ ♂
Ireland/UK, male/female vocal/instrumental group   70 wks

6 Apr 85	A PAIR OF BROWN EYES *Stiff BUY 220*	72 2
22 Jun 85	SALLY MACLENNANE *Stiff BUY 224*	51 4
14 Sep 85	DIRTY OLD TOWN *Stiff BUY 229*	62 3
8 Mar 86	POGUETRY IN MOTION EP *Stiff BUY 243*	29 6
30 Aug 86	HAUNTED *MCA MCA 1084*	42 4
28 Mar 87 ●	THE IRISH ROVER *Stiff BUY 258* [1]	8 8
5 Dec 87 ●	FAIRYTALE OF NEW YORK *Pogue Mahone NY 7* [2]	2 9
5 Mar 88	IF I SHOULD FALL FROM GRACE WITH GOD *Pogue Mahone PG 1*	58 3
16 Jul 88	FIESTA *Pogue Mahone PG 2*	24 5

Left column

17 Dec 88	YEAH YEAH YEAH YEAH YEAH *Pogue Mahone YZ 355*	...43 4
8 Jul 89	MISTY MORNING, ALBERT BRIDGE *PM YZ 407*	...41 3
16 Jun 90	JACK'S HEROES/WHISKEY IN THE JAR *PM YZ 500* [1]	...63 2
15 Sep 90	SUMMER IN SIAM *PM YZ 519*	...64 2
21 Sep 91	A RAINY NIGHT IN SOHO *PM YZ 603*	...67 1
14 Dec 91	FAIRYTALE OF NEW YORK (re-issue) *PM YZ 628* [2]	...36 5
30 May 92	HONKY TONK WOMEN *PM YZ 673*	...56 2
21 Aug 93	TUESDAY MORNING *PM YZ 758 CD*	...18 5
22 Jan 94	ONCE UPON A TIME *PM YZ 771CD*	...66 2

[1] Pogues and the Dubliners [2] Pogues featuring Kirsty MacColl

Tracks on Poguetry in Motion EP: London Girl / The Body of an American / A Rainy Night in Soho / Planxty Noel Hill

POINTER SISTERS ♀ ◑ *US, female vocal group* — 87 wks

3 Feb 79	EVERYBODY IS A STAR *Planet K 12324*	...61 3
17 Mar 79	FIRE *Planet K 12339*	...34 8
22 Aug 81 ●	SLOWHAND *Planet K 12530*	...10 11
5 Dec 81	SHOULD I DO IT? *Reprise K 12578*	...50 5
14 Apr 84 ●	AUTOMATIC *Planet RPS 105*	...2 15
23 Jun 84 ●	JUMP (FOR MY LOVE) *Planet RPS 106*	...6 10
11 Aug 84	I NEED YOU *Planet RPS 107*	...25 9
27 Oct 84	I'M SO EXCITED *Planet RPS 108*	...11 11
12 Jan 85	NEUTRON DANCE *Planet RPS 109*	...31 7
20 Jul 85	DARE ME *RCA PB 49957*	...17 8

POISON ☿ *US, male vocal/instrumental group* — 43 wks

23 May 87	TALK DIRTY TO ME *Music For Nations KUT 125*	...67 1
7 May 88	NOTHIN' BUT A GOOD TIME *Capitol CL 486*	...35 3
5 Nov 88	FALLEN ANGEL *Capitol CL 500*	...59 1
11 Feb 89	EVERY ROSE HAS ITS THORN *Capitol CL 520* ▲	...13 9
29 Apr 89	YOUR MAMA DON'T DANCE *Capitol CL 523*	...13 7
23 Sep 89	NOTHIN' BUT A GOOD TIME (re-issue)	
	Capitol CL 539	...48 3
30 Jun 90	UNSKINNY BOP *Capitol CL 582*	...15 7
27 Oct 90	SOMETHING TO BELIEVE IN *Enigma CL 594*	...35 4
23 Nov 91	SO TELL ME WHY *Capitol CL 640*	...25 2
13 Feb 93	STAND *Capitol CDCL 679*	...25 3
24 Apr 93	UNTIL YOU SUFFER SOME (FIRE AND ICE)	
	Capitol CDCL 685	...32 3

POLECATS *UK, male vocal/instrumental group* — 18 wks

7 Mar 81	JOHN I'M ONLY DANCING/BIG GREEN CAR	
	Mercury POLE 1	...35 8
16 May 81	ROCKABILLY GUY *Mercury POLE 2*	...35 6
22 Aug 81	JEEPSTER/MARIE CELESTE *Mercury POLE 3*	...53 4

POLICE ⚡ *World-famous Anglo-American rock trio: Sting (b. Gordon Sumner) (v/b), Andy Summers (g/v), Stewart Copeland (d/v). These BRIT and Grammy Award winners were one of the 1980s' most popular acts. They had five successive albums enter the UK chart at No 1* — 150 wks

7 Oct 78	CAN'T STAND LOSING YOU *A & M AMS 7381*	...42 5
28 Apr 79	ROXANNE *A & M AMS 7348*	...12 9
7 Jul 79 ●	CAN'T STAND LOSING YOU (re-entry) *A & M AMS 7381*	...2 11
22 Sep 79 ★	MESSAGE IN A BOTTLE *A & M AMS 7474*	...1 11
17 Nov 79	FALL OUT *Illegal IL 001*	...47 4
1 Dec 79 ★	WALKING ON THE MOON *A & M AMS 7494*	...1 10
16 Feb 80 ●	SO LONELY *A & M AMS 7402*	...6 10
14 Jun 80	SIX PACK *A & M AMPP 6001*	...17 4
27 Sep 80 ★	DON'T STAND SO CLOSE TO ME *A & M AMS 7564* ■	...1 10
13 Dec 80 ●	DE DO DO DO, DE DA DA DA *A & M AMS 7578*	...5 8
26 Sep 81 ●	INVISIBLE SUN *A & M AMS 8164*	...2 8
24 Oct 81 ★	EVERY LITTLE THING SHE DOES IS MAGIC	
	A & M AMS 8174	...1 13
12 Dec 81	SPIRITS IN THE MATERIAL WORLD *A & M AMS 8194*	...12 8
28 May 83 ★	EVERY BREATH YOU TAKE *A & M AM 117* ▲	...1 11
23 Jul 83 ●	WRAPPED AROUND YOUR FINGER *A & M AM 127*	...7 7
5 Nov 83	SYNCHRONICITY II *A & M AM 153*	...17 4
14 Jan 84	KING OF PAIN *A & M AM 176*	...17 5
11 Oct 86	DON'T STAND SO CLOSE TO ME '86 (re-mix)	
	A & M AM 354	...24 4
13 May 95	CAN'T STAND LOSING YOU (LIVE) *A & M 5810372*	...27 2

Right column

20 Dec 97	ROXANNE '97 (re-mix) *A & M 5824552* [1]	...17 6

[1] Sting and The Police

Six Pack consists of six separate Police singles as follows: The Bed's Too Big Without You / Roxanne / Message in a Bottle / Walking on the Moon / So Lonely / Can't Stand Losing You. The last five titles were re-issues

Su POLLARD ◑ *UK, female vocalist* — 11 wks

5 Oct 85	COME TO ME (I AM WOMAN) *Rainbow RBR 1*	...71 1
1 Feb 86 ●	STARTING TOGETHER *Rainbow RBR 4*	...2 10

Jimi POLO *US, male producer* — 5 wks

9 Nov 91	NEVER GOIN' DOWN *MCA MCS 1578* [1]	...51 2
1 Aug 92	EXPRESS YOURSELF *Perfecto 74321101827*	...59 2
9 Aug 97	EXPRESS YOURSELF (re-issue) *Perfecto PERF 146CD1*	...62 1

[1] Adamski featuring Jimi Polo

The listed flip side of 'Never Goin' Down' was 'Born to Be Alive' by Adamski featuring Soho

Marco POLO *Italy, male instrumental/production duo* — 1 wk

8 Apr 95	A PRAYER TO THE MUSIC *Hi-Life HICD 7*	...65 1

POLTERGEIST *UK, male producer – Simon Berry* — 2 wks

6 Jul 96	VICIOUS CIRCLES *Manifesto FESCD 8*	...32 2

Peter POLYCARPOU *UK, male vocalist* — 4 wks

20 Feb 93	LOVE HURTS *Soundtrack Music CDEM 259*	...26 4

POLYGON WINDOW *UK, male producer – Richard James* — 1 wk

3 Apr 93	QUOTH *Warp WAP 33CD*	...49 1

See also APHEX TWIN

PONI-TAILS ◑ *US, female vocal group* — 14 wks

19 Sep 58 ●	BORN TOO LATE *HMV POP 516*	...5 11
10 Apr 59	EARLY TO BED *HMV POP 596*	...26 3

Brian POOLE and the TREMELOES ◑
UK, male vocalist, male vocal/instrumental backing group — 90 wks

4 Jul 63 ●	TWIST AND SHOUT *Decca F 11694*	...4 14
12 Sep 63 ★	DO YOU LOVE ME *Decca F 11739*	...1 14
28 Nov 63	I CAN DANCE *Decca F 11771*	...31 8
30 Jan 64	CANDY MAN *Decca F 11823*	...6 13
7 May 64 ●	SOMEONE SOMEONE *Decca F 11893*	...2 17
20 Aug 64	TWELVE STEPS TO LOVE *Decca F 11951*	...32 7
7 Jan 65	THREE BELLS *Decca F 12037*	...17 9
22 Jul 65	I WANT CANDY *Decca F 12197*	...25 8

See also TREMELOES

Glyn POOLE *UK, male vocalist* — 8 wks

20 Oct 73	MILLY MOLLY MANDY *York SYK 565*	...35 8

Iggy POP ✎ ⚡ *US, male vocalist* — 28 wks

13 Dec 86 ●	REAL WILD CHILD (WILD ONE) *A & M AM 368*	...10 11
10 Feb 90	LIVIN' ON THE EDGE OF THE NIGHT	
	Virgin America VUS 18	...51 4
13 Oct 90	CANDY *Virgin America VUS 29*	...67 1
5 Jan 91	WELL DID YOU EVAH! *Chrysalis CHS 3646* [1]	...42 4
4 Sep 93	THE WILD AMERICA (EP) *Virgin America VUSCD 74*	...63 1
21 May 94	BESIDE YOU *Virgin America VUSCD 77*	...47 2
23 Nov 96	LUST FOR LIFE *Virgin America VUSCD 116*	...26 2
7 Mar 98	THE PASSENGER *Virgin VSCDT 1689*	...22 3

[1] Deborah Harry and Iggy Pop

Tracks on The Wild America (EP): Wild America / Credit Card / Come Back Tomorrow / My Angel

---

UK No 1 ★ UK Top 10 ● UK million seller ◆ UK entry at No 1 ■ US No 1 ▲

POP TOPS *Spain, male vocal group*   **6 wks**

| 9 Oct 71 | MAMY BLUE *A & M AMS 859* | 35 | 6 |

POP WILL EAT ITSELF ☹ ☺
UK, male vocal/instrumental group   **43 wks**

30 Jan 88	THERE IS NO LOVE BETWEEN US ANYMORE		
	Chapter 22 CHAP 20	66	1
23 Jul 88	DEF. CON ONE *Chapter 22 PWE 001*	63	4
11 Feb 89	CAN U DIG IT *Chapter 22 PWE 002*	38	4
22 Apr 89	WISE UP! SUCKER *RCA PB 42761*	41	3
2 Sep 89	VERY METAL NOISE POLLUTION EP *RCA PB 42883*	45	3
9 Jun 90	TOUCHED BY THE HAND OF CICCIOLINA *RCA PB 43735*	28	4
13 Oct 90	DANCE OF THE MAD *RCA PB 44023*	32	2
12 Jan 91	X Y & ZEE *RCA PB 44243*	15	4
1 Jun 91	92 DEGREES *RCA PB 44555*	23	3
6 Jun 92	KARMADROME/EAT ME DRINK ME LOVE ME		
	RCA PB 45467	17	2
29 Aug 92	BULLETPROOF! *RCA 74321110137*	24	3
16 Jan 93 ●	GET THE GIRL! KILL THE BADDIES! *RCA 74321128802*	9	4
16 Oct 93	RSVP/FAMILUS HORRIBILUS *Infectious INFECT 1CD*	27	2
12 Mar 94	ICH BIN EIN AUSLANDER *Infectious INFECT 4CD*	28	2
10 Sep 94	EVERYTHING'S COOL *Infectious INFECT 9CD*	23	2

Tracks on Very Metal Noise Pollution EP: Def Con. 1989 AD including the Twilight Zone/Preaching to the Perverted/P.W.E.I.-zation/92 Degrees Fahrenheit
See also VARIOUS ARTISTS (EPs & LPs) – Gimme Shelter (EP)

POPES – *See Shane MacGOWAN and the POPES*

POPPERS presents AURA
UK, male production trio, and UK, female vocalist   **1 wk**

| 25 Oct 97 | EVERY LITTLE TIME *VC VCRD 26* | 44 | 1 |

POPPY FAMILY ◐
Canada, male/female vocal/instrumental group   **14 wks**

| 15 Aug 70 ● | WHICH WAY YOU GOIN' BILLY *Decca F 22976* | 7 | 14 |

PORN KINGS ☺ *UK, male instrumental/production group*   **5 wks**

| 28 Sep 96 | UP TO NO GOOD *All Around The World CDGLOBE 145* | 28 | 2 |
| 21 Jun 97 | AMOUR (C'MON) *All Around The World CDGLOBE 152* | 17 | 3 |

PORNO FOR PYROS *US, male vocal/instrumental group*   **2 wks**

| 5 Jun 93 | PETS *Warner Bros. 0777CDX* | 53 | 2 |

PORTISHEAD ☺ *UK, male/female vocal/instrumental group*   **20 wks**

13 Aug 94	SOUR TIMES *Go.Beat GODCD 116*	57	1
14 Jan 95	GLORY BOX *Go.Beat GODCD 120*	13	7
22 Apr 95	SOUR TIMES (re-entry) *Go.Beat GODCD 116*	13	4
20 Sep 97 ●	ALL MINE *Go.Beat 5715972*	8	4
22 Nov 97	OVER *Go.Beat 5719932*	25	2
14 Mar 98	ONLY YOU *Go.Beat 5694752*	35	2

Gary PORTNOY *US, male vocalist*   **3 wks**

| 25 Feb 84 | THEME FROM 'CHEERS' *Starblend CHEER 1* | 58 | 3 |

PORTRAIT *US, male vocal group*   **6 wks**

27 Mar 93	HERE WE GO AGAIN *Capitol CDCL 683*	37	3
8 Apr 95	I CAN CALL YOU *Capitol CDCL 740*	61	1
8 Jul 95	HOW DEEP IS YOUR LOVE *Capitol CDCL 751*	41	2

PORTSMOUTH SINFONIA *UK, orchestra*   **4 wks**

| 12 Sep 81 | CLASSICAL MUDDLEY *Island WIP 6736* | 38 | 4 |

Sandy POSEY ◐ *US, female vocalist*   **32 wks**

15 Sep 66	BORN A WOMAN *MGM 1321*	24	11
5 Jan 67	SINGLE GIRL *MGM 1330*	15	13
13 Apr 67	WHAT A WOMAN IN LOVE WON'T DO *MGM 1335*	48	3
6 Sep 75	SINGLE GIRL (re-issue) *MGM 2006 533*	35	5

POSIES *US, male vocal/instrumental group*   **1 wk**

| 19 Mar 94 | DEFINITE DOOR *Geffen GFSTD 68* | 67 | 1 |

POSITIVE FORCE ♀ *US, female vocal duo*   **9 wks**

| 22 Dec 79 | WE GOT THE FUNK *Sugarhill SHL 102* | 18 | 9 |

POSITIVE GANG *UK, male/female instrumental/vocal group*   **5 wks**

| 17 Apr 93 | SWEET FREEDOM *PWL Continental PWCD 261* | 34 | 4 |
| 31 Jul 93 | SWEET FREEDOM PART 2 *PWL Continental PWCD 264* | 67 | 1 |

POSITIVE K *US, male rapper*   **2 wks**

| 15 May 93 | I GOT A MAN *Fourth & Broadway BRCD 280* | 43 | 2 |

Mike POST *US, orchestra*   **18 wks**

9 Aug 75	AFTERNOON OF THE RHINO *Warner Bros. K 16588* [1]	48	1
23 Aug 75	AFTERNOON OF THE RHINO (re-entry)		
	Warner Bros. K 16588 [1]	47	1
16 Jan 82	THEME FROM 'HILL STREET BLUES' *Elektron K 12576* [2]	25	11
29 Sep 84	THE A TEAM *RCA 443*	45	5

[1] Mike Post Coalition [2] Mike Post featuring Larry Carlton

POTTERS *UK, male vocal group*   **2 wks**

| 1 Apr 72 | WE'LL BE WITH YOU *Pye JT 100* | 34 | 2 |

P.O.V. – *See JADE*

POWDER *UK, male/female vocal/instrumental group*   **1 wk**

| 24 Jun 95 | AFRODISIAC *Parkway PARK 002CD* | 72 | 1 |

Bryan POWELL *UK, male vocalist*   **3 wks**

13 Mar 93	IT'S ALRIGHT *Talkin Loud TLKCD 34*	73	1
15 May 93	I THINK OF YOU *Talkin Loud TLKCD 38*	61	1
7 Aug 93	NATURAL *Talkin Loud TLKCD 41*	73	1

Cozy POWELL ♪ *UK, male instrumentalist – drums*   **38 wks**

8 Dec 73 ●	DANCE WITH THE DEVIL *RAK 164*	3	15
25 May 74	THE MAN IN BLACK *RAK 173*	18	8
10 Aug 74 ●	NA NA NA *RAK 180*	10	10
10 Nov 79	THEME ONE *Ariola ARO 189*	62	2
19 Jun 93	RESURRECTION *Parlophone CDRS 6351* [1]	23	3

[1] Brian May with Cozy Powell

Kobie POWELL – *See US3*

POWER CIRCLE – *See CHICANE*

POWER OF DREAMS *Ireland, male vocal/instrumental group*   **2 wks**

| 19 Jan 91 | AMERICAN DREAM *Polydor PO 117* | 74 | 1 |
| 11 Apr 92 | THERE I GO AGAIN *Polydor PO 200* | 65 | 1 |

POWER STATION ◐ ♪ *UK/US, male vocal/instrumental group*   **17 wks**

16 Mar 85	SOME LIKE IT HOT *Parlophone R 6091*	14	8
11 May 85	GET IT ON *Parlophone R 6096*	22	7
9 Nov 85	COMMUNICATION *Parlophone R 6114*	75	1
12 Oct 96	SHE CAN ROCK IT *Chrysalis CDCHS 5039*	63	1

POWERCUT featuring NUBIAN PRINZ
US, male vocal/instrumental group   **4 wks**

| 22 Jun 91 | GIRLS *Eternal YZ 570* | 50 | 4 |

POWERHOUSE *UK, male dance group*   **4 wks**

| 20 Dec 97 | RHYTHM OF THE NIGHT *Satellite 74321522592* | 38 | 4 |

POWERPILL *UK, male instrumental/production group*   **3 wks**

| 6 Jun 92 | PAC-MAN *Ffrreedom TABX 110* | 43 | 3 |

Will POWERS ○ *US, female vocalist – Lyn Goldsmith* 9 wks

1 Oct 83	KISSING WITH CONFIDENCE *Island IS 134*	17 9

Hit features uncredited vocals by Carly Simon

Perez PRADO ℂ *Cuba, orchestra* 57 wks

25 Mar 55 ★	CHERRY PINK AND APPLE BLOSSOM WHITE *HMV B 10833* [1] ▲	1 17
25 Jul 58 ●	PATRICIA *RCA 1067*	8 16
10 Dec 94	GUAGLIONE *RCA 74321250192* [2]	41 6
8 Apr 95	GUAGLIONE (re-entry) *RCA 74321250192* [2]	58 2
6 May 95 ●	GUAGLIONE (2nd re-entry) *RCA 74321250192* [2]	2 16

[1] Perez 'Prez' Prado and his Orchestra, the King of the Mambo
[2] Perez 'Prez' Prado and his Orchestra

PRAISE ○ ☺ *UK, male/female vocal/instrumental group* 7 wks

2 Feb 91 ●	ONLY YOU *Epic 6566117*	4 7

PRATT and McCLAIN with BROTHERLOVE
US, male vocal duo with male instrumental group 6 wks

1 Oct 77	HAPPY DAYS *Reprise K 14435*	31 6

PRAXIS
UK, male/female vocal/instrumental group 5 wks

25 Nov 95	TURN ME OUT *Stress CDSTR 40*	44 2
20 Sep 97	TURN ME OUT (TURN TO SUGAR) (re-issue) *ffrr FCD 314* [1]	35 3

[1] Praxis featuring Kathy Brown

PRAYING MANTIS *UK, male vocal/instrumental group* 2 wks

31 Jan 81	CHEATED *Arista ARIST 378*	69 2

PREFAB SPROUT ○
UK, male/female vocal/instrumental group 60 wks

28 Jan 84	DON'T SING *Kitchenware SK 9*	62 2
20 Jul 85	FARON YOUNG *Kitchenware SK 22*	74 1
9 Nov 85	WHEN LOVE BREAKS DOWN *Kitchenware SK 21*	25 10
8 Feb 86	JOHNNY JOHNNY *Kitchenware SK 24*	64 2
13 Feb 88	CARS AND GIRLS *Kitchenware SK 35*	44 5
30 Apr 88 ●	THE KING OF ROCK 'N' ROLL *Kitchenware SK 37*	7 10
23 Jul 88	HEY MANHATTAN! *Kitchenware SK 38*	72 2
18 Aug 90	LOOKING FOR ATLANTIS *Kitchenware SK 47*	51 3
20 Oct 90	WE LET THE STARS GO *Kitchenware SK 48*	50 3
5 Jan 91	JORDAN: THE EP *Kitchenware SK 49*	35 4
13 Jun 92	THE SOUND OF CRYING *Kitchenware SK 58*	23 5
8 Aug 92	IF YOU DON'T LOVE ME *Kitchenware SK 60*	33 4
3 Oct 92	ALL THE WORLD LOVES LOVERS *Kitchenware SK 62*	61 2
9 Jan 93	LIFE OF SURPRISES *Kitchenware SKCD 63*	24 4
10 May 97	A PRISONER OF THE PAST *Columbia SKZD 70*	30 2
2 Aug 97	ELECTRIC GUITARS *Columbia SKZD 71*	53 1

Tracks on Jordan: The EP: Carnival 2000 / The Ice Maiden / One of the Broken / Jordan: The Comeback

PRELUDE *UK, male/female vocal group* 26 wks

26 Jan 74	AFTER THE GOLDRUSH *Dawn DNS 1052*	21 9
26 Apr 80	PLATINUM BLONDE *EMI 5046*	45 7
22 May 82	AFTER THE GOLDRUSH (re-issue) *After Hours AFT 02*	28 7
31 Jul 82	ONLY THE LONELY *After Hours AFT 06*	55 3

AFT 02 was a re-recording of DNS 1052. Both songs are a cappella

PRESENCE *UK, male/female vocal/production group* 1 wk

5 Dec 98	SENSE OF DANGER *Pagan PAGAN 024CDS* [1]	61 1

[1] Presence featuring Shara Nelson

PRESIDENT BROWN – See SABRE featuring PRESIDENT BROWN

PRESIDENTS OF THE UNITED STATES OF AMERICA ✎
US, male vocal/instrumental trio 21 wks

6 Jan 96	LUMP *Columbia 6624962*	15 7
20 Apr 96 ●	PEACHES *Columbia 6631072*	8 7
20 Jul 96	DUNE BUGGY *Columbia 6634892*	15 4
2 Nov 96	MACH 5 *Columbia 6638812*	29 2
1 Aug 98	VIDEO KILLED THE RADIO STAR *Maverick W 0450CD*	52 1

Elvis PRESLEY ♪ *Vocalist/film-star; the most important, most influential and biggest-selling solo artist of the 20th century, b. 8 January, 1935, Mississippi, d. 16 August, 1977. The 'King of Rock'n'Roll' broke and set countless records, won hundreds of awards, and sold an estimated one billion records around the world* 1155 wks

11 May 56 ●	HEARTBREAK HOTEL *HMV POP 182* ▲	2 21
25 May 56 ●	BLUE SUEDE SHOES *HMV POP 213*	9 8
13 Jul 56 ●	I WANT YOU I NEED YOU I LOVE YOU *HMV POP 235* ▲	25 2
3 Aug 56	I WANT YOU I NEED YOU I LOVE YOU (re-entry) *HMV POP 235*	14 9
17 Aug 56	BLUE SUEDE SHOES (re-entry) *HMV POP 213*	26 2
21 Sep 56 ●	HOUND DOG *HMV POP 249* ▲	2 23
26 Oct 56	HEARTBREAK HOTEL (re-entry) *HMV POP 182*	23 1
16 Nov 56 ●	BLUE MOON *HMV POP 272*	9 11
23 Nov 56	I DON'T CARE IF THE SUN DON'T SHINE *HMV POP 272*	29 1
7 Dec 56 ●	LOVE ME TENDER *HMV POP 253* ▲	11 9
21 Dec 56	I DON'T CARE IF THE SUN DON'T SHINE (re-entry) *HMV POP 272*	23 3
15 Feb 57	MYSTERY TRAIN *HMV POP 295*	25 5
8 Mar 57	RIP IT UP *HMV POP 305*	27 1
10 May 57 ●	TOO MUCH *HMV POP 330* ▲	6 8
14 Jun 57	ALL SHOOK UP *HMV POP 359* ▲	24 1
28 Jun 57 ★	ALL SHOOK UP (re-entry) *HMV POP 359*	1 20
12 Jul 57 ●	TEDDY BEAR *RCA 1013* ▲	3 19
12 Jul 57	TOO MUCH (re-entry) *HMV POP 330*	26 1
30 Aug 57 ●	PARALYSED *HMV POP 378*	8 10
4 Oct 57 ●	PARTY *RCA 1020*	2 15
18 Oct 57	GOT A LOT O' LIVIN' TO DO *RCA 1020*	17 4
1 Nov 57	LOVING YOU *RCA 1013*	24 2
1 Nov 57	TRYING TO GET TO YOU *HMV POP 408*	16 4
8 Nov 57	LAWDY MISS CLAWDY *HMV POP 408*	15 5
15 Nov 57	SANTA BRING MY BABY BACK TO ME *RCA 1025*	7 8
17 Jan 58	I'M LEFT YOU'RE RIGHT SHE'S GONE *HMV POP 428*	21 2
24 Jan 58 ★	JAILHOUSE ROCK *RCA 1028* ■ ▲	1 14
31 Jan 58	JAILHOUSE ROCK EP *RCA RCX 106*	18 5
7 Feb 58	I'M LEFT YOU'RE RIGHT SHE'S GONE (re-entry) *HMV POP 428*	29 1
28 Feb 58 ●	DON'T *RCA 1043* ▲	2 11
2 May 58 ●	WEAR MY RING AROUND YOUR NECK *RCA 1058*	3 10
25 Jul 58 ●	HARD HEADED WOMAN *RCA 1070* ▲	2 11
3 Oct 58 ●	KING CREOLE *RCA 1081*	2 15
23 Jan 59 ★	ONE NIGHT/I GOT STUNG *RCA 1100*	1 12
24 Apr 59 ★	A FOOL SUCH AS I/I NEED YOUR LOVE TONIGHT *RCA 1113*	1 15
24 Jul 59 ●	A BIG HUNK O' LOVE *RCA 1136* ▲	4 9
12 Feb 60	STRICTLY ELVIS EP *RCA RCX 175*	26 1
7 Apr 60 ●	STUCK ON YOU *RCA 1187* ▲	3 14
28 Jul 60 ●	A MESS OF BLUES *RCA 1194*	2 18
3 Nov 60 ★	IT'S NOW OR NEVER *RCA 1207* ◆ ■ ▲	1 19
19 Jan 61 ★	ARE YOU LONESOME TONIGHT *RCA 1216* ▲	1 15
9 Mar 61 ★	WOODEN HEART *RCA 1226*	1 27
25 May 61 ★	SURRENDER *RCA 1227* ■ ▲	1 15
7 Sep 61 ●	WILD IN THE COUNTRY/I FEEL SO BAD *RCA 1244*	4 12
2 Nov 61 ★	HIS LATEST FLAME/LITTLE SISTER *RCA 1258*	1 13
1 Feb 62 ★	ROCK A HULA BABY/CAN'T HELP FALLING IN LOVE *RCA 1270*	1 20
10 May 62 ★	GOOD LUCK CHARM *RCA 1280* ▲	1 17
21 Jun 62	FOLLOW THAT DREAM EP *RCA RCX 211*	34 2
30 Aug 62 ★	SHE'S NOT YOU *RCA 1303*	1 14
29 Nov 62 ★	RETURN TO SENDER *RCA 1320*	1 14
28 Feb 63	ONE BROKEN HEART FOR SALE *RCA 1337*	12 9
4 Jul 63 ★	DEVIL IN DISGUISE *RCA 1355*	1 13
24 Oct 63	BOSSA NOVA BABY *RCA 1374*	13 8
19 Dec 63	KISS ME QUICK *RCA 1375*	14 10
12 Mar 64	VIVA LAS VEGAS *RCA 1390*	17 12
25 Jun 64 ●	KISSIN' COUSINS *RCA 1404*	10 11

UK No 1 ★   UK Top 10 ●   UK million seller ◆   UK entry at No 1 ■   US No 1 ▲

20 Aug 64		SUCH A NIGHT *RCA 1411*	13	10
29 Oct 64		AIN'T THAT LOVIN' YOU BABY *RCA 1422*	15	8
3 Dec 64		BLUE CHRISTMAS *RCA 1430*	11	7
11 Mar 65		DO THE CLAM *RCA 1443*	19	8
27 May 65	★	CRYING IN THE CHAPEL *RCA 1455*	1	15
11 Nov 65		TELL ME WHY *RCA 1489*	15	10
24 Feb 66		BLUE RIVER *RCA 1504*	22	7
7 Apr 66		FRANKIE AND JOHNNY *RCA 1509*	21	9
7 Jul 66	●	LOVE LETTERS *RCA 1526*	6	10
13 Oct 66		ALL THAT I AM *RCA 1545*	18	8
1 Dec 66	●	IF EVERY DAY WAS LIKE CHRISTMAS *RCA 1557*	9	7
9 Feb 67		INDESCRIBABLY BLUE *RCA 1565*	21	5
11 May 67		YOU GOTTA STOP / LOVE MACHINE *RCA 1593*	38	5
16 Aug 67		LONG LEGGED GIRL *RCA RCA 1616*	49	2
21 Feb 68		GUITAR MAN *RCA 1663*	19	9
15 May 68		U. S. MALE *RCA 1688*	15	8
17 Jul 68		YOUR TIME HASN'T COME YET BABY *RCA 1714*	22	11
16 Oct 68		YOU'LL NEVER WALK ALONE *RCA 1747*	44	3
26 Feb 69		IF I CAN DREAM *RCA 1795*	11	10
11 Jun 69	●	IN THE GHETTO *RCA 1831*	2	16
6 Sep 69		CLEAN UP YOUR OWN BACK YARD *RCA 1869*	21	7
18 Oct 69		IN THE GHETTO (re-entry) *RCA 1831*	50	1
29 Nov 69	●	SUSPICIOUS MINDS *RCA 1900* ▲	2	14
28 Feb 70		DON'T CRY DADDY *RCA 1916*	8	11
16 May 70		KENTUCKY RAIN *RCA 1949*	21	11
11 Jul 70	★	THE WONDER OF YOU *RCA 1974*	1	20
8 Aug 70		KENTUCKY RAIN (re-entry) *RCA 1949*	46	1
14 Nov 70		I'VE LOST YOU *RCA 1999*	9	12
9 Jan 71		YOU DON'T HAVE TO SAY YOU LOVE ME *RCA 2046*	9	7
23 Jan 71		THE WONDER OF YOU (re-entry) *RCA 1974*	47	1
6 Mar 71		YOU DON'T HAVE TO SAY YOU LOVE ME (re-entry) *RCA 2046*	35	3
20 Mar 71	●	THERE GOES MY EVERYTHING *RCA 2060*	6	11
15 May 71	●	RAGS TO RICHES *RCA 2084*	9	11
17 Jul 71	●	HEARTBREAK HOTEL / HOUND DOG (re-issue) *RCA Maximillion 2104*	10	12
2 Oct 71		I'M LEAVIN' *RCA 2125*	23	9
4 Dec 71	●	I JUST CAN'T HELP BELIEVING *RCA 2158*	6	16
11 Dec 71		JAILHOUSE ROCK (re-issue) *RCA Maximillion 2153*	42	5
1 Apr 72	●	UNTIL IT'S TIME FOR YOU TO GO *RCA 2188*	5	9
17 Jun 72	●	AMERICAN TRILOGY *RCA 2229*	8	11
30 Sep 72	●	BURNING LOVE *RCA 2267*	7	9
16 Dec 72	●	ALWAYS ON MY MIND *RCA 2304*	9	13
26 May 73		POLK SALAD ANNIE *RCA 2359*	23	7
11 Aug 73		FOOL *RCA 2393*	15	10
24 Nov 73		RAISED ON ROCK *RCA 2435*	36	7
16 Mar 74		I'VE GOT A THING ABOUT YOU BABY *RCA APBO 0196*	33	5
13 Jul 74		IF YOU TALK IN YOUR SLEEP *RCA APBO 0280*	40	3
16 Nov 74		MY BOY *RCA 2458*	5	13
18 Jan 75	●	PROMISED LAND *RCA PB 10074*	9	8
24 May 75		T. R. O. U. B. L. E. *RCA 2562*	31	4
29 Nov 75		GREEN GREEN GRASS OF HOME *RCA 2635*	29	7
1 May 76		HURT *RCA 2674*	37	5
4 Sep 76	●	GIRL OF MY BEST FRIEND *RCA 2729*	9	12
25 Dec 76	●	SUSPICION *RCA 2768*	9	12
5 Mar 77	●	MOODY BLUE *RCA PB 0857*	6	9
13 Aug 77	★	WAY DOWN *RCA PB 0998*	1	13
3 Sep 77		ALL SHOOK UP (re-issue) *RCA PB 2694*	41	2
3 Sep 77		ARE YOU LONESOME TONIGHT (re-issue) *RCA PB 2699*	46	1
3 Sep 77		CRYING IN THE CHAPEL (re-issue) *RCA PB 2708*	43	2
3 Sep 77		IT'S NOW OR NEVER (re-issue) *RCA PB 2698*	39	2
3 Sep 77		JAILHOUSE ROCK (2nd re-issue) *RCA PB 2695*	44	2
3 Sep 77		RETURN TO SENDER (re-issue) *RCA PB 2706*	42	3
3 Sep 77		THE WONDER OF YOU (re-issue) *RCA PB 2709*	48	1
3 Sep 77		WOODEN HEART (re-issue) *RCA PB 2700*	49	1
10 Dec 77	●	MY WAY *RCA PB 1165*	9	8
24 Jun 78		DON'T BE CRUEL *RCA PB 9265*	24	12
15 Dec 79		IT WON'T SEEM LIKE CHRISTMAS (WITHOUT YOU) *RCA PB 9464*	13	6
30 Aug 80	●	IT'S ONLY LOVE / BEYOND THE REEF *RCA 4*	3	10
6 Dec 80		SANTA CLAUS IS BACK IN TOWN *RCA 16*	41	6
14 Feb 81		GUITAR MAN *RCA 43*	43	4
18 Apr 81		LOVING ARMS *RCA 48*	47	6
13 Mar 82		ARE YOU LONESOME TONIGHT *RCA 196*	25	7

26 Jun 82		THE SOUND OF YOUR CRY *RCA 232*	59	2
5 Feb 83		JAILHOUSE ROCK (re-entry) *RCA 1028*	27	6
7 May 83		BABY I DON'T CARE *RCA 332*	61	3
3 Dec 83		I CAN HELP *RCA 369*	30	9
10 Nov 84		THE LAST FAREWELL *RCA 459*	48	6
19 Jan 85		THE ELVIS MEDLEY *RCA 476*	51	3
10 Aug 85		ALWAYS ON MY MIND (re-recording) *RCA PB 49944*	59	4
11 Apr 87		AIN'T THAT LOVIN' YOU BABY / BOSSA NOVA BABY *RCA ARON 1*	47	5
22 Aug 87		LOVE ME TENDER / IF I CAN DREAM (re-issue) *RCA ARON 2*	56	3
16 Jan 88		STUCK ON YOU (re-issue) *RCA PB 49595*	58	2
17 Aug 91		ARE YOU LONESOME TONIGHT (LIVE) (re-issue) *RCA PB 49177*	68	2
29 Aug 92		DON'T BE CRUEL (re-issue) *RCA 74321110777*	42	2
11 Nov 95		THE TWELFTH OF NEVER *RCA 74321320122*	21	3
18 May 96		HEARTBREAK HOTEL / I WAS THE ONE (2nd re-issue) *RCA 74321336862*	45	1
24 May 97		ALWAYS ON MY MIND (re-issue of 1972 hit) *RCA 74321485412*	13	6

Tracks on Jailhouse Rock (EP): Jailhouse Rock / Young and Beautiful / I Want to Be Free / Don't Leave Me Now / Baby I Don't Care. On Strictly Elvis (EP): Old Shep / Any Place Is Paradise / Paralysed / Is It So Strange. On Follow That Dream (EP): Follow That Dream / Angel / What a Wonderful Life / I'm Not the Marrying Kind. On 5 July, 1962, a note on the Top 50 for that week stated: "Due to difficulties in assessing returns of Follow That Dream EP, it has been decided not to include it in Britain's Top 50. It is of course No 1 in the EP charts." Therefore this EP only had a two-week run on the chart when its sales would certainly have justified a much longer one. 'Beyond the Reef' listed only 30 Aug to 13 Sep, 1980. It peaked at No 7. 'Are You Lonesome Tonight?' on RCA 196 is a live version. RCA PB 49177 is a re-issue of RCA 196. 'Can't Help Falling in Love' credited from 1 Mar, 1962. Tracks on The Elvis Medley: Jailhouse Rock / Teddy Bear / Hound Dog / Don't Be Cruel / Burning Love / Suspicious Minds. Both sides of RCA ARON 1 are alternate versions to the original hits. RCA PB 49944 is also an alternate version

PRESSURE DROP *UK, male vocal/instrumental duo*   **1 wk**

| 21 Mar 98 | | SILENTLY BAD MINDED *Higher Ground HIGHS6 CD* | 53 | 1 |

Billy PRESTON *US, male vocalist/instrumentalist – keyboards*   **51 wks**

23 Apr 69	★	GET BACK *Apple R 5777* [1]	1	17
2 Jul 69		THAT'S THE WAY GOD PLANNED IT *Apple 12*	11	10
16 Sep 72		OUTA SPACE *A & M AMS 7007*	44	3
3 Apr 76		GET BACK (re-entry) *Apple R 5777* [1]	28	5
15 Dec 79	●	WITH YOU I'M BORN AGAIN *Motown TMG 1159* [2]	2	11
8 Mar 80		IT WILL COME IN TIME *Motown TMG 1175* [2]	47	4
22 Apr 89		GET BACK (2nd re-entry) *Apple R 5777* [1]	74	1

[1] Beatles with Billy Preston [2] Billy Preston and Syreeta

See also VARIOUS ARTISTS (LPs & EPs) – The Apple EP

Johnny PRESTON *US, male vocalist*   **45 wks**

12 Feb 60	★	RUNNING BEAR *Mercury AMT 1079* ▲	1	14
21 Apr 60	●	CRADLE OF LOVE *Mercury AMT 1092*	2	16
2 Jun 60		RUNNING BEAR (re-entry) *Mercury AMT 1079*	41	1
28 Jul 60		I'M STARTING TO GO STEADY *Mercury AMT 1104*	49	1
11 Aug 60		FEEL SO FINE *Mercury AMT 1104*	18	10
8 Dec 60		CHARMING BILLY *Mercury AMT 1114*	34	1
22 Dec 60		CHARMING BILLY (re-entry) *Mercury AMT 1114*	42	2

Mike PRESTON *UK, male vocalist*   **33 wks**

30 Oct 59		MR. BLUE *Decca F 11167*	12	8
25 Aug 60		I'D DO ANYTHING *Decca F 11255*	23	10
22 Dec 60		TOGETHERNESS *Decca F 11287*	41	5
9 Mar 61		MARRY ME *Decca F 11335*	14	10

PRETENDERS / Chrissie HYNDE *Transatlantically successful, British-based post-punk group with an ever-changing line-up, but with ex-NME journalist Chrissie Hynde (b. 7 September, 1951, Ohio, USA) (v/g) as a common factor. Hynde was briefly married to the lead singer of Simple Minds, Jim Kerr*   **165 wks**

| 10 Feb 79 | | STOP YOUR SOBBING *Real ARE 6* | 34 | 9 |

14 Jul 79	KID *Real ARE 9*..	33	7
17 Nov 79 ★	BRASS IN POCKET *Real ARE 11*	1	17
5 Apr 80 ●	TALK OF THE TOWN *Real ARE 12*	8	8
14 Feb 81	MESSAGE OF LOVE *Real ARE 15*....................	11	7
12 Sep 81	DAY AFTER DAY *Real ARE 17*.........................	45	4
14 Nov 81 ●	I GO TO SLEEP *Real ARE 18*	7	10
2 Oct 82	BACK ON THE CHAIN GANG *Real ARE 19*	17	9
26 Nov 83	2000 MILES *Real ARE 20*..............................	15	9
9 Jun 84	THIN LINE BETWEEN LOVE AND HATE *Real ARE 22* ..	49	3
3 Aug 85 ★	I GOT YOU BABE *DEP International DEP 20* [1] ..	1	13
11 Oct 86 ●	DON'T GET ME WRONG *Real YZ 85*	10	9
13 Dec 86 ●	HYMN TO HER *Real YZ 93*	8	12
15 Aug 87	IF THERE WAS A MAN *Real YZ 149* [2]	49	6
18 Jun 88 ●	BREAKFAST IN BED *DEP International DEP 29* [1] ..	6	11
12 Oct 91	SPIRITUAL HIGH (STATE OF INDEPENDENCE) *Arista 114528* [3] ..66		2
23 Jan 93	SPIRITUAL HIGH (STATE OF INDEPENDENCE) (re-issue)		
	Arista 74321127712 [3]	47	2
23 Apr 94 ●	I'LL STAND BY YOU *WEA YZ 815CD*	10	10
2 Jul 94	NIGHT IN MY VEINS *WEA YZ 825CD*	25	5
15 Oct 94	977 *WEA YZ 848CD1*.....................................	66	2
18 Mar 95 ★	LOVE CAN BUILD A BRIDGE *London COCD 1* [4] ..	1	8
14 Oct 95	KID *WEA 014CD*...	73	1
10 May 97	FEVERPITCH THE EP *Blancy Y Negro NEG 104CD* [5]	65	1

[1] UB40 featuring Chrissie Hynde [2] Pretenders For 007 [3] Moodswings featuring Chrissie Hynde [4] Cher, Chrissie Hynde and Neneh Cherry with Eric Clapton [5] Pretenders: La's: Orlando: Nick Hornby

Tracks on Feverpitch the EP: Goin' Back – Pretenders; Here She Goes – LA's; How Can We Hang On to a Dream – Orlando; Football – Neil MacColl; Boo Hewerdine – Nick Hornby
'Kid' in 1995 is a re-recording

PRETTY BOY FLOYD *US, male vocal/instrumental group* — 1 wk

10 Mar 90	ROCK AND ROLL (IS GONNA SET THE NIGHT ON FIRE)		
	MCA MCA 1393	75	1

PRETTY THINGS ✔ *UK, male vocal/instrumental group* — 41 wks

18 Jun 64	ROSALYN *Fontana TF 469*	41	5
22 Oct 64 ●	DON'T BRING ME DOWN *Fontana TF 503*	10	11
25 Feb 65	HONEY I NEED *Fontana TF 537*	13	10
15 Jul 65	CRY TO ME *Fontana TF 585*	28	7
20 Jan 66	MIDNIGHT TO SIX MAN *Fontana TF 647*	46	1
5 May 66	COME SEE ME *Fontana TF 688*	43	5
21 Jul 66	A HOUSE IN THE COUNTRY *Fontana TF 722* ...	50	1
4 Aug 66	A HOUSE IN THE COUNTRY (re-entry) *Fontana TF 722*..	50	1

Alan PRICE ◎ *UK, male vocalist/instrumentalist – keyboards* — 87 wks

31 Mar 66 ●	I PUT A SPELL ON YOU *Decca F 12367* [1]	9	10
14 Jul 66	HI LILI HI LO *Decca F 12442* [1]	11	12
2 Mar 67 ●	SIMON SMITH AND HIS AMAZING DANCING BEAR		
	Decca F 12570 [1]	4	12
2 Aug 67 ●	THE HOUSE THAT JACK BUILT *Decca F 12641* [1] ..	4	10
15 Nov 67	SHAME *Decca F 12691* [1]	45	2
31 Jan 68	DON'T STOP THE CARNIVAL *Decca F 12731* [1] ..	13	8
10 Apr 71	ROSETTA *CBS 7108* [2]	11	10
25 May 74 ●	JARROW SONG *Warner Bros. K 16372*............	6	9
29 Apr 78	JUST FOR YOU *Jet UP 36358*	43	7
17 Feb 79	BABY OF MINE/ JUST FOR YOU (re-issue) *Jet 135* ..32		3
30 Apr 88	CHANGES *Ariola 109911*	54	4

[1] Alan Price Set [2] Fame and Price Together

Kelly PRICE *US, female vocalist* — 3 wks

7 Nov 98	FRIEND OF MINE *Island Black Music CID 723*	25	3

Lloyd PRICE ♩ *US, male vocalist* — 36 wks

13 Feb 59 ●	STAGGER LEE *HMV POP 580* ▲	7	14
15 May 59	WHERE WERE YOU *HMV POP 598*..................	15	6
12 Jun 59 ●	PERSONALITY *HMV POP 626*	9	8
14 Aug 59	PERSONALITY (re-entry) *HMV POP 626*	25	2
11 Sep 59	I'M GONNA GET MARRIED *HMV POP 650*	23	5
21 Apr 60	LADY LUCK *HMV POP 712*	45	1

PRICKLY HEAT *UK, male producer* — 1 wk

26 Dec 98	OOOIE, OOOIE, OOOIE *Virgin VSCDT 1727* ....57†		1

Dickie PRIDE *UK, male vocalist* — 1 wk

30 Oct 59	PRIMROSE LANE *Columbia DB 4340*	28	1

Maxi PRIEST ✔ ◎ *Popular dancehall reggae star, b. Max Elliott, 10 June, 1960, London. This internationally acclaimed vocalist is the only UK reggae act to top the US chart ('Close to You', 1990). A duet with Roberta Flack, 'Set the Night to Music', also reached the US Top 10 in 1991* — 106 wks

29 Mar 86	STROLLIN' ON *10 TEN 84*	32	9
12 Jul 86	IN THE SPRINGTIME *10 TEN 127*....................	54	3
8 Nov 86	CRAZY LOVE *10 TEN 135*..............................	67	5
4 Apr 87	LET ME KNOW *10 TEN 156*............................	49	4
24 Oct 87	SOME GUYS HAVE ALL THE LUCK *10 TEN 198*	12	12
20 Feb 88	HOW CAN WE EASE THE PAIN *10 TEN 207* [1]	41	6
4 Jun 88 ●	WILD WORLD *10 TEN 221*	5	9
27 Aug 88	GOODBYE TO LOVE AGAIN *10 TEN 238*.........	57	3
9 Jun 90 ●	CLOSE TO YOU *10 TEN 294* ▲	7	10
1 Sep 90	PEACE THROUGHOUT THE WORLD *10 TEN 317* [2] ..	41	4
1 Dec 90	HUMAN WORK OF ART *10 TEN 328*................	75	1
15 Dec 90	HUMAN WORK OF ART (re-entry) *10 TEN 328* ..	71	3
24 Aug 91	HOUSECALL *Epic 6573477* [3]	31	7
5 Oct 91	THE MAXI PRIEST EP *Ten TEN 343*	62	3
26 Sep 92	GROOVIN' IN THE MIDNIGHT *Ten TEN 412*......	50	2
28 Nov 92	JUST WANNA KNOW/'FE' REAL *Ten TEN 416* [4] ..	33	3
20 Mar 93	ONE MORE CHANCE *Ten TENCD 420*	40	3
8 May 93 ●	HOUSECALL (re-mix) *Epic 6592842* [3]	8	8
31 Jul 93	WAITING IN VAIN *GRP MCSC 1921* [5]	65	2
22 Jun 96	THAT GIRL *Virgin America VUSCD 106* [6]	15	7
21 Sep 96	WATCHING THE WORLD GO BY		
	Virgin America VUSCD 108	36	2

[1] Maxi Priest featuring Beres Hammond [2] Maxi Priest featuring Jazzie B [3] Shabba Ranks featuring Maxi Priest [4] Maxi Priest/Maxi Priest featuring Apache Indian [5] Lee Ritenour and Maxi Priest [6] Maxi Priest featuring Shaggy

Tracks on The Maxi Priest EP: Just a Little Bit Longer / Best of Me / Searching / Fever

Louis PRIMA *US, male vocalist* — 1 wk

21 Feb 58	BUONA SERA *Capitol CL 14841*	25	1

PRIMA DONNA *UK, male/female vocal group* — 4 wks

26 Apr 80	LOVE ENOUGH FOR TWO *Ariola ARO 221*.........	48	4

PRIMAL SCREAM ☹ ☺ *UK, male vocal/instrumental group* — 44 wks

3 Mar 90	LOADED *Creation CRE 070*	16	9
18 Aug 90	COME TOGETHER *Creation CRE 0778*	26	6
22 Jun 91	HIGHER THAN THE SUN *Creation CRE 096*	40	2
24 Aug 91	DON'T FIGHT IT FEEL IT *Creation CRE 110* [1] ..	41	2
8 Feb 92	DIXIE-NARCO EP *Creation CRE 117*................	11	6
12 Mar 94 ●	ROCKS/FUNKY JAM *Creation CRESCD 129*	7	5
18 Jun 94	JAILBIRD *Creation CRESCD 145*	29	2
10 Dec 94	(I'M GONNA) CRY MYSELF BLIND		
	Creation CRESCD 183	49	2
15 Jun 96	THE BIG MAN AND THE SCREAM TEAM MEET THE BARMY		
	ARMY UPTOWN *Creation CRESCD 194* [2]	17	2
17 May 97 ●	KOWALSKI *Creation CRESCD 245*	8	3
28 Jun 97	STAR *Creation CRESCD 263*	16	3
25 Oct 97	BURNING WHEEL *Creation CRESCD 272*	17	2

[1] Primal Scream featuring Denise Johnson [2] Primal Scream, Irvine Welsh and On-U Sound

Tracks on Dixie-Narco EP: Movin' on Up / Stone My Soul / Carry Me Home / Screamadelica
See also Gary CLAIL ON-U SOUND SYSTEM

PRIME MOVERS *US, male vocal/instrumental group* — 1 wk

8 Feb 86	ON THE TRAIL *Island IS 263*	74	1

What: *Don't You Want Me*   **73**
Who: Human League
When: 1981 (1), 1995 (16 – remix)
Which: Outsold all other singles in the UK in 1981. Six months after topping the UK chart, it repeated that feat Stateside and launched the second 'British Invasion' of the US charts

What: *From Me to You*   **74**
Who: Beatles
When: 1963 (1), 1983 (40)
Which: Was the group's first No 1 and began their unequalled run of 11 No 1s. It was also Lennon and McCartney's first composition to chart Stateside, although Del Shannon sang the hit there

What: *Two Little Boys*   **75**
Who: Rolf Harris
When: 1969 (1)
Which: Stood at No 1 as the 1970s dawned. Thanks to this turn-of-the-century music-hall number, the unique entertainer became the first Australian solo artist to top the chart

What: *The Wonder of You*   **76**
Who: Elvis Presley
When: 1970 (1), 1977 (48)
Which: Unusually lists Presley as co-producer of this live recording. Presley's friend and label associate Ray Peterson first recorded the song (in 1959), and it became The King's last No 1 in his lifetime

PRIMITIVE RADIO GODS
US, male vocalist – Chris O'Connor   **1 wk**

30 Mar 96	STANDING OUTSIDE A BROKEN PHONE BOOTH WITH MONEY IN MY HAND *Columbia 6627692*	74	1

PRIMITIVES ☹ ◐ ✎ UK, male/female vocal/instrumental group   **27 wks**

27 Feb 88	● CRASH *Lazy PB 41761*	5	10
30 Apr 88	OUT OF REACH *Lazy PB 42011*	25	4
3 Sep 88	WAY BEHIND ME *Lazy PB 42209*	36	4
29 Jul 89	SICK OF IT *Lazy PB 42947*	24	4
30 Sep 89	SECRETS *Lazy PB 43173*	49	3
3 Aug 91	YOU ARE THE WAY *RCA PB 44481*	58	2

♀ PRINCE ◐ R&B ✎ Prolific singer/songwriter/producer/
multi-instrumentalist/actor/label- and studio-owner, b. Prince Rogers Nelson, 7 June, 1958, Minneapolis. This often-controversial entertainer has packed stadiums and collected awards worldwide. He is now referred to as The Artist Formerly Known As Prince   **294 wks**

19 Jan 80	I WANNA BE YOUR LOVER *Warner Bros. K 17537*	41	3
29 Jan 83	1999 *Warner Bros. W 9896*	25	7
30 Apr 83	LITTLE RED CORVETTE *Warner Bros. W 9688*	54	6
26 Nov 83	LITTLE RED CORVETTE (re-issue) *Warner Bros. W 9436*	66	2
30 Jun 84	● WHEN DOVES CRY *Warner Bros. W 9286* ▲	4	15
22 Sep 84	PURPLE RAIN *Warner Bros. W 9174*	8	9
8 Dec 84	I WOULD DIE 4 U *Warner Bros. W 9121* [1]	58	6
19 Jan 85	● 1999/LITTLE RED CORVETTE (re-issue) *Warner Bros. W 1999*	2	10
23 Feb 85	● LET'S GO CRAZY/TAKE ME WITH U *Warner Bros. W 2000* [1] ▲	7	9
25 May 85	PAISLEY PARK *WEA W 9052*	18	10
27 Jul 85	RASPBERRY BERET *WEA W 8929* [1]	25	8
26 Oct 85	POP LIFE *Paisley Park W 8858* [1]	60	2
8 Mar 86	● KISS *Paisley Park W 8751* [1] ▲	6	9
14 Jun 86	MOUNTAINS *Paisley Park W 8711* [1]	45	4
16 Aug 86	GIRLS AND BOYS *Paisley Park W 8586* [1]	11	8
1 Nov 86	ANOTHERLOVERHOLENYOHEAD *Paisley Park W 8521* [1]	36	3
14 Mar 87	● SIGN 'O' THE TIMES *Paisley Park W 8399*	10	9
20 Jun 87	IF I WAS YOUR GIRLFRIEND *Paisley Park W 8334*	20	6
15 Aug 87	U GOT THE LOOK *Paisley Park W 8289*	11	9
28 Nov 87	I COULD NEVER TAKE THE PLACE OF YOUR MAN *Paisley Park W 8288*	29	6
7 May 88	● ALPHABET STREET *Paisley Park W 7900*	9	6
23 Jul 88	GLAM SLAM *Paisley Park W 7806*	29	4
5 Nov 88	I WISH U HEAVEN *Paisley Park W 7745*	24	5
24 Jun 89	● BATDANCE *Warner Bros. W 2924* ▲	2	12
9 Sep 89	PARTYMAN *Warner Bros. W 2814*	14	6
18 Nov 89	THE ARMS OF ORION *Warner Bros. W 2757* [2]	27	5
4 Aug 90	● THIEVES IN THE TEMPLE *Paisley Park W 9751*	7	6
10 Nov 90	NEW POWER GENERATION *Paisley Park W 9525*	26	4
31 Aug 91	● GETT OFF *Paisley Park W 0056* [3]	4	8
21 Sep 91	CREAM *Paisley Park W 0061* [3] ▲	15	7
7 Dec 91	DIAMONDS AND PEARLS *Paisley Park W 0075* [3]	25	6
28 Mar 92	MONEY DON'T MATTER 2 NIGHT *Paisley Park W 0091* [3]	19	5
27 Jun 92	THUNDER *Paisley Park W 01132P* [3]	28	3
18 Jul 92	SEXY MF/STROLLIN' *Paisley Park W 0123* [3]	4	7
10 Oct 92	MY NAME IS PRINCE *Paisley Park W 0132* [3]	7	5
14 Nov 92	MY NAME IS PRINCE (re-mix) *Paisley Park W 0142T* [3]	51	1
5 Dec 92	7 *Paisley Park W 0147* [3]	27	6
13 Mar 93	THE MORNING PAPERS *Paisley Park W 0162CD* [3]	52	3
16 Oct 93	PEACH *Paisley Park W 0210CD*	14	5
11 Dec 93	● CONTROVERSY *Paisley Park W 0215CD1*	5	5
9 Apr 94	★ THE MOST BEAUTIFUL GIRL IN THE WORLD *NPG NPG 60155* [4]	1	12
4 Jun 94	THE BEAUTIFUL EXPERIENCE (re-mix) *NPG NPG 60212* [4]	18	3
10 Sep 94	LETITGO *Warner Bros. W 0260CD*	30	4
18 Mar 95	PURPLE MEDLEY *Warner Bros. W 0289CD*	33	2
23 Sep 95	EYE HATE U *Warner Bros. W 0315CD* [4]	20	3
9 Dec 95	● GOLD *Warner Bros. W 0325CD* [4]	10	9
3 Aug 96	DINNER WITH DELORES *Warner Bros. 9362437422*	36	2
14 Dec 96	BETCHA BY GOLLY WOW *NPG CDEM 463*	11	6
8 Mar 97	THE HOLY RIVER *EMI CDEM 467* [5]	19	3

[1] Prince and the Revolution [2] Prince with Sheena Easton [3] Prince and the

New Power Generation [4] ♀ [5] The Artist

Although uncredited, Sheena Easton also vocalises on 'U Got the Look'. 'The Beautiful Experience' was a seven-track CD featuring 'The Most Beautiful Girl in the World' and six further mixes of the track

PRINCE BUSTER ✌ Jamaica, male vocalist   **16 wks**

23 Feb 67	AL CAPONE *Blue Beat BB 324*	18	13
4 Apr 98	WHINE AND GRINE *Island CID 691*	21	3

PRINCE CHARLES and the CITY BEAT BAND
US, male vocalist with male vocal/instrumental group   **2 wks**

22 Feb 86	WE CAN MAKE IT HAPPEN *PRT 7P 348*	56	2

PRINCE NASEEM – *See KALEEF*

PRINCESS ◐ ✎ UK, female vocalist   **44 wks**

3 Aug 85	● SAY I'M YOU'RE NO. 1 *Supreme SUPE 101*	7	12
9 Nov 85	AFTER THE LOVE HAS GONE *Supreme SUPE 103*	28	13
19 Apr 86	I'LL KEEP ON LOVING YOU *Supreme SUPE 105*	16	8
5 Jul 86	TELL ME TOMORROW *Supreme SUPE 106*	34	5
25 Oct 86	IN THE HEAT OF A PASSIONATE MOMENT *Supreme SUPE 109*	74	1
13 Jun 87	RED HOT *Polydor POSP 868*	58	5

PRINCESS IVORI US, female rapper   **2 wks**

17 Mar 90	WANTED *Supreme SUPE 163*	69	2

Patrick PRINZ – *See ARTEMESIA; ETHICS; MOVIN' MELODIES; SUBLIMINAL CUTS*

Maddy PRIOR – *See STATUS QUO*

PRIVATE LIVES UK, male vocal/instrumental duo   **4 wks**

11 Feb 84	LIVING IN A WORLD (TURNED UPSIDE DOWN) *EMI PRIV 2*	53	4

PRIZNA featuring DEMOLITION MAN
UK, male vocal/instrumental group   **2 wks**

29 Apr 95	FIRE *Labello Blanco NLBCDX 18*	33	2

PJ PROBY ◐ US, male vocalist   **91 wks**

28 May 64	● HOLD ME *Decca F 11904*	3	15
3 Sep 64	● TOGETHER *Decca F 11967*	8	11
10 Dec 64	● SOMEWHERE *Liberty LIB 10182*	6	12
25 Feb 65	I APOLOGISE *Liberty LIB 10188*	11	8
8 Jul 65	LET THE WATER RUN DOWN *Liberty LIB 10206*	19	8
30 Sep 65	THAT MEANS A LOT *Liberty LIB 10215*	30	6
25 Nov 65	● MARIA *Liberty LIB 10218*	8	9
10 Feb 66	YOU'VE COME BACK *Liberty LIB 10223*	25	7
16 Jun 66	TO MAKE A BIG MAN CRY *Liberty LIB 10236*	34	3
27 Oct 66	I CAN'T MAKE IT ALONE *Liberty LIB 10250*	37	5
6 Mar 68	IT'S YOUR DAY TODAY *Liberty LBF 15046*	32	5
28 Dec 96	YESTERDAY HAS GONE *EMI Premier CDPRESX 13* [1]	58	1
11 Jan 97	YESTERDAY HAS GONE (re-entry) *EMI Premier CDPRESX 13* [1]	69	1

[1] PJ Proby and Marc Almond

PROCLAIMERS ◐ ♂ UK, male vocal/instrumental duo   **50 wks**

14 Nov 87	● LETTER FROM AMERICA *Chrysalis CHS 3178*	3	10
5 Mar 88	MAKE MY HEART FLY *Chrysalis CLAIM 1*	63	3
27 Aug 88	I'M GONNA BE *Chrysalis CLAIM 2*	11	11
12 Nov 88	SUNSHINE ON LEITH *Chrysalis CLAIM 3*	41	5
11 Feb 89	I'M ON MY WAY *Chrysalis CLAIM 4*	43	4
24 Nov 90	● KING OF THE ROAD EP *Chrysalis CLAIM 5*	9	8
19 Feb 94	LET'S GET MARRIED *Chrysalis CDCLAIMS 6*	21	4
16 Apr 94	WHAT MAKES YOU CRY *Chrysalis CDCLAIMS 7*	38	3
22 Oct 94	THESE ARMS OF MINE *Chrysalis CDCLAIM 8*	51	2

Tracks on King of the Road (EP): King of the Road/Long Black Veil/Lulu Selling Tea/Not Ever

UK No 1 ★   UK Top 10 ●   UK million seller ◆   UK entry at No 1 ■   US No 1 ▲

PROCOL HARUM 🎸 *UK, male vocal/instrumental group*   **56 wks**

25 May 67 ★	A WHITER SHADE OF PALE *Deram DM 126*	1	15
4 Oct 67 ●	HOMBURG *Regal Zonophone RZ 3003*	6	10
24 Apr 68	QUITE RIGHTLY SO *Regal Zonophone RZ 3007*	50	1
18 Jun 69	SALTY DOG *Regal Zonophone RZ 3019*	44	1
2 Jul 69	SALTY DOG (re-entry) *Regal Zonophone RZ 3019*	44	1
16 Jul 69	SALTY DOG (2nd re-entry) *Regal Zonophone RZ 3019*	44	1
22 Apr 72	A WHITER SHADE OF PALE (re-issue)		
	Fly Magnifly ECHO 101	13	13
5 Aug 72	CONQUISTADOR *Chrysalis CHS 2003*	22	7
23 Aug 75	PANDORA'S BOX *Chrysalis CHS 2073*	16	7

Michael PROCTOR – See URBAN BLUES PROJECT present Michael PROCTOR

PRODIGY 🙂 *Confrontational dance-rock collision masterminded by Liam Howlett (k/prog) and featuring charismatic Keith Flint (v). This act has achieved run of 12 successive Top 20 singles, while their 1997 album, Fat of the Land, debuted at No 1 in more than 20 countries, including the UK and the USA*   **137 wks**

24 Aug 91 ●	CHARLY *XL XLS 21*	3	10
4 Jan 92 ●	EVERYBODY IN THE PLACE EP *XL XLS 26*	2	9
26 Sep 92	FIRE/JERICHO *XL XLS 30*	11	4
21 Nov 92 ●	OUT OF SPACE/RUFF IN THE JUNGLE BIZNESS *XL XLS 35*	5	12
17 Apr 93	WIND IT UP (REWOUND) *XL XLS 39CD*	11	7
16 Oct 93	ONE LOVE *XL XLS 47CD*	8	6
28 May 94 ●	NO GOOD (START THE DANCE) *XL XLS 51CD*	4	12
24 Sep 94	VOODOO PEOPLE *XL XLS 54CD*	13	5
18 Mar 95	POISON *XL XLS 58CD*	15	6
30 Mar 96 ★	FIRESTARTER *XL XLS 70CD* ■	1	19
20 Apr 96	OUT OF SPACE/RUFF IN THE JUNGLE BIZNESS (re-entry)		
	XL XLS 35CD	52	2
20 Apr 96	NO GOOD (START THE DANCE) (re-entry) *XL XLS 51CD*	57	2
20 Apr 96	POISON (re-entry) *XL XLS 58CD*	62	1
20 Apr 96	FIRE/JERICHO (re-entry) *XL XLS 30CD*	63	1
20 Apr 96	CHARLY (re-entry) *XL XLS 21CD*	66	1
20 Apr 96	WIND IT UP (REWOUND) (re-entry) *XL XLS 39CD*	71	1
20 Apr 96	VOODOO PEOPLE (re-entry) *XL XLS 54CD*	75	1
27 Apr 96	EVERYBODY IN THE PLACE EP (re-entry) *XL XLS 26CD1*	69	1
23 Nov 96 ★	BREATHE *XL XLS 80CD* ■	1	16
14 Dec 96	FIRESTARTER (re-entry) *XL XLS 70CD*	70	3
25 Jan 97	FIRESTARTER (re-entry) *XL XLS 70CD*	53	1
5 Apr 97	BREATHE (re-entry) *XL XLS 80CD*	71	1
29 Nov 97 ●	SMACK MY BITCH UP *XL XLS 90CD*	8	10

PROFESSIONALS *UK, male vocal/instrumental group*   **4 wks**

11 Oct 80	1-2-3 *Virgin VS 376*	43	4

PROFESSOR – See DJ PROFESSOR

PROFESSOR T – See SHUT UP AND DANCE

PROGRAM 2 BELTRAM – See BELTRAM

PROGRESS FUNK *Italy, male production trio*   **1 wk**

11 Oct 97	AROUND MY BRAIN *Deconstruction 74321518182*	73	1

PROJECT 1 *UK, male producer – Mark Williams*   **3 wks**

16 May 92	ROUGHNECK EP *Rising High RSN 22*	49	2
29 Aug 92	DON CARGON COMIN' *Rising High RSN 35*	64	1

Tracks on Roughneck EP: Come My Selector/Can't Take the Heartbreak/ Live Vibe 4 (Summer Vibes)

PROJECT featuring GERIDEAU *US, male vocal/instrumental duo*   **1 wk**

27 Aug 94	BRING IT BACK 2 LUV *Fruittree FTREE 10CD*	65	1

PRONG *US, male vocal/instrumental group*   **1 wk**

25 Apr 92	WHOSE FIST IS THIS ANYWAY EP *Epic 6580026*	58	1

Tracks on Whose Fist Is This Anyway EP: Prove You Wrong/Hell If I Could/(Get a) Grip (On Yourself)/Prove You Wrong (re-mix)

PROPAGANDA *Germany, male/female vocal/instrumental group*   **35 wks**

17 Mar 84	DR MABUSE *ZTT ZTAS 2*	27	9
4 May 85	DUEL *ZTT ZTAS 8*	21	12
10 Aug 85	P MACHINERY *ZTT ZTAS 12*	50	5
28 Apr 90	HEAVEN GIVE ME WORDS *Virgin VS 1245*	36	5
8 Sep 90	ONLY ONE WORD *Virgin VS 1271*	71	4

PROPELLERHEADS 🙂 *UK, male instrumental/production duo – Alex Gifford and Will White*   **15 wks**

7 Dec 96	TAKE CALIFORNIA *Wall Of Sound WALLD 024*	69	1
17 May 97	SPYBREAK! *Wall Of Sound WALLD 029X*	40	1
18 Oct 97 ●	ON HER MAJESTY'S SECRET SERVICE		
	East West EW 136CD [1]	7	5
20 Dec 97	HISTORY REPEATING *Wall Of Sound WALLD 036* [2]	19	7
27 Jun 98	BANG ON! *Wall Of Sound WALLD 039*	53	1

[1] Propellerheads/David Arnold [2] Propellerheads featuring Miss Shirley Bassey

PROPHETS OF SOUND *UK, male instrumental/production duo*   **1 wk**

14 Nov 98	HIGH *Distinctive DISNCD 47*	73	1

PROSPECT PARK *UK, male/female vocal/production duo*   **1 wk**

8 Aug 98	MOVIN' ON *AM:PM 5827312* [1]	55	1

[1] Prospect Park featuring Carolyn Harding

Brian PROTHEROE *UK, male vocalist*   **6 wks**

7 Sep 74	PINBALL *Chrysalis CHS 2043*	22	6

Dorothy PROVINE © *US, female vocalist*   **15 wks**

7 Dec 61	DON'T BRING LULU *Warner Bros. WB 53*	17	12
28 Jun 62	CRAZY WORDS CRAZY TUNE *Warner Bros. WB 70*	45	3

PSEUDO ECHO ☺ *Australia, male vocal/instrumental group*   **12 wks**

18 Jul 87 ●	FUNKY TOWN *RCA PB 49705*	8	12

PSYCHEDELIC FURS 🎸 *UK, male vocal/instrumental group*   **31 wks**

2 May 81	DUMB WAITERS *CBS 1166*	59	2
27 Jun 81	PRETTY IN PINK *CBS A 1327*	43	5
31 Jul 82	LOVE MY WAY *CBS A 2549*	42	6
31 Mar 84	HEAVEN *CBS A 4300*	29	6
16 Jun 84	GHOST IN YOU *CBS A 4470*	68	2
23 Aug 86	PRETTY IN PINK *CBS A 7242*	18	9
9 Jul 88	ALL THAT MONEY WANTS *CBS FURS 4*	75	1

A 7242 was a re-recording of A 1327

PSYCHIC TV *UK, male/female vocal/instrumental group*   **4 wks**

26 Apr 86	GODSTAR *Temple TOPY 009* [1]	67	2
20 Sep 86	GOOD VIBRATIONS/ROMAN P. *Temple TOPY 23*	65	2

[1] Psychic TV and the Angels of Light

PSYCHOTROPIC – See FREEFALL featuring PSYCHOTROPIC; SALT-N-PEPA

PUBLIC ANNOUNCEMENT *US, male vocal/instrumental group*   **3wks**

9 May 92	SHE'S GOT THAT VIBE *Jive JIVET 292* [1]	57	2
20 Nov 93	SEX ME *Jive JIVECD 346* [1]	75	1

[1] R Kelly and Public Announcement

PUBLIC DEMAND *UK, male vocal group*   **2 wks**

15 Feb 97	INVISIBLE *ZTT ZANG 85CD*	41	2

PUBLIC ENEMY ⬅ *US, male rap group*   **52 wks**

21 Nov 87	REBEL WITHOUT A PAUSE *Def Jam 651245 7*	37	5
2 Jan 88	REBEL WITHOUT A PAUSE (re-entry) *Def Jam 651245 7*	71	2
9 Jan 88	BRING THE NOISE *Def Jam 651335 7*	32	5
2 Jul 88	DON'T BELIEVE THE HYPE *Def Jam 652833 7*	18	5

UK No 1 ★   UK Top 10 ●   UK million seller ◆   UK entry at No 1 ■   US No 1 ▲

15 Oct 88	NIGHT OF THE LIVING BASEHEADS *Def Jam 6530460*	63	2
24 Jun 89	FIGHT THE POWER *Motown ZB 42877*	29	5
20 Jan 90	WELCOME TO THE TERRORDOME *Def Jam 655476 0*	18	4
7 Apr 90	911 IS A JOKE *Def Jam 655830 7*	41	3
23 Jun 90	BROTHERS GONNA WORK IT OUT *Def Jam 656018 1*	46	2
3 Nov 90	CAN'T DO NUTTIN' FOR YA MAN *Def Jam 656385 7*	53	2
12 Oct 91	CAN'T TRUSS IT *Def Jam 6575307*	22	4
25 Jan 92	SHUT 'EM DOWN *Def Jam 6577617*	21	3
11 Apr 92	NIGHTTRAIN *Def Jam 6578647*	55	2
13 Aug 94	GIVE IT UP *Def Jam DEFCD 1*	18	3
29 Jul 95	SO WATCHA GONNA DO NOW *Def Jam DEFCD 5*	50	1
6 Jun 98	HE GOT GAME *Def Jam 5689852*	16	4

PUBLIC IMAGE LTD ✏ *UK, male vocal/instrumental group* — 61 wks

21 Oct 78	● PUBLIC IMAGE *Virgin VS 228*	9	8
7 Jul 79	DEATH DISCO *Virgin VS 274*	20	7
20 Oct 79	MEMORIES *Virgin VS 299*	60	2
4 Apr 81	FLOWERS OF ROMANCE *Virgin VS 397*	24	7
17 Sep 83	● THIS IS NOT A LOVE SONG *Virgin VS 529*	5	10
19 May 84	BAD LIFE *Virgin VS 675*	71	2
1 Feb 86	RISE *Virgin VS 841*	11	8
3 May 86	HOME *Virgin VS 855*	75	1
22 Aug 87	SEATTLE *Virgin VS 988*	47	4
6 May 89	DISAPPOINTED *Virgin VS 1181*	38	5
20 Oct 90	DON'T ASK ME *Virgin VS 1231*	22	5
22 Feb 92	CRUEL *Virgin VS 1390*	49	2

Group often known as P.I.L.
See also John LYDON

Gary PUCKETT – *See UNION GAP featuring Gary PUCKETT*

Tito PUENTE Jr. and the LATIN RHYTHM featuring Tito PUENTE, INDIA and Cali ALEMAN
US, male/female vocal/instrumental group — 3 wks

16 Mar 96	OYE COMO VA *Media MCSTD 40013*	36	2
19 Jul 97	OYE COMA VA (re-issue) *Nukleuz MCSTD 40120*	56	1

PUFF DADDY ◄═ *US, male producer* — 58 wks

29 Mar 97	CAN'T NOBODY HOLD ME DOWN *Arista 74321464552* [1] ▲	19	4
26 Apr 97	NO TIME *Atlantic A 5594CD* [2]	45	1
28 Jun 97	★ I'LL BE MISSING YOU *Puff Daddy 74321499102* [3] ◆ ■ ▲	1	21
9 Aug 97	MO MONEY MO PROBLEMS *Puff Daddy 74321492492* [4]	6	10
13 Sep 97	SOMEONE *RCA 74321513942* [5]	34	2
1 Nov 97	BEEN AROUND THE WORLD *Puff Daddy 74321539442* [6]	20	4
3 Jan 98	BEEN AROUND THE WORLD (re-entry) *Puff Daddy 74321539442* [6]	59	2
7 Feb 98	IT'S ALL ABOUT THE BENJAMINS *Puff Daddy 74321561972* [6]	18	3
1 Aug 98	COME WITH ME (IMPORT) *Epic 34K78954* [7]	75	1
8 Aug 98	● COME WITH ME *Epic 6662842* [7]	2	10

[1] Puff Daddy featuring Mase [2] Lil' Kim featuring Puff Daddy [3] Puff Daddy & Faith Evans [4] Notorious B.I.G. featuring Puff Daddy and Mase [5] SWV featuring Puff Daddy [6] Puff Daddy & The Family [7] Puff Daddy featuring Jimmy Page

PULP ⚫ ☹ *UK, male/female vocal/instrumental group* — 70 wks

27 Nov 93	LIP GLOSS *Island CID 567*	50	2
2 Apr 94	DO YOU REMEMBER THE FIRST TIME *Island CID 574*	33	4
4 Jun 94	THE SISTERS EP *Island CID 595*	19	4
3 Jun 95	● COMMON PEOPLE *Island CID 613*	2	13
7 Oct 95	● MIS-SHAPES/SORTED FOR E'S AND WIZZ *Island CID 620*	2	8
9 Dec 95	● DISCO 2000 *Island CID 623*	7	11
30 Dec 95	MIS-SHAPES/SORTED FOR E'S AND WIZZ (re-entry) *Island CID 620*	62	3
6 Apr 96	● SOMETHING CHANGED *Island CID 632*	10	5
8 Jun 96	SOMETHING CHANGED (re-entry) *Island CID 632*	62	1
22 Jun 96	SOMETHING CHANGED (2nd re-entry) *Island CID 632*	61	1
7 Sep 96	DO YOU REMEMBER THE FIRST TIME (re-entry) *Island CID 574*	73	1
22 Nov 97	● HELP THE AGED *Island CID 679*	8	7
24 Jan 98	HELP THE AGED (re-entry) *Island CID 679*	74	2
28 Mar 98	THIS IS HARDCORE *Island CID 695*	12	4

20 Jun 98	A LITTLE SOUL *Island CID 708*	22	2
19 Sep 98	PARTY HARD *Island CID 719*	29	2

Tracks on The Sisters EP: Babies/Your Sister's Clothes/Seconds/His 'n' Hers

PULSE featuring Antoinette ROBERSON
US, male/female vocal/instrumental duo — 3 wks

25 May 96	THE LOVER THAT YOU ARE *ffrr FCD 278*	22	3

Pulse is David Morales
See also David MORALES

PURE SUGAR *UK, male/female vocal/instrumental trio* — 1 wk

24 Oct 98	DELICIOUS *Geffen GFSTD 22355*	70	1

PURESSENCE *UK, male vocal/instrumental group* — 5 wks

23 May 98	THIS FEELING *Island CID 688*	33	2
8 Aug 98	IT DOESN'T MATTER ANYMORE *Island CID 703*	47	1
21 Nov 98	ALL I WANT *Island CID 722*	39	2

James and Bobby PURIFY ✒ *US, male vocal duo* — 16 wks

24 Apr 76	I'M YOUR PUPPET *Mercury 6167 324*	12	10
7 Aug 76	MORNING GLORY *Mercury 6167 380*	27	6

PURPLE HEARTS *UK, male vocal/instrumental group* — 5 wks

22 Sep 79	MILLIONS LIKE US *Fiction FICS 003*	57	3
8 Mar 80	JIMMY *Fiction FICS 9*	60	2

PURPLE KINGS *UK, male vocal/instrumental duo* — 3 wks

15 Oct 94	THAT'S THE WAY YOU DO IT *Positiva CDTIV 21*	26	3

PUSSYCAT ⊘ *Holland, male/female vocal/instrumental group* — 30 wks

28 Aug 76	★ MISSISSIPPI *Sonet SON 2077*	1	22
25 Dec 76	SMILE *Sonet SON 2096*	24	8

PYRAMIDS *Jamaica, male vocal/instrumental group* — 4 wks

22 Nov 67	TRAIN TOUR TO RAINBOW CITY *President PT 161*	35	4

PYTHON LEE JACKSON 🎸
Australia, male vocal/instrumental group — 12 wks

30 Sep 72	● IN A BROKEN DREAM *Youngblood YB 1002*	3	12

Uncredited lead vocals by Rod Stewart

Q

Q *UK, male instrumental/production duo* — 6 wks

5 Jun 93	GET HERE *Arista 74321145972* [1]	37	4
12 Mar 94	(EVERYTHING I DO) I DO IT FOR YOU *Bell 74321193062* [2]	47	2

[1] Q featuring Tracy Ackerman [2] Q featuring Tony Jackson

Q-BASS *UK, male production/instrumental group* — 1 wk

8 Feb 92	HARDCORE WILL NEVER DIE *Suburban Base SUBBASE 007*	64	1

See also VARIOUS ARTISTS (EPs & LPs) – Subplates Volume 1 EP

Q-CLUB *Italy, male/female vocal/instrumental group*   3 wks

6 Jan 96	TELL IT TO MY HEART *Manifesto FESCD 5*	28	3

Q-TEE *UK, female rapper*   7 wks

21 Apr 90	AFRIKA *SBK SBK 7008* [1]	42	5
10 Feb 96	GIMME THAT BODY *Heavenly HVN 48CD*	40	2

[1] History featuring Q-Tee

Q-TEX *UK, male/female vocal/instrumental group*   7 wks

9 Apr 94	THE POWER OF LOVE *Stoatin' STOAT 002CD*	65	1
26 Nov 94	BELIEVE *23rd Precinct THIRD 2CD*	41	2
15 Jun 96	LET THE LOVE *23rd Precinct THIRD 4CD*	30	2
30 Nov 96	DO YOU WANT ME *23rd Precinct THIRD 5CD*	48	1
28 Jun 97	POWER OF LOVE '97 *23rd Precinct THIRD 7CD*	49	1

Q-Tip – See Janet JACKSON; Joni MITCHELL

Q UNIQUE – See C&C MUSIC FACTORY/CLIVILLES & COLE

QATTARA *UK, male production duo: Andy Kato and Alex Whitcombe*   2 wks

15 Mar 97	COME WITH ME *Positiva CDTIV 71*	31	2

QFX *UK, male vocal / instrumental group*   14 wks

6 May 95	FREEDOM (EP) *Epidemic EPICD 004*	41	3
3 Feb 96	EVERYTIME YOU TOUCH ME *Epidemic EPICD 006*	22	4
3 Aug 96	YOU GOT THE POWER *Epidemic EPICD 007*	33	3
18 Jan 97	FREEDOM 2 (re-mix) *Epidemic EPICD 008*	21	4

Tracks on Freedom (EP): Freedom / Metropolis / Sianora Baby / The Machine

QUAD CITY DJs *US, male rap duo*   1 wk

15 Nov 97	SPACE JAM *Atlantic EW773*	57	1

See also TAG TEAM

QUADROPHONIA ☺
Belgium, male instrumental/production group   15 wks

13 Apr 91	QUADROPHONIA *ARS 6567687*	14	9
6 Jul 91	THE WAVE OF THE FUTURE *ARS 6569937*	40	3
21 Dec 91	FIND THE TIME (PART ONE) *ARS 6576260*	41	3

QUADS *UK, male vocal/instrumental group*   2 wks

22 Sep 79	THERE MUST BE THOUSANDS *Big Bear BB 23*	66	2

QUAKE featuring Marcia RAE
UK, male producer, and UK, female vocalist   1 wk

29 Aug 98	THE DAY WILL COME *ffrr FCD 344*	53	1

QUANTUM JUMP ◐ *UK, male vocal/instrumental group*   10 wks

2 Jun 79	● THE LONE RANGER *Electric WOT 33*	5	10

QUARTERFLASH *US, male/female vocal/instrumental group*   5 wks

27 Feb 82	HARDEN MY HEART *Geffen GEF A 1838*	49	5

QUARTZ ◀ *UK, male instrumental group*   19 wks

17 Mar 90	WE'RE COMIN' AT YA *Mercury ITMR 2* [1]	65	2
2 Feb 91	● IT'S TOO LATE *Mercury ITM 3* [2]	8	14
15 Jun 91	NAKED LOVE (JUST SAY YOU WANT ME) *Mercury ITM 4* [3]	39	3

[1] Quartz featuring Stepz   [2] Quartz introducing Dina Carroll
[3] Quartz and Dina Carroll

Jakie QUARTZ *France, female vocalist*   3 wks

11 Mar 89	A LA VIE, A L'AMOUR *PWL PWL 30*	55	3

QUARTZ LOCK – See Lonnie GORDON

Suzi QUATRO ◐ *Leather-clad US rock singer/guitarist, b. Suzi Quatrocchio, 3 June, 1950, Detroit. Thanks partly to ultra-commercial songs and productions by Nicky Chinn and Mike Chapman, she was a regular hitmaker in Europe. In her homeland, however, only 'Stumblin' In' reached Top 40*   122 wks

19 May 73	★ CAN THE CAN *RAK 150*	1	14
28 Jul 73	● 48 CRASH *RAK 158*	3	9
27 Oct 73	DAYTONA DEMON *RAK 161*	14	13
9 Feb 74	★ DEVIL GATE DRIVE *RAK 167*	1	11
29 Jun 74	TOO BIG *RAK 175*	14	6
9 Nov 74	● THE WILD ONE *RAK 185*	7	10
8 Feb 75	YOUR MAMA WON'T LIKE ME *RAK 191*	31	5
5 Mar 77	TEAR ME APART *RAK 248*	27	6
18 Mar 78	● IF YOU CAN'T GIVE ME LOVE *RAK 271*	4	13
22 Jul 78	THE RACE IS ON *RAK 278*	43	5
11 Nov 78	STUMBLIN' IN *RAK 285* [1]	41	8
20 Oct 79	SHE'S IN LOVE WITH YOU *RAK 299*	11	9
19 Jan 80	MAMA'S BOY *RAK 303*	34	5
5 Apr 80	I'VE NEVER BEEN IN LOVE *RAK 307*	56	3
25 Oct 80	ROCK HARD *Dreamland DLSP 6*	68	2
13 Nov 82	HEART OF STONE *Polydor POSP 477*	60	3

[1] Suzi Quatro and Chris Norman

Finley QUAYE ◐ ☂ *UK, male vocal/instrumentalist*   20 wks

21 Jun 97	SUNDAY SHINING *Epic 6644552*	16	6
13 Sep 97	● EVEN AFTER ALL *Epic 6649712*	10	5
29 Nov 97	IT'S GREAT WHEN WE'RE TOGETHER *Epic 6653382*	29	3
7 Mar 98	YOUR LOVE GETS SWEETER *Epic 6656065*	16	5
15 Aug 98	ULTRA STIMULATION *Epic 6660792*	51	1

QUEEN ✍ *World-renowned, record-breaking British quartet: Freddie Mercury (v) (d. 1991), Brian May (g/v), John Deacon (b/v), Roger Taylor (d/v). The Beatles are the only group to have more UK Top 10 singles than this act, whose Greatest Hits albums sold 25 million copies worldwide*   403 wks

9 Mar 74	SEVEN SEAS OF RHYE *EMI 2121*	10	10
26 Oct 74	● KILLER QUEEN *EMI 2229*	2	12
25 Jan 75	NOW I'M HERE *EMI 2256*	11	7
8 Nov 75	★ BOHEMIAN RHAPSODY *EMI 2375* ◆	1	17
3 Jul 76	● YOU'RE MY BEST FRIEND *EMI 2494*	7	8
27 Nov 76	● SOMEBODY TO LOVE *EMI 2565*	2	9
19 Mar 77	TIE YOUR MOTHER DOWN *EMI 2593*	31	4
4 Jun 77	QUEEN'S FIRST EP *EMI 2623*	17	10
22 Oct 77	● WE ARE THE CHAMPIONS *EMI 2708*	2	11
25 Feb 78	SPREAD YOUR WINGS *EMI 2757*	34	4
28 Oct 78	BICYCLE RACE / FAT BOTTOMED GIRLS *EMI 2870*	11	12
10 Feb 79	DON'T STOP ME NOW *EMI 2910*	9	12
14 Jul 79	LOVE OF MY LIFE *EMI 5022*	11	6
20 Oct 79	● CRAZY LITTLE THING CALLED LOVE *EMI 5001* ▲	2	14
2 Feb 80	SAVE ME *EMI 5022*	11	6
14 Jun 80	PLAY THE GAME *EMI 5076*	14	8
6 Sep 80	● ANOTHER ONE BITES THE DUST *EMI 5102* ▲	7	9
6 Dec 80	FLASH *EMI 5126*	10	13
14 Nov 81	★ UNDER PRESSURE *EMI 5250* [1]	1	11
1 May 82	BODY LANGUAGE *EMI 5293*	25	4
12 Jun 82	LAS PALABRAS DE AMOR *EMI 5316*	17	8
21 Aug 82	BACKCHAT *EMI 5325*	40	4
4 Feb 84	● RADIO GAGA *EMI QUEEN 1*	2	9
14 Apr 84	● I WANT TO BREAK FREE *EMI QUEEN 2*	3	15
28 Jul 84	● IT'S A HARD LIFE *EMI QUEEN 3*	6	9
22 Sep 84	HAMMER TO FALL *EMI QUEEN 4*	13	7
8 Dec 84	THANK GOD IT'S CHRISTMAS *EMI QUEEN 5*	21	6
16 Nov 85	● ONE VISION *EMI QUEEN 6*	7	10
29 Mar 86	● A KIND OF MAGIC *EMI EMI Queen 7*	3	11
21 Jun 86	FRIENDS WILL BE FRIENDS *EMI QUEEN 8*	14	8
27 Sep 86	WHO WANTS TO LIVE FOREVER *EMI QUEEN 9*	24	5
13 May 89	● I WANT IT ALL *Parlophone QUEEN 10*	3	7
1 Jul 89	● BREAKTHRU' *Parlophone QUEEN 11*	7	7
19 Aug 89	THE INVISIBLE MAN *Parlophone QUEEN 12*	12	6
21 Oct 89	SCANDAL *Parlophone QUEEN 14*	25	4
9 Dec 89	THE MIRACLE *Parlophone QUEEN 15*	21	5
26 Jan 91	★ INNUENDO *Parlophone QUEEN 16* ■	1	6
25 May 91	I'M GOING SLIGHTLY MAD *Parlophone QUEEN 17*	22	5
25 May 91	HEADLONG *Parlophone QUEEN 18*	14	4

26 Oct 91	THE SHOW MUST GO ON *Parlophone QUEEN 19*	16	5
7 Dec 91	THE SHOW MUST GO ON (re-entry) *Parlophone QUEEN 19*	27	5
21 Dec 91 ★	BOHEMIAN RHAPSODY (re-issue) / THESE ARE THE DAYS OF OUR LIVES *Parlophone QUEEN 20* ◆ ■	1	14
1 May 93 ★	FIVE LIVE EP *Parlophone CDRS 6340* [2]	1	11
24 Jul 93	FIVE LIVE EP (re-entry) *Parlophone CDRS 6340* [2]	74	1
4 Nov 95 ●	HEAVEN FOR EVERYONE *Parlophone CDQUEEN 21*	2	12
23 Dec 95 ●	A WINTER'S TALE *Parlophone CDQUEEN 22*	6	6
9 Mar 96 ●	TOO MUCH LOVE WILL KILL YOU *Parlophone CDQUEEN 23*	15	6
29 Jun 96 ●	LET ME LIVE *Parlophone CDQUEEN 24*	9	4
30 Nov 96 ●	YOU DON'T FOOL ME *Parlophone CDQUEEN 25*	17	4
17 Jan 98	NO-ONE BUT YOU / TIE YOUR MOTHER DOWN *Parlophone CDQUEEN 27*	13	4
14 Nov 98 ●	ANOTHER ONE BITES THE DUST *Dreamworks DRMCD 22364* [3]	5	6

[1] Queen and David Bowie [2] George Michael and Queen with Lisa Stansfield
[3] Queen with Wyclef Jean featuring Pras Michel/Free

Tracks on Queen's First EP: Good Old Fashioned Lover Boy / Death on Two Legs (Dedicated to...) / Tenement Funster / White Queen (As it Began). Tracks on Five Live EP: Somebody to Love / These Are the Days of Our Lives / Calling You / Papa Was a Rolling Stone – Killer (medley). Queen only appear on the first two tracks. The first credits George Michael and Queen and the second George Michael with Lisa Stansfield

QUEEN LATIFAH 🔽 *US, female rapper* — 17 wks

24 Mar 90	MAMA GAVE BIRTH TO THE SOUL CHILDREN *Gee Street GEE 26* [1]	14	7
26 May 90	FIND A WAY *Ahead Of Our Time CCUT 8* [2]	52	2
31 Aug 91	FLY GIRL *Gee Street GEE 34*	67	1
26 Jun 93	WHAT'CHA GONNA DO *Epic 6593072* [3]	21	4
26 Mar 94	U.N.I.T.Y. *Motown TMGCD 1422*	74	1
12 Apr 97	MR BIG STUFF *Motown 5736572* [4]	31	2

[1] Queen Latifah + De La Soul [2] Coldcut featuring Queen Latifah
[3] Shabba Ranks featuring Queen Latifah [4] Queen Latifah, Shades & Free

QUEEN PEN 🔽 *US, female rapper* — 10 wks

7 Mar 98	MAN BEHIND THE MUSIC *Interscope IND 95562*	38	2
9 May 98	ALL MY LOVE *Interscope IND 95584* [1]	11	5
5 Sep 98	IT'S TRUE *Interscope IND 95597*	24	3

[1] Queen Pen featuring Eric Williams

QUEENSRYCHE 🔽 *US, male vocal/instrumental group* — 21 wks

13 May 89	EYES OF A STRANGER *EMI USA MT 65*	59	1
10 Nov 90	EMPIRE *EMI USA MT 90*	61	1
20 Apr 91	SILENT LUCIDITY *EMI USA MT 94*	34	5
6 Jul 91	BEST I CAN *EMI USA MT 97*	36	3
7 Sep 91	JET CITY WOMAN *EMI USA MT 98*	39	2
8 Aug 92	SILENT LUCIDITY (re-issue) *EMI USA MT 104*	18	4
28 Jan 95	I AM I *EMI CDMT 109*	40	2
25 Mar 95	BRIDGE *EMI CDMT 111*	40	3

QUENCH *Australia, male instrumental/production duo* — 1 wk

17 Feb 96	DREAMS *Infectious INFECT 3CD*	75	1

QUENTIN and ASH *UK, female vocal duo* — 3 wks

6 Jul 96	TELL HIM *East West EW 049CD*	25	3

? (QUESTION MARK) and the MYSTERIANS
US, male vocal/instrumental group — 4 wks

17 Nov 66	96 TEARS *Cameo Parkway C428* ▲	37	4

QUESTIONS *UK, male vocal/instrumental group* — 8 wks

23 Apr 83	PRICE YOU PAY *Respond KOB 702*	56	3
17 Sep 83	TEAR SOUP *Respond KOB 705*	66	1
10 Mar 84	TUESDAY SUNSHINE *Respond KOB 707*	46	4

QUICK *UK, male vocal/instrumental group* — 7 wks

15 May 82	RHYTHM OF THE JUNGLE *Epic EPC A 2013*	41	7

Tommy QUICKLY *UK, male vocalist* — 8 wks

22 Oct 64	WILD SIDE OF LIFE *Pye 7N 15708*	33	8

QUIET FIVE *UK, male vocal/instrumental group* — 3 wks

13 May 65	WHEN THE MORNING SUN DRIES THE DEW *Parlophone R 5273*	45	1
21 Apr 66	HOMEWARD BOUND *Parlophone R 5421*	44	2

QUIET RIOT *US, male vocal/instrumental group* — 5 wks

3 Dec 83	METAL HEALTH/CUM ON FEEL THE NOIZE *Epic A 3968*	45	5

'Cum on Feel the Noize' only credited from 10 Dec, 1983

Eimear QUINN *Ireland, female vocalist* — 2 wks

15 Jun 96	THE VOICE *Polydor 5768842*	40	2

Paul QUINN – See Edwyn COLLINS

QUIREBOYS 🔽 *UK, male vocal/instrumental group* — 27 wks

4 Nov 89	7 O'CLOCK *Parlophone R 6230*	36	4
6 Jan 90	HEY YOU *Parlophone R 6241*	14	7
7 Apr 90	I DON'T LOVE YOU ANYMORE *Parlophone R 6248*	24	6
8 Sep 90	THERE SHE GOES AGAIN/MISLED *Parlophone R 6267*	37	4
10 Oct 92	TRAMPS AND THIEVES *Parlophone RS 6323*	41	3
20 Feb 93	BROTHER LOUIE *Parlophone CDR 6335*	31	3

QUIVER – See SUTHERLAND BROTHERS and QUIVER

QUIVVER *UK, male instrumental/production duo* — 3 wks

5 Mar 94	SAXY LADY *A & M 5805152*	56	2
18 Nov 95	BELIEVE IN ME *Perfecto PERF 111CD*	56	1

QWILO & FELIX DA HOUSECAT
US, male / female vocal / DJ / production duo — 1 wk

6 Sep 97	DIRTY MOTHA *Manifesto FESCD 29*	66	1

R

Eddie RABBITT *US, male vocalist* — 14 wks

27 Jan 79	EVERY WHICH WAY BUT LOOSE *Elektra K 12331*	41	9
28 Feb 81	I LOVE A RAINY NIGHT *Elektra K 12498* ▲	53	5

Steve RACE *UK, male instrumentalist – piano* — 9 wks

28 Feb 63	PIED PIPER (THE BEEJE) *Parlophone R 4981*	29	9

RACEY ✖ *UK, male vocal/instrumental group* — 44 wks

25 Nov 78 ●	LAY YOUR LOVE ON ME *RAK 284*	3	14
31 Mar 79 ●	SOME GIRLS *RAK 291*	2	11
18 Aug 79	BOY OH BOY *RAK 297*	22	9
20 Dec 80	RUNAROUND SUE *RAK 325*	13	10

RACING CARS ✖ *UK, male vocal/instrumental group* — 7 wks

12 Feb 77	THEY SHOOT HORSES DON'T THEY *Chrysalis CHS 2129*	14	7

RACKETEERS – See Elbow BONES and the RACKETEERS

Jimmy RADCLIFFE US, male vocalist   2 wks

| 4 Feb 65 | LONG AFTER TONIGHT IS ALL OVER *Stateside SS 374* | 40 | 2 |

RADHA KRISHNA TEMPLE ☻
Oxford Street, male/female vocal/instrumental group   17 wks

| 13 Sep 69 | HARE KRISHNA MANTRA *Apple 15* | 12 | 9 |
| 28 Mar 70 | GOVINDA *Apple 25* | 23 | 8 |

RADICAL ROB UK, male producer – Rob McLuan   1 wk

| 11 Jan 92 | MONKEY WAH *R&S RSUK 8* | 67 | 1 |

Jack RADICS – See Chaka DEMUS and PLIERS; SUPERCAT

RADIO HEART – See Gary NUMAN

RADIO 1 DJ POSSE – See Liz KERSHAW and Bruno BROOKES

RADIO REVELLERS – See Anthony STEEL and the RADIO REVELLERS

RADIO STARS UK, male vocal/instrumental group   3 wks

| 4 Feb 78 | NERVOUS WRECK *Chiswick NS 23* | 39 | 3 |

RADIOHEAD ✍ ☹ UK, male vocal/instrumental group   43 wks

13 Feb 93		ANYONE CAN PLAY GUITAR *Parlophone CDR 6333*	32	2
22 May 93		POP IS DEAD *Parlophone CDR 6345*	42	2
18 Sep 93	●	CREEP *Parlophone CDR 6359*	7	6
8 Oct 94		MY IRON LUNG *Parlophone CDR 6394*	24	2
11 Mar 95		HIGH AND DRY/PLANET TELEX *Parlophone CDR 6405*	17	4
27 May 95		FAKE PLASTIC TREES *Parlophone CDR 6411*	20	4
2 Sep 95		JUST *Parlophone CDR 6415*	19	3
3 Feb 96	●	STREET SPIRIT (FADE OUT) *Parlophone CDR 6419*	5	4
7 Jun 97	●	PARANOID ANDROID *Parlophone CDODATA 01*	3	4
6 Sep 97	●	KARMA POLICE *Parlophone CDODATAS 03*	8	4
24 Jan 98	●	NO SURPRISES *Parlophone CDODATAS 04*	4	7

RADISH US, male vocal/instrumental group   3 wks

| 30 Aug 97 | LITTLE PINK STARS *Mercury MERCD 494* | 32 | 2 |
| 15 Nov 97 | SIMPLE SINCERITY *Mercury MERCD 498* | 50 | 1 |

Fonda RAE US, female vocalist   4 wks

| 6 Oct 84 | TUCH ME *Streetwave KHAN 28* | 49 | 4 |

Jesse RAE UK, male vocalist   2 wks

| 11 May 85 | OVER THE SEA *Scotland-Video YZ 36* | 65 | 2 |

RAF Italy, male producer – Mauro Picotto   6 wks

14 Mar 92	WE'VE GOT TO LIVE TOGETHER *PWL Continental PWL 218*	34	3
5 Mar 94	TAKE ME HIGHER *Media MRLCD 0012*	71	1
23 Mar 96	TAKE ME HIGHER (re-mix) *Media MCSTD 40026*	59	1
27 Jul 96	ANGEL'S SYMPHONY *Media MCSTD 40051*	73	1

Gerry RAFFERTY ♂ ☻ UK, male vocalist   47 wks

18 Feb 78	●	BAKER STREET *United Artists UP 36346*	3	15
26 May 79	●	NIGHT OWL *United Artists UP 36512*	5	13
18 Aug 79		GET IT RIGHT NEXT TIME *United Artists BP 301*	30	9
22 Mar 80		BRING IT ALL HOME *United Artists BP 340*	54	4
21 Jun 80		ROYAL MILE *United Artists BP 354*	67	2
10 Mar 90		BAKER STREET (re-mix) *EMI EM 132*	53	4

RAGE ☻ ☺ UK, male vocal/instrumental group   15 wks

31 Oct 92	●	RUN TO YOU *Pulse 8 LOSE 33*	3	11
27 Feb 93		WHY DON'T YOU *Pulse 8 CDLOSE 39*	44	2
15 May 93		HOUSE OF THE RISING SUN *Pulse 8 CDLOSE 43*	41	2

RAGE AGAINST THE MACHINE ✈ 👟
US, male vocal/instrumental group   15 wks

27 Feb 93		KILLING IN THE NAME *Epic 6584922*	25	4
8 May 93		BULLET IN THE HEAD *Epic 6592582*	16	4
4 Sep 93		BOMBTRACK *Epic 6594712*	37	2
13 Apr 96	●	BULLS ON PARADE *Epic 6631522*	8	3
7 Sep 96		PEOPLE OF THE SUN *Epic 6636282*	26	2

RAGGA TWINS UK, male vocal group   10 wks

10 Nov 90	ILLEGAL GUNSHOT/SPLIFFHEAD *Shut Up And Dance SUAD 7*	51	2
6 Apr 91	WIPE THE NEEDLE/JUGGLING *Shut Up And Dance SUAD 12S*	71	2
6 Jul 91	HOOLIGAN 69 *Shut Up And Dance SUAD 16S*	56	2
7 Mar 92	MIXED TRUTH/BRING UP THE MIC SOME MORE *Shut Up And Dance SUAD 27S*	65	2
11 Jul 92	SHINE EYE *Shut Up And Dance SUAD 32S* [1]	63	2

[1] Ragga Twins featuring Junior Reid

RAGTIMERS UK, male instrumental group   8 wks

| 16 Mar 74 | THE STING *Pye 7N 45323* | 46 | 1 |
| 30 Mar 74 | THE STING (re-entry) *Pye 7N 45323* | 31 | 7 |

RAH BAND ☻ UK, male/female vocal/instrumental group   50 wks

9 Jul 77	●	THE CRUNCH *Good Earth GD 7*	6	12
1 Nov 80		FALCON *DJM DJS 10954*	35	7
7 Feb 81		SLIDE *DJM DJS 10964*	50	7
1 May 82		PERFUMED GARDEN *KR KR 5*	45	7
9 Jul 83		MESSAGES FROM THE STARS *TMT TMT 5*	42	5
19 Jan 85		ARE YOU SATISFIED? (FUNKA NOVA) *RCA RCA 470*	70	2
30 Mar 85	●	CLOUDS ACROSS THE MOON *RCA PB 40025*	6	10

RAHSAAN – See US3

RAILWAY CHILDREN UK, male vocal/instrumental group   13 wks

24 Mar 90	EVERY BEAT OF THE HEART *Virgin VS 1237*	68	2
2 Jun 90	MUSIC STOP *Virgin VS 1255*	66	2
20 Oct 90	SO RIGHT *Virgin VS 1289*	68	1
2 Feb 91	EVERY BEAT OF THE HEART (re-entry) *Virgin VS 1237*	24	6
20 Apr 91	SOMETHING SO GOOD *Virgin VS 1318*	57	2

RAIN – See Stephanie DE SYKES

RAIN TREE CROW UK, male vocal/instrumental group   1 wk

| 30 Mar 91 | BLACKWATER *Virgin VS 1340* | 62 | 1 |

Group is Japan under an assumed name
See also JAPAN

RAINBOW ✈ UK, male vocal/instrumental group   62 wks

17 Sep 77		KILL THE KING *Polydor 2066 845*	44	3
8 Apr 78		LONG LIVE ROCK 'N' ROLL *Polydor 2066 913*	33	3
30 Sep 78		L. A. CONNECTION *Polydor 2066 968*	40	4
15 Sep 79	●	SINCE YOU'VE BEEN GONE *Polydor POSP 70*	6	10
16 Feb 80	●	ALL NIGHT LONG *Polydor POSP 104*	5	11
31 Jan 81	●	I SURRENDER *Polydor POSP 221*	3	10
20 Jun 81		CAN'T HAPPEN HERE *Polydor POSP 221*	20	8
11 Jul 81		KILL THE KING (re-issue) *Polydor POSP 274*	41	4
3 Apr 82		STONE COLD *Polydor POSP 421*	34	4
27 Aug 83		STREET OF DREAMS *Polydor POSP 631*	52	3
5 Nov 83		CAN'T LET YOU GO *Polydor POSP 654*	43	2

RAINBOW COTTAGE UK, male vocal/instrumental group   4 wks

| 6 Mar 76 | SEAGULL *Penny Farthing PEN 906* | 33 | 4 |

RAINMAKERS ☻ ✍ US, male vocal/instrumental group   11 wks

| 7 Mar 87 | LET MY PEOPLE GO-GO *Mercury MER 238* | 18 | 11 |

Marvin RAINWATER ✈ *US, male vocalist* — 22 wks

7 Mar 58 ★	WHOLE LOTTA WOMAN *MGM 974*.........1	15
6 Jun 58	I DIG YOU BABY *MGM 980*.........19	7

Bonnie RAITT *US, female vocalist* — 9 wks

14 Dec 91	I CAN'T MAKE YOU LOVE ME *Capitol CL 639*.........50	4
9 Apr 94	LOVE SNEAKIN' UP ON YOU *Capitol CDCL 713*.........69	1
18 Jun 94	YOU *Capitol CDCLS 718*.........31	2
11 Nov 95	ROCK STEADY *Capitol CDCL 763* [1].........50	2

[1] Bonnie Raitt and Bryan Adams

RA JA NEE *US, female vocalist* — 2 wks

4 Mar 95	TURN IT UP *Perspective 5874872* 42	2

RAKIM *US, male rapper* — 4 wks

27 Dec 97	GUESS WHO'S BACK *Universal UND 56151* 32	3
22 Aug 98	STAY A WHILE *Universal UND 56203* 53	1

Tony RALLO and the MIDNIGHT BAND
France/US, male vocal/instrumental group — 8 wks

23 Feb 80	HOLDIN' ON *Calibre CAB 150* 34	8

Sheryl Lee RALPH *US, female vocalist* — 2 wks

26 Jan 85	IN THE EVENING *Arista ARIST 595* 64	2

RAM JAM ✪ *US, male vocal/instrumental group* — 20 wks

10 Sep 77 ●	BLACK BETTY *Epic EPC 5492* 7	12
17 Feb 90	BLACK BETTY (re-mix) *Epic 655430 7*.........13	8

RAM JAM BAND – See Geno WASHINGTON and the RAM JAM BAND

RAMBLERS (from the Abbey Hey Junior School) ℃
UK, children's choir — 15 wks

13 Oct 79	THE SPARROW *Decca F 13860*.........11	15

Karen RAMIREZ ✪ ☺ *UK, female vocalist* — 15 wks

28 Mar 98	TROUBLED GIRL *Manifesto FEXCD 31* 50	1
27 Jun 98	LOOKING FOR LOVE *Manifesto FESCD 44* 8	11
21 Nov 98	IF WE TRY *Manifesto FESCD 50*.........23	3

RAMONES ✎ *US, male vocal/instrumental group* — 32 wks

21 May 77	SHEENA IS A PUNK ROCKER *Sire RAM 001* 22	7
6 Aug 77	SWALLOW MY PRIDE *Sire 6078 607* 36	3
30 Sep 78	DON'T COME CLOSE *Sire SRE 1031* 39	5
8 Sep 79	ROCK `N' ROLL HIGH SCHOOL *Sire SIR 4021*.........67	2
26 Jan 80 ●	BABY I LOVE YOU *Sire SIR 4031* 8	9
19 Apr 80	DO YOU REMEMBER ROCK 'N' ROLL RADIO *Sire SIR 4037* 54	3
10 May 86	SOMEBODY PUT SOMETHING IN MY DRINK/SOMETHING TO BELIEVE IN *Beggars Banquet BEG 157* 69	1
19 Dec 92	POISON HEART *Chrysalis CHS 3917*.........69	2

RAMP *UK, male instrumental/production duo* — 1 wk

8 Jun 96	ROCK THE DISCOTEK *Loaded LOADCD 30*.........49	1

RAMPAGE *UK, male vocal/instrumental duo* — 2 wks

25 Nov 95	THE MONKEES *Almo Sounds CDALMOS 017* 51	1
18 Oct 97	TAKE IT TO THE STREETS *Elektra E 3914CD* [1] 58	1

[1] Rampage featuring Billy Lawrence

RAMRODS ✪ *US, male/female instrumental group* — 12 wks

23 Feb 61 ●	RIDERS IN THE SKY *London HLU 9282*.........8	12

RANCID *US, male vocal/instrumental group* — 1 wk

7 Oct 95	TIME BOMB *Out Of Step WOOS 8CDS* 56	1

RANGE – See Bruce HORNSBY and the RANGE

RANGERS FC *UK, male football team vocalists* — 2 wks

4 Oct 97	GLASGOW RANGERS (NINE IN A ROW) *Gers GERSCD 1* 54	2

RANKING ANN – See SCRITTI POLITTI

RANKING ROGER – See Pato BANTON; VARIOUS ARTISTS (EPs & LPs) – Gimme Shelter (EP)

Shabba RANKS ✔ *Jamaica, male vocalist* — 67 wks

16 Mar 91	SHE'S A WOMAN *Virgin VS 1333* [1] 20	7
18 May 91	TRAILER LOAD A GIRLS *Epic 6568747* 63	2
24 Aug 91	HOUSECALL *Epic 6573477* [2] 31	7
8 Aug 92	MR LOVERMAN *Epic 6582517* 23	7
28 Nov 92	SLOW AND SEXY *Epic 6587727* [3] 17	7
6 Mar 93	I WAS A KING *Motown TMGCD 1414* [4] 64	1
13 Mar 93 ●	MR. LOVERMAN (re-issue) *Epic 6590782* 3	11
8 May 93 ●	HOUSECALL (re-mix) *Epic 6592842* [2] 8	8
26 Jun 93	WHAT'CHA GONNA DO *Epic 6593072* [4] 21	4
25 Dec 93	FAMILY AFFAIR *Polydor PZCD 304* [5] 18	8
29 Apr 95	LET'S GET IT ON *Epic 6614122* 22	3
5 Aug 95	SHINE EYE GAL *Epic 6622332* [6] 46	2

[1] Scritti Politti featuring Shabba Ranks [2] Shabba Ranks featuring Maxi Priest [3] Shabba Ranks featuring Johnny Gill [4] Eddie Murphy featuring Shabba Ranks [5] Shabba Ranks featuring Queen Latifah [6] Shabba Ranks featuring Patra and Terry & Monica [7] Shabba Ranks (featuring Mykal Rose)

RAPINATION *Italy, male instrumental/production duo* — 12 wks

26 Dec 92	LOVE ME THE RIGHT WAY *Logic 74321128097* [1] 22	10
10 Jul 93	HERE'S MY A *Logic 74321153092* [1] 69	1
28 Sep 96	LOVE ME THE RIGHT WAY (re-mix) *Logic 7432140442* [1] 55	1

[1] Rapination featuring Kym Mazelle [2] Rapination featuring Carol Kenyon

RAPPIN' 4-TAY *US, male rapper* — 5 wks

24 Jun 95	I'LL BE AROUND *Cooltempo CDCOOL 306* [1] 30	4
30 Sep 95	PLAYAZ CLUB *Cooltempo CDCOOL 310* 63	1

[1] Rappin' 4-Tay featuring the Spinners

The Spinners on 'I'll Be Around' are the Detroit Spinners

RARE *UK, male/female vocal/instrumental group* — 1 wk

17 Feb 96	SOMETHING WILD *Equator AXISCD 011*.........57	1

RARE BIRD *UK, male vocal/instrumental group* — 8 wks

14 Feb 70	SYMPATHY *Charisma CB 120*.........27	8

O. RASBURY – See Rahni HARRIS and F.L.O.

Roland RAT SUPERSTAR ✪ ✈
UK, male rodent vocalist/rapper — 20 wks

19 Nov 83	RAT RAPPING *Rodent RAT 1*.........14	12
28 Apr 84	LOVE ME TENDER *Rodent RAT 2*.........32	7
2 Mar 85	NO. 1 RAT FAN *Rodent RAT 4* 72	1

RATPACK *UK, male instrumental/production duo* — 3 wks

6 Jun 92	SEARCHIN' FOR MY RIZLA *Big Giant BIGT 02* 58	3

RATTLES ✎ *Germany, male vocal/instrumental group* — 15 wks

3 Oct 70 ●	THE WITCH *Decca F 23058*.........8	15

RAVESIGNAL III *UK, male producer – Christian Bolland* — 2 wks

14 Dec 91	HORSEPOWER *R&S RSUK 6* 61	2

See also CJ BOLLAND

RAW – See Erick 'More' MORILLO presents RAW

RAW SILK ♪ US, female vocal group　　12 wks

| 16 Oct 82 | DO IT TO THE MUSIC *KR KR 14* | 18 | 9 |
| 10 Sep 83 | JUST IN TIME *West End WEND 2* | 49 | 3 |

RAW STYLUS UK, male/female vocal/instrumental duo　　1 wk

| 26 Oct 96 | BELIEVE IN ME *Wired WIRED 234* | 66 | 1 |

Lou RAWLS ♪ US, male vocalist　　10 wks

| 31 Jul 76 ● | YOU'LL NEVER FIND ANOTHER LOVE LIKE MINE *Philadelphia Interna PIR 4372* | 10 | 10 |

Gene Anthony RAY – See KIDS FROM FAME

Jimmy RAY ☻ UK, male vocalist　　6 wks

| 25 Oct 97 | ARE YOU JIMMY RAY? *Sony S2 6650125* | 13 | 5 |
| 14 Feb 98 | GOIN' TO VEGAS *Sony S2 6654652* | 49 | 1 |

Johnnie RAY ℂ A sensation in the 1950s, the heart-wrenching vocal delivery of the 'Cry Guy' (b. 10 January, 1927, Oregon, d. 25 February, 1990) influenced many acts, including Elvis, and Ray was the prime target for teen hysteria in pre-Presley days　　152 wks

14 Nov 52	WALKING MY BABY BACK HOME *Columbia DB 3060*	12	1
19 Dec 52 ●	FAITH CAN MOVE MOUNTAINS *Columbia DB 3154* [1]	7	2
9 Jan 53 ●	FAITH CAN MOVE MOUNTAINS (re-entry) *Columbia DB 3154* [1]	9	1
3 Apr 53	MA SAYS PA SAYS *Columbia DB 3242* [2]	12	1
10 Apr 53 ●	SOMEBODY STOLE MY GAL *Philips PB 123*	6	1
17 Apr 53	FULL TIME JOB *Columbia DB 3242* [2]	11	1
24 Apr 53 ●	SOMEBODY STOLE MY GAL (re-entry) *Philips PB 123*	6	4
29 May 53	SOMEBODY STOLE MY GAL (2nd re-entry) *Philips PB 123*	12	1
24 Jul 53 ●	LET'S WALK THAT-A-WAY *Philips PB 157* [2]	4	14
7 Aug 53	SOMEBODY STOLE MY GAL (3rd re-entry) *Philips PB 123*	11	1
9 Apr 54 ★	SUCH A NIGHT *Philips PB 244*	1	18
8 Apr 55	IF YOU BELIEVE *Philips PB 379*	15	1
13 May 55 ●	IF YOU BELIEVE (re-entry) *Philips PB 379*	7	10
20 May 55	PATHS OF PARADISE *Philips PB 441*	20	1
7 Oct 55	HERNANDO'S HIDEAWAY *Philips PB 495*	11	5
14 Oct 55 ●	HEY THERE *Philips PB 495*	5	9
28 Oct 55 ●	SONG OF THE DREAMER *Philips PB 516*	10	5
17 Feb 56	WHO'S SORRY NOW *Philips PB 546*	17	2
20 Apr 56	AIN'T MISBEHAVIN' *Philips PB 580*	17	6
8 Jun 56	AIN'T MISBEHAVIN' (re-entry) *Philips PB 580*	24	1
12 Oct 56 ★	JUST WALKIN' IN THE RAIN *Philips PB 624*	1	19
18 Jan 57	YOU DON'T OWE ME A THING *Philips PB 655*	12	15
8 Feb 57 ●	LOOK HOMEWARD ANGEL *Philips PB 655*	7	16
10 May 57 ★	YES TONIGHT JOSEPHINE *Philips PB 686*	1	16
6 Sep 57	BUILD YOUR LOVE *Philips PB 721*	17	7
4 Oct 57	GOOD EVENING FRIENDS/UP ABOVE MY HEAD I HEAR MUSIC IN THE AIR *Philips PB 708* [3]	25	4
4 Dec 59	I'LL NEVER FALL IN LOVE AGAIN *Philips PB 952*	26	4
8 Jan 60	I'LL NEVER FALL IN LOVE AGAIN (re-entry) *Philips PB 952*	26	1
5 Feb 60	I'LL NEVER FALL IN LOVE AGAIN (2nd re-entry) *Philips PB 952*	28	1

[1] Johnnie Ray and the Four Lads [2] Doris Day and Johnnie Ray
[3] Frankie Laine and Johnnie Ray

The chart history of 'You Don't Owe Me a Thing/Look Homeward Angel' is complicated, as follows: 'You Don't Owe Me a Thing' entered the chart by itself on 18 Jan, 1957. On 8 and 15 Feb, 1957, 'Look Homeward Angel' was coupled with 'You Don't Owe Me a Thing' but from 22 Feb, 1957, the two sides went their individual ways on the chart and were listed separately: 'You Don't Owe Me a Thing' for a further ten weeks and 'Look Homeward Angel' for a further 14 weeks

Nicole RAY US, female vocalist　　5 wks

| 22 Aug 98 | MAKE IT HOT *East West E 3821CD* [1] | 22 | 4 |
| 5 Dec 98 | I CAN'T SEE *East West E 3801CD* | 55 | 1 |

[1] Nicole featuring Missy 'Misdemeanour' Elliott

RAYDIO US, male vocal/instrumental group　　21 wks

| 8 Apr 78 | JACK AND JILL *Arista 161* | 11 | 12 |

| 8 Jul 78 | IS THIS A LOVE THING *Arista 193* | 27 | 9 |

See also Ray PARKER Jr.

RAYVON – See SHAGGY

RAZE ☺ US, male/female vocal/instrumental group　　47 wks

1 Nov 86	JACK THE GROOVE *Champion CHAMP 23*	57	7
3 Jan 87	JACK THE GROOVE (re-entry) *Champion CHAMP 23*	20	8
28 Feb 87	LET THE MUSIC MOVE U *Champion CHAMP 27*	57	3
31 Dec 88	BREAK 4 LOVE *Champion CHAMP 67*	28	11
15 Jul 89	LET IT ROLL *Atlantic A 8866* [1]	27	5
2 Sep 89	BREAK 4 LOVE (re-entry) *Champion CHAMP 67*	59	5
27 Jan 90	ALL 4 LOVE (BREAK 4 LOVE 1990) *Champion CHAMP 228* [2]	30	5
10 Feb 90	CAN YOU FEEL IT/CAN YOU FEEL IT *Champion CHAMP 227* [3]	62	1
24 Sep 94	BREAK 4 LOVE (2nd re-mix) *Champion CHAMPCD 314*	44	2

[1] Raze presents Doug Lazy [2] Raze featuring Lady J and Secretary of Entertainment [3] Raze/Championship Legend

'Can You Feel It' by Championship Legend is a montage of six Raze tracks

Chris REA ✍ ☻ One of the most popular UK singer/songwriters of late 1980s, b. 4 March, 1951, Middlesborough. He was already a major European star by the time he finally cracked the UK Top 10 with his 18th chart entry, 'The Road to Hell (Part 2)'　　120 wks

7 Oct 78	FOOL (IF YOU THINK IT'S OVER) *Magnet MAG 111*	30	7
21 Apr 79	DIAMONDS *Magnet MAG 144*	44	3
27 Mar 82	LOVING YOU *Magnet MAG 215*	65	3
1 Oct 83	I CAN HEAR YOUR HEARTBEAT *Magnet MAG 244*	60	2
17 Mar 84	I DON'T KNOW WHAT IT IS BUT I LOVE IT *Magnet MAG 255*	65	2
30 Mar 85	STAINSBY GIRLS *Magnet MAG 276*	26	10
29 Jun 85	JOSEPHINE *Magnet MAG 280*	67	2
29 Mar 86	IT'S ALL GONE *Magnet MAG 283*	69	1
31 May 86	ON THE BEACH *Magnet MAG 294*	57	3
28 Jun 86	ON THE BEACH (re-entry) *Magnet MAG 294*	75	1
12 Jul 86	ON THE BEACH (2nd re-entry) *Magnet MAG 294*	66	4
6 Jun 87	LET'S DANCE *Magnet MAG 299*	12	10
29 Aug 87	LOVING YOU AGAIN *Magnet MAG 300*	47	4
5 Dec 87	JOYS OF CHRISTMAS *Magnet MAG 314*	67	1
13 Feb 88	QUE SERA *Magnet MAG 318*	73	2
13 Aug 88	ON THE BEACH SUMMER '88 *WEA YZ 195*	12	6
22 Oct 88	I CAN HEAR YOUR HEARTBEAT *WEA YZ 320*	74	2
17 Dec 88	DRIVING HOME FOR CHRISTMAS EP *WEA YZ 325*	53	3
18 Feb 89 ●	WORKING ON IT *WEA YZ 50*	53	3
14 Oct 89 ●	THE ROAD TO HELL (PART 2) *WEA YZ 431*	10	9
10 Feb 90	TELL ME THERE'S A HEAVEN *East West YZ 455*	24	4
5 May 90	TEXAS *East West YZ 468*	69	1
16 Feb 91	AUBERGE *East West YZ 555*	16	6
6 Apr 91	HEAVEN *East West YZ 566*	57	2
29 Jun 91	LOOKING FOR THE SUMMER *East West YZ 584*	49	3
9 Nov 91	WINTER SONG *East West YZ 629*	27	4
24 Oct 92	NOTHING TO FEAR *East West YZ 699*	16	4
28 Nov 92	GOD'S GREAT BANANA SKIN *East West YZ 706*	31	3
30 Jan 93	SOFT TOP HARD SHOULDER *East West YZ 710CD*	53	2
23 Oct 93	JULIA *East West YZ 772CD*	18	5
12 Nov 94	YOU CAN GO YOUR OWN WAY *East West YZ 835CD*	28	3
24 Dec 94	TELL ME THERE'S A HEAVEN (re-issue) *East West YZ 885CD*	70	1
16 Nov 96	'DISCO' LA PASSIONE *East West EW 072CD* [1]	41	1
24 May 97	LET'S DANCE *Magnet EW 112CD* [2]	44	1

[1] Chris Rea and Shirley Bassey
[2] Middlesborough FC featuring Bob Mortimer and Chris Rea

Both 'On the Beach Summer '88' and 'I Can Hear Your Heartbeat' in 1988 are re-recordings. Tracks on Driving Home for Christmas EP: Driving Home for Christmas/Footsteps in the Snow/Joys of Christmas/Smile

REACT 2 RHYTHM UK, male production group　　1 wk

| 28 Jun 97 | INTOXICATION *Jackpot WIN 014CD* | 73 | 1 |

Eileen READ – See CADETS

Eddi READER *UK, female vocalist* — 13 wks

Date	Title	Pos	Wks
4 Jun 94	PATIENCE OF ANGELS *Blanco Y Negro NEG 68CD*	33	5
13 Aug 94	JOKE (I'M LAUGHING) *Blanco Y Negro NEG 72CD*	42	3
5 Nov 94	DEAR JOHN *Blanco Y Negro NEG 75CD1*	48	2
22 Jun 96	TOWN WITHOUT PITY *Blanco Y Negro NEG 90CD*	26	3

READY FOR THE WORLD *US, male vocal/instrumental group* — 8 wks

Date	Title	Pos	Wks
26 Oct 85	OH SHEILA *MCA MCA 1005* ▲	50	5
14 Mar 87	LOVE YOU DOWN *MCA MCA 1110*	60	3

REAL EMOTION *UK, male/female vocal/instrumental group* — 1 wk

Date	Title	Pos	Wks
1 Jul 95	BACK FOR GOOD *Living Beat LBECD 34*	67	1

REAL McCOY ◉ ☺ 👟
Germany/US, male/female vocal/instrumental duo — 36 wks

Date	Title	Pos	Wks
6 Nov 93	ANOTHER NIGHT *Logic 74321173732*	61	1
5 Nov 94 ●	ANOTHER NIGHT (re-issue) *Logic 74321236992* [1]	2	12
28 Jan 95 ●	RUN AWAY *Logic 74321258822* [1]	6	10
22 Apr 95	LOVE AND DEVOTION *Logic 74321272702*	11	8
26 Aug 95	COME AND GET YOUR LOVE *Logic 74321301272*	19	4
11 Nov 95	AUTOMATIC LOVER (CALL FOR LOVE) *Logic 74321325042*	58	1

[1] (MC Sar &) the Real McCoy

REAL PEOPLE *UK, male vocal/instrumental group* — 8 wks

Date	Title	Pos	Wks
16 Feb 91	OPEN UP YOUR MIND (LET ME IN) *CBS 6566127*	70	1
20 Apr 91	THE TRUTH *Columbia 6567877*	73	1
6 Jul 91	WINDOW PANE (EP) *Columbia 6569327*	60	1
11 Jan 92	THE TRUTH (re-issue) *Columbia 6576987*	41	3
23 May 92	BELIEVER *Columbia 6580067*	38	2

Tracks on Window Pane (EP): Window Pane / See Through You / Everything Must Change

REAL ROXANNE 👟 *US, female rapper* — 10 wks

Date	Title	Pos	Wks
28 Jun 86	BANG ZOOM (LET'S GO GO) *Cooltempo COOL 124* [1]	11	9
12 Nov 88	RESPECT *Cooltempo COOL 176*	71	1

[1] Real Roxanne with Hitman Howie Tee

REAL THING 🎸 *Liverpool vocal quartet who have two singles in the All-Time Top 100: brothers Chris and Eddie Amoo, Ray Lake, Dave Smith. They were the UK's best-selling black group of the late 1970s, whose biggest hits returned to the Top 10 (when re-mixed) in the 1980s* — 114 wks

Date	Title	Pos	Wks
5 Jun 76 ★	YOU TO ME ARE EVERYTHING *Pye International 7N 25709*	1	11
4 Sep 76 ●	CAN'T GET BY WITHOUT YOU *Pye 7N 45618*	2	10
12 Feb 77	YOU'LL NEVER KNOW WHAT YOU'RE MISSING *Pye 7N 45662*	16	9
30 Jul 77	LOVE'S SUCH A WONDERFUL THING *Pye 7N 45701*	33	5
4 Mar 78	WHENEVER YOU WANT MY LOVE *Pye 7N 46045*	18	9
3 Jun 78	LET'S GO DISCO *Pye 7N 46078*	39	7
12 Aug 78	RAININ' THROUGH MY SUNSHINE *Pye 7N 46113*	40	8
17 Feb 79 ●	CAN YOU FEEL THE FORCE *Pye 7N 46147*	5	11
21 Jul 79	BOOGIE DOWN (GET FUNKY NOW) *Pye 7P 109*	33	6
22 Nov 80	SHE'S A GROOVY FREAK *Calibre CAB 105*	52	4
8 Mar 86 ●	YOU TO ME ARE EVERYTHING (THE DECADE REMIX 76-86) *PRT 7P 349*	5	12
24 May 86 ●	CAN'T GET BY WITHOUT YOU (THE SECOND DECADE REMIX) *PRT 7P 352*	6	13
7 Jun 86	YOU TO ME ARE EVERYTHING (THE DECADE REMIX 76-86) (re-entry) *PRT 7P 349*	72	1
2 Aug 86	CAN YOU FEEL THE FORCE ('86 REMIX) *PRT 7P 358*	24	6
25 Oct 86	STRAIGHT TO THE HEART *Jive JIVE 129*	71	2

REAL TO REEL *US, male vocal/instrumental group* — 2 wks

Date	Title	Pos	Wks
21 Apr 84	LOVE ME LIKE THIS *Arista ARIST 565*	68	2

REBEL MC 👟 *UK, male vocalist* — 52 wks

Date	Title	Pos	Wks
27 May 89	JUST KEEP ROCKIN' *Desire WANT 9* [1]	11	12
7 Oct 89 ●	STREET TUFF *Desire WANT 18* [2]	3	14
31 Mar 90	BETTER WORLD *Desire WANT 25*	20	6
2 Jun 90	REBEL MUSIC *Desire WANT 31*	53	2
6 Apr 91	WICKEDEST SOUND *Desire WANT 40* [3]	43	6
15 Jun 91	TRIBAL BASE *Desire WANT 44* [4]	20	6
31 Aug 91	BLACK MEANING GOOD *Desire WANT 47*	73	1
21 Mar 92	RICH AH GETTING RICHER *Big Life BLR 70* [5]	48	4
8 Aug 92	HUMANITY *Big Life BLR 78* [6]	62	1

[1] Double Trouble and the Rebel MC [2] Rebel MC and Double Trouble
[3] Rebel MC featuring Tenor Fly [4] Rebel MC featuring Tenor Fly and Barrington Levy [5] Rebel MC introducing Little T [6] Rebel MC featuring Lincoln Thompson

REBEL ROUSERS – See Cliff BENNETT and the REBEL ROUSERS

REBELETTES – See Duane EDDY and the REBELS

REBELS – See Duane EDDY and the REBELS

Ezz RECO and the LAUNCHERS with Boysie GRANT
Jamaica, male vocal/instrumental group — 4 wks

Date	Title	Pos	Wks
5 Mar 64	KING OF KINGS *Columbia DB 7217*	44	4

RECOIL *UK, male vocal/instrumental group* — 1 wk

Date	Title	Pos	Wks
21 Mar 92	FAITH HEALER *Mute MUTE 110*	60	1

RED BOX ◉ *UK, male vocal/instrumental duo* — 28 wks

Date	Title	Pos	Wks
24 Aug 85 ●	LEAN ON ME (AH-LI-AYO) *Sire W 8926*	3	14
25 Oct 86 ●	FOR AMERICA *Sire YZ 84*	10	12
31 Jan 87	HEART OF THE SUN *Sire YZ 100*	71	2

RED CAR AND THE BLUE CAR
UK, male vocal/instrumental group — 4 wks

Date	Title	Pos	Wks
14 Dec 91	HOME FOR CHRISTMAS DAY *Virgin VS 1394*	44	4

RED DRAGON with Brian and Tony GOLD 〽
Jamaica, male vocal group — 15 wks

Date	Title	Pos	Wks
30 Jul 94 ●	COMPLIMENTS ON YOUR KISS *Mango CIDM 820*	2	13
31 Dec 94	COMPLIMENTS ON YOUR KISS (re-entry) *Mango CIDM 820*	49	2

RED EYE *UK, male instrumental/production duo* — 1 wk

Date	Title	Pos	Wks
3 Dec 94	KUT IT *Champion CHAMPCD 315*	62	1

RED 5 ☺ *Germany, male producer – Thomas Kukula* — 10 wks

Date	Title	Pos	Wks
10 May 97	I LOVE YOU … STOP! *Multiply CDMULTY 20*	11	5
20 Dec 97	LIFT ME UP *Multiply CDMULTY 30*	26	5

RED HILL CHILDREN *UK, male/female vocal group* — 2 wks

Date	Title	Pos	Wks
30 Nov 96	WHEN CHILDREN RULE THE WORLD *Really Useful 5797262*	40	2

RED HOT CHILI PEPPERS ◉ 🎸
US, male vocal/instrumental group — 41 wks

Date	Title	Pos	Wks
10 Feb 90	HIGHER GROUND *EMI-USA MT 75*	55	3
23 Jun 90	TASTE THE PAIN *EMI-USA MT 85*	29	3
8 Sep 90	HIGHER GROUND (re-issue) *EMI-USA MT 88*	54	3
14 Mar 92	UNDER THE BRIDGE *Warner Bros. W 0084*	26	4
15 Aug 92	BREAKING THE GIRL *Warner Bros. W 0126*	41	3
5 Feb 94 ●	GIVE IT AWAY *Warner Bros. W 0225CD1*	9	4
30 Apr 94	UNDER THE BRIDGE (re-issue) *Warner Bros. W 0237CD*	13	6
2 Sep 95	WARPED *Warner Bros. W 0316CD*	31	2
21 Oct 95	MY FRIENDS *Warner Bros. W 0317CD*	29	2
17 Feb 96	AEROPLANE *Warner Bros. W 0331CD*	11	3
14 Jun 97 ●	LOVE ROLLERCOASTER *Geffen GFSTD 22188*	7	8

RED JERRY *UK, male producer* — 2 wks

Date	Title	Pos	Wks
13 Jun 98	WIZARDS OF THE SONIC *Wonderboy WBOYD 010* [1]	43	2

[1] Westbam vs Red Jerry

UK No 1 ★   UK Top 10 ●   UK million seller ◆   UK entry at No 1 ■   US No 1 ▲

RED RAW featuring 007 *UK, male vocal/instrumental duo*   **1 wk**

| 28 Oct 95 | OOH LA LA LA *Media MCSTD 2065* | 59 | 1 |

RED SNAPPER
UK, male/female vocal/instrumental/production group   **1 wk**

| 21 Nov 98 | IMAGE OF YOU *Warp WAP 111CD* | 60 | 1 |

REDBONE ✎ *US, male vocal/instrumental group*   **12 wks**

| 25 Sep 71 ● | WITCH QUEEN OF NEW ORLEANS *Epic EPC 7351* | 2 | 12 |

Sharon REDD ◢ ✎ *US, female vocalist*   **32 wks**

28 Feb 81	CAN YOU HANDLE IT *Epic EPC 9572*	31	8
2 Oct 82	NEVER GIVE YOU UP *Prelude PRL A2755*	20	9
15 Jan 83	IN THE NAME OF LOVE *Prelude PRL A2905*	31	5
22 Oct 83	LOVE HOW YOU FEEL *Prelude A3868*	39	5
1 Feb 92	CAN YOU HANDLE IT *EMI EM 219* [1]	17	5

[1] DNA featuring Sharon Redd

REDD KROSS *US, male vocal/instrumental group*   **4 wks**

5 Feb 94	VISIONARY *This Way Up WAY 2733*	75	1
10 Sep 94	YESTERDAY ONCE MORE *A & M 5807932*	45	2
1 Feb 97	GET OUT OF MYSELF *This Way Up WAY 5466*	63	1

The listed flip side of 'Yesterday Once More' was 'Superstar' by Sonic Youth

Otis REDDING ✎ *Peerless sixties singer/songwriter, b. 9 September, 1941, Georgia, d. 10 December, 1967. He was one of the first and most influential sixties soul stars. He replaced Elvis as the World's Top Male Singer in a* Melody Maker *poll shortly before his death in a plane crash*   **124 wks**

25 Nov 65	MY GIRL *Atlantic AT 4050*	11	16
7 Apr 66	SATISFACTION *Atlantic AT 4080*	33	4
14 Jul 66	MY LOVER'S PRAYER *Atlantic 584 019*	37	6
25 Aug 66	I CAN'T TURN YOU LOOSE *Atlantic 584 030*	29	8
24 Nov 66	FA FA FA FA FA (SAD SONG) *Atlantic 584 049*	23	9
26 Jan 67	TRY A LITTLE TENDERNESS *Atlantic 584 070*	46	4
23 Mar 67	DAY TRIPPER *Stax 601 005*	43	6
4 May 67	LET ME COME ON HOME *Stax 601 007*	48	1
15 Jun 67	SHAKE *Stax 601 011*	28	10
19 Jul 67	TRAMP *Stax 601 012* [1]	18	11
11 Oct 67	KNOCK ON WOOD *Stax 601 021* [1]	35	5
14 Feb 68	MY GIRL (re-issue) *Atlantic 584 092*	36	9
21 Feb 68 ●	(SITTIN' ON) THE DOCK OF THE BAY *Stax 601 031* ▲	3	15
29 May 68	HAPPY SONG *Stax 601 040*	24	5
31 Jul 68	HARD TO HANDLE *Atlantic 584 199*	15	12
9 Jul 69	LOVE MAN *Atco 226 001*	43	3

[1] Otis Redding and Carla Thomas

Helen REDDY ◖ *Australia, female vocalist*   **18 wks**

| 18 Jan 75 ● | ANGIE BABY *Capitol CL 15799* ▲ | 5 | 10 |
| 28 Nov 81 | I CAN'T SAY GOODBYE TO YOU *MCA 744* | 43 | 8 |

REDHEAD KINGPIN and the FBI ✎ *US, male vocalist*   **11 wks**

| 22 Jul 89 | DO THE RIGHT THING *10 TEN 271* | 13 | 10 |
| 2 Dec 89 | SUPERBAD SUPERSLICK *10 TEN 286* | 68 | 1 |

REDMAN – *See Beverley KNIGHT; DAS EFX*

REDNEX ☺ *Sweden, male/female vocal/instrumental group*   **23 wks**

17 Dec 94 ★	COTTON EYE JOE *Internal Affairs KGBCD 016*	1	16
25 Mar 95	OLD POP IN AN OAK *Internal Affairs KGBD 019*	12	6
21 Oct 95	WILD 'N FREE *Internal Affairs KGBD 024*	55	1

REDS UNITED ☺ *UK, male vocal group*   **13 wks**

| 6 Dec 97 ● | SING UP FOR THE CHAMPIONS *Music Collection MANUCDP 2* | 12 | 9 |
| 9 May 98 | UNITED CALYPSO '98 *Music Collection MANUCDP 3* | 33 | 4 |

See also MANCHESTER UNITED FOOTBALL CLUB

REDSKINS *UK, male vocal/instrumental duo*   **12 wks**

10 Nov 84	KEEP ON KEEPIN' ON *Decca F 1*	43	5
22 Jun 85	BRING IT DOWN (THIS INSANE THING) *Decca F 2*	33	5
22 Feb 86	THE POWER IS YOURS *Decca F 3*	59	2

Alex REECE *UK, male producer*   **7 wks**

16 Dec 95	FEEL THE SUNSHINE *Blunted Vinyl BLNCD 016*	69	1
11 May 96	FEEL THE SUNSHINE (re-mix) *Fourth & Broadway BRCD 332*	26	3
27 Jul 96	CANDLES *Fourth & Broadway BRCD 333*	33	2
18 Nov 96	ACID LAB *Fourth & Broadway BRCD 344*	64	1

Jimmy REED *US, male vocalist*   **2 wks**

| 10 Sep 64 | SHAME SHAME SHAME *Stateside SS 330* | 45 | 2 |

Lou REED ✎ *US, male vocalist*   **19 wks**

| 12 May 73 ● | WALK ON THE WILD SIDE *RCA 2303* | 10 | 9 |
| 17 Jan 87 | SOUL MAN *A & M AM 364* [1] | 30 | 10 |

[1] Sam Moore and Lou Reed

Dan REED NETWORK *US, male vocal/instrumental group*   **16 wks**

20 Jan 90	COME BACK BABY *Mercury DRN 2*	51	3
17 Mar 90	RAINBOW CHILD *Mercury DRN 3*	60	3
21 Jul 90	STARDATE 1990/RAINBOW CHILD (re-issue) *Mercury DRN 4*	39	4
8 Sep 90	LOVER/MONEY *Mercury DRN 5*	45	3
13 Jul 91	MIX IT UP *Mercury MER 345*	49	2
21 Sep 91	BABY NOW I *Mercury MER 352*	65	1

Michael REED ORCHESTRA – *See Richard HARTLEY / Michael REED ORCHESTRA*

REEF ✎ *UK, male vocal/instrumental group*   **31 wks**

15 Apr 95	GOOD FEELING *Sony S2 6613602*	24	4
3 Jun 95	NAKED *Sony S2 6620622*	11	5
5 Aug 95	WEIRD *Sony S2 6622772*	19	3
2 Nov 96 ●	PLACE YOUR HANDS *Sony S2 6635712*	6	7
25 Jan 97 ●	COME BACK BRIGHTER *Sony S2 6640972*	8	5
5 Apr 97	CONSIDERATION *Sony S2 6643125*	13	4
2 Aug 97	YER OLD *Sony S2 6647032*	21	3

REEL 2 REAL ☺ *US, male vocal/instrumental duo*   **53 wks**

12 Feb 94 ●	I LIKE TO MOVE IT *Positiva CDTIV 10* [1]	5	20
2 Jul 94 ●	GO ON MOVE *Positiva CDTIV 15* [1]	7	9
1 Oct 94	CAN YOU FEEL IT *Positiva CDTIV 22* [1]	13	5
3 Dec 94	RAISE YOUR HANDS *Positiva CDTIV 27* [1]	14	6
1 Apr 95	CONWAY *Positiva CDTIVS 30* [1]	27	4
6 Jul 96	JAZZ IT UP *Positiva CDTIV 59*	7	7
5 Oct 96	ARE YOU READY FOR SOME MORE *Positiva CDTIV 56*	24	2

[1] Reel 2 Real featuring the Mad Stuntman

Maureen REES *UK, female (learner driver) vocalist*   **4 wks**

| 20 Dec 97 | DRIVING IN MY CAR *Eagle EAGXS 014* | 49 | 4 |

Tony REES and the COTTAGERS *UK, male vocal group*   **1 wk**

| 10 May 75 | VIVA EL FULHAM *Sonet SON 2059* | 46 | 1 |

REESE PROJECT *US, male producer – Kevin Saunderson*   **7 wks**

8 Aug 92	THE COLOUR OF LOVE *Network NWK 51*	52	2
12 Dec 92	I BELIEVE *Network NWKT 63*	74	1
13 Mar 93	SO DEEP *Network NWKCD 68*	54	2
24 Sep 94	THE COLOUR OF LOVE (re-mix) *Network NWKCD 81*	55	1
6 May 95	DIRECT-ME *Network NEKCD 87*	44	1

Conner REEVES [R&B] ☺ *UK, male vocalist*   **15 wks**

| 30 Aug 97 | MY FATHER'S SON *Wildstar CDWILD 1* | 12 | 5 |
| 22 Nov 97 | EARTHBOUND *Wildstar CDWILD 2* | 14 | 4 |

11 Apr 98	READ MY MIND *Wildstar CXWILD 4*	19 4
3 Oct 98	SEARCHING FOR A SOUL *Wildstar CDWILD 6*	28 2

Jim REEVES 🎵 *Internationally acclaimed velvet-voiced vocalist b. 20 August, 1924, Texas, d. 31 July, 1964. 'Gentleman Jim' had an impressive portfolio of posthumous hits, including a record-breaking eight albums simultaneously on the UK chart three months after his death*   322 wks

24 Mar 60	HE'LL HAVE TO GO *RCA 1168*	36 1
7 Apr 60	HE'LL HAVE TO GO (re-entry) *RCA 1168*	12 30
16 Mar 61	WHISPERING HOPE *RCA 1223*	50 1
23 Nov 61	YOU'RE THE ONLY GOOD THING *RCA 1261*	17 19
28 Jun 62	ADIOS AMIGO *RCA 1293*	23 21
22 Nov 62	I'M GONNA CHANGE EVERYTHING *RCA 1317*	42 2
13 Jun 63 ●	WELCOME TO MY WORLD *RCA 1342*	6 15
17 Oct 63	GUILTY *RCA 1364*	29 7
20 Feb 64 ●	I LOVE YOU BECAUSE *RCA 1385*	5 39
18 Jun 64 ●	I WON'T FORGET YOU *RCA 1400*	3 25
5 Nov 64 ●	THERE'S A HEARTACHE FOLLOWING ME *RCA 1423*	6 13
7 Jan 65	I WON'T FORGET YOU (re-entry) *RCA 1400*	47 1
4 Feb 65 ●	IT HURTS SO MUCH *RCA 1437*	8 10
15 Apr 65	NOT UNTIL THE NEXT TIME *RCA 1446*	13 12
6 May 65	HOW LONG HAS IT BEEN *RCA 1445*	45 5
15 Jul 65	THIS WORLD IS NOT MY HOME *RCA 1412*	22 9
11 Nov 65	IS IT REALLY OVER *RCA 1488*	17 9
18 Aug 66 ★	DISTANT DRUMS *RCA 1537*	1 25
2 Feb 67	I WON'T COME IN WHILE HE'S THERE *RCA 1563*	12 11
26 Jul 67	TRYING TO FORGET *RCA 1611*	33 5
22 Nov 67	I HEARD A HEART BREAK LAST NIGHT *RCA 1643*	38 6
27 Mar 68	PRETTY BROWN EYES *RCA 1672*	33 5
25 Jun 69	WHEN TWO WORLDS COLLIDE *RCA 1830*	17 17
6 Dec 69	BUT YOU LOVE ME DADDY *RCA 1899*	15 16
21 Mar 70	NOBODY'S FOOL *RCA 1915*	32 5
12 Sep 70	ANGELS DON'T LIE *RCA 1997*	44 1
26 Sep 70	ANGELS DON'T LIE (re-entry) *RCA 1997*	32 2
26 Jun 71	I LOVE YOU BECAUSE/HE'LL HAVE TO GO/ MOONLIGHT & ROSES (re-issue) *RCA Maximillion 2092*	34 8
19 Feb 72	YOU'RE FREE TO GO *RCA 2174*	48 2

Martha REEVES and the VANDELLAS 🎤
US, female vocal group   85 wks

29 Oct 64	DANCING IN THE STREET *Stateside SS 345* [1]	28 8
1 Apr 65	NOWHERE TO RUN *Tamla Motown TMG 502* [1]	26 8
1 Dec 66	I'M READY FOR LOVE *Tamla Motown TMG 582* [1]	29 8
30 Mar 67	JIMMY MACK *Tamla Motown TMG 599* [1]	21 9
17 Jan 68	HONEY CHILE *Tamla Motown TMG 636*	30 9
15 Jan 69 ●	DANCING IN THE STREET (re-issue) *Tamla Motown TMG 684*	4 12
16 Apr 69	NOWHERE TO RUN (re-issue) *Tamla Motown TMG 694*	42 3
29 Aug 70	JIMMY MACK (re-entry) *Tamla Motown TMG 599* ...	21 12
13 Feb 71	FORGET ME NOT *Tamla Motown TMG 762*	11 8
8 Jan 72	BLESS YOU *Tamla Motown TMG 794*	33 5
23 Jul 88	NOWHERE TO RUN (2nd re-issue) *A & M AM 444*	52 3

[1] Martha and the Vandellas

The listed flip side of 'Nowhere to Run' in 1988 was I Got You (I Feel Good) by James Brown

Vic REEVES ○ *UK, male vocalist*   29 wks

27 Apr 91 ●	BORN FREE *Sense SIGH 710* [1]	6 6
26 Oct 91 ★	DIZZY *Sense SIGH 712* [2]	1 12
14 Dec 91	ABIDE WITH ME *Sense SIGH 713*	47 3
8 Jul 95 ●	I'M A BELIEVER *Parlophone CDR 6412* [3]	3 8

[1] Vic Reeves and the Roman Numerals [2] Vic Reeves and the Wonder Stuff [3] EMF and Reeves and Mortimer

RE-FLEX *UK, male vocal/instrumental group*   9 wks

28 Jan 84	THE POLITICS OF DANCING *EMI FLEX 2*	28 9

REFUGEE ALLSTARS – See FUGEES; Wyclef JEAN

Joan REGAN © *UK, female vocalist*   62 wks

11 Dec 53 ●	RICOCHET *Decca F 10193* [1]	8 1

8 Jan 54 ●	RICOCHET (re-entry) *Decca F 10193* [1]	9 4
14 May 54 ●	SOMEONE ELSE'S ROSES *Decca F 10257*	5 8
1 Oct 54	IF I GIVE MY HEART TO YOU *Decca F 10373*	20 1
29 Oct 54 ●	IF I GIVE MY HEART TO YOU (re-entry) *Decca F 10373*	3 10
5 Nov 54	WAIT FOR ME DARLING *Decca F 10362* [2]	18 1
25 Mar 55 ●	PRIZE OF GOLD *Decca F 10432*	6 8
6 May 55	OPEN UP YOUR HEART *Decca F 10474*	19 1
1 May 59 ●	MAY YOU ALWAYS *HMV POP 593*	9 16
5 Feb 60	HAPPY ANNIVERSARY *Pye 7N 15238*	29 1
19 Feb 60	HAPPY ANNIVERSARY (re-entry) *Pye 7N 15238* ...	29 1
28 Jul 60	PAPA LOVES MAMA *Pye 7N 15278*	29 8
24 Nov 60	ONE OF THE LUCKY ONES *Pye 7N 15310*	47 1
5 Jan 61	IT MUST BE SANTA *Pye 7N 15303*	42 1

[1] Joan Regan with the Squadronaires [2] Joan Regan and the Johnston Brothers

See also VARIOUS ARTISTS (EPs & LPs) – All Star Hit Parade

REGENTS ○ *UK, male/female vocal/instrumental group*   14 wks

22 Dec 79	7 TEEN *Rialto TREB 111*	11 12
7 Jun 80	SEE YOU LATER *Arista ARIST 350*	55 2

REGGAE BOYZ *Jamaica, male vocal / instrumental group*   1 wk

27 Jun 98	KICK IT *Universal MCSTD 40167*	59 1

REGGAE PHILHARMONIC ORCHESTRA
UK, male/female vocal/instrumental group   11 wks

19 Nov 88	MINNIE THE MOOCHER *Mango IS 378*	35 9
28 Jul 90	LOVELY THING *Mango MNG 742*	71 2

REGGAE REVOLUTION – See Pato BANTON

REGGIE – See TECHNOTRONIC

REGINA *US, female vocalist*   3 wks

1 Feb 86	BABY LOVE *Funkin' Marvellous MARV 01*	50 3

REID *UK, male vocal group*   12 wks

8 Oct 88	ONE WAY OUT *Syncopate SY 16*	66 2
11 Feb 89	REAL EMOTION *Syncopate SY 24*	65 2
15 Apr 89	GOOD TIMES *Syncopate SY 27*	55 6
21 Oct 89	LOVIN' ON THE SIDE *Syncopate REID 1*	71 2

Ellen REID – See CRASH TEST DUMMIES

John REID – See NIGHTCRAWLERS featuring John REID

Junior REID – See COLDCUT; RAGGA TWINS; SOUPDRAGONS

Mike REID © *UK, male vocalist*   8 wks

22 Mar 75 ●	THE UGLY DUCKLING *Pye 7N 45434*	10 8

Neil REID © *UK, male vocalist*   26 wks

1 Jan 72 ●	MOTHER OF MINE *Decca F 13264*	2 20
8 Apr 72	THAT'S WHAT I WANT TO BE *Decca F 13300*	49 1
22 Apr 72	THAT'S WHAT I WANT TO BE (re-entry) *Decca F 13300*	45 5

Maggie REILLY – See Mike OLDFIELD

Keith RELF *UK, male vocalist*   1 wk

26 May 66	MR. ZERO *Columbia DB 7920*	50 1

R.E.M. ○ 🎸 *"America's Best Rock Band", according to* Rolling Stone: *Michael Stipe (v), Peter Buck (g), Mike Mills (b), Bill Berry (d). This Georgia group went from the US college circuit to packing stadiums worldwide. In 1996, the award-winning, platinum-album-earning quartet signed an $80-million record deal*   134 wks

28 Nov 87	THE ONE I LOVE *IRS IRM 46*	51 8
30 Apr 88	FINEST WORKSONG *IRS IRM 161*	50 2

4 Feb 89	STAND *Warner Bros. W 7577*	51	3
3 Jun 89	ORANGE CRUSH *Warner Bros. W 2960*	28	5
12 Aug 89	STAND (re-issue) *Warner Bros. W 2833*	48	2
9 Mar 91	LOSING MY RELIGION *Warner Bros. W 0015*	19	9
18 May 91 ●	SHINY HAPPY PEOPLE *Warner Bros. W 0027*	6	11
17 Aug 91	NEAR WILD HEAVEN *Warner Bros. W 0055*	27	4
21 Sep 91	THE ONE I LOVE (re-issue) *IRS IRM 178*	16	6
16 Nov 91	RADIO SONG *Warner Bros. W 0072*	28	3
14 Dec 91	IT'S THE END OF THE WORLD AS WE KNOW IT *IRS IRM 180*	39	4
3 Oct 92	DRIVE *Warner Bros. W 0136*	11	5
28 Nov 92	MAN ON THE MOON *Warner Bros. W 0143*	18	8
20 Feb 93	THE SIDEWINDER SLEEPS TONITE *Warner Bros. W 0152CD1*	17	6
17 Apr 93 ●	EVERYBODY HURTS *Warner Bros W 0169CD1*	7	12
24 Jul 93	NIGHTSWIMMING *Warner Bros. W 0184CD*	27	5
11 Dec 93	FIND THE RIVER *Warner Bros. W 0211CD*	54	1
17 Sep 94 ●	WHAT'S THE FREQUENCY, KENNETH *Warner Bros. W 0265CD*	9	7
12 Nov 94	BANG AND BLAME *Warner Bros. W 0275CD*	15	4
4 Feb 95	CRUSH WITH EYELINER *Warner Bros. W 0281CD*	23	3
15 Apr 95 ●	STRANGE CURRENCIES *Warner Bros. W 0290CD*	9	4
29 Jul 95	TONGUE *Warner Bros. W 0308CD*	13	5
31 Aug 96 ●	E-BOW THE LETTER *Warner Bros. W 0369CD*	4	5
2 Nov 96	BITTERSWEET ME *Warner Bros. W 0377CD*	19	2
14 Dec 96	ELECTROLITE *Warner Bros. W 0383CD*	29	2
24 Oct 98 ●	DAYSLEEPER *Warner Brothers W 0455CD*	6	6
19 Dec 98	LOTUS *Warner Brothers W 466CD*	26†	2

REMBRANDTS ◐ ✔ *US, male vocal/instrumental group* 28 wks

2 Sep 95 ●	I'LL BE THERE FOR YOU (THEME FROM FRIENDS) *East West A 4390CD*	3	12
20 Jan 96	THIS HOUSE IS NOT A HOME *East West A 4336CD*	58	1
24 May 97 ●	I'LL BE THERE FOR YOU (THEME FROM FRIENDS) (re-entry) *East West A 4390CD*	5	15

RENAISSANCE ✔ *UK, male/female vocal/instrumental group* 11 wks

15 Jul 78 ●	NORTHERN LIGHTS *Warner Bros. K 17177*	10	11

RENE and ANGELA *US, male/female vocal duo* 15 wks

15 Jun 85	SAVE YOUR LOVE (FOR NUMBER 1) *Club JAB 14* [1]	66	2
7 Sep 85	I'LL BE GOOD *Club JAB 18*	22	10
2 Nov 85	SECRET RENDEZVOUS *Champion CHAMP 5*	54	3

[1] Rene and Angela featuring Kurtis Blow

RENE and YVETTE *UK, male/female vocal duo* 4 wks

22 Nov 86	JE T'AIME (ALLO ALLO)/RENE D.M.C. (DEVASTATING MACHO CHARISMA) *Sedition EDIT 3319*	57	4

Nicole RENEE *US, female vocalist* 1 wk

12 Dec 98	STRAWBERRY *Atlantic AT 0050CD*	55	1

RENEE and RENATO ℂ *UK/Italy, female/male vocal duo* 22 wks

30 Oct 82 ★	SAVE YOUR LOVE *Hollywood HWD 003*	1	16
12 Feb 83	JUST ONE MORE KISS *Hollywood HWD 006*	48	6

RENEGADE SOUNDWAVE *UK, male vocal/instrumental group* 7 wks

3 Feb 90	PROBABLY A ROBBERY *Mute MUTE 102*	38	6
5 Feb 94	RENEGADE SOUNDWAVE *Mute CDMUTE 146*	64	1

REO SPEEDWAGON ✔ ◐ *US, male vocal/instrumental group* 38 wks

11 Apr 81 ●	KEEP ON LOVING YOU *Epic EPC 9544* ▲	7	14
27 Jun 81	TAKE IT ON THE RUN *Epic EPC A 1207*	19	14
16 Mar 85	CAN'T FIGHT THIS FEELING *Epic A 4880* ▲	16	10

REPARATA and the DELRONS ◐ *US, female vocal group* 12 wks

20 Mar 68	CAPTAIN OF YOUR SHIP *Bell 1002*	13	10
18 Oct 75	SHOES *Dart 2066 562* [1]	43	2

[1] Reparata

REPRAZENT – See Roni SIZE/REPRAZENT

REPUBLICA ◐ ☺ *UK, male/female vocal/instrumental group* 18 wks

27 Apr 96	READY TO GO *Deconstruction 74321326132*	43	2
1 Mar 97	READY TO GO *Deconstruction 74321421332*	13	6
3 May 97 ●	DROP DEAD GORGEOUS *Deconstruction 74321408442*	7	7
3 Oct 98	FROM RUSH HOUR WITH LOVE *Deconstruction 74321610472*	20	3

See also SAFFRON

REST ASSURED ☺ ◐ *UK, male vocal/instrumental trio* 7 wks

28 Feb 98	TREAT INFAMY *ffrr FCD 333*	14	7

REUNION *US, male vocal group* 4 wks

21 Sep 74	LIFE IS A ROCK (BUT THE RADIO ROLLED ME) *RCA PB 10056*	33	4

REVILLOS – See REZILLOS

REVIVAL 3000 *UK, male DJ/production trio* 1 wk

1 Nov 97	THE MIGHTY HIGH *Hi-Life 5718092*	47	1

REVOLTING COCKS *US, male vocal/instrumental group* 1 wk

18 Sep 93	DA YA THINK I'M SEXY *Devotion CDDVN 111*	61	1

REVOLUTION – See PRINCE

Debbie REYNOLDS ℂ *US, female vocalist* 17 wks

30 Aug 57 ●	TAMMY *Vogue-Coral Q 72274* ▲	2	17

Jody REYNOLDS *US, male vocalist* 1 wk

14 Apr 79	ENDLESS SLEEP *Lightning LIG 9015*	66	1

'Endless Sleep' was coupled with 'To Know Him Is to Love Him' by the Teddy Bears as a double A-side

LJ REYNOLDS *US, male vocalist* 3 wks

30 Jun 84	DON'T LET NOBODY HOLD YOU DOWN *Club JAB 5*	53	3

REYNOLDS GIRLS ◐ *UK, female vocal duo* 12 wks

25 Feb 89 ●	I'D RATHER JACK *PWL PWL 25*	8	12

REZILLOS ✐ *UK, male/female vocal/instrumental group* 21 wks

12 Aug 78	TOP OF THE POPS *Sire SIR 4001*	17	9
25 Nov 78	DESTINATION VENUS *Sire SIR 4008*	43	4
18 Aug 79	I WANNA BE YOUR MAN/I CAN'T STAND MY BABY *Sensible SAB 1*	71	1
1 Sep 79	I WANNA BE YOUR MAN/I CAN'T STAND MY BABY (re-entry) *Sensible SAB 1*	75	1
26 Jan 80	MOTORBIKE BEAT *Dindisc DIN 5* [1]	45	6

[1] Revillos

RHC *Belgium, male/female vocal/instrumental duo* 1 wk

11 Jan 92	FEVER CALLED LOVE *R&S RSUK 9*	65	1

RHODA – See SPECIALS

Busta RHYMES ◀ *US, male rapper* 36 wks

11 May 96 ●	WOO-HAH!! GOT YOU ALL IN CHECK *Elektra EKR 220CD*	8	7
21 Sep 96	IT'S A PARTY *Elektra EKR 226CD* [1]	23	2
5 Apr 97 ●	HIT 'EM HIGH (THE MONSTARS' ANTHEM) *Atlantic A 5449CD* [2]	8	6
3 May 97	DO MY THING *Elektra EKR 235CD*	39	1
18 Oct 97	PUT YOUR HANDS WHERE MY EYES COULD SEE *Elektra E 3900CD*	16	3
20 Dec 97	DANGEROUS *Elektra E 3877CD*	32	4
18 Apr 98 ●	TURN IT UP/FIRE IT UP *Elektra E 3847CD*	2	10

UK No 1 ★   UK Top 10 ●   UK million seller ◆   UK entry at No 1 ■   US No 1 ▲

| 11 Jul 98 | ONE *Elektra E 3833CD1* [3] | ....23 | 3 |

[1] Busta Rhymes featuring Zhane [2] B Real / Busta Rhymes / Coolio / LL Cool J / Method Man [3] Busta Rhymes featuring Erykah Badu

RHYTHIM IS RHYTHIM *US, male instrumental duo* — 1 wk
| 11 Nov 89 | STRINGS OF LIFE *Kool Kat KOOL 509* | ....74 | 1 |

RHYTHM ETERNITY *UK, male/female vocal/instrumental group* — 1 wk
| 23 May 92 | PINK CHAMPAGNE *Dead Dead Good GOOD 15T* | ....72 | 1 |

RHYTHM FACTOR *US, male/female vocal/instrumental group* — 2 wks
| 29 Apr 95 | YOU BRING ME JOY *Multiply CDMULTY 4* | ....53 | 2 |

RHYTHM MASTERS *UK, male DJ / production duo* — 1 wk
| 16 Aug 97 | COME ON Y'ALL *Faze 2 CDFAZE 37* | ....49 | 1 |

RHYTHM-N-BASS *UK, male rap group* — 4 wks
| 19 Sep 92 | ROSES *Epic 6582907* | ....56 | 2 |
| 3 Jul 93 | CAN'T STOP THIS FEELING *Epic 6592002* | ......59 | 2 |

RHYTHM ON THE LOOSE *UK, male producer – Geoff Hibbert* — 2 wks
| 19 Aug 95 | BREAK OF DAWN *Six6 SIXCD 126* | ....36 | 2 |

RHYTHM QUEST *UK, male producer – Mark Hadfield* — 2 wks
| 20 Jun 92 | CLOSER TO ALL YOUR DREAMS *Network NWK 40* | ......45 | 2 |

RHYTHM SECTION *UK, male vocal/instrumental group* — 1 wk
| 18 Jul 92 | MIDSUMMER MADNESS EP *Rhythm Section RSEC 006* | ....66 | 1 |

Tracks on Midsummer Madness EP: Dreamworld / Burnin' Up / Perfect Love 2am / Perfect Love 8am

RHYTHM SOURCE *UK, male/female vocal/instrumental group* — 1 wk
| 17 Jun 95 | LOVE SHINE *A & M 5810672* | ....74 | 1 |

RHYTHMATIC *UK, male instrumental group* — 3 wks
12 May 90	TAKE ME BACK *Network NWK 8*	74	1
26 May 90	TAKE ME BACK (re-entry) *Network NWK 8*	71	1
3 Nov 90	FREQUENCY *Network NWK 13*	62	1

RIALTO ☺ ◑ *UK, male vocal/instrumental group* — 8 wks
8 Nov 97	MONDAY MORNING 5:19 *East West EW 116CD*	37	2
17 Jan 98	UNTOUCHABLE *East West EW 107CD1*	20	3
28 Mar 98	DREAM ANOTHER DREAM *East West EW 156CD1*	39	2
17 Oct 98	SUMMER'S OVER *China WOKCDR 2099*	60	1

Reva RICE and Greg ELLIS *UK, male/female vocal duo* — 2 wks
| 27 Mar 93 | NEXT TIME YOU FALL IN LOVE *Really Useful RURCD 12* | ....59 | 2 |

Charlie RICH ✒ *US, male vocalist* — 29 wks
16 Feb 74	● THE MOST BEAUTIFUL GIRL *CBS 1897* ▲	2	14
13 Apr 74	BEHIND CLOSED DOORS *Epic EPC 1539*	16	10
1 Feb 75	WE LOVE EACH OTHER *Epic EPC 2868*	37	5

Kelli RICH – See NU SOUL featuring Kelli RICH

Richie RICH *UK, DJ/producer* — 16 wks
16 Jul 88	TURN IT UP *Club JAB 68*	48	3
22 Oct 88	I'LL HOUSE YOU *Gee Street GEE 003* [1]	22	5
10 Dec 88	MY DJ (PUMP IT UP SOME) *Gee Street GEE 7*	74	1
2 Sep 89	SALSA HOUSE *ffrr F 113*	50	3
9 Mar 91	YOU USED TO SALSA *ffrr F 156* [2]	52	3
29 Mar 97	STAY WITH ME *Castle CATX 1001* [3]	58	1

[1] Richie Rich meets the Jungle Brothers [2] Richie Rich's Salsa House featuring Ralphi Rosario [3] Richie Rich and Esera Tuaolo

RICH KIDS *UK, male vocal/instrumental group* — 5 wks
| 28 Jan 78 | RICH KIDS *EMI 2738* | ....24 | 5 |

Tony RICH PROJECT [R&B] *US, male vocalist* — 22 wks
4 May 96	● NOBODY KNOWS *LaFace 74321356422*	4	17
31 Aug 96	LIKE A WOMAN *LaFace 74321401612*	27	4
14 Dec 96	LEAVIN' *LaFace 74321438382*	52	1

Cliff RICHARD ◑ ℭ
Britain's most successful solo vocalist, b. Harry Webb, 14 October, 1940, Lucknow, India. This seemingly ageless entertainer's record number of 64 Top 10 entries now spans 40 years, with worldwide sales of more than 85 million records. He was knighted in 1995 — 1124 wks

12 Sep 58	● MOVE IT *Columbia DB 4178*	2	17
21 Nov 58	● HIGH CLASS BABY *Columbia DB 4203*	7	10
30 Jan 59	LIVIN' LOVIN' DOLL *Columbia DB 4249*	20	6
8 May 59	● MEAN STREAK *Columbia DB 4290*	10	9
15 May 59	NEVER MIND *Columbia DB 4290*	21	2
10 Jul 59	★ LIVING DOLL *Columbia DB 4306*	1	11
9 Oct 59	★ TRAVELLIN' LIGHT *Columbia DB 4351*	1	17
9 Oct 59	DYNAMITE *Columbia DB 4351*	16	2
30 Oct 59	DYNAMITE (re-entry) *Columbia DB 4351*	21	2
11 Dec 59	LIVING DOLL (re-entry) *Columbia DB 4306*	26	1
1 Jan 60	LIVING DOLL (2nd re-entry) *Columbia DB 4306*	28	1
15 Jan 60	EXPRESSO BONGO EP *Columbia SEG 7971*	14	7
22 Jan 60	● VOICE IN THE WILDERNESS *Columbia DB 4398*	2	13
24 Mar 60	● FALL IN LOVE WITH YOU *Columbia DB 4431*	2	15
5 May 60	VOICE IN THE WILDERNESS (re-entry) *Columbia DB 4398*	36	2
30 Jun 60	★ PLEASE DON'T TEASE *Columbia DB 4479*	1	18
22 Sep 60	● NINE TIMES OUT OF TEN *Columbia DB 4506*	3	12
1 Dec 60	★ I LOVE YOU *Columbia DB 4547*	1	16
2 Mar 61	● THEME FOR A DREAM *Columbia DB 4593*	3	14
30 Mar 61	● GEE WHIZ IT'S YOU *Columbia DC 756*	4	14
22 Jun 61	● A GIRL LIKE YOU *Columbia DB 4657*	3	14
19 Oct 61	● WHEN THE GIRL IN YOUR ARMS IS THE GIRL IN YOUR HEART *Columbia DB 4716*	3	15
11 Jan 62	★ THE YOUNG ONES *Columbia DB 4761* ◆ ■	1	21
10 May 62	● I'M LOOKING OUT THE WINDOW/DO YOU WANNA DANCE *Columbia DB 4828*	2	17
6 Sep 62	● IT'LL BE ME *Columbia DB 4886*	2	12
6 Dec 62	★ THE NEXT TIME/BACHELOR BOY *Columbia DB 4950*	1	18
21 Feb 63	★ SUMMER HOLIDAY *Columbia DB 4977*	1	18
9 May 63	● LUCKY LIPS *Columbia DB 7034*	4	15
22 Aug 63	● IT'S ALL IN THE GAME *Columbia DB 7089*	2	13
7 Nov 63	● DON'T TALK TO HIM *Columbia DB 7150*	2	13
6 Feb 64	● I'M THE LONELY ONE *Columbia DB 7203*	8	10
13 Feb 64	DON'T TALK TO HIM (re-entry) *Columbia DB 7150*	50	1
30 Apr 64	● CONSTANTLY *Columbia DB 7272*	4	13
2 Jul 64	● ON THE BEACH *Columbia DB 7305*	7	13
8 Oct 64	● THE TWELFTH OF NEVER *Columbia DB 7372*	8	11
10 Dec 64	● I COULD EASILY FALL *Columbia DB 7420*	9	11
11 Mar 65	★ THE MINUTE YOU'RE GONE *Columbia DB 7496*	1	14
10 Jun 65	ON MY WORD *Columbia DB 7596*	12	10
19 Aug 65	THE TIME IN BETWEEN *Columbia DB 7660*	22	8
4 Nov 65	● WIND ME UP (LET ME GO) *Columbia DB 7745*	2	16
24 Mar 66	BLUE TURNS TO GREY *Columbia DB 7866*	15	9
21 Jul 66	● VISIONS *Columbia DB 7968*	7	12
13 Oct 66	TIME DRAGS BY *Columbia DB 8017*	10	12
15 Dec 66	IN THE COUNTRY *Columbia DB 8094*	6	10
16 Mar 67	● IT'S ALL OVER *Columbia DB 8150*	9	10
8 Jun 67	I'LL COME RUNNING *Columbia DB 8210*	26	8
16 Aug 67	● THE DAY I MET MARIE *Columbia DB 8245*	10	14
15 Nov 67	● ALL MY LOVE *Columbia DB 8293*	6	12
20 Mar 68	★ CONGRATULATIONS *Columbia DB 8376*	1	13
26 Jun 68	I'LL LOVE YOU FOREVER TODAY *Columbia DB 8437*	27	6
25 Sep 68	MARIANNE *Columbia DB 8476*	22	8
27 Nov 68	DON'T FORGET TO CATCH ME *Columbia DB 8503*	21	10
26 Feb 69	GOOD TIMES (BETTER TIMES) *Columbia DB 8548*	12	11
28 May 69	● BIG SHIP *Columbia DB 8581*	8	10
13 Sep 69	● THROW DOWN A LINE *Columbia DB 8615* [1]	7	9
6 Dec 69	WITH THE EYES OF A CHILD *Columbia DB 8641*	20	11
21 Feb 70	JOY OF LIVING *Columbia DB 8657* [1]	25	8
6 Jun 70	● GOODBYE SAM HELLO SAMANTHA *Columbia DB 8685*	6	15

Date	Title	Pos	Wks
5 Sep 70	I AIN'T GOT TIME ANYMORE *Columbia DB 8708*	21	7
23 Jan 71	SUNNY HONEY GIRL *Columbia DB 8747*	19	8
10 Apr 71	SILVERY RAIN *Columbia DB 8774*	27	6
17 Jul 71	FLYING MACHINE *Columbia DB 8797*	37	7
13 Nov 71	SING A SONG OF FREEDOM *Columbia DB 8836*	13	12
11 Mar 72	JESUS *Columbia DB 8864*	35	3
26 Aug 72	LIVING IN HARMONY *Columbia DB 8917*	12	10
17 Mar 73 ●	POWER TO ALL OUR FRIENDS *EMI 2012*	4	12
12 May 73	HELP IT ALONG/TOMORROW RISING *EMI 2022*	29	6
1 Dec 73	TAKE ME HIGH *EMI 2088*	27	12
18 May 74	(YOU KEEP ME) HANGIN' ON *EMI 2150*	13	8
7 Feb 76	MISS YOU NIGHTS *EMI 2376*	15	10
8 May 76 ●	DEVIL WOMAN *EMI 2458*	9	8
21 Aug 76	I CAN'T ASK FOR ANYMORE THAN YOU *EMI 2499*	17	8
4 Dec 76	HEY MR. DREAM MAKER *EMI 2559*	31	5
5 Mar 77	MY KINDA LIFE *EMI 2584*	15	8
16 Jul 77	WHEN TWO WORLDS DRIFT APART *EMI 2633*	46	3
31 Mar 79	GREEN LIGHT *EMI 2920*	57	3
21 Jul 79 ★	WE DON'T TALK ANYMORE *EMI 2975*	1	14
3 Nov 79	HOT SHOT *EMI 5003*	46	5
2 Feb 80 ●	CARRIE *EMI 5006*	4	10
16 Aug 80 ●	DREAMIN' *EMI 5095*	8	10
25 Oct 80	SUDDENLY *Jet 7002* [2]	15	8
24 Jan 81	A LITTLE IN LOVE *EMI 5123*	15	8
29 Aug 81 ●	WIRED FOR SOUND *EMI 5221*	4	9
21 Nov 81 ●	DADDY'S HOME *EMI 5251*	2	12
17 Jul 82 ●	THE ONLY WAY OUT *EMI 5318*	10	9
25 Sep 82	WHERE DO WE GO FROM HERE *EMI 5341*	60	3
4 Dec 82	LITTLE TOWN *EMI 5348*	11	7
19 Feb 83 ●	SHE MEANS NOTHING TO ME *Capitol CL 276* [3]	9	9
16 Apr 83 ●	TRUE LOVE WAYS *EMI 5385* [4]	8	8
4 Jun 83	DRIFTING *DJM SHEIL 1* [5]	64	2
3 Sep 83	NEVER SAY DIE (GIVE A LITTLE BIT MORE) *EMI 5415*	15	7
26 Nov 83 ●	PLEASE DON'T FALL IN LOVE *EMI 5437*	7	9
31 Mar 84	BABY YOU'RE DYNAMITE/OCEAN DEEP *EMI 5457*	27	6
19 May 84	OCEAN DEEP/BABY YOU'RE DYNAMITE (re-entry) *EMI 5457*	72	1
3 Nov 84	SHOOTING FROM THE HEART *EMI RICH 1*	51	4
9 Feb 85	HEART USER *EMI RICH 2*	46	3
14 Sep 85	SHE'S SO BEAUTIFUL *EMI 5531*	17	9
7 Dec 85	IT'S IN EVERY ONE OF US *EMI 5537*	45	6
22 Mar 86 ★	LIVING DOLL *WEA YZ 65* [6]	1	11
4 Oct 86 ●	ALL I ASK OF YOU *Polydor POSP 802* [7]	3	16
29 Nov 86	SLOW RIVERS *Rocket EJS 13* [8]	44	8
20 Jun 87 ●	MY PRETTY ONE *EMI EM 4*	6	10
29 Aug 87 ●	SOME PEOPLE *EMI EM 18*	3	10
31 Oct 87	REMEMBER ME *EMI EM 31*	35	4
13 Feb 88	TWO HEARTS *EMI EM 42*	34	3
3 Dec 88 ●	MISTLETOE AND WINE *EMI EM 78*	1	8
10 Jun 89	THE BEST OF ME *EMI EM 78*	2	7
26 Aug 89 ●	I JUST DON'T HAVE THE HEART *EMI EM 101*	3	8
14 Oct 89	LEAN ON YOU *EMI EM 105*	17	6
9 Dec 89	WHENEVER GOD SHINES HIS LIGHT *Polydor VANS 2* [9]	20	6
24 Feb 90	STRONGER THAN THAT *EMI EM 129*	14	4
25 Aug 90 ●	SILHOUETTES *EMI EM 152*	10	7
13 Oct 90	FROM A DISTANCE *EMI EM 155*	11	6
8 Dec 90 ★	SAVIOUR'S DAY *EMI XMAS 90*	1	7
14 Sep 91	MORE TO LIFE *EMI EM 205*	23	5
7 Dec 91	WE SHOULD BE TOGETHER *EMI XMAS 91*	10	6
11 Jan 92	THIS NEW YEAR *EMI EMS 216*	30	2
5 Dec 92 ●	I STILL BELIEVE IN YOU *EMI EM 255*	7	7
27 Mar 93 ●	PEACE IN OUR TIME *EMI CDEM 265*	8	5
12 Jun 93	HUMAN WORK OF ART *EMI CDEM 267*	24	4
2 Oct 93	NEVER LET GO *EMI CDEM 281*	32	3
18 Dec 93	HEALING LOVE *EMI CDEM 294*	19	5
10 Dec 94	ALL I HAVE TO DO IS DREAM/MISS YOU NIGHTS (re-issue) *EMI CDEM 359* [10]	14	6
25 Feb 95	ALL I HAVE TO DO IS DREAM/MISS YOU NIGHTS (re-entry of re-issue) *EMI CDEM 359* [10]	58	3
2 Oct 95	MISUNDERSTOOD MAN *EMI CDEM 394*	19	3
9 Dec 95	HAD TO BE *EMI CDEM 410* [11]	22	4
30 Mar 96	THE WEDDING *EMI CDEM 422* [12]	40	1
25 Jan 97	BE WITH ME ALWAYS *EMI CDEM 453*	52	1
24 Oct 98 ●	CAN'T KEEP THIS FEELING IN *EMI CDEM 526*	10	4

[1] Cliff and Hank [2] Olivia Newton-John and Cliff Richard [3] Phil Everly and Cliff Richard [4] Cliff Richard with the London Philharmonic Orchestra [5] Sheila Walsh and Cliff Richard [6] Cliff Richard and the Young Ones featuring Hank B Marvin [7] Cliff Richard and Sarah Brightman [8] Elton John and Cliff Richard [9] Van Morrison with Cliff Richard [10] Cliff Richard with Phil Everly/Cliff Richard [11] Cliff Richard and Olivia Newton-John [12] Cliff Richard featuring Helen Hobson

The Shadows appear on all Cliff's hits from 'Move It to a Girl Like You'. After that they are on the following hits: 'The Young Ones', 'Do You Wanna Dance', 'It'll Be Me', 'The Next Time', 'Bachelor Boy', 'Summer Holiday', 'Lucky Lips', 'Don't Talk to Him', 'I'm The Lonely One', 'On the Beach', 'I Could Easily Fall', 'The Time in between', 'Blue Turns to Grey', 'Time Drags By', 'In the Country' and 'Don't Forget to Catch Me'. Tracks on the Expresso Bongo EP: Love / A Voice in the Wilderness / The Shrine on the Second Floor / Bongo Blue. 'Bongo Blues' features only The Shadows. The Shadows were the Drifters on Cliff's hits before 'Living Doll'. 'Bachelor Boy' was listed with 'The Next Time' from 10 Jan, 1963. 'Ocean Deep' listed from 28 Apr, 1984, onwards. It peaked at No 41

Wendy RICHARD – *See Mike SARNE*

Lionel RICHIE ⊕ ✎
Foremost singer/composer/producer, b. 20 June, 1949, Alabama. He launched a solo career in 1982 after 12 years fronting The Commodores. Arguably, he was the most successful US songwriter of the 1980s, who composed at least one chart-topper per year for a record eight successive years **167 wks**

Date	Title	Pos	Wks
12 Sep 81 ●	ENDLESS LOVE *Motown TMG 1240* [1] ▲	7	12
20 Nov 82 ●	TRULY *Motown TMG 1284* ▲	6	11
29 Jan 83	YOU ARE *Motown TMG 1290*	43	7
7 May 83	MY LOVE *Motown TMG 1300*	70	3
1 Oct 83 ●	ALL NIGHT LONG (ALL NIGHT) *Motown TMG 1319* ▲	2	16
3 Dec 83 ●	RUNNING WITH THE NIGHT *Motown TMG 1324*	9	12
10 Mar 84 ★	HELLO *Motown TMG 1330* ▲	1	15
23 Jun 84	STUCK ON YOU *Motown TMG 1341*	12	12
20 Oct 84	PENNY LOVER *Motown TMG 1356*	18	7
16 Nov 85 ●	SAY YOU, SAY ME *Motown ZB 40421* ▲	8	11
26 Jul 86 ●	DANCING ON THE CEILING *Motown L10 1*	7	11
11 Oct 86	LOVE WILL CONQUER ALL *Motown L10 2*	45	5
20 Dec 86	BALLERINA GIRL/DEEP RIVER WOMAN *Motown L10 3*	17	8
28 Mar 87	SELA *Motown L10 4*	43	6
9 May 92	DO IT TO ME *Motown TMG 1407*	33	6
22 Aug 92 ●	MY DESTINY *Motown TMG 1408*	7	13
28 Nov 92	LOVE OH LOVE *Motown TMG 1413*	52	3
26 Dec 92	LOVE OH LOVE (re-entry) *Motown TMG 1413*	73	1
6 Apr 96	DON'T WANNA LOSE YOU *Mercury MERCD 461*	17	5
23 Nov 96	STILL IN LOVE *Mercury MERCD 477*	66	1
27 Jun 98	CLOSEST THING TO HEAVEN *Mercury 5661312*	26	2

[1] Diana Ross and Lionel Richie

'Deep River Woman' was only listed from 17 Jan, 1987. It has the credit: background vocal 'Alabama'

Jonathan RICHMAN and the MODERN LOVERS ✎ ⊕
US, male vocal/instrumental group **27 wks**

Date	Title	Pos	Wks
16 Jul 77	ROADRUNNER *Beserkley BZZ 1*	11	9
29 Oct 77 ●●	EGYPTIAN REGGAE *Beserkley BZZ 2*	5	14
21 Jan 78	MORNING OF OUR LIVES *Beserkley BZZ 7* [1]	29	4

[1] Modern Lovers

Ricky Dillard – *See Farley 'Jackmaster' FUNK*

RICO – *See SPECIALS*

RIDE ☺ *UK, male vocal/instrumental group* **22 wks**

Date	Title	Pos	Wks
27 Jan 90	RIDE EP *Creation CRE 07T2*	71	2
14 Apr 90	PLAY EP *Creation CRE 075T*	32	3
29 Sep 90	FALL EP *Creation CRE 087T*	34	3
16 Mar 91	TODAY FOREVER *Creation CRE 100T*	14	4
15 Feb 92 ●	LEAVE THEM ALL BEHIND *Creation CRE 123T*	9	3
25 Apr 92	TWISTERELLA *Creation CRE 150T*	36	2

30 Apr 94	BIRDMAN *Creation CRESCD 155*	38 2
25 Jun 94	HOW DOES IT FEEL TO FEEL *Creation CRESCD 184*	58 1
8 Oct 94	I DON'T KNOW WHERE IT COMES FROM *Creation CRESCD 189R*	46 1
24 Feb 96	BLACK NITE CRASH *Creation CRESCD 199*	67 1

Tracks on Ride EP: Chelsea Girl / Drive Blind / All I See / Close My Eyes
Tracks on Play EP: Like a Daydream / Silver / Furthest Sense / Perfect Time
Tracks on Fall EP: Dreams Burn Down / Taste / Hear and Now / Nowhere

Andrew RIDGELEY *UK, male vocalist*　　3 wks
31 Mar 90	SHAKE *Epic AJR 1*	58 3

Stan RIDGWAY ☺ ✔ *US, male vocalist*　　12 wks
5 Jul 86 ●	CAMOUFLAGE *IRS IRM 114*	4 12

RIGHEIRA *Italy, male vocal duo*　　3 wks
24 Sep 83	VAMOS A LA PLAYA *A & M AM 137*	53 3

RIGHT SAID FRED ☺ *UK, male vocal/instrumental group*　　61 wks
27 Jul 91 ●	I'M TOO SEXY *Tug SNOG 1* ▲	2 16
7 Dec 91 ●	DON'T TALK JUST KISS *Tug SNOG 2* [1]	3 11
21 Mar 92 ★	DEEPLY DIPPY *Tug SNOG 3*	1 14
1 Aug 92	THOSE SIMPLE THINGS/DAYDREAM *Tug SNOG 4*	29 5
27 Feb 93 ●	STICK IT OUT *Tug CDCOMIC 1* [2]	4 7
23 Oct 93	BUMPED *Tug CDSNOG 7*	32 4
18 Dec 93	HANDS UP (4 LOVERS) *Tug CDSNOG 8*	60 3
19 Mar 94	WONDERMAN *Tug CDSNOG 9*	55 1

[1] Right Said Fred, guest vocals: Jocelyn Brown [2] Right Said Fred and Friends

RIGHTEOUS BROTHERS ☺ ♪ *US, male vocal duo*　　86 wks
14 Jan 65 ★	YOU'VE LOST THAT LOVIN' FEELIN' *London HLU 9943* ▲	1 10
12 Aug 65	UNCHAINED MELODY *London HL 9975*	14 12
13 Jan 66	EBB TIDE *London HL 10011*	48 2
14 Apr 66	(YOU'RE MY) SOUL AND INSPIRATION *Verve VS 535* ▲	15 10
10 Nov 66	WHITE CLIFFS OF DOVER *London HL 10086*	21 9
22 Dec 66	ISLAND IN THE SUN *Verve VS 547*	36 5
12 Feb 69 ●	YOU'VE LOST THAT LOVIN' FEELIN' (re-issue) *London HL 10241*	10 11
19 Nov 77	YOU'VE LOST THAT LOVIN' FEELIN' (2nd re-issue) *Phil Spector Interna 2010 022*	42 4
27 Oct 90 ★	UNCHAINED MELODY (re-issue) *Verve/Polydor PO 101*	1 14
15 Dec 90 ●	YOU'VE LOST THAT LOVIN' FEELIN'/EBB TIDE (3rd re-issue) *Verve/Polydor PO 116*	3 9

Cheryl Pepsii RILEY *US, female vocalist*　　1 wk
28 Jan 89	THANKS FOR MY CHILD *CBS 653153 7*	75 1

Jeannie C RILEY ☛ *US, female vocalist*　　15 wks
16 Oct 68	HARPER VALLEY P. T. A. *Polydor 56748* ▲	12 15

Teddy RILEY *US, male producer*　　5 wks
21 Mar 92	IS IT GOOD TO YOU *MCA MCS 1611* [1]	53 2
19 Jun 93	BABY BE MINE *MCA MCSTD 1772* [2]	37 3

[1] Teddy Riley featuring Tammy Lucas [2] Blackstreet featuring Teddy Riley

LeAnn RIMES ☛ *US, female vocalist*　　39 wks
7 Mar 98 ●	HOW DO I LIVE *Curb CUBCX 30*	7 33
12 Sep 98	LOOKING THROUGH YOUR EYES/COMMITMENT *Curb CUBC 32*	38 2
31 Oct 98	HOW DO I LIVE (re-entry) *Curb CUBCX 30*	72 1
12 Dec 98	BLUE *Curb CUBC 39*	23† 3

RIMSHOTS *US, male instrumental/vocal group*　　5 wks
19 Jul 75	7-6-5-4-3-2-1 (BLOW YOUR WHISTLE) *All Platinum 6146 304*	26 5

RIO and MARS
France/UK, male/female vocal/instrumental duo　　3 wks
28 Jan 95	BOY I GOTTA HAVE YOU *Dome CDDOME 1014*	43 2
13 Apr 96	BOY I GOTTA HAVE YOU (re-issue) *Feverpitch CDFVR 1007*	46 1

Miguel RIOS ℂ *Spain, male vocalist*　　12 wks
11 Jul 70	SONG OF JOY *A & M AMS 790*	16 12

Waldo de los RIOS ℂ *Argentina, orchestra*　　16 wks
10 Apr 71 ●	MOZART SYMPHONY NO. 40 IN G MINOR K550 1ST MOVEMENT (ALLEGRO MOLTO) *A & M AMS 836*	5 16

RIP PRODUCTIONS *UK, production duo*　　1 wk
29 Nov 97	THE CHANT (WE R) / RIP PRODUCTIONS *Satellite 74321534022*	58 1

See also DOUBLE 99

Minnie RIPERTON ♪ *US, female vocalist*　　10 wks
12 Apr 75 ●	LOVING YOU *Epic EPC 3121* ▲	2 10

RITCHIE FAMILY ♫ *US, female vocal group*　　19 wks
23 Aug 75	BRAZIL *Polydor 2058 625*	41 4
18 Sep 76 ●	THE BEST DISCO IN TOWN *Polydor 2058 777*	10 9
17 Feb 79	AMERICAN GENERATION *Mercury 6007 199*	49 6

Lee RITENOUR – See Maxi PRIEST

Tex RITTER ☛ *US, male vocalist*　　14 wks
22 Jun 56 ●	WAYWARD WIND *Capitol CL 14581*	8 14

RIVER CITY PEOPLE ☺ ✔
UK, male/female vocal/instrumental group　　27 wks
12 Aug 89	(WHAT'S WRONG WITH) DREAMING *EMI EM 95*	70 3
3 Mar 90	WALKING ON ICE *EMI EM 130*	62 2
30 Jun 90	CARRY THE BLAME/CALIFORNIA DREAMIN' *EMI EM 145*	13 10
22 Sep 90	(WHAT'S WRONG WITH) DREAMING (re-issue) *EMI EM 156*	40 3
2 Mar 91	WHEN I WAS YOUNG *EMI EM 176*	62 2
28 Sep 91	SPECIAL WAY *EMI EM 207*	44 3
22 Feb 92	STANDING IN THE NEED OF LOVE *EMI EM 216*	36 4

RIVER DETECTIVES *UK, male vocal/instrumental duo*　　4 wks
29 Jul 89	CHAINS *WEA YZ 383*	51 4

RIVER OCEAN – See INDIA

Danny RIVERS *UK, male vocalist*　　3 wks
12 Jan 61	CAN'T YOU HEAR MY HEART *Decca F 11294*	36 3

ROACH MOTEL *UK, male instrumental/production group*　　2 wks
21 Aug 93	AFRO SLEEZE/TRANSATLANTIC *Junior Boy's Own JBO 1412*	73 1
10 Dec 94	HAPPY BIZZNESS/WILD LUV *Junior Boy's Own JBO 24*	75 1

ROACHFORD ☺ ✔
UK, male/female vocal/instrumental group　　59 wks
18 Jun 88	CUDDLY TOY *CBS ROA 2*	61 4
14 Jan 89 ●	CUDDLY TOY (re-issue) *CBS ROA 4*	4 9
18 Mar 89	FAMILY MAN *CBS ROA 5*	25 6
1 Jul 89	KATHLEEN *CBS ROA 6*	43 5
13 Apr 91	GET READY! *Columbia 6567057*	22 8
19 Mar 94	ONLY TO BE WITH YOU *Columbia 6601562*	21 7
18 Jun 94	LAY YOUR LOVE ON ME *Columbia 6603722*	36 5
20 Aug 94	THIS GENERATION *Columbia 6607452*	38 4
3 Dec 94	CRY FOR ME *Columbia 6610742*	46 2
1 Apr 95	I KNOW YOU DON'T LOVE ME *Columbia 6612525*	42 2
11 Oct 97	THE WAY I FEEL *Columbia 6651042*	20 4

14 Feb 98	HOW COULD I? (INSECURITY) *Columbia 6653462*	.....34 3
11 Jul 98	NAKED WITHOUT YOU *Columbia 6659362*	.....53 0

ROB 'N' RAZ – *See Leila K*

Kate ROBBINS and BEYOND ⊕
UK, female/male vocal/instrumental group   **10 wks**

30 May 81	● MORE THAN IN LOVE *RCA 69*	.....2 10

Marty ROBBINS ✒ *US, male vocalist*   **32 wks**

29 Jan 60	EL PASO *Fontana H 233* ▲	.....19 7
7 Apr 60	EL PASO (re-entry) *Fontana H 233*	.....44 1
26 May 60	BIG IRON *Fontana H 229*	.....48 1
27 Sep 62	● DEVIL WOMAN *CBS AAG 114*	.....5 17
17 Jan 63	RUBY ANN *CBS AAG 128*	.....24 6

Antoinette ROBERSON – *See PULSE featuring Antoinette ROBERSON*

Al ROBERTS – *See FOUR ACES*

Austin ROBERTS *US, male vocalist*   **7 wks**

25 Oct 75	ROCKY *Private Stock PVT 33*	.....22 7

Joe ROBERTS *UK, male vocalist*   **17 wks**

28 Aug 93	BACK IN MY LIFE *ffrr FCD 215*	.....59 1
29 Jan 94	LOVER *ffrr FCD 220*	.....22 5
14 May 94	BACK IN MY LIFE (re-issue) *ffrr FCD 230*	.....39 3
6 Aug 94	ADORE *ffrr FCD 240*	.....45 3
18 Feb 95	YOU ARE EVERYTHING *Columbia 6611755* [1]	.....28 4
24 Feb 96	HAPPY DAYS *Grass Green GRASS 10CD* [2]	.....63 1

[1] Melanie Williams and Joe Roberts [2] Sweet Mercy featuring Joe Roberts

Juliet ROBERTS ☺ ✒ *UK, female vocalist*   **24 wks**

31 Jul 93	CAUGHT IN THE MIDDLE *Cooltempo CDCOOL 272*	.....24 6
6 Nov 93	FREE LOVE *Cooltempo CDCOOL 281*	.....25 3
19 Mar 94	AGAIN/I WANT YOU *Cooltempo CDCOOL 285*	.....33 3
2 Jul 94	CAUGHT IN THE MIDDLE (re-mix) *Cooltempo CDCOOL 291*	.....14 5
15 Oct 94	I WANT YOU (re-issue) *Cooltempo CDCOOL 297*	.....28 3
31 Jan 98	SO GOOD/FREE LOVE 98 *Delirious 74321554002*	.....15 4

Malcolm ROBERTS ℭ *UK, male vocalist*   **29 wks**

11 May 67	TIME ALONE WILL TELL *RCA 1578*	.....45 2
30 Oct 68	● MAY I HAVE THE NEXT DREAM WITH YOU	
	Major Minor MM 581	.....8 14
12 Feb 69	MAY I HAVE THE NEXT DREAM WITH YOU (re-entry)	
	Major Minor MM 581	.....45 1
22 Nov 69	LOVE IS ALL *Major Minor MM 637*	.....12 12

B.A. ROBERTSON ⊕ *UK, male vocalist*   **60 wks**

28 Jul 79	● BANG BANG *Asylum K 13152*	.....2 12
27 Oct 79	● KNOCKED IT OFF *Asylum K 12396*	.....8 12
1 Mar 80	KOOL IN THE KAFTAN *Asylum K 12427*	.....17 12
31 May 80	TO BE OR NOT TO BE *Asylum K 12449*	.....9 11
17 Oct 81	HOLD ME *Swansong BAM 1* [1]	.....11 8
17 Dec 83	TIME *Epic A 3983* [2]	.....45 5

[1] B.A. Robertson and Maggie Bell [2] Frida and B.A. Robertson

Don ROBERTSON ℭ *US, male instrumentalist – piano and whistle*   **9 wks**

11 May 56	● THE HAPPY WHISTLER *Capitol CL 14575*	.....8 9

Robbie ROBERTSON ✒ *Canada, male vocalist*   **11 wks**

23 Jul 88	SOMEWHERE DOWN THE CRAZY RIVER *Geffen GEF 40*	.....15 10
11 Apr 98	TAKE YOUR PARTNER BY THE HAND *Polydor 5693272* [1]	.....74 1

[1] Howie B featuring Robbie Robertson

Ivo ROBIC *Yugoslavia, male vocalist*   **1 wk**

6 Nov 59	MORGEN *Polydor 23923*	.....23 1

Floyd ROBINSON ⊕ *US, male vocalist*   **9 wks**

16 Oct 59	● MAKIN' LOVE *RCA 1146*	.....9 9

Smokey ROBINSON ✒ *US, male vocalist*   **41 wks**

23 Feb 74	JUST MY SOUL RESPONDING	
	Tamla Motown TMG 883	.....35 6
24 Feb 79	POPS WE LOVE YOU *Motown TMG 1136* [1]	.....66 5
9 May 81	★ BEING WITH YOU *Motown TMG 1223*	.....1 13
13 Mar 82	TELL ME TOMORROW *Motown TMG 1255*	.....51 4
28 Mar 87	JUST TO SEE HER *Motown ZB 41147*	.....52 6
25 Feb 89	INDESTRUCTIBLE *Arista 112074* [2]	.....30 7

[1] Diana Ross, Marvin Gaye, Smokey Robinson and Stevie Wonder

[2] Four Tops featuring Smokey Robinson

See also Smokey ROBINSON and the MIRACLES

Smokey ROBINSON and the MIRACLES
US, male vocal group   **71 wks**

24 Feb 66	GOING TO A GO-GO *Tamla Motown TMG 547*	.....44 5
22 Dec 66	(COME 'ROUND HERE) I'M THE ONE YOU NEED	
	Tamla Motown TMG 584	.....45 2
27 Dec 67	I SECOND THAT EMOTION *Tamla Motown TMG 631*	.....27 11
3 Apr 68	IF YOU CAN WANT *Tamla Motown TMG 648*	.....50 1
7 May 69	● TRACKS OF MY TEARS *Tamla Motown TMG 696*	.....9 13
1 Aug 70	★ THE TEARS OF A CLOWN *Tamla Motown TMG 745* ▲	.....1 14
30 Jan 71	(COME 'ROUND HERE) I'M THE ONE YOU NEED (re-issue)	
	Tamla Motown TMG 761	.....13 9
5 Jun 71	I DON'T BLAME YOU AT ALL *Tamla Motown TMG 774*	.....11 10
2 Oct 76	THE TEARS OF A CLOWN (re-issue)	
	Tamla Motown TMG 1048	.....34 6

See also MIRACLES; Smokey ROBINSON

Tom ROBINSON ⚥ ✐ *UK, male vocalist*   **41 wks**

22 Oct 77	● 2-4-6-8 MOTORWAY *EMI 2715* [1]	.....5 9
18 Feb 78	DON'T TAKE NO FOR AN ANSWER *EMI 2749* [1]	.....18 6
13 May 78	UP AGAINST THE WALL *EMI 2787* [1]	.....33 6
17 Mar 79	BULLY FOR YOU *EMI 2916* [1]	.....68 2
25 Jun 83	● WAR BABY *Panic NIC 2*	.....6 9
12 Nov 83	LISTEN TO THE RADIO: ATMOSPHERICS *Panic NIC 3*	.....39 6
15 Sep 84	RIKKI DON'T LOSE THAT NUMBER *Castaway TR 2*	.....58 3

[1] Tom Robinson Band

Vicki Sue ROBINSON *US, female vocalist*   **1 wk**

27 Sep 97	HOUSE OF JOY *Logic 74321511492*	.....48 1

ROBSON and JEROME ⊕ *UK, male vocal duo*   **45 wks**

20 May 95	★ UNCHAINED MELODY/(THERE'LL BE BLUEBIRDS OVER)	
	THE WHITE CLIFFS OF DOVER *RCA 74321284362* [1] ◆ ■	.....1 16
4 Nov 95	UNCHAINED MELODY/(THERE'LL BE BLUEBIRDS OVER)	
	THE WHITE CLIFFS OF DOVER (re-entry)	
	RCA 74321284362 [1]	.....63 1
11 Nov 95	★ I BELIEVE/UP ON THE ROOF *RCA 74321326882* ◆ ■	.....1 14
9 Nov 96	★ WHAT BECOMES OF THE BROKENHEARTED/SATURDAY	
	NIGHT AT THE MOVIES/YOU'LL NEVER WALK ALONE	
	RCA 74321424732 ■	.....1 14

[1] Robson Green and Jerome Flynn

ROBYN ⊕ ☺ *Sweden, female vocalist*   **14 wks**

20 Jul 96	YOU'VE GOT THAT SOMETHIN' *RCA 74321393462*	.....54 1
16 Aug 97	DO YOU KNOW (WHAT IT TAKES) *RCA 74321509932*	.....26 3
7 Mar 98	● SHOW ME LOVE *RCA 74321555032*	.....8 6
30 May 98	DO YOU REALLY WANT ME *RCA 74321582982*	.....20 4

John ROCCA – *See FREEEZ*

ROCHELLE *US, female vocalist*   **6 wks**

1 Feb 86	MY MAGIC MAN *Warner Bros. W 8838*	.....27 6

ROCK AID ARMENIA
UK, male vocal/instrumental charity ensemble **5 wks**

16 Dec 89	SMOKE ON THE WATER *Life Aid Armenia ARMEN 001*	39	5

ROCK CANDY *UK, male vocal/instrumental group* **6 wks**

11 Sep 71	REMEMBER *MCA MK 5069*	32	6

Chubb ROCK *US, male rapper* **1 wk**

19 Jan 91	TREAT 'EM RIGHT *Champion CHAMP 272*	67	1

ROCK GODDESS *UK, female vocal/instrumental group* **5 wks**

5 Mar 83	MY ANGEL *A & M AMS 8311*	64	2
24 Mar 84	I DIDN'T KNOW I LOVED YOU (TILL I SAW YOU ROCK 'N' ROLL) *A & M AMS 185*	57	3

Sir Monti ROCK III – See DISCO TEX and the SEX-O-LETTES

ROCKER'S REVENGE 🎸
US, male/female vocal/instrumental group **20 wks**

14 Aug 82	● WALKING ON SUNSHINE *London LON 11* [1]	4	13
29 Jan 83	THE HARDER THEY COME *London LON 18*	30	7

[1] Rocker's Revenge featuring Donnie Calvin

ROCKET FROM THE CRYPT 🎸
US, male vocal/instrumental group **7 wks**

27 Jan 96	BORN IN 69 *Elemental ELM 32CD*	68	1
13 Apr 96	YOUNG LIVERS *Elemental ELM 33CDS*	67	1
14 Sep 96	ON A ROPE *Elemental ELM 38CDS1*	12	4
29 Aug 98	LIPSTICK *Elemental ELM 48CDS1*	64	1

ROCKETS – See Tony CROMBIE and his ROCKETS

ROCKFORD FILES *UK, male instrumental/production duo* **4 wks**

11 Mar 95	YOU SEXY DANCER *Escapade CDJAPE 7*	34	3
6 Apr 96	YOU SEXY DANCER (re-issue) *Escapade CDJAPE 14*	59	1

ROCKIN' BERRIES 🌐 *UK, male vocal/instrumental group* **41 wks**

1 Oct 64	I DIDN'T MEAN TO HURT YOU *Piccadilly 7N 35197*	43	1
15 Oct 64	● HE'S IN TOWN *Piccadilly 7N 35203*	3	13
21 Jan 65	WHAT IN THE WORLD'S COME OVER YOU *Piccadilly 7N 35217*	23	7
13 May 65	● POOR MAN'S SON *Piccadilly 7N 35236*	5	11
26 Aug 65	YOU'RE MY GIRL *Piccadilly 7N 35254*	40	7
6 Jan 66	THE WATER IS OVER MY HEAD *Piccadilly 7N 35270*	43	1
20 Jan 66	THE WATER IS OVER MY HEAD (re-entry) *Piccadilly 7N 35270*	50	1

ROCKNEY – See CHAS and DAVE

ROCKSTEADY CREW 🌐 *US, male/female vocal group* **16 wks**

1 Oct 83	● (HEY YOU) THE ROCKSTEADY CREW *Charisma/Virgin RSC 1*	6	12
5 May 84	UPROCK *Charisma/Virgin RSC 2*	64	4

ROCKWELL 🎸 *US, male vocalist* **11 wks**

4 Feb 84	● SOMEBODY'S WATCHING ME *Motown TMG 1331*	6	11

ROCKY V – See Joey B ELLIS

ROCOCO *UK/Italy, male/female vocal/instrumental group* **5 wks**

16 Dec 89	ITALO HOUSE MIX *Mercury MER 314*	54	5

RODEO JONES
UK/Grenada, male/female vocal/instrumental group **2 wks**

30 Jan 93	NATURAL WORLD *A & M AMCD 0165*	75	1
3 Apr 93	SHADES OF SUMMER *A & M AMCD 212*	59	1

Clodagh RODGERS 🌐 *Ireland, female vocalist* **59 wks**

26 Mar 69	● COME BACK AND SHAKE ME *RCA 1792*	3	14
9 Jul 69	● GOODNIGHT MIDNIGHT *RCA 1852*	4	11
4 Oct 69	GOODNIGHT MIDNIGHT (re-entry) *RCA 1852*	48	1
8 Nov 69	BILJO *RCA 1891*	22	9
4 Apr 70	EVERYBODY GO HOME THE PARTY'S OVER *RCA 1930*	47	2
20 Mar 71	JACK IN THE BOX *RCA 2066*	4	10
9 Oct 71	LADY LOVE BUG *RCA 2117*	28	12

Jimmie RODGERS 🌐 *US, male vocalist* **37 wks**

1 Nov 57	HONEYCOMB *Columbia DB 3986* ▲	30	1
20 Dec 57	● KISSES SWEETER THAN WINE *Columbia DB 4052*	7	11
28 Mar 58	OH OH, I'M FALLING IN LOVE AGAIN *Columbia DB 4078*	18	6
19 Dec 58	WOMAN FROM LIBERIA *Columbia DB 4206*	18	6
14 Jun 62	● ENGLISH COUNTRY GARDEN *Columbia DB 4847*	5	13

Paul RODGERS *UK, male vocalist* **2 wks**

12 Feb 94	MUDDY WATER BLUES *Victory ROGCD 1*	45	2

RODRIGUEZ – See SASH!

RODS – See EDDIE and the HOT RODS

Tommy ROE 🌐 *US, male vocalist* **74 wks**

6 Sep 62	● SHEILA *HMV POP 1060* ▲	3	14
6 Dec 62	SUSIE DARLIN' *HMV POP 1092*	37	5
21 Mar 63	● THE FOLK SINGER *HMV POP 1138*	4	13
26 Sep 63	● EVERYBODY *HMV POP 1207*	9	11
19 Dec 63	EVERYBODY (re-entry) *HMV POP 1207*	49	3
16 Apr 69	★ DIZZY *Stateside SS 2143* ▲	1	19
23 Jul 69	HEATHER HONEY *Stateside SS 2152*	24	9

ROFO *UK, male instrumental/production duo* **3 wks**

1 Aug 92	ROFO'S THEME *PWL Continental PWLT 236*	44	3

ROGER *US, male vocalist* **8 wks**

17 Oct 87	I WANT TO BE YOUR MAN *Reprise W 8229*	61	4
12 Nov 88	BOOM! THERE SHE WAS *Virgin VS 1143* [1]	55	3
13 May 95	HIGH AS A KITE *ffrr FCD 259* [2]	55	1

[1] Scritti Politti featuring Roger [2] One Tribe featuring Roger

Julie ROGERS 🌙 *UK, female vocalist* **38 wks**

13 Aug 64	● THE WEDDING *Mercury MF 820*	3	23
10 Dec 64	LIKE A CHILD *Mercury MF 838*	21	9
25 Mar 65	HAWAIIAN WEDDING SONG *Mercury MF 849*	31	6

Kenny ROGERS 🌐 🎤 *Celebrated crossover country vocalist/actor, who was one of the USA's top-selling artists of the past 30 years, b. 21 August, 1938, Dallas. This Grammy-winning ex-New Christy Minstrel has collected more than 20 US gold albums and is a household name in many countries* **109 wks**

18 Oct 69	● RUBY DON'T TAKE YOUR LOVE TO TOWN *Reprise RS 20829*	2	23
7 Feb 70	● SOMETHING'S BURNING *Reprise RS 20888* [1]	8	14
30 Apr 77	★ LUCILLE *United Artists UP 36242*	1	14
17 Sep 77	DAYTIME FRIENDS *United Artists UP 36289*	39	4
2 Jun 79	SHE BELIEVES IN ME *United Artists UP 36533*	42	7
26 Jan 80	● COWARD OF THE COUNTY *United Artists UP 614*	1	12
15 Nov 80	LADY *United Artists UP635* ▲	12	12
12 Feb 83	WE'VE GOT TONIGHT *Liberty UP 658* [2]	28	7
22 Oct 83	EYES THAT SEE IN THE DARK *RCA 358*	61	1
12 Nov 83	● ISLANDS IN THE STREAM *RCA 378* [3] ▲	7	15

[1] Kenny Rogers and the First Edition [2] Kenny Rogers and Sheena Easton
[3] Kenny Rogers and Dolly Parton

ROKOTTO *UK, male vocal/instrumental group* **10 wks**

22 Oct 77	BOOGIE ON UP *State STAT 62*	40	4
10 Jun 78	FUNK THEORY *State STAT 80*	49	6

UK No 1 ★   UK Top 10 ●   UK million seller ◆   UK entry at No 1 ■   US No 1 ▲

What: *Release Me (And Let Me Love Again)* **77**
Who: Engelbert Humperdinck
When: 1967 (1)
Which: Spent more than one year on the chart and rocketed the balladeer to international stardom. His version of the country standard was the biggest UK hit of 1967

What: *Can't Get By Without You* **78**
Who: Real Thing
When: 1976 (2), 1986 (6)
Which: Reached the Top 10 twice, as did their previous release 'You to Me Are Everything'. Only fellow Liverpudlians The Beatles and Frankie Goes to Hollywood have had more singles in the all-time Top 100

What: *Moulin Rouge* **79**
Who: Mantovani
When: 1953 (1)
Which: Was the first instrumental to top the UK chart. This title song, from a film about the artist Toulouse-Lautrec, also took Mantovani's British-based orchestra into the US Top 10

What: *Should I Stay or Should I Go* **80**
Who: Clash
When: 1982 (17), 1991 (1)
Which: Gave these punk pioneers their only Top 10 single when it was re-issued in 1991 (six years after group had split) following its use in a TV advertisement for Levi 501s

ROLLING STONES ♫ 'World's No 1 rock group': Mick Jagger (v), Keith Richard (g), Brian Jones (g) (d. 1969), Bill Wyman (b), Charlie Watts (d) – Ron Wood (g) joined in 1975. No group has accumulated more UK or US Top 10 albums or grossed more income from touring than this legendary British band

366 wks

25 Jul 63	COME ON *Decca F 11675*	21	14
14 Nov 63	I WANNA BE YOUR MAN *Decca F 11764*	12	16
27 Feb 64 ●	NOT FADE AWAY *Decca F 11845*	3	15
2 Jul 64 ★	IT'S ALL OVER NOW *Decca F 11934*	1	15
19 Nov 64 ★	LITTLE RED ROOSTER *Decca F 12014*	1	12
4 Mar 65 ★	THE LAST TIME *Decca F 12104*	1	13
26 Aug 65 ★	(I CAN'T GET NO) SATISFACTION *Decca F 12220* ▲	1	12
28 Oct 65 ★	GET OFF OF MY CLOUD *Decca F 12263* ▲	1	12
10 Feb 66 ●	NINETEENTH NERVOUS BREAKDOWN *Decca F 12331*	2	8
19 May 66 ●	PAINT IT BLACK *Decca F 12395* ▲	1	10
29 Sep 66 ●	HAVE YOU SEEN YOUR MOTHER BABY STANDING IN THE SHADOW *Decca F 12497*	5	8
19 Jan 67 ●	LET'S SPEND THE NIGHT TOGETHER/RUBY TUESDAY *Decca F 12546*	3	10
23 Aug 67 ●	WE LOVE YOU/DANDELION *Decca F 12654*	8	8
29 May 68 ★	JUMPING JACK FLASH *Decca F 12782*	1	11
9 Jul 69 ★	HONKY TONK WOMEN *Decca F 12952* ▲	1	17
24 Apr 71 ●	BROWN SUGAR/BITCH/LET IT ROCK *Rolling Stones RS 19100* ▲	2	13
3 Jul 71	STREET FIGHTING MAN *Rolling Stones RS 13195*	21	8
29 Apr 72 ●	TUMBLING DICE *Rolling Stones RS 19103*	5	8
1 Sep 73 ●	ANGIE *Rolling Stones RS 19105* ▲	5	10
3 Aug 74 ●	IT'S ONLY ROCK AND ROLL *Rolling Stones RS 19114*	10	7
20 Sep 75	OUT OF TIME *Decca F 13597*	45	2
1 May 76 ●	FOOL TO CRY *Rolling Stones RS 19121*	6	10
3 Jun 78 ●	MISS YOU/FAR AWAY EYES *Rolling Stones EMI 2802* ▲	3	13
30 Sep 78	RESPECTABLE *Rolling Stones EMI 2861*	23	9
5 Jul 80 ●	EMOTIONAL RESCUE *Rolling Stones RSR 105*	9	8
4 Oct 80	SHE'S SO COLD *Rolling Stones RSR 106*	33	6
29 Aug 81 ●	START ME UP *Rolling Stones RSR 108*	7	9
12 Dec 81	WAITING ON A FRIEND *Rolling Stones RSR 109*	50	6
12 Jun 82	GOING TO A GO GO *Rolling Stones RSR 110*	26	6
2 Oct 82	TIME IS ON MY SIDE *Rolling Stones RSR 111*	62	2
12 Nov 83	UNDERCOVER OF THE NIGHT *Rolling Stones RSR 113*	11	9
11 Feb 84	SHE WAS HOT *Rolling Stones RSR 114*	42	4
21 Jul 84	BROWN SUGAR (re-issue) *Rolling Stones SUGAR 1*	58	2
15 Mar 86	HARLEM SHUFFLE *Rolling Stones A 6864*	13	7
2 Sep 89	MIXED EMOTIONS *Rolling Stones 655193 7*	36	5
2 Dec 89	ROCK AND A HARD PLACE *Rolling Stones 655422 7*	63	1
23 Jun 90	PAINT IT, BLACK (re-issue) *London LON 264*	61	3
30 Jun 90	ALMOST HEAR YOU SIGH *Rolling Stones 656065 7*	31	5
30 Mar 91	HIGHWIRE *Rolling Stones 6567567*	29	4
1 Jun 91	RUBY TUESDAY (LIVE) *Rolling Stones 6568927*	59	2
16 Jul 94	LOVE IS STRONG *Virgin VSCDT 1503*	14	5
8 Oct 94	YOU GOT ME ROCKING *Virgin VSCDG 1518*	23	3
10 Dec 94	OUT OF TEARS *Virgin VSCDT 1524*	36	4
15 Jul 95	I GO WILD *Virgin VSCDX 1539*	29	3
11 Nov 95	LIKE A ROLLING STONE *Virgin VSCDT 1562*	12	5
4 Oct 97	ANYBODY SEEN MY BABY? *Virgin VSCDT 1653*	22	3
7 Feb 98	SAINT OF ME *Virgin VSCDT 1667*	26	2
22 Aug 98	OUT OF CONTROL *Virgin VSCDT 1700*	51	1

'Far Away Eye's was listed from 15 Jul, 1978, with a peak position of 10

ROLLINS BAND *US, male vocal/instrumental group*

4 wks

12 Sep 92	TEARING *Imago 72787250187*	54	2
10 Sep 94	LIAR/DISCONNECTED *Imago 74321213052*	27	2

ROLLO *UK, male producer – Rollo Armstrong*

8 wks

29 Jan 94	GET OFF YOUR HIGH HORSE *Cheeky CHEKCD 003* [1]	43	2
1 Oct 94	GET OFF YOUR HIGH HORSE (re-entry) *Cheeky CHEKCD 003* [1]	47	2
10 Jun 95	LOVE LOVE LOVE – HERE I COME *Cheeky CHEKCD 007* [2]	32	2
8 Jun 96	LET THIS BE A PRAYER *Cheeky CHEKCD 013* [3]	26	2

[1] Rollo Goes Camping [2] Rollo Goes Mystic
[3] Rollo Goes Spiritual with Pauline Taylor

ROMAN HOLIDAY ◎ *UK, male vocal/instrumental group*

19 wks

2 Apr 83	STAND BY *Jive JIVE 31*	61	3
2 Jul 83	DON'T TRY TO STOP IT *Jive JIVE 39*	14	9
24 Sep 83	MOTORMANIA *Jive JIVE 49*	40	7

ROMAN NUMERALS – See Vic REEVES

ROMANTICS – See RUBY and the ROMANTICS

Max ROMEO ♉ *Jamaica, male vocalist*

25 wks

28 May 69 ●	WET DREAM *Unity UN 503*	10	24
29 Nov 69	WET DREAM (re-entry) *Unity UN 503*	50	1

RONALDO'S REVENGE *UK, male production duo*

2 wks

1 Aug 98	MAS QUE MANCADA *AM:PM 5827532*	37	2

See also FULL INTENTION

RONDO VENEZIANA *Italy, orchestra*

3 wks

22 Oct 83	LA SERENISSIMA (THEME FROM 'VENICE IN PERIL') *Ferroway 7 RON 1*	58	3

RONETTES ◎ ♉ *US, female vocal group*

34 wks

17 Oct 63 ●	BE MY BABY *London HLU 9793*	4	13
9 Jan 64	BABY I LOVE YOU *London HLU 9826*	11	14
27 Aug 64	BEST PART OF BREAKING UP *London HLU 9905*	43	3
8 Oct 64	DO I LOVE YOU *London HLU 9922*	35	4

RONNETTE – See FIDELFATTI featuring RONNETTE

Mick RONSON with Joe ELLIOTT
UK, male instrumental/vocal duo

1 wk

7 May 94	DON'T LOOK DOWN *Epic 6603582*	55	1

Linda RONSTADT ◎ ♫ *US, female vocalist*

34 wks

8 May 76	TRACKS OF MY TEARS *Asylum K 13034*	42	3
28 Jan 78	BLUE BAYOU *Asylum K 13106*	35	4
26 May 79	ALISON *Asylum K 13149*	66	2
11 Jul 87 ●	SOMEWHERE OUT THERE *MCA MCA 1132* [1]	8	13
11 Nov 89 ●	DON'T KNOW MUCH *Elektra EKR 100*	2	12

[1] Linda Ronstadt and James Ingram

'Don't Know Much' features the uncredited vocals of Aaron Neville

ROOFTOP SINGERS ♫ ◎ *US, male/female vocal group*

12 wks

31 Jan 63 ●	WALK RIGHT IN *Fontana TF 271700* ▲	10	12

ROOTJOOSE *UK male vocal / instrumental group*

3 wks

17 May 97	CAN'T KEEP LIVING THIS WAY *Rage RAGECD 2*	73	1
2 Aug 97	MR FIXIT *Rage RAGECDX 3*	54	1
4 Oct 97	LONG WAY *Rage RAGECD 5*	68	1

ROOTS *US, male vocal / instrumental group*

1 wk

3 May 97	WHAT THEY DO *Geffen GFSTD 22240*	49	1

Ralphi ROSARIO – See Richie RICH

ROSE MARIE *UK, female vocalist*

5 wks

19 Nov 83	WHEN I LEAVE THE WORLD BEHIND *A1 284*	75	1
3 Dec 83	WHEN I LEAVE THE WORLD BEHIND (re-entry) *A1 284*	63	2
24 Dec 83	WHEN I LEAVE THE WORLD BEHIND (2nd re-entry) *A1 284*	66	2

Mykal ROSE – See Shabba RANKS

ROSE OF ROMANCE ORCHESTRA *UK, orchestra*

1 wk

9 Jan 82	TARA'S THEME FROM 'GONE WITH THE WIND' *BBC RESL 108*	71	1

UK No 1 ★   UK Top 10 ●   UK million seller ◆   UK entry at No 1 ■   US No 1 ▲

ROSE ROYCE
♪ The best-selling nine-piece soul/dance combo from Los Angeles, whose biggest hits featured vocalist Gwen Dickey, started as a backing band for Motown acts and topped the UK album chart with their Greatest Hits *collection in 1980* **113 wks**

25 Dec 76	● CAR WASH *MCA 267* ▲	9	12
22 Jan 77	PUT YOUR MONEY WHERE YOUR MOUTH IS *MCA 259*	44	5
2 Apr 77	I WANNA GET NEXT TO YOU *MCA 278*	14	8
24 Sep 77	DO YOUR DANCE *Whitfield K 17006*	30	6
14 Jan 78	● WISHING ON A STAR *Warner Bros. K 17060*	3	14
6 May 78	IT MAKES YOU FEEL LIKE DANCIN' *Warner Bros. K 17148*	16	10
16 Sep 78	● LOVE DON'T LIVE HERE ANYMORE *Whitfield K 17236*	2	10
3 Feb 79	I'M IN LOVE (AND I LOVE THE FEELING) *Whitfield K 17291*	51	4
17 Nov 79	IS IT LOVE YOU'RE AFTER *Whitfield K 17456*	13	13
8 Mar 80	OOH BOY *Whitfield K 17575*	46	7
21 Nov 81	ROSE ROYCE EXPRESS *Warner Bros. K 17875*	52	3
1 Sep 84	MAGIC TOUCH *Streetwave KHAN 21*	43	8
6 Apr 85	LOVE ME RIGHT NOW *Streetwave KHAN 39*	60	3
11 Jun 88	CAR WASH/IS IT LOVE YOU'RE AFTER (re-issue) *MCA MCA 1253*	20	7
31 Oct 98	CAR WASH (re-recording) *MCA MCSTD 48096* [1]	18	3

[1] Rose Royce featuring Gwen Dickey

ROSE TATTOO
Australia, male vocal/instrumental group **4 wks**

11 Jul 81	ROCK 'N' ROLL OUTLAW *Carrere CAR 200*	60	4

Jimmy ROSELLI
US, male vocalist **8 wks**

5 Mar 83	WHEN YOUR OLD WEDDING RING WAS NEW *A1 282*	51	5
20 Jun 87	WHEN YOUR OLD WEDDING RING WAS NEW (re-issue) *First Night SCORE 9*	52	3

Diana ROSS
♪ Perennially popular ex-leader of The Supremes, the most successful female group of all time. B. Diane Earle, 26 March, 1944, Detroit. She sang on at least one hit every year for 33 years (1964–1996) – officially a record **429 wks**

18 Jul 70	REACH OUT AND TOUCH *Tamla Motown TMG 743*	33	5
12 Sep 70	● AIN'T NO MOUNTAIN HIGH ENOUGH *Tamla Motown TMG 751* ▲	6	12
3 Apr 71	● REMEMBER ME *Tamla Motown TMG 768*	7	12
31 Jul 71	★ I'M STILL WAITING *Tamla Motown TMG 781*	1	14
30 Oct 71	● SURRENDER *Tamla Motown TMG 792*	10	11
13 May 72	DOOBEDOOD'NDOOBE DOOBEDOOD'NDOOBE *Tamla Motown TMG 812*	12	9
14 Jul 73	● TOUCH ME IN THE MORNING *Tamla Motown TMG 861* ▲	9	12
13 Oct 73	TOUCH ME IN THE MORNING (re-entry) *Tamla Motown TMG 861*	50	1
5 Jan 74	● ALL OF MY LIFE *Tamla Motown TMG 880*	9	13
23 Mar 74	● YOU ARE EVERYTHING *Tamla Motown TMG 890* [1]	5	12
4 May 74	LAST TIME I SAW HIM *Tamla Motown TMG 893*	35	4
20 Jul 74	STOP LOOK LISTEN (TO YOUR HEART) *Tamla Motown TMG 906* [1]	25	8
28 Sep 74	LOVE ME *Tamla Motown TMG 917*	38	5
29 Mar 75	SORRY DOESN'T ALWAYS MAKE IT RIGHT *Tamla Motown TMG 941*	23	9
3 Apr 76	● THEME FROM MAHOGANY (DO YOU KNOW WHERE YOU'RE GOING TO) *Tamla Motown TMG 1010* ▲	5	8
24 Apr 76	● LOVE HANGOVER *Tamla Motown TMG 1024* ▲	10	10
10 Jul 76	I THOUGHT IT TOOK A LITTLE TIME *Tamla Motown TMG 1032*	32	5
16 Oct 76	I'M STILL WAITING (re-issue) *Tamla Motown TMG 1041*	41	4
19 Nov 77	GETTIN' READY FOR LOVE *Motown TMG 1090*	23	7
22 Jul 78	LOVIN' LIVIN' AND GIVIN' *Motown TMG 1112*	54	6
18 Nov 78	EASE ON DOWN THE ROAD *MCA 396* [2]	45	4
24 Feb 79	POPS WE LOVE YOU *Motown TMG 1136* [3]	66	5
21 Jul 79	THE BOSS *Motown TMG 1150*	40	7
6 Oct 79	NO ONE GETS THE PRIZE *Motown TMG 1160*	59	3
24 Nov 79	IT'S MY HOUSE *Motown TMG 1169*	32	10
19 Jul 80	● UPSIDE DOWN *Motown TMG 1195* ▲	2	12
20 Sep 80	● MY OLD PIANO *Motown TMG 1202*	5	9
15 Nov 80	I'M COMING OUT *Motown TMG 1210*	13	10
17 Jan 81	IT'S MY TURN *Motown TMG 1217*	16	8
28 Mar 81	ONE MORE CHANCE *Motown TMG 1227*	49	5
13 Jun 81	CRYIN' MY HEART OUT FOR YOU *Motown TMG 1233*	58	3
12 Sep 81	● ENDLESS LOVE *Motown TMG 1240* [4] ▲	7	12
7 Nov 81	● WHY DO FOOLS FALL IN LOVE *Capitol CL 226*	4	12
23 Jan 82	TENDERNESS *Motown TMG 1248*	73	1
30 Jan 82	MIRROR MIRROR *Capitol CL 234*	36	5
6 Feb 82	TENDERNESS (re-entry) *Motown TMG 1248*	75	1
29 May 82	● WORK THAT BODY *Capitol CL 241*	7	11
7 Aug 82	IT'S NEVER TOO LATE *Capitol CL 256*	41	4
23 Oct 82	MUSCLES *Capitol CL 268*	15	9
15 Jan 83	SO CLOSE *Capitol CL 277*	43	4
23 Jul 83	PIECES OF ICE *Capitol CL 298*	46	3
7 Jul 84	ALL OF YOU *CBS A 4522* [5]	43	8
15 Sep 84	TOUCH BY TOUCH *Capitol CL 337*	47	6
28 Sep 85	EATEN ALIVE *Capitol CL 372*	71	1
25 Jan 86	★ CHAIN REACTION *Capitol CL 386*	1	17
3 May 86	EXPERIENCE *Capitol CL 400*	47	3
13 Jun 87	DIRTY LOOKS *EMI EM 2*	49	3
8 Oct 88	MR. LEE *EMI EM 73*	58	2
26 Nov 88	LOVE HANGOVER (re-mix) *Motown ZB 42307*	75	1
6 May 89	WORKIN' OVERTIME *EMI EM 91*	32	5
29 Jul 89	PARADISE *EMI EM 94*	61	2
7 Jul 90	I'M STILL WAITING (re-mix) *Motown ZB 43781*	21	6
30 Nov 91	● WHEN YOU TELL ME THAT YOU LOVE ME *EMI EM 217*	2	11
15 Feb 92	THE FORCE BEHIND THE POWER *EMI EM 221*	27	3
20 Jun 92	● ONE SHINING MOMENT *EMI EM 239*	10	8
28 Nov 92	IF WE HOLD ON TOGETHER *EMI EM 257*	11	10
13 Mar 93	HEART (DON'T CHANGE MY MIND) *EMI CDEM 261*	31	3
9 Oct 93	CHAIN REACTION (re-issue) *EMI CDEM 290*	20	5
11 Dec 93	YOUR LOVE *EMI CDEM 299*	14	8
2 Apr 94	THE BEST YEARS OF MY LIFE *EMI CDEM 305*	28	4
9 Jul 94	WHY DO FOOLS FALL IN LOVE/I'M COMING OUT (re-issue of re-mix) *EMI CDEM 332*	36	4
2 Sep 95	TAKE ME HIGHER *EMI CDEM 388*	32	4
25 Nov 95	I'M GONE *EMI CDEM 402*	36	3
17 Feb 96	I WILL SURVIVE *EMI CDEM 415* [6]	14	4
21 Dec 96	IN THE ONES YOU LOVE *EMI CDEM 457*	34	3

[1] Diana Ross and Marvin Gaye [2] Diana Ross and Michael Jackson [3] Diana Ross, Marvin Gaye, Smokey Robinson and Stevie Wonder [4] Diana Ross and Lionel Richie [5] Julio Iglesias and Diana Ross [6] Diana

See also SUPREMES

Ricky ROSS
UK, male vocalist **3 wks**

18 May 96	RADIO ON *Epic 6631352*	35	2
10 Aug 96	GOOD EVENING PHILADELPHIA *Epic 6635335*	58	1

Francis ROSSI
UK, male vocalist **6 wks**

11 May 85	MODERN ROMANCE (I WANT TO FALL IN LOVE AGAIN) *Vertigo FROS 1* [1]	54	4
3 Aug 96	GIVE MYSELF TO LOVE *Virgin VSCDT 1594* [2]	42	2

[1] Francis Rossi and Bernard Frost [2] Francis Rossi of Status Quo

See also STATUS QUO

Nini ROSSO
Ⓒ Italy, male instrumentalist – trumpet **14 wks**

26 Aug 65	● IL SILENZIO *Durium DRS 54000*	8	14

David Lee ROTH
US, male vocalist **15 wks**

23 Feb 85	CALIFORNIA GIRLS *Warner Bros. W 9102*	68	2
5 Mar 88	JUST LIKE PARADISE *Warner Bros. W 8119*	27	7
3 Sep 88	DAMN GOOD/STAND UP *Warner Bros. W 7753*	72	1
12 Jan 91	A LIL' AIN'T ENOUGH *Warner Bros. W 0002*	32	3
19 Feb 94	SHE'S MY MACHINE *Reprise W 0229CD*	64	1
28 May 94	NIGHT LIFE *Reprise W 0249CD*	72	1

ROTTERDAM TERMINATION SOURCE
Holland, male instrumental/production duo **6 wks**

7 Nov 92	POING *SEP EDGE 74*	27	4
25 Dec 93	MERRY X-MESS *React CDREACT 33*	73	2

ROULA – *See 20 FINGERS*

ROULETTES – See Adam FAITH

Robert ROUNSEVILLE – See VARIOUS ARTISTS (EPs & LPs) – Carousel LP

Demis ROUSSOS ℂ *Greece, male vocalist*   44 wks

22 Nov 75	●	HAPPY TO BE ON AN ISLAND IN THE SUN *Philips 6042 033*......5	10
28 Feb 76		CAN'T SAY HOW MUCH I LOVE YOU *Philips 6042 114*......35	5
26 Jun 76	★	THE ROUSSOS PHENOMENON EP *Philips DEMIS 001* 1	12
2 Oct 76	●	WHEN FOREVER HAS GONE *Philips 6042 186*.................2	10
19 Mar 77		BECAUSE *Philips 6042 245*.................................39	4
18 Jun 77		KYRILA EP *Philips Demis 002* 33	3

Tracks on The Roussos Phenomenon EP: Forever and Ever / Sing an Ode to Love / So Dreamy / My Friend the Wind. Tracks on Kyrila EP: Kyrila / I'm Gonna Fall in Love / I Dig You / Sister Emilyne

ROUTERS *US, male instrumental group*   7 wks

27 Dec 62	LET'S GO *Warner Bros. WB 77* 32	7

Maria ROWE *UK, female vocalist*   2 wks

20 May 95	SEXUAL *ffrr FCD 248*.....................................67	2

ROWETTA – See OPEN ARMS featuring ROWETTA; VARIOUS ARTISTS (EPs & LPs) – The Further Adventures of North EP

Kevin ROWLAND – See DEXY'S MIDNIGHT RUNNERS

John ROWLES ℂ *New Zealand, male vocalist*   28 wks

13 Mar 68	●	IF I ONLY HAD TIME *MCA MU 1000* 3	18
19 Jun 68		HUSH NOT A WORD TO MARY *MCA MU 1023*.....................12	10

ROXETTE ❸ *The most successful Scandinavian act on the US singles chart: Marie Fredriksson (v), Per Gessle (v/g). The duo, who have even appeared on postage stamps in their homeland, can claim total worldwide sales in excess of 40 million*   135 wks

22 Apr 89	●	THE LOOK *EMI EM 87* ▲ 7	10
15 Jul 89		DRESSED FOR SUCCESS *EMI EM 96*.........................48	5
28 Oct 89		LISTEN TO YOUR HEART *EMI EM 108* ▲ 62	3
2 Jun 90	●	IT MUST HAVE BEEN LOVE *EMI EM 141* ▲ 3	14
11 Aug 90		LISTEN TO YOUR HEART / DANGEROUS (re-issue) *EMI EM 149* 6	9
27 Oct 90		DRESSED FOR SUCCESS (re-issue) *EMI EM 162*.............18	7
9 Mar 91	●	JOYRIDE *EMI EM 177* ▲ 4	10
11 May 91		FADING LIKE A FLOWER *EMI EM 190*.......................12	6
7 Sep 91		THE BIG L *EMI EM 204* 21	6
23 Nov 91		SPENDING MY TIME *EMI EM 215*...........................22	4
28 Mar 92		CHURCH OF YOUR HEART *EMI EM 227* 21	4
1 Aug 92		HOW DO YOU DO! *EMI EM 241* 13	7
7 Nov 92		QUEEN OF RAIN *EMI EM 253* 28	4
24 Jul 93	●	ALMOST UNREAL *EMI CDEM 268* 7	9
18 Sep 93	●	IT MUST HAVE BEEN LOVE (re-issue) *EMI CDEM 285* 10	8
26 Mar 94		SLEEPING IN MY CAR *EMI CDEM 314*.......................14	6
4 Jun 94		CRASH! BOOM! BANG! *EMI CDEM 324* 26	5
17 Sep 94		FIREWORKS *EMI CDEM 345* 30	4
3 Dec 94		RUN TO YOU *EMI CDEM 360* 27	6
8 Apr 95		VULNERABLE *EMI CDEM 369* 44	2
25 Nov 95		THE LOOK (re-mix) *EMI CDEM 406* 28	3
30 Mar 96		YOU DON'T UNDERSTAND ME *EMI CDEM 418*..................42	2
20 Jul 96		JUNE AFTERNOON *EMI CDEM 437* 52	1

ROXY MUSIC ✍ *Stylish art-rock group perennially regarded as highly influential pioneers. Nucleus of oft-changing group line-up: Bryan Ferry (v), Andy Mackay (sax), Phil Manzanera (g). A major act of its time, this group amassed nine Top 10 albums*   155 wks

19 Aug 72	●	VIRGINIA PLAIN *Island WIP 6144* 4	12
10 Mar 73	●	PYJAMARAMA *Island WIP 6159*...........................10	12
17 Nov 73	●	STREET LIFE *Island WIP 6173* 9	12
12 Oct 74		ALL I WANT IS YOU *Island WIP 6208*....................12	8
11 Oct 75	●	LOVE IS THE DRUG *Island WIP 6248*.....................2	10
27 Dec 75		BOTH ENDS BURNING *Island WIP 6262* 25	7
22 Oct 77		VIRGINIA PLAIN (re-issue) *Polydor 2001 739* 11	6

3 Mar 79		TRASH *Polydor POSP 32*................................40	6
28 Apr 79	●	DANCE AWAY *Polydor POSP 44*...........................2	14
11 Aug 79	●	ANGEL EYES *Polydor POSP 67*...........................4	11
17 May 80		OVER YOU *Polydor POSP 93*.............................5	9
2 Aug 80	●	OH YEAH (ON THE RADIO) *Polydor 2001 972*..............5	8
8 Nov 80		THE SAME OLD SCENE *Polydor ROXY 1*....................12	7
21 Feb 81	★	JEALOUS GUY *EG ROXY 2*................................1	11
3 Apr 82	●	MORE THAN THIS *EG ROXY 3*.............................6	8
19 Jun 82		AVALON *EG ROXY 4*.....................................13	6
25 Sep 82		TAKE A CHANCE WITH ME *EG ROXY 5*......................26	6
27 Apr 96		LOVE IS THE DRUG (re-mix) *EG VSCDT 1580*..............33	2

See also Bryan FERRY

Billy Joe ROYAL *US, male vocalist*   4 wks

7 Oct 65	DOWN IN THE BOONDOCKS *CBS 201802*......................38	4

The Central Band of the ROYAL AIR FORCE, Conductor W/Cdr. A.E. SIMS O.B.E. ℂ *UK, military band*   1 wk

21 Oct 55	THE DAMBUSTERS MARCH *HMV B 10877* 18	1

ROYAL GUARDSMEN ❸ *US, male vocal/instrumental group*   17 wks

19 Jan 67	●	SNOOPY VS. THE RED BARON *Stateside SS 574*..............8	13
6 Apr 67	RETURN OF THE RED BARON *Stateside SS 2010* 37	4

ROYAL HOUSE ☺ *US, male/female vocal/instrumental group*   18 wks

10 Sep 88	CAN YOU PARTY *Champion CHAMP 79* 14	14
7 Jan 89	YEAH! BUDDY *Champion CHAMP 91* 35	4

ROYAL PHILHARMONIC ORCHESTRA arranged and conducted by Louis CLARK ℂ *UK, orchestra and conductor*   19 wks

25 Jul 81	●	HOOKED ON CLASSICS *RCA 109* 2	11
24 Oct 81		HOOKED ON CAN-CAN *RCA 151* 47	3
10 Jul 82		BBC WORLD CUP GRANDSTAND *BBC RESL 116* 61	3
7 Aug 82		IF YOU KNEW SOUSA (AND FRIENDS) *RCA 256* 71	2

Louis Clark did not conduct the third hit
See also Elvis COSTELLO

The Pipes and Drums and Military Band of the ROYAL SCOTS DRAGOON GUARDS ℂ *UK, military band*   43 wks

1 Apr 72	★	AMAZING GRACE *RCA 2191* 1	24
19 Aug 72		HEYKENS SERENADE / THE DAY IS ENDED *RCA 2251*.........30	7
2 Dec 72		LITTLE DRUMMER BOY *RCA 2301*..........................13	9
23 Dec 72		AMAZING GRACE (re-entry) *RCA 2191* 42	3

ROYALLE DELITE *US, female vocal group*   6 wks

14 Sep 85	(I'LL BE A) FREAK FOR YOU *Streetwave KHAN 51* 45	6

Lita ROZA ℂ *UK, female vocalist*   18 wks

13 Mar 53	★	(HOW MUCH IS) THAT DOGGIE IN THE WINDOW *Decca F 10070* 1	11
7 Oct 55		HEY THERE *Decca F 10611* 17	2
23 Mar 56		JIMMY UNKNOWN *Decca F 10679* 15	5

See also VARIOUS ARTISTS (EPs & LPs) – All Star Hit Parade

ROZALLA ☺ ❸ *Zimbabwe, female vocalist*   48 wks

27 Apr 91		FAITH (IN THE POWER OF LOVE) *Pulse 8 LOSE 7*..........65	2
7 Sep 91	●	EVERYBODY'S FREE (TO FEEL GOOD) *Pulse 8 LOSE 13*.......6	11
16 Nov 91		FAITH (IN THE POWER OF LOVE) (re-issue) *Pulse 8 LOSE 15* 11	6
22 Feb 92		ARE YOU READY TO FLY *Pulse 8 LOSE 21* 14	6
9 May 92		LOVE BREAKDOWN *Pulse 8 LOSE 25* 65	2
15 Aug 92		IN 4 CHOONS LATER *Pulse 8 LOSE 29*....................50	2
30 Oct 93		DON'T PLAY WITH ME *Pulse 8 CDLOSE 52* 50	1
5 Feb 94		I LOVE MUSIC *Epic 6598932*............................18	5
6 Aug 94		THIS TIME I FOUND LOVE *Epic 6603742* 33	3
29 Oct 94		YOU NEVER LOVE THE SAME WAY TWICE *Epic 6609052* 16	5

UK No 1 ★   UK Top 10 ●   UK million seller ◆   UK entry at No 1 ■   US No 1 ▲

4 Mar 95	BABY *Epic 6611955*	26	3
31 Aug 96	EVERYBODY'S FREE (re-mix)		
	Pulse 8 CDLOSE 110	30	2

RTE CONCERT ORCHESTRA – See Bill WHELAN featuring ANUNA and the RTE CONCERT ORCHESTRA

RUBBADUBB UK, male/female vocal/instrumental group   1 wk

18 Jul 98	TRIBUTE TO OUR ANCESTORS		
	Perfecto PERF 165CD	56	1

RUBETTES ☯ UK, male vocal/instrumental group   68 wks

4 May 74 ★	SUGAR BABY LOVE *Polydor 2058 442*	1	10
13 Jul 74	TONIGHT *Polydor 2058 499*	12	9
16 Nov 74 ●	JUKE BOX JIVE *Polydor 2058 529*	3	12
8 Mar 75 ●	I CAN DO IT *State STAT 1*	7	9
21 Jun 75	FOE-DEE-O-DEE *State STAT 7*	15	6
22 Nov 75	LITTLE DARLING *State STAT 13*	30	5
1 May 76	YOU'RE THE REASON WHY *State STAT 20*	28	4
25 Sep 76	UNDER ONE ROOF *State STAT 27*	40	3
12 Feb 77 ●	BABY I KNOW *State STAT 37*	10	10

RUBY and the ROMANTICS US, female/male vocal group   6 wks

28 Mar 63	OUR DAY WILL COME *London HLR 9679* ▲	38	6

RUDE BOY OF HOUSE – See HOUSEMASTER BOYZ and the RUDE BOY OF HOUSE

RUDIES – See Freddie NOTES and the RUDIES

RUFF DRIVERZ ☺ UK, male/female vocal/production trio   12 wks

7 Feb 98	DON'T STOP *Inferno CDFERN 003*	30	2
23 May 98	DEEPER LOVE *Inferno CDFERN 006*	19	3
24 Oct 98	SHAME *Inferno CXFERN 9*	51	2
28 Nov 98 ●	DREAMING *Inferno CXFERN 11* [1]	10†	5

[1] Ruff Driverz presents Arrola

Frances RUFFELLE UK, female vocalist   6 wks

16 Apr 94	LONELY SYMPHONY *Virgin VSCDT 1499*	25	6

Bruce RUFFIN ⍒ Jamaica, male vocalist   23 wks

1 May 71	RAIN *Trojan TR 7814*	19	11
24 Jun 72 ●	MAD ABOUT YOU *Rhino RNO 101*	9	12

David RUFFIN 🎤 US, male vocalist   10 wks

17 Jan 76 ●	WALK AWAY FROM LOVE *Tamla Motown TMG 1017*	10	8
21 Sep 85	A NIGHT AT THE APOLLO LIVE! *RCA PB 49935* [1]	58	2

[1] Hall and Oates featuring David Ruffin and Eddie Kendrick

Jimmy RUFFIN 🎤 Major Motown hitmaker, b. 7 May, 1939, Mississippi.

After rejecting a job as the lead vocalist of The Temptations (in favour of his brother David), he had a handful of UK/US hits (several charting twice). He relocated to UK, and was in a one-off hit act, Council Collective   106 wks

27 Oct 66 ●	WHAT BECOMES OF THE BROKENHEARTED		
	Tamla Motown TMG 577	8	15
9 Feb 67	I'VE PASSED THIS WAY BEFORE *Tamla Motown TMG 593*	29	7
20 Apr 67	GONNA GIVE HER ALL THE LOVE I'VE GOT		
	Tamla Motown TMG 603	26	6
9 Aug 69	I'VE PASSED THIS WAY BEFORE (re-issue)		
	Tamla Motown TMG 703	33	6
28 Feb 70 ●	FAREWELL IS A LONELY SOUND *Tamla Motown TMG 726*	8	16
4 Jul 70 ●	I'LL SAY FOREVER MY LOVE *Tamla Motown TMG 740*	7	12
17 Oct 70 ●	IT'S WONDERFUL (TO BE LOVED BY YOU)		
	Tamla Motown TMG 753	6	14
27 Jul 74 ●	WHAT BECOMES OF THE BROKENHEARTED (re-issue)		
	Tamla Motown TMG 911	4	12
2 Nov 74	FAREWELL IS A LONELY SOUND (re-issue)		
	Tamla Motown TMG 922	30	5
16 Nov 74	TELL ME WHAT YOU WANT *Polydor 2058 433*	39	4

3 May 80 ●	HOLD ON TO MY LOVE *RSO 57*	7	8
26 Jan 85	THERE WILL NEVER BE ANOTHER YOU *EMI 5541*	68	1

See also COUNCIL COLLECTIVE

RUFFNECK featuring YAVAHN ☺
US, male/female vocal/instrumental group   5 wks

11 Nov 95	EVERYBODY BE SOMEBODY *Positiva CDTIV 46*	13	4
7 Sep 96	MOVE YOUR BODY *Positiva CDTIV 61*	60	1

RUFUS – See Chaka KHAN

Barbara RUICK – See VARIOUS ARTISTS (EPs & LPs) – Carousel LP

RUKMANI – See SNAP

RUMOUR – See Graham PARKER and the RUMOUR

RUMPLE-STILTS-SKIN
US, male/female vocal/instrumental group   4 wks

24 Sep 83	I THINK I WANT TO DANCE WITH YOU *Polydor POSP 649*	51	4

RUN-DMC ☎ US, male rap group   59 wks

19 Jul 86	MY ADIDAS/PETER PIPER *London LON 101*	62	2
6 Sep 86 ●	WALK THIS WAY *London LON 104*	8	10
7 Feb 87	YOU BE ILLIN' *Profile LON 118*	42	4
30 May 87	IT'S TRICKY *Profile LON 130*	16	7
12 Dec 87	CHRISTMAS IN HOLLIS *Profile LON 163*	56	4
21 May 88	RUN'S HOUSE *London LON 177*	37	4
2 Sep 89	GHOSTBUSTERS *MCA Profile MCA 1360*	65	2
1 Dec 90	WHAT'S IT ALL ABOUT *Profile PROF 315*	48	3
27 Mar 93	DOWN WITH THE KING *Profile PROFCD 39*	69	2
21 Feb 98	IT'S LIKE THAT (IMPORT) *Columbia 6652932* [1]	63	3
21 Mar 98 ★	IT'S LIKE THAT (re-mix)		
	Smile Communications SM 90652 [1] ◆ ■	1	17
18 Apr 98	IT'S TRICKY (re-mix) *Epidrome EPD 6656982* [1]	74	1

[1] Run-DMC vs Jason Nevins

RUN TINGS UK, male instrumental/production duo   1 wk

16 May 92	FIRES BURNING *Suburban Base SUBBASE 009*	58	1

See also VARIOUS ARTISTS (EPs & LPs) – Subplates Volume 1

Todd RUNDGREN US, male vocalist   8 wks

30 Jun 73	I SAW THE LIGHT *Bearsville K 15506*	36	6
14 Dec 85	LOVING YOU'S A DIRTY JOB BUT SOMEBODY'S GOTTA DO IT		
	CBS A 6662 [1]	73	2

[1] Bonnie Tyler, guest vocals Todd Rundgren

RUNRIG ♂ 🎸 UK, male vocal/instrumental group   28 wks

29 Sep 90	CAPTURE THE HEART EP *Chrysalis CHS 3594*	49	2
7 Sep 91	HEARTHAMMER EP *Chrysalis CHS 3754*	25	4
9 Nov 91	FLOWER OF THE WEST *Chrysalis CHS 3805*	43	2
6 Mar 93	WONDERFUL *Chrysalis CDCHS 3952*	29	3
15 May 93	THE GREATEST FLAME *Chrysalis CDCHS 3975*	36	3
7 Jan 95	THIS TIME OF YEAR *Chrysalis CDCHS 5018*	38	2
6 May 95	AN UBHAL AS AIRDE (THE HIGHEST APPLE)		
	Chrysalis CDCHS 5021	18	5
4 Nov 95	THINGS THAT ARE *Chrysalis CDCHS 5029*	40	2
12 Oct 96	RHYTHM OF MY HEART *Chrysalis CDCHS 5035*	24	2
11 Jan 97 ●	THE GREATEST FLAME (re-issue) *Chrysalis CDCHSS 5045*	30	3

Tracks on Capture The Heart EP: Stepping Down the Glory Road / Satellite Flood / Harvest Moon / The Apple Came Down. Tracks on Hearthammer (EP): Hearthammer / Pride of the Summer (Live) / Loch Lomond (Live) / Solus Na Madain.

RuPAUL ☺ ☯ US, male vocalist   19 wks

26 Jun 93	SUPERMODEL (YOU BETTER WORK) *Union City UCRD 21*	39	4
18 Sep 93	HOUSE OF LOVE/BACK TO MY ROOTS *Union City UCRD 23*	40	2
22 Jan 94	SUPERMODEL (RE-MIX)/LITTLE DRUMMER BOY (re-mix)		
	Union City UCRD 25	61	2

26 Feb 94	● DON'T GO BREAKING MY HEART (re-mix)		
	Rocket EJCD 33 [1]	7	7
21 May 94	HOUSE OF LOVE Union City UCRDG 29	68	1
28 Feb 98	IT'S RAINING MEN…THE SEQUEL		
	Logic 74321555412 [2]	21	3

[1] Elton John with RuPaul [2] Martha Wash featuring RuPaul

RUSH ⌁ Canada, male vocal/instrumental group — 43 wks

11 Feb 78	CLOSER TO THE HEART Mercury RUSH 7	36	3
15 Mar 80	SPIRIT OF RADIO Mercury RADIO 7	13	7
28 Mar 81	VITAL SIGNS/A PASSAGE TO BANGKOK		
	Mercury VITAL7	41	4
31 Oct 81	TOM SAWYER Exit EXIT 7	25	6
4 Sep 82	NEW WORLD MAN Mercury RUSH 8	42	3
30 Oct 82	SUBDIVISIONS Mercury RUSH 9	53	2
7 May 83	COUNTDOWN/NEW WORLD MAN		
	Mercury RUSH 10	36	5
26 May 84	THE BODY ELECTRIC Vertigo RUSH 11	56	3
12 Oct 85	THE BIG MONEY Vertigo RUSH 12	46	3
31 Oct 87	TIME STAND STILL Vertigo RUSH 13 [1]	42	3
23 Apr 88	PRIME MOVER Vertigo RUSH 14	43	3
7 Mar 92	ROLL THE BONES Atlantic A 7524	49	1

[1] Rush with Aimee Mann

'New World Man' on RUSH 10 is a live version of RUSH 8

Donell RUSH US, male vocalist — 1 wk

5 Dec 92	SYMPHONY ID 6587977	66	1

Jennifer RUSH ◉ US, female vocalist — 58 wks

29 Jun 85	★ THE POWER OF LOVE CBS A 5003 ◆	1	32
14 Dec 85	RING OF ICE CBS A 4745	14	10
20 Dec 86	THE POWER OF LOVE (re-entry) CBS A 5003	55	4
20 Jun 87	FLAMES OF PARADISE CBS 650865 [1]	59	3
27 May 89	TILL I LOVED YOU CBS 654843 7 [2]	24	9

[1] Jennifer Rush and Elton John [2] Placido Domingo and Jennifer Rush

Patrice RUSHEN ♪ ⚞ US, female vocalist — 25 wks

1 Mar 80	HAVEN'T YOU HEARD Elektra K 12414	62	3
24 Jan 81	NEVER GONNA GIVE YOU UP (WON'T LET YOU BE)		
	Elektra K 12494	66	3
24 Apr 82	● FORGET ME NOTS Elektra K 13173	8	11
10 Jul 82	I WAS TIRED OF BEING ALONE Elektra K 13184	39	5
9 Jun 84	FEELS SO REAL (WON'T LET GO) Elektra E 9742	51	3

Brenda RUSSELL US, female vocalist — 17 wks

19 Apr 80	SO GOOD SO RIGHT/IN THE THICK OF IT		
	A & M AM 7515	51	5
12 Mar 88	PIANO IN THE DARK Breakout USA 623	23	12

RUTH UK, male vocal / instrumental group — 1 wk

12 Apr 97	I DON'T KNOW Arc 5737812	66	1

Paul RUTHERFORD UK, male vocalist — 6 wks

8 Oct 88	GET REAL Fourth & Broadway BRW 113	47	3
19 Aug 89	OH WORLD Fourth & Broadway BRW 136	61	3

RUTHLESS RAP ASSASSINS UK, male rappers — 2 wks

9 Jun 90	JUST MELLOW Syncopate SY 35	75	1
1 Sep 90	AND IT WASN'T A DREAM Syncopate SY 38	75	1

RUTLES UK, male vocal group — 5 wks

15 Apr 78	I MUST BE IN LOVE Warner Bros. K 17125	39	3
13 May 78	I MUST BE IN LOVE (re-entry)		
	Warner Bros. K 17125	64	1
16 Nov 96	SHANGRI-LA Virgin America VUSCD 117	68	1

RUTS ✍ UK, male vocal/instrumental group — 28 wks

16 Jun 79	● BABYLON'S BURNING Virgin VS 271	7	11
8 Sep 79	SOMETHING THAT I SAID Virgin VS 285	29	5
19 Apr 80	STARING AT THE RUDE BOYS Virgin VS 327	22	8
30 Aug 80	WEST ONE (SHINE ON ME) Virgin VS 370	43	4

Barry RYAN ◉ UK, male vocalist — 33 wks

23 Oct 68	● ELOISE MGM 1442	2	12
19 Feb 69	LOVE IS LOVE MGM 1464	25	4
4 Oct 69	HUNT Polydor 56 348	34	5
21 Feb 70	MAGICAL SPIEL Polydor 56 370	49	1
16 May 70	KITSCH Polydor 2001 035	37	6
15 Jan 72	CAN'T LET YOU GO Polydor 2001 256	32	5

See also Paul and Barry RYAN

Marion RYAN ℂ UK, female vocalist — 11 wks

24 Jan 58	● LOVE ME FOREVER Pye Nixa N 15121	5	11

Paul and Barry RYAN ◉ UK, male vocal duo — 43 wks

11 Nov 65	DON'T BRING ME YOUR HEARTACHES		
	Decca F 12260	13	9
3 Feb 66	HAVE PITY ON THE BOY Decca F 12319	18	6
12 May 66	I LOVE HER Decca F 12391	17	8
14 Jul 66	I LOVE HOW YOU LOVE ME Decca F 12445	21	7
29 Sep 66	HAVE YOU EVER LOVED SOMEBODY		
	Decca F 12494	49	1
8 Dec 66	MISSY MISSY Decca F 12520	43	4
2 Mar 67	KEEP IT OUT OF SIGHT Decca F 12567	30	6
29 Jun 67	CLAIRE Decca F 12633	47	2

See also Barry RYAN

Rebekah RYAN UK, female vocalist — 5 wks

18 May 96	YOU LIFT ME UP MCA MCSTD 40022	26	3
7 Sep 96	JUST A LITTLE BIT OF LOVE MCA MCSTD 40063	51	1
17 May 97	WOMAN IN LOVE MCA MCSTD 40109	64	1

Bobby RYDELL ◉ US, male vocalist — 60 wks

10 Mar 60	● WILD ONE Columbia DB 4429	7	14
23 Jun 60	WILD ONE (re-entry) Columbia DB 4429	47	1
30 Jun 60	SWINGING SCHOOL Columbia DB 4471	44	1
1 Sep 60	VOLARE Columbia DB 4495	46	1
15 Sep 60	VOLARE (re-entry) Columbia DB 4495	22	5
15 Dec 60	SWAY Columbia DB 4545	12	13
23 Mar 61	GOOD TIME BABY Columbia DB 4600	42	7
19 Apr 62	TEACH ME TO TWIST Columbia DB 4802 [1]	45	1
20 Dec 62	JINGLE BELL ROCK Cameo Parkway C 205 [1]	40	3
23 May 63	FORGET HIM Cameo Parkway C 108	13	14

[1] Chubby Checker and Bobby Rydell

Mitch RYDER and the DETROIT WHEELS
US, male vocalist, male vocal/instrumental backing group — 5 wks

10 Feb 66	JENNY TAKE A RIDE Stateside SS 481	44	1
24 Feb 66	JENNY TAKE A RIDE (re-entry)		
	Stateside SS 481	33	4

Shaun RYDER – See BLACK GRAPE; HAPPY MONDAYS; HEADS with Shaun RYDER

RYTHM SYNDICATE
US, male vocal/instrumental group — 5 wks

27 Jul 91	P.A.S.S.I.O.N. Impact American EM 197	58	5

Les RYTHMES DIGITALES
UK, male DJ/production project – Jacques Lu Cont — 1 wk

25 Apr 98	MUSIC MAKES YOU LOSE CONTROL		
	Wall Of Sound WALLD 037	69	1

UK No 1 ★   UK Top 10 ●   UK million seller ◆   UK entry at No 1 ■   US No 1 ▲

S

Robin S ☺ *US, female vocalist*   36 wks

16 Jan 93		SHOW ME LOVE *Champion CHAMPCD 300*	59 4
13 Mar 93	●	SHOW ME LOVE (re-entry) *Champion CHAMPCD 300*	6 13
31 Jul 93		LUV 4 LUV *Champion CHAMPCD 301*	11 7
4 Dec 93		WHAT I DO BEST *Champion CHAMPCD 307*	43 2
19 Mar 94		I WANT TO THANK YOU *Champion CHAMPCD 310*	48 1
5 Nov 94		BACK IT UP *Champion CHAMPCD 312*	43 2
8 Mar 97	●	SHOW ME LOVE (re-mix) *Champion CHAMPCD 326*	9 5
12 Jul 97		IT MUST BE LOVE *Atlantic A 5596CD*	37 1
4 Oct 97		YOU GOT THE LOVE *Champion CHAMPCD 330* [1]	62 1

[1] T2 featuring Robin S

S EXPRESS ☺ *UK, male/female vocal/instrumental group*   50 wks

16 Apr 88	★	THEME FROM S-EXPRESS *Rhythm King LEFT 21*	1 13
23 Jul 88	●	SUPERFLY GUY *Rhythm King LEFT 28*	5 9
18 Feb 89		HEY MUSIC LOVER *Rhythm King LEFT 30*	6 10
16 Sep 89		MANTRA FOR A STATE OF MIND *Rhythm King LEFT 35*	21 8
15 Sep 90		NOTHING TO LOSE *Rhythm King SEXY 01*	32 4
30 May 92		FIND 'EM, FOOL 'EM, FORGET 'EM *Rhythm King 6580137*	43 2
11 May 96		THEME FROM S.EXPRESS (re-mix) *Rhythm King SEXY 9CD* [1]	14 4

[1] Mark Moore presents S Express

S-J *UK, female vocalist*   4 wks

11 Jan 97	FEVER *React CDREACT93*	46 1
24 Jan 98	I FEEL DIVINE *React CDREACT 113*	30 2
7 Nov 98	SHIVER *React CDREACT 138*	59 1

Raphael SAADIQ – *See TRIBE CALLED QUEST*

SABRE featuring PRESIDENT BROWN
Jamaica, male vocal duo   1 wk

19 Aug 95	WRONG OR RIGHT *Greensleeves GRECD 485*	71 1

SABRES – *See Denny SEYTON and the SABRES*

SABRES OF PARADISE *UK, male instrumental group*   8 wks

2 Oct 93	SMOKEBELCH II *Sabres Of Paradise PT 009CD*	55 3
9 Apr 94	THEME *Sabres Of Paradise PT 014CD*	56 3
17 Sep 94	WILMOT *Warp WAP 50CD*	36 2

SABRINA ◐ *Italy, female vocalist*   22 wks

6 Feb 88		BOYS (SUMMERTIME LOVE) *IBIZA IBIZ 1*	60 3
11 Jun 88	●	BOYS (SUMMERTIME LOVE) (re-entry) *IBIZA IBIZ 1*	3 11
1 Oct 88		ALL OF ME *PWL PWL 19*	25 7
1 Jul 89		LIKE A YO-YO *Videogram DCUP 1*	72 1

SACRED SPIRIT *European, anonymous male producer*
utilizing Native American chants   5 wks

15 Apr 95	YEHA-NOHA (WISHES OF HAPPINESS AND PROSPERITY) *Virgin VSCDT 1514*	71 1
18 Nov 95	WISHES OF HAPPINESS AND PROSPERITY (YEHA-NOHA) (re-entry) *Virgin VSCDT 1514*	37 2
16 Mar 96	WINTER CEREMONY (TOR-CHENEY-NAHANA) *Virgin VSCDT 1574*	45 2

SAD CAFE ♪ *UK, male vocal/instrumental group*   44 wks

22 Sep 79	●	EVERY DAY HURTS *RCA PB 5180*	3 12
19 Jan 80		STRANGE LITTLE GIRL *RCA PB 5202*	32 5
15 Mar 80		MY OH MY *RCA SAD 3*	14 11
21 Jun 80		NOTHING LEFT TOULOUSE *RCA SAD 4*	62 4
27 Sep 80		LA-DI-DA *RCA SAD 5*	41 6
20 Dec 80		I'M IN LOVE AGAIN *RCA SAD 6*	40 6

SADE ◐ ♪ *UK, female/male vocal/instrumental group*   63 wks

25 Feb 84	●	YOUR LOVE IS KING *Epic A 4137*	6 11
19 May 84		YOUR LOVE IS KING (re-entry) *Epic A 4137*	75 1
26 May 84		WHEN AM I GONNA MAKE A LIVING *Epic A 4437*	36 5
15 Sep 84		SMOOTH OPERATOR *Epic A 4655*	19 10
12 Oct 85		THE SWEETEST TABOO *Epic A 6609*	31 5
11 Jan 86		IS IT A CRIME *Epic A 6742*	49 3
2 Apr 88		LOVE IS STRONGER THAN PRIDE *Epic SADE 1*	44 3
4 Jun 88		PARADISE *Epic SADE 2*	29 7
10 Oct 92		NO ORDINARY LOVE *Epic 6583567*	26 3
28 Nov 92		FEEL NO PAIN *Epic 6588297*	56 2
8 May 93		KISS OF LIFE *Epic 6591162*	44 3
5 Jun 93		NO ORDINARY LOVE (re-entry) *Epic 6583562*	14 8
31 Jul 93		CHERISH THE DAY *Epic 6594812*	53 2

Staff Sergeant Barry SADLER *US, male vocalist*   8 wks

24 Mar 66	BALLAD OF THE GREEN BERETS *RCA 1506* ▲	24 8

SAFFRON *UK, female vocalist*   2 wks

16 Jan 93	CIRCLES *WEA SAFF 9CD*	60 2

See also REPUBLICA

SAFFRONS – *See CINDY and the SAFFRONS*

Mike SAGAR *UK, male vocalist*   5 wks

8 Dec 60	DEEP FEELING *HMV POP 819*	44 5

SAGAT *US, male rapper*   6 wks

4 Dec 93	FUNK DAT *ffrr FCD 224*	25 5
3 Dec 94	LUVSTUFF *ffrr FCD 250*	71 1

Carole Bayer SAGER ◐ *US, female vocalist*   9 wks

28 May 77	● YOU'RE MOVING OUT TODAY *Elektra K 12257*	6 9

Bally SAGOO ☺ 🌐 *India, male producer*   8 wks

3 Sep 94	CHURA LIYA *Columbia 6607092*	64 1
22 Apr 95	CHOLI KE PEECHE *Columbia 6613352*	45 1
19 Oct 96	DIL CHEEZ (MY HEART...) *Higher Ground 6634882*	12 3
1 Feb 97	TUM BIN JIYA *Higher Ground 6641372*	21 3

SAILOR ◐ *UK, male vocal/instrumental group*   24 wks

6 Dec 75	●	GLASS OF CHAMPAGNE *Epic EPC 3770*	2 12
27 Mar 76	●	GIRLS GIRLS GIRLS *Epic EPC 3858*	7 8
19 Feb 77		ONE DRINK TOO MANY *Epic EPC 4804*	35 4

ST. ANDREWS CHORALE *UK, church choir*   5 wks

14 Feb 76	CLOUD 99 *Decca F 13617*	31 5

ST. CECILIA ◐ *UK, male vocal/instrumental group*   17 wks

19 Jun 71	LEAP UP AND DOWN (WAVE YOUR KNICKERS IN THE AIR) *Polydor 2058 104*	12 17

SAINT ETIENNE ☹ ☺
UK, male/female vocal/instrumental group   44 wks

18 May 91	NOTHING CAN STOP US/SPEEDWELL *Heavenly HVN 009*	54 3
7 Sep 91	ONLY LOVE CAN BREAK YOUR HEART/FILTHY *Heavenly HVN 12*	39 4
16 May 92	JOIN OUR CLUB/PEOPLE GET REAL *Heavenly HVN 15*	21 3

17 Oct 92	AVENUE *Heavenly HVN 2312*	40	2
13 Feb 93	YOU'RE IN A BAD WAY *Heavenly HVN 25CD*	12	5
22 May 93	HOBART PAVING/WHO DO YOU THINK YOU ARE *Heavenly HVN 29CD*	23	5
18 Dec 93	I WAS BORN ON CHRISTMAS DAY *Heavenly HVN 36CD*	37	5
19 Feb 94	PALE MOVIE *Heavenly HVN 37CD*	28	3
28 May 94	LIKE A MOTORWAY *Heavenly HVN 40CD*	47	2
1 Oct 94	HUG MY SOUL *Heavenly HVN 42CD*	32	2
11 Nov 95	HE'S ON THE PHONE *Heavenly HVN 50CDR* [1]	11	5
7 Feb 98	SYLVIE *Creation CRESCD 279*	12	3
2 May 98	THE BAD PHOTOGRAPHER *Creation CRESCD 290*	27	2

[1] Saint Etienne featuring Etienne Daho

See also Sarah CRACKNELL; VARIOUS ARTISTS (EPs & LPs) – The Fred EP

ST. GERMAIN *France, male producer* — 1 wk

31 Aug 96	ALABAMA BLUES (REVISITED) *F Communications F 050CD*	50	1

Barry ST. JOHN *UK, female vocalist* — 1 wk

9 Dec 65	COME AWAY MELINDA *Columbia DB 7783*	47	1

ST. JOHN'S COLLEGE SCHOOL CHOIR and the Band of the GRENADIER GUARDS *UK, school choir and military band* — 3 wks

3 May 86	THE QUEEN'S BIRTHDAY SONG *Columbia Q1*	40	3

ST. LOUIS UNION ○ *UK, male vocal/instrumental group* — 10 wks

13 Jan 66	GIRL *Decca F 12318*	11	10

Crispian ST. PETERS ○ *UK, male vocalist* — 31 wks

6 Jan 66 ●	YOU WERE ON MY MIND *Decca F 12287*	2	14
31 Mar 66 ●	PIED PIPER *Decca F 12359*	5	13
15 Sep 66	CHANGES *Decca F 12480*	49	1
29 Sep 66	CHANGES (re-entry) *Decca F 12480*	47	3

ST. PHILIPS CHOIR *UK, choir* — 4 wks

12 Dec 87	SING FOR EVER *BBC RESL 222*	49	4

ST. THOMAS MORE SCHOOL CHOIR – *See Scott FITZGERALD*

ST. WINIFRED'S SCHOOL CHOIR ℂ *UK, school choir* — 11 wks

22 Nov 80 ★	THERE'S NO ONE QUITE LIKE GRANDMA *MFP FP 900*	1	11

Buffy SAINTE-MARIE ♂ *Canada, female vocalist* — 29 wks

17 Jul 71 ●	SOLDIER BLUE *RCA 2081*	7	18
18 Mar 72	I'M GONNA BE A COUNTRY GIRL AGAIN *Vanguard VRS 35143*	34	5
8 Feb 92	THE BIG ONES GET AWAY *Ensign ENY 650*	39	5
4 Jul 92	FALLEN ANGELS *Ensign ENY 655*	57	1

SAINTS *Australia, male vocal/instrumental group* — 4 wks

16 Jul 77	THIS PERFECT DAY *Harvest HAR 5130*	34	4

Kyu SAKAMOTO ℂ *Japan, male vocalist* — 13 wks

27 Jun 63 ●	SUKIYAKI *HMV POP 1171* ▲	6	13

Ryuichi SAKAMOTO – *See David SYLVIAN*

SAKKARIN – *See Jonathan KING*

SALAD *UK/Holland, male/female vocal/instrumental group* — 5 wks

11 Mar 95	DRINK THE ELIXIR *Island Red CIRD 104*	66	1
13 May 95	MOTORBIKE TO HEAVEN *Island Red CIRD 106*	42	1
16 Sep 95	GRANITE STATUE *Island Red CIRD 108*	50	1
26 Oct 96	I WANT YOU *Island CID 646*	60	1
17 May 97	CARDBOY KING *Island CID 654*	65	1

SALFORD JETS *UK, male vocal/instrumental group* — 2 wks

31 May 80	WHO YOU LOOKING AT *RCA PB 5239*	72	2

SALSOUL ORCHESTRA – *See CHARO and the SALSOUL ORCHESTRA*

SALT TANK *UK, male instrumental group* — 2 wks

11 May 96	EUGINA *Internal LIECD 29*	40	2

SALT-N-PEPA ◀ *Rappers Cheryl 'Salt' James (b. 28 March, 1969, Brooklyn, USA) and Sandra 'Pepa' Denton (b. 9 November, 1969, Kingston, Jamaica), backed-up by DJ Dee Dee 'Spinderella' Roper, are the most commercially successful female rap troupe of all time* — 118 wks

26 Mar 88	PUSH IT/I AM DOWN *ffrr FFR 2*	41	6
25 Jun 88 ●	PUSH IT/TRAMP *Champion CHAMP 51 & ffrr FFR 2*	2	13
3 Sep 88	SHAKE YOUR THANG (IT'S YOUR THING) *ffrr FFR 11* [1]	22	8
12 Nov 88 ●	TWIST AND SHOUT *ffrr FFR 16*	4	9
14 Apr 90	EXPRESSION *ffrr F 127*	40	6
25 May 91 ●	DO YOU WANT ME *ffrr F 151*	5	12
31 Aug 91 ●	LET'S TALK ABOUT SEX *ffrr F 162* [2]	2	13
30 Nov 91	YOU SHOWED ME *ffrr F 174*	15	9
28 Mar 92	EXPRESSION (re-mix) *ffrr F 182*	23	6
3 Oct 92	START ME UP *ffrr F 196*	39	3
9 Oct 93	SHOOP *ffrr FCD 219*	29	3
19 Mar 94 ●	WHATTA MAN *ffrr FCD 222* [3]	7	10
28 May 94	SHOOP (re-mix) *ffrr FCD 234*	13	8
12 Nov 94	NONE OF YOUR BUSINESS *ffrr FCD 244*	19	4
7 Jan 95	NONE OF YOUR BUSINESS (re-entry) *ffrr FCD 244*	64	1
21 Dec 96	CHAMPAGNE *MCA MCSTD 48025*	23	5
29 Nov 97	R U READY *ffrr FCDP 322*	24	2

[1] Salt-N-Pepa featuring E.U. [2] Salt-N-Pepa featuring Psychotropic
[3] Salt-N-Pepa with En Vogue

'I Am Down' only listed from 2 April, 1988. The disc re-entered on 25 June when it was made available on Champion with a different flip side. Sales for both discs were amalgamated

SAM and DAVE ♪ *US, male vocal duo* — 39 wks

16 Mar 67	SOOTHE ME *Stax 601 004*	48	2
13 Apr 67	SOOTHE ME (re-entry) *Stax 601 004*	35	6
1 Nov 67	SOUL MAN *Stax 601 023*	24	14
13 Mar 68	I THANK YOU *Stax 601 030*	34	9
29 Jan 69	SOUL SISTER BROWN SUGAR *Atlantic 584 237*	15	8

See also Lou Reed

SAM THE SHAM and the PHARAOHS ○ *US, male vocal/instrumental group* — 18 wks

24 Jun 65	WOOLY BULLY *MGM 1269*	11	15
4 Aug 66	LIL' RED RIDING HOOD *MGM 1315*	48	1
18 Aug 66	LIL' RED RIDING HOOD (re-entry) *MGM 1315*	46	2

Richie SAMBORA *US, male vocalist/instrumentalist – bass* — 4 wks

7 Sep 91	BALLAD OF YOUTH *Mercury MER 350*	59	1
7 Mar 98	HARD TIMES COME EASY *Mercury 5686972*	37	2
1 Aug 98	IN IT FOR LOVE *Mercury 5660632*	58	1

Mike SAMMES SINGERS ℂ *UK, male/female vocal group* — 38 wks

15 Sep 66	SOMEWHERE MY LOVE *HMV POP 1546*	22	19
12 Jul 67	SOMEWHERE MY LOVE (re-entry) *HMV POP 1546*	14	19

Dave SAMPSON *UK, male vocalist* — 6 wks

19 May 60	SWEET DREAMS *Columbia DB 4449*	48	1
2 Jun 60	SWEET DREAMS (re-entry) *Columbia DB 4449*	29	5

SAMSON *UK, male vocal/instrumental group* — 6 wks

4 Jul 81	RIDING WITH THE ANGELS *RCA 67*	55	3
24 Jul 82	LOSING MY GRIP *Polydor POSP 471*	63	2
5 Mar 83	RED SKIES *Polydor POSP 554*	65	1

SAN JOSE featuring Rodriguez ARGENTINA ⊗
UK, male instrumental group   **8 wks**

| 17 Jun 78 | ARGENTINE MELODY (CANCION DE ARGENTINA) *MCA 369* | 14 | 8 |

Rodriguez Argentina is Rod Argent.
See also ARGENT; SILSOE

SAN REMO STRINGS *US, orchestra*   **8 wks**

| 18 Dec 71 | FESTIVAL TIME *Tamla Motown TMG 795* | 39 | 8 |

Chris SANDFORD ⊗ *UK, male vocalist*   **9 wks**

| 12 Dec 63 | NOT TOO LITTLE NOT TOO MUCH *Decca F 11778* | 17 | 9 |

SANDPIPERS ℂ *US, male vocal group*   **33 wks**

15 Sep 66 ●	GUANTANAMERA *Pye International 7N 25380*	7	17
5 Jun 68	QUANDO M'INNAMORO (A MAN WITHOUT LOVE) *A & M AMS 723*	33	6
26 Mar 69	KUMBAYA *A & M AMS 744*	38	1
9 Apr 69	KUMBAYA (re-entry) *A & M AMS 744*	49	1
27 Nov 76	HANG ON SLOOPY *Satril SAT 114*	32	8

SANDRA *Germany, female vocalist*   **8 wks**

| 17 Dec 88 | EVERLASTING LOVE *Siren SRN 85* | 45 | 8 |

Jodie SANDS ⊗ *US, female vocalist*   **10 wks**

| 17 Oct 58 | SOMEDAY (YOU'LL WANT ME TO WANT YOU) *HMV POP 533* | 14 | 10 |

Tommy SANDS *US, male vocalist*   **7 wks**

| 4 Aug 60 | OLD OAKEN BUCKET *Capitol CL 15143* | 25 | 7 |

Samantha SANG ⊗ *Australia, female vocalist*   **13 wks**

| 4 Feb 78 | EMOTION *Private Stock PVT 128* | 11 | 13 |

SANTA CLAUS and the CHRISTMAS TREES ⊗
UK, male vocal/instrumental group   **10 wks**

| 11 Dec 82 | SINGALONG-A-SANTA *Polydor IVY 1* | 19 | 5 |
| 10 Dec 83 | SINGALONG-A-SANTA AGAIN *Polydor IVY 2* | 39 | 5 |

SANTA ESMERALDA and Leroy GOMEZ
US/France, male/female vocal/instrumental group   **5 wks**

| 12 Nov 77 | DON'T LET ME BE MISUNDERSTOOD *Philips 6042 325* | 41 | 5 |

SANTANA ✔ *US, male vocal/instrumental group*   **25 wks**

28 Sep 74	SAMBA PA TI *CBS 2561*	27	7
15 Oct 77	SHE'S NOT THERE *CBS 5671*	11	12
25 Nov 78	WELL ALL RIGHT *CBS 6755*	53	3
22 Mar 80	ALL I EVER WANTED *CBS 8160*	57	3

SANTO and JOHNNY
US, male instrumental duo – steel and electric guitars   **5 wks**

| 16 Oct 59 | SLEEP WALK *Pye International 7N 25037* ▲ | 22 | 4 |
| 31 Mar 60 | TEARDROP *Parlophone R 4619* | 50 | 1 |

Mike SARNE ⊗ *UK, male vocalist*   **43 wks**

10 May 62 ★	COME OUTSIDE *Parlophone R 4902* [1]	1	19
30 Aug 62	WILL I WHAT *Parlophone R 4932* [2]	18	10
10 Jan 63	JUST FOR KICKS *Parlophone R 4974*	22	7
28 Mar 63	CODE OF LOVE *Parlophone R 5010*	29	7

[1] Mike Sarne with Wendy Richard [2] Mike Sarne with Billie Davis

Joy SARNEY *UK, female vocalist*   **6 wks**

| 7 May 77 | NAUGHTY NAUGHTY NAUGHTY *Alaska ALA 2005* | 26 | 6 |

SARR BAND
Italy/UK/France, male/female vocal/instrumental group   **1 wk**

| 16 Sep 78 | MAGIC MANDRAKE *Calendar Day 111* | 68 | 1 |

Peter SARSTEDT ⊗ *UK, male vocalist*   **25 wks**

| 5 Feb 69 ★ | WHERE DO YOU GO TO MY LOVELY *United Artists UP 2262* | 1 | 16 |
| 4 Jun 69 ● | FROZEN ORANGE JUICE *United Artists UP 35021* | 10 | 9 |

Robin SARSTEDT ⊗ *UK, male vocalist*   **9 wks**

| 8 May 76 ● | MY RESISTANCE IS LOW *Decca F 13624* | 3 | 9 |

SARTORELLO *Italy, male/female vocal/instrumental duo*   **1 wk**

| 10 Aug 96 | MOVE BABY MOVE *Multiply CDMULTY 12* | 56 | 1 |

SASH! ☺ *Germany, male DJ/producer*   **70 wks**

1 Mar 97 ●	ENCORE UNE FOIS *Multiply CDMULTY 18*	2	15
5 Jul 97 ●	ECUADOR *Multiply CDMULTY 23* [1]	2	12
18 Oct 97 ●	STAY *Multiply CDMULTY 26* [2]	2	14
4 Apr 98 ●	LA PRIMAVERA *Multiply CXMULTY 32*	3	12
15 Aug 98 ●	MYSTERIOUS TIMES *Multiply CXMULTY 40* [3]	2	12
28 Nov 98 ●	MOVE MANIA *Multiply CDMULTY 45* [4]	8†	5

[1] Sash! featuring Rodriguez [2] Sash! featuring La Trec [3] Sash! featuring Tina Cousins [4] Sash! featuring Shannon

SASHA ☺ *UK, male producer*   **12 wks**

31 Jul 93	TOGETHER *ffrr FCD 212* [1]	57	1
19 Feb 94	HIGHER GROUND *Deconstruction 74321189002* [2]	19	3
27 Aug 94	MAGIC *Deconstruction 74321221862* [2]	32	4
9 Mar 96	BE AS ONE *Deconstruction 74321342962* [3]	17	4

[1] Danny Campbell and Sasha [2] Sasha with Sam Mollison [3] Sasha and Maria

Joe SATRIANI *US, male/vocalist/instrumentalist – guitar*   **1 wk**

| 13 Feb 93 | THE SATCH EP *Relativity 6589532* | 53 | 1 |

Tracks on The Satch EP: The Extremist / Banana Mango / Summer Song / Crazy

SATURDAY NIGHT BAND ◢ *US, male vocal/instrumental group*   **9 wks**

| 1 Jul 78 | COME ON DANCE DANCE *CBS 6367* | 16 | 9 |

Deion SAUNDERS – *See HAMMER*

Kevin SAUNDERSON – *See INNER CITY*

Chantay SAVAGE 〔R&B〕 *US, female vocalist*   **9 wks**

| 4 May 96 | I WILL SURVIVE *RCA 74321377682* | 12 | 8 |
| 8 Nov 97 | REMINDING (OF SEF) *Relativity 6650672* [1] | 59 | 1 |

[1] Common featuring Chantay Savage

Edna SAVAGE ℂ *UK, female vocalist*   **1 wk**

| 13 Jan 56 | ARRIVEDERCI DARLING *Parlophone R 4097* | 19 | 1 |

SAVAGE GARDEN ⊗ ✔
Australia, male vocal/instrumental duo   **50 wks**

21 Jun 97	I WANT YOU *Columbia 6645452*	11	7
27 Sep 97	TO THE MOON AND BACK *Columbia 6648932*	55	1
28 Feb 98 ●	TRULY MADLY DEEPLY *Columbia 6656022* ▲	4	23
22 Aug 98	TO THE MOON AND BACK (re-issue) *Columbia 6662882*	3	16
12 Dec 98	I WANT YOU '98 (re-mix) *Columbia 6667332*	12†	3

Telly SAVALAS ℂ *US, male vocalist*   **12 wks**

| 22 Feb 75 ★ | IF *MCA 174* | 1 | 9 |
| 31 May 75 | YOU'VE LOST THAT LOVIN' FEELING *MCA 189* | 47 | 3 |

SAVANNA *UK, male vocal group*   **4 wks**

| 10 Oct 81 | I CAN'T TURN AWAY *R & B RBS 203* | 61 | 4 |

SAW DOCTORS ♂ ✏ *Ireland, male vocal/instrumental group* 9 wks

12 Nov 94	SMALL BIT OF LOVE *Shamtown SAW 001CD*	24	3
27 Jan 96	WORLD OF GOOD *Shamtown SAW 002CD*	15	3
13 Jul 96	TO WIN JUST ONCE *Shamtown SAW 004CD*	14	2
6 Dec 97	SIMPLE THINGS *Shamtown SAW 006CD*	56	1

SAXON ☝ *UK, male vocal/instrumental group* 61 wks

22 Mar 80	WHEELS OF STEEL *Carrere CAR 143*	20	11
21 Jun 80	747 (STRANGERS IN THE NIGHT) *Carrere CAR 151*	13	9
28 Jun 80	BACKS TO THE WALL *Carrere HM 6*	64	2
28 Jun 80	BIG TEASER/RAINBOW THEME *Carrere HM 5*	66	2
29 Nov 80	STRONG ARM OF THE LAW *Carrere CAR 170*	63	3
11 Apr 81	AND THE BANDS PLAYED ON *Carrere CAR 180*	12	8
18 Jul 81	NEVER SURRENDER *Carrere CAR 204*	18	6
31 Oct 81	PRINCESS OF THE NIGHT *Carrere CAR 208*	57	3
23 Apr 83	POWER AND THE GLORY *Carrere SAXON 1*	32	5
30 Jul 83	NIGHTMARE *Carrere CAR 284*	50	3
31 Aug 85	BACK ON THE STREETS *Parlophone R 6103*	75	1
29 Mar 86	ROCK 'N' ROLL GYPSY *Parlophone R 6112*	71	1
30 Aug 86	WAITING FOR THE NIGHT *EMI EMI 5575*	66	2
5 Mar 88	RIDE LIKE THE WIND *EMI EM 43*	52	4
30 Apr 88	I CAN'T WAIT ANYMORE *EMI EM 54*	71	1

Al SAXON ℂ *UK, male vocalist* 10 wks

16 Jan 59	YOU'RE THE TOP CHA *Fontana H 164*	17	4
28 Aug 59	ONLY SIXTEEN *Fontana H 205*	24	3
22 Dec 60	BLUE-EYED BOY *Fontana H 278*	39	2
7 Sep 61	THERE I'VE SAID IT AGAIN *Piccadilly 7N 35011*	48	1

Leo SAYER ❂ *Distinctive singer/songwriter (b. 21 May, 1948, Sussex) who was a top singles and album act on both sides of the Atlantic in the late 1970s. His first seven hits all reached the Top 10 – a feat first achieved by his manager, Adam Faith* 151 wks

15 Dec 73 ●	THE SHOW MUST GO ON *Chrysalis CHS 2023*	2	13
15 Jun 74 ●	ONE MAN BAND *Chrysalis CHS 2045*	6	9
14 Sep 74 ●	LONG TALL GLASSES *Chrysalis CHS 2052*	4	9
30 Aug 75 ●	MOONLIGHTING *Chrysalis CHS 2076*	2	8
30 Oct 76	YOU MAKE ME FEEL LIKE DANCING *Chrysalis CHS 2119* ▲	2	12
29 Jan 77 ★	WHEN I NEED YOU *Chrysalis CHS 2127* ▲	1	13
9 Apr 77 ●	HOW MUCH LOVE *Chrysalis CHS 2140*	10	8
10 Sep 77	THUNDER IN MY HEART *Chrysalis CHS 2163*	22	8
16 Sep 78 ●	I CAN'T STOP LOVIN' YOU (THOUGH I TRY) *Chrysalis CHS 2240*	6	11
25 Nov 78	RAINING IN MY HEART *Chrysalis CHS 2277*	21	10
5 Jul 80 ●	MORE THAN I CAN SAY *Chrysalis CHS 2442*	2	11
13 Mar 82 ●	HAVE YOU EVER BEEN IN LOVE *Chrysalis CHS 2596*	10	9
19 Jun 82	HEART (STOP BEATING IN TIME) *Chrysalis CHS 2616*	22	10
12 Mar 83	ORCHARD ROAD *Chrysalis CHS 2677*	16	8
15 Oct 83	TILL YOU COME BACK TO ME *Chrysalis LEO 01*	51	3
8 Feb 86	UNCHAINED MELODY *Chrysalis LEO 3*	54	4
13 Feb 93	WHEN I NEED YOU (re-issue) *Chrysalis CDCHS 3926*	65	2
8 Aug 98	YOU MAKE ME FEEL LIKE DANCING (re-mix) *Brothers Org. CDBRUV 8* [1]	32	3

[1] Groove Generation featuring Leo Sayer

Alexei SAYLE ❂ *UK, male vocalist* 8 wks

25 Feb 84	'ULLO JOHN GOT A NEW MOTOR? *Island IS 162*	15	8

SCAFFOLD ❂ *UK, male vocal group* 62 wks

22 Nov 67 ●	THANK U VERY MUCH *Parlophone R 5643*	4	12
27 Mar 68	DO YOU REMEMBER *Parlophone R 5679*	34	5
6 Nov 68 ★	LILY THE PINK *Parlophone R 5734*	1	24
1 Nov 69	GIN GAN GOOLIE *Parlophone R 5812*	38	11
24 Jan 70	GIN GAN GOOLIE (re-entry) *Parlophone R 5812*	50	1
1 Jun 74 ●	LIVERPOOL LOU *Warner Bros. K 16400*	7	9

Boz SCAGGS ✏ 🎤 *US, male vocalist* 31 wks

30 Oct 76	LOWDOWN *CBS 4563*	28	4
22 Jan 77 ●	WHAT CAN I SAY *CBS 4869*	10	10
14 May 77	LIDO SHUFFLE *CBS 5136*	13	9
10 Dec 77	HOLLYWOOD *CBS 5836*	33	8

SCARFACE *US, male rapper* 6 wks

11 Mar 95	HAND OF THE DEAD BODY *Virgin America VUSCD 88* [1]	41	2
5 Aug 95	I SEEN A MAN DIE *Virgin America VUSCD 94*	55	2
5 Jul 97	GAME OVER *Virgin VUSCD 121*	34	2

[1] Scarface featuring Ice Cube

SCARFO *UK, male vocal/instrumental group* 2 wks

19 Jul 97	ALKALINE *Deceptive BLUFF 044CD*	61	1
18 Oct 97	COSMONAUT NO. 7 *Deceptive BLUFF 053CD*	67	1

SCARLET ❂ *UK, female vocal/instrumental duo* 18 wks

21 Jan 95	INDEPENDENT LOVE SONG *WEA YZ 820CD*	12	12
29 Apr 95	I WANNA BE FREE (TO BE WITH HIM) *WEA YZ 913CD*	21	4
5 Aug 95	LOVE HANGOVER *WEA YZ 969CD*	54	1
6 Jul 96	BAD GIRL *WEA WEA 046CD*	54	1

SCARLET FANTASTIC *UK, male/female vocal/instrumental group* 12 wks

3 Oct 87	NO MEMORY *Arista RIS 36*	24	10
23 Jan 88	PLUG ME IN (TO THE CENTRAL LOVE LINE) *Arista 109693*	67	2

SCARLET PARTY *UK, male vocal/instrumental group* 5 wks

16 Oct 82	101 DAM-NATIONS *Parlophone R 6058*	44	5

SCATMAN JOHN ❂ ☺ *US, male vocalist* 19 wks

13 May 95 ●	SCATMAN (SKI-BA-BOP-BA-DOP-BOP) *RCA 74321281712*	3	12
2 Sep 95 ●	SCATMAN'S WORLD *RCA 74321289952*	10	7

Michael SCHENKER GROUP *Germany/UK, male vocal/instrumental group* 9 wks

13 Sep 80	ARMED AND READY *Chrysalis CHS 2455*	53	3
8 Nov 80	CRY FOR THE NATIONS *Chrysalis CHS 2471*	56	3
11 Sep 82	DANCER *Chrysalis CHS 2636*	52	3

Lalo SCHIFRIN ✏ ℂ *Argentina, male conductor and US, orchestra* 11 wks

9 Oct 76	JAWS *CTI CTSP 005*	14	9
21 Oct 97	BULLITT *Warner.esp WESP 002CD*	36	2

Peter SCHILLING *Germany, male vocalist* 6 wks

5 May 84	MAJOR TOM (COMING HOME) *PSP/WEA X 9438*	42	5
16 Jun 84	MAJOR TOM (COMING HOME) (re-entry) *PSP/WEA X 9438*	73	1

Phillip SCHOFIELD *UK, male vocalist* 6 wks

5 Dec 92	CLOSE EVERY DOOR *Really Useful RUR 11*	27	6

SCIENTIST *UK, male instrumentalist* 13 wks

6 Oct 90	THE EXORCIST *Kickin KICK 1*	62	3
1 Dec 90	THE EXORCIST (re-mix) *Kickin KICK 1TR*	46	3
15 Dec 90	THE BEE *Kickin KICK 3S*	52	3
26 Jan 91	THE BEE (re-entry) *Kickin KICK 3S*	47	3
11 May 91	SPIRAL SYMPHONY *Kickin KICK 5*	74	1

SCOOTER ❂ ☺ *UK/Germany, male vocal/instrumental group* 14 wks

21 Oct 95	MOVE YOUR ASS *Club Tools 0061675 CLU*	23	4
17 Feb 96	BACK IN THE UK *Club Tools 0061955 CLU*	18	3
25 May 96	REBEL YELL *Club Tools 0062575 CLU*	30	2
19 Oct 96	I'M RAVING *Club Tools 0063015 CLU*	33	3
17 May 97	FIRE *Club Tools 0060005*	45	2

SCORPIONS ✈ *Germany, male vocal/instrumental group* **35 wks**

26 May 79	IS THERE ANYBODY THERE/ANOTHER PIECE OF MEAT *Harvest HAR 5185* 39	4
25 Aug 79	LOVEDRIVE *Harvest HAR 5188* 69	2
31 May 80	MAKE IT REAL *Harvest HAR 5206* 72	2
20 Sep 80	THE ZOO *Harvest HAR 5212* 75	1
3 Apr 82	NO ONE LIKE YOU *Harvest HAR 5219* 65	3
1 May 82	NO ONE LIKE YOU (re-entry) *Harvest HAR 5219* 64	1
17 Jul 82	CAN'T LIVE WITHOUT YOU *Harvest HAR 5221* 63	2
4 Jun 88	RHYTHM OF LOVE *Harvest HAR 5240* 59	2
18 Feb 89	PASSION RULES THE GAME *Harvest 5242* 74	1
1 Jun 91	WIND OF CHANGE *Vertigo VER 54* 53	3
28 Sep 91 ●	WIND OF CHANGE (re-issue) *Vertigo VER 58* 2	9
30 Nov 91	SEND ME AN ANGEL *Vertigo VER 60* 27	3
28 Dec 91	SEND ME AN ANGEL (re-entry) *Vertigo VER 60* 68	2

SCOTLAND WORLD CUP SQUAD ◐
UK, male football team vocalists **27 wks**

22 Jun 74	EASY EASY *Polydor 2058 452* 20	4
27 May 78 ●	OLE OLA (MULHER BRASILEIRA) *Riva 15* [1] 4	6
1 May 82	WE HAVE A DREAM *WEA K 19145* 5	9
9 Jun 90	SAY IT WITH PRIDE *RCA PB 43791* 45	3
15 Jun 96	PURPLE HEATHER *Warner Bros. W 0354CD* [2] 16	5

[1] Rod Stewart featuring the Scottish World Cup Football Squad
[2] Rod Stewart with the Scottish Euro '96 Squad

Jack SCOTT 🎸 *Canada, male vocalist* **28 wks**

10 Oct 58 ●	MY TRUE LOVE *London HLU 8626* 9	10
25 Sep 59	THE WAY I WALK *London HLL 8912* 30	1
10 Mar 60	WHAT IN THE WORLD'S COME OVER YOU *Top Rank JAR 280* 11	15
2 Jun 60	BURNING BRIDGES *Top Rank JAR 375* 32	2

Linda SCOTT ◐ *US, female vocalist* **14 wks**

18 May 61 ●	I'VE TOLD EVERY LITTLE STAR *Columbia DB 4638* 7	13
14 Sep 61	DON'T BET MONEY HONEY *Columbia DB 4692* 50	1

Mike SCOTT *UK, male vocalist/multi-instrumentalist* **4 wks**

16 Sep 95	BRING 'EM ALL IN *Chrysalis CDCHS 5025* 56	1
11 Nov 95	BUILDING THE CITY OF LIGHT *Chrysalis CDCHS 5026* 60	1
27 Sep 97	LOVE ANYWAY *Chrysalis CDCHS 5064* 50	1
14 Feb 98	RARE, PRECIOUS AND GONE *Chrysalis CDCHSS 5073* 74	1

Millie SCOTT *US, female vocalist* **11 wks**

12 Apr 86	PRISONER OF LOVE *Fourth & Broadway BRW 45* 52	4
23 Aug 86	AUTOMATIC *Fourth & Broadway BRW 51* 56	3
21 Feb 87	EV'RY LITTLE BIT *Fourth & Broadway BRW 58* 63	4

Simon SCOTT *UK, male vocalist* **8 wks**

13 Aug 64	MOVE IT BABY *Parlophone R 5164* 37	8

Tony SCOTT *Holland, male rapper* **6 wks**

15 Apr 89	THAT'S HOW I'M LIVING/THE CHIEF *Champion CHAMP 97* [1] 48	4
10 Feb 90	GET INTO IT/THAT'S HOW I'M LIVING (re-issue) *Champion CHAMP 232* 63	2

[1] Wrongly credited as Toni Scott

'The Chief' only listed from 22 Apr, 1989

SCOTTISH RUGBY TEAM with Ronnie BROWNE
UK, male rugby team vocalists **1 wk**

2 Jun 90	FLOWER OF SCOTLAND *Greentrax STRAX 1001* 73	1

SCREAMING BLUE MESSIAHS
UK, male vocal/instrumental group **6 wks**

16 Jan 88	I WANNA BE A FLINTSTONE *WEA YZ 166* 28	6

SCREAMING TREES *US, male vocal/instrumental group* **2 wks**

6 Mar 93	NEARLY LOST YOU *Epic 6582372* 50	1
1 May 93	DOLLAR BILL *Epic 6591792* 52	1

SCRITTI POLITTI ◐ *UK, male vocal/instrumental group* **77 wks**

21 Nov 81	THE SWEETEST GIRL *Rough Trade RT 091* 64	3
22 May 82	FAITHLESS *Rough Trade RT 101* 56	4
7 Aug 82	ASYLUMS IN JERUSALEM/JACQUES DERRIDA *Rough Trade RT 111* 43	5
10 Mar 84 ●	WOOD BEEZ (PRAY LIKE ARETHA FRANKLIN) *Virgin VS 657* 10	12
9 Jun 84	ABSOLUTE *Virgin VS 680* 17	9
17 Nov 84	HYPNOTIZE *Virgin VS 725* 68	2
11 Sep 85 ●	THE WORD GIRL *Virgin VS 747* [1] 6	12
7 Sep 85	PERFECT WAY *Virgin VS 780* 48	5
7 May 88	OH PATTI (DON'T FEEL SORRY FOR LOVERBOY) *Virgin VS 1006* 13	9
27 Aug 88	FIRST BOY IN THIS TOWN (LOVE SICK) *Virgin VS 1082* 63	3
12 Nov 88	BOOM! THERE SHE WAS *Virgin VS 1143* [2] 55	3
16 Mar 91	SHE'S A WOMAN *Virgin VS 1333* [3] 20	7
3 Aug 91	TAKE ME IN YOUR ARMS AND LOVE ME *Virgin VS 1346* 47	3

[1] Scritti Politti featuring Ranking Ann [2] Scritti Politti featuring Roger
[3] Scritti Politti featuring Shabba Ranks

Sweetie Irie is credited on the sleeve only of 'Take Me In Your Arms and Love Me'

Earl SCRUGGS – See Lester FLATT and Earl SCRUGGS

SEA LEVEL *US, male instrumental group* **4 wks**

17 Feb 79	FIFTY-FOUR *Capricorn POSP 28* 63	4

SEAHORSES ☹ ◐ *UK, male vocal/instrumental group* **26 wks**

10 May 97 ●	LOVE IS THE LAW *Geffen GFSTD 22243* 3	7
26 Jul 97	BLINDED BY THE SUN *Geffen GFSTD 22266* 7	7
11 Oct 97	LOVE ME AND LEAVE ME *Geffen GFSTD 22282* 16	4
13 Dec 97	YOU CAN TALK TO ME *Geffen GFSTD 22297* 15	8

SEAL ◐ ☺ *UK, male vocalist* **70 wks**

8 Dec 90 ●	CRAZY *ZTT ZANG 8* 2	15
4 May 91	FUTURE LOVE EP *ZTT ZANG 11* 12	6
20 Jul 91	THE BEGINNING *ZTT ZANG 21* 24	6
16 Nov 91 ●	KILLER EP *ZTT ZANG 23* 8	8
29 Feb 92	VIOLET *ZTT ZANG 27* 39	2
21 May 94	PRAYER FOR THE DYING *ZTT ZANG 51CD* 14	5
30 Jul 94	KISS FROM A ROSE *ZTT ZANG 52CD1* 20	5
5 Nov 94	NEWBORN FRIEND *ZTT ZANG 58CD* 45	2
15 Jul 95 ●	KISS FROM A ROSE/I'M ALIVE (re-issue) *ZTT ZANG 70CD* ▲ 4	13
9 Dec 95	DON'T CRY/PRAYER FOR THE DYING (re-issue) *ZTT ZANG 75CD* 51	2
29 Mar 97	FLY LIKE AN ANGEL *ZTT ZEAL 1CD* 13	5
14 Nov 98	HUMAN BEINGS *Warner Brothers W 464CD* 50	1

Tracks on Future Love EP: Future Love Paradise / A Minor Groove / Violet
Tracks on Killer (EP): Killer / Hey Joe / Come See What Love Has Done
See also ADAMSKI

SEARCHERS ◐ *Merseybeat combo initially tipped to be as big as the Beatles, formed 1960: Mike Pender (v/g), John McNally (g/v), Tony Jackson (v/b) (left 1964 – replaced by Frank Allen). Chris Curtis (d). Unlike the Beatles, however, most of this influential act's early hits were cover versions of US originals* **128 wks**

27 Jun 63 ★	SWEETS FOR MY SWEET *Pye 7N 15533* 1	16
10 Oct 63	SWEET NOTHINS *Philips BF 1274* 48	1
24 Oct 63 ●	SUGAR AND SPICE *Pye 7N 15566* 2	13
16 Jan 64 ★	NEEDLES AND PINS *Pye 7N 15594* 1	15
16 Apr 64 ★	DON'T THROW YOUR LOVE AWAY *Pye 7N 15630* 1	11
16 Jul 64	SOMEDAY WE'RE GONNA LOVE AGAIN *Pye 7N 15670* 11	9
17 Sep 64 ●	WHEN YOU WALK IN THE ROOM *Pye 7N 15694* 3	12
3 Dec 64	WHAT HAVE THEY DONE TO THE RAIN *Pye 7N 15739* 13	11
4 Mar 65 ●	GOODBYE MY LOVE *Pye 7N 15794* 4	11

8 Jul 65	HE'S GOT NO LOVE *Pye 7N 15878*	12	10
14 Oct 65	WHEN I GET HOME *Pye 7N 15950*	35	3
16 Dec 65	TAKE ME FOR WHAT I'M WORTH *Pye 7N 15992*	20	8
21 Apr 66	TAKE IT OR LEAVE IT *Pye 7N 17094*	31	6
13 Oct 66	HAVE YOU EVER LOVED SOMEBODY *Pye 7N 17170*	48	2

SEASHELLS *UK, female vocal group* 5 wks

9 Sep 72	MAYBE I KNOW *CBS 8218*	32	5

SEB *UK, male instrumentalist – keyboards* 1 wk

18 Feb 95	SUGAR SHACK *React CDREACT 50*	61	1

SEBADOH *US, male vocal/instrumental group* 1 wk

27 Jul 96	BEAUTY OF THE RIDE *Domino RUG 47CD*	74	1

Jon SECADA ☺ *Cuba, male vocalist* 42 wks

18 Jul 92 ●	JUST ANOTHER DAY *SBK SBK 35*	5	15
31 Oct 92	DO YOU BELIEVE IN US *SBK SBK 37*	30	4
6 Feb 93	ANGEL *SBK CDSBK 39*	23	5
17 Jul 93	DO YOU REALLY WANT ME *SBK CDSBK 41*	30	4
16 Oct 93	I'M FREE *SBK CDSBK 44*	50	2
14 May 94	IF YOU GO *SBK CDSBK 51*	39	4
2 Jul 94	IF YOU GO (re-entry) *SBK CDSBK 51*	71	1
4 Feb 95	MENTAL PICTURE *SBK CDSBK 54*	44	2
16 Dec 95	IF I NEVER KNEW YOU (LOVE THEME FROM POCAHONTAS) *Walt Disney WD 7023C* [1]	51	4
14 Jun 97	TOO LATE, TOO SOON *SBK CDSBK 57*	43	1

[1] Jon Secada and Shanice

SECCHI featuring Orlando JOHNSON
Italy/US, male vocal/instrumental duo 3 wks

4 May 91	I SAY YEAH *Epic 6568467*	46	3

Harry SECOMBE ℂ *UK, male vocalist* 35 wks

9 Dec 55	ON WITH THE MOTLEY *Philips PB 523*	16	3
3 Oct 63	IF I RULED THE WORLD *Philips BF 1261*	44	2
21 Nov 63	IF I RULED THE WORLD (re-entry) *Philips BF 1261*	18	15
23 Feb 67 ●	THIS IS MY SONG *Philips BF 1539*	2	15

SECOND CITY SOUND *UK, male instrumental group* 8 wks

20 Jan 66	TCHAIKOVSKY ONE *Decca F 12310*	22	7
2 Apr 69	DREAM OF OLWEN *Major Minor MM 600*	43	1

SECOND IMAGE *UK, male vocal/instrumental group* 11 wks

24 Jul 82	STAR *Polydor POSP 457*	60	2
2 Apr 83	BETTER TAKE TIME *Polydor POSP 565*	67	2
26 Nov 83	DON'T YOU *MCA 848*	68	2
11 Aug 84	SING AND SHOUT *MCA MCA 882*	53	3
2 Feb 85	STARTING AGAIN *MCA 936*	65	2

SECOND PHASE *US, male producer – Joey Beltram* 2 wks

21 Sep 91	MENTASM *R&S RSUK 2*	48	2

SECRET AFFAIR ☺ ✎ *UK, male vocal/instrumental group* 34 wks

1 Sep 79	TIME FOR ACTION *I-Spy SEE 1*	13	10
10 Nov 79	LET YOUR HEART DANCE *I-Spy SEE 3*	32	6
8 Mar 80	MY WORLD *I-Spy SEE 5*	16	9
23 Aug 80	SOUND OF CONFUSION *I-Spy SEE 8*	45	5
17 Oct 81	DO YOU KNOW *I-Spy SEE 10*	57	4

SECRET KNOWLEDGE
UK/US, male/female vocal/instrumental duo 2 wks

27 Apr 96	LOVE ME NOW *Deconstruction 74321342432*	66	1
24 Aug 96	SUGAR DADDY *Deconstruction 74321400242*	75	1

SECRET LIFE *UK, male vocal group* 10 wks

12 Dec 92	AS ALWAYS *Cowboy 7RODEO 9*	45	4
7 Aug 93	LOVE SO STRONG *Cowboy RODEO 18CD*	38	2
7 May 94	SHE HOLDS THE KEY *Pulse 8 CDLOSE 58*	63	1
29 Oct 94	I WANT YOU *Pulse 8 CDLOSE 71*	70	1
28 Jan 95	LOVE SO STRONG (re-mix) *Pulse 8 CDLOSE 79*	37	2

SECRETARY OF ENTERTAINMENT – See RAZE

SECTION-X *France, male instrumental duo* 1 wk

8 Mar 97	ATLANTIS *Perfecto PERF 136*	42	1

Neil SEDAKA ☺ *The man who put the 'Tra-La-La' into 1960s pop, b. 13 March, 1939, New York. Ultra-commercial singer/songwriter/ pianist who enjoyed two separate chart runs as an artist and wrote many hits for numerous other acts* 190 wks

24 Apr 59 ●	I GO APE *RCA 1115*	9	13
13 Nov 59 ●	OH CAROL *RCA 1152*	3	17
14 Apr 60 ●	STAIRWAY TO HEAVEN *RCA 1178*	8	15
1 Sep 60	YOU MEAN EVERYTHING TO ME *RCA 1198*	45	3
2 Feb 61 ●	CALENDAR GIRL *RCA 1220*	8	14
18 May 61 ●	LITTLE DEVIL *RCA 1236*	9	12
21 Dec 61 ●	HAPPY BIRTHDAY SWEET SIXTEEN *RCA 1266*	3	18
19 Apr 62	KING OF CLOWNS *RCA 1282*	23	11
19 Jul 62 ●	BREAKING UP IS HARD TO DO *RCA 1298* ▲	7	16
22 Nov 62	NEXT DOOR TO AN ANGEL *RCA 1319*	29	4
30 May 63	LET'S GO STEADY AGAIN *RCA 1343*	42	1
13 Jun 63	LET'S GO STEADY AGAIN (re-entry) *RCA 1343*	43	2
7 Oct 72	OH CAROL/BREAKING UP IS HARD TO DO/LITTLE DEVIL (re-issue) *RCA Maximillion 2259*	19	14
4 Nov 72	BEAUTIFUL YOU *RCA 2269*	43	3
24 Feb 73	THAT'S WHEN THE MUSIC TAKES ME *RCA 2310*	18	10
2 Jun 73	STANDING ON THE INSIDE *MGM 2006 267*	26	9
25 Aug 73	OUR LAST SONG TOGETHER *MGM 2006 307*	31	8
9 Feb 74	A LITTLE LOVIN' *Polydor 2058 434*	34	6
22 Jun 74	LAUGHTER IN THE RAIN *Polydor 2058 494* ▲	15	9
22 Mar 75	THE QUEEN OF 1964 *Polydor 2058 546*	35	5

SEDUCTION *US, female vocal group* 1 wk

21 Apr 90	HEARTBEAT *Breakout USA 685*	75	1

SEEKERS ♂ ☺ *First Australian act to top UK single or album chart: Judith Durham (v), Keith Potger (g), Bruce Woodley (g), Athol Guy (b). Their unique harmony vocals were displayed on many of their hits, which were penned and produced by Tom Springfield. Durham went solo in 1967, and Potger later went on to form the New Seekers* 120 wks

7 Jan 65 ★	I'LL NEVER FIND ANOTHER YOU *Columbia DB 7431*	1	23
15 Apr 65	A WORLD OF OUR OWN *Columbia DB 7532*	3	18
28 Oct 65 ★	THE CARNIVAL IS OVER *Columbia DB 7711* ◆	1	17
24 Mar 66	SOMEDAY ONE DAY *Columbia DB 7867*	11	11
8 Sep 66 ●	WALK WITH ME *Columbia DB 8000*	10	12
24 Nov 66 ●	MORNINGTOWN RIDE *Columbia DB 8060*	2	15
23 Feb 67 ●	GEORGY GIRL *Columbia DB 8134*	3	11
20 Sep 67	WHEN WILL THE GOOD APPLES FALL *Columbia DB 8273*	11	12
13 Dec 67	EMERALD CITY *Columbia DB 8313*	50	1

Bob SEGER and the SILVER BULLET BAND
US, male vocal/instrumental group 30 wks

30 Sep 78	HOLLYWOOD NIGHTS *Capitol CL 16004*	42	6
3 Feb 79	WE'VE GOT TONITE *Capitol CL 16028*	41	6
24 Oct 81	HOLLYWOOD NIGHTS *Capitol CL 223*	49	3
6 Feb 82	WE'VE GOT TONITE *Capitol CL 235*	60	4
9 Apr 83	EVEN NOW *Capitol CL 284*	73	2
28 Jan 95	WE'VE GOT TONIGHT (re-issue) *Capitol CDCL 734*	22	5
29 Apr 95	NIGHT MOVES *Capitol CDCL 741*	45	2
29 Jul 95	HOLLYWOOD NIGHTS (re-issue) *Capitol CDCL 749*	52	1
10 Feb 96	LOCK AND LOAD *Parlophone CDCL 765*	57	1

Capitol CL 223 and CL 235 were live versions of earlier studio hits

What: *Rose Marie*   **81**
Who: Slim Whitman
When: 1955 (1)
Which: Headed the chart for 11 consecutive weeks – a record that lasted for more than 35 years. It was the title song of an operetta that was first produced in 1924, the year in which country yodeler Whitman was born

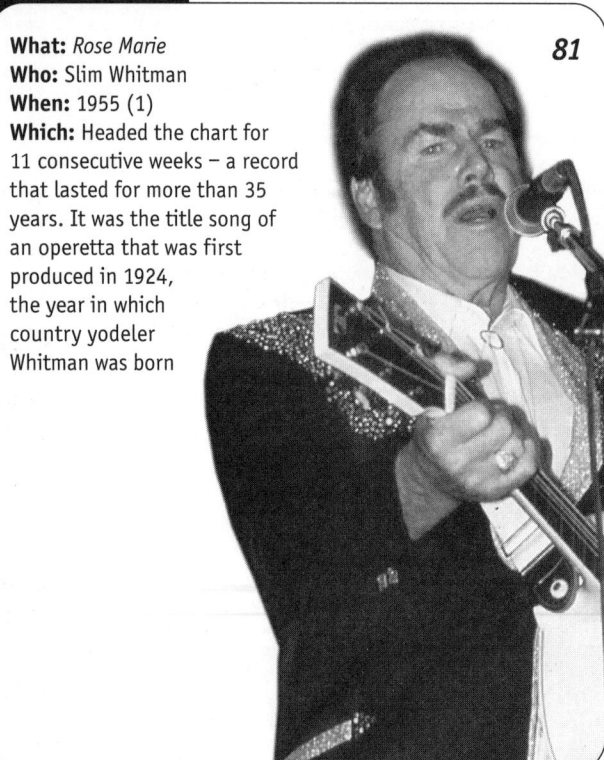

What: *Wannabe*   **82**
Who: Spice Girls
When: 1996 (1)
Which: Catapulted the girl-power quintet to the top around the globe, and was the first of six successive No 1s for Britain's biggest-selling female group of all time

What: *I'll Be There for You*   **83**
Who: Rembrandts
When: 1995 (3), 1997 (5)
Which: Twice journeyed into the Top 5 in less than 20 months. Its continued success was due to its use as the theme tune to the very popular US TV sitcom *Friends*

What: *Side Saddle*   **84**
Who: Russ Conway
When: 1959
Which: Was originally titled 'Come and Dance' by the pianist for a 1956 musical version of *Beauty and the Beast*. He only recorded it himself after Joe 'Mr Piano' Henderson declined to

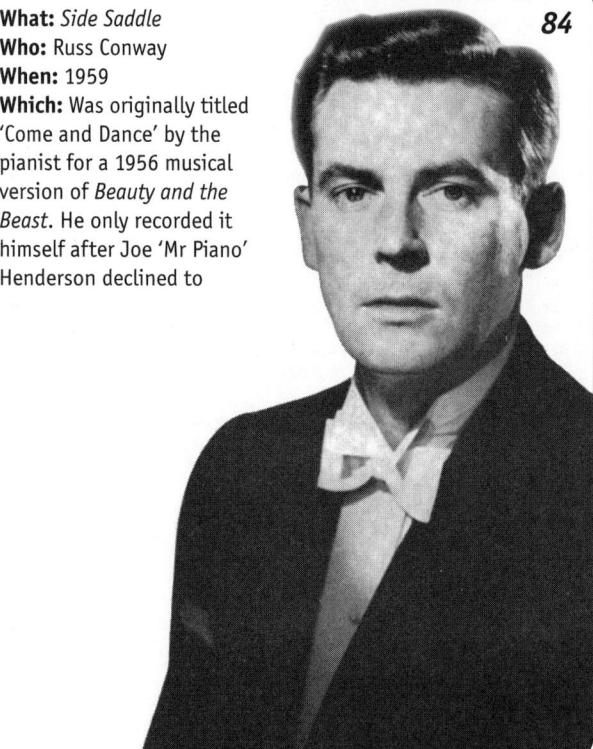

SEIKO and Donnie WAHLBERG
Japan/US, female/male vocal duo **5 wks**

18 Aug 90	THE RIGHT COMBINATION *Epic 656203 7*	44	5

SELECTER ⓞ ⱱ *UK, male/female vocal/instrumental group* **28 wks**

13 Oct 79 ●	ON MY RADIO *2 Tone CHSTT 4*	8	9
2 Feb 80	THREE MINUTE HERO *2 Tone CHSTT 8*	16	6
29 Mar 80	MISSING WORDS *2 Tone CHSTT 10*	23	8
23 Aug 80	THE WHISPER *Chrysalis CHSS 1*	36	5

See also VARIOUS ARTISTS (EPs & LPs) – The Two Tone EP

Peter SELLERS ⓞ *UK, male vocalist* **39 wks**

2 Aug 57	ANY OLD IRON *Parlophone R 4337*	21	3
6 Sep 57	ANY OLD IRON (re-entry) *Parlophone R 4337*	17	8
10 Nov 60 ●	GOODNESS GRACIOUS ME *Parlophone R 4702* [1]	4	14
12 Jan 61	BANGERS AND MASH *Parlophone R 4724* [1]	22	5
23 Dec 65	A HARD DAY'S NIGHT *Parlophone R 5393*	14	7
27 Nov 93	A HARD DAY'S NIGHT (re-issue) *EMI CDEMS 293*	52	2

[1] Peter Sellers and Sophia Loren

Michael SEMBELLO *US, male vocalist* **6 wks**

20 Aug 83	MANIAC *Casablanca CAN 1017* ▲	43	6

SEMPRINI *UK, orchestra* **8 wks**

16 Mar 61	THEME FROM 'EXODUS' *HMV POP 842*	25	8

SENSELESS THINGS ⓞ *UK, male vocal/instrumental group* **19 wks**

22 Jun 91	EVERYBODY'S GONE *Epic 6569807*	73	1
28 Sep 91	GOT IT AT THE DELMAR *Epic 6574497*	50	3
11 Jan 92	EASY TO SMILE *Epic 6576957*	18	4
11 Apr 92	HOLD IT DOWN *Epic 6579267*	19	4
5 Dec 92	HOMOPHOBIC ASSHOLE *Epic 6588337*	52	2
13 Feb 93	PRIMARY INSTINCT *Epic 6589402*	41	2
12 Jun 93	TOO MUCH KISSING *Epic 6592502*	69	1
5 Nov 94	CHRISTINE KEELER *Epic 6609572*	56	1
28 Jan 95	SOMETHING TO MISS *Epic 6611162*	57	1

SENSER *UK, male/female vocal/instrumental group* **5 wks**

25 Sep 93	THE KEY *Ultimate TOPP 019CD*	47	1
19 Mar 94	SWITCH *Ultimate TOPP 022CD*	39	2
23 Jul 94	AGE OF PANIC *Ultimate TOPP 027CD*	52	1
17 Aug 96	CHARMING DEMONS *Ultimate TOPP 045CD*	42	1

SEPULTURA ⱱ *Brazil, male vocal/instrumental group* **12 wks**

2 Oct 93	TERRITORY *Roadrunner RR 23823*	66	2
26 Feb 94	REFUSE-RESIST *Roadrunner RR 23773*	51	2
4 Jun 94	SLAVE NEW WORLD *Roadrunner RR 23745*	46	2
24 Feb 96	ROOTS BLOODY ROOTS *Roadrunner RR 23205*	19	2
17 Aug 96	RATAMAHATTA *Roadrunner RR 23145*	23	2
14 Dec 96	ATTITUDE *Roadrunner RR 22995*	46	2

SERIAL DIVA *UK, male/female dance group* **1 wk**

18 Jan 97	KEEP HOPE ALIVE *Sound Of Ministry SOMCD 26*	57	1

SERIOUS DANGER *UK, male producer – Richard Phillips* **4 wks**

20 Dec 97	DEEPER *Fresh FRSHD 68*	40	3
2 May 98	HIGH NOON *Fresh FRSHD 69*	54	1

SERIOUS INTENTION *US, male vocal/instrumental group* **6 wks**

16 Nov 85	YOU DON'T KNOW (OH-OH-OH) *Important TAN 8*	75	1
5 Apr 86	SERIOUS *Pow Wow LON 93*	51	5

SERIOUS ROPE *UK, male/female vocal/instrumental group* **3 wks**

22 May 93	HAPPINESS *Rumour RUMACD 64* [1]	54	2

---

1 Oct 94	HAPPINESS – YOU MAKE ME HAPPY (re-mix) *Mercury MERCD 407*	70	1

[1] Serious Rope presents Sharon Dee Clarke

SET THE TONE *UK, male/female vocal/instrumental group* **4 wks**

22 Jan 83	DANCE SUCKER *Island WIP 6836*	62	2
26 Mar 83	RAP YOUR LOVE *Island IS 110*	67	2

SETTLERS *UK, male/female vocal/instrumental group* **5 wks**

16 Oct 71	THE LIGHTNING TREE *York SYK 505*	36	5

Taja SEVELLE ⓞ ♪ *US, female vocalist* **13 wks**

20 Feb 88 ●	LOVE IS CONTAGIOUS *Paisley Park W 8257*	7	9
14 May 88	WOULDN'T YOU LOVE TO LOVE ME *Paisley Park W 8127*	59	4

SEVEN GRAND HOUSING AUTHORITY
UK, male producer – Terence Parker **1 wk**

23 Oct 93	THE QUESTION *Olympic ELYCD 010*	70	1

702 *US, female vocal group* **3 wks**

14 Dec 96	STEELO *Motown 8606072*	41	2
29 Nov 97	NO DOUBT *Motown 8607052*	59	1

7669 *US, female rap group* **1 wk**

18 Jun 94	JOY *Motown TMGCD 1429*	60	1

740 BOYZ *US, male vocal/instrumental duo* **1 wk**

4 Nov 95	SHIMMY SHAKE *MCA MCSTD 40002*	54	1

7TH HEAVEN *UK, male vocal group* **5 wks**

14 Sep 85	HOT FUN *Mercury MER 199*	47	5

SEVERINE ℂ *France, female vocalist* **11 wks**

24 Apr 71 ●	UN BANC, UN ARBRE, UNE RUE *Philips 6009 135*	9	11

David SEVILLE ⓞ *US, male vocalist* **6 wks**

23 May 58	WITCH DOCTOR *London HLU 8619* ▲	11	6

See also ALFI and HARRY; CHIPMUNKS

Janette SEWELL – *See DOUBLE TROUBLE*

SEX CLUB featuring BROWN SUGAR
US, male/female vocal/instrumental duo **1 wk**

28 Jan 95	BIG DICK MAN *Club Tools CLU 60775*	67	1

SEX-O-SONIQUE
UK, male production/instrumental duo – Mike Gray, Jon Pearn **3 wks**

6 Dec 97	I THOUGHT IT WAS YOU *ffrr FCD 321*	32	3

See also HUSTLERS CONVENTION; FULL INTENTION

SEX PISTOLS ✐ *UK, male vocal/instrumental group* **88 wks**

18 Dec 76	ANARCHY IN THE U.K. *EMI 2566*	38	4
4 Jun 77 ●	GOD SAVE THE QUEEN *Virgin VS 181*	2	9
9 Jul 77 ●	PRETTY VACANT *Virgin VS 184*	6	8
22 Oct 77 ●	HOLIDAYS IN THE SUN *Virgin VS 191*	8	6
8 Jul 78 ●	NO ONE IS INNOCENT/MY WAY *Virgin VS 220* [1]	7	10
3 Mar 79 ●	SOMETHING ELSE/FRIGGIN' IN THE RIGGIN' *Virgin VS 240*	3	12
7 Apr 79 ●	SILLY THING *Virgin VS 256*	6	8
30 Jun 79 ●	C'MON EVERYBODY *Virgin VS 272*	3	8
13 Oct 79	THE GREAT ROCK 'N' ROLL SWINDLE *Virgin VS 290*	21	6
14 Jun 80	(I'M NOT YOUR) STEPPING STONE *Virgin VS 339*	21	8
3 Oct 92	ANARCHY IN THE UK (re-issue) *Virgin VS 1431*	33	3
5 Dec 92	PRETTY VACANT (re-issue) *Virgin VS 1448*	56	2

UK No 1 ★ UK Top 10 ● UK million seller ◆ UK entry at No 1 ■ US No 1 ▲

| 27 Jul 96 | | PRETTY VACANT (LIVE) *Virgin America VUSCD 113* | 18 | 3 |

[1] Sex Pistols, punk prayer by Ronald Biggs

The listed flip side of 'Silly Thing' was 'Who Killed Bambi' by Ten Pole Tudor. The listed flip side of 'The Great Rock 'n' Roll Swindle' was 'Rock Around the Clock', also by Ten Pole Tudor

SEX-O-LETTES – See DISCO TEX and the SEX-O-LETTES

Denny SEYTON and the SABRES
UK, male vocal/instrumental group   **1 wk**

| 17 Sep 64 | | THE WAY YOU LOOK TONIGHT *Mercury MF 824* | 48 | 1 |

SFX *UK, male instrumental/production duo*   **3 wks**

| 15 May 93 | | LEMMINGS *Parlophone CDR 6343* | 51 | 3 |

SHADES *US, female vocal group*   **3 wks**

| 12 Apr 97 | | MR BIG STUFF *Motown 5736572* [1] | 31 | 2 |
| 20 Sep 97 | | SERENADE *Motown 8606892* | 75 | 1 |

[1] Queen Latifah, Shades & Free

SHADES & FREE – See QUEEN LATIFAH; SHADES

SHADES OF LOVE *US, male instrumental/production duo*   **1 wk**

| 22 Apr 95 | | KEEP IN TOUCH (BODY TO BODY) *Vicious Muzik MUZCD 102* | 64 | 1 |

SHADES OF RHYTHM ☺

UK, male instrumental/production group   **25 wks**

2 Feb 91		HOMICIDE/EXORCIST *ZTT ZANG 13*	53	3
13 Apr 91		SWEET SENSATION *ZTT ZANG 18*	54	4
20 Jul 91		THE SOUND OF EDEN *ZTT ZANG 22*	35	5
30 Nov 91		EXTACY *ZTT ZANG 24*	16	7
20 Feb 93		SWEET REVIVAL (KEEP IT COMIN') *ZTT ZANG 40CD*	61	1
11 Sep 93		SOUND OF EDEN (re-issue) *ZTT ZANG 44CD*	37	3
5 Nov 94		THE WANDERING DRAGON *Public Demand PPDCD 5*	55	1
21 Jun 97		PSYCHO BASE *Coalition CRUM 002CD*	57	1

SHADOWS ⊕ *Britain's most successful instrumental group: Hank Marvin (b. Brian Rankin) (g), Bruce Welch (g), Terence 'Jet' Harris (b), Tony Meehan (d). They were Cliff Richard's one-time backing band and have been headliners for five decades. This band was Britain's most influential and imitated act before The Beatles arrived*   **359 wks**

21 Jul 60	★	APACHE *Columbia DB 4484*	1	21
10 Nov 60	●	MAN OF MYSTERY/THE STRANGER *Columbia DB 4530*	5	15
9 Feb 61	●	F. B. I. *Columbia DB 4580*	6	19
11 May 61		FRIGHTENED CITY *Columbia DB 4637*	3	20
7 Sep 61	★	KON-TIKI *Columbia DB 4698*	1	10
16 Nov 61	●	THE SAVAGE *Columbia DB 4726*	10	8
23 Nov 61		KON-TIKI (re-entry) *Columbia DB 4698*	37	2
1 Mar 62	★	WONDERFUL LAND *Columbia DB 4790*	1	19
2 Aug 62	●	GUITAR TANGO *Columbia DB 4870*	4	15
13 Dec 62	★	DANCE ON *Columbia DB 4948*	1	15
7 Mar 63	★	FOOT TAPPER *Columbia DB 4984*	1	16
6 Jun 63	●	ATLANTIS *Columbia DB 7047*	2	17
19 Sep 63	●	SHINDIG *Columbia DB 7106*	6	12
5 Dec 63		GERONIMO *Columbia DB 7163*	11	12
5 Mar 64		THEME FOR YOUNG LOVERS *Columbia DB 7231*	12	10
7 May 64	●	THE RISE AND FALL OF FLINGEL BUNT *Columbia DB 7261*	5	14
3 Sep 64		RHYTHM AND GREENS *Columbia DB 7342*	22	7
3 Dec 64		GENIE WITH THE LIGHT BROWN LAMP *Columbia DB 7416*	17	10
11 Feb 65		MARY ANNE *Columbia DB 7476*	17	10
10 Jun 65		STINGRAY *Columbia DB 7588*	19	7
5 Aug 65	●	DON'T MAKE MY BABY BLUE *Columbia DB 7650*	10	10
25 Nov 65		WAR LORD *Columbia DB 7769*	18	9
17 Mar 66		I MET A GIRL *Columbia DB 7853*	22	5
7 Jul 66		A PLACE IN THE SUN *Columbia DB 7952*	24	6
3 Nov 66		THE DREAMS I DREAM *Columbia DB 8034*	42	6
13 Apr 67		MAROC 7 *Columbia DB 8170*	24	8
8 Mar 75		LET ME BE THE ONE *EMI 2269*	12	9

16 Dec 78	●	DON'T CRY FOR ME ARGENTINA *EMI 2890*	5	14
28 Apr 79	●	THEME FROM THE DEER HUNTER (CAVATINA) *EMI 2939*	9	14
26 Jan 80		RIDERS IN THE SKY *EMI 5027*	12	12
23 Aug 80		EQUINOXE (PART V) *Polydor POSP 148*	50	3
2 May 81		THE THIRD MAN *Polydor POSP 255*	44	4

All the above hits were instrumentals except for 'Mary Anne, Don't Make My Baby Blue', 'I Met a Girl', 'The Dreams I Dream' and 'Let Me Be the One'
See also Cliff RICHARD

SHAFT ☺ ⊕ *UK, male instrumental/production duo*   **9 wks**

| 21 Dec 91 | ● | ROOBARB AND CUSTARD *Ffrreedom TAB 100* | 7 | 8 |
| 25 Jul 92 | | MONKEY *Ffrreedom TAB 114* | 61 | 1 |

SHAG – See Jonathan KING

SHAGGY ⚐ *Jamaica, male vocalist*   **66 wks**

6 Feb 93	★	OH CAROLINA *Greensleeves GRECD 361*	1	19
10 Jul 93		SOON BE DONE *Greensleeves GRECD 380*	46	3
8 Jul 95	●	IN THE SUMMERTIME *Virgin VSCDT 1542* [1]	5	9
23 Sep 95	★	BOOMBASTIC *Virgin VSCDT 1536* ■	1	12
13 Jan 96		WHY YOU TREAT ME SO BAD *Virgin VSCDT 1566* [2]	11	5
23 Mar 96		SOMETHING DIFFERENT/THE TRAIN IS COMING *Virgin VSCDT 1581* [3]	21	5
22 Jun 96		THAT GIRL *Virgin America VUSCDX 106* [4]	15	7
19 Jul 97	●	PIECE OF MY HEART *Virgin VSCDT 1647* [5]	7	6

[1] Shaggy featuring Rayvon [2] Shaggy featuring Grand Puba
[3] Shaggy featuring Wayne Wonder/Shaggy [4] Maxi Priest featuring Shaggy
[5] Shaggy featuring Marsha

SHAH *UK, female vocalist*   **1 wk**

| 6 Jun 98 | | SECRET LOVE *Evocative EVOKE 5CDS* | 69 | 1 |

SHAI *US, male vocal group*   **6 wks**

| 19 Dec 92 | | IF I EVER FALL IN LOVE *MCA MCS 1727* | 36 | 6 |

SHAKATAK ⊕ ✎ ♪

UK, male/female vocal/instrumental group   **85 wks**

8 Nov 80		FEELS LIKE THE RIGHT TIME *Polydor POSP 188*	41	5
7 Mar 81		LIVING IN THE U.K. *Polydor POSP 230*	52	4
25 Jul 81		BRAZILIAN DAWN *Polydor POSP 282*	48	3
21 Nov 81		EASIER SAID THAN DONE *Polydor POSP 375*	12	17
3 Apr 82	●	NIGHT BIRDS *Polydor POSP 407*	9	8
19 Jun 82		STREETWALKIN' *Polydor POSP 452*	38	6
4 Sep 82		INVITATIONS *Polydor POSP 502*	24	7
6 Nov 82		STRANGER *Polydor POSP 530*	43	3
4 Jun 83		DARK IS THE NIGHT *Polydor POSP 595*	15	8
27 Aug 83		IF YOU COULD SEE ME NOW *Polydor POSP 635*	49	4
7 Jul 84	●	DOWN ON THE STREET *Polydor POSP 688*	9	11
15 Sep 84		DON'T BLAME IT ON LOVE *Polydor POSP 699*	55	3
16 Nov 85		DAY BY DAY *Polydor POSP 770* [1]	53	3
24 Oct 87		MR. MANIC AND SISTER COOL *Polydor MANIC 1*	56	3

[1] Shakatak with Al Jarreau

SHAKESPEARS SISTER ⊕

UK/US, female vocal/instrumental duo   **52 wks**

29 Jul 89	●	YOU'RE HISTORY *ffrr F 112*	7	9
14 Oct 89		RUN SILENT *ffrr F 119*	54	3
10 Mar 90		DIRTY MIND *ffrr F 128*	71	1
12 Oct 91		GOODBYE CRUEL WORLD *London LON 309*	59	2
25 Jan 92	★	STAY *London LON 314*	1	16
16 May 92	●	I DON'T CARE *London LON 318*	7	7
18 Jul 92		GOODBYE CRUEL WORLD (re-issue) *London LON 322*	32	4
7 Nov 92		HELLO (TURN YOUR RADIO ON) *London LONCD 330*	14	6
27 Feb 93		MY 16TH APOLOGY EP *London LONCD 337*	61	1
22 Jun 96		I CAN DRIVE *London LONCD 383*	30	3

Tracks on My 16th Apology (EP): My 16th Apology/Catwoman/Dirty Mind/Hot Love. From 1996 Shakespears Sister was essentially just vocalist Siobhan Fahey

SHAKY and BONNIE – See Shakin' STEVENS; Bonnie TYLER

SHALAMAR 🎵 🎤 *Influential US dance-music vocal trio masterminded by* Soul Train *TV producer Don Cornelius. Line-up 1979-1984: Jeffrey Daniel, Jody Watley, Howard Hewett. Regarded as fashion icons and trend-setters, they helped to introduce 'body-popping' to Britain*

134 wks

14 May 77	UPTOWN FESTIVAL *Soul Train FB 0885*	30	5
9 Dec 78	TAKE THAT TO THE BANK *RCA FB 1379*	20	12
24 Nov 79	THE SECOND TIME AROUND *Solar FB 1709*	45	9
9 Feb 80	RIGHT IN THE SOCKET *Solar SO2*	44	6
30 Aug 80	I OWE YOU ONE *Solar SO 11*	13	10
28 Mar 81	MAKE THAT MOVE *Solar SO 17*	30	10
27 Mar 82 ●	I CAN MAKE YOU FEEL GOOD *Solar K 12599*	7	11
12 Jun 82 ●	A NIGHT TO REMEMBER *Solar K 13162*	5	12
4 Sep 82 ●	THERE IT IS *Solar K 13194*	5	10
27 Nov 82	FRIENDS *Solar CHUM 1*	12	10
11 Jun 83 ●	DEAD GIVEAWAY *Solar E 9819*	8	10
13 Aug 83	DISAPPEARING ACT *Solar E 9807*	18	8
15 Oct 83	OVER AND OVER *Solar E 9792*	23	6
24 Mar 84	DANCING IN THE SHEETS *CBS A 4171*	41	3
31 Mar 84	DEADLINE USA *MCA MCA 866*	52	3
24 Nov 84	AMNESIA *Solar/MCA SHal 1*	61	2
2 Feb 85	MY GIRL LOVES ME *MCA SHal 2*	45	3
26 Apr 86	A NIGHT TO REMEMBER (re-mix) *MCA SHal 3*	52	4

SHAM 69 ✏️ *UK, male vocal/instrumental group*

53 wks

13 May 78	ANGELS WITH DIRTY FACES *Polydor 2059 023*	19	10
29 Jul 78 ●	IF THE KIDS ARE UNITED *Polydor 2059 050*	9	9
14 Oct 78 ●	HURRY UP HARRY *Polydor POSP 7*	10	8
24 Mar 79	QUESTIONS AND ANSWERS *Polydor POSP 27*	18	9
4 Aug 79 ●	HERSHAM BOYS *Polydor POSP 64*	6	9
27 Oct 79	YOU'RE A BETTER MAN THAN I *Polydor POSP 82*	49	5
12 Apr 80	TELL THE CHILDREN *Polydor POSP 136*	45	3

SHAM ROCK ♂ 🌐
Ireland, male/female vocal/instrumental group

8 wks

7 Nov 98	TELL ME MA *Jive 0522352*	13†	8

SHAMEN ☺ *UK, male vocal/instrumental duo*

76 wks

7 Apr 90	PRO-GEN *One Little Indian 36 TP7*	55	4
22 Sep 90	MAKE IT MINE *One Little Indian 46 TP7*	42	5
6 Apr 91	HYPERREAL *One Little Indian 48 TP7*	29	5
27 Jul 91 ●	MOVE ANY MOUNTAIN (re-mix) *One Little Indian 52 TP7*	4	10
18 Jul 92 ●	LSI *One Little Indian 68 TP7*	6	8
5 Sep 92 ★	EBENEEZER GOODE *One Little Indian 78 TP7*	1	10
7 Nov 92 ●	BOSS DRUM *One Little Indian 88 TP7*	4	7
7 Nov 92	BOSS DRUM (re-mix) *One Little Indian 88 TP12*	58	1
19 Dec 92 ●	PHOREVER PEOPLE *One Little Indian 98 TP7*	5	10
6 Mar 93	RE: EVOLUTION *One Little Indian 118 TP7CD* [1]	18	2
6 Nov 93	THE SOS EP *One Little Indian 108 TP7CD*	14	4
19 Aug 95	DESTINATION ESCHATON *One Little Indian 128 TP7CDL*	15	4
21 Oct 95	TRANSAMAZONIA *One Little Indian 138 TP7CD*	28	2
10 Feb 96	HEAL (THE SEPARATION) *One Little Indian 158 TP7CDL*	31	2
21 Dec 96	MOVE ANY MOUNTAIN (2nd re-mix) *One Little Indian 169 TP7CD*	35	2

[1] Shamen with Terence McKenna

'Move Any Mountain' is a re-mix of 'Pro-Gen'. Tracks on The SOS EP: Comin' On/Make It Mine/Possible Worlds. 'Make It Mine' on the EP is a re-mix of their second hit

SHAMPOO 🌐 *UK, female vocal duo*

28 wks

30 Jul 94	TROUBLE *Food CDFOOD 51*	11	12
15 Oct 94	VIVA LA MEGABABES *Food CDFOOD 54*	27	4
18 Feb 95	DELICIOUS *Food CDFOOD 58*	21	4
5 Aug 95	TROUBLE (re-issue) *Food CDFOOD 66*	36	3
13 Jul 96	GIRL POWER *Food CDFOOD 76*	25	4
21 Sep 96	I KNOW WHAT BOYS LIKE *Food CDFOOD 83*	42	1

Jimmy SHAND ℂ *UK, male dance band*

2 wks

23 Dec 55	BLUEBELL POLKA *Parlophone F 3436*	20	2

Paul SHANE and the YELLOWCOATS
UK, male vocalist with male/female vocal group

5 wks

16 May 81	HI DE HI (HOLIDAY ROCK) *EMI 5180*	36	5

SHANGRI-LAS 🌐 *US, female vocal group*

57 wks

8 Oct 64	REMEMBER (WALKIN' IN THE SAND) *Red Bird RB 10008*	14	13
14 Jan 65	LEADER OF THE PACK *Red Bird RB 10014* ▲	11	9
14 Oct 72 ●	LEADER OF THE PACK (re-issue) *Kama Sutra 2013 024*	3	14
5 Jun 76 ●	LEADER OF THE PACK (2nd re-issue) *Charly CS 1009*	7	11
12 Jun 76 ●	LEADER OF THE PACK (3rd re-issue) *Contempo CS 9032*	7	10

From 19 Jun, 1976, until 14 Aug, 1976, the last week of the disc's chart run, the Charly and Contempo releases of 'Leader of the Pack' were bracketed together on the chart

SHANICE 🅡&🅑 🌐 *US, female vocalist*

24 wks

23 Nov 91	I LOVE YOUR SMILE *Motown ZB 44907*	55	4
22 Feb 92 ●	I LOVE YOUR SMILE (re-mix) *Motown TMG 1401*	2	10
14 Nov 92	LOVIN' YOU *Motown TMG 1409*	54	1
16 Jan 93	SAVING FOREVER FOR YOU *Giant W 0148CD*	42	3
13 Aug 94	I LIKE *Motown TMGCD 1427*	49	2
16 Dec 95	IF I NEVER KNEW YOU (LOVE THEME FROM POCAHONTAS) *Walt Disney WD 7023CD* [1]	51	4

[1] Jon Secada and Shanice

SHANNON 🎵 *US, female vocalist*

57 wks

19 Nov 83	LET THE MUSIC PLAY *Club LET 1*	51	3
28 Jan 84	LET THE MUSIC PLAY (re-entry) *Club LET 1*	14	12
7 Apr 84	GIVE ME TONIGHT *Club JAB 1*	24	7
30 Jun 84	SWEET SOMEBODY *Club JAB 3*	25	8
20 Jul 85	STRONGER TOGETHER *Club JAB 15*	46	6
6 Dec 97	IT'S OVER LOVE *Manifesto FESCD 37* [1]	16	16
28 Nov 98 ●	MOVE MANIA *Multiply CDMULTY 45* [2]	8†	5

[1] Todd Terry presents Shannon [2] Sash! featuring Shannon

Del SHANNON 🌐 *Early 1960s chart regular, b. Charles Westover, 30 December, 1934, Michigan, d. 8 February, 1990. This unmistakable singer/songwriter had a falsetto vocal ability. He topped both the UK and US charts with the first of his many hits*

147 wks

27 Apr 61 ★	RUNAWAY *London HLX 9317* ▲	1	22
14 Sep 61 ●	HATS OFF TO LARRY *London HLX 9402*	6	12
7 Dec 61	SO LONG BABY *London HLX 9462*	10	11
15 Mar 62	HEY LITTLE GIRL *London HLX 9515*	2	15
6 Sep 62	CRY MYSELF TO SLEEP *London HLX 9587*	29	6
11 Oct 62 ●	SWISS MAID *London HLX 9609*	2	17
17 Jan 63 ●	LITTLE TOWN FLIRT *London HLX 9653*	4	13
25 Apr 63 ●	TWO KINDS OF TEARDROPS *London HLX 9710*	5	13
22 Aug 63	TWO SILHOUETTES *London HLX 9761*	23	8
24 Oct 63	SUE'S GOTTA BE MINE *London HLU 9800*	21	8
12 Mar 64	MARY JANE *Stateside SS 269*	35	5
30 Jul 64	HANDY MAN *Stateside SS 317*	36	4
14 Jan 65 ●	KEEP SEARCHIN' (WE'LL FOLLOW THE SUN) *Stateside SS 368*	3	11
18 Mar 65	STRANGER IN TOWN *Stateside SS 395*	40	2

Roxanne SHANTE *US, female rapper*

10 wks

1 Aug 87	HAVE A NICE DAY *Breakout USA 612*	58	3
4 Jun 88	GO ON GIRL *Breakout USA 633*	55	3
29 Oct 88	SHARP AS A KNIFE *Club JAB 73* [1]	45	3
14 Apr 90	GO ON GIRL (re-mix) *Breakout USA 689*	74	1

[1] Brandon Cooke featuring Roxanne Shante

Helen SHAPIRO 🌐 *Youngest female chart-topper, b. 28 September, 1946, London. Before she was 16 years old, she amassed four Top 5 hits (including two No 1s) and had been voted Britain's Top Female Singer. She headlined the first UK tour on which The Beatles appeared (as her support act)*

119 wks

23 Mar 61 ●	DON'T TREAT ME LIKE A CHILD *Columbia DB 4589*	3	20
29 Jun 61 ★	YOU DON'T KNOW *Columbia DB 4670*	1	23
28 Sep 61 ★	WALKIN' BACK TO HAPPINESS *Columbia DB 4715*	1	19

15 Feb 62 ●	TELL ME WHAT HE SAID Columbia DB 4782	2	15
3 May 62	LET'S TALK ABOUT LOVE Columbia DB 4824	23	7
12 Jul 62 ●	LITTLE MISS LONELY Columbia DB 4869	8	11
18 Oct 62	KEEP AWAY FROM OTHER GIRLS Columbia DB 4908	40	6
7 Feb 63	QUEEN FOR TONIGHT Columbia DB 4966	33	5
25 Apr 63	WOE IS ME Columbia DB 7026	35	6
24 Oct 63	LOOK WHO IT IS Columbia DB 7130	47	3
23 Jan 64	FEVER Columbia DB 7190	38	4

SHARADA HOUSE GANG
Italy, male/female vocal/instrumental group **4 wks**

12 Aug 95	KEEP IT UP Media MCSTD 2071	36	2
11 May 96	LET THE RHYTHM MOVE YOU Media MCSTD 40035	50	1
18 Oct 97	GYPSY BOY, GYPSY GIRL Gut CXGUT 12	52	1

SHARKEY *UK, male DJ/production duo* **1 wk**

8 Mar 97	REVOLUTIONS EP React CDREACT 95	53	1

Tracks on Revolutions EP: Revolution Part One / Revolution Part Two / Revolution Part Two (remix)

Feargal SHARKEY ○ *UK, male vocalist* **58 wks**

13 Oct 84	LISTEN TO YOUR FATHER Zarjazz JAZZ 1	23	7
29 Jun 85	LOVING YOU Virgin VS 770	26	10
12 Oct 85 ★	A GOOD HEART Virgin VS 808	1	16
4 Jan 86 ●	YOU LITTLE THIEF Virgin VS 840	5	9
5 Apr 86	SOMEONE TO SOMEBODY Virgin VS 828	64	3
16 Jan 88	MORE LOVE Virgin VS 992	44	5
16 Mar 91	I'VE GOT NEWS FOR YOU Virgin VS 1294	12	8

SHARONETTES *US, female vocal group* **8 wks**

26 Apr 75	PAPA OOM MOW MOW Black Magic BM 102	26	5
12 Jul 75	GOING TO A GO-GO Black Magic BM 104	46	3

Debbie SHARP – See DREAM FREQUENCY

Dee Dee SHARP *US, female vocalist* **2 wks**

25 Apr 63	DO THE BIRD Cameo Parkway C 244	46	2

Barrie K. SHARPE – See Diana BROWN and Barrie K. SHARPE

SHARPE and NUMAN – See Gary NUMAN

Rocky SHARPE and the REPLAYS ○
UK, male/female vocal group **41 wks**

16 Dec 78	RAMA LAMA DING DONG Chiswick CHIS 104	17	10
24 Mar 79	IMAGINATION Chiswick CHIS 110	39	6
25 Aug 79	LOVE WILL MAKE YOU FAIL IN SCHOOL Chiswick CHIS 114 [1]	60	4
9 Feb 80	MARTIAN HOP Chiswick CHIS 121 [1]	55	4
17 Apr 82	SHOUT SHOUT (KNOCK YOURSELF OUT) Chiswick DICE 3	19	9
7 Aug 82	CLAP YOUR HANDS RAK 345	54	3
26 Feb 83	IF YOU WANNA BE HAPPY Polydor POSP 560	46	5

[1] Rocky Sharpe and the Replays featuring the Top Liners

Mark SHAW *UK, male vocalist* **1 wk**

17 Nov 90	LOVE SO BRIGHT EMI EM 161	54	1

Sandie SHAW ○ *Barefoot pop princess of the sixties, b. Sandra Goodrich, 26 February, 1947, Essex. This distinctive vocalist, who has a 30-year chart span, was the first UK act to win the Eurovision Song Contest (with 'Puppet on a String' in 1967)* **165 wks**

8 Oct 64 ★	(THERE'S) ALWAYS SOMETHING THERE TO REMIND ME Pye 7N 15704	1	11
10 Dec 64 ●	GIRL DON'T COME Pye 7N 15743	3	12
18 Feb 65 ●	I'LL STOP AT NOTHING Pye 7N 15783	4	9
13 May 65 ★	LONG LIVE LOVE Pye 7N 15841	1	14
23 Sep 65 ●	MESSAGE UNDERSTOOD Pye 7N 15940	6	10
18 Nov 65 ●	HOW CAN YOU TELL Pye 7N 15987	21	9

27 Jan 66 ●	TOMORROW Pye 7N 17036	9	9
19 May 66	NOTHING COMES EASY Pye 7N 17086	14	9
8 Sep 66	RUN Pye 7N 17163	32	5
24 Nov 66	THINK SOMETIMES ABOUT ME Pye 7N 17212	32	4
19 Jan 67	I DON'T NEED ANYTHING Pye 7N 17239	50	1
16 Mar 67 ★	PUPPET ON A STRING Pye 7N 17272	1	18
12 Jul 67	TONIGHT IN TOKYO Pye 7N 17346	21	6
4 Oct 67	YOU'VE NOT CHANGED Pye 7N 17378	18	12
7 Feb 68	TODAY Pye 7N 17441	27	7
12 Feb 69 ●	MONSIEUR DUPONT Pye 7N 17675	6	15
14 May 69	THINK IT ALL OVER Pye 7N 17726	42	4
21 Apr 84	HAND IN GLOVE Rough Trade RT 130	27	5
14 Jun 86	ARE YOU READY TO BE HEARTBROKEN Polydor POSP 793	68	1
12 Nov 94	NOTHING LESS THAN BRILLIANT Virgin VSCDT 1521	66	2

See also VARIOUS ARTISTS (EPs & LPs) – Gimme Shelter (EP)

Tracy SHAW *UK, female vocalist* **1 wk**

4 Jul 98	HAPPENIN' ALL OVER AGAIN Recognition CDREC 2	46	1

Winifred SHAW *US, female vocalist* **4 wks**

14 Aug 76	LULLABY OF BROADWAY United Artists UP 36131	42	4

SHE – See URBAN DISCHARGE featuring SHE

SHE ROCKERS *UK, female rap duo* **2 wks**

13 Jan 90	JAM IT JAM Jive JIVE 233	58	2

George SHEARING ℭ *UK, male instrumentalist – piano* **15 wks**

19 Jul 62	LET THERE BE LOVE Capitol CL 15257 [1]	11	14
4 Oct 62	BAUBLES BANGLES AND BEADS Capitol CL 15269	49	1

[1] Nat 'King' Cole with George Shearing

Gary SHEARSTON ○ *Australia, male vocalist* **8 wks**

5 Oct 74 ●	I GET A KICK OUT OF YOU Charisma CB 234	7	8

SHED SEVEN ○ ✎ *UK, male vocal/instrumental group* **40 wks**

25 Jun 94	DOLPHIN Polydor YORCD 2	28	4
27 Aug 94	SPEAKEASY Polydor YORCD 3	24	3
12 Nov 94	OCEAN PIE Polydor YORCD 4	33	2
13 May 95	WHERE HAVE YOU BEEN TONIGHT Polydor YORCD 5	23	2
27 Jan 96	GETTING BETTER Polydor 5778912	14	3
23 Mar 96 ●	GOING FOR GOLD Polydor 5762152	8	5
18 May 96	BULLY BOY Polydor 5765972	22	3
31 Aug 96	ON STANDBY Polydor 5752732	12	4
23 Nov 96	CHASING RAINBOWS Polydor 5759292	17	5
14 Mar 98	SHE LEFT ME ON FRIDAY Polydor 5695412	11	4
23 May 98	THE HEROES Polydor 5699172	18	3
22 Aug 98	DEVIL IN YOUR SHOES Polydor 5672072	37	2

SHEEP ON DRUGS *UK, male vocal/instrumental duo* **5 wks**

27 Mar 93	15 MINUTES OF FAME Transglobal CID 564	44	2
30 Oct 93	FROM A TO H AND BACK AGAIN Transglobal CID 575	40	2
14 May 94	LET THE GOOD TIMES ROLL Transglobal CID 576	56	1

SHEER BRONZE featuring Lisa MILLETT
UK, male/female vocal/instrumental duo **1 wk**

3 Sep 94	WALKIN' ON Go.Beat GODCD 115	63	1

SHEER ELEGANCE ○ ♪ *UK, male vocal group* **23 wks**

20 Dec 75	MILKY WAY Pye International 7N 25697	18	10
3 Apr 76 ●	LIFE IS TOO SHORT GIRL Pye International 7N 25703	9	9
24 Jul 76	IT'S TEMPTATION Pye International 7N 25715	41	4

SHEILA and B DEVOTION – See Sheila B DEVOTION

Doug SHELDON *UK, male vocalist* **15 wks**

9 Nov 61	RUNAROUND SUE Decca F 11398	36	3

4 Jan 62	YOUR MA SAID YOU CRIED IN YOUR SLEEP LAST NIGHT		
	Decca F 11416	29	6
7 Feb 63	I SAW LINDA YESTERDAY Decca F 11564	36	6

Pete SHELLEY UK, male vocalist — 1 wk

12 Mar 83	TELEPHONE OPERATOR Genetic XX1	66	1

Peter SHELLEY ☺ UK, male vocalist — 20 wks

14 Sep 74	● GEE BABY Magnet MAG 12	4	10
22 Mar 75	● LOVE ME LOVE MY DOG Magnet MAG 22	3	10

Anne SHELTON € UK, female vocalist — 31 wks

16 Dec 55	ARRIVEDERCI DARLING HMV POP 146	17	4
13 Apr 56	SEVEN DAYS Philips PB 567	20	4
24 Aug 56	★ LAY DOWN YOUR ARMS Philips PB 616	1	14
20 Nov 59	VILLAGE OF ST. BERNADETTE Philips PB 969	27	1
26 Jan 61	SAILOR Philips PB 1096	10	8

SHENA UK, female vocalist — 2 wks

2 Aug 97	LET THE BEAT HIT 'EM VC VCRD 24	28	2

Vikki SHEPARD – See SLEAZESISTERS

Vonda SHEPARD ☺ US, female vocalist — 4 wks

5 Dec 98	● SEARCHIN' MY SOUL Epic 6666332	10†	4

SHEPHERD SISTERS ☺ US, female vocal group — 6 wks

15 Nov 57	ALONE HMV POP 411	14	5
3 Jan 58	ALONE (re-entry) HMV POP 411	22	1

SHERBET ☺ Australia, male vocal/instrumental group — 10 wks

25 Sep 76	● HOWZAT Epic EPC 4574	4	10

Tony SHERIDAN – See BEATLES

Allan SHERMAN € US, male vocalist — 10 wks

12 Sep 63	HELLO MUDDAH HELLO FADDAH Warner Bros. WB 106	14	10

Bobby SHERMAN US, male vocalist — 4 wks

31 Oct 70	JULIE DO YA LOVE ME CBS 5144	28	4

SHERRICK US, male vocalist — 10 wks

1 Aug 87	JUST CALL Warner Bros. W 8380	23	8
21 Nov 87	LET'S BE LOVERS TONIGHT Warner Bros. W 8146	63	2

Pluto SHERVINGTON ♈ Jamaica, male vocalist — 20 wks

7 Feb 76	● DAT Opal Pal 5	6	8
10 Apr 76	RAM GOAT LIVER Trojan TR 7978	43	4
6 Mar 82	YOUR HONOUR KR KR 4 [1]	19	8

[1] Pluto

Holly SHERWOOD US, female vocalist — 7 wks

5 Feb 72	DAY BY DAY Bell 1182	29	7

Tony SHEVETON UK, male vocalist — 1 wk

13 Feb 64	MILLION DRUMS Oriole CB 1895	49	1

SHIMMON and WOOLFSON UK, male DJ/production duo — 1 wk

10 Jan 98	WELCOME TO THE FUTURE React CDREACT 119	69	1

SHINEHEAD Jamaica, male vocalist — 6 wks

3 Apr 93	JAMAICAN IN NEW YORK Elektra EKR 161CD	30	5
26 Jun 93	LET 'EM IN Elektra EKR 168CD	70	1

SHIRELLES ♪ US, female vocal group — 29 wks

9 Feb 61	● WILL YOU LOVE ME TOMORROW Top Rank JAR 540 ▲	4	15
31 May 62	SOLDIER BOY HMV POP 1019 ▲	23	9
23 May 63	FOOLISH LITTLE GIRL Stateside SS 181	38	5

SHIRLEY and COMPANY ♪ ◢
US, female vocalist and male vocal/instrumental backing group — 9 wks

8 Feb 75	● SHAME SHAME SHAME All Platinum 6146 301	6	9

SHIVA ☺ UK, male/female vocal/instrumental group — 5 wks

13 May 95	WORK IT OUT ffrr FCD 261	36	2
19 Aug 95	FREEDOM ffrr FCD 263	18	3

SHO NUFF US, male vocal/instrumental group — 4 wks

24 May 80	IT'S ALRIGHT Ensign ENY 37	53	4

Michelle SHOCKED US, female vocalist — 10 wks

8 Oct 88	ANCHORAGE Cooking Vinyl LON 193	60	4
14 Jan 89	IF LOVE WAS A TRAIN Cooking Vinyl LON 212	63	3
11 Mar 89	WHEN I GROW UP Cooking Vinyl LON 219	67	3

SHOCKING BLUE ☺
Holland, male/female vocal/instrumental group — 14 wks

17 Jan 70	● VENUS Penny Farthing PEN 702 ▲	8	11
25 Apr 70	MIGHTY JOE Penny Farthing PEN 713	43	3

Troy SHONDELL US, male vocalist — 11 wks

2 Nov 61	THIS TIME London HLG 9432	22	11

SHONDELLS – See Tommy JAMES and the SHONDELLS

SHOOTING PARTY UK, male vocal duo — 2 wks

31 Mar 90	LET'S HANG ON Lisson DOLE 15	66	2

SHOWADDYWADDY ☺ Rock'n'roll revival octet from Leicester, which included vocalists Dave Bartram and Buddy Gask. At the peak of their career, they had seven successive Top 5 entries with rousing revivals of old US rock'n'roll songs — 209 wks

18 May 74	● HEY ROCK AND ROLL Bell 1357	2	14
17 Aug 74	ROCK 'N' ROLL LADY Bell 1374	15	9
30 Nov 74	HEY MR. CHRISTMAS Bell 1387	13	8
22 Feb 75	SWEET MUSIC Bell 1403	14	9
17 May 75	● THREE STEPS TO HEAVEN Bell 1426	2	11
6 Sep 75	● HEARTBEAT Bell 1450	7	7
15 Nov 75	HEAVENLY Bell 1460	34	6
29 May 76	TROCADERO Bell 1476	32	3
6 Nov 76	★ UNDER THE MOON OF LOVE Bell 1495	1	15
5 Mar 77	● WHEN Arista 91	3	11
23 Jul 77	● YOU GOT WHAT IT TAKES Arista 126	2	10
5 Nov 77	● DANCIN' PARTY Arista 149	4	11
25 Mar 78	● I WONDER WHY Arista 174	2	11
24 Jun 78	● A LITTLE BIT OF SOAP Arista 191	5	12
4 Nov 78	● PRETTY LITTLE ANGEL EYES Arista ARIST 222	5	12
31 Mar 79	REMEMBER THEN Arista 247	17	8
28 Jul 79	SWEET LITTLE ROCK 'N' ROLLER Arista 278	15	9
10 Nov 79	A NIGHT AT DADDY GEE'S Arista 314	39	5
27 Sep 80	WHY DO LOVERS BREAK EACH OTHER'S HEARTS Arista ARIST 359	22	10
29 Nov 80	BLUE MOON Arista ARIST 379	32	9
13 Jun 81	MULTIPLICATION Arista ARIST 416	39	4
28 Nov 81	FOOTSTEPS Bell BELL 1499	31	9
28 Aug 82	WHO PUT THE BOMP (IN THE BOMP-A-BOMP-A-BOMP) RCA 236	37	6

SHOWDOWN – See Garry LEE and SHOWDOWN

SHOWDOWN US, male vocal/instrumental group — 3 wks

17 Dec 77	KEEP DOIN' IT State STAT 63	41	3

SHOWSTOPPERS 🎤 US, male vocal group — 25 wks

Date	Title	Pos	Wks
13 Mar 68	AIN'T NOTHING BUT A HOUSEPARTY *Beacon 3-100*	11	15
13 Nov 68	EENY MEENY *MGM 1436*	33	7
30 Jan 71	AIN'T NOTHING BUT A HOUSEPARTY (re-issue) *Beacon BEA 100*	43	1
13 Feb 71	AIN'T NOTHING BUT A HOUSEPARTY (re-entry of re-issue) *Beacon BEA 100*	33	1
27 Feb 71	AIN'T NOTHING BUT A HOUSEPARTY (2nd re-entry of re-issue) *Beacon BEA 100*	36	1

SHRIEKBACK UK, male vocal/instrumental group — 4 wks

Date	Title	Pos	Wks
28 Jul 84	HAND ON MY HEART *Arista SHRK 1*	52	4

SHRINK Holland, male DJ/production duo — 2 wks

Date	Title	Pos	Wks
10 Oct 98	NERVOUS BREAKDOWN *VC Recordings VCRD42*	42	2

SHUT UP AND DANCE ☺ UK, male vocal/production group — 14 wks

Date	Title	Pos	Wks
21 Apr 90	£20 TO GET IN *Shut Up And Dance SUAD 3*	56	3
28 Jul 90	LAMBORGHINI *Shut Up And Dance SUAD 4*	55	1
8 Feb 92	AUTOBIOGRAPHY OF A CRACKHEAD/THE GREEN MAN *Shut Up And Dance SUAD 21*	43	2
30 May 92 ●	RAVING I'M RAVING *Shut Up And Dance SUAD 30S* [1]	2	2
15 Aug 92	THE ART OF MOVING BUTTS *Shut Up And Dance SUAD 34S* [2]	69	1
1 Apr 95	SAVE IT 'TIL THE MOURNING AFTER *Pulse 8 PULS 84CD*	25	3
8 Jul 95	I LUV U *Pulse 8 PULS 90CD* [3]	68	1

[1] Shut Up and Dance featuring Peter Bouncer [2] Shut Up and Dance featuring Erin
[3] Shut Up and Dance featuring Richie Davis and Professor T

SHY UK, male vocal/instrumental group — 3 wks

Date	Title	Pos	Wks
19 Apr 80	GIRL (IT'S ALL I HAVE) *Gallery GA 1*	60	3

SHY FX – See UK APACHI with SHY FX

SHYHEIM US, male rapper — 1 wk

Date	Title	Pos	Wks
8 Jun 96	THIS IZ REAL *Noo Trybe VUSCD 105*	61	1

Labi SIFFRE ◑ UK, male vocalist — 44 wks

Date	Title	Pos	Wks
27 Nov 71	IT MUST BE LOVE *Pye International 7N 25572*	14	12
25 Mar 72	CRYING LAUGHING LOVING LYING *Pye International 7N 25576*	11	9
29 Jul 72	WATCH ME *Pye International 7N 25586*	29	6
4 Apr 87 ●	(SOMETHING INSIDE) SO STRONG *China WOK 12*	4	13
21 Nov 87	NOTHIN'S GONNA CHANGE *China WOK 16*	52	4

SIGNUM Holland, male vocal/instrumental/production duo — 1 wk

Date	Title	Pos	Wks
28 Nov 98	WHAT YA GOT 4 ME *Tidy Trax TIDY 118CD*	70	1

SIGUE SIGUE SPUTNIK ◑ UK, male vocal/instrumental group — 20 wks

Date	Title	Pos	Wks
1 Mar 86 ●	LOVE MISSILE F1-11 *Parlophone SSS 1*	3	9
7 Jun 86	TWENTY-FIRST CENTURY BOY *Parlophone SSS 2*	20	5
19 Nov 88	SUCCESS *Parlophone SSS 3*	31	3
1 Apr 89	DANCERAMA *Parlophone SSS 5*	50	2
20 May 89	ALBINONI VS STAR WARS *Parlophone SSS 4*	75	1

SIL Holland, male DJ/production duo — 1 wk

Date	Title	Pos	Wks
11 Apr 98	WINDOWS '98 *Hooj Choons HOOJCD 60*	58	1

SILENCERS UK, male vocal/instrumental group — 7 wks

Date	Title	Pos	Wks
25 Jun 88	PAINTED MOON *RCA HUSH 1*	57	4
27 May 89	SCOTTISH RAIN *RCA PB 42701*	71	2
15 May 93	I CAN FEEL IT *RCA 74321147112*	62	1

SILENT UNDERDOG UK, male instrumentalist – Paul Hardcastle — 1 wk

Date	Title	Pos	Wks
16 Feb 85	PAPA'S GOT A BRAND NEW PIGBAG *Kaz KAZ 50*	73	1

SILJE Norway, female vocalist — 6 wks

Date	Title	Pos	Wks
15 Dec 90	TELL ME WHERE YOU'RE GOING *EMI EM 159*	55	6

SILK US, male vocal group — 10 wks

Date	Title	Pos	Wks
24 Apr 93	FREAK ME *Elektra EKR 165CD* ▲	46	5
5 Jun 93	GIRL U FOR ME *Elektra EKR 167CD*	67	2
9 Oct 93	BABY IT'S YOU *Elektra EKR 173CD*	44	2
26 Feb 94	FREAK ME (re-entry) *Elektra EKR 165CD*	72	1

SILKIE UK, male/female vocal/instrumental group — 6 wks

Date	Title	Pos	Wks
23 Sep 65	YOU'VE GOT TO HIDE YOUR LOVE AWAY *Fontana TF 603*	28	6

SILSOE UK, male instrumentalist – keyboards — 4 wks

Date	Title	Pos	Wks
21 Jun 86	AZTEC GOLD *CBS A 7231*	48	4

'Aztec Gold' was the ITV theme to the 1986 World Cup Finals and was performed by Rod Argent under the title Silsoe
See also ARGENT; SAN JOSE featuring Rodriguez ARGENTINA

SILVER BULLET ◀━ ☺ UK, male rap/instrumental duo — 20 wks

Date	Title	Pos	Wks
2 Sep 89	BRING FORTH THE GUILLOTINE *Tam Tam TTT 013*	70	1
9 Dec 89	20 SECONDS TO COMPLY *Tam Tam 7TTT 019*	11	10
3 Mar 90	BRING FORTH THE GUILLOTINE (re-entry) *Tam Tam TTT 013*	45	5
13 Apr 91	UNDERCOVER ANARCHIST *Parlophone R 6284*	33	4

SILVER BULLET BAND – See Bob SEGER and the SILVER BULLET BAND

SILVER CITY UK, male/female vocal/instrumental duo — 1 wk

Date	Title	Pos	Wks
30 Oct 93	LOVE INFINITY *Silver City GFJMCD 1*	62	1

SILVER CONVENTION ☺ Germany/US, female vocal group — 35 wks

Date	Title	Pos	Wks
5 Apr 75	SAVE ME *Magnet MAG 26*	30	7
15 Nov 75	FLY ROBIN FLY *Magnet MAG 43* ▲	28	8
3 Apr 76 ●	GET UP AND BOOGIE *Magnet MAG 55*	7	11
19 Jun 76	TIGER BABY/NO NO JOE *Magnet MAG 69*	41	4
29 Jan 77	EVERYBODY'S TALKIN' 'BOUT LOVE *Magnet MAG 81*	25	5

SILVER SUN ☹ ◑ UK, male vocal/instrumental group — 13 wks

Date	Title	Pos	Wks
2 Nov 96	LAVA *Polydor 5756872*	54	1
22 Feb 97	LAST DAY *Polydor 5732432*	48	1
3 May 97	GOLDEN SKIN *Polydor 5738272*	32	2
5 Jul 97	JULIA *Polydor 5711752*	51	1
18 Oct 97	LAVA *Polydor 5714242*	35	2
20 Jun 98	TOO MUCH, TOO LITTLE, TOO LATE *Polydor 5699152*	20	4
26 Sep 98	I'LL SEE YOU AROUND *Polydor 5674532*	26	2

SILVERCHAIR Australia, male vocal/instrumental group — 7 wks

Date	Title	Pos	Wks
29 Jul 95	PURE MASSACRE *Murmur 6622642*	71	1
9 Sep 95	TOMORROW *Murmur 6623952*	59	2
5 Apr 97	FREAK *Murmur 6640765*	34	2
19 Jul 97	ABUSE ME *Murmur 6647907*	40	2

Dooley SILVERSPOON US, male vocalist — 3 wks

Date	Title	Pos	Wks
31 Jan 76	LET ME BE THE NUMBER 1 (LOVE OF YOUR LIFE) *Seville SEV 1020*	44	3

Harry SIMEONE CHORALE ☾ US, choir — 14 wks

Date	Title	Pos	Wks
13 Feb 59	LITTLE DRUMMER BOY *Top Rank JAR 101*	13	7
22 Dec 60	ONWARD CHRISTIAN SOLDIERS *Ember EMBS 118*	35	1
5 Jan 61	ONWARD CHRISTIAN SOLDIERS (re-entry) *Ember EMBS 118*	38	1
21 Dec 61	ONWARD CHRISTIAN SOLDIERS (2nd re-entry) *Ember EMBS 118*	36	3
20 Dec 62	ONWARD CHRISTIAN SOLDIERS (re-issue) *Ember EMBS 144*	38	2

Gene SIMMONS US, male vocalist — 4 wks

Date	Title	Pos	Wks
27 Jan 79	RADIOACTIVE *Casablanca CAN 134*	41	4

Carly SIMON ♂ ✎ US, female vocalist — 76 wks

16 Dec 72	● YOU'RE SO VAIN Elektra K 12077 ▲	3	15
31 Mar 73	THE RIGHT THING TO DO Elektra K 12095	17	9
16 Mar 74	MOCKINGBIRD Elektra K 12134 [1]	34	5
6 Aug 77	● NOBODY DOES IT BETTER Elektra K 12261	7	12
21 Aug 82	● WHY WEA K 79300	10	13
24 Jan 87	● COMING AROUND AGAIN Arista ARIST 687	10	12
10 Apr 89	WHY (re-issue) WEA U 7501	56	5
20 Apr 91	YOU'RE SO VAIN (re-issue) Elektra EKR 123	41	5

[1] Carly Simon and James Taylor

See also Will POWERS

Joe SIMON ✎ US, male vocalist — 10 wks

16 Jun 73	STEP BY STEP Mojo 2093 030	14	10

Paul SIMON ♂ ✎ US, male vocalist — 85 wks

19 Feb 72	● MOTHER AND CHILD REUNION CBS 7793	5	12
29 Apr 72	ME AND JULIO DOWN BY THE SCHOOLYARD CBS 7964	15	9
16 Jun 73	● TAKE ME TO THE MARDI GRAS CBS 1578	7	11
22 Sep 73	LOVES ME LIKE A ROCK CBS 1700	39	5
10 Jan 76	50 WAYS TO LEAVE YOUR LOVER CBS 3887 ▲	23	6
3 Dec 77	SLIP SLIDIN' AWAY CBS 5770	36	5
6 Sep 80	LATE IN THE EVENING Warner Bros. K 17666	58	4
13 Sep 86	● YOU CAN CALL ME AL Warner Bros. W 8667	4	13
13 Dec 86	THE BOY IN THE BUBBLE Warner Bros. W 8509	26	8
6 Oct 90	THE OBVIOUS CHILD Warner Bros W 9549	15	10
9 Dec 95	SOMETHING SO RIGHT RCA 74321332392 [1]	44	2

[1] Annie Lennox featuring Paul Simon

See also SIMON and GARFUNKEL

Ronni SIMON UK, male vocalist — 2 wks

13 Aug 94	B GOOD 2 ME Network NWKCD 80	73	1
10 Jun 95	TAKE YOU THERE Network NWKCD 85	58	1

Tito SIMON Jamaica, male vocalist — 4 wks

8 Feb 75	THIS MONDAY MORNING FEELING Horse HOSS 57	45	4

SIMON and GARFUNKEL ♂ ✎ US, male vocal duo — 87 wks

24 Mar 66	● HOMEWARD BOUND CBS 202045	9	12
16 Jun 66	I AM A ROCK CBS 202303	17	10
10 Jul 68	● MRS ROBINSON CBS 3443 ▲	4	12
8 Jan 69	● MRS ROBINSON (EP) CBS EP 6400	9	5
30 Apr 69	● THE BOXER CBS 4162	6	14
21 Feb 70	★ BRIDGE OVER TROUBLED WATER CBS 4790 ▲	1	19
15 Aug 70	BRIDGE OVER TROUBLED WATER (re-entry) CBS 4790	45	1
7 Oct 72	AMERICA CBS 8336	25	7
7 Dec 91	A HAZY SHADE OF WINTER/SILENT NIGHT – SEVEN O'CLOCK NEWS Columbia 6576537	30	6
15 Feb 92	THE BOXER (re-issue) Columbia 6578067	75	1

Tracks on Mrs Robinson (EP): Mrs Robinson / Scarborough Fair – Canticle / Sounds of Silence / April Come She Will. This EP would have stayed more than five weeks on chart had a decision to exclude EPs from chart in Feb, 1969, not been taken
See also Paul SIMON; Art GARFUNKEL

SIMONE US, female vocalist — 1 wk

23 Nov 91	MY FAMILY DEPENDS ON ME Strictly Rhythm A 8678	75	1

Nina SIMONE ✎ US, female vocalist — 46 wks

5 Aug 65	I PUT A SPELL ON YOU Philips BF 1415	49	1
16 Oct 68	● AIN'T GOT NO – I GOT LIFE/DO WHAT YOU GOTTA DO RCA 1743	2	18
15 Jan 69	● TO LOVE SOMEBODY RCA 1779	5	9
15 Jan 69	I PUT A SPELL ON YOU (re-issue) Philips BF 1736	28	4
31 Oct 87	● MY BABY JUST CARES FOR ME Charly CYZ 7112	5	11
9 Jul 94	FEELING GOOD Mercury MERCD 403	40	3

'Do What You Gotta Do' was only listed for the first eight weeks of the record's chart run. It peaked at No 7

Victor SIMONELLI presents SOLUTION US, male producer — 1 wk

2 Nov 96	FEELS SO RIGHT Soundproof MCSTD 40068	63	1

SIMPLE MINDS ⊘ ✎ Most successful Scottish band of the 1980s, fronted by Jim Kerr (b. 9 July, 1959, Glasgow), who married Chrissie Hynde, lead singer of Pretenders. Five of the quintet's albums entered UK chart at No 1, and world sales topped 30 million — 187 wks

12 May 79	LIFE IN A DAY Zoom ZUM 10	62	2
23 May 81	THE AMERICAN Virgin VS 410	59	3
15 Aug 81	LOVE SONG Virgin VS 434	47	4
7 Nov 81	SWEAT IN BULLET Virgin VS 451	52	3
10 Apr 82	PROMISED YOU A MIRACLE Virgin VS 488	13	11
28 Aug 82	GLITTERING PRIZE Virgin VS 511	16	11
13 Nov 82	SOMEONE SOMEWHERE (IN SUMMERTIME) Virgin VS 538	36	5
26 Nov 83	WATERFRONT Virgin VS 636	13	10
28 Jan 84	SPEED YOUR LOVE TO ME Virgin VS 649	20	4
24 Mar 84	UP ON THE CATWALK Virgin VS 661	27	5
20 Apr 85	● DON'T YOU (FORGET ABOUT ME) Virgin VS 749 ▲	7	11
17 Aug 85	DON'T YOU (FORGET ABOUT ME) (re-entry) Virgin VS 749	61	8
12 Oct 85	● ALIVE AND KICKING Virgin VS 817	7	9
28 Dec 85	DON'T YOU (FORGET ABOUT ME) (2nd re-entry) Virgin VS 749	74	1
4 Jan 86	ALIVE AND KICKING (re-entry) Virgin VS 817	60	2
1 Feb 86	SANCTIFY YOURSELF Virgin SM 1	10	7
15 Feb 86	DON'T YOU (FORGET ABOUT ME) (3rd re-entry) Virgin VS 779	62	3
15 Mar 86	DON'T YOU (FORGET ABOUT ME) (4th re-entry) Virgin VS 779	68	1
12 Apr 86	● ALL THE THINGS SHE SAID Virgin VS 860	9	8
14 Jun 86	ALL THE THINGS SHE SAID (re-entry) Virgin VS 860	73	1
15 Nov 86	GHOSTDANCING Virgin VS 907	13	6
3 Jan 87	GHOSTDANCING (re-entry) Virgin VS 907	68	2
20 Jun 87	PROMISED YOU A MIRACLE Virgin SM 2	19	7
18 Feb 89	★ BELFAST CHILD Virgin SMX 3	1	11
22 Apr 89	THIS IS YOUR LAND Virgin SMX4	13	4
29 Jul 89	KICK IT IN Virgin SM 5	15	5
9 Dec 89	THE AMSTERDAM EP Virgin SMX 6	18	6
23 Mar 91	● LET THERE BE LOVE Virgin VS 1332	6	7
25 May 91	SEE THE LIGHTS Virgin VS 1343	20	4
31 Aug 91	STAND BY LOVE Virgin VS 1358	13	4
26 Oct 91	REAL LIFE Virgin VS 1382	34	3
10 Oct 92	● LOVE SONG/ALIVE AND KICKING (re-issue) Virgin VS 1440	6	6
28 Jan 95	SHE'S A RIVER Virgin VSCDX 1509	9	5
8 Apr 95	HYPNOTISED Virgin VSCDX 1534	18	5
14 Mar 98	GLITTERBALL Chrysalis CDCHSS 5078	18	2
30 May 98	WAR BABIES Chrysalis CDCHS 5088	43	1

The 1987 version of 'Promised You a Miracle' was a live recording
Tracks on The Amsterdam EP: Let It All Come Down / Jerusalem / Sign of the Times

SIMPLICIOUS US, male vocal group — 9 wks

29 Sep 84	LET HER FEEL IT Fourth & Broadway BRW 13	65	3
2 Feb 85	LET HER FEEL IT (re-issue) Fourth & Broadway BRW 18	34	6

The re-issue of 'Let Her Feel It' was listed with 'Personality' by Eugene Wilde

SIMPLY RED ⊘ The unmistakable Mick Hucknall (b. 8 June, 1960, Manchester) quickly became the representative face and voice of this internationally popular outfit. Their Stars album sold more than two million in the UK and was the biggest British seller in 1991 and 1992 — 205 wks

15 Jun 85	MONEY'S TOO TIGHT (TO MENTION) Elektra EKR 9	13	12
21 Sep 85	COME TO MY AID Elektra EKR 19	66	2
16 Nov 85	HOLDING BACK THE YEARS Elektra EKR 29 ▲	51	4
8 Mar 86	JERICHO WEA YZ 63	53	3
17 May 86	● HOLDING BACK THE YEARS (re-issue) WEA YZ 70	2	13
9 Aug 86	OPEN UP THE RED BOX WEA YZ 75	61	4
14 Feb 87	THE RIGHT THING WEA YZ 103	11	10
23 May 87	INFIDELITY Elektra YZ 114	31	5
28 Nov 87	EV'RY TIME WE SAY GOODBYE Elektra YZ 161	11	9
12 Mar 88	I WON'T FEEL BAD Elektra YZ 172	68	3
28 Jan 89	IT'S ONLY LOVE Elektra YZ 349	13	8
8 Apr 89	● IF YOU DON'T KNOW ME BY NOW Elektra YZ 377 ▲	2	10
8 Jul 89	A NEW FLAME WEA YZ 404	17	8

Date	Title	Pos	Wks
28 Oct 89	YOU'VE GOT IT *Elektra YZ 424*	46	3
21 Sep 91	SOMETHING GOT ME STARTED *East West YZ 614*	11	8
30 Nov 91 ●	STARS *East West YZ 626*	8	10
8 Feb 92 ●	FOR YOUR BABIES *East West YZ 642*	9	8
2 May 92	THRILL ME *East West YZ 671*	33	5
25 Jul 92	YOUR MIRROR *East West YZ 689*	17	4
21 Nov 92	MONTREUX EP *East West YZ 716*	11	10
30 Sep 95 ★	FAIRGROUND *East West EW 001CD1* ■	1	14
16 Dec 95	REMEMBERING THE FIRST TIME *East West EW 015CD1*	22	6
24 Feb 96	NEVER NEVER LOVE *East West EW 029CD1*	18	4
22 Jun 96	WE'RE IN THIS TOGETHER *East West EW 046CD1*	11	6
9 Nov 96 ●	ANGEL *East West EW 074CD1*	4	12
20 Sep 97	NIGHT NURSE *East West EW 129CD1* [1]	14	8
16 May 98 ●	SAY YOU LOVE ME *East West EW 164CD*	7	7
22 Aug 98 ●	THE AIR THAT I BREATHE *East West E 3821CD*	6	7
12 Dec 98	GHETTO GIRL *East West EW 191CD1*	34	2

[1] Sly and Robbie featuring Simply Red

Tracks on Montreux EP: Drowning In My Own Tears / Grandma's Hands / Lady Godiva's Room / Love for Sale

SIMPLY RED AND WHITE *UK, male vocal group*   **4 wks**

Date	Title	Pos	Wks
6 Apr 96	DAYDREAM BELIEVER (CHEER UP PETER REID) *Ropery SHAYISGOD 1D*	41	3
4 May 96	DAYDREAM BELIEVER (CHEER UP PETER REID) (re-entry) *Ropery SHAYISGOD 1D*	74	1

SIMPLY SMOOTH *US, male/female vocal group*   **1 wk**

Date	Title	Pos	Wks
17 Oct 98	LADY (YOU BRING ME UP) *Big Bang CDBANG 07*	70	1

Paul SIMPSON – See ADEVA

Vida SIMPSON *US, female vocalist*   **1 wk**

Date	Title	Pos	Wks
18 Feb 95	OOHHH BABY *Hi-Life HICD 6*	70	1

SIMPSONS ☺ 📀 *US, male/female cartoon group*   **19 wks**

Date	Title	Pos	Wks
26 Jan 91 ★	DO THE BARTMAN *Geffen GEF 87*	1	12
6 Apr 91 ●	DEEP DEEP TROUBLE *Geffen GEF 88* [1]	7	7

[1] Simpsons featuring Bart and Homer

W/Cdr. A.E. SIMS – *See Central Band of the ROYAL AIR FORCE, conductor W/Cdr. A.E. SIMS, O.B.E*

Joyce SIMS ✎ ☺ *US, female vocalist*   **36 wks**

Date	Title	Pos	Wks
19 Apr 86	ALL AND ALL *London LON 94*	16	10
13 Jun 87	LIFETIME LOVE *London LON 137*	34	6
9 Jan 88 ●	COME INTO MY LIFE *London LON 161*	7	9
23 Apr 88	WALK AWAY *London LON 176*	24	6
17 Jun 89	LOOKING FOR A LOVE *ffrr F 109*	39	4
27 May 95	COME INTO MY LIFE (re-mix) *Club Tools 0060435 CLU*	72	1

Kym SIMS ☺ 📀 *US, female vocalist*   **23 wks**

Date	Title	Pos	Wks
7 Dec 91 ●	TOO BLIND TO SEE IT *Atco B 8667*	5	12
28 Mar 92	TAKE MY ADVICE *Atco B 8591*	13	7
27 Jun 92	A LITTLE BIT MORE *Atco B 8528*	30	3
8 Jun 96	WE GOTTA LOVE *Pulse 8 CDLOSE 104*	58	1

SIN WITH SEBASTIAN *Germany, male vocalist – Sebastian Roth*   **2 wks**

Date	Title	Pos	Wks
16 Sep 95	SHUT UP (AND SLEEP WITH ME) *Sing Sing 74321253592*	44	1
27 Jan 96	SHUT UP (AND SLEEP WITH ME) (re-mix) *Sing Sing 74321337972*	46	1

Frank SINATRA Ⓒ

Arguably the greatest song stylist of the 20th century, b. 12 December, 1915, New Jersey, d. 15 May, 1998. The earliest 'teen idol' sang on the first ever US No 1 (1940) and 'My Way' holds the longevity record on the UK chart. His 1956 album, Songs for Swingin' Lovers, *made the Top 20 of the singles chart*   **439 wks**

Date	Title	Pos	Wks
9 Jul 54	YOUNG AT HEART *Capitol CL 14064*	12	1

Date	Title	Pos	Wks
16 Jul 54 ★	THREE COINS IN THE FOUNTAIN *Capitol CL 14120*	1	19
10 Jun 55	YOU MY LOVE *Capitol CL 14240*	13	3
22 Jul 55	YOU MY LOVE (re-entry) *Capitol CL 14240*	17	2
5 Aug 55 ●	LEARNIN' THE BLUES *Capitol CL 14296*	2	13
12 Aug 55	YOU MY LOVE (2nd re-entry) *Capitol CL 14240*	17	2
2 Sep 55	NOT AS A STRANGER *Capitol CL 14326*	18	1
13 Jan 56 ●	LOVE AND MARRIAGE *Capitol CL 14503*	3	8
20 Jan 56 ●	(LOVE IS) THE TENDER TRAP *Capitol CL 14511*	2	9
15 Jun 56	SONGS FOR SWINGING LOVERS LP *Capitol LCT 6106*	12	8
22 Nov 57	ALL THE WAY *Capitol CL 14800*	29	1
29 Nov 57	CHICAGO *Capitol CL 14800*	25	1
6 Dec 57	ALL THE WAY / CHICAGO (re-entry) *Capitol CL 14800*	21	1
13 Dec 57 ●	ALL THE WAY (2nd re-entry) *Capitol CL 14800*	3	17
7 Feb 58	WITCHCRAFT *Capitol CL 14819*	12	8
14 Nov 58	MR. SUCCESS *Capitol CL 14956*	29	1
12 Dec 58	MR. SUCCESS (re-entry) *Capitol CL 14956*	25	2
2 Jan 59	MR. SUCCESS (2nd re-entry) *Capitol CL 14956*	26	1
10 Apr 59	FRENCH FOREIGN LEGION *Capitol CL 14997*	18	5
15 May 59	COME DANCE WITH ME LP *Capitol LCT 6179*	30	1
28 Aug 59	HIGH HOPES *Capitol CL 15052*	28	1
11 Sep 59 ●	HIGH HOPES (re-entry) *Capitol CL 15052*	6	13
10 Mar 60	HIGH HOPES (2nd re-entry) *Capitol CL 15052*	42	1
7 Apr 60	IT'S NICE TO GO TRAV'LING *Capitol CL 15116*	48	2
16 Jun 60	RIVER STAY 'WAY FROM MY DOOR *Capitol CL 15135*	18	9
8 Sep 60	NICE 'N' EASY *Capitol CL 15150*	15	12
24 Nov 60	OL' MACDONALD *Capitol CL 15168*	11	8
20 Apr 61	MY BLUE HEAVEN *Capitol CL 15193*	33	7
28 Sep 61	GRANADA *Reprise R 20010*	15	8
23 Nov 61	THE COFFEE SONG *Reprise R 20035*	39	3
5 Apr 62	EVERYBODY'S TWISTING *Reprise R 20063*	22	12
13 Dec 62	ME AND MY SHADOW *Reprise R 20128* [1]	20	7
7 Feb 63	ME AND MY SHADOW (re-entry) *Reprise R 20128* [1]	47	2
7 Mar 63	MY KIND OF GIRL *Reprise R 20148* [2]	35	6
24 Sep 64	HELLO DOLLY *Reprise R 20351*	47	1
12 May 66 ★	STRANGERS IN THE NIGHT *Reprise R 23052* ▲	1	20
29 Sep 66	SUMMER WIND *Reprise RS 20509*	36	5
15 Dec 66	THAT'S LIFE *Reprise RS 20531*	46	5
23 Mar 67 ★	SOMETHIN' STUPID *Reprise RS 23166* [3] ▲	1	18
23 Aug 67	THE WORLD WE KNEW (OVER AND OVER) *Reprise RS 20610*	33	11
2 Apr 69 ●	MY WAY *Reprise RS 20817*	5	42
4 Oct 69 ●	LOVE'S BEEN GOOD TO ME *Reprise RS 20852*	8	18
31 Jan 70	MY WAY (re-entry) *Reprise RS 20817*	49	1
28 Feb 70	MY WAY (2nd re-entry) *Reprise RS 20817*	30	5
11 Apr 70	MY WAY (3rd re-entry) *Reprise RS 20817*	33	9
27 Jun 70	MY WAY (4th re-entry) *Reprise RS 20817*	28	21
28 Nov 70	MY WAY (5th re-entry) *Reprise RS 20817*	18	16
6 Mar 71	I WILL DRINK THE WINE *Reprise RS 23487*	16	12
27 Mar 71	MY WAY (6th re-entry) *Reprise RS 20817*	22	19
4 Sep 71	MY WAY (7th re-entry) *Reprise RS 20817*	39	8
1 Jan 72	MY WAY (8th re-entry) *Reprise RS 20817*	50	1
20 Dec 75	I BELIEVE I'M GONNA LOVE YOU *Reprise K 14400*	34	7
9 Aug 80	THEME FROM NEW YORK, NEW YORK *Reprise K 14502*	59	4
22 Feb 86 ●	THEME FROM NEW YORK, NEW YORK (re-entry) *Reprise K 14502*	4	10
4 Dec 93 ●	I'VE GOT YOU UNDER MY SKIN *Island CID 578* [4]	4	9
16 Apr 94	MY WAY (re-issue) *Reprise W 0163CD*	45	2

[1] Frank Sinatra and Sammy Davis Jr.   [2] Frank Sinatra with Count Basie
[3] Nancy Sinatra and Frank Sinatra   [4] Frank Sinatra with Bono

Tracks on Songs for Swinging Lovers LP: You Make Me Feel So Young / It Happened In Monterey / You're Getting to Be a Habit With Me / You Brought a New Kind of Love to Me / Too Marvellous for Words / Old Devil Moon / Pennies From Heaven / Love Is Here to Stay / I've Got You Under My Skin / I Thought About You / We'll Be Together Again / Making Whoopee / Swingin' Down the Lane / Anything Goes / How About You. Tracks on Come Dance With Me LP: Something's Gotta Give / Just in Time / Dancing in the Dark / Too Close for Comfort / I Could Have Danced All Night / Saturday Night is the Loneliest Night of the Week / Day In Day Out / Cheek to Cheek / Baubles Bangles and Beads / The Song Is You / The Last Dance. 'All the Way' and 'Chicago', Capitol CL 14800, were at first billed separately, then together for one week, then 'All The Way' on its own. 'I've Got You Under My Skin' was the listed B-side of 'Stay (Faraway So Close)' by U2

Nancy SINATRA 📀 *US, female vocalist*   **99 wks**

Date	Title	Pos	Wks
27 Jan 66 ★	THESE BOOTS ARE MADE FOR WALKING *Reprise R 20432* ▲	1	14

28 Apr 66	HOW DOES THAT GRAB YOU DARLIN'		
	Reprise R 20461 19	8
19 Jan 67 ●	SUGAR TOWN *Reprise RS 20527* 8	10
23 Mar 67 ★	SOMETHIN' STUPID *Reprise RS 23166* [1] ▲ 1	18
5 Jul 67	YOU ONLY LIVE TWICE/JACKSON		
	Reprise RS 20595 [2] 11	19
8 Nov 67	LADYBIRD *Reprise RS 20629* [3] 47	1
29 Nov 69	HIGHWAY SONG *Reprise RS 20869* 21	10
21 Aug 71 ●	DID YOU EVER *Reprise K 14093* [4] 2	19

[1] Nancy Sinatra and Frank Sinatra [2] Nancy Sinatra/Nancy Sinatra and Lee Hazlewood [3] Nancy Sinatra and Lee Hazlewood [4] Nancy and Lee

'Jackson' listed with 'You Only Live Twice' from 12 Jul, 1967

SINCLAIR *UK, male vocalist* — 8 wks

21 Aug 93	AIN'T NO CASANOVA *Dome CDDOME 1004* 28	5
26 Feb 94	(I WANNA KNOW) WHY *Dome CDDOME 1009* 58	2
6 Aug 94	DON'T LIE *Dome CDDOME 1010* 70	1

SINDY *UK, female doll vocalist* — 1 wk

5 Oct 96	SATURDAY NIGHT *Love This LUVTHISCD 13* 70	1

SINE *US, disco aggregation* — 9 wks

10 Jun 78	JUST LET ME DO MY THING *CBS 6351* 33	9

SINFONIA OF LONDON – See Peter AUTY and the SINFONIA OF LONDON

SINGING CORNER – See DONOVAN

SINGING DOGS ☻ *Denmark, canine vocal group* — 4 wks

25 Nov 55	THE SINGING DOGS (MEDLEY) *Nixa N 15009* 13	4

Medley songs: Pat-a-Cake/Three Blind Mice/Jingle Bells/Oh Susanna

SINGING NUN (Soeur Sourire) ℂ *Belgium, female vocalist* — 14 wks

5 Dec 63 ●	DOMINIQUE *Philips BF 1293* ▲ 7	14

SINGING SHEEP *UK, computerized sheep noises* — 5 wks

18 Dec 82	BAA BAA BLACK SHEEP *Sheep BAA 1* 42	5

Maxine SINGLETON *US, female vocalist* — 3 wks

2 Apr 83	YOU CAN'T RUN FROM LOVE *Creole CR 50* 57	3

SINITTA ☻ ☺ As well as a string of Hi-NRG dance hits, disco diva Miquel Brown's daughter Sinitta Malone (b. 19 October, 1966, Washington DC) has starred in several London stage musicals including Mutiny with David Essex and What a Feeling with Luke Goss and Sonia — 104 wks

8 Mar 86	SO MACHO/CRUISING *Fanfare FAN 7* 47	11
28 Jun 86 ●	SO MACHO/CRUISING (re-entry)		
	Fanfare FAN 7 2	17
11 Oct 86	FEELS LIKE THE FIRST TIME *Fanfare FAN 8* 45	5
25 Jul 87 ●	TOY BOY *Fanfare FAN 12* 4	14
12 Dec 87	G.T.O. *Fanfare FAN 14* 15	9
19 Mar 88 ●	CROSS MY BROKEN HEART *Fanfare FAN 15* 6	9
24 Sep 88 ●	I DON'T BELIEVE IN MIRACLES *Fanfare FAN 16* 22	8
3 Jun 89 ●	RIGHT BACK WHERE WE STARTED FROM		
	Fanfare FAN 18 4	10
7 Oct 89	LOVE ON A MOUNTAIN TOP *Fanfare FAN 21* 20	6
21 Apr 90	HITCHIN' A RIDE *Fanfare FAN 24* 24	6
22 Sep 90	LOVE AND AFFECTION *Fanfare FAN 31* 62	3
4 Jul 92	SHAME SHAME SHAME *Arista 74321100327* 28	4
17 Apr 93	THE SUPREME EP *Arista 74321139592* 49	2

Tracks on The Supreme EP: Where Did Our Love Go/Stop! In the Name of Love/ You Can't Hurry Love/Remember Me

SINNAMON *US, male vocal/instrumental group* — 1 wk

28 Sep 96	I NEED YOU NOW *Worx WORXCD 003* 70	1

SIOUXSIE and the BANSHEES ✐ *Long-running commercially successful UK band included Susan 'Siouxsie' Dallion (v), Steve Severin (b) (also recorded as The Glove), Siouxsie's husband, Peter 'Budgie' Clark (d) (who recorded with Siouxsie as The Creatures), and at times Cure front man, Robert Smith (g)* — 150 wks

26 Aug 78 ●	HONG KONG GARDEN *Polydor 2059 052* 7	10
31 Mar 79	THE STAIRCASE (MYSTERY) *Polydor POSP 9* 24	8
7 Jul 79	PLAYGROUND TWIST *Polydor POSP 59* 28	6
29 Sep 79	MITTAGEISEN (METAL POSTCARD) *Polydor 2059 151* 47	3
15 Mar 80	HAPPY HOUSE *Polydor POSP 117* 17	8
7 Jun 80	CHRISTINE *Polydor 2059 249* 22	8
6 Dec 80	ISRAEL *Polydor POSP 205* 41	8
30 May 81	SPELLBOUND *Polydor POSP 273* 22	8
1 Aug 81	ARABIAN KNIGHTS *Polydor POSP 309* 32	7
29 May 82	FIRE WORKS *Polydor POSPG 450* 22	6
9 Oct 82	SLOWDIVE *Polydor POSP 510* 41	4
4 Dec 82	MELT/IL EST NE LE DIVIN ENFANT *Polydor POSP 539* 49	5
1 Oct 83 ●	DEAR PRUDENCE *Wonderland SHE 4* 3	8
24 Mar 84	SWIMMING HORSES *Wonderland SHE 6* 28	4
2 Jun 84	DAZZLE *Wonderland SHE 7* 33	3
27 Oct 84	THE THORN EP *Wonderland SHEEP 8* 47	3
26 Oct 85	CITIES IN DUST *Wonderland SHE 9* 21	6
8 Mar 86	CANDYMAN *Wonderland SHE 10* 34	5
17 Jan 87	THIS WHEEL'S ON FIRE *Wonderland SHE 11* 14	6
28 Mar 87	THE PASSENGER *Wonderland SHE 12* 41	6
25 Jul 87	SONG FROM THE EDGE OF THE WORLD		
	Wonderland SHE 13 59	3
30 Jul 88	PEEK-A-BOO *Wonderland SHE 14* 16	6
8 Oct 88	THE KILLING JAR *Wonderland SHE 15* 41	3
3 Dec 88	THE LAST BEAT OF MY HEART *Wonderland SHE 16* 44	1
25 May 91	KISS THEM FOR ME *Wonderland SHE 19* 32	4
13 Jul 91	SHADOWTIME *Wonderland SHE 20* 57	1
25 Jul 92	FACE TO FACE *Wonderland SHE 21* 21	4
20 Aug 94	INTERLUDE *Parlophone CDR 6365* [1] 25	2
7 Jan 95	O BABY *Wonderland SHECD 22* 34	3
18 Feb 95	STARGAZER *Wonderland SHECD 23* 64	1

[1] Morrissey and Siouxsie

Tracks on The Thorn EP: Overground/Voices/Placebo Effect/Red Over White

SIR DOUGLAS QUINTET ♫
US, male vocal/instrumental group — 10 wks

17 Jun 65	SHE'S ABOUT A MOVER *London HLU 9964* 15	10

SIR MIX-A-LOT *US, male rapper* — 2 wks

8 Aug 92	BABY GOT BACK *Def American DEFA 20* ▲ 56	2

SIRRON – See PLUS ONE featuring SIRRON

SISSEL – See Warren G

SISTA – See VARIOUS ARTISTS (EPs and LPs) – The Dangerous Minds EP

SISTER BLISS with COLETTE
UK, female vocal/instrumental duo — 7 wks

15 Oct 94	CANTGETAMAN CANTGETAJOB (LIFE'S A BITCH)		
	Go.Beat GODCD 124 31	4
15 Jul 95	OH! WHAT A WORLD *Go.Beat GODCD 126* 40	2
29 Jun 96	BADMAN *Junk Dog JDOGCD 1* [1] 51	1

[1] Sister Bliss

SISTER SLEDGE ♫ ♪ *Successful US family group from Philadelphia: Kathy, Debra, Joni and Kim Sledge. They found more fame in the UK than in the USA, and recorded some of the best-known disco records with noted producer/songwriters Nile Rodgers and Bernard Edwards* — 111 wks

21 Jun 75	MAMA NEVER TOLD ME *Atlantic K 10619* 20	6
17 Mar 79 ●	HE'S THE GREATEST DANCER *Atlantic/Cotillion K 11257* 6	11
26 May 79 ●	WE ARE FAMILY *Atlantic/Cotillion K 11293* 8	10
11 Aug 79	LOST IN MUSIC *Atlantic/Cotillion K 11337* 17	10
19 Jan 80	GOT TO LOVE SOMEBODY *Atlantic/Cotillion K 11404* 34	4

28 Feb 81	ALL AMERICAN GIRLS *Atlantic K 11656*	41	5
26 May 84	THINKING OF YOU *Cotillion/Atlantic B 9744*	11	13
8 Sep 84 ●	LOST IN MUSIC (re-mix) *Cotillion/Atlantic B 9718*	4	12
17 Nov 84	WE ARE FAMILY (re-mix) *Cotillion/Atlantic B 9692*	33	4
1 Jun 85 ★	FRANKIE *Atlantic A 9547*	1	16
31 Aug 85	DANCING ON THE JAGGED EDGE *Atlantic A 9520*	50	3
23 Jan 93 ●	WE ARE FAMILY (2nd re-mix) *Atlantic A 4508CD*	5	8
13 Mar 93	LOST IN MUSIC (2nd re-mix) *Atlantic A 4509CD*	14	4
12 Jun 93	THINKING OF YOU (re-mix) *Atlantic A 4515CD*	17	4

SISTERS OF MERCY ☹ ✍
UK, male vocalist Andrew Eldritch and backing musicians **40 wks**

16 Jun 84	BODY AND SOUL/TRAIN *Merciful Release MR 029*	46	3
20 Oct 84	WALK AWAY *Merciful Release MR 033*	45	3
9 Mar 85	NO TIME TO CRY *Merciful Release MR 035*	63	2
3 Oct 87 ●	THIS CORROSION *Merciful Release MR 39*	7	6
27 Feb 88	DOMINION *Merciful Release MR 43*	13	6
18 Jun 88	LUCRETIA MY REFLECTION *Merciful Release MR 45*	20	4
13 Oct 90	MORE *Merciful Release MR 47*	14	4
22 Dec 90	DOCTOR JEEP *Merciful Release MR 51*	37	4
2 May 92 ●	TEMPLE OF LOVE *Merciful Release MR 53*	3	5
28 Aug 93	UNDER THE GUN *Merciful Release MR 59CDX*	19	3

SIVUCA *Brazil, male vocalist* **3 wks**

28 Jul 84	AIN'T NO SUNSHINE *London LON 51*	56	3

SIX BY SEVEN *UK, male vocal/instrumental group* **1 wk**

9 May 98	CANDLELIGHT *Mantra MNT 34CD*	70	1

6 BY SIX *UK, male instrumental/production duo* **1 wk**

4 May 96	INTO YOUR HEART *Six6 SIXCD 130*	51	1

666 *Germany, male/female vocal/instrumental group* **1 wk**

3 Oct 98	ALARMA *Danceteria CDDAN 001*	58	1

60FT DOLLS *UK, male vocal/instrumental group* **4 wks**

3 Feb 96	STAY *Indolent DOLLS 002CD*	48	1
11 May 96	TALK TO ME *Indolent DOLLS 003CD*	37	1
20 Jul 96	HAPPY SHOPPER *Indolent DOLLS 005CD*	38	1
9 May 98	ALISON'S ROOM *Indolent DOLLS 007CD1*	61	1

SIZE 9 *US, male producer – Josh Wink* **4 wks**

17 Jun 95	I'M READY *Virgin America VUSCD 92*	52	1
11 Nov 95	I'M READY (re-issue) *VC VCRD 2* [1]	30	3

[1] Josh Wink's Size 9

See also Josh WINK

Roni SIZE / REPRAZENT ☺
UK, male/female vocal/instrumental **9 wks**

14 Jun 97	SHARE THE FALL *Talkin Loud TLCD 21*	37	2
13 Sep 97	HEROES *Talkin Loud TLCD 25*	31	2
15 Nov 97	BROWN PAPER BAG *Talkin Loud TLCD 28*	20	3
14 Mar 98	WATCHING WINDOWS *Talkin Loud TLCD 31*	28	2

S-J *UK, female vocalist* **1 wk**

7 Nov 98	SHIVER *React CDREACTX 138*	59	1

SKATALITES *Jamaica, male instrumental group* **6 wks**

20 Apr 67	GUNS OF NAVARONE *Island WI 168*	36	6

SKEE-LO 🔊 *US, male rapper* **10 wks**

9 Dec 95	I WISH *Wild Card 5777752*	15	8
27 Apr 96	TOP OF THE STAIRS *Wild Card 5763352*	38	2

Beverli SKEETE – See DE-CODE featuring Beverli SKEETE

Peter SKELLERN ✪ *UK, male vocalist* **24 wks**

23 Sep 72 ●	YOU'RE A LADY *Decca F 13333*	3	11
29 Mar 75	HOLD ON TO LOVE *Decca F 13568*	14	9
28 Oct 78	LOVE IS THE SWEETEST THING *Mercury 6008 603* [1]	60	4

[1] Peter Skellern featuring Grimethorpe Colliery Band

SKID ROW ▼ *US, male vocal/instrumental group* **27 wks**

18 Nov 89	YOUTH GONE WILD *Atlantic A 8935*	42	3
3 Feb 90	18 AND LIFE *Atlantic A 8883*	12	6
31 Mar 90	I REMEMBER YOU *East West A 8836*	36	4
15 Jun 91	MONKEY BUSINESS *Atlantic A 7673*	19	3
14 Sep 91	SLAVE TO THE GRIND *Atlantic A 7603*	43	2
23 Nov 91	WASTED TIME *Atlantic A 7570*	20	3
29 Aug 92	YOUTH GONE WILD/DELIVERING THE GOODS (re-issue) *Atlantic A 7444*	22	4
18 Nov 95	BREAKIN' DOWN *Atlantic A 7135CD1*	48	2

SKIDS ✍ *UK, male vocal/instrumental group* **60 wks**

23 Sep 78	SWEET SUBURBIA *Virgin VS 227*	70	1
7 Oct 78	SWEET SUBURBIA (re-entry) *Virgin VS 227*	71	2
4 Nov 78	THE SAINTS ARE COMING *Virgin VS 232*	48	3
17 Feb 79 ●	INTO THE VALLEY *Virgin VS 241*	10	11
26 May 79	MASQUERADE *Virgin VS 262*	14	9
29 Sep 79	CHARADE *Virgin VS 288*	31	6
24 Nov 79	WORKING FOR THE YANKEE DOLLAR *Virgin VS 306*	20	11
1 Mar 80	ANIMATION *Virgin VS 323*	56	3
16 Aug 80	CIRCUS GAMES *Virgin VS 359*	32	7
18 Oct 80	GOODBYE CIVILIAN *Virgin VS 373*	52	4
6 Dec 80	WOMEN IN WINTER *Virgin VSK 101*	49	3

SKIN ✍ *UK/Germany, male vocal/instrumental group* **19 wks**

25 Dec 93	THE SKIN UP EP *Parlophone CDR 6363*	67	2
12 Mar 94	HOUSE OF LOVE *Parlophone CDR 6374*	45	2
30 Apr 94	MONEY/UNBELIEVEABLE *Parlophone CDR 6381*	18	3
23 Jul 94	TOWER OF STRENGTH *Parlophone CDR 6387*	19	3
15 Oct 94	LOOK BUT DON'T TOUCH EP *Parlophone CDR 6391*	33	3
20 May 95	TAKE ME DOWN TO THE RIVER *Parlophone CDR 6409*	26	2
23 Mar 96	HOW LUCKY YOU ARE *Parlophone CDR 6426*	32	2
18 May 96	PERFECT DAY *Parlophone CDR 6433*	33	2

Tracks on The Skin Up EP: Look But Don't Touch/Shine Your Light/Monkey.
Tracks on Look But Don't Touch EP: Look But Don't Touch/Should I Stay or
Should I Go/Pump It Up/Monkey. The first and last tracks on this EP are,
of course, re-issues of two tracks from The Skin Up EP.

SKIN UP *UK, male producer* **9 wks**

7 Sep 91	IVORY *Love EVOL 4*	48	3
14 Mar 92	A JUICY RED APPLE *Love EVOL 11*	32	4
18 Jul 92	ACCELERATE *Love EVOL 17*	45	2

SKINNER – See LIGHTNING SEEDS

SKINNY
UK, male vocal/instrumental/production duo **2 wks**

11 Apr 98	FAILURE *Cheeky CHEKCD 023*	31	2

SKIPWORTH and TURNER *US, male vocal duo* **12 wks**

27 Apr 85	THINKING ABOUT YOUR LOVE *Fourth & Broadway BRW 23*	24	10
21 Jan 89	MAKE IT LAST *Fourth & Broadway BRW 118*	60	2

SKUNK ANANSIE ✍ ☹
UK, male/female vocal/instrumental group **32 wks**

25 Mar 95	SELLING JESUS *One Little Indian 101 TP7CD*	46	1
17 Jun 95	I CAN DREAM *One Little Indian 121 TP7CD*	41	2
2 Sep 95	CHARITY *One Little Indian 131 TP7CD*	40	2
27 Jan 96	WEAK *One Little Indian 141 TP7CD*	20	5
27 Apr 96	CHARITY (re-issue) *One Little Indian 151 TP7CD*	20	3
28 Sep 96	ALL I WANT *One Little Indian 161 TP7CD*	14	4
30 Nov 96	TWISTED (EVERYDAY HURTS) *One Little Indian 171 TP7CD*	26	4

1 Feb 97		HEDONISM (JUST BECAUSE YOU FEEL GOOD)		
		One Little Indian 181TP7CD 13	6
14 Jun 97		BRAZEN 'WEEP' One Little Indian 191TP7 11	5

SKY ℂ ◐ UK/Australia, male instrumental group   11 wks

5 Apr 80	●	TOCCATA Ariola ARO 300 5	11

SKYHOOKS Australia, male vocal/instrumental group   1 wk

9 Jun 79		WOMEN IN UNIFORM United Artists UP 36508 73	1

SLACKER UK, male production duo   4 wks

26 Apr 97		SCARED XL XLS 84CD 36	2
30 Aug 97		YOUR FACE XL XLS 87CD 33	2

SLADE ◐ Top group of the 1970s: Noddy Holder (v/g), Dave Hill (g), Jimmy Lea (b/p), Don Powell (d). They were the first act to have three singles enter at No 1. All six of the Wolverhampton band's chart-topping stompers were penned by Holder and Lea   277 wks

19 Jun 71		GET DOWN AND GET WITH IT Polydor 2058 112 16	14
30 Oct 71	★	COZ I LUV YOU Polydor 2058 155 1	15
5 Feb 72	●	LOOK WOT YOU DUN Polydor 2058 195 4	10
3 Jun 72	★	TAKE ME BAK 'OME Polydor 2058 231 1	13
2 Sep 72	★	MAMA WEER ALL CRAZEE NOW Polydor 2058 274 1	10
25 Nov 72	●	GUDBUY T'JANE Polydor 2058 312 2	13
3 Mar 73	●	CUM ON FEEL THE NOIZE Polydor 2058 339 ▪ 1	12
30 Jun 73	★	SKWEEZE ME PLEEZE ME Polydor 2058 377 ▪ 1	10
6 Oct 73	●	MY FREND STAN Polydor 2058 407 2	8
15 Dec 73	★	MERRY XMAS EVERYBODY Polydor 2058 422 ◆ ▪ 1	9
6 Apr 74	●	EVERYDAY Polydor 2058 453 3	7
6 Jul 74	●	BANGIN' MAN Polydor 2058 492 3	7
19 Oct 74	●	FAR FAR AWAY Polydor 2058 522 2	6
15 Feb 75		HOW DOES IT FEEL Polydor 2058 547 15	7
17 May 75	●	THANKS FOR THE MEMORY (WHAM BAM THANK YOU MAM)	
		Polydor 2058 585 7	7
22 Nov 75		IN FOR A PENNY Polydor 2058 663 11	8
7 Feb 76		LET'S CALL IT QUITS Polydor 2058 690 11	7
5 Feb 77		GYPSY ROAD HOG Barn 2014 105 48	2
29 Oct 77		MY BABY LEFT ME – THAT'S ALL RIGHT (MEDLEY)	
		Barn 2014 114 32	4
18 Oct 80		SLADE ALIVE AT READING '80 EP Cheapskate CHEAP 5 44	5
27 Dec 80		MERRY XMAS EVERYBODY (re-entry)	
		Cheapskate CHEAP 11 [1] 70	2
31 Jan 81	●	WE'LL BRING THE HOUSE DOWN Cheapskate CHEAP 16 10	9
4 Apr 81		WHEELS AIN'T COMING DOWN Cheapskate CHEAP 21 60	3
19 Sep 81		LOCK UP YOUR DAUGHTERS RCA 124 29	8
19 Dec 81		MERRY XMAS EVERYBODY (re-entry) Polydor 2058 422 32	4
27 Mar 82		RUBY RED RCA 191 51	3
27 Nov 82		(AND NOW – THE WALTZ) C'EST LA VIE RCA 291 50	6
25 Dec 82		MERRY XMAS EVERYBODY (2nd re-entry) Polydor 2058 422 67	3
19 Nov 83	●	MY OH MY RCA 373 2	11
10 Dec 83		MERRY XMAS EVERYBODY (3rd re-entry) Polydor 2058 422 20	5
4 Feb 84	●	RUN RUN AWAY RCA 385 7	10
17 Nov 84		ALL JOIN HANDS RCA 455 15	9
15 Dec 84		MERRY XMAS EVERYBODY (4th re-entry) Polydor 2058 422 47	4
26 Jan 85		7 YEAR BITCH RCA 475 60	3
23 Mar 85		MYZSTERIOUS MIZTER JONES RCA PB 40027 50	5
30 Nov 85		DO YOU BELIEVE IN MIRACLES RCA PB 40449 54	6
21 Dec 85		MERRY XMAS EVERYBODY (re-issue) Polydor POSP 780 48	3
27 Dec 86		MERRY XMAS EVERYBODY (re-entry of re-issue)	
		Polydor POSP 780 71	1
21 Feb 87		STILL THE SAME RCA PB 41137 73	2
19 Oct 91		RADIO WALL OF SOUND Polydor PO 180 21	5
26 Dec 98		MERRY XMAS EVERYBODY '98 (re-mix)	
		Polydor 5633532 [2] ....30†	1

[1] Slade and the Reading Choir [2] Slade vs Flush

Tracks on Slade Alive at Reading '80 EP: When I'm Dancin' I Ain't Fightin'/ Born to Be Wild/ Somethin' Else/ Pistol Packin' Mama/ Keep a Rollin'

SLAMM UK, male vocal/instrumental group   6 wks

17 Jul 93		ENERGIZE PWL International PWCD 266 57	2

---

23 Oct 93		VIRGINIA PLAIN PWL International PWCD 274 60	1
22 Oct 94		THAT'S WHERE MY MIND GOES	
		PWL International PWCD 310 68	1
4 Feb 95		CAN'T GET BY PWL International PWCD 316 47	2

SLAUGHTER US, male vocal/instrumental group   2 wks

29 Sep 90		UP ALL NIGHT Chrysalis CHS 3556 62	1
2 Feb 91		FLY TO THE ANGELS Chrysalis CHS 3634 55	1

SLAVE US, male vocal/instrumental group   3 wks

8 Mar 80		JUST A TOUCH OF LOVE Atlantic/Cotillion K 11442 64	3

SLAYER US, male vocal/instrumental group   3 wks

13 Jun 87		CRIMINALLY INSANE Def Jam LON 133 64	1
26 Oct 91		SEASONS IN THE ABYSS Def American DEFA 9 51	1
9 Sep 95		SERENITY IN MURDER American 74321312482 50	1

SLEAZESISTERS UK, male producer   3 wks

29 Jul 95		SEX Pulse 8 CDLOSE 92 [1] 53	1
30 Mar 96		LET'S WHIP IT UP (YOU GO GIRL) Pulse 8 CDLOSE 102 [1] 46	1
26 Sep 98		WORK IT UP Logic 74321616622 [2] 74	1

[1] Sleazesisters with Vikki Shepard [2] Sleaze Sisters

Kathy SLEDGE ♪ US, female vocalist   7 wks

16 May 92		TAKE ME BACK TO LOVE AGAIN Epic 6579837 62	2
18 Feb 95		ANOTHER STAR NRC DEACD 002 54	1
29 Nov 97		FREEDOM Deconstruction 74321536952 [1] 15	4

[1] Robert Miles featuring Kathy Sledge

Percy SLEDGE ♪ US, male vocalist   34 wks

12 May 66	●	WHEN A MAN LOVES A WOMAN Atlantic 584 001 ▲ 4	17
4 Aug 66		WARM AND TENDER LOVE Atlantic 584 034 34	7
14 Feb 87	●	WHEN A MAN LOVES A WOMAN (re-issue) Atlantic YZ 96 2	10

SLEEPER ☹ ◐ UK, male/female vocal/instrumental group   29 wks

21 May 94		DELICIOUS Indolent SLEEP 003CD 75	1
21 Jan 95		INBETWEENER Indolent SLEEP 006CD 16	4
8 Apr 95		VEGAS Indolent SLEEP 008CD 33	3
7 Oct 95		WHAT DO I DO NOW Indolent SLEEP 009CD1 14	4
4 May 96	●	SALE OF THE CENTURY Indolent SLEEP 011CD 10	5
13 Jul 96	●	NICE GUY EDDIE Indolent SLEEP 013CD 10	5
5 Oct 96		STATUESQUE Indolent SLEEP 014CD1 17	3
4 Oct 97		SHE'S A GOOD GIRL Indolent SLEEP 015CD 28	2
6 Dec 97		ROMEO ME Indolent SLEEP 17CD1 39	2

SLICK ◢ US, male/female vocal/instrumental group   15 wks

16 Jun 79		SPACE BASS Fantasy FTC 176 16	10
15 Sep 79		SEXY CREAM Fantasy FTC 182 47	5

Grace SLICK US, female vocalist   4 wks

24 May 80		DREAMS RCA PB 9534 50	4

SLICK RICK – See Montell JORDAN

SLIK ◐ UK, male vocal/instrumental group   18 wks

17 Jan 76	★	FOREVER AND EVER Bell 1464 1	9
8 May 76		REQUIEM Bell 1478 24	9

SLIM CHANCE – See Ronnie LANE and SLIM CHANCE

SLIPSTREEM ◐ ☺ UK, male vocal group   7 wks

19 Dec 92		WE ARE RAVING – THE ANTHEM Boogie Food 7BF 1 18	7

SLITS UK, female vocal/instrumental group   3 wks

13 Oct 79		TYPICAL GIRLS/I HEARD IT THROUGH THE GRAPEVINE	
		Island WIP 6505 60	3

What: *Things Can Only Get Better*   85
Who: D:ream
When: 1994 (1), 1997 (19)
Which: Can thank New Labour for its second chart run – the political party used this dance anthem as their campaign song in the 1997 General Election

What: *House of the Rising Sun*   86
Who: Animals
When: 1964 (1), 1972 (25), 1982 (11)
Which: Despite the fact that it was about a brothel and was 50 per cent longer in duration than any other hit of its time, topped both the UK and the US charts

What: *Heart of Glass*   87
Who: Blondie
When: 1979 (1), 1995 (15 – remix)
Which: Turned these new wave pioneers into international pop stars and sold one million copies in the UK alone. This electro-disco track was the first of the group's three UK/US No 1s

What: *Heartbreak Hotel*   88
Who: Elvis Presley
When: 1956 (2), 1971 (10), 1996 (45)
Which: Was the follow-up to his first US country-and-western No 1. After a rather slow start, this revolutionary recording topped the US chart, launched The King's worldwide pop career, and helped to change the face of popular music

SLO-MOSHUN UK, male instrumental/production duo — 4 wks

5 Feb 94	BELLS OF NY Six6 SIXCD 108	29	3
30 Jul 94	HELP MY FRIEND Six6 SIXCD 117	52	1

PF SLOAN US, male vocalist — 3 wks

4 Nov 65	SINS OF THE FAMILY RCA 1482	38	3

SLOWDIVE UK, male/female vocal/instrumental group — 2 wks

15 Jun 91	CATCH THE BREEZE/SHINE Creation CRE 112	52	1
29 May 93	OUTSIDE YOUR ROOM EP Creation CRESCD 119	69	1

Tracks on Outside Your Room EP: Outside Your Room / Alison / So Tired / Souvlaki Space Station

SL2 ☺ UK, male instrumental/production duo — 25 wks

2 Nov 91	DJS TAKE CONTROL/WAY IN MY BRAIN XL XLS 24	11	5
4 Jan 92	DJS TAKE CONTROL/WAY IN MY BRAIN (re-entry) XL XLS 24	71	1
18 Apr 92 ●	ON A RAGGA TIP XL XLS 29	2	11
19 Dec 92	WAY IN MY BRAIN/DRUMBEATS (re-mix) XL XLS 36	26	6
15 Feb 97	ON A RAGGA TIP '97 (re-mix) XL XLSR 29CD	31	2

SLY and the FAMILY STONE ♪
US, male/female vocal/instrumental group — 42 wks

10 Jul 68 ●	DANCE TO THE MUSIC Direction 58 3568	7	14
2 Oct 68	M'LADY Direction 58 3707	32	7
19 Mar 69	EVERYDAY PEOPLE Direction 58 3938 ▲	36	1
9 Apr 69	EVERYDAY PEOPLE (re-entry) Direction 58 3938	37	4
8 Jan 72	FAMILY AFFAIR Epic EPC 7632 ▲	15	8
15 Apr 72	RUNNIN' AWAY Epic EPC 7810	17	8

SLY FOX ☻ US, male vocal/instrumental duo — 16 wks

31 May 86 ●	LET'S GO ALL THE WAY Capitol CL 403	3	16

SLY and ROBBIE ⚑ ☺ Jamaica, male vocal/instrumental duo — 23 wks

4 Apr 87	BOOPS (HERE TO GO) Fourth & Broadway BRW 61	12	11
25 Jul 87	FIRE Fourth & Broadway BRW 71	60	4
20 Sep 97	NIGHT NURSE East West EW 129CD1 [1]	13	8

[1] Sly And Robbie featuring Simply Red

SMALL ADS UK, male vocal/instrumental group — 3 wks

18 Apr 81	SMALL ADS Bronze BRO 115	63	3

SMALL FACES ☻ ✎ Revered London-based mod quartet: Steve Marriott (v/g) (d. 1991), Ronnie Lane (b) (d. 1997), Ian McLagan (o), Kenny Jones (d). Marriott and Lane penned most of the act's UK hits. Further international fame came when Marriott formed Humble Pie and the other members formed The Faces — 137 wks

2 Sep 65	WHATCHA GONNA DO ABOUT IT? Decca F 12208	14	12
10 Feb 66 ●	SHA LA LA LA LEE Decca F 12317	3	11
12 May 66 ●	HEY GIRL Decca F 12393	10	9
11 Aug 66 ★	ALL OR NOTHING Decca F 12470	1	12
17 Nov 66	MY MIND'S EYE Decca F 12500	4	11
9 Mar 67	I CAN'T MAKE IT Decca F 12565	26	7
8 Jun 67	HERE COME THE NICE Immediate IM 050	12	10
9 Aug 67 ●	ITCHYCOO PARK Immediate IM 057	3	14
6 Dec 67	TIN SOLDIER Immediate IM 062	9	12
17 Apr 68 ●	LAZY SUNDAY Immediate IM 064	2	11
10 Jul 68	UNIVERSAL Immediate IM 069	16	11
19 Mar 69	AFTERGLOW OF YOUR LOVE Immediate IM 077	36	1
13 Dec 75 ●	ITCHYCOO PARK (re-issue) Immediate IMS 102	9	11
20 Mar 76	LAZY SUNDAY (re-issue) Immediate IMS 106	39	5

Heather SMALL – See M PEOPLE

SMALLER UK, male vocal/instrumental group — 2 wks

28 Sep 96	WASTED Better BETSCD 006	72	1
29 Mar 97	IS Better BETSCD 008	55	1

SMART E'S ☻ ☺ UK, male instrumental/production group — 9 wks

11 Jul 92 ●	SESAME'S TREET Suburban Base SUBBASE 12S	2	9

S*M*A*S*H UK, male vocal/instrumental group — 1 wk

6 Aug 94	(I WANT TO) KILL SOMEBODY Hi-Rise FLATSCD 5	26	1

SMASH MOUTH ☹ ✎ US, male vocal/instrumental group — 4 wks

25 Oct 97	WALKIN ON THE SUN Interscope IND95555	19	4

SMASHING PUMPKINS ✎
US, male/female vocal/instrumental group — 33 wks

5 Sep 92	I AM ONE Hut HUTT 18	73	1
3 Jul 93	CHERUB ROCK Hut HUTCD 31	31	2
25 Sep 93	TODAY Hut HUTCD 37	44	2
5 Mar 94	DISARM Hut HUTCD 43	11	3
28 Oct 95	BULLET WITH BUTTERFLY WINGS Hut HUTCD 63	20	3
10 Feb 96	1979 Hut HUTCD 67	16	3
18 May 96 ●	TONIGHT TONIGHT Hut HUTDX 69	7	6
23 Nov 96	THIRTY THREE Hut HUTCD 78	21	2
14 Jun 97 ●	THE END IS THE BEGINNING IS THE END Warner Bros. W 040CD	10	4
23 Aug 97	THE END IS THE BEGINNING IS THE END Warner Bros. W 0410CD	72	1
30 May 98	AVA ADORE Hut HUTCD 101	11	4
19 Sep 98	PERFECT Hut HUTCD 106	24	2

SMEAR CAMPAIGN – See MR BEAN and SMEAR CAMPAIGN featuring Bruce DICKINSON

SMELLS LIKE HEAVEN Italy, male producer – Fabio Paras — 1 wk

10 Jul 93	LONDRES STRUTT Deconstruction 74321154312	57	1

'Fast' Eddie SMITH – See DJ 'FAST' EDDIE

Ann-Marie SMITH UK, female vocalist — 5 wks

23 Jan 93	MUSIC Synthetic CDR 6334 [1]	34	2
18 Mar 95	ROCKIN' MY BODY Media MCSTD 2021 [2]	31	2
15 Jul 95	(YOU'RE MY ONE AND ONLY) TRUE LOVE Media MCSTD 2060	46	1

[1] Fargetta and Ann-Marie Smith [2] 49ers featuring Ann-Marie Smith

Elliott SMITH US, male vocalist/instrumentalist — 1 wk

19 Dec 98	WALTZ #2 (XO) DreamWorks DRMCD 22347	52	1

Hurricane SMITH ☻ UK, male vocalist — 35 wks

12 Jun 71 ●	DON'T LET IT DIE Columbia DB 8785	2	12
29 Apr 72 ●	OH BABE WHAT WOULD YOU SAY? Columbia DB 8878	4	16
2 Sep 72	WHO WAS IT Columbia DB 8916	23	7

Jimmy SMITH US, male instrumentalist – organ — 3 wks

28 Apr 66	GOT MY MOJO WORKING Verve VS 536	48	2
19 May 66	GOT MY MOJO WORKING (re-entry) Verve VS 536	48	1

Keely SMITH ☾ US, female vocalist — 10 wks

18 Mar 65	YOU'RE BREAKIN' MY HEART Reprise R 20346	14	10

Mandy SMITH UK, female vocalist — 2 wks

20 May 89	DON'T YOU WANT ME BABY PWL PWL 37	59	2

Mark E. SMITH ☹ ✎ UK, male vocalist — 4 wks

5 Mar 94	I WANT YOU Cow DUNG 24CD [1]	18	3
23 Mar 96	PLUG MYSELF IN Coliseum TOGA 001CD1 [2]	50	1

[1] Inspiral Carpets featuring Mark E Smith [2] Dose featuring Mark E Smith

See also FALL

Mel SMITH ☉ *UK, male vocalist* — **10 wks**

5 Dec 87 ●	ROCKIN' AROUND THE CHRISTMAS TREE *10 TEN 2* [1]	3	7
21 Dec 91	ANOTHER BLOOMING CHRISTMAS *Epic 6576877*	59	3

[1] Mel and Kim (Wilde)

Muriel SMITH ℂ *US, female vocalist* — **17 wks**

15 May 53 ●	HOLD ME THRILL ME KISS ME *Philips PB 122*	3	17

OC SMITH ☉ *US, male vocalist* — **23 wks**

29 May 68 ●	SON OF HICKORY HOLLER'S TRAMP *CBS 3343*	2	15
26 Mar 77	TOGETHER *Caribou CRB 4910*	25	8

Rex SMITH – See Rachel SWEET

Richard Jon SMITH *South Africa, male vocalist* — **2 wks**

16 Jul 83	SHE'S THE MASTER OF THE GAME *Jive JIVE 38*	63	2

Rose SMITH – See DELAKOTA

Whistling Jack SMITH ☉ *UK, male whistler* — **12 wks**

2 Mar 67 ●	I WAS KAISER BILL'S BATMAN *Deram DM 112*	5	12

Will SMITH ⬅ ☉ *US, male vocalist/rapper* — **46 wks**

16 Aug 97 ★	MEN IN BLACK *Columbia 6648682* ■	1	16
13 Dec 97	JUST CRUISIN' *Columbia 6653482*	23	6
7 Feb 98 ●	GETTIN' JIGGY WIT IT *Columbia 6655605* ▲	3	10
1 Aug 98 ●	JUST THE TWO OF US *Columbia 6662092*	2	10
5 Dec 98 ●	MIAMI *Columbia 6666782*	3†	4

See also JAZZY JEFF and the FRESH PRINCE

Patti SMITH GROUP 🎸
US, female vocalist, male instrumental backing group — **16 wks**

29 Apr 78 ●	BECAUSE THE NIGHT *Arista 181*	5	12
19 Aug 78	PRIVILEGE (SET ME FREE) *Arista 197*	72	1
2 Jun 79	FREDERICK *Arista 264*	63	3

SMITHS ☹ *Mancunian quartet with loyal fan base: Morrissey (b. Stephen Morrissey) (v), Johnny Marr (g), Andy Rourke (b), Mike Joyce (d). Their achievements include monopolising the top three indie chart placings (February 1984) and having seven albums simultaneously in UK chart (March 1995)* — **105 wks**

12 Nov 83	THIS CHARMING MAN *Rough Trade RT 136*	25	12
28 Jan 84	WHAT DIFFERENCE DOES IT MAKE *Rough Trade RT 146*	12	9
2 Jun 84 ●	HEAVEN KNOWS I'M MISERABLE NOW *Rough Trade RT 156*	10	8
1 Sep 84	WILLIAM, IT WAS REALLY NOTHING *Rough Trade RT 166*	17	6
9 Feb 85	HOW SOON IS NOW? *Rough Trade RT 176*	24	6
30 Mar 85	SHAKESPEARE'S SISTER *Rough Trade RT 181*	26	4
13 Jul 85	THAT JOKE ISN'T FUNNY ANYMORE *Rough Trade RT 186*	49	3
5 Oct 85	THE BOY WITH THE THORN IN HIS SIDE *Rough Trade RT 191*	23	5
31 May 86	BIG MOUTH STRIKES AGAIN *Rough Trade RT 192*	26	4
2 Aug 86	PANIC *Rough Trade RT 193*	11	8
1 Nov 86	ASK *Rough Trade RT 194*	14	5
7 Feb 87	SHOPLIFTERS OF THE WORLD UNITE *Rough Trade RT 195*	12	4
25 Apr 87 ●	SHEILA TAKE A BOW *Rough Trade RT 196*	10	5
22 Aug 87	GIRLFRIEND IN A COMA *Rough Trade RT 197*	13	5
14 Nov 87	I STARTED SOMETHING I COULDN'T FINISH *Rough Trade RT 198*	23	4
19 Dec 87	LAST NIGHT I DREAMT THAT SOMEBODY LOVED ME *Rough Trade RT 200*	30	4
15 Aug 92 ●	THIS CHARMING MAN (re-issue) *WEA YZ 0001*	8	5
12 Sep 92	HOW SOON IS NOW (re-issue) *WEA YZ 0002*	16	4
24 Oct 92	THERE IS A LIGHT THAT NEVER GOES OUT *WEA YZ 0003*	25	3
18 Feb 95	ASK (re-issue) *WEA YZ 0004CDX*	62	1

SMOKE *UK, male vocal/instrumental group* — **3 wks**

9 Mar 67	MY FRIEND JACK *Columbia DB 8115*	45	3

SMOKE CITY ☺ ☉
UK / Brazil, male/female vocal/instrumental group — **5 wks**

12 Apr 97 ●	UNDERWATER LOVE *Jive JIVECD 422*	4	5

SMOKIE ☉ *British group who became European superstars, fronted by easily identifiable vocalist Chris Norman. Especially popular in Germany, many of their hits were penned by Mike Chapman and Nicky Chinn* — **125 wks**

19 Jul 75 ●	IF YOU THINK YOU KNOW HOW TO LOVE ME *RAK 206* [1]	3	9
4 Oct 75 ●	DON'T PLAY YOUR ROCK 'N ROLL TO ME *RAK 217* [1]	8	7
31 Jan 76	SOMETHING'S BEEN MAKING ME BLUE *RAK 227*	17	8
25 Sep 76	I'LL MEET YOU AT MIDNIGHT *RAK 241*	11	9
4 Dec 76 ●	LIVING NEXT DOOR TO ALICE *RAK 244*	5	11
19 Mar 77	LAY BACK IN THE ARMS OF SOMEONE *RAK 251*	12	9
16 Jul 77 ●	IT'S YOUR LIFE *RAK 260*	5	9
15 Oct 77	NEEDLES AND PINS *RAK 263*	10	9
28 Jan 78	FOR A FEW DOLLARS MORE *RAK 267*	17	6
20 May 78 ●	OH CAROL *RAK 276*	5	13
23 Sep 78	MEXICAN GIRL *RAK 283*	19	9
19 Apr 80	TAKE GOOD CARE OF MY BABY *RAK 309*	34	7
13 May 95	LIVING NEXT DOOR TO ALICE (WHO THE F**K IS ALICE) *NOW CDWAG 245* [2]	64	2
12 Aug 95 ●	LIVING NEXT DOOR TO ALICE (WHO THE F**K IS ALICE) (re-entry) *NOW CDWAG 245* [2]	3	17

[1] Smokey [2] Smokie featuring Roy 'Chubby' Brown

'Living Next Door to Alice (Who The F**k Is Alice)' is a re-recorded version of 'Living Next Door to Alice'

SMOKIN BEATS featuring LYN EDEN
UK, male DJ / production duo, and UK, female vocalist — **3 wks**

17 Jan 98	DREAMS *AM:PM 5824711*	23	3

SMOKIN' MOJO FILTERS ☉ 🎸
UK/US, male/female vocal/instrumental group — **5 wks**

23 Dec 95	COME TOGETHER (WAR CHILD) *Go! Discs GODCD 136*	19	5

SMOOTH *US, female vocalist* — **7 wks**

22 Jul 95	MIND BLOWIN' *Jive JIVECD 379*	36	2
7 Oct 95	IT'S SUMMERTIME (LET IT GET INTO YOU) *Jive JIVECD 383*	46	1
16 Mar 96	WE GOT IT *MCA MCSTD 48009* [1]	26	2
16 Mar 96	LOVE GROOVE (GROOVE WITH YOU) *Jive JIVECD 390*	46	1
6 Jul 96	UNDERCOVER LOVER *Jive JIVECD 397*	41	1

[1] Immature featuring Smooth

Joe SMOOTH *US, male vocalist* — **4 wks**

4 Feb 89	PROMISED LAND *DJ International DJIN 6*	56	4

SMOOTH TOUCH *US, male instrumental/production duo* — **1 wk**

2 Apr 94	HOUSE OF LOVE (IN MY HOUSE) *Six6 SIXCD 112*	58	1

SMURFS ☉ *Holland, small blue creatures vocal group* — **52 wks**

3 Jun 78 ●	THE SMURF SONG *Decca F 13759* [1]	2	17
30 Sep 78	DIPPETY DAY *Decca F 13798*	13	12
2 Dec 78	CHRISTMAS IN SMURFLAND *Decca F 13819*	19	7
7 Sep 96 ●	I'VE GOT A LITTLE PUPPY *EMI TV CDSMURF 100*	4	10
21 Dec 96 ●	YOUR CHRISTMAS WISH *EMI TV CDSMURF 102*	8	6

[1] Father Abraham and the Smurfs

Patty SMYTH – See Don HENLEY

SNAKEBITE *Italy, male production trio* — **2 wks**

9 Aug 97	THE BIT GOES ON *Multiply CDMULTY 22*	25	2

SNAP ☺ ☉ *German-based producers Benito Benites (b. Michael Munzing) and John Garrett Virgo III (b. Luca Anzilotti) masterminded a string of world-wide dance hits for this act, which featured a host of mostly US vocalists and rappers including Turbo B, Jackie Harris, Penny Ford and Thea Austin* — **115 wks**

24 Mar 90 ★	THE POWER *Arista 113133*	1	15

UK No 1 ★   UK Top 10 ●   UK million seller ◆   UK entry at No 1 ■   US No 1 ▲

16 Jun 90 ●	OOOPS UP *Arista 113296*	5	12
22 Sep 90 ●	CULT OF SNAP *Arista 113596*	8	7
8 Dec 90 ●	MARY HAD A LITTLE BOY *Arista 113831*	8	10
30 Mar 91 ●	SNAP MEGAMIX *Arista 114169*	10	6
21 Dec 91	THE COLOUR OF LOVE *Arista 114678*	54	3
4 Jul 92 ★	RHYTHM IS A DANCER *Arista 115309*	1	19
9 Jan 93 ●	EXTERMINATE! *Arista 74321106962* [1]	2	11
12 Jun 93 ●	DO YOU SEE THE LIGHT (LOOKING FOR) *Arista 74321147622* [1]	10	8
17 Sep 94 ●	WELCOME TO TOMORROW *Arista 74321223852* [2]	6	13
14 Jan 95	WELCOME TO TOMORROW (re-entry) *Arista 74321223852* [2]	75	1
1 Apr 95	THE FIRST THE LAST ETERNITY (TIL THE END) *Arista 74321254672* [2]	15	7
28 Oct 95 ●	THE WORLD IN MY HANDS *Arista 74321314792* [2]	44	1
13 Apr 96	RAME *Arista 74321369902* [3]	50	1
24 Aug 96	THE POWER *Arista 74321398672* [4]	42	1

[1] Snap featuring Niki Harris [2] Snap featuring Summer [3] Snap featuring Rukmani
[4] Snap featuring Einstein

'The Power' in 1996 is a re-recording

SNEAKER PIMPS ☹ ☺
UK, male/female vocal/instrumental group **16 wks**

19 Oct 96	6 UNDERGROUND *Clean Up CUP 023CDS*	15	4
15 Mar 97	SPIN SPIN SUGAR *Clean Up CUP 033CDS*	21	3
7 Jun 97 ●	6 UNDERGROUND (re-mix) *Clean Up CUP 036CDM*	9	4
30 Aug 97	POST MODERN SLEAZE *Clean Up CUP 038CDM*	22	3
7 Feb 98	SPIN SPIN SUGAR (re-mix) *Clean Up CUP 037*	46	2

SNIFF 'N' THE TEARS *UK, male vocal/instrumental group* **5 wks**

23 Jun 79	DRIVER'S SEAT *Chiswick CHIS 105*	42	5

SNOOP DOGGY DOGG ◄ *US, male rapper* **27 wks**

4 Dec 93	WHAT'S MY NAME? *Death Row A 8337CD*	20	8
12 Feb 94	GIN AND JUICE *Death Row A 8316CD*	39	3
20 Aug 94	DOGGY DOGG WORLD *Death Row A 8289CD*	32	3
14 Dec 96	SNOOP'S UPSIDE YOUR HEAD *Interscope IND 95520* [1]	12	3
26 Apr 97	WANTED DEAD OR ALIVE *Def Jam 5744052* [2]	16	3
3 May 97	VAPORS *Interscope IND 95530*	18	2
20 Sep 97	WE JUST WANNA PARTY WITH YOU *Columbia 6649902* [3]	21	2
24 Jan 98	THA DOGGFATHER *Interscope IND 95550*	36	2
12 Dec 98	COME AND GET WITH ME *Elektra E 3787CD* [4]	58	1

[1] Snoop Doggy Dogg featuring Charlie Wilson [2] 2Pac and Snoop Doggy Dogg
[3] Snoop Doggy Dogg featuring JD [4] Keith Sweat featuring Snoop Dogg

SNOW ⌃ *Canada, male rapper* **18 wks**

13 Mar 93 ●	INFORMER *East West America A 8436CD* ▲	2	15
5 Jun 93	GIRL I'VE BEEN HURT *East West America A 8417CD*	48	2
4 Sep 93	UHH IN YOU *Atlantic A 8378CD*	67	1

Mark SNOW ☺ *US, male instrumentalist – keyboards* **15 wks**

30 Mar 96 ●	THE X-FILES *Warner Bros. W 0341CD*	2	15

Phoebe SNOW *US, female vocalist* **7 wks**

6 Jan 79	EVERY NIGHT *CBS 6842*	37	7

SNOWMAN – See Peter AUTY and the SINFONIA OF LONDON

SNOWMEN ☺ *UK, male vocal/instrumental group* **12 wks**

12 Dec 81	HOKEY COKEY *Stiff ODB 1*	18	8
18 Dec 82	XMAS PARTY *Solid STOP 006*	44	4

SNUG *UK, male vocal/instrumental group* **1 wk**

18 Apr 98	BEATNIK GIRL *WEA WEA 151CDX*	55	1

SO *UK, male vocal/instrumental group* **3 wks**

13 Feb 88	ARE YOU SURE *Parlophone R 6173*	62	3

SOAP *Denmark, female vocal group* **2 wks**

25 Jul 98	THIS IS HOW WE PARTY *Columbia 6661295*	36	2

SOAPY *UK, male instrumental/production duo* **2 wks**

14 Sep 96	HORNY AS FUNK *WEA WEA 074CD*	35	2

Gino SOCCIO *Canada, male instrumentalist – keyboards* **5 wks**

28 Apr 79	DANCER *Warner Bros. K 17357*	46	5

SOEUR SOURIRE – See SINGING NUN

SOFT CELL ☺ ☺ *Successful synth-driven duo from Leeds: Marc Almond (v), David Ball (k). The visually striking pair's revival of Northern soul classic 'Tainted Love' was the Top UK single of 1981 and also broke the longevity record on the US Top 100* **107 wks**

1 Aug 81 ★	TAINTED LOVE *Some Bizarre BZS 2*	1	16
14 Nov 81 ●	BED SITTER *Some Bizarre BZS 6*	4	12
9 Jan 82	TAINTED LOVE (re-entry) *Some Bizarre BZS 2*	43	10
6 Feb 82 ●	SAY HELLO WAVE GOODBYE *Some Bizarre BZS 7*	3	9
29 May 82 ●	TORCH *Some Bizarre BZS 9*	2	9
24 Jul 82	TAINTED LOVE (2nd re-entry) *Some Bizarre BZS 2*	50	4
21 Aug 82 ●	WHAT *Some Bizarre BZS 11*	3	8
4 Dec 82	WHERE THE HEART IS *Some Bizarre BZS 16*	21	7
5 Mar 83	NUMBERS/BARRIERS *Some Bizarre BZS 17*	25	4
24 Sep 83	SOUL INSIDE *Some Bizarre BZS 20*	16	5
25 Feb 84	DOWN IN THE SUBWAY *Some Bizarre BZS 22*	24	6
9 Feb 85	TAINTED LOVE (3rd re-entry) *Some Bizarre BZS 2*	43	6
23 Mar 91	SAY HELLO WAVE GOODBYE '91 *Mercury SOFT 1* [1]	38	3
18 May 91 ●	TAINTED LOVE *Mercury SOFT 2* [1]	5	8

[1] Soft Cell/Marc Almond

SOHO ☺ ☺ *UK, male/female vocal/instrumental group* **11 wks**

5 May 90	HIPPY CHICK *Savage 7SAV 106*	67	1
19 Jan 91	HIPPY CHICK (re-entry) *Savage 7SAV 106*	8	8
9 Nov 91	BORN TO BE ALIVE *MCA MCS 1578* [1]	51	2

[1] Adamski featuring Soho

The listed flip side of 'Born to be Alive' was 'Never Goin' Down' by Adamski featuring Jimi Polo

SOLAR STONE *UK, male DJ/production trio* **1 wk**

21 Feb 98	THE IMPRESSIVE EP *Hooj Choons HOOJCD 57*	75	1

SOLID HARMONIE ☺ *UK/US, female vocal group* **11 wks**

31 Jan 98	I'LL BE THERE FOR YOU *Jive JIVECD 437*	18	3
18 Apr 98	I WANT YOU TO WANT ME *Jive JIVECD 452*	16	3
15 Aug 98	I WANNA LOVE YOU *Jive 0521742*	20	4
21 Nov 98	TO LOVE ONCE AGAIN *Jive 0522472*	55	1

SOLO *UK, male producer – Stuart Crichton* **4 wks**

20 Jul 91	RAINBOW (SAMPLE FREE) *Reverb RVBT 003*	59	2
18 Jan 92	COME ON! *Reverb RVBT 008*	75	1
11 Sep 93	COME ON! (re-mix) *Stoatin' STOAT 003CD*	63	1

SOLO *US, male vocal group* **3 wks**

3 Feb 96	HEAVEN *Perspective 5875212*	35	2
30 Mar 96	WHERE DO U WANT ME TO PUT IT *Perspective 5875312*	45	1

Sal SOLO ☺ *UK, male vocalist* **13 wks**

15 Dec 84	SAN DAMIANO (HEART AND SOUL) *MCA MCA 930*	15	10
6 Apr 85	MUSIC AND YOU *MCA MCA 946* [1]	52	3

[1] Sal Solo with the London Community Gospel Choir

SOLUTION – See Victor SIMONELLI presents SOLUTION

Belouis SOME ☺ *UK, male vocalist* **26 wks**

27 Apr 85	IMAGINATION *Parlophone R 6097*	50	7

18 Jan 86	IMAGINATION (re-issue) *Parlophone R 1986*	17	10
12 Apr 86	SOME PEOPLE *Parlophone R 6130*	33	7
16 May 87	LET IT BE WITH YOU *Parlophone R 6154*	53	2

Jimmy SOMERVILLE ◎ ☺ *UK, male vocalist*   53 wks

11 Nov 89	COMMENT TE DIRE ADIEU *London LON 241* [1]	14	9
13 Jan 90 ●	YOU MAKE ME FEEL (MIGHTY REAL) *London LON 249*	5	8
17 Mar 90	READ MY LIPS (ENOUGH IS ENOUGH) *London LON 254*	26	6
3 Nov 90 ●	TO LOVE SOMEBODY *London LON 281*	8	11
2 Feb 91	SMALLTOWN BOY *London LON 287* [2]	32	4
10 Aug 91	RUN FROM LOVE *London LON 301*	52	2
28 Jan 95	HEARTBEAT *London LONCD 358*	24	4
27 May 95	HURT SO GOOD *London LONCD 364*	15	6
28 Oct 95	BY YOUR SIDE *London LONCD 372*	41	2
13 Sep 97	DARK SKY *Gut CXGUT 11*	66	1

[1] Jimmy Somerville featuring June Miles-Kingston [2] Jimmy Somerville with Bronski Beat

See also BRONSKI BEAT; VARIOUS ARTISTS (EPs & LPs) – Gimme Shelter (EP)

SOMETHIN FOR THE PEOPLE
US, male vocal/instrumental group   1 wk

7 Feb 98	MY LOVE IS THE SHHH! *Warner Bros W 0427CD*	64	1

SOMORE featuring DAMON TRUEITT
US, male production group, and male vocalist   2 wks

24 Jan 98	I REFUSE (WHAT YOU WANT) *XL Recordings XLS 93CD*	21	2

SONIA ◎ *UK, female vocalist*   78 wks

24 Jun 89 ★	YOU'LL NEVER STOP ME LOVING YOU *Chrysalis CHS 3385*	1	13
7 Oct 89	CAN'T FORGET YOU *Chrysalis CHS 3419*	17	6
9 Dec 89 ●	LISTEN TO YOUR HEART *Chrysalis CHS 3465*	10	10
7 Apr 90	COUNTING EVERY MINUTE *Chrysalis CHS 3492*	16	7
23 Jun 90	YOU'VE GOT A FRIEND *Jive CHILD 90* [1]	14	6
25 Aug 90	END OF THE WORLD *Chrysalis/PWL CHS 3557*	18	7
1 Jun 91 ●	ONLY FOOLS (NEVER FALL IN LOVE) *IQ ZB 44613*	10	8
31 Aug 91	BE YOUNG BE FOOLISH BE HAPPY *IQ ZB 44935*	22	5
16 Nov 91	YOU TO ME ARE EVERYTHING *IQ ZB 45121*	13	5
12 Sep 92	BOOGIE NIGHTS *Arista 74321113467*	30	3
1 May 93	BETTER THE DEVIL YOU KNOW *Arista 74321146872*	15	7
30 Jul 94	HOPELESSLY DEVOTED TO YOU *Cockney COCCD 2*	61	1

[1] Big Fun and Sonia featuring Gary Barnacle

SONIC SOLUTION *UK, male/producer – Steve Cop*   1 wk

4 Apr 92	BEATSTIME *R&S RSUK 11*	59	1

SONIC SURFERS *Holland, male instrumental/production duo*   2 wks

20 Mar 93	TAKE ME UP *A & M AMCD 210* [1]	61	1
30 Jul 94	DON'T GIVE IT UP *Brilliant CDBRIL 6*	54	1

[1] Sonic Surfers featuring Jocelyn Brown

SONIC THE HEDGEHOG – See HWA featuring SONIC THE HEDGEHOG

SONIC YOUTH *US, male/female vocal/instrumental group*   14 wks

11 Jul 92	100% *DGC DGCS 11*	28	4
7 Nov 92	YOUTH AGAINST FASCISM *Geffen GFS 26*	52	2
3 Apr 93	SUGAR KANE *Geffen GFSTD 37*	26	3
7 May 94	BULL IN THE HEATHER *Geffen GFSTD 72*	24	2
10 Sep 94	SUPERSTAR *A & M 5807932*	45	2
11 Jul 98	SUNDAY *Geffen GFSTD 22332*	72	1

The listed flip side of 'Superstar' was 'Yesterday Once More' by Redd Kross

SONIQUE *UK, female vocalist / DJ*   5 wks

13 Jun 98	I PUT A SPELL ON YOU *Serious SERR 001CD*	36	2
5 Dec 98	IT FEELS SO GOOD *Serious SERR 004CD*	24	3

SONNY ◎ *US, male vocalist*   11 wks

19 Aug 65 ●	LAUGH AT ME *Atlantic AT 4038*	9	11

See also SONNY and CHER

SONNY and CHER ◎ *US, male/female vocal duo*   78 wks

12 Aug 65 ★	I GOT YOU BABE *Atlantic AT 4035* ▲	1	12
16 Sep 65	BABY DON'T GO *Reprise R 20309*	11	9
21 Oct 65	BUT YOU'RE MINE *Atlantic AT 4047*	17	8
17 Feb 66	WHAT NOW MY LOVE *Atlantic AT 4069*	13	11
30 Jun 66	HAVE I STAYED TOO LONG *Atlantic 584 018*	42	3
8 Sep 66 ●	LITTLE MAN *Atlantic 584 040*	4	10
17 Nov 66	LIVING FOR YOU *Atlantic 584 057*	44	4
2 Feb 67	THE BEAT GOES ON *Atlantic 584 078*	29	8
15 Jan 72	ALL I EVER NEED IS YOU *MCA MU 1145*	8	12
22 May 93	I GOT YOU BABE (re-issue) *Epic 6592402*	66	1

See also SONNY; CHER

SON'Z OF A LOOP DA LOOP ERA
UK, male producer – Danny Breaks   4 wks

15 Feb 92	FAR OUT *Suburban Base SUBBASE 008*	36	3
17 Oct 92	PEACE + LOVEISM *Suburban Base SUBBASE 14*	60	1

See also VARIOUS ARTISTS (EPs & LPs) – Subplates Volume 1 EP

SORROWS *UK, male vocal/instrumental group*   8 wks

16 Sep 65	TAKE A HEART *Piccadilly 7N 35260*	21	8

S.O.S. BAND ◢ ♪ *US, male/female vocal/instrumental group*   46 wks

19 Jul 80	TAKE YOUR TIME (DO IT RIGHT) PART 1 *Tabu TBU 8564*	51	4
26 Feb 83	GROOVIN' (THAT'S WHAT WE'RE DOIN') *Tabu TBU A3120*	72	1
7 Apr 84	JUST BE GOOD TO ME *Tabu A 3626*	13	11
4 Aug 84	JUST THE WAY YOU LIKE IT *Tabu A 4621*	32	7
13 Oct 84	WEEKEND GIRL *Tabu A 4785*	51	5
29 Mar 86	THE FINEST *Tabu A 6997*	17	10
5 Jul 86	BORROWED LOVE *Tabu A 7241*	50	5
2 May 87	NO LIES *Tabu 650444 7*	64	3

David SOUL ◎ *US, male vocalist*   56 wks

18 Dec 76 ★	DON'T GIVE UP ON US *Private Stock PVT 84* ◆ ▲	1	16
26 Mar 77 ●	GOING IN WITH MY EYES OPEN *Private Stock PVT 99*	2	8
27 Aug 77 ★	SILVER LADY *Private Stock PVT 115*	1	14
17 Dec 77 ●	LET'S HAVE A QUIET NIGHT IN *Private Stock PVT 130*	8	9
27 May 78	IT SURE BRINGS OUT THE LOVE IN YOUR EYES *Private Stock PVT 137*	12	9

Jimmy SOUL *US, male vocalist*   5 wks

11 Jul 63	IF YOU WANNA BE HAPPY *Stateside SS 178* ▲	39	2
15 Jun 91	IF YOU WANNA BE HAPPY (re-issue) *Epic 6569647*	68	3

SOUL ASYLUM ◎ ✔ *US, male vocal/instrumental group*   33 wks

19 Jun 93	RUNAWAY TRAIN *Columbia 6593902*	37	8
4 Sep 93	SOMEBODY TO SHOVE *Columbia 6596492*	34	3
13 Nov 93 ●	RUNAWAY TRAIN (re-entry) *Columbia 6593902*	7	11
22 Jan 94	BLACK GOLD *Columbia 6598442*	26	4
26 Mar 94	SOMEBODY TO SHOVE (re-issue) *Columbia 6602245*	32	3
15 Jul 95	MISERY *Columbia 6621092*	30	3
2 Dec 95	JUST LIKE ANYONE *Columbia 6624785*	52	1

SOUL BROTHERS *UK, male vocal/instrumental group*   3 wks

22 Apr 65	I KEEP RINGING MY BABY *Decca F 12116*	42	3

SOUL CITY ORCHESTRA
UK, male instrumental/production group   1 wk

11 Dec 93	IT'S JURASSIC *London JURCD 1*	70	1

SOUL CITY SYMPHONY – See Van McCOY

SOUL FAMILY SENSATION
UK/US, male/female vocal/instrumental group **4 wks**

| 11 May 91 | I DON'T EVEN KNOW IF I SHOULD CALL YOU BABY | | |
| | *One Little Indian 47 TP7* ....49 | 4 |

SOUL FOR REAL *US, male vocal group* **4 wks**

| 8 Jul 95 | CANDY RAIN *Uptown MCSTD 2052* ....23 | 2 |
| 23 Mar 96 | EVERY LITTLE THING I DO *Uptown MCSTD 48005* ....31 | 2 |

SOUL II SOUL [R&B] *UK, male producer – Jazzie B* **89 wks**

21 May 88	FAIRPLAY *10 TEN 228* [1] 63	3
17 Sep 88	FEEL FREE *10 TEN 236* [2] 64	2
18 Mar 89 ●	KEEP ON MOVING *10 TEN 263* [3] 5	12
10 Jun 89 ★	BACK TO LIFE (HOWEVER DO YOU WANT ME) *10 TEN 265* [3] ..1	14
9 Dec 89 ●	GET A LIFE *10 TEN 284* 3	13
5 May 90 ●	A DREAM'S A DREAM *10 TEN 300* 6	6
24 Nov 90	MISSING YOU *10 TEN 345* [4] ● 22	7
4 Apr 92 ●	JOY *Ten TEN 350* 4	7
13 Jun 92	MOVE ME NO MOUNTAIN *Ten TEN 400* [5] 31	4
26 Sep 92	JUST RIGHT *Ten TEN 410* 38	2
6 Nov 93	WISH *Virgin VSCDG 1480* 24	4
22 Jul 95	LOVE ENUFF *Virgin VSCDT 1527* 12	6
21 Oct 95	I CARE (SOUL II SOUL) *Virgin VSCDT 1560* 17	4
19 Oct 96	KEEP ON MOVIN' (re-mix) *Virgin VSCDT 1612* 31	2
30 Aug 97	REPRESENT *Island CID 668* 39	2
8 Nov 97	PLEASURE DOME *Island CID 669* 51	1

[1] Soul II Soul featuring Rose Windross [2] Soul II Soul featuring Do'reen
[3] Soul II Soul featuring Caron Wheeler [4] Soul II Soul featuring Kym Mazelle
[5] Soul II Soul, lead vocals Kofi

SOUL SONIC FORCE – See Afrika BAMBAATAA

S.O.U.L. S.Y.S.T.E.M. introducing Michelle VISAGE ☺
US, male/female vocal/instrumental group **5 wks**

| 16 Jan 93 | IT'S GONNA BE A LOVELY DAY *Arista 74321125692* ....17 | 5 |

SOULED OUT
Italy/US/UK, male/female vocal/instrumental group **1 wk**

| 9 May 92 | IN MY LIFE *Columbia 6578367* ....75 | 1 |

SOUND 9418 – See Jonathan KING

SOUND FACTORY *Sweden, male vocal/instrumental duo* **1 wk**

| 5 Jun 93 | 2 THE RHYTHM *Logic 74321149422* ....72 | 1 |

SOUND OF ONE *US, male/female vocal/instrumental duo* **1 wk**

| 20 Nov 93 | AS I AM *Cooltempo CDCOOL 280* ....65 | 1 |

SOUNDGARDEN ✎ *US, male vocal/instrumental group* **23 wks**

11 Apr 92	JESUS CHRIST POSE *A & M AM 862* 30	3
20 Jun 92	RUSTY CAGE *A & M AM 874* 41	1
21 Nov 92	OUTSHINED *A & M AM 0102* 50	1
26 Feb 94	SPOONMAN *A & M 5805392* 20	3
30 Apr 94	THE DAY I TRIED TO LIVE *A & M 5805952* 42	2
20 Aug 94	BLACK HOLE SUN *A & M 5807532* 12	5
28 Jan 95	FELL ON BLACK DAYS *A & M 5809472* 24	2
18 May 96	PRETTY NOOSE *A & M 5816202* 14	3
28 Sep 96	BURDEN IN MY HAND *A & M 5818552* 33	2
28 Dec 96	BLOW UP THE OUTSIDE WORLD *A & M 5819862* 40	1

SOUNDMAN and David LLOYDIE with Elizabeth TROY
UK, male/female vocal/instrumental group **2 wks**

| 25 Feb 95 | GREATER LOVE *Sound Of Underground SOURCD 016* ....49 | 2 |

SOUNDS INCORPORATED *UK, male instrumental group* **11 wks**

| 23 Apr 64 | THE SPARTANS *Columbia DB 7239* ....30 | 6 |
| 30 Jul 64 | SPANISH HARLEM *Columbia DB 7321* ....35 | 5 |

SOUNDS NICE ☺ *UK, male instrumental group* **11 wks**

| 6 Sep 69 | LOVE AT FIRST SIGHT (JE T'AIME . . . MOI NON PLUS) | | |
| | *Parlophone R 5797* ....18 | 11 |

Has credit: Tim Mycroft on organ

SOUNDS OF BLACKNESS [R&B] ☺
US, male/female gospel choir **32 wks**

22 Jun 91	OPTIMISTIC *Perspective PERSS 786* 45	4
28 Sep 91	THE PRESSURE PART 1 *Perspective PERSS 816* 71	1
15 Feb 92	OPTIMISTIC (re-issue) *Perspective PERSS 849* 28	4
25 Apr 92	THE PRESSURE PART 1 (re-issue) *Perspective PERSS 867* ...49	2
8 May 93	I'M GOING ALL THE WAY *Perspective 5874252* 27	3
26 Mar 94	I BELIEVE *A & M 5874512* 17	4
2 Jul 94	GLORYLAND *Mercury MERCD 404* [1] 36	4
20 Aug 94	EVERYTHING IS GONNA BE ALRIGHT *A & M 5874672* 29	3
14 Jan 95	I'M GOING ALL THE WAY (re-issue) *A & M 5874832* 14	4
7 Jun 97	SPIRIT *A & M 5822292* [2] 35	2
14 Feb 98	THE PRESSURE *AM:PM 5824872* 46	1

[1] Daryl Hall and the Sounds of Blackness [2] Sounds of Blackness / Craig Mack

SOUNDS ORCHESTRAL ☾ *UK, orchestra* **18 wks**

| 3 Dec 64 ● | CAST YOUR FATE TO THE WIND *Piccadilly 7N 35206* ....5 | 16 |
| 8 Jul 65 | MOONGLOW *Piccadilly 7N 35248* ....43 | 2 |

SOUNDSATION *UK, male producer* **1 wk**

| 14 Jan 95 | PEACE AND JOY *Ffrreedom TABCD 224* ....48 | 1 |

SOUNDSCAPE *UK, male DJ / production group* **1 wk**

| 14 Feb 98 | DUBPLATE CULTURE *Satellite 74321552002* ....61 | 1 |

SOUNDSOURCE
Sweden/UK, male instrumental/production group **1 wk**

| 11 Jan 92 | TAKE ME UP *ffrr FX 177* ....62 | 1 |

SOUP DRAGONS ☹ ☺ *UK, male vocal/instrumental group* **23 wks**

20 Jun 87	CAN'T TAKE NO MORE *Raw TV RTV 3* 65	1
5 Sep 87	SOFT AS YOUR FACE *Raw TV RTV 4* 66	2
14 Jul 90 ●	I'M FREE *Raw TV RTV 9* [1] 5	12
20 Oct 90	MOTHER UNIVERSE *Big Life BLR 30* 26	5
11 Apr 92	DIVINE THING *Big Life BLR 68* 53	3

[1] Soup Dragons featuring Junior Reid

SOURCE ☺ *UK, male producer – John Truelove* **22 wks**

2 Feb 91 ●	YOU GOT THE LOVE *Truelove TLOVE 7001* [1] 4	11
26 Dec 92	ROCK THE HOUSE *React 12REACT 12* [2] 63	1
1 Mar 97 ●	YOU GOT THE LOVE *React CDREACT 89* [1] 3	8
23 Aug 97	CLOUDS *XL XLS 83CD* 38	2

[1] Source featuring Candi Staton [2] Source featuring Nicole

Joe SOUTH ☻ *US, male vocalist* **11 wks**

| 5 Mar 69 ● | GAMES PEOPLE PLAY *Capitol CL 15579* ....6 | 11 |

Jeri SOUTHERN *US, female vocalist* **3 wks**

| 21 Jun 57 | FIRE DOWN BELOW *Brunswick 05665* ....22 | 3 |

SOUTHLANDERS ☻ *Jamaica/UK, male vocal group* **10 wks**

| 22 Nov 57 | ALONE *Decca F 10946* ....17 | 10 |

SOUVLAKI *UK, male producer – Mark Summers* **4 wks**

| 15 Feb 97 | INFERNO *Wonderboy WBOYD 003* ....24 | 3 |
| 8 Aug 98 | MY TIME *Wonderboy WBOYD 009* ....63 | 1 |

SOVEREIGN COLLECTION *UK, orchestra* **6 wks**

| 3 Apr 71 | MOZART 40 *Capitol CL 15676* ....27 | 6 |

Red SOVINE 🎵 *US, male vocalist* **8 wks**

| 13 Jun 81 | ● TEDDY BEAR *Starday SD 142* ....4 | 8 |

SOX *UK, female vocal group* **1 wk**

| 15 Apr 95 | GO FOR THE HEART *Living Beat LBECD 33* ....47 | 1 |

Bob B. SOXX and the BLUE JEANS *US, male/female vocal group* **2 wks**

| 31 Jan 63 | ZIP-A-DEE-DOO-DAH *London HLU 9646* ....45 | 2 |

SPACE ☺ *France, male instrumental group* **12 wks**

| 13 Aug 77 | ● MAGIC FLY *Pye International 7N 25746* ....2 | 12 |

SPACE ☻ ☹ *UK, male vocal/instrumental group* **50 wks**

6 Apr 96	NEIGHBOURHOOD *Gut CDGUT 1* 56	1
8 Jun 96	FEMALE OF THE SPECIES *Gut CDGUT 2* 14	10
7 Sep 96	● ME AND YOU VERSUS THE WORLD (re-entry) *Gut CDGUT 4* 9	6
2 Nov 96	NEIGHBOURHOOD (re-issue) *Gut CDGUT 5* 11	6
22 Feb 97	DARK CLOUDS *Gut CDGUT 6* 14	4
10 Jan 98	● AVENGING ANGELS *Gut CDGUT 16* 6	8
4 Jul 98	BEGIN AGAIN *Gut CDGUT 019* 21	4
7 Mar 98	● THE BALLAD OF TOM JONES *Gut CDGUT 18* [1] 4	8
5 Dec 98	THE BAD DAYS EP *Gut CDGUT 22* ....20†	3

[1] Space with Cerys of Catatonia

Tracks on The Bad Days EP: Bad Days / The Unluckiest Man in the World / We Gotta Get Out of This Place

SPACE BABY *UK, male producer – Matt Darey* **1 wk**

| 8 Jul 95 | FREE YOUR MIND *Hooj Choons HOOJ 34CD* ....55 | 1 |

SPACE BROTHERS *UK, male / female vocal / instrumental trio* **10 wks**

| 17 May 97 | SHINE *Manifesto FESCD 23* ....23 | 3 |
| 13 Dec 97 | FORGIVEN (I FEEL YOUR LOVE) *Manifesto FESCD 36* ....27 | 7 |

SPACE KITTENS *UK, male instrumental/production group* **1 wk**

| 13 Apr 96 | STORM *Hooj Choons HOOJCD 41* ....58 | 1 |

SPACE MONKEY *UK, male producer – Paul Goodchild* **4 wks**

| 8 Oct 83 | CAN'T STOP RUNNING *Innervision A 3742* ....53 | 4 |

SPACE RAIDERS *UK, male production trio* **1 wk**

| 28 Mar 98 | GLAM RAID *Skint SKINT 32CD* ....68 | 1 |

SPACE 2000 *UK, male vocal/instrumental duo* **1 wk**

| 12 Aug 95 | DO U WANNA FUNK *Wired WIRED 218* ....50 | 1 |

SPACEDUST ☺ *UK, male production duo* **8 wks**

| 24 Oct 98 | ★ GYM AND TONIC *East West EW 188CD* ■ ....1 | 8 |

SPACEHOG *UK, male vocal/instrumental group* **7 wks**

11 May 96	IN THE MEANTIME *Sire 7559643162* 70	1
28 Dec 96	IN THE MEANTIME (re-entry) *Sire 7559643162* 29	5
7 Feb 98	CARRY ON *Sire W 0428CD* 43	1

SPACEMAID *UK, male vocal/instrumental group* **1 wk**

| 5 Apr 97 | BABY COME ON *Big Star STARC 105* ....70 | 1 |

SPAGHETTI SURFERS *UK, male instrumental/production duo* **1 wk**

| 22 Jul 95 | MISIRLOU (THE THEME TO THE MOTION PICTURE PULP FICTION) *Tempo Toons CDTOON 4* ....55 | 1 |

SPAGNA ☻ *Italy, female vocalist* **23 wks**

25 Jul 87	● CALL ME *CBS 650279 7* 2	12
17 Oct 87	EASY LADY *CBS 651169 7* 62	3
20 Aug 88	EVERY GIRL AND BOY *CBS SPAG 1* 23	8

SPANDAU BALLET ☻ 🎵 *Kilt-clad new-romantic revolutionaries.*
This London band went on to become smart-suited Top 10 regulars: Tony Hadley (v), Gary Kemp (g), Martin Kemp (b), Steve Norman (g/s/prc), John Keeble (d). The Kemp brothers later went into the movies, including lead roles in The Krays (1990) **159 wks**

15 Nov 80	● TO CUT A LONG STORY SHORT *Reformation CHS 2473* 5	11
24 Jan 81	THE FREEZE *Reformation CHS 2486* 17	8
4 Apr 81	● MUSCLEBOUND/GLOW *Reformation CHS 2509* 10	10
18 Jul 81	● CHANT NO. 1 (I DON'T NEED THIS PRESSURE ON) *Reformation CHS 2528* 3	10
14 Nov 81	PAINT ME DOWN *Chrysalis CHS 2560* 30	5
30 Jan 82	SHE LOVED LIKE DIAMOND *Chrysalis CHS 2585* 49	4
10 Apr 82	● INSTINCTION *Chrysalis CHS 2602* 10	11
2 Oct 82	LIFELINE *Chrysalis CHS 2642* 7	9
12 Feb 83	COMMUNICATION *Reformation CHS 2662* 12	10
23 Apr 83	★ TRUE *Reformation SPAN 1* 1	12
13 Aug 83	● GOLD *Reformation SPAN 2* 2	9
9 Jun 84	● ONLY WHEN YOU LEAVE *Reformation SPAN 3* 3	9
18 Aug 84	ONLY WHEN YOU LEAVE (re-entry) *Reformation SPAN 3* 74	1
25 Aug 84	● I'LL FLY FOR YOU *Reformation SPAN 4* 9	9
20 Oct 84	HIGHLY STRUNG *Reformation SPAN 5* 15	5
8 Dec 84	ROUND AND ROUND *Reformation SPAN 6* 18	8
26 Jul 86	FIGHT FOR OURSELVES *Reformation A 7264* 15	7
8 Nov 86	● THROUGH THE BARRICADES *Reformation SPANS 1* 6	10
14 Feb 87	HOW MANY LIES *Reformation SPANS 2* 34	4
3 Sep 88	RAW *CBS SPANS 3* 47	3
26 Aug 89	BE FREE WITH YOUR LOVE *CBS SPANS 4* 42	4

SPARKLE (R&B) *US, female vocalist* **8 wks**

| 18 Jul 98 | ● BE CAREFUL *Jive 0521452* [1] ....7 | 6 |
| 7 Nov 98 | TIME TO MOVE ON *Jive 0522032* ....40 | 2 |

[1] Sparkle featuring R Kelly

SPARKLEHORSE *US, male vocal/instrumental group* **2 wks**

| 31 Aug 96 | RAINMAKER *Capitol CDCL 777* ....61 | 1 |
| 17 Oct 98 | SICK OF GOODBYES *Parlophone CDCLS 808* ....57 | 1 |

SPARKS ☻ 🎵 *US, male vocal/instrumental duo* **81 wks**

4 May 74	● THIS TOWN AIN'T BIG ENOUGH FOR BOTH OF US *Island WIP 6193* 2	10
20 Jul 74	● AMATEUR HOUR *Island WIP 6203* 7	9
19 Oct 74	NEVER TURN YOUR BACK ON MOTHER EARTH *Island WIP 6211* 13	7
18 Jan 75	SOMETHING FOR THE GIRL WITH EVERYTHING *Island WIP 6221* 17	7
19 Jul 75	GET IN THE SWING *Island WIP 6236* 27	7
4 Oct 75	LOOKS LOOKS LOOKS *Island WIP 6249* 26	4
21 Apr 79	THE NUMBER ONE SONG IN HEAVEN *Virgin VS 244* 14	12
21 Jul 79	● BEAT THE CLOCK *Virgin VS 270* 10	9
27 Oct 79	TRYOUTS FOR THE HUMAN RACE *Virgin VS 289* 45	5
29 Oct 94	WHEN DO I GET TO SING 'MY WAY' *Logic 74321234472* 38	3
11 Mar 95	WHEN I KISS YOU (I HEAR CHARLIE PARKER PLAYING) *Logic 74321264272* 36	2
20 May 95	WHEN DO I GET TO SING 'MY WAY' (re-issue) *Logic 74321274002* 32	2
9 Mar 96	NOW THAT I OWN THE BBC *Logic 74321348672* 60	1
25 Oct 97	THE NUMBER ONE SONG IN HEAVEN (re-recording) *Roadrunner RR 22692* 70	1
13 Dec 97	THIS TOWN AIN'T BIG ENOUGH FOR BOTH OF US *Roadrunner RR 22513* [1] 40	2

[1] Sparks Vs Faith No More

Group was a UK / US group for first six hits

SPEAR OF DESTINY 🖊 🎵
UK, male vocal/instrumental group **43 wks**

21 May 83	THE WHEEL *Epic A 3372* 59	5
21 Jan 84	PRISONER OF LOVE *Epic A 4068* 59	3
14 Apr 84	LIBERATOR *Epic A 4310* 67	2
15 Jun 85	ALL MY LOVE (ASK NOTHING) *Epic A 6333* 61	3
10 Aug 85	COME BACK *Epic 6445* 55	3

7 Feb 87	STRANGERS IN OUR TOWN *10 TEN 148*	49	4
4 Apr 87	NEVER TAKE ME ALIVE *10 TEN 162*	14	11
25 Jul 87	WAS THAT YOU *10 TEN 173*	55	4
3 Oct 87	THE TRAVELLER *10 TEN 189*	44	3
24 Sep 88	SO IN LOVE WITH YOU *Virgin VS 1123*	36	5

SPEARHEAD US, male vocal/instrumental group — 5 wks

17 Dec 94	OF COURSE YOU CAN *Capitol CDCL 733*	74	1
22 Apr 95	HOLE IN THE BUCKET *Capitol CDCL 742*	55	1
15 Jul 95	PEOPLE IN THA MIDDLE *Capitol CDCLS 752*	49	2
15 Mar 97	WHY OH WHY *Capital CDCL 785*	45	1

Billie Jo SPEARS ⏺ US, female vocalist — 40 wks

12 Jul 75	● BLANKET ON THE GROUND *United Artists UP 35805*	6	13
17 Jul 76	● WHAT I'VE GOT IN MIND *United Artists UP 36118*	4	13
11 Dec 76	SING ME AN OLD FASHIONED SONG *United Artists UP 36179*	34	9
21 Jul 79	I WILL SURVIVE *United Artists UP 601*	47	5

SPECIALS ❷ ✌ Midlands-based septet who led the early 1980s ska revival and, under Jerry Dammers (k), founded the trailblazing indie label 2 Tone. In 1981, Terry Hall (v), Neville Staples (v) and Lynval Golding (g) broke away to form Fun Boy Three — 101 wks

28 Jul 79	● GANGSTERS *2 Tone CHSTT 1* [1]	6	12
27 Oct 79	● A MESSAGE TO YOU RUDY/NITE CLUB *2 Tone CHSTT 5* [2]	10	14
26 Jan 80	★ THE SPECIAL A.K.A. LIVE EP *2 Tone CHSTT 7* [1]	1	10
24 May 80	● RAT RACE/RUDE BOYS OUTA JAIL *2 Tone CHSTT 11*	5	9
20 Sep 80	● STEREOTYPE/INTERNATIONAL JET SET *2 Tone CHSTT 13*	6	8
13 Dec 80	● DO NOTHING/MAGGIE'S FARM *2 Tone CHSTT 16*	4	11
20 Jun 81	★ GHOST TOWN *2 Tone CHSTT 17*	1	14
23 Jan 82	THE BOILER *2 Tone CHSTT 18* [3]	35	5
3 Sep 83	RACIST FRIEND/BRIGHT LIGHTS *2 Tone CHSTT 25* [1]	60	3
17 Mar 84	● NELSON MANDELA *2 Tone CHSTT 26* [1]	9	10
8 Sep 84	WHAT I LIKE MOST ABOUT YOU IS YOUR GIRLFRIEND *2 Tone CHSTT 27* [1]	51	4
10 Feb 96	HYPOCRITE *Kuff KUFFD 3*	66	1

[1] Special A.K.A. [2] Specials (featuring Rico+) [3] Rhoda with the Special A.K.A.

Tracks on The Special A.K.A. Live EP: Too Much Too Young/Guns of Navarone/ Long Shot Kick De Bucket/Liquidator/Skinhead Moonstomp. 'Maggie's Farm' only listed with 'Do Nothing' from 10 Jan, 1981. Group was male/female for last four hits.
See also VARIOUS ARTISTS (EPs & LPs) – The Two Tone EP

SPECTRUM UK, male instrumental/production group — 1 wk

| 26 Sep 92 | TRUE LOVE WILL FIND YOU IN THE END *Silvertone ORE 44* | 70 | 1 |

Chris SPEDDING ❷ UK, male vocalist/instrumentalist – guitar — 8 wks

| 23 Aug 75 | MOTOR BIKING *RAK 210* | 14 | 8 |

SPEECH US, male vocalist — 2 wks

| 17 Feb 96 | LIKE MARVIN GAYE SAID (WHAT'S GOING ON) *Cooltempo CDCOOL 314* | 35 | 2 |

SPEEDY UK, male vocal/instrumental group — 1 wk

| 9 Nov 96 | BOY WONDER *Boiler House! BOIL 2CD* | 56 | 1 |

SPELLBOUND India, female vocal duo — 1 wk

| 31 May 97 | HEAVEN ON EARTH *East West EW 098CD* | 73 | 1 |

Johnnie SPENCE ♪ UK, orchestra — 15 wks

| 1 Mar 62 | THEME FROM DR. KILDARE *Parlophone R 4872* | 15 | 15 |

Don SPENCER UK, male vocalist — 12 wks

| 21 Mar 63 | FIREBALL *HMV POP 1087* | 32 | 11 |
| 13 Jun 63 | FIREBALL (re-entry) *HMV POP 1087* | 49 | 1 |

Jon SPENCER BLUES EXPLOSION US, male vocal/instrumental group — 1 wk

| 10 May 97 | WAIL *Mute CDMUTE 204* | 66 | 1 |

Tracie SPENCER US, female vocalist — 2 wks

| 4 May 91 | THIS HOUSE *Capitol CL 612* | 65 | 2 |

SPHINX UK/US, male vocal/instrumental group — 2 wks

| 25 Mar 95 | WHAT HOPE HAVE I *Champion CHAMPCD 318* | 43 | 2 |

SPICE GIRLS ❷ ☺ Britain's most successful female vocal group: Geri Halliwell (Ginger Spice), Melanie Chisholm (Mel C/Sporty Spice), Emma Bunton (Baby Spice), Victoria Adams (Posh Spice), Melanie Brown (Mel B/Scary Spice). The girl-power group who made it a Spiceworld — 139 wks

20 Jul 96	★ WANNABE *Virgin VSCDX 1588* ◆ ▲	1	25
26 Oct 96	★ SAY YOU'LL BE THERE *Virgin VSCDT 1601* ■	1	16
28 Dec 96	★ 2 BECOME 1 *Virgin VSCDT 1607* ◆ ■	1	18
15 Mar 97	★ MAMA/WHO DO YOU THINK YOU ARE *Virgin VSCDT 1623* ■	1	15
17 May 97	2 BECOME 1 (re-entry) *Virgin VSCDT 1607*	54	4
25 Oct 97	★ SPICE UP YOUR LIFE *Virgin VSCDT 1660* ■	1	15
27 Dec 97	★ TOO MUCH *Virgin VSCDR 1669* ■	1	15
21 Mar 98	● STOP *Virgin VSCDT 1679*	2	15
11 Jul 98	STOP (re-entry) *Virgin VSCDT 1679*	52	2
1 Aug 98	★ VIVA FOREVER *Virgin VSCDT 1692* ■	1	13
26 Dec 98	★ GOODBYE *Virgin VSCD 1721* ■	1†	13

See also Bryan ADAMS (featuring Melanie C); Melanie B

SPIDER UK, male vocal/instrumental group — 5 wks

| 5 Mar 83 | WHY D'YA LIE TO ME *RCA 313* | 65 | 2 |
| 10 Mar 84 | HERE WE GO ROCK 'N' ROLL *A & M AM 180* | 57 | 3 |

SPIN DOCTORS ❷ ✒ US, male vocal/instrumental group — 28 wks

15 May 93	● TWO PRINCES *Epic 6591452*	3	15
14 Aug 93	LITTLE MISS CAN'T BE WRONG *Epic 6584892*	23	5
9 Oct 93	JIMMY OLSEN'S BLUES *Epic 6597582*	40	2
4 Dec 93	WHAT TIME IS IT *Epic 6599552*	56	1
25 Jun 94	CLEOPATRA'S CAT *Epic 6604192*	29	2
30 Jul 94	YOU LET YOUR HEART GO TOO FAST *Epic 6606612*	66	1
29 Oct 94	MARY JANE *Epic 6609772*	55	1
8 Jun 96	SHE USED TO BE MINE *Epic 6632682*	55	1

SPINAL TAP US/UK, male vocal/instrumental group — 3 wks

| 28 Mar 92 | BITCH SCHOOL *MCA MCS 1624* | 35 | 2 |
| 2 May 92 | THE MAJESTY OF ROCK *MCA MCS 1629* | 61 | 1 |

SPINNERS – See DETROIT SPINNERS

SPIRAL TRIBE UK, male/female vocal/instrumental group — 2 wks

| 29 Aug 92 | BREACH THE PEACE EP *Butterfly BLRT 79* | 66 | 1 |
| 21 Nov 92 | FORWARD THE REVOLUTION *Butterfly BLRT 85* | 70 | 1 |

Tracks on Breach the Peace EP: Breach the Peace/Do It/Seven/ 25 Minute Warning

SPIRITS UK, male/female vocal duo — 5 wks

| 19 Nov 94 | DON'T BRING ME DOWN *MCA MCSTD 2018* | 31 | 3 |
| 8 Apr 95 | SPIRIT INSIDE *MCA MCSTD 2045* | 39 | 2 |

SPIRITUAL COWBOYS – See Dave STEWART (David A Stewart)

SPIRITUALIZED UK, male vocal/instrumental group — 12 wks

30 Jun 90	ANYWAY YOU WANT ME/STEP INTO THE BREEZE *Dedicated ZB 43783*	75	1
17 Aug 91	RUN *Dedicated SPIRIT 002*	59	1
25 Jul 92	MEDICATION *Dedicated SPIRIT 005T*	55	1
23 Oct 93	ELECTRIC MAINLINE *Dedicated SPIRIT 007CD*	49	1
4 Feb 95	LET IT FLOW *Dedicated SPIRIT 009CD* [1]	30	2
9 Aug 97	ELECTRICITY *Dedicated SPIRIT 012CD1*	32	2

UK No 1 ★   UK Top 10 ●   UK million seller ◆   UK entry at No 1 ■   US No 1 ▲

| 14 Feb 98 | I THINK I'M IN LOVE *Dedicated SPIRIT 014CD* | 27 | 2 |
| 6 Jun 98 | THE ABBEY ROAD EP *Dedicated SPIRIT 015CD* | 39 | 2 |

[1] Spiritualized Electric Mainline

Tracks on The Abbey Road EP: Come Together / Broken heart / Death in Vegas

SPIRO and WIX UK, male instrumental duo — 2 wks

| 10 Aug 96 | TARA'S THEME *EMI Premier PRESCD 4* | 29 | 2 |

SPITTING IMAGE ✪ UK, male/female puppets — 18 wks

10 May 86 ★	THE CHICKEN SONG *Virgin SPIT 1*	1	10
26 Jul 86	THE CHICKEN SONG (re-entry) *Virgin SPIT 1*	67	1
6 Dec 86	SANTA CLAUS IS ON THE DOLE/FIRST ATHEIST TABERNACLE CHOIR *Virgin VS 921*	22	7

SPLINTER ✪ UK, male vocal/instrumental duo — 10 wks

| 2 Nov 74 | COSTAFINE TOWN *Dark Horse AMS 7135* | 17 | 10 |

SPLIT ENZ ✪ ✎
New Zealand/UK, male vocal/instrumental group — 15 wks

| 16 Aug 80 | I GOT YOU *A & M AMS 7546* | 12 | 11 |
| 23 May 81 | HISTORY NEVER REPEATS *A & M AMS 8128* | 63 | 4 |

A SPLIT SECOND
Belgium/Italy, male instrumental/production group — 1 wk

| 14 Dec 91 | FLESH *ffrr FX 178* | 68 | 1 |

SPLODGENESSABOUNDS ✎
UK, male vocal/instrumental group — 17 wks

14 Jun 80 ●	SIMON TEMPLAR/TWO PINTS OF LAGER AND A PACKET OF CRISPS PLEASE *Deram BUM 1*	7	8
6 Sep 80	TWO LITTLE BOYS/HORSE *Deram ROLF 1*	26	7
13 Jun 81	COWPUNK MEDLUM *Deram BUM 3*	69	2

SPONGE US, male vocal/instrumental group — 1 wk

| 19 Aug 95 | PLOWED *Work 6623162* | 74 | 1 |

SPOOKY UK, male vocal/instrumental duo — 1 wk

| 13 Mar 93 | SCHMOO *Guerilla GRRR 45CD* | 72 | 1 |

SPOTNICKS ✪ Sweden, male instrumental group — 37 wks

14 Jun 62	ORANGE BLOSSOM SPECIAL *Oriole CB 1724*	29	10
6 Sep 62	ROCKET MAN *Oriole CB 1755*	38	9
31 Jan 63	HAVA NAGILA *Oriole CB 1790*	13	12
25 Apr 63	JUST LISTEN TO MY HEART *Oriole CB 1818*	36	6

Dusty SPRINGFIELD ✪
One of Britain's leading female vocalists of the 1960s, b. Mary O'Brien, 16 April, 1939, London, d. 2 March, 1999. After leaving The Springfields in 1963, she had numerous transatlantic solo hits, and during the sixties was regularly voted UK's Top Female Singer — 211 wks

21 Nov 63 ●	I ONLY WANT TO BE WITH YOU *Philips BF 1292*	4	18
20 Feb 64	STAY AWHILE *Philips BF 1313*	13	10
2 Jul 64 ●	I JUST DON'T KNOW WHAT TO DO WITH MYSELF *Philips BF 1348*	3	12
22 Oct 64 ●	LOSING YOU *Philips BF 1369*	9	13
18 Feb 65	YOUR HURTIN' KIND OF LOVE *Philips BF 1396*	37	4
1 Jul 65 ●	IN THE MIDDLE OF NOWHERE *Philips BF 1418*	8	10
16 Sep 65 ●	SOME OF YOUR LOVIN' *Philips BF 1430*	8	12
27 Jan 66	LITTLE BY LITTLE *Philips BF 1466*	17	9
31 Mar 66 ★	YOU DON'T HAVE TO SAY YOU LOVE ME *Philips BF 1482*	1	13
7 Jul 66 ●	GOING BACK *Philips BF 1502*	10	10
15 Sep 66 ●	ALL I SEE IS YOU *Philips BF 1510*	9	12
23 Feb 67	I'LL TRY ANYTHING *Philips BF 1553*	13	9
25 May 67	GIVE ME TIME *Philips BF 1577*	24	6
10 Jul 68 ●	I CLOSE MY EYES AND COUNT TO TEN *Philips BF 1682*	4	12
4 Dec 68 ●	SON OF A PREACHER MAN *Philips BF 1730*	9	9
20 Sep 69	AM I THE SAME GIRL *Philips BF 1811*	43	3

18 Oct 69	AM I THE SAME GIRL (re-entry) *Philips BF 1811*	46	1
19 Sep 70	HOW CAN I BE SURE *Philips 6006 045*	36	4
20 Oct 79	BABY BLUE *Mercury DUSTY 4*	61	5
22 Aug 87 ●	WHAT HAVE I DONE TO DESERVE THIS *Parlophone R 6163* [1]	2	9
25 Feb 89	NOTHING HAS BEEN PROVED *Parlophone R 6207*	16	7
2 Dec 89	IN PRIVATE *Parlophone R 6234*	14	10
26 May 90	REPUTATION *Parlophone R 6253*	38	6
24 Nov 90	ARRESTED BY YOU *Parlophone R 6266*	70	2
30 Oct 93	HEART AND SOUL *Columbia 6598562* [2]	75	1
10 Jun 95	WHEREVER WOULD I BE *Columbia 6620592* [3]	44	3
4 Nov 95	ROLL AWAY *Columbia 6623682*	68	1

[1] Pet Shop Boys and Dusty Springfield [2] Cilla Black with Dusty Springfield [3] Dusty Springfield and Daryl Hall

See also SPRINGFIELDS

Rick SPRINGFIELD Australia, male vocalist — 13 wks

| 14 Jan 84 | HUMAN TOUCH/SOULS *RCA RICK 1* | 23 | 7 |
| 24 Mar 84 | JESSIE'S GIRL *RCA RICK 2* ▲ | 43 | 6 |

'Souls' only listed from 11 Feb, 1984. It peaked at No 24

SPRINGFIELDS ✎ ✪
UK, male/female vocal/instrumental group — 66 wks

31 Aug 61	BREAKAWAY *Philips BF 1168*	31	8
16 Nov 61	BAMBINO *Philips BF 1178*	16	11
13 Dec 62 ●	ISLAND OF DREAMS *Philips 326557 BF*	5	26
28 Mar 63 ●	SAY I WON'T BE THERE *Philips 326577 BF*	5	15
25 Jul 63	COME ON HOME *Philips BF 1263*	31	6

See also Dusty SPRINGFIELD

Bruce SPRINGSTEEN ✎
'The Boss', b. 23 September, 1949, New Jersey. Singer/songwriter/guitarist/rock superstar, whose legendary stage performances have packed stadiums worldwide. He released the biggest-selling box set, and is one of world's best-selling album artists — 144 wks

22 Nov 80	HUNGRY HEART *CBS 9309*	44	4
13 Jun 81	THE RIVER *CBS A 1179*	35	6
26 May 84	DANCING IN THE DARK *CBS A 4436*	28	7
6 Oct 84	COVER ME *CBS 4662*	38	5
12 Jan 85 ●	DANCING IN THE DARK (re-entry) *CBS A 4436*	4	16
23 Mar 85	COVER ME (re-entry) *CBS A 4662*	16	8
15 Jun 85	I'M ON FIRE/BORN IN THE USA *CBS A 6342*	5	12
3 Aug 85	GLORY DAYS *CBS A 6375*	17	6
14 Dec 85 ●	SANTA CLAUS IS COMIN' TO TOWN/MY HOMETOWN *CBS A 6773*	9	5
29 Nov 86	WAR *CBS 650193 7*	18	7
7 Feb 87	FIRE *CBS 650381 7*	54	2
23 May 87	BORN TO RUN *CBS BRUCE 2*	16	4
3 Oct 87	BRILLIANT DISGUISE *CBS 651141 7*	20	5
12 Dec 87	TUNNEL OF LOVE *CBS 651295 7*	45	4
18 Jun 88	TOUGHER THAN THE REST *CBS BRUCE 3*	13	8
24 Sep 88	SPARE PARTS *CBS BRUCE 4*	32	3
21 Mar 92	HUMAN TOUCH *Columbia 6578727*	11	5
23 May 92	BETTER DAYS *Columbia 6578907*	34	3
25 Jul 92	57 CHANNELS (AND NOTHIN' ON) *Columbia 6581387*	32	4
24 Oct 92	LEAP OF FAITH *Columbia 6583697*	46	3
10 Apr 93	LUCKY TOWN (LIVE) *Columbia 6592282*	48	3
19 Mar 94 ●	STREETS OF PHILADELPHIA *Columbia 6600652*	2	12
22 Apr 95	SECRET GARDEN *Columbia 6612955*	44	3
11 Nov 95	HUNGRY HEART (re-issue) *Columbia 6626252*	28	3
4 May 96	THE GHOST OF TOM JOAD *Columbia 6630315*	26	2
19 Apr 97	SECRET GARDEN (re-issue) *Columbia 6643245*	17	4

SPRINGWATER ✪ UK, male instrumentalist – Phil Cordell — 12 wks

| 23 Oct 71 ● | I WILL RETURN *Polydor 2058 141* | 5 | 12 |

SPRINKLER UK/US, male/female vocal / rap group — 2 wks

| 11 Jul 98 | LEAVE 'EM SOMETHING TO DESIRE *Island CID 706* | 45 | 2 |

UK No 1 ★   UK Top 10 ●   UK million seller ◆   UK entry at No 1 ■   US No 1 ▲

SPYRO GYRA 🎸 🎤 US, male instrumental group | 10 wks

21 Jul 79	MORNING DANCE *Infinity INF 111*	17	10

SQUADRONAIRES – See Joan REGAN

SQUEEZE 🌐 🎸 Critically acclaimed London band, which had several UK/US best sellers. Featured noted singer/songwriters Glenn Tilbrook (g/v) and Chris Difford (v/g). Fluctuating line-up included Jools Holland (k) and Paul Carrack (v/k – also of Ace, and Mike and The Mechanics fame) | 123 wks

8 Apr 78	TAKE ME I'M YOURS *A & M AMS 7335*	19	9
10 Jun 78	BANG BANG *A & M AMS 7360*	49	5
18 Nov 78	GOODBYE GIRL *A & M AMS 7398*	63	2
24 Mar 79 ●	COOL FOR CATS *A & M AMS 7426*	2	11
2 Jun 79 ●	UP THE JUNCTION *A & M AMS 7444*	2	11
8 Sep 79	SLAP AND TICKLE *A & M AMS 7466*	24	8
1 Mar 80	ANOTHER NAIL IN MY HEART *A & M AMS 7507*	17	9
10 May 80	PULLING MUSSELS (FROM THE SHELL) *A & M AMS 7523*	44	6
16 May 81	IS THAT LOVE *A & M AMS 8129*	35	8
25 Jul 81	TEMPTED *A & M AMS 8147*	41	5
10 Oct 81 ●	LABELLED WITH LOVE *A & M AMS 8166*	4	10
24 Apr 82	BLACK COFFEE IN BED *A & M AMS 8219*	51	4
23 Oct 82	ANNIE GET YOUR GUN *A & M AMS 8259*	43	4
15 Jun 85	LAST TIME FOREVER *A & M AM 255*	45	5
8 Aug 87	HOURGLASS *A & M AM 400*	16	10
17 Oct 87	TRUST ME TO OPEN MY MOUTH *A & M AM 412*	72	1
25 Apr 92	COOL FOR CATS (re-issue) *A & M AM 860*	62	2
24 Jul 93	THIRD RAIL *A & M 5803372*	39	3
11 Sep 93	SOME FANTASTIC PLACE *A & M 5803792*	73	1
9 Sep 95	THIS SUMMER *A & M 5811912*	36	3
18 Nov 95	ELECTRIC TRAINS *A & M 5812692*	44	2
15 Jun 96	HEAVEN KNOWS *A & M 5816052*	27	2
24 Aug 96	THIS SUMMER (re-mix) *A & M 5818372*	32	2

Billy SQUIER US, male vocalist | 3 wks

3 Oct 81	THE STROKE *Capitol CL 214*	52	3

Dorothy SQUIRES 🎵 UK, female vocalist | 56 wks

5 Jun 53	I'M WALKING BEHIND YOU *Polygon P 1068*	12	1
24 Aug 61	SAY IT WITH FLOWERS *Columbia DB 4665* [1]	23	10
20 Sep 69	FOR ONCE IN MY LIFE *President PT 267*	24	10
20 Dec 69	FOR ONCE IN MY LIFE (re-entry) *President PT 267*	48	1
21 Feb 70	TILL *President PT 281*	25	10
9 May 70	TILL (re-entry) *President PT 281*	48	1
8 Aug 70	MY WAY *President PT 305*	40	5
19 Sep 70	MY WAY (re-entry) *President PT 305*	34	8
28 Nov 70	MY WAY (2nd re-entry) *President PT 305*	25	10

[1] Dorothy Squires and Russ Conway

STABBS
Finland/US/Cameroon, male instrumental/production group | 1 wk

24 Dec 94	JOY AND HAPPINESS *Hi-Life HICD 3*	65	1

STACCATO UK/Holland, male/female vocal/instrumental duo | 1 wk

20 Jul 96	I WANNA KNOW *Multiply CDMULTY 11*	65	1

Jim STAFFORD 🌐 US, male vocalist | 16 wks

27 Apr 74	SPIDERS AND SNAKES *MGM 2006 374*	14	8
6 Jul 74	MY GIRL BILL *MGM 2006 423*	20	8

Jo STAFFORD 🎵 US, female vocalist | 28 wks

14 Nov 52 ★	YOU BELONG TO ME *Columbia DB 3152* ▲	1	19
19 Dec 52	JAMBALAYA *Columbia DB 3169*	11	2
7 May 54 ●	MAKE LOVE TO ME *Philips PB 233* ▲	8	1
9 Dec 55	SUDDENLY THERE'S A VALLEY *Philips PB 509*	12	5
3 Feb 56	SUDDENLY THERE'S A VALLEY (re-entry) *Philips PB 509*	19	1

Terry STAFFORD US, male vocalist | 9 wks

7 May 64	SUSPICION *London HLU 9871*	31	9

STAIFFI and his MUSTAFAS
France, male vocal/instrumental group | 1 wk

28 Jul 60	MUSTAFA CHA CHA CHA *Pye International 7N 25057*	43	1

STAKKA BO 🌐 ✉ Sweden, male rap/DJ duo | 12 wks

25 Sep 93	HERE WE GO *Polydor PZCD 280*	13	8
18 Dec 93	DOWN THE DRAIN *Polydor PZCD 301*	64	4

Frank STALLONE US, male vocalist | 2 wks

22 Oct 83	FAR FROM OVER *RSO 95*	68	2

STAMFORD BRIDGE UK, male vocal group | 1 wk

16 May 70	CHELSEA *Penny Farthing PEN 715*	47	1

STAN UK, male vocal/instrumental duo | 3 wks

31 Jul 93	SUNTAN *Hug CDBUM 1*	40	3

Lisa STANSFIELD ☺ 🌐 Only UK act to have three US R&B No 1 hits, b. 11 April, 1966, Lancashire. Like Yazz, she was featured vocalist on a Coldcut single before achieving a No 1 in her own right. This multi-BRIT Award winner has sold millions of records all around the world | 125 wks

25 Mar 89	PEOPLE HOLD ON *Ahead Of Our Time CCUT 5* [1]	11	9
12 Aug 89	THIS IS THE RIGHT TIME *Arista 112512*	13	8
28 Oct 89 ★	ALL AROUND THE WORLD *Arista 112693*	1	14
10 Feb 90 ●	LIVE TOGETHER *Arista 112914*	10	6
12 May 90	WHAT DID I DO TO YOU (EP) *Arista 113168*	25	4
19 Oct 91 ●	CHANGE *Arista 114820*	10	7
21 Dec 91	ALL WOMAN *Arista 115000*	20	8
14 Mar 92	TIME TO MAKE YOU MINE *Arista 115113*	14	8
6 Jun 92	SET YOUR LOVING FREE *Arista 74321100587*	28	4
19 Dec 92 ●	SOMEDAY (I'M COMING BACK) *Arista 74321123567*	10	9
1 May 93 ★	FIVE LIVE (EP) *Parlophone CDRS 6340* [2]	1	11
5 Jun 93 ●	IN ALL THE RIGHT PLACES *MCA MCSTD 1780*	8	11
24 Jul 93	FIVE LIVE EP (re-entry) *Parlophone CDRS 6340* [2]	74	1
23 Oct 93	SO NATURAL *Arista 74321169132*	15	5
11 Dec 93	LITTLE BIT OF HEAVEN *Arista 74321178202*	32	4
18 Jan 97 ●	PEOPLE HOLD ON (THE BOOTLEG MIXES) *Arista 74321452012*	4	6
22 Mar 97 ●	THE REAL THING *Arista 74321463222*	9	7
21 Jun 97	NEVER, NEVER GONNA GIVE YOU UP *Arista 74321490392*	25	2
4 Oct 97	THE LINE *RCA 74321511372*	64	1

[1] Coldcut featuring Lisa Stansfield [2] George Michael and Queen with Lisa Stansfield [3] Lisa Stansfield vs The Dirty Rotten Scoundrels

Tracks on What Did I Do to You (EP): What Did I Do to You / My Apple Heart / Lay Me Down / Something's Happenin'. Tracks on Five Live EP: Somebody to Love / These Are the Days of Our Lives / Calling You / Papa Was a Rolling Stone – Killer (medley). Lisa Stansfield appears only on the second track

Viv STANSHALL – See Mike OLDFIELD

STAPLE SINGERS US, male/female vocal group | 14 wks

10 Jun 72	I'LL TAKE YOU THERE *Stax 2025 110* ▲	30	8
8 Jun 74	IF YOU'RE READY (COME GO WITH ME) *Stax 2025 224*	34	6

Cyril STAPLETON 🎵 UK, orchestra | 27 wks

27 May 55	ELEPHANT TANGO *Decca F 10488*	20	2
1 Jul 55	ELEPHANT TANGO (re-entry) *Decca F 10488*	20	1
22 Jul 55	ELEPHANT TANGO (2nd re-entry) *Decca F 10488*	19	1
23 Sep 55 ●	BLUE STAR (THE MEDIC THEME) *Decca F 10559* [1]	2	12
6 Apr 56	THE ITALIAN THEME *Decca F 10703*	18	2
1 Jun 56	THE HAPPY WHISTLER *Decca F 10735* [2]	22	4
19 Jul 57	FORGOTTEN DREAMS *Decca F 10912*	27	5

[1] Cyril Stapleton Orchestra featuring Julie Dawn

[2] Cyril Stapleton Orchestra featuring Desmond Lane, penny whistle

STARDUST ☺ France, male/female vocal/instrumental group — 25 wks

8 Oct 77	ARIANA *Satril SAT 120*	42	3
1 Aug 98	MUSIC SOUNDS BETTER WITH YOU (import) *Roule ROULE 305.*	55	3
22 Aug 98 ●	MUSIC SOUNDS BETTER WITH YOU *Virgin DINSD 175*	2†	19

Alvin STARDUST ◐ Sixties hitmaker who became bill-topping seventies vocalist, b. Bernard Jewry, 27 September, 1942, London. After several minor hits as Shane Fenton, he collected a string of smashes as OTT rocker Stardust, and extended his chart span to almost 25 years — 119 wks

3 Nov 73 ●	MY COO-CA-CHOO *Magnet MAG 1*	2	21
16 Feb 74 ★	JEALOUS MIND *Magnet MAG 5*	1	11
4 May 74 ●	RED DRESS *Magnet MAG 8*	7	8
31 Aug 74 ●	YOU YOU YOU *Magnet MAG 13*	6	10
30 Nov 74	TELL ME WHY *Magnet MAG 19*	16	8
1 Feb 75	GOOD LOVE CAN NEVER DIE *Magnet MAG 21*	11	9
12 Jul 75	SWEET CHEATIN' RITA *Magnet MAG 32*	37	4
5 Sep 81 ●	PRETEND *Stiff BUY 124*	4	10
21 Nov 81	A WONDERFUL TIME UP THERE *Stiff BUY 132*	56	8
5 May 84 ●	I FEEL LIKE BUDDY HOLLY *Chrysalis CHS 2784*	7	11
27 Oct 84 ●	I WON'T RUN AWAY *Chrysalis CHS 2829*	7	13
15 Dec 84	SO NEAR TO CHRISTMAS *Chrysalis CHS 2835*	29	4
23 Mar 85	GOT A LITTLE HEARTACHE *Chrysalis CHS 2856*	55	2

Alvin started his career as Shane Fenton
See also Shane FENTON and the FENTONES

STARGARD ◢ ♪ US, female vocal group — 14 wks

28 Jan 78	THEME FROM 'WHICH WAY IS UP' *MCA 346*	19	7
15 Apr 78	LOVE IS SO EASY *MCA 354*	45	1
9 Sep 78	WHAT YOU WAITING FOR *MCA 382*	39	6

STARGAZERS ℂ UK/Australia, male/female vocal group — 53 wks

13 Feb 53	BROKEN WINGS *Decca F 10047*	11	1
27 Feb 53 ★	BROKEN WINGS (re-entry) *Decca F 10047*	1	11
19 Feb 54 ★	I SEE THE MOON *Decca F 10213*	1	15
9 Apr 54	HAPPY WANDERER *Decca F 10259*	12	1
4 Mar 55	SOMEBODY *Decca F 10437*	20	1
3 Jun 55	CRAZY OTTO RAG *Decca F 10523*	18	3
9 Sep 55	CLOSE THE DOOR *Decca F 10594*	6	9
11 Nov 55	TWENTY TINY FINGERS *Decca F 10626*	4	11
22 Jun 56	HOT DIGGITY *Decca F 10731*	28	1

See also Dickie VALENTINE

STARGAZERS UK, male vocal/instrumental group — 3 wks

6 Feb 82	GROOVE BABY GROOVE EP *Epic EPC A 1924*	56	3

Tracks on Groove Baby Groove EP: Groove Baby Groove / Jump Around / La Rock 'n' Roll (Quelques Uns A La Lune) / Red Light Green Light

STARJETS UK, male vocal/instrumental group — 5 wks

8 Sep 79	WAR STORIES *Epic EPC 7770*	51	5

STARLAND VOCAL BAND ◐ US, male/female vocal group — 10 wks

7 Aug 76	AFTERNOON DELIGHT *RCA 2716* ▲	18	10

STARLIGHT ☺ Italy, male instrumental/production group — 11 wks

19 Aug 89 ●	NUMERO UNO *Citybeat CBE 742*	9	11

STARLITERS – See Joey DEE and the STARLITERS

Edwin STARR ♪ US, male vocalist — 70 wks

12 May 66	STOP HER ON SIGHT (SOS) *Polydor BM 56 702*	35	8
18 Aug 66	HEADLINE NEWS *Polydor 56 717*	39	3
11 Dec 68	STOP HER ON SIGHT (SOS) / HEADLINE NEWS (re-issue) *Polydor 56 753*	11	11
13 Sep 69	25 MILES *Tamla Motown TMG 672*	36	6
24 Oct 70 ●	WAR *Tamla Motown TMG 754* ▲	3	12
20 Feb 71	STOP THE WAR NOW *Tamla Motown TMG 764*	33	1
27 Jan 79 ●	CONTACT *20th Century BTC 2396*	6	12

26 May 79 ●	H.A.P.P.Y. RADIO *RCA TC 2408*	9	11
1 Jun 85	IT AIN'T FAIR *Hippodrome HIP 101*	56	4
30 Oct 93	WAR *Weekend CDWEEK 103* [1]	69	2

[1] Edwin Starr and Shadow

'Headline News' not listed with 'SOS' from 22 Jan, 1969, to 19 Feb, 1969. It therefore peaked at No 16. 'War' in 1993 was a re-recording and was listed with the flip side 'Wild Thing' by the Troggs and Wolf

Freddie STARR ♪ UK, male vocalist — 14 wks

23 Feb 74 ●	IT'S YOU *Tiffany 6121 501*	9	10
20 Dec 75	WHITE CHRISTMAS *Thunderbird THE 102*	41	4

Kay STARR ℂ US, female vocalist — 58 wks

5 Dec 52 ★	COMES A-LONG A-LOVE *Capitol CL 13808*	1	16
24 Apr 53 ●	SIDE BY SIDE *Capitol CL 13871*	7	4
19 Mar 54 ●	CHANGING PARTNERS *Capitol CL 14050*	4	14
15 Oct 54	AM I A TOY OR A TREASURE *Capitol CL 14151*	17	3
12 Nov 54	AM I A TOY OR A TREASURE (re-entry) *Capitol CL 14151*	20	1
17 Feb 56 ★	ROCK AND ROLL WALTZ *HMV POP 168* ▲	1	20

Ringo STARR ◐ UK, male vocalist — 56 wks

17 Apr 71 ●	IT DON'T COME EASY *Apple R 5898*	4	11
1 Apr 72 ●	BACK OFF BOOGALOO *Apple R 5944*	2	10
27 Oct 73 ●	PHOTOGRAPH *Apple R 5992* ▲	8	13
23 Feb 74 ●	YOU'RE SIXTEEN *Apple R 5995* ▲	4	10
30 Nov 74	ONLY YOU *Apple R 6000*	28	11
6 Jun 92	WEIGHT OF THE WORLD *Private Music 115392*	74	1

STARS ON 54 US, female vocal trio — 3 wks

28 Nov 98	IF YOU COULD READ MY MIND *Tommy Boy TBCD 7497* ▲	23	3

STARSHIP ✎ US, female/male vocal/instrumental group — 41 wks

26 Jan 80	JANE *Grunt FB 1750* [1]	21	9
16 Nov 85	WE BUILT THIS CITY *RCA PB 49929* ▲	12	12
8 Feb 86	SARA *RCA FB 49893* ▲	66	3
11 Apr 87 ★	NOTHING'S GONNA STOP US NOW *Grunt FB 49757* ▲	1	17

[1] Jefferson Starship

STARSOUND ◐ Holland, producer Jaap Eggermont with male/female session singers — 37 wks

18 Apr 81 ●	STARS ON 45 *CBS A 1102* ▲	2	14
4 Jul 81 ●	STARS ON 45 VOL.2 *CBS A 1407*	2	10
19 Sep 81	STARS ON 45 VOL.3 *CBS A 1521*	17	6
27 Feb 82	STARS ON STEVIE *CBS A 2041*	14	7

STARTRAX ◐ UK, male/female session group — 8 wks

1 Aug 81	STARTRAX CLUB DISCO *Picksy KSY 1001*	18	8

STARTURN ON 45 (PINTS) ◐ UK, male vocalist — 9 wks

24 Oct 81	STARTURN ON 45 (PINTS) *V Tone V TONE 003*	45	4
30 Apr 88	PUMP UP THE BITTER *Pacific DRINK 1*	12	5

STARVATION
Multi-national, male/female vocal/instrumental charity assembly — 6 wks

9 Mar 85	STARVATION/TAM-TAM POUR L'ETHIOPE *Zarjazz JAZZ 3*	33	6

STARVING SOULS UK, male vocal/instrumental group — 1 wk

21 Oct 95	I BE THE PROPHET *Durban Poison DPCD 1*	66	1

STATE OF MIND UK, male/female vocal/production group — 3 wks

18 Apr 98	THIS IS IT *Ministry Of Sound MOSCDS 123*	30	2
25 Jul 98	TAKE CONTROL *Ministry Of Sound MOSCDS 124*	46	1

STATLER BROTHERS US, male vocal group — 4 wks

24 Feb 66	FLOWERS ON THE WALL *CBS 201976*	38	4

Candi STATON ♪ US, female vocalist — 66 wks

Date	Title	Pos	Wks
29 May 76 ●	YOUNG HEARTS RUN FREE *Warner Bros. K 16730*	2	13
18 Sep 76	DESTINY *Warner Bros. K 16806*	41	3
23 Jul 77 ●	NIGHTS ON BROADWAY *Warner Bros. K 16972*	6	12
3 Jun 78	HONEST I DO LOVE YOU *Warner Bros. K 17164*	48	5
24 Apr 82	SUSPICIOUS MINDS *Sugarhill SH 112*	31	9
31 May 86	YOUNG HEARTS RUN FREE (re-mix) *Warner Bros. W 8680*	47	5
2 Feb 91 ●	YOU GOT THE LOVE *Truelove TLOVE 7001* [1]	4	11
1 Mar 97 ●	YOU GOT THE LOVE *React CDREACT 89* [1]	3	8

[1] Source featuring Candi Staton

STATUS IV US, male vocal group — 3 wks

Date	Title	Pos	Wks
9 Jul 83	YOU AIN'T REALLY DOWN *TMT TMT 4*	56	3

STATUS QUO ♪ Ever popular London boogie band: Francis Rossi (g/v), Rick Parfitt (g/v), Alan Lancaster (b), John Coghlan (d). No group has accumulated more British hits than these head-bangers' heroes, who were chosen to open Live Aid in 1985 — 408 wks

Date	Title	Pos	Wks
24 Jan 68 ●	PICTURES OF MATCHSTICK MEN *Pye 7N 17449*	7	12
21 Aug 68 ●	ICE IN THE SUN *Pye 7N 17581*	8	12
28 May 69	ARE YOU GROWING TIRED OF MY LOVE *Pye 7N 17728*	46	2
18 Jun 69	ARE YOU GROWING TIRED OF MY LOVE (re-entry) *Pye 7N 17728*	50	1
2 May 70 ●	DOWN THE DUSTPIPE *Pye 7N 17907*	12	17
7 Nov 70 ●	IN MY CHAIR *Pye 7N 17998*	21	14
13 Jan 73 ●	PAPER PLANE *Vertigo 6059 071*	8	11
14 Apr 73	MEAN GIRL *Pye 7N 45229*	20	11
8 Sep 73 ●	CAROLINE *Vertigo 6059 085*	5	13
4 May 74 ●	BREAK THE RULES *Vertigo 6059 101*	8	8
7 Dec 74 ★	DOWN DOWN *Vertigo 6059 114*	1	11
17 May 75 ●	ROLL OVER LAY DOWN *Vertigo QUO 13*	9	8
14 Feb 76	RAIN *Vertigo 6059 133*	7	7
10 Jul 76	MYSTERY SONG *Vertigo 6059 146*	11	9
11 Dec 76 ●	WILD SIDE OF LIFE *Vertigo 6059 153*	9	12
8 Oct 77 ●	ROCKIN' ALL OVER THE WORLD *Vertigo 6059 184*	3	16
2 Sep 78	AGAIN AND AGAIN *Vertigo QUO 1*	13	9
25 Nov 78	ACCIDENT PRONE *Vertigo QUO 2*	36	8
22 Sep 79 ●	WHATEVER YOU WANT *Vertigo 6059 242*	4	9
24 Nov 79	LIVING ON AN ISLAND *Vertigo 6059 248*	16	10
11 Oct 80 ●	WHAT YOU'RE PROPOSING *Vertigo QUO 3*	2	11
6 Dec 80	LIES/DON'T DRIVE MY CAR *Vertigo QUO 4*	11	10
28 Feb 81 ●	SOMETHING 'BOUT YOU BABY I LIKE *Vertigo QUO 5*	9	7
28 Nov 81 ●	ROCK 'N' ROLL *Vertigo QUO 6*	8	11
27 Mar 82 ●	DEAR JOHN *Vertigo QUO 7*	10	8
12 Jun 82	SHE DON'T FOOL ME *Vertigo QUO 8*	36	5
30 Oct 82	CAROLINE (LIVE AT THE N.E.C.) *Vertigo QUO 10*	13	7
10 Sep 83 ●	OL' RAG BLUES *Vertigo QUO 11*	9	8
5 Nov 83	A MESS OF THE BLUES *Vertigo QUO 12*	15	6
10 Dec 83 ●	MARGUERITA TIME *Vertigo QUO 14*	3	11
19 May 84	GOING DOWN TOWN TONIGHT *Vertigo QUO 15*	20	6
27 Oct 84 ●	THE WANDERER *Vertigo QUO 16*	7	11
17 May 86 ●	ROLLIN' HOME *Vertigo QUO 18*	9	6
26 Jul 86	RED SKY *Vertigo QUO 19*	19	8
4 Oct 86 ●	IN THE ARMY NOW *Vertigo QUO 20*	2	14
6 Dec 86	DREAMIN' *Vertigo QUO 21*	15	8
26 Mar 88	AIN'T COMPLAINING *Vertigo QUO 22*	19	6
21 May 88	WHO GETS THE LOVE *Vertigo QUO 23*	34	4
20 Aug 88	RUNNING ALL OVER THE WORLD *Vertigo QUAID 1*	17	6
3 Dec 88 ●	BURNING BRIDGES (ON AND OFF AND ON AGAIN) *Vertigo QUO 25*	5	10
28 Oct 89	NOT AT ALL *Vertigo QUO 26*	50	2
29 Sep 90 ●	THE ANNIVERSARY WALTZ – PART 1 *Vertigo QUO 28*	2	9
15 Dec 90	THE ANNIVERSARY WALTZ – PART 2 *Vertigo QUO 29*	16	7
7 Sep 91	CAN'T GIVE YOU MORE *Vertigo QUO 30*	37	3
18 Jan 92	ROCK 'TIL YOU DROP *Vertigo QUO 32*	38	3
10 Oct 92	ROADHOUSE MEDLEY (ANNIVERSARY WALTZ PART 25) *Polydor QUO 33*	21	4
6 Aug 94	I DIDN'T MEAN IT *Polydor QUOCD 34*	21	4
22 Oct 94	SHERRI DON'T FAIL ME NOW *Polydor QUOCD 35*	38	2
3 Dec 94	RESTLESS *Polydor QUOCD 36*	39	2
4 Nov 95	WHEN YOU WALK IN THE ROOM *PolyGram TV 5775122*	34	2
2 Mar 96	FUN FUN FUN *PolyGram TV 5762632* [1]	24	4
13 Apr 96	DON'T STOP *PolyGram TV 5766352*	35	2
9 Nov 96	ALL AROUND MY HAT *PolyGram TV 5759452* [2]	47	1

[1] Status Quo with the Beach Boys
[2] Status Quo with Maddy Prior from Steeleye Span

'Don't Drive My Car' listed from 20 Dec, 1980, only. 'Running All Over the World' is a re-recorded version of 'Rockin' All Over the World', with a slightly changed lyric, released to promote the Race Against Time of 28 Aug, 1988.
See also Francis ROSSI

STAXX ☺ UK, male/female vocal/instrumental group — 11 wks

Date	Title	Pos	Wks
2 Oct 93	JOY *Champion CHAMPCD 303*	25	6
20 May 95	YOU *Champion CHAMPCD 316* [1]	50	1
13 Sep 97	JOY *Champion CHAMPCD 328* [1]	14	4

[1] Staxx featuring Carol Leeming

STEALER'S WHEEL ♂ ♪ UK, male vocal/instrumental group — 22 wks

Date	Title	Pos	Wks
26 May 73 ●	STUCK IN THE MIDDLE WITH YOU *A & M AMS 7036*	8	10
1 Sep 73	EVERYTHING'LL TURN OUT FINE *A & M AMS 7079*	33	6
26 Jan 74	STAR *A & M AMS 7094*	25	6

STEAM ◎ US, male vocal/instrumental group — 14 wks

Date	Title	Pos	Wks
31 Jan 70 ●	NA NA HEY HEY KISS HIM GOODBYE *Fontana TF 1058* ▲	9	14

Anthony STEEL and the RADIO REVELLERS ◖ UK, male vocalist/male instrumental group — 6 wks

Date	Title	Pos	Wks
10 Sep 54	WEST OF ZANZIBAR *Polygon P 1114*	11	6

STEEL PULSE UK, male vocal/instrumental group — 12 wks

Date	Title	Pos	Wks
1 Apr 78	KU KLUX KLAN *Island WIP 6428*	41	4
8 Jul 78	PRODIGAL SON *Island WIP 6449*	35	6
23 Jun 79	SOUND SYSTEM *Island WIP 6490*	71	2

Tommy STEELE ♪ ◎ Britain's first homegrown rock'n'roll star, b. Thomas Hicks, 17 December, 1936, London. Just four months after his chart debut, he was filming his life story. The singer/songwriter/guitarist, who topped the chart before Elvis, starred in many other movies and musicals — 147 wks

Date	Title	Pos	Wks
26 Oct 56	ROCK WITH THE CAVEMAN *Decca F 10795* [1]	13	4
30 Nov 56	ROCK WITH THE CAVEMAN (re-entry) *Decca F 10795* [1]	23	1
14 Dec 56 ★	SINGING THE BLUES *Decca F 10819* [1]	1	13
15 Feb 57	KNEE DEEP IN THE BLUES *Decca F 10849* [1]	15	9
19 Apr 57	SINGING THE BLUES (re-entry) *Decca F 10819* [1]	24	1
3 May 57	BUTTERFINGERS *Decca F 10877* [1]	25	1
17 May 57 ●	BUTTERFINGERS (re-entry) *Decca F 10877* [1]	8	17
17 May 57	SINGING THE BLUES (2nd re-entry) *Decca F 10819* [1]	29	1
16 Aug 57 ●	WATER WATER/HANDFUL OF SONGS *Decca F 10923* [1]	5	16
30 Aug 57	SHIRALEE *Decca F 10896* [1]	11	4
22 Nov 57	HEY YOU *Decca F 10941* [1]	28	1
13 Dec 57	WATER WATER/HANDFUL OF SONGS (re-entry) *Decca F 10923* [1]	28	1
7 Mar 58 ●	NAIROBI *Decca F 10991*	3	11
25 Apr 58	HAPPY GUITAR *Decca F 10976*	20	5
18 Jul 58	THE ONLY MAN ON THE ISLAND *Decca F 11041* [1]	16	8
14 Nov 58 ●	COME ON LET'S GO *Decca F 11072*	10	13
14 Aug 59	TALLAHASSEE LASSIE *Decca F 11152*	16	4
28 Aug 59	GIVE GIVE GIVE *Decca F 11152*	28	2
25 Sep 59	TALLAHASSEE LASSIE (re-entry) *Decca F 11152*	25	1
4 Dec 59 ●	LITTLE WHITE BULL *Decca F 11177*	6	12
10 Mar 60	LITTLE WHITE BULL (re-entry) *Decca F 11177*	30	5
23 Jun 60	WHAT A MOUTH *Decca F 11245*	5	11
29 Dec 60	MUST BE SANTA *Decca F 11299*	40	1
17 Aug 61	WRITING ON THE WALL *Decca F 11372*	30	5

[1] Tommy Steele and the Steelmen

'Handful of Songs' listed together with 'Water Water' from week of 23 Aug, 1957.
See also VARIOUS ARTISTS (EPs & LPs) – All Star Hit Parade No 2

UK No 1 ★   UK Top 10 ●   UK million seller ◆   UK entry at No 1 ■   US No 1 ▲

What: *Diana*   89
Who: Paul Anka
When: 1957 (1)
Which: He penned about his babysitter, Diana Ayoub.
It was the first single by a teenager to earn a British gold disc and has sold more than ten million copies worldwide

What: *Ride on Time*   90
Who: Black Box
When: 1989 (1)
Which: Topped the chart for six weeks and was the work of an Italian group who were unknown in their homeland. The single heavily sampled Loleatta Holloway's 1980 US dance chart-topper, 'Love Sensation'

What: *Tie a Yellow Ribbon Round the Old Oak Tree*   91
Who: Dawn
When: 1973
Which: Was inspired by the true story of a Florida convict. It was the biggest hit of 1973 on both sides of the Atlantic, selling more than six million copies worldwide

What: *Little Things Mean a Lot*   92
Who: Kitty Kallen
When: 1954
Which: Gave the veteran big-band vocalist her only UK hit. The song, which topped the sheet music charts for three months, was co-written by a DJ and a journalist

STEELEYE SPAN ♂ ⊕
UK, male/female vocal/instrumental group **18 wks**

| 8 Dec 73 | GAUDETE *Chrysalis CHS 2007* | 14 | 9 |
| 15 Nov 75 ● | ALL AROUND MY HAT *Chrysalis CHS 2078* | 5 | 9 |

See also STATUS QUO

STEELY DAN ✎
US, male vocal/instrumental group **21 wks**

30 Aug 75	DO IT AGAIN *ABC 4075*	39	4
11 Dec 76	HAITIAN DIVORCE *ABC 4152*	17	9
29 Jul 78	FM (NO STATIC AT ALL) *MCA 374*	49	4
2 Sep 78	FM (NO STATIC AT ALL) (re-entry) *MCA 374*	75	1
10 Mar 79	RIKKI DON'T LOSE THAT NUMBER *ABC 4241*	58	3

Jim STEINMAN *US, male producer* **9 wks**

| 4 Jul 81 | ROCK 'N' ROLL DREAMS COME THROUGH
Epic EPC A 1236 1 | 52 | 7 |
| 23 Jun 84 | TONIGHT IS WHAT IT MEANS TO BE YOUNG
MCA MCA 889 2 | 67 | 2 |

1 Jim Steinman, vocals by Rory Dodd 2 Jim Steinman and Fire Inc

STEINSKI and MASS MEDIA *US, male producer and rapper* **2 wks**

| 31 Jan 87 | WE'LL BE RIGHT BACK *Fourth & Broadway BRW 59* | 63 | 2 |

Mike STEIPHENSON – See BURUNDI STEIPHENSON BLACK

Doreen STEPHENS – See Billy COTTON and his BAND

Richie STEPHENS *Jamaica, male vocalist* **1 wk**

| 9 Aug 97 | COME GIVE ME YOUR LOVE *Delirious 74321450442* | 61 | 1 |

See also MAD COBRA featuring Ritchie STEPHENS

Martin STEPHENSON and the DAINTEES
UK, male vocal/instrumental group **7 wks**

8 Nov 86	BOAT TO BOLIVIA *Kitchenware SL 27*	70	2
17 Jan 87	TROUBLE TOWN *Kitchenware SK 13* 1	58	3
27 Jun 92	BIG SKY NEW LIGHT *Kitchenware SK 57*	71	2

1 Daintees

STEPPENWOLF *US/Canada, male vocal/instrumental group* **9 wks**

| 11 Jun 69 | BORN TO BE WILD *Stateside SS 8017* | 30 | 7 |
| 9 Aug 69 | BORN TO BE WILD (re-entry) *Stateside SS 8017* | 50 | 2 |

STEPS ⊕ ☺ *UK, male / female vocal group* **48 wks**

22 Nov 97	5, 6, 7, 8 *Jive JIVECD 438*	14	17
2 May 98 ●	LAST THING ON MY MIND *Jive 0518492*	6	14
5 Sep 98 ●	ONE FOR SORROW *Jive 0519092*	2	11
21 Nov 98 ●	HEARTBEAT/TRAGEDY *Jive 0519142*	2†	6

STEREO MCs ◀ ☺ *UK, male vocal/rap group* **31 wks**

29 Sep 90	ELEVATE MY MIND *Fourth & Broadway BRW 186*	74	1
9 Mar 91	LOST IN MUSIC *Fourth & Broadway BRW 198*	46	3
26 Sep 92	CONNECTED *Fourth & Broadway BRW 262*	18	6
5 Dec 92	STEP IT UP *Fourth & Broadway BRW 266*	12	12
20 Feb 93	GROUND LEVEL *Fourth & Broadway BRCD 268*	19	5
29 May 93	CREATION *Fourth & Broadway BRCD 276*	19	4

STEREO NATION *UK, male vocal duo* **1 wk**

| 17 Aug 96 | I'VE BEEN WAITING *EMI Premier PRESCD 5* | 53 | 1 |

STEREOLAB *UK/France, male/female vocal/instrumental group* **6 wks**

8 Jan 94	JENNY ONDIOLINE/FRENCH DISKO *Duophonic UHF DUHFD 01*	75	1
30 Jul 94	PING PONG *Duophonic UHF DUHFCD 04*	45	2
12 Nov 94	WOW AND FLUTTER *Duophonic UHF DUHFCD 07*	70	1
2 Mar 96	CYBELE'S REVERIE *Duophonic UHF DUHFCD 10*	62	1
13 Sep 97	MISS MODULAR *Duophonic UHF DUHFCD 16*	60	1

STEREOPHONICS ✎ ⊕ *UK, male vocal/instrumental trio* **19 wks**

29 Mar 97	LOCAL BOY IN THE PHOTOGRAPH *V2 SPHD 2*	51	1
31 May 97	MORE LIFE IN A TRAMP'S VEST *V2 SPHD 4*	33	2
23 Aug 97	A THOUSAND TREES *V2 VVR 5000443*	22	3
8 Nov 97	TRAFFIC *V2 VVR 5000948*	20	3
21 Feb 98	LOCAL BOY IN THE PHOTOGRAPH (re-issue) *V2 VVR 5001263*	14	4
21 Nov 98 ●	THE BARTENDER AND THE THIEF *V2 VVR 5004653*	3†	6

STETSASONIC *US, male rap group* **3 wks**

| 24 Sep 88 | TALKIN' ALL THAT JAZZ *Breakout USA 640* | 73 | 2 |
| 7 Nov 98 | TALKIN ALL THAT JAZZ (re-mix) *Tommy Boy TBCD 7310B* | 54 | 1 |

STEVE and EYDIE – See Steve LAWRENCE; Eydie GORME

April STEVENS – See Nino TEMPO and April STEVENS

Cat STEVENS ⊕ ♂ ✎ *UK, male vocalist* **96 wks**

20 Oct 66	I LOVE MY DOG *Deram DM 102*	28	7
12 Jan 67 ●	MATTHEW AND SON *Deram DM 110*	2	10
30 Mar 67 ●	I'M GONNA GET ME A GUN *Deram DM 118*	6	10
2 Aug 67	A BAD NIGHT *Deram DM 140*	20	8
20 Dec 67	KITTY *Deram DM 156*	47	1
27 Jun 70 ●	LADY D'ARBANVILLE *Island WIP 6086*	8	13
28 Aug 71	MOON SHADOW *Island WIP 6092*	22	11
1 Jan 72 ●	MORNING HAS BROKEN *Island WIP 6121*	9	13
9 Dec 72	CAN'T KEEP IT IN *Island WIP 6152*	13	12
24 Aug 74	ANOTHER SATURDAY NIGHT *Island WIP 6206*	19	8
2 Jul 77	(REMEMBER THE DAYS OF THE) OLD SCHOOL YARD *Island WIP 6387*	44	3

Connie STEVENS ⊕ *US, female vocalist* **20 wks**

5 May 60 ●	SIXTEEN REASONS *Warner Bros. WB 3*	9	11
5 May 60	KOOKIE KOOKIE (LEND ME YOUR COMB) *Warner Bros. WB 5* 1	27	8
4 Aug 60	SIXTEEN REASONS (re-entry) *Warner Bros. WB 3*	45	1

1 Edward Byrnes and Connie Stevens

Ray STEVENS ⊕ *US, male vocalist* **64 wks**

16 May 70 ●	EVERYTHING IS BEAUTIFUL *CBS 4953* ▲	6	16
13 Mar 71 ●	BRIDGET THE MIDGET (THE QUEEN OF THE BLUES) *CBS 7070*	2	14
25 Mar 72	TURN YOUR RADIO ON *CBS 7634*	33	4
25 May 74 ★	THE STREAK *Janus 6146 201* ▲	1	12
21 Jun 75 ●	MISTY *Janus 6146 204*	2	10
27 Sep 75	INDIAN LOVE CALL *Janus 6146 205*	34	4
5 Mar 77	IN THE MOOD *Warner Bros. K 16875*	31	4

*'In the Mood' features Ray Stevens not as a conventional vocalist,
but as a group of chickens*

Ricky STEVENS *UK, male vocalist* **7 wks**

| 14 Dec 61 | I CRIED FOR YOU *Columbia DB 4739* | 34 | 7 |

Shakin' STEVENS ⊕ *Retro rock'n'roll vocalist who was more successful
than the majority of the original rock'n'roll stars. B. Michael Barratt.
4 March, 1948, Glamorgan, Wales. He amassed more Top 20 hits in
the 1980s than any other solo artist* **277 wks**

16 Feb 80	HOT DOG *Epic EPC 8090*	24	9
16 Aug 80	MARIE MARIE *Epic EPC 8725*	19	10
28 Feb 81 ★	THIS OLE HOUSE *Epic EPC 9555*	1	17
2 May 81 ●	YOU DRIVE ME CRAZY *Epic A 1165*	2	12
25 Jul 81 ★	GREEN DOOR *Epic A 1354*	1	12
10 Oct 81 ●	IT'S RAINING *Epic A 1643*	10	9
16 Jan 82 ★	OH JULIE *Epic EPC A 1742*	1	10
24 Apr 82 ●	SHIRLEY *Epic EPC A 2087*	6	6
21 Aug 82	GIVE ME YOUR HEART TONIGHT *Epic EPC A 2656*	11	10
16 Oct 82 ●	I'LL BE SATISFIED *Epic EPC A 2846*	10	8
11 Dec 82 ●	THE SHAKIN' STEVENS EP *Epic SHAKY 1*	2	7
23 Jul 83	IT'S LATE *Epic A 3565*	11	7

5 Nov 83 ●	CRY JUST A LITTLE BIT *Epic A 3774*	3	12
7 Jan 84 ●	A ROCKIN' GOOD WAY *Epic A 4071* [1]	5	9
24 Mar 84 ●	A LOVE WORTH WAITING FOR *Epic A 4291*	2	10
15 Sep 84 ●	A LETTER TO YOU *Epic A 4677*	10	8
24 Nov 84 ●	TEARDROPS *Epic A 4882*	5	9
2 Mar 85	BREAKING UP MY HEART *Epic A 6072*	14	7
12 Oct 85	LIPSTICK POWDER AND PAINT *Epic A 6610*	11	9
7 Dec 85 ★	MERRY CHRISTMAS EVERYONE *Epic A 6769*	1	8
8 Feb 86	TURNING AWAY *Epic A 6819*	15	7
1 Nov 86	BECAUSE I LOVE YOU *Epic SHAKY 2*	14	10
20 Dec 86	MERRY CHRISTMAS EVERYONE (re-entry) *Epic A 6769*	58	3
27 Jun 87	A LITTLE BOOGIE WOOGIE (IN THE BACK OF MY MIND) *Epic SHAKY 3*	12	10
19 Sep 87	COME SEE ABOUT ME *Epic SHAKY 4*	24	6
28 Nov 87 ●	WHAT DO YOU WANT TO MAKE THOSE EYES AT ME FOR *Epic SHAKY 5*	5	8
23 Jul 88	FEEL THE NEED IN ME *Epic SHAKY 6*	26	5
15 Oct 88	HOW MANY TEARS CAN YOU HIDE *Epic SHAKY 7*	47	4
10 Dec 88	TRUE LOVE *Epic SHAKY 8*	23	6
18 Feb 89	JEZEBEL *Epic SHAKY 9*	58	2
13 May 89	LOVE ATTACK *Epic SHAKY 10*	28	4
24 Feb 90	I MIGHT *Epic SHAKY 11*	18	6
12 May 90	YES I DO *Epic SHAKY 12*	60	2
18 Aug 90	PINK CHAMPAGNE *Epic SHAKY 13*	59	2
13 Oct 90	MY CUTIE CUTIE *Epic SHAKY 14*	75	1
15 Dec 90	THE BEST CHRISTMAS OF THEM ALL *Epic SHAKY 15*	19	4
7 Dec 91	I'LL BE HOME THIS CHRISTMAS *Epic 6576507*	34	5
10 Oct 92	RADIO *Epic 6584367* [2]	37	3

[1] Shaky and Bonnie [2] Shaky featuring Roger Taylor

Tracks on The Shakin' Stevens EP: Blue Christmas / Que Sera Sera / Josephine / Lawdy Miss Clawdy

STEVENSON'S ROCKET *UK, male vocal/instrumental group*   **5 wks**

| 29 Nov 75 | ALRIGHT BABY *Magnet MAG 47* | 37 | 2 |
| 20 Dec 75 | ALRIGHT BABY (re-entry) *Magnet MAG 47* | 45 | 3 |

Al STEWART *UK, male vocalist*   **6 wks**

| 29 Jan 77 | YEAR OF THE CAT *RCA 2771* | 31 | 6 |

Amii STEWART *US, female vocalist*   **61 wks**

7 Apr 79 ●	KNOCK ON WOOD *Atlantic/Hansa K 11214* ▲	6	12
16 Jun 79 ●	LIGHT MY FIRE/137 DISCO HEAVEN (MEDLEY) *Atlantic/Hansa K 11278*	5	11
3 Nov 79	JEALOUSY *Atlantic/Hansa K 11386*	58	3
19 Jan 80	THE LETTER/PARADISE BIRD *Atlantic/Hansa K 11424*	39	4
19 Jul 80	MY GUY – MY GIRL (MEDLEY) *Atlantic/Hansa K 11550* [1]	39	5
29 Dec 84	FRIENDS *RCA 471*	12	11
17 Aug 85 ●	KNOCK ON WOOD/LIGHT MY FIRE (re-mix) *Sedition EDIT 3303*	7	12
25 Jan 86	MY GUY – MY GIRL (MEDLEY) *Sedition EDIT 3310* [2]	63	3

[1] Amii Stewart and Johnny Bristol [2] Amii Stewart and Deon Estus

Andy STEWART *UK, male vocalist*   **67 wks**

15 Dec 60	DONALD WHERE'S YOUR TROOSERS *Top Rank JAR 427*	37	1
12 Jan 61	A SCOTTISH SOLDIER *Top Rank JAR 512*	19	38
1 Jun 61	THE BATTLE'S O'ER *Top Rank JAR 565*	28	13
12 Oct 61	A SCOTTISH SOLDIER (re-entry) *Top Rank JAR 512*	43	2
12 Aug 65	DR. FINLAY *HMV POP 1454*	50	1
26 Aug 65	DR. FINLAY (re-entry) *HMV POP 1454*	43	4
9 Dec 89 ●	DONALD WHERE'S YOUR TROOSERS (re-issue) *Stone SON 2353*	4	8

Billy STEWART *US, male vocalist*   **2 wks**

| 8 Sep 66 | SUMMERTIME *Chess CRS 8040* | 39 | 2 |

Dave STEWART ☉ *UK, male instrumentalist – keyboards*   **30 wks**

14 Mar 81	WHAT BECOMES OF THE BROKEN HEARTED *Stiff BROKEN 1* [1]	13	10
19 Sep 81 ★	IT'S MY PARTY *Broken BROKEN 2* [2]	1	13
13 Aug 83	BUSY DOING NOTHING *Broken BROKEN 5* [2]	49	4
14 Jun 86	THE LOCOMOTION *Broken BROKEN 8* [2]	70	3

[1] Dave Stewart Guest vocals Colin Blunstone
[2] Dave Stewart with Barbara Gaskin

Dave STEWART ☉ *UK, male instrumentalist – guitar*   **19 wks**

24 Feb 90 ●	LILY WAS HERE *RCA ZB 43045* [1]	6	12
18 Aug 90	JACK TALKING *RCA PB 43907* [2]	69	2
3 Sep 94	HEART OF STONE *East West YZ 845CD*	36	5

[1] David A Stewart featuring Candy Dulfer
[2] Dave Stewart and the Spiritual Cowboys

Jermaine STEWART ☺ ☉ *US, male vocalist*   **42 wks**

9 Aug 86 ●	WE DON'T HAVE TO . . . *10 TEN 96*	2	14
1 Nov 86	JODY *10 TEN 143*	50	4
16 Jan 88 ●	SAY IT AGAIN *10 TEN 188*	7	12
2 Apr 88	GET LUCKY *Siren SRN 82*	13	9
24 Sep 88	DON'T TALK DIRTY TO ME *Siren SRN 86*	61	3

John STEWART *US, male vocalist*   **6 wks**

| 30 Jun 79 | GOLD *RSO 35* | 43 | 6 |

Rod STEWART ✔ *Legendary British rocker, b. 10 January, 1945, London. Consistently popular gravel-voiced vocalist, who fronted the Faces 1969-1975. He has amassed a vast collection of gold records, and earned a Grammy Living Legend Award in 1989*   **465 wks**

4 Sep 71	REASON TO BELIEVE *Mercury 6052 097*	19	2
18 Sep 71 ★	MAGGIE MAY *Mercury 6052 097* ▲	1	19
12 Aug 72 ★	YOU WEAR IT WELL *Mercury 6052 171*	1	12
18 Nov 72 ●	ANGEL/WHAT MADE MILWAUKEE FAMOUS (HAS MADE A LOSER OUT OF ME) *Mercury 6052 198*	4	11
5 May 73	I'VE BEEN DRINKING *RAK RR 4* [1]	27	6
8 Sep 73 ●	OH NO NOT MY BABY *Mercury 6052 371*	6	9
5 Oct 74 ●	FAREWELL – BRING IT ON HOME TO ME/YOU SEND ME *Mercury 6167 033*	7	7
16 Aug 75 ★	SAILING *Warner Bros. K 16600*	1	11
15 Nov 75 ●	THIS OLD HEART OF MINE *Riva 1*	4	9
5 Jun 76 ●	TONIGHT'S THE NIGHT *Riva 3* ▲	5	9
21 Aug 76 ●	THE KILLING OF GEORGIE *Riva 4*	2	10
4 Sep 76 ●	SAILING (re-entry) *Warner Bros. K 16600*	3	20
20 Nov 76	GET BACK *Riva 6*	11	9
4 Dec 76	MAGGIE MAY (re-entry) *Mercury 6160 006*	31	7
23 Apr 77 ★	I DON'T WANT TO TALK ABOUT IT/FIRST CUT IS THE DEEPEST *Riva 7*	1	13
15 Oct 77 ●	YOU'RE IN MY HEART *Riva 11*	3	10
28 Jan 78 ●	HOTLEGS/I WAS ONLY JOKING *Riva 10*	5	8
27 May 78 ●	OLE OLA (MULHER BRASILEIRA) *Riva 15* [2]	4	6
18 Nov 78 ★	DA YA THINK I'M SEXY? *Riva 17* ▲	1	13
3 Feb 79	AIN'T LOVE A BITCH *Riva 18*	11	8
5 May 79	BLONDES (HAVE MORE FUN) *Riva 19*	63	3
31 May 80	IF LOVING YOU IS WRONG (I DON'T WANT TO BE RIGHT) *Riva 23*	23	9
8 Nov 80	PASSION *Riva 26*	17	10
20 Dec 80	MY GIRL *Riva 28*	32	7
17 Oct 81 ●	TONIGHT I'M YOURS (DON'T HURT ME) *Riva 33*	8	13
12 Dec 81	YOUNG TURKS *Riva 34*	11	9
27 Feb 82	HOW LONG *Riva 35*	41	4
4 Jun 83 ★	BABY JANE *Warner Bros. W 9608*	1	14
27 Aug 83 ●	WHAT AM I GONNA DO (I'M SO IN LOVE WITH YOU) *Warner Bros. W 9564*	3	8
10 Dec 83	SWEET SURRENDER *Warner Bros. W 9440*	23	9
26 May 84	INFATUATION *Warner Bros. W 9256*	27	7
28 Jul 84	SOME GUYS HAVE ALL THE LUCK *Warner Bros. W 9204*	15	10
24 May 86	LOVE TOUCH *Warner Bros. W 8668*	27	5
5 Jul 86	LOVE TOUCH (re-entry) *Warner Bros. W 8668*	69	3
12 Jul 86	EVERY BEAT OF MY HEART *Warner Bros. W 8625*	2	9
20 Sep 86	ANOTHER HEARTACHE *Warner Bros. W 8631*	54	2
28 Mar 87	SAILING (2nd re-entry) *Warner Bros. K 16600*	41	3
28 May 88	LOST IN YOU *Warner Bros. W 7927*	21	6
13 Aug 88	FOREVER YOUNG *Warner Bros. W 7796*	57	3
6 May 89	MY HEART CAN'T TELL YOU NO *Warner Bros. W 7729*	49	4

11 Nov 89		THIS OLD HEART OF MINE *Warner Bros. W 2686* [3]	51	3
13 Jan 90	●	DOWNTOWN TRAIN *Warner Bros. W 2647*	10	12
24 Nov 90	●	IT TAKES TWO *Warner Bros. ROD 1* [4]	5	8
16 Mar 91	●	RHYTHM OF MY HEART *Warner Bros. W 0017*	3	11
15 Jun 91	●	THE MOTOWN SONG *Warner Bros. W 0030*	10	8
7 Sep 91		BROKEN ARROW *Warner Bros. W 0059*	54	3
7 Mar 92		PEOPLE GET READY *Epic 6577567* [1]	49	3
18 Apr 92		YOUR SONG/BROKEN ARROW (re-issue) *Warner Bros. W 0104*	41	4
5 Dec 92	●	TOM TRAUBERT'S BLUES (WALTZING MATILDA) *Warner Bros. W 0144*	6	9
20 Feb 93		RUBY TUESDAY *Warner Bros. W 0158CD*	11	6
17 Apr 93		SHOTGUN WEDDING *Warner Bros. W 0171CD*	21	4
26 Jun 93	●	HAVE I TOLD YOU LATELY *Warner Bros. W 0185CD*	5	9
21 Aug 93		REASON TO BELIEVE *Warner Bros. W 0198CD1*	51	3
18 Dec 93	●	PEOPLE GET READY *Warner Bros. W 0226CD1*	45	4
15 Jan 94	●	ALL FOR LOVE *A & M 5804772* [5] ▲	2	13
20 May 95		YOU'RE THE STAR *Warner Bros. W 0296CD*	19	5
19 Aug 95		LADY LUCK *Warner Bros. W 0310CD1*	56	1
15 Jun 96		PURPLE HEATHER *Warner Bros. W 0354CD* [6]	16	5
14 Dec 96		IF WE FALL IN LOVE TONIGHT *Warner Bros. W 0380CD*	58	1
1 Nov 97	●	DA YA THINK I'M SEXY *All Around The World CDGLOBE 150* [7]	10	7
30 May 98		OOH LA LA *Warner Brothers W 0446CD*	16	5
5 Sep 98		ROCKS *Warner Brothers W 0452CD1*	55	1

[1] Jeff Beck and Rod Stewart [2] Rod Stewart featuring the Scottish World Cup Football Squad [3] Rod Stewart featuring Ronald Isley [4] Rod Stewart and Tina Turner [5] Bryan Adams, Rod Stewart and Sting [6] Rod Stewart with the Scottish Euro '96 Squad [7] N-Trance featuring Rod Stewart

'Reason to Believe' and 'People Get Ready' in 1993 were re-recordings. 'Reason to Believe' additionally credits Ronnie Wood on the sleeve. See also FACES; GLASS TIGER; Python Lee JACKSON

STEX *UK, male/female vocal/instrumental group*   2 wks

19 Jan 91	STILL FEEL THE RAIN *Some Bizarre SBZ 7002*	63	2

STIFF LITTLE FINGERS ✏ 🎸
UK, male vocal/instrumental group   39 wks

29 Sep 79	STRAW DOGS *Chrysalis CHS 2368*	44	4
16 Feb 80	AT THE EDGE *Chrysalis CHS 2406*	15	9
24 May 80	NOBODY'S HERO/TIN SOLDIERS *Chrysalis CHS 2424*	36	5
2 Aug 80	BACK TO FRONT *Chrysalis CHS 2447*	49	4
28 Mar 81	JUST FADE AWAY *Chrysalis CHS 2510*	47	6
30 May 81	SILVER LINING *Chrysalis CHS 2517*	68	3
23 Jan 82	LISTEN EP *Chrysalis CHS 2580*	33	6
18 Sep 82	BITS OF KIDS *Chrysalis CHS 2637*	73	2

Tracks on Listen EP: *That's When Your Blood Bumps/Two Guitars Clash/Listen/ Sad-Eyed People*

Curtis STIGERS 🅾 *US, male vocalist*   34 wks

18 Jan 92	●	I WONDER WHY *Arista 114716*	5	10
28 Mar 92	●	YOU'RE ALL THAT MATTERS TO ME *Arista 115273*	6	12
11 Jul 92		SLEEPING WITH THE LIGHTS ON *Arista 74321102307*	53	4
17 Oct 92		NEVER SAW A MIRACLE *Arista 74321117257*	34	4
3 Jun 95		THIS TIME *Arista 74321286962*	28	3
2 Dec 95		KEEP ME FROM THE COLD *Arista 74321319162*	57	1

Stephen STILLS *US, male vocalist*   4 wks

13 Mar 71	LOVE THE ONE YOU'RE WITH *Atlantic 2091 046*	37	4

See also CROSBY, STILLS, NASH and YOUNG

STILTSKIN 🎸 *UK, male vocal/instrumental group*   15 wks

7 May 94	★	INSIDE *White Water LEV 1CD*	1	13
24 Sep 94		FOOTSTEPS *White Water WWRD 2*	34	2

STING 🅾 🎸 *World's best known ex-Police-man, b. Gordon Sumner, 2 October, 1951, Newcastle. This singer/songwriter/bass-player has amassed more solo hits than as front man of that top-selling trio. As a soloist, he has won both BRIT and Grammy Awards*   137 wks

14 Aug 82	SPREAD A LITTLE HAPPINESS *A & M AMS 8242*	16	8

8 Jun 85		IF YOU LOVE SOMEBODY SET THEM FREE *A & M AM 258*	26	7
24 Aug 85		LOVE IS THE SEVENTH WAVE *A & M AM 272*	41	5
19 Oct 85		FORTRESS AROUND YOUR HEART *A & M AM 286*	49	3
7 Dec 85		RUSSIANS *A & M AM 292*	12	11
15 Feb 86		MOON OVER BOURBON STREET *A & M AM 305*	44	4
1 Mar 86		RUSSIANS (re-entry) *A & M AM 292*	71	1
7 Nov 87		WE'LL BE TOGETHER *A & M AM 410*	41	4
20 Feb 88		ENGLISHMAN IN NEW YORK *A & M AM 431*	51	3
9 Apr 88		FRAGILE *A & M AM 439*	70	2
11 Aug 90		ENGLISHMAN IN NEW YORK (re-mix) *A & M AM 580*	15	7
12 Jan 91		ALL THIS TIME *A & M AM 713*	22	4
9 Mar 91		MAD ABOUT YOU *A & M AM 721*	56	2
4 May 91		THE SOUL CAGES *A & M AM 759*	57	1
29 Aug 92		IT'S PROBABLY ME *A & M AM 883* [1]	30	5
13 Feb 93		IF I EVER LOSE MY FAITH IN YOU *A & M AMCD 0172*	14	6
24 Apr 93		SEVEN DAYS *A & M 5802232*	25	4
19 Jun 93		FIELDS OF GOLD *A & M 5803012*	16	6
4 Sep 93		SHAPE OF MY HEART *A & M 5803532*	57	1
20 Nov 93		DEMOLITION MAN *A & M 5804512*	21	4
15 Jan 94	●	ALL FOR LOVE *A & M 5804772* [2] ▲	2	13
26 Feb 94		NOTHING 'BOUT ME *A & M 5805292*	32	3
29 Oct 94	●	WHEN WE DANCE *A & M 5808612*	9	7
11 Feb 95		THIS COWBOY SONG *A & M 5809652*	15	6
20 Jan 96		SPIRITS IN THE MATERIAL WORLD *MCA MCSTD 2113* [3]	36	2
2 Mar 96		LET YOUR SOUL BE YOUR PILOT *A & M 5813312*	15	4
11 May 96		YOU STILL TOUCH ME *A & M 5815472*	27	3
22 Jun 96		LIVE AT TFI FRIDAY EP *A & M 5817652*	53	2
14 Sep 96		I WAS BROUGHT TO MY SENSES *A & M 5818912*	31	2
30 Nov 96		I'M SO HAPPY I CAN'T STOP CRYING *A & M 5820312*	54	1
20 Dec 97		ROXANNE '97 (re-mix) *A & M 5824552* [4]	17	6

[1] Sting with Eric Clapton [2] Bryan Adams, Rod Stewart and Sting [3] Pato Banton with Sting [4] Sting and The Police

Pato Banton provides uncredited vocals on 'This Cowboy Song'. Tracks on Live at TFI Friday EP: *You Still Touch Me/Lithium Sunset/Message In a Bottle*

STINGERS – See B BUMBLE and The STINGERS

Byron STINGILY ☺ 🎤 *US, male vocalist*   12 wks

25 Jan 97	GET UP (EVERYBODY) *Manifesto FESCD 19*	14	5
1 Nov 97	SING A SONG *Manifesto FESCD 35*	38	2
31 Jan 98	YOU MAKE ME FEEL (MIGHTY REAL) *Manifesto FESCD 38*	13	4
13 Jun 98	TESTIFY *Manifesto FESCD 42*	48	1

STIX 'N' STONED *UK, male instrumental/production duo*   2 wks

20 Jul 96	OUTRAGEOUS *Positiva CDTIV 52*	39	2

Catherine STOCK 🅾 🅒 *UK, female vocalist*   6 wks

18 Oct 86	TO HAVE AND TO HOLD *Sierra FED 29*	17	6

STOCK AITKEN WATERMAN ☺ 🅾 *UK, male producers*   36 wks

25 Jul 87		ROADBLOCK *Breakout USA 611*	13	9
24 Oct 87	●	MR SLEAZE *London NANA 14*	3	10
12 Dec 87		PACKJAMMED (WITH THE PARTY POSSE) *Breakout USA 620*	41	6
21 May 88		ALL THE WAY *MCA GOAL 1* [1]	64	2
3 Dec 88		SS PAPARAZZI *PWL PWL 22*	68	2
20 May 89	★	FERRY 'CROSS THE MERSEY *PWL PWL 41* [2] ■	1	7

[1] England Football Team with the 'sound' of Stock Aitken and Waterman
[2] Christians, Holly Johnson, Paul McCartney, Gerry Marsden and Stock Aitken Waterman

The listed flip side of 'Mr Sleaze' was 'Love In the First Degree' by Bananarama

Rhet STOLLER *UK, male instrumentalist – guitar*   8 wks

12 Jan 61	CHARIOT *Decca F 11302*	26	8

Morris STOLOFF 🅒 *US, orchestra*   11 wks

1 Jun 56	●	MOONGLOW/THEME FROM PICNIC *Brunswick 05553*	7	11

UK No 1 ★   UK Top 10 ●   UK million seller ◆   UK entry at No 1 ■   US No 1 ▲

R & J STONE ◎ UK/US, male/female vocal duo — 9 wks

10 Jan 76 ●	WE DO IT RCA 2616	5	9

STONE ROSES ☹ ◎ UK, male vocal/instrumental group — 74 wks

29 Jul 89	SHE BANGS THE DRUMS Silvertone ORE 6	36	3
25 Nov 89 ●	WHAT THE WORLD IS WAITING FOR/FOOL'S GOLD		
	Silvertone ORE 13	8	14
6 Jan 90	SALLY CINNAMON Revolver REV 36	75	1
20 Jan 90	SALLY CINNAMON (re-entry) Revolver REV 36	46	4
3 Mar 90 ●	ELEPHANT STONE Silvertone ORE 1	8	6
17 Mar 90	MADE OF STONE Silvertone ORE 2	20	4
31 Mar 90	SHE BANGS THE DRUMS (re-entry) Silvertone ORE 6	34	3
14 Jul 90 ●	ONE LOVE Silvertone ORE 17	4	7
15 Sep 90	WHAT THE WORLD IS WAITING FOR/FOOL'S GOLD		
	(re-entry) Silvertone ORE 13	22	5
14 Sep 91	I WANNA BE ADORED Silvertone ORE 31	20	3
11 Jan 92	WATERFALL Silvertone ORE 35	27	4
11 Apr 92	I AM THE RESURRECTION Silvertone ORE 40	33	2
30 May 92	FOOL'S GOLD (re-mix) Silvertone ORET 13	73	1
3 Dec 94 ●	LOVE SPREADS Geffen GFSTD 84	2	8
11 Mar 95	TEN STOREY LOVE SONG Geffen GFSTD 87	11	3
29 Apr 95	FOOL'S GOLD (2nd re-mix) Silvertone ORECD 71	25	3
11 Nov 95	BEGGING YOU Geffen GFSTD 22060	15	3

STONE TEMPLE PILOTS US, male vocal/instrumental group — 11 wks

27 Mar 93	SEX TYPE THING Atlantic A 5769CD	60	2
4 Sep 93	PLUSH Atlantic A 7349CD	23	4
27 Nov 93	SEX TYPE THING (re-issue) Atlantic A 7293CD	55	2
20 Aug 94	VASOLINE Atlantic A 5650CD	48	2
10 Dec 94	INTERSTATE LOVE SONG Atlantic A 7192CD	53	1

STONEBRIDGE McGUINNESS UK, male vocal/instrumental duo — 2 wks

14 Jul 79	OO-EEH BABY RCA PB 5163	54	2

STONEFREE UK, male vocalist — 1 wk

23 May 87	CAN'T SAY 'BYE Ensign ENY 607	73	1

STONKERS – See HALE and PACE and the STONKERS

STOP THE VIOLENCE US, male/female rap charity ensemble — 1 wk

18 Feb 89	SELF DESTRUCTION Jive BDPST 1	75	1

Axel STORDAHL – See June HUTTON and Axel STORDAHL with the BOYS NEXT DOOR

STORM UK, male/female vocal/instrumental group — 10 wks

17 Nov 79	IT'S MY HOUSE Scope SC 10	36	10

STORM Germany, male production duo — 2 wks

29 Aug 98	STORM Positiva CDTIV 94	32	2

See also JAM AND SPOON; TOKYO GHETTO PUSSY

Danny STORM UK, male vocalist — 4 wks

12 Apr 62	HONEST I DO Piccadilly 7N 35025	42	4

Rebecca STORM UK, female vocalist — 13 wks

13 Jul 85	THE SHOW (THEME FROM 'CONNIE') Towerbell TVP 3	22	13

STORYVILLE JAZZ BAND – See Bob WALLIS and his STORYVILLE JAZZ BAND

Izzy STRADLIN' US, male vocalist/instrumentalist – guitar — 2 wks

26 Sep 92	PRESSURE DROP Geffen GFS 25	45	2

Nick STRAKER BAND ◎ ◢
UK, male vocal/instrumental group — 15 wks

2 Aug 80	A WALK IN THE PARK CBS 8525	20	12
15 Nov 80	LEAVING ON THE MIDNIGHT TRAIN CBS 9088	61	3

Peter STRAKER and the HANDS OF DR. TELENY
UK, male vocalist and male vocal/instrumental group — 4 wks

19 Feb 72	THE SPIRIT IS WILLING RCA 2163	40	4

STRANGE BEHAVIOUR – See Jane KENNAWAY and STRANGE BEHAVIOUR

STRANGE FRUIT – see Jimmy NAIL with STRANGE FRUIT

STRANGELOVE UK, male vocal/instrumental group — 8 wks

20 Apr 96	LIVING WITH THE HUMAN MACHINES		
	Food CDFOOD 70	53	1
15 Jun 96	BEAUTIFUL ALONE Food CDFOOD 81	35	2
19 Oct 96	SWAY Food CDFOOD 82	47	1
26 Jul 97	THE GREATEST SHOW ON EARTH Food CDFOODS 97	36	2
11 Oct 97	FREAK Food CDFOOD 105	43	1
21 Feb 98	ANOTHER NIGHT IN Food CDFOOD 110	46	1

STRANGLERS ✐ Most commercially successful and long-lasting group to emerge from the punk/new-wave scene: Hugh Cornwell (v/g), Jean-Jacques Burnel (b/v), Dave Greenfield (k), Jet Black (d). This London-based band had at least one hit every year between 1977 and 1992 — 194 wks

19 Feb 77	(GET A) GRIP (ON YOURSELF) United Artists UP 36211	44	4
21 May 77 ●	PEACHES/GO BUDDY GO United Artists UP 36248	8	14
30 Jul 77 ●	SOMETHING BETTER CHANGE/STRAIGHTEN OUT		
	United Artists UP 36277	9	8
24 Sep 77 ●	NO MORE HEROES United Artists UP 36300	8	9
4 Feb 78	FIVE MINUTES United Artists UP 36350	11	9
6 May 78	NICE 'N SLEAZY United Artists UP 36379	18	8
12 Aug 78	WALK ON BY United Artists UP 36429	21	8
18 Aug 79	DUCHESS United Artists BP 308	14	9
20 Oct 79	NUCLEAR DEVICE (THE WIZARD OF AUS)		
	United Artists BP 318	36	4
1 Dec 79	DON'T BRING HARRY EP United Artists STR 1	41	3
22 Mar 80	BEAR CAGE United Artists BP 344	36	5
7 Jun 80	WHO WANTS THE WORLD United Artists BPX 355	39	4
31 Jan 81	THROWN AWAY Liberty BP 383	42	4
14 Nov 81	LET ME INTRODUCE YOU TO THE FAMILY		
	United Artists BP 405	42	3
9 Jan 82 ●	GOLDEN BROWN Liberty BP 407	2	12
24 Apr 82	LA FOLIE Liberty BP 410	47	3
24 Jul 82 ●	STRANGE LITTLE GIRL Liberty BP 412	7	9
8 Jan 83 ●	EUROPEAN FEMALE Epic EPC A 2893	9	6
26 Feb 83	MIDNIGHT SUMMER DREAM Epic EPC A 3167	35	4
6 Aug 83	PARADISE Epic A 3387	48	3
6 Oct 84	SKIN DEEP Epic A 4738	15	7
1 Dec 84	NO MERCY Epic A 4921	37	7
16 Feb 85	LET ME DOWN EASY Epic A 6045	48	4
23 Aug 86	NICE IN NICE Epic 650057	30	5
18 Oct 86	ALWAYS THE SUN Epic SOLAR 1	30	5
13 Dec 86	BIG IN AMERICA Epic HUGE 1	48	6
7 Mar 87	SHAKIN' LIKE A LEAF Epic SHEIK 1	58	4
9 Jan 88 ●	ALL DAY AND ALL OF THE NIGHT Epic VICE 1	7	7
28 Jan 89	GRIP '89 (GET A) GRIP (ON YOURSELF) (re-mix)		
	EMI EM 84	33	3
17 Feb 90	96 TEARS Epic TEARS 1	17	6
21 Apr 90	SWEET SMELL OF SUCCESS Epic TEARS 2	65	2
5 Jan 91	ALWAYS THE SUN (re-mix) Epic 6564307	29	5
30 Mar 91	GOLDEN BROWN (re-mix) Epic 6567617	68	2
22 Aug 92	HEAVEN OR HELL Psycho WOK 2025	46	2

'Go Buddy Go' credited with 'Peaches' from 11 Jun, 1977. 'Straighten Out' credited with 'Something Better Change' from 13 Aug, 1977. Tracks on Don't Bring Harry (EP): Don't Bring Harry/Wired/Crabs (Live)/In the Shadows (Live)

STRAWBERRY SWITCHBLADE ◎ UK, female vocal duo — 26 wks

17 Nov 84 ●	SINCE YESTERDAY Korova KOW 38	5	17
23 Mar 85	LET HER GO Korova KOW 39	59	5
21 Sep 85	JOLENE Korova KOW 42	53	4

STRAWBS ♂ ◎ ✐ UK, male vocal/instrumental group — 27 wks

28 Oct 72	LAY DOWN A & M AMS 7035	12	13
27 Jan 73 ●	PART OF THE UNION A & M AMS 7047	2	11

6 Oct 73	SHINE ON SILVER SUN A & M AMS 7082	34	3

STRAY CATS ⊕ ♪ US, male vocal/instrumental group — 49 wks

29 Nov 80 ●	RUNAWAY BOYS Arista SCAT 1	9	10
7 Feb 81 ●	ROCK THIS TOWN Arista SCAT 2	9	8
25 Apr 81	STRAY CAT STRUT Arista SCAT 3	11	10
20 Jun 81	THE RACE IS ON Swansong SSK 19425 [1]	34	6
7 Nov 81	YOU DON'T BELIEVE ME Arista SCAT 4	57	3
6 Aug 83	(SHE'S) SEXY AND 17 Arista SCAT 6	29	9
4 Mar 89	BRING IT BACK AGAIN EMI USA MT 62	64	3

[1] Dave Edmunds and the Stray Cats

STRAY MOB – See MC SKAT KAT and the STRAY MOB

STREETBAND ⊕ UK, male vocal/instrumental group — 6 wks

4 Nov 78	TOAST/HOLD ON Logo GO 325	18	6

Barbra STREISAND ℂ The world's best-selling female album artist, b. 24 April, 1942, Brooklyn. This world-renowned MOR vocalist/actress, has collected countless awards for her recordings and her stage and film work, and is a recipient of both Grammy Living Legend and Lifetime Achievement Awards — 149 wks

20 Jan 66	SECOND HAND ROSE CBS 202025	14	13
30 Jan 71	STONEY END CBS 5321	46	1
13 Feb 71	STONEY END (re-entry) CBS 5321	27	10
30 Mar 74	THE WAY WE WERE CBS 1915 ▲	31	6
9 Apr 77 ●	LOVE THEME FROM 'A STAR IS BORN' (EVERGREEN) CBS 4855 ▲	3	19
25 Nov 78 ●	YOU DON'T BRING ME FLOWERS CBS 6803 [1] ▲	5	12
3 Nov 79 ●	NO MORE TEARS (ENOUGH IS ENOUGH) Casablanca CAN 174/ CBS 8000 [2] ▲	3	13
4 Oct 80 ★	WOMAN IN LOVE CBS 8966 ▲	1	16
6 Dec 80	GUILTY CBS 9315 [3]	34	10
30 Jan 82	COMIN' IN AND OUT OF YOUR LIFE CBS A 1789	66	3
20 Mar 82	MEMORY CBS A 1903	34	6
5 Nov 88	TILL I LOVED YOU (LOVE THEME FROM 'GOYA') CBS BARB 2 [4]	16	7
7 Mar 92	PLACES THAT BELONG TO YOU Columbia 6577947	17	5
5 Jun 93	WITH ONE LOOK Columbia 6593422 [5]	30	3
30 Apr 94	AS IF WE NEVER SAID GOODBYE Columbia 6603572	20	3
8 Feb 97 ●	I FINALLY FOUND SOMEONE A&M 5820832 [6]	10	7
15 Nov 97	TELL HIM Epic 6653052 [7]	3	15

[1] Barbra and Neil [2] Donna Summer and Barbra Streisand [3] Barbra Streisand and Barry Gibb [4] Barbra Streisand and Don Johnson [5] Barbra Streisand (duet with Michael Crawford) [6] Barbra Streisand and Bryan Adams [7] Barbra Streisand and Celine Dion

Neil was Neil Diamond. 'No More Tears (Enough Is Enough)' was released simultaneously on two different labels, a 7-inch single on Casablanca and a 12-inch on CBS

STRESS UK, male vocal/instrumental group — 1 wk

13 Oct 90	BEAUTIFUL PEOPLE Eternal YZ 495	74	1

STRETCH ⊕ UK, male vocal/instrumental group — 9 wks

8 Nov 75	WHY DID YOU DO IT Anchor ANC 1021	16	9

STRETCH 'N' VERN present MADDOG ☺ UK, male instrumental/production duo — 14 wks

14 Sep 96 ●	I'M ALIVE ffrr FCD 284	6	9
9 Aug 97	GET UP! GO INSANE! ffrr FCD 304	17	5

STRICT INSTRUCTOR Russia, female vocalist — 1 wk

24 Oct 98	STEP-TWO-THREE-FOUR All Around The World CDGLOBE 155	49	1

STRIKE ☺ UK/Australia, male/female vocal/instrumental group — 23 wks

24 Dec 94	U SURE DO Fresh FRSHD 19	31	5
1 Apr 95 ●	U SURE DO (re-entry) Fresh FRSHD 19	4	9
23 Sep 95	THE MORNING AFTER (FREE AT LAST) Fresh FRSHD 37	38	1
29 Jun 96	INSPIRATION Fresh FRSHD 45	27	2
16 Nov 96	MY LOVE IS FOR REAL Fresh FRSHD 46	35	2
31 May 97	I HAVE PEACE Fresh FRSHCD 58	17	4

STRIKERS US, male vocal/instrumental group — 5 wks

6 Jun 81	BODY MUSIC Epic EPC A 1290	45	5

STRING-A-LONGS ⊕ US, male instrumental group — 16 wks

23 Feb 61 ●	WHEELS London HLU 9278	8	16

STRINGS OF LOVE Italy, male/female vocal/instrumental group — 2 wks

3 Mar 90	NOTHING HAS BEEN PROVED Breakout USA 688	59	2

Joe STRUMMER ✎ ✐ UK, male vocalist — 13 wks

2 Aug 86	LOVE KILLS CBS A 7244	69	1
23 Dec 95	JUST THE ONE China WOKCD 2076 [1]	12	8
29 Jun 96 ●	ENGLAND'S IRIE Radioactive RAXTD 25 [2]	6	4

[1] Levellers, special guest Joe Strummer [2] Black Grape featuring Joe Strummer and Keith Allen

STRYKER – See MANCHESTER UNITED FOOTBALL CLUB

Chad STUART and Jeremy CLYDE UK, male vocal duo — 7 wks

28 Nov 63	YESTERDAY'S GONE Ember EMB S 180	37	7

STUDIO 2 Jamaica, male vocalist – Errol Jones — 1 wk

27 Jun 98	TRAVELLING MAN Multiply CDMULTY 35	40	1

STUMP UK, male vocal/instrumental group — 1 wk

13 Aug 88	CHARLTON HESTON Ensign ENY 614	72	1

STUTZ BEARCATS and the Denis KING ORCHESTRA UK, male/female vocal group with orchestra — 6 wks

24 Apr 82	THE SONG THAT I SING (THEME FROM 'WE'LL MEET AGAIN') Multi-Media Tapes MMT 6	36	6

STYLE COUNCIL ⊕ Eighties chart regulars: Paul Weller (v/g), Mick Talbot (k), and sometimes D C Lee (v – former Wham! backing vocalist and Weller's wife). As with Weller's previous band, The Jam, most of this London act's hits were in their homeland — 103 wks

19 Mar 83 ●	SPEAK LIKE A CHILD Polydor TSC 1	4	8
28 May 83	MONEY GO ROUND (PART 1) Polydor TSC 2	11	6
13 Aug 83 ●	LONG HOT SUMMER/PARIS MATCH Polydor TSC 3	3	9
20 Aug 83	MONEY GO ROUND (PART 1) (re-entry) Polydor TSC 2	74	1
19 Nov 83	SOLID BOND IN YOUR HEART Polydor TSC 4	11	8
18 Feb 84 ●	MY EVER CHANGING MOODS Polydor TSC 5	5	7
26 May 84 ●	GROOVIN' (YOU'RE THE BEST THING)/BIG BOSS GROOVE Polydor TSC 6	5	8
13 Oct 84 ●	SHOUT TO THE TOP Polydor TSC 7	7	8
11 May 85 ●	WALLS COME TUMBLING DOWN! Polydor TSC 8	6	7
6 Jul 85	COME TO MILTON KEYNES Polydor TSC 9	23	5
28 Sep 85	THE LODGERS Polydor TSC 10	13	6
5 Apr 86	HAVE YOU EVER HAD IT BLUE Polydor CINE 1	14	6
17 Jan 87 ●	IT DIDN'T MATTER Polydor TSC 12	9	5
14 Mar 87	WAITING Polydor TSC 13	52	3
31 Oct 87	WANTED Polydor TSC 14	20	4
28 May 88	LIFE AT A TOP PEOPLE'S HEALTH FARM Polydor TSC 15	28	3
23 Jul 88	HOW SHE THREW IT ALL AWAY EP Polydor TSC 16	41	2
18 Feb 89	PROMISED LAND Polydor TSC 17	27	5
27 May 89	LONG HOT SUMMER 89 (re-mix) Polydor LHS 1	48	2

'Paris Match' was listed with 'Long Hot Summer' from 3 Sep, 1983. It peaked at No 7. Tracks on How She Threw It All Away EP: How She Threw It All Away/Love the First Time/Long Hot Summer/I Do Like to Be B-Side the A-Side. The version of 'Long Hot Summer' on the EP is a re-recording of their third hit

UK No 1 ★   UK Top 10 ●   UK million seller ◆   UK entry at No 1 ■   US No 1 ▲

STYLISTICS
Stylish and smooth vocal group from Philadelphia, fronted by falsetto-voiced Russell Thompkins Jr (b. 21 March, 1951), whose UK hits continued after success in their homeland diminished. The quintet's Greatest Hits album topped the UK album chart in 1975 **143 wks**

24 Jun 72	BETCHA BY GOLLY WOW *Avco 6105 011*	13	12
4 Nov 72 ●	I'M STONE IN LOVE WITH YOU *Avco 6105 015*	9	10
17 Mar 73	BREAK UP TO MAKE UP *Avco 6105 020*	34	5
30 Jun 73	PEEK-A-BOO *Avco 6105 023*	35	6
19 Jan 74	ROCKIN' ROLL BABY *Avco 6105 026*	6	9
13 Jul 74 ●	YOU MAKE ME FEEL BRAND NEW *Avco 6105 028*	2	14
19 Oct 74 ●	LET'S PUT IT ALL TOGETHER *Avco 6105 032*	9	9
25 Jan 75	STAR ON A TV SHOW *Avco 6105 035*	12	8
10 May 75 ●	SING BABY SING *Avco 6105 036*	3	10
26 Jul 75 ★	CAN'T GIVE YOU ANYTHING (BUT MY LOVE) *Avco 6105 039*	1	11
15 Nov 75 ●	NA NA IS THE SADDEST WORD *Avco 6105 041*	5	10
14 Feb 76 ●	FUNKY WEEKEND *Avco 6105 044*	10	7
24 Apr 76 ●	CAN'T HELP FALLING IN LOVE *H & L 6105 050*	4	7
7 Aug 76	16 BARS *H & L 6105 059*	7	9
27 Nov 76	YOU'LL NEVER GET TO HEAVEN EP *H & L STYL 001*	24	9
26 Mar 77	7000 DOLLARS AND YOU *H & L 6105 073*	24	7

Tracks on You'll Never Get to Heaven EP: You'll Never Get to Heaven / Country Living / You Are Beautiful / The Miracle

STYX
US, male vocal/instrumental group **18 wks**

5 Jan 80 ●	BABE *A & M AMS 7489* ▲	6	10
24 Jan 81	THE BEST OF TIMES *A & M AMS 8102*	42	5
18 Jun 83	DON'T LET IT END *A & M AM 120*	56	3

SUB MERGE featuring Jan JOHNSTON
US, male producer / instrumentalist, and US, female vocalist **1 wk**

8 Feb 97	TAKE ME BY THE HAND *AM:PM 5821012*	28	1

SUB SUB ☺ *UK, male instrumental/production group* **12 wks**

10 Apr 93 ●	AIN'T NO LOVE (AIN'T NO USE) *Rob's CDROB 9* [1]	3	11
19 Feb 94	RESPECT *Rob's CDROB 19*	49	1

[1] Sub Sub featuring Melanie Williams

SUBCIRCUS *Denmark/UK, male vocal/instrumental group* **2 wks**

26 Apr 97	YOU LOVE YOU *Echo ECSCD 34*	61	1
12 Jul 97	86'D *Echo ECSCX 43*	56	1

SUBLIME *US, male vocal / instrumental group* **1 wk**

5 Jul 97	WHAT I GOT *Gasoline Alley MCSTD 48045*	71	1

SUBLIMINAL CUTS *Holland, male producer – Patrick Prinz* **3 wks**

15 Oct 94	LE VOIE LE SOLEIL *XL XLS 53CD*	69	1
20 Jul 96	LE VOIE LE SOLEIL (re-mix) *XL XLSR 53CD*	23	2

See also ARTEMESIA; ETHICS; MOVIN' MELODIES

SUBSONIC 2 *UK, male rap duo* **3 wks**

13 Jul 91	THE UNSUNG HEROES OF HIP HOP *Unity 6577947*	63	3

SUBTERRANIA featuring Ann CONSUELO
Sweden, male/female vocal/instrumental duo **1 wk**

5 Jun 93	DO IT FOR LOVE *Champion CHAMPCD 297*	68	1

SUEDE ☹ ● *UK, male vocal/instrumental group* **54 wks**

23 May 92	THE DROWNERS / TO THE BIRDS *Nude NUD 1S*	49	2
26 Sep 92	METAL MICKEY *Nude NUD 3S*	17	3
6 Mar 93 ●	ANIMAL NITRATE *Nude NUD 4CD*	7	7
29 May 93	SO YOUNG *Nude NUD 5CD*	22	3
26 Feb 94 ●	STAY TOGETHER *Nude NUD 9CD*	3	6
24 Sep 94	WE ARE THE PIGS *Nude NUD 10CD*	18	3
19 Nov 94	THE WILD ONES *Nude NUD 11CD1*	18	4
11 Feb 95	NEW GENERATION *Nude NUD 12CD1*	21	3
11 Mar 95	NEW GENERATION (re-entry) *Nude NUD 12CD1*	75	1
10 Aug 96 ●	TRASH *Nude NUD 21CD1*	3	6

26 Oct 96 ●	BEAUTIFUL ONES *Nude NUD 23CD1*	8	5
25 Jan 97 ●	SATURDAY NIGHT *Nude NUD 24CD1*	6	4
19 Apr 97 ●	LAZY *Nude NUD 27CD1*	9	3
23 Aug 97 ●	FILMSTAR *Nude NUD 30CD1*	9	4

SUENO LATINO featuring Carolina DAMAS
Italy, male production duo and female vocalist **5 wks**

23 Sep 89	SUENO LATINO *BCM BCM 323*	47	5

SUGAR *US, male vocal/instrumental group* **7 wks**

31 Oct 92	A GOOD IDEA *Creation CRE 143*	65	1
30 Jan 93	IF I CAN'T CHANGE YOUR MIND *Creation CRESCD 149*	30	2
21 Aug 93	TILTED *Creation CRECD 156*	48	1
3 Sep 94	YOUR FAVORITE THING *Creation CRESCD 186*	40	2
29 Oct 94	BELIEVE WHAT YOU'RE SAYING *Creation CRESCD 193*	73	1

SUGAR CANE *US, male/female vocal group* **5 wks**

30 Sep 78	MONTEGO BAY *Ariola Hansa AHA 524*	54	5

SUGAR RAY *US, male vocal/instrumental group* **1 wk**

31 Jan 98	FLY *Atlantic AT 0008CD*	58	1

SUGARCUBES ☹
Iceland, male/female vocal/instrumental group **22 wks**

14 Nov 87	BIRTHDAY *One Little Indian TP 7*	65	3
30 Jan 88	COLD SWEAT *One Little Indian 7TP 9*	56	4
16 Apr 88	DEUS *One Little Indian 7TP 10*	51	3
3 Sep 88	BIRTHDAY *One Little Indian 7TP 11*	65	3
16 Sep 89	REGINA *One Little Indian 26TP7*	55	2
11 Jan 92	HIT *One Little Indian 62 TP7*	17	6
3 Oct 92	BIRTHDAY (re-mix) *One Little Indian 104 TP12*	64	1

7TP 11 is a re-recording of their first hit

SUGARHILL GANG ◄ *US, male rap group* **16 wks**

1 Dec 79 ●	RAPPER'S DELIGHT *Sugarhill SHL 101*	3	11
11 Sep 82	THE LOVER IN YOU *Sugarhill SH 116*	54	3
25 Nov 89	RAPPER'S DELIGHT (re-mix) *Sugarhill SHRD 0007*	58	2

SUGGS ☺ *UK, male vocalist* **46 wks**

12 Aug 95	I'M ONLY SLEEPING / OFF ON HOLIDAY *WEA YZ 975CD*	7	6
14 Oct 95	CAMDEN TOWN *WEA WEA 019CD*	14	6
16 Dec 95	THE TUNE *WEA WEA 031CD*	33	3
13 Apr 96 ●	CECILIA *WEA WEA 042CD1* [1]	4	17
24 Aug 96	CECILIA (re-entry) *WEA WEA 042CD1* [1]	65	1
7 Sep 96	CECILIA (2nd re-entry) *WEA WEA 042CD1* [1]	59	1
21 Sep 96	NO MORE ALCOHOL *WEA WEA 065CD1* [1]	24	4
17 May 97	BLUE DAY *WEA WEA 112CD* [2]	22	5
5 Sep 98	I AM *WEA WEA 174CD*	38	1

[1] Suggs featuring Louchie Lou and Michie One
[2] Suggs & Co featuring Chelsea Team

SULTANA *Italy, male instrumental/production group* **1 wk**

26 Mar 94	TE AMO *Union City UCRD 28*	57	1

SULTANS OF PING *Ireland, male vocal/instrumental group* **12 wks**

8 Feb 92	WHERE'S ME JUMPER *Divine ATHY 01* [1]	67	2
9 May 92	STUPID KID *Divine ATHY 02* [1]	67	1
10 Oct 92	VERONICA *Divine ATHY 03* [1]	69	1
9 Jan 93	YOU TALK TOO MUCH *Rhythm King 6588872* [1]	26	3
11 Sep 93	TEENAGE PUNKS *Epic 6595792*	49	2
30 Oct 93	MICHIKO *Epic 6598222*	43	2
19 Feb 94	WAKE UP AND SCRATCH ME *Epic 6601122*	50	1

[1] Sultans of Ping FC

SUMMER – See SNAP

Donna SUMMER 🎵 ✏️ *'Queen of disco music', b. LaDonna Gaines,*
31 December, 1948, Massachusetts. Germany was the launching pad for this
diva, who had eight successive US Top 5 singles in the late 1970s. She was
also the first female to score three consecutive US No 1 albums **298 wks**

17 Jan 76	●	LOVE TO LOVE YOU BABY *GTO GT 17*	....4 9
29 May 76		COULD IT BE MAGIC *GTO GT 60*	....40 7
25 Dec 76		WINTER MELODY *GTO GT 76*	....27 6
9 Jul 77	★	I FEEL LOVE *GTO GT 100*	....1 11
20 Aug 77	●	DEEP DOWN INSIDE (THEME FROM 'THE DEEP')	
		Casablanca CAN 111	....5 10
24 Sep 77		I REMEMBER YESTERDAY *GTO GT 107*	....14 7
3 Dec 77	●	LOVE'S UNKIND *GTO GT 113*	....3 13
10 Dec 77		I LOVE YOU *Casablanca CAN 114*	....10 9
25 Feb 78		RUMOUR HAS IT *Casablanca CAN 122*	....19 8
22 Apr 78		BACK IN LOVE AGAIN *GTO GT 117*	....29 7
10 Jun 78		LAST DANCE *Casablanca TGIF 2*	....70 1
24 Jun 78		LAST DANCE (re-entry) *Casablanca TGIF 2*	....51 8
14 Oct 78	●	MACARTHUR PARK *Casablanca CAN 131* ▲	....5 10
17 Feb 79		HEAVEN KNOWS *Casablanca CAN 141*	....34 8
12 May 79		HOT STUFF *Casablanca CAN 151* ▲	....11 10
7 Jul 79		BAD GIRLS *Casablanca CAN 155* ▲	....14 10
1 Sep 79		DIM ALL THE LIGHTS *Casablanca CAN 162*	....29 9
3 Nov 79	●	NO MORE TEARS (ENOUGH IS ENOUGH)	
		Casablanca CAN 174/ CBS 8 000 [1] ▲	....3 13
16 Feb 80		ON THE RADIO *Casablanca NB 2236*	....32 6
21 Jun 80		SUNSET PEOPLE *Casablanca CAN 198*	....46 5
27 Sep 80		THE WANDERER *Geffen K 79180*	....48 6
17 Jan 81		COLD LOVE *Geffen K 79193*	....44 3
10 Jul 82		LOVE IS IN CONTROL (FINGER ON THE TRIGGER)	
		Warner Bros. K 79302	....18 11
6 Nov 82		STATE OF INDEPENDENCE *Warner Bros. K 79344*	....14 11
4 Dec 82		I FEEL LOVE (re-mix) *Casablanca FEEL 7*	....21 10
5 Mar 83		THE WOMAN IN ME *Warner Bros. U 9983*	....62 2
18 Jun 83		SHE WORKS HARD FOR THE MONEY *Mercury DONNA 1*	....25 8
24 Sep 83		UNCONDITIONAL LOVE *Mercury DONNA 2*	....14 12
21 Jan 84		STOP LOOK AND LISTEN *Mercury DONNA 3*	....57 2
24 Oct 87		DINNER WITH GERSHWIN *Warner Bros. U 8237*	....13 11
23 Jan 88		ALL SYSTEMS GO *WEA U 8122*	....54 3
25 Feb 89	●	THIS TIME I KNOW IT'S FOR REAL *Warner Bros. U 7780*	....3 14
27 May 89	●	I DON'T WANNA GET HURT *Warner Bros. U 7567*	....7 9
26 Aug 89		LOVE'S ABOUT TO CHANGE MY HEART	
		Warner Bros. U 7494	....20 6
25 Nov 89		WHEN LOVE TAKES OVER YOU *WEA U 7361*	....72 1
17 Nov 90		STATE OF INDEPENDENCE (re-issue) *Warner Bros. U 2857*	....45 3
12 Jan 91		BREAKAWAY *Warner Bros. U 3308*	....49 4
30 Nov 91		WORK THAT MAGIC *Warner Bros. U 5937*	....74 1
12 Nov 94		MELODY OF LOVE (WANNA BE LOVED)	
		Mercury MERCD 418	....21 3
9 Sep 95	●	I FEEL LOVE *Manifesto FESCD 1*	....8 5
6 Apr 96		STATE OF INDEPENDENCE (re-mix)	
		Manifesto FESCD 7 [2]	....13 5
11 Jul 98		CARRY ON *Almighty CDALMY 120* [3]	....65 1

[1] Donna Summer and Barbra Streisand [2] Donna Summer featuring the All Star
Choir [3] Donna Summer and Giorgio Moroder

'No More Tears (Enough Is Enough)' was released simultaneously on two different
labels, a 7-inch single on Casablanca and 12-inch on CBS. 'Unconditional Love'
features the additional vocals of Musical Youth. 'I Feel Love' in 1995 is a re-recording

SUMMER DAZE *UK, male instrumental/production duo* **1 wk**

26 Oct 96		SAMBA MAGIC *VC VCRD 14*	....61 1

Mark SUMMERS *UK, male producer* **6 wks**

26 Jan 91		SUMMER'S MAGIC *Fourth & Broadway BRW 205*	....27 6

SUNDANCE – *See DJ 'FAST' EDDIE*

SUNDANCE *UK, male production duo* **6 wks**

8 Nov 97		SUNDANCE *React CDREACT 109*	....33 2
3 Oct 98		SUNDANCE 98 (re-mix) *React CDREACTX 136*	....49 4

SUNDAYS ☹ *UK, male/female vocal/instrumental group* **12 wks**

11 Feb 89		CAN'T BE SURE *Rough Trade RT 218*	....45 5
3 Oct 92		GOODBYE *Parlophone R 6319*	....27 2
20 Sep 97		SUMMERTIME *Parlophone CDRS 6475*	....15 4
22 Nov 97		CRY *Parlophone CDR 6487*	....43 1

SUNDRAGON *UK, male vocal/instrumental duo* **1 wk**

21 Feb 68		GREEN TAMBOURINE *MGM 1380*	....50 1

SUNFIRE ✏️ 🎵 *US, male vocal/instrumental group* **11 wks**

12 Mar 83		YOUNG, FREE AND SINGLE *Warner Bros. W 9897*	....20 11

SUNNY ◑ *UK, female vocalist* **10 wks**

30 Mar 74	●	DOCTOR'S ORDERS *CBS 2068*	....7 10

SUNSCREEM ☹ ◑ *UK, male/female vocal/instrumental group* **33 wks**

29 Feb 92		PRESSURE *Sony S2 6578017*	....60 2
18 Jul 92		LOVE U MORE *Sony S2 6581727*	....23 6
17 Oct 92		PERFECT MOTION *Sony S2 6584057*	....18 5
9 Jan 93		BROKEN ENGLISH *Sony S2 6589032*	....13 5
27 Mar 93		PRESSURE US (re-mix) *Sony S2 6591102*	....19 5
2 Sep 95		WHEN *Sony S2 6623222*	....47 2
18 Nov 95		EXODUS *Sony S2 6625342*	....40 2
20 Jan 96		WHITE SKIES *Sony S2 6627425*	....25 3
23 Mar 96		SECRETS *Sony S2 6629342*	....36 2
6 Sep 97		CATCH *Pulse-8 CDLOSE 117*	....55 1

Monty SUNSHINE – *See Chris BARBER'S JAZZ BAND*

SUNSHINE BAND – *See KC and the SUNSHINE BAND*

SUPER FURRY ANIMALS ☹ 🖌️
UK, male vocal/instrumental group **21 wks**

9 Mar 96		HOMETOWN UNICORN *Creation CRESCD 222*	....47 1
11 May 96		GOD! SHOW ME MAGIC *Creation CRESCD 231*	....33 2
13 Jul 96		SOMETHING 4 THE WEEKEND *Creation CRESCD 235*	....18 3
12 Oct 96		IF YOU DON'T WANT ME TO DESTROY YOU	
		Creation CRESCD 243	....18 2
14 Dec 96		THE MAN DON'T GIVE A FUCK *Creation CRESCD 247*	....22 2
24 May 97		HERMANN LOVES PAULINE *Creation CRESCD 252*	....26 2
26 Jul 97		THE INTERNATIONAL LANGUAGE OF SCREAMING	
		Creation CRESCD 269	....24 2
4 Oct 97		PLAY IT COOL *Creation CRESCD 275*	....27 2
6 Dec 97		DEMONS *Creation CRESCD 283*	....27 2
6 Jun 98		ICE HOCKEY HAIR *Creation CRESCD 288*	....12 3

SUPERCAT *Jamaica, male vocalist* **5 wks**

1 Aug 92		IT FE DONE *Columbia 6582737*	....66 1
6 May 95		MY GIRL JOSEPHINE *Columbia 6614702* [1]	....22 4

[1] Supercat featuring Jack Radics

SUPERGRASS ☹ ◑ *UK, male vocal/instrumental group* **38 wks**

29 Oct 94		CAUGHT BY THE FUZZ *Parlophone CDR 6396*	....43 2
18 Feb 95		MANSIZE ROOSTER *Parlophone CDR 6402*	....20 3
25 Mar 95		LOSE IT *Sub Pop SP 281*	....75 1
13 May 95	●	LENNY *Parlophone CDR 6410*	....10 3
15 Jul 95	●	ALRIGHT/TIME *Parlophone CDR 6413*	....2 10
9 Mar 96	●	GOING OUT *Parlophone CDR 6428*	....5 6
12 Apr 97	●	RICHARD III *Parlophone CDR 6461*	....2 5
21 Jun 97	●	SUN HITS THE SKY *Parlophone CDR 6469*	....10 4
18 Oct 97		LATE IN THE DAY *Parlophone CDR 6484*	....18 4

SUPERNATURALS *UK, male vocal/instrumental group* **11 wks**

26 Oct 96		LAZY LOVER *Food CDFOOD 85*	....34 2
8 Feb 97		THE DAY BEFORE YESTERDAY'S MAN *Food CDFOODS 88*	....25 2
26 Apr 97		SMILE *Food CDFOOD 92*	....23 2
12 Jul 97		LOVE HAS PASSED AWAY *Food CDFOOD 99*	....38 1
25 Oct 97		PREPARE TO LAND *Food CDFOODS 106*	....48 1

UK No 1 ★ UK Top 10 ● UK million seller ◆ UK entry at No 1 ■ US No 1 ▲

| 1 Aug 98 | I WASN'T BUILT TO GET UP *Food CDFOOD 112* | 25 | 3 |
| 24 Oct 98 | SHEFFIELD SONG *Food CDFOODS 115* | 45 | 1 |

SUPERNOVA *UK, male/female vocal/instrumental duo* — 1 wk

| 11 May 96 | SOME MIGHT SAY *Sing Sing 74321369442* | 55 | 1 |

SUPERSTAR *UK, male vocal/instrumental group* — 2 wks

| 7 Feb 98 | EVERY DAY I FALL APART *Deconstruction CDFAB 003CD* | 66 | 1 |
| 25 Apr 98 | SUPERSTAR *Camp Fabulous CFAB 007CD* | 49 | 1 |

SUPERTRAMP 🎸 *UK/US, male vocal/instrumental group* — 52 wks

15 Feb 75	DREAMER *A & M AMS 7132*	13	10
25 Jun 77	GIVE A LITTLE BIT *A & M AMS 7293*	29	7
31 Mar 79 ●	THE LOGICAL SONG *A & M AMS 7427*	7	11
30 Jun 79 ●	BREAKFAST IN AMERICA *A & M AMS 7451*	9	10
27 Oct 79	GOODBYE STRANGER *A & M AMS 7481*	57	3
30 Oct 82	IT'S RAINING AGAIN *A & M AMS 8255* [1]	26	11

[1] Supertramp featuring vocals by Roger Hodgson

SUPREMES 🎵 *World's most successful female group: Diana Ross, Mary Wilson, Florence Ballard (d. 1976). Before Ross went solo in 1969, this Detroit-based trio had amassed one dozen US No 1s. They were inducted into the Rock and Roll Hall of Fame in 1988* — 306 wks

3 Sep 64 ●	WHERE DID OUR LOVE GO *Stateside SS 327* ▲	3	14
22 Oct 64 ★	BABY LOVE *Stateside SS 350* ▲	1	15
21 Jan 65	COME SEE ABOUT ME *Stateside SS 376* ▲	27	6
25 Mar 65 ●	STOP IN THE NAME OF LOVE *Tamla Motown TMG 501* ▲	7	12
10 Jun 65	BACK IN MY ARMS AGAIN *Tamla Motown TMG 516* ▲	40	5
9 Dec 65	I HEAR A SYMPHONY *Tamla Motown TMG 543* ●	50	1
23 Dec 65	I HEAR A SYMPHONY (re-entry) *Tamla Motown TMG 543*	39	4
8 Sep 66 ●	YOU CAN'T HURRY LOVE *Tamla Motown TMG 575* ▲	3	12
1 Dec 66 ●	YOU KEEP ME HANGIN' ON *Tamla Motown TMG 585* ▲	8	10
2 Mar 67	LOVE IS HERE AND NOW YOU'RE GONE *Tamla Motown TMG 597* ▲	17	10
11 May 67 ●	THE HAPPENING *Tamla Motown TMG 607* ▲	6	12
30 Aug 67 ●	REFLECTIONS *Tamla Motown TMG 616* [1]	5	14
29 Nov 67	IN AND OUT OF LOVE *Tamla Motown TMG 632* [1]	13	13
10 Apr 68	FOREVER CAME TODAY *Tamla Motown TMG 650* [1]	28	8
3 Jul 68	SOME THINGS YOU NEVER GET USED TO *Tamla Motown TMG 662* [1]	34	6
20 Nov 68	LOVE CHILD *Tamla Motown TMG 677* [1] ▲	15	14
29 Jan 69 ●	I'M GONNA MAKE YOU LOVE ME *Tamla Motown TMG 685* [2]	3	11
23 Apr 69	I'M GONNA MAKE YOU LOVE ME (re-entry) *Tamla Motown TMG 685* [2]	49	1
23 Apr 69	I'M LIVING IN SHAME *Tamla Motown TMG 695* [1]	14	9
2 Jul 69	I'M LIVING IN SHAME (re-entry) *Tamla Motown TMG 695* [1]	50	1
16 Jul 69	NO MATTER WHAT SIGN YOU ARE *Tamla Motown TMG 704* [1]	37	7
20 Sep 69	I SECOND THAT EMOTION *Tamla Motown TMG 709* [2]	18	8
13 Dec 69	SOMEDAY WE'LL BE TOGETHER *Tamla Motown TMG 721* [1] ▲	13	13
21 Mar 70	WHY (MUST WE FALL IN LOVE) *Tamla Motown TMG 730* [2]	31	7
2 May 70 ●	UP THE LADDER TO THE ROOF *Tamla Motown TMG 735*	6	15
16 Jan 71 ●	STONED LOVE *Tamla Motown TMG 760*	3	13
26 Jun 71	RIVER DEEP MOUNTAIN HIGH *Tamla Motown TMG 777* [3]	11	10
21 Aug 71 ●	NATHAN JONES *Tamla Motown TMG 782*	5	11
20 Nov 71	YOU GOTTA HAVE LOVE IN YOUR HEART *Tamla Motown TMG 793* [2]	25	10
4 Mar 72 ●	FLOY JOY *Tamla Motown TMG 804*	9	10
15 Jul 72 ●	AUTOMATICALLY SUNSHINE *Tamla Motown TMG 821*	10	9
21 Apr 73	BAD WEATHER *Tamla Motown TMG 847*	37	4
24 Aug 74	BABY LOVE (re-issue) *Tamla Motown TMG 915* [1]	12	10
18 Feb 89	STOP! IN THE NAME OF LOVE (re-issue) *Motown ZB 41963* [1]	62	1

[1] Diana Ross and the Supremes [2] Diana Ross and the Supremes and the Temptations [3] Supremes and the Four Tops

Al B SURE! *US, male vocalist* — 13 wks

16 Apr 88	NITE AND DAY *Uptown W 8192*	44	5
30 Jul 88	OFF ON YOUR OWN (GIRL) *Uptown W 7870*	70	2
10 Jun 89	IF I'M NOT YOUR LOVER *Warner Bros. W 2908*	54	3
31 Mar 90	SECRET GARDEN *Qwest W 9992* [1]	67	1
12 Jun 93	BLACK TIE WHITE NOISE *Arista 74321148682* [2]	36	2

[1] Quincy Jones featuring Al B. Sure!, James Ingram, El DeBarge and Barry White
[2] David Bowie featuring Al B. Sure!

SURFACE *US, male vocal/instrumental duo* — 14 wks

23 Jul 83	FALLING IN LOVE *Salsoul SAL 104*	67	3
23 Jun 84	WHEN YOUR 'EX' WANTS YOU BACK *Salsoul SAL 106*	52	4
28 Feb 87	HAPPY *CBS 650393 7*	56	5
12 Jan 91	THE FIRST TIME *Columbia 6564767* ▲	60	2

SURFACE NOISE *UK, male instrumental group* — 11 wks

| 31 May 80 | THE SCRATCH *WEA K 18291* | 26 | 8 |
| 30 Aug 80 | DANCIN' ON A WIRE *Groove GP102* | 59 | 3 |

SURFARIS ⊗ *US, male instrumental group* — 14 wks

| 25 Jul 63 ● | WIPE OUT *London HLD 9751* | 5 | 14 |

SURPRISE SISTERS *UK, female vocal group* — 3 wks

| 13 Mar 76 | LA BOOGA ROOGA *Good Earth GD 1* | 38 | 3 |

SURVIVOR ⊗ 🎸 *US, male vocal/instrumental group* — 26 wks

| 31 Jul 82 ★ | EYE OF THE TIGER *Scotti Brothers SCT A 2411* ▲ | 1 | 15 |
| 1 Feb 86 ● | BURNING HEART *Scotti Brothers A 6708* | 5 | 11 |

SUTHERLAND BROTHERS and QUIVER ♂ ⊗ 🎸 *UK, male vocal/instrumental group* — 20 wks

3 Apr 76 ●	ARMS OF MARY *CBS 4001*	5	12
20 Nov 76	SECRETS *CBS 4668*	35	4
2 Jun 79	EASY COME EASY GO *CBS 7121* [1]	50	4

[1] Sutherland Brothers

Pat SUZUKI *US, female vocalist* — 1 wk

| 14 Apr 60 | I ENJOY BEING A GIRL *RCA 1171* | 49 | 1 |

Billy SWAN ⊗ 🎵 *US, male vocalist* — 13 wks

| 14 Dec 74 ● | I CAN HELP *Monument MNT 2752* ▲ | 6 | 9 |
| 24 May 75 | DON'T BE CRUEL *Monument MNT 3244* | 42 | 4 |

SWAN LAKE *US, male vocalist/multi-instrumentalist* — 4 wks

| 17 Sep 88 | IN THE NAME OF LOVE *Champion CHAMP 86* | 53 | 4 |

SWANS WAY ⊗ *UK, male/female vocal/instrumental group* — 12 wks

| 4 Feb 84 | SOUL TRAIN *Exit EXT 3* | 20 | 7 |
| 26 May 84 | ILLUMINATIONS *Balgier PH 5* | 57 | 5 |

Patrick SWAYZE featuring Wendy FRASER ⊗ *US, male/female vocal duo* — 11 wks

| 26 Mar 88 | SHE'S LIKE THE WIND *RCA PB 49565* | 17 | 11 |

Keith SWEAT *US, male vocalist* — 22 wks

20 Feb 88	I WANT HER *Vintertainment EKR 68*	26	10
14 May 88	SOMETHING JUST AIN'T RIGHT *Vintertainment EKR 72*	55	3
14 May 94	HOW DO YOU LIKE IT *Elektra EKR 185CD*	71	1
22 Jun 96	TWISTED *Elektra EKR 223CD*	39	2
23 Nov 96	JUST A TOUCH *Elektra EKR 227CD*	35	2
3 May 97	NOBODY *Elektra EKR 233CD* [1]	30	2
6 Dec 97	I WANT HER *Elektra E 3887CD*	44	1
12 Dec 98	COME AND GET WITH ME *Elektra E 3787CD* [2]	58	1

[1] Keith Sweat featuring Athena Cage
[2] Keith Sweat featuring Snoop Dogg

Michelle SWEENEY US, female vocalist — 1 wk

29 Oct 94	THIS TIME Big Beat A 8229CD	57	1

SWEET ○ Glam-rock giants: Brian Connolly (v) (d. 1997), Andy Scott (g), Steve Priest (b), Mick Tucker (d). The flamboyantly attired UK quartet were very popular in Europe and the USA. Despite only topping the chart once, they achieved five No 2 hits — 159 wks

13 Mar 71	FUNNY FUNNY RCA 2051	13	14
12 Jun 71 ●	CO-CO RCA 2087	2	15
16 Oct 71	ALEXANDER GRAHAM BELL RCA 2121	33	5
5 Feb 72	POPPA JOE RCA 2164	11	12
10 Jun 72 ●	LITTLE WILLY RCA 2225	4	14
9 Sep 72 ●	WIG-WAM BAM RCA 2260	4	13
13 Jan 73 ★	BLOCKBUSTER RCA 2305	1	15
5 May 73 ●	HELL RAISER RCA 2357	2	11
22 Sep 73 ●	BALLROOM BLITZ RCA 2403	2	9
19 Jan 74 ●	TEENAGE RAMPAGE RCA LPBO 5004	2	8
13 Jul 74 ●	THE SIX TEENS RCA LPBO 5037	9	7
9 Nov 74	TURN IT DOWN RCA 2480	41	2
15 Mar 75 ●	FOX ON THE RUN RCA 2524	2	10
12 Jul 75	ACTION RCA 2578	15	6
24 Jan 76	LIES IN YOUR EYES RCA 2641	35	4
28 Jan 78 ●	LOVE IS LIKE OXYGEN Polydor POSP 1	9	9
26 Jan 85	IT'S IT'S THE SWEET MIX Anagram ANA 28	45	5

It's It's the Sweet Mix is a medley of the following songs: Blockbuster / Fox on the Run / Teenage Rampage / Hell Raiser / Ballroom Blitz

Rachel SWEET US, female vocalist — 15 wks

9 Dec 78	B-A-B-Y Stiff BUY 39	35	8
22 Aug 81	EVERLASTING LOVE CBS A 1405 [1]	35	7

[1] Rex Smith and Rachel Sweet

SWEET DREAMS ○ UK, male/female vocal duo — 12 wks

20 Jul 74 ●	HONEY HONEY Bradley's BRAD 7408	10	12

SWEET DREAMS UK, male/female vocal group — 7 wks

9 Apr 83	I'M NEVER GIVING UP Ariola ARO 333	21	7

SWEET MERCY – See Joe ROBERTS

SWEET PEOPLE © ○ France, male vocal/instrumental group — 10 wks

4 Oct 80 ●	ET LES OISEAUX CHANTAIENT (AND THE BIRDS WERE SINGING) Polydor POSP 179	4	8
29 Aug 87	ET LES OISEAUX CHANTAIENT (AND THE BIRDS WERE SINGING) (re-entry) Polydor POSP 179	73	2

SWEET PUSSY PAULINE – See CANDY GIRLS

SWEET SENSATION ○ ✎ UK, male vocal group — 17 wks

14 Sep 74 ★	SAD SWEET DREAMER Pye 7N 45385	1	10
18 Jan 75	PURELY BY COINCIDENCE Pye 7N 45421	11	7

SWEET TEE US, female rapper — 8 wks

16 Jan 88	IT'S LIKE THAT Y'ALL/I GOT DA FEELIN' Cooltempo COOL 160	31	6
13 Aug 94	THE FEELING Deep Distraxion OILYCD 029 [1]	32	2

[1] Tin Tin Out featuring Sweet Tee

SWEETBACK UK, male vocal/instrumental group — 1 wk

29 Mar 97	YOU WILL RISE Epic 6643155	64	1

See also SADE

SWEETBOX ○ R&B
Germany / US, male / female vocal / production duo — 12 wks

22 Aug 98 ●	EVERYTHING'S GONNA BE ALRIGHT RCA 74321606842	5	12

Sally SWEETLAND – See Eddie FISHER

SWERVEDRIVER UK, male vocal/instrumental group — 3 wks

10 Aug 91	SANDBLASTED EP Creation CRE 102	67	1
30 May 92	NEVER LOSE THAT FEELING Creation CRE 120	62	1
14 Aug 93	DUEL Creation CRESCD 136	60	1

Tracks on Sandblasted EP: Sandblaster / Flawed / Out / Laze It Up

SWIMMING WITH SHARKS Germany, female vocal duo — 3 wks

7 May 88	CARELESS LOVE WEA YZ 173	63	3

SWING – See DR ALBAN

SWING 52 US, male vocal/instrumental group — 1 wk

25 Feb 95	COLOR OF MY SKIN ffrr FCD 256	60	1

SWING KIDS – See K7

SWING OUT SISTER ✎
UK, male/female vocal/instrumental group — 55 wks

25 Oct 86 ●	BREAKOUT Mercury SWING 2	4	14
10 Jan 87 ●	SURRENDER Mercury SWING 3	7	8
18 Apr 87	TWILIGHT WORLD Mercury SWING 4	32	6
11 Jul 87	FOOLED BY A SMILE Mercury SWING 5	43	4
8 Apr 89	YOU ON MY MIND Fontana SWING 6	28	9
8 Jul 89	WHERE IN THE WORLD Fontana SWING 7	47	4
11 Apr 92	AM I THE SAME GIRL Fontana SWING 9	21	6
20 Jun 92	NOTGONNACHANGE Fontana SWING 10	49	2
27 Aug 94	LA LA (MEANS I LOVE YOU) Fontana SWIDD 11	37	2

SWINGING BLUE JEANS ○
UK, male vocal/instrumental group — 57 wks

20 Jun 63	IT'S TOO LATE NOW HMV POP 1170	30	6
8 Aug 63	IT'S TOO LATE NOW (re-entry) HMV POP 1170	46	3
12 Dec 63 ●	HIPPY HIPPY SHAKE HMV POP 1242	2	17
19 Mar 64	GOOD GOLLY MISS MOLLY HMV POP 1273	11	10
4 Jun 64 ●	YOU'RE NO GOOD HMV POP 1304	3	13
20 Jan 66	DON'T MAKE ME OVER HMV POP 1501	31	8

SWIRL 360 US, male vocal duo — 1 wk

14 Nov 98	HEY NOW NOW Mercury 5665352	61	1

SWITCH US, male vocal/instrumental group — 3 wks

10 Nov 84	KEEPING SECRETS Total Experience RCA XE 502	61	3

SWV R&B US, female vocal group — 43 wks

1 May 93	I'M SO INTO YOU RCA 74321144972	17	6
26 Jun 93	WEAK RCA 74321153352 ▲	33	3
28 Aug 93 ●	RIGHT HERE RCA 74321160482	3	12
26 Feb 94	DOWNTOWN RCA 74321189012	19	5
11 Jun 94	ANYTHING RCA 74321212212	24	3
25 May 96	YOU'RE THE ONE RCA 74321383312	13	3
21 Dec 96	IT'S ALL ABOUT U RCA 74321442152	36	5
12 Apr 97	CAN WE Jive JIVECD 423	18	4
13 Sep 97	SOMEONE RCA 74321513942 [1]	34	2

[1] SWV featuring Puff Daddy

SYBIL ☺ ○ US, female vocalist — 69 wks

1 Nov 86	FALLING IN LOVE Champion CHAMP 22	68	3
25 Apr 87	LET YOURSELF GO Champion CHAMP 42	32	6
29 Aug 87	MY LOVE IS GUARANTEED PWL PPWLCD 277	42	5
22 Jul 89	DON'T MAKE ME OVER Champion CHAMP 213	59	5
14 Oct 89	DON'T MAKE ME OVER (re-entry) Champion CHAMP 213	19	6
27 Jan 90 ●	WALK ON BY PWL PWL 48	6	9
21 Apr 90	CRAZY FOR YOU PWL PWL 53	71	1
16 Jan 93 ●	THE LOVE I LOST PWL Sanctuary PWCD 253 [1]	3	13
20 Mar 93 ●	WHEN I'M GOOD AND READY PWL International PWCD 260	5	13

UK No 1 ★   UK Top 10 ●   UK million seller ◆   UK entry at No 1 ■   US No 1 ▲

6 Mar 76	LONDON BOYS *EMI MARC 13*..40	3
19 Jun 76	I LOVE TO BOOGIE *EMI MARC 14*..13	9
2 Oct 76	LASER LOVE *EMI MARC 15*...41	4
2 Apr 77	THE SOUL OF MY SUIT *EMI MARC 16*...42	3
9 May 81	RETURN OF THE ELECTRIC WARRIOR EP	
	Rarn MBSF 001 [4]...50	4
19 Sep 81	YOU SCARE ME TO DEATH *Cherry Red CHERRY 29* [4] 51	4
27 Mar 82	TELEGRAM SAM (re-entry) *T. Rex 101*.....................................69	2
18 May 85	MEGAREX *Marc On Wax TANX 1* [2].......................................72	2
9 May 87	GET IT ON (re-mix) *Marc On Wax MARC 10* [2] 54	4
24 Aug 91	20TH CENTURY BOY (re-issue) *Marc On Wax MARC 501* [2] 13	8

[1] Tyrannosaurus Rex [2] Marc Bolan and T. Rex [3] T. Rex Disco Party [4] Marc Bolan

Tracks on Return of the Electric Warrior EP: Sing Me a Song / Endless Sleep / The Lilac Hand of Menihol Dan. Megarex is a medley of extracts from the following T. Rex hits: Truck on (Tyke) / The Groover / Telegram Sam / Shock Rock / Metal Guru / 20th Century Boy / Children of the Revolution / Hot Love

T-SHIRT *UK, female vocal duo* — **1 wk**

13 Sep 97	YOU SEXY THING *Eternal WEA 122CD*..63	1

T-SPOON ☺ *Holland, male/female vocal/instrumental group* — **13 wks**

19 Sep 98 ●	SEX ON THE BEACH *Control 0042395 CON*.................................2	13

TABERNACLE *UK, male instrumental/production group* — **2 wks**

4 Mar 95	I KNOW THE LORD *Good Groove CDGG 1*...................................62	1
3 Feb 96	I KNOW THE LORD (re-mix) *Good Groove CDGGX 1* 55	1

TACK HEAD *US, male rapper* — **3 wks**

30 Jun 90	DANGEROUS SEX *SBK SBK 7014*...48	3

TAFFY ✪ ☺ *UK, female vocalist* — **14 wks**

10 Jan 87 ●	I LOVE MY RADIO (MY DEE JAY'S RADIO)	
	Transglobal TYPE 1...6	10
18 Jul 87	STEP BY STEP *Transglobal TYPE 5*...59	4

TAG TEAM *US, male rap duo* — **8 wks**

8 Jan 94	WHOOMP! (THERE IT IS) *Club Tools SHXCD 1* 34	5
29 Jan 94	ADDAMS FAMILY (WHOOMP!) *Atlas PZCD 305* 53	1
10 Sep 94	WHOOMP! (THERE IT IS) (re-mix) *Club Tools SHXR 1* 48	2

See also QUAD CITY DJS

TAK TIX *US, female vocalist* — **2 wks**

20 Jan 96	FEEL LIKE SINGING *A & M 5813212*..33	2

TAKE 5 *US, male vocal group* — **1 wk**

7 Nov 98	I GIVE *Edel 0039635 ERE*..70	1

TAKE THAT ✪ *Record-breaking British boy band: Gary Barlow (v), Robbie Williams (v), Jason Orange (v), Howard Donald (v), Mark Owen (v). They were the first artists since The Beatles to score four consecutive chart-toppers, and the only act to release eight singles entering at No 1* — **158 wks**

23 Nov 91	PROMISES *RCA PB 45085*..38	2
8 Feb 92	ONCE YOU'VE TASTED LOVE *RCA PB 45257* 47	3
6 Jun 92 ●	IT ONLY TAKES A MINUTE *RCA 74321101007*...........................7	8
15 Aug 92	I FOUND HEAVEN *RCA 74321108137*......................................15	6
10 Oct 92 ●	A MILLION LOVE SONGS *RCA 74321116307*..............................7	9
12 Dec 92	COULD IT BE MAGIC *RCA 74321123137*....................................3	12
20 Feb 93 ●	WHY CAN'T I WAKE UP WITH YOU *RCA 74321133102*...............2	10
17 Jul 93 ★	PRAY *RCA 74321154502* ■...1	11
9 Oct 93 ★	RELIGHT MY FIRE *RCA 74321167722* [1] ■..............................1	14
18 Dec 93 ★	BABE *RCA 74321182122* ■..1	10
9 Apr 94 ●	EVERYTHING CHANGES *RCA 74321167732* ■...........................1	10
9 Jul 94 ●	LOVE AIN'T HERE ANYMORE *RCA 74321214832* 3	10
15 Oct 94 ★	SURE *RCA 74321236622* ■...1	15
15 Oct 94	LOVE AIN'T HERE ANYMORE (re-entry)	
	RCA 74321214832..55	2
8 Apr 95 ★	BACK FOR GOOD *RCA 74321271462* ■..1	13

5 Aug 95 ★	NEVER FORGET *RCA 74321299572* ■...1	9
9 Mar 96 ★	HOW DEEP IS YOUR LOVE *RCA 74321355592* ■.........................1	13
15 Jun 96	HOW DEEP IS YOUR LOVE (re-entry) *RCA 74321355592*.........71	1

[1] Take That featuring Lulu

Billy TALBOT – *See Ian McNABB*

TALK TALK ♪ ✪ *UK, male vocal/instrumental group* — **73 wks**

24 Apr 82	TALK TALK *EMI 5284* 52	4
24 Jul 82	TODAY *EMI 5314*..14	13
13 Nov 82	TALK TALK (re-mix) *EMI 5352*...23	10
19 Mar 83	MY FOOLISH FRIEND *EMI 5373* 57	3
14 Jan 84	IT'S MY LIFE *EMI 5443*..46	5
7 Apr 84	SUCH A SHAME *EMI 5433* 49	6
11 Aug 84	DUM DUM GIRL *EMI 5480*..74	1
18 Jan 86	LIFE'S WHAT YOU MAKE IT *EMI EMI 5540*..............................16	9
15 Mar 86	LIVING IN ANOTHER WORLD *EMI EMI 5551*.............................48	4
17 May 86	GIVE IT UP *Parlophone R 6131* 59	3
19 May 90	IT'S MY LIFE (re-issue) *Parlophone R 6254* 13	9
1 Sep 90	LIFE'S WHAT YOU MAKE IT (re-issue) *Parlophone R 6264* 23	6

TALKING HEADS ♪ ☺ *US/UK, male/female vocal/instrumental group* — **54 wks**

7 Feb 81	ONCE IN A LIFETIME *Sire SIR 4048*...14	10
9 May 81	HOUSES IN MOTION *Sire SIR 4050*..50	3
21 Jan 84	THIS MUST BE THE PLACE *Sire W 9451* 51	3
3 Nov 84	SLIPPERY PEOPLE *EMI 5504*..68	2
12 Oct 85 ●	ROAD TO NOWHERE *EMI EMI 5530*...6	16
8 Feb 86	AND SHE WAS *EMI EMI 5543*..17	8
6 Sep 86	WILD WILD LIFE *EMI EMI 5567*...43	4
16 May 87	RADIO HEAD *EMI EM 1* 52	2
13 Aug 88	BLIND *EMI EM 68* 59	3
10 Oct 92	LIFETIME PILING UP *EMI EM 250* 50	3

See also HEADS with Shaun RYDER

TALL PAUL ☺ *UK, male DJ/producer – Paul Newman* — **4 wks**

29 Mar 97	ROCK DA HOUSE *VC VCRD 18* 12	4

See also CAMISRA; ESCRIMA; PARTIZAN

TAMBA TRIO *Argentina, male vocal/instrumental group* — **2 wks**

18 Jul 98	MAS QUE NADA *Talkin Loud TLCD 34* 34	2

TAMPERER featuring MAYA ☺ ✪ *Italy, male production duo, and US, female vocalist* — **24 wks**

25 Apr 98 ★	FEEL IT *Pepper 0530032*...1	17
14 Nov 98 ●	IF YOU BUY THIS RECORD YOUR LIFE WILL BE	
	Pepper 0530082...3†	7

TAMS ♪ *US, male vocal group* — **31 wks**

14 Feb 70	BE YOUNG BE FOOLISH BE HAPPY *Stateside SS 2123*...............32	7
31 Jul 71 ★	HEY GIRL DON'T BOTHER ME *Probe PRO 532*.............................1	17
21 Nov 87	THERE AIN'T NOTHING LIKE SHAGGIN' *Virgin VS 1029*............21	7

Norma TANEGA *US, female vocalist* — **8 wks**

7 Apr 66	WALKING MY CAT NAMED DOG *Stateside SS 496* 22	8

The Children of TANSLEY SCHOOL *UK, children's choir* — **4 wks**

28 Mar 81	MY MUM IS ONE IN A MILLION *EMI 5151*..................................27	4

Jimmy TARBUCK *UK, male vocalist* — **2 wks**

16 Nov 85	AGAIN *Safari SAFE 68*...74	1
30 Nov 85	AGAIN (re-entry) *Safari SAFE 68*..68	1

Lord TARIQ and Peter GUNZ *US, male vocal/rap duo* — **3 wks**

2 May 98	DEJA VU (UPTOWN BABY) *Columbia 6658722*............................21	3

What: *Have You Seen Her*   **93**
Who: Chi-Lites
When: 1972 (3), 1975 (5)
Which: Was a Top 5 hit twice and was composed in 1966 by the group's leader, Eugene Record. He also produced the track and played most of the instruments on it

What: *Those Were the Days*   **94**
Who: Mary Hopkin
When: 1968 (1)
Which: Started life as a Russian folk song. Paul McCartney, who liked the 1965 version by The Limeliters, produced Hopkin's chart-topping rendition, which knocked 'Hey Jude' off the top

What: *Gangsta's Paradise*   **95**
Who: Coolio featuring LV
When: 1995 (1)
Which: Was based on Stevie Wonder's 'Pastime Paradise'. It was the first rap record to enter the chart at No 1 in the UK and the first single to sell more than three million copies in the USA

What: *I Want You Back*   **96**
Who: Jackson Five
When: 1970 (2), 1988 (8 – remix)
Which: The writers initially intended for either Gladys Knight or Diana Ross. Nonetheless, it was the song that introduced the world to 11-year-old Michael Jackson and his brothers

Bill TARMEY ℭ *UK, male vocalist* — **9 wks**

3 Apr 93	ONE VOICE *Arista 74321140852*	16	4
19 Feb 94	WIND BENEATH MY WINGS *EMI CDEM 304*	40	3
19 Nov 94	IOU *EMI CDEM 361*	55	2

TARRIERS ♂ *US, male vocal/instrumental group* — **6 wks**

14 Dec 56	CINDY OH CINDY *London HLN 8340* [1]	26	1
1 Mar 57	BANANA BOAT SONG *Columbia DB 3891*	15	5

[1] Vince Martin and the Tarriers

TARTAN ARMY *UK, male vocal ensemble* — **4 wks**

6 Jun 98	SCOTLAND BE GOOD *The Precious JWLCD 33*	54	4

A TASTE OF HONEY *US, female vocal duo* — **19 wks**

17 Jun 78 ●	BOOGIE OOGIE OOGIE *Capitol CL 15988* ▲	3	16
18 May 85	BOOGIE OOGIE OOGIE (re-mix) *Capitol CL 357*	59	3

TATJANA *Croatia, female vocalist* — **2 wks**

21 Sep 96	SANTA MARIA *Love This LUVTHISCDX 4*	40	2

TAVARES *US, male vocal group* — **77 wks**

10 Jul 76 ●	HEAVEN MUST BE MISSING AN ANGEL *Capitol CL 15876*	4	11
9 Oct 76 ●	DON'T TAKE AWAY THE MUSIC *Capitol CL 15886*	4	10
5 Feb 77	MIGHTY POWER OF LOVE *Capitol CL 15905*	25	6
9 Apr 77 ●	WHODUNIT *Capitol CL 15914*	5	10
2 Jul 77	ONE STEP AWAY *Capitol CL 15930*	16	7
18 Mar 78	THE GHOST OF LOVE *Capitol CL 15968*	29	6
6 May 78 ●	MORE THAN A WOMAN *Capitol CL 15977*	7	11
12 Aug 78	SLOW TRAIN TO PARADISE *Capitol CL 15996*	62	3
22 Feb 86	HEAVEN MUST BE MISSING AN ANGEL (re-mix) *Capitol TAV 1*	12	9
3 May 86	IT ONLY TAKES A MINUTE *Capitol TAV 2*	46	4

TAXMAN – See KICKING BACK with TAXMAN

TAYLOR – See LIBRA presents TAYLOR

Andy TAYLOR *UK, male vocalist* — **2 wks**

20 Oct 90	LOLA *A & M AM 596*	60	2

Dina TAYLOR – See BBG

Felice TAYLOR *US, female vocalist* — **13 wks**

25 Oct 67	I FEEL LOVE COMIN' ON *President PT 155*	11	13

James TAYLOR ♂ *US, male vocalist* — **23 wks**

21 Nov 70	FIRE AND RAIN *Warner Bros. WB 6104*	42	3
28 Aug 71 ●	YOU'VE GOT A FRIEND *Warner Bros. WB 16085* ▲	4	15
16 Mar 74	MOCKINGBIRD *Elektra K 12134* [1]	34	5

[1] Carly Simon and James Taylor

John TAYLOR *UK, male vocalist* — **4 wks**

15 Mar 86	I DO WHAT I DO . . . THEME FOR '9 1/2 WEEKS' *Parlophone R 6125*	42	4

Johnnie TAYLOR *US, male vocalist* — **7 wks**

24 Apr 76	DISCO LADY *CBS 4044* ▲	25	7

JT TAYLOR *US, male vocalist* — **5 wks**

24 Aug 91	LONG HOT SUMMER NIGHT *MCA MCS 1567*	63	2
30 Nov 91	FEEL THE NEED *MCA MCS 1592*	57	1
18 Apr 92	FOLLOW ME *MCA MCS 1617*	59	2

Pauline TAYLOR *UK, female vocalist* — **3 wks**

8 Jun 96	LET THIS BE A PRAYER *Cheeky CHEKCD 013* [1]	26	2
9 Nov 96	CONSTANTLY WAITING *Cheeky CHEKCD 015*	51	1

[1] Rollo Goes Spiritual with Pauline Taylor

R Dean TAYLOR ☉ ✐ *Canada, male vocalist* — **48 wks**

19 Jun 68	GOTTA SEE JANE *Tamla Motown TMG 656*	17	12
3 Apr 71 ●	INDIANA WANTS ME *Tamla Motown TMG 763*	2	15
11 May 74 ●	THERE'S A GHOST IN MY HOUSE *Tamla Motown TMG 896*	3	12
31 Aug 74	WINDOW SHOPPING *Polydor 2058 502*	36	5
21 Sep 74	GOTTA SEE JANE (re-issue) *Tamla Motown TMG 918*	41	4

Roger TAYLOR *UK, male vocalist* — **16 wks**

18 Apr 81	FUTURE MANAGEMENT *EMI 5157*	49	4
16 Jun 84	MAN ON FIRE *EMI 5478*	66	2
10 Oct 92	RADIO *Epic 6584367* [1]	37	3
14 May 94	NAZIS *Parlophone CDR 6379*	22	2
1 Oct 94	FOREIGN SAND *Parlophone CDR 6389* [2]	26	2
26 Nov 94	HAPPINESS *Parlophone CDR 6399*	32	2
10 Oct 98	PRESSURE ON *Parlophone CDRS6507*	45	1

[1] Shaky featuring Roger Taylor [2] Roger Taylor and Yoshiki

James TAYLOR QUARTET – See JTQ

TC *Italy, male instrumental/production duo* — **5 wks**

14 Mar 92	BERRY *Union City UCRT 1* [1]	73	1
21 Nov 92	FUNKY GUITAR *Union City UCRT 13* [2]	40	2
10 Jul 93	HARMONY *Union UCRD 20* [3]	51	2

[1] TC 1991 [2] TC 1992 [3] TC 1993

T-CONNECTION ✇ *US, male vocal/instrumental group* — **27 wks**

18 Jun 77	DO WHAT YOU WANNA DO *TK XC 9109*	11	8
14 Jan 78	ON FIRE *TK TKR 6006*	16	5
10 Jun 78	LET YOURSELF GO *TK TKR 6024*	52	3
24 Feb 79	AT MIDNIGHT *TK TKR 7517*	53	5
5 May 79	SATURDAY NIGHT *TK TKR 7536*	41	6

T-COY – See VARIOUS ARTISTS (EPs & LPs) – The Further Adventures of North EP

Kiri TE KANAWA ♪ *New Zealand, female vocalist* — **11 wks**

28 Sep 91 ●	WORLD IN UNION *Columbia 6574817*	4	11

TEACH-IN ☉ *Holland, male/female vocal/instrumental group* — **7 wks**

12 Apr 75	DING-A-DONG *Polydor 2058 570*	13	7

TEAM *UK, male vocal/instrumental group* — **5 wks**

1 Jun 85	WICKI WACKY HOUSE PARTY *EMI 5519*	55	5

TEAM DEEP *Belgium, male production duo* — **1 wk**

17 May 97	MORNINGLIGHT *Multiply CDMULTY 19*	42	1

TEARDROP EXPLODES ☉ ✐
UK, male vocal/instrumental group — **50 wks**

27 Sep 80	WHEN I DREAM *Mercury TEAR 1*	47	6
31 Jan 81 ●	REWARD *Vertigo TEAR 2*	6	13
2 May 81	TREASON (IT'S JUST A STORY) *Mercury TEAR 3*	18	8
29 Aug 81	PASSIONATE FRIEND *Zoo TEAR 5*	25	10
21 Nov 81	COLOURS FLY AWAY *Mercury TEAR 6*	54	3
19 Jun 82	TINY CHILDREN *Mercury TEAR 7*	44	7
19 Mar 83	YOU DISAPPEAR FROM VIEW *Mercury TEAR 8*	41	3

TEARS FOR FEARS ☉ *Bath-based band at the forefront of the mid-1980s 'British Invasion' of the USA: Roland Orzabal (v/g/k), Curt Smith (v/b; left in 1991). Their first US No 1, 'Everybody Wants to Rule the World', also won the 1986 BRIT Award for Best Single.* — **143 wks**

2 Oct 82 ●	MAD WORLD *Mercury IDEA 3*	3	16
5 Feb 83 ●	CHANGE *Mercury IDEA 4*	4	9
30 Apr 83 ●	PALE SHELTER *Mercury IDEA 5*	5	8
3 Dec 83	THE WAY YOU ARE *Mercury IDEA 6*	24	8

UK No 1 ★   UK Top 10 ●   UK million seller ◆   UK entry at No 1 ■   US No 1 ▲

18 Aug 84		MOTHER'S TALK *Mercury IDEA 7*	14	8
1 Dec 84	●	SHOUT *Mercury IDEA 8* ▲	4	16
30 Mar 85	●	EVERYBODY WANTS TO RULE THE WORLD *Mercury IDEA 9*	2	14
22 Jun 85		HEAD OVER HEELS *Mercury IDEA 10*	12	9
31 Aug 85		SUFFER THE CHILDREN *Mercury IDEA 1*	52	4
7 Sep 85		PALE SHELTER (re-issue) *Mercury IDEA 2*	73	2
12 Oct 85		I BELIEVE (A SOULFUL RE-RECORDING) *Mercury IDEA 11*	23	4
22 Feb 86		EVERYBODY WANTS TO RULE THE WORLD (re-entry) *Mercury IDEA 9* ▲	73	1
31 May 86	●	EVERYBODY WANTS TO RUN THE WORLD *Mercury RACE 1*	5	6
19 Jul 86		EVERYBODY WANTS TO RUN THE WORLD (re-entry) *Mercury RACE 1*	73	1
2 Sep 89	●	SOWING THE SEEDS OF LOVE *Fontana IDEA 12*	5	9
18 Nov 89		WOMAN IN CHAINS *Fontana IDEA 13*	26	4
3 Mar 90		ADVICE FOR THE YOUNG AT HEART *Fontana IDEA 14*	36	4
22 Feb 92		LAID SO LOW (TEARS ROLL DOWN) *Fontana IDEA 17*	17	5
25 Apr 92		WOMAN IN CHAINS (re-issue) *Fontana IDEA 16* [1]	57	1
29 May 93		BREAK IT DOWN AGAIN *Mercury IDECD 18*	20	5
31 Jul 93		COLD *Mercury IDECD 19*	72	1
7 Oct 95		RAOUL AND THE KINGS OF SPAIN *Epic 6624765*	31	3
29 Jun 96		GOD'S MISTAKE *Epic 6634185*	61	1

[1] Tears For Fears featuring Oleta Adams

Mercury RACE 1 was a slightly changed version of Mercury IDEA 9, released to promote the Race Against Time of 15 May, 1986. Oleta Adams is given no label credit on the original release of 'Woman In Chains'. From 1992 Tears For Fears was essentially a male vocalist/multi-instrumentalist – Roland Orzabal

TECHNICIAN 2 *UK, male instrumental/production group*   1 wk

14 Nov 92	PLAYING WITH THE BOY *MCA MCS 1710*	70	1

TECHNO TWINS *UK, male/female vocal duo*   2 wks

16 Jan 82	FALLING IN LOVE AGAIN *PRT 7P 224*	75	1
30 Jan 82	FALLING IN LOVE AGAIN (re-entry) *PRT 7P 224*	70	1

TECHNOCAT – See Tom WILSON

TECHNOHEAD ☺ *UK, male/female vocal/instrumental duo*   20 wks

3 Feb 96	●	I WANNA BE A HIPPY *Mokum DB 17703*	6	14
27 Apr 96		HAPPY BIRTHDAY *Mokum DB 17593*	18	5
12 Oct 96		BANANA-NA-NA (DUMB DI DUMB) *Mokum DB 17473*	64	1

Technohead, Tricky Disco and GTO are all the same act
See also TRICKY DISCO; GTO

TECHNOTRONIC ☺ ☺ *Belgium, male producer – Jo Bogaert*   66 wks

2 Sep 89	●	PUMP UP THE JAM *Swanyard SYR 4* [1]	2	15
3 Feb 90	●	GET UP (BEFORE THE NIGHT IS OVER) *Swanyard SYR 8* [2]	2	10
7 Apr 90		THIS BEAT IS TECHNOTRONIC *Swanyard SYR 9* [3]	14	7
14 Jul 90	●	ROCKIN' OVER THE BEAT *Swanyard SYR 14* [2]	9	9
6 Oct 90		MEGAMIX *Swanyard SYR 19*	6	8
15 Dec 90		TURN IT UP *Swanyard SYD 9* [4]	42	4
25 May 91		MOVE THAT BODY *ARS 6568377* [5]	12	7
3 Aug 91		WORK *ARS 6573317* [5]	40	4
14 Dec 96		PUMP UP THE JAM (re-mix) *Worx WORXCD 004*	36	2

[1] Technotronic featuring Felly [2] Technotronic featuring Ya Kid K
[3] Technotronic featuring MC Eric [4] Technotronic featuring Melissa and Einstein
[5] Technotronic featuring Reggie

See also HI-TEK 3 featuring YA KID K

TEDDY BEARS ☺ *US, male/female vocal group*   17 wks

19 Dec 58	●	TO KNOW HIM IS TO LOVE HIM *London HLN 8733* ▲	2	16
14 Apr 79		TO KNOW HIM IS TO LOVE HIM (re-issue) *Lightning LIG 9015*	66	1

'To Know Him Is to Love Him' re-issue was coupled with 'Endless Sleep' by Jody Reynolds as a double A-side

TEENAGE FANCLUB ☹ ✎

UK, male vocal/instrumental group   20 wks

24 Aug 91	STAR SIGN *Creation CRE 105*	44	2

2 Nov 91		THE CONCEPT *Creation CRE 111*	51	1
8 Feb 92		WHAT YOU DO TO ME EP *Creation CRE 115*	31	2
26 Jun 93		RADIO *Creation CRESCD 130*	31	2
2 Oct 93		NORMAN 3 *Creation CRESCD 142*	50	1
2 Apr 94		FALLIN' *Epic 6602622* [1]	59	1
8 Apr 95		MELLOW DOUBT *Creation CRESCD 175*	34	2
27 May 95		SPARKY'S DREAM *Creation CRESCD 201*	40	2
2 Sep 95		NEIL JUNG *Creation CRESCD 210*	62	1
16 Dec 95		HAVE LOST IT EP *Creation CRESCD 216*	53	1
12 Jul 97		AIN'T THAT ENOUGH *Creation CRESCD 228*	17	3
30 Aug 97		I DON'T WANT CONTROL OF YOU *Creation CRESCD 238*	43	1
29 Nov 97		START AGAIN *Creation CRESCD 280*	54	1

[1] Teenage Fanclub and De La Soul

Tracks on What You Do to Me EP: What You Do to Me/B-Side/Life's a Gas/Filler Tracks On Have Lost It EP: 120 Mins/Don't Look Back/Everything Flows/Star Sign This last track is a re-recorded version of their first hit

TEENAGERS – See Frankie LYMON and the TEENAGERS

Towa TEI *Japan, male DJ/producer*   1 wk

31 Oct 98	GBI *Athrob ART 021CD* [1]	63	1

[1] Towa Tei featuring Kylie Minogue

TEKNO TOO *UK, male instrumental/production duo*   2 wks

13 Jul 91	JET-STAR *D-Zone DANCE 012*	56	2

TELETUBBIES ☺ *UK, male/female cuddly alien vocal group*   32 wks

13 Dec 97	★	TELETUBBIES SAY EH-OH! *BBC Worldwide WMXS 00092* ◆ ■	1	29
18 Jul 98		TELETUBBIES SAY EH-OH! (re-entry) *BBC Worldwide WMXS 00092*	66	2
15 Aug 98		TELETUBBIES SAY EH-OH! (2nd re-entry) *BBC Worldwide WMXS 00092*	72	1

TELEVISION *US, male vocal/instrumental group*   10 wks

16 Apr 77	MARQUEE MOON *Elektra K 12252*	30	4
30 Jul 77	PROVE IT *Elektra K 12262*	25	4
22 Apr 78	FOXHOLE *Elektra K 12287*	36	2

TELEX *Belgium, male vocal/instrumental duo*   7 wks

21 Jul 79	ROCK AROUND THE CLOCK *Sire SIR 4020*	34	7

Sylvia TELLA – See BLOW MONKEYS

TEMPERANCE SEVEN ☺ *UK, male vocal/instrumental band*   45 wks

30 Mar 61	★	YOU'RE DRIVING ME CRAZY *Parlophone R 4757*	1	16
15 Jun 61	●	PASADENA *Parlophone R 4781*	4	17
28 Sep 61		HARD HEARTED HANNAH/CHILI BOM BOM *Parlophone R 4823*	28	4
7 Dec 61		CHARLESTON *Parlophone R 4851*	22	8

'Chili Bom Bom' only listed with 'Hard Hearted Hannah' for the weeks of 12 and 19 Oct, 1961

TEMPLE OF THE DOG *US, male vocal/instrumental group*   2 wks

24 Oct 92	HUNGER STRIKE *A & M AM 0091*	51	2

Nino TEMPO and April STEVENS ☺

US, male/female vocal duo   19 wks

7 Nov 63	DEEP PURPLE *London HLK 9782* ▲	17	11
16 Jan 64	WHISPERING *London HLK 9829*	20	8

TEMPTATIONS ✎ *The world's most successful R&B vocal group: Eddie Kendricks (d. 1992), Otis Williams, Paul Williams (d. 1973), Melvin Franklin (d. 1995), David Ruffin (d. 1991). Detroit quintet, whose biggest UK hit, 'My Girl', was a 27-year-old US No 1. The current line-up of the group is still doing well Stateside*   203 wks

18 Mar 65	MY GIRL *Stateside SS 378* ▲	43	1

Date	Title	Pos	Wks
1 Apr 65	IT'S GROWING *Tamla Motown TMG 504*	49	1
15 Apr 65	IT'S GROWING (re-entry) *Tamla Motown TMG 504*	45	1
14 Jul 66	AIN'T TOO PROUD TO BEG *Tamla Motown TMG 565*	21	11
6 Oct 66	BEAUTY IS ONLY SKIN DEEP *Tamla Motown TMG 578*	18	10
15 Dec 66	(I KNOW) I'M LOSING YOU *Tamla Motown TMG 587*	19	9
6 Sep 67	YOU'RE MY EVERYTHING *Tamla Motown TMG 620*	26	15
6 Mar 68	I WISH IT WOULD RAIN *Tamla Motown TMG 641*	45	1
12 Jun 68	I COULD NEVER LOVE ANOTHER *Tamla Motown TMG 658*	47	1
29 Jan 69 ●	I'M GONNA MAKE YOU LOVE ME *Tamla Motown TMG 685* [1]	3	11
5 Mar 69 ●	GET READY *Tamla Motown TMG 688*	10	9
23 Apr 69	I'M GONNA MAKE YOU LOVE ME (re-entry) *Tamla Motown TMG 685* [1]	49	1
23 Aug 69	CLOUD NINE *Tamla Motown TMG 707*	15	10
20 Sep 69	I SECOND THAT EMOTION *Tamla Motown TMG 709* [1]	18	8
17 Jan 70	I CAN'T GET NEXT TO YOU *Tamla Motown TMG 722* ▲	13	9
21 Mar 70	WHY (MUST WE FALL IN LOVE) *Tamla Motown TMG 730* [1]	31	7
13 Jun 70	PSYCHEDELIC SHACK *Tamla Motown TMG 741*	33	7
19 Sep 70 ●	BALL OF CONFUSION *Tamla Motown TMG 749*	7	12
19 Dec 70	BALL OF CONFUSION (re-entry) *Tamla Motown TMG 749*	48	3
22 May 71 ●	JUST MY IMAGINATION (RUNNING AWAY WITH ME) *Tamla Motown TMG 773* ▲	8	16
5 Feb 72	SUPERSTAR (REMEMBER HOW YOU GOT WHERE YOU ARE) *Tamla Motown TMG 800*	32	5
15 Apr 72	TAKE A LOOK AROUND *Tamla Motown TMG 808*	13	10
13 Jan 73	PAPA WAS A ROLLIN' STONE *Tamla Motown TMG 839* ▲	14	8
29 Sep 73	LAW OF THE LAND *Tamla Motown TMG 866*	41	4
12 Jun 82	STANDING ON THE TOP (PART 1) *Motown TMG 1263* [2]	53	3
17 Nov 84	TREAT HER LIKE A LADY *Motown TMG 1365*	12	10
15 Aug 87	PAPA WAS A ROLLIN' STONE (re-mix) *Motown ZB 41431*	31	6
6 Feb 88	LOOK WHAT YOU STARTED *Motown ZB 41733*	63	2
21 Oct 89	ALL I WANT FROM YOU *Motown ZB 43233*	71	1
15 Feb 92 ●	MY GIRL (re-issue) *Epic 6576767*	2	10
22 Feb 92	THE JONES' *Motown TMG 1403*	69	1

[1] Diana Ross and the Supremes and the Temptations
[2] Temptations featuring Rick James

10 CC ☺ *Multi-talented Manchester supergroup: Graham Gouldman (previously penned hits for Hollies, Yardbirds and Herman's Hermits), Eric Stewart (ex-Mindbenders, Hotlegs), and Lol Creme and Kevin Godley (both ex-Hotlegs). Godley and Creme went on to have hits as a duo and produced award-winning videos* **133 wks**

Date	Title	Pos	Wks
23 Sep 72 ●	DONNA *UK 6*	2	13
19 May 73 ★	RUBBER BULLETS *UK 36*	1	15
25 Aug 73 ●	THE DEAN AND I *UK 48*	10	8
15 Jun 74 ●	WALL STREET SHUFFLE *UK 69*	10	10
14 Sep 74	SILLY LOVE *UK 77*	24	7
5 Apr 75 ●	LIFE IS A MINESTRONE *Mercury 6008 010*	7	8
31 May 75 ★	I'M NOT IN LOVE *Mercury 6008 014*	1	11
29 Nov 75 ●	ART FOR ART'S SAKE *Mercury 6008 017*	5	10
20 Mar 76 ●	I'M MANDY FLY ME *Mercury 6008 019*	6	9
11 Dec 76 ●	THINGS WE DO FOR LOVE *Mercury 6008 022*	6	11
16 Apr 77 ●	GOOD MORNING JUDGE *Mercury 6008 025*	5	12
12 Aug 78 ★	DREADLOCK HOLIDAY *Mercury 6008 035*	1	13
7 Aug 82	RUN AWAY *Mercury MER 113*	50	4
18 Mar 95	I'M NOT IN LOVE *Avex UK AVEXCD 2*	29	2

From 'Things We Do For Love' 10 CC were a male vocal/instrumental duo
'I'm Not In Love' 1995 is a re-recording

TEN CITY ☺ *US, male vocal/instrumental group* **21 wks**

Date	Title	Pos	Wks
21 Jan 89 ●	THAT'S THE WAY LOVE IS *Atlantic A 8963*	8	10
8 Apr 89	DEVOTION *Atlantic A 8916*	29	4
22 Jul 89	WHERE DO WE GO *Atlantic A 8864*	60	1
27 Oct 90	WHATEVER MAKES YOU HAPPY *Atlantic A 7819*	60	2
15 Aug 92	ONLY TIME WILL TELL/MY PEACE OF HEAVEN *East West America A 8516*	63	2
11 Sep 93	FANTASY *Columbia 6595042*	45	2

TEN POLE TUDOR ✐ ☺ *UK, male vocal/instrumental group* **40 wks**

Date	Title	Pos	Wks
7 Apr 79 ●	WHO KILLED BAMBI *Virgin VS 256*	6	8
13 Oct 79	ROCK AROUND THE CLOCK *Virgin VS 290*	21	6
25 Apr 81 ●	SWORDS OF A THOUSAND MEN *Stiff BUY 109*	6	12
1 Aug 81	WUNDERBAR *Stiff BUY 120*	16	9
14 Nov 81	THROWING MY BABY OUT WITH THE BATHWATER *Stiff BUY 129*	49	5

The listed flip side of 'Who Killed Bambi' was 'Silly Thing' by the Sex Pistols.
The listed flip side of 'Rock Around the Clock' was 'The Great Rock 'n' Roll Swindle' also by the Sex Pistols

TEN SHARP ☺ *Holland, male vocal/instrumental duo* **15 wks**

Date	Title	Pos	Wks
21 Mar 92 ●	YOU *Columbia 6566647*	10	13
20 Jun 92	AIN'T MY BEATING HEART *Columbia 6580947*	63	2

10,000 MANIACS *US, female/male vocal/instrumental group* **7 wks**

Date	Title	Pos	Wks
12 Sep 92	THESE ARE DAYS *Elektra EKR 156*	58	3
10 Apr 93	CANDY EVERYBODY WANTS *Elektra EKR 160CD1*	47	3
23 Oct 93	BECAUSE THE NIGHT *Elektra EKR 175CD*	65	1

TEN YEARS AFTER ✐ *UK, male vocal/instrumental group* **18 wks**

Date	Title	Pos	Wks
6 Jun 70 ●	LOVE LIKE A MAN *Deram DM 299*	10	18

Danny TENAGLIA and CELEDA
UK, male DJ/producer, and UK, female vocalist **3 wks**

Date	Title	Pos	Wks
5 Sep 98	MUSIC IS THE ANSWER (DANCIN' AND PRANCIN') *Twisted UK TWCD 10038*	36	3

TENNESSEE THREE – See Johnny CASH

TENOR FLY ✌ *UK, male vocalist* **17 wks**

Date	Title	Pos	Wks
6 Apr 91	WICKEDEST SOUND *Desire WANT 40* [1]	43	6
15 Jun 91	TRIBAL BASE *Desire WANT 44* [2]	20	6
7 Jan 95	BRIGHT SIDE OF LIFE *Mango CIDM 825*	51	2
7 Feb 98	B-BOY STANCE *Freskanova FND 7* [3]	23	3

[1] Rebel MC featuring Tenor Fly [2] Rebel MC featuring Tenor Fly and Barrington Levy
[3] Freestylers featuring Tenor Fly

TERMINATERS – See ARNEE and the TERMINATERS

TERRA FIRMA *Italy, male producer – Claudio Giussani* **1 wk**

Date	Title	Pos	Wks
18 May 96	FLOATING *Platipus PLAT 21CD*	64	1

Tammi TERRELL – See Marvin GAYE

TERRORIZE *UK, male producer – Shaun Imrei* **6 wks**

Date	Title	Pos	Wks
2 May 92	IT'S JUST A FEELING *Hamster STER 1*	52	3
22 Aug 92	FEEL THE RHYTHM *Hamster 12STER 2*	69	1
14 Nov 92	IT'S JUST A FEELING (re-issue) *Hamster STER 8*	47	2

TERRORVISION ✐ *UK, male vocal/instrumental group* **42 wks**

Date	Title	Pos	Wks
19 Jun 93	AMERICAN TV *Total Vegas CDVEGAS 3*	63	1
30 Oct 93	NEW POLICY ONE *Total Vegas CDVEGAS 4*	42	2
8 Jan 94	MY HOUSE *Total Vegas CDVEGAS 5*	29	4
9 Apr 94	OBLIVION *Total Vegas CDVEGAS 6*	21	5
25 Jun 94	MIDDLEMAN *Total Vegas CDVEGAS 7*	25	4
3 Sep 94	PRETEND BEST FRIEND *Total Vegas CDVEGAS 8*	25	3
29 Oct 94	ALICE WHAT'S THE MATTER *Total Vegas CDVEGAS 9*	24	4
18 Mar 95	SOME PEOPLE SAY *Total Vegas CDVEGAS 10*	22	3
2 Mar 96 ●	PERSEVERANCE *Total Vegas CDVEGAS 11*	5	4
4 May 96	CELEBRITY HIT LIST *Total Vegas CDVEGAS 12*	20	3
20 Jul 96 ●	BAD ACTRESS *Total Vegas CDVEGAS 13*	10	3
11 Jan 97	EASY *Total Vegas CDVEGASS 14*	12	4
3 Oct 98	JOSEPHINE *EMI CDVEGAS 15*	23	2

Helen TERRY *UK, female vocalist* **6 wks**

Date	Title	Pos	Wks
12 May 84	LOVE LIES LOST *Virgin VS 678*	34	6

UK No 1 ★   UK Top 10 ●   UK million seller ◆   UK entry at No 1 ■   US No 1 ▲

Todd TERRY PROJECT ☺ *US, male producer* — **32 wks**

12 Nov 88	WEEKEND *Sleeping Bag SBUK 1T*	56	3
14 Oct 95	WEEKEND (re-mix) *Ore AG 13CD*	28	3
13 Jul 96 ●	KEEP ON JUMPIN' *Manifesto FESCD 11* [1]	8	6
12 Jul 97 ●	SOMETHING GOIN' ON *Manifesto FESCD 25* [2]	5	10
6 Dec 97 ●	IT'S OVER LOVE *Manfiesto FESCD 37* [3]	16	8
11 Apr 98 ●	READY FOR A NEW DAY *Manifesto FESCD 40* [2]	20	2

[1] Todd Terry featuring Martha Wash and Jocelyn Brown
[2] Todd Terry [3] Todd Terry presents Shannon

Tony TERRY *US, male vocalist* — **6 wks**

27 Feb 88	LOVEY DOVEY *Epic TONY 2*	44	6

TESLA *US, male vocal/instrumental group* — **1 wk**

27 Apr 91	SIGNS *Geffen GFS 3*	70	1

Joe TEX ♪ *US, male vocalist* — **11 wks**

23 Apr 77 ●	AIN'T GONNA BUMP NO MORE (WITH NO BIG FAT WOMAN) *Epic EPC 5035*	2	11

TEXAS ☺ ♪ *UK, male/female vocal/instrumental group* — **71 wks**

4 Feb 89	I DON'T WANT A LOVER *Mercury TEX 1*	8	11
6 May 89	THRILL HAS GONE *Mercury TEX 2*	60	3
5 Aug 89	EVERYDAY NOW *Mercury TEX 3*	44	5
2 Dec 89	PRAYER FOR YOU *Mercury TEX 4*	73	1
7 Sep 91	WHY BELIEVE IN YOU *Mercury TEX 5*	66	1
26 Oct 91	IN MY HEART *Mercury TEX 6*	74	1
8 Feb 92	ALONE WITH YOU *Mercury TEX 7*	32	4
25 Apr 92	TIRED OF BEING ALONE *Mercury TEX 8*	19	6
11 Sep 93	SO CALLED FRIEND *Vertigo TEXCD 9*	30	3
30 Oct 93	YOU OWE IT ALL TO ME *Vertigo TEXCD 10*	39	3
18 Jan 97	SAY WHAT YOU WANT *Mercury MERCD 480*	3	10
12 Feb 94	SO IN LOVE WITH YOU *Vertigo TEXCD 11*	28	2
9 Aug 97 ●	BLACK EYED BOY *Mercury MERCD 490*	5	6
15 Nov 97 ●	PUT YOUR ARMS AROUND ME *Mercury MERCD 497*	10	5
3 Jan 98	PUT YOUR ARMS AROUND ME (re-entry) *Mercury MERCD 497*	75	1
17 Jan 98	PUT YOUR ARMS AROUND ME (2nd re-entry) *Mercury MERCD 497*	64	2
21 Mar 98 ●	SAY WHAT YOU WANT/INSANE *Mercury MERCD 499* [1]	4	7

[1] Texas featuring Wu-Tang Clan (rap by Method Man and RZA)

THAT KID CHRIS *US, male DJ/producer – Chris Staropoli* — **1 wk**

22 Feb 97	FEEL THA VIBE *Manifesto FESCD 16*	52	1

THAT PETROL EMOTION *UK, male vocal/instrumental group* — **24 wks**

11 Apr 87	BIG DECISION *Polydor TPE 1*	43	7
11 Jul 87	DANCE *Polydor TPE 2*	64	2
17 Oct 87	GENIUS MOVE *Virgin VS 1002*	65	2
31 Mar 90	ABANDON *Virgin VS 1242*	73	1
1 Sep 90	HEY VENUS *Virgin VS 1290*	49	4
9 Feb 91	TINGLE *Virgin VS 1312*	49	4
27 Apr 91	SENSITIZE *Virgin VS 1261*	55	4

The THE ☹ ☺
UK, male vocalist – Matt Johnson and backing musicians — **52 wks**

4 Dec 82	UNCERTAIN SMILE *Epic EPC A 2787*	68	3
17 Sep 83	THIS IS THE DAY *Epic A 3710*	71	3
9 Aug 86	HEARTLAND *Some Bizarre TRUTH 2*	29	10
25 Oct 86	INFECTED *Some Bizarre TRUTH 3*	48	5
24 Jan 87	SLOW TRAIN TO DAWN *Some Bizarre TENSE 1*	64	2
23 May 87	SWEET BIRD OF TRUTH *Epic TENSE 2*	55	2
1 Apr 89	THE BEAT(EN) GENERATION *Epic EMU 8*	18	5
22 Jul 89	GRAVITATE TO ME *Epic EMU 9*	63	3
7 Oct 89	ARMAGEDDON DAYS ARE HERE (AGAIN) *Epic EMU 10*	70	2
2 Mar 91	SHADES OF BLUE EP *Epic 6557968*	54	1
16 Jan 93	DOGS OF LUST *Epic 6584572*	25	4
17 Apr 93	SLOW EMOTION REPLAY *Epic 6590772*	35	3

19 Jun 93	LOVE IS STRONGER THAN DEATH *Epic 6593712*	39	3
15 Jan 94	DIS-INFECTED EP *Epic 6598112*	17	4
4 Feb 95	I SAW THE LIGHT *Epic 6610912*	31	2

Tracks on Shades of Blue EP: Jealous of Youth / Another Boy Drowning (Live) / Solitude / Dolphins. Tracks on Dis-Infected EP: That Was The Day / Dis-Infected / Helpline Operator / Dogs of Lust. 'That Was the Day' and 'Dis-Infected' on the EP are re-recordings of earlier hits. 'Dogs of Lust' is a re-mix

THEATRE OF HATE *UK, male vocal/instrumental group* — **9 wks**

23 Jan 82	DO YOU BELIEVE IN THE WESTWORLD *Burning Rome BRR 2*	40	7
29 May 82	THE HOP *Burning Rome BRR 3*	70	2

THE AUDIENCE *UK, male vocal/instrumental group* — **5 wks**

7 Mar 98	IF YOU CAN'T DO IT WHEN YOU'RE YOUNG, WHEN CAN YOU DO IT? *Mercury AUDCD 2*	48	1
23 May 98	A PESSIMIST IS NEVER DISAPPOINTED *Mercury AUDCD 3*	27	2
8 Aug 98	I KNOW ENOUGH (I DON'T GET ENOUGH) *Elleffe AUCD 4*	25	2

THEM ♪ ♪ *UK, male vocal/instrumental group* — **23 wks**

7 Jan 65 ●	BABY PLEASE DON'T GO *Decca F 12018*	10	9
25 Mar 65 ●	HERE COMES THE NIGHT *Decca F 12094*	2	12
9 Feb 91	BABY PLEASE DON'T GO (re-issue) *London LON 292*	65	2

THEN JERICO ☺ ♪ *UK, male vocal/instrumental group* — **36 wks**

31 Jan 87	LET HER FALL *London LON 97*	65	3
25 Jul 87	THE MOTIVE (LIVING WITHOUT YOU) *London LON 145*	18	12
24 Oct 87	MUSCLE DEEP *London LON 156*	48	4
28 Jan 89	BIG AREA *London LON 204*	13	7
8 Apr 89	WHAT DOES IT TAKE *London LON 223*	33	4
12 Aug 89	SUGAR BOX *London LON 235*	22	6

THERAPY? ♪ ☺ *UK, male vocal/instrumental group* — **33 wks**

31 Oct 92	TEETHGRINDER *A & M AM 0097*	30	2
20 Mar 93 ●	SHORTSHARPSHOCK EP *A & M AMCD 208*	9	4
12 Jun 93	FACE THE STRANGE EP *A & M 5803052*	18	3
28 Aug 93	OPAL MANTRA *A & M 5803612*	14	3
29 Jan 94	NOWHERE *A & M 5805052*	18	4
12 Mar 94	TRIGGER INSIDE *A & M 5805352*	22	3
11 Jun 94	DIE LAUGHING *A & M 5805892*	29	2
27 May 95	INNOCENT X *Volume VOLCD 1*	53	1
3 Jun 95	STORIES *A & M 5811052*	14	3
29 Jul 95	LOOSE *A & M 5811652*	25	3
18 Nov 95	DIANE *A & M 5812912*	26	2
14 Mar 98	CHURCH OF NOISE *A & M 5825392*	29	2
30 May 98	LONELY, CRYIN' ONLY *A&M 0441212*	32	1

Tracks on Shortsharpshock EP: Screamager / Auto Surgery / Totally Random Man / Accelerator. Tracks on Face the Strange EP: Turn / Speedball / Bloody Blue / Neckfreak. The listed flip side of 'Innocent X' was 'Belfast' by Orbital

THESE ANIMAL MEN *UK, male vocal/instrumental group* — **3 wks**

24 Sep 94	THIS IS THE SOUND OF YOUTH *Hi-Rise FLATSCD 7*	72	1
8 Feb 97	LIFE SUPPORT MACHINE *Hut HUTCD 76*	62	1
12 Apr 97	LIGHT EMITTING ELECTRICAL WAVE *Hut HUTCD 81*	72	1

THEY MIGHT BE GIANTS ☹ ☺
US, male vocal/instrumental duo — **13 wks**

3 Mar 90 ●	BIRDHOUSE IN YOUR SOUL *Elektra EKR 104*	6	11
2 Jun 90	ISTANBUL (NOT CONSTANTINOPLE) *Elektra EKR 110*	61	2

THIN LIZZY ✁ *Accomplished Irish hard-rock group (which at times included noted guitarists Gary Moore, Snowy White and Midge Ure) was built around distinctive singer/bass-guitarist Phil Lynott (d. 1986). After a slow start, they wrote their own chapter in British rock history* — **128 wks**

20 Jan 73 ●	WHISKEY IN THE JAR *Decca F 13355*	6	12
29 May 76 ●	THE BOYS ARE BACK IN TOWN *Vertigo 6059 139*	8	10
14 Aug 76	JAILBREAK *Vertigo 6059 150*	31	4
15 Jan 77	DON'T BELIEVE A WORD *Vertigo Lizzy 001*	12	7

13 Aug 77	DANCIN' IN THE MOONLIGHT (IT'S CAUGHT ME IN THE SPOTLIGHT) *Vertigo 6059 177*	14 8
13 May 78	ROSALIE – COWGIRLS' SONG (MEDLEY) *Vertigo LIZZY 2*	20 13
3 Mar 79 ●	WAITING FOR AN ALIBI *Vertigo LIZZY 003*	9 8
16 Jun 79	DO ANYTHING YOU WANT TO *Vertigo LIZZY 004*	14 9
20 Oct 79	SARAH *Vertigo LIZZY 5*	24 13
24 May 80	CHINATOWN *Vertigo LIZZY 6*	21 9
27 Sep 80 ●	KILLER ON THE LOOSE *Vertigo LIZZY 7*	10 7
2 May 81	KILLERS LIVE EP *Vertigo LIZZY 8*	19 7
8 Aug 81	TROUBLE BOYS *Vertigo LIZZY 9*	53 4
6 Mar 82	HOLLYWOOD (DOWN ON YOUR LUCK) *Vertigo LIZZY 10*	53 3
12 Feb 83	COLD SWEAT *Vertigo LIZZY 11*	27 5
7 May 83	THUNDER AND LIGHTNING *Vertigo LIZZY 12*	39 2
6 Aug 83	THE SUN GOES DOWN *Vertigo LIZZY 13*	52 3
26 Jan 91	DEDICATION *Vertigo LIZZY 14*	35 3
23 Mar 91	THE BOYS ARE BACK IN TOWN (re-issue) *Vertigo LIZZY 15*	63 1

Tracks on Killers Live EP: Bad Reputation / Are You Ready / Dear Miss Lonely Hearts

3RD BASS *US, male rap group* — 5 wks

10 Feb 90	THE GAS FACE *Def Jam 655627 0*	71 1
7 Apr 90	BROOKLYN-QUEENS *Def Jam 655830 7*	61 2
22 Jun 91	POP GOES THE WEASEL *Def Jam 6569547*	64 2

THIRD DIMENSION featuring Julie McDERMOTT
UK, male/female vocal/instrumental group — 2 wks

12 Oct 96	DON'T GO *Soundproof MCSTD 40082*	34 2

THIRD EYE BLIND *US, male vocal/instrumental group* — 6 wks

27 Sep 97	SEMI-CHARMED LIFE *Elektra E 3907CD*	37 5
21 Mar 98	HOW'S IT GOING TO BE *Elektra E 3863CD*	51 1

THIRD WORLD *Jamaica, male vocal/instrumental group* — 53 wks

23 Sep 78 ●	NOW THAT WE'VE FOUND LOVE *Island WIP 6457*	10 9
6 Jan 79	COOL MEDITATION *Island WIP 6469*	17 10
16 Jun 79	TALK TO ME *Island WIP 6496*	56 5
6 Jun 81 ●	DANCING ON THE FLOOR (HOOKED ON LOVE) *CBS A 1214*	10 15
17 Apr 82	TRY JAH LOVE *CBS A 2063*	47 6
9 Mar 85	NOW THAT WE'VE FOUND LOVE (re-issue) *Island IS 219*	22 8

THIRST *UK, male vocal/instrumental group* — 2 wks

6 Jul 91	THE ENEMY WITHIN *Ten TEN 379*	61 2

1300 DRUMS featuring the UNJUSTIFIED ANCIENTS OF MU ⓧ
UK, male instrumental/production group — 4 wks

18 May 96	OOH! AAH! CANTONA *Dynamo DYND 5*	11 4

THIS ISLAND EARTH
UK, male/female vocal/instrumental group — 5 wks

5 Jan 85	SEE THAT GLOW *Magnet MAG 266*	47 5

THIS MORTAL COIL *UK, male/female vocal/instrumental group* — 3 wks

22 Oct 83	SONG TO THE SIREN *4AD AD 310*	66 2
12 Nov 83	SONG TO THE SIREN (re-entry) *4AD AD 310*	75 1

THIS WAY UP *UK, male vocal/instrumental duo* — 2 wks

22 Aug 87	TELL ME WHY *Virgin VS 954*	72 2

THIS YEAR'S BLONDE
UK, male/female vocal/instrumental group — 8 wks

10 Oct 81	PLATINUM POP *Creole CR 19*	46 5
14 Nov 87	WHO'S THAT MIX *Debut DEBT 3034*	62 3

BJ THOMAS *US, male vocalist* — 4 wks

21 Feb 70	RAINDROPS KEEP FALLING ON MY HEAD *Wand WN1* ▲	38 3
2 May 70	RAINDROPS KEEP FALLING ON MY HEAD (re-entry) *Wand WN1*	49 1

Carla THOMAS – See Otis REDDING

Evelyn THOMAS ♫ ✍ *US, female vocalist* — 29 wks

24 Jan 76	WEAK SPOT *20th Century BTC 1014*	26 7
17 Apr 76	DOOMSDAY *20th Century BTC 1017*	41 1
1 May 76	DOOMSDAY (re-entry) *20th Century BTC 1017*	45 1
21 Apr 84 ●	HIGH ENERGY *Record Shack SOHO 18*	5 17
25 Aug 84	MASQUERADE *Record Shack SOHO 25*	60 3

Jamo THOMAS *US, male vocalist* — 2 wks

26 Feb 69	I SPY FOR THE FBI *Polydor 56755*	48 1
12 Mar 69	I SPY FOR THE FBI (re-entry) *Polydor 56755*	44 1

Kenny THOMAS Ⓡⓑ ⓧ *UK, male vocalist* — 54 wks

26 Jan 91	OUTSTANDING *Cooltempo COOL 227*	12 10
1 Jun 91 ●	THINKING ABOUT YOUR LOVE *Cooltempo COOL 235*	4 13
5 Oct 91	BEST OF YOU *Cooltempo COOL 243*	11 7
30 Nov 91	TENDER LOVE *Cooltempo COOL 247*	26 6
10 Jul 93	STAY *Cooltempo CDCOOL 271*	22 6
4 Sep 93	TRIPPIN' ON YOUR LOVE *Cooltempo CDCOOL 277*	17 5
6 Nov 93	PIECE BY PIECE *Cooltempo CDCOOL 283*	36 3
14 May 94	DESTINY *Cooltempo CDCOOL 289*	59 1
2 Sep 95	WHEN I THINK OF YOU *Cooltempo CDCOOL 309*	27 1

Lillo THOMAS *US, male vocalist* — 10 wks

27 Apr 85	SETTLE DOWN *Capitol CL 356*	66 2
21 Mar 87	SEXY GIRL *Capitol CL 445*	23 5
30 May 87	I'M IN LOVE *Capitol CL 450*	54 3

Mickey THOMAS – See Elvin BISHOP

Nicky THOMAS *Jamaica, male vocalist* — 14 wks

13 Jun 70 ●	LOVE OF THE COMMON PEOPLE *Trojan TR 7750*	9 14

Rufus THOMAS *US, male vocalist* — 12 wks

11 Apr 70	DO THE FUNKY CHICKEN *Stax 144*	18 12

Tasha THOMAS *US, female vocalist* — 3 wks

20 Jan 79	SHOOT ME (WITH YOUR LOVE) *Atlantic LV 4*	59 3

Timmy THOMAS *US, male vocalist* — 20 wks

24 Feb 73	WHY CAN'T WE LIVE TOGETHER *Mojo 2027 012*	12 11
28 Dec 85	NEW YORK EYES *Portrait A 6805* [1]	41 7
14 Jul 90	WHY CAN'T WE LIVE TOGETHER (re-mix) *TK TKR 1*	54 2

[1] Nicole with Timmy Thomas

THOMAS and TAYLOR *US, male/female vocal duo* — 5 wks

17 May 86	YOU CAN'T BLAME LOVE *Cooltempo COOL 123*	53 5

Amanda THOMPSON – See Lesley GARRETT and Amanda THOMPSON

Carroll THOMPSON – See MOVEMENT 98 featuring Carroll THOMPSON; Courtney PINE

Chris THOMPSON *UK, male vocalist* — 5 wks

27 Oct 79	IF YOU REMEMBER ME *Planet K 12389*	42 5

Gina THOMPSON – See MC Lyte

Sue THOMPSON *US, female vocalist* — 9 wks

2 Nov 61	SAD MOVIES *Polydor NH 66967*	46 1
16 Nov 61	SAD MOVIES (re-entry) *Polydor NH 66967*	48 1
21 Jan 65	PAPER TIGER *Hickory 1284*	50 1
11 Feb 65	PAPER TIGER (re-entry) *Hickory 1284*	30 6

UK No 1 ★   UK Top 10 ●   UK million seller ◆   UK entry at No 1 ■   US No 1 ▲

THOMPSON TWINS ◐ *British-based synth-rock trio: Tom Bailey (v/syn), New Zealand-born Alannah Currie (v/prc/s), Joe Leeway (prc). Named after characters in a Tin Tin cartoon, they were joined on stage at Live Aid by Madonna and were at the fore of second so-called 'British Invasion'* **110 wks**

6 Nov 82		LIES *Arista ARIST 486*	67	3
29 Jan 83	●	LOVE ON YOUR SIDE *Arista ARIST 504*	9	12
16 Apr 83	●	WE ARE DETECTIVE *Arista ARIST 526*	7	9
16 Jul 83		WATCHING *Arista TWINS 1*	33	6
19 Nov 83	●	HOLD ME NOW *Arista TWINS 2*	4	15
4 Feb 84	●	DOCTOR DOCTOR *Arista TWINS 3*	3	10
31 Mar 84	●	YOU TAKE ME UP *Arista TWINS 4*	2	9
7 Jul 84		SISTER OF MERCY *Arista TWINS 5*	11	8
8 Sep 84		SISTER OF MERCY (re-entry) *Arista TWINS 5*	66	1
8 Dec 84		LAY YOUR HANDS ON ME *Arista TWINS 6*	13	9
31 Aug 85		DON'T MESS WITH DOCTOR DREAM *Arista TWINS 9*	15	6
19 Oct 85		KING FOR A DAY *Arista TWINS 7*	22	6
7 Dec 85		REVOLUTION *Arista TWINS 10*	56	3
4 Jan 86		REVOLUTION (re-entry) *Arista TWINS 10*	75	1
21 Mar 87		GET THAT LOVE *Arista TWINS 12*	68	2
11 Apr 87		GET THAT LOVE (re-entry) *Arista TWINS 12*	66	1
15 Oct 88		IN THE NAME OF LOVE '88 *Arista 111808*	46	3
28 Sep 91		COME INSIDE *Warner Bros. W 0058*	56	4
25 Jan 92		THE SAINT *Warner Bros. W 0080*	53	2

Tracey THORN – See EVERYTHING BUT THE GIRL; MASSIVE ATTACK

David THORNE *US, male vocalist* **8 wks**

24 Jan 63		ALLEY CAT SONG *Stateside SS 141*	21	8

Ken THORNE ℂ *UK, orchestra* **15 wks**

18 Jul 63	●	THEME FROM THE FILM 'THE LEGION'S LAST PATROL' *HMV POP 1176*	4	15

THOSE 2 GIRLS *UK, female vocal duo* **4 wks**

5 Nov 94		WANNA MAKE YOU GO . . . UUH! *Final Vinyl 74321233782*	74	1
4 Mar 95		ALL I WANT *Final Vinyl 74321254202*	36	3

THOUSAND YARD STARE *UK, male vocal/instrumental group* **5 wks**

26 Oct 91		SEASONSTREAM EP *Stifled Aardvark AARD 5T*	65	1
8 Feb 92		COMEUPPANCE *Stifled Aardvark AARD 007*	37	2
11 Jul 92		SPINDRIFT EP *Stifled Aardvark AARDT 010*	58	1
8 May 93		VERSION OF ME *Polydor AARDC 012*	57	1

Tracks on Seasonstream EP: O-O AET / Village End / Keepsake / Worse for Wear
Tracks on Spindrift EP: Wideshire Two / Hand, Son / Happenstance / Mocca Pune

THRASHING DOVES *UK, male vocal/instrumental group* **3 wks**

24 Jan 87		BEAUTIFUL IMBALANCE *A & M TDOVE 1*	50	3

3 COLOURS RED ☹ *UK, male vocal/instrumental group* **9 wks**

18 Jan 97		NUCLEAR HOLIDAY *Creation CRESCD 250*	22	2
15 Mar 97		SIXTY MILE SMILE *Creation CRESCD 254*	20	3
10 May 97		PURE *Creation CRESCD 265*	28	1
12 Jul 97		COPPER GIRL *Creation CRESCD 270*	30	2
8 Nov 97		THIS IS MY HOLLYWOOD *Creation CRESCD 277*	48	1

THREE DEGREES ♪ *US R&B vocal group, who became top UK stars in the 1970s: Sheila Ferguson, Valerie Holiday, Fayette Pinkney. The trio, tagged by the media as "Prince Charles's favourites", were the first girl group to top the UK chart since The Supremes in 1964* **112 wks**

13 Apr 74		YEAR OF DECISION *Philadelphia Interna PIR 2073*	13	10
27 Apr 74		TSOP (THE SOUND OF PHILADELPHIA) *Philadelphia Interna PIR 2289* [1] ▲	22	9
13 Jul 74	★	WHEN WILL I SEE YOU AGAIN *Philadelphia Interna PIR 2155*	1	16
2 Nov 74		GET YOUR LOVE BACK *Philadelphia Interna PIR 2737*	34	4
12 Apr 75	●	TAKE GOOD CARE OF YOURSELF *Philadelphia Interna PIR 3177*	9	9
5 Jul 75		LONG LOST LOVER *Philadelphia Interna PIR 3352*	40	4

1 May 76		TOAST OF LOVE *Epic EPC 4215*	36	4
7 Oct 78		GIVIN' UP GIVIN' IN *Ariola ARO 130*	12	10
13 Jan 79	●	WOMAN IN LOVE *Ariola ARO 141*	3	11
24 Mar 79	●	THE RUNNER *Ariola ARO 154*	10	10
23 Jun 79		THE GOLDEN LADY *Ariola ARO 170*	56	3
29 Sep 79		JUMP THE GUN *Ariola ARO 183*	48	5
24 Nov 79	●	MY SIMPLE HEART *Ariola ARO 202*	9	11
5 Oct 85		THE HEAVEN I NEED *Supreme SUPE 102*	42	5
26 Dec 98		LAST CHRISTMAS *Wildstar CDWILD 15* [2]	54	1

[1] MFSB featuring the Three Degrees [2] Alien Voices featuring the Three Degrees

THREE DOG NIGHT ♪ *US, male vocal/instrumental group* **23 wks**

8 Aug 70	●	MAMA TOLD ME NOT TO COME *Stateside SS 8052* ▲	3	14
29 May 71		JOY TO THE WORLD *Probe PRO 523* ▲	24	9

THREE DRIVES ON A VINYL *Holland, male DJ/production group* **1 wk**

27 Jun 98		GREECE 2000 *Hooj Choons HOOJCD 63*	44	1

THREE GOOD REASONS *UK, male vocal/instrumental group* **3 wks**

10 Mar 66		NOWHERE MAN *Mercury MF 899*	47	3

THREE KAYES – See KAYE SISTERS

THREE 'N ONE *Germany, male production duo* **1 wk**

7 Jun 97		REFLECT *ffrr FCD 301*	66	1

3T ◐ (R&B) *US, male vocal trio* **40 wks**

27 Jan 96	●	ANYTHING *MJJ 6627152*	2	14
4 May 96		24/7 *MJJ 6631995*	11	7
24 Aug 96	●	WHY *MJJ 6636482* [1]	2	9
11 Jan 97		I NEED YOU *Epic 6639912*	20	5
5 Apr 97	●	GOTTA BE YOU *Epic 6643645*	10	5

[1] 3T featuring Michael Jackson

THREE TONS OF JOY – See Johnny OTIS SHOW

THROWING MUSES *US, male/female vocal/instrumental group* **6 wks**

9 Feb 91		COUNTING BACKWARDS *4AD AD 1001*	70	2
1 Aug 92		FIREPILE EP *4AD BAD 2012*	46	1
24 Dec 94		BRIGHT YELLOW GUN *4AD BAD 4018CD*	51	2
10 Aug 96		SHARK *4AD BAD 6016CD*	53	1

Tracks on Firepile (EP): Firepile / Manic Depression / Snailhead / City of the Dead

THS – THE HORN SECTION
US, male/female vocal/instrumental group **3 wks**

18 Aug 84		LADY SHINE (SHINE ON) *Fourth & Broadway BRW 10*	54	3

Harry THUMANN *Germany, male instrumentalist – keyboards* **6 wks**

21 Feb 81		UNDERWATER *Decca F 13901*	41	6

THUNDER ♪ *UK/US, male vocal/instrumental group* **51 wks**

17 Feb 90		DIRTY LOVE *EMI EM 126*	32	4
12 May 90		BACKSTREET SYMPHONY *EMI EM 137*	25	4
14 Jul 90		GIMME SOME LOVIN' *EMI EM 148*	36	3
29 Sep 90		SHE'S SO FINE *EMI EM 158*	34	3
23 Feb 91		LOVE WALKED IN *EMI EM 175*	21	4
15 Aug 92		LOW LIFE IN HIGH PLACES *EMI EM 242*	22	5
10 Oct 92		EVERYBODY WANTS HER *EMI EM 249*	36	4
13 Feb 93		A BETTER MAN *EMI CDBETTER 1*	18	4
19 Jun 93		LIKE A SATELLITE EP *EMI CDEM 272*	28	2
7 Jan 95		STAND UP *EMI CDEM 365*	23	4
25 Feb 95		RIVER OF PAIN *EMI CDEM 367*	31	2
6 May 95		CASTLES IN THE SAND *EMI CDEM 372*	30	3
23 Sep 95		IN A BROKEN DREAM *EMI CDEM 384*	26	2
25 Jan 97		DON'T WAIT UP *Raw Power RAWX 1020*	27	2
5 Apr 97		LOVE WORTH DYING FOR *Raw Power RAWX 1043*	60	1
7 Feb 98		THE ONLY ONE *Eagle EAGXA 016*	31	2

27 Jun 98	PLAY THAT FUNKY MUSIC *Eagle EAGXS 030*	39	2

Tracks on Like a Satellite (EP): *Like a Satellite / The Damage Is Done / Like a Satellite (Live) / Gimme Shelter*
See also VARIOUS ARTISTS (EPs & LPs) – Gimme Shelter (EP)

THUNDERBIRDS – See Chris FARLOWE

THUNDERCLAP NEWMAN ☉
UK, male vocal/instrumental group   **13 wks**

11 Jun 69	★ SOMETHING IN THE AIR *Track 604-031*	1	12
27 Jun 70	ACCIDENTS *Track 2094 001*	46	1

THUNDERTHIGHS *UK, female vocal group*   **5 wks**

22 Jun 74	CENTRAL PARK ARREST *Philips 6006 386*	30	5

Bobby THURSTON ◢ 🎤 *US, male vocalist*   **10 wks**

29 Mar 80	● CHECK OUT THE GROOVE *Epic EPC 8348*	10	10

TIFFANY ☉ *US, female vocalist*   **45 wks**

16 Jan 88	★ I THINK WE'RE ALONE NOW *MCA MCA 1211* ▲	1	13
19 Mar 88	● COULD'VE BEEN *MCA TIFF 2* ▲	4	9
4 Jun 88	● I SAW HIM STANDING THERE *MCA TIFF 3*	8	7
6 Aug 88	FEELINGS OF FOREVER *MCA TIFF 4*	52	2
12 Nov 88	RADIO ROMANCE *MCA TIFF 5*	13	11
11 Feb 89	ALL THIS TIME *MCA TIFF 6*	47	3

TIGER *UK/Ireland, male/female vocal/instrumental group*   **3 wks**

16 Nov 96	MY PUPPET PAL *Trade 2 TRDCD 005*	62	1
22 Feb 97	ON THE ROSE *Trade 2 TRDCD 008*	57	1
22 Aug 98	FRIENDS *Trade 2 TRDCD 013*	72	1

TIGERTAILZ *US, male vocal/instrumental group*   **2 wks**

24 Jun 89	LOVE BOMB BABY *Music For Nations KUT 132*	75	1
16 Feb 91	HEAVEN *Music For Nations KUT 137*	71	1

TIGHT FIT ☉ *UK, male/female vocal group*   **49 wks**

18 Jul 81	● BACK TO THE SIXTIES *Jive JIVE 002*	4	11
26 Sep 81	BACK TO THE SIXTIES PART 2 *Jive JIVE 005*	33	5
23 Jan 82	★ THE LION SLEEPS TONIGHT *Jive JIVE 9*	1	15
1 May 82	● FANTASY ISLAND *Jive JIVE 13*	5	12
31 Jul 82	SECRET HEART *Jive JIVE 20*	41	6

TIJUANA BRASS – See Herb ALPERT

TIK and TOK *UK, male vocal duo*   **2 wks**

8 Oct 83	COOL RUNNING *Survival SUR 016*	69	2

Tanita TIKARAM ☉ *UK, female vocalist*   **31 wks**

30 Jul 88	● GOOD TRADITION *WEA YZ 196*	10	10
22 Oct 88	TWIST IN MY SOBRIETY *WEA YZ 321*	22	8
14 Jan 89	CATHEDRAL SONG *WEA YZ 331*	48	3
18 Mar 89	WORLD OUTSIDE YOUR WINDOW *WEA YZ 363*	58	2
13 Jan 90	WE ALMOST GOT IT TOGETHER *WEA YZ 443*	52	3
9 Feb 91	ONLY THE ONES WE LOVE *East West YZ 558*	69	1
4 Feb 95	I MIGHT BE CRYING *East West YZ 879CD*	64	2
6 Jun 98	STOP LISTENING *Mother MUMCD 102*	67	1
29 Aug 98	I DON'T WANNA LOSE AT LOVE *Mother MUMCD 105*	73	1

Johnny TILLOTSON ☉ *US, male vocalist*   **50 wks**

1 Dec 60	★ POETRY IN MOTION *London HLA 9231*	1	15
2 Feb 61	JIMMY'S GIRL *London HLA 9275*	50	1
16 Feb 61	JIMMY'S GIRL (re-entry) *London HLA 9275*	43	1
12 Jul 62	IT KEEPS RIGHT ON A HURTIN' *London HLA 9550*	31	10
4 Oct 62	SEND ME THE PILLOW YOU DREAM ON *London HLA 9598*	21	10
27 Dec 62	I CAN'T HELP IT *London HLA 9642*	42	1
10 Jan 63	I CAN'T HELP IT (re-entry) *London HLA 9642*	47	1
24 Jan 63	I CAN'T HELP IT (2nd re-entry) *London HLA 9642*	41	4

9 May 63	OUT OF MY MIND *London HLA 9695*	34	5
14 Apr 79	POETRY IN MOTION (re-issue) *Lightning LIG 9016*	67	2

TILT *UK, male instrumental/production group*   **4 wks**

2 Dec 95	I DREAM *Perfecto PERF 112CD*	69	1
10 May 97	MY SPIRIT *Perfecto PERF 139CD*	61	1
13 Sep 97	PLACES *Perfecto PERF 149CD*	64	1
7 Feb 98	BUTTERFLY *Perfecto PERF 154CD1* 1	41	1

1 Tilt featuring Zee

TIMBUK 3 *US, male/female vocal/instrumental duo*   **7 wks**

31 Jan 87	THE FUTURE'S SO BRIGHT I GOTTA WEAR SHADES *IRS IRM 126* ∷	21	7

TIME FREQUENCY ☺ *UK, male instrumental/production group*   **33 wks**

6 Jun 92	REAL LOVE *Jive JIVET 307*	60	1
9 Jan 93	NEW EMOTION *Internal Affairs KGBCD 009*	36	6
12 Jun 93	THE ULTIMATE HIGH / THE POWER ZONE *Internal Affairs KGBD 010*	17	11
6 Nov 93	● REAL LOVE (re-mix) *Internal Affairs KGBCD 011*	8	6
1 Jan 94	REAL LOVE (re-entry of re-mix) *Internal Affairs KGBCD 011*	71	1
28 May 94	SUCH A PHANTASY *Internal Affairs KGBD 013*	25	4
8 Oct 94	DREAMSCAPE '94 *Internal Affairs KGBD 015*	32	3

TIME OF THE MUMPH *UK, male producer – Mark Mumford*   **1 wk**

11 Feb 95	CONTROL *Fresh FRSHD 24*	69	1

TIME UK *UK, male vocal/instrumental group*   **3 wks**

8 Oct 83	THE CABARET *Red Bus/Aroadia TIM 123*	63	3

TIME ZONE *UK/US, male instrumental duo*   **9 wks**

19 Jan 85	WORLD DESTRUCTION *Virgin VS 743*	44	9

TIMEBOX *UK, male vocal/instrumental group*   **4 wks**

24 Jul 68	BEGGIN' *Deram DM 194*	38	4

TIMELORDS ☺ ☉ *UK, male vocal/instrumental group*   **9 wks**

4 Jun 88	★ DOCTORIN' THE TARDIS *KLF Communications KLF 003*	1	9

See also KLF

TIMEX SOCIAL CLUB R&B ◢
US, male vocal/instrumental group   **9 wks**

13 Sep 86	RUMORS *Cooltempo COOL 133*	13	9

TIN MACHINE *US/UK, male vocal/instrumental group*   **10 wks**

1 Jul 89	UNDER THE GOD *EMI-USA MT 68*	51	2
9 Sep 89	TIN MACHINE/MAGGIE'S FARM (LIVE) *EMI-USA MT 73*	48	2
24 Aug 91	YOU BELONG IN ROCK 'N' ROLL *London LON 305*	33	3
2 Nov 91	BABY UNIVERSAL *London LON 310*	48	3

TIN TIN OUT ☺ ☉ *UK, male instrumental/production duo*   **27 wks**

13 Aug 94	THE FEELING *Deep Distraxion OILYCD 029* 1	32	2
25 Mar 95	ALWAYS SOMETHING THERE TO REMIND ME *WEA YZ 911CD* 2	14	5
8 Feb 97	ALL I WANNA DO *VC VCRD 15*	31	1
10 May 97	DANCE WITH ME *VC VCRD 17* 3	35	2
20 Sep 97	STRINGS FOR YASMIN *VC VCRD 20*	31	3
28 Mar 98	● HERE'S WHERE THE STORY ENDS *VC Recordings VCRD 30* 4	7	10
12 Sep 98	SOMETIMES *VC Recordings VCRD 34* 4	20	4

1 Tin Tin Out featuring Sweet Tee   2 Tin Tin Out featuring Espiritu
3 Tin Tin Out featuring Tony Hadley   4 Tin Tin Out featuring Shelley Nelson

TINA – See Tina TURNER

UK No 1 ★   UK Top 10 ●   UK million seller ◆   UK entry at No 1 ■   US No 1 ▲

TINDERSTICKS UK, male vocal/instrumental group — 5 wks

5 Feb 94	KATHLEEN EP This Way Up WAY 2833CD	61	1
18 Mar 95	NO MORE AFFAIRS This Way Up WAY 3833	58	1
12 Aug 95	TRAVELLING LIGHT This Way Up WAY 4533	51	1
7 Jun 97	BATHTIME This Way Up WAY 6166	38	1
1 Nov 97	RENTED ROOMS This Way Up WAY 6566	56	1

Tracks on Kathleen (EP): Kathleen / Summat Moon / A Sweet Man / E-Type Joe

TINGO TANGO UK, male instrumental group — 2 wks

| 21 Jul 90 | IT IS JAZZ Champion CHAMP 250 | 68 | 2 |

TINMAN ☺ UK, male producer – Paul Dakeyne — 9 wks

| 20 Aug 94 ● | EIGHTEEN STRINGS ffrr FCD 242 | 9 | 8 |
| 3 Jun 95 | GUDVIBE ffrr FCD 262 | 49 | 1 |

TINY TIM US, male vocalist — 1 wk

| 5 Feb 69 | GREAT BALLS OF FIRE Reprise RS 20802 | 45 | 1 |

TITANIC ● Norway/UK, male instrumental group — 12 wks

| 25 Sep 71 ● | SULTANA CBS 5365 | 5 | 12 |

TITIYO Sweden, female vocalist — 6 wks

3 Mar 90	AFTER THE RAIN Arista 112722	60	3
6 Oct 90	FLOWERS Arista 113212	71	1
5 Feb 94	TELL ME I'M NOT DREAMING Arista 74321185622	45	2

Cara TIVEY – See Billy BRAGG

TJR UK, male instrumental / production group — 1 wk

| 27 Sep 97 | JUST GETS BETTER Multiply CDMULTY 25 | 28 | 2 |

[1] TJR featuring Xavier

TLC (R&B) US, female vocal group — 44 wks

20 Jun 92	AIN'T 2 PROUD 2 BEG Arista 115265	13	5
22 Aug 92	BABY-BABY-BABY LaFace 74321111297	55	3
24 Oct 92	WHAT ABOUT YOUR FRIENDS LaFace 74321118177	59	2
21 Jan 95	CREEP LaFace 74321254212 ▲	22	4
22 Apr 95	RED LIGHT SPECIAL LaFace 74321273662	18	4
5 Aug 95 ●	WATERFALLS LaFace 74321298812 ▲	4	14
4 Nov 95	DIGGIN' ON YOU LaFace 74321319252	18	5
13 Jan 96 ●	CREEP (re-issue) LaFace 74321340942	6	7

See also T-BOZ

T99 ☺ Belgium, male instrumental/production group — 10 wks

| 11 May 91 | ANASTHASIA XL XLS 19 | 14 | 6 |
| 19 Oct 91 | NOCTURNE Emphasis 6574097 | 33 | 4 |

TOADS – See Stan FREBERG

Art and Dotty TODD ℂ US, male/female vocal duo — 7 wks

| 13 Feb 53 ● | BROKEN WINGS HMV B 10399 | 6 | 7 |

TOGETHER ☺ UK, male vocal/instrumental group — 8 wks

| 4 Aug 90 | HARDCORE UPROAR ffrr F 143 | 12 | 8 |

TOKENS ● US, male vocal group — 12 wks

| 21 Dec 61 | THE LION SLEEPS TONIGHT (WIMOWEH) RCA 1263 ▲ | 11 | 12 |

TOKYO GHETTO PUSSY
Germany, male instrumental/production duo — 4 wks

| 16 Sep 95 | EVERYBODY ON THE FLOOR (PUMP IT) Epic 6611132 | 26 | 2 |
| 16 Mar 96 | I KISS YOUR LIPS Epic 6623212 | 55 | 2 |

Duo are also known as Jam and Spoon
See also JAM AND SPOON featuring PLAVKA; STORM

TOL and TOL Holland, male vocal/instrumental duo — 2 wks

| 14 Apr 90 | ELENI Dover ROJ 5 | 73 | 2 |

TOM TOM CLUB ☺ ●
US, female/male vocal/instrumental group — 20 wks

20 Jun 81 ●	WORDY RAPPINGHOOD Island WIP 6694	7	9
10 Oct 81	GENIUS OF LOVE Island WIP 6735	65	2
7 Aug 82	UNDER THE BOARDWALK Island WIP 6762	22	9

Satoshi TOMIIE – See Frankie KNUCKLES

TOMSKI UK, male producer – Tom Jankiewicz — 1 wk

| 18 Apr 98 | 14 HOURS TO SAVE THE EARTH Xtravaganza 0091515 EXT | 42 | 1 |

TONGUE 'N' CHEEK ☺ ✎
UK, male/female vocal/instrumental group — 28 wks

27 Feb 88	NOBODY (CAN LOVE ME) Criminal BUS 6 [1]	59	6
25 Nov 89	ENCORE Syncopate SY 33	41	4
14 Apr 90	TOMORROW Syncopate SY 34	20	7
4 Aug 90	NOBODY Syncopate SY 37	37	5
19 Jan 91	FORGET ME NOTS Syncopate SY 39	26	6

[1] Tongue In Cheek

TONIGHT ● UK, male vocal/instrumental group — 10 wks

| 28 Jan 78 | DRUMMER MAN Target TDS 1 | 14 | 8 |
| 20 May 78 | MONEY THAT'S YOUR PROBLEM Target TDS 2 | 66 | 2 |

TONY TONI TONE US, male vocal group — 12 wks

30 Jun 90	OAKLAND STROKE Wing WING 7	50	5
9 Mar 91	IT NEVER RAINS (IN SOUTHERN CALIFORNIA) Wing WING 10	69	2
4 Sep 93	IF I HAD NO LOOT Polydor PZCD 292	44	3
3 May 97	LET'S GET DOWN Mercury MERCD 485	33	2

TOO TOUGH TEE – See DYNAMIX II featuring TOO TOUGH TEE

TOP UK, male vocal/instrumental group — 2 wks

| 20 Jul 91 | NUMBER ONE DOMINATOR Island IS 496 | 67 | 2 |

TOP LINERS – See Rocky SHARPE and the REPLAYS

TOPOL ℂ Israel, male vocalist — 20 wks

| 20 Apr 67 ● | IF I WERE A RICH MAN CBS 202651 | 9 | 20 |

Mel TORME ℂ US, male vocalist — 32 wks

27 Apr 56	MOUNTAIN GREENERY Vogue/Coral Q 72150	15	11
27 Jul 56 ●	MOUNTAIN GREENERY (re-entry) Vogue/Coral Q 72150	4	13
3 Jan 63	COMING HOME BABY London HLK 9643	13	8

TORNADOS ● UK, male instrumental group — 59 wks

30 Aug 62 ★	TELSTAR Decca F 11494 ▲	1	25
10 Jan 63	GLOBETROTTER Decca F 11562	5	11
21 Mar 63	ROBOT Decca F 11606	17	12
6 Jun 63	THE ICE CREAM MAN Decca F 11662	18	9
10 Oct 63	DRAGONFLY Decca F 11745	41	2

Mitchell TOROK ● US, male vocalist — 19 wks

28 Sep 56 ●	WHEN MEXICO GAVE UP THE RUMBA Brunswick 05586	6	17
11 Jan 57	RED LIGHT GREEN LIGHT Brunswick 05626	29	1
1 Feb 57	WHEN MEXICO GAVE UP THE RUMBA (re-entry) Brunswick 05586	30	1

Peter TOSH Jamaica, male vocalist — 12 wks

| 21 Oct 78 | (YOU GOTTA WALK) DON'T LOOK BACK Rolling Stones 2859 | 43 | 7 |
| 2 Apr 83 | JOHNNY B. GOODE EMI RIC 115 | 48 | 5 |

TOTAL [R&B] US, female vocal group — 10 wks

15 Jul 95	CAN'T YOU SEE Tommy Boy TBCD 700 [1]	43	2
14 Sep 96	KISSIN' YOU Arista 7432140 4172	29	2
15 Feb 97	DO YOU THINK ABOUT US Puff Daddy 74321458492	49	1
18 Apr 98	WHAT YOU WANT Puff Daddy 74321578772 [2]	15	5

[1] Total featuring Notorious BIG [2] Mase featuring Total

TOTAL CONTRAST ☺ 🎸 UK, male vocal/instrumental duo — 22 wks

3 Aug 85	TAKES A LITTLE TIME London LON 71	17	10
19 Oct 85	HIT AND RUN London LON 76	41	5
1 Mar 86	THE RIVER London LON 83	44	3
10 May 86	WHAT YOU GONNA DO ABOUT IT London LON 95	63	4

TOTO 🎸 US, male vocal/instrumental group — 35 wks

10 Feb 79	HOLD THE LINE CBS 6784	14	11
5 Feb 83 ●	AFRICA CBS A 2510 ▲	3	10
9 Apr 83	ROSANNA CBS A 2079	12	8
18 Jun 83	I WON'T HOLD YOU BACK CBS A 3392	37	5
18 Nov 95	I WILL REMEMBER Columbia 6626552	64	1

TOTO COELO 🌐 UK, female vocal group — 14 wks

7 Aug 82 ●	I EAT CANNIBALS PART 1 Radialchoice TIC 10	8	10
13 Nov 82	DRACULA'S TANGO/MUCHO MACHO Radialchoice TIC 11	54	4

TOTTENHAM HOTSPUR F.A. CUP FINAL SQUAD 🌐
UK, male football team vocalists — 23 wks

9 May 81 ●	OSSIE'S DREAM (SPURS ARE ON THEIR WAY TO WEMBLEY) Shelf SHELF 1	5	8
1 May 82	TOTTENHAM TOTTENHAM Shelf SHELF 2	19	7
9 May 87	HOT SHOT TOTTENHAM! Rainbow RBR 16	18	5
11 May 91	WHEN THE YEAR ENDS IN 1 A1 A 1324	44	3

All hits feature the vocal and instrumental talents of Chas and Dave

TOUCH AND GO ☺ 🌐 UK, male/female vocal/production group — 8 wks

7 Nov 98 ●	WOULD YOU...? Oval VVR 5003083	3†	8

TOUCH OF SOUL UK, male/female vocal/instrumental group — 3 wks

19 May 90	WE GOT THE LOVE Cooltempo COOL 204	46	3

TOUR DE FORCE UK, male production trio — 1 wk

16 May 98	CATALAN East West EW 161CD	71	1

TOURISTS 🌐 🎸 UK, male/female vocal/instrumental group — 40 wks

9 Jun 79	BLIND AMONG THE FLOWERS Logo GO 350	52	5
8 Sep 79	THE LONELIEST MAN IN THE WORLD Logo GO 360	32	7
10 Nov 79 ●	I ONLY WANT TO BE WITH YOU Logo GO 370	4	14
9 Feb 80 ●	SO GOOD TO BE BACK HOME AGAIN Logo TOUR 1	8	9
18 Oct 80	DON'T SAY I TOLD YOU SO RCA TOUR 2	40	5

Carol Lynn TOWNES US, female vocalist — 7 wks

4 Aug 84	99 1/2 Polydor POSP 693	47	4
19 Jan 85	BELIEVE IN THE BEAT Polydor POSP 720	56	3

Fuzz TOWNSHEND UK, male producer — 1 wk

6 Sep 97	HELLO DARLIN Echo ECSCD 46	51	1

Pete TOWNSHEND UK, male vocalist — 17 wks

5 Apr 80	ROUGH BOYS Atco K 11460	39	6
21 Jun 80	LET MY LOVE OPEN YOUR DOOR Atco K 11486	46	6
21 Aug 82	UNIFORMS (CORPS D'ESPRIT) Atco K 11751	48	5

TOXIC TWO ☺ US, male instrumental/production duo — 6 wks

7 Mar 92	RAVE GENERATOR PWL International PWL 223	13	6

TOY DOLLS 🌐 ✐ UK, male vocal/instrumental group — 12 wks

1 Dec 84 ●	NELLIE THE ELEPHANT Volume VOL 11	4	12

TOYAH 🌐 ✐ UK, female vocalist — 87 wks

14 Feb 81 ●	FOUR FROM TOYAH EP Safari TOY 1	4	14
16 May 81 ●	I WANT TO BE FREE Safari SAFE 34	8	11
3 Oct 81 ●	THUNDER IN THE MOUNTAINS Safari SAFE 38	4	9
28 Nov 81	FOUR MORE FROM TOYAH EP Safari TOY 2	14	9
22 May 82	BRAVE NEW WORLD Safari SAFE 45	21	8
17 Jul 82	IEYA Safari SAFE 28	48	5
9 Oct 82	BE LOUD BE PROUD (BE HEARD) Safari SAFE 52	30	7
24 Sep 83	REBEL RUN Safari SAFE 56	24	5
19 Nov 83	THE VOW Safari SAFE 58	50	5
27 Apr 85	DON'T FALL IN LOVE (I SAID) Portrait A 6160	22	6
29 Jun 85	SOUL PASSING THROUGH SOUL Portrait A 6359	57	3
25 Apr 87	ECHO BEACH EG EGO 31	54	5

Tracks on Four From Toyah EP: It's a Mystery/Revelations/War Boys/Angels and Demons. Tracks on Four More From Toyah EP: Good Morning Universe/Urban Tribesman/In the Fairground/The Furious Futures

TOYS ✐ 🌐 US, female vocal group — 17 wks

4 Nov 65 ●	A LOVER'S CONCERTO Stateside SS 460	5	13
27 Jan 66	ATTACK Stateside SS 483	36	4

T'PAU 🌐 🎸 UK, male/female vocal/instrumental group — 77 wks

8 Aug 87 ●	HEART AND SOUL Siren SRN 41	4	13
24 Oct 87 ★	CHINA IN YOUR HAND Siren SRN 64	1	15
30 Jan 88 ●	VALENTINE Siren SRN 69	9	8
2 Apr 88	SEX TALK (LIVE) Siren SRN 80	23	7
25 Jun 88	I WILL BE WITH YOU Siren SRN 87	14	6
1 Oct 88	SECRET GARDEN Siren SRN 93	18	7
3 Dec 88	ROAD TO OUR DREAM Siren SRN 100	42	6
25 Mar 89	ONLY THE LONELY Siren SRN 107	28	6
18 May 91	WHENEVER YOU NEED ME Siren SRN 140	16	6
27 Jul 91	WALK ON AIR Siren SRN 142	62	2
20 Feb 93	VALENTINE (re-issue) Virgin VALEG 1	53	1

TRACIE 🌐 UK, female vocalist — 24 wks

26 Mar 83 ●	THE HOUSE THAT JACK BUILT Respond KOB 701	9	8
16 Jul 83	GIVE IT SOME EMOTION Respond KOB 704	24	9
14 Apr 84	SOUL'S ON FIRE Respond KOB 708	73	2
9 Jun 84	(I LOVE YOU) WHEN YOU SLEEP Respond KOB 710	59	3
17 Aug 85	I CAN'T LEAVE YOU ALONE Respond SBS 1 [1]	60	2

[1] Tracie Young

TRACY – See MASSIVO featuring TRACY

Jeanie TRACY US, female vocalist — 3 wks

11 Jun 94	IF THIS IS LOVE Pulse 8 CDLOSE 63	73	1
5 Nov 94	DO YOU BELIEVE IN THE WONDER Pulse 8 CDLOSE 74	57	1
13 May 95	IT'S A MAN'S MAN'S MAN'S WORLD Pulse 8 CDLOSE 89 [1]	73	1

[1] Jeanie Tracy and Bobby Womack

TRAFFIC 🎸 UK, male vocal/instrumental group — 40 wks

1 Jun 67 ●	PAPER SUN Island WIP 6002	5	10
6 Sep 67 ●	HOLE IN MY SHOE Island WIP 6017	2	14
29 Nov 67 ●	HERE WE GO ROUND THE MULBERRY BUSH Island WIP 6025	8	12
6 Mar 68	NO FACE, NO NAME, NO NUMBER Island WIP 6030	40	4

TRAMAINE US, female vocalist — 2 wks

5 Oct 85	FALL DOWN (SPIRIT OF LOVE) A & M AM 281	60	2

TRAMMPS ✐ ☺ US, male vocal group — 55 wks

23 Nov 74	ZING WENT THE STRINGS OF MY HEART Buddah BDS 405	29	10
1 Feb 75	SIXTY MINUTE MAN Buddah BDS 415	40	4
11 Oct 75 ●	HOLD BACK THE NIGHT Buddah BDS 437	5	8

UK No 1 ★   UK Top 10 ●   UK million seller ◆   UK entry at No 1 ■   US No 1 ▲

13 Mar 76	THAT'S WHERE THE HAPPY PEOPLE GO *Atlantic K 10703* 35	8
24 Jul 76	SOUL SEARCHIN' TIME *Atlantic K 10797* 42	3
14 May 77	DISCO INFERNO *Atlantic K 10914* 16	7
24 Jun 78	DISCO INFERNO (re-issue) *Atlantic K 11135* 47	10
12 Dec 92	HOLD BACK THE NIGHT *Network NWK 65* [1] 30	5

[1] KWS featuring guest vocals from the Trammps

TRANSA *UK, male DJ / production duo* — 2 wks

30 Aug 97	PROPHASE *Perfecto PERF 147CD* 65	1
21 Feb 98	ENERVATE *Perfecto PERF 155CD* 42	1

TRANSATLANTIC SOUL *UK, male producer – Roger Sanchez* — 1 wk

22 Mar 97	RELEASE YO SELF *Deconstruction 74321459102* 43	1

TRANSFORMER 2
Belgium/Holland, male/female vocal/instrumental group — 1 wk

24 Feb 96	JUST CAN'T GET ENOUGH *Positiva CDTIV 49* 45	1

TRANSISTER *UK / US, male / female vocal/instrumental group* — 1 wk

28 Mar 98	LOOK WHO'S PERFECT NOW *Virgin VSCDT 1678* 56	1

TRANSVISION VAMP
UK, female/male vocal/instrumantal group — 59 wks

16 Apr 88	TELL THAT GIRL TO SHUT UP *MCA TVV 2* 45	3
25 Jun 88	I WANT YOUR LOVE *MCA TVV 3* 5	13
17 Sep 88	REVOLUTION BABY *MCA TVV 4* 30	5
19 Nov 88	SISTER MOON *MCA TVV 5* 41	5
1 Apr 89	BABY I DON'T CARE *MCA TVV 6* 3	11
10 Jun 89	THE ONLY ONE *MCA TVV 7* 15	6
5 Aug 89	LANDSLIDE OF LOVE *MCA TVV 8* 14	5
4 Nov 89	BORN TO BE SOLD *MCA TVV 9* 22	4
13 Apr 91	(I JUST WANNA) B WITH U *MCA TVV 10* 30	4
22 Jun 91	IF LOOKS COULD KILL *MCA TVV 11* 41	3

TRANS-X *Canada, female/male vocal/instrumental group* — 9 wks

13 Jul 85	LIVING ON VIDEO *Boiling Point POSP 650* 9	9

TRASH *UK, male vocal/instrumental group* — 3 wks

25 Oct 69	GOLDEN SLUMBERS/CARRY THAT WEIGHT *Apple 17* 35	3

TRASH CAN SINATRAS *UK, male vocal/instrumental group* — 1 wk

24 Apr 93	HAYFEVER *Go! Discs GODCD 98* 61	1

TRAVELING WILBURYS *UK/US, male vocal/instrumental group* — 19 wks

29 Oct 88	HANDLE WITH CARE *Wilbury W 7732* 21	13
11 Mar 89	END OF THE LINE *Wilbury W 7637* 52	4
30 Jun 90	NOBODY'S CHILD *Wilbury W 9773* 44	2

TRAVIS *UK, male vocal/instrumental group* — 11 wks

12 Apr 97	U16 GIRLS *Independiente ISOM 1MS* 40	2
28 Jun 97	ALL I WANT TO DO IS ROCK *Independiente ISOM 3MS* 39	2
23 Aug 97	TIED TO THE 90'S *Independiente ISOM 5MS* 30	2
25 Oct 97	HAPPY *Independiente ISOM 6MS* 38	2
11 Apr 98	MORE THAN US EP *Independiente ISOM 11MS* 16	3

Tracks on More Than Us EP: More Than Us / Give Me Some Truth / All I Want to Do
Is Rock / Funny Thing

Randy TRAVIS *US, male vocalist* — 6 wks

21 May 88	FOREVER AND EVER, AMEN *Warner Bros. W 8384* 55	6

John TRAVOLTA *US, male vocalist* — 90 wks

20 May 78	★ YOU'RE THE ONE THAT I WANT *RSO 006* [1] ◆ ▲ 1	26
16 Sep 78	★ SUMMER NIGHTS *RSO 18* [1] ◆ 1	19
7 Oct 78	SANDY *Polydor POSP 6* 2	15
2 Dec 78	GREASED LIGHTNIN' *Polydor POSP 14* 11	9
22 Dec 90	GREASE MEGAMIX *Polydor PO 114* [1] 3	10

23 Mar 91	GREASE – THE DREAM MIX *PWL/Polydor PO 136* [2] 47	2
25 Jul 98	YOU'RE THE ONE THAT I WANT *Polydor 0441332* [1] 4	9

[1] John Travolta and Olivia Newton-John [2] Frankie Valli, John Travolta and Olivia
Newton-John

TREMELOES
*Early-1960s backing band who become late-1960s stars:
Len 'Chip' Hawkes (v/b), Rick West (g), Alan Blakely (g), Dave Munden (d).
After supporting Brian Poole on his many hits, this Essex group went on
to score even more in their own right. Hawkes is the father of 1991
chart-topper Chesney Hawkes* — 131 wks

2 Feb 67	HERE COMES MY BABY *CBS 202519* 4	11
27 Apr 67	★ SILENCE IS GOLDEN *CBS 2723* 1	15
2 Aug 67	EVEN THE BAD TIMES ARE GOOD *CBS 2930* 4	13
8 Nov 67	BE MINE *CBS 3043* 39	2
17 Jan 68	SUDDENLY YOU LOVE ME *CBS 3234* 6	11
8 May 68	HELULE HELULE *CBS 2889* 14	9
18 Sep 68	MY LITTLE LADY *CBS 3680* 6	12
11 Dec 68	I SHALL BE RELEASED *CBS 3873* 29	5
19 Mar 69	HELLO WORLD *CBS 4065* 14	8
1 Nov 69	(CALL ME) NUMBER ONE *CBS 4582* 2	14
21 Mar 70	BY THE WAY *CBS 4815* 35	6
12 Sep 70	ME AND MY LIFE *CBS 5139* 4	18
10 Jul 71	HELLO BUDDY *CBS 7294* 32	7

See also Brian POOLE and the TREMELOES

Jackie TRENT *UK, female vocalist* — 17 wks

22 Apr 65	★ WHERE ARE YOU NOW (MY LOVE) *Pye 7N 15776* 1	11
1 Jul 65	WHEN THE SUMMERTIME IS OVER *Pye 7N 15865* 39	2
2 Apr 69	I'LL BE THERE *Pye 7N 17693* 38	4

Ralph TRESVANT [R&B] *US, male vocalist* — 21 wks

12 Jan 91	SENSITIVITY *MCA MCS 1462* 18	8
15 Aug 92	THE BEST THINGS IN LIFE ARE FREE *Perspective PERSS 7400* [1] 2	13

[1] Luther Vandross and Janet Jackson with special guests BBD and Ralph Tresvant

TRI *UK, male vocal/instrumental group* — 1 wk

2 Sep 95	WE GOT THE LOVE *Epic 6623642* 61	1

TRIBAL HOUSE *US, male vocal/instrumental group* — 2 wks

3 Feb 90	MOTHERLAND-A-FRI-CA *Cooltempo COOL 198* 57	2

Tony TRIBE *Jamaica, male vocalist* — 2 wks

16 Jul 69	RED RED WINE *Downtown DT 419* 50	1
9 Aug 69	RED RED WINE (re-entry) *Downtown DT 419* 46	1

A TRIBE CALLED QUEST *US, male rap group* — 18 wks

18 Aug 90	BONITA APPLEBUM *Jive JIVE 256* 47	3
19 Jan 91	CAN I KICK IT *Jive JIVE 265* 15	7
11 Jun 94	OH MY GOD *Jive JIVECD 355* 68	1
13 Jul 96	1NCE AGAIN *Jive JIVECD 399* 34	2
23 Nov 96	STRESSED OUT *Jive JIVECD 404* [1] 33	2
23 Aug 97	THE JAM EP *Jive JIVECD 427* 61	1
29 Aug 98	FIND A WAY *Jive 0518982* 41	2

[1] Tribe Called Quest featuring Faith Evans and Raphael Saadiq

Tracks on The Jam EP: Jam / Get a Hold / Mardi Gras at Midnight / Same Ol' Thing

TRIBE OF TOFFS *UK, male vocal/instrumental group* — 5 wks

24 Dec 88	JOHN KETTLEY (IS A WEATHERMAN) *Completely Different DAFT 1* 21	5

TRICKBABY *UK, female vocal/instrumental group* — 2 wks

12 Oct 96	INDIE-YARN *Logic 74321423152* 47	2

TRICKSTER *UK, male producer* — 3 wks

4 Apr 98	MOVE ON UP *AM:PM 5825812* 19	3

UK No 1 ★   UK Top 10 ●   UK million seller ◆   UK entry at No 1 ■   US No 1 ▲

TRICKY ☺ *UK, male vocalist/multi-instrumentalist* — 27 wks

5 Feb 94	AFTERMATH *Fourth & Broadway BRCD 288*	69 1
28 Jan 95	OVERCOME *Fourth & Broadway BRCD 304*	34 3
15 Apr 95	BLACK STEEL *Fourth & Broadway BRCD 320*	28 3
5 Aug 95	THE HELL EP *Fourth & Broadway BRCD 326* [1]	12 3
11 Nov 95	PUMPKIN *Fourth & Broadway BRCD 330*	26 2
9 Nov 96	CHRISTIANSANDS *Fourth & Broadway BRCD 340*	36 2
23 Nov 96 ●	MILK *Mushroom D 1494* [2]	10 6
11 Jan 97	TRICKY KID *Fourth & Broadway BRCD 341*	28 2
18 Jan 97	MILK (re-entry) *Mushroom D 1494* [2]	74 1
3 May 97	MAKES ME WANNA DIE *Fourth & Broadway BRCD 348*	29 2
30 May 98	MONEY GREEDY/BROKEN HOMES *Island CID 701*	25 2

[1] Tricky vs the Gravediggaz [2] Garbage featuring Tricky
[2] Garbage featuring Tricky

Tracks on The Hell EP: Hell Is Round the Corner / Hell Is Round the Corner (remix) / Psychosis / Tonite Is a Special Nite

TRICKY DISCO ☺ *UK, male/female instrumental/production duo* — 10 wks

28 Jul 90	TRICKY DISCO *Warp WAP 7*	14 8
20 Apr 91	HOUSE FLY *Warp 7WAP 11*	55 2

See also GTO; TECHNOHEAD. All three are the same act

TRIFFIDS *New Zealand, male vocal/instrumental group* — 1 wk

6 Feb 88	A TRICK OF THE LIGHT *Island IS 350*	73 1

TRINIDAD OIL COMPANY
Trinidad, male/female vocal/instrumental group — 5 wks

21 May 77	THE CALENDAR SONG *Harvest HAR 5122*	34 5

TRINITY – See Julie DRISCOLL, Brian AUGER and the TRINITY

TRIO ☻ *Germany, male vocal/instrumental group* — 10 wks

3 Jul 82 ●	DA DA DA *Mobile Suit Corporation CORP 5*	2 10

TRIPPING DAISY *US, male vocal/instrumental group* — 1 wk

30 Mar 96	PIRANHA *Island CID 638*	72 1

TRIUMPH *Canada, male vocal/instrumental group* — 2 wks

22 Nov 80	I LIVE FOR THE WEEKEND *RCA 13*	59 2

TROGGS ☻ *UK, male vocal/instrumental group* — 87 wks

5 May 66 ●	WILD THING *Fontana TF 689* ▲	2 12
14 Jul 66 ★	WITH A GIRL LIKE YOU *Fontana TF 717*	1 12
29 Sep 66 ●	I CAN'T CONTROL MYSELF *Page One POF 001*	2 14
15 Dec 66 ●	ANY WAY THAT YOU WANT ME *Page One POF 010*	8 10
16 Feb 67	GIVE IT TO ME *Page One POF 015*	12 10
1 Jun 67	NIGHT OF THE LONG GRASS *Page One POF 022*	17 6
26 Jul 67	HI HI HAZEL *Page One POF 030*	42 3
18 Oct 67 ●	LOVE IS ALL AROUND *Page One POF 040*	5 14
28 Feb 68	LITTLE GIRL *Page One POF 056*	37 4
30 Oct 93	WILD THING *Weekend CDWEEK 103* [1]	69 2

[1] Troggs and Wolf

'Wild Thing' in 1993 is a re-recording and was listed with the flip side, 'War', by Edwin Starr and Shadow

TRONIKHOUSE *US, male producer – Kevin Saunderson* — 1 wk

14 Mar 92	UP TEMPO *KMS UK KMSUK 1*	68 1

TROUBADOURS DU ROI BAUDOUIN
Zaire, male/female vocal group — 11 wks

19 Mar 69	SANCTUS (MISSA LUBA) *Philips BF 1732*	28 6
7 May 69	SANCTUS (MISSA LUBA) (re-entry) *Philips BF 1732*	37 5

TROUBLE FUNK *US, male vocal/instrumental group* — 3 wks

27 Jun 87	WOMAN OF PRINCIPLE *Fourth & Broadway BRW 70*	65 3

Roger TROUTMAN – See 2PAC

Doris TROY *US, female vocalist* — 12 wks

19 Nov 64	WHATCHA GONNA DO ABOUT IT *Atlantic AT 4011*	37 7
21 Jan 65	WHATCHA GONNA DO ABOUT IT (re-entry) *Atlantic AT 4011*	38 5

Elizabeth TROY – See SOUNDMAN and David LLOYDIE featuring Elizabeth TROY

TRUBBLE *UK, female vocalist* — 1 wk

26 Dec 98	DANCING BABY (OOGA-CHAKA) *Island YYCD 1*	21† 1

TRUCE ®&® *UK, female vocal group* — 6 wks

2 Sep 95	THE FINEST *Big Life BLRD 118*	54 1
30 Mar 96	CELEBRATION OF LIFE *Big Life BLRD 126*	51 1
29 Nov 97	NOTHIN' BUT A PARTY *Big Life BLRD 138*	71 1
5 Sep 98	EYES DON'T LIE *Big Life BLRD 146*	20 3

TRUCKIN' CO. – See Garnet MIMMS and TRUCKIN' CO.

Andrea TRUE CONNECTION ☺
US, female vocalist, male instrumental backing group — 16 wks

17 Apr 76 ●	MORE MORE MORE *Buddah BDS 442*	5 10
4 Mar 78	WHAT'S YOUR NAME WHAT'S YOUR NUMBER *Buddah BDS 467*	34 6

TRUE FAITH with FINAL CUT
US, male/female vocal/instrumental group — 4 wks

2 Mar 91	TAKE ME AWAY *Network NWK 20*	51 4

TRUE IMAGE – See Monie LOVE

Damon TRUEITT – See SOMORE

TRUMAN and WOLFF featuring STEEL HORSES
UK, male production duo, and UK male rap group — 1 wk

22 Aug 98	COME AGAIN *Multiply CDMULTY 38*	57 1

TRUSSEL *US, male vocal/instrumental group* — 4 wks

8 Mar 80	LOVE INJECTION *Elektra K 12412*	43 4

TRUTH *UK, male vocal duo* — 6 wks

3 Feb 66	GIRL *Pye 7N 17035*	27 6

TRUTH *UK, male vocal/instrumental group* — 16 wks

11 Jun 83	CONFUSION (HITS US EVERY TIME) *Formation TRUTH 1*	22 7
27 Aug 83	A STEP IN THE RIGHT DIRECTION *Formation TRUTH 2*	32 7
4 Feb 84	NO STONE UNTURNED *Formation TRUTH 3*	66 2

TSD *UK, female vocal group* — 2 wks

17 Feb 96	HEART AND SOUL *Avex UK AVEXCD 21*	69 1
30 Mar 96	BABY I LOVE YOU *Avex UK AVEXCD 34*	64 1

T2 *US, male production duo* — 1 wk

4 Oct 97	YOU GOT THE LOVE *Champion CHAMPCD 330* [1]	62 1

[1] T2 featuring Robin S

Esera TUAOLO – See Richie RICH

TUBES *US, male vocal/instrumental group* — 18 wks

19 Nov 77	WHITE PUNKS ON DOPE *A & M AMS 7323*	28 4
28 Apr 79	PRIME TIME *A & M AMS 7423*	34 10
12 Sep 81	DON'T WANT TO WAIT ANYMORE *Capitol CL 208*	60 4

TUBEWAY ARMY – See Gary NUMAN

Barbara TUCKER US, female vocalist — 8 wks

Date	Title	Label	Pos	Wks
5 Mar 94	BEAUTIFUL PEOPLE *Positiva CDTIV 11*		23	3
26 Nov 94	I GET LIFTED *Positiva CDTIV 23*		33	2
23 Sep 95	STAY TOGETHER *Positiva CDTIV 39*		46	1
8 Aug 98	EVERYBODY DANCE (THE HORN SONG) *Positiva CDTIV 96*		28	2

Junior TUCKER UK, male vocalist — 2 wks

Date	Title	Label	Pos	Wks
2 Jun 90	DON'T TEST *10 TEN 299*		54	2

Louise TUCKER UK, female vocalist — 5 wks

Date	Title	Label	Pos	Wks
9 Apr 83	MIDNIGHT BLUE *Ariola ARO 289*		59	5

Tommy TUCKER US, male vocalist — 10 wks

Date	Title	Label	Pos	Wks
26 Mar 64	HI-HEEL SNEAKERS *Pye 7N 25238*		23	10

TUFF JAM UK, male production duo — 1 wk

Date	Title	Label	Pos	Wks
10 Oct 98	NEED GOOD LOVE *Locked On LOX 99CD*		44	1

Claramae TURNER – See VARIOUS ARTISTS (EPs & LPs) – Carousel LP

Ike and Tina TURNER ✎
US, male/female vocal instrumental duo — 44 wks

Date	Title	Label	Pos	Wks
9 Jun 66	● RIVER DEEP MOUNTAIN HIGH *London HL 10046*		3	13
28 Jul 66	TELL HER I'M NOT HOME *Warner Bros. WB 5753*		48	1
27 Oct 66	A LOVE LIKE YOURS *London HL 10083*		16	10
12 Feb 69	RIVER DEEP MOUNTAIN HIGH (re-issue) *London HLU 10242*		33	7
8 Sep 73	● NUTBUSH CITY LIMITS *United Artists UP 35582*		4	13

See also Tina TURNER

Ruby TURNER UK, female vocalist — 31 wks

Date	Title	Label	Pos	Wks
25 Jan 86	IF YOU'RE READY (COME GO WITH ME) *Jive JIVE 109* [1]		30	7
29 Mar 86	I'M IN LOVE *Jive JIVE 118*		61	4
13 Sep 86	BYE BABY *Jive JIVE 126*		52	3
14 Mar 87	I'D RATHER GO BLIND *Jive RTS 1*		24	8
16 May 87	I'M IN LOVE (re-issue) *Jive RTS 2*		57	2
13 Jan 90	IT'S GONNA BE ALRIGHT *Jive RTS 7*		57	3
5 Feb 94	STAY WITH ME BABY *M & G MAGCD 53*		39	3
9 Dec 95	SHAKABOOM! *Telstar HUNTCD 1* [2]		64	1

[1] Ruby Turner featuring Jonathan Butler [2] Hunter featuring Ruby Turner

Sammy TURNER US, male vocalist — 2 wks

Date	Title	Label	Pos	Wks
13 Nov 59	ALWAYS *London HLX 8963*		26	2

Tina TURNER ✎
Supreme soul singer-cum-rock legend, b. Anna Mae Bullock, 26 November, 1939, Tennessee. After a successful, if stormy, partnership with husband Ike, she went to greater heights as a soloist. Thus Grammy-winning singer is still one of world's top music stars — 213 wks

Date	Title	Label	Pos	Wks
19 Nov 83	● LET'S STAY TOGETHER *Capitol CL 316*		6	13
25 Feb 84	HELP *Capitol CL 325*		40	6
16 Jun 84	● WHAT'S LOVE GOT TO DO WITH IT *Capitol CL 334* ▲		3	16
15 Sep 84	BETTER BE GOOD TO ME *Capitol CL 338*		45	5
17 Nov 84	PRIVATE DANCER *Capitol CL 343*		26	9
2 Mar 85	I CAN'T STAND THE RAIN *Capitol CL 352*		57	3
20 Jul 85	● WE DON'T NEED ANOTHER HERO (THUNDERDOME) *Capitol CL 364*		3	12
12 Oct 85	ONE OF THE LIVING *Capitol CL 376*		55	2
2 Nov 85	IT'S ONLY LOVE *A & M AM 285* [1]		29	6
23 Aug 86	TYPICAL MALE *Capitol CL 419*		33	6
8 Nov 86	TWO PEOPLE *Capitol CL 430*		43	4
14 Mar 87	WHAT YOU GET IS WHAT YOU SEE *Capitol CL 439*		30	7
13 Jun 87	BREAK EVERY RULE *Capitol CL 452*		43	3
20 Jun 87	TEARING US APART *Duck W 8299* [2]		56	3
19 Mar 88	ADDICTED TO LOVE (LIVE) *Capitol CL 484*		71	2
2 Sep 89	● THE BEST *Capitol CL 543*		5	12
18 Nov 89	● I DON'T WANNA LOSE YOU *Capitol CL 553*		8	11
17 Feb 90	STEAMY WINDOWS *Capitol CL 560*		13	6
11 Aug 90	LOOK ME IN THE HEART *Capitol CL 584*		31	6
13 Oct 90	BE TENDER WITH ME BABY *Capitol CL 593*		28	4
24 Nov 90	● IT TAKES TWO *Warner Bros. ROD 1* [3]		5	8
21 Sep 91	NUTBUSH CITY LIMITS *Capitol CL 630*		23	5
23 Nov 91	WAY OF THE WORLD *Capitol CL 637*		13	7
15 Feb 92	LOVE THING *Capitol CL 644*		29	4
6 Jun 92	I WANT YOU NEAR ME *Capitol CL 659*		22	4
22 May 93	● I DON'T WANNA FIGHT *Parlophone CDRS 6346*		7	9
28 Aug 93	DISCO INFERNO *Parlophone CDR 6357*		12	6
30 Oct 93	WHY MUST WE WAIT UNTIL TONIGHT *Parlophone CDR 6366*		16	4
18 Nov 95	● GOLDENEYE *Parlophone CDR 0071001*		10	9
23 Mar 96	WHATEVER YOU WANT *Parlophone CDR 6429*		23	6
8 Jun 96	ON SILENT WINGS *Parlophone CDR 6434*		13	6
27 Jul 96	MISSING YOU *Parlophone CDR 6441* [4]		12	5
19 Oct 96	SOMETHING BEAUTIFUL REMAINS *Parlophone CDR 6448*		27	2
21 Dec 96	IN YOUR WILDEST DREAMS *Parlophone CDR 6451* [5]		32	2

[1] Bryan Adams and Tina Turner [2] Eric Clapton and Tina Turner [3] Rod Stewart and Tina Turner [4] Tina [5] Tina Turner featuring Barry White

See also Ike and Tina TURNER

TURNTABLE ORCHESTRA US, male vocal/instrumental duo — 4 wks

Date	Title	Label	Pos	Wks
21 Jan 89	YOU'RE GONNA MISS ME *Republic LIC 012*		52	4

TURTLES ☺ ✎ US, male vocal/instrumental group — 39 wks

Date	Title	Label	Pos	Wks
23 Mar 67	HAPPY TOGETHER *London HL 10115* ▲		12	12
15 Jun 67	SHE'D RATHER BE WITH ME *London HLU 10135*		4	15
30 Oct 68	ELENORE *London HL 10223*		7	12

TUXEDOS – See Bobby ANGELO and the TUXEDOS

T.W.A UK, male instrumental/production group — 1 wk

Date	Title	Label	Pos	Wks
16 Sep 95	NASTY GIRLS *Mercury MERCD 441*		51	1

Shania TWAIN ✿ US, female vocalist — 19 wks

Date	Title	Label	Pos	Wks
28 Feb 98	● YOU'RE STILL THE ONE *Mercury 5684932*		10	10
13 Jun 98	WHEN *Mercury 5661192*		18	4
28 Nov 98	● FROM THIS MOMENT ON *Mercury 5665632*		9†	5

TWEETS ☺ UK, male instrumental group — 34 wks

Date	Title	Label	Pos	Wks
12 Sep 81	● THE BIRDIE SONG (BIRDIE DANCE) *PRT 7P 219*		2	23
5 Dec 81	LET'S ALL SING LIKE THE BIRDIES SING *PRT 7P 226*		44	6
18 Dec 82	THE BIRDIE SONG (BIRDIE DANCE) (re-entry) *PRT 7P 219*		46	5

20 FINGERS ☺ US, male instrumental/production duo — 14 wks

Date	Title	Label	Pos	Wks
26 Nov 94	SHORT DICK MAN *Multiply CDMULT 12* [1]		21	4
30 Sep 95	SHORT SHORT MAN (re-mix) *Multiply CXMULTY 7* [1]		11	7
30 Sep 95	LICK IT *Zyx ZYX 75908* [2]		48	3

[1] 20 Fingers featuring Gillette [2] 20 Fingers featuring Roula

TWENTY 4 SEVEN – See CAPTAIN HOLLYWOOD PROJECT

TWICE AS MUCH UK, male vocal duo — 9 wks

Date	Title	Label	Pos	Wks
16 Jun 66	SITTIN' ON A FENCE *Immediate IM 033*		25	9

TWIGGY ☺ UK, female vocalist — 10 wks

Date	Title	Label	Pos	Wks
14 Aug 76	HERE I GO AGAIN *Mercury 6007 100*		17	10

TWIN HYPE US, male rap duo — 2 wks

Date	Title	Label	Pos	Wks
15 Jul 89	DO IT TO THE CROWD *Profile PROF 255*		65	2

TWINKLE ☺ UK, female vocalist — 20 wks

Date	Title	Label	Pos	Wks
26 Nov 64	● TERRY *Decca F 12013*		4	15
25 Feb 65	GOLDEN LIGHTS *Decca F 12076*		21	5

TWISTED SISTER ⚔ US, male vocal/instrumental group — 28 wks

Date	Title	Label	Pos	Wks
26 Mar 83	I AM (I'M ME) *Atlantic A 9854*		18	9

UK No 1 ★ UK Top 10 ● UK million seller ◆ UK entry at No 1 ■ US No 1 ▲

28 May 83	THE KIDS ARE BACK *Atlantic A 9827*	32	6
20 Aug 83	YOU CAN'T STOP ROCK 'N' ROLL *Atlantic A 9792*	43	4
2 Jun 84	WE'RE NOT GONNA TAKE IT *Atlantic A 9657*	58	6
18 Jan 86	LEADER OF THE PACK *Atlantic A 9478*	47	3

Conway TWITTY 🎸 🎤 *US, male vocalist* — 36 wks

14 Nov 58	★ IT'S ONLY MAKE BELIEVE *MGM 992* ▲	1	15
27 Mar 59	STORY OF MY LOVE *MGM 1003*	30	1
21 Aug 59	● MONA LISA *MGM 1029*	5	14
21 Jul 60	IS A BLUE BIRD BLUE *MGM 1082*	43	3
23 Feb 61	C'EST SI BON *MGM 1118*	40	3

2 BAD MICE *UK, male instrumental/production group* — 4 wks

15 Feb 92	HOLD IT DOWN *Moving Shadow SHADOW 14*	70	1
8 Aug 92	HOLD IT DOWN (re-entry) *Moving Shadow SHADOW 14*	48	2
7 Sep 96	BOMBSCARE *Arista 74321397662*	46	1

TWO COWBOYS ● ☺ *Italy, male instrumental/production duo* — 11 wks

| 9 Jul 94 | ● EVERYBODY GONFI-GON *3 Beat TABCD 221* | 7 | 11 |

2 ELVISSA ☺ ● *Germany, vocal duo* — 6 wks

| 4 Oct 97 | ● OH LA LA LA *Club Tools 0063475 CLU* | 13 | 6 |

2 FOR JOY *UK, male instrumental/production duo* — 3 wks

| 1 Dec 90 | IN A STATE *Mercury MER 333* | 61 | 1 |
| 9 Nov 91 | LET THE BASS KICK *All Around The World GLOBE 102* | 67 | 2 |

2 FUNKY 2 starring Katherine DION
UK, male/female vocal/instrumental group — 4 wks

| 6 Nov 93 | BROTHERS AND SISTERS *Logic 74321170772* | 56 | 2 |
| 30 Nov 96 | BROTHERS AND SISTERS (re-mix) *All Around The World CDGLOBE 138* | 36 | 2 |

2 HOUSE *US, male instrumental/production duo* — 1 wk

| 21 Mar 92 | GO TECHNO *Atlantic A 7519* | 65 | 1 |

2 MAD *UK, male vocal/instrumental duo* — 4 wks

| 9 Feb 91 | THINKING ABOUT YOUR BODY *Big Life BLR 37* | 43 | 4 |

TWO MAN SOUND *Belgium, male vocal/instrumental group* — 7 wks

| 20 Jan 79 | QUE TAL AMERICA *Miracle M 1* | 46 | 7 |

TWO MEN, A DRUM MACHINE AND A TRUMPET ☺ ●
UK, male instrumental duo — 17 wks

| 9 Jan 88 | I'M TIRED OF GETTING PUSHED AROUND *London LON 141* | 18 | 8 |
| 25 Jun 88 | HEAT IT UP *Jive JIVE 174* [1] | 21 | 9 |

[1] Wee Papa Girl Rappers featuring Two Men and a Drum Machine

TWO NATIONS *UK, male vocal/instrumental group* — 1 wk

| 20 Jun 87 | THAT'S THE WAY IT FEELS *10 TEN 168* | 74 | 1 |

TWO PEOPLE *UK, male vocal/instrumental group* — 2 wks

| 31 Jan 87 | HEAVEN *Polydor POSP 844* | 63 | 2 |

2 IN A ROOM ☺ ● *US, male vocal duo* — 15 wks

18 Nov 89	SOMEBODY IN THE HOUSE SAY YEAH! *Big Life BLR 12*	66	1
26 Jan 91	● WIGGLE IT *SBK SBK 19*	3	8
6 Apr 91	SHE'S GOT ME GOING CRAZY *SBK SBK 23*	54	2
22 Oct 94	EL TRAGO (THE DRINK) *Positiva CDTIV 18*	34	2
8 Apr 95	AHORA ES (NOW IS THE TIME) *Positiva CDTIV 32*	43	1
17 Aug 96	GIDDY-UP *Encore CDCOR 008*	74	1

2 IN A TENT *UK, male instrumental/production duo* — 7 wks

| 17 Dec 94 | WHEN I'M CLEANING WINDOWS (TURNED OUT NICE AGAIN) *Love This SPONCD 1* | 25 | 5 |

| 13 May 95 | BOOGIE WOOGIE BUGLE BOY (DON'T STOP) *Bald Cat BALDCD 1* [1] | 48 | 1 |
| 6 Jan 96 | WHEN I'M CLEANING WINDOWS (TURNED OUT NICE AGAIN) (re-entry) *Love This SPONCD 1* | 62 | 1 |

[1] 2 In a Tank

First hit features the vocals of George FORMBY
See also George FORMBY

2WO THIRD3 ● ☺ *UK, male vocal/instrumental group* — 15 wks

19 Feb 94	HEAR ME CALLING *Epic 6600642*	48	3
11 Jun 94	EASE THE PRESSURE *Epic 6604782*	45	2
8 Oct 94	I WANT THE WORLD *Epic 6608542*	20	5
17 Dec 94	I WANT TO BE ALONE *Epic 6610852*	29	5

2 UNLIMITED ● ☺ *The brainchild of Jean-Paul de Coster and Phil Wilde, fronted by the minimalist vocals/chants/raps of Dutch duo Ray Slijngaard and Anita Dels. Their youth-aimed, infectious dance tracks sold millions around Europe and gave them 11 successive UK Top 20 hits* — 112 wks

5 Oct 91	● GET READY FOR THIS *PWL Continental PWL 206*	2	15
25 Jan 92	● TWILIGHT ZONE *PWL Continental PWL 211*	2	10
2 May 92	● WORKAHOLIC *PWL Continental PWL 228*	4	7
15 Aug 92	THE MAGIC FRIEND *PWL Continental PWL 240*	11	7
30 Jan 93	★ NO LIMIT *PWL Continental PWCD 256*	1	16
8 May 93	● TRIBAL DANCE *PWL Continental PWCD 262*	4	11
4 Sep 93	● FACES *PWL Continental PWCD 268*	8	7
20 Nov 93	MAXIMUM OVERDRIVE *PWL Continental PWCD 276*	15	8
19 Feb 94	● LET THE BEAT CONTROL YOUR BODY *PWL Continental PWCD 280*	6	9
21 May 94	● THE REAL THING *PWL Continental PWCD 306*	6	7
1 Oct 94	NO ONE *PWL Continental PWCD 314*	17	6
25 Mar 95	HERE I GO *PWL Continental PWCD 317*	22	3
21 Oct 95	DO WHAT'S GOOD FOR ME *PWL Continental PWL 322CD1*	16	4
11 Jul 98	WANNA GET UP *Big Life BLRD 143*	38	2

2K *UK, male production duo* — 2 wks

| 25 Oct 97 | ***K THE MILLENNIUM *Blast First BFFP 146CDK* [1] | 28 | 2 |

[1] This act is the KLF under an assumed name

2PAC 🎤 *US, male rapper* — 38 wks

13 Apr 96	● CALIFORNIA LOVE *Death Row DRWCD 3* [1] ▲	6	8
27 Jul 96	HOW DO YOU WANT IT *Death Row DRWCD 4* [2]	17	4
30 Nov 96	I AIN'T MAD AT CHA *Death Row DRWCD 5* [2]	13	10
26 Apr 97	WANTED DEAD OR ALIVE *Def Jam 5744052* [3]	16	3
10 Jan 98	I WONDER IF HEAVEN GOT A GHETTO *Jive JIVECD 446*	21	4
13 Jun 98	DO FOR LOVE *Jive 0518512*	12	4
18 Jul 98	RUNNIN' *Black Jam BJAM 9005* [4]	15	3
28 Nov 98	HAPPY HOME *Eagle EAGXS 058*	17	2

[1] 2Pac featuring Dr. Dre and Roger Troutman [2] 2Pac featuring KC and Jojo
[3] 2Pac and Snoop Doggy Dogg [4] 2Pac and Notorious B.I.G.

See also MAKAVELI

TYGERS OF PAN TANG *UK, male vocal/instrumental group* — 15 wks

14 Feb 81	HELLBOUND *MCA 672*	48	3
27 Mar 82	LOVE POTION NO. 9 *MCA 769*	45	6
10 Jul 82	RENDEZVOUS *MCA 777*	49	4
11 Sep 82	PARIS BY AIR *MCA 790*	63	2

Bonnie TYLER ● *UK, female vocalist* — 81 wks

30 Oct 76	● LOST IN FRANCE *RCA 2734*	9	10
19 Mar 77	MORE THAN A LOVER *RCA PB 5008*	27	6
3 Dec 77	● IT'S A HEARTACHE *RCA PB 5057*	4	12
30 Jun 79	MARRIED MEN *RCA PB 5164*	35	6
19 Feb 83	★ TOTAL ECLIPSE OF THE HEART *CBS TYLER 1* ▲	1	12
7 May 83	FASTER THAN THE SPEED OF NIGHT *CBS A 3338*	43	4
25 Jun 83	HAVE YOU EVER SEEN THE RAIN *CBS A 3517*	47	3
7 Jan 84	● A ROCKIN' GOOD WAY *Epic A 4071* [1]	5	9
31 Aug 85	● HOLDING OUT FOR A HERO *CBS A 4251*	2	13

UK No 1 ★ UK Top 10 ● UK million seller ◆ UK entry at No 1 ■ US No 1 ▲

14 Dec 85	LOVING YOU'S A DIRTY JOB BUT SOMEBODY'S GOTTA DO IT		
	CBS A 6662 [2]	73	2
28 Dec 91	HOLDING OUT FOR A HERO (re-issue) *Total TYLER 10*	69	2
27 Jan 96	MAKING LOVE (OUT OF NOTHING AT ALL)		
	East West EW 010CD	45	2

[1] Shaky and Bonnie [2] Bonnie Tyler, guest vocalist Todd Rundgren

TYMES 🎵 *US, male vocal group* 41 wks

25 Jul 63	SO MUCH IN LOVE *Cameo Parkway P 871* ▲	21	8
15 Jan 69	PEOPLE *Direction 58 3903*	16	10
21 Sep 74	YOU LITTLE TRUSTMAKER *RCA 2456*	18	9
21 Dec 74	★ MS GRACE *RCA 2493*	1	11
17 Jan 76	GOD'S GONNA PUNISH YOU *RCA 2626*	41	3

TYPICALLY TROPICAL ✪ *UK, male vocal/instrumental duo* 11 wks

5 Jul 75	★ BARBADOS *Gull GULS 14*	1	11

TYREE *US, male producer* 10 wks

25 Feb 89	TURN UP THE BASS *ffrr FFR 24* [1]	12	7
6 May 89	HARDCORE HIP HOUSE *DJ International DJIN 11*	70	2
2 Dec 89	MOVE YOUR BODY *CBS 655470 7* [2]	72	1

[1] Tyree featuring Kool Rock Steady [2] Tyree featuring JMD

TYRREL CORPORATION ☺ 👟
UK, male vocal/instrumental duo 9 wks

14 Mar 92	THE BOTTLE *Volante TYR 1*	71	1
15 Aug 92	GOING HOME *Volante TYR 2*	58	2
10 Oct 92	WAKING WITH A STRANGER/ONE DAY *Volante TYRS 3*	59	1
24 Sep 94	YOU'RE NOT HERE *Cooltempo CDCOOL 292*	42	2
14 Jan 95	BETTER DAYS AHEAD *Cooltempo CDCOOL 303*	29	3

TZANT ☺ *UK, male/female rap/vocal/instrumental duo* 10 wks

7 Sep 96	HOT AND WET (BELIEVE IT) *Logic 74321376832*	36	2
25 Apr 98	SOUNDS OF WICKEDNESS *Logic 74321568842*	11	6
22 Aug 98	BOUNCE WITH THE MASSIVE *Logic 74321602102*	39	2

Judie TZUKE ✪ *UK, female vocalist* 10 wks

14 Jul 79	STAY WITH ME TILL DAWN *Rocket XPRES 17*	16	10

UB40 ✪ 🌿 *Reggae's most successful transatlantic act: includes brothers Ali (v/g) and Robin (v/g) Campbell, and Earl Falconer (b). Only three groups can claim more chart hits than this act, named after the number of the UK unemployment benefit form* 324 wks

8 Mar 80	● KING/FOOD FOR THOUGHT *Graduate GRAD 6*	4	13
14 Jun 80	● MY WAY OF THINKING/I THINK IT'S GOING TO RAIN		
	Graduate GRAD 8	6	10
1 Nov 80	● THE EARTH DIES SCREAMING/DREAM A LIE		
	Graduate GRAD 10	10	12
23 May 81	DON'T LET IT PASS YOU BY/DON'T SLOW DOWN		
	DEP International DEP 1	16	9
8 Aug 81	● ONE IN TEN *DEP International DEP 2*	7	10
13 Feb 82	I WON'T CLOSE MY EYES *DEP International DEP 3*	32	6
15 May 82	LOVE IS ALL IS ALRIGHT *DEP International DEP 4*	29	7

28 Aug 82	SO HERE I AM *DEP International DEP 5*	25	9
5 Feb 83	I'VE GOT MINE *DEP International 7 DEP 6*	45	4
20 Aug 83	★ RED RED WINE *DEP International 7 DEP 7* ▲	1	14
15 Oct 83	● PLEASE DON'T MAKE ME CRY *DEP International 7 DEP 8*	10	8
10 Dec 83	MANY RIVERS TO CROSS *DEP International 7 DEP 9*	16	8
17 Mar 84	CHERRY OH BABY *DEP International DEP 10*	12	8
22 Sep 84	● IF IT HAPPENS AGAIN *DEP International DEP 11*	9	8
1 Dec 84	RIDDLE ME *DEP International DEP 15*	59	2
3 Aug 85	★ I GOT YOU BABE *DEP International DEP 20* [1]	1	13
26 Oct 85	DON'T BREAK MY HEART *DEP International DEP 22*	3	13
12 Jul 86	● SING OUR OWN SONG *DEP International DEP 23*	5	9
27 Sep 86	ALL I WANT TO DO *DEP International DEP 24*	41	4
17 Jan 87	RAT IN MI KITCHEN *DEP International DEP 25*	12	7
9 May 87	WATCHDOGS *DEP International DEP 26*	39	4
10 Oct 87	MAYBE TOMORROW *DEP International DEP 27*	14	8
27 Feb 88	RECKLESS *EMI EM 41* [2]	17	8
18 Jun 88	● BREAKFAST IN BED *DEP International DEP 29* [1]	6	11
20 Aug 88	WHERE DID I GO WRONG *DEP International DEP 30*	26	6
17 Jun 89	I WOULD DO FOR YOU *DEP International DEP 32*	45	4
18 Nov 89	HOMELY GIRL *DEP International DEP 33*	6	10
27 Jan 90	HERE I AM (COME AND TAKE ME) *DEP International DEP 34*	46	3
31 Mar 90	● KINGSTON TOWN *DEP International DEP 35*	4	12
28 Jul 90	WEAR YOU TO THE BALL *DEP International DEP 36*	35	6
3 Nov 90	● I'LL BE YOUR BABY TONIGHT *EMI EM 167* [3]	6	10
1 Dec 90	IMPOSSIBLE LOVE *DEP International DEP 37*	47	2
2 Feb 91	THE WAY YOU DO THE THINGS YOU DO		
	DEP International DEP 38	49	3
12 Dec 92	ONE IN TEN *ZTT ZANG 39* [4]	17	8
22 May 93	★ (I CAN'T HELP) FALLING IN LOVE WITH YOU		
	DEP International DEPDG 40 ▲	1	16
21 Aug 93	● HIGHER GROUND *DEP International DEPD 41*	8	9
11 Dec 93	BRING ME YOUR CUP *DEP International DEPD 42*	24	6
2 Apr 94	C'EST LA VIE *DEP International DEPD 43*	37	3
27 Aug 94	REGGAE MUSIC *DEP International DEPDG 44*	28	2
4 Nov 95	UNTIL MY DYING DAY *DEP International DEPD 45*	15	6
30 Aug 97	TELL ME IT IS TRUE *DEP International DEP 48*	14	4
15 Nov 97	ALWAYS THERE *DEP International DEPD 49*	53	1
10 Oct 98	● COME BACK DARLING *DEP International DEPD 50*	10	6
19 Dec 98	HOLLY HOLY *DEP International DEPD 51*	31†	2

[1] UB40 featuring Chrissie Hynde [2] Afrika Bambaataa with UB40 and Family [3] Robert Palmer and UB40 [4] 808 State vs UB40

UBM *Germany, male / female vocal / instrumental group* 1 wk

23 May 98	LOVIN' YOU *Logic 74321571692*	46	1

UCC – See URBAN COOKIE COLLECTIVE

UFO *UK/Germany, male vocal/instrumental group* 31 wks

5 Aug 78	ONLY YOU CAN ROCK ME *Chrysalis CHS 2241*	50	4
27 Jan 79	DOCTOR DOCTOR *Chrysalis CHS 2287*	35	6
31 Mar 79	SHOOT SHOOT *Chrysalis CHS 2318*	48	5
12 Jan 80	YOUNG BLOOD *Chrysalis CHS 2399*	36	5
17 Jan 81	LONELY HEART *Chrysalis CHS 2482*	41	5
30 Jan 82	LET IT RAIN *Chrysalis CHS 2576*	62	3
19 Mar 83	WHEN IT'S TIME TO ROCK *Chrysalis CHS 2672*	70	3

U4EA featuring BERRI – See NEW ATLANTIC

UGLY KID JOE 🎸 *US, male vocal/instrumental group* 28 wks

16 May 92	● EVERYTHING ABOUT YOU *Mercury MER 367*	3	9
22 Aug 92	NEIGHBOR *Mercury MER 374*	28	4
31 Oct 92	SO DAMN COOL *Mercury MER 383*	44	2
13 Mar 93	● CATS IN THE CRADLE *Mercury MERCD 385*	7	9
19 Jun 93	BUSY BEE *Mercury MERCD 389*	39	2
8 Jul 95	MILKMAN'S SON *Mercury MERCD 435*	39	2

UHF *US, male instrumental/production group* 4 wks

14 Dec 91	UHF/EVERYTHING *XL XLS 25*	46	4

UK *UK, male vocal/instrumental group* 2 wks

30 Jun 79	NOTHING TO LOSE *Polydor POSP 55*	67	2

UK No 1 ★ UK Top 10 ● UK million seller ◆ UK entry at No 1 ■ US No 1 ▲

UK *Canada/Spain, male vocal/instrumental group*   **1 wk**

3 Aug 96	SMALL TOWN BOY *Media MCSTD 400*	74	1

UK APACHI with SHY FX *UK, male vocal/instrumental duo*   **3 wks**

1 Oct 94	ORIGINAL NUTTAH		
	Sound Of Underground SOUR 008CD	39	3

UK MIXMASTERS ☉ *UK, male producer – Nigel Wright*   **15 wks**

2 Feb 91	THE NIGHT FEVER MEGAMIX *IQ ZB 44339* [1]	23	5
27 Jul 91	LUCKY 7 MEGAMIX *IQ ZB 44731*	43	3
14 Dec 91	BARE NECESSITIES MEGAMIX *Connect ZB 35135*	14	7

[1] Mixmasters

UK PLAYERS *UK, male vocal/instrumental group*   **3 wks**

14 May 83	LOVE'S GONNA GET YOU *RCA 326*	52	3

UK SUBS *UK, male vocal/instrumental group*   **39 wks**

23 Jun 79	STRANGLEHOLD *Gem GEMS 5*	26	8
8 Sep 79	TOMORROW'S GIRLS *Gem GEMS 10*	28	6
1 Dec 79	SHE'S NOT THERE/KICKS EP *Gem GEMS 14*	36	7
8 Mar 80	WARHEAD *Gem GEMS 23*	30	4
17 May 80	TEENAGE *Gem GEMS 30*	32	5
25 Oct 80	PARTY IN PARIS *Gem GEMS 42*	37	4
18 Apr 81	KEEP ON RUNNIN' (TILL YOU BURN)		
	Gem GEMS 45	41	5

Tracks on She's Not There/Kicks EP: She's Not There/Kicks/Victim/The Same Thing

Tracey ULLMAN ☉ *UK, female vocalist*   **49 wks**

19 Mar 83	● BREAKAWAY *Stiff BUY 168*	4	11
24 Sep 83	● THEY DON'T KNOW *Stiff BUY 180*	2	11
3 Dec 83	● MOVE OVER DARLING *Stiff BUY 195*	8	9
3 Mar 84	MY GUY *Stiff BUY 197*	23	6
28 Jul 84	SUNGLASSES *Stiff BUY 205*	18	9
27 Oct 84	HELPLESS *Stiff BUY 211*	61	3

ULTIMATE KAOS ☉ (R&B) *UK, male vocal group*   **27 wks**

22 Oct 94	● SOME GIRLS *Wild Card CARDD 12*	9	8
7 Jan 95	SOME GIRLS (re-entry) *Wild Card CARDD 12*	67	1
21 Jan 95	HOOCHIE BOOTY *Wild Card CARDD 14*	17	4
1 Apr 95	SHOW A LITTLE LOVE *Wild Card CARDW 18*	23	5
1 Jul 95	RIGHT HERE *Wild Card 5795832*	18	4
8 Mar 97	CASANOVA *Polydor 5759312*	24	3
18 Jul 98	CASANOVA (re-issue) *Mercury MERCD 505*	29	2

ULTRA ☉ *UK, male vocal / instrumental group*   **15 wks**

18 Apr 98	SAY YOU DO *East West EW 124CD*	11	7
4 Jul 98	SAY IT ONCE *East West EW 171CD1*	16	6
10 Oct 98	THE RIGHT TIME *East West EW 182CD*	28	2

ULTRA HIGH *UK, male vocalist – Michael McCloud*   **3 wks**

2 Dec 95	STAY WITH ME *MCA MCSTD 40007*	36	2
20 Jul 96	ARE YOU READY FOR LOVE *MCA MCSTD 40039*	45	1

ULTRA NATE ☺ *US, female vocalist*   **36 wks**

9 Dec 89	IT'S OVER NOW *Eternal YZ 440*	62	3
23 Feb 91	IS IT LOVE *Eternal YZ 509*	71	1
29 Jan 94	SHOW ME *Warner Bros. W 0219CD*	62	1
14 Jun 97	● FREE *AM:PM 5822432*	4	17
24 Jan 98	FREE (THE MIXES) *AM:PM 5825012*	33	2
18 Apr 98	● FOUND A CURE *AM:PM 5826452*	6	7
25 Jul 98	NEW KIND OF MEDICINE *AM:PM 5827492*	14	5

ULTRA-SONIC *UK, male instrumental/production duo*   **2 wks**

3 Sep 94	OBSESSION *Clubscene DCSRT 027*	75	1
21 Sep 96	DO YOU BELIEVE IN LOVE *Clubscene DCSRT 070*	47	1

ULTRACYNIC *UK, male/female vocal/instrumental group*   **3 wks**

29 Aug 92	NOTHING IS FOREVER *380 PEW 2*	50	2
19 Apr 97	NOTHING IS FOREVER *All Around The World CDGLOBE 139*	47	1

ULTRAMARINE *UK, male instrumental duo*   **4 wks**

24 Jul 93	KINGDOM *Blanco Y Negro NEG 65CD*	46	2
29 Jan 94	BAREFOOT EP *Blanco Y Negro NEG 67CD*	61	1
27 Apr 96	HYMN *Blanco Y Negro NEG 87CD* [1]	65	1

[1] Ultramarine featuring David McAlmont

Tracks on Barefoot EP: Hooter/The Badger/Urf/Happy Land

ULTRASOUND *UK, male/female vocal/instrumental group*   **3 wks**

7 Mar 98	BEST WISHES *Nude NUD 33CD*	68	1
13 Jun 98	STAY YOUNG *Nude NUD 35CD1*	30	2

ULTRAVOX ☉ ☺ *Groundbreaking British electro-rock quartet: Midge Ure (v/g) (replaced John Foxx in 1979), Billy Currie (k/syn), Chris Cross (b/syn), Warren Cann (d). Ex-Slik and Visage vocalist Ure was a driving force behind Band Aid hits, Live Aid and Nelson Mandela birthday concerts*   **142 wks**

5 Jul 80	SLEEPWALK *Chrysalis CHS 2441*	29	11
18 Oct 80	PASSING STRANGERS *Chrysalis CHS 2457*	57	4
17 Jan 81	● VIENNA *Chrysalis CHS 2481*	2	14
28 Mar 81	SLOW MOTION *Island WIP 6691*	33	4
6 Jun 81	● ALL STOOD STILL *Chrysalis CHS 2522*	8	10
22 Aug 81	THE THIN WALL *Chrysalis CHS 2540*	14	8
7 Nov 81	THE VOICE *Chrysalis CHS 2559*	16	12
25 Sep 82	REAP THE WILD WIND *Chrysalis CHS 2639*	12	9
27 Nov 82	HYMN *Chrysalis CHS 2657*	11	11
19 Mar 83	VISIONS IN BLUE *Chrysalis CHS 2676*	15	6
4 Jun 83	WE CAME TO DANCE *Chrysalis VOX 1*	18	7
11 Feb 84	ONE SMALL DAY *Chrysalis VOX 2*	27	6
19 May 84	● DANCING WITH TEARS IN MY EYES *Chrysalis UV 1*	3	10
7 Jul 84	LAMENT *Chrysalis UV 2*	22	6
4 Aug 84	DANCING WITH TEARS IN MY EYES (re-entry)		
	Chrysalis UV 1	74	1
25 Aug 84	LAMENT (re-entry) *Chrysalis UV 2*	73	1
20 Oct 84	LOVE'S GREAT ADVENTURE *Chrysalis UV 3*	12	9
27 Sep 86	SAME OLD STORY *Chrysalis UV 4*	31	4
22 Nov 86	ALL FALL DOWN *Chrysalis UV 5*	30	5
6 Feb 93	VIENNA (re-issue) *Chrysalis CDCHSS 3936*	13	4

UMBOZA ☺ *UK, male instrumental/production duo*   **9 wks**

23 Sep 95	CRY INDIA *Positiva CDTIV 43*	19	4
20 Jul 96	SUNSHINE *Positiva CDTIV 47*	14	5

Piero UMILIANI ℂ *Italy, orchestra and chorus*   **8 wks**

30 Apr 77	● MAH NA MAH NA *EMI International INT 530*	8	8

UNATION *UK, male/female vocal/instrumental group*   **3 wks**

5 Jun 93	HIGHER AND HIGHER *MCA MCSTD 1773*	42	2
7 Aug 93	DO YOU BELIEVE IN LOVE *MCA MCSTD 1796*	75	1

UNBELIEVABLE TRUTH *UK, male vocal / instrumental group*   **5 wks**

14 Feb 98	HIGHER THAN REASON *Virgin VSCDT 1676*	38	2
9 May 98	SOLVED *Virgin VSCDT 1684*	39	2
18 Jul 98	SETTLE DOWN/DUNE SEA *Virgin VSCDT 1697*	46	1

UNCANNY ALLIANCE *US, male/female vocal/instrumental duo*   **5 wks**

19 Dec 92	I GOT MY EDUCATION *A & M AM 0128*	39	5

UNCLE SAM *US, male vocalist*   **2 wks**

16 May 98	I DON'T EVER WANT TO SEE YOU AGAIN *Epic 6656382*	30	2

UNDERCOVER ☉ ☺ *UK, male vocal/instrumental group*   **29 wks**

15 Aug 92	● BAKER STREET *PWL International PWL 239*	2	14
14 Nov 92	● NEVER LET HER SLIP AWAY *PWL International PWL 255*	5	11
6 Feb 93	I WANNA STAY WITH YOU *PWL International PWCD 258*	28	3

UK No 1 ★   UK Top 10 ●   UK million seller ◆   UK entry at No 1 ■   US No 1 ▲

14 Aug 93   **LOVESICK** *PWL International PWCD 271* [1] 62   1

[1] Undercover featuring John Matthews

UNDERTAKERS *UK, male vocal/instrumental group*   **1 wk**

9 Apr 64   **JUST A LITTLE BIT** *Pye 7N 15607* 49   1

UNDERTONES ✏ ☺ *UK, male vocal/instrumental group*   **67 wks**

21 Oct 78   **TEENAGE KICKS** *Sire SIR 4007* 31   6
3 Feb 79   **GET OVER YOU** *Sire SIR 4010* 57   4
28 Apr 79   **JIMMY JIMMY** *Sire SIR 4015* 16 10
21 Jul 79   **HERE COMES THE SUMMER** *Sire SIR 4022* 34   6
20 Oct 79   **YOU'VE GOT MY NUMBER (WHY DON'T YOU USE IT?)**
         Sire SIR 4024 32   6
5 Apr 80 ● **MY PERFECT COUSIN** *Sire SIR 4038* 9 10
5 Jul 80   **WEDNESDAY WEEK** *Sire SIR 4042* 11   9
2 May 81   **IT'S GOING TO HAPPEN!** *Ardeck AROS 8* 18   9
25 Jul 81   **JULIE OCEAN** *Ardeck ARDS 9* 41   5
9 Jul 83   **TEENAGE KICKS** (re-issue) *Ardeck ARDS 1* 60   2

UNDERWORLD ☺ *UK, male instrumental/vocal group*   **30 wks**

18 Dec 93   **SPIKEE/DOGMAN GO** *Junior Boy's Own JBO 17CD* 63   1
25 Jun 94   **DARK AND LONG** *Junior Boy's Own JBO 19CDS* 57   1
13 May 95   **BORN SLIPPY** *Junior Boy's Own JBO 29CDS* 52   2
18 May 96   **PEARL'S GIRL** *Junior Boy's Own JBO 38CDS1* 24   2
13 Jul 96 ● **BORN SLIPPY** (re-mix) *Junior Boy's Own JBO 44CDS* 2 16
9 Nov 96   **PEARL'S GIRL** (re-issue) *Junior Boy's Own JBO 45CDS1* 22   3
28 Dec 96   **BORN SLIPPY** (re-entry of re-mix)
         Junior Boy's Own JBO 44CDS 58   5

UNDISPUTED TRUTH *US, male/female vocal group*   **4 wks**

22 Jan 77   **YOU + ME = LOVE** *Warner Bros. K 16804* 43   4

U96 ☺ *Germany, male producer – Alex Christiansen*   **7 wks**

29 Aug 92   **DAS BOOT** *M & G MAGS 28* 18   5
4 Jun 94   **INSIDE YOUR DREAMS** *Logic 74321209722* 44   1
29 Jun 96   **CLUB BIZARRE** *Urban 5750152* 70   1

UNION featuring the ENGLAND WORLD CUP SQUAD ☺
UK/Holland, male instrumental group with UK rugby team vocalists   **7 wks**

12 Oct 91   **SWING LOW (RUN WITH THE BALL)** *Columbia 6575317* 16   7

UNION GAP featuring Gary PUCKETT ☺
US, male vocal/instrumental group   **47 wks**

17 Apr 68 ★ **YOUNG GIRL** *CBS 3365* 1 17
7 Aug 68 ● **LADY WILLPOWER** *CBS 3551* 5 16
28 Aug 68   **WOMAN WOMAN** *CBS 3110* [1] 48   1
15 Jun 74 ● **YOUNG GIRL** *CBS 8202* [1] 6 13

[1] Gary Puckett and the Union Gap

UNIQUE *US, male/female vocal/instrumental group*   **7 wks**

10 Sep 83   **WHAT I GOT IS WHAT YOU NEED** *Prelude A 3707* 27   7

UNIQUE 3 *UK, male rap/scratch group*   **12 wks**

4 Nov 89   **THE THEME** *10 TEN 285* 61   3
14 Apr 90   **MUSICAL MELODY/WEIGHT FOR THE BASS** *10 TEN 298* 29   5
10 Nov 90   **RHYTHM TAKES CONTROL** *10 TEN 327* [1] 41   3
16 Nov 91   **NO MORE** *10 TEN 387* 74   1

[1] Unique 3 featuring Karin

UNIT FOUR PLUS TWO ☺ *UK, male vocal/instrumental group*   **29 wks**

13 Feb 64   **GREEN FIELDS** *Decca F 11821* 48   2
25 Feb 65 ★ **CONCRETE AND CLAY** *Decca F 12071* 1 15
13 May 65   **YOU'VE NEVER BEEN IN LOVE LIKE THIS BEFORE**
         Decca F 12144 ....14 11
17 Mar 66   **BABY NEVER SAY GOODBYE** *Decca F 12333* 49   1

UNITED CITIZEN FEDERATION *UK, male production duo*   **1 wk**

14 Feb 98   **STARSHIP TROOPERS** *Coalition COLA 040CD* [1] 58   1

[1] United Citizen Federation featuring Sarah Brightman

UNITED KINGDOM SYMPHONY *UK, orchestra*   **4 wks**

27 Jul 85   **SHADES (THEME FROM THE CROWN PAINT TELEVISION
         COMMERCIAL)** *Food For Thought YUM 108* 68   4

UNITONE – See Laurel AITKEN and the UNITONE

UNITONE ROCKERS featuring STEEL
UK, male vocal/instrumental group   **1 wk**

26 Jun 93   **CHILDREN OF THE REVOLUTION** *The Hit Label HLC 4* 60   1

UNITY *UK, male/female vocal/instrumental group*   **2 wks**

31 Aug 91   **UNITY** *Cardiac CNY 6* 64   2

UNIVERSAL ☺ *Australia, male vocal group*   **6 wks**

2 Aug 97   **ROCK ME GOOD** *London LONCD 397* 19   4
18 Oct 97   **MAKE IT WITH YOU** *London LONCD 404* 33   2

UNO CLIO featuring Martine McCUTCHEON
UK, male/female vocal/instrumental group   **1 wk**

18 Nov 95   **ARE YOU MAN ENOUGH** *Avex UK AVEXCD 14* 62   1

UNTOUCHABLES *US, male vocal/instrumental group*   **16 wks**

6 Apr 85   **FREE YOURSELF** *Stiff BUY 221* 26 11
27 Jul 85   **I SPY FOR THE FBI** *Stiff BUY 227* 59   5

UP YER RONSON featuring Mary PEARCE
UK, male/female vocal/instrumental group   **7 wks**

5 Aug 95   **LOST IN LOVE** *Hi-Life 5795572* 27   3
30 Mar 96   **ARE YOU GONNA BE THERE** *Hi-Life 5763272* 27   2
19 Apr 97   **I WILL BE RELEASED** *Hi-Life 5737352* 32   2

Phil UPCHURCH COMBO
US, male instrumental group, Phil Upchurch – bass guitar   **2 wks**

5 May 66   **YOU CAN'T SIT DOWN** *Sue WI 4005* 39   2

UPSETTERS ⍋ *Jamaica, male instrumental group*   **15 wks**

4 Oct 69 ● **RETURN OF DJANGO/DOLLAR IN THE TEETH**
         Upsetter US 301 ....5 15

UPSIDE DOWN ☺ *UK, male vocal group*   **16 wks**

20 Jan 96   **CHANGE YOUR MIND** *World CDWORLD 1A* 11   7
13 Apr 96   **EVERY TIME I FALL IN LOVE** *World CDWORLD 2A* 18   3
8 Jun 96   **EVERY TIME I FALL IN LOVE** (re-entry)
         World CDWORLD 2A 71   1
29 Jun 96   **NEVER FOUND A LOVE LIKE THIS BEFORE**
         World CDWORLD 3A 19   3
23 Nov 96   **IF YOU LEAVE ME NOW** *World CDWORLD 4A* 27   2

URBAN ALL STARS *UK, male producer,*
US, male/female vocal/instrumental group   **2 wks**

27 Aug 88   **IT BEGAN IN AFRICA** *Urban URB 23* 64   2

URBAN BLUES PROJECT present Michael PROCTOR
US, male vocal/instrumental group   **1 wk**

10 Aug 96   **LOVE DON'T LIVE** *AM:PM 5817932* 55   1

URBAN COOKIE COLLECTIVE ☺ ☺
UK, male/female vocal/instrumental group   **37 wks**

10 Jul 93 ● **THE KEY THE SECRET** *Pulse 8 CDLOSE 48* 2 16
13 Nov 93 ● **FEELS LIKE HEAVEN** *Pulse 8 CDLOSE 55* 5   9
19 Feb 94   **SAIL AWAY** *Pulse 8 CDLOSE 56* 18   4

23 Apr 94	HIGH ON A HAPPY VIBE *Pulse 8 CDLOSE 60*	31	3
15 Oct 94	BRING IT ON HOME *Pulse 8 CDLOSE 73*	56	1
27 May 95	SPEND THE DAY *Pulse 8 CDLOSE 85*	59	1
9 Sep 95	REST OF MY LOVE *Pulse 8 CDLOSE 93*	67	1
16 Dec 95	SO BEAUTIFUL *Pulse 8 CDLOSE 100*	68	1
24 Aug 96	THE KEY THE SECRET (re-mix) *Pulse 8 CDLOSE 109* [1]	52	1

[1] UCC

URBAN DISCHARGE featuring SHE
US, male/female vocal/instrumental group — **1 wk**

| 27 Jan 96 | WANNA DROP A HOUSE (ON THAT BITCH) *MCA MCSTD 40020* | 51 | 1 |

URBAN HYPE *UK, male production/instrumental group* — **12 wks**

11 Jul 92 ●	A TRIP TO TRUMPTON *Faze 2 FAZE 5*	6	8
17 Oct 92	THE FEELING *Faze 2 FAZE 10*	67	1
9 Jan 93	LIVING IN A FANTASY *Faze 2 CDFAZE 13*	57	3

URBAN SHAKEDOWN featuring Micky FINN
UK/Italy, male vocal/instrumental group — **8 wks**

27 Jun 92	SOME JUSTICE *Urban Shakedown URBST 1*	23	5
12 Sep 92	BASS SHAKE *Urban Shakedown URBST 2*	59	2
10 Jun 95	SOME JUSTICE *Urban Shakedown URBCD 3* [1]	49	1

[1] Urban Shakedown featuring D Bo General

'Some Justice' in 1995 is a re-recording

URBAN SOUL *UK, male / female vocal / production group* — **11 wks**

30 Mar 91	ALRIGHT *Cooltempo COOL 231*	60	4
21 Sep 91	ALRIGHT (re-mix) *Cooltempo COOL 244*	43	3
28 Mar 92	ALWAYS *Cooltempo COOL 251*	41	3
13 Jun 98	LOVE IS SO NICE *VC Recordings VCRD 33*	75	1

URBAN SPECIES *UK, male vocal/instrumental group* — **9 wks**

12 Feb 94	SPIRITUAL LOVE *Talkin Loud TLKCD 45*	35	4
16 Apr 94	BROTHER *Talkin Loud TLKCD 47*	40	3
20 Aug 94	LISTEN *Talkin Loud TLKCD 50* [1]	47	2

[1] Urban Species featuring MC Solaar

Midge URE ☺ *UK, male vocalist* — **56 wks**

12 Jun 82 ●	NO REGRETS *Chrysalis CHS 2618*	9	10
9 Jul 83	AFTER A FASHION *Musicfest FEST 1* [1]	39	4
14 Sep 85 ★	IF I WAS *Chrysalis URE 1*	1	11
16 Nov 85	THAT CERTAIN SMILE *Chrysalis URE 2*	28	4
8 Feb 86	WASTELANDS *Chrysalis URE 3*	46	3
7 Jun 86	CALL OF THE WILD *Chrysalis URE 4*	27	8
20 Aug 88	ANSWERS TO NOTHING *Chrysalis URE 5*	49	4
19 Nov 88	DEAR GOD *Chrysalis URE 6*	55	4
17 Aug 91	COLD COLD HEART *Arista 114555*	17	7
25 May 96	BREATHE *Arista 74321371172*	70	1

[1] Midge Ure and Mick Karn

URGE OVERKILL *US, male vocal/instrumental group* — **6 wks**

21 Aug 93	SISTER HAVANA *Geffen GFSTD 51*	67	1
16 Oct 93	POSITIVE BLEEDING *Geffen GFSTD 57*	61	1
19 Nov 94	GIRL YOU'LL BE A WOMAN SOON *MCA MCSTD 2024*	37	4

URUSEI YATSURA *UK, male/female vocal / instrumental group* — **4 wks**

22 Feb 97	STRATEGIC HAMLETS *Che CHE 67CD*	64	1
28 Jun 97	FAKE FUR *Che CHE 70CD*	58	1
21 Feb 98	HELLO TIGER *Che CHE 75CD1*	40	1
6 Jun 98	SLAIN BY ELF *Che CHE 80CD1*	63	1

US3 *UK, male instrumental/production duo* — **15 wks**

10 Jul 93	RIDDIM *Blue Note CDCL 686* [1]	34	6
25 Sep 93	CANTALOOP *Blue Note CDCL 696* [2]	23	5
28 May 94	I GOT IT GOIN' ON *Blue Note CDCL 708* [3]	52	2

| 1 Mar 97 | COME ON EVERYBODY (GET DOWN) *Blue Note CDCL 784* | 38 | 2 |

[1] Us3 featuring Tukka Yoot   [2] Us3 featuring Rahsaan
[3] Us3 featuring Kobie Powell and Rahsaan

USA FOR AFRICA ☻ *US, male/female vocal ensemble* — **9 wks**

| 13 Apr 85 ★ | WE ARE THE WORLD *CBS USAID 1* ▲ | 1 | 9 |

USHER [R&B] *US, male vocalist* — **19 wks**

18 Mar 95	THINK OF YOU *LaFace 74321269252*	70	1
31 Jan 98 ★	YOU MAKE ME WANNA... *LaFace 74321560652* ■	1	12
2 May 98	YOU MAKE ME WANNA... (re-entry) *LaFace 74321560652*	70	1
2 May 98	NICE & SLOW *LaFace 74321579102*	24	5

USURA ☺ *Italy, male/female vocal/instrumental group* — **15 wks**

23 Jan 93 ●	OPEN YOUR MIND *Deconstruction 74321128042*	7	9
10 Jul 93	SWEAT *Deconstruction 74321154602*	29	3
6 Dec 97	OPEN YOUR MIND 97 (re-mix) *Malarky MLKD 4* [1]	21	3

[1] U.S.U.R.A.

UTAH SAINTS ☺ *UK, male instrumental/production duo* — **35 wks**

24 Aug 91 ●	WHAT CAN YOU DO FOR ME *ffrr F 164*	10	11
6 Jun 92 ●	SOMETHING GOOD *ffrr F 187*	4	9
8 May 93 ●	BELIEVE IN ME *ffrr FCD 209*	8	6
17 Jul 93	I WANT YOU *ffrr FCD 213*	25	5
25 Jun 94	I STILL THINK OF YOU *ffrr FCD 225*	32	2
2 Sep 95	OHIO *ffrr FCD 264*	42	2

U2 ✎ ☻ *Giants of contemporary rock: Bono (b. Paul Hewson) (v), The Edge (b. David Evans) (g), Adam Clayton (b), Larry Mullen Jr. (d). Stadium-packing, award-winning Irish supergroup, who have smashed countless records for sales and live appearances around the globe* — **207 wks**

8 Aug 81	FIRE *Island WIP 6679*	35	6
17 Oct 81	GLORIA *Island WIP 6733*	55	4
3 Apr 82	A CELEBRATION *Island WIP 6770*	47	4
22 Jan 83 ●	NEW YEARS DAY *Island UWIP 6848*	10	8
2 Apr 83	TWO HEARTS BEAT AS ONE *Island IS 109*	18	5
15 Sep 84 ●	PRIDE (IN THE NAME OF LOVE) *Island IS 202*	3	11
4 May 85 ●	THE UNFORGETTABLE FIRE *Island IS 220*	6	6
28 Mar 87 ●	WITH OR WITHOUT YOU *Island IS 319* ▲	4	11
6 Jun 87 ●	I STILL HAVEN'T FOUND WHAT I'M LOOKING FOR *Island IS 328* ▲	6	11
12 Sep 87 ●	WHERE THE STREETS HAVE NO NAME *Island IS 340*	4	6
26 Dec 87	IN GOD'S COUNTRY (IMPORT) *Island 7-99385*	48	4
1 Oct 88 ★	DESIRE *Island IS 400*	1	8
17 Dec 88 ●	ANGEL OF HARLEM *Island IS 402*	9	6
15 Apr 89 ●	WHEN LOVE COMES TO TOWN *Island IS 411* [1]	6	6
24 Jun 89 ●	ALL I WANT IS YOU *Island IS 422*	4	6
2 Nov 91 ★	THE FLY *Island IS 500* ■	1	5
4 Jan 92	MYSTERIOUS WAYS *Island IS 509*	13	7
14 Dec 91	THE FLY (re-entry) *Island IS 500*	62	1
7 Mar 92 ●	ONE *Island IS 515*	7	6
20 Jun 92	EVEN BETTER THAN THE REAL THING *Island IS 525*	12	6
11 Jul 92	EVEN BETTER THAN THE REAL THING (re-mix) *Island REAL U2*	8	7
5 Dec 92	WHO'S GONNA RIDE YOUR WILD HORSES *Island IS 550*	14	8
4 Dec 93 ●	STAY (FARAWAY, SO CLOSE) *Island CID 578*	4	9
17 Jun 95 ●	HOLD ME THRILL ME KISS ME KILL ME / *Atlantic A 7131CD*	2	14
15 Feb 97 ★	DISCOTHEQUE *Island CID 649* ■	1	9
26 Apr 97 ●	STARING AT THE SUN *Island CID 658*	3	6
17 May 97	DISCOTHEQUE (re-entry) *Island CID 649*	72	2
2 Aug 97 ●	LAST NIGHT ON EARTH *Island CID 664*	10	4
4 Oct 97 ●	PLEASE *Island CID 673*	7	4
20 Dec 97 ●	IF GOD WILL SEND HIS ANGELS *Island CID 684*	12	6
31 Oct 98 ●	SWEETEST THING *Island CID 727*	3†	9

[1] U2 featuring B.B. King

'Stay (Faraway, So Close)' was listed with 'I've Got You Under My Skin' by Frank Sinatra with Bono, which was featured on many but not all formats

VAGABONDS – See Jimmy JAMES and the VAGABONDS

Ricky VALANCE ◎ *UK, male vocalist*   **16 wks**

| 25 Aug 60 | ★ TELL LAURA I LOVE HER *Columbia DB 4493* | 1 | 16 |

Ritchie VALENS *US, male vocalist*   **5 wks**

| 6 Mar 59 | DONNA *London HL 8803* | 29 | 1 |
| 1 Aug 87 | LA BAMBA *RCA PB 41435* | 49 | 4 |

Caterina VALENTE ℂ *France, female vocalist*   **14 wks**

| 19 Aug 55 | ● THE BREEZE AND I *Polydor BM 6002* | 5 | 14 |

Dickie VALENTINE ℂ *UK, male vocalist*   **92 wks**

20 Feb 53	BROKEN WINGS *Decca F 9954*	12	1
13 Mar 53	● ALL THE TIME AND EVERYWHERE *Decca F 10038*	9	3
5 Jun 53	● IN A GOLDEN COACH *Decca F 10098*	7	1
5 Nov 54	ENDLESS *Decca F 10346*	19	1
17 Dec 54	● MR. SANDMAN *Decca F 10415*	5	12
17 Dec 54	★ FINGER OF SUSPICION *Decca F 10394* [1]	1	15
18 Feb 55	A BLOSSOM FELL *Decca F 10430*	9	9
29 Apr 55	A BLOSSOM FELL (re-entry) *Decca F 10430*	18	1
3 Jun 55	● I WONDER *Decca F 10493*	4	15
25 Nov 55	★ CHRISTMAS ALPHABET *Decca F 10628*	1	7
16 Dec 55	OLD PIANNA RAG *Decca F 10645*	15	5
7 Dec 56	CHRISTMAS ISLAND *Decca F 10798*	8	5
27 Dec 57	SNOWBOUND FOR CHRISTMAS *Decca F 10950*	28	1
13 Mar 59	VENUS *Pye Nixa 7N 15192*	28	1
3 Apr 59	VENUS (re-entry) *Pye Nixa 7N 15192*	25	1
17 Apr 59	VENUS (2nd re-entry) *Pye Nixa 7N 15192*	20	4
22 May 59	VENUS (3rd re-entry) *Pye Nixa 7N 15192*	25	1
19 Jun 59	VENUS (4th re-entry) *Pye Nixa 7N 15192*	28	1
23 Oct 59	ONE MORE SUNRISE (MORGEN) *Pye 7N 15221*	14	8

[1] Dickie Valentine with the Stargazers

See also VARIOUS ARTISTS (EPs & LPs) – All Star Hit Parade

VALENTINE BROTHERS *US, male vocal duo*   **1 wk**

| 23 Apr 83 | MONEY'S TOO TIGHT (TO MENTION) *Energy NRG 1* | 73 | 1 |

Joe VALINO *US, male vocalist*   **2 wks**

| 18 Jan 57 | GARDEN OF EDEN *HMV POP 283* | 23 | 2 |

Frankie VALLI ◎ *US, male vocalist*   **52 wks**

12 Dec 70	YOU'RE READY NOW *Philips 320226*	11	13
1 Feb 75	● MY EYES ADORED YOU *Private Stock PVT 1* ▲	5	11
21 Jun 75	SWEARIN' TO GOD *Private Stock PVT 21*	31	5
17 Apr 76	FALLEN ANGEL *Private Stock PVT 51*	11	7
26 Aug 78	● GREASE *RSO 012* ▲	3	14
23 Mar 91	GREASE – THE DREAM MIX *PWL/Polydor PO 136* [1]	47	2

[1] Frankie Valli, John Travolta and Olivia Newton-John

See also FOUR SEASONS

Mark VAN DALE with ENRICO *Belgium, male production duo*   **1 wk**

| 3 Oct 98 | WATER WAVE *Club Tools 0065815 CLU* | 71 | 1 |

David VAN DAY *UK, male vocalist*   **3 wks**

| 14 May 83 | YOUNG AMERICANS TALKING *WEA DAY 1* | 43 | 3 |

George VAN DUSEN *UK, male vocalist*   **4 wks**

| 17 Dec 88 | IT'S PARTY TIME AGAIN *Bri-Tone 7BT 001* | 43 | 4 |

Paul VAN DYK *Germany, male DJ*   **6 wks**

17 May 97	FORBIDDEN FRUIT *Deviant DVNT 18CDR*	69	1
15 Nov 97	WORDS *Deviant DVNT 26CDS* [1]	54	1
5 Sep 98	FOR AN ANGEL *Deviant DVT 24CDS*	28	4

[1] Paul Van Dyk featuring Toni Halliday

Leroy VAN DYKE ☜ *US, male vocalist*   **20 wks**

| 4 Jan 62 | ● WALK ON BY *Mercury AMT 1166* | 5 | 17 |
| 26 Apr 62 | BIG MAN IN A BIG HOUSE *Mercury AMT 1173* | 34 | 3 |

VAN HALEN ⤳ *US/Holland, male vocal/instrumental group*   **51 wks**

28 Jun 80	RUNNIN' WITH THE DEVIL *Warner Bros. HM 10*	52	3
4 Feb 84	● JUMP *Warner Bros. W 9384* ▲	7	13
19 May 84	PANAMA *Warner Bros. W 9273*	61	2
5 Apr 86	● WHY CAN'T THIS BE LOVE *Warner Bros. W 8740*	8	14
12 Jul 86	DREAMS *Warner Bros. W 8642*	62	2
6 Aug 88	WHEN IT'S LOVE *Warner Bros. W 7816*	28	7
1 Apr 89	FEELS SO GOOD *Warner Bros. W 7565*	63	1
22 Jun 91	POUNDCAKE *Warner Bros. W 0045*	74	1
19 Oct 91	TOP OF THE WORLD *Warner Bros. W 0066*	63	1
27 Mar 93	JUMP (LIVE) *Warner Bros. W 0155CD*	26	3
21 Jan 95	DON'T TELL ME *Warner Bros. W 0280CD*	27	2
1 Apr 95	CAN'T STOP LOVIN' YOU *Warner Bros. W 0288CD*	33	2

Armand VAN HELDEN *US, male producer*   **3 wks**

| 8 Mar 97 | THE FUNK PHENOMENA *ZYX ZYX 8523U8* | 38 | 2 |
| 8 Nov 97 | ULTRAFUNKULA *ffrr FCD 317* | 46 | 1 |

VAN TWIST
Zaire/Belgium, male/female vocal/instrumental group   **2 wks**

| 16 Feb 85 | SHAFT *Polydor POSP 729* | 57 | 2 |

VANDELLAS – See Martha REEVES and the VANDELLAS

Luther VANDROSS ♪ *Superior soul singer/songwriter and producer,
b. 20 April, 1951, New York. Ex-David Bowie backing vocalist, who fronted
chart group Change before embarking on a solo career that earned
him ten successive US platinum albums and a stack of awards*   **146 wks**

19 Feb 83	NEVER TOO MUCH *Epic EPC A 3101*	44	6
26 Jul 86	GIVE ME THE REASON *Epic A 7288*	60	3
21 Feb 87	GIVE ME THE REASON (re-issue) *Epic 650216 7*	71	2
28 Mar 87	SEE ME *Epic LUTH 1*	60	4
11 Jul 87	I REALLY DIDN'T MEAN IT *Epic LUTH 3*	16	10
5 Sep 87	STOP TO LOVE *Epic LUTH 2*	24	7
7 Nov 87	SO AMAZING *Epic LUTH 4*	33	6
23 Jan 88	GIVE ME THE REASON (2nd re-issue) *Epic LUTH 5*	26	6
16 Apr 88	I GAVE IT UP (WHEN I FELL IN LOVE) *Epic LUTH 6*	28	5
9 Jul 88	THERE'S NOTHING BETTER THAN LOVE *Epic LUTH 7* [1]	72	1
8 Oct 88	ANY LOVE *Epic LUTH 8*	31	4
4 Feb 89	SHE WON'T TALK TO ME *Epic LUTH 9*	34	4
22 Apr 89	COME BACK *Epic LUTH 10*	53	3
28 Oct 89	NEVER TOO MUCH (re-mix) *Epic LUTH 12*	13	7
6 Jan 90	HERE AND NOW *Epic LUTH 13*	43	3
27 Apr 91	POWER OF LOVE – LOVE POWER *Epic 6568227*	46	5
18 Jan 92	THE RUSH *Epic 6577237*	53	3
15 Aug 92	● THE BEST THINGS IN LIFE ARE FREE *Perspective PERSS 7400* [2]	2	13
22 May 93	LITTLE MIRACLES (HAPPEN EVERY DAY) *Epic 6590442*	28	3
18 Sep 93	HEAVEN KNOWS *Epic 6596522*	34	3
4 Dec 93	LOVE IS ON THE WAY *Epic 6599592*	38	2
17 Sep 94	● ENDLESS LOVE *Epic 6608062* [3]	3	10
26 Nov 94	LOVE THE ONE YOU'RE WITH *Epic 6610612*	31	4

7 Jan 95	ENDLESS LOVE (re-entry) Epic 6608062 [3]	70	2
4 Feb 95	ALWAYS AND FOREVER Epic 6611942	20	5
4 Feb 95	ENDLESS LOVE (2nd re-entry) Epic 6608062 [3]	55	4
15 Apr 95	AIN'T NO STOPPING US NOW Epic 6614242	22	3
11 Nov 95	POWER OF LOVE – LOVE POWER (re-mix) Epic 6625902	31	3
16 Dec 95 ●	THE BEST THINGS IN LIFE ARE FREE (re-mix) A & M 5813092 [4]	7	7
23 Dec 95	EVERY YEAR EVERY CHRISTMAS Epic 6627762	43	2
12 Oct 96	YOUR SECRET LOVE Epic 6638385	14	5
28 Dec 96	I CAN MAKE IT BETTER Epic 6640632	44	1

[1] Luther Vandross, duet with Gregory Hines [2] Luther Vandross and Janet Jackson with special guests BBD and Ralph Tresvant [3] Luther Vandross and Mariah Carey [4] Luther Vandross and Janet Jackson

VANESSA-MAE ℂ ♪ Singapore, female instrumentalist – violin   20 wks

28 Jan 95	TOCCATA AND FUGUE EMI Classics MAE 8816812	16	10
20 May 95	RED HOT EMI CDMAE 2	37	2
18 Nov 95	CLASSICAL GAS EMI CDEM 404	41	2
26 Oct 96	I'M A DOUN FOR LACK O' JOHNNIE (A LITTLE SCOTTISH FANTASY) EMI CDMAE 3	28	2
25 Oct 97	STORM EMI CDEM 497	54	1
20 Dec 97	I FEEL LOVE EMI CDEM 553	41	2
5 Dec 98	DEVIL'S TRILL / REFLECTION EMI CDEM 530	53	1

VANGELIS ◉ ℂ Greece, male instrumentalist – keyboards   25 wks

9 May 81	CHARIOTS OF FIRE – TITLES Polydor POSP 246 ▲	12	10
11 Jul 81	HEAVEN AND HELL, THIRD MOVEMENT (THEME FROM THE BBC-TV SERIES, THE COSMOS) BBC 1	48	6
24 Apr 82	CHARIOTS OF FIRE – TITLES (re-entry) Polydor POSP 246	41	7
31 Oct 92	CONQUEST OF PARADISE East West YZ 704	60	2

See also JON and VANGELIS

VANILLA ◉ UK, female vocal group   10 wks

22 Nov 97	NO WAY NO WAY EMI CDEM 487	75	1
27 Dec 97	NO WAY NO WAY (re-entry) EMI CDEM 487	14	7
23 May 98	TRUE TO US EMI CDEM 509	36	2

VANILLA FUDGE ⅄ US, male vocal/instrumental group   11 wks

9 Aug 67	YOU KEEP ME HANGIN' ON Atlantic 584 123	18	11

VANILLA ICE ◀ US, male rapper   32 wks

24 Nov 90 ★	ICE ICE BABY SBK SBK 18 ▲	1	13
2 Feb 91 ●	PLAY THAT FUNKY MUSIC SBK SBK 20	10	6
30 Mar 91	I LOVE YOU SBK SBK 22	45	5
29 Jun 91	ROLLIN' IN MY 5.0 SBK SBK 27	27	4
10 Aug 91	SATISFACTION SBK SBK 29	22	4

VANITY FARE ◉ UK, male vocal/instrumental group   34 wks

28 Aug 68	I LIVE FOR THE SUN Page One POF 075	20	9
23 Jul 69 ●	EARLY IN THE MORNING Page One POF 142	8	12
27 Dec 69	HITCHIN' A RIDE Page One POF 158	16	13

Joe T. VANNELLI PROJECT Italy, male producer   2 wks

17 Jun 95	SWEETEST DAY OF MAY Positiva CDTIV 36	45	2

Randy VANWARMER ◉ US, male vocalist   11 wks

4 Aug 79 ●	JUST WHEN I NEEDED YOU MOST Bearsville WIP 6516	8	11

VAPORS ◉ ✐ UK, male vocal/instrumental group   23 wks

9 Feb 80 ●	TURNING JAPANESE United Artists BP 334	3	13
5 Jul 80	NEWS AT TEN United Artists BP 345	44	4
11 Jul 81	JIMMIE JONES Liberty BP 401	44	6

VARDIS UK, male vocal/instrumental group   4 wks

27 Sep 80	LET'S GO Logo VAR 1	59	4

VARIOUS ARTISTS (EPs and LPs)   60 wks

15 Jun 56	CAROUSEL – ORIGINAL SOUNDTRACK LP Capitol LCT 6105	27	1
29 Jun 56 ●	ALL STAR HIT PARADE Decca F 10752	2	9
6 Jul 56	CAROUSEL – ORIGINAL SOUNDTRACK LP (re-entry) Capitol LCT 6105	26	1
26 Jul 57	ALL STAR HIT PARADE NO. 2 Decca F 10915	15	7
9 Dec 89	THE FOOD CHRISTMAS EP Food FOOD 23	63	1
20 Jan 90	THE FURTHER ADVENTURES OF NORTH EP Deconstruction PT 43372	64	2
2 Nov 91	THE APPLE EP Apple APP 1	60	1
11 Jul 92	FOURPLAY EP XL XLFP 1	45	2
7 Nov 92	THE FRED EP Heavenly HVN 19	26	3
24 Apr 93	GIMME SHELTER EP Food CDORDERA 1	23	4
5 Jun 93	SUBPLATES VOLUME 1 EP Suburban Base SUBBASE 24CD	69	1
9 Oct 93	THE TWO TONE EP 2 Tone CHSTT 31	30	3
4 Nov 95	HELP EP Go! Discs GODCD 135	51	2
16 Mar 96	NEW YORK UNDERCOVER EP Uptown MCSTD 48002	39	1
30 Mar 96	DANGEROUS MINDS EP MCA MCSTD 48007	35	1
29 Nov 97 ★	PERFECT DAY Chrysalis CDNEED 01 ◆ ■	1	19
12 Sep 98	THE FULL MONTY-MONSTER MIX RCA Victor 74321602582	62	1
26 Sep 98	TRADE EP (DISC 2) Tidy Trax TREP2	75	1

Tracks and artists on Carousel are as follows: Carousel Waltz – Orchestra conducted by Alfred Newman; You're a Queer One Julie Jordan – Barbara Ruick and Shirley Jones; Mister Snow – Barbara Ruick; If I Loved You – Shirley Jones and Gordon MacRae; June Is Busting Out All Over – Claramae Turner; Soliloquy – Gordon MacRae; Blow High Blow Low – Cameron Mitchell; When the Children Are Asleep – Robert Rounseville and Barbara Ruick; This Was a Real Nice Clambake – Barbara Ruick, Claramae Turner, Robert Rounseville and Cameron Mitchell; Stonecutters Cut It On Stone (There's Nothing So Bad For a Woman) – Cameron Mitchell; What's the Use of Wonderin' – Shirley Jones; You'll Never Walk Alone – Claramae Turner; If I Loved You – Gordon MacRae; You'll Never Walk Alone – Shirley Jones.

Tracks on All Star Hit Parade: Theme From The Threepenny Opera – Winifred Atwell; No Other Love – Dave King; My September Love – Joan Regan; A Tear Fell – Lita Roza; Out of Town – Dickie Valentine; It's Almost Tomorrow – David Whitfield.

Tracks on All Star Hit Parade No 2: Around the World – Johnston Brothers; Puttin' On the Style – Billy Cotton; When I Fall In Love – Jimmy Young; A White Sport Coat – Max Bygraves; Freight Train – Beverley Sisters; Butterfly – Tommy Steele.

Tracks on The Food Christmas EP: Like Princes Do – Crazyhead; I Don't Want That Kind of Love – Jesus Jones; Info Freako – Diesel Park West.

Tracks on The Further Adventures of North EP: Dream 17 – Annette; Carino 90 – T-Coy; The Way I Feel – Frequency 9; Stop This Thing – Dynasty of Two featuring Rowetta.

Tracks on The Apple EP: Those Were the Days – Mary Hopkin; That's the Way God Planned It – Billy Preston; Sour Milk Sea – Jackie Lomax; Come and Get It – Badfinger.

Tracks on Fourplay EP: DJs Unite; Alright – Glide; Be Free – Noisy Factory; True Devotion – EQ.

Tracks on The Fred EP: Deeply Dippy – Rockingbirds; Don't Talk Just Kiss – Flowered Up; I'm Too Sexy – Saint Etienne.

Gimme Shelter EP was available on all four formats, each featuring an interview with the featured artist plus the following artists performing versions of Gimme Shelter; (cassette) Jimmy Somerville and Voice of the Beehive; Heaven 17; (12") Blue Pearl, 808 State and Robert Owens; Pop Will Eat Itself vs Gary Clail; Ranking Roger and the Mighty Diamonds; (CD) Thunder; Little Angels; Hawkwind and Sam Fox; (2nd CD) Cud with Sandie Shaw; Kingmaker; New Model Army and Tom Jones.

Tracks on Subplates Volume 1 EP: Style Warz – Son'z of a Loop Da Loop Era; Funky Dope Track – Q-Bass; The Chopper – DJ Hype; Look No Further – Run Tings.

Tracks on The Two Tone EP: Gangsters – Special AKA; The Prince – Madness; On My Radio – Selecter; Tears of a Clown – Beat.

Tracks on Help EP: Lucky – Radiohead; 50ft Queenie (Live) PJ Harvey; Momentum – Guru featuring Big Shug; an untitled piece of incidental music.

Tracks on New York Undercover EP: Tell Me What You Like – Guy; Dom Perignon – Little Shawn; I Miss You – Monifah; Jeeps, Lex Coups, Bimax & Menz – Lost Boys.

Tracks on Dangerous Minds EP: Curiosity – Aaron Hall; Gin & Dance – De Vante; It's Alright – Sista featuring Craig Mack.

Artists on Perfect Day are as follows: BBC Symphony Orchestra and Andrew Davis, Bono (U2), Boyzone, Brett Anderson (Suede), Brodsky Quartet, Burning Spear, Courtney Pine, David Bowie, Dr John, Elton John, Emmylou Harris, Evan Dando (Lemonheads), Gabrielle, Heather Small (M People), Huey (Fun Lovin' Criminals), Ian Broudie (Lightning Seeds), Joan Armatrading, Laurie Anderson, Lesley Garrett, Lou Reed, Robert Cray, Shane McGowan, Sheona White, Skye (Morcheeba), Suzanne Vega, Tammy Wynette, Thomas Allen, Tom Jones, Visual Ministry Orchestra

Tracks on The Full-Monty Monster Mix (medley): You Sexy Thing – Hot Chocolate;

Hot Stuff – Donna Summer; You Can Leave Your Hat On – Tom Jones. CD also
has a full version of 'You Can Leave Your Hat On' by Tom Jones and 'The Stripper'
by David Rose.
Tracks on Trade EP (disc 2): Put Your House in Order – Steve Thomas; The Dawn –
Tony De Vit

VARIOUS ARTISTS (MONTAGES) — 31 wks

17 May 80	CALIBRE CUTS *Calibre CAB 502*	75	2
25 Nov 89	DEEP HEAT '89 *Deep Heat DEEP 10*	12	11
3 Mar 90 ●	THE BRITS 1990 *RCA PB 43565*	2	7
28 Apr 90	THE SIXTH SENSE *Deep Heat DEEP 12*	49	2
10 Nov 90	TIME TO MAKE THE FLOOR BURN *Megabass MEGAX 1*	16	9

The following tracks are sampled:
Calibre Cuts: Big Apples Rock – Black Ivory; Don't Hold Back – Chanson; The River
Drive – Jupiter Beyond; Dancing In the Disco – LAX; Mellow Mellow Right On –
Lowrell; Pata Pata – Osibisa; I Like It – Players Association; We Got the Funk –
Positive Force; Holdin' On – Tony Rallo and the Midnight Band; Can You Feel the
Force – Real Thing; Miami Heatwave – Seventh Avenue; Rappers Delight – Sugarhill
Gang; Que Tal America – Two Man Sound; Remakes by session musicians: Ain't No
Stoppin' Us Now, Bad Girls, We Are Family
Deep Heat '89 (credited to Latino Rave): Pump Up the Jam – Technotronics; Stakker
Humanoid – Humanoid; A Day in the Life – Black Riot; Work it to the Bone – LNR;
I Can Make U Dance – DJ 'Fast' Eddie; Voodoo Ray – A Guy Called Gerald; Numero
Uno – Starlight; Bango (To the Batmobile) – Todd Terry; Break 4 Love – Raze;
Don't Scandalize Mine – Sugar Bear.
The Brits 1990: Street Tuff – Double Trouble and the Rebel MC; Voodoo Ray –
A Guy Called Gerald; Theme From S-Express – S-Express; Hey DJ I Can't Dance to
That Music You're Playing – Beatmasters; Eve of the War – Jeff Wayne; Pacific
State – 808 State; We Call It Acieed – D Mob; Got to Keep On – Cookie Crew.
The Sixth Sense (credited to Megabass): Get Up – Technotronic; The Magic
Number – De La Soul; G'Ding G'Ding (Do Wanna Wanna) – Anna G; Show 'M
the Bass – MC Miker G; Turn It Out (Go Base) – Rob Base; Eve of the War (War
of the Worlds) – Project D; Moments In Love – 2 to the Power.
Time to Make the Floor Burn (credited to Megabass): Do This My Way – Kid 'N' Play;
Street Tuff – Double Trouble and the Rebel MC; Ride On Time – Black Box; Ride On
Time – Black Box; Make My Body Rock – Jomanda; Don't Miss the Partyline – Bizz
Nizz; Pump Pump It Up – Hypnotek; Big Fun – Inner City; Pump That Body – Mr Lee;
Pump Up the Jam – Technotronic; This Beat Is Technotronic – Technotronic; Get
Busy – Mr Lee; Touch Me – 49ers; Thunderbirds Are Go – FAB

Junior VASQUEZ *US, male producer* — 5 wks

15 Jul 95	GET YOUR HANDS OFF MY MAN! *Positiva CDTIV 37*	22	3
31 Aug 96	IF MADONNA CALLS *Multiply CDMULTY 13*	24	2

Elaine VASSELL – See BEATMASTERS

Sven VATH *Germany, male producer* — 5 wks

24 Jul 93	L'ESPERANZA *Eye Q YZ 757*	63	2
6 Nov 93	AN ACCIDENT IN PARADISE *Eye Q YZ 778CD*	57	2
22 Oct 94	HARLEQUIN – THE BEAUTY AND THE BEAST *Eye Q YZ 857*	72	1

Frankie VAUGHAN ● ℂ *High-kicking fifties heartthrob vocalist.*
*b. Frank Abelson, 3 February, 1928, Liverpool. This variety-show veteran,
who received an OBE in 1965 for his charity work, was one of the
most popular performers of the 1950s* — 232 wks

29 Jan 54	ISTANBUL *HMV B 10599*	11	1
28 Jan 55	HAPPY DAYS AND LONELY NIGHTS *HMV B 10783*	12	3
22 Apr 55	TWEEDLE DEE *Philips PB 423*	17	1
2 Dec 55	SEVENTEEN *Philips PB 511*	18	3
3 Feb 56	MY BOY FLAT TOP *Philips PB 544*	20	2
9 Nov 56 ●	GREEN DOOR *Philips PB 640*	2	15
11 Jan 57 ★	GARDEN OF EDEN *Philips PB 660*	1	13
4 Oct 57 ●	MAN ON FIRE/WANDERIN' EYES *Philips PB 729*	6	11
1 Nov 57 ●	GOTTA HAVE SOMETHING IN THE BANK FRANK *Philips PB 751* [1]	8	11
20 Dec 57 ●	KISSES SWEETER THAN WINE *Philips PB 775*	8	11
7 Mar 58	CAN'T GET ALONG WITHOUT YOU/WE ARE NOT ALONE *Philips PB 793*	11	6
9 May 58 ●	KEWPIE DOLL *Philips PB 825*	10	12
1 Aug 58	WONDERFUL THINGS *Philips PB 834*	22	3
12 Sep 58	WONDERFUL THINGS (re-entry) *Philips PB 834*	27	3
10 Oct 58	AM I WASTING MY TIME ON YOU *Philips PB 865*	25	2
9 Jan 59	AM I WASTING MY TIME ON YOU (re-entry) *Philips PB 865*	27	2
30 Jan 59	THAT'S MY DOLL *Philips PB 895*	28	2
1 May 59 ●	COME SOFTLY TO ME *Philips PB 913* [1]	9	9
24 Jul 59 ●	THE HEART OF A MAN *Philips PB 930*	5	14
18 Sep 59	WALKIN' TALL *Philips PB 931*	28	1
2 Oct 59	WALKIN' TALL (re-entry) *Philips PB 931*	29	1
29 Jan 60	WHAT MORE DO YOU WANT *Philips PB 985*	25	2
22 Sep 60	KOOKIE LITTLE PARADISE *Philips PB 1054*	31	5
27 Oct 60	MILORD *Philips PB 1066*	34	6
9 Nov 61 ★	TOWER OF STRENGTH *Philips PB 1195*	1	13
1 Feb 62	DON'T STOP TWIST *Philips 1219*	22	7
27 Sep 62	HERCULES *Philips 326542 BF*	42	4
24 Jan 63 ●	LOOP-DE-LOOP *Philips 326566 BF*	5	12
20 Jun 63	HEY MAMA *Philips BF 1254*	21	9
4 Jun 64	HELLO DOLLY *Philips BF 1339*	18	11
11 Mar 65	SOMEONE MUST HAVE HURT YOU A LOT *Philips BF 1394*	46	1
23 Aug 67 ●	THERE MUST BE A WAY *Columbia DB 8248*	7	21
15 Nov 67	SO TIRED *Columbia DB 8298*	21	9
28 Feb 68	NEVERTHELESS *Columbia DB 8354*	29	5

[1] Frankie Vaughan and the Kaye Sisters

Malcolm VAUGHAN ℂ *Arguably the last of the hitmaking big-voiced
tenors, b. 1930, Glamorgan, Wales. He was the straight man in a comedy
duo with Kenny Earle, while enjoying his enviable run of UK ballad hits
(at the height of the rock'n'roll explosion)* — 106 wks

1 Jul 55 ●	EVERY DAY OF MY LIFE *HMV B 10874*	5	16
27 Jan 56	WITH YOUR LOVE *HMV POP 130*	20	1
10 Feb 56	WITH YOUR LOVE (re-entry) *HMV POP 130*	18	1
2 Mar 56	WITH YOUR LOVE (2nd re-entry) *HMV POP 130*	20	1
26 Oct 56	ST. THERESE OF THE ROSES *HMV POP 250*	27	1
16 Nov 56 ●	ST. THERESE OF THE ROSES (re-entry) *HMV POP 250*	3	19
12 Apr 57	THE WORLD IS MINE *HMV POP 303*	30	1
3 May 57	THE WORLD IS MINE (re-entry) *HMV POP 303*	29	2
10 May 57	CHAPEL OF THE ROSES *HMV POP 325*	13	8
31 May 57	THE WORLD IS MINE (2nd re-entry) *HMV POP 303*	26	1
29 Nov 57 ●	MY SPECIAL ANGEL *HMV POP 419*	3	14
21 Mar 58	TO BE LOVED *HMV POP 459* [1]	14	12
17 Oct 58 ●	MORE THAN EVER (COME PRIMA) *HMV POP 538* [1]	5	14
27 Feb 59	WAIT FOR ME/WILLINGLY *HMV POP 590*	28	1
13 Mar 59	WAIT FOR ME (re-entry) *HMV POP 590*	13	14

[1] Malcolm Vaughan with the Michael Sammes Singers

Norman VAUGHAN *UK, male vocalist* — 5 wks

17 May 62	SWINGING IN THE RAIN *Pye 7N 15438*	34	5

Sarah VAUGHAN ✒ *US, female vocalist* — 34 wks

27 Sep 57	PASSING STRANGERS *Mercury MT 164* [1]	22	2
11 Sep 59 ●	BROKEN HEARTED MELODY *Mercury AMT 1057*	7	13
29 Dec 60	LET'S/SERENATA *Columbia DB 4542*	37	3
2 Feb 61	LET'S/SERENATA (re-entry) *Columbia DB 4542*	47	1
12 Mar 69	PASSING STRANGERS (re-issue) *Mercury MF 1082* [1]	20	15

[1] Billy Eckstine and Sarah Vaughan

Billy VAUGHN ℂ *US, orchestra and chorus* — 8 wks

27 Jan 56	SHIFTING WHISPERING SANDS *London HLD 8205* [1]	20	1
23 Mar 56	THEME FROM THE 'THREEPENNY OPERA' *London HLD 8238*	12	7

[1] Billy Vaughn Orchestra and Chorus, narration by Ken Nordene

VDC – See BLAST featuring VDC

Bobby VEE ● *Early 1960s teen idol, b. Robert Velline, 30 April, 1943,
North Dakota. This photogenic, Buddy Holly-influenced teenaged vocalist
(whose backing band once included Bob Dylan) was rarely away
from the UK or US charts in the pre-Beat Boom years* — 134 wks

19 Jan 61 ●	RUBBER BALL *London HLG 9255*	4	11
13 Apr 61 ●	MORE THAN I CAN SAY/STAYING IN *London HLG 9316*	4	16
3 Aug 61 ●	HOW MANY TEARS *London HLG 9389*	10	13
26 Oct 61 ●	TAKE GOOD CARE OF MY BABY *London HLG 9438* ▲	3	16

21 Dec 61	●	RUN TO HIM *London HLG 9470*	6	15
8 Mar 62		PLEASE DON'T ASK ABOUT BARBARA		
		Liberty LIB 55419	29	9
7 Jun 62	●	SHARING YOU *Liberty LIB 55451*	10	13
27 Sep 62		A FOREVER KIND OF LOVE *Liberty LIB 10046*	13	19
7 Feb 63	●	THE NIGHT HAS A THOUSAND EYES		
		Liberty LIB 10069	3	12
20 Jun 63		BOBBY TOMORROW *Liberty LIB 55530*	21	10

*'Staying In' listed with 'More Than I Can Say' from 13 Apr to 4 May, 1961.
It peaked at No 13*

Louie VEGA and Marc ANTHONY
US, male vocal/instrumental duo **4 wks**

5 Oct 91	RIDE ON THE RHYTHM *Atlantic A 7602* [1]	71	1
23 May 92	RIDE ON THE RHYTHM (re-issue) *Atlantic A 7486*	70	1
31 Jan 98	RIDE ON THE RHYTHM *Perfecto PERF 151CD1* [2]	36	2

[1] Little Louie Vega and Marc Anthony [2] Little Louie and Mark Anthony

Suzanne VEGA ♂ ☺ *US, female vocalist* **52 wks**

18 Jan 86	SMALL BLUE THING *A & M AM 294*	65	3
22 Mar 86	MARLENE ON THE WALL *A & M AM 309*	21	9
7 Jun 86	LEFT OF CENTER *A & M AM 320* [1]	32	9
23 May 87	LUKA *A & M VEGA 1*	23	8
18 Jul 87	TOM'S DINER *A & M VEGA 2*	58	3
19 May 90	BOOK OF DREAMS *A & M AM 559*	66	1
28 Jul 90	● TOM'S DINER *A & M AM 592* [2]	2	10
22 Aug 92	IN LIVERPOOL *A & M AM 0029*	52	2
24 Oct 92	99.9 F *A & M AM 0085*	46	2
19 Dec 92	BLOOD MAKES NOISE *A & M AM 0112*	60	3
6 Mar 93	WHEN HEROES GO DOWN *A & M AMCD 0158*	58	1
22 Feb 97	NO CHEAP THRILL *A & M 5818692*	40	1

[1] Suzanne Vega featuring Joe Jackson [2] DNA featuring Suzanne Vega

Tata VEGA *US, female vocalist* **4 wks**

26 May 79	GET IT UP FOR LOVE/I JUST KEEP THINKING ABOUT YOU BABY		
	Motown TMG 1140	52	4

VEGAS *UK, male vocal/instrumental duo* **10 wks**

19 Sep 92	POSSESSED *RCA 74321110437*	32	4
28 Nov 92	SHE *RCA 74321124657*	43	4
3 Apr 93	WALK INTO THE WIND *RCA 74321122462*	65	2

Rosie VELA *US, female vocalist* **7 wks**

17 Jan 87	MAGIC SMILE *A & M AM 369*	27	7

Wil VELOZ – See LOS DEL MAR featuring Wil VELOZ

VELVELETTES *US, female vocal group* **7 wks**

31 Jul 71	THESE THINGS WILL KEEP ME LOVING YOU		
	Tamla Motown TMG 780	34	7

VELVET UNDERGROUND
UK/US, male/female vocal/instrumental group **1 wk**

12 Mar 94	VENUS IN FURS *Sire W 0224CD*	71	1

VELVETS *US, male vocal group* **2 wks**

11 May 61	THAT LUCKY OLD SUN *London HLU 9328*	46	1
17 Aug 61	TONIGHT (COULD BE THE NIGHT) *London HLU 9372*	50	1

VENGABOYS ☺ ☻ *Holland / Spain / Hungary / Brazil,
male/female vocal/production group* **5 wks**

28 Nov 98	● UP AND DOWN *Positiva CDTIV 105* ....4†	5

VENT 414 *UK, male vocal/instrumental group* **1 wk**

28 Sep 96	FIXER *Polydor 5753292*	71	1

VENTURES ☻ *US, male instrumental group* **31 wks**

8 Sep 60	●	WALK DON'T RUN *Top Rank JAR 417*	8	13
1 Dec 60	●	PERFIDIA *London HLG 9232*	4	13
9 Mar 61		RAM-BUNK-SHUSH *London HLG 9292*	45	1
11 May 61		LULLABY OF THE LEAVES *London HLG 9344*	43	4

Al VERLAINE – See PING PING and Al VERLAINE

VERNONS GIRLS ☻ *UK, female vocal group* **31 wks**

17 May 62	LOVER PLEASE *Decca F 11450*	16	9
23 Aug 62	LOVER PLEASE (RE-ENTRY)/YOU KNOW WHAT I MEAN		
	(re-entry) *Decca F 11450*	39	7
6 Sep 62	LOCO-MOTION *Decca F 11495*	47	1
18 Oct 62	YOU KNOW WHAT I MEAN (re-entry) *Decca F 11450*	37	3
15 Nov 62	YOU KNOW WHAT I MEAN (2nd re-entry) *Decca F 11450*	50	1
3 Jan 63	FUNNY ALL OVER *Decca F 11549*	31	8
18 Apr 63	DO THE BIRD *Decca F 11629*	50	1
2 May 63	DO THE BIRD (re-entry) *Decca F 11629*	44	1

*'You Know What I Mean' was not coupled with 'Lover Please' on the chart of
23 Aug, 1962, but both sides of this record were listed for the following six weeks*

VERNON'S WONDERLAND
Germany, male producer – Matthias Hoffmann **1 wk**

25 May 96	VERNON'S WONDERLAND *Eye-Q Classics EYECL 004CD*	59	1

VERUCA SALT *US, male/female vocal/instrumental group* **5 wks**

2 Jul 94	SEETHER *Scared Hitless FRET 003CD*	61	1
3 Dec 94	SEETHER (re-issue) *Hi-Rise FLATSDG 12*	73	1
4 Feb 95	NUMBER ONE BLIND *Hi-Rise FLATSCD 16*	68	1
22 Feb 97	VOLCANO GIRLS *Outpost OPRCD 22197*	56	1
30 Aug 97	BENJAMIN *Outpost OPRCD 22261*	75	1

VERVE ☹ ✎ ☻ *UK, male vocal/instrumental group* **50 wks**

4 Jul 92		SHE'S A SUPERSTAR *Hut HUT 16*	66	1
22 May 93		BLUE *Hut HUTCD 29*	69	1
13 May 95		THIS IS MUSIC *Hut HUTCD 54*	35	3
24 Jun 95		ON YOUR OWN *Hut HUTCD 55*	28	2
30 Sep 95		HISTORY *Hut HUTCD 59*	24	3
28 Jun 97	●	BITTER SWEET SYMPHONY *Virgin HUTDG 82*	2	11
13 Sep 97	★	THE DRUGS DON'T WORK *Hut HUTDG 88* ■	1	12
6 Dec 97	●	LUCKY MAN *Hut HUTDG 92*	7	13
3 Jan 98		THE DRUGS DON'T WORK (re-entry) *Hut HUTDG 88*	66	1
3 Jan 98		BITTER SWEET SYMPHONY (re-entry) *Hut HUTDG 82*	70	2
30 May 98		SONNET *Hut 8950752*	74	1

VIBRATIONS – See Tony JACKSON and the VIBRATIONS

VIBRATORS ☹ ✎ ☻ *UK, male vocal/instrumental group* **8 wks**

18 Mar 78	AUTOMATIC LOVER *Epic EPC 6137*	35	5
17 Jun 78	JUDY SAYS (KNOCK YOU IN THE HEAD) *Epic EPC 6393*	70	3

VICE SQUAD *UK, male/female vocal/instrumental group* **1 wk**

13 Feb 82	OUT OF REACH *Zonophone Z 26*	68	1

VICIOUS PINK *UK, male/female vocal/instrumental duo* **4 wks**

15 Sep 84	CCCAN'T YOU SEE *Parlophone R 6074*	67	4

Mike VICKERS – See Kenny EVERETT

Maria VIDAL ☻ ☺ *US, female vocalist* **13 wks**

24 Aug 85	BODY ROCK *EMI America EA 189*	11	13

VIDEO KIDS *Holland, male/female vocal duo* **1 wk**

5 Oct 85	WOODPECKERS FROM SPACE *Epic A 6504*	72	1

VIDEO SYMPHONIC *UK, orchestra* **3 wks**

24 Oct 81	THE FLAME TREES OF THIKA *EMI EMI 5222*	42	3

VIENNA PHILHARMONIC ORCHESTRA ℂ 𝄞
Austria, orchestra — **14 wks**

18 Dec 71	THEME FROM 'THE ONEDIN LINE' *Decca F 13259*	15	14

VIEW FROM THE HILL
UK, male/female vocal/instrumental group — **6 wks**

19 Jul 86	NO CONVERSATION *EMI EMI 5565*	58	3
21 Feb 87	I'M NO REBEL *EMI EM 5580*	59	3

VIKKI
UK, female vocalist — **3 wks**

4 May 85	LOVE IS . . . *PRT 7P 326*	49	3

VILLAGE PEOPLE ⚓ *US, male vocal/instrumental group* — **63 wks**

3 Dec 77	SAN FRANCISCO (YOU'VE GOT ME) *DJM DJS 10817*	45	5
25 Nov 78	★ Y.M.C.A. *Mercury 6007 192* ◆	1	16
17 Mar 79	● IN THE NAVY *Mercury 6007 209*	2	9
16 Jun 79	GO WEST *Mercury 6007 221*	15	8
9 Aug 80	CAN'T STOP THE MUSIC *Mercury MER 16*	11	11
9 Feb 85	SEX OVER THE PHONE *Record Shack SOHO 34*	59	5
4 Dec 93	Y.M.C.A. (re-mix) *Bell 74321177182*	12	7
28 May 94	IN THE NAVY (re-mix) *Bell 74321198192*	36	2

V.I.M. *UK, male instrumental/production group* — **1 wk**

26 Jan 91	MAGGIE'S LAST PARTY *F2 BOZ 1*	68	1

Gene VINCENT 🎸 *US, male vocalist* — **51 wks**

13 Jul 56	BE BOP A LULA *Capitol CL 14599*	30	2
24 Aug 56	BE BOP A LULA (re-entry) *Capitol CL 14599*	16	3
28 Sep 56	BE BOP A LULA (2nd re-entry) *Capitol CL 14599*	23	2
12 Oct 56	RACE WITH THE DEVIL *Capitol CL 14628*	28	1
19 Oct 56	BLUE JEAN BOP *Capitol CL 14637*	16	5
8 Jan 60	WILD CAT *Capitol CL 15099*	21	3
10 Mar 60	MY HEART *Capitol CL 15115*	16	6
10 Mar 60	WILD CAT (re-entry) *Capitol CL 15099*	39	3
28 Apr 60	MY HEART (re-entry) *Capitol CL 15115*	47	1
19 May 60	MY HEART (2nd re-entry) *Capitol CL 15115*	36	1
16 Jun 60	PISTOL PACKIN' MAMA *Capitol CL 15136*	15	9
1 Jun 61	SHE SHE LITTLE SHEILA *Capitol CL 15202*	22	10
17 Aug 61	SHE SHE LITTLE SHEILA (re-entry) *Capitol CL 15202*	44	1
31 Aug 61	I'M GOING HOME *Capitol CL 15215*	36	4

VINDALOO SUMMER SPECIAL
UK, male/female vocal/instrumental group — **3 wks**

19 Jul 86	ROCKIN' WITH RITA (HEAD TO TOE) *Vindaloo UGH 13*	56	3

Bobby VINTON ℂ *US, male vocalist* — **29 wks**

2 Aug 62	ROSES ARE RED *Columbia DB 4878* ▲	15	8
19 Dec 63	THERE I'VE SAID IT AGAIN *Columbia DB 7179* ▲	34	10
29 Sep 90	● BLUE VELVET *Epic 6505240* ▲	2	10
17 Nov 90	ROSES ARE RED (MY LOVE) (re-issue) *Epic 6564677*	71	1

VIOLINSKI ☻ *UK, male instrumental group* — **9 wks**

17 Feb 79	CLOG DANCE *Jet 136*	17	9

V.I.P.s *UK, male instrumental/production group* — **4 wks**

6 Sep 80	THE QUARTER MOON *Gem GEMS 39*	55	4

VIPER *Belgium, production group* — **1 wk**

7 Feb 98	THE TWISTER *Hooj Choons HOOJCD 59*	55	1

VIPERS SKIFFLE GROUP ☻
UK, male vocal/instrumental group — **18 wks**

25 Jan 57	● DON'T YOU ROCK ME DADDY-O *Parlophone R 4261*	10	9
22 Mar 57	● CUMBERLAND GAP *Parlophone R 4289*	10	6
31 May 57	STREAMLINE TRAIN *Parlophone R 4308*	23	3

VIRUS *UK, male instrumental/production duo* — **3 wks**

26 Aug 95	SUN *Perfecto PERF 107CD*	62	1
25 Jan 97	MOON *Perfecto PERF 134CD*	36	2

VISAGE ☻ ☺ *UK, male vocal/instrumental group* — **56 wks**

20 Dec 80	● FADE TO GREY *Polydor POSP 194*	8	15
14 Mar 81	MIND OF A TOY *Polydor POSP 236*	13	8
11 Jul 81	VISAGE *Polydor POSP 293*	21	7
13 Mar 82	DAMNED DON'T CRY *Polydor POSP 390*	11	8
26 Jun 82	NIGHT TRAIN *Polydor POSP 441*	12	10
13 Nov 82	PLEASURE BOYS *Polydor POSP 523*	44	3
1 Sep 84	LOVE GLOVE *Polydor POSP 691*	54	3
28 Aug 93	FADE TO GREY (re-mix) *Polydor PZCD 282*	39	2

Michelle VISAGE – *See S.O.U.L. S.Y.S.T.E.M. introducing Michelle VISAGE*

VISCOUNTS ☻ *UK, male vocal group* — **18 wks**

13 Oct 60	SHORT'NIN' BREAD *Pye 7N 15287*	16	8
14 Sep 61	WHO PUT THE BOMP *Pye 7N 15379*	21	10

VISION *UK, male vocal/instrumental group* — **1 wk**

9 Jul 83	LOVE DANCE *MVM MVM 2886*	74	1

VISIONMASTERS – *See Kylie MINOGUE*

VIXEN *US, female vocal/instrumental group* — **21 wks**

3 Sep 88	EDGE OF A BROKEN HEART *Manhattan MT 48*	51	4
4 Mar 89	CRYIN' *EMI Manhattan MT 60*	27	4
3 Jun 89	LOVE MADE ME *EMI-USA MT 66*	36	4
2 Sep 89	EDGE OF A BROKEN HEART (re-entry) *EMI-USA MT 48*	59	2
28 Jul 90	HOW MUCH LOVE *EMI-USA MT 87*	35	3
20 Oct 90	LOVE IS A KILLER *EMI-USA MT 91*	41	2
16 Mar 91	NOT A MINUTE TOO SOON *EMI America MT 93*	37	2

VOGGUE *Canada, female vocal duo* — **6 wks**

18 Jul 81	DANCIN' THE NIGHT AWAY *Mercury MER 76*	39	6

VOICE OF THE BEEHIVE ☹ ☻
US/UK, male/female vocal/instrumental group — **51 wks**

14 Nov 87	I SAY NOTHING *London LON 151*	45	5
5 Mar 88	I WALK THE EARTH *London LON 169*	42	4
14 May 88	DON'T CALL ME BABY *London LON 175*	15	10
23 Jul 88	I SAY NOTHING (re-issue) *London LON 190*	22	6
22 Oct 88	I WALK THE EARTH (re-issue) *London LON 206*	46	4
13 Jul 91	MONSTERS AND ANGELS *London LON 302*	17	10
28 Sep 91	I THINK I LOVE YOU *London LON 308*	25	6
11 Jan 92	PERFECT PLACE *London LON 312*	37	6

See also VARIOUS ARTISTS (EPs & LPs) – Gimme Shelter (EP)

VOICES OF LIFE *US, male/female vocal/production duo* — **2 wks**

21 Mar 98	THE WORD IS LOVE (SAY THE WORD) *AM:PM 5825272*	26	2

Sterling VOID *UK, male vocalist* — **3 wks**

4 Feb 89	RUNAWAY GIRL/IT'S ALRIGHT *ffrr FFR 21*	53	3

VOLCANO *Norway/UK, male/female vocal/instrumental group* — **4 wks**

23 Jul 94	MORE TO LOVE *Deconstruction 74321221832*	32	3
18 Nov 95	THAT'S THE WAY LOVE IS *EXP EXPCD 002* [1]	72	1

[1] Volcano with Sam Cartwright

VOYAGE ⚓ *UK/France, disco aggregation* — **27 wks**

17 Jun 78	FROM EAST TO WEST/SCOTS MACHINE *GTO GT 224*	13	13
25 Nov 78	SOUVENIRS *GTO GT 241*	56	7
24 Mar 79	LET'S FLY AWAY *GTO GT 245*	38	7

'Scots Machine' credited from 24 Jun, 1978, until end of record's chart run

VOYAGER *UK, male vocal/instrumental group*   **8 wks**

| 26 May 79 | HALFWAY HOTEL *Mountain VOY 001* | 33 | 8 |

VYBE *US, female vocal group*   **1 wk**

| 7 Oct 95 | WARM SUMMER DAZE *Fourth & Broadway BRCD 315* | 60 | 1 |

Kristine W *US, female vocalist*   **8 wks**

21 May 94	LOVE COME HOME *Triangle BLUESCD 001* [1]	73	1
25 Jun 94	FEEL WHAT YOU WANT *Champion CHAMPCD 304*	33	3
25 May 96	ONE MORE TRY *Champion CHAMPCD 317*	41	1
21 Dec 96	LAND OF THE LIVING *Champion CHAMPCD 324*	57	1
5 Jul 97	FEEL WHAT YOU WANT *Champion CHAMPCD 329*	40	2

[1] Our Tribe with Franke Pharoah and Kristine W

Bill WADDINGTON – *See CORONATION STREET CAST featuring Bill WADDINGTON*

Adam WADE *US, male vocalist*   **6 wks**

| 8 Jun 61 | TAKE GOOD CARE OF HER *HMV POP 843* | 38 | 1 |
| 22 Jun 61 | TAKE GOOD CARE OF HER (re-entry) *HMV POP 843* | 38 | 5 |

WAG YA TAIL *UK, male vocal/instrumental group*   **1 wk**

| 3 Oct 92 | XPAND YA MIND (EXPANSIONS) *PWL International PWL 238* | 49 | 1 |

WAH! ☹ ☺ *UK, male vocal/instrumental group*   **26 wks**

25 Dec 82 ●	THE STORY OF THE BLUES *Eternal JF 1*	3	12
19 Mar 83	HOPE (I WISH YOU'D BELIEVE ME) *WEA X 9880*	37	5
30 Jun 84	COME BACK *Beggars Banquet BEG 111* [1]	20	9

[1] Mighty Wah

Donnie WAHLBERG – *See SEIKO and Donnie WAHLBERG*

WAIKIKIS *Belgium, male instrumental group*   **2 wks**

| 11 Mar 65 | HAWAII TATTOO *Pye International 7N 25286* | 41 | 2 |

WAILERS – *See Bob MARLEY and the WAILERS*

John WAITE ☺ *UK, male vocalist*   **13 wks**

| 29 Sep 84 ● | MISSING YOU *EMI America EA 182* ▲ | 9 | 11 |
| 13 Feb 93 | MISSING YOU (re-issue) *Chrysalis CDCHS 3938* | 56 | 2 |

WAITRESSES *UK, female vocal group*   **4 wks**

| 18 Dec 82 | CHRISTMAS WRAPPING *Ze/Island WIP 6821* | 45 | 4 |

Johnny WAKELIN ☺ *UK, male vocalist*   **20 wks**

| 18 Jan 75 ● | BLACK SUPERMAN (MUHAMMAD ALI) *Pye 7N 45420* [1] | 7 | 10 |
| 24 Jul 76 ● | IN ZAIRE *Pye 7N 45595* | 4 | 10 |

[1] Johnny Wakelin and the Kinshasa Band

Narada Michael WALDEN *US, male vocalist/producer*   **28 wks**

| 23 Feb 80 | TONIGHT I'M ALRIGHT *Atlantic K 11437* | 34 | 9 |
| 26 Apr 80 ● | I SHOULDA LOVED YA *Atlantic K 11413* | 8 | 9 |

| 23 Apr 88 ● | DIVINE EMOTIONS *Reprise W 7967* [1] | 8 | 10 |

[1] Narada

Gary WALKER *US, male vocalist*   **12 wks**

| 24 Feb 66 | YOU DON'T LOVE ME *CBS 202036* | 26 | 6 |
| 26 May 66 | TWINKIE LEE *CBS 202081* | 26 | 6 |

See also WALKER BROTHERS

John WALKER *US, male vocalist*   **6 wks**

| 5 Jul 67 | ANNABELLA *Philips BF 1593* | 48 | 1 |
| 19 Jul 67 | ANNABELLA (re-entry) *Philips BF 1593* | 24 | 5 |

See also WALKER BROTHERS

Junior WALKER and the ALL-STARS 🎷
US, male instrumental/vocal group   **59 wks**

18 Aug 66	HOW SWEET IT IS *Tamla Motown TMG 571*	22	10
2 Apr 69	(I'M A) ROAD RUNNER *Tamla Motown TMG 691*	12	12
18 Oct 69	WHAT DOES IT TAKE (TO WIN YOUR LOVE) *Tamla Motown TMG 712*	13	12
26 Aug 72	WALK IN THE NIGHT *Tamla Motown TMG 824*	16	11
27 Jan 73	TAKE ME GIRL I'M READY *Tamla Motown TMG 840*	16	9
30 Jun 73	WAY BACK HOME *Tamla Motown TMG 857*	35	5

Scott WALKER 🎤 *US, male vocalist*   **30 wks**

6 Dec 67	JACKIE *Philips BF 1628*	22	9
1 May 68 ●	JOANNA *Philips BF 1662*	7	11
11 Jun 69	LIGHTS OF CINCINATTI *Philips BF 1793*	13	10

See also WALKER BROTHERS

WALKER BROTHERS ☺ *US, male vocal group*   **93 wks**

29 Apr 65	LOVE HER *Philips BF 1409*	20	13
19 Aug 65 ★	MAKE IT EASY ON YOURSELF *Philips BF 1428*	1	14
2 Dec 65 ●	MY SHIP IS COMING IN *Philips BF 1454*	3	12
3 Mar 66 ★	THE SUN AIN'T GONNA SHINE ANYMORE *Philips BF 1473*	1	11
14 Jul 66	(BABY) YOU DON'T HAVE TO TELL ME *Philips BF 1497*	13	8
22 Sep 66	ANOTHER TEAR FALLS *Philips BF 1514*	12	8
15 Dec 66	DEADLIER THAN THE MALE *Philips BF 1537*	34	6
9 Feb 67	STAY WITH ME BABY *Philips BF 1548*	26	6
18 May 67	WALKING IN THE RAIN *Philips BF 1576*	26	6
17 Jan 76 ●	NO REGRETS *GTO GT 42*	7	9

See also Gary WALKER; John WALKER; Scott WALKER

WALL OF SOUND featuring Gerald LETHAN
US, male vocal/instrumental group   **1 wk**

| 31 Jul 93 | CRITICAL (IF YOU ONLY KNEW) *Positiva CDTIV 4* | 73 | 1 |

WALL OF VOODOO *US, male vocal/instrumental group*   **3 wks**

| 19 Mar 83 | MEXICAN RADIO *Illegal ILS 36* | 64 | 3 |

Jerry WALLACE *US, male vocalist*   **1 wk**

| 23 Jun 60 | YOU'RE SINGING OUR LOVE SONG TO SOMEBODY ELSE *London HLH 9110* | 46 | 1 |

WALLFLOWERS *US, male vocal / instrumental group*   **1 wk**

| 12 Jul 97 | ONE HEADLIGHT *Interscope IND 95532* | 54 | 1 |

Bob WALLIS and his STORYVILLE JAZZ BAND
UK, male jazz band, Bob Wallis vocalist/instrumentalist – trumpet   **7 wks**

| 6 Jul 61 | I'M SHY MARY ELLEN I'M SHY *Pye Jazz 7NJ 2043* | 44 | 2 |
| 4 Jan 62 | COME ALONG PLEASE *Pye Jazz 7NJ 2048* | 33 | 5 |

Joe WALSH 🎸 *US, male vocalist*   **15 wks**

| 16 Jul 77 | ROCKY MOUNTAIN WAY EP *ABC ABE 12002* | 39 | 4 |
| 8 Jul 78 | LIFE'S BEEN GOOD *Asylum K 13129* | 14 | 11 |

Tracks on Rocky Mountain Way EP: Rocky Mountain Way / Turn to Stone / Meadows / Walk Away

Maureen WALSH – See MAUREEN

Sheila WALSH – See Cliff RICHARD

Steve WALSH ☺ ✧ UK, male vocalist — 18 wks

Date	Title	Pos	Wks
18 Jul 87	I FOUND LOVIN' *A1 A1 299*	74	1
29 Aug 87 ●	I FOUND LOVIN' (re-entry) *A1 A1 299*	9	12
12 Dec 87	LET'S GET TOGETHER TONITE *A1 A1 303*	74	1
30 Jul 88	AIN'T NO STOPPING US NOW (PARTY FOR THE WORLD) *A1 A1 304*	44	4

Trevor WALTERS ✧ UK, male vocalist — 22 wks

Date	Title	Pos	Wks
24 Oct 81	LOVE ME TONIGHT *Magnet MAG 198*	27	8
21 Jul 84 ●	STUCK ON YOU *Sanity IS 002*	9	12
1 Dec 84	NEVER LET HER SLIP AWAY *Polydor POSP 716*	73	2

WANG CHUNG UK, male vocal/instrumental group — 12 wks

Date	Title	Pos	Wks
28 Jan 84	DANCE HALL DAYS *Geffen A 3837*	21	12

WANNADIES ☹ Sweden, male/female vocal/instrumental group — 11 wks

Date	Title	Pos	Wks
18 Nov 95	MIGHT BE STARS *Indolent DIE 003CD1*	51	2
24 Feb 96	HOW DOES IT FEEL *Indolent DIE 004CD1*	53	1
20 Apr 96	YOU AND ME SONG *Indolent DIE 005CD*	18	3
7 Sep 96	SOMEONE SOMEWHERE *Indolent DIE 006CD*	38	1
26 Apr 97	HIT *Indolent DIE 009CD1*	20	2
5 Jul 97	SHORTY *Indolent DIE 010CD1*	41	2

Dexter WANSELL US, male instrumentalist – keyboards — 3 wks

Date	Title	Pos	Wks
20 May 78	ALL NIGHT LONG *Philadelphia Interna PIR 6255*	59	3

WAR ♀ US/Canada/Denmark, male vocal/instrumental group — 32 wks

Date	Title	Pos	Wks
24 Jan 76	LOW RIDER *Island WIP 6267*	12	7
26 Jun 76	ME AND BABY BROTHER *Island WIP 6303*	21	7
14 Jan 78	GALAXY *MCA 339*	14	7
15 Apr 78	HEY SENORITA *MCA 359*	40	2
10 Apr 82	YOU GOT THE POWER *RCA 201*	58	4
6 Apr 85	GROOVIN' *Bluebird BR 16*	43	5

Anita WARD ◢ US, female vocalist — 11 wks

Date	Title	Pos	Wks
2 Jun 79 ★	RING MY BELL *TK TKR 7543* ▲	1	11

Billy WARD and HIS DOMINOES ♀ US, male vocal group — 13 wks

Date	Title	Pos	Wks
13 Sep 57	STARDUST *London HLU 8465*	13	11
29 Nov 57	DEEP PURPLE *London HLU 8502*	30	1
3 Jan 58	STARDUST (re-entry) *London HLU 8465*	26	1

Chrissy WARD US, female vocalist — 2 wks

Date	Title	Pos	Wks
24 Jun 95	RIGHT AND EXACT *Ore AG 6CD*	62	1
8 Feb 97	RIGHT AND EXACT (re-mix) *Ore AG 21CD*	59	1

Clifford T WARD ◑ UK, male vocalist — 16 wks

Date	Title	Pos	Wks
30 Jun 73 ●	GAYE *Charisma CB 205*	8	11
26 Jan 74	SCULLERY *Charisma CB 221*	37	5

Michael WARD ℂ UK, male vocalist — 13 wks

Date	Title	Pos	Wks
29 Sep 73	LET THERE BE PEACE ON EARTH (LET IT BEGIN WITH ME) *Philips 6006 340*	15	10
15 Dec 73	LET THERE BE PEACE ON EARTH (LET IT BEGIN WITH ME) (re-entry) *Philips 6006 340*	50	3

WARD BROTHERS UK, male vocal/instrumental group — 8 wks

Date	Title	Pos	Wks
10 Jan 87	CROSS THAT BRIDGE *Siren SIREN 37*	32	8

Justin WARFIELD – See BOMB THE BASS

WARM JETS UK/Canada, male vocal/instrumental group — 4 wks

Date	Title	Pos	Wks
14 Feb 98	NEVER NEVER *Island WAY 6766*	37	2
25 Apr 98	HURRICANE *Island CID 697*	34	2

WARM SOUNDS UK, male vocal duo — 6 wks

Date	Title	Pos	Wks
4 May 67	BIRDS AND BEES *Deram DM 120*	27	6

Toni WARNE UK, female vocalist — 4 wks

Date	Title	Pos	Wks
25 Apr 87	BEN *Mint CHEW 110*	50	4

Jennifer WARNES ◑ US, female vocalist — 37 wks

Date	Title	Pos	Wks
15 Jan 83 ●	UP WHERE WE BELONG *Island WIP 6830* [1] ▲	7	13
25 Jul 87	FIRST WE TAKE MANHATTAN *Cypress PB 49709*	74	1
31 Oct 87 ●	(I'VE HAD) THE TIME OF MY LIFE *RCA PB 49625* [2] ▲	6	12
15 Dec 90	(I'VE HAD) THE TIME OF MY LIFE (re-entry) *RCA PB 49625* [2]	8	11

[1] Joe Cocker and Jennifer Warnes [2] Bill Medley and Jennifer Warnes

WARRANT US, male vocal/instrumental group — 7 wks

Date	Title	Pos	Wks
17 Nov 90	CHERRY PIE *CBS 6562587*	59	2
9 Mar 91	CHERRY PIE (re-issue) *Columbia 6566867*	35	5

Alysha WARREN UK, female vocalist — 4 wks

Date	Title	Pos	Wks
24 Sep 94	I'M SO IN LOVE *Wild Card CARDD 10*	61	1
25 Mar 95	I THOUGHT I MEANT THE WORLD TO YOU *Wild Card CARDD 16*	40	1
27 Jul 96	KEEP ON PUSHING OUR LOVE *Arista 74321390422* [1]	30	2

[1] Nightcrawlers featuring John Reid and Alysha Warren

Ann WARREN – See Ruby MURRAY

Nikita WARREN Italy, female vocalist — 1 wk

Date	Title	Pos	Wks
13 Jul 96	I NEED YOU *VC VCRD 12*	48	1

Dionne WARWICK ✧ ℂ Super-stylish soul diva, b. 12 December, 1940, New Jersey, whose classy and unmistakable vocals on songs written by Burt Bacharach and Hal David produced more than 30 US hits for her between 1962 and 1972 for her. She is a cousin of Whitney Houston — 101 wks

Date	Title	Pos	Wks
13 Feb 64	ANYONE WHO HAD A HEART *Pye International 7N 25234*	42	3
16 Apr 64 ●	WALK ON BY *Pye International 7N 25241*	9	14
30 Jul 64	YOU'LL NEVER GET TO HEAVEN *Pye International 7N 25256*	20	8
8 Oct 64	REACH OUT FOR ME *Pye International 7N 25265*	23	7
1 Apr 65	YOU CAN HAVE HIM *Pye International 7N 25290*	37	5
13 Mar 68	VALLEY OF THE DOLLS *Pye International 7N 25445*	28	8
15 May 68 ●	DO YOU KNOW THE WAY TO SAN JOSE *Pye International 7N 25457*	8	10
19 Oct 74	THEN CAME YOU *Atlantic K 10495* [1] ▲	29	6
23 Oct 82	HEARTBREAKER *Arista ARIST 496*	2	13
11 Dec 82 ●	ALL THE LOVE IN THE WORLD *Arista ARIST 507*	10	10
26 Feb 83	YOURS *Arista ARIST 518*	66	2
28 May 83	I'LL NEVER LOVE THIS WAY AGAIN *Arista ARIST 530*	62	3
9 Nov 85	THAT'S WHAT FRIENDS ARE FOR *Arista ARIST 638* [2] ▲	16	9
15 Aug 87	LOVE POWER *Arista RIS 27* [3]	63	3

[1] Dionne Warwick and the Detroit Spinners [2] Dionne Warwick and Friends featuring Elton John, Stevie Wonder and Gladys Knight [3] Dionne Warwick and Jeffrey Osborne

WAS (NOT WAS) ☺ ◑ US, male vocal/instrumental duo — 58 wks

Date	Title	Pos	Wks
3 Mar 84	OUT COME THE FREAKS *Ze/Geffen A 4178*	41	5
18 Jul 87	SPY IN THE HOUSE OF LOVE *Fontana WAS 2*	51	7
3 Oct 87 ●	WALK THE DINOSAUR *Fontana WAS 3*	10	10
6 Feb 88	SPY IN THE HOUSE OF LOVE (re-entry) *Fontana WAS 2*	21	8
7 May 88	OUT COME THE FREAKS (AGAIN) *Fontana WAS 4*	44	3
16 Jul 88	ANYTHING CAN HAPPEN *Fontana WAS 5*	67	3
26 May 90	PAPA WAS A ROLLING STONE *Fontana WAS 7*	12	7
11 Aug 90	HOW THE HEART BEHAVES *Fontana WAS 8*	53	3

23 May 92		LISTEN LIKE THIEVES *Fontana WAS 10*	58	2
11 Jul 92	●	SHAKE YOUR HEAD *Fontana WAS 11*	4	9
26 Sep 92		SOMEWHERE IN AMERICA (THERE'S A STREET NAMED AFTER MY DAD) *Fontana WAS 12*	57	1

Fontana WAS 4 was a re-recorded version of their first hit. 'Shake Your Head' features uncredited vocals by Ozzy Osbourne and Kim Basinger
See also OZZY OSBOURNE

Martha WASH ☺ 🎤 *US, female vocalist* — 20 wks

28 Nov 92	CARRY ON *RCA 74321125457*	74	1
6 Mar 93	GIVE IT TO YOU *RCA 74321136562*	37	4
10 Jul 93	RUNAROUND/CARRY ON (re-mix) *RCA 74321153702*	49	2
18 Feb 95	I FOUND LOVE *Columbia 6612112* [1]	26	2
13 Jul 96	● KEEP ON JUMPIN' *Manifesto FESCD 11* [2]	8	6
25 Oct 97	CARRY ON (2nd re-mix) *Delirious DELICD 6*	49	1
28 Feb 98	IT'S RAINING MEN…THE SEQUEL *Logic 74321555412* [3]	21	3
15 Aug 98	CATCH THE LIGHT *Logic 74321587912*	45	1

[1] C & C Music Factory featuring Martha Wash [2] Todd Terry featuring Martha Wash and Jocelyn Brown [3] Martha Wash featuring RuPaul

The listed flip side of 'I Found Love' was 'Take a Toke' by C & C Music Factory
See also C & C MUSIC FACTORY

Dinah WASHINGTON *US, female vocalist* — 8 wks

30 Nov 61	SEPTEMBER IN THE RAIN *Mercury AMT 1162*	35	3
18 Jan 62	SEPTEMBER IN THE RAIN (re-entry) *Mercury AMT 1162*	49	1
4 Apr 92	MAD ABOUT THE BOY *Mercury DINAH 1*	41	4

Geno WASHINGTON and the RAM JAM BAND
US, male vocalist, and UK, male instrumental backing group — 20 wks

19 May 66	WATER *Piccadilly 7N 35312*	39	8
21 Jul 66	HI HI HAZEL *Piccadilly 7N 35329*	45	3
25 Aug 66	HI HI HAZEL (re-entry) *Piccadilly 7N 35329*	48	1
6 Oct 66	QUE SERA SERA *Piccadilly 7N 35346*	43	3
2 Feb 67	MICHAEL *Piccadilly 7N 35359*	39	5

Grover WASHINGTON Jr. *US, male instrumentalist – saxophone* — 7 wks

| 16 May 81 | JUST THE TWO OF US *Elektra K 12514* | 34 | 7 |

Although uncredited, Bill Withers vocalises on 'Just the Two of Us'

Keith WASHINGTON – See Kylie MINOGUE

Sarah WASHINGTON ☻ ☺ *UK, female vocalist* — 13 wks

14 Aug 93	I WILL ALWAYS LOVE YOU *Almighty CDALMY 33*	12	7
27 Nov 93	CARELESS WHISPER *Almighty CDALMY 43*	45	2
25 May 96	HEAVEN *AM:PM 5815352*	28	2
12 Oct 96	EVERYTHING *AM:PM 5818872*	30	2

W.A.S.P. ✈ *US, male vocal/instrumental group* — 38 wks

31 May 86	WILD CHILD *Capitol CL 388*	71	2
11 Oct 86	95 – NASTY *Capitol CL 432*	70	1
29 Aug 87	SCREAM UNTIL YOU LIKE IT *Capitol CL 458*	32	5
31 Oct 87	I DON'T NEED NO DOCTOR (LIVE) *Capitol CL 469*	31	5
20 Feb 88	LIVE ANIMAL (F**K LIKE A BEAST) *Music For Nations KUT 109*	61	3
4 Mar 89	MEAN MAN *Capitol CL 521*	21	5
27 May 89	THE REAL ME *Capitol CL 534*	23	5
9 Sep 89	FOREVER FREE *Capitol CL 546*	25	5
4 Apr 92	CHAINSAW CHARLIE (MURDERS IN THE NEW MORGUE) *Parlophone RS 6308*	17	2
6 Jun 92	THE IDOL *Parlophone RPD 6314*	41	2
31 Oct 92	I AM ONE *Parlophone 10RG 6324*	56	1
23 Oct 93	SUNSET AND BABYLON *Capitol CDCL 698*	38	2

WATERBOYS 🎸 ♂ *UK/Ireland, male vocal/instrumental group* — 33 wks

2 Nov 85	THE WHOLE OF THE MOON *Ensign ENY 520*	26	7
14 Jan 89	FISHERMAN'S BLUES *Ensign ENY 621*	32	6
1 Jul 89	AND A BANG ON THE EAR *Ensign ENY 624*	51	4

6 Apr 91	●	THE WHOLE OF THE MOON (re-issue) *Ensign ENY 642*	3	9
8 Jun 91		FISHERMAN'S BLUES (re-issue) *Ensign ENY 645*	75	1
15 May 93		THE RETURN OF PAN *Geffen GFSTD 42*	24	3
24 Jul 93		GLASTONBURY SONG *Geffen GFSTD 49*	29	3

WATERFRONT ☻ *UK, male vocal/instrumental duo* — 19 wks

15 Apr 89	BROKEN ARROW *Polydor WON 3*	63	2
27 May 89	CRY *Polydor WON 1*	17	13
9 Sep 89	NATURE OF LOVE *Polydor WON 2*	63	4

Dennis WATERMAN ☻ *UK, male vocalist* — 17 wks

| 25 Oct 80 | ● I COULD BE SO GOOD FOR YOU *EMI 5009* [1] | 3 | 12 |
| 17 Dec 83 | WHAT ARE WE GONNA GET 'ER INDOORS *EMI MIN 101* [2] | 21 | 5 |

[1] Dennis Waterman with the Dennis Waterman Band
[2] Dennis Waterman and George Cole

Crystal WATERS ☺ *US, female vocalist* — 35 wks

18 May 91	● GYPSY WOMAN (LA DA DEE) *A & M AM 772*	2	10
7 Sep 91	MAKIN' HAPPY *A & M AM 790*	18	6
11 Jan 92	MEGAMIX *A & M AM 843*	39	3
3 Oct 92	GYPSY WOMAN (re-mix) *Epic 6584377*	35	2
23 Apr 94	100% PURE LOVE *A & M 8586692*	15	7
2 Jul 94	GHETTO DAY *A & M 8589592*	40	2
25 Nov 95	RELAX *Manifesto FESCD 4*	37	2
24 Aug 96	IN DE GHETTO *Manifesto FESCD 12* [1]	35	2
19 Apr 97	SAY …IF YOU FEEL ALRIGHT *Mercury 5742912*	45	1

[1] David Morales and the Bad Yard Club featuring Crystal Waters and Delta

The listed flip side of 'Gypsy Woman' (re-mix) was 'Peace' (re-mix) by Sabrina Johnston

Muddy WATERS *US, male vocalist/instrumentalist – guitar* — 6 wks

| 16 Jul 88 | MANNISH BOY *Epic MUD 1* | 51 | 6 |

Roger WATERS *UK, male vocalist/instrumentalist* — 8 wks

30 May 87	RADIO WAVES *Harvest EM 6*	74	1
26 Dec 87	THE TIDE IS TURNING (AFTER LIVE AID) *Harvest EM 37*	54	4
5 Sep 92	WHAT GOD WANTS PART 1 *Columbia 6581390*	35	3

Michael WATFORD *US, male vocalist* — 2 wks

| 26 Feb 94 | SO INTO YOU *East West A 8309CD* | 53 | 2 |

Jody WATLEY 🎤 ☺ *US, female vocalist* — 35 wks

9 May 87	LOOKING FOR A NEW LOVE *MCA MCA 1107*	13	11
17 Oct 87	DON'T YOU WANT ME *MCA MCA 1198*	55	3
8 Apr 89	REAL LOVE *MCA MCA 1324*	31	7
12 Aug 89	FRIENDS *MCA MCA 1352* [1]	21	6
10 Feb 90	EVERYTHING *MCA MCA 1395*	74	2
11 Apr 92	I'M THE ONE YOU NEED *MCA MCS 1608*	50	3
21 May 94	WHEN A MAN LOVES A WOMAN *MCA MCSTD 1964*	33	2
25 Apr 98	OFF THE HOOK *Atlantic AT 0024CD1*	51	1

[1] Jody Watley with Eric B and Rakim

Johnny 'Guitar' WATSON
US, male vocalist / instrumentalist – guitar — 8 wks

| 28 Aug 76 | I NEED IT *DJM DJS 10694* | 35 | 5 |
| 23 Apr 77 | A REAL MOTHER FOR YA *DJM DJT 10762* | 44 | 3 |

WAVELENGTH ☻ *UK, male vocal group* — 12 wks

| 10 Jul 82 | HURRY HOME *Ariola ARO 281* | 17 | 12 |

WAX ☻ *US/UK, male vocal/instrumental duo* — 16 wks

| 12 Apr 86 | RIGHT BETWEEN THE EYES *RCA PB 40509* | 60 | 5 |
| 1 Aug 87 | BRIDGE TO YOUR HEART *RCA PB 41405* | 12 | 11 |

Anthony WAY *UK, choirboy* — 2 wks

| 15 Apr 95 | PANIS ANGELICUS *Decca 4481642* | 55 | 2 |

UK No 1 ★   UK Top 10 ●   UK million seller ◆   UK entry at No 1 ■   US No 1 ▲

A WAY OF LIFE US, male/female vocal/instrumental group — 3 wks

21 Apr 90	TRIPPIN' ON YOUR LOVE Eternal YZ 464	55	3

WAY OF THE WEST ☺ UK, male vocal/instrumental group — 5 wks

25 Apr 81	DON'T SAY THAT'S JUST FOR WHITE BOYS		
	Mercury MER 66	54	5

WAY OUT WEST ☺ UK, male instrumental/production duo — 12 wks

3 Dec 94	AJARE Deconstruction 74321243802	52	1
2 Mar 96	DOMINATION Deconstruction 74321342822	38	2
14 Sep 96	THE GIFT Deconstruction 74321401912 [1]	15	5
30 Aug 97	BLUE Deconstruction 74321477512	41	2
29 Nov 97	AJARE (re-mix) Deconstruction 74321521352	36	2

[1] Way Out West featuring Miss Joanna Law

Bruce WAYNE Germany, male DJ — 2 wks

13 Dec 97	READY Logic 74321527012	44	1
4 Jul 98	NO GOOD FOR ME Logic 74321587052	70	1

Jeff WAYNE ✪ ✎ US, orchestra — 3 wks

10 Jul 82	MATADOR CBS A 2493	57	3

See also Jeff WAYNE'S WAR OF THE WORLDS

Jeff WAYNE'S WAR OF THE WORLDS
US/UK, male/female vocal/instrumental cast — 18 wks

9 Sep 78	EVE OF THE WAR CBS 6496	36	8
25 Nov 89 ●	EVE OF THE WAR (re-mix) CBS 6551267	3	10

See also Jeff WAYNE

WEATHER GIRLS ☺ ♪ US, female vocal duo — 14 wks

27 Aug 83	IT'S RAINING MEN CBS A 2924	73	3
3 Mar 84 ●	IT'S RAINING MEN (re-entry) CBS A 2924	2	11

WEATHER PROPHETS UK, male vocal/instrumental group — 2 wks

28 Mar 87	SHE COMES FROM THE RAIN Elevation ACID 1	62	2

WEATHERMEN – See Jonathan KING

Marti WEBB ☾ UK, female vocalist — 42 wks

9 Feb 80 ●	TAKE THAT LOOK OFF YOUR FACE Polydor POSP 100	3	12
19 Apr 80	TELL ME ON A SUNDAY Polydor POSP 111	67	2
20 Sep 80	YOUR EARS SHOULD BE BURNING NOW		
	Polydor POSP 166	61	4
8 Jun 85 ●	BEN Starblend STAR 6	5	11
20 Sep 86	ALWAYS THERE BBC RESL 190	13	12
6 Jun 87	I CAN'T LET GO Rainbow RBR 12	65	1

'Always There' features the Simon May Orchestra
See also Simon MAY

Joan WEBER ☾ US, female vocalist — 1 wk

18 Feb 55	LET ME GO LOVER Philips PB 389 ▲	16	1

WEDDING PRESENT ☹ UK, male vocal/instrumental group — 38 wks

5 Mar 88	NOBODY'S TWISTING YOUR ARM Reception REC 009	46	2
1 Oct 88	WHY ARE YOU BEING SO REASONABLE NOW		
	Reception REC 011	42	2
7 Oct 89	KENNEDY RCA PB 43117	33	3
17 Feb 90	BRASSNECK RCA PB 43403	24	3
29 Sep 90	3 SONGS EP RCA PB 44021	25	4
11 May 91	DALLIANCE RCA PB 44495	29	3
27 Jul 91	LOVENEST RCA PT 44750	58	1
18 Jan 92	BLUE EYES RCA PB 45185	26	2
15 Feb 92	GO-GO DANCER RCA PB 45183	20	1
14 Mar 92	THREE RCA PB 45181	14	2
18 Apr 92	SILVER SHORTS RCA PB 45311	14	1
16 May 92 ●	COME PLAY WITH ME RCA PB 45313	10	2

13 Jun 92	CALIFORNIA RCA PB 45315	16	1
18 Jul 92	FLYING SAUCER RCA 74321101157	22	1
15 Aug 92	BOING! RCA 74321101177	19	1
19 Sep 92	LOVE SLAVE RCA 743211101167	17	1
17 Oct 92	STICKY RCA 74321116917	17	1
14 Nov 92	THE QUEEN OF OUTER SPACE RCA 74321116927	23	1
19 Dec 92	NO CHRISTMAS RCA 74321116937	25	1
10 Sep 94	YEAH YEAH YEAH YEAH YEAH Island CID 585	51	2
26 Nov 94	IT'S A GAS Island CID 591	71	1
31 Aug 96	2, 3, GO Cooking Vinyl FRYCD 048	67	1
25 Jan 97	MONTREAL Cooking Vinyl FRYCD 053	40	1

Tracks on 3 Songs EP: Corduroy / Crawl / Make Me Smile (Come Up and See Me)

Fred WEDLOCK ✪ UK, male vocalist — 10 wks

31 Jan 81 ●	OLDEST SWINGER IN TOWN Rocket XPRES 46	6	10

WEE PAPA GIRL RAPPERS ◀ UK, female rap/vocal duo — 27 wks

12 Mar 88	FAITH Jive JIVE 164	60	4
25 Jun 88	HEAT IT UP Jive JIVE 174 [1]	21	9
1 Oct 88 ●	WEE RULE Jive JIVE 185	6	9
24 Dec 88	SOULMATE Jive JIVE 193	45	4
25 Mar 89	BLOW THE HOUSE DOWN Jive JIVE 197	65	1

[1] Wee Papa Girl Rappers featuring Two Men and a Drum Machine

Bert WEEDON ✪ UK, male instrumentalist – guitar — 38 wks

15 May 59 ●	GUITAR BOOGIE SHUFFLE Top Rank JAR 117	10	9
20 Nov 59	NASHVILLE BOOGIE Top Rank JAR 221	29	2
10 Mar 60	BIG BEAT BOOGIE Top Rank JAR 300	37	3
7 Apr 60	BIG BEAT BOOGIE (re-entry) Top Rank JAR 300	49	1
9 Jun 60	TWELFTH STREET RAG Top Rank JAR 360	47	2
28 Jul 60	APACHE Top Rank JAR 415	44	1
11 Aug 60	APACHE (re-entry) Top Rank JAR 415	24	3
27 Oct 60	SORRY ROBBIE Top Rank JAR 517	28	11
2 Feb 61	GINCHY Top Rank JAR 537	35	5
4 May 61	MR. GUITAR Top Rank JAR 559	47	1

WEEKEND International, male/female vocal/instrumental group — 5 wks

14 Dec 85	CHRISTMAS MEDLEY / AULD LANG SYNE Lifestyle XY 1	47	5

Michelle WEEKS US, female vocalist — 6 wks

2 Aug 97	MOMENT OF MY LIFE Ministry Of Sound MOSCDS 1 [1]	23	3
8 Nov 97	DON'T GIVE UP Ministry Of Sound MOSCDS 2	28	2
11 Jul 98	GIVE ME LOVE VC Recordings VCRD 37 [2]	59	1

[1] Bobby D'Ambrosio featuring Michelle Weeks [2] DJ Dado vs Michelle Weeks

WEEZER ✎ US, male vocal/instrumental group — 12 wks

11 Feb 95	UNDONE – THE SWEATER SONG Geffen GFSTD 85	35	2
6 May 95	BUDDY HOLLY Geffen GFSTD 88	12	7
22 Jul 95	SAY IT AIN'T SO Geffen GFSTD 95	37	2
5 Oct 96	EL SCORCHO Geffen GFSTD 22167	50	1

Frank WEIR UK, orchestra — 4 wks

15 Sep 60	CARIBBEAN HONEYMOON Oriole CB 1559	42	4

See also Vera LYNN

Eric WEISSBERG – See 'DELIVERANCE' SOUNDTRACK

Denise WELCH UK, female vocalist — 3 wks

4 Nov 95	YOU DON'T HAVE TO SAY YOU LOVE ME / CRY ME A RIVER		
	Virgin VSCDT 1569	23	3

Paul WELLER ✪ ✎ UK, male vocalist — 58 wks

18 May 91	INTO TOMORROW Freedom High FHP 1 [1]	36	3
15 Aug 92	UH HUH OH YEH Go! Discs GODCD 107	18	5
10 Oct 92	ABOVE THE CLOUDS Go! Discs GOD 91	47	2
17 Jul 93	SUNFLOWER Go! Discs GODCD 102	16	5
4 Sep 93	WILD WOOD Go! Discs GODCD 104	14	3

13 Nov 93		THE WEAVER EP *Go! Discs GODCD 107*	18 3
9 Apr 94		HUNG UP *Go! Discs GODCD 111*	11 3
5 Nov 94		OUT OF THE SINKING *Go! Discs GODCD 121*	20 3
6 May 95	●	THE CHANGINGMAN *Go! Discs GODCD 127*	7 4
22 Jul 95	●	YOU DO SOMETHING TO ME *Go! Discs GODCD 130*	9 6
30 Sep 95		BROKEN STONES *Go! Discs GODCD 132*	20 4
9 Mar 96		OUT OF THE SINKING *Go! Discs GODCD 143*	16 2
17 Aug 96	●	PEACOCK SUIT *Go! Discs GODCD 149*	5 5
9 Aug 97		BRUSHED *Island CID 666*	14 3
11 Oct 97		FRIDAY STREET *Island CID 676*	21 2
6 Dec 97		MERMAIDS *Island CID 683*	30 2
14 Nov 98		BRAND NEW START *Island CID 711*	16 3

[1] Paul Weller Movement

Tracks on The Weaver (EP): *The Weaver / There Is No Time / Another New Day / Ohio.*
'Out of the Sinking' in 1996 is a re-recording

See also JAM; STYLE COUNCIL

Brandi WELLS *US, female vocalist* — 1 wk

20 Feb 82	WATCH OUT *Virgin VS 479*	74 1

Houston WELLS *UK, male vocalist* — 10 wks

1 Aug 63	ONLY THE HEARTACHES *Parlophone R 5031*	22 10

Mary WELLS ✗ *US, female vocalist* — 25 wks

21 May 64	●	MY GUY *Stateside SS 288* ▲	5 14
30 Jul 64		ONCE UPON A TIME *Stateside SS 316* [1]	50 1
8 Jul 72		MY GUY (re-issue) *Tamla Motown TMG 820*	14 10

[1] Marvin Gaye and Mary Wells

Terri WELLS ✗ ◢ *US, female vocalist* — 9 wks

2 Jul 83	YOU MAKE IT HEAVEN *Phillyworld PWS 111*	53 2
5 May 84	I'LL BE AROUND *Phillyworld LON 48*	17 7

Alex WELSH *UK, male instrumentalist – trumpet* — 4 wks

10 Aug 61	TANSY *Columbia DB 4686*	45 4

Irvine WELSH – See PRIMAL SCREAM

WENDY and LISA *US, female vocal duo* — 31 wks

5 Sep 87	WATERFALL *Virgin VS 999*	66 4
16 Jan 88	SIDE SHOW *Virgin VS 1012*	49 5
18 Feb 89	ARE YOU MY BABY *Virgin VS 1156*	70 3
29 Apr 89	LOLLY LOLLY *Virgin VS 1175*	64 3
8 Jul 89	SATISFACTION *Virgin VS 1194*	27 8
18 Nov 89	WATERFALL (re-mix) *Virgin VS 1223*	69 2
30 Jun 90	STRUNG OUT *Virgin VS 1272*	44 5
10 Nov 90	RAINBOW LAKE *Virgin VS 1280*	70 1

WES ⊛ ❸ *France, male vocalist* — 7 wks

14 Feb 98	ALANE *Epic 6654682*	11 6
27 Jun 98	I LOVE FOOTBALL *Epic 6660772*	75 1

Dodie WEST *UK, female vocalist* — 4 wks

14 Jan 65	GOING OUT OF MY HEAD *Decca F 12046*	39 4

Keith WEST ❸ *UK, male vocalist* — 18 wks

9 Aug 67	●	EXCERPT FROM A TEENAGE OPERA *Parlophone R 5623*	2 15
22 Nov 67		SAM *Parlophone R 5651*	38 3

Kit WEST – See DEGREES OF MOTION featuring BITI

WEST END – See SYBIL

WEST END *UK, female vocal group* — 2 wks

19 Aug 95	LOVE RULES *RCA 74321292702*	44 2

WEST HAM UNITED CUP SQUAD
UK, male football team vocalists — 2 wks

10 May 75	I'M FOREVER BLOWING BUBBLES *Pye 7N 45470*	31 2

WEST STREET MOB *US, male DJ/producers* — 3 wks

8 Oct 83	BREAK DANCIN'– ELECTRIC BOOGIE *Sugarhill SH 128*	71 1
22 Oct 83	BREAK DANCIN'– ELECTRIC BOOGIE (re-entry) *Sugarhill SH 128*	64 2

WESTBAM *Germany, male producer* — 9 wks

9 Jul 94	CELEBRATION GENERATION *Low Spirit PQCD 5*	48 2
19 Nov 94	BAM BAM BAM *Low Spirit PZCD 329*	57 1
3 Jun 95	WIZARDS OF THE SONIC *Urban PZCD 344*	32 2
23 Mar 96	ALWAYS MUSIC *Low Spirit 5779152* [1]	51 1
13 Jun 98	WIZARDS OF THE SONIC *Wonderboy WBOYD 010* [2]	43 2
28 Nov 98	ROOF IS ON FIRE *Logic 74321633162*	58 1

[1] Westbam/Koon + Stephenson [2] Westbam vs Red Jerry

Kim WESTON – See Marvin GAYE

WESTWORLD ❸
UK/US, male/female vocal/instrumental group — 23 wks

21 Feb 87	SONIC BOOM BOY *RCA BOOM 1*	11 7
2 May 87	BA-NA-NA-BAM-BOO *RCA BOOM 2*	37 5
25 Jul 87	WHERE THE ACTION IS *RCA BOOM 3*	54 4
17 Oct 87	SILVERMAC *RCA BOOM 4*	42 5
15 Oct 88	EVERYTHING GOOD IS BAD *RCA PB 42243*	72 2

WET WET WET ❸ *Perennially popular Glasgow quartet fronted by vocalist Marti Pellow (b. Mark McLoughlin, 23 March, 1966). They were voted Best British Newcomers at the 1988 BRIT Awards. 'Love Is All Around' holds the record for most weeks at No 1 by a UK single (15)* — 207 wks

11 Apr 87	●	WISHING I WAS LUCKY *Precious JEWEL 3*	6 14
25 Jul 87	●	SWEET LITTLE MYSTERY *Precious JEWEL 4*	5 12
5 Dec 87	●	ANGEL EYES (HOME AND AWAY) *Precious JEWEL 6*	5 12
19 Mar 88		TEMPTATION *Precious JEWEL 7*	12 8
14 May 88	★	WITH A LITTLE HELP FROM MY FRIENDS *Childline CHILD 1*	1 11
30 Sep 89	●	SWEET SURRENDER *Precious JEWEL 9*	6 8
9 Dec 89		BROKE AWAY *Precious JEWEL 10*	19 7
10 Mar 90		HOLD BACK THE RIVER *Precious JEWEL 11*	31 4
11 Aug 90		STAY WITH ME HEARTACHE/I FEEL FINE *Precious JEWEL 13*	30 4
14 Sep 91		MAKE IT TONIGHT *Precious JEWEL 15*	37 3
2 Nov 91		PUT THE LIGHT ON *Precious JEWEL 16*	56 2
4 Jan 92	★	GOODNIGHT GIRL *Precious JEWEL 17*	1 11
21 Mar 92		MORE THAN LOVE *Precious JEWEL 18*	19 5
11 Jul 92		LIP SERVICE EP *Precious JEWEL 19*	15 5
8 May 93		BLUE FOR YOU/THIS TIME (LIVE) *Precious JWLCD 20*	38 2
6 Nov 93		SHED A TEAR *Precious JWLCD 21*	22 5
8 Jan 94		COLD COLD HEART *Precious JWLCD 22*	23 4
21 May 94	★	LOVE IS ALL AROUND *Precious JWLCD 23* ◆	1 37
25 Mar 95	●	JULIA SAYS *Precious JWLDD 24*	3 9
17 Jun 95	●	DON'T WANT TO FORGIVE ME NOW *Precious JWLDD 25*	7 8
30 Sep 95	●	SOMEWHERE SOMEHOW *Precious JWLDD 26*	7 7
2 Dec 95		SHE'S ALL ON MY MIND *Precious JWLDD 27*	17 7
30 Mar 96		MORNING *Precious JWLDD 28*	16 4
22 Mar 97	●	IF I NEVER SEE YOU AGAIN *Precious JWLCD 29*	3 8
14 Jun 97		STRANGE *Precious JWLCD 30*	13 4
16 Aug 97	●	YESTERDAY *Precious JWLCD 31*	4 6

The listed A-side with With a Little Help From My Friends was She's Leaving Home
by Billy Bragg with Cara Tivey. Tracks on Lip Service (EP): *Lip Service / High On the
Happy Side / Lip Service (Live) / More Than Love (Live)*

WE'VE GOT A FUZZBOX AND WE'RE GONNA USE IT ❸ ✐
UK, female vocal/instrumental group — 39 wks

26 Apr 86	XX SEX/RULES AND REGULATIONS *Vindaloo UGH 11*	41 7
15 Nov 86	LOVE IS THE SLUG *Vindaloo UGH 14*	31 4
7 Feb 87	WHAT'S THE POINT *Vindaloo YZ 101*	51 2
25 Feb 89	INTERNATIONAL RESCUE *WEA YZ 347* [1]	11 10

UK No 1 ★   UK Top 10 ●   UK million seller ◆   UK entry at No 1 ■   US No 1 ▲

| 20 May 89 | PINK SUNSHINE *WEA YZ 401* [1] | 14 10 |
| 5 Aug 89 | SELF! *WEA YZ 408* [1] | 24 6 |

[1] Fuzzbox

WHALE ☺ 🎸 *Sweden, male/female vocal/instrumental group*   8 wks

19 Mar 94	HOBO HUMPIN' SLOBO BABE *East West YZ 798CD*	46 2
15 Jul 95	I'LL DO YA *Hut HUTDG 51*	53 1
25 Nov 95	HOBO HUMPIN' SLOBO BABE (re-issue) *Hut HUTCD 64*	15 4
4 Jul 98	FOUR BIG SPEAKERS *Hut HUTCD 96* [1]	69 1

[1] Whale featuring Bus 75

WHALERS – *See Hal PAGE and the WHALERS*

WHAM! ☺ *Teen-dream duo with a feel-good, pure pop sound: George Michael (v), Andrew Ridgeley (g). They were the only British group to have three chart-toppers in the UK and the USA during the 1980s, a feat George later equalled as a solo artist*   137 wks

16 Oct 82	● YOUNG GUNS (GO FOR IT) *Innervision IVL A2766*	3 17
15 Jan 83	● WHAM RAP *Innervision IVL A2442*	8 11
14 May 83	● BAD BOYS *Innervision A 3143*	2 14
30 Jul 83	● CLUB TROPICANA *Innervision A 3613*	4 11
3 Dec 83	CLUB FANTASTIC MEGAMIX *Innervision A 3586*	15 8
26 May 84	★ WAKE ME UP BEFORE YOU GO GO *Epic A 4440* ▲	1 16
13 Oct 84	★ FREEDOM *Epic A 4743*	1 14
15 Dec 84	● LAST CHRISTMAS/EVERYTHING SHE WANTS *Epic A 4949* ◆ ▲	2 13
23 Nov 85	★ I'M YOUR MAN *Epic A 6716*	1 12
14 Dec 85	● LAST CHRISTMAS (re-issue) *Epic WHAM 1*	6 7
21 Jun 86	★ THE EDGE OF HEAVEN/WHERE DID YOUR HEART GO *Epic FIN 1*	1 10
20 Dec 86	LAST CHRISTMAS (2nd re-issue) *Epic 650269 7*	45 4

'Where Did Your Heart Go' only listed from 2 August, 1986, with a peak No of 28

WHATNAUTS – *See MOMENTS*

Caron WHEELER 🎤 [R&B] *UK, female vocalist*   42 wks

18 Mar 89	● KEEP ON MOVING *10 TEN 263* [1]	5 12
10 Jun 89	★ BACK TO LIFE (HOWEVER DO YOU WANT ME) *10 TEN 265* [1]	1 14
8 Sep 90	LIVIN' IN THE LIGHT *RCA PB 43939*	14 6
10 Nov 90	UK BLAK *RCA PB 43719*	40 4
9 Feb 91	DON'T QUIT *RCA PB 44259*	53 3
7 Nov 92	I ADORE YOU *Perspective PERSS 7407*	59 2
11 Sep 93	BEACH OF THE WAR GODDESS *EMI CDEM 282*	75 1

[1] Soul II Soul featuring Caron Wheeler

Bill WHELAN featuring ANUNA and the RTE CONCERT ORCHESTRA ♂ *Ireland, male composer, male/female choir and orchestra*   16 wks

| 17 Dec 94 | ● RIVERDANCE *Son RTEBUACD 1* | 9 16 |

WHEN IN ROME *UK, male vocal/instrumental group*   3 wks

| 28 Jan 89 | THE PROMISE *10 TEN 244* | 58 3 |

WHIGFIELD ❂ ☺ *Denmark, female vocalist*   52 wks

17 Sep 94	★ SATURDAY NIGHT *Systematic SYSCD 3* ◆ ■	1 18
10 Dec 94	● ANOTHER DAY *Systematic SYSCD 4*	7 10
10 Jun 95	● THINK OF YOU *Systematic SYSCDP 10*	7 11
9 Sep 95	CLOSE TO YOU *Systematic SYSCDP 18*	13 7
16 Dec 95	LAST CHRISTMAS/BIG TIME *Systematic SYSCD 24*	21 5
10 Oct 98	SEXY EYES – REMIXES *ZYX ZYX 8085R8*	68 1

WHIPPING BOY *Ireland, male vocal/instrumental group*   4 wks

14 Oct 95	WE DON'T NEED NOBODY ELSE *Columbia 6622205*	51 1
3 Feb 96	WHEN WE WERE YOUNG *Columbia 6628062*	46 2
25 May 96	TWINKLE *Columbia 6632272*	55 1

Nancy WHISKEY – *See Charles McDEVITT SKIFFLE GROUP featuring Nancy WHISKEY*

WHISPERS ☺ 🎤 *US, male vocal group*   52 wks

2 Feb 80	● AND THE BEAT GOES ON *Solar SO 1*	2 12
10 May 80	LADY *Solar SO 4*	55 3
12 Jul 80	MY GIRL *Solar SO 8*	26 6
14 Mar 81	● IT'S A LOVE THING *Solar SO 16*	9 11
13 Jun 81	I CAN MAKE IT BETTER *Solar SO 19*	44 5
19 Jan 85	CONTAGIOUS *MCA MCA 937*	56 3
28 Mar 87	AND THE BEAT GOES ON (re-issue) *Solar MCA 1126*	45 4
23 May 87	ROCK STEADY *Solar MCA 1152*	38 6
15 Aug 87	SPECIAL F/X *Solar MCA 1178*	69 2

WHISTLE 🚙 ❂ *US, male rap group*   8 wks

| 1 Mar 86 | ● (NOTHIN' SERIOUS) JUST BUGGIN' *Champion CHAMP 12* | 7 8 |

Alex WHITCOMBE and BIG C *UK, male DJ, and UK, male vocalist*   1 wk

| 23 May 98 | ICE RAIN *Xtravaganza 0091075 EXT* | 44 1 |

Barry WHITE 🎤 ☺ *1970s soul and disco icon, b. 12 September, 1944, Texas. This singer/songwriter/pianist/producer/arranger was behind best sellers by Love Unlimited and Love Unlimited Orchestra. His unmistakable deep voice has been in the charts for more than three decades*   135 wks

9 Jun 73	I'M GONNA LOVE YOU JUST A LITTLE BIT MORE BABY *Pye International 7N 25610*	23 7
26 Jan 74	NEVER NEVER GONNA GIVE YA UP *Pye International 7N 25633*	14 11
17 Aug 74	● CAN'T GET ENOUGH OF YOUR LOVE BABE *Pye International 7N 25661* ▲	8 12
2 Nov 74	★ YOU'RE THE FIRST THE LAST MY EVERYTHING *20th Century BTC 2133*	1 14
8 Mar 75	● WHAT AM I GONNA DO WITH YOU *20th Century BTC 2177*	5 8
24 May 75	(FOR YOU) I'LL DO ANYTHING YOU WANT ME TO *20th Century BTC 2208*	20 6
27 Dec 75	● LET THE MUSIC PLAY *20th Century BTC 2265*	9 8
6 Mar 76	● YOU SEE THE TROUBLE WITH ME *20th Century BTC 2277*	2 10
21 Aug 76	BABY WE BETTER TRY TO GET IT TOGETHER *20th Century BTC 2298*	15 7
13 Nov 76	DON'T MAKE ME WAIT TOO LONG *20th Century BTC 2309*	17 8
5 Mar 77	I'M QUALIFIED TO SATISFY *20th Century BTC 2328*	37 5
15 Oct 77	IT'S ECSTASY WHEN YOU LAY DOWN NEXT TO ME *20th Century BTC 2350*	40 3
16 Dec 78	JUST THE WAY YOU ARE *20th Century BTC 2380*	12 12
24 Mar 79	SHA LA LA MEANS I LOVE YOU *20th Century BTC 1041*	55 6
7 Nov 87	SHO' YOU RIGHT *Breakout USA 614*	14 7
16 Jan 88	NEVER NEVER GONNA GIVE YOU UP (re-mix) *Club JAB 59*	63 2
31 Mar 90	SECRET GARDEN *Qwest W 9992* [1]	67 1
21 Jan 95	PRACTICE WHAT YOU PREACH/LOVE IS THE ICON *A & M 5808992*	20 4
8 Apr 95	I ONLY WANT TO BE WITH YOU *A & M 5810252*	36 2
21 Dec 96	IN YOUR WILDEST DREAMS *Parlophone CDR 6451* [2]	32 2

[1] Quincy Jones featuring Al B. Sure!, James Ingram, El DeBarge and Barry White
[2] Tina Turner featuring Barry White

Chris WHITE *UK, male vocalist*   4 wks

| 20 Mar 76 | SPANISH WINE *Charisma CB 272* | 37 4 |

Karyn WHITE 🎤 ☺ *US, female vocalist*   38 wks

5 Nov 88	THE WAY YOU LOVE ME *Warner Bros. W 7773*	42 5
18 Feb 89	SECRET RENDEZVOUS *Warner Bros. W 7562*	52 3
10 Jun 89	SUPERWOMAN *Warner Bros. W 2920*	11 13
9 Sep 89	SECRET RENDEZVOUS (re-issue) *Warner Bros. W 2855*	22 9
17 Aug 91	ROMANTIC *Warner Bros. W 0028* ▲	23 5
18 Jan 92	THE WAY I FEEL ABOUT YOU *Warner Bros. W 0073*	65 2
24 Sep 94	HUNGAH *Warner Bros. W 0264CD*	69 1

Snowy WHITE 🎸 ❂ *UK, male vocalist/instrumentalist – guitar*   12 wks

| 24 Dec 83 | ● BIRD OF PARADISE *Towerbell TOW 42* | 6 10 |

| 28 Dec 85 | FOR YOU *R4 FOR 3*............ | 65 | 1 |
| 18 Jan 86 | FOR YOU (re-entry) *R4 FOR 3*............ | 72 | 1 |

Tam WHITE *UK, male vocalist*   **4 wks**

| 15 Mar 75 | WHAT IN THE WORLD'S COME OVER YOU *RAK 193*............ | 36 | 4 |

Tony Joe WHITE *US, male vocalist*   **10 wks**

| 6 Jun 70 | GROUPIE GIRL *Monument MON 1043*............ | 22 | 10 |

WHITE and TORCH *UK, male vocal/instrumental duo*   **4 wks**

| 2 Oct 82 | PARADE *Chrysalis CHS 2641*............ | 54 | 4 |

WHITE PLAINS ☺ *UK, male vocal group*   **56 wks**

7 Feb 70 ●	MY BABY LOVES LOVIN' *Deram DM 280*............	9	11
18 Apr 70 ●	I'VE GOT YOU ON MY MIND *Deram DM 291*............	17	11
24 Oct 70 ●	JULIE DO YA LOVE ME *Deram DM 315*............	8	14
12 Jun 71	WHEN YOU ARE A KING *Deram DM 333*............	13	11
17 Feb 73	STEP INTO A DREAM *Deram DM 371*............	21	9

WHITE TOWN ☺ ☺
UK, male vocalist/instrumentalist/producer   **10 wks**

| 25 Jan 97 ★ | YOUR WOMAN *Chrysalis CDCHS 5052* ■ .... | 1 | 9 |
| 24 May 97 | UNDRESSED *Chrysalis CDCHS 5058*............ | 57 | 1 |

WHITE ZOMBIE *US, male vocal/instrumental group*   **4 wks**

| 20 May 95 | MORE HUMAN THAN HUMAN *Geffen GFSTD 92*............ | 51 | 2 |
| 18 May 96 | ELECTRIC HEAD PART 2 (THE ECSTASY) *Geffen GFSXD 22140*............ | 31 | 2 |

WHITEHEAD BROS. *US, male vocal duo*   **5 wks**

| 14 Jan 95 | YOUR LOVE IS A 187 *Motown TMGCD 1434*............ | 32 | 3 |
| 13 May 95 | FORGET I WAS A G *Motown TMGCD 1441*............ | 40 | 2 |

WHITEHOUSE *US/UK, male vocal/instrumental/production duo*   **1 wk**

| 15 Aug 98 | AIN'T NO MOUNTAIN HIGH ENOUGH *Beautiful Noise BNOISE 2CD*............ | 60 | 1 |

WHITEOUT *UK, male vocal/instrumental group*   **2 wks**

| 24 Sep 94 | DETROIT *Silvertone ORECD 66*............ | 73 | 1 |
| 18 Feb 95 | JACKIE'S RACING *Silvertone ORECD 68*............ | 72 | 1 |

WHITESNAKE ✔ *Leading 1980s British rock group founded by ex-Deep Purple vocalist, David Coverdale (b. 22 September, 1949, Cleveland), but with an ever-changing line-up. Whitesnake (1987), their most successful album, shifted more than ten million copies worldwide*   **112 wks**

24 Jun 78	SNAKE BITE EP *EMI International INEP 751* [1]	61	3
10 Nov 79	LONG WAY FROM HOME *United Artists BP 324*............	55	2
26 Apr 80	FOOL FOR YOUR LOVING *United Artists BP 352*............	13	9
12 Jul 80	READY AN' WILLING (SWEET SATISFACTION) *United Artists BP 363*............	43	4
22 Nov 80	AIN'T NO LOVE IN THE HEART OF THE CITY *Sunburst/Liberty BP 381*............	51	4
11 Apr 81	DON'T BREAK MY HEART AGAIN *Liberty BP 395*............	17	9
6 Jun 81	WOULD I LIE TO YOU *Liberty BP 399*............	37	6
6 Nov 82	HERE I GO AGAIN/BLOODY LUXURY *Liberty BP 416* ▲............	34	10
13 Aug 83	GUILTY OF LOVE *Liberty BP 420*............	31	5
14 Jan 84	GIVE ME MORE TIME *Liberty BP 422*............	29	4
28 Apr 84	STANDING IN THE SHADOW *Liberty BP 423*............	62	2
9 Feb 85	LOVE AIN'T NO STRANGER *Liberty BP 424*............	44	4
28 Mar 87	STILL OF THE NIGHT *EMI EMI 5606*............	16	8
6 Jun 87 ●	IS THIS LOVE *EMI EM 3*............	9	11
31 Oct 87 ●	HERE I GO AGAIN (re-mix) *EMI EM 35*............	9	11
6 Feb 88	GIVE ME ALL YOUR LOVE *EMI EM 23*............	18	6
2 Dec 89	FOOL FOR YOUR LOVING *EMI EM 123*............	43	2
10 Mar 90	THE DEEPER THE LOVE *EMI EM 128*............	35	3
25 Aug 90	NOW YOU'RE GONE *EMI EM 150*............	31	4
6 Aug 94	IS THIS LOVE (RE-ISSUE) /SWEET LADY LUCK *EMI CDEM 329*............	25	4

| 7 Jun 97 | TOO MANY TEARS *EMI CDEM 471* [2] .... | 46 | 1 |

[1] David Coverdale's Whitesnake [2] David Coverdale and Whitesnake

Tracks on Snake Bite EP: Bloody Mary / Steal Away / Ain't No Love In the Heart of the City / Come On. EM 123 is a re-recording of their third hit

David WHITFIELD ℂ *Most successful UK male singer in the USA during the pre-rock years, b. 2 February, 1925, Yorkshire, d. 16 January, 1980. This operatic-style tenor had a formidable and predominantly female fan following in the 1950s*   **181 wks**

2 Oct 53 ●	BRIDGE OF SIGHS *Decca F 10129*............	9	1
16 Oct 53 ★	ANSWER ME *Decca F 10192*............	1	13
11 Dec 53	RAGS TO RICHES *Decca F 10207* [1]	12	1
8 Jan 54	RAGS TO RICHES (re-entry) *Decca F 10207* [1]	3	10
29 Jan 54	ANSWER ME (re-entry) *Decca F 10192*............	12	1
19 Feb 54 ●	THE BOOK *Decca F 10242*............	5	12
28 May 54	THE BOOK (re-entry) *Decca F 10242*............	10	3
18 Jun 54 ★	CARA MIA *Decca F 10327* [2]	1	25
12 Nov 54	SANTO NATALE *Decca F 10399*............	2	10
11 Feb 55 ●	BEYOND THE STARS *Decca F 10458*............	8	9
27 May 55	MAMA *Decca F 10515*............	20	1
24 Jun 55	MAMA (re-entry) *Decca F 10515*............	19	2
8 Jul 55	EV'RYWHERE *Decca F 10515* [3]	3	20
29 Jul 55	MAMA (2nd re-entry) *Decca F 10515*............	12	8
25 Nov 55 ●	WHEN YOU LOSE THE ONE YOU LOVE *Decca F 10627* [2]	7	11
2 Mar 56	MY SEPTEMBER LOVE *Decca F 10690*............	19	2
23 Mar 56	MY SEPTEMBER LOVE (re-entry) *Decca F 10690*............	18	1
6 Apr 56 ●	MY SEPTEMBER LOVE (2nd re-entry) *Decca F 10690*............	3	20
24 Aug 56	MY SON JOHN *Decca F 10769*............	22	4
31 Aug 56	MY UNFINISHED SYMPHONY *Decca F 10769*............	29	1
7 Sep 56	MY SEPTEMBER LOVE (3rd re-entry) *Decca F 10690*............	25	1
25 Jan 57 ●	ADORATION WALTZ *Decca F 10833* [3]	9	11
5 Apr 57	I'LL FIND YOU *Decca F 10864*............	28	2
7 Jun 57	I'LL FIND YOU (re-entry) *Decca F 10864*............	27	2
14 Feb 58	CRY MY HEART *Decca F 10978* [2]	22	3
16 May 58	ON THE STREET WHERE YOU LIVE *Decca F 11018* [4]	16	14
8 Aug 58	THE RIGHT TO LOVE *Decca F 11039*............	30	1
24 Nov 60	I BELIEVE *Decca F 11289*............	49	1

[1] David Whitfield with Stanley Buick and his Orchestra [2] David Whitfield with chorus and Mantovani and his Orchestra [3] David Whitfield with the Roland Shaw Orchestra [4] David Whitfield with Cyril Stapleton and his Orchestra

See also MANTOVANI; VARIOUS ARTISTS (EPs & LPs) – All-Star Hit Parade

Slim WHITMAN 🎸 *US, male vocalist*   **77 wks**

15 Jul 55 ★	ROSE MARIE *London HL 8061*............	1	19
29 Jul 55 ●	INDIAN LOVE CALL *London L 1149*............	7	12
23 Sep 55	CHINA DOLL *London L 1149*............	15	2
9 Mar 56	TUMBLING TUMBLEWEEDS *London HLU 8230*............	19	2
13 Apr 56	I'M A FOOL *London HLU 8252*............	16	3
11 May 56	I'M A FOOL (re-entry) *London HLU 8252*............	29	1
22 Jun 56	SERENADE *London HLU 8287*............	24	3
27 Jul 56 ●	SERENADE (re-entry) *London HLU 8287*............	8	12
12 Apr 57 ●	I'LL TAKE YOU HOME AGAIN KATHLEEN *London HLP 8403*............	7	13
5 Oct 74	HAPPY ANNIVERSARY *United Artists UP 35728*............	14	10

Roger WHITTAKER ℂ *Kenya, male vocalist*   **85 wks**

8 Nov 69	DURHAM TOWN (THE LEAVIN') *Columbia DB 8613*............	12	18
11 Apr 70 ●	I DON'T BELIEVE IN IF ANYMORE *Columbia DB 8664*............	8	18
10 Oct 70	NEW WORLD IN THE MORNING *Columbia DB 8718*............	17	14
3 Apr 71	WHY *Columbia DB 8752*............	47	1
2 Oct 71	MAMMY BLUE *Columbia DB 8822*............	31	10
26 Jul 75 ●	THE LAST FAREWELL *EMI 2294*............	2	14
8 Nov 86 ●	THE SKYE BOAT SONG *Tembo TML 119* [1]	10	10

[1] Roger Whittaker and Des O'Connor

WHO 🎸 *Legendary live band from London, whose Tommy album (1969) popularised rock opera: Roger Daltrey (v), Pete Townshend (g), John Entwistle (b), Keith Moon (d. 1978). These gold-record collectors have spent four decades breaking both guitars and box-office records*   **247 wks**

| 18 Feb 65 ● | I CAN'T EXPLAIN *Brunswick 05926*............ | 8 | 13 |

UK No 1 ★   UK Top 10 ●   UK million seller ◆   UK entry at No 1 ■   US No 1 ▲

27 May 65 ●	**ANYWAY ANYHOW ANYWHERE** *Brunswick 05935* 10	12
4 Nov 65 ●	**MY GENERATION** *Brunswick 05944* 2	13
10 Mar 66 ●	**SUBSTITUTE** *Reaction 591 001*...5	13
24 Mar 66	**A LEGAL MATTER** *Brunswick 05956*...32	6
1 Sep 66 ●	**I'M A BOY** *Reaction 591 004*...2	13
1 Sep 66	**THE KIDS ARE ALRIGHT** *Brunswick 05965*..41	2
22 Sep 66	**THE KIDS ARE ALRIGHT (re-entry)** *Brunswick 05965*.............48	1
15 Dec 66 ●	**HAPPY JACK** *Reaction 591 010*..3	11
27 Apr 67 ●	**PICTURES OF LILY** *Track 604 002*...4	10
26 Jul 67	**THE LAST TIME/UNDER MY THUMB** *Track 604 006*............44	3
18 Oct 67 ●	**I CAN SEE FOR MILES** *Track 604 011*..10	12
19 Jun 68	**DOGS** *Track 604 023*...25	5
23 Oct 68	**MAGIC BUS** *Track 604 024*...26	6
19 Mar 69 ●	**PINBALL WIZARD** *Track 604 027*...4	13
4 Apr 70	**THE SEEKER** *Track 604 036*...19	11
8 Aug 70	**SUMMERTIME BLUES** *Track 2094 002*...38	4
10 Jul 71 ●	**WON'T GET FOOLED AGAIN** *Track 2094 009*.................................9	12
23 Oct 71	**LET'S SEE ACTION** *Track 2094 012*..16	12
24 Jun 72 ●	**JOIN TOGETHER** *Track 2094 102*...9	9
13 Jan 73	**RELAY** *Track 2094 106*...21	5
13 Oct 73	**5:15** *Track 2094 115*...20	6
24 Jan 76 ●	**SQUEEZE BOX** *Polydor 2121 275*...10	9
30 Oct 76 ●	**SUBSTITUTE (re-issue)** *Polydor 2058 803*.......................................7	7
22 Jul 78	**WHO ARE YOU** *Polydor WHO 1*...18	12
28 Apr 79	**LONG LIVE ROCK** *Polydor WHO 2*..48	5
7 Mar 81	**YOU BETTER YOU BET** *Polydor WHO 004*...9	8
9 May 81	**DON'T LET GO THE COAT** *Polydor WHO 005*...................................47	4
2 Oct 82	**ATHENA** *Polydor WHO 6*..40	4
26 Nov 83	**READY STEADY WHO EP** *Polydor WHO 7*...58	2
20 Feb 88	**MY GENERATION (re-issue)** *Polydor POSP 907*...........................68	2
27 Jul 96	**MY GENERATION (2nd re-issue)** *Polydor 8546372* 31	2

Tracks on Ready Steady Who EP: Disguises / Circles / Batman / Bucket 'T' /
Barbara Ann.
See also HIGH NUMBERS

WHODINI *US, male rap/scratch duo* 10 wks

25 Dec 82	**MAGIC'S WAND** *Jive JIVE 28* 47	6
17 Mar 84	**MAGIC'S WAND (THE WHODINI ELECTRIC EP)** *Jive JIVE 61* 63	4

Tracks on The Whodini Electric EP: Jive Magic Wand / Nasty Lady / Rap Machine /
The Haunted House of Rock

WHOOLIGANZ *US, male rap duo* 2 wks

13 Aug 94	**PUT YOUR HANDZ UP** *Positiva CDTIV 17* 53	2

WHOOSH *UK, male production trio* 1 wk

13 Sep 97	**WHOOSH** *Wonderboy WBOYD 006*...72	1

WHYCLIFFE *UK, male vocalist* 2 wks

20 Nov 93	**HEAVEN** *MCA MCSTD 1944* 56	1
2 Apr 94	**ONE MORE TIME** *MCA MCSTD 1955*..72	1

Jane WIEDLIN ◐ *US, female vocalist* 14 wks

6 Aug 88	**RUSH HOUR** *Manhattan MT 36*...12	11
29 Oct 88	**INSIDE A DREAM** *Manhattan MT 55* 64	3

WIGAN'S CHOSEN FEW 🎵
Canada, male vocal/instrumental group and UK crowd chants 11 wks

18 Jan 75 ●	**FOOTSEE** *Pye Disco Demand DDS 111* 9	11

WIGAN'S OVATION ◐ *UK, male vocal/instrumental group* 19 wks

15 Mar 75	**SKIING IN THE SNOW** *Spark SRL 1122*...12	10
28 Jun 75	**PER-SO-NAL-LY** *Spark SRL 1129*..38	6
29 Nov 75	**SUPER LOVE** *Spark SRL 1133*...41	3

Jack WILD *UK, male vocalist* 2 wks

2 May 70	**SOME BEAUTIFUL** *Capitol CL 15635* 46	2

WILD BOYS – See HEINZ

WILD CHERRY ◐ 🎵 *US, male vocal/instrumental group* 11 wks

9 Oct 76 ●	**PLAY THAT FUNKY MUSIC** *Epic EPC 4593* ▲ 7	11

WILD COLOUR *UK, male/female vocal/instrumental group* 2 wks

14 Oct 95	**DREAMS** *Perfecto PERF 105CD* 25	2

WILD PAIR – See Paula ABDUL

WILD WEEKEND *UK, male vocal/instrumental group* 2 wks

29 Apr 89	**BREAKIN' UP** *Parlophone R 6204* 74	1
5 May 90	**WHO'S AFRAID OF THE BIG BAD LOVE** *Parlophone R 6249* 70	1

WILDCHILD ☺ *UK, male producer – Roger McKenzie* 20 wks

22 Apr 95	**LEGENDS OF THE DARK BLACK PART 2** *Hi-Life HICD 9* 34	3
21 Oct 95	**RENEGADE MASTER (re-issue)** *Hi-Life 5771312*...........................11	4
23 Nov 96	**JUMP TO MY BEAT** *Hi-Life 5757372*..30	2
17 Jan 98 ●	**RENEGADE MASTER '98 (re-mix)** *Hi-Life 5692792*.........................3	10
25 Apr 98	**BAD BOY** *Polydor 5716072* [1] 38	1

[1] Wildchild featuring Jomalski

Although titled differently, first two hits are identical

Eugene WILDE 🎵 ☺ *US, male vocalist* 15 wks

13 Oct 84	**GOTTA GET YOU HOME TONIGHT** *Fourth & Broadway BRW 15*18	9
2 Feb 85	**PERSONALITY** *Fourth & Broadway BRW 18*.....................................34	6

'Personality' was coupled with 'Let Her Feel It' by Simplicious

Kim WILDE ◐ *Most charted British female vocalist in the 1980s, b. Kim Smith, 18 November, 1960, London. Like her father, rock'n'roll star Marty Wilde, she never managed a UK No 1, but topped the US chart* 194 wks

21 Feb 81 ●	**KIDS IN AMERICA** *RAK 327* 2	13
9 May 81 ●	**CHEQUERED LOVE** *RAK 330*..4	9
1 Aug 81	**WATER ON GLASS/BOYS** *RAK 334*...11	8
14 Nov 81	**CAMBODIA** *RAK 336*...12	12
17 Apr 82	**VIEW FROM A BRIDGE** *RAK 342* 16	7
16 Oct 82	**CHILD COME AWAY** *RAK 352*...43	4
30 Jul 83	**LOVE BLONDE** *RAK 360*...23	8
12 Nov 83	**DANCING IN THE DARK** *RAK 365*..67	2
13 Oct 84	**THE SECOND TIME** *MCA KIM 1* 29	6
8 Dec 84	**THE TOUCH** *MCA KIM 2*...56	3
27 Apr 85	**RAGE TO LOVE** *MCA KIM 3*...19	8
25 Oct 86 ●	**YOU KEEP ME HANGIN' ON** *MCA KIM 4* ▲ 2	14
4 Apr 87 ●	**ANOTHER STEP (CLOSER TO YOU)** *MCA KIM 5* [1] 6	11
8 Aug 87	**SAY YOU REALLY WANT ME** *MCA KIM 6* 29	5
5 Dec 87 ●	**ROCKIN' AROUND THE CHRISTMAS TREE** *10 TEN 2* [2] 3	7
14 May 88	**HEY MISTER HEARTACHE** *MCA KIM 7* 31	5
16 Jul 88 ●	**YOU CAME** *MCA KIM 8*...3	11
1 Oct 88 ●	**NEVER TRUST A STRANGER** *MCA KIM 9* 7	9
3 Dec 88 ●	**FOUR LETTER WORD** *MCA KIM 10* 6	12
4 Mar 89	**LOVE IN THE NATURAL WAY** *MCA KIM 11*.......................................32	6
14 Apr 90	**IT'S HERE** *MCA KIM 12*..42	4
16 Jun 90	**TIME** *MCA KIM 13*...71	3
15 Dec 90	**I CAN'T SAY GOODBYE** *MCA KIM 14* 51	3
2 May 92	**LOVE IS HOLY** *MCA KIM 15*...16	6
27 Jun 92	**HEART OVER MIND** *MCA KIM 16* 34	2
12 Sep 92	**WHO DO YOU THINK YOU ARE** *MCA KIM 17*....................................49	3
10 Jul 93	**IF I CAN'T HAVE YOU** *MCA KIMTD 18* 12	8
13 Nov 93	**IN MY LIFE** *MCA KIMTD 19*...54	1
14 Oct 95	**BREAKIN' AWAY** *MCA KIMTD 21* 43	2
10 Feb 96	**THIS I SWEAR** *MCA KIMTD 22* 46	1

[1] Kim Wilde and Junior [2] Mel and Kim (Mel is Mel Smith)

Marty WILDE 🎵 *Early British rock'n'roll singing idol, b. Reginald Smith, 15 April, 1939, London. Although most of his best sellers were cover versions (the normal practice at the time), he later penned hits for Lulu, Casuals, Status Quo and many for his daughter, Kim Wilde* 117 wks

11 Jul 58 ●	**ENDLESS SLEEP** *Philips PB 835* 4	14
6 Mar 59 ●	**DONNA** *Philips PB 902* 3	16
5 Jun 59 ●	**A TEENAGER IN LOVE** *Philips PB 926*...2	17

3 Jul 59	DONNA (re-entry) *Philips PB 902*	25 2
25 Sep 59 ●	SEA OF LOVE *Philips PB 959*	3 12
11 Dec 59 ●	BAD BOY *Philips PB 972*	7 8
10 Mar 60	JOHNNY ROCCO *Philips PB 1002*	30 4
19 May 60	THE FIGHT *Philips PB 1022*	47 1
22 Dec 60	LITTLE GIRL *Philips PB 1078*	16 9
26 Jan 61 ●	RUBBER BALL *Philips PB 1101*	9 9
27 Jul 61	HIDE AND SEEK *Philips PB 1161*	47 2
9 Nov 61	TOMORROW'S CLOWN *Philips PB 1191*	33 5
24 May 62	JEZEBEL *Philips PB 1240*	19 11
25 Oct 62	EVER SINCE YOU SAID GOODBYE *Philips 326546 BF*	31 7

Matthew WILDER ◐ *US, male vocalist* — 11 wks

21 Jan 84 ●	BREAK MY STRIDE *Epic A 3908*	4 11

WILDHEARTS ✍ *UK, male vocal/instrumental group* — 24 wks

20 Nov 93	TV TAN *Bronze YZ 784CD*	53 2
19 Feb 94	CAFFEINE BOMB *Bronze YZ 794CD*	31 3
9 Jul 94	SUCKERPUNCH *Bronze YZ 828CD*	38 2
28 Jan 95	IF LIFE IS LIKE A LOVE BANK I WANT AN OVERDRAFT/ GEORDIE IN WONDERLAND *East West YZ 874CD*	31 3
6 May 95	I WANNA GO WHERE THE PEOPLE GO *East West YZ 923CD*	16 3
29 Jul 95	JUST IN LUST *East West YZ 967CD*	28 2
20 Apr 96	SICK OF DRUGS *Round WILD 1CD*	14 3
29 Jun 96	RED LIGHT – GREEN LIGHT EP *Round WILD 2CD*	30 2
16 Aug 97	ANTHEM *Mushroom MUSH 6CD*	21 2
18 Oct 97	URGE *Mushroom MUSH 14CD*	26 2

Tracks on Red Light – Green Light (EP): Red Light – Green Light / Got It On Tuesday / Do Anything / The British All-American Homeboy Crowd

Sue WILKINSON *UK, female vocalist* — 8 wks

2 Aug 80	YOU GOTTA BE A HUSTLER IF YOU WANNA GET ON *Cheapskate CHEAP 2*	25 8

WILL TO POWER ◐ *US, male/female vocal/instrumental duo* — 18 wks

7 Jan 89 ●	BABY I LOVE YOUR WAY – FREEBIRD *Epic 653094 7* ▲	6 9
22 Dec 90	I'M NOT IN LOVE *Epic 6565377*	29 9

Alyson WILLIAMS ✎ ☺ *US, female vocalist* — 28 wks

4 Mar 89	SLEEP TALK *Def Jam 654656 7*	17 9
6 May 89	MY LOVE IS SO RAW *Def Jam 654898 7* [1]	34 5
19 Aug 89 ●	I NEED YOUR LOVIN' *Def Jam 655143 7*	8 11
18 Nov 89	I SECOND THAT EMOTION *Def Jam 655456 7* [2]	44 3

[1] Alyson Williams featuring Nikki D [2] Alyson Williams with Chuck Stanley

Andy WILLIAMS ◐ ℂ *Leading MOR vocalist, who hosted top-rated 1960s TV series, b. 3 December, 1928, Iowa. He left the noted family act The Williams Brothers in 1951 and had an enviable portfolio of UK and US hit singles and albums in the 1950s and the 1960s* — 228 wks

19 Apr 57 ★	BUTTERFLY *London HLA 8399*	1 15
21 Jun 57	I LIKE YOUR KIND OF LOVE *London HLA 8437*	16 10
30 Aug 57	BUTTERFLY (re-entry) *London HLA 8399*	29 1
14 Jun 62	STRANGER ON THE SHORE *CBS AAG 103*	30 10
21 Mar 63 ●	CAN'T GET USED TO LOSING YOU *CBS AAG 138*	2 18
27 Feb 64	A FOOL NEVER LEARNS *CBS AAG 182*	40 4
16 Sep 65 ●	ALMOST THERE *CBS 201813*	2 17
24 Feb 66	MAY EACH DAY *CBS 202042*	19 8
22 Sep 66	IN THE ARMS OF LOVE *CBS 202300*	33 7
4 May 67	MUSIC TO WATCH GIRLS BY *CBS 2675*	33 6
2 Aug 67	MORE AND MORE *CBS 2886*	45 1
13 Mar 68 ●	CAN'T TAKE MY EYES OFF YOU *CBS 3298*	5 18
7 May 69	HAPPY HEART *CBS 4062*	47 1
21 May 69	HAPPY HEART (re-entry) *CBS 4062*	19 9
14 Mar 70 ●	CAN'T HELP FALLING IN LOVE *CBS 4818*	3 17
1 Aug 70	IT'S SO EASY *CBS 5113*	13 13
7 Nov 70	IT'S SO EASY (re-entry) *CBS 5113*	49 1
21 Nov 70	HOME LOVIN' MAN *CBS 5267*	7 12
20 Mar 71 ●	(WHERE DO I BEGIN) LOVE STORY *CBS 7020*	4 17
24 Jul 71	(WHERE DO I BEGIN) LOVE STORY (re-entry) *CBS 7020*	49 1
5 Aug 72	LOVE THEME FROM THE GODFATHER *CBS 8166*	50 1
2 Sep 72	LOVE THEME FROM THE GODFATHER (re-entry) *CBS 8166*	44 3
30 Sep 72	LOVE THEME FROM THE GODFATHER (2nd re-entry) *CBS 8166*	42 5
8 Dec 73 ●	SOLITAIRE *CBS 1824*	4 18
18 May 74	GETTING OVER YOU *CBS 2181*	35 5
31 May 75	YOU LAY SO EASY ON MY MIND *CBS 3167*	32 7
6 Mar 76	THE OTHER SIDE OF ME *CBS 3903*	42 3

Andy and David WILLIAMS *US, male vocal duo* — 5 wks

24 Mar 73	I DON'T KNOW WHY *MCA MUS 1183*	37 5

Do not see Andy Williams. This Andy is the nephew of the other Andy

Billy WILLIAMS *US, male vocalist* — 9 wks

2 Aug 57	I'M GONNA SIT RIGHT DOWN AND WRITE MYSELF A LETTER *Vogue Coral Q 72266*	22 8
18 Oct 57	I'M GONNA SIT RIGHT DOWN AND WRITE MYSELF A LETTER (re-entry) *Vogue Coral Q 72266*	28 1

Danny WILLIAMS ℂ *UK, male vocalist* — 74 wks

25 May 61	WE WILL NEVER BE AS YOUNG AS THIS AGAIN *HMV POP 839*	44 3
6 Jul 61	THE MIRACLE OF YOU *HMV POP 885*	41 8
2 Nov 61 ★	MOON RIVER *HMV POP 932*	1 19
18 Jan 62	JEANNIE *HMV POP 968*	14 14
12 Apr 62 ●	WONDERFUL WORLD OF THE YOUNG *HMV POP 1002*	8 13
5 Jul 62	TEARS *HMV POP 1035*	22 7
28 Feb 63	MY OWN TRUE LOVE *HMV POP 1112*	45 3
30 Jul 77	DANCIN' EASY *Ensign ENY 3*	30 7

Deniece WILLIAMS ✎ *US, female vocalist* — 59 wks

2 Apr 77 ★	FREE *CBS 4978*	1 10
30 Jul 77 ●	THAT'S WHAT FRIENDS ARE FOR *CBS 5432*	8 11
12 Nov 77	BABY BABY MY LOVE'S ALL FOR YOU *CBS 5779*	32 5
25 Mar 78 ●	TOO MUCH TOO LITTLE TOO LATE *CBS 6164* [1] ▲	3 14
29 Jul 78	YOU'RE ALL I NEED TO GET BY *CBS 6483* [1]	45 6
5 May 84 ●	LET'S HEAR IT FOR THE BOY *CBS A 4319* ▲	2 12
4 Aug 84	LET'S HEAR IT FOR THE BOY (re-entry) *CBS A 4319*	75 1

[1] Johnny Mathis and Deniece Williams

Diana WILLIAMS *US, female vocalist* — 3 wks

25 Jul 81	TEDDY BEAR'S LAST RIDE *Capitol CL 207*	54 3

Don WILLIAMS ⬥ *US, male vocalist* — 16 wks

19 Jun 76	I RECALL A GYPSY WOMAN *ABC 4098*	13 10
23 Oct 76	YOU'RE MY BEST FRIEND *ABC 4144*	35 6

Eric WILLIAMS – See QUEEN PEN

Freedom WILLIAMS ☺ ⬛ *US, male rapper* — 31 wks

15 Dec 90 ●	GONNA MAKE YOU SWEAT (EVERYBODY DANCE NOW) *CBS 6564540* [1]	3 12
30 Mar 91	HERE WE GO *Columbia 6567537* [1]	20 7
6 Jul 91 ●	THINGS THAT MAKE YOU GO HMMM . . . *Columbia 6566907* [1]	4 11
5 Jun 93	VOICE OF FREEDOM *Columbia 6593342*	62 1

[1] C & C Music Factory (featuring Freedom Williams)

Geoffrey WILLIAMS *UK, male vocalist* — 8 wks

11 Apr 92	IT'S NOT A LOVE THING *EMI EM 228*	63 2
22 Aug 92	SUMMER BREEZE *EMI EM 245*	56 3
18 Jan 97	DRIVE *Hands On CDHOR 11*	52 2
19 Apr 97	SEX LIFE *Hands On CDHOR 12*	71 1

Iris WILLIAMS ℂ *UK, female vocalist* — 8 wks

27 Oct 79	HE WAS BEAUTIFUL (CAVATINA) (THE THEME FROM 'THE DEER HUNTER') *Columbia DB 9070*	18 8

UK No 1 ★ UK Top 10 ● UK million seller ◆ UK entry at No 1 ■ US No 1 ▲

John WILLIAMS ℂ *UK, male instrumentalist – guitar* **11 wks**

| 19 May 79 | CAVATINA *Cube BUG 80* .... | 13 | 11 |

John WILLIAMS *US, orchestra leader with US, orchestra* **12 wks**

| 18 Dec 82 | THEME FROM 'E.T.' (THE EXTRA-TERRESTRIAL) *MCA 800* ....17 | 10 |
| 14 Aug 93 | THEME FROM JURASSIC PARK *MCA MCSTD 1927* ....45 | 2 |

Kenny WILLIAMS *US, male vocalist* **7 wks**

| 19 Nov 77 | (YOU'RE) FABULOUS BABE *Decca FR 13731* ....35 | 7 |

Larry WILLIAMS ♪ *US, male vocalist* **18 wks**

| 20 Sep 57 | SHORT FAT FANNIE *London HLN 8472* ....21 | 8 |
| 17 Jan 58 | BONY MORONIE *London HLU 8532* ....11 | 10 |

Lenny WILLIAMS *US, male vocalist* **7 wks**

| 5 Nov 77 | SHOO DOO FU FU OOH *ABC 4194* ....38 | 4 |
| 16 Sep 78 | YOU GOT ME BURNING *ABC 4228* ....67 | 3 |

Mark WILLIAMS – See Karen BODDINGTON and Mark WILLIAMS

Mason WILLIAMS ℂ *US, male instrumentalist – guitar* **13 wks**

| 28 Aug 68 | ● CLASSICAL GAS *Warner Bros. WB 7190* ....9 | 13 |

Maurice WILLIAMS and the ZODIACS ♫ *US, male vocal group* **9 wks**

| 5 Jan 61 | STAY *Top Rank JAR 526* ▲ ....14 | 9 |

Melanie WILLIAMS ☺ *UK, female vocalist* **21 wks**

10 Apr 93	● AIN'T NO LOVE (AIN'T NO USE) *Rob's CDROB 9* [1] 3	11
9 Apr 94	ALL CRIED OUT *Columbia 6601872* 60	2
11 Jun 94	EVERYDAY THANG *Columbia 6604712* 38	3
17 Sep 94	NOT ENOUGH *Columbia 6607752* 65	1
18 Feb 95	YOU ARE EVERYTHING *Columbia 6611755* [2] 28	4

[1] Sub Sub featuring Melanie Williams [2] Melanie Williams and Joe Roberts

Robbie WILLIAMS ♥ *UK, male vocalist* **83 wks**

10 Aug 96	● FREEDOM *Chrysalis CDFREE 1* 2	10
26 Oct 96	FREEDOM (re-entry) *Chrysalis CDFREE 1* 56	4
16 Apr 97	● OLD BEFORE I DIE *Chrysalis CDCHS 5055* 2	9
5 Jul 97	OLD BEFORE I DIE (re-entry) *Chrysalis CDCHS 5055* 72	1
26 Jul 97	● LAZY DAYS *Chrysalis CDCHS 5063* 8	5
27 Sep 97	SOUTH OF THE BORDER *Chrysalis CDCHS 5068* 14	4
13 Dec 97	● ANGELS *Chrysalis CDCHS 5072* ◆ 4	20
28 Mar 98	● LET ME ENTERTAIN YOU *Chrysalis CDCHS 5080* 3	12
19 Sep 98	★ MILLENNIUM *Chrysalis CDCHS 5099* ■ 1	15
12 Dec 98	● NO REGRETS *Chrysalis CDCHS 5100* ....4†	1

Vanessa WILLIAMS ♥ ♪ *US, female vocalist* **24 wks**

20 Aug 88	THE RIGHT STUFF *Wing WING 3* 71	1
25 Mar 89	DREAMIN' *Wing WING 4* 74	2
19 Aug 89	THE RIGHT STUFF (re-mix) *Wing WINR 3* 62	2
21 Mar 92	● SAVE THE BEST FOR LAST *Polydor PO 192* ▲ 3	11
8 Apr 95	THE SWEETEST DAYS *Mercury MERCD 422* 41	2
8 Jul 95	THE WAY THAT YOU LOVE *Mercury MERCD 439* 52	1
18 Sep 95	COLOURS OF THE WIND *Walt Disney WD 7677CD* 21	5

Vesta WILLIAMS ♪ ☺ *US, female vocalist* **13 wks**

| 20 Dec 86 | ONCE BITTEN TWICE SHY *A & M AM 362* ....14 | 13 |

Wendell WILLIAMS *US, male rapper* **6 wks**

| 6 Oct 90 | EVERYBODY (RAP) *Deconstruction PB 44701* [1] ....30 | 4 |
| 18 May 91 | SO GROOVY *Deconstruction PB 44567* ....74 | 2 |

[1] Criminal Element Orchestra and Wendell Williams

WILLING SINNERS – See Marc ALMOND

Bruce WILLIS ✪ *US, male vocalist* **30 wks**

7 Mar 87	● RESPECT YOURSELF *Motown ZB 41117* 7	10
30 May 87	● UNDER THE BOARDWALK *Motown ZB 41349* 2	15
12 Sep 87	SECRET AGENT MAN – JAMES BOND IS BACK *Motown ZB 41437* 43	4
23 Jan 88	COMIN' RIGHT UP *Motown ZB 41453* 73	1

Chill WILLS – See LAUREL and HARDY with the AVALON BOYS featuring Chill WILLS

Viola WILLS ◢ *US, female vocalist* **16 wks**

| 6 Oct 79 | ● GONNA GET ALONG WITHOUT YOU NOW *Ariola/Hansa AHA 546* ....8 | 10 |
| 15 Mar 86 | BOTH SIDES NOW/DARE TO DREAM *Streetwave KHAN 66* ....35 | 6 |

Al WILSON *US, male vocalist* **5 wks**

| 23 Aug 75 | THE SNAKE *Bell 1436* ....41 | 5 |

Charlie WILSON – See SNOOP DOGGY DOGG

Dooley WILSON ℂ *US, male vocalist* **9 wks**

| 3 Dec 77 | AS TIME GOES BY *United Artists UP 36331* ....15 | 9 |

Disc has credit: 'With the voices of Humphrey Bogart and Ingrid Bergman'

Jackie WILSON ♪ ♥ *US, male vocalist* **97 wks**

15 Nov 57	● REET PETITE *Coral Q 72290* 6	14
14 Mar 58	TO BE LOVED *Coral Q 72306* 27	1
28 Mar 58	TO BE LOVED (re-entry) *Coral Q 72306* 23	6
16 May 58	TO BE LOVED (2nd re-entry) *Coral Q 72306* 23	1
15 Sep 60	(YOU WERE MADE FOR) ALL MY LOVE *Coral Q 72407* 33	6
3 Nov 60	(YOU WERE MADE FOR) ALL MY LOVE (re-entry) *Coral Q 72407* 47	1
22 Dec 60	ALONE AT LAST *Coral Q 72412* 50	1
14 May 69	(YOUR LOVE KEEPS LIFTING ME) HIGHER AND HIGHER *MCA BAG 2* 11	11
29 Jul 72	● I GET THE SWEETEST FEELING *MCA MU 1160* 9	13
3 May 75	I GET THE SWEETEST FEELING/(YOUR LOVE KEEPS LIFTING ME) HIGHER AND HIGHER (re-issue) *Brunswick BR 18* 25	8
29 Nov 86	★ REET PETITE (re-issue) *SMP SKM 3* 1	17
28 Feb 87	● I GET THE SWEETEST FEELING (2nd re-issue) *SMP SKM 1* 3	11
4 Jul 87	HIGHER AND HIGHER (2nd re-issue) *SMP SKM 10*..................15	7

'Higher and Higher' was not listed together with 'I Get the Sweetest Feeling' on Brunswick until 17 May, 1975

Mari WILSON ✪ *UK, female vocalist* **34 wks**

6 Mar 82	BEAT THE BEAT *Compact PINK 2* 59	3
8 May 82	BABY IT'S TRUE *Compact PINK 3* 42	6
11 Sep 82	● JUST WHAT I ALWAYS WANTED *Compact PINK 4* 8	10
13 Nov 82	(BEWARE) BOYFRIEND *Compact PINK 5* 51	4
19 Mar 83	CRY ME A RIVER *Compact PINK 6* 27	7
11 Jun 83	WONDERFUL *Compact PINK 7* 47	4

Meri WILSON ✪ *US, female vocalist* **10 wks**

| 27 Aug 77 | ● TELEPHONE MAN *Pye International 7N 25747* ....6 | 10 |

Mike 'Hitman' WILSON *US, male producer* **1 wk**

| 22 Sep 90 | ANOTHER SLEEPLESS NIGHT *Arista 113506*...........................74 | 1 |

Precious WILSON – See ERUPTION; MESSIAH

Tom WILSON *UK, male producer* **4 wks**

| 2 Dec 95 | TECHNOCAT *Pukka CDPUKKA 4* [1] ....33 | 3 |
| 16 Mar 96 | LET YOUR BODY GO *Clubscene DCSRT 050* ....60 | 1 |

[1] Technocat featuring Tom Wilson

Victoria WILSON JAMES *US, female vocalist* **1 wk**

| 9 Aug 97 | REACH 4 THE MELODY *Sony S3 VWJCD1*..................................72 | 1 |

WILSON PHILLIPS ☺ *US, female vocal group*   **33 wks**

26 May 90	● HOLD ON *SBK SBK 6* ▲	6	12
18 Aug 90	RELEASE ME *SBK SBK 11* ▲	36	5
10 Nov 90	IMPULSIVE *SBK SBK 16*	42	3
11 May 91	YOU'RE IN LOVE *SBK SBK 25* ▲	29	5
23 May 92	YOU WON'T SEE ME CRY *SBK SBK 34*	18	5
22 Aug 92	GIVE IT UP *SBK SBK 36*	36	3

Chris WILTSHIRE – See CLASS ACTION featuring Chris WILTSHIRE

WIMBLEDON CHORAL SOCIETY – See Des LYNAM

WIN *UK, male vocal/instrumental group*   **3 wks**

| 4 Apr 87 | SUPER POPOID GROOVE *Swamplands LON 128* | 63 | 3 |

WINANS *US, male vocal group*   **1 wk**

| 30 Nov 85 | LET MY PEOPLE GO (PART 1) *Qwest W 8874* | 71 | 1 |

BeBe WINANS – See ETERNAL

Ce Ce WINANS – See Whitney HOUSTON

WINDJAMMER ◢ *US, male vocal/instrumental group*   **12 wks**

| 30 Jun 84 | TOSSING AND TURNING *MCA MCA 897* | 18 | 12 |

Rose WINDROSS – See SOUL II SOUL

WING AND A PRAYER FIFE AND DRUM CORPS ◢
US, male/female vocal/instrumental group   **7 wks**

| 24 Jan 76 | BABY FACE *Atlantic K 10705* | 12 | 7 |

WINGER *US, male vocal/instrumental group*   **3 wks**

| 19 Jan 91 | MILES AWAY *Atlantic A 7802* | 56 | 3 |

Pete WINGFIELD ☺ 🎤 *UK, male vocalist*   **7 wks**

| 28 Jun 75 | ● EIGHTEEN WITH A BULLET *Island WIP 6231* | 7 | 7 |

WINGS – See Paul McCARTNEY

Josh WINK ☺ *US, male producer*   **26 wks**

6 May 95	DON'T LAUGH *XL XLS 62CD* [1]	38	2
21 Oct 95	● HIGHER STATE OF CONCIOUSNESS *Manifesto FESCD 3*	8	8
30 Dec 95	HIGHER STATE OF CONCIOUSNESS (re-entry) *Manifesto FESCD 3*	60	4
2 Mar 96	HYPNOTIZIN' *XL XLS 71CD* [1]	35	2
27 Jul 96	● HIGHER STATE OF CONCIOUSNESS (re-mix) *Manifesto FESCD 9* [1]	7	10

[1] Winx

See also SIZE 9

Edgar WINTER GROUP ✍ *US, male instrumental group*   **9 wks**

| 26 May 73 | FRANKENSTEIN *Epic EPC 1440* ▲ | 18 | 9 |

Ruby WINTERS 🎤 *US, female vocalist*   **35 wks**

5 Nov 77	● I WILL *Creole CR 141*	4	13
29 Apr 78	COME TO ME *Creole CR 153*	11	12
26 Aug 78	I WON'T MENTION IT AGAIN *Creole CR 160*	45	5
16 Jun 79	BABY LAY DOWN *Creole CR 171*	43	5

Steve WINWOOD ☺ ✍ *UK, male vocalist*   **33 wks**

17 Jan 81	WHILE YOU SEE A CHANCE *Island WIP 6655*	45	5
9 Oct 82	VALERIE *Island WIP 6818*	51	4
28 Jun 86	HIGHER LOVE *Island IS 288* ▲	13	9
13 Sep 86	FREEDOM OVERSPILL *Island IS 294*	69	1
24 Jan 87	BACK IN THE HIGH LIFE AGAIN *Island IS 303*	53	2
19 Sep 87	VALERIE (re-issue) *Island IS 336*	19	8
11 Jun 88	ROLL WITH IT *Virgin VS 1085* ▲	53	4

WINX – See Josh WINK

WIRE *UK, male vocal/instrumental group*   **4 wks**

| 27 Jan 79 | OUTDOOR MINER *Harvest HAR 5172* | 51 | 3 |
| 13 May 89 | EARDRUM BUZZ *Mute MUTE 87* | 68 | 1 |

WIRELESS *UK, male vocal/instrumental group*   **2 wks**

| 28 Jun 97 | I NEED YOU *Chrysalis CDCHS 5059* | 68 | 1 |
| 7 Feb 98 | IN LOVE WITH THE FAMILIAR *Chrysalis CDCHS 5075* | 69 | 1 |

Norman WISDOM ℂ *UK, male vocalist*   **20 wks**

| 19 Feb 54 | ● DON'T LAUGH AT ME *Columbia DB 3133* | 3 | 15 |
| 15 Mar 57 | WISDOM OF A FOOL *Columbia DB 3903* | 13 | 5 |

WISEGUYS *UK, male DJ/producer – Theo Keating*   **2 wks**

| 6 Jun 98 | OOH LA LA *Wall Of Sound WALLD 038* | 55 | 1 |
| 12 Sep 98 | START THE COMMOTION *Wall Of Sound WALLD 044* | 66 | 1 |

Bill WITHERS 🎤 *US, male vocalist*   **29 wks**

12 Aug 72	LEAN ON ME *A & M AMS 7004* ▲	18	9
14 Jan 78	● LOVELY DAY *CBS 5773*	7	8
25 May 85	OH YEAH! *CBS A 6154*	60	3
10 Sep 88	● LOVELY DAY (re-mix) *CBS 653001 7*	4	9

See also Grover WASHINGTON Jr

WIX – See SPIRO and WIX

WIZZARD ☺ *UK, male vocal/instrumental group*   **77 wks**

9 Dec 72	● BALL PARK INCIDENT *Harvest HAR 5062*	6	12
21 Apr 73	★ SEE MY BABY JIVE *Harvest HAR 5070*	1	17
1 Sep 73	★ ANGEL FINGERS *Harvest HAR 5076*	1	10
8 Dec 73	I WISH IT COULD BE CHRISTMAS EVERYDAY *Harvest HAR 5079* [1]	4	9
27 Apr 74	ROCK 'N' ROLL WINTER *Warner Bros. K 16357*	6	7
10 Aug 74	THIS IS THE STORY OF MY LOVE (BABY) *Warner Bros. K 16434*	34	4
21 Dec 74	ARE YOU READY TO ROCK *Warner Bros. K 16497*	8	10
19 Dec 81	I WISH IT COULD BE CHRISTMAS EVERYDAY (re-issue) *Harvest HAR 5173* [1]	41	4
15 Dec 84	I WISH IT COULD BE CHRISTMAS EVERYDAY (re-entry of re-issue) *Harvest HAR 5173* [1]	23	4

[1] Wizzard featuring vocal backing by the Suedettes plus the Stockland Green Bilateral School First Year Choir with additional noises by Miss Snob and Class 3C

Jah WOBBLE'S INVADERS OF THE HEART
UK, male vocalist/multi-instrumentalist   **10 wks**

1 Feb 92	VISIONS OF YOU *Oval OVAL 103*	35	5
30 Apr 94	BECOMING MORE LIKE GOD *Island CID 571*	36	2
25 Jun 94	THE SUN DOES RISE *Island CIDX 587*	41	3

First hit features the uncredited vocals of Sinead O'Connor

Terry WOGAN *Ireland, male vocalist*   **5 wks**

| 7 Jan 78 | FLORAL DANCE *Philips 6006 592* | 21 | 5 |

WOLFSBANE *US, male vocal/instrumental group*   **1 wk**

| 5 Oct 91 | EZY *Def American DEFA 11* | 68 | 1 |

Bobby WOMACK *US, male vocalist*   **21 wks**

16 Jun 84	TELL ME WHY *Motown TMG 1339*	60	3
5 Oct 85	I WISH HE DIDN'T TRUST ME SO MUCH *MCA MCA 994*	64	2
26 Sep 87	SO THE STORY GOES *Chrysalis LIB 3* [1]	34	8
7 Nov 87	LIVING IN A BOX *MCA MCA 1210*	70	2
3 Apr 93	I'M BACK FOR MORE *Dome CDDOME 1002* [2]	27	5
13 May 95	IT'S A MAN'S MAN'S MAN'S WORLD *Pulse 8 CDLOSE 89* [3]	73	1

[1] Living In a Box featuring Bobby Womack [2] Lulu and Bobby Womack [3] Jeanie Tracy and Bobby Womack

See also Wilton FELDER

WOMACK and WOMACK 🎤 US, male/female vocal duo | 51 wks

Date	Title	Pos	Wks
28 Apr 84	LOVE WARS *Elektra E 9799*	14	10
30 Jun 84	BABY I'M SCARED OF YOU *Elektra E 9733*	72	2
6 Dec 86	SOUL LOVE – SOUL MAN *Manhattan MT 16*	58	6
6 Aug 88 ●	TEARDROPS *Fourth & Broadway BRW 101*	3	17
12 Nov 88	LIFE'S JUST A BALLGAME *Fourth & Broadway BRW 116*	32	5
25 Feb 89	CELEBRATE THE WORLD *Fourth & Broadway BRW 125*	19	8
5 Feb 94	SECRET STAR *Warner Bros. W 0222CD* [1]	46	3

[1] House of Zekkariyas A.K.A. Womack and Womack

WOMBLES ☺

UK, furry vocal / instrumental litter-gatherers, led by Mike Batt | 95 wks

Date	Title	Pos	Wks
26 Jan 74 ●	THE WOMBLING SONG *CBS 1794*	4	23
6 Apr 74 ●	REMEMBER YOU'RE A WOMBLE *CBS 2241*	3	16
22 Jun 74 ●	BANANA ROCK *CBS 2465*	9	13
12 Oct 74	MINUETTO ALLEGRETTO *CBS 2710*	16	9
7 Dec 74 ●	WOMBLING MERRY CHRISTMAS *CBS 2842*	2	8
10 May 75	WOMBLING WHITE TIE AND TAILS *CBS 3266*	22	7
9 Aug 75	SUPER WOMBLE *CBS 3480*	20	6
13 Dec 75	LET'S WOMBLE TO THE PARTY TONIGHT *CBS 3794*	34	5
21 Mar 98	REMEMBER YOU'RE A WOMBLE (re-issue) *Columbia 6656202*	13	5
13 Jun 98	THE WOMBLING SONG (re-entry) *Columbia 6660412*	27	3

Stevie WONDER 🎤 Consistently successful multi-Grammy winner,

b. Steveland Judkins, 13 May, 1950, Michigan. He was the youngest singer to top the US album chart (aged 13), and he also recorded Motown's biggest UK seller, 'I Just Called to Say I Love You' | 415 wks

Date	Title	Pos	Wks
3 Feb 66	UPTIGHT *Tamla Motown TMG 545*	14	10
18 Aug 66	BLOWIN' IN THE WIND *Tamla Motown TMG 570*	36	5
5 Jan 67	A PLACE IN THE SUN *Tamla Motown TMG 588*	20	5
26 Jul 67	I WAS MADE TO LOVE HER *Tamla Motown TMG 613*	5	15
25 Oct 67	I'M WONDERING *Tamla Motown TMG 626*	22	8
8 May 68	SHOO BE DOO BE DOO DA DAY *Tamla Motown TMG 653*	46	4
18 Dec 68 ●	FOR ONCE IN MY LIFE *Tamla Motown TMG 679*	3	13
19 Mar 69	I DON'T KNOW WHY (I LOVE YOU) *Tamla Motown TMG 690*	14	10
9 Jul 69	I DON'T KNOW WHY (I LOVE YOU) (re-entry) *Tamla Motown TMG 690*	43	1
16 Jul 69 ●	MY CHERIE AMOUR *Tamla Motown TMG 690*	4	15
15 Nov 69 ●	YESTER-ME YESTER-YOU YESTERDAY *Tamla Motown TMG 717*	2	13
28 Mar 70 ●	NEVER HAD A DREAM COME TRUE *Tamla Motown TMG 731*	6	12
18 Jul 70	SIGNED SEALED DELIVERED I'M YOURS *Tamla Motown TMG 744*	15	9
26 Sep 70	SIGNED SEALED DELIVERED I'M YOURS (re-entry) *Tamla Motown TMG 744*	49	1
21 Nov 70	HEAVEN HELP US ALL *Tamla Motown TMG 757*	29	11
15 May 71	WE CAN WORK IT OUT *Tamla Motown TMG 772*	27	7
22 Jan 72	IF YOU REALLY LOVE ME *Tamla Motown TMG 798*	20	7
3 Feb 73	SUPERSTITION *Tamla Motown TMG 841* ▲	11	9
19 May 73 ●	YOU ARE THE SUNSHINE OF MY LIFE *Tamla Motown TMG 852*	7	11
13 Oct 73	HIGHER GROUND *Tamla Motown TMG 869*	29	5
12 Jan 74	LIVING FOR THE CITY *Tamla Motown TMG 881*	15	9
13 Apr 74 ●	HE'S MISSTRA KNOW IT ALL *Tamla Motown TMG 892*	10	9
19 Oct 74	YOU HAVEN'T DONE NOTHIN' *Tamla Motown TMG 921* ▲	30	5
11 Jan 75	BOOGIE ON REGGAE WOMAN *Tamla Motown TMG 928*	12	8
18 Dec 76 ●	I WISH *Tamla Motown TMG 1054* ▲	5	10
9 Apr 77 ●	SIR DUKE *Motown TMG 1068* ▲	2	9
10 Sep 77	ANOTHER STAR *Motown TMG 1083*	29	5
24 Feb 79	POPS WE LOVE YOU *Motown TMG 1136* [1]	66	5
24 Nov 79	SEND ONE YOUR LOVE *Motown TMG 1149*	52	3
26 Jan 80	BLACK ORCHID *Motown TMG 1173*	63	3
29 Mar 80	OUTSIDE MY WINDOW *Motown TMG 1179*	52	4
13 Sep 80 ●	MASTERBLASTER (JAMMIN') *Motown TMG 1204*	2	10
27 Dec 80 ●	I AIN'T GONNA STAND FOR IT *Motown TMG 1215*	10	10
7 Mar 81 ●	LATELY *Motown TMG 1226*	3	13
25 Jul 81 ●	HAPPY BIRTHDAY *Motown TMG 1235*	2	11
23 Jan 82	THAT GIRL *Motown TMG 1254*	39	6
10 Apr 82 ★	EBONY AND IVORY *Parlophone R 6054* [2] ▲	1	10
5 Jun 82 ●	DO I DO *Motown TMG 1269*	10	8
25 Sep 82	RIBBON IN THE SKY *Motown TMG 1280*	45	4
25 Aug 84 ★	I JUST CALLED TO SAY I LOVE YOU *Motown TMG 1349* ▲ ◆	1	24
1 Dec 84	LOVE LIGHT IN FLIGHT *Motown TMG 1364*	44	5

Date	Title	Pos	Wks
29 Dec 84	DON'T DRIVE DRUNK *Motown TMG 1372*	71	1
12 Jan 85	DON'T DRIVE DRUNK (re-entry) *Motown TMG 1372*	62	2
7 Sep 85 ●	PART-TIME LOVER *Motown ZB 40351* ▲	3	12
9 Nov 85	THAT'S WHAT FRIENDS ARE FOR *Arista ARIST 638* [3]	16	9
23 Nov 85	GO HOME *Motown ZB 40501*	67	2
28 Dec 85	I JUST CALLED TO SAY I LOVE YOU (re-entry) *Motown TMG 1349*	64	2
8 Mar 86	OVERJOYED *Motown ZB 40567*	17	8
17 Jan 87	STRANGER ON THE SHORE OF LOVE *Motown WOND 2*	55	3
31 Oct 87	SKELETONS *Motown ZB 41439*	59	3
28 May 88	GET IT *Motown ZB 41883* [4]	37	4
6 Aug 88 ●	MY LOVE *CBS JULIO 2* [5]	5	11
20 May 89	FREE *Motown ZB 42855*	49	5
12 Oct 91	FUN DAY *Motown ZB 44957*	63	1
25 Feb 95	FOR YOUR LOVE *Motown TMGCD 1437*	23	4
22 Jul 95	TOMORROW ROBINS WILL SING *Motown 8603732*	71	1
19 Jul 97 ●	HOW COME, HOW LONG *EPIC 6646202* [6]	10	5
31 Oct 98	TRUE TO YOUR HEART *Motown 8608832* [7]	51	1

[1] Diana Ross, Marvin Gaye, Smokey Robinson and Stevie Wonder [2] Paul McCartney with Stevie Wonder [3] Dionne Warwick and Friends featuring Elton John, Gladys Knight and Stevie Wonder [4] Stevie Wonder and Michael Jackson [5] Julio Iglesias featuring Stevie Wonder [6] Babyface featuring Stevie Wonder [7] 98 Degrees featuring Stevie Wonder

Wayne WONDER – See SHAGGY

WONDER DOGS UK, canine vocal group | 7 wks

Date	Title	Pos	Wks
21 Aug 82	RUFF MIX *Flip FLIP 001*	31	7

WONDER STUFF ☹ ☺ 🎸 UK, male vocal/instrumental group | 66 wks

Date	Title	Pos	Wks
30 Apr 88	GIVE GIVE GIVE ME MORE MORE MORE *Polydor GONE 3*	72	2
16 Jul 88	A WISH AWAY *Polydor GONE 4*	43	5
24 Sep 88	IT'S YER MONEY I'M AFTER BABY *Polydor GONE 5*	40	3
11 Mar 89	WHO WANTS TO BE THE DISCO KING *Polydor GONE 6*	28	3
23 Sep 89	DON'T LET ME DOWN GENTLY *Polydor GONE 7*	19	4
11 Nov 89	GOLDEN GREEN/GET TOGETHER *Polydor GONE 8*	33	3
12 May 90	CIRCLESQUARE *Polydor GONE 10*	20	4
13 Apr 91 ●	THE SIZE OF A COW *Polydor GONE 11*	5	7
25 May 91	CAUGHT IN MY SHADOW *Polydor GONE 12*	18	3
7 Sep 91	SLEEP ALONE *Polydor GONE 13*	43	2
26 Oct 91 ★	DIZZY *Sense SIGH 712* [1]	1	12
25 Jan 92 ●	WELCOME TO THE CHEAP SEATS (EP) *Polydor GONE 14*	8	5
25 Sep 93 ●	ON THE ROPES EP *Polydor GONCD 15*	10	4
27 Nov 93	FULL OF LIFE (HAPPY NOW) *Polydor GONCD 16*	28	3
26 Mar 94	HOT LOVE NOW *Polydor GONCD 17*	19	3
10 Sep 94	UNBEARABLE *Polydor GONCD 18*	16	3

[1] Vic Reeves and the Wonder Stuff

Tracks on Welcome to the Cheap Seats (EP): *Welcome to the Cheap Seats / Me, My Mom, My Dad and My Brother / Will the Circle Be Unbroken / That's Entertainment.*
Tracks on On the Ropes (EP): *On the Ropes / Professional Disturber of the Peace / Hank and John*

WONDERS US, male vocal/instrumental group | 3 wks

Date	Title	Pos	Wks
22 Feb 97	THAT THING YOU DO! *Play-Tone 6640552*	22	3

WONDRESS – See MANTRONIX

Brenton WOOD 🎤 US, male vocalist | 14 wks

Date	Title	Pos	Wks
27 Dec 67 ●	GIMME LITTLE SIGN *Liberty LBF 15021*	8	14

Roy WOOD ☺ 🎸 UK, male vocalist/multi-instrumentalist | 41 wks

Date	Title	Pos	Wks
11 Aug 73	DEAR ELAINE *Harvest HAR 5074*	18	8
1 Dec 73 ●	FOREVER *Harvest HAR 5078*	8	13
15 Jun 74	GOING DOWN THE ROAD *Harvest HAR 5083*	13	7
31 May 75	OH WHAT A SHAME *Jet 754*	13	7
22 Nov 86	WATERLOO *IRS IRM 125* [1]	45	4
23 Dec 95	I WISH IT COULD BE CHRISTMAS EVERYDAY *Woody WOODY 001CD* [2]	59	2

[1] Doctor and the Medics featuring Roy Wood [2] Roy Wood Big Band

WOODENTOPS *UK, male vocal/instrumental group* — **1 wk**

11 Oct 86	EVERYDAY LIVING *Rough Trade RT 178*	72	1

Edward WOODWARD *UK, male vocalist* — **2 wks**

16 Jan 71	THE WAY YOU LOOK TONIGHT *DJM DJS 232*	50	1
30 Jan 71	THE WAY YOU LOOK TONIGHT (re-entry) *DJM DJS 232*	42	1

Sheb WOOLEY ☉ *US, male vocalist* — **8 wks**

20 Jun 58	PURPLE PEOPLE EATER *MGM 981* ▲	12	8

WOOLPACKERS ☉ 👟 *UK, male vocal group* — **23 wks**

16 Nov 96 ●	HILLBILLY ROCK HILLBILLY ROLL *RCA 74321425412*	7	13
29 Nov 97	LINE DANCE PARTY *RCA 74321512262*	25	10

WORKING WEEK *UK, male/female vocal/instrumental group* — **2 wks**

9 Jun 84	VENCEREMOS – WE WILL WIN *Virgin VS 684*	64	2

WORLD – See LIL' LOUIS

WORLD PARTY ☉ 🖋
Ireland/UK, male vocal/instrumental group — **29 wks**

14 Feb 87	SHIP OF FOOLS *Ensign ENY 606*	42	6
16 Jun 90	MESSAGE IN THE BOX *Ensign ENY 631*	39	6
15 Sep 90	WAY DOWN NOW *Ensign ENY 634*	66	2
18 May 91	THANK YOU WORLD *Ensign ENY 643*	68	1
10 Apr 93	IS IT LIKE TODAY *Ensign CDENY 658*	19	6
10 Jul 93	GIVE IT ALL AWAY *Ensign CDENY 659*	43	3
2 Oct 93	ALL I GAVE *Ensign CDENYS 660*	37	3
7 Jun 97	BEAUTIFUL DREAM *Chrysalis CDCHS 5053*	31	2

WORLD PREMIERE *US, male vocal/instrumental group* — **4 wks**

28 Jan 84	SHARE THE NIGHT *Epic A 4133*	64	4

WORLD OF TWIST *UK, male/female vocal/instrumental group* — **12 wks**

24 Nov 90	THE STORM *Circa YR 55*	42	3
5 Jan 91	THE STORM (re-entry) *Circa YR 55*	74	2
23 Mar 91	SONS OF THE STAGE *Circa YR 62*	47	3
12 Oct 91	SWEETS *Circa YR 72*	58	2
22 Feb 92	SHE'S A RAINBOW *Circa YR 82*	62	2

WORLD WARRIOR *UK, male producer – Simon Harris* — **1 wk**

16 Apr 94	STREET FIGHTER II *Living Beat LBECD 27*	70	1

See also Simon HARRIS

WORLDS APART ☉ *UK, male vocal group* — **17 wks**

27 Mar 93	HEAVEN MUST BE MISSING AN ANGEL *Arista 74321139362*	29	3
3 Jul 93	WONDERFUL WORLD *Arista 74321153402*	51	1
25 Sep 93	EVERLASTING LOVE *Bell 74321164802*	20	4
26 Mar 94	COULD IT BE I'M FALLING IN LOVE *Bell 74321189952*	15	6
4 Jun 94	BEGGIN' TO BE WRITTEN *Bell 74321211982*	29	3

WORLD'S FAMOUS SUPREME TEAM ☺ 👟
US, male vocal/scratch group — **18 wks**

4 Dec 82 ●	BUFFALO GALS *Charisma MALC 1* [1]	9	12
25 Feb 84	HEY DJ *Charisma TEAM 1*	52	5
8 Dec 90	OPERAA HOUSE *Virgin VS 1273* [2]	75	1

[1] Malcolm McLaren and the World's Famous Supreme Team
[2] World's Famous Supreme Team Show

WRECKX-N-EFFECT *US, male rap group* — **18 wks**

13 Jan 90	JUICY *Motown ZB 43295* [1]	29	7
5 Dec 92	RUMP SHAKER *MCA MCS 1725*	24	7
7 May 94	WRECKX SHOP *MCA MCSTD 1969*	26	2
13 Aug 94	RUMP SHAKER (re-issue) *MCA MCSTD 1989*	40	2

[1] Wrecks-N-Effect

Betty WRIGHT *US, female vocalist* — **23 wks**

25 Jan 75	SHOORAH SHOORAH *RCA 2491*	27	7
19 Apr 75	WHERE IS THE LOVE *RCA 2548*	25	7
8 Feb 86	PAIN *Cooltempo COOL 117*	42	6
9 Sep 89	KEEP LOVE NEW *Sure Delight SD 11*	71	3

Ian WRIGHT *UK, male vocalist* — **2 wks**

28 Aug 93	DO THE RIGHT THING *M & G MAGCD 45*	43	2

Linda WRIGHT – See NEW ATLANTIC

Ruby WRIGHT ☉ 👟 *US, female vocalist* — **15 wks**

16 Apr 54 ●	BIMBO *Parlophone R 3816*	7	4
21 May 54	BIMBO (re-entry) *Parlophone R 3816*	12	1
22 May 59	THREE STARS *Parlophone R 4556*	19	10

'Three Stars' is narrated by Dick Pike

Steve WRIGHT *UK, male vocalist* — **10 wks**

27 Nov 82	I'M ALRIGHT *RCA 296* [1]	40	6
15 Oct 83	GET SOME THERAPY *RCA RCA 362* [2]	75	1
1 Dec 84	THE GAY CAVALIEROS (THE STORY SO FAR) *MCA 925*	61	3

[1] Young Steve and the Afternoon Boys [2] Steve Wright and the Sisters of Soul

WU-TANG CLAN 👟 *US, male rap/instrumental band* — **8 wks**

16 Aug 97	TRIUMPH *Loud 74321510212* [1]	46	1
21 Mar 98 ●	SAY WHAT YOU WANT/INSANE *Mercury MERCD 499* [2]	4	7

[1] Wu-Tang Clan featuring Cappadonna [2] Texas featuring Wu-Tang Clan
(rap by Method Man and RZA)

WUBBLE-U *UK, male production group* — **1 wk**

7 Mar 98	PETAL *Indolent DGOL 003CD1*	55	1

WURZELS ☉ *UK, male vocal/instrumental group* — **28 wks**

2 Feb 67	DRINK UP THY ZIDER *Columbia DB 8081* [1]	45	1
15 May 76 ★	COMBINE HARVESTER (BRAND NEW KEY) *EMI 2450*	1	13
11 Sep 76 ●	I AM A CIDER DRINKER (PALOMA BLANCA) *EMI 2520*	3	9
25 Jun 77	FARMER BILL'S COWMAN (I WAS KAISER BILL'S BATMAN) *EMI 2637*	32	5

[1] Adge Cutler and the Wurzels

WWF SUPERSTARS ☉ *US/UK, male wrestling vocalists* — **15 wks**

12 Dec 92 ●	SLAM JAM *Arista 74321124887*	4	8
13 Feb 93	SLAM JAM *Arista 74321124887*	75	1
3 Apr 93	WRESTLEMANIA *Arista 74321136832*	14	5
10 Jul 93	USA *Arista 74321153092*	71	1

Robert WYATT *UK, male vocalist* — **11 wks**

28 Sep 74	I'M A BELIEVER *Virgin VS 114*	29	5
7 May 83	SHIPBUILDING *Rough Trade RT 115*	35	6

Michael WYCOFF *US, male vocalist* — **2 wks**

23 Jul 83	(DO YOU REALLY LOVE ME) TELL ME LOVE *RCA 348*	60	2

Pete WYLIE ☹ ☉ *UK, male vocalist* — **18 wks**

3 May 86	SINFUL *Eternal MDM 7*	13	10
13 Sep 86	DIAMOND GIRL *Eternal MDM 12*	57	3
13 Apr 91	SINFUL! *Siren SRN 138* [1]	28	5

[1] Pete Wylie with the Farm

Bill WYMAN ☉ *UK, male vocalist* — **13 wks**

25 Jul 81	(SI SI) JE SUIS UN ROCK STAR *A & M AMS 8144*	14	9
20 Mar 82	A NEW FASHION *A & M AMS 8209*	37	4

Jane WYMAN – See Bing CROSBY

Tammy WYNETTE 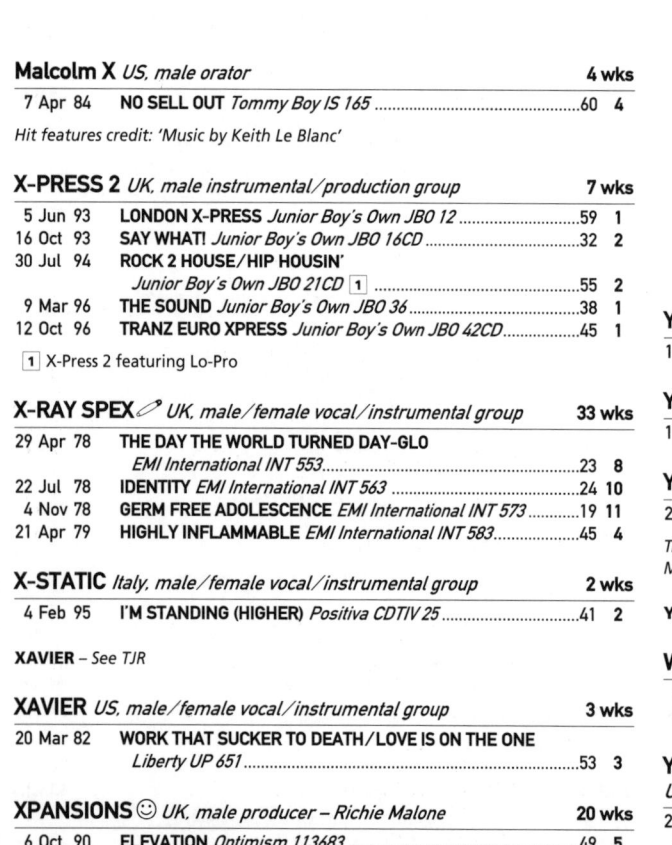 US, female vocalist — 35 wks

26 Apr 75	★ STAND BY YOUR MAN Epic EPC 7137	1	12
28 Jun 75	D. I. V. O. R. C. E. Epic EPC 3361	12	7
12 Jun 76	I DON'T WANNA PLAY HOUSE Epic EPC 4091	37	4
7 Dec 91	● JUSTIFIED AND ANCIENT KLF Communications KLF 099 [1]	2	12

[1] KLF, guest vocals: Tammy Wynette

Mark WYNTER ⊙ UK, male vocalist — 80 wks

25 Aug 60	IMAGE OF A GIRL Decca F 11263	11	10
10 Nov 60	KICKING UP THE LEAVES Decca F 11279	24	10
9 Mar 61	DREAM GIRL Decca F 11323	27	5
8 Jun 61	EXCLUSIVELY YOURS Decca F 11354	32	7
4 Oct 62	● VENUS IN BLUE JEANS Pye 7N 15466	4	15
13 Dec 62	● GO AWAY LITTLE GIRL Pye 7N 15492	6	11
6 Jun 63	SHY GIRL Pye 7N 15525	28	6
14 Nov 63	IT'S ALMOST TOMORROW Pye 7N 15577	12	12
9 Apr 64	ONLY YOU Pye 7N 15626	38	4

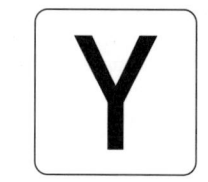

Malcolm X US, male orator — 4 wks

7 Apr 84	NO SELL OUT Tommy Boy IS 165	60	4

Hit features credit: 'Music by Keith Le Blanc'

X-PRESS 2 UK, male instrumental/production group — 7 wks

5 Jun 93	LONDON X-PRESS Junior Boy's Own JBO 12	59	1
16 Oct 93	SAY WHAT! Junior Boy's Own JBO 16CD	32	2
30 Jul 94	ROCK 2 HOUSE/HIP HOUSIN' Junior Boy's Own JBO 21CD [1]	55	2
9 Mar 96	THE SOUND Junior Boy's Own JBO 36	38	1
12 Oct 96	TRANZ EURO XPRESS Junior Boy's Own JBO 42CD	45	1

[1] X-Press 2 featuring Lo-Pro

X-RAY SPEX ✐ UK, male/female vocal/instrumental group — 33 wks

29 Apr 78	THE DAY THE WORLD TURNED DAY-GLO EMI International INT 553	23	8
22 Jul 78	IDENTITY EMI International INT 563	24	10
4 Nov 78	GERM FREE ADOLESCENCE EMI International INT 573	19	11
21 Apr 79	HIGHLY INFLAMMABLE EMI International INT 583	45	4

X-STATIC Italy, male/female vocal/instrumental group — 2 wks

4 Feb 95	I'M STANDING (HIGHER) Positiva CDTIV 25	41	2

XAVIER – See TJR

XAVIER US, male/female vocal/instrumental group — 3 wks

20 Mar 82	WORK THAT SUCKER TO DEATH/LOVE IS ON THE ONE Liberty UP 651	53	3

XPANSIONS ☺ UK, male producer – Richie Malone — 20 wks

6 Oct 90	ELEVATION Optimism 113683	49	5
23 Feb 91	● MOVE YOUR BODY Arista 113 683	7	9
15 Jun 91	WHAT YOU WANT Arista 114 246 [1]	55	2

26 Aug 95	MOVE YOUR BODY (re-mix) Arista 74321294982 [2]	14	4

[1] Xpansions featuring Dale Joyner   [2] Xpansions 95

'Move Your Body' is a re-mix of 'Elevation'

XSCAPE US, female vocal group — 15 wks

20 Nov 93	JUST KICKIN' IT Columbia 6598622	49	2
5 Nov 94	JUST KICKIN' IT (re-issue) Columbia 6608642	54	2
7 Oct 95	FEELS SO GOOD Columbia 6625022	34	2
27 Jan 96	WHO CAN I RUN TO Columbia 6628112	31	3
29 Jun 96	KEEP ON KEEPIN' ON East West A 4287CD	39	2
19 Apr 97	KEEP ON KEEPIN' ON (re-issue) East West A 3950CD1 [1]	27	2
22 Aug 98	THE ARMS OF THE ONE WHO LOVES YOU Columbia 6662522	46	2

[1] MC Lyte featuring Xscape

XTC ✐ 🎸 UK, male vocal/instrumental group — 70 wks

12 May 79	LIFE BEGINS AT THE HOP Virgin VS 259	54	4
22 Sep 79	MAKING PLANS FOR NIGEL Virgin VS 282	17	11
6 Sep 80	GENERALS AND MAJORS/DON'T LOSE YOUR TEMPER Virgin VS 365	32	8
18 Oct 80	TOWERS OF LONDON Virgin VS 372	31	5
24 Jan 81	SGT ROCK (IS GOING TO HELP ME) Virgin VS 384	16	9
23 Jan 82	● SENSES WORKING OVERTIME Virgin VS 462	10	9
27 Mar 82	BALL AND CHAIN Virgin VS 482	58	4
15 Oct 83	LOVE ON A FARMBOY'S WAGES Virgin VS 613	50	4
29 Sep 84	ALL YOU PRETTY GIRLS Virgin VS 709	55	5
28 Jan 89	MAYOR OF SIMPLETON Virgin VS 1158	46	5
4 Apr 92	THE DISAPPOINTED Virgin VS 1404	33	5
13 Jun 92	THE BALLAD OF PETER PUMPKINHEAD Virgin VS 1415	71	1

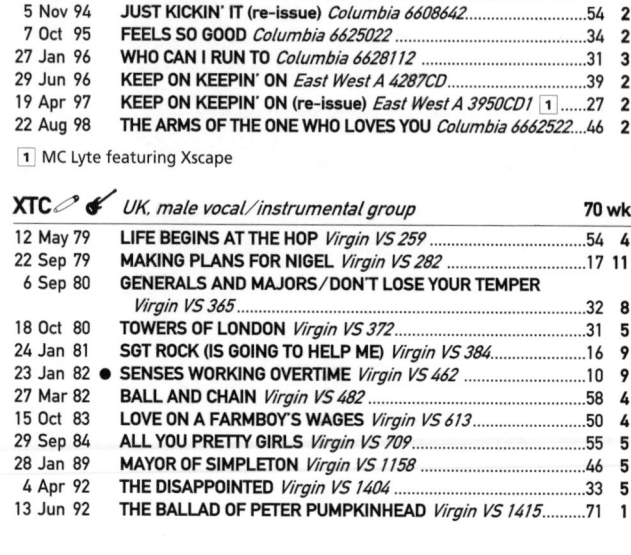

Y & T US, male vocal/instrumental group — 4 wks

13 Aug 83	MEAN STREAK A & M AM 135	41	4

Y?N-VEE US, female vocal group — 1 wk

17 Dec 94	CHOCOLATE RAL RALCD 2	65	1

Y-TRAXX Belgium, male producer – Frederique De Backer — 1 wk

24 May 97	MYSTERY LAND EP ffrr FCD 292	63	1

Tracks on Mystery Land EP: Mystery Land (radio edit) / Trance Piano / Kiss the Sound / Mystery Land

YA KID K – See HI-TEK 3 featuring YA KID K; TECHNOTRONIC

Weird Al YANKOVIC US, male vocalist — 8 wks

7 Apr 84	EAT IT Scotti Bros./Epic A 4257	36	7
4 Jul 92	SMELLS LIKE NIRVANA Scotti Bros PO 219	58	1

YARBROUGH and PEOPLES 🔌 ✐

US, male/female vocal/instrumental duo — 20 wks

27 Dec 80	● DON'T STOP THE MUSIC Mercury MER 53	7	12
5 May 84	DON'T WASTE YOUR TIME Total Experience XE 501	60	3
11 Jan 86	GUILTY Total Experience FB 49905	53	3
5 Jul 86	I WOULDN'T LIE Total Experience FB 49841	61	2

YARDBIRDS ✔ *UK, male vocal/instrumental group* — 62 wks

12 Nov 64	GOOD MORNING LITTLE SCHOOLGIRL *Columbia DB 7391*	44	4
18 Mar 65 ●	FOR YOUR LOVE *Columbia DB 7499*	3	12
17 Jun 65 ●	HEART FULL OF SOUL *Columbia DB 7594*	2	13
14 Oct 65 ●	EVIL HEARTED YOU/STILL I'M SAD *Columbia DB 7706*	3	10
3 Mar 66 ●	SHAPES OF THINGS *Columbia DB 7848*	3	9
2 Jun 66 ●	OVER UNDER SIDEWAYS DOWN *Columbia DB 7928*	10	9
27 Oct 66	HAPPENINGS TEN YEARS TIME AGO *Columbia DB 8024*	43	5

YAVAHN – See RUFFNECK featuring YAVAHN

YAZOO ❂ ☺ *UK, female/male vocal/instrumental duo* — 53 wks

17 Apr 82 ●	ONLY YOU *Mute MUTE 020*	2	14
17 Jul 82 ●	DON'T GO *Mute YAZ 001*	3	11
20 Nov 82	THE OTHER SIDE OF LOVE *Mute YAZ 002*	13	9
21 May 83 ●	NOBODY'S DIARY *Mute YAZ 003*	3	11
8 Dec 90	SITUATION *Mute YAZ 4*	14	8

YAZZ ☺ ❂ *UK, female vocalist* — 69 wks

20 Feb 88 ●	DOCTORIN' THE HOUSE *Ahead Of Our Time CCUT 27* [1]	6	9
23 Jul 88 ★	THE ONLY WAY IS UP *Big Life BLR 4* [2]	1	15
29 Oct 88 ●	STAND UP FOR YOUR LOVE RIGHTS *Big Life BLR 5*	2	12
4 Feb 89 ●	FINE TIME *Big Life BLR 6*	9	8
29 Apr 89	WHERE HAS ALL THE LOVE GONE *Big Life BLR 8*	16	6
23 Jun 90	TREAT ME GOOD *Big Life BLR 24*	20	5
28 Mar 92	ONE TRUE WOMAN *Polydor PO 198*	60	2
31 Jul 93	HOW LONG *Polydor PZCD 252* [3]	31	5
2 Apr 94	HAVE MERCY *Polydor PZCD 309*	42	3
9 Jul 94	EVERYBODY'S GOT TO LEARN SOMETIME *Polydor PZCD 316*	56	2
28 Sep 96	GOOD THING GOING *East West EW 062CD*	53	1
22 Mar 97	NEVER CAN SAY GOODBYE *East West EW 081CD*	61	1

[1] Coldcut featuring Yazz and the Plastic Population [2] Yazz and the Plastic Population [3] Yazz and Aswad

Trisha YEARWOOD *US, female vocalist* — 1 wk

9 Aug 97	HOW DO I LIVE *MCA MCSTD 48064*	66	1

YELL! ❂ *UK, male vocal duo* — 8 wks

20 Jan 90 ●	INSTANT REPLAY *Fanfare FAN 22*	10	8

YELLO ☺ *Switzerland, male vocal/instrumental duo* — 42 wks

25 Jun 83	I LOVE YOU *Stiff BUY 176*	41	4
26 Nov 83	LOST AGAIN *Stiff BUY 191*	73	1
9 Aug 86	GOLDRUSH *Mercury MER 218*	54	3
22 Aug 87	THE RHYTHM DIVINE *Mercury MER 253* [1]	54	2
27 Aug 88 ●	THE RACE *Mercury YELLO 1*	7	11
17 Dec 88	TIED UP *Mercury YELLO 2*	60	5
25 Mar 89	OF COURSE I'M LYING *Mercury YELLO 3*	23	8
22 Jul 89	BLAZING SADDLES *Mercury YELLO 4*	47	2
8 Jun 91	RUBBERBANDMAN *Mercury YELLO 5*	58	2
5 Sep 92	JUNGLE BILL *Mercury MER 376*	61	2
7 Nov 92	THE RACE/BOSTITCH (re-issue) *Mercury MER 382*	55	1
15 Oct 94	HOW HOW *Mercury MERCD 414*	59	1

[1] Yello featuring Shirley Bassey

YELLOW DOG ❂ *US/UK, male vocal/instrumental group* — 13 wks

4 Feb 78 ●	JUST ONE MORE NIGHT *Virgin VS 195*	8	9
22 Jul 78	WAIT UNTIL MIDNIGHT *Virgin VS 217*	54	4

YELLOW MAGIC ORCHESTRA ◢ ☺
Japan, male instrumental group — 11 wks

14 Jun 80	COMPUTER GAME (THEME FROM 'THE INVADERS') *A & M AMS 7502*	17	11

YELLOWCOATS – See Paul SHANE and the YELLOWCOATS

YES ✔ *UK/South Africa, male vocal/instrumental group* — 31 wks

17 Sep 77 ●	WONDEROUS STORIES *Atlantic K 10999*	7	9
26 Nov 77	GOING FOR THE ONE *Atlantic K 11047*	24	4
9 Sep 78	DON'T KILL THE WHALE *Atlantic K 11184*	36	4
12 Nov 83	OWNER OF A LONELY HEART *Atco B 9817* ▲	28	9
31 Mar 84	LEAVE IT *Atco B 9787*	56	4
3 Oct 87	LOVE WILL FIND A WAY *Atco A 9449*	73	1

Group were UK only for first three hits

Melissa YIANNAKOU – See DESIYA featuring Melissa YIANNAKOU

YIN and YAN *UK, male vocal duo* — 5 wks

29 Mar 75	IF *EMI 2282*	25	5

YO-HANS – See JODE featuring YO-HANS

Tukka YOOT – See US3

YOSH presents LOVEDEEJAY AKEMI *Holland, male producer* — 5 wks

29 Jul 95	IT'S WHAT'S UPFRONT THAT COUNTS *Limbo LIMB 46CD*	69	1
2 Dec 95	IT'S WHAT'S UPFRONT THAT COUNTS (re-mix) *Limbo LIMB 50CD*	31	2
20 Apr 96	THE SCREAMER *Limbo LIMB 54CD*	38	2

YOSHIKI – See Roger TAYLOR

YOTHU YINDI *Australia, male vocal/instrumental group* — 1 wk

15 Feb 92	TREATY *Hollywood HWD 116*	72	1

Faron YOUNG ⬤ *US, male vocalist* — 23 wks

15 Jul 72 ●	IT'S FOUR IN THE MORNING *Mercury 6052 140*	3	23

Jimmy YOUNG ☾ *UK, male vocalist* — 88 wks

9 Jan 53	FAITH CAN MOVE MOUNTAINS *Decca F 9986*	11	1
21 Aug 53 ●	ETERNALLY *Decca F 10130*	8	9
6 May 55 ★	UNCHAINED MELODY *Decca F 10502*	1	19
16 Sep 55 ★	THE MAN FROM LARAMIE *Decca F 10597*	1	12
23 Dec 55	SOMEONE ON YOUR MIND *Decca F 10640*	13	5
16 Mar 56 ●	CHAIN GANG *Decca F 10694*	9	6
8 Jun 56	WAYWARD WIND *Decca F 10736*	27	1
22 Jun 56	RICH MAN POOR MAN *Decca F 10736*	25	1
28 Sep 56 ●	MORE *Decca F 10774*	4	17
3 May 57	ROUND AND ROUND *Decca F 10875*	30	1
10 Oct 63	MISS YOU *Columbia DB 7119*	15	13
26 Mar 64	UNCHAINED MELODY *Columbia DB 7234*	43	3

The versions of 'Unchained Melody' on Decca and on Columbia are different recordings. 'Round and Round' is with the Michael Sammes Singers
See also VARIOUS ARTISTS (EPs & LPs) – All-Star Hit Parade No 2

John Paul YOUNG ❂ *Australia, male vocalist* — 16 wks

29 Apr 78 ●	LOVE IS IN THE AIR *Ariola ARO 117*	5	13
14 Nov 92	LOVE IS IN THE AIR (re-mix) *Columbia 6587697*	49	3

Karen YOUNG ❂ *US, female vocalist* — 21 wks

6 Sep 69 ●	NOBODY'S CHILD *Major Minor MM 625*	6	21

Karen YOUNG *US, female vocalist* — 9 wks

19 Aug 78	HOT SHOT *Atlantic K 11180*	34	7
24 Feb 79	HOT SHOT (re-issue) *Atlantic LV 8*	75	1
15 Nov 97	HOT SHOT '97 (re-mix) *Distinctive DISNCD 37*	68	1

Neil YOUNG ✔ *Canada, male vocalist* — 22 wks

11 Mar 72 ●	HEART OF GOLD *Reprise K 14140* ▲	10	11
6 Jan 79	FOUR STRONG WINDS *Reprise K 14493*	57	4
27 Feb 93	HARVEST MOON *Reprise W 0139CD*	36	3
17 Jul 93	THE NEEDLE AND THE DAMAGE DONE *Reprise W 0191CD*	75	1
30 Oct 93	LONG MAY YOU RUN (LIVE) *Reprise W 0207CD*	71	1
9 Apr 94	PHILADELPHIA *Reprise W 0242CD*	62	2

See also CROSBY, STILLS, NASH and YOUNG

Paul YOUNG ◉ *Soulful-sounding pop singer/songwriter (b. 17 January, 1956, Bedfordshire) who earlier fronted The Q-Tips and chart act Streetband. This multi-BRIT Award winner sold seven million copies of No Parlez album (including more than one million in the UK)* **134 wks**

18 Jun 83	★ WHEREVER I LAY MY HAT (THAT'S MY HOME) *CBS A 3371*	1	15
10 Sep 83	● COME BACK AND STAY *CBS A 3636*	4	9
19 Nov 83	● LOVE OF THE COMMON PEOPLE *CBS A 3585*	2	13
13 Oct 84	● I'M GONNA TEAR YOUR PLAYHOUSE DOWN *CBS A 4786*	9	7
8 Dec 84	● EVERYTHING MUST CHANGE *CBS A 4972*	9	11
9 Mar 85	● EVERYTIME YOU GO AWAY *CBS A 6300* ▲	4	11
22 Jun 85	TOMB OF MEMORIES *CBS A 6321*	16	7
17 Aug 85	TOMB OF MEMORIES (re-entry) *CBS A 6321*	74	1
4 Oct 86	WONDERLAND *CBS YOUNG 1*	24	5
29 Nov 86	SOME PEOPLE *CBS YOUNG 2*	56	3
7 Feb 87	WHY DOES A MAN HAVE TO BE STRONG *CBS YOUNG 3*	63	2
12 May 90	SOFTLY WHISPERING I LOVE YOU *CBS YOUNG 4*	21	6
7 Jul 90	OH GIRL *CBS YOUNG 5*	25	6
6 Oct 90	HEAVEN CAN WAIT *CBS YOUNG 6*	71	2
12 Jan 91	CALLING YOU *CBS YOUNG 7*	57	2
30 Mar 91	● SENZA UNA DONNA (WITHOUT A WOMAN) *London LON 294* [1]	4	12
10 Aug 91	BOTH SIDES NOW *MCA MCS 1546* [2]	74	1
26 Oct 91	DON'T DREAM IT'S OVER *Columbia 6574117*	20	5
25 Sep 93	NOW I KNOW WHAT MADE OTIS BLUE *Columbia 6596412*	14	7
27 Nov 93	HOPE IN A HOPELESS WORLD *Columbia 6598652*	42	3
23 Apr 94	IT WILL BE YOU *Columbia 6602812*	34	4
17 May 97	I WISH YOU LOVE *East West EW 100CD1*	33	2

[1] Zucchero and Paul Young [2] Clannad and Paul Young

Retta YOUNG *US, female vocalist* **7 wks**

24 May 75	SENDING OUT AN S. O. S. *All Platinum 6146 305*	28	7

Leon YOUNG STRING CHORALE – See Mr Acker BILK and his PARAMOUNT JAZZ BAND

Tracie YOUNG – See TRACIE

YOUNG and COMPANY ⚓
US, male/female vocal/instrumental group **12 wks**

1 Nov 80	I LIKE (WHAT YOU'RE DOING TO ME) *Excalibur EXC 501*	20	12

YOUNG BLACK TEENAGERS *US, male rap group* **3 wks**

9 Apr 94	TAP THE BOTTLE *MCA MCSTD 1967*	39	3

YOUNG DISCIPLES [R&B] ☺
UK/US, male/female vocal/instrumental group **17 wks**

13 Oct 90	GET YOURSELF TOGETHER *Talkin Loud TLK 2*	68	1
23 Feb 91	APPARENTLY NOTHIN' *Talkin Loud TLK 5*	46	4
3 Aug 91	APPARENTLY NOTHIN' (re-entry) *Talkin Loud TLK 5*	13	7
5 Oct 91	GET YOURSELF TOGETHER (re-issue) *Talkin Loud TLK 15*	65	2
5 Sep 92	YOUNG DISCIPLES EP *Talkin Loud TLKX 18*	48	3

Tracks on Young Disciples EP: Move On/Freedom/All I Have In Me/Move On (re-mix)

YOUNG IDEA ◉ *UK, male vocal duo* **6 wks**

29 Jun 67	● WITH A LITTLE HELP FROM MY FRIENDS *Columbia DB 8205*	10	6

YOUNG MC *US, male rapper* **7 wks**

15 Jul 89	BUST A MOVE *Delicious Vinyl BRW 137*	73	2
17 Feb 90	PRINCIPAL'S OFFICE *Delicious Vinyl BRW 161*	54	3
17 Aug 91	THAT'S THE WAY LOVE GOES *Capitol CL 623*	65	2

YOUNG AND MOODY BAND *UK, male vocal/instrumental group* **4 wks**

10 Oct 81	DON'T DO THAT *Bronze BRO 130*	63	4

YOUNG OFFENDERS *Ireland, male vocal/instrumental group* **1 wk**

7 Mar 98	THAT'S WHY WE LOSE CONTROL *Columbia 6651942*	60	1

YOUNG ONES – See Cliff RICHARD

YOUNG RASCALS ◉ ⚓ *US, male vocal/instrumental group* **17 wks**

25 May 67	● GROOVIN' *Atlantic 584 111* ▲	8	13
16 Aug 67	A GIRL LIKE YOU *Atlantic 584 128*	37	4

Sydney YOUNGBLOOD ◉ ☺ *US, male vocalist* **31 wks**

26 Aug 89	● IF ONLY I COULD *Circa YR 34*	3	14
9 Dec 89	SIT AND WAIT *Circa YR 40*	16	8
31 Mar 90	I'D RATHER GO BLIND *Circa YR 43*	44	5
29 Jun 91	HOOKED ON YOU *Circa YR 65*	72	2
20 Mar 93	ANYTHING *RCA 74321138672*	48	2

Z

Z FACTOR *UK, male DJ/producer – Dave Lee* **1 wk**

21 Feb 98	GOTTA KEEP PUSHIN' *ffrr FCD 329*	47	1

See also Joey NEGRO

Helmut ZACHARIAS Ⓒ *Germany, orchestra* **11 wks**

29 Oct 64	● TOKYO MELODY *Polydor NH 52341*	9	11

Pia ZADORA *US, female vocalist* **6 wks**

27 Oct 84	WHEN THE RAIN BEGINS TO FALL *Arista ARIST 584* [1]	68	2
12 Nov 88	DANCE OUT OF MY HEAD *Epic 6528867* [2]	65	4

[1] Jermaine Jackson and Pia Zadora [2] Pia

Michael ZAGER BAND ⚓
US, male/female vocal/instrumental group **12 wks**

1 Apr 78	● LET'S ALL CHANT *Private Stock PVT 143*	8	12

ZAGER and EVANS ◉ *US, male vocal duo* **13 wks**

9 Aug 69	★ IN THE YEAR 2525 (EXORDIUM AND TERMINUS) *RCA 1860* ▲	1	13

Georghe ZAMFIR Ⓒ *Romania, male instrumentalist – pipes* **9 wks**

21 Aug 76	● (LIGHT OF EXPERIENCE) DOINA DE JALE *Epic EPC 4310*	4	9

Tommy ZANG *US, male vocalist* **1 wk**

16 Feb 61	HEY GOOD LOOKING *Polydor NH 66957*	45	1

ZAPP *US, male vocal/instrumental group* **6 wks**

25 Jan 86	IT DOESN'T REALLY MATTER *Warner Bros. W 8879*	57	3
24 May 86	COMPUTER LOVE (PART 1) *Warner Bros. W 8805*	64	3

Francesco ZAPPALA *Italy, male producer* **3 wks**

10 Aug 91	WE GOTTA DO IT *Fourth & Broadway BRW 225* [1]	57	2
2 May 92	NO WAY OUT *PWL Continental PWL 230*	69	1

[1] DJ Professor featuring Francesco Zappala

Lena ZAVARONI Ⓒ *UK, female vocalist* **14 wks**

9 Feb 74	● MA HE'S MAKING EYES AT ME *Philips 6006 367*	10	11
1 Jun 74	PERSONALITY *Philips 6006 391*	33	3

ZEE UK, female vocalist — 4 wks

6 Jul 96	DREAMTIME Perfecto PERF 122CD	31	2
22 Mar 97	SAY MY NAME Perfecto PERF 135CD	36	1
7 Feb 98	BUTTERFLY Perfecto PERF 154CD1 [1]	41	1

[1] Tilt featuring Zee

ZEPHYRS UK, male vocal/instrumental group — 1 wk

18 Mar 65	SHE'S LOST YOU Columbia DB 7481	48	1

ZERO B UK, male instrumentalist – keyboards — 6 wks

22 Feb 92	THE EP Ffrreedom TAB 102	32	4
24 Jul 93	RECONNECTION EP Internal LIECD 6	54	2

Tracks on The EP: Lock Up/Spinning Wheel/Module/Eclipse. Tracks on
Reconnection EP: Lock Up/Lock Up (re-mix)/Ou Est Le Spoon/Love to Be
In Love. All three versions of 'Lock Up' are different mixes of the same track

ZERO VU UK, male/female vocal/production group — 1 wk

15 Mar 97	FEELS SO GOOD Avex UK AVEXCD 53 [1]	69	1

[1] Zero Vu featuring Lorna B

ZERO ZERO UK, male instrumental/production duo — 1 wk

10 Aug 91	ZEROXED Kickin KICK 9	71	1

ZHANE US, female vocal duo — 17 wks

11 Sep 93	HEY MR. DJ Epic 6596102	26	3
4 Dec 93	HEY MR. DJ (re-entry) Epic 6596102	50	2
19 Mar 94	GROOVE THANG Motown TMGCD 1423	34	3
20 Aug 94	VIBE Motown TMGCD 1430	67	1
25 Feb 95	SHAME Jive JIVECD 372	66	1
21 Sep 96	IT'S A PARTY Elektra EKR 226CD [1]	23	2
8 Mar 97	4 MORE Tommy Boy TBCD 7779A [2]	52	1
26 Apr 97	REQUEST LINE Motown 8606452	22	3
30 Aug 97	CRUSH Motown 5716712	44	1

[1] Busta Rhymes featuring Zhane [2] De La Soul featuring Zhane

ZIG and ZAG ☺ Ireland, male puppet duo — 12 wks

24 Dec 94	● THEM GIRLS THEM GIRLS RCA 74321251042	5	9
1 Jul 95	HANDS UP! HANDS UP! RCA 74321284392	21	3

ZIGZAG JIVE FLUTES – See ELIAS and his ZIGZAG JIVE FLUTES

ZION TRAIN UK, male/female vocal/instrumental group — 1 wk

27 Jul 96	RISE China WOKCD 2085	61	1

ZODIAC MINDWARP and the LOVE REACTION ✍
UK, male/female vocal/instrumental group — 11 wks

9 May 87	PRIME MOVER Mercury ZOD 1	18	6
14 Nov 87	BACKSEAT EDUCATION Mercury ZOD 2	49	3
2 Apr 88	PLANET GIRL Mercury ZOD 3	63	2

ZODIACS – See Maurice WILLIAMS and the ZODIACS

ZOE ☺ UK, female vocalist — 22 wks

10 Nov 90	SUNSHINE ON A RAINY DAY M & G MAGS 6	53	5
24 Aug 91	● SUNSHINE ON A RAINY DAY (re-mix) M & G MAGS 14	4	11
2 Nov 91	LIGHTNING M & G MAGS 18	37	4
29 Feb 92	HOLY DAYS M & G MAGS 21	72	2

Rob ZOMBIE US, male vocalist — 1 wk

26 Dec 98	DRAGULA Geffen GFSTD 22367	44†	1

ZOMBIES ✍ UK, male vocal/instrumental group — 16 wks

13 Aug 64	SHE'S NOT THERE Decca F 11940	12	11
11 Feb 65	TELL HER NO Decca F 12072	42	5

ZODIACS – See Maurice WILLIAMS and the ZODIACS

ZOE ☺ UK, female vocalist — 22 wks

10 Nov 90	SUNSHINE ON A RAINY DAY M & G MAGS 6	53	5
24 Aug 91	● SUNSHINE ON A RAINY DAY (re-mix) M & G MAGS 14	4	11
2 Nov 91	LIGHTNING M & G MAGS 18	37	4
29 Feb 92	HOLY DAYS M & G MAGS 21	72	2

Rob ZOMBIE US, male vocalist — 1 wk

26 Dec 98	DRAGULA Geffen GFSTD 22367	44†	1

ZOMBIES ✍ UK, male vocal/instrumental group — 16 wks

13 Aug 64	SHE'S NOT THERE Decca F 11940	12	11
11 Feb 65	TELL HER NO Decca F 12072	42	5

ZOO EXPERIENCE featuring DESTRY
UK, male instrumental group, and US, male vocalist — 1 wk

22 Aug 92	LOVE'S GOTTA HOLD ON ME Cooltempo COOL 261	66	1

ZUCCHERO ☾
Italy, male vocalist/instrumentalist – guitar, Adelmo Fornaciari — 24 wks

30 Mar 91	● SENZA UNA DONNA (WITHOUT A WOMAN) London LON 294 [1]	4	12
18 Jan 92	DIAMANTE London LON 313 [2]	44	7
24 Oct 92	MISERERE London LON 329 [3]	15	5

[1] Zucchero and Paul Young [2] Zucchero with Randy Crawford
[3] Zucchero with Luciano Pavarotti

ZZ TOP ✈ US, male vocal/instrumental group — 91 wks

3 Sep 83	GIMME ALL YOUR LOVIN' Warner Bros. W 9693	61	3
26 Nov 83	SHARP DRESSED MAN Warner Bros. W 9576	53	3
31 Mar 84	TV DINNERS Warner Bros. W 9334	67	3
6 Oct 84	● GIMME ALL YOUR LOVIN' (re-entry) Warner Bros. W 9693	10	15
15 Dec 84	SHARP DRESSED MAN (re-entry) Warner Bros. W 9576	22	10
23 Feb 85	LEGS Warner Bros. W 9272	16	7
13 Jul 85	SUMMER HOLIDAY EP Warner Bros. W 8946	51	5
19 Oct 85	SLEEPING BAG Warner Bros. W 2001	27	5
15 Feb 86	STAGES Warner Bros. W 2002	43	3
19 Apr 86	ROUGH BOY Warner Bros. W 2003	23	9
4 Oct 86	VELCRO FLY Warner Bros. W 8650	54	3
21 Jul 90	DOUBLEBACK Warner Bros. W 9812	29	6
13 Apr 91	MY HEAD'S IN MISSISSIPPI Warner Bros W 0009	37	5
11 Apr 92	VIVA LAS VEGAS Warner Bros. W 0098	10	7
20 Jun 92	ROUGH BOY (re-issue) Warner Bros. W 0111	49	3
29 Jan 94	PINCUSHION RCA 74321184732	15	3
7 May 94	BREAKAWAY RCA 74321192282	60	1
29 Jun 96	WHAT'S UP WITH THAT RCA 74321394822	58	1

Tracks on Summer Holiday EP: Tush/Got Me Under Pressure/Beer Drinkers and Hell
Raisers/I'm Bad, I'm Nationwide

What: *In the Summertime*   **97**
Who: Mungo Jerry
When: 1970 (1)
Which: Sold more than seven million copies around the world and topped the chart in 26 countries. It was also the first three-track single to reach No 1 in the UK

What: *Mary's Boy Child*   **98**
Who: Harry Belafonte
When: 1957 (1), 1958 (10), 1959 (30)
Which: Passed the one-million sales mark in (what was then) a record of six weeks and also charted during the following two years. The song hit the top again and sold another million when recorded by Boney M in 1978

What: *The Best Things in Life Are Free*   **99**
Who: Luther Vandross and Janet Jackson
When: 1992 (2), 1995 (7 – remix)
Which: Also features R&B trio Bell Biv DeVoe and New Edition's Ralph Tresvant. This two-time Top 10 hit was also featured on the film soundtrack for *Mo' Money*

What: *What a Wonderful World*   **100**
Who: Louis Armstrong
When: 1968 (1), 1988 (53)
Which: Headed the chart for one month shortly before Satchmo's 68th birthday. Twenty years later, in 1988 (and 17 years after his death), this classic finally reached the US Top 40

4 - Alphabetical-by-title

This section contains an alphabetical list of every hit since 1952 in order of title, act name, highest position hit reached on the chart and the year(s) in which it charted.

Covers: Different songs with the same title are differentiated by a letter in brackets after the song title: [A], [B], etc. Cover versions of the same song share the same letter. For example, there are six versions of 'Around the World'. Four of these titles share the letter [A], which indicates that they are all covers of the same song (recorded individually and in different years by Bing Crosby, Ronnie Hilton, Gracie Fields, and Mantovani). However, the fifth version is followed by the letter [B], which indicates that it is a different song (recorded by East 17). If the original version of a cover was never a chart hit, it will not be listed here.

Non-singles: Individual titles of songs on EP, LP, medley or megamix singles that made the chart are not listed here, although full track listings are included in the artist entries in Section 3.

Multiple chart entries: Remixes, reissues, re-entries, imports and second recordings of songs are not listed individually here (although they appear as separate chart entries under artist listings in Section 3). If a hit charted more than once the information is combined to include the highest position the hit reached and each of the years in which it charted. Thus, although 'Cigarettes and Alcohol' by Oasis re-entered the chart nine times from 1994 to 1996, it is listed just once with combined information for all of those entries. If a hit re-charted very briefly, this information may be omitted. Thus Cliff Richard's original version of 'Living Doll', which re-entered the charts for one brief week in 1960 after topping the charts in 1959, is only shown as a hit in 1959.

Duets: Most duets list both artists involved (e.g. 'Don't Let the Sun Go Down On Me' by Elton John and George Michael), but some hits are only credited to the main artist. For example, 'Zing a Little Zong' is credited to Bing Crosby. But if you look up his entry in Section 3, a footnote for the hit explains that it was, in fact, a duet with Jane Wyman.

Looking up acts: Act names use **bold** type to indicate their alphabetical order in Section 3. Groups, bands, orchestras, and ensembles are alphabetized according to the whole act name, while individual artists are ordered according to their surnames. Thus, **Brock Landers** is a group and appears under 'B', while Cyndi **Lauper** is an individual and appears under 'L'.

PJ Harvey

445

462

467

468

472

476

480

491

493

510

Picture credits

Guinness Publishing Ltd would like to thank Rex Features and all companies and individuals who gave permission for use of their images

004		Pepper Records
005		East West
008	tl	Rex Features
008	tr	Simon Fowler/Parlophone
008	bl	Rex Features
008	br	Rex Features
009		Columbia/Warren Du Preez
010		Diamond
011		Rex Features
012		Rex Features
013		Rex Features
014		Parlophone Rhythm/Tim Brett Day
015		Chrysalis/Hamish Brown
016		Hut/Scarlet Page
018		Mushroom Records/Stephane Sednaoui
019		Deconstruction
020		Epic/Mitch Ikeda
021		Island/Joseph Cultice
022		Echo/Mike Diver
023		Stockholm Records
024		Serious Records
025		Skint Records
026		Virgin/Kevin Westenberg
027		One Little Indian
028		Virgin
029		Sony
030		Polygram/Elleffe/Rankin
031		Paul Postle/Food
032	tl	Rex Features
032	tr	Rex Features/Sipa Press/Interfoto
032	bl	Wea
032	br	Wea
033		Maverick/WB Records/Mario Testino
035		London
036		EMI
037		Rex Features/Sipa Press
039		Sony
040		Hamish Brown
041		Dean Freeman/Virgin
042		Chris Cuffaro
043		East West
045		Rex Features
049		Rex Features
054		Arista
055		RCA
056		Mario Testino/Rocket/Polygram
057		Rex Features
059		Mike Diver
060		Rex Features/Magnus
061		Rex Features
063		Telstar
064		Paul Postle
065		Rankin/RCA
066		Mike Diver
067		Heather Favell/Innocent
068		Amanda Searle
069		Mercury
071		Unique Group
073		Hut/Kevin Westenberg
075		London
076		Arista
077		Sony
078		Steven Stickler
079		Linda McCartney/MPL/Parlophone
080		Rex Features/Harry Goodwin
081		Kevin Westenberg/Virgin
082	tl	Rex Features/Stills
082	tr	Danny Clinch/A & M/Mercury/Polygram
082	bl	Rex Features/Michele Taylor
082	br	Rex Features/Fotex/R Drechsler
083		Ian Macmillan/Lenono Photo Archive/Parlophone
098	tl	Brian Aris/Mercury
098	tr	Parlophone
098	bl	Lorenzo Agvis
098	br	Frank Micelotta
114	tl	Rex Features
114	tr	Rex Features
114	bl	John Dove/Apple/Parlophone
114	br	Coral Q
130	tl	Ian Macmillan/Lenono Photo Archive/Parlophone
130	tr	Rex Features
130	bl	RCA
130	br	Some Bizzare
146	tl	Island
146	tr	Rex Features
146	bl	Circus
146	br	Rex Features/Magnus
162	tl	Rex Features
162	tr	Rex Features
162	bl	London
162	br	Sony
178	tl	Maverick/WB Records/Mario Testino
178	tr	Rex Features
178	bl	Arista
178	br	Mercury
194	tl	Rex Features/Dezo Hoffman
194	tr	Rex Features
194	bl	Kama-Sutra
194	br	Rex Features
210	tl	Capitol
210	tr	Decca
210	bl	Rex Features
210	br	Rex Features/Dezo Hoffman
222	tl	Rex Features/Fotos International
222	tr	Rex Features
222	bl	Apple/Parlophone
222	br	RCA
238	tl	Rex Features
238	tr	Rex Features
238	bl	Rex Features
238	br	Timothy White/Virgin
254	tl	EMI
254	tr	Andy Gotts/Virgin
254	bl	Decca
254	br	Rex Features
270	tl	Columbia
270	tr	Epic
270	bl	Rex Features/Harry Goodwin/F Ballard
270	br	Rex Features
286	tl	Michael Lavine
286	tr	London
286	bl	Capitol
286	br	Mario Testino/Rocket/Polygram
296	tl	Linda McCartney/MPL/Parlophone
296	tr	Rex Features
296	bl	London
296	br	Ian Macmillan/Lenono Photo Archive/Capitol
314	tl	Rex Features
314	tr	Arista
314	bl	Rex Features
314	br	RCA
330	tl	Rex Features/F Gray
330	tr	Rex Features
330	bl	Rex Features
330	br	Rex Features
348	tl	Rex Features
348	tr	Rex Features
348	bl	Decca
348	br	Rex Features
360	tl	Rex Features
360	tr	Dean Freeman/Virgin
360	bl	Caroline Greyshock/East West
360	br	Columbia
372	tl	Magnet
372	tr	Rex Features
372	bl	Nitin Vadukul/Beyond/RCA
372	br	Rex Features/Sipa Press
384	tl	Rex Features/Harry Goodwin
384	tr	Rex Features/P Swirc
384	bl	Rex Features
384	br	Brunswick
396	tl	Rex Features
396	tr	Rex Features/Harry Goodwin
396	bl	Steven Stickler
396	br	Rex Features/Globe
436	tl	Rex Features
436	tr	Rex Features
436	bl	Rex Features/Sipa Press
436	br	Rex Features
437		Richard Sylvarnes

Key: t = top b = bottom r = right l = left